Koren Talmud Bavli

THE NOÉ EDITION

ZEVAḤIM

Steinsaltz Center

KOREN

תלמוד בבלי

KOREN TALMUD BAVLI

THE NOÉ EDITION

זבחים

ZEVAḤIM

Daf 98b through Daf 120b

COMMENTARY BY

Rabbi Adin Even-Israel Steinsaltz

EDITOR-IN-CHIEF

Rabbi Dr Tzvi Hersh Weinreb

SENIOR CONTENT EDITOR

Rabbi Dr Shalom Z Berger

EXECUTIVE EDITOR

Rabbi Joshua Schreier

STEINSALTZ CENTER

KOREN PUBLISHERS JERUSALEM

Supported by the Matanel Foundation

Koren Talmud Bavli, The Noe Edition
Vol. 29f: Tractate Zevaḥim, Daf 98b through Daf 120b
Paperback, ISBN, 978-965-7767-22-1

First Hebrew/English paperback edition, 2021

Koren Publishers Jerusalem Ltd.
PO Box 4044, Jerusalem 91040, ISRAEL
PO Box 8531, New Milford, CT 06776, USA
www.korenpub.com

Steinsaltz Center

Steinsaltz Center is the parent organization of institutions established by Rabbi Adin Even-Israel Steinsaltz

PO Box 45187, Jerusalem 91450 ISRAEL
Telephone: +972 2 646 0900, Fax +972 2 624 9454
www.steinsaltz-center.org

הִנֵּה יָמִים בָּאִים, נְאֻם אֲדֹנָי יֱהוִה, וְהִשְׁלַחְתִּי רָעָב בָּאָרֶץ,
לֹא־רָעָב לַלֶּחֶם וְלֹא־צָמָא לַמַּיִם, כִּי אִם־לִשְׁמֹעַ אֵת דִּבְרֵי יהוה.

Behold, days are coming – says the Lord God – I will send a hunger to the land, not a hunger for bread nor a thirst for water, but to hear the words of the Lord. (AMOS 8:11)

The Noé edition of the Koren Talmud Bavli
with the commentary of Rabbi Adin Even-Israel Steinsaltz
is dedicated to all those who open its covers
to quench their thirst for Jewish Knowledge,
in our generation of Torah renaissance.

This beautiful edition is for the young, the aged,
the novice and the savant alike,
as it unites the depth of Torah knowledge
with the best of academic scholarship.

Within its exquisite and vibrant pages,
words become worlds.

It will claim its place in the library of classics,
in the bookcases of the Beit Midrash,
the classrooms of our schools,
and in the offices of professionals and business people
who carve out precious time to grapple with its timeless wisdom.

For the Student and the Scholar

DEDICATED BY LEO AND SUE NOÉ

Steinsaltz Center

Executive Director, Steinsaltz Center

Rabbi Meni Even-Israel

Managing Editor

Rabbi Jason Rappoport

Senior Content Editor

Rabbi Dr. Shalom Z. Berger

Editors

Rabbi Dr. Joshua Amaru, *Coordinating Editor*
Rabbi Yehoshua Duker, *Senior Editor*
Rabbi Yedidya Naveh, *Content Curator*
Rabbi Avishai Magence, *Content Curator*
Rabbi Yehonatan Eliav, *Hebrew Edition*
Rabbi Gershon Kitsis, *Hebrew Edition*
Menucha Chwat
Rabbi Yonatan Shai Freedman
Rabbi Ayal Geffon
Rabbi Uri Goldstein
Noam Harris
Yisrael Kalker
Rabbi Tzvi Chaim Kaye
Rabbi Yonatan Kohn
Sholom Licht
Catriel Lev
Elisha Loewenstern
Rafi Miller
Rabbi Jonathan Mishkin
Rabbi Eli Ozarowski
Rabbi David Sedley
Rabbi Jonathan Shulman
Rabbi Michael Siev
Avi Steinhart
Rabbi David Strauss

Copy Editors

Aliza Israel, *Coordinator*
Ita Olesker
Debbie Ismailoff
Shira Finson
Ilana Sobel
Deena Nataf
Eliana Kurlantzick Yorav
Erica Hirsch Edvi
Sara Henna Dahan
Oritt Sinclair

Language Consultants

Dr. Stéphanie E. Binder, *Greek & Latin*
Rabbi Yaakov Hoffman, *Arabic*
Dr. Shai Secunda, *Persian*
Shira Shmidman, *Aramaic*

Technical Staff

Tani Bednarsh
Adena Frazer
Yaakov Shmidman
Shaltiel Shmidman
Nava Wieder

KOREN

Design & Typesetting

Dena Landowne Bailey, *Typesetting*
Tani Bayer, *Jacket Design*
Raphaël Freeman, *Design & Typography*

Images

Eliahu Misgav, *Illustration & Image Acquisition*
Daniel Gdalevich, *Illustration & Image Acquisition*

Introduction by the Publisher

The Talmud has sustained and inspired Jews for thousands of years. Throughout Jewish history, an elite cadre of scholars has absorbed its learning and passed it on to succeeding generations. The Talmud has been the fundamental text of our people.

Beginning in the 1960s, Rabbi Adin Even-Israel Steinsaltz שליט״א created a revolution in the history of Talmud study. His translation of the Talmud, first into modern Hebrew and then into other languages, as well the practical learning aids he added to the text, have enabled millions of people around the world to access and master the complexity and context of the world of Talmud.

It is thus a privilege to present the *Koren Talmud Bavli*, an English translation of the talmudic text with the brilliant elucidation of Rabbi Steinsaltz. The depth and breadth of his knowledge are unique in our time. His rootedness in the tradition and his reach into the world beyond it are inspirational.

Working with Rabbi Steinsaltz on this remarkable project has been not only an honor, but a great pleasure. Never shy to express an opinion, with wisdom and humor, Rabbi Steinsaltz sparkles in conversation, demonstrating his knowledge (both sacred and worldly), sharing his wide-ranging interests, and, above all, radiating his passion. I am grateful for the unique opportunity to work closely with him, and I wish him many more years of writing and teaching.

Our intentions in publishing this new edition of the Talmud are threefold. First, we seek to fully clarify the talmudic page to the reader – textually, intellectually, and graphically. Second, we seek to utilize today's most sophisticated technologies, both in print and electronic formats, to provide the reader with a comprehensive set of study tools. And third, we seek to help readers advance in their process of Talmud study.

To achieve these goals, the *Koren Talmud Bavli* is unique in a number of ways:

- The classic *tzurat hadaf* of Vilna, used by scholars since the 1800s, has been reset for great clarity, and opens from the Hebrew "front" of the book. Full *nikkud* has been added to both the talmudic text and Rashi's commentary, allowing for a more fluent reading with the correct pronunciation; the commentaries of *Tosafot* have been punctuated. Upon the advice of many English-speaking teachers of Talmud, we have separated these core pages from the translation, thereby enabling the advanced student to approach the text without the distraction of the translation. This also reduces the number of volumes in the set. At the bottom of each *daf*, there is a reference to the corresponding English pages. In addition, the Vilna edition was read against other manuscripts and older print editions, so that texts which had been removed by non-Jewish censors have been restored to their rightful place.
- The English translation, which starts on the English "front" of the book, reproduces the *menukad* Talmud text alongside the English translation (in bold) and commentary and explanation (in a lighter font). The Hebrew and Aramaic text is presented in logical paragraphs. This allows for a fluent reading of the text for the non-Hebrew or non-Aramaic reader. It also allows for the Hebrew reader to refer easily to the text alongside. Where the original text features dialogue or poetry, the English text is laid out in a manner appropriate to the genre. Each page refers to the relevant *daf*.

- Critical contextual tools surround the text and translation: personality notes, providing short biographies of the Sages; language notes, explaining foreign terms borrowed from Greek, Latin, Persian, or Arabic; and background notes, giving information essential to the understanding of the text, including history, geography, botany, archaeology, zoology, astronomy, and aspects of daily life in the talmudic era.
- Halakhic summaries provide references to the authoritative legal decisions made over the centuries by the rabbis. They explain the reasons behind each halakhic decision as well as the ruling's close connection to the Talmud and its various interpreters.
- Photographs, drawings, and other illustrations have been added throughout the text – in full color in the Standard and Electronic editions, and in black and white in the Daf Yomi edition – to visually elucidate the text.

This is not an exhaustive list of features of this edition, it merely presents an overview for the English-speaking reader who may not be familiar with the "total approach" to Talmud pioneered by Rabbi Steinsaltz.

Several professionals have helped bring this vast collaborative project to fruition. My many colleagues are noted on the Acknowledgments page, and the leadership of this project has been exceptional.

RABBI MENACHEM EVEN-ISRAEL, DIRECTOR OF THE STEINSALTZ CENTER, was the driving force behind this enterprise. With enthusiasm and energy, he formed the happy alliance with Koren and established close relationships among all involved in the work.

RABBI DR. TZVI HERSH WEINREB שליט״א, EDITOR-IN-CHIEF, brought to this project his profound knowledge of Torah, intellectual literacy of Talmud, and erudition of Western literature. It is to him that the text owes its very high standard, both in form and content, and the logical manner in which the beauty of the Talmud is presented.

RABBI JOSHUA SCHREIER, EXECUTIVE EDITOR, assembled an outstanding group of scholars, translators, editors, and proofreaders, whose standards and discipline enabled this project to proceed in a timely and highly professional manner.

RABBI MEIR HANEGBI, EDITOR OF THE HEBREW EDITION OF THE STEINSALTZ TALMUD, lent his invaluable assistance throughout the work process, supervising the reproduction of the Vilna pages.

RAPHAËL FREEMAN, EXECUTIVE EDITOR OF KOREN, created this Talmud's unique typographic design which, true to the Koren approach, is both elegant and user friendly.

It has been an enriching experience for all of us at Koren Publishers Jerusalem to work with the Steinsaltz Center to develop and produce the *Koren Talmud Bavli*. We pray that this publication will be a source of great learning and, ultimately, greater *avodat Hashem* for all Jews.

Matthew Miller, Publisher
Koren Publishers Jerusalem
Jerusalem 5772

Contents

Zevaḥim **199**

Image Credits **348**

For the vocalized Vilna Shas layout, please open as a Hebrew book.

Introduction to **Perek XII**

As is the sin offering, so is the guilt offering; there is one law for them; the priest that effects atonement with it, he shall have it to himself.

(Leviticus 7:7)

And of it he shall present one out of each offering for a gift unto the Lord; it shall be the priest's that sprinkles the blood of the peace offering against the altar.

(Leviticus 7:14)

And Aaron spoke unto Moses: Behold, today have they sacrificed their sin offering and their burnt offering before the Lord, and there have befallen me such things as these; and if I had consumed the sin offering today, would it have been good in the eyes of the Lord?

(Leviticus 10:19)

And the bull of the sin offering, and the goat of the sin offering, whose blood was brought in to make atonement in the Sanctuary, they shall be carried forth outside the camp; and they shall burn in the fire their hides, and their flesh, and their dung. And he who burns them shall wash his garments, and bathe his flesh in water, and afterward he may come into the camp.

(Leviticus 16:27–28)

This chapter addresses two main topics: The portions of offerings that priests acquire, and the *halakhot* of sin offerings of bulls and goats that are burned, of which the priests have no portion.

For almost all offerings, the priests receive a portion of meat, which they and their families may consume. On the one hand, the Torah grants the priest who sacrifices an offering the right to the priestly portion. On the other hand, it is agreed that all the priests of the patrilineal family serving in the Temple that day receive a share in the portions of that day's offerings. This chapter attempts to resolve this tension by discussing which priests have a right to receive a share of sacrificial meat. Do priests who may not serve at the time of the offering due to various disqualifications receive a share? For this purpose, does the *halakha* distinguish between a permanent disqualification, e.g., a blemish, and a temporary one, such as ritual impurity or acute mourning? Does a priest's right to a share of the meat depend on his being fit to partake of it at the time, or may he receive a share at that time that he will be able to partake of only later, e.g., when he will become pure? These discussions lead to a lengthy analysis of the disqualifications of priests, both from serving in the Temple and from partaking of sacrificial meat. This analysis deals mainly with the various principles of acute mourning for priests, by both Torah law and rabbinic law.

Just as a priest who sacrifices an offering has a right to those portions that are eaten, the Torah also states that he has a right to the hide of a burnt offering. This principle raises several questions, e.g., whether it applies only to burnt offerings, or to other offerings as well. The Gemara also examines the relationship between a priest's right to the meat, the consumption of which is part of an offering's mitzva, and his right to the hide, which becomes his personal property. If an offering is disqualified and its flesh cannot be burned on the altar, do the priests still have a right to the hide?

The second part of the chapter discusses offerings from which the priests receive neither meat nor hide, namely, those sin offerings whose blood is sprinkled on the inner altar. These sin offerings are known as bulls and goats that are burned, because the Torah states that their flesh and hides must be burned "outside the camp." Various questions arise in this context, e.g., what is considered to be outside the camp, and whether the word camp refers to the camp of the Tabernacle or the camp of the Israelites. As well, the Gemara must determine if there is a designated place for the burning of these offerings, and what happens if they are disqualified.

The Torah also states that the priests who burn these sin offerings render their garments ritually impure. The Gemara discusses questions that follow from this principle: From what point do the sin offerings cause impurity, and at what point do they no longer cause impurity? Is the priest who burns the offering the only one who renders his garments impure, or do other priests who are involved with sacrificing the offering render their garments impure as well? The details of this impurity are the primary subject of the second part of the chapter.

מתני׳ טְבוּל יוֹם וּמְחוּסַּר כִּיפּוּרִים אֵינָן חוֹלְקִין בַּקֳּדָשִׁים לֶאֱכוֹל לָעֶרֶב.

MISHNA A priest who was ritually impure **who immersed that day**[NH] and is waiting for nightfall for the purification process to be completed, **and a** priest **who has not yet brought an atonement** offering[N] to complete the purification process, e.g., a *zav* and a leper who did not bring their requisite atonement offerings, who are not yet permitted to partake of sacrificial meat, **do not receive a share of sacrificial** meat along with the other members of the patrilineal priestly family serving in the Temple that day, in order **to partake** of it **in the evening** after the offerings were sacrificed, even though after nightfall he would be permitted to partake of the offerings.

אוֹנֵן (אֵינוֹ) נוֹגֵעַ וְאֵינוֹ מַקְרִיב, וְאֵינוֹ חוֹלֵק לֶאֱכוֹל לָעֶרֶב.

A priest who is **an acute mourner,**[B] i.e., if one of his relatives for whom he is obligated to mourn died that day, is permitted to **touch** sacrificial meat,[H] as he is not ritually impure. **But he may not sacrifice** offerings,[H] **and he does not receive a share**[H] of sacrificial meat in order **to partake** of it **in the evening.**

בַּעֲלֵי מוּמִין, בֵּין בַּעֲלֵי מוּמִין עוֹבְרִין בֵּין בַּעֲלֵי מוּמִין קְבוּעִין – חוֹלְקִין וְאוֹכְלִין, אֲבָל לֹא מַקְרִיבִין.

Blemished priests, **whether** they are **temporarily blemished** or **whether** they are **permanently blemished, receive a share and partake**[H] of the offerings with their priestly brethren, **but do not sacrifice**[H] the offerings.

כָּל שֶׁאֵינוֹ רָאוּי לַעֲבוֹדָה – אֵינוֹ חוֹלֵק בְּבָשָׂר, וְכָל שֶׁאֵין לוֹ בְּבָשָׂר – אֵין לוֹ בָּעוֹרוֹת.

The principle is: **Any** priest **who is unfit for the service**[H] that specific day **does not receive a share of the** sacrificial **meat, and anyone who has no share of the meat has no share in the hides**[H] of the animals, to which the priests are entitled as well.

אֲפִילּוּ טָמֵא בִּשְׁעַת זְרִיקַת דָּמִים וְטָהוֹר בִּשְׁעַת הֶקְטֵר חֲלָבִים – אֵינוֹ חוֹלֵק בְּבָשָׂר, שֶׁנֶּאֱמַר: ״הַמַּקְרִיב אֶת דַּם הַשְּׁלָמִים [וְאֶת הַחֵלֶב מִבְּנֵי אַהֲרֹן] לוֹ (יִהְיֶה) [תִהְיֶה שׁוֹק הַיָּמִין לְמָנָה]״.

Even if the priest was **ritually impure** only **at the time of the sprinkling of the blood**[H] of the offering **and** he was **pure at the time of the burning of the fats**[N] of that offering, he still **does not receive a share of the meat, as it is stated: "He that sacrifices the blood of the peace offerings and the fat, from among the sons of Aaron, shall have the right thigh for a portion"** (Leviticus 7:33). One who cannot sprinkle the blood does not receive a share in the meat.

BACKGROUND

Acute mourner – אוֹנֵן: The period of acute mourning is observed on the day of the death of a spouse, parent, child, or sibling. The mourner is exempt from all positive mitzvot from the time of the death of the close relative until after the burial. At that point his status changes from that of an acute mourner to that of a mourner.

NOTES

A priest who immersed that day, etc. – טְבוּל יוֹם וכו׳: A priest who immersed that day, a priest who has not yet brought an atonement offering, an acute mourner, and a blemished priest are all unfit for the Temple service, as is taught in a mishna (15b). It is also prohibited for priests in two of these categories, one who immersed that day and one who has not yet brought an atonement offering, to touch sacrificial meat, because they are ritually impure.

A priest who has not yet brought an atonement offering – מְחוּסַּר כִּפּוּרִים: By Torah law, one who has not yet brought an atonement offering may partake of sacrificial meat as soon as his offering is offered on the eighth day, as the Torah states with regard to a woman after childbirth (see Leviticus 12:8 and *Yevamot* 74b). By rabbinic law, he must immerse before partaking of sacrificial meat (see *Ḥagiga* 21a).

Tosafot discuss at length the phrasing in the mishna: In order to partake of it in the evening after the offerings were sacrificed, which seems to indicate that even after his offering was brought, the priest may not partake of sacrificial meat until the evening. While the Sages did require waiting until sunset in other cases where they required immersion, e.g., one who is impure by rabbinic law, *Tosafot* conclude that in this case, the one who brought his atonement offering does not need to wait until sunset. The mishna specifies the evening only with regard to the previous case, one who immersed that day, who must wait until sunset before partaking of sacrificial meat.

Others explain that the mishna means that even one whose atonement offering is sacrificed must wait until evening before partaking of sacrificial meat. They explain that since he gives the money for his offering to the priest and does not know precisely when it will be sacrificed, he must wait until the evening, or at least until the afternoon daily offering is sacrificed, which is the last offering of the day (*Tiferet Yisrael*, citing *Pesaḥim* 90b).

The *Birkat HaZevaḥ* explains that because the Sages required one whose atonement offering is sacrificed to immerse, he may not receive a share of the sacrificial meat until he immerses. The *Panim Meirot* disagrees, and holds that because he is fit by Torah law to partake of the sacrificial meat as soon as his offering is sacrificed, he may receive a share of the sacrificial meat even before he immerses. *Tosefot Rabbi Akiva Eiger* concurs.

Pure at the time of the burning of the fats – טָהוֹר בִּשְׁעַת הֶקְטֵר חֲלָבִים: Most of the burning of the fats takes place during the night, at which time one who immersed that day or one whose atonement offering was brought is fully pure (Rashi).

HALAKHA

A priest who immersed that day, etc. – טְבוּל יוֹם וכו׳: A priest who immersed that day and a priest who has not yet brought an atonement offering do not receive a share of sacrificial meat to partake of it in the evening (Rambam *Sefer Avoda, Hilkhot Ma'aseh HaKorbanot* 10:19).

An acute mourner is permitted to touch – אוֹנֵן נוֹגֵעַ: By rabbinic law, when an ordinary priest finishes a period of acute mourning, he must immerse before partaking of sacrificial meat, in case his mind was distracted from avoiding ritual impurity. It is permitted for him to touch sacrificial meat before he immerses, as the Sages restricted him only with regard to partaking and not with regard to contact (Rambam *Sefer Tahara, Hilkhot She'ar Avot HaTumot* 12:15).

An acute mourner…may not sacrifice offerings – אוֹנֵן...אֵינוֹ מַקְרִיב: If an ordinary priest was in the Temple performing the service, and he heard that a relative for whom he must mourn had died, he must stop serving, though he need not leave the Temple. If he continued to perform the service, his service is not valid. The High Priest performs the service even when he is an acute mourner (Rambam *Sefer Avoda, Hilkhot Biat HaMikdash* 2:6–7).

An acute mourner…does not receive a share – אוֹנֵן...אֵינוֹ חוֹלֵק: It is prohibited by Torah law for an acute mourner to partake of sacrificial meat on the day of his relative's death, whether he is an ordinary priest or a High Priest. Therefore, he does not receive a share of the sacrificial meat to partake of it in the evening (Rambam *Sefer Avoda, Hilkhot Biat HaMikdash* 2:8 and *Hilkhot Ma'aseh HaKorbanot* 10:19).

Blemished priests…receive a share and partake – בַּעֲלֵי מוּמִין...חוֹלְקִין וְאוֹכְלִין: A blemished priest, whether he has a temporary or permanent blemish, and whether he was born with the blemish or it developed later, may receive a share and partake of sacrificial meat. If a priest is impure, he does not receive a share of the meat to partake of it in the evening (Rambam *Sefer Avoda, Hilkhot Ma'aseh HaKorbanot* 10:17 and *Hilkhot Biat HaMikdash* 6:12).

Blemished priests…do not sacrifice – בַּעֲלֵי מוּמִין...לֹא מַקְרִיבִין: It is prohibited for a blemished priest, even with a temporary blemish, to perform the Temple service. If he served, his service is not valid and he receives lashes (Rambam *Sefer Avoda, Hilkhot Biat HaMikdash* 6:1–2).

Any priest who is unfit for the service – כָּל שֶׁאֵינוֹ רָאוּי לַעֲבוֹדָה: A priest who is fit for Temple service at the time an offering is sacrificed receives a share of the sacrificial meat. A priest who is unfit has no share, with the exception of a blemished priest (Rambam *Sefer Avoda, Hilkhot Ma'aseh HaKorbanot* 10:14, 20).

Anyone who has no share of the meat has no share in the hides – כָּל שֶׁאֵין לוֹ בְּבָשָׂר אֵין לוֹ בָּעוֹרוֹת: A priest who receives no share in the meat of an offering receives no share in the hides (Rambam *Sefer Avoda, Hilkhot Ma'aseh HaKorbanot* 10:21).

Even if the priest was ritually impure at the time of the sprinkling of the blood – אֲפִילּוּ טָמֵא בִּשְׁעַת זְרִיקַת דָּמִים: If a priest was ritually impure at the time the blood was sprinkled, then even if he was pure at the time the fats were burned, he receives no share of the meat (Rambam *Sefer Avoda, Hilkhot Ma'aseh HaKorbanot* 10:21).

גמ׳ מְנָא הָנֵי מִילֵּי? אָמַר רֵישׁ לָקִישׁ: דְּאָמַר קְרָא ״הַכֹּהֵן הַמְחַטֵּא אֹתָהּ יֹאכְלֶנָּה״, כֹּהֵן הַמְחַטֵּא – יֹאכַל, שֶׁאֵינוֹ מְחַטֵּא – אֵינוֹ אוֹכֵל.

GEMARA The mishna teaches that a priest who is unfit for the Temple service does not receive a share of the sacrificial meat. The Gemara asks: **From where are these matters** derived? **Reish Lakish said:** It is derived from a verse, **as the verse states** about a sin offering: "**The priest who effects atonement shall eat it;** in a sacred place shall it be eaten, in the court of the Tent of Meeting" (Leviticus 6:19). This teaches that only **a priest who effects atonement** by performing the rites of the offering **shall partake** of its meat, but a priest **who does not effect atonement does not partake** of its meat.

וּכְלָלָא הוּא? וַהֲרֵי מִשְׁמָרָה כּוּלָּהּ, דְּאֵין מְחַטְּאִין, וְאוֹכְלִין! רָאוּי לְחִיטּוּי קָאָמְרִינַן.

The Gemara challenges: **And is** this an established **principle? But** there are **all the** priests of the **priestly watch**[N] of that week in the Temple, **who do not effect atonement** for that offering, because the blood of a specific sin offering is presented by just one priest, **and** yet they all **partake** of its meat. The Gemara explains: **We** mean to **say** that any priest who is **fit for effecting atonement** may partake of it, even one who did not participate in the service.

הֲרֵי קָטָן, דְּאֵינוֹ רָאוּי לְחִיטּוּי, וְאוֹכֵל! אֶלָּא: מַאי ״יֹאכְלֶנָּה״ – יְחַלְּקֶנָּה; רָאוּי לְחִיטּוּי – חוֹלֵק, שֶׁאֵינוֹ רָאוּי לְחִיטּוּי – אֵינוֹ חוֹלֵק.

The Gemara objects: **But** there is the case of **a minor, who is unfit for effecting atonement, and** who nevertheless **partakes** of sacrificial meat. The Gemara explains: **Rather, what** is meant by the term: **"Shall eat it"?** It means that he **shall receive a share of it.** The *halakha* is therefore that a priest who is **fit for effecting atonement receives a share** of the meat,[H] but a priest **who is unfit for effecting atonement does not receive a share** of the meat. Minors do not receive a share, though they may partake of meat given to them by others.

הֲרֵי בַּעַל מוּם, דְּאֵינוֹ רָאוּי לְחִיטּוּי, וְחוֹלֵק! בַּעַל מוּם רַחֲמָנָא רַבְּיֵיהּ: ״כׇּל זָכָר בַּכֹּהֲנִים״ – לְרַבּוֹת בַּעַל מוּם.

The Gemara objects: But there is **a blemished priest, who is unfit for effecting atonement, and** yet he **receives a share** of its meat. The Gemara replies: **The Merciful One included a blemished** priest[H] as an exception, as the verse that states: "**Every male among the priests** shall eat it" (Leviticus 6:22), serves **to include a blemished** priest.

וְאֵימָא: ״כׇּל זָכָר״ – לְרַבּוֹת טְבוּל יוֹם! מִסְתַּבְּרָא, בַּעַל מוּם הֲוָה לֵיהּ לְרַבּוּיֵי, שֶׁכֵּן אוֹכֵל.

The Gemara suggests: **But say** that the phrase **"every male"** serves **to include one who immersed that day,** teaching that he may also receive a share in the sacrificial meat. Why should it be understood as referring specifically to a blemished priest? The Gemara replies: **It stands to reason** that the Torah **should include a blemished** priest for receiving his own share of the meat, **because** he may **partake** of sacrificial meat in any event. By contrast, one who immersed that day is impure and may not touch or partake of sacrificial meat.

אַדְּרַבָּה, טְבוּל יוֹם הֲוָה לֵיהּ לְרַבּוּיֵי, דִּלְאוּרְתָּא מִיחְזָא חֲזֵי! הַשְׁתָּא מִיהָא הָא לָא חֲזֵי.

The Gemara rejects this: **On the contrary,** the Torah **should include one who immersed that day, because,** unlike a blemished priest, **in the evening he will be fit** to perform the service. The Gemara replies: **Now, in any event,** the one who immersed himself **is not fit.**

NOTES

All the priests of the priestly watch – וַהֲרֵי מִשְׁמָרָה כּוּלָּהּ: In practice, the sacrificial meat would be shared not by the entire watch, but by the family that performed the service that day.

HALAKHA

A priest who is fit for effecting atonement receives a share of the meat – רָאוּי לְחִיטּוּי חוֹלֵק: The verse states with regard to a sin offering: "The priest who effects atonement shall eat it," teaching that only a priest who is fit for service receives a share of the meat. A priest who is not fit at the time of the service, e.g., because he is impure, does not receive a share of the meat, even if he will be fit in the evening (Rambam *Sefer Avoda, Hilkhot Ma'aseh HaKorbanot* 10:14).

The Merciful One included a blemished priest – בַּעַל מוּם רַחֲמָנָא רַבְּיֵיהּ: Any priest who is unfit to serve is also unfit to partake of sacrificial meat, except for blemished priests, who are permitted explicitly in the Torah (Rambam *Sefer Avoda, Hilkhot Ma'aseh HaKorbanot* 10:20, and see 10:17).

רב יוסף אמר: מכדי מאי "יאכלנה" – יחלקנה, לכתוב רחמנא "יחלקנה", מאי "יאכלנה"? שמע מינה: ראוי לאכילה – חולק, שאינו ראוי לאכילה – אינו חולק.

Rav Yosef said another explanation: **Now what** is meant by the term: **"Shall eat it"?** It means: He **shall receive a share of it.** But if so, **let the Merciful One write: Shall receive a share of it. What** is the reason for writing: **"Shall eat it"? Learn from it** that only a priest who is **fit for partaking** of sacrificial meat, which includes a blemished priest, **receives a share** in the meat;[H] but a priest **who is not fit for partaking** of sacrificial meat, e.g., one who immersed that day, **does not** receive a **share** in the meat.

בעי ריש לקיש: בעל מום והוא טמא, מהו שיחלקו לו? כיון דלא חזי ורחמנא רבייה – לא שנא, מה לי טמא מה לי בעל מום. או דלמא: ראוי לאכילה – חולק, שאינו ראוי לאכילה – אינו חולק?

§ **Reish Lakish raises a dilemma:** If a priest is **blemished and he is impure,**[H] **what is the** *halakha*? Must the other priests **give him a share** of the meat? Perhaps we say that **since he is not fit** to perform the rite as a blemished priest **and** nevertheless **the Merciful One included him** to receive a share in the meat, there **is no difference: What** is the difference **to me** if he is **impure,** and **what** is the difference **to me** if he is only **blemished?** In any event he is not fit, yet the Torah allows him to receive a share in the meat. **Or perhaps** he may not receive a share in the meat, because only a priest who is **fit for partaking** of sacrificial meat **receives a share** of the meat, but a priest **who is not fit for partaking** of sacrificial meat **does not receive a share** of the meat.

אמר רבה, תא שמע: כהן גדול מקריב אונן, ואינו אוכל, ואינו חולק לאכול לערב. שמע מינה: ראוי לאכילה בעינן, שמע מינה.

Rabba said: Come and **hear** a resolution to this dilemma from a *baraita*: If a **High Priest** is serving in the Temple and one of his immediate relatives dies, **he sacrifices** offerings even as **an acute mourner.**[H] **But he does not partake** of sacrificial meat, **and he does not receive a share to partake** of it **in the evening. Conclude from** the *baraita* that in order for the priest to receive a share in sacrificial meat, **we require** that he be **fit for partaking** of it, and accordingly, a blemished priest who is impure does not receive a share. The Gemara affirms: **Conclude from** the *baraita* that this is so.

בעי רב אושעיא: טמא בקרבנות ציבור, מהו שיחלקו לו? מי אמרינן: "המחטא" אמר רחמנא, והאי נמי מחטא הוא. או דלמא ראוי לאכילה – חולק, שאין ראוי לאכילה – אינו חולק?

§ **Rav Oshaya raises a dilemma:** If a priest is **impure,** then **in** a case **of communal offerings,**[H] which may be offered by an impure priest, **what is the** *halakha*? Do the other priests **give him a share** of the meat, so that he may partake of it in the evening when he becomes pure? **Do we say** that **the Merciful One states:** "The priest **who effects atonement,"** and therefore any priest who is fit for effecting atonement receives a share, as derived earlier, and **this** priest **is also** one who may **effect atonement,** since this is a communal offering? **Or perhaps** he may not, due to the principle that only a priest who is **fit for partaking** of sacrificial meat **receives a share** of the meat, but a priest **who is unfit for partaking** of sacrificial meat **does not receive a share.**

אמר רבינא, תא שמע: כהן גדול מקריב אונן, ואינו אוכל, ואינו חולק לאכול לערב. שמע מינה: ראוי לאכילה בעינן, שמע מינה.

Ravina said: Come and **hear** a resolution to this dilemma from a *baraita*: If a **High Priest** is serving in the Temple and one of his relatives dies, **he sacrifices** offerings even as **an acute mourner, but he does not partake** of sacrificial meat **and he does not receive a share** of it **to partake in the evening. Conclude from** the *baraita* that in order for a priest to receive a share in sacrificial meat, **we require** that he be **fit for partaking** of it at the time of the service, without regard to whether he can perform the service. The Gemara affirms: **Conclude from** the *baraita* that this is so.

HALAKHA

A priest who is fit for partaking of sacrificial meat receives a share in the meat – ראוי לאכילה חולק: Any priest who is fit to partake of sacrificial meat at the time of the sacrifice receives a share of the meat. But any priest who is unfit to partake of sacrificial meat at the time of the sacrifice, even if he is fit for the service, or even if he will be fit to partake in the evening, does not receive a share of the meat (Rambam *Sefer Avoda, Hilkhot Ma'aseh HaKorbanot* 10:19).

A priest is blemished and he is impure – בעל מום והוא טמא: A blemished priest shares and partakes of sacrificial meat. But if he is impure, he does not receive a share of the meat to partake of it in the evening, in accordance with the statement of Rabba (Rambam *Sefer Avoda, Hilkhot Ma'aseh HaKorbanot* 10:17).

A High Priest sacrifices the offerings even as an acute mourner, etc. – כהן גדול מקריב אונן וכו׳: A High Priest serves in the Temple when he is an acute mourner, but it is prohibited for him to partake of sacrificial meat, and he does not receive a share of the meat to partake of it in the evening (Rambam *Sefer Avoda, Hilkhot Biat HaMikdash* 2:8).

If a priest is impure in a case of communal offerings – טמא בקרבנות ציבור: When a communal offering is brought in a state of impurity, impure priests may sacrifice it but do not receive a share of the sacrificial meat to partake of it in the evening, in accordance with the statement of Ravina (Rambam *Sefer Avoda, Hilkhot Ma'aseh HaKorbanot* 10:23).

״אוֹנֵן נוֹגֵעַ וְאֵינוֹ מַקְרִיב״ כו׳. אוֹנֵן נוֹגֵעַ? וּרְמִינְהִי: אוֹנֵן וּמְחוּסַּר כִּיפּוּרִים צְרִיכִין טְבִילָה לַקּוֹדֶשׁ!

§ The mishna teaches: A priest who is **an acute mourner** is permitted to **touch** sacrificial meat, **but he may not sacrifice** offerings. The Gemara asks: Is it in fact permitted for **an acute mourner** to **touch** sacrificial meat? **And** the Gemara **raises a contradiction** from another mishna (*Ḥagiga* 21a): **An acute mourner and one who has not yet** brought **an atonement** offering, even after their respective disqualifications have expired, **require immersion**[H] in order **to** eat **sacrificial** food. According to that mishna, an acute mourner who did not immerse may not touch sacrificial meat.

אֲמַר רַבִּי אַמִּי אֲמַר רַבִּי יוֹחָנָן: לָא קַשְׁיָא, כָּאן – בְּשֶׁטָּבַל, כָּאן – בְּשֶׁלֹּא טָבַל.

Rabbi Ami said that **Rabbi Yoḥanan said:** This is **not difficult. Here,** the ruling of the mishna is stated **with regard to** a case **where** the mourner **immersed** during his day of acute mourning. This is why he is permitted to touch the sacrificial meat. **There,** the ruling of the mishna in tractate *Ḥagiga* is stated **with regard to** a case **where** the mourner **did not immerse.**

וְכִי טָבַל מַאי הָוֵי? הָא הָדְרָא עֲלֵיהּ אֲנִינוּת. דְּאָמַר רַבָּה בַּר רַב הוּנָא: אוֹנֵן שֶׁטָּבַל – אֲנִינוּתוֹ חוֹזֶרֶת עָלָיו!

The Gemara asks: **And** even **if** he **immersed, what of it? But doesn't his acute mourning return to him? As Rabba, son of Rav Huna, says:** In a case of **an acute mourner who immersed** during his day of his acute mourning, **his acute mourning returns to him.**

לָא קַשְׁיָא; הָא – דְּאַסַּח דַּעְתֵּיהּ, הָא – דְּלָא אַסַּח דַּעְתֵּיהּ.

The Gemara answers: This is **not difficult. That** case, in tractate *Ḥagiga,* is one **where he was distracted**[N] from safeguarding his state of purity, so he may not touch sacrificial meat in the event that he is impure. **This** case, in the mishna here, is one **where he was not distracted.**

הֶיסַּח הַדַּעַת, שְׁלִישִׁי וּשְׁבִיעִי בָּעֵי. דְּאָמַר רַבִּי יוּסְטַאי בְּרַבִּי מָתוּן אָמַר רַבִּי יוֹחָנָן: הֶיסַּח הַדַּעַת צָרִיךְ הַזָּאָה שְׁלִישִׁי וּשְׁבִיעִי!

The Gemara counters: If the mishna in tractate *Ḥagiga* is discussing a case of **distraction,** then his status is like that of one who contracted ritual impurity imparted by a corpse, who **requires** sprinkling with water of purification on the **third and seventh** days of his impurity. **As Rabbi Yustai, son of Rabbi Matun, says** that **Rabbi Yoḥanan says:** One who experienced **a distraction requires sprinkling** with water of purification on the **third and seventh** days.

לָא קַשְׁיָא; הָא – דְּאַסַּח דַּעְתֵּיהּ מִטְּמֵא מֵת, הָא – דְּאַסַּח דַּעְתֵּיהּ מִטְּמֵא שֶׁרֶץ.

The Gemara responds: This is **not difficult. That** statement, that he requires sprinkling, is discussing a case **where he was distracted** and careless **about** contracting **impurity imparted by a corpse. This** mishna in tractate *Ḥagiga,* stating that he requires immersion but not sprinkling, is discussing a case **where he was distracted** and careless **about** contracting **impurity imparted by** the carcass of **a creeping animal.**[H]

טְמֵא שֶׁרֶץ טָמֵא מְעַלְּיָיא הוּא, הַעֲרֵב שֶׁמֶשׁ בָּעֵי! וְעוֹד: אֲפִילּוּ תְּרוּמָה נָמֵי!

The Gemara counters: One who was careless about becoming **impure due to** the carcass of **a creeping animal is fully impure,** and so he requires not only immersion to become pure, but he also **requires sunset. And furthermore,** if the mishna in tractate *Ḥagiga* is discussing this case, the mourner should be prohibited from touching **even *teruma*,** not just sacrificial meat. Why does the mishna mention only the latter?

אֲמַר רַבִּי יִרְמְיָה, בְּאוֹמֵר: ״נִשְׁמַרְתִּי מִדָּבָר הַמְטַמְּאֵנִי, וְלֹא נִשְׁמַרְתִּי מִדָּבָר הַפּוֹסְלֵנִי״.

Rabbi Yirmeya said: The mishna is discussing a case **where he says: I safeguarded myself from anything that would render me impure,**[N] so I am certain that I did not contract impurity that requires waiting until sunset; **but I did not safeguard myself from anything that would render me unfit** for touching sacrificial meat.

HALAKHA

An acute mourner and one who has not yet brought an atonement offering require immersion – אוֹנֵן וּמְחוּסַּר כִּפּוּרִים צְרִיכִים טְבִילָה: An acute mourner whose period of acute mourning has ended and one whose atonement offering was brought on that day must immerse before they may partake of sacrificial food. The reason is that they may not have been careful to avoid impurity while sacrificial food was forbidden to them. Nevertheless, they may partake of *teruma* even before they immerse (Rambam *Sefer Tahara, Hilkhot She'ar Avot HaTumot* 12:15).

NOTES

That case in *Ḥagiga* is one where he was distracted – לָא קַשְׁיָא הָא דְּאַסַּח דַּעְתֵּיהּ: Rashi's version of the text introduces this answer with the word rather. Accordingly, the Gemara rejects Rabbi Yoḥanan's resolution of the two *mishnayot*, that the difference between them is whether or not the mourner had immersed, and now presents a different distinction between the cases. *Tosafot* have the standard version of the text, which does not include the term rather. Accordingly, the Gemara explains that one's status of acute mourning returns after immersion only if he was distracted, and the discussion continues according to this understanding (see *Ḥok Natan*).

From anything that would render me impure – מִדָּבָר הַמְטַמְּאֵנִי: The distinction is between items that render a person impure to the degree that he now renders others impure through contact, and items that render a person unfit, meaning that he may not partake of sacrificial meat, even though he does not render others impure.

According to Rashi, Rabbi Yirmeya answers the first challenge: Doesn't one who was distracted from avoiding contracting impurity imparted by the carcass of a creeping animal need both immersion and sunset? Rabbi Yirmeya answers that this person was distracted only from becoming unfit by rabbinic law, which requires only immersion and not sunset. This does not address the Gemara's second challenge, that contact with *teruma* is also prohibited.

Tosafot suggest that the text should read: I safeguarded myself from anything that would render me unfit for touching *teruma*, but not from anything that would render me unfit for touching sacrificial meat. This would apply to third-degree impurity, which disqualifies sacrificial meat, but not *teruma* (see *Ḥagiga* 20b).

HALAKHA

Where he was distracted, etc. – הָא דְּאַסַּח דַּעְתֵּיהּ וכו׳: If one was distracted from safeguarding his purity for the purpose of partaking of *teruma*, and all the more so for partaking of sacrificial food, then he is considered impure. He must immerse before he partakes, but need not wait until sunset. If one was distracted from safeguarding himself from contracting impurity imparted by a corpse, and he does not know for certain that he is pure, then he must be sprinkled with water of purification on the third and seventh days of his impurity. If one was distracted from safeguarding himself from other forms of impurity, he must immerse and wait for sunset (Rambam *Sefer Tahara, Hilkhot She'ar Avot HaTumot* 13:3).

ומי איכא נטירותא לפלגא? אין, והתניא: עודהו הסל על ראשו,

The Gemara asks: **But is there** such a concept of **partial care,** that one can claim to have safeguarded himself from one form of impurity but not another? The Gemara answers: **Yes, and it is taught** in a *baraita*: If one was carrying a basket, and **the basket was still on his head,**

Perek **XII**
Daf **99**. Amud **b**

ומגריפה בתוכו, ואמר: "לבי על הסל ואין לבי על המגריפה" – הסל טהור והמגריפה טמאה.

and a shovel[B] was **in the basket, and he said: I am minding the basket,**[H] that it not become impure, **but I am not minding the shovel,** then **the basket is pure, and the shovel is impure.**

ותטמא מגריפה לסל! אין כלי מטמא כלי. ותטמא מה שבתוכו! אמר רבא, באומר: "שמרתיה מדבר המטמאה ולא שמרתיה מדבר הפוסלה".

The Gemara challenges the ruling of the *baraita*: **But** wouldn't **the shovel render the basket impure?** The Gemara answers: There is a principle that **a vessel does not render** another **vessel** ritually **impure.** The Gemara challenges: **But** wouldn't **the shovel render that which is in** the basket, e.g., figs, **impure? Rava said:** The case is **where he says: I safeguarded it,**[N] the shovel, **from anything that** would allow it to **render** another item **impure, but I did not safeguard it from anything that would render it** itself **unfit,**[N] i.e., impure.

איגלגל מילתא ומטאי לקמיה דרבי אבא בר ממל, אמר להו: לא שמיע להו הא דאמר רבי יוחנן אמר רבי: האוכל שלישי של תרומה – אסור לאכול ומותר ליגע.

The Gemara returns to discuss the contradiction between the mishna, which permits an acute mourner to touch sacrificial meat, and the mishna in tractate *Ḥagiga*, which requires him to immerse. The Gemara relates: **The matter circulated and came before Rabbi Abba bar Memel. He said to** the Sages before him: **Have they not heard that which Rabbi Yoḥanan says** that **Rabbi** Yehuda HaNasi **says: One who partakes of** *teruma* that has **third**-degree impurity,[H] i.e., *teruma* disqualified through contact with an item with second-degree impurity, **is prohibited from partaking** of *teruma*, **but permitted to touch** *teruma*.

אלמא: באכילה עבוד רבנן מעלה, בנגיעה לא עבוד רבנן מעלה.

Rabbi Abba bar Memel continued: **Apparently,** in a case of **partaking, the Sages imposed a higher standard,** whereas **in a** case of **touching, the Sages did not impose a higher standard.**[H] Similarly, in a case of an acute mourner, the Sages require him to immerse before he may partake of sacrificial meat, as taught in tractate *Ḥagiga*, but they do not impose this standard for touching the meat, as taught in the mishna here.

"ואינו חולק לאכול" כו'. מיפלג הוא דלא פליג, וכי מזמני ליה – אכיל.

§ The mishna teaches with regard to an acute mourner: **And he does not receive a share** of sacrificial meat in order **to partake** of it in the evening. The Gemara comments: The mishna indicates only that **he may not receive a share** of the meat, **but when** other priests **invite him** to join in their portions, **he may partake** of them in the evening.

BACKGROUND

Shovel – מגריפה: A number of tools are referred to as shovels. When associated with a basket, this is a wood or metal tool with a long handle and wide head used for raking clay. A common secondary use was raking dried figs (Rashi).

HALAKHA

I am minding the basket, etc. – לבי על הסל וכו׳: If a person had a basket on his shoulder, and there was a shovel in the basket, and he said: I safeguarded the shovel from anything that would render it impure, but I did not safeguard it from anything that would render it unfit, then the basket is pure and the shovel is impure. The shovel renders any *teruma* in the basket unfit. This is in accordance with Rava's explanation of the *baraita* (Rambam *Sefer Tahara, Hilkhot Metamei Mishkav UMoshav* 13:6).

One who partakes of *teruma* that has third-degree impurity – האוכל שלישי של תרומה: If one partakes of *teruma*, or non-sacred food that one is accustomed to keep pure like *teruma*, when that food has third-degree impurity, then it is prohibited for him to partake of *teruma* until he immerses. It is permitted for him to touch *teruma*, and any *teruma* that he touches remains pure, because the Sages imposed a higher standard only with regard to partaking. This is in accordance with the statement of Rabbi Yoḥanan, as explained by Rabbi Abba bar Memel (Rambam *Sefer Tahara, Hilkhot She'ar Avot HaTumot* 11:11).

In a case of partaking the Sages imposed a higher standard, etc. – באכילה עבוד רבנן מעלה וכו׳: In the cases of an acute mourner whose period of acute mourning has ended, and one who brought an atonement offering, although the Sages required them to immerse before partaking of sacrificial meat, the Sages did not impose this higher standard with regard to touching sacrificial meat. This is in accordance with the statement of Rabbi Abba bar Memel. Although the Gemara states this only with regard to an acute mourner, the Rambam applies this *halakha* to the case of one who has not yet brought an atonement offering, as the two cases are taught together (Rambam *Sefer Avoda, Hilkhot Biat HaMikdash* 2:8 and *Kesef Mishne* there).

NOTES

I safeguarded it – שמרתיה: The commentary here follows the interpretation of Rashi, who explains that when the person says: I safeguarded it [*shemartiha*], he is referring to safeguarding the shovel. Rava therefore explains why the contents of the basket remain pure.

The Rambam understands that when the person says: I safeguarded it from anything that would allow it to render another item impure, the word: It, refers to the *teruma* inside the basket. In other words, the shovel does render the *teruma* inside unfit, but does not cause it to transmit impurity. Rava's answer to the Gemara's challenge is that the *baraita* discusses impurity alone; and since the unfit *teruma* does not transmit impurity, the *baraita* does not address it (*Kesef Mishne*).

But I did not safeguard it from anything that would render it unfit – ולא שמרתיה מדבר הפוסלה וכו׳: When the *baraita* states that the shovel is impure, it means it is unfit for use with sacrificial food *ab initio*, even though it does not transmit impurity (Rashi; see *Shita Mekubbetzet*). In tractate *Ḥagiga* (20a), Rashi explains that the only consequence of a vessel becoming unfit is that any food that adheres to it also becomes unfit.

וּרְמִינְהִי: אוֹנֵן (וּמְחוּסַּר כִּיפּוּרִים) טוֹבֵל וְאוֹכֵל אֶת פִּסְחוֹ לָעֶרֶב, אֲבָל לֹא בְּקָדָשִׁים!

And the Gemara **raises a contradiction** from a mishna (*Pesaḥim* 91b): **An acute mourner immerses and partakes of his Paschal offering**[BH] **in the evening, but** he may **not** partake **of** other **sacrificial** meat.

אָמַר רַב יִרְמְיָה מִדִּיפְתִּי: לָא קַשְׁיָא, כָּאן – בְּפֶסַח, כָּאן – בִּשְׁאָר יְמוֹת הַשָּׁנָה.

Rav Yirmeya of Difti said: This is **not difficult. Here,** the ruling of the mishna is stated **with regard to** the first night of **Passover,** whereas **there,** in tractate *Pesaḥim*, the ruling of the mishna is stated **with regard to the rest of the days of the year.**

בְּפֶסַח, אַיְּידֵי דְּאָכֵיל פֶּסַח – אָכֵיל נַמִּי קָדָשִׁים. בִּשְׁאָר יְמוֹת הַשָּׁנָה, דְּלָא חֲזֵי – לָא חֲזֵי. וּמַאי ״אֲבָל לֹא בְּקָדָשִׁים״ – אֲבָל לֹא בְּקָדָשִׁים שֶׁל כׇּל הַשָּׁנָה.

What is the reason for the distinction between the two? **On the** first night of **Passover, since he partakes of the Paschal offering, he may also partake of** other **sacrificial** meat. But **on the rest of the days of the year, when he is unfit** to partake of sacrificial meat, **he is unfit. And what** does the mishna in *Pesaḥim* mean when it states: **But** he may **not** partake **of** other **sacrificial** meat? It means: **But** he may **not** partake **of sacrificial** meat **of all** of the rest of **the year,** other than the first night of Passover.

רַב אַסִּי אָמַר: לָא קַשְׁיָא, כָּאן – שֶׁמֵּת לוֹ מֵת בְּאַרְבָּעָה עָשָׂר וּקְבָרוֹ בְּאַרְבָּעָה עָשָׂר, כָּאן – שֶׁמֵּת לוֹ מֵת בִּשְׁלֹשָׁה עָשָׂר וּקְבָרוֹ בְּאַרְבָּעָה עָשָׂר; יוֹם קְבוּרָה לָא תָּפֵיס לֵילוֹ מִדְּרַבָּנַן.

Rav Asi said there is a different resolution to the contradiction between the *mishnayot*: This is **not difficult. Here,** in the ruling of the mishna in tractate *Pesaḥim*, which prohibits an acute mourner from partaking of sacrificial meat, it is referring to a case **where his** relative **died on the fourteenth** day of Nisan, **and he buried him on the fourteenth** itself, in which case he is still considered an acute mourner by rabbinic law that evening. **There,** in the ruling of the mishna in this chapter, it is referring to a case **where his** relative **died on the thirteenth** of Nisan,[H] **and he buried him on the fourteenth** of Nisan. The reason the mourner may partake is that since **the day of burial** is not the day of death, it **does not take hold of its** following **night by rabbinic law.**

מַאן תְּנָא אֲנִינוּת לַיְלָה מִדְּרַבָּנַן – רַבִּי שִׁמְעוֹן הִיא. דְּתַנְיָא: אֲנִינוּת לַיְלָה מִדִּבְרֵי תוֹרָה, דִּבְרֵי רַבִּי יְהוּדָה. רַבִּי שִׁמְעוֹן אוֹמֵר: אוֹנֵן אֵינוֹ מִדִּבְרֵי תוֹרָה אֶלָּא מִדִּבְרֵי סוֹפְרִים. תֵּדַע, שֶׁהֲרֵי אָמְרוּ: אוֹנֵן טוֹבֵל וְאוֹכֵל אֶת פִּסְחוֹ לָעֶרֶב, אֲבָל לֹא בְּקָדָשִׁים.

The Gemara clarifies: **Who is the** *tanna* who **taught** that **acute mourning** the following **night is by rabbinic law,**[H] as opposed to by Torah law? This **is** the opinion of **Rabbi Shimon, as it is taught** in a *baraita*: **Acute mourning at night is by Torah law;** this is **the statement of Rabbi Yehuda. Rabbi Shimon says:** His status as an **acute mourner** at night **is not by Torah law, but by rabbinic law.** Know that this so, as the Sages said:[N] **An acute mourner immerses and partakes of his Paschal offering in the evening, but** he may still **not** partake **of** other **sacrificial** meat. If acute mourning at night were by Torah law, he would not be permitted to partake of the Paschal offering.

וְסָבַר רַבִּי שִׁמְעוֹן אֲנִינוּת לַיְלָה מִדְּרַבָּנַן? וְהָתַנְיָא, רַבִּי שִׁמְעוֹן אוֹמֵר: אוֹנֵן אֵינוֹ מְשַׁלֵּחַ קׇרְבְּנוֹתָיו; מַאי לָאו וַאֲפִילּוּ בְּפֶסַח? לָא, לְבַר מִפֶּסַח.

The Gemara asks: **And does Rabbi Shimon hold** that **acute mourning at night is by rabbinic law** and that consequently an acute mourner partakes of his Paschal offering in the evening? **But isn't it taught** in a *baraita*: **Rabbi Shimon says: An acute mourner does not send his offerings**[H] to the Temple to be sacrificed? **What, is it not** referring **even to a Paschal offering?** The Gemara rejects this: **No,** the *baraita* is referring to all offerings **other than a Paschal offering.**

וְהָתַנְיָא, רַבִּי שִׁמְעוֹן אוֹמֵר: ״שְׁלָמִים״ – כְּשֶׁהוּא שָׁלֵם מֵבִיא, וְאֵינוֹ מֵבִיא כְּשֶׁהוּא אוֹנֵן; מִנַּיִן לְרַבּוֹת אֶת הַתּוֹדָה? מְרַבֶּה אֲנִי אֶת הַתּוֹדָה שֶׁכֵּן נֶאֱכֶלֶת בְּשִׂמְחָה כִּשְׁלָמִים;

The Gemara counters: **But isn't it taught** in a *baraita*: With regard to the verse: "And if his offering be a sacrifice of peace offerings [*shelamim*]" (Leviticus 3:1), **Rabbi Shimon says:** The offering is called ***shelamim*** to teach that **when** a person **is whole** [***shalem***],[N] i.e., in a state of contentment, **he brings** his offering, **but he does not bring it when he is an acute mourner. From where** is it derived **to include** that an acute mourner does not bring even **a thanks offering? I include the thanks offering because it is consumed in** a state of **joy, like a peace offering.**

BACKGROUND

Paschal offering – פֶּסַח: The Torah commands that all adult Jews bring an offering to the Temple on the afternoon of the fourteenth of Nisan to be consumed that evening after nightfall. The Paschal offering, which may be a male lamb or goat in its first year (see Exodus, chapter 12, and Deuteronomy 16:2), is an offering of lesser sanctity and may be slaughtered anywhere within the Temple courtyard. Its blood is poured on the base of the altar. It is brought by groups of individuals acting in partnership, and some of its *halakhot* resemble those of the communal offerings; for example, it is sacrificed even on Shabbat or when the majority of the community is in a state of ritual impurity.

Pilgrims carrying their Paschal offerings after slaughter

HALAKHA

An acute mourner immerses and partakes of his Paschal offering – אוֹנֵן טוֹבֵל וְאוֹכֵל אֶת פִּסְחוֹ: Just as it is prohibited by Torah law for an acute mourner to partake of sacrificial meat on the day of his relative's death, it is prohibited by rabbinic law for him to partake of sacrificial meat the following night. Nevertheless, he may immerse and partake of the Paschal offering at night, as the Sages did not institute a decree in the case of an obligation whose neglect is punished by *karet* (Rambam *Sefer Avoda*, *Hilkhot Biat HaMikdash* 2:8 and *Sefer Korbanot*, *Hilkhot Korban Pesaḥ* 6:9).

His relative died on the thirteenth day of Nisan – מֵת לוֹ מֵת בִּשְׁלֹשָׁה עָשָׂר: One whose relative died and was buried the following day is an acute mourner on the day of burial by rabbinic law. He may not sacrifice or partake of sacred offerings. He immerses and partakes of sacrificial meat in the evening, whether from the Paschal offering or other offerings, in accordance with the opinion of the Rabbis on 100b and Rav Asi (Rambam *Sefer Avoda*, *Hilkhot Biat HaMikdash* 2:10 and *Sefer Korbanot*, *Hilkhot Korban Pesaḥ* 6:9).

Acute mourning at night is by rabbinic law – אֲנִינוּת לַיְלָה מִדְּרַבָּנַן: One whose relative died is an acute mourner by Torah law only on the day of the death, and the following night he is an acute mourner by rabbinic law. The *halakha* is in accordance with the opinion of Rabbi Shimon, because Rabbi Yehuda HaNasi (100b) and the unattributed opinion in tractate *Pesaḥim* (91b) hold in accordance with his opinion (Rambam *Sefer Avoda*, *Hilkhot Biat HaMikdash* 2:9).

An acute mourner does not send his offerings to the Temple to be sacrificed – אוֹנֵן אֵינוֹ מְשַׁלֵּחַ קׇרְבְּנוֹתָיו: A mourner does not send offerings to the Temple during the seven-day mourning period, even voluntary offerings of wine, wood, or frankincense (Rambam *Sefer Avoda*, *Hilkhot Biat HaMikdash* 2:11).

NOTES

Know that this so, as they said, etc. – תֵּדַע שֶׁהֲרֵי אָמְרוּ וכו׳: Rabbi Shimon cites the mishna from *Pesaḥim* 91a to support his opinion in his dispute with Rabbi Yehuda. Rabbi Yehuda holds that the *halakha* does not accord with that mishna. Alternatively, Rabbi Yehuda may explain that although acute mourning at night is by Torah law, the obligation of the Paschal offering overrides it, as neglecting the Paschal offering carries the punishment of *karet*, excision from the World-to-Come (see *Panim Meirot* and *Sefat Emet*).

When a person is whole – כְּשֶׁהוּא שָׁלֵם: Rashi explains in tractate *Moed Katan* (15b) that this means a person must have a settled mind. The *Shita Mekubbetzet* there explains that it means a person's family must be whole, i.e., a relative has not recently died. The text in *Moed Katan*, and more explicitly in the *Tosefta*, teaches Rabbi Shimon's statement not just with regard to the time of acute mourning, but also for the seven-day period of mourning.

מִנַּיִן לְרַבּוֹת אֶת הָעוֹלָה? מְרַבֶּה אֲנִי אֶת הָעוֹלָה, שֶׁכֵּן בָּאָה בְּנֶדֶר וּבִנְדָבָה כִּשְׁלָמִים; מִנַּיִן לְרַבּוֹת [בְּכוֹר וּמַעֲשֵׂר וּפֶסַח? מְרַבֶּה אֲנִי] בְּכוֹר וּמַעֲשֵׂר וּפֶסַח שֶׁכֵּן אֵינָן בָּאִין עַל חֵטְא; מִנַּיִן לְרַבּוֹת חַטָּאת וְאָשָׁם – תַּלְמוּד לוֹמַר: ״זֶבַח״.

From where is it derived that the verse also serves **to include a burnt offering? I include the burnt offering because it comes as** a vow offering **and as a gift** offering, **like a peace offering. From where** is it derived that the verse also serves **to include a firstborn** offering, **and** an animal **tithe** offering, **and a Paschal offering,** which are not brought voluntarily? **I include a firstborn** offering, **and** an animal **tithe** offering, **and a Paschal offering, because they** too, like a peace offering, **do not come** to atone **for a sin. From where** is it derived **to include a sin offering and a guilt offering,** which atone for sins? **The verse states:** "And if his offering be a **sacrifice** [*zevaḥ*] of peace offerings," which teaches that an acute mourner may not sacrifice any slaughtered offering [*zevaḥ*].

מִנַּיִן לְרַבּוֹת הָעוֹפוֹת וְהַמְּנָחוֹת וְהַיַּיִן וְהָעֵצִים וְהַלְּבוֹנָה – תַּלְמוּד לוֹמַר: ״שְׁלָמִים קׇרְבָּנוֹ״, כׇּל קׇרְבָּנוֹת שֶׁהוּא מֵבִיא, כְּשֶׁהוּא שָׁלֵם מֵבִיא, וְאֵינוֹ מֵבִיא כְּשֶׁהוּא אוֹנֵן.

From where is it derived **to include** even **the bird offerings, and the meal offerings, and the wine, and the wood, and the frankincense** brought for the Temple service? **The verse states:** "And if **his offering** be a sacrifice of **peace offerings** [***shelamim korbano***]," teaching that for **all offerings** [***korbanot***] **that** a person **brings, he brings** them **when he is whole** [***shalem***], **but he does not bring** them **when he is an acute mourner.**

קָתָנֵי מִיהָא פֶּסַח!

The Gemara explains: **In any event,** Rabbi Shimon **teaches** that it is prohibited for an acute mourner to bring **a Paschal offering,** even though he will cease to be an acute mourner that night; this contradicts the first *baraita*.

אָמַר רַב חִסְדָּא: פֶּסַח כְּדִי נַסְבֵיהּ.

Rav Ḥisda said: The latter *baraita* mentions **a Paschal offering for no purpose.** In other words, the *halakha* that an acute mourner does not bring an offering does not actually apply to a Paschal offering, and the *baraita* mentions it only out of habit, since a firstborn-animal offering, the animal tithe offering, and a Paschal offering are frequently mentioned together.

רַב שֵׁשֶׁת אָמַר: מַאי ״פֶּסַח״ – שַׁלְמֵי פֶּסַח. אִי הָכִי, הַיְינוּ שְׁלָמִים! תְּנָא שְׁלָמִים הַבָּאִין מֵחֲמַת פֶּסַח, וּתְנָא שְׁלָמִים הַבָּאִין מֵחֲמַת עַצְמָן.

Rav Sheshet said: What is meant in this *baraita* by the term: **Paschal offering?** It is referring to **the peace offerings of Passover,**[N] i.e., the peace offering that is sacrificed along with the Paschal offering. The Gemara objects: **If so,** that **is** the same as **a peace offering,** which Rabbi Shimon already mentioned. The Gemara answers: He **taught** the *halakha* with regard to **peace offerings that come on account of** the **Paschal offering, and he taught** separately the *halakha* with regard to **peace offerings that come on their own account.**

דְּאִי לָא תְּנָא שְׁלָמִים הַבָּאִין מֵחֲמַת פֶּסַח – סָלְקָא דַּעְתָּךְ אָמֵינָא: הוֹאִיל וּמֵחֲמַת פֶּסַח אָתֵי – כְּגוּפֵיהּ דְּפֶסַח דָּמֵי, קָא מַשְׁמַע לַן.

The Gemara explains: Rabbi Shimon needed to teach both cases explicitly, **because if he did not teach** the *halakha* with regard to **peace offerings that come on account of** the **Paschal offering,** it would **enter your mind to say: Since they come on account of the Paschal offering, they are considered like** the **Paschal offering itself,** and the acute mourner offers them as well. Therefore, Rabbi Shimon **teaches us** that these peace offerings are also forbidden to an acute mourner.

רַב מָרִי אָמַר:

Rav Mari said a different resolution to the contradiction between the statements of Rabbi Shimon:

NOTES

The peace offerings of Passover – שַׁלְמֵי פֶּסַח: Rashi here explains that this refers to peace offerings that were brought with the Paschal offering. Large groups of people sharing a Paschal offering would fulfill their obligation of consuming it on a full stomach by partaking of meat of peace offerings first (see *Pesaḥim* 70a). Rashi in tractate *Rosh HaShana* (5a) explains that this refers to an offering that was set aside as a Paschal offering but was ultimately not used for that purpose, which is brought as a peace offering.

Pilgrims in Jerusalem partaking of a peace offering and Paschal offering

לָא קַשְׁיָא, כָּאן – שֶׁמֵּת לוֹ מֵת בְּאַרְבָּעָה עָשָׂר וּקְבָרוֹ בְּאַרְבָּעָה עָשָׂר, כָּאן – שֶׁמֵּת לוֹ מֵת בִּשְׁלֹשָׁה עָשָׂר וּקְבָרוֹ בְּאַרְבָּעָה עָשָׂר.

It is **not difficult. Here,** in the *baraita* where Rabbi Shimon holds an acute mourner may not send a Paschal offering, since acute mourning at night is by Torah law, it is referring to a case **where his** relative **died on the fourteenth** day of Nisan **and he buried him on the fourteenth** itself. **There,** the ruling in the mishna in tractate *Pesaḥim,* which teaches that an acute mourner immerses and partakes of the Paschal offering in the evening, since acute mourning at night is by rabbinic law, is referring to a case **where his** relative **died on the thirteenth** day of Nisan **and he buried him on the fourteenth** of Nisan.

מֵת לוֹ מֵת בְּאַרְבָּעָה עָשָׂר וּקְבָרוֹ בְּאַרְבָּעָה עָשָׂר – יוֹם מִיתָה תּוֹפֵס לֵילוֹ מִדְּאוֹרַיְיתָא. מֵת לוֹ מֵת בִּשְׁלֹשָׁה עָשָׂר וּקְבָרוֹ בְּאַרְבָּעָה עָשָׂר – יוֹם קְבוּרָה מִדְּרַבָּנַן, אֵינוֹ תּוֹפֵס לֵילוֹ אֶלָּא מִדְּרַבָּנַן.

Rav Mari explains: In a case where **his** relative **died on the fourteenth** day of Nisan **and he buried him on the fourteenth** itself, his acute mourning is due to **the day of death** and is therefore by Torah law. Consequently, it **takes hold of its** following **night by Torah law,** and the mitzva of the Paschal offering does not override it. By contrast, in a case where **his** relative **died on the thirteenth** day of Nisan **and he buried him on the fourteenth** of Nisan, the fourteenth is only **the day of burial,** and his acute mourning is therefore **by rabbinic law.** Consequently, **it takes hold of its** following **night only by rabbinic law,** and the mitzva of the Paschal offering overrides it.

אֲמַר לֵיהּ רַב אַשִׁי לְרַב מָרִי: וְאֶלָּא הָא דְּקָתָנֵי, אָמַר לוֹ רַבִּי שִׁמְעוֹן: תֵּדַע, שֶׁהֲרֵי אָמְרוּ: אוֹנֵן טוֹבֵל וְאוֹכֵל אֶת פִּסְחוֹ אֲבָל לֹא בְּקָדָשִׁים. נֵימָא לֵיהּ: קָאָמִינָא לָךְ אֲנָא יוֹם מִיתָה דְּאוֹרַיְיתָא, וְאָמְרַתְּ לִי אַתְּ יוֹם קְבוּרָה דְּרַבָּנַן! קַשְׁיָא.

Rav Ashi said to Rav Mari: But if so, it is difficult to understand **that which** the *baraita* **teaches: Rabbi Shimon said to** Rabbi Yehuda: **Know** that this so, as the Sages **said: An acute mourner immerses** on the fourteenth of Nisan **and partakes of his Paschal offering** in the evening, **but** he may **not** partake **of** other **sacrificial** meat. According to your explanation of this statement, **let** Rabbi Yehuda **say to** Rabbi Shimon that this is no proof: **I am telling you** a *halakha* about **the day of death,** when acute mourning is **by Torah law, and you tell me** that you have a proof from a mishna that deals with **the day of burial,** when acute mourning is **by rabbinic law.** The Gemara concludes: This indeed poses **a difficulty** for Rav Mari.

אַבַּיֵי אֲמַר: לָא קַשְׁיָא, כָּאן – שֶׁמֵּת קוֹדֶם חֲצוֹת, כָּאן – שֶׁמֵּת לְאַחַר חֲצוֹת. קוֹדֶם חֲצוֹת, דְּלָא אִיחֲזֵי לְפֶסַח – חָיְילָא עֲלֵיהּ אֲנִינוּת, אַחַר חֲצוֹת, דְּאִיחֲזֵי לְפֶסַח – לָא חָיְילָא עֲלֵיהּ אֲנִינוּת.

Abaye said a different resolution to the contradiction between the statements of Rabbi Shimon: It is **not difficult. Here,** in the *baraita* where Rabbi Shimon holds that an acute mourner may not send a Paschal offering, it is referring to a case **where** his relative **died before midday**[H] on the fourteenth of Nisan. **There,** the ruling in the mishna in tractate *Pesaḥim,* which teaches that an acute mourner immerses and partakes of the Paschal offering in the evening, it is a case **where** his relative **died after midday** on the fourteenth of Nisan. When his relative died **before midday,** in which case **he was not** ever **fit for** bringing **a Paschal offering** since the obligation begins at midday, the status of **acute mourning applies to him,** and it is prohibited for him to bring a Paschal offering. But if his relative dies **after midday, when he is** already **fit for** bringing **a Paschal offering,** the status of **acute mourning does not apply to him** with regard to this matter, so he may immerse and partake of the Paschal offering in the evening.

וּמְנָא תֵּימְרָא דְּשַׁנֵּי לֵיהּ בֵּין קוֹדֶם חֲצוֹת בֵּין לְאַחַר חֲצוֹת? דְּתַנְיָא: ״לָהּ יִטַּמָּא״ – מִצְוָה, לֹא רָצָה – מְטַמְּאִין אוֹתוֹ עַל כָּרְחוֹ. וּמַעֲשֶׂה בְּיוֹסֵף הַכֹּהֵן שֶׁמֵּתָה אִשְׁתּוֹ בְּעֶרֶב הַפֶּסַח וְלֹא רָצָה לִיטַּמֵּא, וְנִמְנוּ אֶחָיו הַכֹּהֲנִים וְטִימְּאוּהוּ בְּעַל כָּרְחוֹ.

The Gemara explains: **And from where do you say that** the *halakha* **is different** depending on **whether** his relative died **before midday** on the fourteenth of Nisan or **whether** he died **after midday? As it is taught** in a *baraita*: The Torah states with regard to a priest: "And for his sister a virgin, that is near unto him, that has had no husband, **for her may he become impure**" (Leviticus 21:3). From here it is derived that it is **a mitzva** for a priest to become impure in order to bury his deceased relatives, and if he **did not want** to do so, others must **render him impure against his will.**[H] **And an incident** occurred **involving Yosef the priest, where his wife died on Passover eve, and he did not want to become impure,** as he wanted to offer the Paschal offering; **and his brethren the priests voted and rendered him impure against his will.**

HALAKHA

Where his relative died before midday, etc. – שֶׁמֵּת קוֹדֶם חֲצוֹת וכו׳: A Paschal offering is slaughtered for an acute mourner, and he partakes of it in the evening. This is the *halakha* when his relative died after midday on the fourteenth of Nisan, since the acute mourner had already become obligated to fulfill the mitzva of the Paschal offering. But if his relative died before midday, a Paschal offering is not slaughtered for him, and he fulfills the mitzva with the second Pesaḥ, one month later on the fourteenth of Iyyar. This is in accordance with the opinion of Abaye (Rambam *Sefer Korbanot, Hilkhot Korban Pesaḥ* 6:9).

If he did not want to do so, others must render him impure against his will – לֹא רָצָה מְטַמְּאִין אוֹתוֹ עַל כָּרְחוֹ: A priest must become impure to bury his deceased wife, even if he does not want to do so. This obligation is by rabbinic law (Rambam *Sefer Shofetim, Hilkhot Evel* 2:7; *Shulḥan Arukh, Yoreh De'a* 373:3–4).

וּרְמִינְהִי: "וּלְאַחוֹתוֹ" מַה תַּלְמוּד לוֹמַר? הֲרֵי שֶׁהָלַךְ לִשְׁחוֹט אֶת פִּסְחוֹ וְלָמוּל אֶת בְּנוֹ, וְשָׁמַע שֶׁמֵּת לוֹ מֵת, יָכוֹל יִטַּמֵּא? אָמַרְתָּ: "לֹא יִטַּמָּא".

And the Sages raise a contradiction from another *baraita*: **What** is the meaning when **the verse states** with regard to a nazirite: "He shall not become impure for his father, or for his mother, for his brother, **or for his sister** when they die; because his consecration unto God is upon his head" (Numbers 6:7)? If a nazirite **went to slaughter his Paschal offering or to circumcise his son,**[N] mitzvot for which failure to fulfill them is punishable by *karet*, **and he heard that** a relative **of his died,** one **might** have thought that he should **become impure** in order to bury his relative even if this will result in his not bringing the Paschal offering. **You** rather **say,** based on this verse, that **"he shall not become impure."**

יָכוֹל כְּשֵׁם שֶׁלֹּא יִטַּמֵּא לַאֲחוֹתוֹ כָּךְ אֵין מִטַּמֵּא לְמֵת מִצְוָה? תַּלְמוּד לוֹמַר: "וּלְאַחוֹתוֹ" – לַאֲחוֹתוֹ הוּא דְּאֵינוֹ מִטַּמֵּא, אֲבָל מִטַּמֵּא הוּא לְמֵת מִצְוָה.

One **might** have thought that **just as he may not become impure** to bury **his sister, so too he may not become impure to** bury **a corpse with no one to bury it** [*met mitzva*].[B] **The verse states: "Or for his sister,"** teaching that **it is** only **to** bury **his sister that he may not become impure, but he does become impure to** bury **a** ***met mitzva*.**

לָאו שְׁמַע מִינָּהּ: כָּאן – קוֹדֶם חֲצוֹת, כָּאן – לְאַחַר חֲצוֹת?

In the first *baraita*, contracting impurity from a dead relative is obligatory, and in the second *baraita* it is forbidden. Do you **not learn from** this contradiction that there must be a distinction between the cases? **Here,** in the first *baraita* concerning a priest, it must be referring to a case where the relative died **before midday,** so he was obligated to become impure before the obligation for the Paschal offering took effect. **There,** in the second *baraita* concerning a nazirite, it must be referring to a case where the relative died **after midday.** This distinction, between death before and after midday, also applies to acute mourning.

מִמַּאי? דִּילְמָא לְעוֹלָם אֵימָא לָךְ: אִידִי וְאִידִי אַחַר חֲצוֹת, וְהָא – רַבִּי יִשְׁמָעֵאל, וְהָא – רַבִּי עֲקִיבָא. דְּתַנְיָא: "לָהּ יִטַּמָּא" – רְשׁוּת, דִּבְרֵי רַבִּי יִשְׁמָעֵאל. רַבִּי עֲקִיבָא אוֹמֵר: חוֹבָה!

The Gemara rejects this explanation: **From where** do you infer that this is the resolution to the contradiction? **Actually, perhaps I will say to you:** Both **this** *baraita* **and that** *baraita* are discussing deaths that occurred **after midday. And this** *baraita*, about a nazirite, is in accordance with the opinion of **Rabbi Yishmael, and that** *baraita*, about Yosef the priest, is in accordance with the opinion of **Rabbi Akiva. As it is taught** in a *baraita*: The Torah states with regard to a priest: "And for his sister a virgin, that is near unto him, that has had no husband, **for her may he become impure"** (Leviticus 21:3). This is **optional,** i.e., a priest is not obligated to become impure to bury his sister; this is **the statement of Rabbi Yishmael. Rabbi Akiva says:** It is **mandatory.**

לָא סָלְקָא דַּעְתָּךְ, דְּרֵישָׁא דְּהַהִיא רַבִּי עֲקִיבָא קָתָנֵי לַהּ. דְּתַנְיָא, רַבִּי עֲקִיבָא אוֹמֵר: "נֶפֶשׁ" – אֵלּוּ הַקְּרוֹבִים, "מֵת" – אֵלּוּ הָרְחוֹקִים,

The Gemara responds: This should **not enter your mind, because** it is **Rabbi Akiva** who **teaches the first clause of** the *baraita* about a nazirite. **As it is taught** in the full version of that *baraita*: The Torah states: "All the days that he consecrates himself unto the Lord he shall not come near to a dead body. He shall not become impure for his father, or for his mother, for his brother, or for his sister when they die; because his consecration unto God is upon his head" (Numbers 6:7). **Rabbi Akiva says:** The term **"body [*nefesh*]"** is referring to **relatives.**[N] The term **"dead [*met*]"** is referring to **non-relatives.**

NOTES

Or to circumcise his son – וְלָמוּל אֶת בְּנוֹ: Rashi explains that circumcising his son is necessary for sacrificing the Paschal offering, because one who has an uncircumcised male in his household is not permitted to bring the Paschal offering.

Body is referring to relatives – נֶפֶשׁ אֵלּוּ הַקְּרוֹבִים: Rashi explains that the meaning of the words *"nefesh"* and *"met"* do not themselves specify relatives and non-relatives. Rather, once there are two words, one of which refers to relatives and the other to non-relatives, it is reasonable that *"nefesh,"* which also means soul, refers to those who are related to the nazirite, as they are closest to his soul.

BACKGROUND

A corpse with no one to bury it [*met mitzva*] – מֵת מִצְוָה: It is an important religious obligation to take part in the burial of the dead. If the deceased has no friends or relatives to bury him, everyone is obligated to assist in his burial. According to the *halakha*, a corpse with no one available to bury it acquires its place, i.e., the body must be interred where it was found. This is the *halakha* provided that it is an honorable location; otherwise, the body must be buried in the nearest cemetery. This religious duty is so important that even priests and nazirites, who are ordinarily prohibited to come in contact with a corpse, must bury a deserted corpse if there is no one else available to bury it. Similarly, the obligation to bury this corpse takes precedence over nearly all other religious obligations.

"לאביו" – אינו מטמא, אבל מטמא הוא למת מצוה. "לאמו" – היה כהן והוא נזיר, לאמו הוא דאינו מטמא, אבל מטמא הוא למת מצוה. "לאחיו" – שאם היה כהן גדול והוא נזיר, לאחיו הוא דאינו מטמא, אבל מטמא הוא למת מצוה.

The verse specifies: **"For his father,"** even though his father is included among his relatives, to teach that **he may not become impure** to bury his father, **but he does become impure to bury a** ***met mitzva.*** The verse states: **"For his mother,"** to teach that even if **he was a priest and he was a nazirite,** and therefore doubly prohibited from becoming impure, nevertheless, **he may not become impure to bury his mother but he does become impure to** bury a ***met mitzva.*** The verse states: **"For his brother,"** to teach **that** even **if he was a High Priest,** who may not become impure even for his relatives, **and he** was also **a nazirite,** nevertheless, **he may not become impure to** bury **his brother but he does become impure to** bury **a** ***met mitzva.***[H]

"ולאחותו" – מה תלמוד לומר? הרי שהלך לשחוט את פסחו ולמול את בנו, ושמע שמת לו מת, יכול יטמא? אמרת: "לא יטמא". יכול כשם שאין מטמא לאחותו כך אינו מטמא למת מצוה? תלמוד לומר "ולאחותו", לאחותו לא יטמא, אבל יטמא הוא למת מצוה.

What is the meaning when **the verse states: "Or for his sister"?** If a nazirite **went to slaughter his Paschal offering or to circumcise his son, and he heard that** a relative **of his died,** one **might** have thought that he should **become impure. You** rather **say** that **he may not become impure.** One **might** have thought that **just as he may not become impure to** bury **his sister, so too he may not become impure to bury a** ***met mitzva.*** **The verse states: "Or for his sister,"** to teach that **he may not become impure to** bury **his sister but he does become impure to** bury **a** ***met mitzva.*** **Consequently,** the statement of the *baraita* concerning a nazirite represents the opinion of Rabbi Akiva.

HALAKHA

He does become impure to bury a ***met mitzva*** **– מטמא הוא למת מצוה:** It is a mitzva for one to become impure to bury a corpse that has no one else to bury it. Even if one is a High Priest and a nazirite, and on his way to bring the Paschal offering or to circumcise his son, he becomes impure in order to bury the corpse (Rambam *Sefer Shofetim, Hilkhot Evel* 3:8; *Shulḥan Arukh, Yoreh De'a* 374:1).

Perek XII
Daf 100 Amud b

רבא אמר: אידי ואידי אחר חצות, ולא קשיא: כאן – קודם ששחטו וזרקו עליו, כאן – לאחר ששחטו וזרקו עליו.

Rava said there is a different resolution to the contradiction between the statements of Rabbi Shimon. Both **this** *baraita* **and that** *baraita* are discussing cases where the relative died **after midday**[N] on the fourteenth of Nisan, **and** still it is **not difficult. Here,** his relative died **before** the priests would have **slaughtered** the Paschal offering **and sprinkled**[H] its blood **on his account,** and he may not send the offering. **There,** the relative died **after** the priests **slaughtered** the Paschal offering **and sprinkled** its blood **on his account.** Since acute mourning at night is by rabbinic law, it is suspended to allow him to consume an offering that was already sacrificed.

אמר ליה רב אדא בר מתנה לרבא: אחר ששחטו וזרקו את דמו – מה דהוה הוה! אמר ליה רבינא: אכילת פסחים מעכבא, מדרבה בר רב הונא. אמר ליה: צייית מאי דקאמר לך רבך.

Rav Adda bar Mattana said to Rava: In a case where one's relative died **after** the priests **slaughtered** the Paschal offering **and sprinkled its blood,** why should he be permitted to partake of the Paschal offering? **What was, was,** and although the offering was sacrificed, isn't he still an acute mourner by rabbinic law? **Ravina said to** Rav Adda bar Mattana: **Partaking of the Paschal offering is indispensable** for the mitzva, as is seen **from that which Rabba bar Rav Huna** taught, as the Gemara will explain. Therefore, the Sages did not prohibit the acute mourner from partaking of the Paschal offering as they do for other offerings, for which consumption of the meat is dispensable. Rava **said to** Rav Adda bar Mattana: **Listen to what your master,** Ravina, **told you,** as his explanation is correct.

HALAKHA

Here his relative died before the priests slaughtered and sprinkled, etc. – כאן קודם ששחטו וזרקו וכו׳: If one's relative died before midday on the eve of Passover, the Paschal offering is not slaughtered for him. But if the offering is slaughtered and its blood sprinkled, then he immerses and partakes of his Paschal offering in the evening (Rambam *Sefer Korbanot, Hilkhot Korban Pesaḥ* 6:9).

NOTES

Both this and that are where the relative died after midday – אידי ואידי אחר חצות: Rashi explains that Rava, like Abaye, understands that Rabbi Shimon holds that acute mourning at night is by rabbinic law, and that an acute mourner is prohibited from sending a Paschal offering. This dispute is that Abaye says that the obligation of the Paschal offering overrides the prohibition if the relative dies after midday. According to Rava, the obligation does not override the prohibition; the mishna in *Pesaḥim* permits an acute mourner to partake of the Paschal offering only if the blood of the offering is sprinkled before the relative dies.

The Rambam understands that Abaye and Rava agree that an acute mourner sends a Paschal offering if his relative dies after midday. Rava's distinction of whether the relative dies before or after the sprinkling of the blood applies only if the relative died before midday (*Kesef Mishne*). A number of commentaries therefore assume that the Rambam had a different version of the text, which reads: This *baraita* and that mishna are discussing a case where the relative died before midday on the fourteenth of Nisan (*Ḥok Natan*; *Haggahot HaGra*; see *Or Same'aḥ*).

מַאי דְּרַבָּה בַּר רַב הוּנָא? דְּתַנְיָא: יוֹם שְׁמוּעָה כְּיוֹם קְבוּרָה לְמִצְוַת שִׁבְעָה וּשְׁלֹשִׁים, וְלַאֲכִילַת פְּסָחִים – כְּיוֹם לִיקּוּט עֲצָמוֹת. אֶחָד זֶה וְאֶחָד זֶה טוֹבֵל וְאוֹכֵל בַּקֳּדָשִׁים לָעֶרֶב.

What is the statement of **Rabba bar Rav Huna** that teaches that partaking of the Paschal offering is indispensable? **As it is taught** in a *baraita*: **The day** that a person receives **tidings**[N] that his relative died is considered **as if it were the day of burial**[H] with regard **to the mitzva of** the **seven**-day mourning period, when he may not bathe or wear shoes, **and** with regard to the **thirty**-day period when he may not wear ironed garments. **And with regard to partaking of the Paschal offering**, the day he receives the tidings is **like the day of the gathering of** the **bones**[NB] of the deceased after the flesh decomposed (see *Pesaḥim* 92a). In **both this and that** case, **he immerses and partakes of sacrificial** meat **in the evening.**[H]

הָא גּוּפָא קַשְׁיָא: אָמְרַתְּ יוֹם שְׁמוּעָה כְּיוֹם קְבוּרָה לְמִצְוַת שִׁבְעָה וּשְׁלֹשִׁים, וְלַאֲכִילַת פְּסָחִים כְּיוֹם לִיקּוּט עֲצָמוֹת. מִכְּלָל דְּיוֹם קְבוּרָה – אֲפִילּוּ לָעֶרֶב נַמִי לָא אָכֵיל. וַהֲדַר תָּנֵי: אֶחָד זֶה וְאֶחָד זֶה טוֹבֵל וְאוֹכֵל בַּקֳּדָשִׁים לָעֶרֶב!

The Gemara challenges: **This** *baraita* **itself** is **difficult.** At first **you say: The day of tidings** is considered **as if it were the day of burial for the mitzva of the seven**-day **and thirty**-day mourning periods; **and with regard to partaking of** the **Paschal offering,** it is **like the day of the gathering of bones,** when one may immerse and partake of sacrificial meat in the evening. **By inference,** one concludes **that** on **the day of burial,** he may **not partake** of the Paschal offering **even in the evening,** and all the more so other sacrificial meat. **And then** it is **taught:** In **both this and that** case, i.e., on both the day of burial and the day of the gathering of bones, **he immerses and partakes of sacrificial** meat **in the evening.**

אֲמַר רַב חִסְדָּא: תַּנָּאֵי הִיא.

Rav Ḥisda said: Whether it is permitted to partake of sacrificial meat the night after the day of burial **is a dispute between** ***tanna'im***, as the Gemara will explain.

רַבָּה בַּר רַב הוּנָא אֲמַר: לָא קַשְׁיָא; כָּאן – שֶׁשָּׁמַע שְׁמוּעָה עַל מֵתוֹ סָמוּךְ לִשְׁקִיעַת הַחַמָּה, וְכֵן שֶׁלִּיקְּטוּ לוֹ עֲצָמוֹת סָמוּךְ לִשְׁקִיעַת הַחַמָּה, וְכֵן שֶׁמֵּת לוֹ מֵת וּקְבָרוֹ סָמוּךְ לִשְׁקִיעַת הַחַמָּה. וְכָאן – לְאַחַר שְׁקִיעַת הַחַמָּה.

Rabba bar Rav Huna said: This is **not difficult. Here,** in the latter clause, where the *baraita* teaches that on both the day of burial and the day of the gathering of bones he immerses and partakes of sacrificial meat in the evening, it is referring to a case **where he heard tidings of his dead** relative **just before sunset, and likewise** a case **where they gathered** the **bones for him just before sunset, and likewise** a case **where his** relative **died and he buried him just before sunset. But there,** in the first clause, from which it is inferred that he may not consume any sacrificial meat the night after the day of burial, the burial occurred **after sunset,**[N] i.e., on the night of the fifteenth of Nisan itself.

לְאַחַר שְׁקִיעַת הַחַמָּה מַאי דַּהֲוָה הֲוָה! אֶלָּא שְׁמַע מִינָּהּ: אֲכִילַת פְּסָחִים מְעַכְּבָא.

The Gemara objects: If so, why not say that even if he gathered bones **after sunset,** then **what was, was?** Why did the Sages permit him to partake of the Paschal offering, as opposed to other sacrificial meat? **Rather, learn from** this *baraita* that **partaking of the Paschal offering is indispensable** to fulfilling the obligation, and due to the severity of the mitzva, the Sages suspended their decree prohibiting one from partaking of it.

BACKGROUND

Gathering of bones – לִיקּוּט עֲצָמוֹת: In the period of the Second Temple and for hundreds of years thereafter, the custom was to bury the deceased in the ground temporarily and to wait a few years until all the flesh decayed. The bones would then be collected and placed in a stone ossuary, which was then placed in a niche in a family burial cave.

Interior of a burial cave unearthed in Beit She'arim, Israel

Ossuary from the Second Temple period

NOTES

The day that a person receives tidings – יוֹם שְׁמוּעָה: If one received tidings of his relative's death within thirty days of the day of death, he observes all the *halakhot* of mourning, including rending his garments, the seven-day mourning period, and the thirty-day mourning period. If a person received tidings more than thirty days after his relative's death, he performs a symbolic gesture of mourning, e.g., removing his shoes or overturning his bed (see *Moed Katan* 20a and Jerusalem Talmud, *Pesaḥim* 8:8).

Like the day of the gathering of bones – כְּיוֹם לִיקּוּט עֲצָמוֹת: This refers to a case where others gathered one's relative's bones for him, because if he gathered the bones himself, he would be impure for seven days and would need to undergo sprinkling with water of purification (*Pesaḥim* 92a).

After sunset – לְאַחַר שְׁקִיעַת הַחַמָּה: In other words, if one received tidings of a relative's death after sunset or his parent's bones were gathered after sunset, he may nevertheless partake of the Paschal offering in the evening, though he may not partake of other sacrificial meat. This is not so for burial: If one's relative was buried during the evening of Passover, e.g., by gentiles, then he may not consume his Paschal offering, as it is considered the day of burial.

Rashi explains that the relative must have died on the thirteenth of Nisan and was buried on the fourteenth, because if he died on the fourteenth, then the evening following the fourteenth would be the night following the day of death, and the mourner would be forbidden to partake of the Paschal offering in any event.

Rabbeinu Ḥananel explains the resolution differently. The first clause of the *baraita* refers to a case where the relative was buried before sunset. In this case, acute mourning overrides the obligation of the Paschal offering, and the mourner does not partake of it in the evening. The second clause of the *baraita* refers to a case where the relative was buried after sunset, when the obligation to eat the Paschal offering had already taken effect, so the acute mourning does not override it.

HALAKHA

The day a person receives tidings that his relative died is as if it were the day of burial – יוֹם שְׁמוּעָה כְּיוֹם קְבוּרָה: If one received tidings that his relative died within thirty days of the death, he must rend his garments and observe the seven- and thirty-day mourning periods (Rambam *Sefer Shofetim, Hilkhot Evel* 7:1; *Shulḥan Arukh, Yoreh De'a* 402:1).

In both this and that case he immerses and partakes of sacrificial meat in the evening – אֶחָד זֶה וְאֶחָד זֶה טוֹבֵל וְאוֹכֵל בַּקֳּדָשִׁים לָעֶרֶב: The day upon which one receives tidings that his relative died and the day of the gathering of bones of his relative for burying are considered like the day of burial. Therefore, if one of these days falls on the fourteenth of Nisan a Paschal offering is slaughtered for him, and he immerses and partakes of it in the evening. This is in accordance with the opinion of the Rabbis, who say that the day of burial does not take hold of its following night (Rambam *Sefer Avoda, Hilkhot Biat HaMikdash* 2:10 and *Sefer Korbanot, Hilkhot Korban Pesaḥ* 6:9).

רב אשי אמר: מאי "אחד זה ואחד זה" – הכי קאמר: אחד יום שמועה ואחד יום ליקוט – טובל ואוכל בקדשים לערב.

Rav Ashi said there is another resolution to this question: **What** is meant by the latter clause in the *baraita*: In **both this and that** case? It does not mean both the day of burial and the day of the gathering of bones. Rather, **this** is what the *baraita* **is saying: Both** on **the day of tidings and** on **the day of** the **gathering** of bones, the mourner **immerses and partakes of sacrificial** meat **in the evening.** But after the day of burial, he may not partake of the Paschal offering, and all the more so of other sacrificial meat, as indicated in the first clause in the *baraita*.

והא דרב אשי בדותא היא; מכדי עלה קאי, "זה וזה" מיבעי ליה. אלא שמע מינה בדותא היא.

The Gemara notes: **And this** resolution **of Rav Ashi is a mistake, since** the *tanna* is already **discussing those** two cases and equating them. According to Rav Ashi's resolution, it is extraneous to say: In both this and that case; the *tanna* **should have** simply said: In **this and that** case. **Rather, learn from** the language of the *baraita* that Rav Ashi's resolution **is a mistake.**

ומאי תנאי? דתניא: עד מתי מתאונן עליו – כל היום, רבי אומר: כל זמן שלא נקבר.

The Gemara returns to discuss Rav Ḥisda's resolution: **And what** is the dispute between ***tanna'im*** with regard to the night following the day of burial? **As it is taught** in a *baraita*: **Until when does a person mourn acutely for** his relative, such that he is prohibited to partake of sacrificial meat? **The entire day. Rabbi** Yehuda HaNasi **says: As long as** his relative **has not been buried.**

במאי עסקינן? אילימא ביום מיתה, מי איכא דלית ליה דיום מיתה דתפיס לילו מדרבנן?

The Gemara asks: **What are we dealing with? If we say** we are dealing **with the day of death, is there** a *tanna* **who does not hold that the day of death takes hold of its** following **night,** at least **by rabbinic law?** In accordance with whose opinion is the statement of the first *tanna*, who says that the acute mourning is only during the day, and not at night?

ותו, רבי אומר: כל זמן שלא נקבר; הא קברו – אישתרי ליה. ומי איכא דלית ליה "ואחריתה כיום מר"?

And furthermore, if we are dealing with the day of death, then when **Rabbi** Yehuda HaNasi **says: As long as** his relative **has not been buried,** it indicates that **consequently,** once he **has buried him, it becomes permitted for him** to partake of sacrificial meat, even on the day of death itself. **But is there** a *tanna* **who does not hold** that acute mourning extends for the entire day of death, even after burial? The verse states: "And I will turn your feasts into mourning, and all your songs into lamentation; and I will bring up sackcloth upon all loins, and baldness upon every head; and I will make it as the mourning for an only son, **and the end thereof as a bitter day**" (Amos 8:10).

אמר רב ששת: איום קבורה קאי.

Rav Sheshet said: The *tanna* of this *baraita* is **discussing the day of burial** when it is not the day of death. The *tanna'im* disagree whether the acute mourning lasts only until the burial, or until the end of the day of burial.

מתקיף רב יוסף: אלא הא דקתני: השומע על מתו כמלקט עצמות, טובל ואוכל בקדשים לערב; מכלל דיום קבורה – אפילו לערב נמי לא אכיל, הא מני? אלא תריץ: עד מתי מתאוננין עליו – כל אותו היום ולילו. רבי אומר: כל זמן שלא נקבר. [אבל נקבר] – בלא לילו.

Rav Yosef objects to this: **But** there is **that which is taught** in a *baraita*: **One who hears** tidings **of his dead** relative is considered **as one who gathers** his relative's **bones,** in that he may **immerse and partake of sacrificial** meat **in the evening. By inference,** on **the day of burial he may not partake even in the evening.** In accordance with **whose** opinion **is this?** This is the opinion of neither the first *tanna* nor Rabbi Yehuda HaNasi. **Rather,** one must **answer** that the *baraita* means: **Until when** does a person **mourn acutely for** his relative? **That entire day** of burial **and its** following **night. Rabbi** Yehuda HaNasi **says:** He continues into the night only **as long as** his relative **has not been buried; but** once he **is buried,** the acute mourning lasts only for the rest of the day, **without its night.**

אמרוה קמיה דרבי ירמיה, אמר: גברא רבה כרב יוסף לימא הכי? לימא דרבי לקולא? והתניא: עד מתי מתאונן עליו – כל זמן שאינו נקבר, אפילו מכאן ועד עשרה ימים, דברי רבי. וחכמים אומרים: אין מתאונן עליו אלא אותו היום בלבד!

The Sages **said this** statement of Rav Yosef **before Rabbi Yirmeya.** Rabbi Yirmeya **said** in surprise: **Would a great man like Rav Yosef say this? Would he say** that the opinion **of Rabbi** Yehuda HaNasi is the more **lenient** of the two? **But isn't it taught** in a *baraita*: **Until when** does a person **mourn acutely for** his relative? **As long as** his relative **has not been buried, even** if he remains unburied **from now until ten days** from now. This is **the statement of Rabbi** Yehuda HaNasi. **And the Sages say: He mourns acutely for** his relative **only on that** same **day.** The opinion of Rabbi Yehuda HaNasi is more stringent than that of the Sages.

אלא תריץ הכי: עד מתי הוא מתאונן עליו – כל אותו היום בלא לילו. רבי אומר: כל זמן שלא נקבר, ואם נקבר – תופס לילו.

Rather, answer like this: Until when does a person **mourn acutely**[H] for his relative? **That entire day** of burial, **without its night. Rabbi** Yehuda HaNasi **says:** The acute mourning continues **as long as** his relative **has not been buried,** even for ten days, **and once he is buried,** that day **takes hold of its night.** This is the dispute to which Rav Ḥisda referred.

אמרוה קמיה דרבא: מדקאמר רבי יום קבורה תופס לילו מדרבנן – מכלל דיום מיתה תופס לילו מדאורייתא.

The Sages **said this** statement **before Rava.** Rava said: **Since Rabbi** Yehuda HaNasi **says** that **the day of burial,** when acute mourning is by rabbinic law, **takes hold of its night by rabbinic law, by inference,** he must hold **that the day of death,** when acute mourning is by Torah law, **takes hold of its night by Torah law.** The Sages would not be more stringent with their ordinance than the parallel law of the Torah.

וסבר רבי אנינות לילה דאורייתא? והתניא: "הן היום" – אני היום אסור ולילה מותר, ולדורות – בין ביום ובין בלילה אסור, דברי רבי יהודה. רבי אומר: אנינות לילה אינה מדברי תורה אלא מדברי סופרים!

The Gemara objects: **And does Rabbi** Yehuda HaNasi **hold** that **acute mourning at night is by Torah law? But isn't it taught** in a *baraita*: On the last day of the inauguration of the Tabernacle,[B] after two of Aaron's sons died, Aaron said to Moses: **"Behold,** today… there have befallen me such things as these; and if I had consumed the sin offering today, would it have been good in the eyes of the Lord?" (Leviticus 10:19). The word "today" teaches that Aaron is saying: **I am prohibited** from partaking **today but permitted** to partake at **night;**[N] **but for future generations,** an acute mourner is **prohibited** from partaking of sacrificial meat **whether during the day or at night.** This is **the statement of Rabbi Yehuda. Rabbi** Yehuda HaNasi **says:** For future generations, **acute mourning at night is not by Torah law,** but **rather by rabbinic law.**

לעולם דרבנן היא,

The Gemara answers: **Actually,** Rabbi Yehuda HaNasi holds that acute mourning on the night after death **is by rabbinic law,** not Torah law.

NOTES

I am prohibited from partaking today but permitted at night – אני היום אסור ולילה מותר: Rashi explains that Rabbi Yehuda derives this from the word "behold," which indicates uniqueness; only in Aaron's case was an acute mourner permitted to partake of the sin offering at night, and not in future cases. He adds that Aaron's case was unique because during the inauguration of the Tabernacle there were no other priests who could consume the meat of the sin offering. But in later generations, when there are many priests to consume the meat, one who is an acute mourner is prohibited from partaking of it the night after the death.

Perek **XII**
Daf **101** Amud **a**

וחכמים עשו חיזוק לדבריהם יותר משל תורה.

And the same holds for the night after the day of burial, even though the acute mourning of that day itself is by rabbinic law, because **the Sages reinforced their pronouncements with greater** severity **than Torah** law.[N]

NOTES

The Sages reinforced their pronouncements with greater severity than Torah law – חכמים עשו חיזוק לדבריהם יותר משל תורה: This expression appears a number of times in the Talmud, usually meaning that the Sages issued decrees to prevent people from transgressing rabbinic law to a greater extent than they did for Torah law. The rationale for this is that there is less concern that someone will transgress a mitzva by Torah law. This is not the meaning here, as the Sages also instituted acute mourning for the night following the day of death, when acute mourning is by Torah law. Rather, the expression here means that the Sages reinforced their ordinance more than the Torah reinforced its own, as the day of death does not take hold of its night by Torah law (*Ḥok Natan*, citing *Tosafot*; see *Tzon Kodashim*).

HALAKHA

Until when does a person mourn acutely – עד מתי הוא מתאונן: One is an acute mourner by Torah law on the day of his relative's death, and by rabbinic law for the following night. If his relative is not buried for several days, his acute mourning continues by rabbinic law until the burial, and the day of burial does not take hold of its following night (Rambam *Sefer Avoda, Hilkhot Biat HaMikdash* 2:9–10).

BACKGROUND

Inauguration of the Tabernacle – שבעת ימי המלואים: This term refers to the week of preparation after construction of the Tabernacle was complete. During these days the structure and its utensils were sanctified for service, as were Aaron and his sons. The Tabernacle was assembled on the first day of Nisan in the second year following the exodus from Egypt. For seven days prior to that, Aaron the High Priest and his sons entered the courtyard of the Tabernacle. There the men and the vessels were anointed with the specially prepared oil, and offerings were sacrificed to mark the consecration of the Tabernacle. On each of the seven days Moses assembled the structure of the Tabernacle, immersed Aaron and his sons in a ritual bath, and dressed them in their priestly garments.

תנו רבנן: "כי כן צויתי", "כאשר צויתי", "כאשר צוה ה'". "כי כן צויתי" – באנינות יאכלוה, "כאשר צויתי" – בשעת מעשה אמר להן, "כאשר צוה ה'" – לא מאליי אני אומר.

§ **The Sages taught** in a *baraita*: On the eighth day of the inauguration of the Tabernacle, on which two of Aaron's sons died, Moses spoke to Aaron and his sons using three different forms of the word command: **"For so I am commanded** [*tzuveiti*]**"** (Leviticus 10:13), **"as I commanded** [*tziveiti*]**"** (Leviticus 10:18), and **"as the Lord has commanded** [*tziva*]**"** (Leviticus 10:15).[N] Moses said to Aaron: "And you shall eat it… **for so I am commanded,"** to teach that Aaron and his remaining sons **shall partake of** the offerings even **in acute mourning.** The statement: "You should certainly have eaten it… **as I commanded,"** Moses **said to them at the time of** the **incident,**[N] when Aaron and his sons burned the sin offering for the New Moon. Moses said: **"As the Lord has commanded,"**[N] to emphasize that it is **not of my own** initiative[N] that **I say** this, but it is from the word of God.

ורמינהי: מפני אנינות נשרפה, לכך נאמר "כאלה"!

And the Sages **raise a contradiction** from another *baraita*: The sin offering **was burned due to** the **acute mourning** of Aaron and his sons, since they felt they could not partake of it. **Therefore,** it **is stated** in Aaron's explanation: "There have befallen me such things **as these;** and if I had consumed the sin offering today, would it have been good in the eyes of the Lord?" (Leviticus 10:19). Moses conceded to Aaron that he was correct (see Leviticus 10:20), indicating that it was not permitted for Aaron to partake of the sin offering in acute mourning.

אמר שמואל: לא קשיא; הא – רבי יהודה, הא – רבי נחמיה.

Shmuel said: This is **not difficult. This** first *baraita*, according to which Moses commanded Aaron and his sons to consume the sacrificial meat in acute mourning, is in accordance with the opinion of **Rabbi Yehuda;** and **that** *baraita*, according to which they acted properly in refraining from eating it, is in accordance with the opinion of **Rabbi Neḥemya.**[N]

דתניא: מפני אנינות שרפוה, לכך נאמר "כאלה", דברי רבי נחמיה. רבי יהודה ורבי שמעון אומרים: מפני טומאה נשרפה, שאם אתה אומר: מפני אנינות נשרפה – היו לשלשתן שישרפוה. דבר אחר: היו ראוי לאוכלן לערב. דבר אחר: והלא פינחס היה עמהן.

This is **as it is taught** in a *baraita*: Aaron and his sons **burned** the sin offering **due to** their **acute mourning. Therefore, it is stated: "As these";** this is **the statement of Rabbi Neḥemya. Rabbi Yehuda and Rabbi Shimon say:** The sin offering **was burned due to ritual impurity. As, if you say** that it **was burned due to acute mourning,** they **should have burned** all **three of** the sin offerings offered that day. **Alternatively,** if it was burned due to acute mourning, **they would have been fit to partake of** the sin offerings **in the evening,**[N] and there would have been no need to burn them. **Alternatively,** if it was burned due to acute mourning, **wasn't Pinehas,** son of Elazar the priest, **with them?** He was not in mourning, and he could have partaken of the sin offering.

NOTES

For so I am commanded, as I commanded, etc. – כי כן צויתי כאשר צויתי וכו׳: The Sages seek to explain why Moses repeats the idea of being commanded, seemingly unnecessarily, and with different language each time, first Moses being commanded, then God commanding, then Moses commanding (*Korban Aharon*).

He said to them at the time of the incident – בשעת מעשה אמר להן: The commentaries disagree as to which incident the *baraita* is referring to. Rashi explains that it refers to the death of two of Aaron's sons, when Aaron and his remaining sons became acute mourners. Moses immediately told them that they should nevertheless consume the meal offering as well as other sacrificial food. Others explain that the *baraita* refers to when they burned the sin offering. Moses told them then that they should have eaten it rather than burn it, as he commanded them earlier with regard to the meal offering (Ra'avad's commentary on *Torat Kohanim*; *Korban Aharon*; Malbim).

As the Lord has commanded – כאשר צוה ה׳: Moses said this with regard to the consumption of the breast and thigh of the special peace offerings of that day. The three verses here are not quoted in order, as this command was stated before the incident where the sin offering was burned. Some explain that the *baraita* grouped: "For so I am commanded [*tzuveiti*]" with: "As I commanded [*tziveiti*]" because they sound similar (commentary attributed to Ra'avad on *Torat Kohanim*). Others explain that there is no absolute chronological order in the Torah, and this command from Moses actually came after the incident (see *Korban Aharon*).

It is not of my own initiative, etc. – לא מאליי וכו׳: Some explain that Moses meant that he did not derive this command using hermeneutical principles but rather received an explicit command from God (*Or HaYashar*).

That *baraita* is in accordance with the opinion of Rabbi Neḥemya – הא רבי נחמיה: Rashi explains that according to Shmuel, as opposed to Rava, Rabbi Neḥemya holds that Moses was not commanded to have Aaron and his sons consume the offerings that day in acute mourning. Moreover, Moses did not even know that partaking of offerings is generally prohibited to an acute mourner. Only after Aaron explained why he burned the sin offering did Moses concede that he had acted correctly.

Accordingly, Rashi explains that for this opinion the statement "for so I am commanded" refers not to the *halakha* that an acute mourner may not partake of offerings but to the very mitzva of consuming a meal offering. See also *Tosafot*, who explain that this opinion agrees that Moses was commanded that the meal offering should be consumed in acute mourning, but he erred in thinking that this was the *halakha* for all the sacrificial food.

To partake of the sin offerings in the evening – לאוכלן לערב: Although Rabbi Yehuda holds that acute mourning at night is by Torah law, he concedes that the offerings of the inaugural days of the Tabernacle were permitted to acute mourners at night. They would certainly be permitted according to Rabbi Shimon, who holds that for all generations, acute mourning at night is by rabbinic law (Rashi).

רָבָא אָמַר: אִידִי וְאִידִי רַבִּי נְחֶמְיָה, וְלָא קַשְׁיָא; כָּאן – בְּקָדְשֵׁי שָׁעָה, כָּאן – בְּקָדְשֵׁי דוֹרוֹת.

Rava said: Both **this** *baraita* **and that** *baraita* are in accordance with the opinion of **Rabbi Neḥemya,** who holds that the sin offering was burned due to acute mourning. **And** this is **not difficult. Here,** the *baraita* according to which Moses commanded that Aaron and his sons partake of the offering as acute mourners is referring **to the offerings of** a particular **time,** i.e., the meal offering, which was unique to the inauguration ceremony. **There,** the *baraita* according to which they rightly burned the sin offering, due to acute mourning, is referring **to the offerings of** all future **generations.** That sin offering was brought for the New Moon of Nisan, and such an offering would be brought at every New Moon from that day onward. Moses conceded that such offerings should not be consumed by acute mourners.

רַבִּי נְחֶמְיָה הֵיכִי מְתָרֵיץ לְהָנֵי קְרָאֵי, וְרַבָּנַן הֵיכִי מְתָרְצִי לְהוּ לְהָנֵי קְרָאֵי?

The Gemara asks: **How would Rabbi Neḥemya reconcile these** apparently contradictory **verses** about the sin offering, **and how would the Sages reconcile these verses** (see Leviticus 10:17–20)?

רַבִּי נְחֶמְיָה מְתָרֵיץ לְהוּ הָכִי: ״מַדּוּעַ לֹא אֲכַלְתֶּם״, אָמַר לוֹ מֹשֶׁה לְאַהֲרֹן: שֶׁמָּא נִכְנַס דָּמָהּ לִפְנַי וְלִפְנִים? אָמַר לוֹ: ״הֵן לֹא הוּבָא אֶת דָּמָהּ״. שֶׁמָּא חוּץ לִמְחִיצָתָהּ יָצָאת? אָמַר לוֹ: בַּקֹּדֶשׁ הָיְתָה.

Rabbi Neḥemya would **reconcile them like this:**[N] When Moses asked: **"Why have you not eaten** the sin offering?" (Leviticus 10:17), this is what **Moses said to Aaron: Perhaps the blood of** this sin offering **entered the innermost sanctum,** thereby disqualifying it (see Leviticus 6:23). Is this why you burned it? Aaron **said to him: "Behold, the blood of it was not brought** into the Sanctuary within" (Leviticus 10:18). Moses then asked: **Perhaps it went outside its partition,**[N] i.e., it exited the courtyard of the Tabernacle, and was thereby disqualified? Aaron **said to him: It was inside the sacred** area at all times.

וְדִלְמָא בַּאֲנִינוּת אַקְרֵיבְתּוּהָ וּפְסַלְתּוּהָ? אָמַר לוֹ: מֹשֶׁה, וְכִי הֵם הִקְרִיבוּ? אֲנִי הִקְרַבְתִּי! וְאָמַר לוֹ: הֵן לֹא הוּבָא אֶת דָּמָהּ, וּבַקֹּדֶשׁ הָיְתָה – ״אָכוֹל תֹּאכְלוּ אֹתָהּ כַּאֲשֶׁר צִוֵּיתִי״ בַּאֲנִינוּת יֹאכְלוּהָ!

Moses then suggested: **But perhaps you sacrificed it in acute mourning,** which is prohibited for ordinary priests, **and disqualified it.** Aaron **said to him: Moses, was it they,** i.e., my sons, **who sacrificed** the offering?[N] **I sacrificed** the offering, and as High Priest, I may serve even as an acute mourner (see Leviticus 21:10–12). **And** Moses **said to him: "Behold, the blood of it was not brought** into the Sanctuary within," **and it was inside the sacred** area at all times; therefore: **"You should certainly have consumed it** in the sacred area, **as I commanded"** (Leviticus 10:18), i.e., just as I commanded that the priests should **consume** today's meal offering **in acute mourning.**

אָמַר לוֹ: ״וַתִּקְרֶאנָה אֹתִי כָּאֵלֶּה וְאָכַלְתִּי חַטָּאת הַיּוֹם הַיִּיטַב בְּעֵינֵי ה׳״? שֶׁמָּא לֹא שָׁמַעְתָּ אֶלָּא בְּקָדְשֵׁי שָׁעָה.

Aaron **said to him:** "Behold, today have they sacrificed their sin offering and their burnt offering before the Lord, **and there have befallen me such things as these; and if I had consumed the sin offering today, would it have been good in the eyes of the Lord?"** (Leviticus 10:19). **Perhaps you heard** the command to consume the offering **only with regard to offerings of** a particular **time,** i.e., the meal offering, which was unique to that day.

דְּאִי בְּקָדְשֵׁי דוֹרוֹת – קַל וָחוֹמֶר מִמַּעֲשֵׂר הַקַּל: וּמָה מַעֲשֵׂר הַקַּל אָמְרָה תּוֹרָה: ״לֹא אָכַלְתִּי בְאֹנִי מִמֶּנּוּ״ – בְּקָדְשֵׁי דוֹרוֹת לֹא כָּל שֶׁכֵּן?

As, if you claim that it also applies **to the offerings of** all **generations,** then one can prove this is not so via **an *a fortiori*** inference **from** the second **tithe,**[B] for **which** the *halakha* **is** more **lenient** than for sacrificial meat: **Just as** with regard to the second **tithe,** for **which** the *halakha* **is** more **lenient, the Torah stated: "I have not eaten thereof in my mourning** [*ve'oni*]" (Deuteronomy 26:14), teaching that an acute mourner [*onen*] is prohibited from partaking of it, **all the more so** is it **not** clear that **with regard to the offerings of** all **generations,** an acute mourner is prohibited from partaking of them?

מִיָּד – ״וַיִּשְׁמַע מֹשֶׁה וַיִּיטַב בְּעֵינָיו״, הוֹדָה וְלֹא בוֹשׁ מֹשֶׁה לוֹמַר ״לֹא שָׁמַעְתִּי״, אֶלָּא אָמַר: ״שָׁמַעְתִּי וְשָׁכַחְתִּי״.

Moses **immediately conceded** to Aaron, as the verse states: **"And Moses heard, and it was good in his eyes"** (Leviticus 10:20). **And Moses was not embarrassed** and did not attempt to justify himself **by saying: I did not hear** of this *halakha* until now. **Rather, he said: I heard** it, **and I forgot** it, as the verse indicates by stating: "Moses heard."

NOTES

Rabbi Neḥemya would reconcile them like this – רַבִּי נְחֶמְיָה מְתָרֵיץ לְהוּ הָכִי: Rashi explains this passage in accordance with Rava's opinion only, as Rava holds that Rabbi Neḥemya distinguishes between the offerings of the inaugural days of the Tabernacle and the offerings of future generations. See *Tosafot*, who explain this passage in accordance with the opinion of Shmuel as well.

Perhaps it went outside its partition – שֶׁמָּא חוּץ לִמְחִיצָתָהּ יָצָאת: The Gemara infers that Moses asked this from the superfluous word "within" in Aaron's response (Rashi on 16a).

Was it they who sacrificed the offering – וְכִי הֵם הִקְרִיבוּ: The Gemara understands Aaron's words: "Behold, today have they sacrificed their sin offering and their burnt offering before the Lord" (Leviticus 10:19), as a rhetorical question: But was it they, the ordinary priests, who sacrificed the sin offering?

BACKGROUND

Second tithe – מַעֲשֵׂר שֵׁנִי: This is a tithe that is separated after the *teruma* is given to the priests and the first tithe is given to the Levites. Second tithe is separated during the first, second, fourth, and fifth years of the Sabbatical cycle, and afterward it is brought to Jerusalem to be eaten there by its owner. If the journey to Jerusalem is too long, making it difficult to transport all of the second tithe there, or if the produce becomes ritually impure, it can be redeemed for an equivalent sum of money, which is brought to Jerusalem and spent on food. If the owner redeems his own produce, he is required to add one-fifth of its value. Second tithe can be redeemed only with minted coins bearing an imprint; unstamped coins and promissory notes cannot be used. Today second tithe is still redeemed, but for a nominal sum, since in the absence of the Temple it is no longer brought to Jerusalem. The *halakhot* of second tithe are discussed in tractate *Ma'aser Sheni*.

NOTES

Or perhaps due to your bitterness, etc. – וְדִילְמָא אַגַּב מְרָרַייכוּ וכו׳: According to the opinion of Rabbi Yehuda and Rabbi Shimon, that acute mourning was not the reason the sin offering was burned, an alternate explanation is necessary as to why Aaron referred to the death of his sons in the context of the sin offering: "There have befallen me such things as these." They would explain that Moses asked Aaron an additional question: Perhaps your neglect led to the offering becoming disqualified? Aaron replied not by saying: There have befallen me these things, but rather by saying: "There have befallen me such things as these," meaning that he would not be careless with consecrated offerings after any tragedy.

וְרַבִּי יְהוּדָה וְרַבִּי שִׁמְעוֹן הֵיכִי מְתָרְצִי לְהוּ? הָכִי מְתָרְצִי לְהוּ: ״מַדּוּעַ לֹא אֲכַלְתֶּם אֶת הַחַטָּאת בִּמְקוֹם [הַקֹּדֶשׁ]״, שֶׁמָּא נִכְנַס דָּמָהּ לִפְנַי וְלִפְנִים? אָמַר לוֹ: ״הֵן לֹא הוּבָא אֶת דָּמָהּ אֶל הַקֹּדֶשׁ פְּנִימָה״.

The Gemara continues: **And how** would **Rabbi Yehuda and Rabbi Shimon,** who hold that the sin offering was burned due to ritual impurity, **reconcile those** verses? **They** would **reconcile them like this:** When Moses said to Aaron and his sons: **"Why have you not eaten the sin offering in the place of the Sanctuary?"** (Leviticus 10:17), he meant: **Perhaps its blood entered the innermost sanctum,** disqualifying the offering. Aaron **said to him** in response: **"Behold, the blood of it was not brought into the Sanctuary within"** (Leviticus 10:18).

שֶׁמָּא חוּץ לִמְחִיצָתָהּ יָצָאת? אָמַר לוֹ: הֵן בַּקּוֹדֶשׁ הָיְתָה. וְדִילְמָא בַּאֲנִינוּת אַקְרִיבְתּוּהָ וּפְסַלְתּוּהָ? אָמַר לוֹ: מֹשֶׁה, הֵן הִקְרִיבוּהָ דְּפָסְלָה בְּהוּ אֲנִינוּת? אֲנִי הִקְרַבְתִּיהָ!

Moses then asked: **Perhaps it went outside its partition,** i.e., the courtyard of the Tabernacle, and was thereby disqualified? Aaron **said to him: It was inside the sacred** area at all times. Moses then asked: **But perhaps you sacrificed it in acute mourning and disqualified it?** Aaron **said to him: Moses,** was it my sons who **sacrificed** the offering, **that** their **acute mourning** would **disqualify** the offering? **I,** the High Priest, **sacrificed** the offering, and I may serve even in acute mourning.

וְדִילְמָא אַגַּב מְרָרַייכוּ פְּשַׁעְתּוּ בָּהּ וְאִיטַּמַּאי! אָמַר לוֹ: מֹשֶׁה, כָּךְ אֲנִי בְּעֵינֶיךָ שֶׁאֲנִי מְבַזֶּה קָדְשֵׁי שָׁמַיִם? ״וַתִּקְרֶאנָה אֹתִי כָּאֵלֶּה״ – וַאֲפִילּוּ אֵלֶּה וְכָאֵלֶּה – אֵין אֲנִי מְבַזֶּה קָדְשֵׁי שָׁמַיִם!

Moses then asked: **Or perhaps, due to your bitterness** in mourning, **were you neglectful of** the offering **and it became impure?** Aaron **said to him: Moses, am I in your eyes such** a person, that I would **treat** an offering **consecrated to Heaven with contempt?** **"There have befallen me such things as these"** (Leviticus 10:19), i.e., **even** if **these** tragedies **and** more **such as them** should befall me, **I** would **not treat** an offering **consecrated to Heaven with contempt.**

אָמַר לוֹ: וְאִי הֵן לֹא הוּבָא אֶת דָּמָהּ, וּבַקּוֹדֶשׁ הָיְתָה – ״אָכוֹל תֹּאכְלוּ אֹתָהּ בַּקּוֹדֶשׁ כַּאֲשֶׁר צִוֵּיתִי״ בַּאֲנִינוּת יֹאכְלוּהָ!

Moses **said to him:** If so, **and if,** as you say: **"Behold, the blood of it was not brought** into the Sanctuary within," **and** it was **inside the sacred** area at all times, then: **"You should certainly have eaten it in the sacred area, as I commanded,"** i.e., as I commanded that the priests should **consume** the meal offering even **in acute mourning.**

אָמַר לוֹ: שֶׁמָּא לֹא שָׁמַעְתָּ אֶלָּא בַּלַּיְלָה, דְּאִי בַּיּוֹם – קַל וָחוֹמֶר מִמַּעֲשֵׂר הַקַּל, וּמַה מַּעֲשֵׂר הַקַּל אָמְרָה תּוֹרָה: ״לֹא אָכַלְתִּי בְאֹנִי מִמֶּנּוּ״, קוֹדֶשׁ חָמוּר לֹא כׇּל שֶׁכֵּן?

Aaron **said to him: Perhaps you heard** the command to consume the offering **only with regard to the night** following the day of acute mourning, but during the day itself the prohibition stands. **As, if** you claim that it may be consumed **during the day** itself, I can prove that this is not so via **an** *a fortiori* inference **from** the second **tithe,** for which the *halakha* is more **lenient** than for sacrificial meat: **Just as** with regard to the second **tithe,** for which the *halakha* is more **lenient, the Torah stated: I have not eaten thereof in my mourning, all the more so** is it **not** clear that in the **stringent** case of **sacrificial** meat, an acute mourner is prohibited from partaking of it?

מִיָּד – ״וַיִּשְׁמַע מֹשֶׁה

Moses **immediately** conceded to Aaron, as the verse states: **"And Moses heard,**

Perek **XII**
Daf **101** Amud **b**

וַיִּיטַב בְּעֵינָיו״, לֹא בּוֹשׁ מֹשֶׁה לוֹמַר: ״לֹא שָׁמַעְתִּי״, אֶלָּא: ״שָׁמַעְתִּי וְשָׁכַחְתִּי״.

and it was good in his eyes" (Leviticus 10:20). **Moses was not embarrassed** and did not attempt to justify himself **by saying: I did not hear** this *halakha* until now. **Rather,** he said: **I heard** it, **and I forgot** it.

אִיבָּעֵי לְהוּ לְשַׁהוּיֵיהּ וּלְמֵיכְלָא בְּאוּרְתָּא. טוּמְאָה בְּאוֹנֶס בָּאתָה.

The Gemara asks: According to this opinion, why was the sin offering burned? **They should have delayed its** consumption **and consumed** it that **night.** The Gemara answers: **Ritual impurity came** upon this sin offering **due to circumstances beyond** the priests' **control,** and they were forced to burn it.

בִּשְׁלָמָא לְרַבָּנַן, הַיְינוּ דִּכְתִיב: ״הַיּוֹם״, אֶלָּא לְרַבִּי נְחֶמְיָה מַאי ״הַיּוֹם״? חוֹבַת הַיּוֹם.

The Gemara asks: **Granted, according to the Rabbis,** i.e., Rabbi Yehuda and Rabbi Shimon, **this is as it is written:** "And if I had consumed the sin offering **today,** would it have been good in the eyes of the Lord"? The verse indicates that Aaron could have eaten it at night. **But according to Rabbi Neḥemya,** who holds that Aaron distinguished between the offerings of that particular time and the offerings of all later generations, **what** did Aaron mean by the word **"today"?**[N] The Gemara answers: He meant: And if I had eaten the sin offering of the New Moon, which is **today's obligation,** would it have been good in the eyes of the Lord?

בִּשְׁלָמָא לְרַבִּי נְחֶמְיָה, הַיְינוּ דִּכְתִיב: ״הֵן הַיּוֹם״, אֶלָּא לְרַבָּנַן מַאי ״הֵן הַיּוֹם״? הָכִי קָאָמַר: הֵן הִקְרִיבוּ? אֲנִי הִקְרַבְתִּי.

The Gemara asks: **Granted, according to Rabbi Neḥemya, this is as it is written: "Behold, today**[N] have they sacrificed their sin offering and their burnt offering before the Lord," i.e., they offered it as the obligation of the day. **But according to the Rabbis,** i.e., Rabbi Yehuda and Rabbi Shimon, **what** did Aaron mean by the phrase **"behold [*hen*], today"?** The Gemara answers: **This** is what Aaron **is saying: Did they [*hen*],** my sons, **sacrifice** the offering today, which would have been prohibited to them in acute mourning? No, **I sacrificed** the offering, and as High Priest, I may perform the service in acute mourning.

אָמַר מָר: הָיוּ לִשְׁלָשְׁתָּן שֶׁיִּשָּׂרְפוּ. מַאי ״שְׁלָשְׁתָּן״?

§ The Gemara continues to analyze the *baraita*. **The Master says:** If the sin offering was burned due to acute mourning, then the priests **should have burned** all **three of** the sin offerings offered that day. The Gemara asks: **What** is meant by: All **three of** the sin offerings?

דְּתַנְיָא: ״וְאֵת שְׂעִיר הַחַטָּאת דָּרֹשׁ דָּרַשׁ מֹשֶׁה״, ״שְׂעִיר״ – זוֹ שְׂעִיר נַחְשׁוֹן, ״חַטָּאת״ – זוֹ חַטַּאת שְׁמִינִי, ״דָּרֹשׁ״ – שָׂעִיר שֶׁל רֹאשׁ חוֹדֶשׁ.

The Gemara responds: **As it is taught** in a *baraita*: The verse states: **"And Moses diligently inquired for the goat of the sin offering,** and behold, it was burned" (Leviticus 10:16). When the verse states: "The **goat," this** is referring to **the goat of Nahshon,** son of Amminadav, the prince of the tribe of Judah, who brought the offering on the first day of the Tabernacle's inauguration (see Numbers 7:12). When the verse states: "The **sin offering," this** is referring to the **sin offering** that the people brought on the **eighth** day of the inauguration (see Leviticus 9:13). The term **"inquired"** is referring to the **goat** sacrificed at every **New Moon** (see Numbers 28:15). The Tabernacle was erected on the New Moon of Nisan (see Exodus 40:17). These are the three goats that were sacrificed that day.

יָכוֹל שְׁלָשְׁתָּן נִשְׂרְפוּ? תַּלְמוּד לוֹמַר: ״וְהִנֵּה שֹׂרָף״ – אֶחָד נִשְׂרַף וְלֹא שְׁלָשְׁתָּן נִשְׂרְפוּ. ״דָּרֹשׁ דָּרַשׁ״ – שְׁתֵּי דְּרִישׁוֹת לָמָּה? אָמַר לְהוּ: מִפְּנֵי מָה חַטָּאת זוֹ נִשְׂרְפָה וְאֵלּוּ מוּנָּחוֹת? וְאֵינִי יוֹדֵעַ אֵיזֶהוּ, כְּשֶׁהוּא אוֹמֵר: ״וְאֹתָהּ נָתַן לָכֶם לָשֵׂאת אֶת עֲוֹן הָעֵדָה״ – הֱוֵי אוֹמֵר: זֶה שָׂעִיר שֶׁל רֹאשׁ חוֹדֶשׁ.

One **might** have thought that all **three of them were burned.** Therefore, **the verse states:** "And Moses diligently inquired for the goat of the sin offering, **and, behold, it was burned,"** to teach that **one** of the offerings **was burned, but not all three of them were burned.** The verse states: "And Moses **diligently inquired** [*darosh darash*]." **Why** were there **two inquiries? Moses said to them: For what** reason is **this sin offering burned, and** secondly, for what reason are **those left** unburned? The *baraita* comments: Still, **I do not know which of them** was burned. **When it states** with regard to the burned goat: **"And He has given it to you to bear the iniquity of the congregation"** (Leviticus 10:17), **you must say: This is the goat of the New Moon,**[NB] which atones for impurity in the Temple.

שַׁפִּיר קָאָמְרִי לֵיהּ! רַבִּי נְחֶמְיָה לְטַעְמֵיהּ, דְּאָמַר: קָדְשֵׁי שָׁעָה לָא פָּסְלָה בְּהוּ אֲנִינוּת.

The Gemara comments: Rabbi Yehuda and Rabbi Shimon **say well to** Rabbi Neḥemya; if the sin offering was burned due to acute mourning, then all three goats should have been burned. How would Rabbi Neḥemya respond? The Gemara explains: **Rabbi Neḥemya** conforms **to his** line of **reasoning, as he says: Acute mourning does not disqualify offerings of** a particular **time.** Therefore, they burned only the New Moon sin offering, which applies to future generations as well.

אָמַר מָר: הָיָה לוֹ לְאׇכְלָהּ לָעֶרֶב. שַׁפִּיר קָאָמְרִי לֵיהּ! קָסָבַר: אֲנִינוּת לַיְלָה דְּאוֹרַיְיתָא.

The Master says in the *baraita*: If the sin offering was burned due to acute mourning, why was it burned at all? **He should have eaten it in the evening.** The Gemara comments: Rabbi Yehuda and Rabbi Shimon **say well to** Rabbi Neḥemya in posing this difficulty. How would he respond? The Gemara explains: He **holds** that **acute mourning in the evening** is **by Torah law,** and therefore the priests were not permitted to eat it even then.

NOTES

But according to Rabbi Neḥemya what did Aaron mean by today – לְרַבִּי נְחֶמְיָה מַאי הַיּוֹם: The difficulty is that according to Rabbi Neḥemya, there is no distinction between day and night. The offerings of that particular time were permitted even during the day, and the offerings of future generations, including the sin offering of the New Moon, were forbidden even at night.

Granted according to Rabbi Neḥemya this is as it is written: Behold, today – בִּשְׁלָמָא לְרַבִּי נְחֶמְיָה הַיְינוּ דִּכְתִיב הֵן הַיּוֹם: Rashi explains that according to Rabbi Neḥemya, Aaron is stating that the priests sacrificed the offering that was the obligation of the day. According to Rabbi Yehuda and Rabbi Shimon, it makes no difference which offering was sacrificed. The Gemara therefore explains that according to them, the word *hen* in this verse does not mean: Behold, but rather: They, and Aaron is asking rhetorically: Is it so that my sons sacrificed the offering?

Later commentaries find difficulty with Rashi's interpretation, as on 101a, the Gemara explains that Aaron gave this latter answer according to the opinion of Rabbi Neḥemya. They explain that the Gemara's interpretation there is based on its conclusions here, and this conclusion accords with all opinions (Rabbi Eliyahu Mizraḥi; *Korban Aharon*; see *Tosafot*).

This is the goat of the New Moon – זֶה שָׂעִיר שֶׁל רֹאשׁ חוֹדֶשׁ: The goat of the New Moon atones for defiling of the Temple that occurred by entering it while ritually impure, or for defiling of its sacrificial foods that occurred by partaking of them while ritually impure (see *Shevuot* 2a). The other two goats sacrificed that day were not for atonement (see Rashi's commentary on that verse and on 48b).

BACKGROUND

Goat of the New Moon – שְׂעִיר שֶׁל רֹאשׁ חוֹדֶשׁ: The Torah (see Numbers 28:15) requires a goat to be sacrificed on the New Moon as a communal sin offering. Its sacrifice followed the same procedure as that used for sin offerings of a private individual, and it was intended to atone for certain transgressions involving the defiling of the Temple or its sacrificial foods.

דָּבָר אַחֵר: וַהֲלֹא פִּינְחָס הָיָה עִמָּהֶן. שַׁפִּיר קָאָמְרִי לֵיהּ! סָבַר לָהּ כְּרַבִּי אֶלְעָזָר. דְּאָמַר רַבִּי אֶלְעָזָר אָמַר רַבִּי חֲנִינָא: לֹא נִתְכַּהֵן פִּינְחָס עַד שֶׁהֲרָגוֹ לְזִמְרִי, דִּכְתִיב: ״וְהָיְתָה לּוֹ וּלְזַרְעוֹ אַחֲרָיו בְּרִית כְּהֻנַּת עוֹלָם״.

Rabbi Yehuda and Rabbi Shimon also stated: **Alternatively, wasn't Pinehas,** son of Elazar the priest, **with them?** He was not an acute mourner. The Gemara comments: Rabbi Yehuda and Rabbi Shimon **say well to** Rabbi Neḥemya. The Gemara explains: **He holds in accordance with** the opinion of **Rabbi Elazar. As Rabbi Elazar says** that **Rabbi Ḥanina says: Pinehas did not become a priest until he killed Zimri,** who had engaged in intercourse with a Midianite woman (see Numbers 25:6–8). **As it is written** only after that incident concerning Pinehas: **"And it shall be unto him and to his seed after him the covenant of an everlasting priesthood"** (Numbers 25:13). Before that incident, at the time of the inauguration of the Tabernacle, the only priests were Aaron and his sons.

רַב אַשִׁי אָמַר: עַד שֶׁשָּׂם שָׁלוֹם בֵּין הַשְּׁבָטִים, שֶׁנֶּאֱמַר: ״וַיִּשְׁמַע פִּינְחָס הַכֹּהֵן וּנְשִׂיאֵי הָעֵדָה וְרָאשֵׁי אַלְפֵי יִשְׂרָאֵל״ וגו׳.

Rav Ashi said: Pinehas did not become a priest **until he made peace among the tribes** at the time of the conquest of Eretz Yisrael, when the tribes east of the Jordan River built their own altar and nearly provoked a civil war. Before this, Pinehas was always referred to as: Son of Elazar the priest, but during this incident he is himself referred to as a priest for the first time, **as it is stated: "And Pinehas the priest, and the princes of the congregation, and the heads of the thousands of Israel** that were with him, **heard** the words that the children of Reuben and the children of Gad and the children of Manasseh spoke, and it pleased them well" (Joshua 22:30).

וְאִידָךְ נַמִי, וְהָכְתִיב ״וְהָיְתָה לּוֹ וּלְזַרְעוֹ אַחֲרָיו״! כִּי כְּתִיב הַהוּא – בִּבְרָכָה הוּא דִּכְתִיב.

The Gemara asks: **And** for **the other** Sage, Rav Ashi, **as well, isn't it written: "And it shall be unto him, and to his seed after him,** the covenant of an everlasting priesthood"? Apparently, Pinehas became a priest after he killed Zimri. The Gemara responds: **When that** verse **is written,** it is **with regard to** the **blessing that it is written,**[N] that his descendants would always be priests. It did not indicate that Pinehas became a priest immediately.

וְאִידָךְ נַמִי, הָא כְּתִיב: ״וַיִּשְׁמַע פִּינְחָס הַכֹּהֵן״! הַהוּא לְיַחֵס זַרְעוֹ אַחֲרָיו.

The Gemara asks: **And** for **the other** Sages **as well,** who hold that Pinehas became a priest immediately after he killed Zimri, **isn't it written: "And Pinehas the priest… heard"?** Apparently he became a priest only after the conquest of Eretz Yisrael. The Gemara answers: **That** verse serves **to entitle his descendants after him,**[N] that they would continue as High Priests through his merit.

אָמַר רַב: מֹשֶׁה רַבֵּינוּ כֹּהֵן גָּדוֹל, וְחוֹלֵק בְּקָדְשֵׁי שָׁמַיִם הָיָה, שֶׁנֶּאֱמַר: ״מֵאֵיל הַמִּלֻּאִים לְמֹשֶׁה הָיָה לְמָנָה״.

§ **Rav says: Moses, our teacher,** was **a High Priest and would receive a share of offerings** consecrated **to Heaven, as it is stated:** "And Moses took the breast, and waved it for a wave offering before the Lord; **it was Moses' portion of the ram of inauguration,** as the Lord commanded Moses" (Leviticus 8:29).

מֵיתִיבֵי: וַהֲלֹא פִּינְחָס הָיָה עִמָּהֶן. וְאִם אִיתָא, לֵימָא: ״וַהֲלֹא מֹשֶׁה רַבֵּינוּ הָיָה עִמָּהֶן״! דִּילְמָא שָׁאנֵי מֹשֶׁה דִּטְרִיד בַּשְּׁכִינָה, דְּאָמַר מָר: מֹשֶׁה בְּהַשְׁכָּמָה עָלָה וּבְהַשְׁכָּמָה יָרַד.

The Gemara **raises an objection:** In the *baraita*, Rabbi Yehuda and Rabbi Shimon claim that acute mourning was not the reason the sin offering was burned by asking: **Wasn't Pinehas with them? And if it is so** that Moses could partake of sacrificial meat, **let them say: Wasn't Moses, our teacher, with them?** The Gemara responds: **Perhaps Moses is different,** since as a prophet, **he was preoccupied with the Divine Presence,** and was not available. **As the Master says: Moses ascended** Mount Sinai **early in the morning, and he descended early in the morning.**

NOTES

It is with regard to the blessing that it is written – בִּבְרָכָה הוּא דִּכְתִיב: Rashi understands that the opinion discussed here is that of Rav Ashi, who holds that Pinehas became a priest when he made peace among the tribes. The blessing at the time of Zimri was a promise for the future, and did not apply immediately.

Rabbeinu Tam does not accept that Pinehas could receive this blessing without thereby becoming a priest. He explains that Pinehas was eligible for the priesthood at that time, and all the special prohibitions of a priest applied to him. Nevertheless, the people refused to anoint him as a priest, because they were angry that he had killed Zimri, the prince of the tribe of Simeon. Only after he made peace among the tribes did they accept him as a priest.

To entitle his descendants after him – לְיַחֵס זַרְעוֹ אַחֲרָיו: *Tosafot* explain that calling Pinehas himself "the priest" indicates that his descendants served as High Priests, because they traced their lineage back to him. *Ben Yehoyada* clarifies that "the priest," with the definite article, indicates that he was the progenitor of the High Priesthood. Although some High Priests were descendants of Itamar, son of Aaron, this did not last (see Rashi on I Samuel 2:30). From the dedication of the Temple and on, the High Priests were descended from Tzadok, who was a descendant of Pinehas (see I Chronicles 5:38).

Some explain that the Israelites cast doubt on Pinehas's lineage after he committed an act of violence and killed Zimri, and therefore the Torah needed to say that he was "Pinehas, son of Elazar, son of Aaron the priest" (see Rashi on Numbers 25:11, citing *Bava Batra* 109b). After he made peace among the tribes, this was no longer necessary, and he was called simply "the priest" (*Iyyun Ya'akov*).

מֵיתִיבֵי: ״לֶחֶם אֱלֹהָיו מִקָּדְשֵׁי הַקֳּדָשִׁים וּמִן הַקֳּדָשִׁים יֹאכֵל״, אִם נֶאֶמְרוּ קָדְשֵׁי קָדָשִׁים, לָמָּה נֶאֱמַר קָדָשִׁים קַלִּים? וְאִם נֶאֶמְרוּ קָדָשִׁים קַלִּים, לָמָּה נֶאֱמַר קָדְשֵׁי קָדָשִׁים?

The Gemara **raises an objection** to Rav's statement from another *baraita*: The verse states with regard to a blemished priest: **"He may eat the bread of his God, both of the most sacred, and of the sacred"** (Leviticus 21:22). **If offerings of the most sacred order are stated,** that a blemished priest may eat them, then **why** are **offerings of lesser sanctity** also **stated? And if offerings of lesser sanctity are stated, why are offerings of the most sacred order stated?**

אִילּוּ לֹא נֶאֱמַר קָדָשִׁים קַלִּים – הָיִיתִי אוֹמֵר: קָדְשֵׁי קָדָשִׁים הוּא דְּאוֹכֵל, שֶׁהֲרֵי הוּתְּרוּ לְזָר וְלַכֹּהֵן, קָדָשִׁים קַלִּים לֹא יֹאכַל. וְאִילּוּ לֹא נֶאֶמְרוּ קָדְשֵׁי קָדָשִׁים – הָיִיתִי אוֹמֵר: בְּקָדָשִׁים קַלִּים יְהֵא אוֹכֵל שֶׁהֵן קַלִּים, בְּקָדְשֵׁי קָדָשִׁים לֹא יְהֵא אוֹכֵל. לְכָךְ נֶאֶמְרוּ קָדְשֵׁי קָדָשִׁים וּלְכָךְ נֶאֱמַר קָדָשִׁים קַלִּים.

The *baraita* answers: **Had offerings of lesser sanctity not been stated, I would have said: It is** only **offerings of the most sacred order that** a blemished priest **may eat, as they were permitted** both **to a non-priest and to** the priests, but a blemished priest **may not eat offerings of lesser sanctity,** which were not permitted to non-priests. **And had offerings of the most sacred order not been stated, I would have said:** A blemished priest **may eat offerings of lesser sanctity, as they are of lesser sanctity,** but **he may not eat of offerings of the most sacred order,** as they are of higher sanctity. **Therefore, offerings of the most sacred order are stated, and therefore, offerings of lesser sanctity** are **stated.**

קָתָנֵי מִיהָא: ״שֶׁהֲרֵי הוּתְּרוּ לְזָר וְלַכֹּהֵן״, לָאו מֹשֶׁה? אָמַר רַב שֵׁשֶׁת: לָא, בְּבָמָה לְזָר, וּכְדִבְרֵי הָאוֹמֵר: יֵשׁ מִנְחָה בְּבָמָה.

The Gemara explains the objection: **In any event,** the *baraita* **teaches: As they were permitted** both **to a non-priest and to** the priests. What non-priest is permitted to eat offerings of the most sacred order? Is this **not** referring to **Moses?** This indicates that Moses was not considered a High Priest, contrary to Rav's statement. **Rav Sheshet said: No,** this is referring **to a non-priest** sacrificing **on** a private **altar.** Once the Jewish people entered Eretz Yisrael, it was permitted for a time for them to build private altars, on which even non-priests could serve. **And** although only offerings of lesser sanctity were offered on private altars, this *baraita* is **in accordance with the statement of the** Sage **who says: There is a meal offering** that may be offered **on** a private **altar.** Meal offerings are of the most sacred order.

מֵיתִיבֵי: מִרְיָם מִי הִסְגִּירָהּ? אִם תֹּאמַר מֹשֶׁה הִסְגִּירָהּ – מֹשֶׁה זָר הוּא,

The Gemara **raises an objection** to Rav's statement: When **Miriam** became a leper (see Numbers 12:10), **who** diagnosed and **quarantined her?**[N] **If you say** that **Moses quarantined her,** that is difficult, as **Moses** was **a non-priest,**

NOTES

Who diagnosed and quarantined her – **מִי הִסְגִּירָהּ**: Unlike other forms of ritual impurity, which take effect due to an incident, e.g., a bodily emission or contact with an impure item, the signs of leprosy do not on their own render a person impure. A priest must examine the signs and declare that the person must be quarantined or is a confirmed leper. The purification from leprosy is also effected by the priest.

Perek **XII**
Daf **102** Amud **a**

וְאֵין זָר רוֹאֶה אֶת הַנְּגָעִים. וְאִם תֹּאמַר: אַהֲרֹן הִסְגִּירָהּ – אַהֲרֹן קָרוֹב הוּא, וְאֵין קָרוֹב רוֹאֶה אֶת הַנְּגָעִים! אֶלָּא, כָּבוֹד גָּדוֹל חָלַק לָהּ הַקָּדוֹשׁ בָּרוּךְ הוּא לְמִרְיָם אוֹתָהּ שָׁעָה: אֲנִי כֹּהֵן, וַאֲנִי מַסְגִּירָהּ, אֲנִי חוֹלְטָהּ, וַאֲנִי פּוֹטְרָהּ.

and a non-priest may not inspect the shades of leprous **marks**[H] to diagnose them. **And if you say** that **Aaron quarantined her,** that is difficult, as **Aaron** was **a relative,** Miriam's brother, **and a relative may not inspect the** shades of leprous **marks.**[H] **Rather, the Holy One, Blessed be He, bestowed a great honor on Miriam at that time,** and said: **I** Myself **am a priest, and I will quarantine her** for seven days to see if the shades of leprous marks persist, and **I will declare her** a leper if she is impure, **and I will exempt her** if she is not impure.

קָתָנֵי מִיהַת: מֹשֶׁה זָר, וְאֵין זָר רוֹאֶה אֶת הַנְּגָעִים!

In any event, the midrash **teaches: Moses** was **a non-priest, and a non-priest may not inspect the** shades of leprous **marks,** which contradicts the statement of Rav that Moses was a priest.

אָמַר רַב נַחְמָן בַּר יִצְחָק: שָׁאנֵי מַרְאוֹת נְגָעִים, דְּאַהֲרֹן וּבָנָיו כְּתוּבִין בַּפָּרָשָׁה.

Rav Naḥman bar Yitzḥak said: The *halakhot* of the examination of **shades of** leprous **marks are different, because** specifically **Aaron and his sons,** and not Moses, **are written in the passage** that discusses them: "Then he shall be brought unto Aaron the priest, or unto one of his sons the priests" (Leviticus 13:2). Therefore, there is no proof from this *baraita* that Moses was not a priest.

HALAKHA

A non-priest may not inspect the leprous marks – **אֵין זָר רוֹאֶה נְגָעִים**: Although anyone may inspect another for leprosy, its purity and impurity depends only on the pronouncement of a priest. If a priest does not know how to identify leprous marks, one who does know may tell him: Pronounce this impure, and the priest says: It is impure. Or he may tell him: Pronounce this pure, and the priest says: It is pure. The priest must also quarantine or confirm a person as a leper; a leper's status depends on the pronouncement of the priest (Rambam *Sefer Tahara*, *Hilkhot Tumat Tzara'at* 9:2).

And a relative may not inspect the marks – **וְאֵין קָרוֹב רוֹאֶה אֶת הַנְּגָעִים**: The *halakha* is in accordance with the opinion of the Rabbis (*Nega'im* 2:5), who say that any priest may inspect leprous marks, including a relative of the one afflicted. A priest may not inspect only his own leprous marks (Rambam *Sefer Tahara*, *Hilkhot Tumat Tzara'at* 9:1).

מֵיתִיבֵי: חָמֵשׁ שְׂמָחוֹת הָיְתָה אֱלִישֶׁבַע יְתֵירָה עַל בְּנוֹת יִשְׂרָאֵל: יְבָמָהּ מֶלֶךְ, אִישָׁהּ כֹּהֵן גָּדוֹל, בְּנָהּ סְגָן, בֶּן בְּנָהּ מְשׁוּחַ מִלְחָמָה, וְאָחִיהָ נְשִׂיא שֵׁבֶט – וַאֲבֵילָה עַל שְׁנֵי בָנֶיהָ.

The Gemara **raises an objection** to Rav's statement from a *baraita*: **Elisheva,** the daughter of Amminadav and the wife of Aaron, **had five more** reasons for **joy than** the other **daughters of Israel** on the day the Tabernacle was dedicated: **Her brother-in-law,** Moses, was **a king; her husband,** Aaron, was the **High Priest; her son,** Elazar, was the **deputy** High Priest; **her son's son,** Pinehas, was the priest **anointed for war,**[BN] who would lead the army out to battle; **and her brother,** Nahshon, son of Amminadav, was **the prince of** the **tribe** of Judah, who brought his offering on that day, as the first of all the princes. **But** on that same day of joy she was **in mourning for her two sons,** Nadav and Avihu, who died on that day.

קָתָנֵי מִיהַת: "יְבָמָהּ מֶלֶךְ", מֶלֶךְ – אִין, כֹּהֵן גָּדוֹל – לָא! אֵימָא: אַף מֶלֶךְ.

In any event, the *baraita* **teaches: Her brother-in-law,** Moses, was **a king.** From this one can infer that **yes,** he was **a king,** but he was **not a High Priest,** contrary to Rav's statement. The Gemara responds: **Say** that the *baraita* means: Moses was **a king as well,** in addition to being a High Priest.

כְּתַנָּאֵי: "וַיִּחַר אַף ה׳ בְּמֹשֶׁה", רַבִּי יְהוֹשֻׁעַ בֶּן קָרְחָה אוֹמֵר: כָּל חֲרוֹן אַף שֶׁבַּתּוֹרָה נֶאֱמַר בּוֹ רוֹשֶׁם, וְזֶה לֹא נֶאֱמַר בּוֹ רוֹשֶׁם.

The Gemara comments: The question of whether Moses was a High Priest is **subject to** a dispute among *tanna'im*, as is taught in a *baraita*: When Moses was at the burning bush and expressed hesitation to deliver God's message to Pharaoh, the verse states: **"And the anger of the Lord burned against Moses,** and He said: Is there not Aaron your brother the Levite? I know that he can speak well. And also, behold, he comes forth to meet you, and when he sees you, he will be glad in his heart" (Exodus 4:14). **Rabbi Yehoshua ben Korha says:** For **every burning anger that** is stated **in the Torah, its effect is** also **stated,** i.e., the Torah records an action or pronouncement as a consequence of that anger, **but** in **this** case **no effect of** the anger **is stated.**

רַבִּי שִׁמְעוֹן בֶּן יוֹחַי אוֹמֵר: אַף זֶה נֶאֱמַר בּוֹ רוֹשֶׁם, שֶׁנֶּאֱמַר: "הֲלֹא אַהֲרֹן אָחִיךָ הַלֵּוִי", וַהֲלֹא כֹּהֵן הוּא! הָכִי קָאָמַר, אֲנִי אָמַרְתִּי: אַתָּה כֹּהֵן וְהוּא לֵוִי, עַכְשָׁיו הוּא כֹּהֵן וְאַתָּה לֵוִי.

Rabbi Shimon ben Yohai says: Even in this case the anger's **effect is stated, as it is stated** there: **"Is there not Aaron your brother the Levite?** I know that he can speak well." **But isn't** Aaron **a priest?** Why is he referred to as a Levite? **This** is what God **is saying** to Moses: **I** initially **said** that **you** would be the **priest and he** would be the **Levite; now he** will be the **priest and you** will be the **Levite.**[N]

וַחֲכָמִים אוֹמְרִים: לֹא נִתְכַּהֵן מֹשֶׁה אֶלָּא שִׁבְעַת יְמֵי הַמִּלּוּאִים בִּלְבַד. וְיֵשׁ אוֹמְרִים: לֹא פָּסְקָה כְּהוּנָּה אֶלָּא מִזַּרְעוֹ שֶׁל מֹשֶׁה, שֶׁנֶּאֱמַר: "וּמֹשֶׁה אִישׁ הָאֱלֹהִים בָּנָיו יִקָּרְאוּ עַל שֵׁבֶט הַלֵּוִי", וְאוֹמֵר: "מֹשֶׁה וְאַהֲרֹן בְּכֹהֲנָיו וּשְׁמוּאֵל בְּקֹרְאֵי שְׁמוֹ".

And the Rabbis say: Moses became a priest for **the seven days of inauguration alone,** and after that his priesthood expired. **And some say:** The **priesthood expired only for the descendants of Moses,** but Moses himself remained a priest, **as it is stated: "But as for Moses the man of God, his sons are named among the tribe of Levi"** (1 Chronicles 23:14). This verse indicates that it was his sons who were Levites, but he himself remained a priest. **And** so too the verse **states: "Moses and Aaron among His priests, and Samuel among them that call upon His name,** did call upon the Lord, and He answered them" (Psalms 99:6).

מַאי "וְאוֹמֵר"? וְכִי תֵּימָא לְדוֹרוֹת הוּא דִּכְתִיב – וְאוֹמֵר: "מֹשֶׁה וְאַהֲרֹן בְּכֹהֲנָיו".

The Gemara asks: **What** is meant by: **And** so too the verse **states?** Why did the *tanna* need to cite a second proof? The Gemara explains: **And if you would say** the first verse **is written only for** future **generations,** to include Moses' descendants in the tribe of Levi but not to exclude him, then there is a second proof: **And** so too, the verse **states: "Moses and Aaron among His priests."** The statement of Rav that Moses was a High Priest is in accordance with the opinion in this *baraita*.

וְכָל חֲרוֹן אַף שֶׁבַּתּוֹרָה נֶאֱמַר בּוֹ רוֹשֶׁם? וְהָכְתִיב: "וַיֵּצֵא מֹשֶׁה מֵעִם פַּרְעֹה בָּחֳרִי אָף", וְלָא אֲמַר לֵיהּ וְלָא מִידֵּי! אֲמַר רֵישׁ לָקִישׁ: סְטָרוֹ וְיָצָא.

The Gemara challenges the statement of Rabbi Yehoshua ben Korha: **And** is it true that for **every burning anger that** is stated **in the Torah, its effect is** also **stated? But isn't it written with** regard to Moses: **"And he went out from Pharaoh in hot anger"** (Exodus 11:8)? **And** Moses **did not say anything to** Pharaoh. **Reish Lakish said:** Moses **slapped him and left.**

BACKGROUND

Anointed for war – מְשׁוּחַ מִלְחָמָה: Before the Jewish people set out to war, a priest was appointed to perform certain duties in connection with the war. This priest, who was inaugurated with special anointing oil, was called: The priest anointed for war. He was responsible for reminding those exempt from fighting to return home, and for encouraging the other soldiers to fight with faith in their mission and trust in their Protector, as stated in the Torah (see Deuteronomy, chapter 20). The oracular stones in the breastplate that this priest wore would be consulted before the army went out to battle. The same prohibitions that apply to a High Priest applied to the priest anointed for war, although he did not bring the sacrifices brought by a High Priest, and his position was not bequeathed to his sons. The institution of the priest anointed for war ceased to exist as far back as the beginning of the Second Temple period.

NOTES

Her son's son Pinehas was the priest anointed for war – בֶּן בְּנָהּ מְשׁוּחַ מִלְחָמָה: In tractate *Sota* (43a), the Sages derive that Pinehas was the priest anointed for war from the verse: "And Moses sent them, a thousand of every tribe, to the war, them and Pinehas, son of Elazar the priest, to the war, with the sacred vessels and the trumpets for the alarm in his hand" (Numbers 31:6).

He will be the priest and you will be the Levite – הוּא כֹּהֵן וְאַתָּה לֵוִי: Although Moses performed the Tabernacle service in the role of High Priest during the seven days of inauguration, this was not because he was a priest, but because he had a special command to serve despite being a non-priest. He did not wear the garments of a High Priest (see Rashi and *Tosafot* on *Avoda Zara* 34a).

וּמִי אָמַר רֵישׁ לָקִישׁ הָכִי? וְהָכְתִיב: "וְנִצַּבְתָּ לִקְרָאתוֹ עַל שְׂפַת הַיְאֹר", וְאָמַר רֵישׁ לָקִישׁ: מֶלֶךְ הוּא, וְהַסְבֵּיר לוֹ פָּנִים. וְרַבִּי יוֹחָנָן אָמַר: רָשָׁע הוּא, וְהָעֵיז פָּנֶיךָ בּוֹ! אֵיפוּךְ.

The Gemara challenges: **And does Reish Lakish** actually **say this? But isn't it written:** "Go unto Pharaoh in the morning; lo, he goes out unto the water; **and you shall stand by the river's brink to meet him,**[N] and the rod which was turned to a serpent shall you take in your hand" (Exodus 7:15); **and Reish Lakish says:** God meant: Pharaoh **is a king, and** so you should **be amiable toward him, and Rabbi Yoḥanan says:** God meant: Pharaoh **is wicked, and** so you should **be insolent toward him.** If according to Reish Lakish Moses was commanded to greet Pharaoh with respect, how could he say that Moses slapped Pharaoh? The Gemara answers: **Reverse** the names of the Sages in this dispute; it is Reish Lakish who says that Moses was commanded to be insolent.

אָמַר רַבִּי יַנַּאי: לְעוֹלָם תְּהֵא אֵימַת מַלְכוּת עָלֶיךָ, דִּכְתִיב: "וְיָרְדוּ כָל עֲבָדֶיךָ אֵלֶּה אֵלַי", וְאִילּוּ לְדִידֵיהּ לָא קָאָמַר לֵיהּ.

With regard to the respect accorded to a king, **Rabbi Yannai says: Fear of** the **kingship should always be upon you,**[N] even when the king does not deserve respect, **as it is written** that Moses said to Pharaoh: **"And all these your servants shall come down unto me** and bow down unto me, saying: Get you out, and all the people that follow you, and after that I will go out" (Exodus 11:8). He mentioned Pharaoh's servants, **but he did not say** this **of** Pharaoh **himself,** even though this was the eventual outcome. Rather, he spoke to Pharaoh with the respect due to a king.

רַבִּי יוֹחָנָן אָמַר, מֵהָכָא: "וְיַד ה׳ הָיְתָה אֶל אֵלִיָּהוּ וַיְשַׁנֵּס מָתְנָיו וַיָּרָץ לִפְנֵי אַחְאָב".

Rabbi Yoḥanan says: Derive the principle **from here: "And the hand of the Lord was on Elijah, and he girded up his loins and ran before Ahab**[N] to the entrance of Jezreel" (I Kings 18:46). Elijah the prophet ran before the evil king Ahab out of respect.

אָמַר עוּלָּא: בִּקֵּשׁ מֹשֶׁה מַלְכוּת, וְלֹא נָתְנוּ לוֹ, דִּכְתִיב: "אַל תִּקְרַב הֲלֹם", וְאֵין "הֲלוֹם" אֶלָּא מַלְכוּת, שֶׁנֶּאֱמַר: "מִי אָנֹכִי ה׳ אֱלֹהִים [וגו׳] כִּי הֲבִיאֹתַנִי עַד הֲלֹם".

The Gemara continues to discuss the roles of Moses: **Ulla says: Moses requested** that he be given the **kingship, but it was not given to him, as it is written: "Do not draw hither"** (Exodus 3:5); **and** the word **"hither"** refers to **nothing other than kingship,**[N] **as it is stated:** "Then David the king went in and sat before the Lord, and he said: **Who am I, O Lord God,** and what is my house, **that You have brought me hither"**? (II Samuel 7:18).

מְתִיב רָבָא, רַבִּי יִשְׁמָעֵאל אוֹמֵר: יְבָמָהּ מֶלֶךְ! אֲמַר רָבָא: לוֹ וּלְזַרְעוֹ קָאָמַר.

Rava raises an objection from the *baraita* cited earlier: **Rabbi Yishmael says:** Elisheva's **brother-in-law,** Moses, was **a king.** This teaches that Moses was in fact granted kingship. **Rava said:** Ulla **is saying** that Moses did not receive kingship **for himself and for his descendants,** i.e., it was not bequeathed to his sons.

וְכָל הֵיכָא דִּכְתִיב "הֲלוֹם" לְדוֹרוֹת הוּא? וְהָא גַּבֵּי שָׁאוּל, דִּכְתִיב: "הֲבָא עוֹד הֲלֹם אִישׁ", הוּא – אִין, זַרְעוֹ – לָא!

The Gemara counters: **And** is it so that **anywhere that it is written "hither"** the verse **is** referring to kingship **for** future **generations** as well? **But isn't it written about** the kingship of **Saul:** "They asked of the Lord further: **Is there yet a man who comes hither"** (I Samuel 10:22), and Saul was **indeed** a king, but **his descendants** were **not.**

אִיבָּעֵית אֵימָא: הָא הֲוָה אִישׁ בֹּשֶׁת. וְאִיבָּעֵית אֵימָא: שָׁאנֵי שָׁאוּל, דַּאֲפִילּוּ בְּגַוֵּיהּ לָא קָאֵים.

The Gemara responds: **If you wish, say: There was Ish-Bosheth,** Saul's son, who was a king (see II Samuel 2:10), indicating that Saul's kingship did pass to his son. **And if you wish, say** instead: **Saul is different, because** the kingship **did not stand even for himself,** and this is why it did not pass on to his descendants.

כְּדְרַבִּי אֶלְעָזָר אָמַר רַבִּי חֲנִינָא: בְּשָׁעָה שֶׁפּוֹסְקִים גְּדוּלָּה לְאָדָם – פּוֹסְקִים לוֹ וּלְזַרְעוֹ עַד סוֹף כָּל הַדּוֹרוֹת, שֶׁנֶּאֱמַר: "לֹא יִגְרַע מִצַּדִּיק עֵינָיו וְאֶת מְלָכִים לַכִּסֵּא" וגו׳. וְאִם הֵגִיס דַּעְתּוֹ – הַקָּדוֹשׁ בָּרוּךְ הוּא מַשְׁפִּילוֹ, שֶׁנֶּאֱמַר: "וְאִם אֲסוּרִים בַּזִּקִּים יִלָּכְדוּן בְּחַבְלֵי עֹנִי".

The second response is **in accordance with** that which **Rabbi Elazar** says that **Rabbi Ḥanina says: When greatness is apportioned to a person** in Heaven, it **is apportioned to him and to his descendants until the end of all generations, as it is stated: "He withdraws not His eyes from the righteous; but with kings upon the throne** He sets them forever, and they are exalted" (Job 36:7). **But if he** then **became arrogant, the Holy One, Blessed be He, humiliates him, as is stated** in the next verse: **"And if they be bound in fetters, and be held in cords of affliction"** (Job 36:8). This was the case with Saul.

NOTES

And you shall stand by the river's brink to meet him – וְנִצַּבְתָּ לִקְרָאתוֹ עַל שְׂפַת הַיְאֹר: The term used here for "stand" [*venitzavta*] is employed to connote standing before a king, e.g., in the verse that states: "You are standing [*nitzavim*] this day all of you before the Lord your God" (Deuteronomy 29:9). But the term also has a sense of standing in defiance, as in the verse: "And Dathan and Abiram came out, and stood [*nitzavim*] at the door of their tents" (Numbers 16:27).

Fear of the kingship should always be upon you – לְעוֹלָם תְּהֵא אֵימַת מַלְכוּת עָלֶיךָ: It is stated: If not for the fear of the government, a man would swallow his neighbor alive (*Avot* 3:2). Furthermore, kingship in this world is comparable to the kingship in heaven, so making light of the honor of a king is similar to disrespecting God (Maharsha).

And ran before Ahab – וַיָּרָץ לִפְנֵי אַחְאָב: Elijah did this to escort Ahab, as it is not honorable for a king to walk alone (Rashi). Radak explains that part of a king's honor is people running before him (see I Kings 1:5 and *Sanhedrin* 95b).

And hither refers to nothing other than kingship – וְאֵין הֲלוֹם אֶלָּא מַלְכוּת: The verse does not use the usual word: Here [*po*], but the unusual word "hither [*halom*]," which is used in contexts of kingship and grandeur (Maharsha). The Sages also use the term *halom* to mean that something is worthy or appropriate (see *Avoda Zara* 44a).

״בַּעֲלֵי מוּמִין, בֵּין בַּעֲלֵי מוּמִין״ כו׳. מְנָא הָנֵי מִילֵּי? דְּתָנוּ רַבָּנַן: ״כׇּל זָכָר״ – לְרַבּוֹת בַּעֲלֵי מוּמִין.

§ The mishna teaches: **Blemished** priests, **whether** they are temporarily **blemished** or permanently blemished, receive a share and partake of offerings, but do not sacrifice them. The Gemara explains: **From where are these matters** derived? **As the Sages taught** in a *baraita*: The verse states with regard to the meal offering: "**Every male** among the sons of Aaron shall eat it" (Leviticus 6:11). The phrase "every male" serves **to include blemished** priests.

לְמַאי? אִי לַאֲכִילָה – הֲרֵי כְּבָר נֶאֱמַר: ״לֶחֶם אֱלֹהָיו מִקׇּדְשֵׁי הַקֳּדָשִׁים יֹאכֵל״. אֶלָּא לַחֲלוּקָּה.

The Gemara clarifies: **For what** matter is this derivation necessary? **If** one suggests it is **for** the matter of **consumption, it is already stated** explicitly: "Any man of the seed of Aaron the priest who has a blemish… **He may eat the bread of his God, of the most sacred,** and of the sacred" (Leviticus 21:21–22). **Rather,** Leviticus 6:11 is necessary **for** the matter of **receiving a share,** teaching that blemished priests may do so along with the other priests. This is the source for the mishna's statement.

תַּנְיָא אִידָּךְ: ״כׇּל זָכָר״ – לְרַבּוֹת בַּעֲלֵי מוּמִין. לְמַאי? אִי לַאֲכִילָה – הֲרֵי כְּבָר אָמוּר, אִי לַחֲלוּקָּה – הֲרֵי כְּבָר אָמוּר! שֶׁיָּכוֹל אֵין לִי אֶלָּא תָּם וְנַעֲשָׂה בַּעַל מוּם, בַּעַל מוּם מֵעִיקָּרוֹ מִנַּיִן? תַּלְמוּד לוֹמַר: ״כׇּל זָכָר״.

It **is taught in another** *baraita*: The verse states with regard to the sin offering: "**Every male** among the priests may eat thereof" (Leviticus 6:22). The phrase "every male" serves **to include blemished** priests. The Gemara explains: **For what** matter is this derivation necessary? **If** one suggests it is **for** the matter of **consumption, isn't** that **already stated** in Leviticus, chapter 21? **If** one suggests it is **for** the matter of **receiving a share, isn't** that **already stated** in verse 6:11? Rather, the verse is necessary **because** one **might** have thought that **I have** derived **only** the *halakha* with regard to a priest who was at first **unblemished and** later **became blemished. From where** is it derived that one **blemished from birth** also receives a share? **The verse states** here: "**Every male.**"

תַּנְיָא אִידָּךְ: ״כׇּל זָכָר״ – לְרַבּוֹת בַּעַל מוּם. לְמַאי? אִי לַאֲכִילָה – הֲרֵי כְּבָר אָמוּר, וְאִי לַחֲלוּקָּה – הֲרֵי כְּבָר אָמוּר, וְאִי לְבַעַל מוּם מֵעִיקָּרוֹ – הֲרֵי כְּבָר אָמוּר! שֶׁיָּכוֹל אֵין לִי אֶלָּא בַּעַל מוּם קָבוּעַ, בַּעַל מוּם עוֹבֵר מִנַּיִן? תַּלְמוּד לוֹמַר ״כׇּל זָכָר״.

It **is taught** in **another** *baraita*: The verse states with regard to the guilt offering: "**Every male** among the priests may eat thereof" (Leviticus 7:6). The phrase "every male" serves **to include a blemished** priest. The Gemara explains: **For what** matter is this derivation necessary? **If** one suggests it is **for** the matter of **eating, isn't** that **already stated? And if** one suggests it is **for** the matter of **receiving a share, isn't** that **already stated? And if** one suggests it is **for** a priest **blemished from birth, isn't** that **already stated?** Rather, the verse is necessary **because** one **might** have thought that **I have** derived **only** the *halakha* with regard to **a permanently blemished** priest. **From where** is it derived that a **temporarily blemished** priest also receives a share? **The verse states** here: "**Every male.**"

כְּלַפֵּי לַיָּיא? אֲמַר רַב שֵׁשֶׁת: אֵיפּוֹךְ.

The Gemara objects: **Isn't it the opposite** [*kelapei layya*]?[L] Wouldn't I have thought that a priest with a permanent blemish would be treated more stringently than one with a temporary blemish? **Rav Sheshet said: Reverse** the wording as follows: One might have thought that I have derived only the *halakha* with regard to a priest with a temporary blemish; from where is it derived that one with a permanent blemish also receives a share?

רַב אַשִׁי אֲמַר: לְעוֹלָם לָא תֵּיפוֹךְ. וְאִיצְטְרִיךְ, סָלְקָא דַּעְתָּךְ אָמִינָא

Rav Ashi said: Actually, do not reverse the wording, **and** this is not difficult. It **was necessary** to teach that even a priest with a temporary blemish receives a share, because it might **enter your mind to say**

LANGUAGE

Isn't it the opposite [*kelapei layya*] – כְּלַפֵּי לַיָּיא: This expression, *kelapei layya*, is usually understood to mean literally: Facing which way? In other words, in which direction do you face, or how do you understand this matter, as your understanding appears to be the opposite of the correct understanding. Some commentaries had a different version of the text, in which the expression read *kelapei alya*, literally: Facing the tail, i.e., the statement is focusing on the tail instead of the head.

כִּי טָמֵא, מָה טָמֵא כַּמָּה דְּלָא טָהוֹר לָא אָכֵיל, אַף הַאי נַמִי, כַּמָּה דְּלָא מִתְקַן לָא אָכֵיל, קָא מַשְׁמַע לַן.

that the *halakha* of this priest is **like** that of **a ritually impure** priest: **Just as an impure** priest **may not partake as long as he is not pure, so too, this** priest with a temporary blemish **may not partake as long as he does not become fit.**[N] The verse therefore **teaches us** that he may receive a share even before his blemish heals.

"כָּל שֶׁאֵינוֹ רָאוּי" וכו׳. וְלָא? וַהֲרֵי בַּעַל מוּם, דְּלָא רָאוּי לַעֲבוֹדָה, וְחוֹלֵק! וְתוּ: הָא רָאוּי לַעֲבוֹדָה חוֹלֵק; הֲרֵי טָמֵא בְּקָרְבְּנוֹת צִיבּוּר, דְּרָאוּי לַעֲבוֹדָה, וְאֵינוֹ חוֹלֵק!

§ The mishna teaches: The principle is: **Any** priest **who is unfit** for the service that day does not receive a share of the sacrificial meat. The Gemara objects: **But doesn't** he? **Isn't there a blemished** priest, **who is not fit for the service and** who nevertheless **receives a share** of the meat, as the mishna itself teaches? **And furthermore,** this principle indicates that only priests unfit for the service do not receive a share, **but** any priest who is **fit for the service** does **receive a share.** But **isn't** there **an impure** priest, **who, with regard to offerings of the community, is fit for the service, and** who nevertheless **does not receive a share?**

רָאוּי לַאֲכִילָה קָאָמַר.

The Gemara answers: The mishna **is saying** that any priest who is not **fit for partaking** of sacrificial meat does not receive a share.[N] Blemished priests may partake of sacrificial meat, and impure priests may not.

וַהֲרֵי קָטָן, דְּרָאוּי לַאֲכִילָה, וְאֵינוֹ חוֹלֵק! הָא לָא קָתָנֵי.

The Gemara objects: This indicates that any priest who is fit to partake may receive a share. **But isn't** there is **a minor, who is fit for partaking and** who **does not receive a share?** The Gemara answers: **This** inverse principle, that any priest who is fit to partake may receive a share, **is not taught.** The mishna means to teach only that any priest who is unfit does not receive a share.

הַשְׁתָּא דְּאָתֵית לְהָכִי, לְעוֹלָם כִּדְקָאָמַר מֵעִיקָּרָא: אִי מִשּׁוּם טָמֵא – טָמֵא לָא קָתָנֵי, וְאִי מִשּׁוּם בַּעַל מוּם – רַחֲמָנָא רַבְּיֵיהּ.

The Gemara notes: **Now that you have arrived at this** conclusion, that the mishna's statement only teaches what it says explicitly, one can say that the mishna **actually** means **what** the Gemara **said at the outset,** that no priest unfit for the service receives a share. **If** one raises an objection **with regard to an impure** priest, who is fit for the service of communal offerings but does not receive a share, answer that the mishna **does not teach** that every fit priest, even **an impure** one, receives a share, only the inverse. **And if** you raise an objection **with regard to a blemished** priest, who is unfit for the service but nevertheless receives a share, answer that **the Merciful One included him** as an exception by the phrase: Every male, as derived above (102a).

"אֲפִילּוּ טָמֵא בִּשְׁעַת זְרִיקַת דָּמִים וְטָהוֹר בִּשְׁעַת הֶקְטֵר חֲלָבִים אֵינוֹ חוֹלֵק". הָא טָהוֹר בִּשְׁעַת זְרִיקַת דָּמִים וְטָמֵא בִּשְׁעַת הֶקְטֵר חֲלָבִים – חוֹלֵק.

§ The mishna teaches: **Even** if the priest was **ritually impure** only **at the time of the sprinkling of the blood** of the offering, **and** he was **pure at the time of the burning of the fats,** he still **does not receive a share** of the meat. The Gemara notes: **Consequently,** one can infer that a priest who was **pure at the time of the sprinkling of the blood,** even one who was **impure at the time of the burning of the fats, does receive a share.**

מַתְנִיתִין דְּלָא כְּאַבָּא שָׁאוּל, דְּתַנְיָא, אַבָּא שָׁאוּל אוֹמֵר: לְעוֹלָם אֵינוֹ אוֹכֵל עַד שֶׁיְּהֵא טָהוֹר מִשְּׁעַת זְרִיקָה עַד שְׁעַת הֶקְטֵר חֲלָבִים, דְּאָמַר קְרָא: "הַמַּקְרִיב אֶת דַּם הַשְּׁלָמִים וְאֶת הַחֵלֶב" – דַּאֲפִילּוּ הֶקְטֵר חֲלָבִים נַמִי בָּעֵי.

The Gemara comments: **The mishna is not in accordance with** the opinion of **Abba Shaul, as it is taught** in a *baraita*: **Abba Shaul says:** A priest **never partakes,**[H] i.e., receives a share, of sacrificial meat, **unless he is pure from the time of sprinkling until the time of the burning of the fats, as the verse states:** "He among the sons of Aaron **who sacrifices the blood of the peace offerings and the fat**[N] shall have the right thigh for a portion" (Leviticus 7:33). The verse **requires** that the priest be pure **even** at the time of **the burning of the fats.**

NOTES

He may not partake as long as he does not become fit – כַּמָּה דְּלָא מִתְקַן לָא אָכֵיל: A priest with a permanent blemish may partake of sacrificial meat, because the Torah had compassion on him for not having any remedy (Rashi on 102a).

The mishna is saying any priest not fit for partaking of sacrificial meat does not receive a share – רָאוּי לַאֲכִילָה קָאָמַר: Although the mishna states: Any priest who is unfit for the service, it should be understood to mean: Any priest who is unfit to partake at the time of the service (see 99b).

Who sacrifices the blood of the peace offerings and the fat – הַמַּקְרִיב אֶת דַּם הַשְּׁלָמִים וְאֶת הַחֵלֶב: The reasoning of the *tanna* of the mishna is that the essential rite of an offering is the sprinkling of the blood, whereas the burning of the fats does not disqualify the offering if omitted (*Sefat Emet*). Furthermore, the *halakha* that a priest must be fit in order to receive a share of sacrificial meat was derived on 99a from the verse: "The priest who effects atonement shall eat it" (Leviticus 6:19), and the sprinkling of the blood is the atonement. Rashi writes that according to this *tanna*, the term "and the fat" (Leviticus 7:33) cited here by Abba Shaul is not meant to teach a *halakha* about the meat of offerings; rather, it teaches the *halakha* that any priest who does not believe in the mitzva of the Temple service is unfit to partake of sacrificial meat (see *Ḥullin* 132b).

HALAKHA

A priest never partakes, etc. – לְעוֹלָם אֵינוֹ אוֹכֵל וכו׳: A priest does not receive a share of the sacrificial meat unless he is pure and fit for the service from the time of sprinkling until the time of the burning of the fats. The *halakha* is in accordance with the statement of Abba Shaul, because the discussion of the Gemara follows his opinion (Rambam *Sefer Avoda*, *Hilkhot Ma'aseh HaKorbanot* 10:21).

בָּעֵי רַב אַשִׁי: נִטְמָא בֵּינְתַיִים, מַהוּ? בִּשְׁעַת זְרִיקָה וּבִשְׁעַת הַקְטָרָה בָּעֵינַן – וְהָאִיכָּא, אוֹ דִּלְמָא: עַד שֶׁיְּהֵא טָהוֹר מִשְּׁעַת זְרִיקָה וְעַד שְׁעַת הֶקְטֵר חֲלָבִים? תֵּיקוּ.

Rav Ashi raises a dilemma: According to the opinion of Abba Shaul, in a case where the priest **became impure between** the sprinkling of the blood and the burning of the fats[H] but became pure again before the latter, **what is the** *halakha*? **Do we require** only that he be pure both **at the time of sprinkling and at the time of** the **burning** of the fats, **and there is** purity at these times? **Or perhaps** Abba Shaul meant that the priest may not receive a share in the meat **unless he is pure from the time of sprinkling until the time of the burning of the fats,** without interruption. The Gemara concludes: The dilemma **shall stand** unresolved.

אָמַר רָבָא: הַאי דִּינָא מֵרַבִּי אֶלְעָזָר בְּרַבִּי שִׁמְעוֹן גְּמִירְנָא, דַּאֲמַר בְּבֵית הַכִּסֵּא: דַּנְתָּה, בָּא טְבוּל יוֹם וְאָמַר: ״תֵּן לִי מִמִּנְחָה וְאוֹכַל״.

§ The mishna teaches that an impure priest who immersed that day, such that he will not be pure until sunset, and likewise an acute mourner and one who has not yet brought an atonement offering, do not receive a share of sacrificial meat in order to partake of it in the evening. **Rava says: I learned this** *halakha* **from Rabbi Elazar, son of Rabbi Shimon, who said in the bathroom: You** can **contend** by way of a story:[N] A priest **who immersed that day came and said** to a pure priest of the same patrilineal priestly family serving in the Temple that day, who was apportioning the sacrificial food: **Give me** a share **of a meal offering, and I will partake** of it in the evening.

אָמַר לוֹ: וּמָה אִם בְּמָקוֹם שֶׁיָּפֶה כֹּחֲךָ, בְּחַטָּאתְךָ – דְּחִיתִיךָ מֵחַטַּאת יִשְׂרָאֵל, מָקוֹם שֶׁהוּרַע כֹּחֲךָ, בְּמִנְחָתְךָ – אֵינוֹ דִּין שֶׁאֲדִיחֲךָ מִמִּנְחַת יִשְׂרָאֵל?

The pure priest **said** an *a fortiori* inference **to him: Just as with** regard to a matter **where your right is superior,** i.e., **in** the case of **your** own **sin offering,**[N] to which you have a right even when your family is not serving in the Temple, I can nevertheless **deny you** a share **of the sin offering of an Israelite** because you immersed today; **is it not logical that** with regard to a matter **where your right is inferior,** i.e., **in** the case of **your** own **meal offering,** as the meal offering of a priest is not eaten at all, that I can **deny you** a share **of the meal offering of an Israelite?**

וּמָה אִם דְּחִיתָנִי מֵחַטַּאת יִשְׂרָאֵל, שֶׁכְּשֵׁם שֶׁיָּפֶה כֹּחִי – כָּךְ יָפֶה כֹּחֲךָ, תִּדְחֵינִי מִמִּנְחָה? שֶׁכְּשֵׁם שֶׁהוּרַע כֹּחִי – כָּךְ הוּרַע כֹּחֲךָ!

The priest who immersed that day responded: But even **if you** can **deny me** a share **of the sin offering of an Israelite** on the day I immersed, perhaps this is **since just as my right is superior** in the case of my own sin offering, **so too, your right is superior** in the case of your own sin offering. If so, is it necessarily so that **you** can **refuse me** a share **of** the **meal offering** of an Israelite, **where just as my right is inferior, so your right is inferior,** as neither of us may eat from our own meal offerings?

הֲרֵי הוּא אוֹמֵר: ״לַכֹּהֵן הַמַּקְרִיב אֹתָהּ לוֹ תִהְיֶה״, בֹּא הַקְרֵב וֶאֱכוֹל.

The pure priest responded: The verse **states:** "And every meal offering that is baked in the oven, and all that is dressed in the stewing pan, and on the griddle, **shall be the priest's that offers it**" (Leviticus 7:9). If you wish to receive a share of a meal offering, **come sacrifice and partake** of one. Since you cannot sacrifice a meal offering, having immersed only today, neither can you receive a share.

״תֵּן לִי מֵחַטַּאת יִשְׂרָאֵל וְאוֹכַל״.

The priest who immersed that day made another demand: **Give me** a share **of the sin offering of an Israelite, and I will partake** of it in the evening when I am pure.

אָמַר לוֹ: וּמָה בְּמָקוֹם שֶׁהוּרַע כֹּחִי, בְּמִנְחָתִי – דְּחִיתִיךָ מִמִּנְחַת יִשְׂרָאֵל, מָקוֹם שֶׁיָּפֶה כֹּחִי, בְּחַטָּאתִי – אֵינוֹ דִּין שֶׁאֲדִיחֲךָ מֵחַטַּאת יִשְׂרָאֵל?

The pure priest **said to him: Just as with regard to** a matter **where my right is inferior,** i.e., **in** the case of **my** own **meal offering,** which is not eaten, **I** can **deny you** a share **of the meal offering of an Israelite,** as I explained; so too, **is it not logical that** with regard to a matter **where my right is superior,** i.e., **in** the case of **my** own **sin offering,** to which I have a right even when my family is not serving in the Temple, **I** can **deny you** a share **of the sin offering of an Israelite?**

אָמַר לוֹ: וּמָה אִם שֶׁדְּחִיתָנִי מִמִּנְחַת יִשְׂרָאֵל – שֶׁכְּשֵׁם שֶׁהוּרַע כֹּחֲךָ כָּךְ הוּרַע כֹּחִי, תִּדְחֵינִי מֵחַטַּאת יִשְׂרָאֵל? שֶׁכְּשֵׁם שֶׁיָּפֶה כֹּחֲךָ כָּךְ יָפֶה כֹּחִי!

The priest who immersed that day **said to him: But if you** can **deny me** a share **of the meal offering of an Israelite, where just as your right is inferior, so too my right is inferior,** is it necessarily so that **you** can **deny me** a share **of the sin offering of an Israelite, where just as your right is superior** in the case of your own sin offering, **so too my right is superior** in the case of my own sin offering?

HALAKHA

The priest became impure between the sprinkling and the burning of the fats – נִטְמָא בֵּינְתַיִים: In a case where the priest became impure after the sprinkling and became pure again before the burning of the fats, it is uncertain if he receives a share of the sacrificial meat, as the dilemma is not resolved in the Gemara. If he seizes a portion of the meat, it is not taken away (Rambam *Sefer Avoda*, *Hilkhot Ma'aseh HaKorbanot* 10:22).

NOTES

You can contend by way of a story – דַּנְתָּה: Rabbi Elazar, son of Rabbi Shimon, is explaining why the Torah states three times that only a priest fit for service receives a share in the sacrificial meat: With regard to a meal offering, a sin offering, and the breast and thigh of a peace offering. He explains through a dialogue that each of these offerings has an aspect that allows its *halakha* to be derived logically from another offering, and another aspect that prevents a logical derivation. Therefore, the Torah must teach the *halakha* in each case (Malbim).

Where your right is superior in the case of your own sin offering – שֶׁיָּפֶה כֹּחֲךָ בְּחַטָּאתְךָ: A priest may sacrifice his own offerings at any time, and has the right to the meat and hides, as taught in a midrash cited by Rashi. This is the *halakha* for any offering; a sin offering is mentioned here specifically only because it is the example under discussion (*Sefer HaYashar*).

הֲרֵי הוּא אוֹמֵר: ״הַכֹּהֵן הַמְחַטֵּא אֹתָהּ יֹאכְלֶנָּה״, בֹּא חַטֵּא וֶאֱכוֹל.

The pure priest responded: The verse **states** with regard to the sin offering: **"The priest who effects atonement shall eat it"** (Leviticus 6:19). If you wish to receive a share of a sin offering, **come effect atonement and partake** of one. Since you cannot perform the service of a sin offering, having immersed only today, you cannot receive a share in its meat either.

אֲמַר לֵיהּ: תֵּן לִי מֵחָזֶה וָשׁוֹק וְאוֹכַל.

The priest who immersed that day made another demand, and **said to him: Give me** a share **of the breast and thigh,** the portions that priests receive of peace offerings, **and I will partake** of it in the evening when I am pure.

אֲמַר לֵיהּ: וּמָה בְּמָקוֹם שֶׁיָּפֶה כֹּחֲךָ בְּחַטָּאתְךָ – דְּחִיתִיךָ [מֵחַטַּאת יִשְׂרָאֵל] (מֵחָזֶה וָשׁוֹק), מָקוֹם שֶׁהוּרַע כֹּחֲךָ בִּשְׁלָמִים, שֶׁאֵין לְךָ בָּהֶן אֶלָּא חָזֶה וָשׁוֹק – אֵינוֹ דִּין שֶׁאַדִּיחֲךָ?

The pure priest **said to him: Just as with regard to** a matter **where your right is superior,** i.e., **in** the case of **your** own **sin offering,** to which you have a right to its meat in its entirety, **I** can **deny you** a share **of the sin offering of an Israelite,** as I explained, so too **is it not logical that** with regard to a matter **where your right is inferior,** i.e., **in** the case of **a peace offering, of which you have only** the right to a share of the **breast and thigh, I** can **deny you** a share?

מָה אִם דְּחִיתַנִי מֵחַטָּאת – שֶׁכֵּן הוּרַע כֹּחִי אֵצֶל נָשַׁיי וַעֲבָדַיי, תִּדְחֵינִי מֵחָזֶה וָשׁוֹק? שֶׁכֵּן יָפֶה כֹּחִי אֵצֶל נָשַׁיי וַעֲבָדַי!

The priest who immersed that day responded: But **if you** can **deny me** a share **of a sin offering, where my right is inferior with regard to my wives and my slaves,** as a sin offering can be consumed only by male priests, is it necessarily so that **you** can **deny me** a share of the **breast and thigh** of a peace offering, **where my right is superior with regard to my wives and my slaves,** who may also partake of them?

הֲרֵי הוּא אוֹמֵר: ״לַכֹּהֵן הַזּוֹרֵק אֶת דַּם הַשְּׁלָמִים לוֹ יִהְיֶה״, בֹּא זְרוֹק וֶאֱכוֹל.

The pure priest responded: The verse **states** with regard to the peace offering: **"It shall be the priest's that sprinkles the blood of the peace offerings** against the altar" (Leviticus 7:14). If you wish to partake of a peace offering, **come sprinkle** its blood **and partake** of it. Since you cannot perform this service, having immersed only today, you cannot receive a share of its meat either.

יָצָא טְבוּל יוֹם קוּלָּיו וַחֲמוּרָיו עַל רֹאשׁוֹ, אוֹנֵן מִימִינוֹ, מְחוּסַּר כַּפָּרָה מִשְּׂמֹאלוֹ.

The story concludes: The priest **who immersed that day left** in disappointment, with **his *a fortiori*** inferences **upon his head,** as they did not help him. And along with him walked **an acute mourner on his right**[N] and a priest **who had not yet** brought an **atonement** offering **on his left.** They too were denied shares, because they were unfit for the Temple service.

פָּרֵיךְ רַב אַחַאי, לֵימָא לֵיהּ: תֵּן לִי מִבְּכוֹר וְאוֹכַל!

Rav Aḥai refutes this: Rabbi Elazar, son of Rabbi Shimon, could have added to the contentions described in the story. **Let** the priest who immersed that day **say to** the pure priest: **Give me** a share **of a firstborn** offering,[N] **and I will partake** of it in the evening.

מִשּׁוּם דַּאֲמַר לֵיהּ: וּמָה בְּמָקוֹם שֶׁהוּרַע כֹּחִי בְּחַטָּאת אֵצֶל נָשַׁיי וַעֲבָדַיי – דְּחִיתִיךָ מֵחַטַּאת יִשְׂרָאֵל, מָקוֹם שֶׁיָּפֶה כֹּחִי בִּבְכוֹר, דְּכוּלֵּיהּ דִּילִי הִיא – אֵינוֹ דִּין שֶׁאַדְּחֲךָ מִמֶּנּוּ?

Perhaps it is **because** the pure priest could **say to him: Just as with regard to a sin offering, where my right is inferior with regard to my wives and my slaves,** since it may be eaten only by male priests, I can nevertheless **deny you** a share **of the sin offering of an Israelite,** as I explained; so too **is it not logical that with regard to a firstborn, where my right is superior because all of** its meat **is mine,** as firstborn offerings are given to a specific priest, **I** can **deny you** a share **of it?**

וּמָה אִם דְּחִיתַנִי מֵחַטָּאת – שֶׁכְּשֵׁם שֶׁהוּרַע כֹּחֲךָ כָּךְ הוּרַע כֹּחִי, תִּדְחֵנִי מִבְּכוֹר? שֶׁכְּשֵׁם שֶׁיָּפֶה כֹּחֲךָ כָּךְ יָפֶה כֹּחִי!

But the priest who immersed that day could respond: **But if you** can **deny me** a share **of a sin offering, where just as your right is inferior, so is my right inferior;** is it necessarily so that **you** can **deny me** a share **of a firstborn** offering, **where just as your right is superior, so my right is superior?**

הֲרֵי הוּא אוֹמֵר: ״אֶת דָּמָם תִּזְרֹק עַל הַמִּזְבֵּחַ וְאֶת חֶלְבָּם תַּקְטִיר...וּבְשָׂרָם יִהְיֶה לָּךְ״, בֹּא זְרוֹק וֶאֱכוֹל.

The pure priest could respond: The verse **says** with regard to a firstborn offering: **"You shall sprinkle their blood on the altar and shall make their fat smoke** for an offering made by fire, for a pleasing aroma to the Lord. **And the flesh of them shall be yours,** as the breast and as the thigh, it shall be yours" (Numbers 18:17–18). If you wish to receive a share in the meat of a firstborn, **come sprinkle** its blood **and partake** of it. Why did Rabbi Elazar, son of Rabbi Shimon, not include this exchange as another stage in his story?

NOTES

An acute mourner on his right – **אוֹנֵן מִימִינוֹ:** The acute mourner walked on the right because the *halakha* is stricter with regard to him, as he may not partake of sacrificial meat even after nightfall. The priest who had not yet brought an atonement offering walked on his left because the *halakha* is more lenient with regard to him, as he may partake of sacrificial meat as soon as he completes his purification process and does not need to wait for nightfall (Malbim; see *Korban Aharon*).

Give me a share of a firstborn offering – **תֵּן לִי מִבְּכוֹר:** The owner of a firstborn offering can give it to any priest of his choosing to eat. The Gemara discusses whether he may give it to a priest who has immersed on the day the offering is slaughtered.

ואידך פריך: מי כתיב "ובשרם לכהן הזורק"? "ובשרם יהיה לך" כתיב, אפילו לכהן אחר.

The Gemara responds: **But the other** priest, the one who immersed that day, could **refute** this proof: **Is it written: And the flesh of them shall be for the priest who sprinkles,** as is written with regard to a meal offering, a sin offering, and a peace offering? Rather, it **is written: "And the flesh of them shall be yours,"** indicating that it can be given **even to a priest other** than the one who sacrificed it. This is why Rabbi Elazar, son of Rabbi Shimon, did not include this exchange in his story.

והיכי עביד הכי? והאמר רבה בר בר חנה אמר רבי יוחנן: בכל מקום מותר להרהר, חוץ ממרחץ ומבית הכסא! לאונסו שאני.

The Gemara returns to Rava's statement that Rabbi Elazar, son of Rabbi Shimon, taught this *halakha* in the bathroom. **And how did** Rabbi Elazar, son of Rabbi Shimon, **do this? But doesn't Rabba bar bar Ḥana say** that **Rabbi Yoḥanan says:** It is **permitted to contemplate** matters of Torah **in all places except the bathhouse and the bathroom?**[H] The Gemara answers: A case where the matter was **involuntary is different.** Rabbi Elazar, son of Rabbi Shimon, was so preoccupied by the issue that he taught it even though he was in the bathroom.

HALAKHA

Except the bathhouse and the bathroom – חוץ ממרחץ ומבית הכסא: It is prohibited to contemplate matters of Torah in a bathhouse, bathroom, or place that has feces or urine, in accordance with the statement of Rabbi Yoḥanan. The *Beit Yosef* writes, citing Rabbeinu Manoaḥ, that if a person's Torah learning arises naturally in his mind, he has not violated a prohibition. He should push the thoughts from his mind *ab initio*. Some commentaries rule that once he contemplates Torah involuntarily, he may also say his thoughts out loud, as the Gemara states that Rabbi Elazar, son of Rabbi Shimon, did. Others rule that when Rava said that Rabbi Elazar, son of Rabbi Shimon, stated this story, he meant that he contemplated it (Rambam *Sefer Ahava, Hilkhot Keriat Shema* 3:4; *Shulḥan Arukh, Oraḥ Ḥayyim* 85:2 and *Mishna Berura* there).

Perek **XII**
Daf **103** Amud **a**

מתני׳ כל שלא זכה המזבח בבשרה – לא זכו כהנים בעורה, שנאמר: "עולת איש" – עולה שעלתה לאיש.

MISHNA In the case of **any burnt offering for which the altar did not acquire its flesh,** e.g., if it was disqualified prior to the sprinkling of its blood, the **priests did not acquire its hide,**[H] **as it is stated** with regard to the burnt offering: "And the priest that sacrifices **a man's burnt offering,** the priest shall have to himself the hide of the burnt offering that he has sacrificed" (Leviticus 7:8), indicating that the priest acquires only the hide of **a burnt offering that satisfied** the obligation **of a man.**[N]

עולה שנשחטה שלא לשמה, אף על פי שלא עלתה לבעלים – עורה לכהנים. אחד עולת האיש ואחד עולת האשה – עורותיהן לכהנים.

Nevertheless, in a case of **a burnt offering that was slaughtered not for its sake**[H] but for the sake of another offering, **although it did not satisfy** the obligation **of the owner, its hide** goes **to the priests.** In addition, although the verse states: "A man's burnt offering," in the case of **both the burnt offering of a man and the burnt offering of a woman, their hides** go **to the priests.**

עורות קדשים קלים – לבעלים, עורות קדשי קדשים – לכהנים. קל וחומר: ומה אם עולה שלא זכו בבשרה – זכו בעורה, קדשי קדשים שזכו בבשרה – אינו דין שיזכו בעורה? אין מזבח יוכיח, שאין לו עור בכל מקום.

The hides of offerings of lesser sanctity belong **to the owners;**[H] **the hides of offerings of the most sacred order** belong **to the priests.** The right of priests to hides of offerings of the most sacred order is derived via **an *a fortiori* inference: If for a burnt offering, for which** the priests **do not acquire its flesh,** as it is burned in its entirety, **they acquire its hide,** then for other **offerings of the most sacred order, for which** the priests **acquire its flesh, is it not right that they should acquire its hide?** And **there is no** room to contend that the **altar will prove** that this is not a valid inference, as it acquires the flesh of a burnt offering but not its hide, **since it does not have** the right to the **hide** of an offering **in any place.**[N]

HALAKHA

Any burnt offering for which the altar did not acquire its flesh, etc. – כל שלא זכה המזבח בבשרה וכו׳: With regard to any burnt offering for which the altar did not acquire its flesh, the priests did not acquire its hide, as taught in the mishna (Rambam *Sefer Avoda, Hilkhot Ma'aseh HaKorbanot* 5:19).

A burnt offering that was slaughtered not for its sake, etc. – עולה שנשחטה שלא לשמה וכו׳: If an offering of the most sacred order was slaughtered not for its sake but for the sake of another offering, then despite the fact that the offering did not satisfy the obligation of its owner, the hide goes to the priest. If an offering of lesser sanctity was slaughtered not for its sake, the hide goes to the owner of the offering (Rambam *Sefer Avoda, Hilkhot Pesulei HaMukdashin* 19:9).

The hides of offerings of lesser sanctity belong to the owners, etc. – עורות קדשים קלים לבעלים וכו׳: The hides of offerings of the most sacred order belong to the priests, whether they are from individual or communal offerings. The hide of an offering of lesser sanctity belongs to the owner (Rambam *Sefer Avoda, Hilkhot Ma'aseh HaKorbanot* 5:19).

NOTES

A burnt offering that satisfied the obligation [*alta*] of a man – עולה שעלתה לאיש: This derivation teaches that the offering must satisfy the obligation of the one who brought it, not only that the altar acquire the flesh of the offering. How does this serve as proof for the principle taught in the mishna? It seems from the *baraita* cited in the Gemara that the proof is not from the derivation itself but from the continuation: In the case of a burnt offering that was slaughtered not for its sake but for the sake of another offering, although it did not satisfy the obligation of its owner, its hide goes to the priests. The *baraita* derives this principle from verses.

Other commentaries explain that the derivation does support the first principle taught in the mishna. In the Rambam's Commentary on the Mishna, he explains that the word "*alta*" should be translated as going up to the top of the altar, not as satisfying an obligation. The *Melekhet Shlomo* adds that the word "man [*ish*]" should be read here as: An offering brought by fire [*esh*] on the altar.

Since it does not have the right to the hide of an offering in any place – שאין לו עור בכל מקום: If the altar had the right to the hides of any offering, then from the fact that it acquires the flesh of the burnt offering but not the hide, one could prove that priests as well do not have the right to the hides of offerings of the most sacred order. The altar does not have the right to the hides of any offering at all, and the Torah explicitly gives the priests the right to the hides of burnt offerings, so there is no proof from one case to the other.

גמ׳ תָּנוּ רַבָּנַן: ״עֹלַת אִישׁ״ – פְּרָט לְעוֹלַת הֶקְדֵּשׁ, דִּבְרֵי רַבִּי יְהוּדָה. רַבִּי יוֹסֵי בְּרַבִּי יְהוּדָה אוֹמֵר: פְּרָט לְעוֹלַת גֵּרִים.

GEMARA **The Sages taught** in a *baraita*: The phrase **"a man's burnt offering"** in the verse mentioned above serves **to exclude the burnt offering of consecrated** property,[H] meaning that the priests do not acquire the hides of such offerings. This is **the statement of Rabbi Yehuda. Rabbi Yosei, son of Rabbi Yehuda, says:** The phrase serves **to exclude the burnt offering of converts.**

מַאי ״פְּרָט לְעוֹלַת הֶקְדֵּשׁ״? אָמַר רַבִּי חִיָּיא בַּר יוֹסֵף: פְּרָט לְעוֹלָה הַבָּאָה מִן הַמּוֹתָרוֹת.

The Gemara clarifies: **What** does Rabbi Yehuda mean when he says that the phrase serves **to exclude the burnt offering of consecrated** property? **Rabbi Ḥiyya bar Yosef says:** He means it serves **to exclude a burnt offering that comes from** property that was **left over.** For example, if an animal consecrated as a guilt offering remains alive after its owner has achieved atonement by sacrificing another animal, the owner must wait until it acquires a blemish and then sell it. The proceeds are used to purchase a communal gift offering, which is sacrificed when there are no other offerings to be burned on the altar (see *Temura* 20b). Because it is a communal offering, it is not considered a man's burnt offering, and the priests therefore have no right to the hide.

הָנִיחָא לְמַאן דְּאָמַר: מוֹתָרוֹת לִנְדָבַת צִיבּוּר אָזְלִי. אֶלָּא לְמַאן דְּאָמַר: מוֹתָרוֹת לִנְדָבַת יָחִיד אָזְלִי, מַאי אִיכָּא לְמֵימַר?

The Gemara asks: **This works out well according to the one who says: Leftover** consecrated property **goes toward communal gift** offerings. **But according to the one who says: Leftover** consecrated property **goes toward an individual's gift** offering, **what can be said?** As this is a man's burnt offering, the priests should have a right to the hides.

כִּדְאָמַר רָבָא: ״הָעֹלָה״ – עוֹלָה רִאשׁוֹנָה, הָכָא נַמִי, ״הָעֹלָה״ – עוֹלָה רִאשׁוֹנָה.

The Gemara answers: According to that opinion, the *halakha* is **as Rava says:** The verse states: "And the priest shall kindle wood on it every morning; and he shall lay **the burnt offering** in order upon it" (Leviticus 6:5). The verse states: "The burnt offering," with the definite article, to teach that the daily burnt offering is the **first burnt offering** sacrificed each day in the Temple. **Here too,** the verse states: "The priest shall have to himself the hide of **the burnt offering** which he has offered," to teach that the priest acquires the hide of **a first burnt offering,** i.e., an animal that was initially designated as a burnt offering, but not of a burnt offering purchased from proceeds left over from another offering.

רַבִּי אַיְיבוּ אָמַר רַבִּי יַנַּאי: פְּרָט לְמַתְפִּיס עוֹלָה לְבֶדֶק הַבַּיִת.

Rabbi Aivu says that **Rabbi Yannai says:** Rabbi Yehuda's statement can be interpreted differently. The phrase "a man's burnt offering" serves **to exclude** a case of **one who consecrates a burnt offering for Temple maintenance.**[N] Since the owner seeks to shift its ownership to the Temple, the priests have no right to its hides.

לָא מִיבַּעְיָא לְמַאן דְּאָמַר: קָדְשֵׁי בֶּדֶק הַבַּיִת תָּפְסִי מִדְּאוֹרַיְיתָא, אֶלָּא אֲפִילּוּ לְמַאן דְּאָמַר: לָא תָּפְסִי – הָנֵי מִילֵּי בָּשָׂר, אֲבָל עוֹר תָּפֵיס.

The Gemara comments: **It is not necessary** to teach this *halakha* **according to the one who says** that **consecration for Temple maintenance applies by Torah law** to offerings already consecrated to the altar, as the animal in fact ceases to belong to the individual, and the priests clearly have no claim to its hide. **Rather, even according to the one who says** that it **does not apply** by Torah law, because the offering is already consecrated for the altar, **this matter** applies only to the **meat; but** as for the **hide,** the consecration for Temple maintenance **applies** and nullifies the priests' claim to it.

NOTES

One who consecrates a burnt offering for Temple maintenance – מַתְפִּיס עוֹלָה לְבֶדֶק הַבַּיִת: This is known as consecration by valuation (see *Temura* 32a). An offering that is consecrated for the altar must be sacrificed on the altar. Therefore, if an animal consecrated as an offering is then consecrated for Temple maintenance, its monetary value is appraised, and the owner pays that amount to the Temple treasury.

The monetary value of the burnt offering is appraised as follows. If the owner consecrated the animal as a vow offering, in which case he is obligated to pay restitution if the animal dies or is stolen, then he pays the full value of the animal. If he consecrated the animal as a gift offering, in which case he is exempt if the animal dies or is stolen, then he pays the monetary value of his benefit of discretion, i.e., his discretion to give the offering to any priest of his choice (see *Arakhin* 28b).

HALAKHA

To exclude the burnt offering of consecrated property – פְּרָט לְעוֹלַת הֶקְדֵּשׁ: If one consecrates a burnt offering for Temple maintenance, or if one consecrates all his property, including an animal that is fit for a burnt offering, then the priest does not acquire the hide of the burnt offering. Rather, the hide is sold, and the money is allocated for Temple maintenance. This is in accordance with the statement of Rabbi Yehuda and its interpretation by Rabbi Yannai and Rav Hamnuna (Rambam *Sefer Avoda, Hilkhot Ma'aseh HaKorbanot* 5:21).

וכן אמר רב נחמן אמר רבה בר אבוה: פרט לעולה הבאה מן המותרות.

The Gemara returns to the explanation of Rabbi Ḥiyya bar Yosef and comments: **And so says Rav Naḥman that Rabba bar Avuh says:** The phrase "a man's burnt offering" serves **to exclude a burnt offering that comes from** property that was **left over.**

אמר ליה רב המנונא לרב נחמן: כמאן – כרבי יהודה? הא הדר ביה! דתניא: "ששה לנדבה" – לעולה הבאה מן המותרות, שלא יהו כהנים זכאין בעורה, דברי רבי יהודה.

Rav Hamnuna said to Rav Naḥman: In accordance with whose statement is your opinion? It is **in accordance with** the opinion of **Rabbi Yehuda.** But **didn't** Rabbi Yehuda **retract** this statement? **As it is taught** in a *baraita*: The mishna in tractate *Shekalim* (6:5) states that the Temple had **six** collection boxes shaped like horns, **for** communal **gift** offerings.[NH] These funds would go **toward burnt offerings that come from** money that was **left over.** For example, if someone dedicated money to purchasing an offering, and after his purchase some of the sum remained, he would put it in these boxes. The *halakha* **is that the priests have no right to the hide of** such an offering.[N] This is **the statement of Rabbi Yehuda.**

אמר לו רבי נחמיה, ואמרי לה רבי שמעון: אם כן, ביטלת מדרשו של יהוידע הכהן. דתניא, זה מדרש דרש יהוידע הכהן: "אשם הוא אשם אשם לה'" – כל שבא משום חטאת ומשום אשם, ילקח בו עולות, הבשר – לשם, עורה – לכהנים.

Rabbi Neḥemya said to Rabbi Yehuda, **and some say** that **Rabbi Shimon** said to him: **If so, you have nullified the interpretation of Jehoiada the priest.**[N] **As it is taught** in a mishna (*Shekalim* 6:6) that **Jehoiada the priest taught this interpretation:** The verse states: **"It is a guilt offering; he is certainly guilty before the Lord"** (Leviticus 5:19). The phrase "before the Lord" teaches that if **any** money **comes on account of a sin offering or on account of a guilt offering,** i.e., it is left over after their purchase, **burnt offerings must be purchased with it,** and their **flesh** must be burned on the altar **to the Lord.** But **its hide** shall go **to the priests.** Rabbi Yehuda did not respond, indicating that he conceded that the hides of such offerings go to the priests.

אמר ליה: אלא מר במאי מוקים לה? אמר ליה: מוקמינא ליה במקדיש נכסיו,

Rav Naḥman **said to** Rav Hamnuna: **But how does the Master interpret** the phrase: "A man's burnt offering," as meaning? Rav Hamnuna **said to him: I interpret it** as referring **to one who consecrates** all **his property,** including animals fit for burnt offerings. If these animals are later sacrificed as burnt offerings, the priests do not acquire the hides, since the offerings are consecrated property.

וכדרבי יהושע. דתנן: המקדיש נכסיו והיו בהן בהמות הראויות לגבי מזבח, זכרים ונקבות, רבי אליעזר אומר: זכרים – ימכרו לצורכי עולות, נקבות – ימכרו לצורכי זבחי שלמים, ודמיהן יפלו עם שאר נכסים לבדק הבית.

And this is **in accordance with** the opinion **of Rabbi Yehoshua, as we learned** in a mishna (*Shekalim* 4:7): If **one consecrates his property**[H] without specifying the purpose, generally speaking, it goes toward Temple maintenance. **But** if **among it were animals fit to** be sacrificed on the **altar,** either **male or female,** then **Rabbi Eliezer says:** Animals that are fit for offerings must be sacrificed. Therefore, the **male** animals **shall be sold for the purpose of burnt offerings** to those who need to bring such offerings, and the **female** animals, which cannot be brought as burnt offerings, **shall be sold for the purpose of peace offerings** to those who need to bring such offerings. **And** because they were consecrated for Temple maintenance, **their proceeds shall be allocated with the rest of** the person's **property for Temple maintenance.**

רבי יהושע אומר: זכרים עצמם – יקרבו עולות, ונקבות – ימכרו לצורכי שלמים, ויביא בדמיהן עולות, ושאר נכסים – יפלו לבדק הבית.

Rabbi Yehoshua says: The donor intended that all animals fit for sacrifice be brought as burnt offerings, and the rest of his property be given for Temple maintenance. Therefore, the **males shall be sacrificed themselves** as **burnt offerings; and the females shall be sold for the purpose of** being sacrificed as **peace offerings, and he shall bring burnt offerings with their proceeds;**[N] **and the rest** of his **property shall be allocated for Temple maintenance.**

ואפילו לרבי יהושע דאמר אדם חולק הקדישו – הני מילי בשר, אבל עור תפיס.

Rav Hamnuna explains: **And even according to** the opinion of **Rabbi Yehoshua, who says** that **a person divides his consecrated** property, as he rules that the animals are themselves sacrificed while the other property is given for Temple maintenance, **this statement** applies specifically to the **flesh,** which is fit to be burned on the altar; **but** as for the **hide,** which is not, the fund for Temple maintenance **acquires** it from the outset, and the priests therefore have no right to it. This is the *halakha* that Rabbi Yehuda derives from the phrase "a man's burnt offering."

NOTES

Six boxes for communal gift offerings – ששה לנדבה: As described in tractate *Shekalim* (6:5), there were thirteen collection boxes in the Temple. They were referred to as horns because they were narrow at the top to prevent people from reaching inside. The Mishna details how the funds from the various boxes were allocated, including six boxes whose funds went to communal gift offerings. See tractate *Menaḥot* (107b), where the Sages discuss why there were six collection boxes.

That the priests have no right to the hide – שלא יהו הכהנים זכאין בעורה: Some ask what is done with the hide. They answer that it is sold, and the funds go to purchasing a communal burnt offering to be sacrificed when there are no other offerings on the altar (*Shita Mekubbetzet*).

The interpretation of Jehoiada the priest – מדרשו של יהוידע הכהן: Jehoiada was the High Priest during the reign of Jehoash, who reformed the system of collection and maintenance in the Temple (see II Kings 12:5–17). The verse there states: "The money for guilt offerings and the money for sin offerings was not brought into the House of the Lord; it was for the priests" (II Kings 12:17). The verse cannot be interpreted according to its literal meaning, that money dedicated for offerings was given to the priests. Rather, money that was left over after purchasing sin offerings and guilt offerings was used to purchase burnt offerings, and the priests acquired their hides.

The mishna explains (*Shekalim* 6:6) that Jehoiada interpreted the verse: "It is a guilt offering; he is certainly guilty before the Lord" (Leviticus 5:19), which contains an apparent contradiction, as, if it is a guilt offering, it belongs to the priests (see Leviticus 7:7), yet the offering is "before the Lord." Jehoiada explained that this verse refers to money left over from purchasing a guilt offering, which is used to purchase a burnt offering. Its flesh goes on the altar to the Lord and its hide goes to the priests.

And he shall bring burnt offerings with their proceeds – ויביא בדמיהן עולות: He does not bring the female animals themselves as peace offerings. Rabbi Yehoshua holds that when one apportions his property without specifying, the assumption is that he wants everything to go entirely to God, with no portion going to the priests. Therefore, the female animals are not sacrificed themselves as peace offerings, whose meat is shared by the owner and the priests. Rather, the owner sells the female animals to others for them to use as peace offerings, then uses the money to purchase burnt offerings, which are consumed entirely on the altar.

HALAKHA

Six boxes for communal gift offerings – ששה לנדבה: There were thirteen collection boxes in the Temple, shaped like horns. The last six of them were designated for money that was left over after purchasing offerings: The eighth for money left over after purchasing sin offerings, the ninth for money left over after purchasing guilt offerings, etc. All the money in these six boxes was used to purchase animals for burnt offerings, and their hides went to the priests like all burnt offerings (Rambam *Sefer Zemanim, Hilkhot Shekalim* 2:3 and *Sefer Avoda, Hilkhot Pesulei HaMukdashin* 5:9).

If one consecrates his property – המקדיש נכסיו: If one consecrates all his animals, or all his property, without specifying for what purpose, then they are consecrated for Temple maintenance. Of the unblemished animals that are fit for offerings, the males are sold for the purpose of being sacrificed as burnt offerings, and the females are sold for the purpose of being sacrificed as peace offerings. The money from the sale is allocated for Temple maintenance. The *halakha* is in accordance with the opinion of Rabbi Eliezer, because Rabbi Akiva ruled in accordance with his opinion in tractate *Shekalim* (Rambam *Sefer Hafla'a, Hilkhot Arakhin* 5:7 and Radbaz there).

רַבִּי יוֹסֵי בְּרַבִּי יְהוּדָה אוֹמֵר: פְּרָט לְעוֹלַת גֵּרִים. אֲמַר לֵיהּ רַב סִימַאי בַּר חִילְקַאי לְרָבִינָא: אַטּוּ גֵּר לָאו ״אִישׁ״ הוּא? אֲמַר לֵיהּ: פְּרָט לְגֵר שֶׁמֵּת וְאֵין לוֹ יוֹרְשִׁים.

The *baraita* states: **Rabbi Yosei, son of Rabbi Yehuda, says:** The phrase "a man's burnt offering" serves **to exclude the burnt offering of converts.** The priests do not acquire the hides of such offerings. **Rav Simai bar Ḥilkai said to Ravina: Is that to say** that **a convert is not** included in the category of **a man?** Ravina **said to him:** Rabbi Yosei, son of Rabbi Yehuda, meant that the verse serves **to exclude** the burnt offering of **a convert who died and has no heirs.**[N] The offering has no owner, and therefore the priests do not acquire its hide.

תָּנוּ רַבָּנַן: ״עֹלַת אִישׁ״ – אֵין לִי אֶלָּא עוֹלַת אִישׁ, עוֹלַת גֵּרִים נָשִׁים וַעֲבָדִים מִנַּיִן? תַּלְמוּד לוֹמַר: ״עוֹר הָעֹלָה״ – רִיבָּה.

§ **The Sages taught** in a *baraita*: The verse states: "And the priest that offers **a man's burnt offering,** the priest shall have to himself the hide of the burnt offering that he has sacrificed" (Leviticus 7:8). From this verse **I have derived** the *halakha* **only** with regard to a **man's burnt offering,** i.e., that of a born-Jewish male. **From where** is the same derived with regard to **the burnt offering of converts, women, or** Canaanite **slaves?**[NH] **The verse states: "The hide of the burnt offering,"**[N] and it thereby **included** these as well.

וְאִם כֵּן, מָה תַּלְמוּד לוֹמַר ״עֹלַת אִישׁ״ – עוֹלָה שֶׁעָלְתָה לְאִישׁ, פְּרָט לְשֶׁנִּשְׁחֲטָה חוּץ לִזְמַנָּהּ וְחוּץ לִמְקוֹמָהּ, שֶׁלֹּא יְהוּ הַכֹּהֲנִים זַכָּאִין בְּעוֹרָהּ.

And if so, why must **the verse state: "A man's burnt offering"?** It serves to teach that the priests acquire the hide only of **a burnt offering that satisfied** the obligation **of a man,**[N] i.e., **to exclude** a burnt offering **that was slaughtered** with the intention of consuming it **beyond its** designated **time or outside its** designated **area**[H] and was thereby disqualified. The verse teaches **that the priests have no right to the hide of** such an offering.

יָכוֹל שֶׁאֲנִי מְרַבֶּה שֶׁנִּשְׁחֲטָה שֶׁלֹּא לִשְׁמָהּ, הוֹאִיל וְלֹא עָלְתָה לִבְעָלִים

One **might** have thought **that I include** a burnt offering **that was not slaughtered for its own sake** but for the sake of another offering. **Since it does not satisfy** the obligation **of the owner,**

NOTES

A convert who died and has no heirs – גֵּר שֶׁמֵּת וְאֵין לוֹ יוֹרְשִׁים: A typical born Jew certainly has heirs. If he has no children, his father inherits from him; if his father is not alive, his brothers inherit from him; if he has no brothers, his father's brothers inherit from him, and so on. But a convert no longer has any legal connection to his original biological family, so if he has no children, he has no heirs. In that case, his property becomes ownerless, and anyone who seizes it acquires it.

The burnt offering of converts, women, or slaves – עוֹלַת גֵּרִים נָשִׁים וַעֲבָדִים: Rashi removes converts from this list, as Rabbi Yosei, son of Rabbi Yehuda, taught that a convert is included in the phrase "a man's burnt offering." Others write that converts are listed here out of a habit of language even though they do not belong, as they are frequently mentioned together with women and slaves in *Torat Kohanim* (Rabbi Shimshon of Saens on *Torat Kohanim*). The Ra'avad writes that this refers to a convert who died without heirs, and this *tanna* disagrees with Rabbi Yosei, son of Rabbi Yehuda, and holds that the priests acquire the hide of that convert's burnt offering.

The *Kesef Mishne* writes that the Rambam's text of the Gemara reads: Gentiles, instead of converts. That is, if a gentile brings a burnt offering, the priests acquire the hide. The Mahari Kurkus writes that the text of the Rambam should be emended to read: Converts.

Slaves are included together with women because they are compared through a verbal analogy between the terms "to her" (Leviticus 19:20) and "to her" (Deuteronomy 24:3), teaching that they share the same *halakhot* (*Tosafot*).

The verse states: The hide of the burnt offering – תַּלְמוּד לוֹמַר עוֹר הָעֹלָה: The verse could have simply stated: Its hide, as it is already discussing the burnt offering of a man. The longer phrase: "The hide of the burnt offering," serves to include the burnt offerings of all people.

A burnt offering that satisfied the obligation of a man – עוֹלָה שֶׁעָלְתָה לְאִישׁ: In some circumstances, the term man indicates an owner (Malbim). An offering that was slaughtered beyond its designated time and outside its designated area is not considered to belong to its owner, as it did not satisfy his obligation (*Korban Aharon*).

HALAKHA

The burnt offering of converts, women, or slaves – עוֹלַת גֵּרִים נָשִׁים וַעֲבָדִים: The hide of a burnt offering goes to the priests, whether it was brought by a man, woman, Canaanite slave, or gentile, as taught in Rambam's version of the *baraita*, which lists gentiles instead of converts (Rambam *Sefer Avoda, Hilkhot Ma'aseh HaKorbanot* 5:19 and *Kesef Mishne* there).

Beyond its designated time or outside its designated area – חוּץ לִזְמַנָּהּ וְחוּץ לִמְקוֹמָהּ: If an offering was disqualified because it was slaughtered with the intention of performing part of its rite beyond its designated time or outside its designated area, then because the offering did not satisfy its owner's obligation, the hide must be burned. This applies both to offerings of the most sacred order and to offerings of lesser sanctity, as taught in the *baraita* (Rambam *Sefer Avoda, Hilkhot Pesulei HaMukdashin* 19:9).

לֹא יְהוּ כֹּהֲנִים זַכָּאִין בְּעוֹרָהּ? תַּלְמוּד לוֹמַר: ״עוֹר הָעֹלָה״, מִכׇּל מָקוֹם.

I might have thought that **the priests have no right to its hide.** Therefore, **the verse states: "The hide of the burnt offering,"**[N] to teach that **in any case** where the offering is not disqualified, the priests acquire its hide, even if it did not satisfy the owner's obligation.

״עוֹר הָעֹלָה״ – אֵין לִי אֶלָּא עוֹר הָעוֹלָה, עוֹרוֹת קׇדְשֵׁי קֳדָשִׁים מִנַּיִן? תַּלְמוּד לוֹמַר: ״עוֹר הָעֹלָה אֲשֶׁר הִקְרִיב״. יָכוֹל שֶׁאֲנִי מְרַבֶּה אַף קֳדָשִׁים קַלִּים? תַּלְמוּד לוֹמַר: ״עֹלָה״, מָה עוֹלָה קׇדְשֵׁי קֳדָשִׁים – אַף כׇּל קׇדְשֵׁי קֳדָשִׁים.

And from the phrase **"the hide of the burnt offering" I have** derived **only** that the priests acquire **the hide of the burnt offering. From where** do I derive that they acquire **the hides of** all **offerings of the most sacred order? The verse states: "The hide of the burnt offering which he has offered,"** which serves to include any offering that the priests sacrifice. If so, one **might** have thought **that I include even offerings of lesser sanctity.** Therefore, **the verse states: "Burnt offering,"** and not simply: Offering, to teach that **just as a burnt offering is an offering of the most sacred order, so too** the priests acquire the hides only of **all offerings of the most sacred order;** they do not acquire the hides of offerings of lesser sanctity.

רַבִּי יִשְׁמָעֵאל אוֹמֵר: ״עוֹר הָעֹלָה״ – אֵין לִי אֶלָּא הָעוֹלָה, עוֹרוֹת קׇדְשֵׁי קֳדָשִׁים מִנַּיִן? וְדִין הוּא: וּמָה עוֹלָה שֶׁלֹּא זָכוּ בִּבְשָׂרָהּ – זָכוּ בְּעוֹרָהּ, קׇדְשֵׁי קֳדָשִׁים שֶׁזָּכוּ בִּבְשָׂרָן – אֵינוֹ דִּין שֶׁזָּכוּ בְּעוֹרָן?

The *baraita* continues: **Rabbi Yishmael says** there is a different derivation. From the phrase **"the hide of the burnt offering," I have** derived **only** that the priests acquire the hide of **the burnt offering. From where** is it derived that they acquire **the hides of** all **offerings of the most sacred order? It is** based on **a logical inference: Just as** in the case of **a burnt offering, for which** the priests **do not acquire its meat,** the priests nevertheless **acquire its hide,** then in the case of **offerings of the most sacred order, for which** the priests **do acquire its meat, is it not logical that** they **acquire their hides?**

מִזְבֵּחַ יוֹכִיחַ, שֶׁזָּכָה בַּבָּשָׂר וְלֹא זָכָה בָּעוֹר! מַה לְּמִזְבֵּחַ שֶׁכֵּן לֹא זָכָה בְּמִקְצָת, תֹּאמַר בְּכֹהֲנִים שֶׁזָּכוּ בְּמִקְצָת; הוֹאִיל וְזָכוּ בְּמִקְצָת – זָכוּ בְּכוּלֵּיהּ.

One may counter: Let the **altar prove** that this is not a valid *a fortiori* inference, **as it acquires the meat, and** still **it does not acquire the hide.** One may respond: **What is notable about the altar?** It is notable **in that it does not acquire** hides **in any** instance. **Will you say** the *halakha* concerning the altar should teach the *halakha* **concerning** the **priests, who acquire** hides of **some of** the offerings, as the Torah explicitly grants them the hides of burnt offerings? Rather say: **Since** the priests **acquire** hides of **some of** the offerings, **they acquire** the hides of **all** offerings of the most sacred order.

רַבִּי אוֹמֵר: כׇּל עַצְמוֹ לֹא הוּצְרַכְנוּ אֶלָּא לְעוֹר הָעוֹלָה בִּלְבַד. שֶׁבְּכׇל מָקוֹם הָעוֹר מְהַלֵּךְ אַחַר הַבָּשָׂר.

Rabbi Yehuda HaNasi **says:** There is no need to derive that hides of offerings of the most sacred order go to the priests. **We need** the verse **itself only to** teach that this is the *halakha* with regard to **the hide of the burnt offering. As** the Torah does not generally require that an offering be flayed, **in all** other **cases the hide** of the offering **follows the flesh** of the offering.

פָּרִים הַנִּשְׂרָפִין וּשְׂעִירִים הַנִּשְׂרָפִין – הֵן וְעוֹרוֹתֵיהֶן [נִשְׂרָפִין] עִמָּהֶן; חַטָּאת וְאָשָׁם וְזִבְחֵי שַׁלְמֵי צִיבּוּר מַתָּנָה לַכֹּהֵן, רָצוּ – מַפְשִׁיטִין אוֹתָן, לֹא רָצוּ – אוֹכְלִין אוֹתָן עַל גַּבֵּי עוֹרָן; קֳדָשִׁים קַלִּים לַבְּעָלִים, רָצוּ – מַפְשִׁיטִין אוֹתָן, רָצוּ – אוֹכְלִין אוֹתָן עַל גַּב עוֹרָן.

For example, **bulls that are burned**[B] **and goats that are burned**[H] must be burned **themselves, and their hides burned with them,** as the Torah states explicitly (see Leviticus 4:11–12). **A sin offering, and a guilt offering, and a communal peace offering** are given as **a gift to the priest** (see Leviticus 7:7); if the priests **want,** they may **flay them** and use the hides, and if they **do not want** to use the hides, they may **eat** the offerings **together with their hides. Offerings of lesser sanctity** are given **to the owners;** if they **want,** they may **flay them** and use the hides, and if they **want,** they may **eat** the offerings **together with their hides.**

אֲבָל עוֹלָה נֶאֱמַר בָּהּ: ״וְהִפְשִׁיט אֶת הָעֹלָה וְנִתַּח אֹתָהּ לִנְתָחֶיהָ״, יָכוֹל לֹא יְהוּ הַכֹּהֲנִים זַכָּאִין בְּעוֹרָהּ? תַּלְמוּד לוֹמַר: ״עוֹר הָעֹלָה אֲשֶׁר הִקְרִיב״.

But with regard to a burnt offering it is stated: "And he shall flay the burnt offering, and cut it into its pieces" (Leviticus 1:6). One **might** have thought that, because all the flesh of the burnt offering is burned on the altar, **the priests have no right to its hide.** Therefore, **the verse states:** "The priest shall have to himself **the hide of the burnt offering that he has sacrificed"** (Leviticus 7:8).

NOTES

The verse states: The hide of the burnt offering – תַּלְמוּד לוֹמַר עוֹר הָעֹלָה: The derivation for the *halakha* concerning a burnt offering of women and slaves also was from this phrase, but that was from fact that the verse did not state: Its hide. Here, the derivation is from the fact that the verse did not state: The hide of his burnt offering (*Korban Aharon*). The offering that was slaughtered not for the sake of his obligation is not entirely his, in that he did not satisfy his obligation, but nevertheless it is considered his gift offering (Malbim).

BACKGROUND

Bulls that are burned – פָּרִים הַנִּשְׂרָפִין: There are two kinds of sin offerings: Outer sin offerings and inner sin offerings. An outer sin offering, whose blood is presented on the external altar, is brought by an individual who unwittingly violates a prohibition whose intentional violation is punishable by *karet*. This offering may be either a lamb or a goat. If a king brings the offering, it must be a goat. The blood of the offering is presented on the corners of the external altar, and its fats and sacrificial portions are burned on that altar. The remainder of the meat is eaten by priests. Inner sin offerings, whose blood is presented inside the Sanctuary, are brought by the community or the High Priest for following a mistaken halakhic ruling. These offerings are bulls, and their blood is sprinkled toward the Curtain and on the golden altar. Their fats and sacrificial portions are burned on the altar, and the rest of the animal is burned outside the camp or the city of Jerusalem. The bull and goat of Yom Kippur, known as bulls that are burned and goats that are burned, are subject to the same procedures as inner sin offerings. Therefore, the *halakhot* of inner sin offerings apply to them.

Burning of the bull of Yom Kippur outside Jerusalem

HALAKHA

Bulls that are burned and goats that are burned, etc. – פָּרִים הַנִּשְׂרָפִין וּשְׂעִירִים הַנִּשְׂרָפִין וכו׳: The hides of all offerings are flayed, and then the portions to be consumed on the altar are removed. The exception is sin offerings that are burned, which are not flayed at all (Rambam *Sefer Avoda*, *Hilkhot Ma'aseh HaKorbanot* 5:18).

״לוֹ יִהְיֶה״ – פְּרָט לִטְבוּל יוֹם וּמְחוּסַּר כִּיפּוּרִים וְאוֹנֵן. שֶׁיָּכוֹל, לֹא יִזְכּוּ בַּבָּשָׂר שֶׁהוּא לַאֲכִילָה, יִזְכּוּ בָּעוֹר שֶׁאֵינוֹ לַאֲכִילָה! תַּלְמוּד לוֹמַר: ״לוֹ יִהְיֶה״ – פְּרָט לִמְחוּסַּר כִּיפּוּרִים וּטְבוּל יוֹם וְאוֹנֵן.

The phrase "the priest **shall have to himself**" serves **to exclude** a priest **who immersed that day and** a priest **who has not yet** brought **an atonement** offering, **and an acute mourner,** i.e., meaning that they do not receive a share of the hides, just as they do not receive a share of the meat. **As** one **might** have thought that although these priests **will not acquire the meat,** this is **because it is for consumption,** and they are not permitted to partake of it; but **they will acquire the hide, because it is not for consumption.** Therefore, **the verse states: "Shall have to himself," to exclude** a priest **who has not yet** brought **an atonement** offering, **and** a priest **who immersed that day, and an acute mourner.**

וְתַנָּא קַמָּא נַמִי, תֵּיפּוֹק לִי מִדִּינָא! מִילְּתָא דְּאָתְיָא בְּקַל וָחוֹמֶר, טָרַח וְכָתַב לָהּ קְרָא.

The Gemara asks: **But let the first** ***tanna*** **also derive** the *halakha* **logically,** as Rabbi Yishmael did. Why did he cite a verse? The Gemara answers: Often when there is **a matter that can be derived through an** ***a fortiori*** inference, the **verse** nevertheless **takes the trouble and writes it** explicitly.

וְרַבִּי יִשְׁמָעֵאל, הַאי ״אֲשֶׁר הִקְרִיב״ מַאי עָבֵיד לֵיהּ? פְּרָט לִטְבוּל יוֹם וּמְחוּסַּר כִּיפּוּרִים וְאוֹנֵן.

And as for **Rabbi Yishmael, what does he do with this** phrase: "The hide of the burnt offering **that he has sacrificed,"** from which the first *tanna* derives the *halakha*? He holds that it serves **to exclude** a priest **who immersed that day, and** a priest **who has not yet** brought **an atonement** offering, **and an acute mourner,** who do not receive a share in the hides.

וְתֵיפּוֹק לֵיהּ מִ״לּוֹ יִהְיֶה״! רַבִּי יִשְׁמָעֵאל לְטַעְמֵיהּ, דְּאָמַר רַבִּי יוֹחָנָן מִשּׁוּם רַבִּי יִשְׁמָעֵאל: נֶאֱמַר בָּעוֹלָה ״לוֹ יִהְיֶה״, וְנֶאֱמַר בָּאָשָׁם ״לוֹ יִהְיֶה״, מָה לְהַלָּן עַצְמוֹתָיו מוּתָּרִין – אַף כָּאן עַצְמוֹתָיו מוּתָּרִין.

The Gemara challenges: **But let** Rabbi Yishmael **derive** this *halakha* **from** the phrase: **"Shall have to himself,"** as does Rabbi Yehuda HaNasi. The Gemara explains: **Rabbi Yishmael** conforms **to his** line **of reasoning,** that the phrase teaches a different *halakha*. **As Rabbi Yoḥanan says in the name of Rabbi Yishmael:** It **is stated: "Shall have to himself"** (Leviticus 7:8), **with regard to a burnt offering, and it is stated:** "The priest that makes atonement, **he shall have to himself"** (Leviticus 7:7), **with regard to a guilt offering.** The following verbal analogy is derived from here: **Just as there,** after the blood of a guilt offering is presented, **its bones** become **permitted** to the priest for any use, since only the portions intended for consumption on the altar are sacrificed whereas the rest of the animal is given to the priests, **so too here,** with regard to a burnt offering, **its bones** that are not attached to the flesh and are therefore not intended for the altar **are permitted.**

מוּפְנֵי, דְּאִי לָא מוּפְנֵי, אִיכָּא לְמִיפְרַךְ: מָה לְאָשָׁם שֶׁכֵּן בְּשָׂרוֹ מוּתָּר! ״לוֹ יִהְיֶה״ קְרָא יְתֵירָא הוּא.

With regard to this verbal analogy the Gemara comments: It must be that those terms **are free,** i.e., superfluous in their context and therefore available for the purpose of establishing a verbal analogy. **As, if they are not free,** the verbal analogy **can be refuted** as follows: **What** is notable **about a guilt offering?** It is notable **in that its meat is permitted** to the priests, unlike the flesh of a burnt offering, which is burned upon the altar, and perhaps this is why the bones of a guilt offering are also permitted. Since the phrase: **"Shall have it to himself,"** is **a superfluous** term in each **verse,** the analogy stands, because a verbal analogy based on free terms cannot be refuted logically.

מתני׳ כָּל הַקֳּדָשִׁים שֶׁאֵירַע בָּהֶן פְּסוּל קוֹדֶם לְהֶפְשֵׁיטָן – אֵין עוֹרוֹתֵיהֶן לַכֹּהֲנִים, לְאַחַר הֶפְשֵׁיטָן – עוֹרוֹתֵיהֶן לַכֹּהֲנִים. אָמַר רַבִּי חֲנִינָא סְגַן הַכֹּהֲנִים: מִיָּמַי לֹא רָאִיתִי עוֹר שֶׁיּוֹצֵא לְבֵית הַשְּׂרֵיפָה.

MISHNA If any **offerings** of the most sacred order **were disqualified**[H] **prior to their flaying, their hides do not** go **to the priests;** rather, they are burned together with the flesh in the place of burning. If they were disqualified **after their flaying, their hides** go **to the priests. Rabbi Ḥanina, the deputy High Priest, said: In all my days, I never saw a hide going out to the place of burning.**

אָמַר רַבִּי עֲקִיבָא: מִדְּבָרָיו לָמַדְנוּ, שֶׁהַמַּפְשִׁיט אֶת הַבְּכוֹר וְנִמְצָא טְרֵיפָה – שֶׁיֵּאוֹתוּ הַכֹּהֲנִים בְּעוֹרוֹ. וַחֲכָמִים אוֹמְרִים: אֵין ״לֹא רָאִינוּ״ רְאָיָה, אֶלָּא יֵצֵא לְבֵית הַשְּׂרֵיפָה.

Rabbi Akiva said: From the statement of Rabbi Ḥanina, the deputy High Priest, **we learned that** in a case where **one flays the firstborn** offering, **and the** animal is later **discovered to have a wound that would have caused it to die within twelve months** [***tereifa***], the *halakha* **is that the priests may derive benefit** [***sheye'otu***][L] **from its hide.**[H] **And the Rabbis say:** The claim: **We did not see, is no proof;**[N] **rather,** if after flaying it is discovered that the animal was unfit before it was flayed, the hide **goes out to the place of burning.**

HALAKHA

Any offerings of the most sacred order were disqualified, etc. – כָּל הַקֳּדָשִׁים שֶׁאֵירַע בָּהֶן פְּסוּל וכו׳: If an offering of the most sacred order was disqualified prior to its flaying, the hide does not go to the priests. If an offering of lesser sanctity was disqualified prior to its flaying, the hide does not go to the owner. In both cases, the hides are burned with the flesh. If the offerings were disqualified after the hides were flayed, the hides go to the priests or owners, in accordance with the opinion of the Rabbis in the mishna (Rambam *Sefer Avoda, Hilkhot Ma'aseh HaKorbanot* 5:20 and *Hilkhot Pesulei HaMukdashin* 19:9).

One flays the firstborn, etc. – הַמַּפְשִׁיט אֶת הַבְּכוֹר וכו׳: If an unblemished firstborn animal is found to be a *tereifa* after its hide is flayed, the hide is burned and the flesh is buried, in accordance with the opinion of the Rabbis (Rambam *Sefer Korbanot, Hilkhot Bekhorot* 3:10).

LANGUAGE

Derive benefit [*ye'otu*] – יֵאוֹתוּ: Apparently related to the word sign [*ot*], this term is used in the Bible with the meaning: To consent or agree. The Sages use it with an additional meaning: Utilize or derive benefit.

NOTES

The claim: We did not see, is no proof – אֵין לֹא רָאִינוּ רְאָיָה: Perhaps there never happened to be this case of *tereifa* in the Temple, or perhaps it happened and the hide was burned, but Rabbi Ḥanina, the deputy High Priest, did not happen to witness it. This principle applies to almost all areas of testimony, excepting a few cases in rabbinic law where the incident would be expected to be very well known, in which case the claim: We did not see, is given weight.

GEMARA The previous mishna (103a) teaches: In the case of **any** burnt offering **for which the altar did not acquire its flesh,** e.g., if it was disqualified prior to the sprinkling of its blood, **the priests did not acquire its hide.** The mishna does not state any qualification, indicating that this is the *halakha* **even if** the priest **flayed the hide before** the **sprinkling** of the blood on the altar. The Gemara posits: **Whose** opinion is this? **It is** the opinion of **Rabbi Elazar, son of Rabbi Shimon, who says: The blood does not effect acceptance of the hide by itself;** i.e., it effects acceptance of the hide only together with the flesh. Since the flesh is disqualified and the sprinkling does not effect its acceptance, the sprinkling does not effect acceptance for the hide either.

גמ׳ כל שלא זכה המזבח בבשרה, לא זכו הכהנים בעורה – ואף על גב דאפשטיה לעור קודם זריקה; מני – רבי אלעזר ברבי שמעון היא, דאמר: אין הדם מרצה על העור בפני עצמו.

The Gemara challenges: **Say the latter clause,** i.e., the mishna here: If **any offerings** of the most sacred order **were disqualified prior to their flaying, their hides do not** go **to the priests.** If they were disqualified **after their flaying, their hides** go **to the priests.** This indicates that once the hides are flayed, they go to the priests even if the flesh was disqualified before the sprinkling of the blood. If so, **we arrive at the** opinion **of Rabbi** Yehuda HaNasi,[N] **who says: The blood effects acceptance of the hide,** i.e., renders the hide permitted to the priests, **by itself.**[NH] Can it be that **the former clause** of the mishna is in accordance with the opinion of **Rabbi Elazar, son of Rabbi Shimon,** and **the latter clause** is in accordance with the opinion of **Rabbi** Yehuda HaNasi?

אימא סיפא: כל הקדשים שאירע בהן פסול קודם הפשיטן – אין עורותיהן לכהנים, לאחר הפשיטן – עורותיהן לכהנים; אתאן לרבי, דאמר: הדם מרצה על העור בפני עצמו. רישא רבי אלעזר ברבי שמעון, סיפא רבי?

Abaye said: Since the latter clause is the opinion of **Rabbi** Yehuda HaNasi, it must be that **the former clause is also** the opinion of **Rabbi** Yehuda HaNasi. **And** although Rabbi Yehuda HaNasi holds that in principle the priests should acquire the hides if they are removed before the flesh is disqualified, in any case **Rabbi** Yehuda HaNasi **concedes that** the **flaying is not** done **before** the **sprinkling.**[NH] Since the offering cannot be disqualified before the hide is removed, practically speaking, the priests will never acquire the hides unless the altar acquires the flesh, as taught in the former clause.

אמר אביי: מדסיפא רבי היא – רישא נמי רבי היא, ומודה רבי שאין הפשט קודם זריקה.

Rava said: On the contrary, **since the former clause** is the opinion of **Rabbi Elazar, son of Rabbi Shimon,** it must be that **the latter clause is also** the opinion of **Rabbi Elazar, son of Rabbi Shimon.** When the mishna states that the priests acquire the hides if the flesh was disqualified after the flaying, it must mean that the flesh was disqualified after the sprinkling. Therefore, **what** does the mishna mean by the phrase: **Before flaying,**

רבא אמר: מדרישא רבי אלעזר ברבי שמעון – סיפא נמי רבי אלעזר ברבי שמעון; מאי ״קודם הפשט״,

and what does it mean by the phrase: **After flaying?** It means **before** the moment the offerings **became fit for flaying,** and **after** the moment **they became fit for flaying,** i.e., before and after the sprinkling of the blood.

ומאי ״אחר הפשט״ – קודם שנראו להפשט, אחר שנראו להפשט.

The Gemara clarifies: **What** is the opinion of **Rabbi** Yehuda HaNasi, **and what** is the opinion of **Rabbi Elazar, son of Rabbi Shimon?** Their opinions are **as it is taught** in a *baraita*: **Rabbi** Yehuda HaNasi **says: The blood effects acceptance of the hide by itself,** after it has been flayed, even if the flesh is disqualified. **And if, when** the hide is still **with the flesh, a disqualification appears on** the flesh, **whether before** the **sprinkling** of the blood **or after** the **sprinkling** of the blood, then the *halakha* with regard to the hide **is parallel to** the *halakha* with regard to the flesh: Both are burned.

מאי רבי ומאי רבי אלעזר ברבי שמעון? דתניא, רבי אומר: הדם מרצה על העור בפני עצמו. וכשהוא עם הבשר, נולד בו פסול, בין קודם זריקה בין לאחר זריקה – הרי הוא כיוצא בו.

NOTES

We arrive at the opinion of Rabbi Yehuda HaNasi – **אתאן לרבי**: The essential dispute is that Rabbi Elazar, son of Rabbi Shimon, holds that the hide does not go to the priests if the flesh is disqualified before the sprinkling of the blood, even if it has already been flayed. Rabbi Yehuda HaNasi holds that it depends on whether the hide is flayed; if it has been flayed, then it is permitted even if the offering is disqualified before the sprinkling of the blood.

See Rabbeinu Ḥananel, who explains the dispute in another manner, based on a version of the Gemara rejected by Rashi. He explains that the dispute is in a case where the flesh was disqualified after the sprinkling of the blood and the hide was not yet flayed. Rabbi Yehuda HaNasi holds that the hide is not permitted to the priests, as the blood effects acceptance of the hide on its own only if it is already flayed. Rabbi Elazar, son of Rabbi Shimon, holds that the hide is permitted to the priests, as the hide was permitted along with the flesh before the offering was disqualified.

The blood effects acceptance of the hide by itself – **מרצה על העור בפני עצמו**: Rabbi Yehuda HaNasi disagrees with Rabbi Elazar, son of Rabbi Shimon, only when the hide has already been flayed (see 104a). Before the hide is flayed, its status follows that of the flesh.

Rabbi Yehuda HaNasi concedes that the flaying is not before the sprinkling – **מודה רבי שאין הפשט קודם זריקה**: This is because it is forbidden to let the blood sit, lest the blood coagulate, while the hide is being flayed. Therefore, in practice the priests always flayed the hide after sprinkling the blood.

HALAKHA

The blood effects acceptance of the hide by itself – **הדם מרצה על העור בפני עצמו**: If offerings of the most sacred order are disqualified prior to being flayed, their hides do not go to the priests. If they are disqualified after their flaying, their hides go to the priests. The Rambam does not distinguish between a case where the offering was disqualified before the sprinkling of the blood and a case where it was disqualified after the sprinkling of the blood, in accordance with the opinion of Rabbi Yehuda HaNasi (Rambam *Sefer Avoda, Hilkhot Ma'aseh HaKorbanot* 5:20; see *Likkutei Halakhot*).

The flaying is not before the sprinkling – **אין הפשט קודם זריקה**: With regard to all offerings, the blood is first sprinkled, then the hide is flayed and the portions to be consumed on the altar are removed. If the hide is flayed before the blood is sprinkled, the offering is not disqualified, in accordance with the opinion of Rabbi Yehuda HaNasi (Rambam *Sefer Avoda, Hilkhot Ma'aseh HaKorbanot* 5:18 and *Kesef Mishne* there, and *Hilkhot Pesulei HaMukdashin* 19:9).

רַבִּי אֶלְעָזָר בְּרַבִּי שִׁמְעוֹן אוֹמֵר: אֵין הַדָּם מְרַצֶּה עַל הָעוֹר בִּפְנֵי עַצְמוֹ. וּכְשֶׁהוּא עִם הַבָּשָׂר, נוֹלַד בּוֹ פְּסוּל קוֹדֶם זְרִיקָה – הֲרֵי הוּא כַּיּוֹצֵא בּוֹ, אַחַר זְרִיקָה – הוּרְצָה בָּשָׂר שָׁעָה אַחַת, יַפְשִׁיטֶנּוּ וְעוֹרוֹ לַכֹּהֲנִים.

Rabbi Elazar, son of Rabbi Shimon, says: The blood does not effect acceptance of the hide by itself. And if, **when** the hide **is** still **with the flesh, a disqualification appears on** the flesh **before** the **sprinkling** of the blood, then the *halakha* with regard to the hide **is parallel to** the *halakha* with regard to the flesh: Both are burned. If a disqualification develops on the flesh **after** the **sprinkling** of the blood, the **flesh was** already **accepted for a time.** Therefore, even though the flesh is disqualified, the priest **may flay** the animal before it is burned, **and its hide** goes **to the priests.**

לֵימָא בִּדְרַבִּי אֱלִיעֶזֶר וְרַבִּי יְהוֹשֻׁעַ קָמִיפַּלְגִי; ״וְעָשִׂיתָ עֹלֹתֶיךָ הַבָּשָׂר וְהַדָּם״, רַבִּי יְהוֹשֻׁעַ אוֹמֵר: אִם אֵין דָּם – אֵין בָּשָׂר, אִם אֵין בָּשָׂר – אֵין דָּם.

The Gemara suggests: **Shall we say** that Rabbi Yehuda HaNasi and Rabbi Elazar **disagree about** the same principle as do **Rabbi Eliezer and Rabbi Yehoshua?**[N] As it is taught in a *baraita*: The verse states: **"And you shall offer your burnt offerings, the flesh and the blood,** upon the altar of the Lord your God" (Deuteronomy 12:27). **Rabbi Yehoshua says:** The verse teaches that **if there is no blood** sprinkled on the altar, **no flesh** may be burned[H] on the altar, and **if there is no flesh** to be burned on the altar, **no blood** may be sprinkled on the altar.

רַבִּי אֱלִיעֶזֶר אוֹמֵר: דָּם אַף עַל פִּי שֶׁאֵין בָּשָׂר, שֶׁנֶּאֱמַר: ״וְדַם זְבָחֶיךָ יִשָּׁפֵךְ״. אִם כֵּן, מַה תַּלְמוּד לוֹמַר ״וְעָשִׂיתָ עֹלֹתֶיךָ הַבָּשָׂר וְהַדָּם״? לוֹמַר לְךָ: מַה דָּם בִּזְרִיקָה – אַף בָּשָׂר בִּזְרִיקָה. הָא לָמַדְתָּ, שֶׁרֶיוַח יֵשׁ בֵּין כֶּבֶשׁ לַמִּזְבֵּחַ.

Rabbi Eliezer says: The **blood** must be sprinkled **even if there is no flesh, as it is stated** in the continuation of the verse: **"And the blood of your sacrifices shall be poured out** against the altar of the Lord your God, and you shall eat the flesh." **If so, what** is taught when **the verse states: "And you shall offer your burnt offerings, the flesh and the blood"?** It is stated **to tell you: Just as blood** is placed on the altar **by sprinkling, so too,** the **flesh** is placed on the altar **by tossing. Consequently, you learn that there is a space between** the **ramp and the altar,** such that the priest must toss the flesh from the edge of the ramp.[B]

לֵימָא מַאן דְּאָמַר הוּרְצָה – כְּרַבִּי אֱלִיעֶזֶר, וּמַאן דְּאָמַר לֹא הוּרְצָה – כְּרַבִּי יְהוֹשֻׁעַ?

The Gemara explains: **Shall we say** that **the one who says** that the hide **is accepted** independent of the flesh holds **in accordance with** the opinion of **Rabbi Eliezer,** that the blood is sprinkled independent of the flesh, **and the one who says** that the hide **is not accepted** independent of the flesh holds **in accordance with** the opinion of **Rabbi Yehoshua,**[N] that if there is no flesh then the blood is not sprinkled?

אַלִּיבָּא דְּרַבִּי אֱלִיעֶזֶר כּוּלֵּי עָלְמָא לָא פְּלִיגִי, כִּי פְּלִיגִי – אַלִּיבָּא דְּרַבִּי יְהוֹשֻׁעַ;

The Gemara rejects this: **According to** the opinion **of Rabbi Eliezer,** who holds that the blood may be sprinkled even if the flesh is disqualified, **everyone agrees** that this sprinkling effects acceptance of the hide. **When they disagree,** it is **according to** the opinion **of Rabbi Yehoshua.**

HALAKHA

If there is no blood no flesh may be burned, etc. – אִם אֵין דָּם אֵין בָּשָׂר וכו׳: If an olive-bulk is not extant from an animal being brought as an offering, its blood is not sprinkled, and if it is sprinkled the offering is not accepted after the fact. This is in accordance with the opinion of Rabbi Yehoshua, as the *halakha* is in accordance with his opinion in his disputes with Rabbi Eliezer (Rambam *Sefer Avoda, Hilkhot Pesulei HaMukdashin* 1:31).

BACKGROUND

Tossing the flesh from the ramp to the altar – זְרִיקַת בָּשָׂר מֵהַכֶּבֶשׁ לַמִּזְבֵּחַ:

Priests standing on the ramp, tossing pieces of the burnt offering onto the altar

NOTES

Shall we say they disagree about the same principle as do Rabbi Eliezer and Rabbi Yehoshua – לֵימָא בִּדְרַבִּי אֱלִיעֶזֶר וְרַבִּי יְהוֹשֻׁעַ קָמִיפַּלְגִי: The dispute between Rabbi Eliezer and Rabbi Yehoshua is discussed at length in tractate *Pesaḥim* (see 77a). The conclusion there is that Rabbi Eliezer holds that the blood is sprinkled regardless of what happens to the flesh. Rabbi Yehoshua distinguishes between a case where the flesh was lost or burned and a case where the flesh was disqualified. If the flesh was lost or burned, he holds that sprinkling the blood is not effective even after the fact. If the flesh was disqualified, the blood should not be sprinkled *ab initio*, but if it is sprinkled, it is accepted after the fact, as stated in the *baraita* here.

Rashi explains that the dispute between Rabbi Yehuda HaNasi and Rabbi Elazar, son of Rabbi Shimon, about a flayed hide also applies in a case where the flesh was lost, and it is specifically in the case where the flesh was lost that the Gemara compares their dispute to the dispute between Rabbi Eliezer and Rabbi Yehoshua, where Rabbi Yehoshua holds that the sprinkling of the blood is not effective even after the fact.

Tosafot explain that the discussion here is about the case found in the mishna, where the flesh was disqualified, and Rabbi Yehoshua holds that the sprinkling of the blood is effective after the fact, but not performed *ab initio*. Each of these interpretations has advantages and difficulties.

The one who says it is not accepted holds in accordance with Rabbi Yehoshua – מַאן דְּאָמַר לֹא הוּרְצָה כְּרַבִּי יְהוֹשֻׁעַ: Rashi explains that Rabbi Elazar, son of Rabbi Shimon, could say: Just as Rabbi Yehoshua holds that if the flesh is lost, the sprinkling of the blood does not effect acceptance of the offering even after the fact, so too, the sprinkling of the blood does not render the hides permitted.

Tosafot explain, in accordance with their interpretation, that just as Rabbi Yehoshua holds that if the flesh is disqualified, by rabbinic law the blood should not be sprinkled, so too, by rabbinic decree, the sprinkling of the blood does not render the hides permitted to the priests.

מַאן דְּאָמַר לֹא הוּרְצָה – כְּרַבִּי יְהוֹשֻׁעַ. מַאן דְּאָמַר הוּרְצָה – אָמַר לָךְ: עַד כָּאן לָא קָאָמַר רַבִּי יְהוֹשֻׁעַ הָתָם אֶלָּא בְּבָשָׂר, דְּלֵיכָּא פְּסֵידָא לַכֹּהֲנִים, אֲבָל עוֹר, דְּאִיכָּא פְּסֵידָא לַכֹּהֲנִים – אֲפִילּוּ רַבִּי יְהוֹשֻׁעַ מוֹדֶה.

The one who says that the hide **is not accepted** independently, i.e., Rabbi Elazar, son of Rabbi Shimon, holds **in accordance with** the straightforward meaning of the statement of **Rabbi Yehoshua**; once the flesh is disqualified, the blood cannot be sprinkled and does not effect acceptance of the hide. **The one who says** that the hide **is accepted,** i.e., Rabbi Yehuda HaNasi, could **say to you: Rabbi Yehoshua says only there** that the blood may not be sprinkled **in** a case where nothing but the **flesh** was at stake, **where there is no loss for the priests,**[N] who never receive meat from burnt offerings. **But** in cases where the **hide** would go to waste, **where there is a loss for the priests,** perhaps **even Rabbi Yehoshua concedes** that the blood effects acceptance.

מִידֵּי דַּהֲוָה אַדִּיעֲבַד. דִּתְנַן: נִטְמָא בָּשָׂר אוֹ נִפְסַל, אוֹ שֶׁיָּצָא חוּץ לַקְּלָעִים, רַבִּי אֱלִיעֶזֶר אוֹמֵר: יִזְרוֹק, רַבִּי יְהוֹשֻׁעַ אוֹמֵר: לֹא יִזְרוֹק. וּמוֹדֶה רַבִּי יְהוֹשֻׁעַ שֶׁאִם זָרַק – הוּרְצָה.

This latter interpretation of Rabbi Yehoshua's opinion with regard to the hides is **just as it is with regard to** disqualified flesh **after the fact.**[N] **As we learned** in a *baraita*: If the **flesh contracted ritual impurity or was disqualified,**[H] **or** if it **emerged beyond the curtains** delineating its designated area, **Rabbi Eliezer says:** The priest must nevertheless **sprinkle** the blood on the altar. **Rabbi Yehoshua says:** The priest **may not sprinkle** the blood on the altar. **And Rabbi Yehoshua concedes that if** the priest nevertheless **sprinkled** the blood, the offering **is accepted** after the fact. Apparently, the sprinkling is sufficiently valid to effect acceptance of the hide.

״אָמַר רַבִּי חֲנִינָא סְגַן הַכֹּהֲנִים״ כו׳. וְלֹא? הֲרֵי פָּרִים הַנִּשְׂרָפִים וּשְׂעִירִים הַנִּשְׂרָפִים!

§ The mishna teaches: **Rabbi Ḥanina, the deputy High Priest, said:** In all my days, I never saw a hide going out to the place of burning. The Gemara challenges: **And** is it so that he did **not** see? **Aren't there bulls that are burned and goats that are burned** together with their hides as a matter of course?

לְמִצְוָתָן לָא קָאָמְרִינַן.

The Gemara answers: **We are not saying** that Rabbi Ḥanina never saw hides go out to be burned **in accordance with their mitzva;** he certainly did. Rather, he never saw hides being burned because the offering was disqualified.

הֲרֵי קוֹדֶם הֶפְשֵׁט וְקוֹדֶם זְרִיקָה! חָלוּץ קָאָמְרִינַן.

The Gemara challenges: But **isn't there** a case where an offering is disqualified **before flaying and before** the **sprinkling** of the blood, in which case all agree that the animal is burned with its hide? The Gemara answers: **We are saying** that Rabbi Ḥanina never saw a hide go out **stripped** from its flesh.

וְהָאִיכָּא אַחַר הֶפְשֵׁט וְקוֹדֶם זְרִיקָה, לְרַבִּי אֶלְעָזָר בְּרַבִּי שִׁמְעוֹן, דְּאָמַר: אֵין הַדָּם מְרַצֶּה עַל הָעוֹר בִּפְנֵי עַצְמוֹ!

The Gemara challenges: **But isn't there** a case where an offering is disqualified **after** the **flaying** of the hide **and before** the **sprinkling** of the blood, in which case the hide is burned **according to** the opinion of **Rabbi Elazar, son of Rabbi Shimon, who says: The blood does not effect acceptance of the hide by itself?**

רַבִּי חֲנִינָא כְּרַבִּי סְבִירָא לֵיהּ. וְאִיבָּעֵית אֵימָא: אֲפִילּוּ תּוּקְמָהּ כְּרַבִּי אֶלְעָזָר בְּרַבִּי שִׁמְעוֹן, מוֹדֶה רַבִּי שֶׁאֵין הֶפְשֵׁט קוֹדֶם זְרִיקָה.

The Gemara answers: **Rabbi Ḥanina holds in accordance with** the opinion of **Rabbi** Yehuda HaNasi, that the blood does effect acceptance of the hide in such a case, and so it would not be burned. **And if you wish, say** instead that you can **even interpret** the opinion of Rabbi Ḥanina **in accordance with** the opinion of **Rabbi Elazar, son of Rabbi Shimon,** as **Rabbi** Yehuda HaNasi **concedes that** the **flaying is not** done **before** the **sprinkling,** and so in practice Rabbi Ḥanina never saw a hide that was flayed before the offering was disqualified.

וְהָאִיכָּא נִמְצֵאת טְרֵיפָה בִּבְנֵי מֵעַיִים!

The Gemara challenges: **But isn't there** the case of an animal that, after the hide was flayed and the blood was sprinkled, **was found** to have a wound **in** its **intestines** rendering it **a** ***tereifa,*** in which case the offering was already disqualified when the blood was sprinkled?

NOTES

Nothing but the flesh was at stake where there is no loss for the priests, etc. – **אֶלָּא בְּבָשָׂר דְּלֵיכָּא פְּסֵידָא לַכֹּהֲנִים וכו׳**: Rashi explains that Rabbi Yehuda HaNasi could say: Rabbi Yehoshua holds that the sprinkling of the blood is not effective only in a case where the blood has not yet been sprinkled, as the priests do not yet have a loss. But if the blood has been sprinkled, then the priests have acquired the hide, in accordance with the verse: "The priest shall have to himself the hide of the burnt offering that he has sacrificed" (Leviticus 7:8). To deny the priests the hides at that point would entail a loss for them (and see *Tosafot*).

Just as it is with regard to disqualified flesh after the fact – **מִידֵּי דַּהֲוָה אַדִּיעֲבַד**: Rashi may have had a different version of the text, which read: Just as it is for disqualified flesh that emerged from the courtyard (see *Shita Mekubbetzet*). He explains that just as sprinkling the blood is not effective after the fact for permitting the flesh if the flesh emerged from the courtyard, but it is effective for permitting the hides, so too in a case where the flesh was lost, where the sprinkling of the blood is not effective after the fact, it is effective for permitting the hides.

Tosafot explain, in accordance with their interpretation: Just as there is a rabbinic decree that the sprinkling of the blood is not effective after the fact for flesh that was burned or lost, but there is no decree for flesh that was disqualified, so too, there is no decree for the hides if they were flayed before the flesh was disqualified, and the priests acquire them after the fact.

HALAKHA

If the flesh contracted ritual impurity or was disqualified, etc. – **נִטְמָא בָּשָׂר אוֹ נִפְסַל וכו׳**: If the flesh was disqualified or emerged from the Temple courtyard before the sprinkling of the blood, its blood should not be sprinkled. If it was sprinkled, it is accepted after the fact, in accordance with the opinion of Rabbi Yehoshua (Rambam *Sefer Avoda, Hilkhot Pesulei HaMukdashin* 1:31).

קסבר: נמצאת טריפה בבני מעיים – מרצה. דיקא נמי, דקתני אמר רבי עקיבא: מדבריו למדנו, שהמפשיט את הבכור ונמצא טריפה שיאותו הכהנים בעורו, שמע מינה.

The Gemara answers: Rabbi Ḥanina **holds** that in the case of an animal that **was found** to be **a** ***tereifa*** due to a wound **in** its **intestines,** the sprinkling of the blood nevertheless **effects acceptance,** because the wound was unknown at the time of the sprinkling. The language of the mishna **is also precise, as it teaches: Rabbi Akiva said: From the statement of** Rabbi Ḥanina, the deputy High Priest, **we learned that** in a case where **one flays the firstborn** offering, **and** the animal is later **discovered** to be **a** ***tereifa,*** the *halakha* **is that the priests may derive benefit from its hide.** This indicates that the sprinkling of the blood effects acceptance if the wound was unknown. The Gemara affirms: Indeed, **learn from** the mishna that this is so.

ואלא מאי קא משמע לן רבי עקיבא? הא קא משמע לן: אפילו בגבולין.

The Gemara challenges: **But** if this is what Rabbi Ḥanina meant, then **what is Rabbi Akiva teaching us?** His statement seems unnecessary. The Gemara answers: **This** is what Rabbi Akiva is **teaching us:** This *halakha* applies not just in the Temple but **even in the outlying areas,** e.g., with regard to a blemished firstborn animal, which is slaughtered outside the Temple. If it is discovered to be a *tereifa* before its slaughter, it must be buried with its hide, but if it is slaughtered and later discovered to be a *tereifa,* then its slaughter renders the hide permitted to the priests, just as the sprinkling of the blood renders the hide permitted in the Temple.

אמר רבי חייא בר אבא אמר רבי יוחנן: הלכה כרבי עקיבא. ואף רבי עקיבא לא אמר אלא כשהתירו מומחה, אבל לא התירו מומחה – לא.

Rabbi Ḥiyya bar Abba says that Rabbi Yoḥanan says: The ***halakha*** **is in accordance** with the opinion **of Rabbi Akiva.** The Gemara adds: **And even Rabbi Akiva said** this *halakha* **only** in a case **where an expert** verified the firstborn animal's blemish and **permitted it** to be slaughtered. **But if an expert did not permit it,** then its slaughter does **not** render the hide permitted to the priest.

והלכתא כדברי חכמים, בשר בקבורה, והעור בשריפה.

The Gemara concludes: **And the** ***halakha*** is **in accordance with the statement of the Rabbis,** not Rabbi Akiva. Therefore, the **flesh** is discarded **by burial and the hide by burning.**[N][H]

מתני׳ פרים הנשרפים ושעירים הנשרפים, בזמן שהן נשרפין כמצותן – נשרפים בבית הדשן, ומטמאין בגדים. ואם אינן נשרפין כמצותן – נשרפין בבית הבירה, ואינן מטמאין בגדים.

MISHNA With regard to **bulls that are burned,**[H] i.e., the bull of Yom Kippur, the bull of the anointed priest, and the bull brought for an unwitting communal sin, which are burned after their blood is sprinkled and their sacrificial portions burned on the altar, **and goats that are burned,** i.e., the goat of Yom Kippur and the goat brought for the unwitting communal transgression of the prohibition against idol worship, **when they are burned in accordance with their mitzva, they are burned in the place of the ashes**[N] (see Leviticus 4:12) outside of Jerusalem, **and they render** the **garments** of the priests who tend to their burning **impure**[H] (see Leviticus 4:25). **And if** these offerings **are not burned in accordance with their mitzva** because they were disqualified, and offerings that are disqualified are also burned, **they are burned in the place of** burning in **the** ***bira,***[H] **and they do not render** the **garments** of the priests who tend to their burning **impure.**

NOTES

The flesh is discarded by burial and the hide by burning – בשר בקבורה והעור בשריפה: The straightforward interpretation is that this statement is referring to a blemished firstborn offering that was slaughtered outside the Temple and later discovered to be a *tereifa*.

Rashi finds it difficult to understand why the hide is not buried as well, as only offerings that were disqualified in the Temple are burned (see *Pesaḥim* 23b). He therefore considers this line to be a mistaken addition to the text. In his interpretation, the Rabbis agree with Rabbi Akiva, and dispute only the statement of Rabbi Ḥanina, the deputy High Priest, who said that the hides of offerings that were flayed before the offering was disqualified are not burned.

The Rambam's text apparently includes the line: The flesh is discarded by burial and the hide by burning. He interprets it as referring to an unblemished firstborn offering in the Temple that was discovered to be a *tereifa* after the hide was flayed. Since it is not considered to have been disqualified in the Temple, as its disqualification is unrelated to the Temple service, it is not burned, but rather buried. But the Rabbis teach that the hide must still be burned, because it does not decompose quickly and the priests might come to derive benefit from it (see *Ḥok Natan* and *Keneset HaRishonim*).

In accordance with their mitzva they are burned in the place of the ashes – כמצותן נשרפים בבית הדשן: This is as the verse states with regard to the bull brought for an unwitting communal sin: "And the whole bull shall he carry forth outside the camp unto a clean place, where the ashes are poured out, and burn it on wood with fire; where the ashes are poured out shall it be burned" (Leviticus 4:12). In the wilderness, the main place of ashes was outside the Israelite camp; in Jerusalem, it was outside the city walls.

HALAKHA

The flesh is discarded by burial and the hide by burning – בשר בקבורה והעור בשריפה: If an unblemished firstborn offering is discovered to be a *tereifa* after its hide is flayed, then its flesh is buried and its hide is burned. If it was a blemished firstborn offering, then its flesh is buried and the priests acquire the hide. This is in accordance with the opinion of the Rabbis.

The *Kesef Mishne* writes that according to the Rambam, the Rabbis do not disagree with Rabbi Akiva; Rabbi Akiva was discussing a blemished firstborn offering, and the Rabbis were discussing an unblemished firstborn offering. The Rosh writes, citing Rashi, that the hide of a blemished firstborn is also buried (Rambam *Sefer Korbanot, Hilkhot Bekhorot* 3:10; *Shulḥan Arukh, Yoreh De'a* 307:2).

Bulls that are burned, etc. – פרים הנשרפים וכו׳: With regard to sin offerings that are burned, when they are burned in accordance with their mitzva, they are burned in the place of the ashes outside Jerusalem (Rambam *Sefer Avoda, Hilkhot Ma'aseh HaKorbanot* 7:4).

And they render the garments impure – מטמאין בגדים: Sin offerings that are burned render the garments of the priests who tend to their burning ritually impure, from the time they are burned until they become ash (Rambam *Sefer Tahara, Hilkhot Para Aduma* 5:4).

They are burned in the place of burning in the Temple [*bira*] courtyard – נשרפין בבית הבירה: If sin offerings of a type that are burned are disqualified, they are burned in the Temple courtyard, like all disqualified offerings. They do not render the garments of the priests who tend to their burning ritually impure (Rambam *Sefer Avoda, Hilkhot Para Aduma* 5:4).

הָיוּ סוֹבְלִין אוֹתוֹ בְּמוֹטוֹת. יָצְאוּ הָרִאשׁוֹנִים חוּץ לְחוֹמַת הָעֲזָרָה וְהָאַחֲרוֹנִים לֹא יָצְאוּ – הָרִאשׁוֹנִים מְטַמְּאִין בְּגָדִים, וְהָאַחֲרוֹנִים אֵינָן מְטַמְּאִין בְּגָדִים עַד שֶׁיֵּצְאוּ. יָצְאוּ – אֵלּוּ וְאֵלּוּ מְטַמְּאִין בְּגָדִים. רַבִּי שִׁמְעוֹן אוֹמֵר: אֵינָן מְטַמְּאִין עַד שֶׁיּוּצַּת הָאוּר בְּרוּבָּן. נִיתַּךְ הַבָּשָׂר – אֵין הַשּׂוֹרֵף מְטַמֵּא בְּגָדִים.

The priests **would carry** the bulls and the goats that are burned suspended **on poles.**[H] When **the first** priests, carrying the front of the pole, **emerged outside the wall of the Temple courtyard and the latter** priests **did not** yet **emerge, the first** priests **render** their **garments impure, and the latter** priests **do not render** their **garments impure until they emerge.** When both **these and those** priests **emerged, they render** their **garments impure. Rabbi Shimon says: They do not render** their **garments impure,** as this *halakha* applies only to those who burn the offerings. And even then their garments do not become ritually impure **until the fire is ignited in the majority of** the offerings. Once **the flesh is** completely **scorched,** with no moisture remaining, **one who** then **burns** the remains **does not render** his **garments impure.**

גמ׳ מַאי ״בִּירָה״? אָמַר רַבָּה בַּר בַּר חָנָה, אָמַר רַבִּי יוֹחָנָן: מָקוֹם יֵשׁ בְּהַר הַבַּיִת, וּבִירָה שְׁמוֹ. וְרֵישׁ לָקִישׁ אָמַר: כָּל הַבַּיִת כּוּלּוֹ קָרוּי בִּירָה, שֶׁנֶּאֱמַר: ״(וְאֶל) הַבִּירָה אֲשֶׁר הֲכִינוֹתִי״.

GEMARA The mishna teaches that if offerings of a type that are burned were disqualified, they are burned in a place of burning called the *bira*. The Gemara asks: **What is the *bira*? Rabba bar bar Ḥana says** that **Rabbi Yoḥanan says: There is a place on the Temple Mount, and its name is *bira*,** and this is where they would burn these offerings. **And Reish Lakish says: The entire Temple is called** the ***bira*,** as **it is stated** in the prayer of David: "And give unto Solomon my son a whole heart, to keep Your commandments, Your testimonies, and Your statutes, and to do all this, and to build **the Temple [*bira*] for which I have made provision"** (I Chronicles 29:19).

אָמַר רַב נַחְמָן אָמַר רַבָּה בַּר אֲבוּהּ, שְׁלֹשָׁה בֵּית הַדְּשָׁנִין הֵן: בֵּית הַדֶּשֶׁן גָּדוֹל הָיָה בָּעֲזָרָה, שֶׁשָּׁם שׂוֹרְפִין פְּסוּלֵי קָדְשֵׁי קֳדָשִׁים, וְאֵימוּרֵי קֳדָשִׁים קַלִּים, וּפָרִים הַנִּשְׂרָפִין וּשְׂעִירִים הַנִּשְׂרָפִין שֶׁאֵירַע בָּהֶן פְּסוּל קוֹדֶם זְרִיקָה.

§ **Rav Naḥman says** that **Rabba bar Avuh says: There are three places of the ashes.** First was the **great place of the ashes** that **was in the** Temple **courtyard,**[N] **where** the priests would **burn the disqualified offerings of the most sacred order, and the** disqualified **sacrificial portions of offerings of lesser sanctity, and bulls that are burned and goats that are burned** if **they were disqualified prior to** the **sprinkling** of the blood.

וּבֵית הַדֶּשֶׁן אַחֵר הָיָה בְּהַר הַבַּיִת, שֶׁשָּׁם שׂוֹרְפִין פָּרִים הַנִּשְׂרָפִים וּשְׂעִירִים הַנִּשְׂרָפִים שֶׁאֵירַע בָּהֶן פְּסוּל אַחַר זְרִיקָה. וּכְמִצְוָתָן – חוּץ לְשָׁלֹשׁ מַחֲנוֹת.

And there was another place of the ashes on the Temple Mount, where the priests would **burn bulls that are burned and goats that are burned** if **they were disqualified after** the **sprinkling** of the blood. **And** the third place of the ashes was for the bulls and goats that were burned **in accordance with their mitzva, outside** the **three camps,**[NB] i.e., outside the walls of Jerusalem.

HALAKHA

They would carry on poles – הָיוּ סוֹבְלִין אוֹתוֹ בְּמוֹטוֹת: Those who carry the bulls and goats that are burned render their garments ritually impure from the time they emerge from the wall of the Temple courtyard. They would carry the animal suspended on poles, and once some of them emerged but others did not yet emerge, the ones who emerged rendered their garments ritually impure and the ones who did not yet emerge did not (Rambam *Sefer Tahara*, *Hilkhot Para Aduma* 5:5).

NOTES

The great place of the ashes that was in the Temple courtyard – בֵּית הַדֶּשֶׁן גָּדוֹל הָיָה בָּעֲזָרָה: There was also a smaller place of ashes in the Temple courtyard on the eastern side of the ramp to the altar, where the crop of a bird burnt offering, the ashes from the inner altar, and the ashes from the Candelabrum were deposited (see 64a and *Yoma* 43b).

Outside the three camps – חוּץ לְשָׁלֹשׁ מַחֲנוֹת: This refers to the three concentric zones of varying sanctity into which the Israelites' camp in the wilderness was divided: The camp of the Tabernacle, the camp of the Levites, and the camp of the Israelites. In the era of the Temple in Jerusalem, the city itself was considered equivalent to the camp of the Israelites.

BACKGROUND

Three camps – שָׁלֹשׁ מַחֲנוֹת: Various *halakhot* are derived from the Torah's account of the activities of the Jews in the wilderness. The halakhic discussions of these topics in the Talmud employ terms appropriate for the time they sojourned in the wilderness, despite the fact that those precise terms were not relevant in talmudic times. It was prohibited by Torah law for ritually impure people to enter certain areas, depending on the degree of impurity and sanctity, and halakhic discussions with regard to these areas adopt the terminology used to describe the three camps of Israel in the wilderness, which had parallels in Eretz Yisrael in later periods.

The camp of the Divine Presence, which was the area within the courtyard of the Tent of Meeting, was paralleled by the Temple and its courtyard inside the Gate of Nicanor. The camp of the Levites, which was the area where the Levites encamped around the Tabernacle, was paralleled by the rest of the Temple Mount. The camp of the Israelites, which was the area where the twelve tribes lived, was paralleled by the city of Jerusalem outside the Temple Mount and, according to many authorities, all walled cities in Eretz Yisrael. The Sages subdivided these areas further and differentiated within the Temple Mount between the different courtyards, the rampart, and the like (see *Kelim* 1:1).

The first image depicts the three camps set up during the Jewish people's travels in the wilderness: In the center is the Tabernacle, the camp of the Divine Presence. Immediately surrounding it is the camp of the Levites; the outermost camp is the camp of Israel.

Left: Three camps in the wilderness

Above: Temple in Jerusalem

תָּנֵי לֵוִי: שְׁלֹשָׁה בֵּית הַדְּשָׁנִין הֵן: בֵּית הַדֶּשֶׁן גָּדוֹל הָיָה בָּעֲזָרָה, שֶׁשָּׁם שׂוֹרְפִין פְּסוּלֵי קׇדְשֵׁי קֳדָשִׁים וְאֵימוּרֵי קֳדָשִׁים קַלִּים, וּפָרִים הַנִּשְׂרָפִים וּשְׂעִירִים הַנִּשְׂרָפִים שֶׁאֵירַע בָּהֶן פְּסוּל, בֵּין קוֹדֶם זְרִיקָה בֵּין לְאַחַר זְרִיקָה. וּבֵית הַדֶּשֶׁן אַחֵר הָיָה בְּהַר הַבַּיִת, שֶׁשָּׁם שׂוֹרְפִין פָּרִים הַנִּשְׂרָפִין וּשְׂעִירִים הַנִּשְׂרָפִין שֶׁאֵירַע בָּהֶן פְּסוּל בִּיצִיאָתָן. וּכְמִצְוָתָן – חוּץ לְשָׁלֹשׁ מַחֲנוֹת.

Levi teaches a different version of this *baraita*:[N] **There are three places of the ashes.**[H] First was the **great place of the ashes** that **was in the** Temple **courtyard, where** the priests would **burn the disqualified offerings of the most sacred order, and the** disqualified **sacrificial portions of offerings of lesser sanctity, and bulls that are burned and goats that are burned** if they **were disqualified, whether prior to the sprinkling** of the blood **or after the sprinkling** of the blood. **And there was another place of the ashes on the Temple Mount, where** the priests would **burn bulls that are burned and goats that are burned** if they **were disqualified upon emerging** from the Temple courtyard. **And** the third was for bulls and goats burned **in accordance with their mitzva, outside** the **three camps.**

בָּעֵי רַבִּי יִרְמְיָה: לִינָה מַהוּ שֶׁתּוֹעִיל בְּפָרִים הַנִּשְׂרָפִים וּבִשְׂעִירִים הַנִּשְׂרָפִים? מִי אָמְרִינַן: כִּי מְהַנְיָא לִינָה – בְּבָשָׂר דְּבַר אֲכִילָה, אֲבָל הָנֵי דְּלָאו בְּנֵי אֲכִילָה נִינְהוּ – לָא. אוֹ דִּלְמָא לָא שְׁנָא?

§ **Rabbi Yirmeya raises a dilemma:** The flesh of most offerings is disqualified by being left overnight.[B] **What is the** *halakha* as to whether **being left overnight is effective**[H] to disqualify **bulls that are burned and goats that are burned?** Given that their flesh is neither eaten nor burned on the altar, **do we say: When being left overnight is effective** to disqualify flesh, this is only **in** a case of **flesh that is fit for consumption,** either by the altar or by human beings; **but** in the case of **these** bulls and goats that are burned, **which are not fit for consumption,** being left overnight does **not** disqualify the flesh? **Or perhaps** this case **is no different,** and being left overnight disqualifies the flesh.

אֲמַר רָבָא: הָא מִילְּתָא אִיבַּעְיָא לֵיהּ לְאַבָּיֵי, וּפְשַׁטְנָא לֵיהּ מֵהָא: וְשָׁוִין שֶׁאִם חִישֵּׁב בַּאֲכִילַת פָּרִים וּבִשְׂרֵיפָתָן – שֶׁלֹּא עָשָׂה כְּלוּם. מַאי לָאו, מִדְּמַחֲשָׁבָה לָא פָּסְלָה, לִינָה נַמִי לָא פָּסְלָה?

Rava said: This matter, Rabbi Yirmeya's **dilemma, was raised by Abaye, and I resolved it from this** *baraita*: The mishna (43a) records a dispute as to whether the sacrificial portions of bulls that are burned are subject to disqualification by intent to burn them beyond their designated time [*piggul*]. **But** the disputants **agree that if** the priest **intended for the consumption of the bulls'** meat[H] **or their burning** to be beyond their designated time, **he did nothing,** as the flesh of these bulls is not meant to be eaten or burned on the altar. Only their sacrificial portions are burned on the altar, and *piggul* applies only to flesh that ought to be consumed by human beings or the altar. **What, is it not** the case that **since** the **intention** of burning after the designated time **does not disqualify** bulls that are burned, one can infer that **being left overnight also does not disqualify** bulls that are burned?

וְדִלְמָא מַחֲשָׁבָה הוּא דְּלָא פָּסְלָה, אֲבָל לִינָה פָּסְלָה!

The Gemara responds: **But perhaps it is** only improper **intention that does not disqualify**[N] such offerings, **but being left overnight does disqualify** them.

תָּא שְׁמַע: פָּרִים הַנִּשְׂרָפִים וּשְׂעִירִים הַנִּשְׂרָפִין מוֹעֲלִין בָּהֶן מִשֶּׁהוּקְדְּשׁוּ. נִשְׁחֲטוּ – הוּכְשְׁרוּ לִיפָּסֵל בִּטְבוּל יוֹם וּבִמְחוּסַּר כִּיפּוּרִים וּבְלִינָה. מַאי לָאו לִינַת בָּשָׂר?

The Gemara suggests: **Come and hear** a mishna (*Me'ila* 9a): With regard to **bulls that are burned and goats that are burned,** one who benefits **from them** is liable for **misuse** of consecrated property **from the time that they were consecrated.**[H] Once **they have been slaughtered, they are susceptible to be rendered disqualified** for sacrifice **through** contact with **one who immersed that day, and through** contact with **one who has not yet** brought **an atonement** offering, **and through** being **left overnight** without the requirements of the offering having been fulfilled. **What, is it not** referring to the **flesh** of bulls, indicating that the flesh is disqualified if **left overnight?**

HALAKHA

There are three places of the ashes – שְׁלֹשָׁה בֵּית הַדְּשָׁנִין הֵן: There are three places where offerings were burned: One was the great place of the ashes that was in the Temple courtyard, where the priests would burn disqualified offerings of the most sacred order, and disqualified portions to be consumed on the altar of offerings of lesser sanctity. Also burned there were bulls that are burned and goats that are burned that were disqualified, whether prior to the sprinkling of the blood or whether after the sprinkling of the blood, e.g., if they were rendered ritually impure, or if they emerged from the courtyard before the designated time, or if the flesh or portions to be consumed on the altar were left overnight. The second place of ashes, called the *bira*, was on the Temple Mount, where the sin offerings that were disqualified after emerging from the Temple courtyard were burned. The third was outside Jerusalem, where the priests would burn sin offerings that are burned in accordance with their mitzva. This is in accordance with the *baraita* taught by Levi (Rambam *Sefer Avoda, Hilkhot Ma'aseh HaKorbanot* 7:3–4).

What is the ***halakha*** **as to whether being left overnight is effective** – לִינָה מַהוּ שֶׁתּוֹעִיל: There is an unresolved dilemma as to whether being left overnight is effective to disqualify the flesh of a sin offering that is burned, so the *halakha* is that one should be stringent and burn it in the courtyard (Rambam *Sefer Avoda, Hilkhot Pesulei HaMukdashin* 19:3).

Intention concerning the consumption of bulls – מַחֲשָׁבָה בַּאֲכִילַת פָּרִים: With regard to the flesh of bulls or goats that are burned, if one had intention to partake of it outside the designated time or beyond the designated area, the offerings are still valid, since they are not consumed. Similarly, even if he intended to burn outer sin offerings outside the designated time or beyond the designated area, they are valid (Rambam *Sefer Avoda, Hilkhot Pesulei HaMukdashin* 13:8, 14:8).

One who benefits from them is liable for misuse from the time that they were consecrated – מוֹעֲלִין בָּהֶן מִשֶּׁהוּקְדְּשׁוּ: One who derives benefit from sin offerings that are burned is liable for misuse of consecrated property from the time they were consecrated until their flesh is completely incinerated in the place of the ashes (Rambam *Sefer Avoda, Hilkhot Me'ila* 2:4).

BACKGROUND

Left overnight – לִינָה: The blood of an offering must be sprinkled the same day that the animal is slaughtered. If it is not sprinkled on the altar before sunset, the blood is disqualified, as is the offering itself. Once the blood is presented, the sacrificial portions must be burned that day or during the subsequent night. This principle also applies to meal offerings, which become disqualified if they are not sacrificed on the same day they are sanctified.

NOTES

Levi teaches a different version of this ***baraita*** – תָּנֵי לֵוִי: The difference between the version where Rav Naḥman cites Rabba bar Avuh and the version of Levi is with regard to bulls and goats that are burned that were disqualified after the sprinkling of the blood. According to Rav Naḥman they are burned on the Temple Mount, because they reached their time to emerge from the Temple courtyard. According to Levi they are burned in the Temple courtyard, because any offering that was disqualified in the courtyard does not emerge from there.

It is only intention that does not disqualify – מַחֲשָׁבָה הוּא דְּלָא פָּסְלָה: Not all improper intentions serve to disqualify an offering. For example, an offering is not disqualified if the priest has the intention to render it ritually impure. This is the *halakha* even in a case of intent to leave over an offering beyond its designated time, as one who intends to disqualify portions of an offering that are consumed on the altar by leaving them overnight is not liable for *piggul* (see 27b).

לָא, לִינַת אֵימוּרִין.

The Gemara responds: **No,** the mishna indicates only that the offerings' **sacrificial portions** are disqualified if **left overnight,** since they must be burned on the altar.

וְהָא מִדְּקָתָנֵי סֵיפָא: כּוּלָּן מוֹעֲלִין בָּהֶן בְּבֵית הַדֶּשֶׁן עַד שֶׁיּוּתַּךְ הַבָּשָׂר; מִדְּסֵיפָא בָּשָׂר – רֵישָׁא נַמִי בָּשָׂר! מִידֵּי אִירְיָא? סֵיפָא בָּשָׂר רֵישָׁא אֵימוּרִין.

The Gemara responds: **But** evidence to the contrary can be adduced **from** the fact **that the latter clause** of the mishna **teaches:** In **all of those** cases, one who benefits **from them** is liable for **misuse** of consecrated property if he derives benefit while they are burned **in the place of the ashes, until the flesh is** completely **incinerated.** The Gemara explains: **From** the fact **that the latter clause** is discussing **flesh,** infer that **the first clause also** discusses **flesh,** and not the sacrificial portions. The Gemara rejects this: **Are the cases comparable? The latter clause** discusses **flesh,** and **the first clause** discusses **sacrificial portions.**

תָּא שְׁמַע, דְּתָנֵי לֵוִי: שֶׁאֵירַע בָּהֶן פְּסוּל בִּיצִיאָתָן. מַאי לָאו לִינָה? לָא, פְּסוּל טוּמְאָה וּפְסוּל יְצִיאָה.

The Gemara suggests: **Come** and **hear** that **which Levi teaches** in the *baraita*: There was another place of the ashes on the Temple Mount, where the priests would burn bulls that are burned and goats that are burned if they were **disqualified upon emerging** from the Temple courtyard. **What, is it not** referring to offerings disqualified by being **left overnight?** The Gemara rejects this: **No,** it is referring to **disqualification by** contracting **ritual impurity or disqualification by leaving** the courtyard before the blood was sprinkled on the altar. The dilemma of Rabbi Yirmeya stands unresolved.

בָּעֵי רַבִּי אֶלְעָזָר: יְצִיאָה מַהוּ שֶׁתּוֹעִיל בְּפָרִים הַנִּשְׂרָפִים וּשְׂעִירִים הַנִּשְׂרָפִים?

§ **Rabbi Elazar raises a dilemma:** In general, the flesh of offerings is disqualified by leaving the Temple courtyard. **What is** the *halakha* as to whether **leaving is effective**[H] to disqualify **bulls that are burned and goats that are burned?**

מַאי קָמִיבָּעֲיָא לֵיהּ? אֲמַר רַבִּי יִרְמְיָה בַּר אַבָּא: אַלִּיבָּא דְּמַאן דְּאָמַר עֲדַיִין לֹא הִגִּיעַ זְמַנּוֹ לָצֵאת;

The Gemara asks: **What is the dilemma he is raising?** Here it is a mitzva to burn the flesh of these offerings outside the Temple courtyard. **Rabbi Yirmeya bar Abba said:** Rabbi Elazar raises his dilemma **in accordance with** the opinion **of the one who says:** With regard to offerings of lesser sanctity, even though the flesh may be consumed anywhere in Jerusalem, nevertheless, if it emerges from the Temple courtyard before the sprinkling of the blood, it is disqualified, because **its time to leave** from the Temple courtyard **has not yet arrived.** Perhaps the same *halakha* applies to bulls and goats that are burned: Even though the flesh must eventually leave the Temple, if it leaves before its designated time, it is disqualified.

מִי אָמְרִינַן: הָנֵי מִילֵּי – בָּשָׂר דְּאֵין סוֹפוֹ לָצֵאת חוֹבָה, אֲבָל הָנֵי דְּסוֹפָן לָצֵאת חוֹבָה – לָא. אוֹ דִּלְמָא הָכָא נַמִי לֹא הִגִּיעַ זְמַנּוֹ לָצֵאת?

The dilemma is: **Do we say** that **this matter,** disqualification by leaving the Temple courtyard prematurely, applies only to **flesh that need not eventually leave** due to an **obligation?** One may consume the meat of offerings of lesser sanctity in the Temple courtyard if he wishes. **But** perhaps **these** bulls and goats that are burned, **which** must **eventually leave** due to an **obligation,** are **not** disqualified by emerging prematurely. **Or perhaps here too** the flesh is disqualified if **its time to leave has not** yet **arrived.**

תָּא שְׁמַע, דְּתָנֵי לֵוִי: שֶׁאֵירַע בּוֹ פְּסוּל בִּיצִיאָתוֹ. מַאי לָאו פְּסוּל יְצִיאָה? לָא, פְּסוּל טוּמְאָה וּפְסוּל לִינָה.

The Gemara suggests: **Come** and **hear** that **which Levi teaches** in the *baraita*: There was another place of the ashes on the Temple Mount, where the priests would burn bulls that are burned and goats that are burned if **they were disqualified upon emerging** from the Temple courtyard. **What, is it not** referring to **disqualification by leaving** the Temple courtyard before the sprinkling of the blood? The Gemara responds: **No,** it is referring to **disqualification by** contracting **ritual impurity or disqualification by being left overnight.** The dilemma of Rabbi Elazar stands unresolved.

HALAKHA

What is the *halakha* as to whether leaving is effective – יְצִיאָה מַהוּ שֶׁתּוֹעִיל: There is an unresolved dilemma as to whether emerging from the courtyard before the designated time is effective to disqualify the flesh of a sin offering that is burned, so the *halakha* is that one should be stringent and burn it in the courtyard (Rambam *Sefer Avoda, Hilkhot Pesulei HaMukdashin* 19:3).

בָּעֵי רַבִּי אֶלְעָזָר: פָּרִים הַנִּשְׂרָפִים וּשְׂעִירִים הַנִּשְׂרָפִים שֶׁיָּצָא רוּבּוֹ בְּמִיעוּט אֵבֶר, מַהוּ? הַךְ מִיעוּטָא דְּאֵבֶר בָּתַר רוּבָּא שָׁדֵינַן לֵיהּ – וְהָא לָא נְפַקָא לֵיהּ, אוֹ דִלְמָא בָּתַר רוּבָּא דִּבְהֵמָה שָׁדֵינַן?

§ **Rabbi Elazar raises** another **dilemma:** With regard to **bulls that are burned and goats that are burned, if the majority of** the animal's body **emerged**[N] from the Temple courtyard, but it consists of a majority only **by** inclusion of **the minority of a limb,**[N] the majority of which remains inside the courtyard, **what is the** ***halakha*****? Do** we determine the status of **this minority of a limb by casting it after the majority** of that limb, **and** the majority of **that** limb **did not leave? Or perhaps** we determine its status by **casting** it **after the majority of** the **animal,** and therefore a majority of the animal has left?

פְּשִׁיטָא, דְּלָא שָׁבְקִינַן רוּבָּא דִּבְהֵמָה וְאָזְלִינַן בָּתַר רוּבָּא דְּאֵבָרִים! אֶלָּא, שֶׁיָּצָא חֶצְיוֹ בְּרוֹב אֵבֶר; הַאי מִיעוּטָא דְּאֵבֶר

The Gemara clarifies: Isn't it **obvious that we do not disregard the majority of the animal and** instead **follow the majority of the limbs? Rather,** Rabbi Elazar's dilemma must be as follows: In a case **where half of** the animal **emerged** from the courtyard such that **the majority of** a certain **limb** emerged,[NH] but a minority of the limb remained inside, what is the *halakha*? Do we determine the status of **this minority of a limb**

NOTES

Where the majority of its body emerged – שֶׁיָּצָא רוּבּוֹ: The Rambam interprets this dilemma as a continuation of the discussion with regard to the disqualification of emerging from the Temple courtyard: Is the animal disqualified? Rashi and Rabbeinu Ḥananel explain that the dilemma is whether the garments of those who carry the animal become ritually impure, as this depends on the majority of the animal emerging from the courtyard (see 105b). *Tosafot* explain that the dilemma is whether or not the bulls or goats that are burned should be burned inside or outside the courtyard (see *Shita Mekubbetzet* and Mahari Kurkus).

By inclusion of the minority of a limb – בְּמִיעוּט אֵבֶר: Rashi explains the dilemma: Is this minority of a limb included with the majority of the animal, or the majority of the limb? Rabbeinu Ḥananel's version of the text reads: A minority of limbs, and he explains the case as one where the majority of the animal's body emerged while the majority of its limbs were still inside. The Gemara responds that it is obvious that the animal's status is determined by following the majority of the limbs.

Where half of it emerged such that the majority of a limb emerged – שֶׁיָּצָא חֶצְיוֹ בְּרוֹב אֵבֶר: The commentaries explain this according to their explanations of the dilemma. Rashi explains that half the animal emerged, including the majority of a certain limb, and the dilemma is whether the minority of that limb that remains inside follows the majority of the limb, so that the majority of the animal is considered to have emerged. Rabbeinu Ḥananel explains the term: Half of [*ḥetzyo*] as referring to the one carrying the animal, and explains that the dilemma is whether he is considered as having emerged with the majority of the animal's limbs, and is impure, or if he is considered as remaining inside with the minority of the animal's limbs. The masculine pronominal suffix of this term [*ḥetzyo*] supports his interpretation, as an animal would be indicated with a feminine suffix [*ḥetzyah*].

HALAKHA

Half of it emerged such that the majority of a limb emerged – יָצָא חֶצְיָן בְּרֹב אֵבֶר: If a bull that is burned emerged from the courtyard before its designated time, and half the animal emerged in a way that most of a certain limb emerged, then it is uncertain whether the animal is considered to have emerged entirely, so the *halakha* is that one should be stringent and burn it in the courtyard.

The Rambam interprets Rabbi Elazar's dilemma with regard to the disqualification of the animal that is emerging. The Ra'avad disagrees, and holds that the dilemma is with regard to whether those carrying the animal render their garments impure (Rambam *Sefer Avoda, Hilkhot Pesulei HaMukdashin* 19:3).

Perek **XII**
Daf **105** Amud **a**

בָּתַר רוֹב אֵבֶר שָׁדֵינַן לֵיהּ, וְהָא נְפַק לֵיהּ, אוֹ דִלְמָא בָּתַר בְּהֵמָה שָׁדֵינַן לֵיהּ? תֵּיקוּ.

by casting it after the majority of that **limb, and** the majority of that limb **did leave? Or perhaps** we determine its status **by casting it after** the half of **the animal,** which did not leave the courtyard. The Gemara concludes: The dilemma of Rabbi Elazar **shall stand** unresolved.

רַבָּה בַּר רַב הוּנָא מַתְנֵי לָהּ בְּגַבְרֵי, בְּמִתְעַסְּקִין בּוֹ חֲמִשָּׁה בְּנֵי אָדָם, וּנְפַקוּ תְּלָתָא וּפָשׁוּ לְהוּ תְּרֵי, מַאי? בָּתַר רוֹב מִתְעַסְּקִין אָזְלִינַן, אוֹ בָּתַר בְּהֵמָה אָזְלִינַן? תֵּיקוּ.

Rabba bar Rav Huna teaches this dilemma **with regard to people:**[N] In a case where **five people are handling** an offering and carrying it out to be burned, **and three** of them **emerged and two of them remained** in the Temple courtyard, such that the animal is partly inside and partly outside, **what is the** ***halakha*****?** Do **we follow the majority of the people handling** the offering,[H] who have left the courtyard, **or** do **we follow the animal,** the majority of which did not yet leave? The Gemara concludes: The dilemma **shall stand** unresolved.

HALAKHA

The majority of the people handling the offering, etc. – רוֹב מִתְעַסְּקִין וכו׳: If several people carried the bulls that are burned out of the Temple courtyard, and a majority of them emerged, and half the animal emerged, then the animal is disqualified due to uncertainty, as the dilemma in the Gemara was not resolved. The Rambam understands this dilemma as addressing the disqualification of the animal emerging before its time, while the Ra'avad understands that the dilemma is addressing whether the people render their garments impure (Rambam *Sefer Avoda, Hilkhot Pesulei HaMukdashin* 19:3 and *Kesef Mishne* there).

NOTES

Rabba bar Rav Huna teaches this with regard to people – רַבָּה בַּר רַב הוּנָא מַתְנֵי לָהּ בְּגַבְרֵי: The commentaries disagree as to how to interpret this dilemma. Rabbeinu Ḥananel explains the question as being whether those carrying the animal render their garments impure if the majority of the animal did not yet emerge. *Tosafot* find this difficult, as it is clear that they do not render their garments impure until the majority of the animal emerges. They therefore explain that the dilemma is whether we also follow the majority of the people. Although the mishna states that each one individually renders his garments impure as he emerges, perhaps once the majority of them have emerged, the garments of those inside are rendered impure as well.

Rashi explains that the dilemma is not with regard to the ritual impurity of the garments, but rather whether the animal should be burned inside or outside if it was disqualified at this point, in accordance with the *baraita* taught by Levi on 104b.

The Rambam explains that this dilemma also addresses the disqualification of emerging before the designated time. The dilemma is whether, if half the animal emerged, one follows the majority of the people to consider the animal as fully emerged or not, just as was considered with regard to the majority of a specific limb (see *Keren Ora*).

בָּעֵי רַבִּי אֶלְעָזָר: פָּרִים וּשְׂעִירִים הַנִּשְׂרָפִים שֶׁיָּצְאוּ וְחָזְרוּ, מַהוּ? מִי אָמְרִינַן: כֵּיוָן דְּנָפְקִי לְהוּ – אִיטַּמּוּ לְהוּ, אוֹ דִּלְמָא כֵּיוָן דַּהֲדוּר – הֲדוּר?

Rabbi Elazar raises another **dilemma: If bulls and goats that are burned left** the Temple courtyard **and returned,**[NH] **what is** the *halakha* with regard to the garments of those who carry them inside the courtyard? **Do we say: Once they left, they became impure? Or perhaps once they return, they return** and do not render garments impure?

אֲמַר רַבִּי אַבָּא בַּר מֶמֶל: תָּא שְׁמַע, הָיוּ סוֹבְלִין אוֹתָן בְּמוֹטוֹת, הָרִאשׁוֹנִים יָצְאוּ חוּץ לְחוֹמַת הָעֲזָרָה וְהָאַחֲרוֹנִים לֹא יָצְאוּ – הָרִאשׁוֹנִים שֶׁיָּצְאוּ חוּץ לְחוֹמַת הָעֲזָרָה מְטַמְּאִין בְּגָדִים, וְהָאַחֲרוֹנִים אֵין מְטַמְּאִין בְּגָדִים עַד שֶׁיֵּצְאוּ. וְאִי סָלְקָא דַּעְתָּךְ כֵּיוָן דְּנָפְקִי לְהוּ אִיטַּמּוּ – הָנָךְ דְּאִיכָּא גַּוַּאי לִיטַּמֵּא!

Rabbi Abba bar Memel says: Come and **hear** the mishna: **They would carry** the bulls and the goats that are burned suspended **on poles.** When **the first** priests, carrying the front of the pole, **emerged beyond the wall of the** Temple **courtyard and the latter** ones **did not** yet **emerge, the first** ones, **who emerged beyond the wall of the** Temple **courtyard, render** their **garments impure, but the latter** ones **do not render** their **garments impure until they emerge.** Rabbi Abba bar Memel explains: **And if it enters your mind** to say that **once they leave, they become impure, these** latter ones mentioned in the mishna **who are** still **inside should be rendered impure,** since the offering itself has emerged. It follows that if the offering returns, their garments are not rendered impure.

אֲמַר רָבִינָא: וְתִסְבְּרָא, הָא בָּעֵינָא ״וְאַחַר יָבֹא אֶל הַמַּחֲנֶה״, וְלֵיכָּא!

Ravina said: And can you understand this as a proof? The reason that the latter ones' garments are not rendered impure is that **I require** the fulfillment of the verse: "And he who burns them shall wash his garments, and bathe his flesh in water, **and afterward he may come into the camp"** (Leviticus 16:28). **And** since they have **not** yet left the camp, they cannot come into it, and therefore they do not contract the impurity described in the verse.

אֶלָּא רַבִּי אֶלְעָזָר הֵיכִי בָּעֵי לָהּ? כְּגוֹן דְּנָקְיטִי לָהּ בְּבַקּוּלְסֵי.

The Gemara asks: **But** if they can become impure only after they leave, **how did Rabbi Elazar raise this dilemma?** The Gemara answers: He raised the dilemma with regard to a case **where they take** the offering **with staffs** [***bevakulsei***],[L] i.e., after the offering is returned to the Temple courtyard, other people stand outside the courtyard and bring it out again using staffs. Does the offering render these people impure, even though they are standing outside the courtyard? The dilemma of Rabbi Elazar remains unresolved.

תָּנוּ רַבָּנַן: פָּרִים וּפָרָה וְשָׂעִיר הַמִּשְׁתַּלֵּחַ – הַמְשַׁלֵּחַ הַשּׂוֹרְפָן וְהַמּוֹצִיאָן מְטַמֵּא בְּגָדִים, וְהֵן עַצְמָן אֵין מְטַמְּאִין בְּגָדִים, אֲבָל מְטַמְּאִין אוֹכָלִין וּמַשְׁקִין, דִּבְרֵי רַבִּי מֵאִיר. וַחֲכָמִים אוֹמְרִים: פָּרָה וּפָרִים – מְטַמְּאִין אוֹכָלִין וּמַשְׁקִין, שָׂעִיר הַמִּשְׁתַּלֵּחַ – אֵינוֹ מְטַמֵּא, שֶׁהוּא חַי, וְהַחַי אֵינוֹ מְטַמֵּא אוֹכָלִין וּמַשְׁקִין.

§ **The Sages taught** in a *baraita*: With regard to **bulls** that are burned, **and** a red **heifer, and the scapegoat** of the Yom Kippur service,[NH] **the one who sends** them, **the one who burns them, and the one who takes them out** of the Temple courtyard **render** their **garments impure. And** the animals **themselves,**[N] after they emerge from the Temple courtyard, **do not render garments** that they touch **impure, but they render food and drink** that they touch **impure.** This is **the statement of Rabbi Meir. And the Rabbis say:** A red **heifer and bulls** that are burned **render food and drink impure,** but **the scapegoat does not transmit impurity** at all, **as it is** still **alive** when it leaves the Temple, **and a living being does not render food and drink impure.**

NOTES

Bulls and goats that are burned left the Temple courtyard and returned – פָּרִים וּשְׂעִירִים הַנִּשְׂרָפִים שֶׁיָּצְאוּ וְחָזְרוּ: Rashi explains that the Gemara assumes at this point that the dilemma is not with regard to the animal itself, but those carrying the animal, as they are the ones who render their garments impure (see 105b). The Gemara concludes that the dilemma is with regard to the animals themselves, once they are brought back inside. *Tosafot* find this difficult: Could the Gemara have assumed that the Temple courtyard is like a ritual bath, in that the people become pure when they enter? They explain that the Gemara assumes that the dilemma is whether the animal continues, if it returns to the courtyard, to cause those who handle it to render their garments impure.

Bulls that are burned and a red heifer and the scapegoat of the Yom Kippur service, etc. – פָּרִים וּפָרָה וְשָׂעִיר הַמִּשְׁתַּלֵּחַ וכו׳: The version of this *baraita* in the *Tosefta* states: The one who burns a red heifer and bulls that are burned, and the one who sends the scapegoat of the Yom Kippur service, and the one who takes them out of the Temple courtyard renders his garments impure.

The rite of the red heifer is taught in Numbers, chapter 19. The *halakha* for bulls that are burned is derived on 83a from a verse. The one who sends the scapegoat of the Yom Kippur service out to the wilderness renders his garments impure from the time he emerges with the scapegoat from Jerusalem (see Leviticus 16:26 and *Yoma* 67a).

And the animals themselves, etc. – וְהֵן עַצְמָן וכו׳: In other words, because the animals were slaughtered properly, they do not have the impurity of unslaughtered animal carcasses, which transmit impurity to people and vessels. The impurity mandated by the Torah for these offerings is only that those who handle the animals need to immerse and launder their garments, but other people who touch them are not rendered impure. In any event, the animals render food and drink that they touch impure, as is the *halakha* concerning any item fit for consumption that was rendered impure by a primary source of impurity.

LANGUAGE

Staffs [*bakulsei*] – בַּקּוּלְסֵי: From the Latin baculum and the Greek βάκλον, *baklon*, meaning staff, stick, or pole.

HALAKHA

Left the Temple courtyard and returned – יָצְאוּ וְחָזְרוּ: If bulls that are burned and goats that are burned emerged from the Temple courtyard and then returned inside, then one who carries them while inside is pure until he emerges with them. If one stood outside the Temple courtyard and pulled the bulls or goats out after they returned inside, it is uncertain if he is impure, as the Gemara leaves this dilemma unresolved (Rambam *Sefer Tahara, Hilkhot Para Aduma* 5:5, and see Ra'avad there).

Bulls that are burned and a red heifer and the scapegoat of the Yom Kippur service, etc. – פָּרִים וּפָרָה וְשָׂעִיר הַמִּשְׁתַּלֵּחַ וכו׳: Bulls and goats that are burned, a red heifer, and the scapegoat of the Yom Kippur service do not render people or vessels impure through contact. They transmit impurity only to those who handle them. A red heifer renders people impure from the time it is slaughtered until it is burned, bulls and goats that are burned render people impure from the time they emerge from the Temple courtyard until they are burned, and the scapegoat renders people impure from the time it emerges from Jerusalem until it is pushed off the cliff.

The Rambam writes that bulls and goats that are burned and the scapegoat of the Yom Kippur service do not render food impure. This indicates that a red heifer does render food impure, but there appears to be a contradiction in the Rambam's writings with regard to this *halakha* (Rambam *Sefer Tahara, Hilkhot Para Aduma* 5:2, 7 and *Hilkhot She'ar Avot HaTumot* 6:15; see *Birkat HaZevaḥ*).

בִּשְׁלָמָא לְרַבִּי מֵאִיר – כִּדְתָנָא דְּבֵי רַבִּי יִשְׁמָעֵאל, דְּתָנָא דְּבֵי רַבִּי יִשְׁמָעֵאל: ״עַל כָּל זֶרַע זֵרוּעַ״,

The Gemara comments. **Granted, according to Rabbi Meir** there is no difficulty, as his opinion is **in accordance with** that **which the school of Rabbi Yishmael taught. As the school of Rabbi Yishmael taught** in a *baraita*: The verse states that seeds can contract impurity from the carcass of a creeping animal only if they first come in contact with water: "And if any part of their carcass fall **upon any sowing seed** which is to be sown, it is pure. But if water be put upon the seed, and any part of their carcass fall thereon, it is impure unto you" (Leviticus 11:37–38).

מַה זְּרָעִים שֶׁאֵין סוֹפָן לִיטַּמֵּא טוּמְאָה חֲמוּרָה וּצְרִיכִין הֶכְשֵׁר – אַף כָּל שֶׁאֵין סוֹפָן לִיטַּמֵּא טוּמְאָה חֲמוּרָה צְרִיכִין הֶכְשֵׁר. יָצְתָה נִבְלַת עוֹף טָהוֹר, שֶׁסּוֹפָהּ לִיטַּמֵּא טוּמְאָה חֲמוּרָה, וְאֵין צְרִיכָה הֶכְשֵׁר.

Just as is the case for **seeds, which,** like any food, **can never contract impurity severe** enough to transmit it to human beings, **and they need** exposure to liquid to be **rendered susceptible** to their less severe level of impurity,[B] **so too, all** items **that can never contract impurity severe** enough to transmit it to human beings **need** exposure to liquid to be **rendered susceptible** to their less severe level of impurity and to transmit it. This serves to **exclude the carcass of a kosher bird,**[H] **which can contract impurity severe** enough to be transmitted to a human being who swallows it, **and** therefore **does not need** to be **rendered susceptible** to ritual impurity in order to transmit ritual impurity. According to this *baraita*, bulls that are burned, a red heifer, and a scapegoat, which are all sources of impurity for human beings, are able to transmit impurity to food and drink on their own, even if they have not been exposed to liquid and have not come in contact with any source of impurity. Rabbi Meir's opinion accords with this principle.

אֶלָּא לְרַבָּנַן, אִי אִית לְהוּ דְּתָנָא דְּבֵי רַבִּי יִשְׁמָעֵאל – אֲפִילּוּ שָׂעִיר הַמִּשְׁתַּלֵּחַ, אִי לֵית לֵיהּ – אֲפִילּוּ פָּרָה וּפָרִים מְנָלַן?

But for the opinion of **the Rabbis,** who disagree with Rabbi Meir and say that a scapegoat does not transmit impurity to food and drink, this is difficult. **If they accept** that **which the school of Rabbi Yishmael taught,** then **even the scapegoat** should transmit impurity to food and drink. And **if they do not accept** that statement, then **from where do we** derive that **even** a red **heifer and bulls** that are burned transmit impurity to food and drink?

כִּי אֲתָא רַב דִּימִי אֲמַר, אָמְרִי בְּמַעֲרָבָא: צְרִיכִין הֶכְשֵׁר טוּמְאָה מִמָּקוֹם אַחֵר.

When Rav Dimi came to Babylonia from Eretz Yisrael he **said:** The Sages **in the West,** Eretz Yisrael, **say:** The opinion of the Rabbis who disagree with Rabbi Meir is that bulls that are burned and a red heifer **need to contract impurity from somewhere else** to be able to transmit impurity[NH] to foods. Since the scapegoat cannot contract impurity, as it is alive, it cannot transmit impurity.

בָּעֵי רַבִּי אֶלְעָזָר: פָּרִים וּשְׂעִירִים הַנִּשְׂרָפִים, מַהוּ שֶׁיְּטַמְּאוּ אוֹכָלִין וּמַשְׁקִין בִּפְנִים כְּבַחוּץ? מְחוּסַּר יְצִיאָה כִּמְחוּסַּר מַעֲשֶׂה דָּמֵי, אוֹ לָא?

§ **Rabbi Elazar raises a dilemma:** With regard to **bulls and goats that are burned, what is the** *halakha* as to **whether they can transmit impurity to food and drink inside** the Temple courtyard,[H] before they leave, **as** they do **outside** afterward? Is an offering **that has not yet left** the Temple **considered as** if it were an item for which a necessary **action has not yet** been performed, i.e., because it has not yet become a source of impurity to those who carry it, it also does not transmit impurity to food without being rendered susceptible by coming into contact with a liquid and then coming into contact with a source of impurity? **Or** perhaps **no,** because the offering will become a source of impurity to those who carry it once it leaves the Temple courtyard, it already transmits impurity to food without being rendered susceptible.

בָּתַר דְּבַעְיָא הֲדַר פַּשְׁטַהּ: מְחוּסַּר יְצִיאָה כִּמְחוּסַּר מַעֲשֶׂה דָּמֵי.

After Rabbi Elazar **raised the dilemma, he then resolved it:** An offering **that has not yet left is considered as** if it were an item for which a necessary **action has not yet** been performed, and it does not transmit impurity to food without being rendered susceptible.

BACKGROUND

Rendered susceptible to impurity – הֶכְשֵׁר: In order for agricultural produce to become capable of contracting ritual impurity, it must be detached from the earth and then come into contact with water or certain other liquids. The owner of the produce must approve of the fact that the produce became wet. If the owner was not pleased, the produce still cannot contract ritual impurity. The Talmud contains numerous discussions about specific instances in which there is uncertainty whether or not the conditions have been fulfilled.

NOTES

Need to contract impurity from somewhere else to be able to transmit impurity – צְרִיכִין הֶכְשֵׁר טוּמְאָה מִמָּקוֹם אַחֵר: The early commentaries disagree as to how to interpret this statement. See *Tosafot* on *Bava Kamma* 77a, who quote a version of this text that reads: Do not need to contract impurity, instead of: Need to contract impurity.

Rashi explains that this statement refers to the seeds mentioned in the *baraita* of the school of Rabbi Yishmael. Seeds must be rendered impure from another place, i.e., they do not transmit impurity to food until they come into contact with the carcass of a creeping animal. Only items that are not in and of themselves a source of ritual impurity require contact with liquid to be susceptible to impurity. But an item that is itself a source of impurity, e.g., a bull that is burned or a red heifer, does not need to become impure from an outside source for it to transmit impurity to food. The scapegoat is excluded from this principle because a living being cannot be rendered impure.

The Ra'avad explains that this statement refers to the bulls and a red heifer. An item that is itself a source of impurity does not need to contract impurity from another source, such as the carcass of a creeping animal, in order to render food impure. But this is the *halakha* only if it can in theory contract impurity from another source. A scapegoat, which cannot contract impurity from another source since it is alive, is excluded from the principle in the *baraita*.

The Ra'avad also suggests an entirely different explanation. According to the Sages of Eretz Yisrael, the Rabbis reject the *baraita* of the school of Rabbi Yishmael. A red heifer or bull that is burned renders food impure only if it contracted impurity from another source, such as the carcass of a creeping animal. This is not possible in the case of a scapegoat, which is alive. From the dilemma of Rabbi Abba bar Shmuel and the discussion later (105b), this interpretation appears to be the most straightforward explanation of the statement and is reflected in the commentary here (see *Yad David*, *Sefat Emet*, and *Zevaḥ Toda*).

HALAKHA

The carcass of a kosher bird – נִבְלַת עוֹף טָהוֹר: The carcass of a kosher bird that one intends to consume renders foods impure. It is considered as a food with first-degree impurity, even though it had no exposure to liquid and did not come in contact with other impurity (Rambam *Sefer Tahara*, *Hilkhot She'ar Avot HaTumot* 3:2).

Need to contract impurity from somewhere else to be able to transmit impurity – צְרִיכִין הֶכְשֵׁר טוּמְאָה מִמָּקוֹם אַחֵר: If one intended to consume bulls and goats that are burned or a red heifer, then even though they render the priests who handle them impure, they do not render food impure unless an impure item renders them impure. See *Kesef Mishne*, who explains how this is based on the discussion here. The *Keren Ora* explains that the source is the Jerusalem Talmud (Rambam *Sefer Tahara*, *Hilkhot She'ar Avot HaTumot* 3:3, and see Ra'avad there).

What is the *halakha* as to whether they can transmit impurity to food and drink inside the Temple courtyard – מַהוּ שֶׁיְּטַמְּאוּ אוֹכָלִין וּמַשְׁקִין בִּפְנִים: The Rambam writes that bulls and goats do not render people, vessels, food, or drink impure even after they emerge. This indicates that the same applies all the more so when the animals are inside (Rambam *Sefer Tahara*, *Hilkhot Para Aduma* 5:7).

NOTES

According to Rabbi Meir…the carcass of a kosher bird, etc. – **נבלת עוף טהור לרבי מאיר וכו׳**: According to Rashi, everyone agrees that if there is an egg-bulk of an animal carcass, then it renders food impure without being rendered susceptible by exposure to liquid and contact with the carcass of a creeping animal, as taught in the *baraita* of the school of Rabbi Yishmael. But if there is merely an olive bulk, then only according to Rabbi Meir could it transmit impurity as it is, as he holds that a scapegoat can render food impure even though it is a living being. According to the Rabbis, who say that the scapegoat cannot render food impure at all, the *halakha* would be the same for an olive-bulk of the carcass of a kosher bird, which is also not susceptible to impurity.

The *Sefat Emet* finds this comparison difficult, as the scapegoat is not susceptible to any impurity whatsoever, whereas olive-bulks of a carcass could combine to become an egg-bulk. Therefore, this dilemma could also be posed in accordance with the opinion of the Rabbis. He notes that this supports the second interpretation of the Ra'avad, that the Rabbis disagree with the *baraita* of the school of Rabbi Yishmael and hold that the carcass of a kosher bird does not render food impure without first being rendered susceptible to impurity.

BACKGROUND

Olive-bulk – **כזית**: An olive-bulk is one of the most significant units of volume. By Torah law, the act of eating is defined as consuming one olive-bulk, and almost every Torah law that either commands or prohibits eating relates to this measure. The measure is defined in terms of the water displacement of a particular strain of olive, but the precise measurement is not clear. One talmudic passage indicates that it is almost half an egg-bulk, and another indicates that it is less than one-third of an egg-bulk. Given the range of opinions concerning the measure of an egg-bulk, the opinions with regard to the measure of an olive-bulk range from 7 cc to 50 cc.

בעא מיניה רבי אבא בר שמואל מרבי חייא בר אבא: נבלת עוף טהור לרבי מאיר, מהו שיטמא בכזית?

§ **Rabbi Abba bar Shmuel posed** another **dilemma to Rabbi Ḥiyya bar Abba:** Food transmits impurity to other food or drink only if it is the volume of at least one egg-bulk and it is first rendered susceptible to impurity. The carcass of a kosher bird transmits impurity to a person who swallows it even if it is of the volume of at least one olive-bulk, and even if it has not been rendered susceptible to impurity. **According to** the opinion of **Rabbi Meir,** that the carcass of a kosher bird transmits impurity to other food without first being rendered susceptible to impurity, **what is** the *halakha* as to the requisite measure? Does **the carcass of a kosher bird**[N] **transmit impurity** to food even if it is of the volume of **an olive-bulk,**[B] as it would to a person?

דמחתא לארעא – לא תיבעי לך, דנקיט בפומיה – לא תיבעי לך. כי תיבעי לך – דנקיט ליה בידיה; מחוסר קריבה כמחוסר מעשה דמי, או לא?

The Gemara clarifies: **Do not raise the dilemma** in a case **where** the carcass **lies on the ground,** as in that case it certainly must be of the volume of an egg-bulk, like any other impure food. And **do not raise the dilemma** in a case **where** a person **holds** the bird's flesh **in his mouth,** as it may be swallowed and transmit impurity to him even if it is of the volume of only an olive-bulk; in this case it certainly transmits impurity to food in the same measure. **When you raise the dilemma,** raise it in a case **where he holds** the bird's flesh **in his hand.** When the flesh **has not yet been brought close** to being swallowed, is it **considered** to be **like** an item for which a necessary **action has not yet** been performed, in which case it is considered a normal food and must be of the volume of an egg-bulk, **or** perhaps **not?**

בתר דבעיא הדר פשטה:

After Abba bar Shmuel **raised the dilemma, he then resolved it:**

Perek **XII**
Daf **105** Amud **b**

HALAKHA

It requires a person's intention that it be eaten and it does not need to be rendered susceptible by contact with liquid – **צריכה מחשבה ואין צריכה הכשר**: The unslaughtered carcass of a kosher bird that one had intention to consume transmits impurity of food and does not need to be made susceptible by contact with liquid. It is considered to have first-degree impurity even if it did not come in contact with other impurity (Rambam *Sefer Tahara, Hilkhot She'ar Avot HaTumot* 3:2).

BACKGROUND

Egg-bulk – **ביצה**: This unit of measurement of volume is the minimum unit with regard to the ritual impurity of food, i.e., a smaller quantity of food than this does not transmit ritual impurity; nor, according to certain authorities, does it contract ritual impurity. The egg-bulk measurement is also used in many other contexts. Opinions as to the volume of an egg-bulk range from 50 cc to 100 cc.

מחוסר קריבה לאו כמחוסר מעשה דמי.

Even if the carcass of a kosher bird **has not yet been brought close** to being swallowed, it is still **not considered as** if a necessary **action has not yet** been performed, and an olive-bulk is sufficient to transmit impurity to food and drink.

איתיביה: שלשה עשר דברים נאמרו בנבלת עוף טהור, וזה אחד מהן: צריכה מחשבה, ואין צריכה הכשר, ומטמא טומאת אוכלין בכביצה. מאי לאו רבי מאיר היא?

Rabbi Ḥiyya bar Abba **raised an objection to** Rabbi Abba bar Shmuel, based on a mishna (*Teharot* 1:1): **Thirteen matters were stated with regard to the carcass of a kosher bird, and this is one of them:** In order to be susceptible to impurity as a food, it **requires** a person's **intention** that it be eaten; **and it does not need** to be **rendered susceptible** to such impurity by contact with liquid;[H] **and it transmits ritual impurity of food in** the amount of **an egg-bulk.**[BN] In accordance with whose opinion is this mishna? **What, is it not** the opinion of **Rabbi Meir?** If so, he holds that an egg-bulk of a carcass of a kosher bird is necessary to transmit impurity.

לא, רבנן היא.

The Gemara responds: **No,** the mishna **is** the opinion of **the Rabbis.**

NOTES

And it transmits ritual impurity of food in the amount of an egg-bulk – **ומטמא טומאת אוכלין בכביצה**: The mishna must be discussing a case where the carcass was in a person's hand. If it is on the ground, then it certainly requires exposure to liquid to be rendered susceptible to impurity of food, as it is not known that it will become a source of severe impurity. If it is in the person's mouth, then it does not require intention, as the person clearly shows with the act of putting it in his mouth that it is food. But if it is in his hand, then it requires intention but not exposure to liquid.

וְהָא קָתָנֵי רֵישָׁא: צְרִיכָה מַחֲשָׁבָה וְאֵין צְרִיכָה הֶכְשֵׁר; וּמַאן שָׁמְעַתְּ לֵיהּ הַאי סְבָרָא – רַבִּי מֵאִיר. וּמִדְּרֵישָׁא רַבִּי מֵאִיר – סֵיפָא נַמִי רַבִּי מֵאִיר!

The Gemara challenges: **But the first clause** of that mishna **teaches:** In order to be susceptible to impurity as a food, it **requires** a person's **intention** that it be eaten **and it does not need** to be **rendered susceptible** by contact with liquid. **And** from **whom do you learn this reasoning?** From **Rabbi Meir,** as was taught in the *baraita* (105a). **And since the first clause** is the opinion of **Rabbi Meir,** it follows that **the latter clause** is **also** the opinion of **Rabbi Meir.**

מִידֵי אִירְיָא? הָא כִּדְאִיתָא וְהָא כִּדְאִיתָא.

The Gemara responds: **Are the cases comparable?** Must both clauses be the opinion of the same *tanna*? **This** case is **as it is, and that** case is **as it is.**[B]

וְהָא מִדְּקָתָנֵי סֵיפָא: שְׁחִיטָתָהּ וּמְלִיקָתָהּ מְטַהֶרֶת טְרֵיפָתָהּ מִטּוּמְאָתָהּ; מַאן שָׁמְעַתְּ לֵיהּ הַאי סְבָרָא – רַבִּי מֵאִיר, רֵישָׁא וְסֵיפָא רַבִּי מֵאִיר וּמְצִיעֲתָא רַבָּנַן?

The Gemara challenges: **But** one can still infer this **from** the fact **that the latter clause** of that mishna **teaches: The slaughter or the pinching** of the nape **of** a bird offering **purifies it from its impurity,** i.e., prevents it from assuming the impure status of a carcass, even if it is found to **have a wound that would have caused it to die within twelve months** [*tereifa*].[H] **And from whom did you learn this reasoning?** From **Rabbi Meir** (see 67a). Could it be that **the first clause and the last clause** represent the opinion of **Rabbi Meir, and the middle clause** represents the opinion of **the Rabbis?**

אִין, רֵישָׁא וְסֵיפָא רַבִּי מֵאִיר וּמְצִיעֲתָא רַבָּנַן.

The Gemara responds: **Yes, the first clause and the last clause** represent the opinion of **Rabbi Meir, and the middle clause** represents the opinion of **the Rabbis.**

אֲמַר לֵיהּ רַב הַמְנוּנָא לְרַבִּי זֵירָא: לָא תֵּיתִיב אַכַּרְעָךְ עַד דְּאָמְרַתְּ לִי הָא מִילְּתָא: נִבְלַת עוֹף טָהוֹר לְרַבִּי מֵאִיר, מוֹנִין לָהּ רִאשׁוֹן וְשֵׁנִי, אוֹ אֵין מוֹנִין רִאשׁוֹן וְשֵׁנִי?

§ **Rav Hamnuna said to Rabbi Zeira: Do not sit down**[N] **until you tell me** the resolution of **this matter:** In general, when a food touches a primary source of ritual impurity after having been rendered susceptible to impurity by contact with a liquid, it contracts first-degree impurity. If it then touches another food, it imparts to it second-degree impurity. **The carcass of a kosher bird, according to** the opinion of **Rabbi Meir,** transmits impurity to food without being rendered susceptible. Does one **count its first and second** degrees of impurity when it touches food or drink, treating it like a primary source of impurity? **Or** perhaps one **does not count first and second** degrees of impurity, but rather treats it as a food with first-degree impurity, which imparts second-degree impurity?

אֲמַר לֵיהּ: כָּל הֵיכָא דִּמְטַמֵּא אָדָם בְּמַגָּע – מוֹנִין בּוֹ רִאשׁוֹן וְשֵׁנִי, כָּל הֵיכָא דְּאֵין מְטַמֵּא אָדָם בְּמַגָּע – אֵין מוֹנִין בּוֹ רִאשׁוֹן וְשֵׁנִי.

Rabbi Zeira **said to him: Wherever** an item **can render a person impure through contact,** it is considered a primary source of impurity, and one **counts its first and second** degrees of impurity. And **wherever it cannot render a person impure through contact,** one **does not count its first and second** degrees of impurity. Since the carcass of a kosher bird does not render a person impure through contact, but only by being swallowed, it is treated as a food with first-degree impurity.

BACKGROUND

This case is as it is and that case is as it is – הָא כִּדְאִיתָא וְהָא כִּדְאִיתָא: This expression is employed to reject conclusions reached from the fact that two cases are juxtaposed in a single source. The circumstances in each case are different, and consequently, no inference may be drawn from their juxtaposition.

HALAKHA

The slaughter and the pinching of the nape of a bird offering purifies it from its impurity if it is found to be a *tereifa* – שְׁחִיטָתָהּ וּמְלִיקָתָהּ מְטַהֶרֶת טְרֵיפָתָהּ מִטּוּמְאָתָהּ: A kosher bird that is a *tereifa* and slaughtered according to *halakha* does not have the ritual impurity of an unslaughtered carcass, even if it is slaughtered in the Temple courtyard. But if the bird's nape is pinched and it is found to be a *tereifa*, it has the ritual impurity of an unslaughtered carcass, in accordance with the statements of Rabbi Yosei and Rabbi Yehuda in the mishna on 68b (Rambam *Sefer Tahara, Hilkhot She'ar Avot HaTumot* 3:12).

NOTES

Do not sit down – לָא תֵּיתִיב אַכַּרְעָךְ: Literally, do not sit down on your feet, as he would sit on the ground. *Tosafot* in tractate *Nazir* (24b) explain this phrase as an abbreviation, as if he said: Do not sit; rather, stand on your feet.

בעא מיניה רבי זירא מרבי אמי בר חייא, ואמרי לה מרבי אבין בר כהנא: הא דתנן: חיבורי אוכלין על ידי משקין – חיבור לטומאה קלה ואין חיבור לטומאה חמורה;

Rabbi Zeira posed a dilemma to Rabbi Ami bar Ḥiyya, and some say to Rabbi Avin bar Kahana concerning **that which we learned** in a mishna (*Teharot* 8:8): **Connections between foods by liquid,** i.e., liquids in contact with two foods, a situation that causes the impurity of one food to be transmitted to the other and their sizes to be combined toward the minimum measure for transmitting impurity, are considered **a connection for the lenient impurity** of foods, **but** are **not** considered **a connection for impurity severe** enough to be transmitted to a human being. If two pieces of animal carcass are connected by a liquid, they do not combine to form the minimum measure for transmitting their impurity to a person, but they can transmit impurity to food.

מונין בו ראשון ושני, או אין מונין בו ראשון ושני?

Rabbi Zeira asks: If these two pieces of animal carcass come in contact with food, does one **count its first and second** degrees of impurity[H] and treat the pieces as a primary source of impurity, such that the food will impart second-degree impurity to other food? **Or** does one **not count its first and second** degrees of impurity, and treat the animal carcass as food with first-degree impurity?

אמר ליה: כל היכא דמטמא אדם – מונין בו ראשון ושני, אין מטמא אדם – אין מונין בו ראשון ושני.

Rabbi Zeira **said to him: Wherever** an item **can render a person impure,** one **counts its first and second** degrees of impurity. And wherever it **cannot render a person impure,** one **does not count its first and second** degrees of impurity. Since the pieces of carcass cannot transmit their impurity to a person, they are treated as food with first-degree impurity.

״יצאו אלו ואלו״. מנא הני מילי? דתנו רבנן: להלן הוא אומר חוץ לשלש מחנות, כאן – למחנה אחת, לומר לך: כיון שיצא חוץ למחנה אחת – מטמא בגדים.

§ The mishna teaches: When both **these** priests **and those** priests **emerged,** all of their garments were rendered ritually impure. The Gemara explains: **From where are these matters** derived? **As the Sages taught** in a *baraita*: The verse states with regard to the bull and goat that are burned on Yom Kippur: "They shall be carried forth outside the camp" (Leviticus 16:27). **There,** elsewhere, the verse **states** that such bulls and goats are burned **outside three camps,**[N] those of the Tabernacle, the Levites, and the Israelites, whereas **here,** the verse states only that they are taken outside **one camp,** i.e., the Tabernacle. This serves **to tell you: Once** the offering **emerges beyond one camp,** one who carries it **renders** his **garments impure,** as the next verse states: "And he who burns them shall wash his garments" (Leviticus 16:28).

והיא גופה מנלן? דתנו רבנן: ״והוציא את כל הפר אל מחוץ למחנה״ – חוץ לשלש מחנות. אתה אומר: חוץ לשלש מחנות, או אינו אלא מחנה אחת?

The Gemara explains further: **And from where do we** derive **that** *halakha* **itself,** that the bulls and goats are burned outside the three camps? **As the Sages taught** in a *baraita*: It is stated about the bull brought as a sin offering of the High Priest: **"Even the whole bull shall he carry outside the camp** unto a pure place, where the ashes are poured out, and burn it" (Leviticus 4:12), meaning that he should take it **outside** the **three camps. Do you say** that he takes it **outside** the **three camps, or** is he required to take it outside **only one camp?**

HALAKHA

Does one count its first and second degrees of impurity, etc. – מונין בו ראשון ושני וכו׳: If two pieces of food are connected by liquid, then together they transmit impurity of food. It is uncertain whether they are considered a single piece with regard to degrees of impurity, so that if they contact a primary source of impurity they have first-degree impurity, or perhaps only the first piece of food has first-degree impurity, and the second piece connected to it has second-degree impurity. This is in accordance with the explanation of Rabbeinu Ḥananel. The Ra'avad objects that the dilemma here is resolved, but the *Kesef Mishne* explains that it appears to remain unresolved in *Menaḥot* 24a. The dilemma is also unresolved in most manuscripts of the text here (Rambam *Sefer Tahara, Hilkhot She'ar Avot HaTumot* 11:6).

NOTES

There it states that bulls and goats are burned outside three camps, etc. – להלן הוא אומר חוץ לשלש מחנות וכו׳: All sin offerings that are burned are juxtaposed with each other, to teach that the location of burning and the *halakhot* of ritual impurity are the same for all of them (see 83a). The *baraita* later on in the *amud* derives from verses that all sin offerings are burned outside three camps. The *baraita* here serves to explain why the verse states that the bull and goat that are burned on Yom Kippur are brought "outside the camp" (Leviticus 16:27), i.e., just one camp, since they are burned outside three camps. The *baraita* explains that this phrase relates to the next verse: "And he who burns them shall wash his garments" (Leviticus 16:28), teaching that the priests render their garments impure once they emerge from one camp. Because sin offerings that are burned are juxtaposed, this *halakha* applies to all of them: The priests render their garments impure once they emerge from one camp.

כְּשֶׁהוּא אוֹמֵר בְּפַר הָעֵדָה "מִחוּץ לַמַּחֲנֶה", שֶׁאֵין צָרִיךְ לוֹמַר, שֶׁהֲרֵי כְּבָר נֶאֱמַר: "כַּאֲשֶׁר שָׂרַף אֵת הַפָּר הָרִאשׁוֹן" – לִיתֵּן לוֹ מַחֲנֶה שְׁנִיָּה.

When the verse **states with regard to the bull** brought as **a communal** sin offering: "He shall carry the bull **outside the camp,** and burn it as he burned the first bull" (Leviticus 4:21), it requires explanation, **as there is no need** for the verse **to state** "outside the camp," **since it is already stated** at the end of that same verse: **"And burn it as he burned the first bull,"** which indicates that all the *halakhot* of the bull brought as a sin offering of a High Priest apply to the bull brought as a communal sin offering. What then does the verse mean when it states "outside the camp"? **To give it a second camp,** i.e., it indicates that it must be removed not only from the camp of the Divine Presence, corresponding to the Temple, but also from the Levite camp, corresponding to the Temple Mount.

כְּשֶׁהוּא אוֹמֵר "מִחוּץ לַמַּחֲנֶה" בַּדֶּשֶׁן, שֶׁאֵין צָרִיךְ לוֹמַר, שֶׁהֲרֵי כְּבָר נֶאֱמַר: "עַל שֶׁפֶךְ הַדֶּשֶׁן יִשָּׂרֵף" – לִיתֵּן לוֹ מַחֲנֶה שְׁלִישִׁית.

And **when** another verse **states with regard to** the removal of **the ash:** "And he shall put off his garments, and put on other garments, and carry forth the ashes **outside the camp** to a pure place" (Leviticus 6:4), that verse also requires an explanation, **as there is no need** for the verse **to state** this, **since it is already stated** with regard to the bull brought as a sin offering of a High Priest: "Even the whole bull shall he carry outside the camp to a pure place, where the ashes are poured out, and burn it on wood with fire; **where the ashes are poured out shall it be burned"** (Leviticus 4:12). The repetition of "outside the camp" indicates that he is required **to give it a third camp,** i.e., teaching that it is burned when outside the Israelite camp, corresponding to the land outside the walls of Jerusalem.

וְרַבִּי שִׁמְעוֹן, הַאי "מִחוּץ לַמַּחֲנֶה" מַאי עָבֵיד לֵיהּ? מִיבָּעֵי לֵיהּ לִכְדְתַנְיָא, רַבִּי אֱלִיעֶזֶר אוֹמֵר: נֶאֱמַר כָּאן: "חוּץ לַמַּחֲנֶה" וְנֶאֱמַר לְהַלָּן: "חוּץ לַמַּחֲנֶה", מַה לְּהַלָּן חוּץ לְשָׁלֹשׁ מַחֲנוֹת – אַף כָּאן חוּץ לְשָׁלֹשׁ מַחֲנוֹת. וּמַה לְּהַלָּן לְמִזְרָחָהּ שֶׁל יְרוּשָׁלַיִם

The Gemara asks: **And what does Rabbi Shimon do with this** phrase, stated with regard to the bull and goat of Yom Kippur: **"Outside the camp"** (Leviticus 16:27), given that he holds that the garments do not become impure until the offering is burning? The Gemara answers: **He requires it for** that **which is taught** in a *baraita*: **Rabbi Eliezer says: It is stated here: "Outside the camp," and it is stated there,** with regard to the red heifer: "He shall bring it **outside the camp"** (Numbers 19:3). **Just as here,** the bull and goat of Yom Kippur are burned **outside three camps, so too there,** the red heifer is burned **outside three camps.**[H] **And just as there,** the red heifer is burned **east of Jerusalem,** since it must be burned "toward the front of the Tent of Meeting" (Numbers 19:4), opposite the entrance of the Temple, which is to its east,

HALAKHA

The place of burning the red heifer – מְקוֹם שְׂרֵפַת פָּרָה אֲדֻמָּה: The red heifer must be burned outside the Temple Mount, as is stated: "He shall bring it outside the camp" (Numbers 19:3). They would burn it on the Mount of Olives, east of the Temple. The *Kesef Mishne* explains based on the Gemara that the Rambam did not state the *halakha* precisely, as the heifer must be burned outside Jerusalem (Rambam *Sefer Tahara, Hilkhot Para Aduma* 3:2).

Perek **XII**
Daf **106** Amud **a**

אַף כָּאן לְמִזְרָחָהּ שֶׁל יְרוּשָׁלַיִם.

so too here, the bull and goat of Yom Kippur are burned **east of Jerusalem.**

אֶלָּא לְרַבָּנַן הֵיכָא שָׂרֵיף לְהוּ? כִּדְתַנְיָא: הֵיכָן נִשְׂרָפִין – לִצְפוֹן יְרוּשָׁלַיִם, חוּץ לְשָׁלֹשׁ מַחֲנוֹת. רַבִּי יוֹסֵי הַגְּלִילִי אוֹמֵר: אַבֵּית הַדֶּשֶׁן נִשְׂרָפִין.

But according to the Rabbis, then, **where** outside Jerusalem **do they burn them?** The Gemara responds: **As it is taught** in a *baraita*: **Where** are the bulls and goats **burned?** They are burned **north of Jerusalem,**[N] **outside of** the **three camps. Rabbi Yosei HaGelili says: They are burned on the place of the ashes,**[H] where the ashes from the altar were poured.

NOTES

North of Jerusalem – לִצְפוֹן יְרוּשָׁלַיִם: Because sin offerings are slaughtered on the north side of the Temple courtyard, this is apparently the appropriate direction to take them for burning (Rashi).

HALAKHA

They are burned on the place of the ashes – אַבֵּית הַדֶּשֶׁן נִשְׂרָפִין: When sin offerings whose blood is sprinkled on the inner altar are burned in accordance with their mitzva, they are burned in the place of the ashes outside Jerusalem. This is in accordance with the statement of Rabbi Yosei HaGelili (Rambam *Sefer Avoda, Hilkhot Ma'aseh HaKorbanot* 7:4).

Rava said: Who is the *tanna* who disagrees with Rabbi Yosei HaGelili?[N] It is Rabbi Eliezer ben Yaakov, as it is taught in a *baraita*: The verse states with regard to bulls that are burned: "Where the ashes are poured out [*shefekh hadeshen*] shall it be burned" (Leviticus 4:12). This teaches that ashes must be there[N] already when the bulls are burned. Rabbi Eliezer ben Yaakov says: This verse teaches that its place should slope [*meshupakh*] downward so that ashes from the burning will slide downhill.

אֲמַר רָבָא: מַאן תַּנָּא דִּפְלִיג עֲלֵיהּ דְּרַבִּי יוֹסֵי הַגְּלִילִי – רַבִּי אֱלִיעֶזֶר בֶּן יַעֲקֹב הִיא. דְּתַנְיָא: "עַל שֶׁפֶךְ הַדֶּשֶׁן יִשָּׂרֵף" – שֶׁיְּהֵא שָׁם דֶּשֶׁן (שֶׁיִּקְדִּים לְשָׁם דֶּשֶׁן). רַבִּי אֱלִיעֶזֶר בֶּן יַעֲקֹב אוֹמֵר: שֶׁיְּהֵא מְקוֹמוֹ מְשׁוּפָּךְ.

Abaye said to Rava: Perhaps they disagree only about whether the place must slope, but Rabbi Eliezer ben Yaakov agrees that it must be the place where the ashes from the altar were deposited.

אֲמַר לֵיהּ אַבַּיֵי: דִּילְמָא בִּמְקוֹמוֹ מְשׁוּפָּךְ פְּלִיגִי!

§ The Sages taught in a *baraita*: The verse states with regard to the bull and goat of Yom Kippur: "And he who burns them shall wash his garments" (Leviticus 16:28). This teaches that only the one who burns them renders his garments impure, but the one who kindles the fire does not render his garments impure, and the one who sets up the arrangement of wood does not render his garments impure. And who is considered the one who burns? One who assists at the actual time of burning.[H]

תָּנוּ רַבָּנַן: הַשּׂוֹרֵף מְטַמֵּא בְּגָדִים, וְלֹא הַמַּצִּית אֶת הָאוּר מְטַמֵּא בְּגָדִים, וְלֹא הַמְסַדֵּר אֶת הַמַּעֲרָכָה מְטַמֵּא בְּגָדִים. וְאֵיזֶהוּ הַשּׂוֹרֵף – הַמְסַיֵּיעַ בִּשְׁעַת שְׂרֵיפָה.

One might have thought that this priest renders his garments impure even after the bull and goat become ash. Therefore, the verse states: "And he who burns them" (Leviticus 16:28), teaching that they, the whole bull and goat, render garments impure, but they do not render garments impure once they become ash.[H] Rabbi Shimon says: The word "them" teaches that they render garments impure, but once the flesh is incinerated they do not render garments impure.

יָכוֹל אַף מִשֶּׁנַּעֲשׂוּ אֵפֶר מְטַמֵּא בְּגָדִים? תַּלְמוּד לוֹמַר "אוֹתָם", אוֹתָם מְטַמְּאִין בְּגָדִים, וּמִשֶּׁנַּעֲשִׂין אֵפֶר אֵין מְטַמְּאִין בְּגָדִים. רַבִּי שִׁמְעוֹן אוֹמֵר: אוֹתָם מְטַמְּאִין בְּגָדִים, נִיתַּךְ הַבָּשָׂר – אֵין מְטַמְּאִין בְּגָדִים.

The Gemara asks: What is the difference between the opinion of the first *tanna* and the opinion of Rabbi Shimon? Rava said: The difference between them is when he turned it into a charred mass, and the form of the animal has become distorted, but has not actually become ash. The first *tanna* holds that at this stage the offering still transmits impurity, whereas Rabbi Shimon holds that it does not.

מַאי בֵּינַיְיהוּ? אֲמַר רָבָא: אִיכָּא בֵּינַיְיהוּ דְּשַׁוְּיֵיהּ חֲרוּכָא.

הדרן עלך טבול יום

NOTES

Who is the *tanna* who disagrees with Rabbi Yosei HaGelili – מַאן תַּנָּא דִּפְלִיג עֲלֵיהּ דְּרַבִּי יוֹסֵי הַגְּלִילִי: From the fact that the first *tanna* said only that the bulls and goats are burned north of Jerusalem, and Rabbi Yosei HaGelili then specified the place of the ashes, the first *tanna* must disagree with him. If so, it must be explained how this *tanna* interprets the verse: "Where the ashes are poured out shall it be burned" (Leviticus 4:12).

That ashes must be there – שֶׁיְּהֵא שָׁם דֶּשֶׁן: Rashi apparently understands this to be the opinion of Rabbi Yosei HaGelili. The intention is that the bull must be burned in a place where ashes were previously poured, and not necessarily that ashes already be there at the time (*Korban Aharon*). According to the commentary attributed to Ra'avad on *Torat Kohanim*, there must be ashes already there at the time, and if there are none then some must be brought from the place of the ashes on the Temple Mount. Rabbi Eliyahu Mizrahi objects that *Torat Kohanim* explicitly states that there do not need to be ashes already there at the time, and explains that there is a difference between what is required *ab initio* and what is sufficient after the fact.

HALAKHA

One who assists at the actual time of burning – הַמְסַיֵּיעַ בִּשְׁעַת שְׂרֵיפָה: For all sin offerings that are burned, the priest who burns them renders his garments impure from the time of burning. And who is considered one who burns? It is one who assists at the actual time of burning, e.g., by turning the flesh, adding firewood, or stoking the fire. The priests who light the fire or set up the arrangement of wood remain pure (Rambam *Sefer Tahara*, *Hilkhot Para Aduma* 5:4).

But they do not render garments impure once they become ash – וּמִשֶּׁנַּעֲשִׂין אֵפֶר אֵין מְטַמְּאִין בְּגָדִים: A priest who is involved with burning a sin offering of a type that is burned does not render his garments impure from the time the offering becomes ash (Rambam *Sefer Tahara*, *Hilkhot Para Aduma* 5:4).

Summary of **Perek XII**

After discussing the right of priests to a share of sacrificial meat, the Gemara concludes that every priest from the patrilineal family serving that day in the Temple may receive a share, provided he is fit to perform the service from the time the offering's blood is sprinkled until its fats are burned on the altar. Nevertheless, if he is fit to perform the service but not fit to partake of sacrificial meat, e.g., in the case of a High Priest in acute mourning, then he does not receive a share. Anyone who is not fit during the necessary time period does not receive a share, even if he will be fit in the evening, e.g., if he was impure and immersed or he was an acute mourner. There is an exception to this in that blemished priests may receive a share of sacrificial meat whether their blemish is permanent or temporary, even though they are not fit for service.

The Gemara examines at length the subject of a priest in acute mourning, who is prohibited by Torah law to perform the service or to partake of sacrificial meat on the day his relative dies. The Sages disagree as to whether this prohibition extends to the following night by Torah law, and the discussion concludes that the prohibition at night is by rabbinic law. Therefore, if a person is an acute mourner on the fourteenth of Nisan, the day the Paschal offering is sacrificed, then because the essential mitzva is to consume the Paschal offering at night, the Sages rendered it permitted for him in certain circumstances to sacrifice it during the day while in acute mourning and consume it at night. The Gemara also concludes that if one's relative is not buried on the day he died, then acute mourning continues by rabbinic law until the end of the day of burial. In the course of this discussion, the Gemara also analyzes the narrative of the eighth day of the inauguration of the Tabernacle, on which Aaron's sons Nadav and Avihu died.

With regard to the right of the priests to the offering's hide, the chapter concludes that the priests acquire not only the hide of a burnt offering, which the Torah teaches explicitly, but also that of any offering where the priests acquire the meat. Any priest who has a right to the meat has a right to the hide, and those priests who have no right to the meat have no right to the hide.

The chapter also clarifies that the priests acquire the hide of a burnt offering whenever its flesh is burned on the altar, even if the offering was not slaughtered for its sake. If a burnt offering is disqualified, the priests do not acquire its hide. The chapter also concludes that although the verse specifies "a man's burnt offering," the principle applies to burnt offerings of women, converts, and Canaanite slaves as well, since the verse means to exclude only burnt offerings of consecrated property.

Although the priests do not acquire the hide of a disqualified burnt offering, the Sages disagree with regard to a case where the hide was flayed before the disqualification, whether the sprinkling of the blood is effective to permit the hide to the priests. There is also a dispute with regard to a case where the animal is found to be a *tereifa* after the hide was flayed and the blood was sprinkled. The Gemara concludes that the priests do not acquire the hide, and it is burned along with the flesh. But in the case of a blemished firstborn offering that is consumed outside the Temple, the priests acquire the hide even if it is found to be a *tereifa*.

When sin offerings of bulls and goats that are burned outside the Temple are burned in accordance with their mitzva, they must be burned in the place of the ashes outside the Israelite camp in the wilderness, or outside Jerusalem in the era of the Temple. The Sages also derive from the Torah that the garments of both the priest who burns the offering and all priests involved in the burning are rendered impure. So too are the garments of those who carry the offering out of the Temple, from the time they emerge from the Temple courtyard until the offering becomes ash.

These sin offerings are unique in that their flesh is consumed neither by people nor by the altar, and in the course of discussing these offerings, the Gemara explores whether the disqualifications of *piggul* and being left overnight apply to them, given that the Torah mentions these disqualifications specifically in the context of offerings that are consumed. The Gemara similarly addresses the question whether the disqualification of emerging from the Temple courtyard before the designated time applies to the flesh of these offerings. These dilemmas are not resolved.

Other discussions of ritual impurity are included tangentially, as well as a discussion of the unique standing of Moses and Pinehas as priests, both during and following the inauguration of the Temple.

Introduction to **Perek XIII**

And the Lord spoke unto Moses, saying: Speak to Aaron, and to his sons, and to all the children of Israel, and say to them: This is the matter that the Lord has commanded, saying: Any man of the house of Israel that slaughters an ox, or lamb, or goat, in the camp, or that slaughters it outside the camp, and he did not bring it to the entrance of the Tent of Meeting, to sacrifice an offering to the Lord, before the Tabernacle of the Lord, blood shall be imputed to that man, he has shed blood, and that man shall be cut off from among his people. In order that the children of Israel shall bring their sacrifices, which they slaughter upon the open field, and they shall bring them to the Lord, to the entrance of the Tent of Meeting, to the priest, and slaughter them as sacrifices of peace offerings to the Lord. And the priest shall sprinkle the blood upon the altar of the Lord at the entrance of the Tent of Meeting, and burn the fat for a pleasing aroma to the Lord. And they shall not slaughter anymore their sacrifices to the se'irim after whom they go astray. This shall be for them an eternal statute, throughout their generations. And to them you shall say: Any man of the house of Israel, or of the stranger that sojourns among them, that offers up a burnt offering or sacrifice, and he will not bring it to the entrance of the Tent of Meeting, to sacrifice it to the Lord, and that man shall be cut off from his people.

(Leviticus 17:1–9)

This chapter will discuss the prohibitions against slaughtering an offering outside the Temple courtyard and offering it up by placing it on an altar outside the Temple courtyard. These prohibitions are independent of the general prohibition of idol worship and apply even if one performed these acts for the sake of God. Both prohibitions carry the punishment of *karet*.

Although they are considered two distinct prohibitions, such that a person who violates both is liable twice, the fact that the Torah presents them together and that there is clearly a logical connection between the prohibitions leads to an important question about the relationship between them. It appears from the verses that one is liable for offering up an offering outside the Temple courtyard only if it was fit to have been offered up inside the courtyard. In light of this, the Gemara will consider a case in which one both slaughtered an offering and offered it up outside the courtyard. When one slaughters an offering outside the courtyard, it is thereby rendered unfit; is one therefore exempt from liability for subsequently offering it up?

This chapter will raise various other issues in delineating the scope of these prohibitions. Is one liable only for slaughtering an offering or offering it up on an altar, or is one also liable for performing other sacrificial rites? The verses refer to slaughtering and offering up inside or outside "the camp." What are the boundaries of this camp? Which types of offerings are subject to these prohibitions? This latter question will be the main focus of the chapter.

Although, as noted, it appears from the verses that one is liable for offering up an offering outside the courtyard only if it was fit to have been offered up inside, the chapter will discuss certain cases of disqualifications where even though the offering should not be offered inside the Temple, one may still be liable for offering it up outside.

Also to be discussed in this chapter are those elements that render one liable when offering up an offering outside the Temple courtyard. Is liability incurred only for a complete offering or also for parts of offerings? Is one liable when part of an offering is sacrificed inside the Temple and the rest is sacrificed outside the Temple?

מתני׳ הַשּׁוֹחֵט וְהַמַּעֲלֶה בַּחוּץ – חַיָּיב עַל הַשְּׁחִיטָה, וְחַיָּיב עַל הָעֲלָאָה.

MISHNA **One who slaughters** an offering outside the Temple courtyard **and one who offers it up outside**[H] the Temple courtyard is **liable for the slaughter and liable for** the **offering up,**[N] as each act involves an independent prohibition. If done intentionally, he is liable to receive excision from the World-to-Come [*karet*] for each act, and if done unwittingly, he is liable to bring a sin offering for each act.

רַבִּי יוֹסֵי הַגְּלִילִי אוֹמֵר: שָׁחַט בִּפְנִים וְהֶעֱלָה בַּחוּץ. שָׁחַט בַּחוּץ וְהֶעֱלָה בַּחוּץ – פָּטוּר, שֶׁלֹּא הֶעֱלָה אֶלָּא דָּבָר פָּסוּל. אָמְרוּ לוֹ: אַף הַשּׁוֹחֵט בִּפְנִים וּמַעֲלֶה בַּחוּץ, כֵּיוָן שֶׁהוֹצִיאוֹ – פְּסָלוֹ.

Rabbi Yosei HaGelili says: If **he slaughtered** an offering **inside** the courtyard **and** then **offered** it **up outside**[H] the courtyard, he is liable. But if **he slaughtered** it **outside,** thereby rendering it unfit, **and** then **he offered** it **up outside,** he is **exempt** for the offering up, **as he offered up only an item** that is **unfit,** and one is liable only for offering up an item that is fit to be offered up inside the Temple. The Rabbis **said to him:** According to your reasoning, **even** in a case where **he slaughters** it **inside and offers** it **up outside,** he should be exempt, **since** the moment **that he took it outside** the courtyard, he thereby **rendered it unfit.** Yet, in such a case, he is certainly liable for offering it up. So too, one who slaughters an offering outside and then offers it up outside is liable.

הַטָּמֵא שֶׁאָכַל בֵּין קֹדֶשׁ טָמֵא בֵּין קֹדֶשׁ טָהוֹר – חַיָּיב. רַבִּי יוֹסֵי הַגְּלִילִי אוֹמֵר: טָמֵא שֶׁאָכַל טָהוֹר – חַיָּיב. וְטָמֵא שֶׁאָכַל טָמֵא – פָּטוּר, שֶׁלֹּא אָכַל אֶלָּא דָּבָר טָמֵא. אָמְרוּ לוֹ: אַף טָמֵא שֶׁאָכַל אֶת הַטָּהוֹר, כֵּיוָן שֶׁנָּגַע בּוֹ – טִמְּאוֹהוּ.

One who is ritually impure who ate sacrificial food, **whether** it was **ritually impure** sacrificial food **or ritually pure sacrificial** food, is **liable** to receive *karet* if he did so intentionally and to bring a sliding-scale offering if he did so unwittingly. **Rabbi Yosei HaGelili says: An impure** person **who ate pure** sacrificial food is **liable. But an impure** person **who ate impure**[H] sacrificial food is **exempt, as he merely ate an impure item,** and the prohibition against eating sacrificial food while one is impure applies only to pure sacrificial food. The Rabbis **said to him:** According to your logic, this *halakha* would apply **even** in a case of **an impure** person **who ate** what had been **pure** sacrificial food, because **once he touched it, he** thereby **rendered it ritually impure.** Yet, in such a case, he is certainly liable for eating it. So too, an impure person who ate impure sacrificial food is liable.

וְטָהוֹר שֶׁאָכַל טָמֵא – פָּטוּר, שֶׁאֵינוֹ חַיָּיב אֶלָּא עַל טוּמְאַת הַגּוּף.

And a pure person **who ate impure** sacrificial food[H] is **exempt, as** one is **liable** for eating sacrificial food in impurity **only due to the impurity of** one's **body,** but not due to the impurity of the food.

NOTES

Liable for the slaughter and liable for the offering up – חַיָּיב עַל הַשְּׁחִיטָה וְחַיָּיב עַל הָעֲלָאָה: Despite the similarity between the two prohibitions, which both involve the sacrifice of an animal outside of the Temple courtyard, they are nevertheless counted as two independent prohibitions. One relates to the slaughter of a consecrated animal and the other concerns the performance of the subsequent sacrificial rites. Therefore, even if one performed both in a single lapse of awareness, e.g., if he was not aware that the prohibition still applies nowadays, he would nevertheless be liable for each action.

HALAKHA

One who slaughters an offering and one who offers it up outside – הַשּׁוֹחֵט וְהַמַּעֲלֶה בַּחוּץ: One who unwittingly slaughters an offering outside the Temple courtyard, and then offers it up outside the Temple courtyard, is liable to bring two sin offerings, one for the slaughtering and one for the offering up (Rambam *Sefer Avoda, Hilkhot Ma'aseh HaKorbanot* 18:5).

He slaughtered inside and offered up outside – שָׁחַט בִּפְנִים וְהֶעֱלָה בַּחוּץ: One who slaughters an offering inside the Temple and then offers it up outside is liable for the offering up. Conversely, one who slaughters an offering outside and then offers it up inside is liable for the slaughtering (Rambam *Sefer Avoda, Hilkhot Ma'aseh HaKorbanot* 18:5).

An impure person who ate impure – טָמֵא שֶׁאָכַל טָמֵא: If a ritually impure person eats an olive-bulk of sacrificial food, he is liable, even if that food is impure. He is liable only if he was impure with a degree of impurity for which he would be liable to receive *karet* if he entered the Temple. If the eating of the sacrificial food was intentional, he is liable to receive *karet*. If it was unwitting, he is liable to bring a sin offering (Rambam *Sefer Avoda, Hilkhot Pesulei HaMukdashin* 18:13).

A pure person who ate impure sacrificial food – טָהוֹר שֶׁאָכַל טָמֵא: A ritually pure person who intentionally ate an olive-bulk of impure sacrificial food is liable to receive lashes but is not liable to receive *karet* (Rambam *Sefer Avoda, Hilkhot Pesulei HaMukdashin* 18:12).

BACKGROUND

Mercury – מַרְקוּלִיס: The reference here is to the Roman god Mercurius, which corresponds to the Greek god Hermes. In Aramaic this idol is referred to as Markulis, i.e., the *r* phoneme has been replaced with an *l* phoneme. This is a common phenomenon, and it is possible that in this case it was done intentionally in order to avoid having to pronounce the proper name of the deity.

This deity was considered by its adherents to provide protection for travelers and merchants. Because of this, travelers and merchants would erect statues of it at crossroads. Frequently, the statue would not be whole, but rather just a head placed on top of a pillar, a structure that was called a herm. The usual form of worship of this idol was to cast stones toward the statue. Over the course of time a large pile of rocks would accumulate, and those rocks would then be considered part of the idol itself.

From the Mishna and other sources it appears that sometimes there was no statue present at all. Rather, people would erect a symbolic pile of three stones, two side by side and the third above them, as a representation of the idol.

Some have suggested that the Gemara is referring specifically to a syncretistic amalgamation of Mercury and an ancient Near Eastern deity.

Relief of Mercurius with worshipper sacrificing a goat

גמ׳ בִּשְׁלָמָא הֶעֱלָה – כְּתִיב עוֹנֶשׁ וּכְתִיב אַזְהָרָה; עוֹנֶשׁ – דִּכְתִיב: ״וְאֶל פֶּתַח אֹהֶל מוֹעֵד לֹא הֱבִיאוֹ״, אַזְהָרָה – דִּכְתִיב: ״הִשָּׁמֶר לְךָ פֶּן תַּעֲלֶה עוֹלוֹתֶיךָ״. וְכִי הָא דְּאָמַר רַבִּי אָבִין אָמַר רַבִּי אֶלְעָזָר: כׇּל מָקוֹם שֶׁנֶּאֱמַר ״הִשָּׁמֵר״ ״פֶּן״ וְ״אַל״ – אֵינוֹ אֶלָּא לֹא תַעֲשֶׂה.

GEMARA The mishna teaches that if one both slaughters and offers up an offering outside the Temple courtyard, he is liable for each act, as they are independent prohibitions. The Gemara asks: **Granted** that one is liable for the **offering up,** as the **punishment** for this act **is written** in the Torah **and** the **prohibition** concerning this act **is** also **written** in the Torah. The **punishment** is **as it is written:** "Any man…that offers up a burnt offering or sacrifice, **and will not bring it to the entrance of the Tent of Meeting,** to sacrifice it to the Lord, and that man shall be cut off from his people" (Leviticus 17:8–9). The **prohibition** is **as it is written: "Take heed to yourself lest you offer up your burnt offerings** in every place that you see" (Deuteronomy 12:13). **And** this is **in accordance with that which Rabbi Avin says** that **Rabbi Elazar says: Wherever it is stated** in the Torah: **Observe,** or: **Lest,** or: **Do not, it is nothing other than a prohibition.** Accordingly, the verse in Deuteronomy is understood as issuing a prohibition.

אֶלָּא שְׁחִיטָה, בִּשְׁלָמָא עוֹנֶשׁ – דִּכְתִיב: ״וְאֶל פֶּתַח אֹהֶל מוֹעֵד לֹא הֱבִיאוֹ״, אֶלָּא אַזְהָרָה מְנָלַן? אָמַר קְרָא: ״וְלֹא יִזְבְּחוּ עוֹד״.

But for the **slaughtering,** why is one liable? **Granted** that the **punishment is stated in the Torah, as it is written:** "Any man…that slaughters it outside the camp, **and he did not bring it to the entrance of the Tent of Meeting,** to sacrifice an offering to the Lord, before the Tabernacle of the Lord…that man shall be cut off from among his people" (Leviticus 17:3–4). **But from where do we** derive its **prohibition?** One is liable only in a case where the Torah specifies both the prohibition and the punishment. The Gemara answers: **The verse states** in the continuation of that passage: **"And they shall not slaughter anymore** their offerings to the *se'irim* after whom they go astray" (Leviticus 17:7).

הַאי מִיבְּעֵי לֵיהּ לְכִדְרַבִּי אֶלְעָזָר, דְּאָמַר: מִנַּיִן לַזּוֹבֵחַ בְּהֵמָה לְמַרְקוּלִיס שֶׁהוּא חַיָּיב – דִּכְתִיב: ״וְלֹא יִזְבְּחוּ עוֹד אֶת זִבְחֵיהֶם״, אִם אֵינוֹ עִנְיָן לְכְדַרְכָּהּ, דִּכְתִיב ״אֵיכָה יַעַבְדוּ״ – תְּנֵהוּ עִנְיָן לְשֶׁלֹּא כְּדַרְכָּהּ!

The Gemara questions the use of this verse as a source: But **this** verse is **necessary for** the purpose of expounding **in accordance with** the statement **of Rabbi Elazar, as he says: From where** is it derived with regard to **one who slaughters an animal** as an offering **to Mercury,**[BH] a pagan deity, **that he is liable** even though this is not the established manner in which that deity is worshipped? **As it is written:** "And **they shall not slaughter anymore their offerings** to the *se'irim.*" **If** the verse **is not** needed to teach the **matter of** worshipping a deity **in accordance with its established manner,** as it is already taught that one is liable for this, **as it is written:** "Take heed to yourself…lest you inquire after their gods, saying: **How do these** nations **serve** their gods, so too will I do likewise" (Deuteronomy 12:30), then **apply it** to the **matter of** worshipping a deity in a way **that is not in accordance with its established manner.**

אֲמַר רַבָּה: קְרֵי בֵּיהּ: ״וְלֹא יִזְבְּחוּ״, וּקְרֵי בֵּיהּ: ״וְלֹא עוֹד״.

Rabba said: Both *halakhot* can be derived from the same verse. **Read into** the verse as though it stops after the phrase: **"And they shall not slaughter"** (Leviticus 17:7), and relates to the prohibition against slaughtering outside the Temple courtyard, which was mentioned in the previous verses. **And** also **read into** the verse as relating to the verse's continuation: **And not anymore** their offerings to the *se'irim,* which serves as the source for the prohibition against sacrificing offerings to false deities.

אַכַּתִּי מִיבְּעֵי לֵיהּ לְכִדְתַנְיָא: עַד כָּאן הוּא מְדַבֵּר בְּקָדָשִׁים שֶׁהִקְדִּישָׁן בִּשְׁעַת אִיסּוּר הַבָּמוֹת, וְהִקְרִיבָן בִּשְׁעַת אִיסּוּר הַבָּמוֹת,

The Gemara challenges: But the verse is **still necessary for** the purpose of expounding **that which is taught** in a *baraita*: The verse states: "Any man…that slaughters it outside the camp, and he did not bring it to the entrance of the Tent of Meeting, to sacrifice an offering to the Lord" (Leviticus 17:3–4). **Until this point,** the verse is **speaking about sacrificial** animals **that one consecrated during a period when the prohibition against** sacrificing on private **altars** was in effect, i.e., after the Tabernacle was erected, **and** then he also **sacrificed them during a period when the prohibition against** sacrificing on private **altars** was in effect.

HALAKHA

One who slaughters an animal to Mercury – זוֹבֵחַ בְּהֵמָה לְמַרְקוּלִיס: If one pours a libation to Ba'al-Peor or slaughters an animal as an offering to Mercury, even though these actions are not the established manner in which these idols are worshipped, one is liable for performing an act of idol worship since he performed a service for them in the same manner as that which is done in the Temple (Rambam *Sefer HaMadda, Hilkhot Avoda Zara* 3:3).

שֶׁהֲרֵי עוֹנְשָׁן אָמוּר – ״וְאֶל פֶּתַח אֹהֶל מוֹעֵד״, אַזְהָרָה – דִּכְתִיב: ״הִשָּׁמֶר לְךָ פֶּן תַּעֲלֶה עֹלֹתֶיךָ״.

This is apparent, **as the punishment for** sacrificing **them is stated**[N] in this verse: "**And** he did not bring it **to the entrance of the Tent of Meeting,** to sacrifice an offering to the Lord, before the Tabernacle of the Lord…that man shall be cut off from among his people." The **prohibition** is also explicit, **as it is written: "Take heed**[N] **to yourself lest you offer up your burnt offerings** in every place that you see" (Deuteronomy 12:13).

מִכָּאן וָאֵילָךְ – בִּזְבָחִים שֶׁהִקְדִּישָׁן בִּשְׁעַת הֶיתֵּר הַבָּמוֹת וְהִקְרִיבָן בִּשְׁעַת אִיסּוּר הַבָּמוֹת,

From that point **onward,** the verse is speaking **about sacrificial** animals **that one consecrated during a period when** there was **permission** to sacrifice offerings on private **altars,** i.e., before the Tabernacle was erected, **and** then **he sacrificed them** outside the Tabernacle **during a period when the prohibition against** sacrificing on private **altars** was in effect.

שֶׁנֶּאֱמַר: ״לְמַעַן אֲשֶׁר יָבִיאוּ בְּנֵי יִשְׂרָאֵל אֶת זִבְחֵיהֶם אֲשֶׁר הֵם זֹבְחִים״ – זְבָחִים שֶׁהִתַּרְתִּי לְךָ כְּבָר, ״עַל פְּנֵי הַשָּׂדֶה״ – לוֹמַר לְךָ: הַזּוֹבֵחַ בִּשְׁעַת אִיסּוּר הַבָּמוֹת מַעֲלֶה עָלָיו הַכָּתוּב כְּאִילּוּ הִקְרִיב עַל פְּנֵי הַשָּׂדֶה.

This is apparent, **as it is stated: "In order that the children of Israel shall bring their sacrifices, which they slaughter** upon the open field, that they shall bring them to the Lord, to the entrance of the Tent of Meeting" (Leviticus 17:5). The phrase "their sacrifices, which they slaughter" is interpreted as referring to **offerings that I have previously permitted for you** to slaughter on private altars. This verse teaches that those offerings may now be sacrificed only inside the Tabernacle. The phrase "**upon the open field" tells you** that in the case of **one who slaughters** an offering on a private altar **during a period when the prohibition against** sacrificing on private **altars** is in effect, even if he sacrifices the offering to God, **the verse ascribes him** blame **as if he sacrificed** it **upon the open field**[N] in idolatrous worship.

״וֶהֱבִיאֻם לַה׳״ – זוֹ מִצְוַת עֲשֵׂה, לֹא תַעֲשֶׂה מִנַּיִין? תַּלְמוּד לוֹמַר: ״וְלֹא יִזְבְּחוּ עוֹד״.

The verse continues: "**That they shall bring them to the Lord." This is a positive mitzva** to sacrifice in the Tabernacle even offerings that were consecrated before the Tabernacle was erected. **From where** is it derived that there is **a prohibition** against sacrificing them outside the Tabernacle? **The verse states: "And they shall not slaughter anymore** their offerings to the *se'irim* after whom they go astray; this shall be to them an eternal statute, throughout their generations" (Leviticus 17:7).

יָכוֹל יְהֵא עָנוּשׁ כָּרֵת? תַּלְמוּד לוֹמַר: ״חֻקַּת עוֹלָם תִּהְיֶה זֹּאת לָהֶם לְדֹרֹתָם״, ״זֹאת לָהֶם״ – וְלֹא אַחֶרֶת לָהֶם!

One **might** have thought that sacrificing these offerings outside the Tabernacle **would be punishable** by *karet*, as is the *halakha* with regard to offerings consecrated after the Tabernacle was erected. Therefore, **the verse states: "This shall be to them an eternal statute, throughout their generations"** (Leviticus 17:7). One can infer from this verse that **this,** the punishment for transgressing a positive mitzva and a prohibition, applies **to them, but no other** punishment applies **to them.** It is clear from this *baraita* that the verse "And they shall not slaughter anymore" is used to teach about the prohibition against sacrificing outside the Tabernacle those offerings that were consecrated while there was permission to sacrifice on private altars, and not those offerings that were consecrated while it was prohibited to sacrifice on private altars.

אֶלָּא אָמַר רַבִּי אָבִין: קַל וָחוֹמֶר, וּמַה בְּמָקוֹם שֶׁלֹּא עָנַשׁ – הִזְהִיר, מָקוֹם שֶׁעָנַשׁ – אֵינוֹ דִּין שֶׁהִזְהִיר?

Rather, Rabbi Avin says: The prohibition against slaughtering an offering outside the Temple is derived through **an *a fortiori*** inference: **Just as in a case** in **which** the Torah **did not** prescribe **punishment** for a certain action, it nevertheless **prohibited** it, as is the case with regard to sacrificing outside the Temple an offering consecrated while there was permission to sacrifice on private altars, so too, in **a case** in **which** the Torah **did prescribe punishment** for a certain action, as is the case with regard to slaughtering outside the Temple an offering consecrated while it was prohibited to sacrifice on private altars, **is it not logical that** the Torah **prohibited** the action?

NOTES

As the punishment for them is stated – שֶׁהֲרֵי עוֹנְשָׁן אָמוּר: There is no clear indication in these verses that they refer specifically to offerings that were consecrated during a period when the use of private altars was prohibited. Rashi alludes to this by explaining simply that since there is no indication to the contrary, the verses are assumed to be referring to such offerings. Accordingly, the *baraita* is not to be understood as offering a proof that the verse is referring to such a case, but merely noting the source of the punishment and prohibition for that case.

Rabbeinu Hillel, in his commentary to *Torat Kohanim*, claims the *baraita* is offering a proof. He suggests that the phrase: "And he did not bring it to the entrance of the Tent of Meeting" (Leviticus 17:4), indicates that the verse is referring to a time when there is an expectation to bring the offerings to the Tabernacle. Accordingly, it is clear that it is referring to a time when the Tabernacle exists and the prohibition of private altars is already in force.

The prohibition, as it is written: Take heed – אַזְהָרָה דִּכְתִיב הִשָּׁמֶר: The verse refers to offering up, not to slaughtering. How then can the *baraita* claim that this verse is the source of the prohibition against slaughtering an offering outside the Temple? *Tosafot* suggest that this *baraita* assumes the existence of the verbal analogy that the Gemara cites later on, according to which it can be derived from the prohibition against offering up outside the Temple that there is also a prohibition against slaughtering an offering outside the Temple.

As if he sacrificed it upon the open field – כְּאִילּוּ הִקְרִיב עַל פְּנֵי הַשָּׂדֶה: Rashi in tractate *Avoda Zara* (51b) explains that sacrificing "upon the open field" is a reference to a sacrifice to an idol. Rashi here explains that it refers to any case where the offering was slaughtered without any specific purpose, i.e., neither for God nor for idol worship. According to Rashi here it is understandable why the verse must highlight the fact that sacrificing such an offering is a violation of both positive mitzvot and prohibitions.

אֲמַר לֵיהּ רָבִינָא לְרַב אַשִׁי: אִם כֵּן, לֹא יֹאמַר לָאו בְּחֵלֶב, וְתֵיתֵי קַל וָחוֹמֶר מִנְּבֵילָה: מַה נְּבֵילָה שֶׁלֹּא עָנַשׁ – הִזְהִיר, חֵלֶב שֶׁעָנַשׁ – אֵינוֹ דִּין שֶׁהִזְהִיר?

Ravina said to Rav Ashi: If so, that whenever the Torah states a punishment for a certain action, there is no need for it to state the prohibition, then **let** the Torah **not state a prohibition with regard to** eating forbidden **fat** of a kosher animal, **and** then **derive** the fact that it is prohibited through **an *a fortiori* inference from** the prohibition against eating **an unslaughtered animal carcass: Just as** with regard to **a carcass,** even though the Torah **did not prescribe punishment** for consuming it, it nevertheless **prohibited** consuming it, so too, with regard to animal **fat, for which** the Torah **did prescribe punishment, is it not logical that** the Torah **prohibited** its consumption?

אֲתָא לְקַמֵּיהּ דְּרָבָא, אֲמַר לֵיהּ: מִנְּבֵלָה נַמִי לָא אָתְיָא, דְּאִיכָּא לְמִיפְרַךְ: מַה לִּנְבֵלָה – שֶׁכֵּן מְטַמָּא.

Rav Ashi **came before Rava and said to him:** The prohibition against eating animal fat **can also not be derived from** the prohibition of **a carcass, as** the *a fortiori* inference **can be refuted** as follows: **What** is notable **about a carcass?** It is notable **in that** it **renders** other items **ritually impure** through contact with it. Forbidden fat does not share this stringency. The existence of a unique stringency undermines the possibility of using an *a fortiori* inference.

מִשְּׁרָצִים טְמֵאִין! מַה לִּשְׁרָצִים טְמֵאִין שֶׁמְּטַמְּאִין בְּמַשֶּׁהוּ.

Rav Ashi raises the possibility of deriving the prohibition against eating forbidden fat through an *a fortiori* inference from various other prohibitions that, like forbidden fat, do not carry the stringency of being punishable by *karet*, and Rava rejects each one. Can one derive the prohibition against eating forbidden fat **from** the prohibition against eating carcasses of **ritually impure creeping animals** (see Leviticus 11:41)? One cannot, as **what** is notable **about ritually impure creeping animals?** They are notable in **that they render** other items **ritually impure though** contact with **any amount**[N] of them. Forbidden fat does not share this stringency.

מִשְּׁרָצִים טְהוֹרִים! מַה לִּשְׁרָצִים טְהוֹרִים שֶׁאִיסּוּרָן בְּמַשֶּׁהוּ.

Can one derive it **from** the prohibition against eating the carcasses of **ritually pure creeping animals** (see Leviticus 11:41), which do not have the capacity to render other items ritually impure? One cannot, as **what** is notable **about ritually pure creeping animals?** They are notable in **that** with regard to **their prohibition** there is liability **for** consuming **any amount**[N] of them. Forbidden fat does not share this stringency, as one is liable only if he eats an olive-bulk of it.

מֵעָרְלָה וְכִלְאֵי הַכֶּרֶם! מַה לְּעָרְלָה וְכִלְאֵי הַכֶּרֶם שֶׁכֵּן אֲסוּרִין בַּהֲנָאָה.

Can one derive it **from** the prohibition against eating **the fruit of a tree during the first three years after its planting** [*orla*] **or** from the prohibition against eating **diverse kinds in a vineyard,** for which one is liable only if he eats an olive-bulk of them, just like with regard to animal fat? One cannot, as **what** is notable **about *orla* and diverse kinds in a vineyard?** They are notable **in that they are items from which** deriving **benefit is prohibited.** Forbidden fat does not share this stringency.

מִשְּׁבִיעִית! מַה לִּשְׁבִיעִית שֶׁכֵּן תּוֹפֶסֶת דָּמֶיהָ.

Can one derive it **from** the prohibition against eating **Sabbatical** Year produce, from which benefit is permitted just like with regard to animal fat? One cannot, as **what** is notable **about Sabbatical** Year produce? It is notable **in that it transfers** its sanctity to the **money** with which **it** is purchased. Forbidden fat does not share this stringency.

מִתְּרוּמָה! שֶׁכֵּן לֹא הוּתַּר מִכְּלָלָהּ. מִכּוּלְּהוּ נַמִי, שֶׁכֵּן לֹא הוּתְּרוּ מִכְּלָלָן.

Can one derive it **from** the prohibition of a non-priest partaking of **the portion of the produce that is designated for the priest** [*teruma*]? One cannot, **as** in the case of *teruma* there are **no** circumstances in which **its general prohibition was permitted.** The prohibition concerning *teruma* applies broadly, unlike in the case of forbidden fat, where the prohibition applies only to the fat of domesticated animals but not to the fat of undomesticated animals. Rava notes that the possibility of deriving the prohibition against eating forbidden fat **from all of those** prohibitions can **also** be refuted based on this claim, **as** in those cases, too, there are **no** circumstances in which **their general prohibition was permitted.**

NOTES

That they render other items ritually impure through contact with any amount – שֶׁמְּטַמְּאִין בְּמַשֶּׁהוּ: Rashi and Rabbeinu Ḥananel both note that even though the Gemara states that any amount renders other items ritually impure, there is still a minimum size requirement, albeit a very small one. This is equal to the size of a skink, the smallest of the eight ritually impure creeping animals, which when it is born is as small as a lentil-bulk. This teaches a *halakha* for all of the creeping animals; a piece of their carcasses will render other items ritually impure only if it is at least the size of a lentil-bulk.

Ritually pure creeping animals, that their prohibition is for consuming any amount – שְׁרָצִים טְהוֹרִים שֶׁאִיסּוּרָן בְּמַשֶּׁהוּ: Only the eight creeping animals cited in Leviticus 11:29–30 render other items ritually impure through contact with their carcasses. Consumption of all other creeping animals is forbidden, but their carcasses do not render other items ritually impure.

Rashi explains that with regard to ritually pure creeping animals, one is liable for eating even a lentil-bulk. This is based on the Gemara in *Me'ila* 16b, where it is derived with regard to ritually impure creeping animals that liability is incurred for eating an amount that can render other items ritually impure, which is a lentil-bulk. Rashi assumes that liability for eating ritually pure creeping animals is also subject to this minimum size requirement. *Tosafot* disagree; they note that according to the conclusion of that Gemara in *Me'ila*, the derivation is restricted to ritually impure creeping animals, but liability for eating ritually pure creeping animals is incurred only for eating an olive-bulk, which is the standard quantity for liability with regard to most prohibited foods. Therefore, *Tosafot* interpret the Gemara here as referring to a case where one eats a whole creeping animal. In such a case, the fact that the animal is whole, as it was formed initially, lends significance to it such that one is liable for eating it even if it is far smaller than an olive-bulk. *Tzon Kodashim* defends Rashi's explanation by noting that it is possible to understand the Gemara in *Me'ila* as equating ritually impure and ritually pure creeping animals, even according to its conclusion, and indeed, that is how Rashi there explains that Gemara.

Skink, one of the impure creeping animals listed in Leviticus

אָמַר רָבָא: אִי קַשְׁיָא לִי – הָא קַשְׁיָא לִי, הָא דִּתְנַן: פֶּסַח וּמִילָה מִצְוֹת עֲשֵׂה,

Rava said: If there is **a difficulty for me** in accepting Rabbi Avin's claim that the prohibition against slaughtering an offering outside the Temple can be derived via an *a fortiori* inference, **this is difficult for me: That which we learned** in a mishna (*Karetot* 2a), which enumerates the thirty-six cases for which one is liable to receive *karet*. The end of that mishna lists: One who neglects sacrificing the **Paschal offering and** one who does not undergo **circumcision,** which are **positive mitzvot,** unlike the other cases enumerated in the mishna, which are all prohibitions.

תֵּיתֵי בְּקַל וָחוֹמֶר מִמּוֹתִיר: מָה מוֹתִיר שֶׁלֹּא עָנַשׁ – הִזְהִיר, פֶּסַח וּמִילָה שֶׁעָנַשׁ – אֵינוֹ דִּין שֶׁהִזְהִיר?

Rava explains his difficulty: If Rabbi Avin is correct, **derive** that there is a prohibition against neglecting the sacrifice of the Paschal offering and not undergoing circumcision **via an *a fortiori*** inference **from the case of one who leaves over**[N] sacrificial meat[B] beyond the allotted period for its consumption (see Leviticus 22:30): **Just as** in the case of **one who leaves over** sacrificial meat, **where** the Torah **did not prescribe punishment** but nevertheless **prohibited** this act, so too, with regard to neglecting the sacrifice of the Paschal offering and not undergoing circumcision, for **which** the Torah **did prescribe punishment, is it not logical that** the Torah actually **prohibited** neglecting them as well?

אָמַר רַב אַשִׁי: אֲמַרִיתָהּ לִשְׁמַעְתָּא קַמֵּיהּ דְּרַב כָּהֲנָא, וַאֲמַר לִי: מִמּוֹתִיר לָא אָתְיָא, דְּאִיכָּא לְמִיפְרַךְ: מָה לְמוֹתִיר – שֶׁכֵּן אֵין לוֹ תַּקָּנָה, תֹּאמַר פֶּסַח יֵשׁ לוֹ תַּקָּנָה.

Rav Ashi said: I stated this very **discussion before Rav Kahana, and he said to me: One cannot derive** a prohibition against neglecting the sacrifice of the Paschal offering **from** the case of **one who leaves over** sacrificial meat via an *a fortiori* inference, **as it can be refuted: What** is notable **about one who leaves over** sacrificial meat? He is notable **in that there is no remedy** once the prohibition has been violated. **Shall you say** the same about the neglect of the **Paschal offering,** for which **there is a remedy?**[N] One who fails to bring it on the first *Pesaḥ* must bring it on the second *Pesaḥ*.[B]

וְכִי מַזְהִירִין מִן הַדִּין? אֲפִילּוּ לְמַאן דְּאָמַר עוֹנְשִׁין מִן הַדִּין, אֵין מַזְהִירִין מִן הַדִּין!

The Gemara challenges the very premise of Rabbi Avin's claim: **But can one** derive that the Torah **prohibits** an action **via** an *a fortiori* **inference? Even the one who says** that the court **administers punishment** based **on** an *a fortiori* **inference** concedes that **one does not** derive **a prohibition from** an *a fortiori* **inference.**[B] Therefore, Rabbi Avin's claim is refuted.

אֶלָּא כִּדְרַבִּי יוֹחָנָן, דְּאָמַר: אָתְיָא הֲבָאָה הֲבָאָה,

Rather, the prohibition against slaughtering an offering outside the Temple courtyard can be derived **in accordance with** the statement **of Rabbi Yoḥanan, who says:** It is **derived** from the prohibition against offering up outside the Temple through a verbal analogy between the reference to **bringing** stated with regard to slaughtering outside the Temple, and the reference to **bringing** stated with regard to offering up outside the Temple.

מָה לְהַלָּן לֹא עָנַשׁ אֶלָּא אִם כֵּן הִזְהִיר – אַף כָּאן לֹא עָנַשׁ אֶלָּא אִם כֵּן הִזְהִיר.

With regard to slaughtering, it is stated: "Or that slaughters it outside the camp, and he did not bring it to the entrance of the Tent of Meeting" (Leviticus 17:3–4), and with regard to offering up, it is stated: "That offers up a burnt offering or sacrifice, and he will not bring it to the entrance of the Tent of Meeting" (Leviticus 17:8–9). The verbal analogy teaches that **just as there,** with regard to offering up, the Torah **did not prescribe punishment** for an action **unless** it also explicitly **prohibited** the action, **so too here,** with regard to slaughtering, the Torah **did not prescribe punishment unless it** also **prohibited** it. Therefore, even though the Torah does not explicitly state the prohibition, it is evident that it is prohibited.

BACKGROUND

One who leaves over sacrificial meat – מוֹתִיר: Any offering whose meat is eaten has a set time for the consumption of the meat. For example, the meat of a thanks offering and of a sin offering must be eaten before the morning following their sacrifice, while the meat of a peace offering may be eaten until the evening of the following day. After that time has passed, any remaining meat is deemed *notar*, leftover, and it is prohibited to derive benefit from it. One who eats leftover meat is liable to receive *karet*.

Second *Pesaḥ* – פֶּסַח שֵׁנִי: One who fails to sacrifice the Paschal offering on the fourteenth of Nisan, the first *Pesaḥ*, may compensate by bringing the offering on the fourteenth of Iyyar, the second *Pesaḥ*. This is the *halakha* both if he was prevented from sacrificing it, e.g., he was too far from the Temple to reach it in time, or if he was ritually impure at the time, and even if he intentionally neglected to sacrifice the Paschal offering.

All the *halakhot* that apply to the sacrifice of the Paschal offering on the first *Pesaḥ* apply on the second *Pesaḥ*, with one exception: There is no prohibition against eating or possessing leaven on that day. Nevertheless, leaven may still not be eaten together with the Paschal offering itself.

One does not derive a prohibition from an inference – אֵין מַזְהִירִין מִן הַדִּין: This is due to the principle that a court may not administer punishment unless there is a Torah prohibition concerning the act performed. Although that prohibition cannot be deduced through an *a fortiori* inference alone, it may be deduced through a verbal analogy or one of the other hermeneutical principles. Some suggest that the reason one cannot use an *a fortiori* inference is because one can never know for certain the particular reasoning behind a given prohibition. Therefore, although an action may be prohibited based on the logic of an *a fortiori* inference, that logic cannot necessarily be relied upon in order to administer a punishment.

NOTES

Derive via an *a fortiori* inference from one who leaves over – תֵּיתֵי בְּקַל וָחוֹמֶר מִמּוֹתִיר: It is reasonable to derive an *a fortiori* inference from the case of one who leaves over sacrificial meat, as it is similar to the Paschal offering and circumcision in that they are all violated though inaction (*Tosafot*).

Paschal offering for which there is a remedy – פֶּסַח יֵשׁ לוֹ תַּקָּנָה: This claim can also be applied to circumcision. Even if one neglected the mitzva and is liable to receive *karet*, if he subsequently circumcises himself he thereby exempts himself from the punishment (*Tzon Kodashim*).

HALAKHA

It is derived through: There, there – **אָתְיָא שָׁם שָׁם**: The prohibition against slaughtering an offering outside the Temple is derived through a juxtaposition in the verse: "There you shall offer up your burnt offerings and there you shall do all that I command you." The offering up mentioned in the first part is juxtaposed to the sacrifice of the offering in the second part, indicated by the phrase "there you shall do." The sacrifice of an offering includes its slaughter. The juxtaposition teaches that just as with regard to offering up, the Torah does not prescribe punishment unless it also prohibits it, so too, with regard to slaughtering, the Torah does not prescribe punishment unless it also prohibits it. This is in accordance with the opinion of Rava and Rabbi Yona (Rambam *Sefer Avoda*, *Hilkhot Ma'aseh HaKorbanot* 18:4).

NOTES

Offerings that are to be burned outside that one then offered up outside – **מוּקְטְרֵי חוּץ שֶׁהֶעֱלָן לַחוּץ**: The Gemara here disagrees with the opinion of Rabbi Yosei HaGelili recorded in the mishna. There, Rabbi Yosei HaGelili states that one is exempt if he offered up, outside the Temple, an offering that was slaughtered outside the Temple.

רָבָא אָמַר: כִּדְרַבִּי יוֹנָה, דְּאָמַר רַבִּי יוֹנָה: אָתְיָא ״שָׁם״ ״שָׁם״, מָה לְהַלָּן לֹא עָנַשׁ אֶלָּא אִם כֵּן הִזְהִיר – אַף כָּאן לֹא עָנַשׁ אֶלָּא אִם כֵּן הִזְהִיר.

Rava said: The prohibition can be derived **in accordance with** the statement **of Rabbi Yona, as Rabbi Yona says:** It is **derived** from the verse: "But in the place that the Lord will choose in one of your tribes, there you shall offer up your burnt offerings and there you shall do all that I command you" (Deuteronomy 12:14), through the juxtaposition of the word **"there"** in the first part of the verse to the word **"there"**[H] in the second part of the verse. This serves to juxtapose the offering up, mentioned in the first part, to the sacrifice of an offering, mentioned in the second part, which includes slaughtering it. Accordingly, it teaches that **just as there,** with regard to offering up, the Torah **did not prescribe punishment unless** it also **prohibited** it, **so too here,** with regard to slaughtering, the Torah **did not prescribe punishment unless** it also **prohibited** it. Therefore, even though the Torah does not explicitly state the prohibition, it is evident that it is prohibited.

אַשְׁכְּחַן מוּקְטְרֵי פְּנִים שֶׁהֶעֱלָן לַחוּץ, מוּקְטְרֵי חוּץ שֶׁהֶעֱלָן לַחוּץ מְנַיִן?

§ The Gemara (106a) states that the source for the liability for offering up outside the Temple is the verse: "Any man…that offers up a burnt offering or sacrifice, and he will not bring it to the entrance of the Tent of Meeting, to sacrifice it to the Lord, and that man shall be cut off from his people" (Leviticus 17:8–9). The Gemara asks: **We have found** that one is liable only for offerings that are fit to be **burned inside** the Temple courtyard, having been appropriately slaughtered inside the Temple courtyard, **which** one then **offered up outside** the courtyard. The verse states: "He will not bring it to the entrance of the Tent of Meeting," which indicates that they were fit to be brought to the Temple. **From where** is it derived that one is also liable with regard to offerings that are unfit and are to be **burned outside** the Temple as they were unlawfully slaughtered outside the Temple courtyard, **that** one then **offered up outside?**[N]

אָמַר רַב כָּהֲנָא, אָמַר קְרָא: ״וַאֲלֵהֶם תֹּאמַר״ – עַל הַסְּמוּכִין תֹּאמַר.

Rav Kahana said: The beginning of that **verse states: "And to them [*va'alehem*] you shall say"** (Leviticus 17:8). The term "*alehem*," to them, written with the letter *alef*, is phonetically similar to the term *alehem*, about them, written with the letter *ayin*. Therefore, the verse can be understood as saying: **About that which is** written in the **adjacent** passage **you shall say.** The preceding passage discusses offerings that were slaughtered outside the Temple, so the liability for offering up outside the Temple mentioned in this verse is also referring to those offerings.

מַתְקִיף לַהּ רָבָא: מִי כְּתִיב ״וַעֲלֵיהֶם״? ״וַאֲלֵיהֶם״ כְּתִיב! אֶלָּא כִּדְתָנָא דְּבֵי רַבִּי יִשְׁמָעֵאל: ״וַאֲלֵהֶם תֹּאמַר״ – לְעָרֵב פָּרָשִׁיּוֹת.

Rava objects to this: Is it written: And about them? "And to them" is written, and it means that the command should be relayed to Aaron, his sons, and the Jewish people, who are mentioned in the beginning of the passage. **Rather,** liability in this case is derived **as the school of Rabbi Yishmael taught:** The opening phrase: **"And to them you shall say,"** starts with the conjunction "and" **to mix** the **passages** of slaughtering outside the Temple and offering up outside the Temple, in order to teach that one is liable for the latter even after having done the former.

רַבִּי יוֹחָנָן אָמַר: אָתְיָא ״הֲבָאָה״ ״הֲבָאָה״, מָה לְהַלָּן מוּקְטְרֵי חוּץ – אַף כָּאן מוּקְטְרֵי חוּץ.

Rabbi Yoḥanan said: Liability in this case **is derived** through a verbal analogy between the reference to **bringing** stated with regard to slaughtering (see Leviticus 17:4), and the reference to **bringing** stated with regard to offering up (see Leviticus 17:9). The verbal analogy teaches that **just as there,** with regard to slaughtering, one is liable for offerings that are going to be **burned outside** the Temple, since one slaughtered them there, **so too here,** with regard to offering up, one is liable even for offerings that are unfit and so will be **burned outside** the Temple, having been slaughtered there.

מַתְקִיף לָהּ רַב בֵּיבָי: הָא דִּתְנַן שְׁלֹשִׁים וָשֵׁשׁ כָּרֵיתוֹת בַּתּוֹרָה – תְּלָתִין וְשַׁב הָוְיָין, דְּאִיכָּא הַמַּעֲלֶה וְהַמַּעֲלֶה! קַשְׁיָא.

Rav Beivai objects to these suggestions: But what about **that which we learned** in a mishna (*Karetot* 2a): There are **thirty-six** cases **in the Torah** for which one is liable to receive *karet*. The mishna enumerates all thirty-six, and offering up outside the Temple is counted as only one of them. According to these suggestions, **there are thirty-seven, as there is** one case of **one who offers up** an offering that was slaughtered inside the Temple, **and** the other case of **one who offers up**[N] an offering that was slaughtered outside the Temple, which are considered two independent prohibitions. The Gemara concedes: This is **difficult.**

וְהָדְתְנַן: הַזּוֹרֵק מִקְצָת דָּמִים בַּחוּץ – חַיָּיב, מְנָלַן? נָפְקָא לֵיהּ מִדְּתַנְיָא: "דָּם יֵחָשֵׁב" – לְרַבּוֹת הַזּוֹרֵק, דִּבְרֵי רַבִּי יִשְׁמָעֵאל. רַבִּי עֲקִיבָא אוֹמֵר: "אוֹ זָבַח" – לְרַבּוֹת אֶת הַזּוֹרֵק.

§ The Gemara considers the source for other prohibitions. **And** concerning **that which we learned** in a mishna (110a): **One who sprinkles part of** the **blood** of an offering, e.g., if he sprinkles one sprinkling instead of four, **outside**[H] the Temple courtyard, is **liable; from where do we** derive this? The *tanna* **derives it from that which is taught** in a *baraita*: The verse states with regard to one who slaughters outside the Temple courtyard: **"Blood shall be imputed** to that man, he has shed blood, and that man shall be cut off from among his people" (Leviticus 17:4). This serves **to include** liability for **one who sprinkles** sacrificial blood outside the Temple courtyard; this is **the statement of Rabbi Yishmael. Rabbi Akiva says:** It is derived from the verse: "Any man…that offers up a burnt offering **or sacrifice"** (Leviticus 17:8). The term "or" serves **to include** liability for **one who sprinkles** blood outside the Temple courtyard.

וְרַבִּי יִשְׁמָעֵאל, הַאי "אוֹ זָבַח" מַאי עָבֵיד לֵיהּ? לְחַלֵּק.

The Gemara asks: **And** as for **Rabbi Yishmael, what does he do with this** term "or" in "a burnt offering **or sacrifice"?**[N] It serves **to divide** them into two independent cases, such that liability is incurred even if one offered up only one of them.

וְרַבִּי עֲקִיבָא לְחַלֵּק מְנָא לֵיהּ? נָפְקָא לֵיהּ מִ"לֹּא יְבִיאֶנּוּ".

The Gemara asks: **And** as for **Rabbi Akiva, from where does he** derive the *halakha* **to divide** them into two cases? **He derives it from** the next verse: "And **he will not bring it** to the entrance of the Tent of Meeting" (Leviticus 17:9). The term "it" is written in the singular to indicate that one is liable even if he offered up only one of them.

וְרַבִּי יִשְׁמָעֵאל: הַהוּא מִיבָּעֵי לֵיהּ: עַל הַשָּׁלֵם הוּא חַיָּיב, וְאֵינוֹ חַיָּיב עַל הֶחָסֵר. וְרַבִּי עֲקִיבָא? נָפְקָא לֵיהּ מִ"לַּעֲשׂוֹת אֹתוֹ".

And as for **Rabbi Yishmael,** why does he not derive that *halakha* from the term "it"? The Gemara answers: According to him, **that** term **is necessary** as the source for the *halakha* that one **is liable for** offering up **a complete** animal, **but** one **is not liable for** offering up **an incomplete** animal.[N] The term "it" indicates an animal in its entirety. **And** as for **Rabbi Akiva, he derives** this **from** the repetition of "it" in the continuation of the verse: "He will not bring it…**to sacrifice it** to the Lord" (Leviticus 17:9).

וְרַבִּי יִשְׁמָעֵאל: חַד לְמוּקְטְרֵי פְּנִים שֶׁחָסְרוּ וְהֶעֱלוּ בַּחוּץ, וְחַד לְמוּקְטְרֵי חוּץ שֶׁחָסְרוּ וְהֶעֱלוּ בַּחוּץ. וְהָא תַּנְיָא, רַבִּי יִשְׁמָעֵאל אוֹמֵר: יָכוֹל מוּקְטְרֵי פְּנִים שֶׁחָסְרוּ וְהֶעֱלוּ בַּחוּץ חַיָּיב? תַּלְמוּד לוֹמַר: "לַעֲשׂוֹת אֹתוֹ" – עַל הַשָּׁלֵם חַיָּיב, וְאֵינוֹ חַיָּיב עַל הֶחָסֵר.

And as for **Rabbi Yishmael,** how does he explain the repetition of "it"? He holds that each mention teaches about a different case: **One** is referring **to** offerings that are fit to be **burned inside**[N] the Temple courtyard **that became incomplete**[H] **and were** then **offered up outside. And** the other **one** is referring **to** offerings that are unfit and so will be **burned outside** the Temple as they were unlawfully slaughtered outside the Temple courtyard, **that became incomplete and were offered up outside.** In both cases one is exempt. **And so it is taught** in a *baraita*: **Rabbi Yishmael says:** One **might** have thought that with regard to offerings that were fit to be **burned inside** the Temple courtyard and **that became incomplete and were** instead **offered up outside,** one would be **liable.** To dispel this notion, **the verse states: "To sacrifice it,"** which indicates that **for** offering up **a complete** animal one is **liable, but** one is **not liable for an incomplete** animal.

וְרַבִּי עֲקִיבָא: מוּקְטְרֵי פְּנִים שֶׁחָסְרוּ וְהֶעֱלוּ בַּחוּץ חַיָּיב.

And Rabbi Akiva, who has already expounded both mentions of "it," disagrees with Rabbi Yishmael and holds that one is **liable** for offerings that are fit to be **burned inside that became incomplete and were** instead **offered up outside.**

NOTES

There is one who offers up and the other one who offers up – דְּאִיכָּא הַמַּעֲלֶה וְהַמַּעֲלֶה: Rashi explains that a prohibition derived through a verbal analogy or juxtaposition is regarded as independent of the prohibition it was derived from. Therefore, one who violates both prohibitions in a single lapse of awareness is liable to bring two sin offerings.

Or sacrifice – אוֹ זָבַח: A burnt offering is entirely burned on the altar. The term "sacrifice" is used in this verse as a generic term for all other types of offerings. In contrast to a burnt offering, only select parts of other offerings are burned on the altar, while the rest of their parts are eaten by the priests or the owner of the offering.

But one is not liable for offering up an incomplete animal – וְאֵינוֹ חַיָּיב עַל הֶחָסֵר: The Gemara (108b) cites a dispute as to whether this refers to an incomplete limb or an incomplete animal. Another opinion holds that this derivation refers not to an animal offering at all; rather, it refers to offering up an incomplete meal offering (see 109b).

One is referring to offerings that are fit to be burned inside, etc. – חַד לְמוּקְטְרֵי פְּנִים וכו׳: There are two independent sources, in order to teach that a person is exempt both where the incomplete offering is fit, as it was slaughtered inside the Temple, and where it is unfit, having been slaughtered outside. Had there been only one source, it would have been applied to the case of an offering slaughtered outside the Temple, teaching that only in that case one is exempt; one would still be liable, though, for offering up an incomplete offering that was slaughtered inside the Temple. The reason for this is that the mishna (86a) states that limbs of an offering that were dislodged from the altar should be restored to the altar, despite the fact that, having already been consumed by the altar's fire, they are now incomplete. The essential condition of liability for offering up outside the Temple is that one is liable only if the offering is fit to be offered upon the altar inside the Temple (see 109a). Therefore, since there exists a case in which one is required to place incomplete limbs upon the altar, one might have thought that a person would be liable for offering up incomplete limbs outside the Temple. To counter this, the Torah provides an independent source to indicate that even in this case one is exempt.

HALAKHA

One who sprinkles part of the blood outside – הַזּוֹרֵק מִקְצָת דָּמִים בַּחוּץ: One who sprinkles part of the blood of an offering outside the Temple courtyard is liable, in accordance with the ruling of the mishna on 110a (Rambam *Sefer Avoda*, *Hilkhot Ma'aseh HaKorbanot* 19:13).

Offerings that are fit to be burned inside that became incomplete, etc. – מוּקְטְרֵי פְּנִים שֶׁחָסְרוּ וכו׳: With regard to items that are supposed to be offered up on the altar, e.g., the handful from the meal offering, the frankincense, the sacrificial portions of an offering, the burnt offering, the meal offering of a priest, or the libations, if any of them became incomplete inside the Temple and then one offered them up outside, he is exempt from liability. This is derived from the verse: "He will not bring it…to sacrifice it to the Lord" (Leviticus 17:9), which indicates that one is liable only in a case where he offered up the complete item outside. This is in accordance with the opinion of Rabbi Yishmael, which is also the opinion expressed in the unattributed mishna on 109b (Rambam *Sefer Avoda*, *Hilkhot Ma'aseh HaKorbanot* 19:9, and *Kesef Mishne* and *Leḥem Mishne* there).

וְרַבִּי עֲקִיבָא, הַאי "דָּם יֵחָשֵׁב" מַאי עָבֵיד לֵיהּ? לְרַבּוֹת שְׁחִיטַת הָעוֹף. וְרַבִּי יִשְׁמָעֵאל? נָפְקָא לֵיהּ מֵ"אוֹ אֲשֶׁר יִשְׁחַט".

Rabbi Yishmael derives the liability for sprinkling part of the blood of an offering outside the Temple courtyard from the verse "Blood shall be imputed to that man." The Gemara asks: **And as for Rabbi Akiva, what does he do with this** verse: **"Blood shall be imputed** to that man"? He expounds it **to include** liability for the **slaughter of a bird** offering outside the courtyard. One is liable despite the fact that inside the Temple, a bird is sacrificed by pinching the nape of its neck, not by slaughtering it. **And as for Rabbi Yishmael, he derives** this *halakha* **from: "Or that slaughters**[N] it outside the camp" (Leviticus 17:3).

וְרַבִּי עֲקִיבָא אָמַר לָךְ, הַהוּא מִיבָּעֵי לֵיהּ: עַל הַשּׁוֹחֵט הוּא חַיָּיב, וְלֹא עַל הַמּוֹלֵק. וְרַבִּי יִשְׁמָעֵאל? נָפְקָא לֵיהּ מִ"זֶּה הַדָּבָר".

And Rabbi Akiva could have **said to you** that he does not derive it from **that** verse, as he holds that it is **necessary to** teach that only **one who slaughters** a bird offering outside **is liable, but** one is **not liable for pinching its nape**[H] outside. **And** as for **Rabbi Yishmael,** from where does he derive that one is exempt if he pinches? **He derives it from** the phrase at the beginning of the passage about slaughtering outside: **"This is the matter"** (Leviticus 17:2), which indicates that one is liable only for slaughtering and not for any other method of killing.

דְּתַנְיָא: "אֲשֶׁר יִשְׁחַט" – אֵין לִי אֶלָּא שׁוֹחֵט בְּהֵמָה, שָׁחַט עוֹף מְנָא לַן? תַּלְמוּד לוֹמַר "אוֹ אֲשֶׁר יִשְׁחַט".

Rabbi Yishmael's opinion is **as it is taught** in a *baraita*: The verse states: "Any man of the house of Israel **that slaughters** an ox, or lamb, or goat, in the camp, or that slaughters it outside the camp" (Leviticus 17:3). From this verse **I have** derived liability **only** for one who **slaughters an animal** offering outside; **from where do we** derive that one is liable if he **slaughtered a bird** offering outside? **The verse states: "Or that slaughters,"** to include liability for slaughtering a bird.

יָכוֹל אַף הַמּוֹלֵק? וְדִין הוּא: מָה שְׁחִיטָה דְּאֵין דֶּרֶךְ הֶכְשֵׁירָהּ בִּפְנִים – חַיָּיב, מְלִיקָה שֶׁדֶּרֶךְ הֶכְשֵׁירָהּ בִּפְנִים – אֵינוֹ דִּין שֶׁהוּא חַיָּיב? תַּלְמוּד לוֹמַר "זֶה הַדָּבָר".

One **might** have thought that **even one who pinches** the nape of a bird offering outside would be liable. **And** there **is a logical inference** to support this: **If** with regard to the **slaughter** of a bird offering, **which is not** the valid **method of preparation inside** the Temple, one is nevertheless **liable** if he did it outside, then with regard to **pinching** the nape of a bird offering, **which is** the valid **method of preparation inside** the Temple, **is it not logical that** one **is liable** if he did it outside? To counter this, **the verse states: "This is the matter"** (Leviticus 17:2), which indicates one is liable only for slaughtering, not for any other method of killing.

וְרַבִּי עֲקִיבָא אָמַר לָךְ: הַהוּא מִיבָּעֵי לֵיהּ לִגְזֵירָה שָׁוָה.

And Rabbi Akiva could have **said to you** that he does not derive it from **that** verse, as he holds that it is **necessary for** expounding as part of **a verbal analogy**[N] with the passage with regard to vows, where it is written: "This is the matter that the Lord has commanded" (Numbers 30:2).

וְהָא דִּתְנַן: הַקּוֹמֵץ וְהַמְקַבֵּל דָּמִים בַּחוּץ – פָּטוּר, מְנָלַן? וּמֵהֵיכָא תֵּיתֵי דְּחַיָּיב?

§ The Gemara considers the source for other prohibitions. **And** concerning **that which we learned** in a mishna (112b): **One who takes a handful** from a meal offering outside the Temple courtyard but does not burn it, **and one who collects the blood**[H] of an offering in a vessel **outside** the Temple courtyard but does not sprinkle it on an altar, he is **exempt; from where do we** derive this, that one is not liable unless he also completes the subsequent sacrificial rites? The Gemara is surprised by the question: **But from where would** it **be derived that** one is **liable** for these acts, necessitating a source for the fact that he is exempt?

תֵּיתֵי מִשְּׁחִיטָה – מַה לִּשְׁחִיטָה שֶׁכֵּן נִפְסֶלֶת שֶׁלֹּא לְאוֹכְלִין בְּפֶסַח!

The Gemara demonstrates that there is no reason to have assumed that one would be liable: If you suggest **deriving** it **through** a comparison to **slaughtering** outside the Temple, where one is liable even if he does not perform the subsequent sacrificial rites, this can be refuted: **What** is notable **about slaughtering?** It is notable **in that with regard to a Paschal offering,** if one slaughters it with the intent that it be **for the** sake of **those who cannot eat** it, it is thereby **disqualified.**[N] The cases in the mishna do not share this stringency.

NOTES

Or that slaughters – אוֹ אֲשֶׁר יִשְׁחַט: The verse states: "Any man of the house of Israel that slaughters an ox, or lamb, or goat, in the camp, or that slaughters it outside the camp." The derivation is based on the unnecessary repetition of the phrase "that slaughters" in the second part of the verse (see Rashi).

For expounding as part of a verbal analogy – לִגְזֵירָה שָׁוָה: This verbal analogy, which is elucidated in tractate *Nedarim* (78a) and tractate *Bava Batra* (120b), associates the phrase "this is the matter" written with regard to slaughtering an offering outside the Temple with the identical phrase in the passage detailing the annulment of vows (see Numbers 30:2). The verbal analogy teaches two *halakhot*. First, the passage in Numbers is addressed specifically to the leaders of the tribes. One might have thought that only a panel of expert judges, like those leaders, can annul vows. The verbal analogy teaches that just as the passage concerning slaughtering outside the Temple is addressed to all of the Jewish people, as it begins: "Speak to Aaron, and to his sons, to all the children of Israel" (Leviticus 17:2), the same applies with regard to the annulment of vows, and even a panel of three common people has the power to annul a vow. A second *halakha* derived via the verbal analogy is that the consecration of an animal, which is done by verbal declaration, is also regarded as a vow to the extent that just as a vow may be annulled, so too, the consecration of an animal may be annulled. Accordingly, if one slaughtered an offering outside the Temple and then had the consecration annulled, he would not be liable for his act because it is found that the original consecration of the animal never took effect, and so he did nothing more than slaughter a non-sacred animal outside the Temple, which is permitted.

For the sake of those who cannot eat it, it is disqualified – נִפְסֶלֶת שֶׁלֹּא לְאוֹכְלִין: This disqualification is a unique facet of the Paschal offering. An essential goal of the Paschal offering is that it be consumed. Therefore, if it is slaughtered exclusively for the sake of those who are unable to partake of it, for example, for elderly or unwell people who will not each be able to consume an olive-bulk of its meat, then the offering is disqualified (see *Pesaḥim* 66a).

HALAKHA

One who slaughters a bird outside is liable but one is not liable for pinching its nape – עַל הַשּׁוֹחֵט הוּא חַיָּיב וְלֹא עַל הַמּוֹלֵק: One who pinches the nape of a bird offering outside the courtyard is exempt. If he then proceeds to offer up that bird outside the courtyard, he is exempt. But if one slaughters a bird outside the courtyard and then offers it up outside the courtyard, he is liable to bring two sin offerings. This is because slaughtering is the valid method of killing outside the courtyard and so it stands in place of the pinching of the nape done inside the courtyard (Rambam *Sefer Avoda, Hilkhot Ma'aseh HaKorbanot* 18:18, and see Ra'avad there).

One who takes a handful and one who collects the blood, etc. – הַקּוֹמֵץ וְהַמְקַבֵּל דָּמִים וכו׳: One who takes a handful from a meal offering outside the Temple courtyard, and one who collects the blood of an offering in a vessel outside the courtyard, is exempt. This is because neither of these acts complete a sacrificial rite. This *halakha* is in accordance with the *baraita* cited on 115b (Rambam *Sefer Avoda, Hilkhot Ma'aseh HaKorbanot* 19:6 and Mahari Kurkus there).

תֵּיתֵי מִזְּרִיקָה – מָה לִזְּרִיקָה שֶׁכֵּן זָר חַיָּיב עָלֶיהָ מִיתָה!

And if you suggest **deriving** it **through** a comparison to **sprinkling** blood outside the Temple, as one is liable for sprinkling the blood even though it is only one of the sacrificial rites of the offering that should have been performed inside the Temple, this can be refuted: **What** is notable **about sprinkling?** It is notable **in that a non-priest** who sprinkles blood in the Temple is **liable** to be punished with **death** at the hand of Heaven **for** this act.[N] The cases in the mishna do not share this stringency.

NOTES

In that a non-priest is liable to be punished with death for this act – **שֶׁכֵּן זָר חַיָּיב עָלֶיהָ מִיתָה**: Even though a non-priest who takes a handful from a meal offering or collects the blood of an offering certainly disqualifies the offering, he is not liable to be punished with death at the hand of Heaven (see 15b and *Menaḥot* 6a). The reason is that the Sages derive that a non-priest is liable to be punished with death at the hand of Heaven only for completing a sacrificial rite. Neither the taking of a handful nor the collection of the blood fulfills this requirement. After taking a handful from a meal offering, the rites of consecration in a service vessel and of burning are still required. After collecting the blood, the rites of carrying the blood of the sacrifice to the altar and sprinkling it are still required (see 112b).

Perek **XIII**
Daf **107** Amud **b**

תֵּיתֵי מִבֵּינַיָּא.

Given that each suggestion has a different refutation, the Gemara suggests: **Derive it through** a comparison to **the common element** shared by these two cases. Slaughtering and sprinkling are each just one of the sacrificial rites that are performed with an offering, and yet one is liable for performing them outside the Temple. Since the derivation is based on a comparison to both cases, the refutations offered for each individual case are no longer relevant.

אִם כֵּן, לֹא יֹאמַר בִּזְרִיקָה, וְתֵיתֵי מִבֵּינַיָּא.

The Gemara rejects this: **If** that were **so,** and one can derive liability for one rite through a comparison to the common element shared by two other rites, then **let** the Torah **not state** that one is liable **for sprinkling** blood outside the Temple, **and** instead **derive** it **from the common element** shared by slaughtering and offering up outside the Temple.

וְתֵיתֵי מִשְּׁחִיטָה – מָה לִשְׁחִיטָה שֶׁכֵּן נִפְסֶלֶת שֶׁלֹּא לְשֵׁם אוֹכְלִין בְּפֶסַח! תֵּיתֵי מֵהַעֲלָאָה – מָה לְהַעֲלָאָה שֶׁכֵּן יֶשְׁנָהּ בְּמִנְחָה! וְתֵיתֵי מִבֵּינַיָּא

The derivation would be as follows: **And** if you suggest **deriving** liability for sprinkling **from** the liability for **slaughtering,** that could be refuted. **What** is notable **about slaughtering?** It is notable **in that, with regard to a Paschal offering,** if one slaughters it with the intent that it be **for the sake of those who cannot eat,** it is thereby **disqualified.** Sprinkling does not share this stringency. And if you suggest **deriving** liability for sprinkling **from** the liability for **offering up,** that could also be refuted. **What** is notable **about offering up?** It is notable **in that** liability for offering up also **exists with regard to a meal offering.** Sprinkling does not share this stringency. **But** it should still be possible to **derive** liability for sprinkling **from the common element** shared by the two cases. Since the derivation is based on a comparison to both cases, the refutations offered above for each individual case are no longer relevant.

לְהָכִי כְּתִיב קְרָא, לְמֵימַר דְּלָא אָתְיָא מִבֵּינַיָּא.

The Gemara explains: It is **for this** very reason that **a verse is written** to teach the liability for sprinkling outside the Temple, **to say** to you **that** liability for performing sacrificial rites outside the Temple **cannot be derived from the common element** shared by two other cases; rather, it must be directly derived from a verse. Accordingly, the Gemara has demonstrated that there is no basis to have assumed that one who takes a handful from a meal offering, or collects blood, outside the Temple is liable.

אמר רבי אבהו: שחט וזרק, לדברי רבי ישמעאל – חייב אחת, לדברי רבי עקיבא – חייב שתים.

§ The Gemara cited a dispute concerning the source for the liability for sprinkling part of the blood of an offering outside the Temple courtyard. According to Rabbi Yishmael, it is derived from the verse in the passage about slaughtering outside the Temple: "Blood shall be imputed to that man" (Leviticus 17:4). According to Rabbi Akiva, it is derived from the verse in the passage about offering up outside the Temple: "Any man…that offers up a burnt offering or sacrifice" (Leviticus 17:8). **Rabbi Abbahu says:** One who **slaughtered** an offering **and sprinkled** its blood outside the Temple in a single lapse of awareness, **according to the statement of Rabbi Yishmael,** is **liable** to bring **one** sin offering, as liability for each transgression is derived from the same passage and they are subcategories of the same prohibition. **According to the statement of Rabbi Akiva,** one is **liable** to bring **two** sin offerings, as the liability for each transgression is derived from a different passage and they are considered independent prohibitions.

אביי אמר: אפילו [לדברי] רבי עקיבא אינו חייב אלא אחת, דאמר קרא: "שם תעשה" – הכתוב עשאן לכולן עבודה אחת.

Abaye said: Even according to the statement of Rabbi Akiva, he is **liable** to bring **only one** sin offering, **as the verse states** with regard to performing sacrificial rites outside the Temple courtyard: "But in the place that the Lord will choose in one of your tribes, there you shall offer up your burnt offerings, and **there you shall do** all that I command you" (Deuteronomy 12:14). Since the first part of the verse makes reference to offering up, by inference, the term "you shall do" in the second part must be referring to all the other sacrificial rites. Therefore, **the verse has regarded all of** the sacrificial rites apart from offering up as **one rite** with regard to the prohibition against performing them outside the Temple courtyard.

זרק והעלה, לדברי רבי ישמעאל – חייב שתים, לדברי רבי עקיבא אינו חייב אלא אחת.

Rabbi Abbahu also said: One who **sprinkled** the blood of an offering **and offered** it **up**[H] outside, in a single lapse of awareness, **according to the statement of Rabbi Yishmael** is **liable** to bring **two** sin offerings. **According to the statement of Rabbi Akiva,** he is **liable** to bring **only one** sin offering.

אביי אמר: אפילו [לדברי] רבי עקיבא חייב שתים, להכי פלגינהו קרא "שם תעלה…ושם תעשה".

Abaye said: Even according to the statement of Rabbi Akiva he is **liable** to bring **two** sin offerings, as it is **for this** reason that **the verse differentiated** between the offering up and the slaughtering, as it states: "**There you shall offer up** your burnt offerings, **and there you shall do,**" in order to teach that one who performs both is liable for each one.

שחט וזרק והעלה – לדברי הכל חייב שתים.

Finally, Rabbi Abbahu adds the logical conclusion that with regard to one who **slaughtered** an offering **and sprinkled** its blood **and offered** it **up** outside, in a single lapse of awareness, **all agree** that he is **liable** to bring **two** sin offerings.

תנו רבנן: "במחנה", יכול השוחט עולה בדרום יהא חייב? תלמוד לומר: "אל מחוץ למחנה".

§ **The Sages taught** in a *baraita*: The verse states: "Any man of the house of Israel that slaughters an ox, or lamb, or goat, in the camp, or that slaughters it outside the camp" (Leviticus 17:3). Based on the first part of the verse: "That slaughters… **in the camp,**" one **might** have thought that **one who slaughters a burnt offering in the south** of the courtyard, instead of in the north, where it should be slaughtered, **will be liable,** as he has slaughtered it outside the area in which it should be slaughtered. To counter this, **the** next part of the **verse states:** "That slaughters it **outside the camp,**" indicating that liability is incurred only for slaughtering an offering outside the Temple courtyard.

HALAKHA

Sprinkled and offered up – זרק והעלה: One who sprinkles the blood of an offering outside of the courtyard and offers it up outside of the courtyard is liable to bring two sin offerings. This is because the Torah differentiates between the prohibition against offering up outside the courtyard and the prohibition against performing other sacrificial rites outside. Although the Rambam does not state the *halakha* with regard to one who, while outside, slaughters an offering and sprinkles its blood, nor with regard to one who, while outside, slaughters an offering, sprinkles its blood, and offers it up, the *halakha* is in accordance with the opinion of Abaye in both cases. In the former case, the person is liable to bring one sin offering, and in the latter case, two sin offerings. This ruling is also in accordance with the ruling of Rav Ashi cited in *Sanhedrin* 34b (Rambam *Sefer Avoda*, *Hilkhot Ma'aseh HaKorbanot* 19:11, and see *Mishne LaMelekh* there; see *Likkutei Halakhot*).

יָכוֹל חוּץ לְשָׁלֹשׁ מַחֲנוֹת? (תַּלְמוּד לוֹמַר: ״אוֹ עֵז בַּמַּחֲנֶה״). מִנַּיִן אַף בְּמַחֲנֵה לְוִיָּה? תַּלְמוּד לוֹמַר ״בַּמַּחֲנֶה״.

The *baraita* continues: Three concentric areas, so-called camps, arranged according to decreasing level of sanctity, encompassed the Tabernacle and Temple: The camp of the Divine Presence comprised the courtyard of the Tabernacle, and later on, of the Temple. Surrounding that was the Levite camp and then the Israelite camp. If the verse had stated only: "That slaughters it outside the camp," one **might** have thought that a person would be liable only for slaughtering an offering **outside** all **three** of the **camps.**[N] To dispel this notion, the first part of **the verse states:** "That slaughters an ox, or lamb, **or goat, in the camp,"**[N] which indicates that liability is incurred even for slaughtering inside these camps. **From where** is it derived that one is liable **even** if he slaughters **inside the Levite camp? The verse states:** "That slaughters… **in the camp,"** which indicates that liability is incurred even for slaughtering inside the three camps.

אִי ״בַּמַּחֲנֶה״, יָכוֹל הַשּׁוֹחֵט עוֹלָה בַּדָּרוֹם יְהֵא חַיָּיב? תַּלְמוּד לוֹמַר: ״אוֹ אֶל מִחוּץ לַמַּחֲנֶה״.

If the verse stated only the term **"in the camp,"**[N] which indicates that one is liable even for slaughtering inside the three camps, one **might** have thought that **one who slaughters a burnt offering in the south** of the courtyard, which is regarded as being outside of the holier northern section of the courtyard, where such an offering should be slaughtered, **will** also **be liable.** To counter this, **the verse states:** **"Or** that slaughters it **outside the camp."**

מַה חוּץ לַמַּחֲנֶה מְיוּחָד, שֶׁאֵין רָאוּי לִשְׁחִיטַת קָדָשִׁים וְלִשְׁחִיטַת כָּל זֶבַח; יָצָא דָּרוֹם, שֶׁאַף עַל פִּי שֶׁאֵין רָאוּי לִשְׁחִיטַת קָדְשֵׁי קָדָשִׁים – רָאוּי לִשְׁחִיטַת קָדָשִׁים קַלִּים.

This indicates that **just as** the phrase **"outside the camp"** is **distinctive** in that it is referring to an area **that is not fit for slaughtering offerings** of the most sacred order **or for slaughtering any** other type of **offering,** so too, the term "in the camp" is referring to an area unfit for the slaughter of any offering. This **excludes** the **south** of the courtyard, **as even though** it is an area that is **not fit for slaughtering offerings of the most sacred order,** it **is fit for slaughtering offerings of lesser sanctity.** Therefore, no liability is incurred for slaughtering an offering in the south of the courtyard, even if it should have been slaughtered in the north.

אָמַר עוּלָּא: הַשּׁוֹחֵט עַל גַּגּוֹ שֶׁל הֵיכָל – חַיָּיב, הוֹאִיל וְאֵין רָאוּי לִשְׁחִיטַת כָּל זֶבַח. מַתְקִיף לַהּ רָבָא: אִם כֵּן, נִיכְתּוֹב קְרָא: (אֶל) ״מִחוּץ לַמַּחֲנֶה״ וְלָא בָּעֵי ״אֶל פֶּתַח אֹהֶל מוֹעֵד״, ״אֶל פֶּתַח אֹהֶל מוֹעֵד״ לָמָּה לִי? לָאו לְמַעוּטֵי גַּגּוֹ?

Based on this *baraita,* **Ulla says: One who slaughters** an offering **on the roof of** the **Sanctuary**[N] **is liable** for slaughtering outside the Temple courtyard, **since** the roof is an area that is **not fit for the slaughter of any offering. Rava objects to this: If so, let the verse write** only: "Or that slaughters it **outside the camp,"** and it would **not be necessary** to write: "And he did not bring it **to the entrance of the Tent of Meeting"** (Leviticus 17:4). **Why do I** need the verse to also write: "And he did not bring it **to the entrance of the Tent of Meeting"**? Is it **not to exclude the roof of** the Sanctuary,[H] as in the Temple the Sanctuary corresponded to the Tent of Meeting? Although the roof is an area that is not fit for slaughtering any offering, one should not be liable for slaughtering there since the offering was nevertheless brought to the Tent of Meeting.

וּלְרָבָא, אִם כֵּן נִכְתּוֹב: ״אֶל פֶּתַח אֹהֶל מוֹעֵד״, ״בַּמַּחֲנֶה״ (וְאֶל) ״מִחוּץ לַמַּחֲנֶה״ לָמָּה לִי? לָאו לְאַתּוּיֵי גַּגּוֹ?

The Gemara questions Rava's claim: **But according to Rava, if** that is **so** and one is exempt if he slaughtered on the roof of the Sanctuary as ultimately the offering was brought to the Tent of Meeting, then **let** the verse **write** only: **"And** he did not bring it **to the entrance of the Tent of Meeting." Why do I** need the verse to also write **"in the camp"** and **"outside the camp"**? Is it **not** that the term "in the camp" indicates that there is a case where one is liable even when slaughtering inside the courtyard, which serves **to include** liability for slaughtering on **the roof of** the Sanctuary? According to this, the term "outside the camp" would then be necessary to exclude liability for slaughtering a burnt offering in the south of the courtyard.

HALAKHA

To exclude the roof of the Sanctuary – לְמַעוּטֵי גַּגּוֹ: One who slaughters an offering on the roof of the Sanctuary is exempt even though the roof is an area that is not fit for slaughtering any offering, in accordance with the opinion of Rava (Rambam *Sefer Avoda, Hilkhot Ma'aseh HaKorbanot* 18:15).

NOTES

One might have thought outside all three camps – יָכוֹל חוּץ לְשָׁלֹשׁ מַחֲנוֹת: Rashi explains that this assumption would be based on the verbal analogy cited in *Sanhedrin* (42b): The Torah states with regard to the sacrificial bulls whose flesh is burned outside the city, i.e., outside all three camps, that they are to be burned: "Outside the camp" (Leviticus 4:12). Similarly, the Torah states with regard to a blasphemer: "Remove the blasphemer to outside the camp" (Leviticus 24:14). A verbal analogy between these two instances of "outside the camp" teaches that the blasphemer must also be taken outside of all three camps. It would appear then that the phrase "outside the camp" mentioned with regard to slaughtering outside the Temple also refers to outside all three camps. Therefore, it is necessary for the Torah to indicate that this is not so, as the *baraita* explains.

The verse states: Or goat in the camp, etc. – תַּלְמוּד לוֹמַר אוֹ עֵז בַּמַּחֲנֶה וכו׳: The Gemara's text of the *baraita* is clearly corrupted and it combines two incompatible versions of the *baraita.* According to the version held by Rashi, the *baraita* rejects the notion that one is liable only when slaughtering outside all three camps by citing the verse: "In the camp." The next question, concerning liability for slaughtering inside the Levite camp, does not appear at all. By contrast, in the version that appears in *Torat Kohanim,* the *baraita* responds to the suggestion that one is liable only for slaughtering outside the three camps by asking for the source that one is liable for slaughtering inside the Levite camp. *Korban Aharon* explains the version in *Torat Kohanim* as follows: Since the verse states that the prohibition applies both "in the camp" and "outside the camp," it is apparent that the term "outside the camp" is referring to a camp that is outside of another camp, namely the Levite camp, which surrounds the camp of the Divine Presence. A different explanation is offered by Rabbeinu Hillel. He explains that according to the *baraita* the term "camp" refers specifically to the Levite camp. Accordingly, the verse is understood as follows: It is forbidden to slaughter in the Levite camp or to slaughter outside the Levite camp, i.e., in the Israelite camp.

If the verse stated only: In the camp, etc. – אִי בַּמַּחֲנֶה וכו׳: It would appear that the *baraita* is returning here to an issue that it already addressed. Indeed, some commentaries emend the text to avoid this difficulty. Rashi, for example, had a version that states: One might have though one would be liable for slaughtering in the camp of the Divine Presence. This also fits more naturally into the progression of the *baraita.*

Whatever the correct version is, it is clear that ultimately the terms "in the camp" and "outside the camp" are stated in order to counterbalance each other. The term "outside the camp" alone indicates an area outside of all three camps. The term "in the camp" alone would appear to include even the camp of the Divine Presence. The fact they are written together teaches that neither extreme is being described. The term "in the camp" modifies the term "outside the camp," to refer even to an area inside the three camps. Likewise, the term "outside the camp" modifies the term "in the camp," to refer only to an area in which it is not valid for sacrificing any offering (*Korban Aharon*).

The roof of the Sanctuary – גַּגּוֹ שֶׁל הֵיכָל: The roofs and upper stories of the Sanctuary were not consecrated with the sanctity of the Temple courtyard. Therefore, one may neither slaughter offerings of lesser sanctity nor eat offerings of the most sacred order there. Similarly, a ritually impure person who enters these areas is exempt (see *Shevuot* 17b).

HALAKHA

Its body is entirely inside but its neck is outside – כּוּלָּהּ בִּפְנִים וְצַוָּארָהּ בַּחוּץ: With regard to the prohibition against slaughtering an offering outside of the courtyard, one is liable both where the animal's body stands entirely outside of the courtyard but its neck is inside the courtyard, and where its body stands inside of the courtyard but its neck is outside the courtyard (Rambam *Sefer Avoda, Hilkhot Ma'aseh HaKorbanot* 18:15).

One who offers up outside the courtyard today – הַמַּעֲלֶה בִּזְמַן הַזֶּה: One who slaughters or offers up an offering outside the Temple courtyard in the present day, when there is no Temple, is liable. This is because the initial consecration of Jerusalem and the Temple area sanctified it for its time and forever, so it is still possible to bring offerings to be sacrificed in the former Temple area, in accordance with the opinion of Rabbi Yoḥanan (Rambam *Sefer Avoda, Hilkhot Ma'aseh HaKorbanot* 19:15).

One sacrifices offerings even if there is no Temple – מַקְרִיבִין אַף עַל פִּי שֶׁאֵין בַּיִת: King Solomon's consecration of the Temple courtyard and the city of Jerusalem sanctified it for its time and forever. Therefore, it is possible to bring offerings there even though there is no Temple structure. Nevertheless, one may sacrifice an offering only if one first erects an altar (*Likkutei Halakhot*). Furthermore, offerings of the most sacred order may be eaten in the courtyard area even though there are no curtains, and one may eat offerings of lesser sanctity and second-tithe produce in Jerusalem, even if there is no wall surrounding the city. This is in accordance with the opinion of Rabbi Yehoshua (Rambam *Sefer Avoda, Hilkhot Beit HaBeḥira* 6:15, and see Ra'avad there; *Shulḥan Arukh, Yoreh De'a* 331:2 and *Beur HaGra* there).

אָמַר רַב מָרִי: לְאִיתוּיֵי כּוּלָּהּ בִּפְנִים וְצַוָּארָהּ בַּחוּץ.

Rav Mari said in defense of Rava: No, the term "in the camp" is written **to include** liability for slaughtering an offering in a case where **its** body is **entirely inside** the courtyard **but its neck is outside**[H] the courtyard.

[צַוָּארָהּ] בַּחוּץ פְּשִׁיטָא, אַמַּאי קָפֵיד רַחֲמָנָא – אַשְּׁחִיטָה, וּשְׁחִיטָה בַּחוּץ הִיא! אֶלָּא לְאִיתוּיֵי כּוּלָּהּ בַּחוּץ וְצַוָּארָהּ בִּפְנִים.

The Gemara modifies Rav Mari's statement: If **its neck is outside** the courtyard, it is **obvious** that one is liable, as **about what** is **the Merciful One particular? The** Merciful One is particular **about** the **slaughter. And** in this case, the **slaughter is** done **outside** the courtyard. **Rather,** say instead that the term "in the camp" is written **to include** liability for slaughtering an offering where **its** body is **entirely outside** the courtyard **but its neck is inside** the courtyard.

אִיתְּמַר, הַמַּעֲלֶה בִּזְמַן הַזֶּה, רַבִּי יוֹחָנָן אָמַר: חַיָּיב, רֵישׁ לָקִישׁ אָמַר: פָּטוּר.

§ An amoraic dispute **was stated** with regard to **one who offers up** an offering outside the courtyard **today,**[H] when there is no Temple: **Rabbi Yoḥanan says:** He is **liable. Reish Lakish says:** He is **exempt.**

רַבִּי יוֹחָנָן אָמַר: חַיָּיב, קְדוּשָּׁה רִאשׁוֹנָה קִידְּשָׁה לִשְׁעָתָהּ וְקִידְּשָׁה לֶעָתִיד לָבֹא. רֵישׁ לָקִישׁ אָמַר: פָּטוּר, קְדוּשָּׁה רִאשׁוֹנָה קִידְּשָׁה לִשְׁעָתָהּ וְלֹא קִידְּשָׁה לֶעָתִיד לָבֹא.

The Gemara elaborates: **Rabbi Yoḥanan says** that he is **liable,** as he holds that the **initial consecration** of the Temple **sanctified** it **for its time and sanctified it forever,** and the location of the Temple remains sacred even after the Temple was destroyed. Accordingly, it is still possible now to build an altar there and bring offerings upon it; therefore, one is liable if he instead offers up an offering outside the Temple courtyard area. **Reish Lakish says** that he is **exempt,** as he holds that the **initial consecration** of the Temple **sanctified** it **for its time but did not sanctify** it **forever.** Accordingly, one can no longer bring offerings there; therefore, one is not liable for offering up outside that area.

נֵימָא דְּבִפְלוּגְתָּא דְּרַבִּי אֱלִיעֶזֶר וְרַבִּי יְהוֹשֻׁעַ קָמִיפַּלְגִי. דִּתְנַן, אָמַר רַבִּי אֱלִיעֶזֶר: כְּשֶׁהָיוּ בּוֹנִין בַּהֵיכָל, הָיוּ עוֹשִׂים קְלָעִים בַּהֵיכָל קְלָעִים בָּעֲזָרוֹת, אֶלָּא שֶׁבַּהֵיכָל בּוֹנִין מִבַּחוּץ וּבָעֲזָרָה בּוֹנִין מִבִּפְנִים.

The Gemara suggests: **Let us say** that Rabbi Yoḥanan and Reish Lakish **disagree with regard to** the issue that is the subject of **the dispute between Rabbi Eliezer and Rabbi Yehoshua, as we learned** in a mishna (*Eduyyot* 8:6): **Rabbi Eliezer said:** I heard that **when they were building the Sanctuary** in the Second Temple, **they would fashion** temporary **curtains for the Sanctuary**[N] and temporary **curtains for the courtyards** to serve as partitions until the construction of the stone walls was completed. The difference was **only that in the Sanctuary,** the workers **built** the walls **outside** the curtains, without entering, **and in the courtyards,** the workers **built** the walls **within** the curtains.

אָמַר רַבִּי יְהוֹשֻׁעַ: שָׁמַעְתִּי שֶׁהָיוּ מַקְרִיבִין אַף עַל פִּי שֶׁאֵין בַּיִת, וְאוֹכְלִים קָדְשֵׁי קָדָשִׁים אַף עַל פִּי שֶׁאֵין קְלָעִים, קָדָשִׁים קַלִּים וּמַעֲשֵׂר שֵׁנִי אַף עַל פִּי שֶׁאֵין חוֹמָה, מִפְּנֵי שֶׁקְּדוּשָּׁה רִאשׁוֹנָה קִידְּשָׁה לִשְׁעָתָהּ וְקִידְּשָׁה לֶעָתִיד לָבֹא.

The mishna continues: **Rabbi Yehoshua said: I heard that one sacrifices** offerings on the altar **even if there is no Temple,**[HN] **and one partakes of offerings of the most sacred order** in the Temple courtyard **even if there are no curtains, and** one partakes of **offerings of lesser sanctity and second-tithe** produce in Jerusalem **even if there is no wall** surrounding the city. This is **due to the fact that the initial consecration sanctified** the Temple and Jerusalem **for their time and** also **sanctified** them **forever.**

NOTES

They would fashion curtains for the Sanctuary – הָיוּ עוֹשִׂים קְלָעִים בַּהֵיכָל: The construction of the Second Temple began during the reign of Cyrus, but it was not completed until some twenty-two years later during the third year of the reign of Darius II. Concerning this period, the book of Ezra reports: "From the first day of the seventh month they began to sacrifice burnt offerings to the Lord, but the foundation of the Temple of the Lord was not yet laid" (Ezra 3:6). According to the Gemara's initial understanding of the mishna, Rabbi Eliezer holds that setting up curtains was necessary in order to delineate and consecrate the Sanctuary and the courtyard, so that the area could be regarded as the Temple and the sacrifice of offerings would be permitted there.

One sacrifices offerings even if there is no Temple – מַקְרִיבִין אַף עַל פִּי שֶׁאֵין בַּיִת: Even if it is not necessary to have a Temple structure in order to sacrifice offerings in the area of the Temple courtyard, it is still necessary to construct an altar. This is because the slaughter of an offering is invalid in the absence of an altar upon which one can later offer it up (see 59a).

Sacrificial service during the construction of the Second Temple

לָאו מִכְּלָל דְּרַבִּי אֱלִיעֶזֶר סָבַר לֹא קִידְּשָׁה?

The Gemara concludes: From the fact that Rabbi Yehoshua based his opinion on the principle that the initial consecration sanctified the Temple and Jerusalem forever, can one **not** learn **by inference** that **Rabbi Eliezer maintains** that **it did not sanctify** them forever? The dispute between Rabbi Yoḥanan and Reish Lakish would then directly parallel the dispute between Rabbi Yehoshua and Rabbi Eliezer.

אֲמַר לֵיהּ רָבִינָא לְרַב אַשִׁי: מִמַּאי? דִּלְמָא דְּכוּלֵּי עָלְמָא קְדוּשָּׁה רִאשׁוֹנָה קִידְּשָׁה לִשְׁעָתָהּ וְקִידְּשָׁה לֶעָתִיד לָבֹא, וּמָר מַאי דִּשְׁמִיעַ לֵיהּ קָאָמַר, וּמָר מַאי דִּשְׁמִיעַ לֵיהּ קָאָמַר! וְכִי תֵּימָא, קְלָעִים לְרַבִּי אֱלִיעֶזֶר לָמָּה לִי – לִצְנִיעוּתָא בְּעָלְמָא.

Ravina said to Rav Ashi: From where do you draw this inference? **Perhaps everyone** maintains that the **initial consecration sanctified** the Temple and Jerusalem **for their time** and also **sanctified** them **forever. And one Sage,** Rabbi Eliezer, **stated that** tradition, **which he heard** from his teachers, **and one Sage,** Rabbi Yehoshua, **stated that** tradition, **which he heard** from his teachers, and there is no dispute between them. **And if you would say: Why do I** need **curtains** at all **according to Rabbi Eliezer?** The original sanctity remained when Jerusalem was not surrounded by walls, and similarly, the presence or absence of curtains is irrelevant to the sanctity of the Temple area as well. The Gemara answers: The curtains were established **merely for seclusion,** as it would have been unbecoming for the activity in this most sacred venue to have been visible to all.

אִיתְּמַר, הַמַּעֲלֶה וְאֵין בּוֹ כַּזַּיִת, וְעֶצֶם מַשְׁלִימוֹ לְכַזַּיִת, רַבִּי יוֹחָנָן אָמַר: חַיָּיב, רֵישׁ לָקִישׁ אָמַר: פָּטוּר.

§ An amoraic dispute **was stated** with regard to **one who offers up** outside the Temple a limb of an offering **and** it **does not have** on it **an olive-bulk** of flesh,[H] **but** the **bone completes** the measure **to make an olive-bulk. Rabbi Yoḥanan says:** He is **liable. Reish Lakish says:** He is **exempt.**

רַבִּי יוֹחָנָן אָמַר: חַיָּיב – חִיבּוּרֵי עוֹלִין כְּעוֹלִין דָּמֵי. רֵישׁ לָקִישׁ אָמַר: פָּטוּר – חִיבּוּרֵי עוֹלִין לָאו כְּעוֹלִין דָּמוּ.

The Gemara elaborates: **Rabbi Yoḥanan says** that he is **liable,** as he holds that an item **attached to** flesh that must be **offered up** on the altar, e.g., a bone attached to sacrificial flesh, is also regarded **as** an item that must be **offered up** on the altar. Even though if it were to become detached, there would be no requirement to offer it up, nevertheless, as long as it is attached it is considered part of the flesh and it contributes to the required measure of an olive-bulk. **Reish Lakish says** that he is **exempt,** as he holds that an item **attached to** flesh that must be **offered up** on the altar is **not** regarded **as** an item that must be **offered up** on the altar.

בָּעֵי רָבָא: הַמַּעֲלֶה

Rava raises a dilemma: With regard to **one who offers up** outside the Temple courtyard

HALAKHA

One who offers up a limb and it does not have an olive-bulk of flesh – הַמַּעֲלֶה וְאֵין בּוֹ כַּזַּיִת: One who offers up a limb of an offering outside the Temple, and it does not have on it an olive-bulk of flesh, but the bone connected to the flesh completes the measure to make an olive-bulk, that person is liable, in accordance with the opinion of Rabbi Yoḥanan (Rambam *Sefer Avoda, Hilkhot Ma'aseh HaKorbanot* 19:10).

Perek **XIII**
Daf **108** Amud **a**

רֹאשׁ בֶּן יוֹנָה שֶׁאֵין בּוֹ כַּזַּיִת, וּמֶלַח מַשְׁלִימוֹ לְכַזַּיִת, מַהוּ?

the **head of a pigeon** burnt offering **that does not have** on it **an olive-bulk** of flesh, **but the salt** that adheres to it, after it was salted in accordance with the requirement to salt it (see Leviticus 2:13), **completes** the measure **to make an olive-bulk,**[H] **what is** the *halakha*? Is one liable for offering it up outside?

אֲמַר לֵיהּ רָבָא מִפַּרְזְקִיָא לְרַב אַשִׁי: לָאו הַיְינוּ פְּלוּגְתַּיְיהוּ דְּרַבִּי יוֹחָנָן וְרֵישׁ לָקִישׁ? תִּיבָּעֵי לְרַבִּי יוֹחָנָן, וְתִיבָּעֵי לְרֵישׁ לָקִישׁ;

Rava from Parzakya said to Rav Ashi: Is this not identical to **the dispute between Rabbi Yoḥanan and Reish Lakish** with regard to a bone attached to sacrificial flesh? Rav Ashi responded: No. **The dilemma can be raised according to Rabbi Yoḥanan and the dilemma can be raised according to Reish Lakish.**

HALAKHA

The salt completes the measure to make an olive-bulk – מֶלַח מַשְׁלִימוֹ לְכַזַּיִת: With regard to one who offers up, outside the Temple courtyard, the limb of an animal in which the amount of flesh is less than an olive-bulk, but the salt completes the measure to make an olive-bulk, it is uncertain whether he is liable or not. This is because the Gemara never resolves its question on the issue. Therefore, one does not receive lashes for this act (Rambam *Sefer Avoda, Hilkhot Ma'aseh HaKorbanot* 19:10).

תִּיבָּעֵי לְרַבִּי יוֹחָנָן: עַד כָּאן לָא קָאָמַר רַבִּי יוֹחָנָן הָתָם אֶלָּא עֶצֶם, דְּמִינָא דְּבָשָׂר הוּא, אֲבָל מֶלַח דְּלָאו מִינָא דְּבַר יוֹנָה הוּא – לָא. תִּיבָּעֵי לְרֵישׁ לָקִישׁ: עַד כָּאן לָא קָאָמַר רֵישׁ לָקִישׁ הָתָם אֶלָּא דְּאִי פָּרֵישׁ מִינָּהּ לָאו מִצְוָה לְאַסּוּקֵי, אֲבָל הָכָא, דְּאִי פָּרֵישׁ מִצְוָה לְאַסּוּקֵי – לָא. אוֹ דִּלְמָא, לָא שְׁנָא?

The Gemara elaborates: **The dilemma can be raised according to Rabbi Yoḥanan:** Perhaps **Rabbi Yoḥanan states** his opinion **only there,** with regard to **a bone,** claiming that it contributes to the measure of an olive-bulk **as it is of the** same **kind that flesh** is, i.e., they are both animal parts. **But** in the case of **salt, which is not of the** same **kind as a pigeon,** perhaps it would **not** contribute to the measure. And **the dilemma can** also **be raised according to Reish Lakish:** Perhaps **Reish Lakish states** his opinion **only there,** with regard to a bone, claiming that it does not contribute to the measure of an olive-bulk, **as if** the bone **separates from** the flesh, there is **no mitzva to offer** the bone **up** on the altar. **But here,** with regard to salt, concerning **which if it separates** from the pigeon there is **a mitzva to offer** it **up,** he would **not** rule as he does concerning a bone attached to flesh. **Or perhaps** there **is no difference** between the cases.

תֵּיקוּ.

The Gemara concludes: The dilemma **shall stand** unresolved.

"רַבִּי יוֹסֵי הַגְּלִילִי אוֹמֵר" כו׳.

§ The mishna teaches: **Rabbi Yosei HaGelili says:** If he slaughtered an offering inside the courtyard and then offered it up outside the courtyard, he is liable. But if he slaughtered it outside, thereby rendering it unfit, and then he offered it up outside, he is exempt for the offering up, as he offered up only an item that is unfit, and one is liable only for offering up an item that is fit to be offered up inside the Temple. The Rabbis said to him: According to your reasoning, even in a case where he slaughters it inside and offers it up outside, he should be exempt, since he rendered it unfit the moment that he took it outside the courtyard. Yet, in such a case, he is certainly liable for offering it up. So too, one who slaughters an offering outside and then offers it up outside is liable.

הֵשִׁיב רַבִּי תַּחַת רַבִּי יוֹסֵי הַגְּלִילִי: מַה לְּשׁוֹחֵט בִּפְנִים וּמַעֲלֶה בַּחוּץ – שֶׁהָיְתָה לוֹ שְׁעַת הַכּוֹשֶׁר, תֹּאמַר בְּשׁוֹחֵט חוּץ וּמַעֲלֶה בַּחוּץ – שֶׁלֹּא הָיְתָה לוֹ שְׁעַת הַכּוֹשֶׁר?

While a defense of Rabbi Yosei HaGelili's opinion is not presented in the mishna, various possibilities are recorded in a *baraita*: **Rabbi** Yehuda HaNasi **responded** to this challenge **on behalf of Rabbi Yosei HaGelili: What** is notable **about slaughtering** an offering **inside** the courtyard **and** then **offering** it **up outside?** It is notable in **that** the offering **had a period of fitness.**[N] **Can you say** the same **about slaughtering** an offering **outside and** then **offering** it **up outside, where** the offering **never had a period of fitness?** It was disqualified as soon as it was slaughtered and so it is reasonable that one is not liable for offering it up.

הֵשִׁיב רַבִּי אֶלְעָזָר בְּרַבִּי שִׁמְעוֹן תַּחַת רַבִּי יוֹסֵי הַגְּלִילִי: מַה לְּשׁוֹחֵט בִּפְנִים וּמַעֲלֶה בַּחוּץ – שֶׁכֵּן קוֹדֶשׁ מְקַבְּלוֹ, תֹּאמַר בְּשׁוֹחֵט בַּחוּץ – שֶׁאֵין קוֹדֶשׁ מְקַבְּלוֹ?

Rabbi Elazar, son of Rabbi Shimon, responded to this challenge **on behalf of Rabbi Yosei HaGelili: What** is notable **about slaughtering** an offering **inside** the courtyard **and** then **offering** it **up outside?** It is notable **in that** even though the offering was taken outside the courtyard and thereby disqualified, if it is, albeit unlawfully, placed on the altar, the **sanctity** of the altar **renders** the offering **acceptable** and it should not be removed from the altar because the disqualification occurred in sanctity, i.e., during the course of the Temple service (see 84a). **Can you say** the same **about slaughtering** an offering **outside** and then offering it up outside, **where** the disqualification did not occur in sanctity and so the **sanctity** of the altar **does not render** the offering **acceptable?** Therefore, even if it were placed there, it must be removed.

מַאי בֵּינַיְיהוּ? אָמַר זְעֵירִי: שְׁחִיטַת לַיְלָה אִיכָּא בֵּינַיְיהוּ.

The Gemara asks: **What** is the practical difference **between these** two responses? **Ze'eiri said:** The practical difference **between them is** a case of **slaughtering** an offering **at night** inside the courtyard and then offering it up outside. According to Rabbi Yehuda HaNasi's response, one would be exempt, as slaughtering at night disqualifies the offering from its very outset; whereas according to the response of Rabbi Elazar, one would be liable as this is a disqualification that occurs in sanctity.

NOTES

That it had a period of fitness – שֶׁהָיְתָה לוֹ שְׁעַת הַכּוֹשֶׁר: The principle concerning sacrificing an offering outside the courtyard is that one is liable only for an offering that has been fit to be sacrificed on the altar inside the courtyard. Accordingly, the fact that an offering had a period when it was fit to be sacrificed inside is a reason to assume that one should be liable for sacrificing it outside. Based on this logic, since an offering that was slaughtered outside the courtyard is immediately disqualified, one should not be liable for then sacrificing it outside the courtyard, since there was never a point when it was fit to be offered up on the altar inside the courtyard. This is indeed the opinion of Rabbi Yosei HaGelili. Although the Rabbis agree with this logic, they derive (see 107a) from a verse that a case where the same offering is both slaughtered and offered up outside the courtyard is an exception to the rule.

רַבָּה אָמַר: קַבָּלָה בִּכְלִי חוֹל אִיכָּא בֵּינַיְיהוּ.

Rabba said: The practical difference **between them is** a case in which, after slaughtering the offering in the courtyard, the **collection** of the blood was done there **in a non-sacred vessel** and then the animal was offered up outside the courtyard. According to Rabbi Yehuda HaNasi's defense, one would be exempt, as collecting the blood in a non-sacred vessel disqualifies the offering from its very outset; whereas according to the response of Rabbi Elazar, one would be liable as this is a disqualification that occurs in sanctity.

״טָמֵא שֶׁאָכַל בֵּין קוֹדֶשׁ״ כו׳.

§ The mishna teaches: One who is **ritually impure who ate** sacrificial food, **whether** it was ritually impure **sacrificial** food or ritually pure sacrificial food, is liable to receive *karet* if he did so intentionally, and to bring a sliding-scale offering if he did so unwittingly. Rabbi Yosei HaGelili says: An impure person who ate pure sacrificial food is liable. But an impure person who ate impure sacrificial food is exempt, as he merely ate an impure item, and the prohibition against eating sacrificial food while one is impure applies only to pure sacrificial food. The Rabbis said to him: According to your logic, even in a case of an impure person who ate what had been pure sacrificial food, once he has touched it, he has thereby rendered it ritually impure. Yet, in such a case, he is certainly liable for eating it. So too, an impure person who ate impure sacrificial food is liable.

שַׁפִּיר קָאָמְרִי לֵיהּ רַבָּנַן לְרַבִּי יוֹסֵי הַגְּלִילִי!

The Gemara notes: **The Rabbis are saying well to Rabbi Yosei HaGelili;** why does Rabbi Yosei HaGelili disagree?

אֲמַר רָבָא: כָּל הֵיכָא דְּנִטְמָא טוּמְאַת הַגּוּף וְאַחַר כָּךְ נִטְמָא בָּשָׂר – דְּכוּלֵּי עָלְמָא לָא פְּלִיגִי דְּחַיָּיב, שֶׁכֵּן טוּמְאַת הַגּוּף בְּכָרֵת.

Rava said in elaboration of the dispute: **Wherever** one is first **rendered impure** with **impurity of the body and** then **afterward** the sacrificial **meat is rendered impure, everyone agrees that** he is **liable** if he eats the meat. This is **because** the prohibition due to the **impurity of** one's **body,** which carries the punishment **of *karet*,** took effect while the meat was still ritually pure, and so this prohibition is not abrogated even when the meat is later rendered impure.

כִּי פְּלִיגִי – כְּשֶׁנִּטְמָא בָּשָׂר וְאַחַר כָּךְ נִטְמָא הַגּוּף,

When they disagree is in a case where first the **meat is rendered impure and** then **afterward the** person's **body is rendered impure.** In general, once an item has become subject to a prohibition, it cannot then become subject to an additional prohibition. In this case, once the meat is rendered impure, it is prohibited for anyone to eat it, even if that person is ritually pure. If that person is later rendered impure, the meat should not become subject to the additional prohibition against a ritually impure person eating sacrificial meat.

דְּרַבָּנַן סָבְרִי: אָמְרִינַן מִיגּוֹ, וְרַבִּי יוֹסֵי הַגְּלִילִי סָבַר: לָא אָמְרִינַן מִיגּוֹ.

Rava explains that Rabbi Yosei HaGelili and the Rabbis disagree as to whether this case is an exception to that principle, **as the Rabbis hold** that **we say** that **since** the prohibition due to the ritual impurity of one's body is a more inclusive prohibition, as it prohibits that person from eating all sacrificial meat, both pure and impure, it therefore takes effect also with regard to this meat, even though it was already rendered impure before the person was. **And Rabbi Yosei HaGelili says** that **we do not say** that **since** it is a more inclusive prohibition, it takes effect.

וְרַבִּי יוֹסֵי, נְהִי דְּמִיגּוֹ לָא אָמְרִינַן, תֵּיתֵי טוּמְאַת הַגּוּף דַּחֲמִירָא וְתָחוּל עַל טוּמְאַת בָּשָׂר!

The Gemara asks: **But** even according to **Rabbi Yosei** HaGelili, **granted that we do not say** that **since** it is a more inclusive prohibition it will take effect. But still, the prohibition due to the **impurity of** a person's **body, which** is **a more stringent** prohibition as it carries the punishment of *karet*, **should come**[N] **and take effect upon** the prohibition due to the **ritual impurity** of the **meat** itself, as that prohibition is less stringent as it carries only the punishment of lashes. One exception to the principle that a second prohibition does not take effect is that even if an item or person is already subject to a prohibition, a more stringent prohibition will still take effect with regard to it.

NOTES

The prohibition due to the impurity of a person's body, which is a more stringent prohibition, should come – תֵּיתֵי טוּמְאַת הַגּוּף דַּחֲמִירָא: According to the straightforward reading of the Gemara, while Rabbi Yosei HaGelili holds that a more inclusive prohibition does not take effect in addition to a more limited preexisting prohibition, he concedes that a more stringent prohibition takes effect in addition to a less stringent prohibition. This is how Rabbeinu Ḥananel interprets the Gemara.

Rashi (*Ḥullin* 101a) offers a different interpretation. He explains that Rabbi Yosei HaGelili holds that if the additional prohibition is both more inclusive and more stringent, it will take effect on the more limited and less stringent preexisting prohibition.

BACKGROUND

Ritual bath – מקוה: The Torah provides that, in certain cases, a person or item that became ritually impure may be purified by being immersed in water: "Only a spring or a pit, a collection of water, will be pure" (Leviticus 11:36). "A collection of water" refers to a stationary body of water, translated here as ritual bath. The bath must contain at least forty *se'a* of water in order to be valid. Furthermore, the water must gather by itself, and must not have been transported to its location using a vessel. In some circumstances, the presence of a small amount of drawn water in even a large bath can invalidate it. Consequently, ritual baths are usually filled directly from rainfall.

Ritual bath from the Second Temple period unearthed at Qumran

HALAKHA

One who slaughters for an ordinary purpose – השוחט להדיוט: One who slaughters an offering outside the Temple courtyard is liable even if he did not slaughter the offering for the sake of God (Rambam *Sefer Avoda, Hilkhot Ma'aseh HaKorbanot* 18:16).

One who offers up for an ordinary purpose – המעלה להדיוט: One is liable for offering up an offering outside the courtyard only if he does so for the sake of God (Rambam *Sefer Avoda, Hilkhot Ma'aseh HaKorbanot* 19:1).

Two who grasped a knife and slaughtered, etc. – שנים שאחזו בסכין ושחטו וכו׳: Two people who grasp a knife and together slaughter an offering outside the courtyard are exempt. If two grasp a limb from an offering and together offer it up outside, they are liable (Rambam *Sefer Avoda, Hilkhot Ma'aseh HaKorbanot* 18:16, 19:12).

If one unwittingly offered up part of an offering and then offered up other parts – העלה חזר והעלה: One who offered up a limb of an offering outside the Temple courtyard and then offered up another limb is liable for each limb. This *halakha* is in accordance with Rabbi Yoḥanan's understanding (108b) of Rabbi Yosei's ruling in the mishna (Rambam *Sefer Avoda, Hilkhot Ma'aseh HaKorbanot* 19:11).

Once he offers it up at the top of an altar – עד שיעלה לראש המזבח: One is liable for offering up an offering outside the courtyard only if he offered it up upon the top of an altar that was erected there, but not if he offered it up on a rock or a stone (Rambam *Sefer Avoda, Hilkhot Ma'aseh HaKorbanot* 19:1).

אמר רב אשי: ממאי דטומאת הגוף חמורה? דלמא טומאת בשר חמורה, שכן אין לה טהרה במקוה!

Rav Ashi said: From where is it apparent **that** the prohibition due to the **impurity of the** person's **body is more stringent? Perhaps** the prohibition due to the **impurity of the meat is more stringent, as** impure meat **does not have** the possibility of **purification in a ritual bath,**[B] whereas a ritually impure person does. Since the prohibition due to the person's impurity is not more stringent in every regard, it cannot take effect upon meat that is already prohibited due to its own impurity.

מתני׳ חומר בשחיטה מבעלייה, ובעלייה מבשחיטה.

MISHNA There is **a greater stringency with regard to slaughtering** outside the Temple courtyard **than with regard to offering up** outside, **and** there is a greater stringency **with regard to offering up** outside **than with regard to slaughtering** outside.

חומר בשחיטה: שהשוחט להדיוט – חייב, והמעלה להדיוט – פטור. חומר בעלייה: שנים שאחזו בסכין ושחטו – פטורין, אחזו באבר והעלו – חייבין.

The mishna elaborates: The **greater stringency with regard to slaughtering** outside is **that one who slaughters** an offering outside the Temple courtyard even **for** the sake of **an ordinary** purpose,[H] not for the sake of God, **is liable.**[N] **But one who offers up** an offering outside the courtyard **for** the sake of **an ordinary** purpose[H] is **exempt.**[N] The **greater stringency with regard to offering up** outside is that **two** people **who grasped a knife and** together **slaughtered**[H] an offering outside the courtyard are **exempt.** But if two **grasped a limb** from an offering **and** together **offered** it **up** outside, they are **liable.**

העלה, חזר והעלה, וחזר והעלה – חייב על כל עלייה, דברי רבי שמעון. רבי יוסי אומר: אינו חייב אלא אחת.

If one unwittingly **offered up** part of an offering outside the courtyard **and then** in a different lapse of awareness **offered up** other parts[H] of that offering **and then** again, in another lapse of awareness, **offered up** yet other parts, he is **liable** to bring a sin offering **for each** act of **offering up;** this is **the statement of Rabbi Shimon. Rabbi Yosei says:** He is **liable** to bring **only one** sin offering.

ואינו חייב עד שיעלה לראש המזבח, רבי שמעון אומר: אפילו העלה על הסלע או על האבן – חייב.

Rabbi Yosei adds: **And** one is **liable** for offering up an offering outside the courtyard **only once he offers** it **up at the top of an altar**[H] that was erected there. **Rabbi Shimon says: Even if he offered** it **up on a rock or on a stone,** not an altar, **he is liable.**

גמ׳ מאי שנא המעלה להדיוט דפטור – דכתיב ״לה׳״, בשחיטה נמי הכתיב ״לה׳״!

GEMARA The Gemara analyzes the first *halakha* of the mishna: **What is different** about **one who offers up** outside **for** the sake of **an ordinary** purpose, **that he is exempt? As it is written:** "And he will not bring it to the entrance of the Tent of Meeting, to sacrifice it **to the Lord**" (Leviticus 17:9), which indicates that the liability applies only to offering up for the sake of the Lord. The Gemara questions this: But **with regard to slaughtering, isn't it also written:** "Or that slaughters it outside the camp, and he did not bring it to the entrance of the Tent of Meeting to sacrifice an offering **to the Lord**" (Leviticus 17:3–4)?

NOTES

One who slaughters outside for an ordinary purpose is liable – השוחט להדיוט חייב: Some commentaries explain that the intention is with regard to one who slaughters an offering in an act of idol worship (commentary attributed to Ra'avad on *Torat Kohanim*). Rashi explains that the reference is even to one who slaughters an offering in order that a person eat its meat. By contrast, the Rambam emphasizes that the key issue is not the purpose it was slaughtered for; rather, what matters is that it was not specifically slaughtered for the sake of God. This opinion of the Rambam's mirrors his ruling with regard to offering up outside the Temple. There he rules that one is liable only if he offers up an offering with the explicit intention that it be for the sake of God. Although when offering up inside the Temple, the offering is valid even if one fails to have any intention, that is because within the context of the Temple all offerings are presumed to be offered to God. Outside the Temple, no such presumption can be made and therefore in order to be liable one's intention must be clear (*Minḥat Ḥinnukh* 440).

One who offers up outside for an ordinary purpose is exempt – המעלה להדיוט פטור: Even though Rashi explains that the case of one who slaughters an offering for the sake of an ordinary purpose refers to a case where the animal was slaughtered for its meat, with regard to offering up outside for an ordinary purpose, Rashi writes that it refers specifically to an act of idol worship. Apparently, the reason for this distinction is that simply placing an animal upon an altar for an ordinary purpose cannot be regarded as an act of offering up that parallels what is done inside the Temple. Therefore, it cannot carry any liability (see *Sefat Emet*). Accordingly, one who unwittingly offered up an offering to an idol outside the Temple, even though he is not liable to bring a sin offering for offering up outside the Temple, as the Gemara derives elsewhere, would be liable to bring a sin offering for the unwitting act of idol worship (see *Tosafot*).

שָׁאנֵי הָתָם, דְּאָמַר קְרָא: "אִישׁ אִישׁ". גַּבֵּי הַעֲלָאָה נַמִּי כְּתִיב: "אִישׁ אִישׁ"! מִיבָּעֵי לֵיהּ לִשְׁנַיִם שֶׁהֶעֱלוּ בְּאֵבֶר – חַיָּיבִין.

The Gemara explains: It is **different there,** with regard to slaughtering, **as the verse states: "Any man** [*ish ish*] of the house of Israel…that slaughters it outside the camp" (Leviticus 17:3). The amplification indicated by the phrase "*ish ish*" teaches that one is liable even for slaughtering for the sake of an ordinary purpose. The Gemara challenges: But **also with regard to offering up it is written: "Any man** [*ish ish*] of the house of Israel…that offers up a burnt offering" (Leviticus 17:8). The Gemara explains: **That** amplification **is necessary to** teach that **two people who offered up a limb** of an offering together outside the courtyard are **liable.**

אִי הָכִי, הָכָא נַמִּי מִיבָּעֵי לֵיהּ לִשְׁנַיִם שֶׁאָחֲזוּ בְּסַכִּין וְשָׁחֲטוּ שֶׁחַיָּיבִין! שָׁאנֵי הָתָם, דְּאָמַר קְרָא: "הַהוּא" – אֶחָד וְלֹא שְׁנַיִם.

The Gemara asks: **If so, here too,** with regard to slaughtering, the phrase "*ish ish*" **should be** used **to** teach that **two** people **who grasped a knife and** together **slaughtered** an offering outside the courtyard are **liable,** contrary to the ruling of the mishna. Why are the two parallel phrases expounded in different ways? The Gemara explains: **It is different there,** with regard to slaughtering, **as the verse states:** "And **that** man shall be cut off from among his people" (Leviticus 17:4). The term "that man," which is in the singular, indicates that only **one** who acts alone is liable, **but not two** who act together.

אִי הָכִי, גַּבֵּי הַעֲלָאָה נַמִּי, הָא כְּתִיב: "הַהוּא"! מִיבָּעֵי לֵיהּ

The Gemara challenges: But **if so, also with regard to offering up, isn't it written: "That** man shall be cut off from his people" (Leviticus 17:9)? Why isn't that term also expounded to teach that only one who acts alone is liable? The Gemara explains: **That** term **is necessary**

Perek **XIII**
Daf **108** Amud **b**

לְמַעוּטֵי שׁוֹגֵג, אָנוּס וּמוּטְעֶה. אִי הָכִי, הָכָא נַמִּי מִיבָּעֵי לְמַעוּטֵי אָנוּס שׁוֹגֵג וּמוּטְעֶה!

to exclude from the liability for *karet* one whose violation was **unwitting,**[N] or who was **compelled to act, or** who was **mistaken.**[N] The term "that man" teaches that only one who offered up with intent is liable to receive *karet*. The Gemara challenges: **If so, here too,** with regard to slaughtering outside, the term is **necessary to exclude** one whose violation was **unwitting,** or who was **compelled to act, or** who was **mistaken.** How can the term be used to teach that only one who acts alone is liable?

תְּרֵי "הַהוּא" כְּתִיבִי.

The Gemara explains: With regard to slaughtering outside, **two** instances of the term **"that** man" **are written:** "Blood shall be imputed to that man, he has shed blood, and that man shall be cut off from among his people" (Leviticus 17:4). One instance teaches that only one who acts with intent is liable to receive *karet*, and the other teaches that only one who acts alone is liable.

NOTES

To exclude one whose violation was unwitting – לְמַעוּטֵי שׁוֹגֵג: The term "that man" (Leviticus 17:9) is understood to be referring to a person in his standard state, i.e., with full awareness and who performs acts intentionally.

Or who was mistaken – וּמוּטְעֶה: The early commentaries discuss the difference between one who acts unwittingly and one who is mistaken. Rashi explains that acting unwittingly refers to a case where the person himself misreads the situation, while being mistaken refers to a case where others gave him misinformation, i.e., he was misled. Rabbi Shimshon of Saens explains that if one transgresses because he misunderstood the facts of the case, then he is considered to be unwitting, but if he misunderstood the *halakha*, he is considered mistaken. A third possible distinction is offered by the Meiri. If one does not realize the severity of a transgression and thinks that he will not be liable to bring an offering for transgressing, he is considered to be unwitting, but if he thinks that the act is entirely permitted then he is called mistaken.

וְאֶלָּא "לַה'" לָמָּה לִי? לְהוֹצִיא שָׂעִיר הַמִּשְׁתַּלֵּחַ.

The Gemara has now justified its claim that the liability of one who slaughters an offering outside for the sake of an ordinary purpose is derived from the phrase "*ish ish*." Accordingly, the Gemara asks: **But why do I need** the term **"to the Lord"?** The Gemara explains: It is written **to exclude** from liability one who slaughters the Yom Kippur **scapegoat**[BH] outside the courtyard.

"חוֹמֶר בְּהַעֲלָאָה" כו'.

§ The mishna teaches: The **greater stringency** with regard to **offering up** outside is that two people who grasped a knife and together slaughtered an offering outside the courtyard are exempt. But if two grasped a limb from an offering and together offered it up outside, they are liable.

תָּנוּ רַבָּנַן: "אִישׁ אִישׁ" מַה תַּלְמוּד לוֹמַר? שְׁנַיִם שֶׁאָחֲזוּ בְּאֵבֶר וְהֶעֱלוּ – שֶׁחַיָּיבִין. שֶׁיָּכוֹל, וַהֲלֹא דִּין הוּא: וּמַה הַשּׁוֹחֵט לְהֶדְיוֹט שֶׁחַיָּיב, שְׁנַיִם שֶׁאָחֲזוּ בְּסַכִּין וְשָׁחֲטוּ – פְּטוּרִין. הַמַּעֲלֶה לְהֶדְיוֹט שֶׁפָּטוּר – אֵינוֹ דִּין שֶׁשְּׁנַיִם שֶׁאָחֲזוּ פְּטוּרִין? תַּלְמוּד לוֹמַר: "אִישׁ אִישׁ", דִּבְרֵי רַבִּי שִׁמְעוֹן.

The Sages taught in a *baraita*: **What** *halakha* is alluded to when **the verse states: "Any man** [*ish ish*] **...** that offers up a burnt offering or sacrifice" (Leviticus 17:8)? The verse teaches that **two people who grasped a limb** of an offering **and offered** it **up** together outside the courtyard are **liable.** It is necessary for the verse to teach this, **as one might** have thought to say: **Could this not be** derived through an *a fortiori* **inference: If** with regard to slaughtering outside the courtyard, **one who slaughters for** the sake of **an ordinary** purpose is **liable,** and nevertheless, **two who grasped a knife and** together **slaughtered** an offering are **exempt,** then with regard to offering up outside the courtyard, where **one who offers up for** the sake of **an ordinary** purpose is **exempt, is it not logical that two who grasped** a limb and offered it up will also be **exempt?** To counter this, **the verse states "*ish ish*"** to teach that they are liable for offering up together; this is **the statement of Rabbi Shimon.**

רַבִּי יוֹסֵי אוֹמֵר: "הַהוּא" – אֶחָד וְלֹא שְׁנַיִם. אִם כֵּן, מַה תַּלְמוּד לוֹמַר "אִישׁ אִישׁ"? דִּבְּרָה תוֹרָה כִּלְשׁוֹן בְּנֵי אָדָם.

Rabbi Yosei says that the *halakha* concerning this case is derived from a different verse. The term **"that** [*hahu*] man" (Leviticus 17:9), which is in the singular, indicates that only **one** who acts alone is liable, **but not two** who act together. The *baraita* asks: **If so, what** *halakha* is alluded to when **the verse states "*ish ish*"?** The *baraita* explains: Rabbi Yosei holds that the reason the Torah uses the doubled term "*ish ish*" is that **the Torah spoke in the language of people,**[B] and no *halakhot* are to be derived from it.

וְרַבִּי שִׁמְעוֹן? הַאי "הַהוּא" מִיבָּעֵי לֵיהּ לְמַעוּטֵי שׁוֹגֵג אָנוּס מוּטְעֶה. וְרַבִּי יוֹסֵי: מֵ"הוּא" "הַהוּא". וְרַבִּי שִׁמְעוֹן: "הוּא" "הַהוּא" לָא דָּרֵישׁ.

The Gemara asks: **And Rabbi Shimon,** what does he derive from the term "that man"? The Gemara explains: **This** term: **"That** man," **is necessary to exclude** from liability one whose violation was **unwitting,** or who was **compelled to act, or** who was **mistaken.** The Gemara notes: **And Rabbi Yosei** derives that *halakha* **from** the fact that the verse could have stated ***hu*** and instead stated **"*hahu*."** The Hebrew word for: That, *hahu*, is formed of the definite article *ha* and the pronoun *hu*. **And Rabbi Shimon does not expound** any *halakhot* **from** the fact that the verse could have stated ***hu*** and instead stated **"*hahu*."** He holds that the expanded form is used because the Torah spoke in the language of people.

BACKGROUND

Scapegoat – שָׂעִיר הַמִּשְׁתַּלֵּחַ: The Torah requires that on Yom Kippur lots be drawn concerning two goats, one to be sacrificed as a sin offering in the Temple, and one to be used as the scapegoat and sent to Azazel (see Leviticus, chapter 16). The latter was ultimately thrown from a high cliff some 12 to 15 km from Jerusalem. Before sending the goat to its death, the High Priest would burden it with all the sins of the Jewish people, including their intentional and unwitting violations. This was done via the High Priest placing his hands on the animal's head and confessing the Jewish people's sins. During the confession the High Priest pronounced the name of God three times, leading all present to fall down to the ground in reverence. Afterward, he sent the goat to the desert with a person specifically designated for this task. A strip of crimson that had earlier been tied to the goat's horns was removed and the goat was pushed off the cliff. It was hoped that this thread would miraculously turn white, indicating that God had forgiven the nation's sins. The service associated with this goat, an essential part of the Yom Kippur ritual, atoned for sins not atoned for by any other offering.

Scapegoat at the top of the cliff

The Torah spoke in the language of people – דִּבְּרָה תוֹרָה כִּלְשׁוֹן בְּנֵי אָדָם: Although phrased as a comprehensive principle, this concept is applied in only very specific cases. Frequently, doubled verbs are used in the Torah to provide an emphatic effect. According to Rabbi Yishmael they have no exegetical significance as the doubling of a verb is simply a linguistic form of emphasis, or in the words of the Talmud: The Torah spoke in the language of people. By contrast, Rabbi Akiva saw these forms as superfluous and drew halakhic inferences from them. Although the principle is used is a very limited way by the Gemara, early commentaries broadened its application to explain such phenomena as the anthropomorphic expressions referring to God in the Torah.

HALAKHA

To exclude the scapegoat – לְהוֹצִיא שָׂעִיר הַמִּשְׁתַּלֵּחַ: With regard to the two goats of the Yom Kippur service that were slaughtered unlawfully outside the Temple courtyard, if they were slaughtered before the High Priest had made his confession upon the scapegoat, then liability is incurred for each of them. This is because at that point, either goat could potentially serve as a sin offering inside the Temple. After the confession, liability is incurred only for the goat that is designated to be brought as a sin offering, but not for the one that will be sent away as the scapegoat, which can no longer serve as a sin offering inside the Temple. This is in accordance with the ruling of the Rambam. The Ra'avad holds that the critical factor is not the confession of the High Priest; rather, it is the lottery, as this determines what each goat will be used for. This is also the opinion of Rashi and *Tosafot* (Rambam *Sefer Avoda*, *Hilkhot Ma'aseh HaKorbanot* 18:1, 19:7).

וְרַבִּי יוֹסֵי, מִדְּהַאי "אִישׁ אִישׁ" דִּבְּרָה תּוֹרָה כִּלְשׁוֹן בְּנֵי אָדָם, הַהוּא "אִישׁ אִישׁ" נַמִּי דִּבְּרָה תּוֹרָה כִּלְשׁוֹן בְּנֵי אָדָם, וְאֶלָּא הַשּׁוֹחֵט לְהֶדְיוֹט מְנָא לֵיהּ דְּחַיָּיב? נָפְקָא לֵיהּ מִ"דָּם יֵחָשֵׁב לָאִישׁ הַהוּא דָּם שָׁפָךְ" – וַאֲפִילּוּ הַשּׁוֹחֵט לָאִישׁ.

The Gemara asks: **And as for Rabbi Yosei, from the fact that** he holds that nothing is to be derived from the phrase **"*ish ish*"** written with regard to offering up, as he holds that **the Torah spoke in the language of people,** then **also** with regard to **that** phrase: "**Any man** [*ish ish*]" (Leviticus 17:3), written with regard to slaughtering, since he holds that **the Torah spoke in the language of people,** he should not derive any *halakhot* from it. **But** if so, **from where** does he derive **that one who slaughters** outside **for** the sake of **an ordinary** purpose is **liable?** The Gemara answers: **He derives it from** the verse: **"Blood shall be imputed to that man;**[N] **he has shed blood"** (Leviticus 17:4), which teaches that **even one who slaughters for** the sake of an ordinary **man** is liable.

"הֶעֱלָה וְחָזַר וְהֶעֱלָה" כו׳.

§ The mishna teaches: If one unwittingly **offered up** part of an offering outside the courtyard **and then** in a different lapse of awareness **offered up** other parts[H] of that offering and then again, in another lapse of awareness, offered up yet other parts, he is liable to bring a sin offering for each act of offering up; this is the statement of Rabbi Shimon. Rabbi Yosei says: He is liable to bring only one sin offering.

אָמַר רֵישׁ לָקִישׁ: מַחְלוֹקֶת בְּאַרְבָּעָה וַחֲמִשָּׁה אֵבָרִים, דְּמָר סָבַר: כִּי כְּתִיב "לַעֲשׂוֹת אֹתוֹ", עַל הַשָּׁלֵם הוּא חַיָּיב וְאֵינוֹ חַיָּיב עַל הֶחָסֵר – אַכּוֹל בְּהֵמָה כְּתִיב. וּמָר סָבַר: אַכָּל אֵבֶר וְאֵבֶר כְּתִיב. אֲבָל אֵבֶר אֶחָד – דִּבְרֵי הַכֹּל אֵינוֹ חַיָּיב אֶלָּא אַחַת.

The Gemara cites two opinions concerning the case under dispute. **Reish Lakish says:** The **dispute** in the mishna **concerns four or five limbs** that were offered up in different lapses of awareness. **As** one **Sage,** Rabbi Yosei, **holds: When it is written: "To sacrifice it"** (Leviticus 17:9), which teaches the *halakha* that **for** offering up **a complete** item one is **liable but** that one is **not liable for** offering up **an incomplete** item, **it is written with regard to a whole animal.**[N] Accordingly, liability to bring a sin offering is incurred only once one offers up the entire animal, even if that was done limb by limb. **And the other Sage,** Rabbi Shimon, **holds** that that verse **is written with regard to each and every limb** of an animal. Accordingly, one is liable for each limb he offered up. **But** with regard to the offering up of **one limb** in parts, **everyone agrees**[N] that a person is **liable** to bring **only one** sin offering. According to Rabbi Shimon this would apply even if that were the only limb that was offered up; according to Rabbi Yosei this would apply only if the rest of the animal had already been offered up.

HALAKHA

One offered up part and then offered up other parts – הֶעֱלָה וְחָזַר וְהֶעֱלָה: If one unwittingly offered up a limb of an offering outside the courtyard and then in a different lapse of awareness offered up another limb, he is liable for each limb. But if one offered up an incomplete limb, he is exempt. This is in accordance with Rabbi Yoḥanan's understanding of Rabbi Yosei's opinion (Rambam *Sefer Avoda, Hilkhot Ma'aseh HaKorbanot* 19:11, and see Ra'avad and commentaries there).

NOTES

From the verse: Blood shall be imputed to that man, etc. – מִדָּם יֵחָשֵׁב לָאִישׁ הַהוּא וכו׳: The Rambam offers two different explanations as to how this *halakha* is derived from the verse. In Rambam's Commentary on the Mishna he explains that the verse "Blood shall be imputed to that man" should be read as though it says: Blood shall be imputed even for one who slaughters for a man. In *Mishne Torah* (*Sefer Avoda, Hilkhot Ma'aseh HaKorbanot* 18:16), he offers a different interpretation, explaining that the verse should be understood as teaching: Although that man, i.e., the one who slaughtered the animal, considers it merely an act of spilling blood since he slaughtered it for an ordinary purpose, not intending for it to be an offering, he is nevertheless liable for his action, as stated by the continuation of the verse: "And that man shall be cut off from among his people."

It is written with regard to a whole animal – אַכּוֹל בְּהֵמָה כְּתִיב: Rashi explains that according to Reish Lakish, Rabbi Yosei holds that one is liable only if he offers up an entire animal. Although Reish Lakish speaks of four or five limbs, the intention is that those constitute all the limbs of the entire animal. The later commentaries question this explanation. They claim that even if ultimately all the animal's limbs are offered up, each act should be considered distinct from the others and they should not combine to render one liable, because each limb was offered up during a different lapse of awareness (see *Ḥok Natan*, *Keren Ora*, and *Zevaḥ Toda*). Avoiding this difficulty, *Tosafot* explain that Rabbi Yosei does not require that the entire animal be offered up in order to render one liable. Rather, he holds that one is liable even for a single limb, but only if it is taken from a complete animal. Accordingly, one is liable only for the first limb that is taken and offered up.

But with regard to one limb everyone agrees – אֲבָל אֵבֶר אֶחָד דִּבְרֵי הַכֹּל: According to Rashi, Rabbi Yosei holds that one is liable only once the entire animal has been offered up, and Rabbi Shimon holds that one is liable only once an entire limb has been offered up. Therefore, Rashi explains that the case in which all agree is where all but one of the limbs of an animal were already offered up and then the last limb was offered up in parts. In such a case, all will agree that one is liable only once that entire limb, and thereby the entire animal, has been offered up.

Tosafot disagree with Rashi's explanation of both opinions. They claim that Rabbi Yosei and Rabbi Shimon agree that one can be liable for offering up even a single olive-bulk, and they both agree that in order to be liable, that olive-bulk must be taken from a complete entity. According to Rabbi Yosei, it must be taken from a complete animal, while according to Rabbi Shimon, it must be taken from a complete limb. Therefore, they explain that the case in which all agree is where an olive-bulk was taken from a limb of a complete animal and then the rest of that limb was also offered up. Accordingly, all agree that one is liable for the first olive-bulk. With regard to the second olive-bulk, since the animal and the limb were both incomplete by the time it was taken, all agree that one is no longer liable for offering it up (see *Panim Meirot*).

Rabbeinu Ḥananel offers an entirely different explanation. He explains that the case is where the same limb was offered up multiple times; all agree that one is liable to bring only one sin offering.

וְרַבִּי יוֹחָנָן אָמַר: מַחֲלוֹקֶת בְּאֵבָר אֶחָד, דְּמָר סָבַר: מוּקְטְרֵי פְּנִים שֶׁחָסְרוּ וְהֶעֱלָה בַּחוּץ – חַיָּיב, וּמָר סָבַר: פָּטוּר. אֲבָל בְּאַרְבָּעָה וַחֲמִשָּׁה אֵיבָרִין – דִּבְרֵי הַכֹּל חַיָּיב עַל כָּל אֵבֶר וְאֵבֶר.

And Rabbi Yoḥanan says: Everyone agrees that one is liable even for offering up a single limb. Furthermore, if an offering is slaughtered outside the courtyard, everyone agrees that one is liable only once an entire limb has been offered up. The **dispute** in the mishna **concerns one limb**[N] from an offering that was slaughtered inside the courtyard that was then taken outside and offered up in parts, during different lapses of awareness. **As** one **Sage,** Rabbi Shimon, **holds** that for offerings **that are** fit to be **burned inside** the Temple, **that became incomplete and were** instead **offered up outside** the Temple, one is **liable.** Accordingly, one is liable for each part of the limb. **And** the other **Sage,** Rabbi Yosei, **holds** that one is **exempt** for offering up part of a limb outside the courtyard. Accordingly, liability is incurred only once all the parts of the limb have been offered up. **But with regard to** offering up **four or five limbs, everyone agrees** that one is **liable for each and every limb,** as they understand that the phrase "to sacrifice it" is written with regard to each and every limb.

וּפְלִיגָא דְּעוּלָּא, דְּאָמַר עוּלָּא: הַכֹּל מוֹדִים בְּמוּקְטְרֵי פְּנִים שֶׁחָסְרוּ וְהֶעֱלוּ בַּחוּץ – שֶׁחַיָּיב, לֹא נֶחְלְקוּ אֶלָּא בְּמוּקְטְרֵי בַּחוּץ שֶׁחָסְרוּ וְהֶעֱלוּ בַּחוּץ, דְּמָר סָבַר: פָּטוּר, וּמָר סָבַר: חַיָּיב.

And Rabbi Yoḥanan **disagrees** with the opinion **of Ulla, as Ulla says: Everyone** in the mishna **concedes with regard to** offerings **that are** fit to be **burned inside**[N] the Temple courtyard **that became incomplete and were** instead **offered up outside** the courtyard, **that** one is **liable. They disagree only with regard to** offerings that, having been slaughtered outside **are** unfit and so will be **burned outside, that became incomplete and were offered up outside. As** one **Sage,** Rabbi Yosei, **holds** that one is **exempt, and** the other **Sage,** Rabbi Shimon, **holds** that one is **liable.**

אִיכָּא דְּאָמְרִי, אָמַר עוּלָּא: הַכֹּל מוֹדִים בְּמוּקְטְרֵי חוּץ שֶׁחָסְרוּ וְהֶעֱלוּ בַּחוּץ – שֶׁהוּא פָּטוּר. לֹא נֶחְלְקוּ אֶלָּא בְּמוּקְטְרֵי פְּנִים שֶׁחָסְרוּ וְהֶעֱלוּ בַּחוּץ, דְּמָר סָבַר פָּטוּר וּמָר סָבַר חַיָּיב.

There are those **who say** there is a different version of Ulla's statement, according to which he agrees with his teacher, Rabbi Yoḥanan. **Ulla says: Everyone** in the mishna **concedes with regard to** offerings that, having been slaughtered outside the Temple **are** unfit and so will be **burned outside, that became incomplete and were offered up outside, that one is exempt. They disagree only with regard to** offerings **that are** fit to be **burned inside that became incomplete and were** instead **offered up outside. As one Sage,** Rabbi Yosei, **holds** that one is **exempt, and** the other **Sage,** Rabbi Shimon, **holds** that one is **liable.**

וּפְלִיגֵי דַּאֲבוּהּ דִּשְׁמוּאֵל אַלִּישָּׁנָא קַמָּא דְּעוּלָּא, דְּאָמַר אֲבוּהּ דִּשְׁמוּאֵל: כְּמַאן מְהַדְּרִינַן פּוֹקְעִין לְגַבֵּי מִזְבֵּחַ? כְּמַאן – דְּלָא כְּרַבִּי יוֹסֵי.

And the statement **of Shmuel's father disagrees with the first version of Ulla's** statement, **as Shmuel's father says: In accordance with whose** opinion **do we restore** limbs **that were dislodged** from upon the altar **to the altar? In accordance with whose** opinion? It is **not in accordance with** the opinion of **Rabbi Yosei** recorded in the mishna. Shmuel's father assumes that Rabbi Yosei holds that incomplete limbs are never offered up on the altar, even if they were dislodged from the altar. Accordingly, he holds that one is not liable for offering them up outside the Temple courtyard. This is contrary to the first version of Ulla's opinion, according to which one is liable for offering up incomplete offerings that were slaughtered inside the courtyard. Evidently, Ulla holds that an incomplete limb that was dislodged from the altar is to be restored to the altar.

NOTES

And Rabbi Yoḥanan says: The dispute concerns one limb – **וְרַבִּי יוֹחָנָן אָמַר מַחֲלוֹקֶת בְּאֵבָר אֶחָד:** According to Rabbi Yoḥanan, everyone agrees that there are cases in which one is exempt if he offered up an incomplete limb. According to Rabbi Yosei, one is always exempt, whereas according to Rabbi Shimon one is exempt only if the offering was also slaughtered outside the courtyard. Where an offering was slaughtered inside the Temple, Rabbi Shimon holds that one is liable, because he compares it to the case of a limb of a fit offering that was dislodged from upon the altar. In that case, the limb, despite being incomplete, is returned to the altar. Similarly, whenever a limb is taken from an otherwise fit offering, one is liable for offering it up outside even if it is incomplete. Rabbi Yosei disagrees with Rabbi Shimon here because he also disagrees with him with regard to a limb that was dislodged from upon the altar. He holds that an incomplete limb is never restored to the altar.

Rashi notes that according to Rabbi Yoḥanan, the dispute between Rabbi Yosei and Rabbi Shimon is the same as the one between Rabbi Akiva and Rabbi Yishmael cited by the Gemara earlier (107a).

Rabbeinu Ḥananel, consistent with his explanation of the previous lines of the Gemara, explains that the dispute is with regard to a case where the same limb was offered up multiple times. Since after the first time the limb is already somewhat incomplete, Rabbi Yosei holds that one is liable only for the first time, whereas Rabbi Shimon holds that one is liable for each and every time. Were four of five different complete limbs to be offered up, all would agree that one is liable for each one.

Ulla says: Everyone concedes with regard to offerings that are fit to be burned inside, etc. – **אָמַר עוּלָּא הַכֹּל מוֹדִים בְּמוּקְטְרֵי פְּנִים וכו׳:** According to Ulla, both Rabbi Shimon and Rabbi Yosei agree that a limb that was dislodged from upon the altar should be restored to the altar. Furthermore, they agree that one is liable even for offering up a single limb outside the courtyard. Rabbi Yosei interprets the phrase "to sacrifice it" as teaching that one is liable only if one offered up a complete limb, whereas Rabbi Shimon holds that one is liable even for an incomplete limb. Rashi explains that Rabbi Shimon interprets that the term "to sacrifice it" does not require that the item offered up be complete, only that it be at least the volume of an olive-bulk.

״וְאֵינוֹ חַיָּיב עַד שֶׁיַּעֲלֶה״ כו׳. אָמַר רַב הוּנָא: מַאי טַעְמָא דְּרַבִּי יוֹסֵי? דִּכְתִיב: ״וַיִּבֶן נֹחַ מִזְבֵּחַ לַה׳״.	§ The mishna teaches: Rabbi Yosei says: **And** one is **liable** for offering up an offering outside the courtyard **only once he offers** it **up** upon the top of an altar that was erected there. Rabbi Shimon says: Even if he offered it up on a rock or on a stone, not an altar, he is liable. **Rav Huna says: What is the reason of Rabbi Yosei? As it is written: "And Noah built an altar to the Lord,**[H] and took of every pure animal, and of every pure bird, and offered up burnt offerings on the altar" (Genesis 8:20). Noah was particular to use an altar rather than one of the available rocks. Apparently, this was because placing an item upon an altar is the only act that can be considered offering up.
אֲמַר רַבִּי יוֹחָנָן: מַאי טַעְמָא דְּרַבִּי שִׁמְעוֹן? דִּכְתִיב: ״וַיִּקַּח מָנוֹחַ אֶת גְּדִי הָעִזִּים וְאֶת הַמִּנְחָה וַיַּעַל עַל הַצּוּר לַה׳״.	**Rabbi Yoḥanan said: What is the reason of Rabbi Shimon? As it is written: "And Manoah took the kid with the meal offering, and offered it up upon the rock, to the Lord"** (Judges 13:19). Evidently, even placing an offering upon a rock is considered an act of offering up.
וְאִידָךְ נַמִי, וְהָכְתִיב ״וַיִּבֶן מִזְבֵּחַ לַה׳״! הַהוּא גּוֹבַהּ בְּעָלְמָא. וְאִידָךְ נַמִי, הָא כְּתִיב ״וַיִּקַּח מָנוֹחַ״! הוֹרָאַת שָׁעָה הָיְתָה.	The Gemara explains how each *tanna* interprets the verse that supports the other. **But also** according to **the other** opinion, Rabbi Shimon's, **isn't it written: "And Noah built an altar to the Lord"?** How does he explain that verse? The Gemara answers: **That** verse is referring **merely** to **an elevated place** and not specifically to an altar. **But also** according to **the other** opinion, Rabbi Yosei's, **isn't it written: "And Manoah took**…and offered it up upon the rock"? How does he explain that verse? The Gemara answers: The use of a rock in **that** case **was a provisional edict**[NB] issued in exigent circumstances, by the angel who visited Manoah, and so one cannot derive normative *halakha* from it.
וְאִיבָּעֵית אֵימָא: הַיְינוּ טַעְמָא דְּרַבִּי שִׁמְעוֹן – כִּדְתַנְיָא, רַבִּי שִׁמְעוֹן אוֹמֵר: ״מִזְבַּח פֶּתַח אֹהֶל מוֹעֵד״ וְאֵין מִזְבֵּחַ בְּבָמָה. לְפִיכָךְ, הֶעֱלָה עַל הַסֶּלַע אוֹ עַל הָאֶבֶן – חַיָּיב;	**And if you wish, say** instead that **the reason of Rabbi Shimon is as it is taught** in a *baraita*: **Rabbi Shimon says** that the verse states: "And the priest shall sprinkle the blood upon the **altar** of the Lord **at the entrance of the Tent of Meeting**" (Leviticus 17:6). From here it is apparent that only in the Sanctuary is there a requirement for an altar, **but** a specifically erected **altar is not** required in order to offer up **on** a private **altar** during periods when it is permitted to do so. **Therefore, one who offered up** outside the courtyard **on a rock or on a stone** is **liable.**
״יָצָא״ מִיבְּעֵי לֵיהּ! הָכִי קָאָמַר: לְפִיכָךְ בִּשְׁעַת אִיסּוּר הַבָּמוֹת הֶעֱלָה עַל הַסֶּלַע אוֹ עַל הָאֶבֶן – חַיָּיב.	The Gemara questions the formulation of the *baraita*: If the *baraita* was referring to offering up during a period when the use of private altars is permitted, it **should have** concluded: One who offered up outside on a rock or on a stone has **fulfilled** his obligation. Why does it state instead that he is liable? The Gemara explains: **This** is what the *baraita* **is saying:** Since there is no requirement for a specifically erected altar during a period when private altars are permitted, **therefore, during a period when** the use of private **altars is prohibited,** one who **offers up** outside **on a rock or on a stone** is **liable.**
בָּעֵי רַבִּי יוֹסֵי בְּרַבִּי חֲנִינָא: קֶרֶן וְכֶבֶשׁ וִיסוֹד וְרִיבּוּעַ, מַהוּ שֶׁיְּעַכְּבוּ בְּבָמָה?	**Rabbi Yosei, son of Rabbi Ḥanina, raises a dilemma:** Features that are indispensable with regard to the altar in the Temple are the **corner,** the **ramp** leading to the altar, the **base** of the altar, **and** the **square shape. What is** the *halakha* with regard to **whether they are** also **indispensable for** the validity of a private **altar** during a period when it is permitted to use private altars?
אֲמַר לֵיהּ רַבִּי יִרְמְיָה: תַּנְיָא, קֶרֶן וְכֶבֶשׁ וְרִיבּוּעַ וִיסוֹד מְעַכְּבִין בְּבָמָה גְּדוֹלָה, וְאֵין מְעַכְּבִין בְּבָמָה קְטַנָּה.	**Rabbi Yirmeya said to him: It is taught** in a *baraita*: **The corner,** the **ramp,** the **square shape, and** the **base** are all **indispensable for** the validity of a **great** public **altar,**[N] **but they are not indispensable for** the validity of **a small** private **altar.**

HALAKHA

And Noah built an altar to the Lord – וַיִּבֶן נֹחַ מִזְבֵּחַ לַה׳: One who offers up an offering outside the courtyard is liable only if he does so on top of an altar. If one offers up upon a rock or a stone he is exempt, as only offering up upon an altar is considered to be a sacrificial act, as it states: "And Noah built an altar to the Lord." This is in accordance with the opinion of Rabbi Yosei (Rambam *Sefer Avoda*, *Hilkhot Ma'aseh HaKorbanot* 19:1).

NOTES

That case was a provisional edict – הוֹרָאַת שָׁעָה הָיְתָה: During Manoah's lifetime, the Tabernacle was located in Shiloh. Rabbi Yosei holds that it was prohibited to use private altars while the Tabernacle stood in Shiloh, and that in any event the actions of Manoah must have been due to a provisional edict issued by the angel. Accordingly, he explains that the use of a rock was also part of that provisional edict, and so its use does not demonstrate whether or not it is normally required to use an altar. Rabbi Shimon disagrees; he holds that it was permitted to have private altars while the Tabernacle stood in Shiloh (see 119b). Accordingly, there was no need for a provisional edict to permit Manoah to use an altar, and it is reasonable to assume that the use of a rock was not due to a provisional edict either.

The Gemara goes on to offer an alternative explanation of Rabbi Shimon's opinion, according to which he does not derive his opinion from Manoah's use of a rock. Apparently, that alternative explanation follows the opinion in the Gemara (119b) that even Rabbi Shimon agrees that private altars were prohibited while the Tabernacle stood in Shiloh and that the use of an altar would be due to a provisional edict. Therefore, no normative *halakha* can be derived from Manoah's actions (*Yad David*; *Keren Ora*).

Great public altar – בָּמָה גְּדוֹלָה: A great altar is an altar that is erected for the sake of the public. Just like a private altar, it was permitted for use only when there was no established Tabernacle or Temple. The Gemara delineates precisely when such altars were permitted and when they were not. The first public altar was established in Gilgal when the Jewish people first entered Eretz Yisrael under the leadership of Joshua. Later, following the destruction of the Tabernacle in Shiloh, another one was established in Nov and then in Gibeon (see 113a and 119b).

Tabernacle in Shiloh

BACKGROUND

Provisional edict – הוֹרָאַת שָׁעָה: This concept explains numerous incidents described in the Torah that do not conform to normative halakhic guidelines. In these instances, a command was given as a temporary measure. Since the command was issued specifically with regard to the situation it was given for, normative *halakha* cannot be derived from it. There are also some examples of provisional edicts instituted by the Sages when the unique needs of the time required acting more leniently or more strictly than the *halakha* generally allows or requires. The principle derived from the verse: "It is time to act for the Lord; they have made void Your law" (Psalms 119:126), dictates that at times even Torah law may be violated when broader Torah values are at stake.

מתני׳ אֶחָד קָדָשִׁים כְּשֵׁרִין, וְאֶחָד קָדָשִׁים פְּסוּלִין שֶׁהָיָה פְּסוּלָן בַּקּוֹדֶשׁ, וְהִקְרִיבָן בַּחוּץ – חַיָּיב.

MISHNA With regard to **both fit sacrificial** animals, **and unfit sacrificial** animals **whose disqualification occurred in sanctity,**[NH] i.e., in the course of the Temple service, **and one sacrificed them outside** the Temple courtyard, he is **liable.**

הַמַּעֲלֶה כַּזַּיִת מִן הָעוֹלָה וּמִן הָאֵימוּרִין בַּחוּץ – חַיָּיב.

One who offers up outside the courtyard **an olive-bulk** made up of the flesh of **a burnt offering and of** its **sacrificial portions**[NH] **is liable.**

גמ׳ תָּנוּ רַבָּנַן: ״אֲשֶׁר יַעֲלֶה עֹלָה אוֹ זָבַח״, אֵין לִי אֶלָּא עוֹלָה, מִנַּיִן לְרַבּוֹת אֵימוּרֵי אָשָׁם, וְאֵימוּרֵי חַטָּאת, וְאֵימוּרֵי קָדְשֵׁי קָדָשִׁים, וְאֵימוּרֵי קָדָשִׁים קַלִּים? תַּלְמוּד לוֹמַר ״זָבַח״.

GEMARA **The Sages taught** in a *baraita*: The verse states with regard to offering up outside the courtyard: **"That offers up a burnt offering or sacrifice,**[H] and he will not bring it to the entrance of the Tent of Meeting, to sacrifice it to the Lord" (Leviticus 17:8–9). From the term "burnt offering" **I have** derived **only** that one is liable for offering up a **burnt offering,** which is burned entirely on the altar. **From where** do I derive **to include** that one is liable for offering up outside the courtyard **the sacrificial portions of a guilt offering,**[N] **the sacrificial portions of a sin offering, the sacrificial portions of offerings of the most sacred order,**[N] **or the sacrificial portions of offerings of lesser sanctity? The verse states: "Sacrifice,"** which includes the sacrificial portions of all other offerings that are to be burned on the altar.

מִנַּיִן לְרַבּוֹת הַקּוֹמֶץ, וְהַלְּבוֹנָה, וְהַקְּטוֹרֶת, וּמִנְחַת כֹּהֲנִים, וּמִנְחַת כֹּהֵן מָשִׁיחַ, וְהַמְנַסֵּךְ שְׁלֹשֶׁת לוּגִּין יַיִן וּשְׁלֹשֶׁת לוּגִּין מַיִם? תַּלְמוּד לוֹמַר: ״וְאֶל פֶּתַח אֹהֶל מוֹעֵד לֹא יְבִיאֶנּוּ״, כֹּל הַבָּא לְפֶתַח אֹהֶל מוֹעֵד – חַיָּיבִין עָלָיו בַּחוּץ.

From where is it derived **to include** that one is liable for offering up outside the courtyard **the handful** taken from a meal offering; **the frankincense** that was to be offered with it; **the incense,** which was offered each day in the Sanctuary; **the meal offering of priests; the meal offering of the anointed priest,** i.e., the High Priest, which he offered daily; **and** to include as liable **one who pours as a libation three** *log* **of wine,** which is the volume of the smallest wine libation used in the Temple; **or** one who pours as a libation **three** *log* **of water** that was consecrated to be used as a libation during the festival of *Sukkot*? **The verse states: "And he will not bring it to the entrance of the Tent of Meeting"** (Leviticus 17:9), which indicates that with regard to **any** offering that is fit to be **brought to the entrance of the Tent of Meeting** to be offered there upon the altar, one is **liable for** offering it up **outside** the courtyard.

וְאֵין לִי אֶלָּא קָדָשִׁים כְּשֵׁרִים, מִנַּיִן לְרַבּוֹת פְּסוּלִין,

I have derived **only** that one is liable for offering up **fit offerings; from where** do I derive **to** also **include** liability for **unfit** offerings whose disqualification occurred in sanctity?

NOTES

Whose disqualification occurred in sanctity – שֶׁהָיָה פְּסוּלָן בַּקּוֹדֶשׁ: This ruling is based upon the principle established by Rabbi Shimon in the mishna on 84a. There, he explains that if an offering becomes disqualified during the course of Temple service, then although it should not be placed on the altar *ab initio*, if it was placed there, it is thereby rendered acceptable and should not be removed. The early commentaries disagree as to the precise application of this principle. Rashi explains that it refers to any disqualification that occurs once the offering has been brought into the Temple courtyard. *Tosafot* on 68b disagree and explain it refers to disqualifications that occurred to the offering after it was slaughtered inside the courtyard.

Based on that ruling, the mishna here states that since a situation exists in which such an offering is acceptable on the altar inside the Temple, one who offers it up outside the Temple is liable.

The mishna on 84a records that Rabbi Yehuda disagrees with Rabbi Shimon's principle and holds that certain disqualified offerings, although their disqualification was in sanctity, are not allowed to remain upon the altar. Ostensibly, he would also disagree with the mishna's ruling here and hold that one is not liable for offering up an unfit offering whose disqualification was in sanctity.

An olive-bulk of the flesh of a burnt offering and of its sacrificial portions – כַּזַּיִת מִן הָעוֹלָה וּמִן הָאֵימוּרִין: The Gemara established that liability is incurred only when one offers up a complete item, but cited a dispute as to whether that requires that the entire animal be complete or whether it is sufficient that one offers up a complete limb. The mishna here would appear to stand in contrast to both opinions as it considers the possibility of being liable for an olive-bulk comprising two different parts of the animal. Rashi notes this difficulty and explains that the mishna indeed represents a third opinion that holds that one is liable even if the item offered up is not a complete animal or limb.

Tosafot offer a different interpretation according to which the requirement for the animal or limb to be complete means only that the flesh that is offered up must come from a complete animal or limb, not that a whole animal or limb must be offered up. Accordingly, the mishna here is entirely consistent with the earlier discussion and refers to a case in which an olive-bulk comprising meat and sacrificial portions was taken from a complete animal.

Sacrificial portions of a guilt offering, etc. – אֵימוּרֵי אָשָׁם וכו׳: The sacrificial portions of all these offerings are to be burned upon the altar inside the Temple. Therefore, one is liable for offering them up outside the Temple. The meat of these offerings is to be eaten, not burned on the altar. Indeed, even if that meat was placed upon the altar in the Temple, it should be removed (see 85b). Accordingly, one is not liable if one offers it up outside the Temple (see 112b).

Sacrificial portions of offerings of the most sacred order – אֵימוּרֵי קָדְשֵׁי קָדָשִׁים: Even though a sin offering and a guilt offering are included in the category of offerings of the most sacred order, offerings of the most sacred order are mentioned separately in order to include the sheep offered on *Shavuot* as communal peace offerings (Rashi).

HALAKHA

Unfit sacrificial animals whose disqualification occurred in sanctity – קָדָשִׁים פְּסוּלִין שֶׁהָיָה פְּסוּלָן בַּקּוֹדֶשׁ: Unfit offerings whose disqualification occurred in sanctity should be burned outside the Temple. This includes sacrificial flesh that was left overnight, taken out of the Temple courtyard, rendered ritually impure, or rendered *piggul*. One who, instead of burning them outside the Temple, offers them up outside the Temple, is liable, as the verse states: "To sacrifice it to the Lord" (Leviticus 17:9), which indicates that concerning any offering that was made for the Lord, one is liable for offering it up outside the Temple courtyard (Rambam *Sefer Avoda, Hilkhot Ma'aseh HaKorbanot* 19:7).

Of the flesh of a burnt offering and of its sacrificial portions – מִן הָעוֹלָה וּמִן הָאֵימוּרִין: The flesh of a burnt offering and its sacrificial portions combine such that one who offers up outside the Temple courtyard an olive-bulk comprising both of them is liable (Rambam *Sefer Avoda, Hilkhot Ma'aseh HaKorbanot* 19:10).

That offers up a burnt offering or sacrifice, etc. – עֹלָה אוֹ זָבַח וכו׳: Liability for offering up outside the Temple courtyard is incurred for offerings that should have been burned on the altar in the Temple. This is derived from the phrase "that offers up a burnt offering or sacrifice," which indicates that the only items that one is liable for are those similar to a burnt offering, i.e., that are burned on the altar. In addition, one who sprinkles sacrificial blood; or who burns the limbs of a burnt offering, the sacrificial portions of an offering, the handful of a meal offering, the frankincense, the incense, the meal offering of priests, or the meal offering of a wine libation; or who pours a libation of three *log* of wine or three *log* of water, outside the courtyard, is liable, as the verse states: "And he did not bring it to the entrance of the Tent of Meeting," which indicates that one is liable for any offering that could be accepted inside the courtyard (Rambam *Sefer Avoda, Hilkhot Ma'aseh HaKorbanot* 19:2–3).

כְּגוֹן הַלָּן, וְהַיּוֹצֵא, וְהַטָּמֵא, וְשֶׁנִּשְׁחַט חוּץ לִזְמַנּוֹ, וְחוּץ לִמְקוֹמוֹ, וְשֶׁקִּבְּלוּ פְּסוּלִין וְזָרְקוּ אֶת דָּמוֹ, וְהַנִּיתָּנִין לְמַטָּה שֶׁנְּתָנָן לְמַעְלָה, וְהַנִּיתָּנִין לְמַעְלָה שֶׁנְּתָנָן לְמַטָּה, וְהַנִּיתָּנִין בַּחוּץ שֶׁנְּתָנָן בִּפְנִים, וְהַנִּיתָּנִין בִּפְנִים שֶׁנְּתָנָן בַּחוּץ, וּפֶסַח וְחַטָּאת שֶׁנְּתָנָן שֶׁלֹּא לִשְׁמָן,

For example: Sacrificial meat **that was left overnight, or** an offering **that went outside** the courtyard, **or** an offering **that is impure, or** an offering **that was slaughtered** with intent to consume it **beyond its** designated **time or outside its** designated **area, or** an offering **that an unfit** person **collected and sprinkled its blood, or if one placed** the blood **that is** to be **placed above** the red line encircling the altar **below** it, **or if one placed** the blood **that is** to be **placed below** the red line **above** it, **or if one placed** the blood **that is** to be **placed inside** the Sanctuary **outside** on the external altar, **or if one placed** the blood **that is** to be **placed outside** the Sanctuary **inside** it, **or a Paschal offering or sin offering whose** blood **was placed not for their sake?**

מִנַּיִן? תַּלְמוּד לוֹמַר: ״לֹא יְבִיאֶנּוּ לַעֲשׂוֹת״, כָּל הַמִּתְקַבֵּל בְּפֶתַח אֹהֶל מוֹעֵד – חַיָּיבִין עָלָיו בַּחוּץ.

Since the disqualification of these offerings occurred in sanctity, if they were to be, albeit unlawfully, placed upon the altar, the altar would render them acceptable such that they should not be removed from upon it. **From where** is it derived to also include liability for these unfit offerings? **The verse states:** "And **he will not bring it** to the entrance of the Tent of Meeting, **to sacrifice it**[N] to the Lord," which indicates that with regard to **any** item **that is** rendered **acceptable** upon the altar **at the entrance of the Tent of Meeting,** even if it should not have been brought there *ab initio*, one is **liable** for offering **it** up **outside** the courtyard.

״הַמַּעֲלֶה כַּזַּיִת מִן הָעוֹלָה״ כו׳. עוֹלָה וְאֵימוּרֶיהָ – אִין, שְׁלָמִים וְאֵימוּרֵיהֶן – לָא.

§ The mishna teaches: **One who offers up outside** the courtyard **an olive-bulk** made up **of** the flesh **of a burnt offering** and of its sacrificial portions is liable. The Gemara infers: The mishna states that for an olive-bulk combined of the flesh of **a burnt offering and** of **its sacrificial portions, yes,** one is liable. By inference, for an olive-bulk combined of the meat of **a peace offering and of its sacrificial portions,** one is **not** liable, because its meat is eaten, not burned on the altar.

תַּנְיָא לְהָא דְּתָנוּ רַבָּנַן: עוֹלָה וְאֵימוּרֶיהָ מִצְטָרְפִין לְכַזַּיִת לְהַעֲלוֹתָן בַּחוּץ, וּלְחַיֵּיב עֲלֵיהֶן מִשּׁוּם פִּיגּוּל נוֹתָר וְטָמֵא.

We learn in the mishna **that which the Sages taught**[N] explicitly in a *baraita* (*Tosefta, Me'ila* 1:28): The flesh of **a burnt offering and its sacrificial portions combine to** form the minimum measure, of **an olive-bulk,** to render one liable **for offering them up outside** the courtyard, **and to render** one **liable** for eating **them due to** ***piggul***, i.e., if the sacrificial rites were performed with the intent of sacrificing the offering after its designated time; ***notar***, i.e., if its flesh remained after the period in which it was permitted to sacrifice it; **or** for eating them while he was **ritually impure.** This *baraita*, too, states that only the flesh and sacrificial portions of a burnt offering combine. This indicates that the meat and sacrificial portions of a peace offering do not combine.

בִּשְׁלָמָא הַעֲלָאַת עוֹלָה דְּכָלִיל – אִין, שְׁלָמִים – לָא. אֶלָּא פִּיגּוּל וְנוֹתָר וְטָמֵא מַאי טַעְמָא?

The Gemara asks: **Granted,** with regard to **offering up** outside the courtyard, it is logical that for **a burnt offering, which is** entirely **consumed** upon the altar, that **yes,** everything will combine, and that for **peace offerings,** whose meat is not burned on the altar, the meat and sacrificial portions will **not** combine. **But** with regard to liability for ***piggul***, ***notar***, **and** eating while **ritually impure, what is the reason** that the *baraita* differentiates between a burnt offering and a peace offering?

וְהָא תְּנַן: כָּל הַפִּגּוּלִין מִצְטָרְפִין, וְכָל הַנּוֹתָרִין מִצְטָרְפִין; קַשְׁיָא פִּיגּוּל אַפִּיגּוּל, קַשְׁיָא נוֹתָר אַנּוֹתָר!

The Gemara compounds its questions: **And didn't we learn** in a mishna (*Me'ila* 15a): **Anything that is** ***piggul*** **combines** together,[H] **and anything that is** ***notar*** **combines** together, to form the measure of an olive-bulk to render one liable? The mishna indicates that this *halakha* applies to all types of offerings. Accordingly, the Gemara notes: The ruling about ***piggul*** in the *baraita* is **difficult,** as it is contradicted **by** the ruling about ***piggul*** in the mishna, and the ruling about ***notar*** in the *baraita* is **difficult,** as it is contradicted **by** the ruling about ***notar*** in the mishna.

NOTES

He will not bring it to sacrifice it – לֹא יְבִיאֶנּוּ לַעֲשׂוֹת: The phrase "to sacrifice it" teaches that not only is liability incurred for offerings that should have been brought to the Temple, but also for any offering concerning which a situation exists in which some form of sacrifice upon the altar is required. Since the disqualifications that are listed all occurred in sanctity, were such offerings to be placed on the altar they would thereby be rendered acceptable and in order to facilitate their burning a priest would have to turn them over. That action is sufficient to include them in the sacrificing referred to by the verse (Rashi).

We learn that which the Sages taught – תַּנְיָא לְהָא דְּתָנוּ רַבָּנַן: This expression is often used by the Gemara to indicate that a ruling alluded to in a mishna is also stated explicitly in a *baraita*, thereby demonstrating that the *baraita* is considered reliable and that the other rulings contained in it should also be given validity (*Yad David*; see Rashi on *Ḥagiga* 2b).

HALAKHA

Anything that is *piggul* combines together, etc. – כָּל הַפִּגּוּלִין מִצְטָרְפִין וכו׳: Any item that is *piggul* combines with other *piggul* items to form the minimum measure of an olive-bulk, such that one who eats it will be liable to receive *karet* if he did so intentionally, and to bring a sin offering if he did so unwittingly. Similarly, any item that is *notar* combines with other *notar* items, and so too, *piggul* and *notar* combine together. This is in accordance with the mishna in *Me'ila* 15a (Rambam *Sefer Avoda, Hilkhot Pesulei HaMukdashin* 18:11).

פִּיגּוּל אַפִּיגּוּל לָא קַשְׁיָא: כָּאן – בְּפִיגּוּל, כָּאן – בְּמַחְשֶׁבֶת פִּיגּוּל.

The Gemara resolves the difficulties: That the ruling about ***piggul*** in the *baraita* is contradicted **by** the ruling about ***piggul*** in the mishna is **not difficult. Here,** in the mishna, the ruling that they combine **concerns** liability for eating ***piggul,*** whereas **there,** in the *baraita*, the ruling that only the parts of a burnt offering combine **concerns *piggul* intention.** An offering is rendered *piggul* only if one intends to eat an olive-bulk of it after the designated time for eating it or to sacrifice an olive-bulk of it after the designated time for sacrificing it. The *baraita* rules that for a burnt offering, if one has such intention for both half an olive-bulk of its meat and half an olive-bulk of its sacrificial portions, that is sufficient for the entire offering to be rendered *piggul*. For a peace offering, the offering is rendered *piggul* only if one has such intention about an olive-bulk comprised only of meat or only of sacrificial portions.

נוֹתָר אַנּוֹתָר לָא קַשְׁיָא: כָּאן – בְּנוֹתָר, כָּאן – בְּשֶׁנִּיתּוֹתְרוּ עַד שֶׁלֹּא נִזְרַק הַדָּם.

The Gemara resolves the second difficulty: That the ruling about ***notar*** in the *baraita* is contradicted **by** the ruling about ***notar*** in the mishna is **not difficult. Here,** in the mishna, the ruling that they combine **concerns** liability for eating ***notar,*** whereas **there,** in the *baraita*, the ruling that only the parts of a burnt offering combine **concerns** a case in **which** only an olive-bulk combined of both the flesh and the sacrificial portions **remained** from the offering, the rest having been destroyed, **before** its **blood was sprinkled.** Blood may not be sprinkled unless an olive-bulk of the offering remains. And if the blood is not sprinkled, the offering will never be rendered *notar*. The *baraita* rules that in the case of a burnt offering, the different parts of it combine to form an olive-bulk to permit the sprinkling of the blood. This does not apply to a peace offering, for which an olive-bulk of only meat or of only sacrificial portions must remain in order to permit the sprinkling of the blood.

וּמַנִּי – רַבִּי יְהוֹשֻׁעַ הִיא. דְּתַנְיָא, רַבִּי יְהוֹשֻׁעַ אוֹמֵר: כׇּל הַזְּבָחִים שֶׁבַּתּוֹרָה, שֶׁנִּשְׁתַּיֵּיר בָּהֶן כַּזַּיִת בָּשָׂר

The Gemara asks: **And whose** opinion is expressed by the *baraita*? **It is** the opinion of **Rabbi Yehoshua, as it is taught** in a *baraita*: **Rabbi Yehoshua says:** With regard to **all the offerings that** are mentioned **in the Torah from which there remains** only **an olive-bulk of meat,** the rest having been destroyed or rendered impure,

וְכַזַּיִת חֵלֶב – זוֹרֵק אֶת הַדָּם,

or from which there remains only **an olive-bulk of** sacrificial portions, e.g., **fat** to be burned on the altar, one still **sprinkles the blood**[H] of the offering on the altar and one thereby fulfills his obligation.

חֲצִי זַיִת בָּשָׂר וַחֲצִי זַיִת חֵלֶב – אֵינוֹ זוֹרֵק אֶת הַדָּם. וּבְעוֹלָה, חֲצִי זַיִת בָּשָׂר וַחֲצִי זַיִת חֵלֶב – זוֹרֵק אֶת הַדָּם, מִפְּנֵי שֶׁכּוּלָּהּ כָּלִיל. וּמִנְחָה, אֲפִילּוּ כּוּלָּהּ קַיֶּימֶת – לֹא יִזְרוֹק.

But if all that remains is **half an olive-bulk of meat and half an olive-bulk of fat, one may not sprinkle the blood,** as since the meat and the sacrificial portions are used differently, the former being eaten and the latter being burned on the altar, they cannot combine to form the minimum requirement of an olive-bulk. This applies only to offerings whose meat is eaten. **But for a burnt offering,** even if all that remains is **half an olive-bulk of flesh and half an olive-bulk of fat, one sprinkles the blood, because** since the offering is **consumed** upon the altar **in its entirety,** all of its parts combine together. **And** with regard to **a meal offering, even if all of it** still **exists, one does not sprinkle** the blood. It is apparent that Rabbi Yehoshua's opinion in this *baraita* is the one expressed in the *baraita*.

מִנְחָה מַאי עֲבִידְתָּהּ? אָמַר רַב פָּפָּא: מִנְחַת נְסָכִים הַבָּאָה עִם הַזֶּבַח.

The Gemara clarifies the final clause of the *baraita*: **What is the relevance of a meal offering** to the sprinkling of blood? In a meal offering there is no blood at all. **Rav Pappa said:** The *baraita* is referring to **a meal offering** brought with the **libations that accompany** an animal **offering.** If the entire body of the offering was destroyed but the meal offering that accompanied it remains, one might have thought that it would be sufficient to allow for the sprinkling of the blood. The *baraita* teaches that this is incorrect.

HALAKHA

Sprinkles the blood – זוֹרֵק אֶת הַדָּם: With regard to all offerings, if the meat of the offering is lost or burned before the blood has been sprinkled, then as long as an olive-bulk of the meat or an olive-bulk of the sacrificial portions remains, the blood may be sprinkled. If less than that remains, the blood may not be sprinkled. With regard to a burnt offering, even if all that remains is half an olive-bulk of flesh and half an olive-bulk of sacrificial portions, they combine to fulfill the requirement of an olive-bulk since both will be burned on the altar; therefore, the blood may be sprinkled on the altar (Rambam *Sefer Avoda*, *Hilkhot Pesulei HaMukdashin* 1:30).

מתני׳ הַקּוֹמֶץ, וְהַלְּבוֹנָה, וְהַקְּטוֹרֶת, וּמִנְחַת כֹּהֲנִים, וּמִנְחַת כֹּהֵן מָשִׁיחַ, וּמִנְחַת נְסָכִים שֶׁהִקְרִיב מֵאַחַת מֵהֶן כַּזַּיִת בַּחוּץ – חַיָּיב. רַבִּי אֱלִיעֶזֶר פּוֹטֵר עַד שֶׁיַּקְרִיב אֶת כּוּלָּן. וְכוּלָּן שֶׁהִקְרִיב בִּפְנִים, וְשִׁיֵּיר מֵהֶן כַּזַּיִת וְהִקְרִיבוֹ בַּחוּץ – חַיָּיב.

MISHNA With regard to **the handful** of a meal offering, **the frankincense,**[B] **the incense, the meal offering of priests, the meal offering of** the **anointed priest, and the meal offering** brought with the **libations** that accompany animal offerings, in a case **where one sacrificed** even **an olive-bulk from** any **one of these,** which should be sacrificed on the altar, **outside**[H] the Temple, he is **liable,**[N] as the burning of an olive-bulk is considered a proper burning. **Rabbi Eliezer deems** him **exempt unless he sacrifices the whole of** any one of these[N] items outside the Temple. **But** Rabbi Eliezer concedes that with regard to **any of them that one sacrificed inside** the courtyard **but left over an olive-bulk from them** and then **sacrificed that** olive-bulk **outside** the courtyard, he is **liable.**

וְכוּלָּן שֶׁחָסְרוּ כׇּל שֶׁהוּ וְהִקְרִיבוֹ בַּחוּץ – פָּטוּר.

And with regard to **any of these** offerings **that were lacking any amount,** if **one sacrifices it outside** the courtyard, he is **exempt.**

הַמַּקְרִיב קֳדָשִׁים וְאֵימוּרִים בַּחוּץ – חַיָּיב.

One who sacrifices sacrificial meat, which is eaten, **and sacrificial portions,** i.e., those that are to be burned on the altar, **outside**[H] the courtyard, is **liable** for the sacrifice of the sacrificial portions. But he is not liable for sacrificing the meat.

גמ׳ תָּנוּ רַבָּנַן: הַמַּקְטִיר כַּזַּיִת בַּחוּץ – חַיָּיב, חֲצִי פְּרָס בִּפְנִים – פָּטוּר.

GEMARA **The Sages taught** in a *baraita*: Each morning and afternoon, a *peras*, i.e., half a *maneh*, of incense must be burned in the Sanctuary. Nevertheless, **one who burns** only **an olive-bulk** of incense **outside** the courtyard is **liable.** If one burns **half a** ***peras*** **inside** the Temple, he is **exempt.**

קָא סָלְקָא דַּעְתִּין, מַאי ״פָּטוּר״ – פָּטוּר זָר. אַמַּאי? הַקְטָרָה הִיא!

The Gemara addresses the latter clause of the *baraita*: **It enters our mind** to explain: **What** is meant by: He is **exempt?** It means that **a non-priest,** for whom it is prohibited to perform the sacrificial rites in the Temple, is **exempt** if he burns incense inside the Temple. The Gemara rejects this: **Why** should he be exempt; this **is** an act of **sacrificial burning?** Even though he burned less than a *peras*, it is apparent from the first clause of the *baraita* that burning even an olive-bulk is considered an act of sacrificial burning.

אֲמַר רַבִּי זֵירָא אֲמַר רַב חִסְדָּא אֲמַר רַב יִרְמְיָה בַּר אַבָּא אֲמַר רַב: מַאי ״פָּטוּר״ – פָּטוּר צִיבּוּר.

Rabbi Zeira said that **Rav Ḥisda said** that **Rav Yirmeya, son of Abba, said** that **Rav said: What** is meant by: He is **exempt?** It means that if a priest burns half a *peras* inside the Temple, the **community** is thereby **exempt** from its obligation to burn incense despite the fact that less than the required amount was burned.

NOTES

The handful, the frankincense…where one sacrificed an olive-bulk from one of these outside he is liable – הַקּוֹמֶץ וְהַלְּבוֹנָה...שֶׁהִקְרִיב מֵאַחַת מֵהֶן כַּזַּיִת בַּחוּץ חַיָּיב: This mishna is a continuation of the previous mishna on 109a. Both *mishnayot* state that one is liable for offering up even an olive-bulk of an offering outside. Rashi explains that the *tanna* of these *mishnayot* derives this from the term "to sacrifice it" (Leviticus 17:9). This is different from the way this term was expounded on 108b; according to Rashi there, it teaches that one is liable only if he offers up a complete entity, which according to one opinion means a whole animal, and according to another opinion means even a whole limb. *Tosafot* disagree with Rashi's explanation of the way the term is expounded on 108b. According to *Tosafot* the derivations in the Gemara there are consistent with the mishna here, i.e., one is liable for offering up even an olive-bulk of an offering. The term teaches only that the olive-bulk must be taken from a complete entity, be it a whole animal or a whole limb. A third opinion emerges from the rulings of the Rambam. He distinguishes between items that are naturally whole units, such as animals and limbs, and the items mentioned in the mishna here, such a meal offerings and incense, which are aggregations of many small pieces. It is only for the latter that the measurement of an olive-bulk is relevant, whereas for the former, one is liable only if the item was complete and was offered up in its entirety (*Ḥok Natan*).

Unless he sacrifices the whole of one of these – עַד שֶׁיַּקְרִיב אֶת כּוּלָּן: It would appear that Rabbi Eliezer disagrees with the previous mishna, which rules that one is liable for offering up even an olive-bulk of an offering outside; rather, he holds one must offer up the entire offering. Rashi explains that Rabbi Eliezer actually agrees with the previous mishna, but makes a distinction between the cases. The mishna here concerns offerings that are disqualified if they lack any amount. Therefore, Rabbi Eliezer rules that one is liable only if he offers up the offering in its entirety. By contrast, the previous mishna concerns a burnt offering, which remains valid even if some of its flesh is lacking. Therefore, Rabbi Eliezer agrees that one is liable even if he offers up only an olive-bulk.

BACKGROUND

Frankincense – לְבוֹנָה: Frankincense is an aromatic spice that was used in various Temple services. An addition to most meal offerings, except for the meal offering of a sinner and the meal offering of jealousy, it was sacrificed on the altar together with the handful of flour.

Frankincense is generally identified as the sap derived from *Boswellia sacra*, the frankincense tree.

Frankincense pellets

HALAKHA

Where one sacrificed an olive-bulk from one of these outside – שֶׁהִקְרִיב מֵאַחַת מֵהֶן כַּזַּיִת בַּחוּץ: In a case where it is prohibited to offer up an offering outside the Temple courtyard, one is liable even for offering up an olive-bulk of that offering. This applies both if the rest of the offering was first offered up appropriately inside the Temple, and even if the offering was not offered up, but an olive-bulk of it was removed, taken outside, and offered up there. But if, while inside the Temple courtyard, the offering was lacking any amount, then even if one takes all that remains and offers it up outside, he is not liable. For example, if the handful, or the frankincense, or the incense, or the meal offering of priests or of the High Priest, or the libations, were lacking any amount, then one who took it outside and offered it up would be exempt, as the verse states: "To sacrifice it," which teaches that one is liable for offering up an item that is complete, but not an item that is lacking (Rambam *Sefer Avoda, Hilkhot Ma'aseh HaKorbanot* 19:8).

One who sacrifices sacrificial meat and sacrificial portions outside – הַמַּקְרִיב קֳדָשִׁים וְאֵימוּרִים בַּחוּץ: One who offers up an animal offering in its entirety outside the Temple courtyard is liable on account of the fact that the animal contains the sacrificial portions. One is liable despite the fact that those portions were never separated from the rest of the animal (Rambam *Sefer Avoda, Hilkhot Ma'aseh HaKorbanot* 19:5).

אֲמַר רַבִּי זֵירָא: אִי קַשְׁיָא לִי – הָא קַשְׁיָא לִי, הָא דַּאֲמַר רַב עֲלָהּ: בְּהָא אֲפִילּוּ רַבִּי אֱלִיעֶזֶר מוֹדֶה. דְּהָא רַבִּי אֱלִיעֶזֶר לָאו הַקְטָרָה הִיא קָאָמַר!

Rabbi Zeira said: If there is something **difficult for me** with regard to this *baraita*, **this is difficult for me: That which Rav said concerning** this *baraita*: **With regard to this** *halakha*, that if a priest burns less than a *peras* of incense the community fulfills its obligation, **even Rabbi Eliezer concedes.** Rabbi Zeira explains: This is difficult for me **as Rabbi Eliezer** rules in the mishna that one who burns an olive-bulk of incense outside is exempt. Effectively, he is **saying** that burning less than the required amount **is not** an act of **sacrificial burning.** How then can he hold that the community fulfills its obligation by the burning of less than a *peras*?

אֲמַר רַבָּה: בְּהַקְטָרָה דְּהֵיכָל – דְּכוּלֵּי עָלְמָא לָא פְּלִיגִי.

Rabba said: With regard to the **burning of** incense designated to be burned in the **Sanctuary** upon the golden altar, **everyone,** i.e., the Rabbis and Rabbi Eliezer, **agrees** that the Torah does not specify the amount to be burned; the requirement to burn a *peras* is rabbinic. Accordingly, the obligation is fulfilled even if only an olive-bulk of incense is burned there, as the *baraita* states, and one who burns an olive-bulk of that incense outside the Temple is liable.

כִּי פְּלִיגִי – בְּהַקְטָרָה דִּפְנִים, דְּמָר סָבַר: "מְלֹא חָפְנָיו" דַּוְקָא, וּמָר סָבַר: "מְלֹא חָפְנָיו" לָאו דַּוְקָא.

When they disagree in the mishna, it is **with regard to** the **burning of** incense in the **inner** sanctum, i.e., in the Holy of Holies, on Yom Kippur.[H] Concerning that obligation, the verse states: "And he shall take… his handful of sweet incense, beaten small, and bring it within the Curtain" (Leviticus 16:12). **As one Sage,** Rabbi Eliezer, **holds** that **"his handful"** indicates that **specifically** that measure must be burned in order to fulfill the obligation. Accordingly, he also holds that one who burns only an olive-bulk of that incense outside the courtyard is exempt. **And** the other **Sage,** the Rabbis who disagree with Rabbi Eliezer, **holds** that **"his handful"** does **not** indicate that **specifically** that measure must be burned, and the obligation can be fulfilled even with a lesser amount. Accordingly, they also hold that one who burns even an olive-bulk of that incense outside the courtyard is liable.

אֲמַר לֵיהּ אַבַּיֵי: וְהָא כִּי קָא כְּתִיבָא "חֻקָּה" – בְּהַקְטָרָה דִּפְנִים הוּא דִּכְתִיב!

Abaye said to Rabba: **But when** the term **"statute" is written** with regard to the Yom Kippur Temple service (see Leviticus 16:29), **it is** also **written with regard to** the **burning of** incense in the **inner** sanctum. The term "statute" stated with regard to a rite indicates that it is valid only if performed precisely in accordance with all the details mentioned in the Torah concerning it. Accordingly, the term "his handful" must be specific.

אֶלָּא אֲמַר אַבַּיֵי: בְּהַקְטָרָה בִּפְנִים – כּוּלֵּי עָלְמָא לָא פְּלִיגִי.

Rather, Abaye said:[N] **With regard to** the **burning** of incense **in** the **inner** sanctum, i.e., in the Holy of Holies, on Yom Kippur, **everyone agrees** that the obligation is only fulfilled if a handful of incense is burned. Also, everyone agrees with regard to burning incense in the Sanctuary that the obligation is fulfilled even with an olive-bulk, as the *baraita* states, and one who burns an olive-bulk of incense outside the Temple is liable.

כִּי פְּלִיגִי – בְּהַקְטָרָה דְּחוּץ, מָר סָבַר: יָלְפִינַן פְּנִים מִחוּץ, וּמָר סָבַר לָא יָלְפִינַן.

When they disagree in the mishna, it is **with regard to** the **burning of** incense of the Holy of Holies **outside** the Temple courtyard. One **Sage,** the Rabbis, **holds** that **we derive** the measure for liability for incense of the **inner** sanctum **from** incense of the **outer** sanctum, i.e., the Sanctuary. Just as for the latter one is liable for an olive-bulk, so too, for the former one is liable for an olive-bulk. **And** the other **Sage,** Rabbi Eliezer, **holds** that **we do not derive** one from the other. Rather, since the obligation inside the Holy of Holies is fulfilled only with a handful of incense, one is liable for burning that incense outside the Temple only if he burns that amount.

אֲמַר רָבָא: הַשְׁתָּא חוּץ מִחוּץ לָא יָלְפִי רַבָּנַן, פְּנִים מִחוּץ מִיבָּעֵי?!

Rava said in rejection of Abaye's understanding: **Now, if the Rabbis do not derive** the measure for liability for offering up outside the Temple courtyard, with regard to other rites performed in the **outer** sanctum, **from** incense of the **outer** sanctum, is it **necessary** to question whether they would derive the measure for liability for incense of the **inner** sanctum **from** incense of the **outer** sanctum? Certainly, they would not.

HALAKHA

The burning of incense in the inner sanctum on Yom Kippur – הַקְטָרָה דִּפְנִים: A non-priest who burns an olive-bulk of incense on the golden altar is liable. If he burned there the incense that was designated for use in the Holy of Holies on Yom Kippur, he is liable only if he burns the full measure prescribed by the Torah, i.e., his handful. This is in accordance with the opinion of the Rabbis as explained by Abaye. For burning incense outside the Temple courtyard, one is liable for burning even an olive-bulk, whether he burns the incense of the Sanctuary or that of the Holy of Holies (Rambam *Sefer Avoda*, *Hilkhot Biat Mikdash* 9:4 and *Hilkhot Avodat Yom HaKippurim* 5:26 and Radbaz there).

NOTES

Rather Abaye said, etc. – אֶלָּא אָמַר אַבַּיֵי וכו׳: Rashi explains that according to both Abaye and Rabba the only disagreement between Rabbi Eliezer and the Rabbis concerns the burning of the incense of the Holy of Holies outside the courtyard: Is one liable for burning even an olive-bulk, or is one liable only for the full measure? The difference between Abaye's opinion and Rabba's opinion is only with regard to how they explain the rationale behind the dispute. According to Rabba, the disagreement is about whether "his handful" is specific or not, whereas according to Abaye it is about whether it is possible derive the measure for liability for incense of the inner sanctum, i.e., the Holy of Holies, from the incense of the outer sanctum, i.e., the Sanctuary, concerning which all agree one is liable even for burning an olive-bulk.

Rabbeinu Hananel disagrees with Rashi. He explains that according to Abaye everyone agrees that with regard to both incense of the Sanctuary and incense of the Holy of Holies, if one burns them outside the courtyard he is liable even if he burns an olive-bulk. The dispute between Rabbi Eliezer and the Rabbis concerns the burning of the incense of the Holy of Holies inside the Sanctuary. Since that incense was supposed to be burned inside the Holy of Holies, burning it in the Sanctuary is considered a violation of the prohibition against offering up outside. It is with regard to this case that they disagree as to whether one is liable only if he burns the full measure, or whether he is liable even for just one olive-bulk.

From the rulings of the Rambam it would appear that he had a third understanding of the dispute, which relates to a case where a non-priest offers up incense inside the Temple. The dispute concerns the quantity of incense he must burn in order to be liable for this action.

מַה הִיא? דְּתַנְיָא: יָכוֹל הַמַּעֲלֶה פָּחוֹת מִכַּזַּיִת קוֹמֶץ, וּפָחוֹת מִכַּזַּיִת אֵימוּרִין, וְהַמְנַסֵּךְ פָּחוֹת מִשְּׁלֹשֶׁת לוּגִּין יַיִן, [פָּחוֹת מִשְּׁלֹשָׁה לוּגִּין מַיִם, יְהֵא חַיָּיב? תַּלְמוּד לוֹמַר: ״לַעֲשׂוֹת״ – עַל הַשָּׁלֵם חַיָּיב, וְאֵינוֹ חַיָּיב עַל הֶחָסֵר.

The Gemara asks: **What is** the rite that Rava is referring to in his response to Abaye? It is **as it is taught** in a *baraita*: One **might** have thought that **one who offers up** outside the courtyard **less than an olive-bulk of** the **handful** taken from a meal offering **or less than an olive-bulk of** the **sacrificial portions, or who pours as a libation** outside the courtyard **less than three** ***log*** **of wine** or who pours as a libation on *Sukkot* **less than three** ***log*** **of water,** that **he would be liable.** To counter this, **the verse states:** "And he will not bring it to the entrance of the Tent of Meeting, **to sacrifice it**" (Leviticus 17:9). The term "to sacrifice it" indicates that one is **liable for the** sacrifice of **a complete** offering outside the courtyard **but one is not liable for the** sacrifice of **an incomplete** offering outside.

וְהָא פָּחוֹת מִשְּׁלֹשֶׁת לוּגִּין, דְּאִית בְּהוּ כַּמָּה זֵיתִים, וְלָא יָלְפִי רַבָּנַן חוּץ מֵחוּץ!

The Gemara explains Rava's inference: **But** the *baraita* states that for a libation of **less than three** ***log*** outside the courtyard one is exempt despite the fact **that** the libation still **contains a few olive-bulks. And** it is apparent then, that **the Rabbis do not derive** the measure for liability for the rite of libation that should be performed in the **outer** sanctum **from** incense that should be burned in the **outer** sanctum. Certainly then, they would not derive the measure for liability for incense of the inner sanctum from incense of the outer sanctum.

אֶלָּא אָמַר רָבָא: כְּגוֹן דְּקַבְעִינְהוּ שְׁנֵי חֲצָאֵי פְרָס

Rather, Rava said[N] to resolve Rabbi Zeira's difficulty: Rabbi Eliezer and the Rabbis agree with regard to the incense of the Sanctuary, that the Torah does not specify an amount to be burned, and the community fulfills its obligation even if only an olive-bulk is burned, as is taught in the *baraita*. When they disagree in the mishna, it is in a case **where, for example, one designated two half-*****peras*** portions[N] of incense, in accordance with the rabbinic requirement to burn one *peras*,

NOTES

Rather Rava said – אֶלָּא אָמַר רָבָא: Rava holds that with regard to the incense of the Holy of Holies, everyone agrees that burning any less than the full measure of a handful is of no significance. Furthermore, he holds that with regard to the incense of the Sanctuary, everyone agrees that the Torah does not require any specific amount to be burned. Accordingly, offering up even one olive-bulk of incense is considered an act of sacrificial burning, and one is liable when this is done outside the Temple. Rava therefore explains that the dispute between the Rabbis and Rabbi Eliezer concerns the unique case in which due to the fact that a certain quantity of incense was designated for use, burning any less than that quantity is no longer regarded as a valid act of sacrificial burning, and one would not be liable for burning any less than that quantity outside. This designation is achieved by removing a quantity of incense from the mortar in which it was ground and placing it in the bowls in which it is to be brought into the Sanctuary (see *Tamid* 32b–33a). According to Rabbi Eliezer, once the measure required by rabbinic law, i.e., a *peras*, or for that matter any amount greater than an olive-bulk, is placed in the bowl, one is no longer liable for offering up merely an olive-bulk outside.

Where, for example, one designated two half-***peras*** **portions – כְּגוֹן דְּקַבְעִינְהוּ שְׁנֵי חֲצָאֵי פְרָס:** The Gemara refers to a whole *peras* because that is the measure of incense required by rabbinic law. For the purposes of the present discussion the Gemara could have referred to any quantity greater than an olive-bulk. Indeed, the *Shita Mekubbetzet* has a version of the text that states: Half a *peras*, and *Tosafot* cites a text that excludes any mention of a specific measure (see *Sefat Emet*).

Perek **XIII**
Daf **110** Amud **a**

בְּמָנָא; מָר סָבַר: קְבִיעוּת מָנָא מִילְּתָא הִיא, וּמָר סָבַר: לָאו מִילְּתָא הִיא.

by placing them **in a vessel.** One **Sage,** Rabbi Eliezer, **holds** that the **designation of** a measure of incense larger than an olive-bulk by placing it in **a vessel is** a significant **matter** that renders one obligated to burn all the incense that was placed there. Therefore, one who then burned only an olive-bulk of that incense outside the courtyard is exempt. **And** one **Sage,** the Rabbis, **holds** that it **is nothing** and does not render one obligated to burn all the incense that was placed in the vessel. Therefore, one who then burned an olive-bulk of that incense outside the courtyard is liable.

אָמַר רָבָא: הַשְׁתָּא לְמַאן דְּאָמַר קְבִיעוּתָא דְּמָנָא וְלָא כְּלוּם הוּא, קָבַע שִׁשָּׁה לְפָר, וּמָשַׁךְ מֵהֶן אַרְבָּעָה וְהִקְרִיבָן בַּחוּץ – חַיָּיב, שֶׁרְאוּיִין לְאַיִל.

Rava said: Now, according to the one who says that **designation** by placing in a **vessel is nothing,** if **one designated** in a vessel **six** *log* of wine **as** a libation to accompany the sacrificing of **a bull,** which is the required amount, **and** then **removed four** *log* **from** it **and brought those** four *log* as a libation **outside** the courtyard, he would be **liable,** as a libation of four *log* of wine is **fit for** the sacrificing **of a ram** (see Numbers 28:14).

קָבַע אַרְבָּעָה לְאַיִל, וּמָשַׁךְ מֵהֶן שְׁלֹשָׁה וְהִקְרִיבָן בַּחוּץ – חַיָּיב, שֶׁרְאוּיִין לְכֶבֶשׂ.

Similarly, if one **designated** by placing in a vessel **four** *log* of wine **for** a libation to accompany the sacrificing of **a ram and** then **removed three** *log* **of** wine from it **and brought those** three *log* as a libation **outside** the courtyard, he would be **liable, as** three *log* of wine is a **fit** libation **for** the sacrificing of **a lamb** (see Numbers 28:14).

חִסְּרוּ כׇּל שֶׁהוּא, וְהִקְרִיבָן בַּחוּץ – פָּטוּר.

But if those three *log* **were lacking any amount, and one brought them** as a libation **outside** the courtyard, he would be **exempt** because less than three *log* of wine is never a fit libation.

NOTES

Even though it involves deriving outer from inner – אַף עַל גַּב דְּחוּץ מִפְּנִים: The text of the Gemara is clearly inverted and should read as Rashi's text reads: Even though it involves deriving the *halakhot* of a rite performed in the inner sanctum from one performed in the outer sanctum.

HALAKHA

A lack that occurs to an offering outside – חִסָּרוֹן דְּחוּץ: One who offers up, outside the Temple courtyard, an offering that became lacking while it was still inside the courtyard, is exempt. This is in accordance with the mishna. If the offering is taken out of the courtyard while it is still complete and it becomes incomplete only once it is outside and then one offers it up, it is uncertain whether one is liable or not; therefore, it is prohibited to offer it up but one is not punished for doing so. The *halakha* in this case is uncertain as it is the subject of an unresolved dilemma in the Gemara (Rambam *Sefer Avoda, Hilkhot Ma'aseh HaKorbanot* 19:9).

רַב אָשֵׁי אָמַר: נִיסּוּךְ מֵהַקְטָרָה לָא יָלְפִי רַבָּנַן.

Rava inferred from the *baraita* that the Rabbis do not derive the measure for liability for a rite performed in the outer sanctum, i.e., the pouring of a libation, from one performed in the outer sanctum, i.e., the burning of incense. From that he concluded that the Rabbis would certainly not derive the measure for liability for a rite performed in the inner sanctum from a rite performed in the outer sanctum. This refuted Abaye's claim that the Rabbis derive the measure for liability for burning outside the incense of the inner sanctum from the measure for liability for burning outside the incense of the outer sanctum. **Rav Ashi said** in defense of Abaye's opinion: Indeed, as is indicated by the *baraita*, **the Rabbis do not derive** the measure for liability for **pouring a libation** outside the courtyard **from** the measure for liability for **burning** incense, which are two different rites performed in the outer sanctum.

אַף עַל גַּב דְּחוּץ מִחוּץ לָא יָלְפִי, הַקְטָרָה מֵהַקְטָרָה יָלְפִי, אַף עַל גַּב דְּחוּץ מִפְּנִים.

Rav Ashi continues: **Even though** the Rabbis **do not derive** the *halakhot* of a rite performed in the **outer** sanctum **from** a different rite performed in the **outer** sanctum, **they do derive** the measure for liability for **burning** the incense of the outer sanctum **from** the identical rite of **burning** of the incense of the inner sanctum, **even though** it involves deriving the *halakhot* of a rite performed in the **outer** sanctum **from** one performed in the **inner**[N] sanctum.

״וְכוּלָּן שֶׁחָסְרוּ״. אִיבַּעְיָא לְהוּ: חִסָּרוֹן דְּחוּץ שְׁמֵיהּ חִסָּרוֹן, אוֹ לָא שְׁמֵיהּ חִסָּרוֹן?

§ After enumerating various items that are burned entirely on the altar, the mishna states: **And** with regard to **any of these** offerings **that were lacking** any amount, if one sacrifices it outside the courtyard, he is exempt. Concerning this ruling, **a dilemma was raised before** the Sages: Is **a lack that** occurs to an offering **outside**[H] the courtyard **considered a lack** in order to exempt one who sacrifices the remainder outside the courtyard? **Or** is it **not considered a lack?**

מִי אָמְרִינַן: כֵּיוָן דִּנְפַק אִיפְּסִלוּ לְהוּ, מָה לִי חָסֵר מָה לִי יָתֵר. אוֹ דִּילְמָא: יוֹצֵא דְּאִיתֵיהּ בְּעֵינֵיהּ – אִין, דְּלֵיתֵיהּ בְּעֵינֵיהּ – לָא?

Do we say that **once** an offering **emerges** from the courtyard **it is** in any event **disqualified,** and yet the Torah deems one liable for offering it there, so **what** difference is there **to me** if there is an additional disqualification of being **lacking** and **what** difference is there **to me** if it is still **complete? Or perhaps** it is only with regard to **emerging** from the courtyard, **where it is** still **in its original state,** that **yes,** one is liable despite the fact that it was disqualified by emerging from the courtyard, but where it is **not in its original state,** one would **not** be liable.

אָמַר אַבַּיֵי: תָּא שְׁמַע, רַבִּי אֱלִיעֶזֶר פּוֹטֵר, עַד שֶׁיַּקְרִיב אֶת כּוּלָּן.

Abaye said: Come and **hear** a resolution from the mishna: **Rabbi Eliezer deems** him **exempt unless he sacrifices the whole of** any one of these items outside the Temple. It is apparent then that the offering must remain complete.

אֲמַר לֵיהּ רַבָּה בַּר רַב חָנָן לְאַבַּיֵי: מִדְּרַבִּי אֱלִיעֶזֶר פָּשֵׁיט מָר?

Rabba bar Rav Ḥanan said to Abaye: Can the **Master resolve** the dilemma **from** the opinion **of Rabbi Eliezer?** The Rabbis disagree with Rabbi Eliezer, and hold that one is liable for sacrificing even an olive-bulk, and the dilemma was raised according to their opinion.

אֲמַר לֵיהּ: בְּפֵירוּשׁ שְׁמִיעַ לִי מִינֵּיהּ דְּרַב: עַד כָּאן לָא פְּלִיגִי רַבָּנַן עֲלֵיהּ דְּרַבִּי אֱלִיעֶזֶר – אֶלָּא דְּאִיתֵיהּ בְּעֵינֵיהּ, אֲבָל בְּחִסָּרוֹן – מוֹדוּ לֵיהּ; לָאו דְּחָסֵר בַּחוּץ? לָא, דְּחָסֵר בִּפְנִים.

Abaye **said to him: I heard explicitly from Rav** that **the Rabbis disagree with Rabbi Eliezer only where** the offering **is** still **in its original form,** i.e., complete. **But where** it is **lacking, they concede to him** that one is not liable. The Gemara attempts to bring a proof from here: Was Rav **not** referring to a case **where it became lacking outside** the courtyard? If so, it is evident that even according to the Rabbis a lack that occurs outside is considered a lack. The Gemara rejects this: **No,** he was referring to a case **where it became lacking inside** the courtyard. Accordingly, this mishna cannot serve as a proof.

תָּא שְׁמַע: וְכוּלָּן שֶׁחָסְרוּ וְהִקְרִיבָן בַּחוּץ – פָּטוּר; לָאו דְּחָסֵר בַּחוּץ? לָא, דְּחָסֵר בִּפְנִים.

The Gemara suggests: **Come** and **hear** a resolution from the continuation of the mishna: **And** with regard to **any of these** offerings **that were lacking** any amount, if **one sacrifices them outside** the courtyard, he is **exempt.** The Gemara attempts to bring a proof from here: Is the mishna **not** referring to a case **where it became lacking outside** the courtyard? If so, it is evident that even a lack that occurs outside is considered a lack. The Gemara rejects this: **No,** it is referring to a case **where it became lacking inside** the courtyard. Accordingly, this cannot serve as a proof.

"הַמַּקְרִיב קָדָשִׁים". אַמַּאי? וְהָאִיכָּא חֲצִיצָה!

§ The mishna teaches: **One who sacrifices sacrificial** meat, which is eaten, and sacrificial portions, i.e., those that are to be burned on the altar, outside the courtyard, is liable for the sacrifice of the sacrificial portions, but not for the meat. The Gemara asks: **Why** is he liable? If the meat is placed directly on the altar's fire and then the sacrificial portions are placed upon the meat, **isn't there an interposition** between the altar and the sacrificial portions? Since if they were offered in the Temple in that manner, one would not have fulfilled the obligation, one should not be liable if he offers them up in this manner outside the Temple.

אָמַר שְׁמוּאֵל: כְּשֶׁהֲפָכָן.

Shmuel said: The mishna is referring to a case **where he turned them over** and the sacrificial portions lay directly on the altar's fire.

וְרַבִּי יוֹחָנָן אָמַר: אֲפִילּוּ תֵּימָא שֶׁלֹּא הֲפָכָן, וְהָא מַנִּי – רַבִּי שִׁמְעוֹן הִיא, דְּאָמַר: אֲפִילּוּ הֶעֱלָה עַל הַסֶּלַע – חַיָּיב.

Rabbi Yoḥanan said there is another explanation: **You may even say** that the mishna is referring to a case **where they did not turn them over. And** in accordance with **whose** opinion **is this** mishna? It **is** in accordance with the opinion of **Rabbi Shimon, who says** (108a) that **even if one offered it up on a rock** he is **liable.** According to him, it is clear that in order for one to be liable, the mode of offering up performed outside the Temple does not need to entirely parallel the mode of offering up in the Temple.

רַב אָמַר: מִין בְּמִינוֹ אֵינוֹ חוֹצֵץ.

Rav said there is another explanation: Even in the Temple, burning the sacrificial meat and sacrificial portions in this manner would be valid as both items are from the same animal, and **a substance** in contact **with the same** type of **substance does not interpose.**[H]

מתני׳ מִנְחָה שֶׁלֹּא נִקְמְצָה, וְהִקְרִיבָהּ בַּחוּץ – פָּטוּר. קְמָצָהּ, וְחָזַר קוֹמְצָהּ לְתוֹכָהּ וְהִקְרִיבוֹ בַּחוּץ – חַיָּיב.

MISHNA If there is **a meal offering** from **which a handful was not removed,**[H] **and one sacrificed it outside** the Temple courtyard, he is **exempt** from liability, because until the handful is actually removed it is not fit to be burned on the altar inside the Temple. But if a priest **took a handful from it and** then **returned its handful into** the remainder of the meal offering, **and one sacrificed** the entire mixture **outside** the courtyard, he is **liable,** as once the handful has been removed it is fit to be burned on the altar inside the Temple, and one is liable for offering it up outside even though it is mixed into the remainder.

גמ׳ וְאַמַּאי? לִיבַטְלִי שִׁירַיִם לְקוֹמֶץ!

GEMARA The Gemara asks about the final clause: **But why** is he liable? **Let the remainder** of the meal offering, which is certainly the majority of the mixture, **nullify the handful.**

אָמַר רַבִּי זֵירָא: נֶאֶמְרָה הַקְטָרָה בְּקוֹמֶץ וְנֶאֶמְרָה הַקְטָרָה בְּשִׁירַיִם, מָה הַקְטָרַת קוֹמֶץ – אֵין קוֹמֶץ מְבַטֵּל חֲבֵירוֹ, אַף הַקְטָרַת שִׁירַיִם – אֵין שִׁירַיִם מְבַטְּלִין קוֹמֶץ.

Rabbi Zeira said: A term of **burning is stated with regard to the handful** removed from the meal offering, **and** a term of **burning is stated with regard to the remainder** of the meal offering. With regard to the handful, referred to by the Torah as "the memorial part," it is written: "And the priest shall burn the memorial part upon the altar" (Leviticus 2:2), and with regard to the remainder of the meal offering it is written: "Do not burn it as a fire to the Lord" (Leviticus 2:11). This provides a verbal analogy that teaches that **just as** with regard to the **burning of the handful,** if two handfuls are mixed together one **handful does not nullify another,**[N] **so too,** with regard to the **burning of the remainder,** if the remainder and the handful are mixed together, the **remainder does not nullify** the **handful.**

NOTES

One handful does not nullify another – אֵין קוֹמֶץ מְבַטֵּל חֲבֵירוֹ: The Torah instructs that on Yom Kippur the blood of the bull and goat offerings are to be mixed together and then sprinkled together inside the Sanctuary. Evidently, even though the quantity of the bull's blood was inevitably greater than the quantity of the goat's blood, the goat's blood is not considered to have been nullified. The Sages derive from here that items placed on the altar do not nullify one another when mixed together (see *Menaḥot* 22a–b).

HALAKHA

A substance in contact with the same substance does not interpose – מִין בְּמִינוֹ אֵינוֹ חוֹצֵץ: One who offers up an animal offering in its entirety outside the Temple courtyard is liable on account of the fact that the animal contains the sacrificial portions that should have been burned on the altar. One is liable despite the fact that those portions were never separated from the rest of the animal. This other meat of the offering is not considered an interposition between the sacrificial portions and the altar because they are all of the same substance (Rambam *Sefer Avoda, Hilkhot Ma'aseh HaKorbanot* 19:5).

A meal offering from which a handful was not removed – מִנְחָה שֶׁלֹּא נִקְמְצָה: One who offers up outside the courtyard a meal offering from which a handful was not removed is exempt because until the handful is removed it is not fit to be burned on the altar inside the Temple. But if a priest took a handful from it and then returned its handful into the remainder of the meal offering and one sacrificed the entire mixture outside the courtyard, he is liable (Rambam *Sefer Avoda, Hilkhot Ma'aseh HaKorbanot* 19:5).

מתני׳ הקומץ והלבונה שהקריב את אחד מהן בחוץ – חייב, רבי אליעזר פוטר עד שיקריב את השני. אחד בפנים ואחד בחוץ – חייב.

MISHNA The burning of both the handful and the frankincense permits the consumption of the remainder of the meal offering by the priests. With regard to **the handful and the frankincense,** in a case **where one sacrificed** only **one of them outside** the Temple courtyard, he is **liable. Rabbi Eliezer exempts** from liability one who burns only one of them **until he** also **sacrifices the second.** Since the remainder of the meal offering becomes permitted only once both have been burned, he considers each one alone to be an incomplete offering, and he holds one is not liable for sacrificing only one of them. Rabbi Eliezer concedes that if one sacrificed **one inside** the courtyard **and one outside** the courtyard, he is **liable.**

שני בזיכי לבונה שהקריב את אחד מהם בחוץ – חייב, רבי אליעזר פוטר עד שיקריב את השני. אחד בפנים ואחד בחוץ – חייב.

The burning of two bowls of frankincense permits the consumption of the shewbread. With regard to the **two bowls of frankincense,**[H] in a case **where one sacrificed** only **one of them outside** the courtyard, he is **liable. Rabbi Eliezer exempts** from liability one who burns only one of them **until he** also **sacrifices the second,** since the shewbread becomes permitted only once both bowls of frankincense are burned. Rabbi Eliezer concedes that if one sacrificed **one inside** the courtyard **and one outside** the courtyard, he is **liable.**

גמ׳ בעי רבי יצחק נפחא: קומץ מהו שיתיר כנגדו בשירים? מישרא שרי, או קלושי מיקלש?

GEMARA The mishna is based on the fact that it is permitted for the priests to consume the remainder of the meal offering only once both the handful and the frankincense have been burned. With regard to this, **Rabbi Yitzḥak Nappaḥa raises a dilemma:** If one burned the **handful** but not the frankincense, **what is** the *halakha* with regard to **whether** this **will permit** the consumption of **the corresponding** half **of the remainder?** Since the burning of both the handful and the frankincense permits the entire remainder, it seems that each one of them affects half of the remainder. Accordingly, it is unclear whether burning one of them will entirely **permit** half of the remainder, **or** whether it will merely **weaken**[N] the prohibition concerning the remainder, and it will still be prohibited to eat any of it.

אליבא דמאן? אי אליבא דרבי מאיר דאמר: מפגלין בחצי מתיר – מישרא שרי!

The Gemara asks: **In accordance with whose** opinion did Rabbi Yitzḥak Nappaḥa raise this dilemma? **If** it is **in accordance with** the opinion **of Rabbi Meir, who says: One can render** an offering ***piggul***[N] by having *piggul* intention **during half** of two acts that together **permit** the offering for consumption, i.e., during either one of them, then it should be obvious that the offering of the handful alone should entirely **permit** half of the remainder. The fact that Rabbi Meir holds that intention during just one of the acts can render the offering *piggul* demonstrates that he holds that each act alone has the power to permit part of the offering. It is apparent, then, the dilemma was not raised according to Rabbi Meir's opinion.

אי אליבא דרבנן דאמרי: אין מפגלין בחצי מתיר – לא מישרא שרי ולא מקלש קליש!

If it is **in accordance with** the opinion **of the Rabbis, who say: One cannot render** an offering *piggul* by having *piggul* intention **during half** of two acts that together **permit** the offering for consumption; rather, one must have *piggul* intention during both acts, then it is evident that neither act alone has the power to affect the offering, and so the burning of the handful alone should **neither permit** any of the remainder **nor weaken** the prohibition that applies to it. It is apparent, then, the dilemma was not raised according to the Rabbis' opinion.

אלא, אליבא דרבי אליעזר – רבי אליעזר כרבנן סבירא ליה, דאמר: אין מפגלין בחצי מתיר!

Rather, the dilemma was raised **in accordance with** the opinion **of Rabbi Eliezer** as taught in the mishna. Rabbi Eliezer rules that one who sacrifices outside only the handful or the frankincense is not liable. Evidently, he holds that neither of these alone can permit the consumption of the meal offering. The Gemara rejects this suggestion as well: **Rabbi Eliezer holds in accordance with** the opinion of **the Rabbis, who say: One cannot render** an offering *piggul* by having *piggul* intention **during half** of two acts that together **permit** the offering for consumption. Accordingly, he would hold that the offering of only the handful neither permits any of the remainder, nor weakens the prohibition concerning it, and it would not make sense to raise the dilemma according to him.

HALAKHA

Two bowls of frankincense – שני בזיכי לבונה: If one sacrificed both the handful and the frankincense of a meal offering outside the Temple courtyard, and even if he sacrificed one inside and the other outside, he is liable. Similarly, with regard to the two bowls of frankincense that are arranged together with the shewbread, if one sacrifices one inside and one outside, he is liable. This is in accordance with the opinion of the Rabbis in the mishna (Rambam *Sefer Avoda*, *Hilkhot Ma'aseh HaKorbanot* 19:14).

NOTES

Permit or weaken – מישרא שרי או קלושי מיקלש: Rashi explains the dilemma as follows: Does the burning of only the handful permit half of the remainder for eating, or does it weaken the prohibition against eating the entire remainder? *Tosafot* disagree with Rashi, insisting that there is no possibility that it would be permitted to eat half of the remainder. Rather, they explain the dilemma as follows: Does the burning of the handful alone effect only half of the remainder, such that if half of the remainder was of the volume of an olive-bulk he would receive lashes for eating the remainder? Or does the burning of the handful weaken the prohibition of the entire remainder such that one who ate from any part of the remainder would be exempt from receiving lashes?

One can render an offering *piggul*, etc. – מפגלין וכו׳: An offering is rendered *piggul* only in a case where were it not for the *piggul* intention during a rite, the performance of that rite would have permitted the consumption of the offering (see 29b). Accordingly, one who holds that one can render an offering *piggul* by having *piggul* intention during half of two acts that together permit the offering for consumption must certainly hold that each act alone has the power to permit the consumption of part of the offering.

אֶלָּא, אַלִּיבָּא דְּרַבָּנַן דְּהָכָא, מַאי? מִישְׁרָא שָׁרֵי, אוֹ קָלֵישׁ מְקַלֵּשׁ?

Rather, it must be that the dilemma was raised **in accordance with** the opinion **of the Rabbis that** is taught **here** in the mishna. They hold that one is liable even for sacrificing outside only the handful or only the frankincense. Evidently, they hold that each one alone has the power to affect the status of the remainder. Accordingly, Rabbi Yitzḥak Nappaḥa asked concerning a case where one of them is burned on the altar in the Temple, **what** is the *halakha*? Does it entirely **permit** half of the remainder, **or** does it **weaken** the prohibition concerning the entire remainder?

תֵּיקוּ.

The Gemara concludes: The dilemma **shall stand** unresolved.

מתני׳ הַזּוֹרֵק מִקְצָת דָּם בַּחוּץ

MISHNA **One who sprinkles part of** the **blood**[H] of an offering, e.g., one sprinkling instead of four, **outside** the Temple courtyard

HALAKHA

One who sprinkles part of the blood – הַזּוֹרֵק מִקְצָת דָּם: One who sprinkles part of the blood of an offering outside the Temple courtyard is liable (Rambam *Sefer Avoda, Hilkhot Ma'aseh HaKorbanot* 19:13).

Perek **XIII**
Daf **110** Amud **b**

חַיָּיב. רַבִּי אֱלִיעֶזֶר אוֹמֵר: אַף הַמְנַסֵּךְ מֵי הֶחָג בֶּחָג בַּחוּץ חַיָּיב. רַבִּי נְחֶמְיָה אוֹמֵר: שְׁיָרֵי הַדָּם שֶׁהִקְרִיבוֹ בַּחוּץ – חַיָּיב.

is liable. Rabbi Elazar says: So too, one who pours as a libation water consecrated for the libation **of the festival** of *Sukkot*, **during the Festival, outside** the courtyard, **is liable. Rabbi Neḥemya says:** For the **remainder of the blood** of an offering that was supposed to be poured at the base of the altar and **that** instead **one sacrificed outside** the courtyard, one is **liable.**

גמ׳ אָמַר רָבָא: וּמוֹדֶה רַבִּי אֱלִיעֶזֶר בְּדָמִים.

GEMARA **Rava says:** Rabbi Elazar generally holds that one is liable for sacrificing outside only when he sacrifices a complete offering, **but Rabbi Elazar concedes with regard to** the sprinkling of the **blood**[N] of an offering, that one is liable for sprinkling outside even part of the blood, e.g., one sprinkling instead of four. This is clearly the *halakha* with regard to offerings whose blood is sprinkled on the external altar, as a single sprinkling renders such an offering valid (see 36b), and it can be regarded as a complete offering. Rabbi Elazar concedes that this is the *halakha* even with regard to offerings whose blood is sprinkled on the inner altar, despite the fact that such offerings are valid only once all the sprinklings have been completed.

דְּתַנְיָא, רַבִּי אֱלִיעֶזֶר וְרַבִּי שִׁמְעוֹן אוֹמְרִים: מִמָּקוֹם שֶׁפָּסַק הוּא מַתְחִיל.

The fact that Rabbi Elazar concedes this point is apparent from that **which is taught** in a mishna (*Yoma* 60a) with regard to the numerous sprinklings of blood performed in the Holy of Holies, upon the Curtain, and on the inner altar, as part of the Yom Kippur Temple service: If during the sprinklings the blood spills and it is necessary to bring the blood of a second animal in order to complete them, **Rabbi Elazar and Rabbi Shimon say: From the place that** the High Priest **stopped** sprinkling the blood of the first animal, there **he begins** to sprinkle the blood of the second animal; it is unnecessary to repeat any of the sprinklings that have already been performed. From this ruling it is apparent that each sprinkling is considered an independent and complete act of service, and one will be liable for even a single act of sprinkling done outside the Temple.

״רַבִּי אֱלִיעֶזֶר אוֹמֵר: אַף הַמְנַסֵּךְ מֵי הֶחָג [בֶּחָג] בַּחוּץ״. אָמַר רַבִּי יוֹחָנָן מִשּׁוּם רַבִּי מְנַחֵם יוֹדְפָאָה: רַבִּי אֱלִיעֶזֶר בְּשִׁיטַת רַבִּי עֲקִיבָא רַבּוֹ אֲמָרָהּ, דְּאָמַר: נִיסּוּךְ הַמַּיִם דְּאוֹרַיְיתָא. דְּתַנְיָא, רַבִּי עֲקִיבָא אוֹמֵר: ״וּנְסָכֶיהָ״ – בִּשְׁנֵי נִיסּוּכִים הַכָּתוּב מְדַבֵּר, אֶחָד נִיסּוּךְ הַמַּיִם וְאֶחָד נִיסּוּךְ הַיַּיִן.

§ The mishna teaches: **Rabbi Elazar says: So too, one who pours as a libation water** consecrated for the libation **of the festival** of *Sukkot*, **during the Festival, outside** the courtyard, is liable. **Rabbi Yoḥanan said in the name of Rabbi Menaḥem Yodfa'a: Rabbi Elazar said that** *halakha* **in accordance with the opinion of Rabbi Akiva, his teacher, who says: The water libation** on *Sukkot* is a mitzva **by Torah law. As it is taught** in a *baraita* that **Rabbi Akiva says** concerning the verse: "Beside the daily burnt offering, its meal offering, **and its libations**" (Numbers 29:31), the fact that the Torah makes reference to "libations" in the plural indicates that **the verse is speaking of two** types of **libations. One is the water libation,** which is unique to the festival of *Sukkot*; **and** the other **one** is **the wine libation,** which always accompanies the daily offering. If the water libation was not a mitzva by Torah law, one would not be liable for pouring it as a libation outside the Temple courtyard.

NOTES

But Rabbi Elazar concedes with regard to sprinkling blood – וּמוֹדֶה רַבִּי אֱלִיעֶזֶר בְּדָמִים: The Gra, in his commentary on the Mishna, explains that Rava is referring here to Rabbi Eliezer and not Rabbi Elazar, and that the text in both the Gemara and the mishna should be emended accordingly. Since Rabbi Eliezer said in the previous mishna that one who sacrifices only the handful or only the frankincense is exempt, it was necessary for Rava to explain that Rabbi Eliezer concedes that one who sprinkles the blood only once outside the courtyard is liable.

אֲמַר לֵיהּ רֵישׁ לָקִישׁ לְרַבִּי יוֹחָנָן: אִי מַה לְּהַלָּן שְׁלֹשֶׁת לוּגִּין – אַף כָּאן שְׁלֹשֶׁת לוּגִּין; וְהָא רַבִּי אֱלִיעֶזֶר ״מֵי הֶחָג״ קָאָמַר! אִי מַה לְּהַלָּן בִּשְׁאָר יְמוֹת הַשָּׁנָה – אַף כָּאן בִּשְׁאָר יְמוֹת הַשָּׁנָה; [וְרַבִּי אֱלִיעֶזֶר] בֶּחָג קָאָמַר!

Reish Lakish said to Rabbi Yoḥanan: If Rabbi Elazar derives the mitzva of the water libation through the derivation taught by Rabbi Akiva, according to which both the wine libation and water libation are derived from the same word, then he should hold that **just as there,** with regard to wine, one is liable only if he pours **three *log*, so too here,** with regard to water, one should be liable only if he pours **three *log*. But** in the mishna, **Rabbi Elazar says** simply: **Water of the festival** of *Sukkot*,[N] which seems to include any amount. Furthermore, he should hold that **just as** with regard to pouring a libation of wine outside the Temple, one is liable for pouring a libation **during the rest of the days of the year** and not only on *Sukkot*, **so too,** with regard to pouring a libation of water, one should be liable for pouring a libation **during the rest of the days of the year. But** in the mishna **Rabbi Elazar says** that one is liable only if he pours the water libation **during the Festival.** It is apparent that Rabbi Elazar derived the mitzva of the water libation from a different source.

אִישְׁתְּמִיטְתֵיהּ הָא דְּאָמַר רַבִּי אַסִי, דְּאָמַר רַבִּי אַסִי אָמַר רַבִּי יוֹחָנָן מִשּׁוּם רַבִּי נְחוּנְיָא אִישׁ בִּקְעַת בֵּית חוֹרְתָן: עֶשֶׂר נְטִיעוֹת, עֲרָבָה וְנִיסּוּךְ הַמַּיִם הֲלָכָה לְמֹשֶׁה מִסִּינַי.

That which Rabbi Asi says escaped him,[N] **as Rabbi Asi says** that **Rabbi Yoḥanan says in the name of Rabbi Neḥunya, a man of the valley of Beit Ḥortan:** The *halakha* of **ten saplings,**[H] the practice of taking **a willow**[H] in the Temple during *Sukkot*, **and** the obligation to perform **the water libation**[H] during *Sukkot*, each of these is **a *halakha*** transmitted **to Moses from Sinai.**[B] According to Rabbi Asi, the mitzva of the water libation is not derived from the same source as the wine libation, and it is possible that there will be differences in the *halakhot* that apply to them.

תָּנוּ רַבָּנַן: הַמְנַסֵּךְ שְׁלֹשֶׁת לוּגִּין מַיִם בֶּחָג בַּחוּץ – חַיָּיב. רַבִּי אֱלְעָזָר (בְּרַבִּי שִׁמְעוֹן) אוֹמֵר: אִם מִלְּאָן לְשֵׁם חַג – חַיָּיב.

§ **The Sages taught** in a *baraita*: **One who pours as a libation three *log*** **of water during the festival** of *Sukkot* **outside**[H] the courtyard is **liable. Rabbi Elazar, son of Rabbi Shimon, says: If he filled** a service vessel with the three *log* in order to consecrate **them for the sake of the Festival,** he is **liable.**

NOTES

But Rabbi Elazar says: Water of the festival of *Sukkot* – וְהָא רַבִּי אֱלִיעֶזֶר מֵי הֶחָג קָאָמַר: Rashi explains that since there is a dispute with regard to the minimum measurement of the water libation, if Rabbi Elazar held that three *log* are required he would have said so explicitly.

That which Rabbi Asi says escaped him – אִישְׁתְּמִיטְתֵיהּ הָא דְּאָמַר רַבִּי אַסִי: The early commentaries discuss who it was that overlooked Rabbi Asi's statement, as well as how to explain the significance of this statement.

Rashi explains that it was Rabbi Menaḥem Yodfa'a who overlooked Rabbi Asi's statement. He therefore assumed that Rabbi Elazar's ruling was based on the derivation of his teacher, Rabbi Akiva, who explains that the water libation is derived from the same verse as the wine libation.

Tosafot explain that it was Reish Lakish who overlooked Rabbi Asi's statement. He therefore presumed that the statement of Rabbi Menaḥem Yodfa'a refers not only to the fact that Rabbi Akiva holds that the mitzva of the water libation is by Torah law, but also to the source of that mitzva. In fact, Rabbi Menaḥem Yodfa'a was stating that Rabbi Elazar agrees with his teacher that the water libation is by Torah law, but Rabbi Menaḥem Yodfa'a disagrees concerning the source of the mitzva, concerning which he agrees with Rabbi Asi.

Both Rashi and *Tosafot* explain that since Rabbi Elazar's statement is based on Rabbi Asi's explanation that the mitzva of the water libation is a *halakha* transmitted to Moses from Sinai, there is no reason that the *halakhot* of the water libation should parallel those of the wine libation, and it is possible that the water libation may be performed even with a minimal amount. Rabbeinu Ḥananel explains further that not only was the actual mitzva of the water libation transmitted to Moses from Sinai, but the *halakhot* pertaining to it were as well. These include the *halakha* that the libation is one that is relevant only during the festival of *Sukkot*. Therefore, one who pours a water libation during the rest of the year would not be liable (see *Sefat Emet* and *Zevaḥ Toda*).

In Rambam's Commentary on the Mishna it is explained that there is a practical difference whether the water libation is derived from a verse in the Torah or whether it is a *halakha* transmitted to Moses from Sinai. One is liable for performing it outside only if it is derived from a verse in Torah, and then only if he pours the standard measure of three *log*, as less than that amount is not regarded by Torah law as a libation.

BACKGROUND

***Halakha* transmitted to Moses from Sinai – הֲלָכָה לְמֹשֶׁה מִסִּינַי:** This phrase refers to a *halakha* that is not derived from a verse in the Torah, but which, according to tradition, was transmitted orally by God to Moses together with the Written Torah. These *halakhot* have the status of Torah law.

HALAKHA

Ten saplings – עֶשֶׂר נְטִיעוֹת: In addition to the prohibition against working the land in Eretz Yisrael during the Sabbatical Year, it is prohibited to work the land during the last thirty days of the preceding year. This prohibition is a *halakha* transmitted to Moses from Sinai. But if ten saplings are planted in the area of a *beit se'a*, 2,500 square cubits, the entire field may be plowed, on account of the saplings, until the start of the Sabbatical Year. This ruling is also a *halakha* transmitted to Moses from Sinai (Rambam *Sefer Zera'im*, *Hilkhot Shemitta VeYovel* 3:1, 5).

Willow – עֲרָבָה: Each day of *Sukkot*, willow branches would be brought to the Temple and placed upright against the altar with the tops of the branches leaning over the top of the altar. This is a *halakha* transmitted to Moses from Sinai. The mitzva can be fulfilled with even a single branch that bears a single leaf (Rambam *Sefer Zemanim*, *Hilkhot Shofar VeSukka VeLulav* 7:20).

Willow branches placed against the altar in the Temple

The water libation – נִיסּוּךְ הַמַּיִם: Each day during the seven days of *Sukkot*, a water libation was poured on the altar at the same time as the wine libation that was poured during the sacrifice of the daily morning offering. This is a *halakha* transmitted to Moses from Sinai (Rambam *Sefer Avoda*, *Hilkhot Temidin UMusafin* 10:6).

One who pours as a libation three *log* of water during the festival of *Sukkot* outside – הַמְנַסֵּךְ שְׁלֹשֶׁת לוּגִּין מַיִם בֶּחָג בַּחוּץ: One who poured three *log* of wine or water as a libation outside the courtyard is liable because such a libation is acceptable as an offering inside the Temple. One who poured less than three *log* of wine or water outside the courtyard is exempt, whether he did so during *Sukkot* or the rest of the year. This is in accordance with the opinion of the first *tanna* of the *baraita*. If one placed more than three *log* of water in a vessel, the water is consecrated and so one who pours that water as a libation outside the courtyard is liable (Rambam *Sefer Avoda*, *Hilkhot Ma'aseh HaKorbanot* 19:3–4 and *Hilkhot Me'ila* 2:9).

מַאי בֵּינַיְיהוּ? אָמַר רַב נַחְמָן בַּר יִצְחָק: בְּיֵשׁ שִׁיעוּר בְּמַיִם קָמִיפַּלְגִי.

The Gemara asks: **What** is the difference **between** these two opinions? **Rav Naḥman bar Yitzḥak said: They disagree with regard to** whether **there is** a precise **measure of water**[N] that can be consecrated as a libation. The first *tanna* holds that even if one fills a service vessel with more than three *log*, the water is thereby consecrated. Therefore, if one then pours at least three *log* of that water outside the courtyard, he is liable. Rabbi Elazar holds that if one attempts to consecrate more than three *log*, the consecration of the water is ineffective. Therefore, if one then pours three *log* of that water as a libation outside the courtyard, he is not liable.

רַב פָּפָּא אָמַר:

Rav Pappa said:

NOTES

They disagree with regard to whether there is a measure of water – בְּיֵשׁ שִׁיעוּר בְּמַיִם קָמִיפַּלְגִי: The commentaries differ in how they explain the dispute. Rashi explains that the first *tanna* holds that if one consecrated even more than three *log*, the consecration would be effective, and one who poured that water as a libation outside the Temple courtyard would be liable. Rabbi Elazar, son of Rabbi Shimon, disagrees and holds that since the libation in the Temple must be three *log*, even if one tries to consecrate more than that amount the consecration would be ineffective and one would not be liable for pouring that water as a libation outside the courtyard.

Rabbeinu Ḥananel explains the dispute in the opposite manner as Rashi. He explains that the first *tanna* holds that since the libation must be at least three *log*, it is not possible to consecrate less than that quantity. Therefore, if one tried to consecrate less than three *log* and then poured it as a libation outside the Temple courtyard, he would not be liable. Rabbi Elazar, son of Rabbi Shimon, holds that it is possible to consecrate even less than three *log*, and one who then pours it as a libation is liable (see *Tosafot*).

An entirely different explanation is offered by the *Keren Ora*, based on the Jerusalem Talmud (*Sukka* 4:6). He suggests that the dispute is not based on how much water can be consecrated but rather on how much water may be poured inside the Temple in fulfillment of the mitzva of the libation. The first *tanna* holds that only three *log* may be poured, but no more. Therefore, once those three *log* have been poured, any more is meaningless, and if one then poured water as a libation outside the Temple courtyard he would not be liable. Rabbi Elazar, son of Rabbi Shimon, holds that one may add to the amount of water poured inside the Temple courtyard. Therefore, even after pouring three *log* inside the Temple, there is still significance to the pouring of more water. Consequently, if one were to then pour water outside the courtyard, he would be liable.

Perek **XIII**
Daf **111** Amud **a**

בְּקָרְבוּ נְסָכִים בַּמִּדְבָּר פְּלִיגִי.

They disagree with regard to whether one is liable for pouring a libation outside the courtyard that was not first consecrated in a service vessel. This dispute is based on a disagreement **with regard to** whether wine **libations were offered** in the Tabernacle **in the wilderness** before the Jewish people entered Eretz Yisrael. The Gemara will soon explain the logical connection between the two issues.

רָבִינָא אָמַר: בִּלְמֵדִין נִיסּוּךְ הַמַּיִם מִנִּיסּוּךְ הַיַּיִן פְּלִיגִי.

Ravina said: Everyone agrees that wine libations are valid even if they are not first consecrated in a sacred service vessel. Therefore, one who pours a wine libation outside the courtyard is liable even if it was not first consecrated in a service vessel. **They disagree with regard to** whether the liability for pouring **a water libation can be derived from** that of **a wine libation.** The first *tanna* holds that it can; Rabbi Elazar, son of Rabbi Shimon, holds that it cannot.

תָּנוּ רַבָּנַן: הַמְנַסֵּךְ שְׁלֹשָׁה לוּגִּין יַיִן בַּחוּץ – חַיָּיב, רַבִּי אֶלְעָזָר בְּרַבִּי שִׁמְעוֹן אוֹמֵר: וְהוּא שֶׁקִּדְּשָׁן בִּכְלִי.

§ **The Sages taught** in a *baraita*: **One who pours as a libation three** *log* **of wine outside**[H] the courtyard is **liable. Rabbi Elazar, son of Rabbi Shimon, says: And that is** in a case **where he first consecrated** the wine **in** a sacred service **vessel.**

HALAKHA

One who pours as a libation three *log* of wine outside – הַמְנַסֵּךְ שְׁלֹשָׁה לוּגִּין יַיִן בַּחוּץ: One who pours as a libation three *log* of wine outside the Temple is liable. This is in accordance with the opinion of the first *tanna*. The Rambam does not note any distinctions based on whether or not the libation was first consecrated in a service vessel. This indicates that one is liable even if it was not first consecrated (Rambam *Sefer Avoda, Hilkhot Ma'aseh HaKorbanot* 19:3; see *Likkutei Halakhot*).

מאי בינייהו? אמר רב אדא בר רב יצחק: בירוצי מידות איכא בינייהו.

What is the difference **between them? Rav Adda bar Rav Yitzḥak said:** The difference **between them is** with regard to whether the **overfill of measuring vessels**[N] is also consecrated. Both agree that one is liable for pouring a libation outside the courtyard only if it was first consecrated in a service vessel. The first *tanna* holds that the liquid that rises above the rim of a vessel is also consecrated, and if one collects three *log* of that liquid and pours it as a libation outside the courtyard he is liable. Rabbi Elazar, son of Rabbi Shimon, holds that only the wine within the walls of the vessel itself is consecrated.

רבא בריה דרבה אמר: קרבו נסכים בבמה איכא בינייהו.

Rava, son of Rabba, said: The difference **between them is** with regard to whether one is liable for pouring a libation outside the courtyard that was not first consecrated in a service vessel. This dispute is based on a disagreement as to whether wine **libations were offered on** private **altars.**

ובפלוגתא דהני תנאי, דתניא: במת יחיד אינה צריכה נסכים, דברי רבי. וחכמים אומרים: טעונה נסכים.

He explains: **And** they disagree **with regard to** the issue that is the subject of **the dispute between these *tanna'im*, as it is taught** in a *baraita*: An offering sacrificed on **a private altar does not need** to be accompanied by wine **libations; this is the statement of Rabbi** Yehuda HaNasi. **And the Rabbis say:** It does **require** wine **libations.** Service vessels are not used in the context of private altars. Therefore, if libations are brought on private altars then it is apparent that libations can be valid even if they were not first consecrated in a service vessel. Accordingly, one would be liable for pouring a libation outside the Temple even if it had not first been consecrated in a service vessel. If libations are not brought on private altars, then there is no precedent of a libation that was not first consecrated in a service vessel, and one would not be liable for pouring a non-consecrated libation outside the Temple.

והני תנאי כהני תנאי, דתניא: "כי תבאו" – להטעינה נסכים בבמה גדולה הכתוב מדבר.

And the opinion of **these *tanna'im* is like** the opinion of **those *tanna'im*, as it is taught** in a *baraita*: In introducing the mitzva to bring wine libations together with animal offerings, the verse states: "**When you come** into the land of your dwellings, which I give to you" (Numbers 15:2), which indicates that the mitzva to bring libations began only once the Jewish people entered Eretz Yisrael. **The verse speaks** in order **to require** that **libations** be brought with animal offerings that are brought **upon a great** public **altar.** This assumes libations were not brought on a public altar in the wilderness. Therefore, it is necessary to teach that upon entering Eretz Yisrael they are required.

אתה אומר בבמה גדולה, או אינו אפילו בבמה קטנה? כשהוא אומר: "אל ארץ מושבתיכם אשר אני נתן לכם" – הרי בבמה הנוהגת לכולכם הכתוב מדבר, דברי רבי ישמעאל.

Do you say that the verse is referring **to** offerings brought on **a great** public **altar, or is it even** referring **to** offerings brought on **a small** private **altar?** Perhaps libations were brought on the public altar in the wilderness, and it is therefore unnecessary to state that after entering Eretz Yisrael libations should continue to be brought on a public altar. Accordingly, the verse must be teaching that after the Jewish people have entered Eretz Yisrael, libations are required even on private altars. This suggestion is rejected: **When** the verse **states:** "**Into the land of your dwellings, which I give to you [*lakhem*],**" using the plural form of the word "you," it is apparent that **the verse is speaking of** a public **altar that is used by everyone;** this is **the statement of Rabbi Yishmael.**

NOTES

The difference between them is with regard to the overfill of measuring vessels – בירוצי מידות איכא בינייהו: When a liquid is placed into a service vessel in order to measure the quantity necessary for a libation, it is thereby consecrated for that purpose. The overfill of a measuring vessel refers to the liquid that rests above the rim of the vessel when it is full. The Gemara in *Menaḥot* (88a and 90a) cites a tannaitic dispute concerning whether that extra quantity is also consecrated by the vessel, or whether only the liquid actually contained within the walls of the vessel is consecrated.

Rashi explains that the first *tanna* and Rabbi Elazar, son of Rabbi Shimon, also disagree about this issue. They are discussing a case where one collected the overfill of a number of measuring vessels, thereby obtaining three *log* (*Ḥazon Ish*), or a case where the measuring vessel itself held only three *log*, including the overfill (*Shita Mekubbetzet*).

According to Rashi's explanation, all opinions agree that one is liable only if the liquid was indeed consecrated by the vessel. The *Sefat Emet* suggests a different explanation, according to which the dispute concerns the very question of whether the liquid needs to be consecrated in order for one to be liable. He explains that the standard measuring vessel would hold precisely three *log*, including the overfill. The first *tanna* holds that although the overfill is not consecrated by the vessel, nevertheless, it is valid for the mitzva. Evidently, a liquid does not require consecration in order to be a valid libation, and accordingly, one who pours unconsecrated liquid as a libation outside is liable. Rabbi Elazar disagrees and holds that the overfill is consecrated by the vessel. Therefore, there is no precedent for the notion that an unconsecrated liquid can be a valid libation. Therefore, he rules that one is liable only in a case where he pours a libation of a consecrated liquid.

רַבִּי עֲקִיבָא אוֹמֵר: ״כִּי תָבֹאוּ״ – לְהַטְעִינָה נְסָכִים בְּבָמָה קְטַנָּה הַכָּתוּב מְדַבֵּר.

Rabbi Akiva says: Through its introductory clause: **"When you come," the verse speaks** in order **to require** that **libations** be brought with animal offerings that are brought **upon a small** private **altar.** This assumes libations were already brought in the wilderness, and the verse must be teaching that libations are required even on private altars.

אַתָּה אוֹמֵר לְבָמָה קְטַנָּה, אוֹ אֵינוֹ אֶלָּא לְבָמָה גְּדוֹלָה? כְּשֶׁהוּא אוֹמֵר: ״אֶל אֶרֶץ מוֹשְׁבֹתֵיכֶם״ – הֲרֵי בְּבָמָה הַנּוֹהֶגֶת בְּכׇל מוֹשְׁבוֹת הַכָּתוּב מְדַבֵּר.

Do you say that the verse is speaking of **a small** private **altar** outside the Temple? **Or is it only** referring **to a great** public **altar?** Perhaps libations were not brought on the public altar in the wilderness and the verse is necessary in order to teach that upon entering Eretz Yisrael they are required. **When** the verse **states: "Into the land of your dwellings,"** it is apparent that **the verse is speaking of an altar that is used in all your dwellings,** which certainly must be referring to private altars, as there was only one central public altar.

כְּשֶׁתִּמְצָא לוֹמַר, לְדִבְרֵי רַבִּי יִשְׁמָעֵאל – לֹא קָרְבוּ נְסָכִים בַּמִּדְבָּר, וּלְדִבְרֵי רַבִּי עֲקִיבָא – קָרְבוּ נְסָכִים בַּמִּדְבָּר.

The Gemara explains: **When** you analyze the matter **you will find** that you can **say** that **according to the statement of Rabbi Yishmael, libations were not offered in the wilderness.** Therefore, it is necessary to teach that upon entering Eretz Yisrael they are required. **And according to the statement of Rabbi Akiva libations were offered in the wilderness.** Therefore, the verse must be teaching that libations are required even on private altars.

רַבִּי נְחֶמְיָה אוֹמֵר: שְׁיָרֵי הַדָּם שֶׁהִקְרִיבָן בַּחוּץ – חַיָּיב.

§ The mishna teaches: **Rabbi Neḥemya says:** For the **remainder of the blood** of an offering that was supposed to be poured at the base of the altar and **that** instead **one sacrificed outside**[H] the courtyard, one is **liable.**

אָמַר רַבִּי יוֹחָנָן: [תְּנָא] רַבִּי נְחֶמְיָה כְּדִבְרֵי הָאוֹמֵר שִׁירַיִם מְעַכְּבִין.

Rabbi Yoḥanan said: Rabbi Neḥemya taught this *halakha* **in accordance with the statement of the one who says** that failure to pour the **remainder** of the blood at the base of the altar **disqualifies** the offering.

מֵיתִיבִי, רַבִּי נְחֶמְיָה אוֹמֵר: שְׁיָרֵי הַדָּם שֶׁהִקְרִיבָן בַּחוּץ – חַיָּיב. אָמַר לוֹ רַבִּי עֲקִיבָא: וַהֲלֹא שְׁיָרֵי הַדָּם שְׁיָרֵי מִצְוָה הֵם! אָמַר לוֹ: אֵיבָרִין וּפְדָרִין יוֹכִיחוּ, שֶׁהֵן שְׁיָרֵי מִצְוָה וְהַמַּקְרִיבָן בַּחוּץ חַיָּיב. אָמַר לוֹ: לֹא, אִם אָמַרְתָּ בְּאֵיבָרִים וּפְדָרִים – שֶׁהֵן תְּחִלַּת עֲבוֹדָה, תֹּאמַר בִּשְׁיָרֵי הַדָּם שֶׁאֵינָן תְּחִלַּת עֲבוֹדָה?

The Gemara **raises an objection** from a *baraita*: **Rabbi Neḥemya says** that for the **remainder of the blood** of an offering **that one sacrificed outside** the courtyard, one is **liable. Rabbi Akiva said to him: Isn't** pouring **the remainder of the blood** considered **a non-essential mitzva,** which is not indispensable to the validity of the offering? Accordingly, one should not be liable for sacrificing the blood outside the Temple courtyard. Rabbi Neḥemya **said to him:** Sacrificial **limbs and fats** of a burnt offering **will prove** the matter, **as they are** considered **a non-essential mitzva, and** yet **one who sacrifices them outside** the courtyard **is liable.** Rabbi Akiva **said to him: No, if you said** that one is liable **with regard to** the burning of the **limbs and fats, which is the start of** a sacrificial **rite,**[N] i.e., burning them is sacrificial rite in and of itself, **shall you** also **say** that this is the *halakha* **with regard to** the pouring of the **remainder of the blood, which is not the start of** a sacrificial **rite,** but is just the conclusion of the sprinkling of the blood?

וְאִם אִיתָא, לֵימָא לֵיהּ: הָנֵי נָמֵי מְעַכְּבִי! תְּיוּבְתָּא.

The Gemara explains the challenge from the *baraita*: **And if it is so** that Rabbi Neḥemya holds that that failure to pour the remainder of the blood at the base of the altar disqualifies the offering, **let** Rabbi Neḥemya **say** in response **to** Rabbi Akiva: **These too,** i.e., the pouring of the remainder of the blood, are considered to be a sacrificial rite in and of themselves because failure to pour out the remainder **disqualifies** the offering. The Gemara concludes: Indeed, this is **a conclusive refutation.**

HALAKHA

The remainder of the blood that one sacrificed outside – שְׁיָרֵי הַדָּם שֶׁהִקְרִיבָן בַּחוּץ: One who pours the remainder of the blood of an offering outside the courtyard is exempt because pouring the remainder of the blood is a non-essential mitzva. This applies even with regard to the remainder of blood that was presented on the inner altar. This is in accordance with the opinion of Rav Adda bar Ahava, who explains that Rabbi Akiva and Rabbi Neḥemya disagree with regard to blood that was presented on the inner altar. The *halakha* is in accordance with the opinion of Rabbi Akiva in his disputes with any other individual Sage (Rambam *Sefer Avoda, Hilkhot Ma'aseh HaKorbanot* 19:4).

NOTES

Burning of limbs and fats, which is the start of a sacrificial rite – אֵיבָרִים וּפְדָרִים שֶׁהֵן תְּחִילַּת עֲבוֹדָה: Rabbi Akiva highlights a fundamental distinction between these two mitzvot: Even though failure to burn the limbs and fats on the altar does not disqualify the offering, nevertheless, burning them is an important component of the sacrifice of an offering and is regarded as a rite in and of itself. Therefore, one who burns the limbs and fats outside the courtyard has certainly performed a sacrificial act, and is liable. By contrast, the pouring of the remainder of the blood upon the base of the altar is an act that is performed only in the event that some blood remains after the blood was sprinkled. Since the blood was consecrated, it cannot simply be discarded; rather, it is respectfully poured upon the base of the altar. It follows that there is no requirement to ensure that any blood remains for this purpose. Furthermore, it is clear that the pouring of the blood is not regarded as a significant sacrificial act in and of itself, and one would not be liable for carrying it out on an altar outside the Temple courtyard (*Ḥiddushei Batra*).

והשתא דאמר רב אדא בר אהבה: מחלוקת בשיריים הפנימיים, אבל בשיריים החיצונים – דברי הכל לא מעכבי; כי קאמר רבי נחמיה – בשיריים הפנימים, כי תניא ההיא – בשיריים החיצונים.

The Gemara qualifies its rejection: **And now that Rav Adda bar Ahava says:** The **dispute** between the *tanna'im* with regard to whether failure to pour the remainder of the blood disqualifies the offering is only **with regard to** the **remainder of** blood that was presented on **the inner** altar, **but with regard to** the **remainder of** blood that was presented on **the external** altar **everyone agrees** that failure to pour it **does not disqualify** the offering; the apparent contradiction between Rabbi Yoḥanan's statement and the *baraita* can therefore be resolved. **When Rabbi Neḥemya says** in the mishna that one is liable for sacrificing the remainder of the blood outside the courtyard, he is referring **to** the **remainder of** blood that was presented on **the inner** altar. The pouring of that blood is considered a rite in and of itself, and one is liable for sacrificing it outside the Temple. **When that** statement of Rabbi Neḥemya **is taught** in the *baraita*, it is referring **to the remainder of** blood that was presented on **the external** altar. Concerning such blood, Rabbi Neḥemya concedes that the pouring is not considered a rite in and of itself.

ורבי עקיבא לא ידע מאי קאמר רבי נחמיה. הוא סבר: רבי נחמיה שיריים חיצונים אמר, וקא מהדר ליה שיריים החיצונים. ורבי נחמיה לדבריו דרבי עקיבא קאמר.

In light of this, the Gemara explains the discussion between Rabbi Akiva and Rabbi Neḥemya: **And Rabbi Akiva did not know**[N] **what Rabbi Neḥemya was saying.** Rabbi Akiva **thought that Rabbi Neḥemya was stating** a ruling about the pouring of the **remainder of** blood that was presented on the **external** altar. Therefore, Rabbi Akiva **responded to him** with a claim relating to the **remainder of** blood that was presented on **the external** altar and said that it is a non-essential mitzva. **And** then **Rabbi Neḥemya** answered him by **saying** a defense of his opinion **in accordance with** the misconception underlying **the statement of Rabbi Akiva.**

מתני׳ המולק את העוף בפנים והעלה בחוץ – חייב, מלק בחוץ והעלה בחוץ – פטור. השוחט את העוף בפנים והעלה בחוץ – פטור,

MISHNA **One who pinches** the nape of **a bird** offering[H] **inside** the Temple courtyard **and** then **offers it up outside** the courtyard is **liable.** But if **one pinched** its nape **outside** the courtyard **and** then **offered** it **up outside** the courtyard he is **exempt,** as pinching the nape of a bird outside the courtyard is not considered valid pinching. **One who slaughters,** with a knife, **a bird** offering **inside**[H] the courtyard **and offers** it **up outside** the courtyard is **exempt,** as slaughtering a bird offering in the Temple courtyard disqualifies it as an offering.

Perek **XIII**
Daf **111** Amud **b**

שחט בחוץ והעלה בחוץ – חייב.

But if one **slaughtered** a bird offering **outside** the courtyard **and** then **offered** it **up outside,**[H] he is **liable.**[N]

נמצא, דרך הכשירו בפנים – פטורו בחוץ, דרך הכשירו מבחוץ – פטורו בפנים.

Evidently, the manner of its preparation inside the courtyard, i.e., pinching, effects **its exemption outside** the courtyard, and **the manner of its preparation outside** the courtyard, i.e., slaughter, effects **its exemption inside** the courtyard.

רבי שמעון אומר: כל שחייבין עליו בחוץ – חייבין על כיוצא בו בפנים שהעלה בחוץ, חוץ מן השוחט בפנים ומעלה בחוץ.

Rabbi Shimon says: With regard to **any** act of killing an animal concerning **which,** when it was performed **outside** the courtyard, one is **liable for** subsequently offering **it** up outside the courtyard, one is also **liable for** having **offered** the animal **up outside** the courtyard after performing **a similar** act of killing **inside** the courtyard. This is the *halakha* **except with regard to one who slaughters** a bird **inside** the courtyard **and offers** it **up outside** the courtyard; he is exempt.

NOTES

And Rabbi Akiva did not know, etc. – ורבי עקיבא לא ידע וכו׳: From Rashi's commentary it would appear that he had a different version of the Gemara's text, according to which the Gemara rejects the distinction between the pouring of the remainder of blood that was presented on the inner and external altars. According to this, Rabbi Neḥemya agrees that pouring the remainder of the blood that was presented on the external altar is indispensable to the validity of the offering, which he why he rules that one is liable for sacrificing this blood outside the Temple courtyard. His response in the *baraita* is that even according to Rabbi Akiva, who holds that the pouring of the remainder is not indispensable, nevertheless, one is liable for sacrificing the blood outside the courtyard (see also *Tosafot*, citing Rabbeinu Tam).

HALAKHA

One who pinches the nape of a bird offering, etc. – המולק את העוף וכו׳: One who pinches the nape of a bird offering inside the courtyard and then sacrifices it outside is liable. If he pinched its nape outside the courtyard he is exempt, and so too, if he then offers up that bird outside the courtyard he is exempt (Rambam *Sefer Avoda, Hilkhot Ma'aseh HaKorbanot* 18:18).

One who slaughters a bird offering inside – השוחט את העוף בפנים: One who slaughters a bird offering inside the Temple courtyard and then offers it up outside the courtyard is exempt, because by slaughtering it he has disqualified it from being brought as an offering inside the Temple (Rambam *Sefer Avoda, Hilkhot Ma'aseh HaKorbanot* 18:18).

HALAKHA

One slaughtered a bird offering outside and offered it up outside – שחט בחוץ והעלה בחוץ: One who slaughters a bird offering outside the courtyard and then offers it up outside the courtyard is liable to bring two sin offerings (Rambam *Sefer Avoda, Hilkhot Ma'aseh HaKorbanot* 18:18, and see Ra'avad there).

NOTES

If one slaughtered outside and offered it up outside he is liable – שחט בחוץ והעלה בחוץ חייב: Even though slaughtering is not a valid method of killing a bird offering inside the courtyard, nevertheless the Gemara derives (107a) that one is liable if he slaughters it outside the courtyard. Furthermore, even though by slaughtering it one renders the bird unfit, one is still liable for offering it up outside the courtyard. This is because, as the Gemara explains based on the verse: "And to them you shall say" (Leviticus 17:8), with regard to any offering that one is liable for slaughtering outside, one is also liable if he then offers it up outside.

גמ׳ הַאי ״הֶכְשֵׁירוֹ״, ״חִיּוּבוֹ״ הוּא! תְּנֵי: ״חִיּוּבוֹ״.

GEMARA In summarizing its rulings the mishna states: The manner of its preparation outside the courtyard effects its exemption inside the courtyard. The Gemara comments: **This** term: The manner of **its preparation,** is inappropriate when referring to the slaughter of a bird offering, as a bird offering is not prepared by slaughtering; on the contrary, it is disqualified if slaughtered. The slaughter of a bird offering outside the courtyard **is** the reason for **its liability.** The Gemara concedes: Emend the mishna and **teach: Its liability.**

״רַבִּי שִׁמְעוֹן אוֹמֵר״ [וכו׳]. אַהֵיכָא קָאֵי?

§ The mishna cites the ruling of Rabbi Shimon: **Rabbi Shimon says:** With regard to any act of killing an animal concerning which, when it was performed outside the courtyard, one is liable for subsequently offering it up outside the courtyard, one is also liable for having offered the animal up outside the courtyard after performing a similar act of killing inside the courtyard. This is the *halakha* except with regard to one who slaughters a bird inside the courtyard and offers it up outside the courtyard; he is exempt. The Gemara asks: **To what does he refer?**

אִילֵימָא אַרֵישָׁא קָאֵי: הַמּוֹלֵק עוֹף בִּפְנִים וְהֶעֱלָה בַּחוּץ – חַיָּיב, מָלַק בַּחוּץ וְהֶעֱלָה בַּחוּץ – פָּטוּר; וְאָמַר לֵיהּ רַבִּי שִׁמְעוֹן: כִּי הֵיכִי דִּפְנִים מִיחַיַּיב – בַּחוּץ נַמִי מִיחַיַּיב. הַאי ״כׇּל שֶׁחַיָּיבִין עָלָיו בַּחוּץ״, ״כׇּל שֶׁחַיָּיבִין עָלָיו בִּפְנִים״ מִיבְּעֵי לֵיהּ!

If we say that he is referring to the first clause of the mishna, which states: **One who pinches** the nape of the **bird** offering **inside and** then **offers** it **up outside** is **liable,** but if **one pinched** its nape **outside and** then **offered** it **up outside,** he is **exempt;** and it is with the second part of this clause that **Rabbi Shimon** disagrees and **says to** the first *tanna*: **Just as** one who pinches the nape of a bird offering **inside** and then offers it up outside is **liable, so too** one who pinches its nape **outside** and then offers it up outside is **liable,** this is difficult. If **that** is what Rabbi Shimon intended, then instead of saying in the mishna: With regard to **any** act of killing an animal concerning **which,** when it was performed **outside** the courtyard, one is **liable for** subsequently offering **it** up outside the courtyard, **he should have** said: With regard to **any** act of killing an animal concerning **which,** when it was performed **inside** the courtyard, one is **liable for** subsequently offering **it** up outside the courtyard, one is also liable for a similar act of killing done outside the courtyard. Evidently, Rabbi Shimon does not disagree with the first *tanna* on this issue.

אֶלָּא: כִּי הֵיכִי דְּבַחוּץ לָא מִיחַיַּיב – בִּפְנִים נַמִי לָא לִיחַיַּיב. הַאי ״כׇּל שֶׁאֵין חַיָּיבִין עָלָיו בַּחוּץ״ מִיבְּעֵי לֵיהּ!

Rather, perhaps Rabbi Shimon disagrees with the first part of the first clause and says to the first *tanna*: **Just as** one who pinches the nape of a bird offering **outside** and then offers it up outside is **not liable, so too** one who pinches its nape **inside** and then offers it up outside is **not liable.** The Gemara rejects this: If **that** is what Rabbi Shimon intended, then **he should have** said: With regard to **any** act of killing an animal concerning **which,** when it was performed **outside** the courtyard, one is **not liable for** subsequently offering **it** up outside the courtyard, one is also not liable for having offered the animal up outside the courtyard after performing a similar act of killing inside the courtyard. Evidently, Rabbi Shimon does not disagree with the first *tanna* on this issue either.

אֶלָּא אַסֵּיפָא קָאֵי: הַשּׁוֹחֵט עוֹף בִּפְנִים וְהֶעֱלָה בַּחוּץ – פָּטוּר, שָׁחַט בַּחוּץ וְהֶעֱלָה בַּחוּץ – חַיָּיב; וְאָמַר לֵיהּ רַבִּי שִׁמְעוֹן: כִּי הֵיכִי דְּבִפְנִים לָא מִיחַיַּיב – בַּחוּץ נַמִי לָא מִיחַיַּיב. הַאי ״כׇּל שֶׁאֵין חַיָּיבִין״ מִיבְּעֵי לֵיהּ!

Rather, he is referring to the latter clause of the mishna: **One who slaughters a bird** offering **inside and offers** it **up outside is exempt,** but if **one slaughtered** a bird offering **outside and** then **offered** it **up outside,** he is **liable. And** it is with the second part of this clause that **Rabbi Shimon** disagrees and **says to** the first *tanna*: **Just as** one who slaughters a bird offering **inside** and then offers it up outside is **not liable, so too** one who slaughters it **outside** and then offers it up outside is **not liable.** The Gemara rejects this: If **that** is what Rabbi Shimon intended, then **he should have** said: With regard to **any** act of killing an animal concerning **which,** when it was performed inside the courtyard, one is **not liable for** subsequently offering **it** up outside the courtyard, one is also not liable for having offered the animal up outside the courtyard after performing a similar act of killing outside the courtyard. Evidently, Rabbi Shimon does not disagree with the first *tanna* on this issue.

אֶלָּא, כִּי הֵיכִי דְּבַחוּץ מִיחַיַּיב – בִּפְנִים נַמִי מִיחַיַּיב. הָא קָתָנֵי: חוּץ מִן הַשּׁוֹחֵט בִּפְנִים וְהַמַּעֲלֶה בַּחוּץ!

Rather, perhaps Rabbi Shimon disagrees with the first part of the latter clause and says to the first *tanna*: **Just as** one who slaughters a bird offering **outside** and then offers it up outside is **liable, so too** one who slaughters it **inside** and then offers it up outside is **liable.** The Gemara rejects this: Rabbi Shimon clearly does not hold **this,** as the mishna **teaches** that he concludes: This is the *halakha* **except with regard to one who slaughters** a bird **inside** the courtyard **and offers it up outside** the courtyard; he is exempt.

אָמַר זְעֵירִי: שְׁחִיטַת בְּהֵמָה בַּלַּיְלָה אִיכָּא בֵּינַיְיהוּ, וְהָכִי קָאָמַר: [וְכֵן] הַשּׁוֹחֵט בְּהֵמָה בִּפְנִים בַּלַּיְלָה וְהֶעֱלָה בַּחוּץ – פָּטוּר, שָׁחַט בַּחוּץ בַּלַּיְלָה וְהֶעֱלָה בַּחוּץ – חַיָּיב.

If Rabbi Shimon is not referring to any of the rulings mentioned in the mishna, he must be disagreeing with the first *tanna* with regard to another issue. **Ze'eiri said:** The difference **between** the first *tanna* and Rabbi Shimon **is** with regard to the **slaughter of an animal** offering **at night** inside the courtyard, **and this** is what the mishna **is saying:** The first *tanna* said: **And so too, one who slaughters an animal** offering **inside** the courtyard **at night and** then **offers** it **up outside**[H] is **exempt,** as by slaughtering the animal at night he caused it to become disqualified. But one who **slaughtered** an animal **outside** the courtyard **at night and** then **offered** it **up outside**[H] is **liable.**

רַבִּי שִׁמְעוֹן אוֹמֵר: כָּל שֶׁחַיָּיבִין עָלָיו בַּחוּץ – חַיָּיבִין עַל כַּיּוֹצֵא בּוֹ בִּפְנִים וְהֶעֱלָה בַּחוּץ, חוּץ מִן הַשּׁוֹחֵט עוֹף בִּפְנִים וְהֶעֱלָה בַּחוּץ.

It is with this ruling that **Rabbi Shimon** disagrees and **says:** With regard to **any** act of killing an animal concerning **which,** when it was performed **outside** the courtyard, one is **liable for** subsequently offering **it** up outside the courtyard, one is also **liable for** having **offered** the animal **up outside** the courtyard after performing **a similar** act of killing **inside** the courtyard. This is the *halakha* **except with regard to one who slaughters** a bird **inside** the courtyard **and offers** it **up outside** the courtyard; he is exempt.

רָבָא אָמַר: קַבָּלָה בִּכְלִי חוֹל אִיכָּא בֵּינַיְיהוּ, וְהָכִי קָאָמַר: [וְכֵן] הַמְקַבֵּל בִּכְלִי חוֹל בִּפְנִים וְהֶעֱלָה בַּחוּץ – פָּטוּר, הַמְקַבֵּל בִּכְלִי חוֹל בַּחוּץ וְהֶעֱלָה בַּחוּץ – חַיָּיב.

The Gemara provides another suggestion: **Rava said** that the difference **between** the first *tanna* and Rabbi Shimon **is** with regard to the **collection** of the blood of an offering **in a non-sacred vessel,**[H] **and this** is what the mishna **is saying:** The first *tanna* said: **And so too, one who collects** the blood of an offering **in a non-sacred vessel inside** the courtyard **and** then **offers up** that offering **outside** is **exempt,** as receiving blood in a non-sacred vessel disqualifies the offering. But **one who collects** the blood of an offering **in a non-sacred vessel outside** the courtyard **and** then **offers up** that offering **outside** is **liable.**

רַבִּי שִׁמְעוֹן אוֹמֵר: כָּל שֶׁחַיָּיבִין עָלָיו בַּחוּץ – חַיָּיבִין עַל כַּיּוֹצֵא בּוֹ בִּפְנִים וְהֶעֱלוֹ בַּחוּץ, חוּץ מִן הַשּׁוֹחֵט עוֹף בִּפְנִים וְהֶעֱלוֹ בַּחוּץ.

It is with this ruling that **Rabbi Shimon** disagrees and **says:** With regard to **any** act done with an animal, i.e., the collecting of its blood, concerning **which,** when it was performed **outside** the courtyard, one is **liable for** subsequently offering **it** up outside the courtyard, one is also **liable for** having **offered** the animal **up outside** the courtyard after performing **a similar** act **inside** the courtyard. This is the *halakha* **except with regard to one who slaughters** a bird **inside** the courtyard **and offers** it **up outside** the courtyard; he is exempt.

HALAKHA

One who slaughters an animal inside at night and offers it up outside – הַשּׁוֹחֵט בְּהֵמָה בִּפְנִים בַּלַּיְלָה וְהֶעֱלָה בַּחוּץ: One who slaughters an animal inside the courtyard at night and then offers it up outside is exempt because by slaughtering it at night he has caused the offering to become disqualified. This is in accordance with the understanding of Ze'eiri of the dispute between Rabbi Shimon and the Rabbis, and the *halakha* is in accordance with the opinion of the Rabbis (Rambam *Sefer Avoda, Hilkhot Ma'aseh HaKorbanot* 18:17 and Radbaz there).

One who slaughtered outside at night and then offered it up outside – שָׁחַט בַּחוּץ בַּלַּיְלָה וְהֶעֱלָה בַּחוּץ: One who slaughters an animal offering outside the courtyard at night is liable because outside of the courtyard, slaughter is a valid method of preparation even at night. So too, if one then offered up that animal outside the courtyard at night, he is liable. Ra'avad disagrees and claims that from the Gemara it appears that liability for offering up outside the courtyard is incurred only during the day (Rambam *Sefer Avoda, Hilkhot Ma'aseh HaKorbanot* 18:17).

The collection of the blood in a non-sacred vessel – קַבָּלָה בִּכְלִי חוֹל: One who collects the blood of an offering in a non-consecrated vessel inside the courtyard and then offers up that offering outside the courtyard is exempt. This is in accordance with Rava's understanding of the dispute between Rabbi Shimon and the Rabbis, and the *halakha* is in accordance with the opinion of the Rabbis (Rambam *Sefer Avoda, Hilkhot Ma'aseh HaKorbanot* 18:17 and Radbaz there).

הַשְׁתָּא דְּתָנֵי אֲבוּהּ דִּשְׁמוּאֵל בַּר רַב יִצְחָק: הַמּוֹלֵק עוֹף בִּפְנִים וְהֶעֱלוֹ בַּחוּץ – חַיָּיב, מָלַק בַּחוּץ וְהֶעֱלָה בַּחוּץ – פָּטוּר, וְרַבִּי שִׁמְעוֹן מְחַיֵּיב; רַבִּי שִׁמְעוֹן הָתָם קָאֵי, וּתְנֵי: כׇּל שֶׁחַיָּיבִין עָלָיו בִּפְנִים וְהֶעֱלָה בַּחוּץ – חַיָּיבִין עָלָיו בַּחוּץ.

The Gemara comments: **Now that Shmuel's father, son of Rav Yitzḥak, has taught** a *baraita*, another explanation can be provided. The *baraita* teaches: **One who pinches** the nape of a **bird inside** the courtyard **and** then **offers it up outside is liable,** but one who **pinched** the nape of a bird **outside and** then **offered** it **up outside is exempt. And Rabbi Shimon** says that he **is liable.** It is apparent then that **Rabbi Shimon** in the mishna **is referring to there,** i.e., to the first clause of the mishna, and disagreeing with it. Therefore, one should emend the mishna **and teach:** With regard to **any** act of killing an animal concerning **which,** when it was performed **inside** the courtyard, one is **liable for** subsequently offering **it** up **outside** the courtyard, one is also **liable** for having offered the animal up **outside** the courtyard after performing a similar act of killing outside the courtyard.

מתני׳ חַטָּאת שֶׁקִּבֵּל דָּמָהּ בְּכוֹס אֶחָד; נָתַן בַּחוּץ וְחָזַר וְנָתַן בִּפְנִים, בִּפְנִים וְחָזַר וְנָתַן בַּחוּץ – חַיָּיב, שֶׁכּוּלּוֹ רָאוּי בִּפְנִים.

MISHNA With regard to **a sin offering where one collected its blood**[N] **in one cup,**[H] if he first **placed** its blood on an altar **outside** the courtyard **and then placed** the remaining blood on the altar **inside** the courtyard, or if he first placed its blood on the altar **inside** the courtyard **and then placed** the remaining blood on an altar **outside** the courtyard, in both cases he is **liable** for placing the blood outside the courtyard, **as** the blood in **its entirety is fit** to be placed on the altar **inside** the courtyard.

קִבֵּל דָּמָהּ בִּשְׁתֵּי כוֹסוֹת; נָתַן שְׁנֵיהֶם בִּפְנִים – פָּטוּר, שְׁנֵיהֶם בַּחוּץ – חַיָּיב. אֶחָד בִּפְנִים וְאֶחָד בַּחוּץ – פָּטוּר. אֶחָד בַּחוּץ וְאֶחָד בִּפְנִים – חַיָּיב עַל הַחִיצוֹן, וְהַפְּנִימִי מְכַפֵּר.

If **one collected its blood in two cups**[H] and **placed** the blood from **both of them** on the altar **inside** the courtyard he is **exempt** as he acted appropriately. If he placed the blood from **both of them** on an altar **outside** the courtyard, he is **liable,**[N] as both are fit to be placed inside. If he first placed the blood from **one** cup **inside and** then placed the blood from the other **one outside,** he is **exempt.**[N] By using the blood of the first cup to perform the mitzva of placing the blood on the altar, he thereby rendered the blood in the second cup unfit to be placed on the altar; therefore, there is no liability for placing it on an altar outside. If he first placed the blood from **one** cup **outside and** then placed the blood from the other **one inside,** he is **liable for the external** placement as that blood was fit to be placed inside, **and the internal** placement **atones** for the transgression for which the sin offering was brought.

NOTES

A sin offering where one collected its blood – חַטָּאת שֶׁקִּבֵּל דָּמָהּ: This *halakha* applies not only to a sin offering but to other offerings as well. Indeed, the *Tosefta* (12:9) states this *halakha* with regard to a burnt offering. It would appear that the only reason the mishna presents this *halakha* specifically with regard to a sin offering is that it goes on to teach the case of a sin offering that was separated and then lost, which applies only in the case of a sin offering.

If he placed the blood from both of them outside he is liable – שְׁנֵיהֶם בַּחוּץ חַיָּיב: Rashi explains that if one placed both of them in a single lapse of awareness he is liable to bring only one sin offering. If he placed them in two separate lapses of awareness he is liable to bring two sin offerings.

One cup inside and one outside, he is exempt – אֶחָד בִּפְנִים וְאֶחָד בַּחוּץ פָּטוּר: When the blood is collected in one cup, any blood that was not placed is a remainder. Whether one is liable for sacrificing such blood outside the courtyard is dependent on whether or not the pouring of the remainder on the base of the altar is indispensable to the validity of the offering, as the Gemara explains. But in a case where the blood is collected in two cups, the Gemara explains that the blood in the second cup is considered to have been disqualified. Therefore, even according to the opinion that the pouring of the remainder is indispensable, one would not be liable for sacrificing such blood outside the courtyard (Rashi).

The Rambam had a different version of the Gemara's text according to which in a case where the blood is collected in two cups one is liable for sacrificing the blood of the second cup outside the courtyard.

HALAKHA

A sin offering where one collected its blood in one cup – חַטָּאת שֶׁקִּבֵּל דָּמָהּ בְּכוֹס אֶחָד: If one collects the blood of a sin offering in a single cup and first places some of the blood on an altar outside the courtyard and then places the remaining blood on the altar inside the courtyard, he is liable for placing the blood outside the courtyard, as it was fit to have been placed on the altar inside the courtyard. If one first places some of the blood on the altar inside the courtyard and then places the remaining blood on an altar outside the courtyard, he is exempt, as once part of the blood has been placed on the altar inside the courtyard the rest of the blood is regarded as a mere remainder. This is not in accordance with the mishna, as the mishna expresses the opinion of Rabbi Neḥemya, who holds that one is liable for placing the remainder on an altar outside the courtyard, as he holds that the pouring of the remainder of the blood on the base is indispensable to the validity of an offering (Rambam *Sefer Avoda, Hilkhot Ma'aseh HaKorbanot* 19:13).

One collected its blood in two cups – קִבֵּל דָּמָהּ בִּשְׁתֵּי כוֹסוֹת: If the blood of a sin offering was collected in two cups and then one placed the blood from both of them on an altar outside the courtyard, or the blood of one outside and then the blood of the other inside, or the blood of one inside and then the blood of the other outside, he is liable. The Ra'avad questions why one is liable even when he places the blood of one inside and then the blood of the other outside, since the blood of the second cup should be regarded as disqualified. It appears that the Rambam had a version of the mishna that explicitly stated that one is liable in that case (Rambam *Sefer Avoda, Hilkhot Ma'aseh HaKorbanot* 19:13, and see *Kesef Mishne* there).

לְמָה הַדָּבָר דּוֹמֶה? לְמַפְרִישׁ חַטָּאתוֹ וְאָבְדָה, וְהִפְרִישׁ אַחֶרֶת תַּחְתֶּיהָ, וְאַחַר כָּךְ נִמְצֵאת הָרִאשׁוֹנָה, וַהֲרֵי שְׁתֵּיהֶן עוֹמְדוֹת; שָׁחַט שְׁתֵּיהֶן בִּפְנִים – פָּטוּר, שְׁתֵּיהֶן בַּחוּץ – חַיָּיב, אַחַת בִּפְנִים וְאַחַת בַּחוּץ – פָּטוּר, אַחַת בַּחוּץ וְאַחַת בִּפְנִים – חַיָּיב עַל הַחִיצוֹנָה, וְהַפְּנִימִית מְכַפֶּרֶת.

To what is this matter comparable? It is comparable **to** a case where one **separated** an animal for **his sin offering and it was lost, and he separated another** animal **in its place, and thereafter, the first** animal **was found.** In that case, **both of them stand** before him and he must sacrifice one as his sin offering. If **he slaughtered both of them inside** the courtyard, he is **exempt.** If he slaughtered **both of them outside** the courtyard, he is **liable,** as each was fit to be slaughtered in the courtyard. If he first slaughtered **one inside and** then slaughtered the other **one outside** he is **exempt** from liability for slaughtering the second, as he has already fulfilled his obligation with the first, thereby rendering the second one unfit for sacrifice. If he first slaughtered **one outside and** then slaughtered the other **one inside** he is **liable for** slaughtering **the external** animal outside the courtyard, as it was fit to be slaughtered inside, **and the internal** animal **atones** for the transgression for which the sin offering was brought.

כְּשֵׁם שֶׁדָּמָהּ פּוֹטֵר אֶת בְּשָׂרָהּ כָּךְ הִיא פּוֹטֶרֶת אֶת בְּשַׂר חֲבֵירְתָּהּ.

The mishna adds: In a case where one slaughtered both inside the courtyard, **just as** placing **the blood of** the first animal[H] **exempts** one who consumes **its meat**[N] from liability for misuse of consecrated property, **so too, it exempts** one who consumes **the meat of its counterpart,** the second animal, from liability.

HALAKHA

Just as placing the blood of the first animal, etc. – כְּשֵׁם שֶׁדָּמָהּ וכו׳: With regard to one who separated a sin offering and it was subsequently lost and he separated another sin offering as a replacement, and then the first sin offering was found, and he slaughtered both sin offerings simultaneously, once the blood of one of the sin offerings has been placed, a person who consumes the meat of that offering does not incur liability for the misuse of consecrated property, and neither does one who consumes the meat of the other offering. This is despite the fact that the placement of the blood of one offering does not permit the consumption of the meat of the other offering. Nevertheless, since before the blood was placed the meat of both offerings could have been permitted by the placement of their blood, one who consumes the meat of either of them does not incur liability for misuse of consecrated property.

If the sin offerings were slaughtered consecutively, then since after the slaughter of the first one, the meat of the second one could no longer be permitted by the placement of its blood, one who consumes its meat is liable for misuse of consecrated property. This is based on the Gemara in *Me'ila* 7a (Rambam *Sefer Avoda, Hilkhot Me'ila* 3:6, and see *Kesef Mishne* there).

NOTES

Just as placing the blood of the first exempts its meat, etc. – כְּשֵׁם שֶׁדָּמָהּ פּוֹטֵר אֶת בְּשָׂרָהּ וכו׳: Rashi explains that this statement of the mishna should not be understood as the continuation of the previous clause. The previous clause concerns a case in which the second sin offering was slaughtered outside the courtyard. Since it died without being appropriately slaughtered, it is obvious that its meat is not subject to the prohibition of misuse of consecrated property (see *Me'ila* 2b). Rather, this statement is independent and concerns a case in which both animals are slaughtered inside the courtyard. In such a case, the placement of the blood of the first sin offering exempts one who consumes the meat of the other sin offering from liability for misuse of consecrated property. This is because by placing the blood of the first sin offering, the owner achieves atonement, and the *halakha* is that there is no liability for misuse of consecrated property in a case where benefit is derived from a sin offering whose owner has already achieved atonement through a different sin offering (see *Me'ila* 3a).

Tosafot explain that this clause concerns a case where both sin offerings were slaughtered simultaneously. Since the two animals are viewed as one unit, the placement of the blood of one affects the other and exempts one who consumes the meat of either animal from liability for misuse of consecrated property (see Rambam's Commentary on the Mishna and *Tiferet Yisrael*).

Perek **XIII**
Daf **112** Amud **a**

גמ׳ בִּשְׁלָמָא בַּחוּץ וְחָזַר וְנָתַן בִּפְנִים – שֶׁכּוּלּוֹ רָאוּי לִהְיוֹת בִּפְנִים. אֲבָל בִּפְנִים וְהֶעֱלָן בַּחוּץ – שִׁירַיִים נִינְהוּ!

GEMARA The Gemara discusses the first clause of the mishna: **Granted** that one is liable in a case where he first placed the blood on an altar **outside** the courtyard **and then placed** the remaining blood on the altar **inside** the courtyard; that is because, as the mishna explains: **As the blood in its entirety is fit to be** placed **inside** the courtyard. **But** in a case where he first placed its blood on the altar **inside** the courtyard **and then offered up** the remaining blood on an altar **outside** the courtyard, why he is liable? That blood **is** merely **a remainder,** and one should not be liable for offering it up outside.

הָא מַנִּי – רַבִּי נְחֶמְיָה הִיא, דְּאָמַר: שִׁירֵי הַדָּם שֶׁהִקְרִיבָן בַּחוּץ – חַיָּיב.

The Gemara explains: In accordance with **whose** opinion **is this** mishna? It **is** in accordance with the opinion of **Rabbi Neḥemya,**[N] **who says:** For the **remainder of the blood** of an offering that was supposed to be poured at the base of the altar and **that** instead **one sacrificed outside** the courtyard, one is **liable.**

NOTES

It is Rabbi Neḥemya – רַבִּי נְחֶמְיָה הִיא: From the Gemara's discussion on the previous mishna it emerges that Rabbi Neḥemya holds that the pouring of the remainder of the blood on the base of the altar is indispensable only with regard to the remainder of blood that was placed on the inner altar. Accordingly, some of the commentaries explain that this mishna should also be understood as referring specifically to offerings whose blood is placed on the inner altar.

אי רבי נחמיה, אימא סיפא: קבל דמה בשני כוסות, נתן שניהם בפנים – פטור, שניהם בחוץ – חייב, אחד בפנים ואחד בחוץ – פטור. והאמר רבי נחמיה: שירי הדם שהקריבן בחוץ – חייב!

The Gemara asks: **If the mishna is in accordance with the opinion of Rabbi Neḥemya,** then **say the latter clause: If one collected its blood in two cups and placed** the blood from **both of them** on the altar **inside** the courtyard, he is **exempt.** If he placed the blood from **both of them** on an altar **outside** the courtyard, he is **liable. If** he first placed the blood from **one** cup **inside and** then placed the blood from the other **one outside,** he is **exempt.** By using the blood of the first cup to perform the mitzva of placing the blood on the altar, he thereby rendered the blood in the second cup a mere remainder. The Gemara asks: How can this clause be attributed to Rabbi Neḥemya? **But doesn't Rabbi Neḥemya say:** For **the remainder of the blood** of an offering **that one offered outside** the courtyard, he is **liable?**

סיפא אתאן לתנא קמא דרבי אלעזר ברבי שמעון, דאמר: כוס עושה דחוי לחבירו.

The Gemara answers: In **the latter clause we arrive at** the opinion of **the first** *tanna*, who disagrees with **Rabbi Elazar, son of Rabbi Shimon.**[N] **As** that *tanna* **says:** The placement of the blood from one **cup renders** the blood of **the other** cup **as disqualified.**[H] Since it is actually disqualified and not merely a remainder, one is not liable for offering it up outside.

״למה הדבר דומה? למפריש חטאתו ואבדה והפריש אחרת תחתיה ואחר כך נמצאת הראשונה״.

§ The mishna presents an analogy for its ruling: **To what is this matter comparable?** It is comparable **to** a case where one **separated** an animal for **his sin offering and it was lost, and he separated another** animal **in its place, and thereafter, the first** animal **was found.**

״למה הדבר דומה״ למה לי? הא מני – רבי היא, דאמר: אבודה בשעת הפרשה – מתה.

The Gemara asks: **Why do I** need to ask: **To what is this matter comparable,** and provide an analogy to the mishna's rulings? What does the analogy add? The Gemara explains: In accordance with **whose** opinion **is this** mishna? It **is** in accordance with the opinion of **Rabbi**[N] Yehuda HaNasi, **who says** (see *Temura* 22b): A sin offering that was **lost during the time of the separation**[H] of a substitute, if it is later found and one of them is slaughtered as the person's sin offering, the other one is **put to death.** Accordingly, it is actually disqualified from being used as an offering, and one is therefore not liable for offering it up outside.

HALAKHA

One cup renders the blood of the other cup as disqualified – כוס עושה דחוי לחבירו: If the blood of a sin offering was collected in four cups, then if all the presentations were sprinkled from one cup, the remainder of blood in that cup must be poured on the base of the altar, whereas the blood in the other cups is poured into the channel running through the Temple. This is in accordance with the opinion of the first *tanna*, who disagrees with Rabbi Elazar, son of Rabbi Shimon (Rambam *Sefer Avoda, Hilkhot Pesulei HaMukdashin* 2:21).

A sin offering that was lost during the time of the separation – אבודה בשעת הפרשה: With regard to one who separated an animal as a sin offering and it was lost, and he separated another animal as a sin offering and then the first one was found: If he selected one of the sin offerings and sacrificed it, the other is rendered unfit and it is put to death. If the person inquired as to which offering it is preferable to sacrifice, he should be told to sacrifice the one he separated first and allow the other to graze until it develops a blemish, at which point it should be sold and the proceeds used to purchase a voluntary offering. This is in accordance with the opinion of the Rabbis who disagree with Rabbi Yehuda HaNasi, as explained by Rav Huna, citing Rav (Rambam *Sefer Avoda, Hilkhot Pesulei HaMukdashin* 4:3).

NOTES

In the latter clause we arrive at the opinion of the first *tanna* who disagrees with Rabbi Elazar son of Rabbi Shimon – סיפא אתאן לתנא קמא דרבי אלעזר ברבי שמעון: The latter clause discusses a case in which all the blood presentations were placed on the altar using blood from one cup. According to Rabbi Elazar, son of Rabbi Shimon, it is then a mitzva to pour the rest of the blood in that cup, as well as all of the blood in the other cup, on the base of the altar. The first *tanna* holds that through the use of the blood of one cup for the blood presentations, the blood in the other cup is rendered disqualified for use. Therefore, it may not even be poured on the base of the altar; rather, it must be poured away into the channel running through the Temple.

Rashi had a different version of the Gemara's text, according to which the first *tanna*, who disagrees with Rabbi Elazar, son of Rabbi Shimon, is actually Rabbi Neḥemya. According to Rabbi Neḥemya's opinion, with regard to the pouring of the blood on the base of the altar, it is only the blood in the cup from which the presentations were made that is indispensable to the validity of the offering. Therefore, one is liable for sacrificing only that blood outside the courtyard, but not the blood from the second cup. According to the standard version of the Gemara's text it appears that the first *tanna* and Rabbi Neḥemya express two distinct opinions.

Whose opinion is this? It is Rabbi, etc. – הא מני רבי היא וכו׳: The mishna in *Temura* (22b) records a dispute between Rabbi Yehuda HaNasi and the Rabbis concerning a case in which a sin offering was lost and another was separated as a replacement. According to the Rabbis, the only case in which one of the animals is put to death is a case where the one that was lost is found only after the replacement had already been sacrificed. If it is found beforehand, then the offering that was not sacrificed is left to graze until it develops a blemish. Rabbi Yehuda HaNasi disagrees and holds that even if it is found before either one was sacrificed, once one of them is sacrificed the other is put to death. The rationale behind Rabbi Yehuda HaNasi's opinion is that as soon as one of the sin offerings is sacrificed, the other is considered disqualified for use.

The Gemara explains that the mishna here is in accordance with the opinion of Rabbi Yehuda HaNasi, and that is why it rules that once one sin offering was appropriately sacrificed inside the Temple courtyard, a person is not liable if he sacrifices the second one outside the courtyard. By attributing this ruling to the opinion of Rabbi Yehuda HaNasi, the Gemara highlights the fact that one is exempt from liability for sacrificing an offering outside only if that offering was disqualified for use, but not in a case where it was merely unfit to the extent that it should be left to graze. This serves to limit the scope of the mishna's ruling concerning two cups, i.e., one is exempt only if the second cup of blood was rendered disqualified for use.

וְהָכִי קָאָמַר: טַעְמָא דְּאָבְדָה, הָא הִפְרִישׁ שְׁתֵּי חַטָּאוֹת לְאַחֲרָיוּת – חֲדָא מִינַּיְיהוּ מֵעִיקָּרָא עוֹלָה הִיא.

And this is what the mishna **is saying** by presenting its analogy: **The reason** that one is exempt from liability for offering up the unused sin offering outside is **that** it **was lost** at the time its substitute was separated and therefore it is considered disqualified. **But** if **one separated two sin offerings** from the outset **as a guarantee,**[H] so that even if one is lost he can use the other, then if neither is lost and he sacrifices one of them, the other one is not put to death. Rather, it is left to graze until it becomes blemished, at which point it is sold and the proceeds used to purchase a voluntary burnt offering. It emerges that **from the outset, one of these** two animals, i.e., the one that was not ultimately sacrificed as his sin offering, **is a burnt offering,** and therefore if one offers it up outside the courtyard he is liable. The analogy teaches that with regard to blood collected in two cups, if one offers up blood from the unused cup outside, he is exempt only because the blood in that cup is considered disqualified, but he would not be exempt if it was considered a remainder.

וְכִדְרַב הוּנָא אָמַר רַב, דְּאָמַר רַב הוּנָא אָמַר רַב: אָשָׁם שֶׁנִּיתַּק לִרְעִיָּיה וּשְׁחָטוֹ סְתָם – כָּשֵׁר לְעוֹלָה.

And this is **in accordance with** the statement that **Rav Huna** says that **Rav says, as Rav Huna says** that **Rav says: A guilt offering that was consigned to grazing**[HN] per the *halakha* to leave it to graze if its owner dies or achieves atonement through another guilt offering, **and** then instead of being left to develop a blemish, at which point it could be sold and the proceeds used to purchase a voluntary burnt offering, one **slaughtered it,** even with **unspecified** intent, the animal itself is **fit** to be sacrificed **as a burnt offering.** Similarly, the mishna assumes that in any case where an animal is consigned to grazing it is considered fit, and one would be liable for slaughtering it outside the courtyard.

מִי דָּמֵי? הָתָם אָשָׁם זָכָר וְעוֹלָה זָכָר, אֲבָל חַטָּאת נְקֵבָה הִיא! אָמַר רַב חִיָּיא מִיּוֹסְתִּינְיָא: בִּשְׂעִיר נָשִׂיא.

The Gemara asks: **Are** these cases **comparable? There,** in Rav's ruling, it is logical that the animal is considered fit, as **a guilt offering** is **a male** animal **and a burnt offering** is **a male** animal, so it is possible to bring an animal as the latter even if it had been designated as the former. Therefore, a guilt offering left to graze is still considered fit. **But** in the mishna's case, just because the animal is left to graze does not necessarily indicate that it itself is fit to be brought, as **a sin offering is a female** animal, which can never be brought as a burnt offering. Therefore, it should be considered unfit. **Rav Ḥiyya from Yostiniyya said:** The ruling of the mishna is **with regard to the goat of the** ***Nasi,***[B] which is a male sin offering. Therefore, in a case where it is left to graze it is still considered fit, as it can be brought as a burnt offering.

הדרן עלך השוחט והמעלה

HALAKHA

One separated two sin offerings as a guarantee – הִפְרִישׁ שְׁתֵּי חַטָּאוֹת לְאַחֲרָיוּת: One who separated two animals as sin offerings as a guarantee may sacrifice either one as his sin offering. The other animal is sent out to graze in the field until it develops a blemish, at which point it is sold and the proceeds used to purchase a voluntary offering (Rambam *Sefer Avoda, Hilkhot Pesulei HaMukdashin* 4:5).

A guilt offering that was consigned to grazing – אָשָׁם שֶׁנִּיתַּק לִרְעִיָּיה: If the owner of a guilt offering dies or achieves atonement through a different guilt offering, the animal is left to graze until it develops a blemish. If one instead slaughtered it as a burnt offering, it is valid. This is in accordance with the opinion of Rav Huna, citing Rav (Rambam *Sefer Avoda, Hilkhot Pesulei HaMukdashin* 4:15).

NOTES

A guilt offering that was consigned to grazing – אָשָׁם שֶׁנִּיתַּק לִרְעִיָּיה: If the owner of a guilt offering dies or achieves atonement through a different guilt offering, the court consigns the animal to grazing until it develops a blemish, at which point it is sold and the proceeds are used to purchase a burnt offering. At the point it was consigned, if one were to offer the animal itself as a burnt offering it would be valid. The Gemara (5b) notes that this is the *halakha* only if the court explicitly consigned the animal to grazing in order to eventually use it for the purchase of a burnt offering. The early commentaries discuss whether the requirement that the court be involved is by Torah law or rabbinic law (see commentaries to 5b).

BACKGROUND

Goat of the *Nasi* – שְׂעִיר נָשִׂיא: The Torah refers to a case in which a *Nasi* commits a transgression (Leviticus 4:22). This is understood to refer to the transgression of a king. In order to atone for his sin, he does not bring a female goat or lamb like a commoner would; rather, he brings a young male goat. In all other respects, this sacrifice follows a procedure identical to that of the standard sin offering.

Summary of **Perek XIII**

This chapter discussed two distinct prohibitions: That of slaughtering an offering outside the Temple courtyard and that of offering up an offering by placing it upon an altar outside the Temple courtyard. Since they are considered two distinct prohibitions, one is liable even if he performs only one of them, and he is liable twice if he performs both.

While the slaughter of an animal is a single act that can be performed only once on each animal, it is possible to offer up an animal in many parts. Therefore, the Gemara discussed when one would incur liability in such cases. According to its conclusion, one is liable separately for offering up each and every limb of an offering, but one is not liable separately for offering up one limb in many parts.

A further distinction between slaughtering and offering up is that one is liable for slaughtering in any place, whereas in order for an act to be defined as offering up, the offering must be raised upon some type of sacrificial platform. This leads to the question of whether it is necessary to offer it up specifically on an altar or whether any high place will suffice. The Gemara concludes that in order to become liable one must use an altar, but the altar does not need to conform to all the requirements of the altar inside the Temple.

A basic condition of liability for offering up outside the Temple is that the offering is fit to have been offered up inside the Temple. The Gemara expanded this to include offerings that were rendered unfit during the course of the Temple service. Even though it is prohibited to sacrifice such offerings, one is liable if he offers them up outside the Temple, since if they are placed, albeit unlawfully, upon the altar in the Temple, they are thereby rendered acceptable. Additionally, one is liable for offering up only those parts of the offering that were supposed to have been offered up on the Temple altar. Accordingly, while one is liable for offering up the sacrificial portions of an offering, he is not liable for offering up its meat, which should have been eaten by the priests or the owner of the offering.

In order to be liable, it is not necessary to offer up the entire offering that would have been brought inside the Temple. Rather, one is liable even if he offers up an olive-bulk of the offering. This applies only in a case where the offering is still fit to be offered up inside. Therefore, if a lack in the quantity of the offering disqualifies it, one would no longer be liable for offering it up outside.

This chapter also considered the application of these prohibitions to the slaughter and sacrifice of birds, and to the sacrifice of meal offerings and incense.

These prohibitions applied only during the times when there was a fixed place for the Tabernacle, and subsequently, once the Temple was constructed. During these periods, the use of any form of private altar was prohibited. Clearly, the prohibitions were not in effect during periods when the use of private altars was permitted. Therefore, one might have assumed that if an offering was consecrated during one of those periods, it would still be permitted to sacrifice that offering even once the use of private altars became prohibited. The Gemara derived that this is incorrect and that the prohibitions also apply to such offerings.

Whether or not the prohibitions still apply nowadays depends on whether theoretically it is still possible to sacrifice offerings today. That question depends primarily on whether the initial consecration of Jerusalem and the Temple area sanctified those areas only for their time, while the Temple stood, or whether it also sanctified them forever, even following the Temple's destruction. If the areas are still consecrated, then it is theoretically still possible to construct an altar there and bring offerings upon it. Accordingly, the prohibition against offering up offerings in a different location would remain in effect.

Introduction to **Perek XIV**

You shall not do all that we do here this day, every man whatsoever is fitting in his own eyes. For you have not as yet come to the rest and to the inheritance, which the Lord your God has given you. But when you go over the Jordan, and dwell in the land that the Lord your God causes you to inherit, and He gives you rest from all your enemies round about, so that you dwell in safety. Then it shall come to pass that the place that the Lord your God shall choose to cause His name to dwell there, there you shall bring all that I command you: Your burnt offerings, and your sacrifices, your tithes, and the offering of your hand, and all your choice vow offerings that you vow to the Lord. And you shall rejoice before the Lord your God, you, and your sons, and your daughters, and your slaves, and your maidservants, and the Levite who is within your gates, as he has no portion or inheritance with you. Take heed to yourself that you do not offer your burnt offerings in every place that you see. But in the place that the Lord shall choose in one of your tribes, there you shall offer your burnt offerings, and there you shall do all that I command you.

(Deuteronomy 12:8–14)

The major issues with regard to the prohibitions against slaughtering and sacrificing offerings outside the Temple courtyard were discussed in the previous chapter. Several outstanding matters remain to be clarified, particularly those cases where the prohibitions do not apply, either entirely or in part.

This chapter can be divided into two main parts. In the first, the Gemara discusses sacrificial animals that are not classified as offerings or which suffer from a fundamental disqualification that prevents them from being sacrificed in the Temple, either permanently or temporarily. Consequently, one is not punished for sacrificing these animals outside the Temple.

It is therefore necessary to define precisely which offerings are unfit for sacrifice on the altar because of their disqualification. In this regard, one must also clarify the status of offerings that were initially fit for sacrifice but which were disqualified after they were consecrated. The same applies to the reverse case of offerings that are currently disqualified but will later be fit for sacrifice due to forthcoming changes in the animal or its owner. Even in the case of an offering for which one is not liable either to receive *karet* if he intentionally sacrificed it outside the Temple or to bring a sin offering if he did so unwittingly, it must be established whether he is entirely exempt or if he has violated a prohibition by Torah law.

The second section of the chapter primarily involves defining those periods in history in which the prohibition against sacrificing offerings outside the Temple was in effect, an issue that was only touched upon in the previous chapter. The verses indicate that this prohibition applies only when the Temple is standing. During times when there was no Temple it was permitted to sacrifice offerings on private altars. It is therefore necessary to determine which offerings may be sacrificed on these altars and how the service at private altars was performed.

Clarifying the details of these issues and various other related matters is the central focus of this chapter.

מתני׳ פָּרַת חַטָּאת שֶׁשְּׂרָפָהּ חוּץ מִגִּתָּהּ, וְכֵן שָׂעִיר הַמִּשְׁתַּלֵּחַ שֶׁהִקְרִיב בַּחוּץ – פָּטוּר,

MISHNA With regard to **the red heifer of purification**[BH] **that one burned**[N] **outside its pit,** the pit being an excavation on the Mount of Olives opposite the entrance to the Sanctuary designated for its slaughter and its burning, **and likewise the scapegoat that one sacrificed outside** the Temple courtyard rather than casting it off a cliff as prescribed, he is **exempt** from punishment for violating the transgression of slaughtering and sacrificing outside the Temple courtyard.

שֶׁנֶּאֱמַר: ״וְאֶל פֶּתַח אֹהֶל מוֹעֵד לֹא הֱבִיאוֹ״, כׇּל שֶׁאֵין רָאוּי לָבֹא אֶל פֶּתַח אֹהֶל מוֹעֵד – אֵין חַיָּיבִין עָלָיו.

The source for this is **as it is stated** with regard to slaughter of sacrificial animals outside the courtyard: "Whatever man…that slaughters outside the camp, **and to the entrance of the Tent of Meeting he did not bring it,** to present it as an offering to the Lord before the Tabernacle of the Lord" (Leviticus 17:3–4). From that verse it is derived: For **any** offering **that is not fit to come to the entrance of the Tent of Meeting** for sacrifice on the altar, e.g., the red heifer and the scapegoat, **one is not liable for its** slaughter and sacrifice outside its place.

הָרוֹבֵעַ, וְהַנִּרְבָּע, וְהַמּוּקְצֶה, וְהַנֶּעֱבָד, וְהַמְּחִיר, [וְהָאֶתְנַן], וְהַכִּלְאַיִם, וְהַטְּרֵיפָה, וְיוֹצֵא דוֹפֶן, שֶׁהִקְרִיבָן בַּחוּץ – פָּטוּר,

With regard to **an animal that** actively **copulated with a person, or an animal that was the object of bestiality, or** an animal **that** was **set aside** for idol worship, **or** an animal **that was worshipped** as a deity, **or** an animal given as **the price** of a dog that was purchased, **or** an animal that was given as **payment** to a prostitute, **or** an animal born of a mixture of **diverse kinds, or an animal with a wound that will cause it to die within twelve months** [*tereifa*], **or** an animal **born by caesarean section,** any of **which one sacrificed outside** the Temple courtyard, he is **exempt.**[H]

שֶׁנֶּאֱמַר: ״לִפְנֵי מִשְׁכַּן ה׳״, כׇּל שֶׁאֵין רָאוּי לָבֹא לִפְנֵי מִשְׁכַּן ה׳ – אֵין חַיָּיבִין עָלָיו.

The source for this is **as it is stated:** "And to the entrance of the Tent of Meeting he did not bring it to present it as an offering to the Lord **before the Tabernacle of the Lord.**" From this verse, it is derived: For **any** animal **that is not fit to come to the entrance of the Tent of Meeting**[N] for sacrifice on the altar, **one is not liable for its** slaughter and sacrifice outside the courtyard.

בַּעֲלֵי מוּמִין, בֵּין בַּעֲלֵי מוּמִין קְבוּעִין בֵּין

For **blemished** animals, **whether** they are **permanently blemished** or **whether** they are

BACKGROUND

Red heifer of purification – פָּרַת חַטָּאת: Purification from ritual impurity imparted by a corpse is achieved by means of water mixed with the ashes of a red heifer (see Numbers, chapter 19). This heifer and all of its hairs must be entirely red; even two black hairs disqualify it for this ritual. Similarly, it may not have any blemishes, nor may it have been used for any labor.

The red heifer was slaughtered on the Mount of Olives outside Jerusalem, and its blood was sprinkled seven times in the direction of the Temple. Its body was then burned on a special pyre, to which cedar wood, hyssop, and crimson wool were added. Afterward, the ashes from this pyre were gathered and mixed in a vessel with water drawn from a spring. Three hyssop branches were dipped in the water, which was then sprinkled on the impure person, on the third and seventh days of their impurity. A single drop from the mixture that lands anywhere on the person's body suffices to purify him.

Grinding the charred remains of the red heifer into ash

HALAKHA

Red heifer of purification – פָּרַת חַטָּאת: If a red heifer was burned outside the location designated for its burning, or a scapegoat was sacrificed outside the Temple courtyard after it had been confessed upon, one is exempt, as it is stated: "And has not brought it to the entrance of the Tent of Meeting" (Leviticus 17:4). From here it is derived that if the animal is not fit to be brought to the Tent of Meeting one is not liable for slaughtering it outside the Temple courtyard (Rambam *Sefer Avoda, Hilkhot Ma'aseh HaKorbanot* 18:11, 19:7).

With regard to an animal that copulated with a person…which one sacrificed outside the Temple courtyard, he is exempt – הָרוֹבֵעַ...שֶׁהִקְרִיבָן בַּחוּץ פָּטוּר: One is liable for slaughtering an offering outside the Temple courtyard only if that animal was fit to be sacrificed upon the altar. If one slaughtered an animal that it is prohibited to sacrifice upon the altar, or a sin offering that is left to die, he is exempt, as it is stated: "Before the Tabernacle of the Lord" (Leviticus 17:4). This indicates that if an animal is not fit to be brought to the Tabernacle one is not liable for slaughtering it outside the courtyard (Rambam *Sefer Avoda, Hilkhot Ma'aseh HaKorbanot* 18:6).

NOTES

That one burned – שֶׁשְּׂרָפָהּ: According to some commentaries, including Rashi, this should read: That one slaughtered. This would accord with the verse cited as proof for this *halakha*, which is taken from the Torah's discussion of animals slaughtered outside the courtyard. The Rambam places this *halakha* in the context of the *halakhot* pertaining to the burning of offerings, and cites as proof the verse: "And to the entrance of the Tent of Meeting he did not bring it" (Leviticus 17:4), which appears in that context as well. In any event, with regard to the discussion in the mishna, the *halakha* of slaughter is equivalent to that of sacrifice.

For any animal that is not fit to come to the entrance of the Tent of Meeting – כׇּל שֶׁאֵין רָאוּי לָבֹא לִפְנֵי מִשְׁכַּן ה׳: In this context, the term: Not fit, does not refer to an offering that is inherently not brought to the entrance of the Tent of Meeting, e.g., a red heifer or a scapegoat, but to an animal that is disqualified from serving as an offering due to its unseemliness (Rabbeinu Ḥananel). According to Rashi, the emphasis is upon the words: "To present it as an offering to the Lord before the Tabernacle of the Lord." If a consecrated animal that is, in principle, fit to be brought to the Temple, becomes disqualified and can no longer be sacrificed, one who slaughters it outside the courtyard is not liable.

בַּעֲלֵי מוּמִין עוֹבְרִין, שֶׁהִקְרִיבָן בַּחוּץ – פָּטוּר. רַבִּי שִׁמְעוֹן אוֹמֵר: בַּעֲלֵי מוּמִין קְבוּעִין – פָּטוּר, בַּעֲלֵי מוּמִין עוֹבְרִין – חַיָּיב בְּלֹא תַעֲשֶׂה.

temporarily blemished, which one sacrificed outside the Temple courtyard, one is **exempt. Rabbi Shimon says:** For **permanently blemished** animals one is **exempt;** for **temporarily blemished** animals one is **liable for** violation of **a prohibition,** but it is not the type of prohibition for which he will receive *karet*, because ultimately the animal will be fit for sacrifice.

תּוֹרִים שֶׁלֹּא הִגִּיעַ זְמַנָּן, וּבְנֵי יוֹנָה שֶׁעָבַר זְמַנָּן, שֶׁהִקְרִיבָן בַּחוּץ – פָּטוּר; רַבִּי שִׁמְעוֹן אוֹמֵר: בְּנֵי יוֹנָה שֶׁעָבַר זְמַנָּן – פָּטוּר, וְתוֹרִים שֶׁלֹּא הִגִּיעַ זְמַנָּן – בְּלֹא תַעֲשֶׂה.

With regard to **doves whose time** of fitness for sacrifice **has not arrived,**[H] as they are fit for sacrifice only when they are older, after their wings assume a golden hue; **and pigeons whose time** of fitness **has passed,** as they are fit only when they are young and their wings did not yet assume a yellowish tint, **that one sacrificed outside** the Temple courtyard, he is **exempt. Rabbi Shimon says:** For **pigeons whose time** of fitness **has passed** one is **exempt, and** for **doves whose time** of fitness **has not** yet **arrived** he is **in** violation of **a prohibition.**

אוֹתוֹ וְאֶת בְּנוֹ וּמְחוּסַּר זְמַן – פָּטוּר, רַבִּי שִׁמְעוֹן אוֹמֵר: הֲרֵי זֶה בְּלֹא תַעֲשֶׂה. שֶׁרַבִּי שִׁמְעוֹן אוֹמֵר: כָּל שֶׁהוּא רָאוּי לָבֹא לְאַחַר זְמַן – הֲרֵי זֶה בְּלֹא תַעֲשֶׂה, וְאֵין בּוֹ כָּרֵת. וַחֲכָמִים אוֹמְרִים: כָּל שֶׁאֵין בּוֹ כָּרֵת – אֵין בּוֹ לֹא תַעֲשֶׂה.

With regard to an animal **itself and its offspring**[B] that were slaughtered on the same day, where one violates a prohibition for slaughtering the second, **and** an animal **whose time has not yet** arrived,[B] if one sacrificed it outside the Temple courtyard he is **exempt. Rabbi Shimon says:** For an animal whose time has not yet arrived, **that** person is **in** violation of a mere **prohibition, as Rabbi Shimon says:** With regard to **any** sacrificial animal **that is fit to come** and be sacrificed **after** the passage of **time,** if one sacrificed it outside the courtyard, **that** person is **in** violation of **a prohibition but there is no** liability for *karet*. **And the Rabbis say: In any case in which there is no** liability for *karet* **there is no** violation of **a prohibition.**

מְחוּסַּר זְמַן, בֵּין בְּגוּפוֹ בֵּין בִּבְעָלָיו.

The mishna adds: An animal is defined as one **whose time has not yet** arrived, **whether** it is **intrinsically** premature, e.g., doves whose wings have not yet assumed a golden hue or an animal less than seven days old (see Leviticus 22:27), or **whether** it is premature **for its owner.**

אֵיזֶהוּ מְחוּסַּר זְמַן בִּבְעָלָיו – הַזָּב וְהַזָּבָה וְהַיּוֹלֶדֶת וְהַמְּצוֹרָע שֶׁהִקְרִיבוּ חַטָּאתָם וַאֲשָׁמָם בַּחוּץ – פְּטוּרִין, עוֹלוֹתֵיהֶן וְשַׁלְמֵיהֶן בַּחוּץ – חַיָּיבִין.

Which is the animal **whose time has not yet** arrived because it is premature **for its owner?**[H] It is the animal of **a man who experiences a gonorrhea-like discharge** [***zav***], **and a woman who experiences a discharge of uterine blood after her menstrual period** [***zava***],[N] **and a woman after childbirth, and a leper** whose period of impurity is not yet complete, **where** these owners, who are ritually impure, **sacrificed their sin offerings or guilt offerings outside** the Temple courtyard. In this case **they are exempt,** as they are neither obligated nor permitted to bring those offerings. But if they sacrificed **their burnt offerings or their peace offerings outside** the courtyard **they are liable,** as those offerings may be brought as gift offerings even if their owner is ritually impure.

BACKGROUND

Itself and its offspring – אוֹתוֹ וְאֶת בְּנוֹ: The Torah prohibits the slaughter of a mother animal and its young on the same day, as it is stated: "You shall not slaughter it and its offspring both in one day" (Leviticus 22:28). Although in the Torah "it and its offspring" uses masculine pronouns, the Sages ruled that the essential prohibition refers to a mother animal and any of its offspring, whether male or female. In addition, some opinions extend the prohibition to a father animal and its offspring in cases where the paternity of the animal is clear.

With regard to the order of the animals slaughtered, the *halakha* is that it is irrelevant whether the mother animal or the offspring is slaughtered first. With regard to the definition of the term "slaughter" used in the verse, the Sages disagreed as to whether the prohibition applies only when the animals are ritually slaughtered and rendered fit for consumption, or whether slaughter that does not render the animal fit for consumption, such as when it is a *tereifa*, is also included.

Whose time has not yet arrived – מְחוּסַּר זְמַן: This term refers to an offering that may not be sacrificed because its time to be sacrificed has not yet arrived. Usually this term is applied to an animal that is not yet eight days old (see Leviticus 22:27).

NOTES

A *zav* and a *zava* – הַזָּב וְהַזָּבָה: Although the mishna does not differentiate, there are in fact differences in the offerings brought by each person listed here. A *zav*, a *zava*, a woman after childbirth, and a leper each bring a sin offering and a burnt offering, and the leper brings a guilt offering as well. The peace offering that is mentioned alludes to the case of a nazirite, who must bring a sin offering, a burnt offering, and a peace offering at the end of his term of naziriteship.

HALAKHA

Temporarily blemished animals…doves whose time of fitness has not yet arrived – בַּעֲלֵי מוּמִין עוֹבְרִין...תּוֹרִים שֶׁלֹּא הִגִּיעַ זְמַנָּן: If one slaughters outside the Temple courtyard an animal whose time has not yet arrived because it is intrinsically lacking, e.g., a dove whose time of fitness has not yet arrived or an animal within seven days of its birth, or if he slaughters outside the Temple courtyard an animal and its offspring on the same day, he is exempt, as these animals were not fit for sacrifice at that time. This ruling is in accordance with the opinion of the Rabbis (Rambam *Sefer Avoda*, *Hilkhot Ma'aseh HaKorbanot* 18:7–8).

The animal whose time has not yet arrived because it is premature for its owner – מְחוּסַּר זְמַן בִּבְעָלָיו: If one slaughters outside the Temple courtyard an animal whose time has not yet arrived because it is premature for the owner, he is exempt. It is considered premature for the owner if his time to bring his offering has not yet arrived. Therefore, a *zav*, a *zava*, and a woman after childbirth who slaughtered their sin offerings outside the Temple courtyard during their days of counting are exempt. Likewise, a leper who slaughters his sin offering or guilt offering outside the Temple courtyard during the days of counting is exempt. The reason is that none of the aforementioned individuals is fit to bring an offering for atonement at that time. But if they slaughtered their burnt offerings outside the Temple courtyard during their days of counting, they are liable. This is because unlike the sin offering or guilt offering, which facilitate atonement, the burnt offering is a gift offering.

Likewise, if a nazirite slaughtered his sin offering outside the Temple courtyard during his term of naziriteship, he is exempt, since the sin offering is the primary offering and is necessary to achieve full atonement. But if he sacrificed a burnt offering or peace offering outside the Temple courtyard he is liable (Rambam *Sefer Avoda*, *Hilkhot Ma'aseh HaKorbanot* 18:9).

הַמַּעֲלֶה מִבְּשַׂר חַטָּאת, מִבְּשַׂר אָשָׁם, מִבְּשַׂר קׇדְשֵׁי קֳדָשִׁים, מִבְּשַׂר קֳדָשִׁים קַלִּים, וּמוֹתַר הָעוֹמֶר, וּשְׁתֵּי הַלֶּחֶם, וְלֶחֶם הַפָּנִים, וּשְׁיָרֵי מְנָחוֹת,

One who offers up outside the Temple courtyard a portion **of the meat of a sin offering**[H] that is eaten; **of the meat of a guilt offering; of the meat of** other **offerings of the most sacred order** that are eaten, e.g., the sheep sacrificed on the festival of *Shavuot*, or **of the meat of offerings of lesser sanctity,** is exempt, as all these are eaten by the priests and not sacrificed on the altar. **And** for the same reason, one who sacrificed a portion of **the surplus of the *omer* offering,** a measure of barley brought as a communal offering on the sixteenth of the Hebrew month of Nisan, after the handful was removed; **or the two loaves,** i.e., the public offering on *Shavuot* of two loaves from the new wheat; **or the shewbread** arranged on the Table each Shabbat in the Sanctuary; **or the remainder of meal offerings,** is also exempt.

וְהַיּוֹצֵק, וְהַפּוֹתֵת, וְהַבּוֹלֵל, וְהַמּוֹלֵחַ, וְהַמֵּנִיף, וְהַמַּגִּישׁ, וְהַמְסַדֵּר אֶת הַשּׁוּלְחָן, וְהַמֵּטִיב אֶת הַנֵּרוֹת, וְהַקּוֹמֵץ, וְהַמְקַבֵּל דָּמִים, בַּחוּץ – פָּטוּר,

And likewise with regard to **one who pours** oil onto a meal offering; **and one who breaks**[H] the loaves of a meal offering into pieces; **and one who mixes** oil into the flour of a meal offering;[N] **and one who salts** a meal offering or other offerings; **and one who waves** a meal offering; **and one who brings** a meal offering to the corner of an altar,[B] if he performs these actions outside the courtyard; **and one who arranges** shewbread on **the table** outside the Sanctuary; **and one who removes the ashes** from **the lamps** of the Candelabrum;[N] **and one who removes a handful** from a meal offering; **and one who collects** the **blood** of an offering in a vessel, if he did so **outside** the Temple courtyard: In all of these cases he is **exempt.** This is because one is liable only if he performs an action similar to sacrifice that completes the sacrificial service, while all of these actions are ones that are normally followed by additional sacrificial rites.

וְאֵין חַיָּיבִין עָלָיו לֹא מִשּׁוּם זָרוּת, וְלֹא מִשּׁוּם טוּמְאָה, וְלֹא מִשּׁוּם מְחוּסַּר בְּגָדִים, וְלֹא מִשּׁוּם [שֶׁלֹּא] רָחוּץ יָדַיִם וְרַגְלַיִם.

And one is likewise **not liable for** any of these actions, **neither due to** the prohibition against **a non-priest**[HN] performing the Temple service, **nor due to** the prohibition against performing the Temple service in a state of **ritual impurity,**[HN] **nor due to** the prohibition against a priest **lacking** the requisite priestly **vestments** while performing the Temple service, **nor due to** the prohibition against performing the Temple service **without washing** one's **hands and feet.**

NOTES

One who pours oil onto a meal offering…one who mixes oil into the flour of a meal offering – הַיּוֹצֵק...הַבּוֹלֵל: The sacrificial rites listed here are not concluding rites, and one is not liable for performing a rite outside its place unless it is the concluding rite of the sacrificial service. The rite for which one is liable must be akin to sacrificing on the altar, sprinkling the blood, or sacrificing the handful of a meal offering, as noted in the previous chapter. Similarly, a non-priest who performs any of these rites is not liable to receive death at the hand of Heaven, since for that purpose only a concluding rite is defined as a rite (see *Yoma* 24a).

Pouring oil on a meal offering

And one who removes the ashes from the lamps of the Candelabrum – וְהַמֵּטִיב אֶת הַנֵּרוֹת: The same *halakha* applies to one who performs any of the rites associated with the Candelabrum. Even lighting it, which ostensibly is the concluding rite, does not engender liability, as it is not deemed a bona fide rite (*Tosafot* on *Sanhedrin* 82b, citing *Yoma* 24b).

One is not liable…neither due to a non-priest – אֵין חַיָּיבִין...לֹא מִשּׁוּם זָרוּת: Rashi explains that this statement applies not only to one who performs the listed rites, such as pouring and mixing oil, but also to one who sacrifices meat of a sin offering or the like, as a non-priest is not liable for burning items that are not fit to be burned.

Nor due to ritual impurity – וְלֹא מִשּׁוּם טוּמְאָה: A priest who performs the Temple service while ritually impure has a status identical to that of a non-priest who performs the service: Both prohibitions are derived from the same verse (Leviticus 22:2; see 15b). Moreover, a priest who performs the service while lacking the requisite priestly vestments also has the status of a non-priest (see 17b). This is derived by means of a verbal analogy that the same applies to a priest who performs the service without first washing his hands and feet. A priest who violates these *halakhot* is liable for desecrating his service, and receives the punishment of death at the hand of Heaven (Rashi).

HALAKHA

One who offers up a portion of the meat of a sin offering – הַמַּעֲלֶה מִבְּשַׂר חַטָּאת: If one sacrifices outside the Temple courtyard a portion of the meat of a sin offering, a guilt offering, or a peace offering, whether it is a peace offering of an individual or a communal peace offering, or if he sacrifices the remainder of a meal offering, or the two loaves brought on the festival of *Shavuot*, or the shewbread, he is exempt, as these are all intended to be eaten, not sacrificed (Rambam *Sefer Avoda*, *Hilkhot Ma'aseh HaKorbanot* 19:4).

One who pours and one who breaks – הַיּוֹצֵק וְהַפּוֹתֵת: One who does any of the following outside the Temple courtyard is exempt: Pours oil onto a meal offering, breaks the loaves of a meal offering into pieces, mixes oil into the flour of a meal offering, salts a meal offering or other offerings, waves a meal offering, brings a meal offering to the corner of an altar that he constructs outside the courtyard, removes the ashes from the lamps of the Candelabrum, removes a handful from a meal offering, or collects the blood of an offering in a vessel. This also applies to one who arranges the shewbread on the table outside the Sanctuary. For all these rites, the reason he is exempt is that none of these completes a sacrificial service (Rambam *Sefer Avoda*, *Hilkhot Ma'aseh HaKorbanot* 19:6).

One is not liable…due to the prohibition against a non-priest – אֵין חַיָּיבִים...מִשּׁוּם זָרוּת: If a non-priest performs any of the following rites he violates a prohibition, he is liable to receives lashes, and his service is disqualified, but he is not liable to receive death at the hand of Heaven: Pours oil onto the meal offering, breaks the loaves of the meal offering into pieces, mixes the oil into the flour of the meal offering, salts the meal offering or other offerings, waves the meal offering, brings the meal offering to the corner of an altar, arranges the shewbread or the bowls of frankincense on the Table, removes the ashes from the lamps of the Candelabrum, kindles the fire on the altar, removes a handful from a meal offering, or collects the blood of an offering in a vessel (Rambam *Sefer Avoda*, *Hilkhot Biat HaMikdash* 9:5).

Nor due to ritual impurity – וְלֹא מִשּׁוּם טוּמְאָה: If a priest who is impure or blemished or who did not wash his hands and feet performed the Temple service, he is liable only if he performed a rite that, if performed by a non-priest, would incur death at the hand of Heaven. For other rites he is in violation of an ordinary prohibition (Rambam *Sefer Avoda*, *Hilkhot Biat HaMikdash* 9:10).

BACKGROUND

One who brings a meal offering to the corner of an altar – הַמַּגִּישׁ: Bringing refers to a ritual involved in the sacrifice of most meal offerings in the Temple. The priests were required to carry the offering in their hands and to bring it to the corner of the altar. This is performed before the priest takes a handful of the meal offering.

Bringing a meal offering to the corner of the altar

עַד שֶׁלֹּא הוּקַם הַמִּשְׁכָּן – הָיוּ הַבָּמוֹת מוּתָּרוֹת, וַעֲבוֹדָה בַּבְּכוֹרוֹת, וּמִשֶּׁהוּקַם הַמִּשְׁכָּן – נֶאֶסְרוּ הַבָּמוֹת, וַעֲבוֹדָה בַּכֹּהֲנִים. קׇדְשֵׁי קֳדָשִׁים נֶאֱכָלִין לִפְנִים מִן הַקְּלָעִים, וְקׇדָשִׁים קַלִּים בְּכׇל מַחֲנֵה יִשְׂרָאֵל. בָּאוּ לְגִלְגָּל – הוּתְּרוּ הַבָּמוֹת, קׇדְשֵׁי קֳדָשִׁים נֶאֱכָלִין לִפְנִים מִן הַקְּלָעִים, וְקׇדָשִׁים קַלִּים בְּכׇל מָקוֹם.

Until the Tabernacle was established, private **altars**[N] **were permitted and** the sacrificial **service** was performed **by the firstborn.**[N] **And from** the time **that the Tabernacle was established,** private **altars were prohibited and** the sacrificial **service** was performed **by the priests. Offerings of the most sacred order were** then **eaten within the curtains** surrounding the courtyard of the Tabernacle in the wilderness **and offerings of lesser sanctity** were eaten **throughout the camp of Israel.** When the Jewish people **arrived at Gilgal**[N] private **altars were permitted, offerings of the most sacred order were** then **eaten within the curtains, and offerings of lesser sanctity** were eaten **anywhere.**

בָּאוּ לְשִׁילֹה – נֶאֶסְרוּ הַבָּמוֹת. וְלֹא הָיָה שָׁם תִּקְרָה, אֶלָּא בֵּית אֲבָנִים בִּלְבַד מִלְּמַטָּן, וְהַיְרִיעוֹת מִלְמַעְלָן. וְהִיא הָיְתָה ״מְנוּחָה״. קׇדְשֵׁי קֳדָשִׁים נֶאֱכָלִין לִפְנִים מִן הַקְּלָעִים, וְקׇדָשִׁים קַלִּים וּמַעֲשֵׂר שֵׁנִי בְּכׇל הָרוֹאֶה.

When **they arrived at Shiloh,**[N] private **altars were prohibited. And there was no roof** of wood or stone **there,** i.e., in the Tabernacle in Shiloh; **rather there was only a building of stone below and the curtains** of the roof of the Tabernacle were spread **above it. And** the period that the Tabernacle was in Shiloh **was** characterized in the Torah as **"rest"** in the verse: "For you have not as yet come to the rest and to the inheritance, which the Lord your God has given you" (Deuteronomy 12:9). **Offerings of the most sacred order were** then **eaten within the curtains** in the courtyard of the Tent of Meeting, **and offerings of lesser sanctity and second tithe** were eaten **in any** place **that overlooks** Shiloh.[N]

בָּאוּ לְנוֹב וְגִבְעוֹן – הוּתְּרוּ הַבָּמוֹת: קׇדְשֵׁי קֳדָשִׁים נֶאֱכָלִין לִפְנִים מִן הַקְּלָעִים, קׇדָשִׁים קַלִּים בְּכׇל עָרֵי יִשְׂרָאֵל.

When Shiloh was destroyed (see I Samuel 4:18), the Jewish people **arrived** with the Tabernacle **at Nov, and** later at **Gibeon,** and private **altars were permitted.**[N] **Offerings of the most sacred order were** then **eaten within the curtains** in the courtyard of the Tent of Meeting, and **offerings of lesser sanctity** were eaten **in all the cities of Eretz Yisrael.**[N]

NOTES

Private altars [*bamot*] – בָּמוֹת: The term *bama*, which also means platform, refers to a place higher than its surroundings. These places were often used for sacrificing offerings. The word is used to describe all of the places that sacrifices were brought outside of the Temple (see I Kings 3:2).

Sacrificial service was performed by the firstborn – עֲבוֹדָה בַּבְּכוֹרוֹת: Initially the Torah states: "Sanctify to Me every firstborn" (Exodus 13:2). Subsequently, Aaron and his sons were inaugurated into the priesthood with the establishment of the Tabernacle, as it is written: "And I have taken the Levites from among the children of Israel instead of every firstborn that opens the womb among the children of Israel; and the Levites shall be Mine" (Numbers 3:12). The Sages explain that as a consequence of the firstborns having worshipped the golden calf, the right to perform the service in the Tabernacle was taken from them and given to the priests (see Jerusalem Talmud, *Megilla* 1:13). A dissenting opinion with regard to this matter is cited in the Gemara (115b).

When they arrived at Gilgal – בָּאוּ לְגִלְגָּל: This is where the Jewish people encamped upon their arrival in Eretz Yisrael, and where the Tabernacle stood for fourteen years (see 118a). The Tabernacle in Gilgal also had a courtyard enclosed with curtains, as the mishna states: Offerings of the most sacred order were then eaten within the curtains.

There was no prohibition against sacrificing outside the Tabernacle at that time, as the prohibition is predicated upon the existence of an Israelite camp, as derived from the verse: "Whatever man of the house of Israel that kills an ox, or lamb, or goat, in the camp" (Leviticus 17:3). There was no Israelite camp during the period of Gilgal because the nation was engaged in conquering and settling Eretz Yisrael. For the same reason, offerings of lesser sanctity, which generally are to be eaten in the Israelite camp, could be eaten anywhere (Rambam's Commentary on the Mishna; see Rashi).

The *Tosefta* (13:18) indicates that since at the time of the conquest of Eretz Yisrael the Ark traveled before the people and was not permanently located in the Tent of Meeting, the Tabernacle did not have the status of the Tabernacle of the Lord, but of a great public altar (see Ramban on Deuteronomy 10:1; 117b; Jerusalem Talmud, *Megilla* 1:12; and *Meshekh Ḥokhma* on Deuteronomy 12:8).

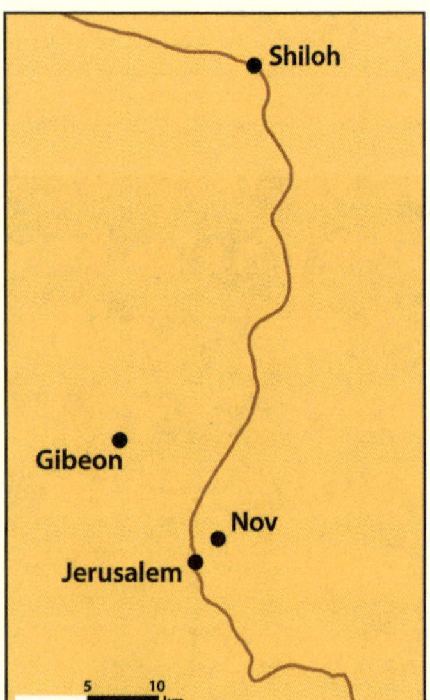

Map showing Jerusalem, Nov, Gibeon, and Shiloh, with the ancient north-south highway

NOTES

When they arrived at Shiloh – בָּאוּ לְשִׁילֹה: After describing the conquest and division of the land, the verse states: "And the whole congregation of the children of Israel assembled themselves together at Shiloh, and set up the Tent of Meeting there; and the land was subdued before them" (Joshua 18:1). It was there that the Ark was located on a permanent basis and the Divine Presence was manifest for 369 years, until the death of Eli the Priest (see I Samuel 3:3).

The Tabernacle in Shiloh was not the portable one that had been utilized in the wilderness; it is referred to as "the house of the Lord" (I Samuel 1:24) and "Temple" (I Samuel 3:3), and it had doors. It was still called "Tent of Meeting" (I Samuel 2:22) and "Tabernacle," e.g., "And He forsook the Tabernacle of Shiloh, the tent that He had made to dwell among men" (Psalms 78:60). Shiloh is located in the hills of Samaria, north of Jerusalem, and archaeological excavations have been undertaken there in recent years.

Tel Shiloh and the surrounding hills

Offerings of lesser sanctity and second tithe were eaten in any place that overlooks Shiloh – קׇדָשִׁים קַלִּים וּמַעֲשֵׂר שֵׁנִי בְּכׇל הָרוֹאֶה: Second tithe was not mentioned in the context of Gilgal; there was no obligation to bring it until Eretz Yisrael was conquered and divided, which took place immediately before the period of Shiloh.

They arrived at Nov and Gibeon, and private altars were permitted – בָּאוּ לְנוֹב וְגִבְעוֹן הוּתְּרוּ הַבָּמוֹת: When the Ark of the Lord was captured by the Philistines and Eli the Priest died (see I Samuel 4:22), the Tabernacle was destroyed and the Divine Presence did not return to it, as the verse states: "And He forsook the Tabernacle of Shiloh" (Psalms 78:60; see Jeremiah 7:12). The Tabernacle was subsequently located in the priestly city of Nov. Yet the Ark was not there but in Kiriath Jearim, and later in the City of David (see I Samuel 7:1; II Samuel, chapter 6). After Saul wiped out the priests of Nov (see I Samuel, chapter 22), the verse mentions the great public altar in Gibeon, which was the location of the Tabernacle during the reign of King David (see I Chronicles 16:39; II Chronicles 2:4), and to which Solomon traveled from Jerusalem to sacrifice his offerings (I Kings 3:4; see 59a). During this period offerings were sacrificed at other locations as well (see II Samuel, chapter 6).

The Sages identify a source for the permitting of private altars during this period in the Torah's specifying only "rest," i.e., Shiloh, and "inheritance," i.e., Jerusalem, which allows for a period between Shiloh and Jerusalem during which private altars were permitted. Additionally, private altars were permitted because the Ark was not located in the Tabernacle during this period (see Jerusalem Talmud, *Megilla* 1:12).

Offerings of lesser sanctity were eaten in all the cities of Eretz Yisrael – קׇדָשִׁים קַלִּים בְּכׇל עָרֵי יִשְׂרָאֵל: According to the version of the mishna utilized by Rashi and the Rambam, this should read: Offerings of lesser sanctity and second tithe were eaten in all the cities of Eretz Yisrael (see 119a).

בָּאוּ לִירוּשָׁלַיִם – נֶאֶסְרוּ הַבָּמוֹת, וְלֹא הָיָה לָהֶן הֶיתֵּר, וְהִיא הָיְתָה "נַחֲלָה". קָדְשֵׁי קָדָשִׁים נֶאֱכָלִין לִפְנִים מִן הַקְּלָעִים, קָדָשִׁים קַלִּים וּמַעֲשֵׂר שֵׁנִי לִפְנִים מִן הַחוֹמָה.

When the Jewish people **arrived at Jerusalem** and built the Temple during the reign of Solomon, private **altars were prohibited,**[H] and private altars **did not have** a subsequent period when they were **permitted. And the** Temple in Jerusalem **was** characterized as **"inheritance"**[N] in the verse: "For you have not as yet come to the rest and to the inheritance, which the Lord your God has given you." **Offerings of the most sacred order were** then **eaten within the curtains,**[HN] i.e., in the Temple courtyard, and **offerings of lesser sanctity and second tithe** were eaten **within the walls** of the city, whose legal status was that of the Israelite camp in the wilderness.

כָּל הַקֳּדָשִׁים שֶׁהִקְדִּישָׁן בִּשְׁעַת אִיסּוּר הַבָּמוֹת וְהִקְרִיבָן בִּשְׁעַת אִיסּוּר הַבָּמוֹת מִבַּחוּץ – הֲרֵי אֵלּוּ בַּעֲשֵׂה וְלֹא תַעֲשֶׂה, וְחַיָּיבִין עָלָיו כָּרֵת.

With regard to **all offerings that one consecrated during a period of prohibition of** private **altars and sacrificed during a period of prohibition of** private **altars,** if he sacrificed them **outside** their designated area, for **these** animals he is **in** violation of both the **positive mitzva** to sacrifice the offering in the place chosen by God **and the prohibition** against sacrificing them on a private altar, **and he is liable** to receive *karet* for doing **it.**[N]

הִקְדִּישָׁן בִּשְׁעַת הֶיתֵּר הַבָּמוֹת וְהִקְרִיבָן בִּשְׁעַת אִיסּוּר הַבָּמוֹת בַּחוּץ – הֲרֵי אֵלּוּ בַּעֲשֵׂה וְלֹא תַעֲשֶׂה, וְאֵין חַיָּיבִין עֲלֵיהֶן כָּרֵת. הִקְדִּישָׁן בִּשְׁעַת אִיסּוּר הַבָּמוֹת וְהִקְרִיבָן בִּשְׁעַת הֶיתֵּר הַבָּמוֹת – הֲרֵי אֵלּוּ בַּעֲשֵׂה, וְאֵין בָּהֶן לֹא תַעֲשֶׂה.

If **one consecrated** the animals **during a period of permitting of** private **altars and sacrificed them during a period of prohibition** of private **altars, outside** their designated area, for **these** animals he is **in** violation of **a positive mitzva and a prohibition, but he is not liable to** receive *karet* **for** sacrificing **them. If he consecrated** the animals **during a period of prohibition of** private **altars and sacrificed them during a period of permitting of** private **altars,** outside their designated area, for **these** animals he is **in** violation of **a positive mitzva**[HN] for failure to bring it to the Tabernacle, **but these** animals **are not subject to a prohibition,** as it is permitted to sacrifice on a private altar.

וְאֵלּוּ קֳדָשִׁים קְרֵבִין בַּמִּשְׁכָּן: קָדָשִׁים שֶׁהוּקְדְּשׁוּ לַמִּשְׁכָּן. קָרְבְּנוֹת צִיבּוּר קְרֵבִין בַּמִּשְׁכָּן, וְקָרְבְּנוֹת הַיָּחִיד בְּבָמָה. קָרְבְּנוֹת הַיָּחִיד שֶׁהוּקְדְּשׁוּ לַמִּשְׁכָּן – יִקְרִיבוּ בַּמִּשְׁכָּן, וְאִם הִקְרִיבָן בְּבָמָה – פָּטוּר.

And these are the sacrificial items that **are sacrificed** only **in the Tabernacle** even when private altars are permitted: **Sacrificial** animals **that were** presumed to be **consecrated for** sacrifice in **the Tabernacle.** Therefore, **communal offerings are sacrificed in the Tabernacle, but offerings of an individual** may be sacrificed **on a** private **altar.** In addition, with regard to **offerings of an individual that were consecrated** expressly **for** sacrifice in **the Tabernacle, one must sacrifice** them **in the Tabernacle. But if he sacrificed** them **on a** private **altar,** he is **exempt.**

וּמָה בֵּין בָּמַת יָחִיד לְבָמַת צִיבּוּר? סְמִיכָה, וּשְׁחִיטַת צָפוֹן,

And what is the difference **between the** private **altar of an individual and the public altar** at the site of the Tabernacle when it was located in Gilgal, Nov, and Gibeon? It is that on a private altar there is no **placing** of **hands** on the head of an offering, no **slaughter in the north,**

HALAKHA

When they arrived at Jerusalem private altars were prohibited – בָּאוּ לִירוּשָׁלַיִם נֶאֶסְרוּ הַבָּמוֹת: After the Temple was built in Jerusalem, it was prohibited to build a house for the Lord or to sacrifice offerings in any other place (Rambam *Sefer Avoda, Hilkhot Beit HaBeḥira* 1:3).

Offerings of the most sacred order were eaten within the curtains – קָדְשֵׁי קָדָשִׁים נֶאֱכָלִין לִפְנִים מִן הַקְּלָעִים: Offerings of the most sacred order are eaten in the Temple courtyard. Offerings of lesser sanctity are eaten in the Israelite camp, which, once the Temple was built, corresponded to the city of Jerusalem. Second tithe is also eaten in Jerusalem (Rambam *Sefer Avoda, Hilkhot Ma'aseh HaKorbanot* 10:3, 5 and *Sefer Zera'im, Hilkhot Ma'aser Sheni* 2:1; *Shulḥan Arukh, Yoreh De'a* 331:132).

He is in violation of a positive mitzva – הֲרֵי אֵלּוּ בַּעֲשֵׂה: There is a positive mitzva to sacrifice all offerings, whether animals, birds, or meal offerings, in the Temple, as it is stated: "And there you shall do all that I command you" (Deuteronomy 12:14). One who sacrifices an offering outside the Temple courtyard has violated both this positive mitzva and a prohibition, as it is stated: "Take heed to yourself that you offer not your burnt offerings in every place that you see" (Deuteronomy 12:13). One who did so intentionally is liable to receive *karet*, as it is stated: "And you shall say to them: Whatever man there is of the house of Israel, or of the strangers that sojourn among them, that offers a burnt offering or sacrifice and brings it not to the entrance of the Tent of Meeting, to sacrifice it to the Lord, that man shall be cut off from his people" (Leviticus 17:8–9). If it was done unintentionally, one brings a sin offering (Rambam *Sefer Avoda, Hilkhot Ma'aseh HaKorbanot* 18:1–2).

NOTES

And the Temple was characterized as inheritance – וְהִיא הָיְתָה נַחֲלָה: It was characterized in this way because its sanctity is permanent and eternal, like an inheritance. The reason is that once God chose to dwell permanently in Jerusalem, the Divine presence does not leave the city, as it is stated in Psalms 94:14: "Neither will He forsake His inheritance" (Rambam's Commentary on the Mishna). This sanctity is no longer dependent on the presence of the Ark, as it had been previously. Indeed, it is generally accepted that during the Second Temple period the Ark was not present in the Holy of Holies (see *Yoma* 21b and *Horayot* 12a).

Within the curtains – לִפְנִים מִן הַקְּלָעִים: This means within the walls of the Temple courtyard (Rambam's Commentary on the Mishna). The walls are called curtains in this context either because at the time of the return to Eretz Yisrael, before the walls were built, curtains were made for the Temple and its courtyard (see 107b), or because the walls of the courtyard were named after the curtains of the courtyard of the Tabernacle (*Tiferet Yisrael*).

Violation of the positive mitzva and the prohibition, and he is liable to receive *karet* for it – עֲשֵׂה וְלֹא תַעֲשֶׂה וְחַיָּיבִין עָלָיו כָּרֵת: Rashi explains that the source of the positive mitzva is: "That they may bring them to the Lord, to the entrance of the Tent of Meeting" (Leviticus 17:5), while the Rambam states that it is the verse: "Then it shall come to pass that the place that the Lord your God shall choose to cause His name to dwell there, there shall you bring all that I command you" (Deuteronomy 12:11). Rabbi Ovadya Bartenura explains that the positive mitzva is essentially a prohibition against sacrificing on private altars, but there is a principle that a prohibition that is inferred from a positive mitzva is classified as a positive mitzva. The prohibition in this case is: "Take heed to yourself that you offer not your burnt offerings in every place that you see" (Deuteronomy 12:13), as the term "take heed" denotes a prohibition (see 106a). The liability to receive *karet* is derived from the verse: "Whatever man of the house of Israel or of the strangers that sojourn among them, that sacrifices a burnt offering or sacrifice, and brings it not to the entrance of the Tent of Meeting, to sacrifice it to the Lord, that man shall be cut off [*venikhrat*] from his people" (Leviticus 17:8–9).

If he consecrated them during a period of prohibition of private altars…he is in violation of a positive mitzva – הִקְדִּישָׁן בִּשְׁעַת אִיסּוּר...הֲרֵי אֵלּוּ בַּעֲשֵׂה: Rashi explains that by not bringing the offerings at the time that private altars were prohibited, he is in violation of the positive mitzva: "That they may bring them" (Leviticus 17:5). The *Sefat Emet* notes that if this was, in fact, the intention of the mishna it would be unnecessary to state that he sacrificed it during a period of permitting of private altars. He therefore suggests that this offering must be sacrificed upon a great public altar, and only if it was sacrificed upon a small private altar is one in violation of the positive mitzva. This is also the ruling in the *Tosefta* (see Rashash).

וּמַתַּן סָבִיב, וּתְנוּפָה וְהַגָּשָׁה. רַבִּי יְהוּדָה אוֹמֵר: אֵין מִנְחָה בְּבָמָה. וְכִיהוּן, וּבִגְדֵי שָׁרֵת, וּכְלֵי שָׁרֵת, וְרֵיחַ נִיחוֹחַ, וּמְחִיצָה לַדָּמִים, וְרִיחוּץ יָדַיִם וְרַגְלַיִם.

no **placement** of blood **around** all sides of the altar[N] in offerings for which this is required, no **waving** of meal offerings, **and** no **bringing** of meal offerings to the corner of the altar prior to removal of the handful. **Rabbi Yehuda says: There is no meal offering** sacrificed **on an altar** outside the Temple. **And** requiring a member of the **priesthood** to perform the sacrificial rites, the priestly **service vestments,** the **service vessels,** the **pleasing aroma**[N] to God, the **partition for the blood,** i.e., the red line dividing the upper and lower halves of the altar, **and** the priest's **washing of hands and feet** before his service all do not apply to sacrifice on private altars, as the service there need not be performed by priests nor follow all the protocols of the Temple service.

אֲבָל הַזְּמַן, הַנּוֹתָר וְהַטָּמֵא – שָׁוִין בָּזֶה וּבָזֶה.

But the intent to sacrifice or partake of the offering beyond its designated **time,**[N] which renders the offering *piggul*; the *halakha* of portions of **the** offering **left over** ⌊*notar*⌋ beyond the time it may be eaten; **and the** prohibition against eating consecrated meat while **ritually impure are equal in this,** a private altar, **and that,** a public altar.

גמ׳ מַאי ״חוּץ מִגִּתָּהּ״? אָמַר רֵישׁ לָקִישׁ: חוּץ מִמָּקוֹם הַבָּדוּק לָהּ. אָמַר לוֹ רַבִּי יוֹחָנָן: וַהֲלֹא כׇּל אֶרֶץ יִשְׂרָאֵל בְּדוּקָה הִיא!

GEMARA The mishna teaches that one who burns the red heifer outside its pit is not liable for sacrificing outside the Temple courtyard. The Gemara clarifies: **What** is the meaning of: **Outside its pit?**[N] **Reish Lakish said:** It means **outside the place that was inspected** to ensure that it is not a gravesite, which would render it impure. **Rabbi Yoḥanan said to him: But is not all of Eretz Yisrael inspected** for impurity? Therefore, there is no need for the site of the burning of the red heifer to be specially inspected.

אֶלָּא אָמַר רַבִּי יוֹחָנָן: כְּגוֹן שֶׁשְּׁחָטָהּ לִפְנִים מִן חוֹמַת יְרוּשָׁלַיִם.

Rather, Rabbi Yoḥanan said: The term: Outside its pit, is referring to a case **where** the priest **slaughtered** the red heifer **within the walls of Jerusalem**[H] and not in the place outside the walls, as the Torah prescribes: "And it shall be brought outside the camp, and it shall be slaughtered before him" (Numbers 19:3).

וְלוֹקְמָהּ כְּגוֹן שֶׁשְּׁחָטָהּ חוּץ לַחוֹמָה שֶׁלֹּא כְּנֶגֶד הַפֶּתַח. דְּאָמַר רַב אַדָּא בַּר אַהֲבָה: שְׁחָטָהּ שֶׁלֹּא כְּנֶגֶד הַפֶּתַח – פְּסוּלָה, שֶׁנֶּאֱמַר: ״וְשָׁחַט...וְהִזָּה״,

The Gemara challenges: **But let** Rabbi Yoḥanan **interpret it** to be a case **where** the priest **slaughtered it outside the wall** but **not opposite,** i.e., not in the direction of, **the entrance**[H] to the Temple, **as Rav Adda bar Ahava says:** If **he slaughtered it** in a location **not opposite the entrance,** it is **disqualified, as it is stated** with regard to the red heifer: "And you shall give it to Elazar the priest, and it shall be brought outside the camp, **and it shall be slaughtered** before him. And Elazar the priest shall take of its blood with his finger, **and sprinkle** of its blood toward the front of the Tent of Meeting seven times" (Numbers 19:3–4).

מַה הַזָּאָתָהּ כְּנֶגֶד הַפֶּתַח – אַף שְׁחִיטָתָהּ כְּנֶגֶד הַפֶּתַח! וְכִי תֵּימָא דְּלָא מַקִּישׁ – וְהָא אִתְּמַר: שְׁחָטָהּ שֶׁלֹּא כְּנֶגֶד הַפֶּתַח, רַבִּי יוֹחָנָן אוֹמֵר: פְּסוּלָה – ״וְשָׁחַט...וְהִזָּה״. רֵישׁ לָקִישׁ אָמַר: כְּשֵׁרָה – ״אֶל מִחוּץ לַמַּחֲנֶה וְשָׁחַט״.

The slaughter of the red heifer and the sprinkling of its blood are juxtaposed so that one will draw the following conclusion: **Just as its sprinkling** must be performed **opposite the entrance, so too, its slaughter** must be performed **opposite the entrance. And if you would say that** Rabbi Yoḥanan does **not juxtapose** the two verses for the purpose of this comparison, that is difficult: **But it was stated** with regard to a red heifer **slaughtered** in a location **not opposite the entrance** that **Rabbi Yoḥanan says:** It is **disqualified,** as **"and it shall be slaughtered"** is juxtaposed with **"and sprinkle." Reish Lakish says:** It is **fit,** since it is stated: "And it shall be brought **outside the camp, and it shall be slaughtered,"** indicating that it may be slaughtered in any location outside the camp.

NOTES

Placement around all sides of the altar – וּמַתַּן סָבִיב: This refers to that which is stated with regard to the burnt offering: "And sprinkle the blood roundabout against the altar" (Leviticus 1:5). According to the Sages, this means that the blood was sprinkled on the northeast and southwest corners of the altar, so that the blood would be sprinkled on all four sides of the altar (see 53b). On a small private altar, one sprinkles the blood onto the altar only one time.

Pleasing aroma – רֵיחַ נִיחוֹחַ: The Sages understand that the Torah's description of offerings as producing a "pleasing aroma" mandates that only flesh that has not yet been roasted may be sacrificed upon the altar, as flesh that has already been roasted does not produce a pleasing aroma. The mishna teaches that this does not apply on a private altar; flesh that has been roasted, and therefore does not emit a pleasing aroma, may be sacrificed *ab initio* (Rabbi Ovadya Bartenura).

The time – הַזְּמַן: Rabbeinu Ḥananel explains that the term: Time, refers here to the age of the offering. Animal offerings are fit to be sacrificed only from the eighth day and on, and young doves and older pigeons are not fit to be sacrificed.

What is the meaning of outside its pit – מַאי חוּץ מִגִּתָּהּ: The Gemara is asking: Which place would disqualify the red heifer if the rite were performed there instead of in the pit, and therefore would have thought that liability is incurred for slaughtering it outside the Temple? The reasoning behind this question is that everyone agrees that the rite of the red heifer was performed in a pit, as is explained in tractate *Para* (4:2), but the pit is not mentioned in the Torah. It is therefore necessary to clarify the precise nature of the pit. It appears from the discussion here that the version of the mishna utilized by the Gemara reads: That one slaughtered outside its pit, as Rashi emended the text of the mishna, and not: That one burned outside its pit.

HALAKHA

Slaughtered the red heifer within the walls of Jerusalem – שְׁחָטָהּ לִפְנִים מִן חוֹמַת יְרוּשָׁלַיִם: If the red heifer was slaughtered outside the place of its burning, even if it was slaughtered within the walls of Jerusalem, it is disqualified, in accordance with the opinion of Rabbi Yoḥanan (Rambam *Sefer Tahara, Hilkhot Para Aduma* 4:10).

Not opposite the entrance – שֶׁלֹּא כְּנֶגֶד הַפֶּתַח: If a red heifer was slaughtered or burned in a location that was not facing the Sanctuary it is disqualified, in accordance with the opinion of Rabbi Yoḥanan (Rambam *Sefer Tahara, Hilkhot Para Aduma* 4:5).

וְאִיתְּמַר נַמִי: שְׂרָפָהּ שֶׁלֹּא כְּנֶגֶד הַפֶּתַח, רַבִּי יוֹחָנָן אָמַר: פְּסוּלָה, וְרַבִּי אוֹשַׁעְיָא אָמַר: כְּשֵׁרָה. רַבִּי יוֹחָנָן אָמַר פְּסוּלָה – "וְשָׂרַף" "וְהִזָּה",

And it was also stated that *amora'im* disagree with regard to a red heifer that the priest **burned not opposite the entrance** to the Temple. **Rabbi Yoḥanan says:** It is **disqualified, and Rabbi Oshaya says:** It is **fit.** The Gemara explains their reasoning: **Rabbi Yoḥanan says** that it is **disqualified** because of an additional juxtaposition. It is stated: **"And** the heifer **shall be burned** in his sight; its skin, and its flesh, and its blood, with its dung, shall be burned" (Numbers 19:5), while in the previous verse it is stated: **"And sprinkle** of its blood toward the front of the Tent of Meeting." This teaches that just as the sprinkling of the blood must be done opposite the entrance, so too must the burning be done opposite the entrance.

וְרַבִּי אוֹשַׁעְיָא אָמַר: כְּשֵׁרָה – "עַל פִּרְשָׁהּ יִשְׂרֹף", מָקוֹם שֶׁפּוֹרֶשֶׁת לְמִיתָה שָׁם תְּהֵא שְׂרֵיפָתָהּ!

And Rabbi Oshaya says that a red heifer that was burned in a location not opposite the entrance is **fit,** as the verse states: **"With its dung** [*pirshah*], **shall be burned,"** which is interpreted homiletically to mean: In **the place that** its soul **departs** [*poreshet*] **for death, there shall be its burning.** Just as no specific location is given for the soul's departing, so too, the burning need not be performed in a specific location. Since Rabbi Yoḥanan holds that the red heifer must be slaughtered opposite the entrance to the Temple, why does he not understand the term: Outside of its pit, to be referring to its slaughter in any location not opposite the Temple entrance?

אָמְרִי: לֹא מִיבַּעְיָא קָאָמַר; לֹא מִיבַּעְיָא חוּץ לַחוֹמָה דְּרַחוֹקֵי רַחֲקָהּ, אֶלָּא אֲפִילּוּ לִפְנִים מִן הַחוֹמָה, דְּקָרוֹבֵי קָרְבָהּ, וְאֵימָא תִּתְכַּשַּׁר – קָא מַשְׁמַע לַן.

The Gemara answers: **Say** that Rabbi Yoḥanan **is speaking** utilizing the style of: **It is not necessary,** as follows: **It is not necessary** for the mishna to teach that in slaughtering a red heifer **outside the wall** in a location not opposite the entrance, one does not transgress the prohibition against slaughtering outside the Temple courtyard. In that case it is clearly disqualified, **as he has distanced it** from where it is meant to be slaughtered. **But even** if one slaughtered it **inside the wall** of Jerusalem, so **that he brings it closer** to the Temple, **and** one might **say** that **it is a valid** way of slaughtering the red heifer, Rabbi Yoḥanan **teaches us** that nevertheless it is disqualified.

אָמַר מָר, אָמַר לוֹ רַבִּי יוֹחָנָן: וַהֲלֹא כׇּל אֶרֶץ יִשְׂרָאֵל בְּדוּקָה הִיא. בְּמַאי קָמִיפַּלְגִי? מָר סָבַר: יָרַד מַבּוּל לְאֶרֶץ יִשְׂרָאֵל, וּמָר סָבַר: לֹא יָרַד.

§ The Gemara returns to the disagreement cited earlier: **The Master says** that **Rabbi Yoḥanan said to** Reish Lakish: **But is not all of Eretz Yisrael inspected** for impurity? Since Reish Lakish's response to this question is not mentioned, the Gemara clarifies: **With regard to what do they disagree?** One **Sage,** Reish Lakish, **holds** that **the flood** in the time of Noah **descended upon Eretz Yisrael,** and its residents perished. It is therefore necessary to inspect the place where the red heifer is burned to ascertain whether it is a gravesite. **And one Sage,** Rabbi Yoḥanan, **holds** that the flood **did not descend** upon Eretz Yisrael, and there is no reason to suspect there are lost graves there.

אָמַר רַב נַחְמָן בַּר יִצְחָק, וּשְׁנֵיהֶם מִקְרָא אֶחָד דָּרְשׁוּ: "בֶּן אָדָם אֱמׇר לָהּ אַתְּ אֶרֶץ לֹא מְטֹהָרָה הִיא לֹא גֻשְׁמָהּ בְּיוֹם זָעַם".

Rav Naḥman bar Yitzḥak says: And both of them, Rabbi Yoḥanan and Reish Lakish, **interpreted the same verse,** stated by Ezekiel with regard to Eretz Yisrael, to derive their opinions. The verse states: **"Son of man, say to her: You are a land that is not cleansed, nor rained upon in the day of indignation"** (Ezekiel 22:24).

רַבִּי יוֹחָנָן סָבַר אַתְמוֹהֵי מִתְמַהּ קְרָא: אֶרֶץ יִשְׂרָאֵל מִי לֹא מְטוֹהָרָה אַתְּ? כְּלוּם יָרְדוּ עָלַיִךְ גְּשָׁמִים בְּיוֹם זַעַם? וְרֵישׁ לָקִישׁ סָבַר כִּפְשָׁטֵיהּ: אֶרֶץ לֹא מְטוֹהָרָה אַתְּ, מִי לֹא יָרְדוּ עָלַיִךְ גְּשָׁמִים בְּיוֹם זַעַם?

Rabbi Yoḥanan holds that **the verse is asking** a rhetorical **question: Eretz Yisrael, are you not cleansed** from the impurity imparted by corpses? **Did** the **rains** of the flood **fall upon you on the day of indignation? And Reish Lakish holds** that this verse should be read **in accordance with its straightforward meaning,** i.e., as a statement, not a question: **You are a land that is not cleansed. Didn't rains fall upon you on the day of indignation?** Therefore, the bodies of all of those who perished in the flood are somewhere in the ground.

אֵיתִיבֵיהּ רֵישׁ לָקִישׁ לְרַבִּי יוֹחָנָן: חֲצֵירוֹת הָיוּ בִּירוּשָׁלַיִם בְּנוּיוֹת עַל הַסֶּלַע, וְתַחְתֵּיהֶן חָלוּל מִפְּנֵי קֶבֶר הַתְּהוֹם, וּמְבִיאִין נָשִׁים מְעוּבָּרוֹת וְיוֹלְדוֹת וּמְגַדְּלוֹת שָׁם בְּנֵיהֶם לַפָּרָה,

Reish Lakish raised an objection to Rabbi Yoḥanan from a mishna (*Para* 3:2): **Courtyards were built in Jerusalem on stone,**[H] **and beneath** these courtyards there was a hollow **space due to** the concern that there was a lost **grave in the depths.** The space served as a barrier preventing the impurity from reaching the courtyards above. **And they** would **bring pregnant women, and** those women would **give birth** in those courtyards. **And** those women would **raise their children there,** thereby ensuring that the children never became impure. This would enable the children **to** assist in the rite **of the** red **heifer.**

HALAKHA

Courtyards were built in Jerusalem on stone – חֲצֵירוֹת הָיוּ בִּירוּשָׁלַיִם בְּנוּיוֹת עַל הַסֶּלַע: Among the higher standards of ritual purity that were established for the red heifer was the construction of courtyards in Jerusalem that were built on stone, beneath which were hollow spaces, due to concern that there might be a grave in the depths. Pregnant women would be brought to these courtyards, where they would give birth and raise their children. When it was necessary to sprinkle purification water on the priest who burned the red heifer, the children would be seated upon doors that were placed on the backs of oxen, and they would take stone cups to the Siloam pool. There they would fill the cups with water and then sit upon the doors again (Rambam *Sefer Tahara, Hilkhot Para Aduma* 2:7).

וּמְבִיאִין שְׁוָורִים וְעַל גַּבֵּיהֶן דְּלָתוֹת, וְתִינוֹקוֹת יוֹשְׁבִין עֲלֵיהֶן וְכוֹסוֹת שֶׁל אֶבֶן בְּיָדָן. וּמִלְאוּ, וְיָשְׁבוּ בִּמְקוֹמָן!

And once the children reached the appropriate age, the priests would **bring oxen** there. **And on the backs of** these oxen, they would place **doors, and the children** would **sit upon** the doors, so that the doors would serve as a barrier between them and any impurity in the depths, **and** they would hold **cups of stone,** which are not susceptible to ritual impurity, **in their hands,** and they would ride upon the oxen to the Siloam pool. **And** they **filled** the cups with water **and would sit** back **in their places** upon the oxen and be taken to the Temple Mount. The water in the cups would be used for the rite of the red heifer. Apparently, there is concern that hidden sources of impurity exist in Eretz Yisrael.

אֲמַר רַב הוּנָא בְּרֵיהּ דְּרַב יְהוֹשֻׁעַ: מַעֲלָה עָשׂוּ בְּפָרָה.

Rav Huna, son of Rav Yehoshua, said that Rabbi Yoḥanan would reply: The Sages **established a higher standard** for purity **in the** case of **the red heifer,**[N] but generally speaking there is no concern for hidden sources of impurity in Eretz Yisrael caused by those who perished in the flood.

אֵיתִיבֵיהּ רַבִּי יוֹחָנָן לְרֵישׁ לָקִישׁ: פַּעַם אַחַת מָצְאוּ עֲצָמוֹת בְּלִשְׁכַּת דִּיר הָעֵצִים וּבִקְּשׁוּ לִגְזוֹר טוּמְאָה עַל יְרוּשָׁלַיִם. עָמַד רַבִּי יְהוֹשֻׁעַ עַל רַגְלָיו וְאָמַר: לֹא בּוּשָׁה וּכְלִימָה הִיא לָנוּ שֶׁנִּגְזוֹר טוּמְאָה עַל עִיר אֲבוֹתֵינוּ? אַיֵּה מֵתֵי מַבּוּל, אַיֵּה מֵתֵי נְבוּכַדְנֶצַּר?

Rabbi Yoḥanan raised an objection to Reish Lakish from a *baraita* (see *Tosefta, Eduyyot* 3:3): **Once,** human **bones were found in the Chamber of the Woodshed,**[N] and the Sages **sought to decree impurity upon Jerusalem,**[N] i.e., to proclaim all who go there to be impure, as if a corpse can be found in a chamber of the Temple there is reason to be concerned that there are lost graves in other places as well. **Rabbi Yehoshua stood upon his feet and said: Is it not a shame and disgrace for us to decree impurity upon the city of our fathers** because of this concern? Show me: **Where are the dead of the flood,**[N] and **where are** all of **the dead** killed by **Nebuchadnezzar?**

מִדְּקָאָמַר הָכִי, לָאו לְמֵימְרָא דְּלָא הֲווּ? וּלְטַעֲמֵיךְ, הֲרוּגֵי נְבוּכַדְנֶצַּר הָכִי נַמִי דְּלָא הֲווּ? אֶלָּא, הֲווּ וּפַנִּינְהוּ. הָכָא נַמִי – הֲווּ וּפַנִּינְהוּ. וְאִי אִפַּנּוּ,

Rabbi Yoḥanan infers: **From the fact that** Rabbi Yehoshua **said this,** is this **not to say that there were no** lost graves in Jerusalem from the flood, because the flood did not take place there? Reish Lakish responds: **And according to your reasoning, so too were there not those killed by Nebuchadnezzar,** in and around Jerusalem, who were mentioned by Rabbi Yehoshua? Certainly there were, as Nebuchadnezzar killed many people in Jerusalem. **Rather,** there **were, and** others **removed** the bodies. **Here too,** with regard to the dead of the flood, **there were, and** others **removed** the bodies. **And** it is possible to ask: **If they were removed,** why is it necessary to be concerned that there may be impurity in the place of the red heifer,

NOTES

The Sages established a higher standard in the case of the red heifer – מַעֲלָה עָשׂוּ בְּפָרָה: The reason for this is because the rite of the red heifer is valid even if performed by one who immersed himself that day and is waiting for nightfall for the purification process to be completed. In fact, Rashi explains, citing *Yoma* 2a, that the priest who performed the rite of the red heifer would be intentionally rendered impure so that he would immerse and perform the rite on that day. This was done in order to refute the Sadducees, who claimed that the rite is not valid if performed by one who immersed himself that day. Due to this practice, the Sages were concerned that the rite's purity might become demeaned. They therefore instituted thirteen areas where the red heifer is held to a higher standard of purity than other consecrated matters (see *Hagiga* 18b).

Bones were found in the Chamber of the Woodshed – עֲצָמוֹת בְּלִשְׁכַּת דִּיר הָעֵצִים: The fact that this place is designated a chamber indicates that it may refer to the Chamber of the Wood that was in the Women's Courtyard in the Temple (see *Middot* 2:5). The version in the *Tosefta* (*Eduyyot* 3:3) reads: There was an incident where bones were found in Jerusalem in a woodshed, which accords better with the Gemara's discussion with regard to the purity of Jerusalem (*Or HaYashar*).

And the Sages sought to decree impurity upon Jerusalem – וּבִקְּשׁוּ לִגְזוֹר טוּמְאָה עַל יְרוּשָׁלַיִם: The decree would have been that Jerusalem is impure in the same sense that land outside Eretz Yisrael is impure. Alternatively, they would have decreed that it has the status of a field in which a corpse is buried, concerning which the *halakha* is that one who walks there has uncertain impure status (see Rabbeinu Ḥananel).

Where are the dead of the flood, etc. – אַיֵּה מֵתֵי מַבּוּל וכו׳: In other words, show us the dead of the flood or of those who were slain by Nebuchadnezzar. Since no one can identify the location of their corpses, there is no concern for impurity imparted by them (Rabbeinu Ḥananel).

Perek **XIV**
Daf **113** Amud **b**

הָא אִפַּנִּי! נְהִי דְּאִפַּנִּי מִירוּשָׁלַיִם, מִכּוּלָּהּ אֶרֶץ יִשְׂרָאֵל לָא אִפַּנִּי.

as **they were** already **removed.** One can respond: This *baraita* deals exclusively with Jerusalem. **Granted that** the bones of those who perished in the flood and at the hands of Nebuchadnezzar **were removed from Jerusalem,** but they **were not removed from all of Eretz Yisrael.** Therefore, outside Jerusalem, the red heifer may be slaughtered only in a place that has been inspected.

אִיכָּא דְּאָמְרִי, אֵיתִיבֵיהּ רֵישׁ לָקִישׁ לְרַבִּי יוֹחָנָן: ״אַיֵּה מֵתֵי מַבּוּל אַיֵּה מֵתֵי נְבוּכַדְנֶאצַּר״? מַאי לָאו מִדְּהָנֵי הָווּ – הָנֵי נַמִי הָווּ? מִידֵּי אִירְיָא? הָא כִּדְאִיתֵיהּ וְהָא כִּדְאִיתֵיהּ.

There are those **who say** the discussion should be inverted, and **Reish Lakish raised an objection to Rabbi Yoḥanan,** who holds that the flood did not affect Eretz Yisrael, from that *baraita*, as Rabbi Yehoshua said: **Where are the dead of the flood,** and **where are** all of **the dead** killed by **Nebuchadnezzar?** Reish Lakish said: **What, is it not** possible to infer from this question that **since those** slaughtered by Nebuchadnezzar **were** in Eretz Yisrael, **those** who perished in the flood **were also** there? Rabbi Yoḥanan responds: **Are the cases comparable? This is as it is and that is as it is,** i.e., the dead of Nebuchadnezzar were indeed in Eretz Yisrael, but the dead of the flood were not, as there was no flood there.

אֵיתִיבֵיהּ: "מִכֹּל אֲשֶׁר בֶּחָרָבָה מֵתוּ"; בִּשְׁלָמָא לְדִידִי דְּאָמֵינָא יָרַד מַבּוּל לְאֶרֶץ יִשְׂרָאֵל – מִשּׁוּם הָכִי מֵתוּ, אֶלָּא לְדִידָךְ אַמַּאי מֵתוּ? מִשּׁוּם הַבְלָא,

Reish Lakish **raised an objection to** Rabbi Yoḥanan: With regard to the flood, it is stated: "All in whose nostrils was the breath of the spirit of life, **whatsoever was on the dry land, died**" (Genesis 7:22). **Granted, according to my** opinion, **that I say the flood descended upon Eretz Yisrael, due to that** reason all living creatures on Earth **died**, even those in Eretz Yisrael. **But according to your** opinion that the flood did not descend on Eretz Yisrael, **why did they die** there? Rabbi Yoḥanan responds: They died **due to the heat** that accompanied the floodwaters, and that spread to Eretz Yisrael as well. Those corpses were then buried in known locations.

כִּדְרַב חִסְדָּא. דְּאָמַר רַב חִסְדָּא: בְּרוֹתְחִין קִלְקְלוּ וּבְרוֹתְחִין נִידּוֹנוּ, דִּכְתִיב הָכָא: "וַיָּשֹׁכּוּ הַמָּיִם", וּכְתִיב הָתָם: "וַחֲמַת הַמֶּלֶךְ שָׁכָכָה".

The Gemara notes that this is **in accordance with** the statement **of Rav Ḥisda, as Rav Ḥisda says:** The generation of the flood **sinned with boiling** heat, i.e., forbidden sexual intercourse, **and they were punished with the boiling** heat of the flood waters. **As it is written here,** with regard to the flood: "And God remembered Noah and every living creature and all the cattle that were with him in the ark; and God made a wind to pass over the earth **and the waters calmed** [*vayashoku hamayim*]" (Genesis 8:1); **and it is written there,** with regard to the execution of Haman: "So they hanged Haman on the gallows that he had prepared for Mordecai. **Then the king's boiling anger was assuaged** [*shakhakha*]" (Esther 7:10). This latter verse indicates that a matter is assuaged from heat; similarly, the flood waters were hot.

אִיכָּא דְּאָמְרִי, אֵיתִיבֵיהּ רַבִּי יוֹחָנָן לְרֵישׁ לָקִישׁ: "מִכֹּל אֲשֶׁר בֶּחָרָבָה מֵתוּ"; בִּשְׁלָמָא לְדִידִי דְּאָמֵינָא לֹא יָרַד מַבּוּל לְאֶרֶץ יִשְׂרָאֵל – מִשּׁוּם הָכִי הֲוֵי חָרָבָה, אֶלָּא לְדִידָךְ מַאי חָרָבָה? חָרָבָה שֶׁהָיְתָה מֵעִיקָּרָא.

There are those **who say** that this discussion should be inverted, and in fact **Rabbi Yoḥanan raised an objection to Reish Lakish** from that verse: It is stated that "**whatsoever was on the dry land, died**" (Genesis 7:22). **Granted, according to my** opinion, **that I say** that the **flood did not descend upon Eretz Yisrael, due to that** reason, **there was** an area of **dry land** even during the flood, and all living creatures there died from the heat. **But according to your** opinion that the flood did descend upon Eretz Yisrael, **what** is the meaning of "**dry land**"? There was no dry land anywhere. Reish Lakish responds: The verse is referring to **land that had been dry initially,** before the flood.

וְאַמַּאי קָרֵי לֵיהּ חָרָבָה – כִּדְרַב חִסְדָּא. דְּאָמַר רַב חִסְדָּא: בְּדוֹר הַמַּבּוּל לֹא נִגְזְרָה גְּזֵרָה עַל דָּגִים שֶׁבַּיָּם, שֶׁנֶּאֱמַר: "מִכֹּל אֲשֶׁר בֶּחָרָבָה מֵתוּ", וְלֹא דָּגִים שֶׁבַּיָּם.

And why does the Torah **call it "dry land"** during the flood? There was no dry land during the flood. It is **in accordance with** the opinion **of Rav Ḥisda, as Rav Ḥisda says: During the generation of the flood no decree was decreed upon the fish in the sea, as it is stated: "Whatsoever was on the dry land, died"** (Genesis 7:22), i.e., only those creatures that had been on dry land, **but not the fish in the sea.**

בִּשְׁלָמָא לְמַאן דְּאָמַר לֹא יָרַד מַבּוּל לְאֶרֶץ יִשְׂרָאֵל – הַיְינוּ דְּקָם רֵימָא הָתָם. אֶלָּא לְמַאן דְּאָמַר יָרַד, רֵימָא הֵיכָא קָם? אָמַר רַבִּי יַנַּאי: גּוּרִיּוֹת הִכְנִיסוּ בַּתֵּיבָה.

The Gemara asks: **Granted, according to the one who says the flood did not descend upon Eretz Yisrael,** i.e., Rabbi Yoḥanan, **this is** the explanation of the fact **that the *reima* remained there,** in Eretz Yisrael, and survived the flood. **But according to the one who says** the flood **descended** upon Eretz Yisrael, i.e., Reish Lakish, **how did the *reima* remain?**[N] Given its large size, it clearly could not have fit into Noah's ark. **Rabbi Yannai says:** They **brought** *reima* **cubs into the ark,** and they survived the flood.

וְהָאָמַר רַבָּה בַּר בַּר חָנָה: לְדִידִי חֲזִי לִי אוּרְזִילָא דְּרֵימָא בַּת יוֹמָא, וַהֲוֵי כְּהַר תָּבוֹר, וְהַר תָּבוֹר כַּמָּה הָוְיָא – אַרְבְּעִין פַּרְסֵי. מַשְׁכָּא דְּצַוָּארֵיהּ – תְּלָתָא פַּרְסֵי, מַרְבַּעְתָּא דְּרֵישָׁא – פַּרְסָא וּפַלְגָּא, רְמָא כָּבָא וּסְכַר יַרְדְּנָא!

The Gemara asks: **But doesn't Rabba bar bar Ḥana say: I have seen a day-old offspring of the *reima*,**[N] **and** it was as large **as Mount Tabor. And how large is Mount Tabor?** It is **forty parasangs.**[B] **And the** length of the cub's **neck** was **three parasangs,** and **the place where its head rests,** i.e., its neck, was **a parasang and a half. It cast feces,** and thereby **dammed up the Jordan** river. Even the cub would have been too large for the ark.

אָמַר רַבִּי יוֹחָנָן: רֹאשׁוֹ הִכְנִיסוּ לַתֵּיבָה. וְהָאָמַר מָר: מַרְבַּעְתָּא דְּרֵישָׁא פַּרְסָא וּפַלְגָּא! אֶלָּא: רֹאשׁ חוֹטְמוֹ הִכְנִיסוּ לַתֵּיבָה.

Rabbi Yoḥanan says: They brought only **the head of** the cub **into the ark,** while its body remained outside. The Gemara asks: **But doesn't the Master,** i.e., Rabba bar bar Ḥana, **say** that the size of **the place where its head rests was a parasang and a half?** Consequently, even its head alone would not fit into the ark. **Rather, they brought the head,** i.e., edge, **of its nose into the ark,** so that it might breathe.

NOTES

How did the *reima* remain – רֵימָא הֵיכָא קָם: Onkelos translates the word *dishon* (Deuteronomy 14:5) as the Aramaic word *reima*. *Tosafot* cite a suggestion that the *reima* is the buffalo, but also cite Rabbeinu Tam as rejecting this identification, as this discussion in the Talmud indicates that is describing a creature far larger than any known animal.

Day-old offspring of the *reima* – אוּרְזִילָא דְּרֵימָא בַּת יוֹמָא: The standard version of the text is a combination of several versions of the early commentaries. Rashi's version reads: An *urzila* of the sea [*urzila deyama*], and he understands that an *urzila* is a *reima*. The Rashbam in *Bava Batra* (73b) has a version that reads: A day-old *urzila* [*urzila bat yoma*], and understands *urzila* in the same manner. *Tosafot* cite an opinion that this refers to a fish in the sea (see Ri Migash and Rashbam). Rabbeinu Tam does not accept any of these versions. In his opinion the Gemara should read: *Urzila dereima*. Based on the *Targum* on Song of Songs, he explains that *urzila dereima* means the offspring of the *re'em* animal. In any case, the Gemara's question remains the same according to all of the commentaries: Even the young offspring was too large for Noah's ark.

BACKGROUND

Parasang – פַּרְסָה: From the Persian; a specific measure of distance. In the Talmud, this measurement is equal to four *mil*, or approximately 4 km.

Map of Persia, with scale in parasangs, 1814

NOTES

Because it shakes [*shemena'eret*] its wealthy people – שֶׁמְּנָעֶרֶת עֲשִׁירֶיהָ: This is a reference to the wealthy Jews of Babylonia, who the Gemara says will descend to Gehenna because they do not have mercy upon others (*Beitza* 32b). The Maharsha connects this to the statement in the Gemara in tractate *Yoma* (9b) that because most of the Babylonian exiles did not ascend to Eretz Yisrael before the building of the Second Temple, they are like cedars, which are susceptible to rotting, and not like silver, which is not susceptible to rotting.

וְהָא אָמַר רַבִּי יוֹחָנָן: לֹא יָרַד מַבּוּל לְאֶרֶץ יִשְׂרָאֵל! לְדִבְרֵי רֵישׁ לָקִישׁ קָאָמַר.

The Gemara wonders why Rabbi Yoḥanan was compelled to give this answer: **But doesn't Rabbi Yoḥanan say** that **the flood did not descend upon Eretz Yisrael?** According to his opinion, perhaps the *reima* survived by remaining there during the flood. The Gemara answers that Rabbi Yoḥanan **said** his answer **in accordance with the statement of Reish Lakish.**

וְהָא קָסַגְיָא תֵּיבָה! אָמַר רֵישׁ לָקִישׁ: קַרְנָיו קָשְׁרוּ בַּתֵּיבָה. וְהָאָמַר רַב חִסְדָּא: אַנְשֵׁי דוֹר הַמַּבּוּל בְּרוֹתְחִין קִלְקְלוּ, וּבְרוֹתְחִין נִידּוֹנוּ!

The Gemara challenges: **But the ark was moving** upon the water. How it was possible to keep the nose of the *reima* in the ark? **Reish Lakish says: They tied its horns to the ark,** so that the *reima* would move with it. The Gemara asks: **But doesn't Rav Ḥisda say** that **the people of the generation of the flood sinned with boiling** heat **and were punished with boiling** heat? How could the *reima* have survived the boiling water?

וּלְטַעֲמֵיךְ, תֵּיבָה הֵיכִי סַגְיָא? וְעוֹד, עוֹג מֶלֶךְ הַבָּשָׁן הֵיכָא קָאֵי? אֶלָּא, נֵס נַעֲשָׂה לָהֶם, שֶׁנִּצְטַנְּנוּ בְּצִידֵּי הַתֵּיבָה.

The Gemara replies: **And according to your reasoning,** that it was impossible to survive the boiling water, **how did** the **ark** itself **move?** It was covered with pitch, which melts in boiling water. **Moreover, how did Og, king of the Bashan** (see Numbers 21:33–35), who according to tradition was of the generation of the flood, **stand,** i.e., survive the boiling water? **Rather,** it must be that **a miracle was performed for them,** namely **that** the water **on the sides of the ark cooled,** allowing the ark, the *reima*, and Og to survive.

וּלְרַבִּי שִׁמְעוֹן [בֶּן לָקִישׁ], נְהִי נַמִּי דְּיָרַד מַבּוּל לְאֶרֶץ יִשְׂרָאֵל, וְהָא לָא פַּשׁ! דְּאָמַר רֵישׁ לָקִישׁ: לָמָּה נִקְרָא שְׁמָהּ ״מְצוּלָה״ – שֶׁכָּל מֵתֵי מַבּוּל נִצְטַלְּלוּ שָׁם. וְרַבִּי יוֹחָנָן אָמַר: לָמָּה נִקְרָא שְׁמָהּ ״שִׁנְעָר״ – שֶׁכָּל מֵתֵי מַבּוּל נִנְעֲרוּ שָׁם! אִי אֶפְשָׁר דְּלָא אִידַּבְקוּ.

The Gemara challenges: But even **according to** the opinion of **Rabbi Shimon ben Lakish,** that the flood descended upon Eretz Yisrael and the corpses of those who perished in the flood might impart impurity there, **though** the **flood did indeed descend upon Eretz Yisrael, no** trace of the dead **remains** there. **As Reish Lakish says: Why** is Babylonia **called Metzula** (see Isaiah 44:27)? It is **because all the dead of the flood,** throughout the world, **sank** [*nitztalelu*] **there. And Rabbi Yoḥanan says: Why is** Babylonia **called Shinar?** It is **because all the dead of the flood were deposited** [*ninaru*] **there.** Evidently, even Reish Lakish says that all who died in the flood, including those from Eretz Yisrael, sank in Babylonia. The Gemara responds: **It is impossible that** the corpses of some of those in Eretz Yisrael who perished in the flood **were not stuck** in the mud and remained there.

אָמַר רַבִּי אַבָּהוּ: לָמָּה נִקְרָא שְׁמָהּ ״שִׁנְעָר״ – שֶׁמְּנָעֶרֶת עֲשִׁירֶיהָ. וְהָא קָחָזֵינַן דְּהָווּ! תְּלָתָא דָּרֵי לָא מָשְׁכִי.

Having mentioned some explanations for the names of Babylonia, the Gemara adds: **Rabbi Abbahu says: Why is it called Shinar? Because it shakes** [*shemena'eret*] **its wealthy** people,[N] i.e., they do not remain wealthy. The Gemara asks: **But we see that there are** wealthy people in Babylonia who remain wealthy. The Gemara responds: Their wealth **does not extend** for **three generations.**

אָמַר רַבִּי אַמִי: כָּל הָאוֹכֵל מֵעֲפָרָהּ שֶׁל בָּבֶל, כְּאִילּוּ אוֹכֵל בְּשַׂר אֲבוֹתָיו. תַּנְיָא נַמִּי הָכִי: כָּל הָאוֹכֵל מֵעֲפָרָהּ שֶׁל בָּבֶל – כְּאִילּוּ אוֹכֵל בְּשַׂר אֲבוֹתָיו, וְיֵשׁ אוֹמְרִים: כְּאִילּוּ אוֹכֵל שְׁקָצִים וּרְמָשִׂים.

With regard to the statement that the corpses of those who perished in the flood came to Babylonia, **Rabbi Ami says:** Concerning **anyone who eats the dust of Babylonia,** it is **as if he eats the flesh of his ancestors,** since there is a great deal of dust from the dead there. **This is also taught** in a *baraita*: Concerning **anyone who eats the dust of Babylonia,** it is **as if he eats the flesh of his ancestors. And some say:** It is **as if he eats repugnant creatures and crawling things,**[B] which also died in the flood and were absorbed by the ground of Babylonia.

״שָׂעִיר הַמִּשְׁתַּלֵּחַ״.

§ The mishna teaches that if one sacrificed **the scapegoat** of Yom Kippur outside the Temple he is exempt from the prohibition against sacrificing outside, since the Torah states: "And to the entrance of the Tent of Meeting he did not bring it" (Leviticus 17:3–4), and the scapegoat is not fit to be brought to the entrance of the Tent of Meeting.

BACKGROUND

Repugnant creatures and crawling things – שְׁקָצִים וּרְמָשִׂים: This term refers to various types of non-kosher animals. *Tosefot Yom Tov* distinguishes between the two words, suggesting that the designation: Repugnant creatures [*shekatzim*], refers to small creatures in the sea and land, as well as birds and insects labeled as *shekatzim* in the Torah. Crawling things [*remasim*], by contrast, refers to worms and other creatures that infect produce and that were believed to form through spontaneous generation.

There is a halakhic principle that a forbidden item or creature whose original form has been completely destroyed or altered is no longer forbidden. Therefore, the Gemara's statement about the flesh of the corpses and repugnant creatures in Babylonia was intended metaphorically, to underscore that one should not eat Babylonian soil for other reasons.

וּרְמִינְהִי: "אוֹ קָרְבָּן", שׁוֹמֵעַ אֲנִי אֲפִילּוּ קׇדְשֵׁי בֶדֶק הַבַּיִת שֶׁנִּקְרְאוּ קׇרְבָּן, שֶׁנֶּאֱמַר: "וַנַּקְרֵב אֶת קׇרְבַּן ה'"?

And the Gemara **raises a contradiction**[N] from a *baraita*: The verse states: "To present it as an offering to the Lord" (Leviticus 17:4), and it is derived from the word "offering" that one who slaughters non-sacred animals inside the Temple is not liable. The *baraita* asks: **Or** perhaps from the word **"offering"** I would **derive** that the prohibition against slaughtering outside the Temple applies **even** to items **consecrated for Temple maintenance, as** they too **are called offerings, as it is stated** with regard to the spoils of the war against Midian: **"And we have brought the Lord's offering,** what every man has gotten, of jewels of gold, armlets, and bracelets, signet rings, earrings, and girdles, to make atonement for our souls before the Lord" (Numbers 31:50). These were certainly not items consecrated for the altar.

תַּלְמוּד לוֹמַר: "וְאֶל פֶּתַח אֹהֶל מוֹעֵד לֹא הֱבִיאוֹ" – מִי שֶׁרָאוּי לָבֹא בְּאֹהֶל מוֹעֵד, יָצְאוּ קׇדְשֵׁי בֶדֶק הַבַּיִת שֶׁאֵינָן רְאוּיִן.

Therefore, **the verse states: "And to the entrance of the Tent of Meeting he did not bring it"** (Leviticus 17:4), which teaches that this *halakha* applies only to **that which is fit to come to** the entrance of the **Tent of Meeting,** i.e., is fit to be sacrificed. **Excluded** are items **consecrated for Temple maintenance, which are not fit** for sacrifice.

אוֹצִיא אֶת אֵלּוּ שֶׁאֵינָן רְאוּיִן, וְלֹא אוֹצִיא אֶת שָׂעִיר הַמִּשְׁתַּלֵּחַ שֶׁהוּא רָאוּי לָבֹא אֶל פֶּתַח אֹהֶל מוֹעֵד! תַּלְמוּד לוֹמַר: "לַה'", לְהוֹצִיא שָׂעִיר הַמִּשְׁתַּלֵּחַ שֶׁאֵינוֹ מְיוּחָד לַה'!

The *baraita* continues: Perhaps **I shall exclude these,** i.e., items consecrated for Temple maintenance, **which are not fit** to be sacrificed upon the altar, from the prohibition against slaughtering outside the Temple, **but I shall not exclude the scapegoat, which is fit to come to the entrance of the Tent of Meeting.** Therefore, **the verse states:** "To present it as an offering **to the Lord,"** which serves **to exclude** from this prohibition **the scapegoat, which is not designated** as a sacrifice **to the Lord,** but is rather sent to Azazel. According to the *baraita,* the scapegoat is fit to be brought to the entrance of the Tent of Meeting.

לָא קַשְׁיָא, כָּאן – קוֹדֶם הַגְרָלָה, כָּאן – לְאַחַר הַגְרָלָה. אַחַר הַגְרָלָה נַמִי, הָאִיכָּא וִידּוּי!

The Gemara answers: This is **not difficult. Here,** the *baraita* that states that the scapegoat is fit to be brought to the entrance of the Tent of Meeting is referring to **before** the **lottery,** wherein the two goats of the Day of Atonement are brought into the Temple courtyard, and the High Priest draws lots to determine which is to be sacrificed to the Lord, and which is for Azazel. **There,** the mishna that states that the scapegoat is not fit to be brought to the entrance of the Tent of Meeting is referring to **after** the **lottery,** at which point it is no longer fit for the Temple. The Gemara challenges: **After** the **lottery** it is **also** fit to be brought inside, as **there is** still an obligation for the High Priest to recite **confession** upon it in the Temple courtyard.

אֶלָּא אֲמַר רַב מָנִי, לָא קַשְׁיָא: כָּאן – קוֹדֶם וִידּוּי, כָּאן – לְאַחַר וִידּוּי.

Rather, Rav Mani said: This is **not difficult,** as **here,** the *baraita* that states that the scapegoat may be brought to the entrance of the Tent of Meeting is referring to **before** the **confession,**[NH] when it is still fit to enter the Temple. **There,** the mishna that states that it is not fit to be brought to the entrance of the Tent of Meeting is referring to **after** the **confession,** at which point it is no longer fit to be brought inside.

"הָרוֹבֵעַ וְהַנִּרְבָּע".

§ The mishna teaches that with regard to **an animal that** actively **copulated with a person, or an animal that was the object of bestiality,** or another disqualified offering such as an animal that was designated for idol worship, or one that was worshipped: If one sacrificed it outside the Temple courtyard, he is exempt. This is because with regard to the prohibition against slaughtering outside, the Torah states: "He did not bring it, to present it as an offering to the Lord before the Tabernacle of the Lord" (Leviticus 17:4), which teaches that there is no liability for slaughtering outside the Temple courtyard an animal that is not fit to be sacrificed.

וְהָא נַמִי תֵּיפוֹק לִי מִ"פֶּתַח אֹהֶל מוֹעֵד"!

The Gemara asks: **And** with regard to **this too, derive from** the first part of that verse: **"To the entrance of the Tent of Meeting,"** that, as in the case of the red heifer and the scapegoat, if an animal is not fit to be brought to the entrance of the Tent of Meeting, one is not liable for slaughtering it outside.

NOTES

The scapegoat…and the Gemara raises a contradiction – שָׂעִיר הַמִּשְׁתַּלֵּחַ וּרְמִינְהִי: There are two primary explanations of this discussion, which are rooted in different versions of the text. According to Rashi, there is a contradiction between the mishna's statement that the scapegoat is not fit to be brought to the entrance of the Tent of Meeting, and consequently one is not liable for slaughtering it outside; and that which is taught in the *baraita,* that the scapegoat is fit to be brought to the entrance of the Tent of Meeting and the scapegoat is excluded from the prohibition against slaughtering outside due to the fact that the verse states: "To the Lord." The resolution is that these two sources are discussing different circumstances: The mishna is discussing a case where the animal is not fit to be brought to the entrance of the Tent of Meeting; the *baraita* is discussing a case where it is fit to be brought there, and the verse: "To the Lord," is therefore necessary to exclude it.

Rabbeinu Ḥananel's version of the *baraita* states the opposite, teaching that "to the Lord" serves to include the scapegoat. According to this version, the Gemara refers to a contradiction between the mishna, which rules that one who slaughters the scapegoat outside the Temple is exempt, and the *baraita,* which holds one liable for slaughtering it there. The Gemara then resolves the contradiction by distinguishing between circumstances in which one is liable for slaughtering outside and circumstances in which one who does so is exempt. This appears to be the version of the text utilized by the Rambam as well, whose ruling on the matter has been difficult for many commentaries to explain. This also appears to be the version utilized in *Piskei HaRid.*

Here is referring to before confession – כָּאן קוֹדֶם וִידּוּי: This explanation appears to indicate that at any point before confession, including before the lottery, the scapegoat is fit to be brought to the entrance of the Tent of Meeting, but is excluded from the prohibition due to the verse: "To the Lord." *Tosafot* note that a *baraita* in tractate *Yoma* (62b) states that one who slaughters either of the goats of Yom Kippur outside the Temple courtyard is liable. They explain that according to the conclusion of this Gemara, the verses indicating that one who slaughters the scapegoat outside the Temple is exempt pertain to after the lottery, but before the lottery one would be liable (see *Tosafot Yeshanim* on *Yoma* 62b). It appears from the ruling of the Rambam that in his opinion, unlike *Tosafot,* there is a contradiction between the two talmudic discussions, and he ruled in accordance with the Gemara here (see Ritva on *Yoma* 62b).

HALAKHA

Here is referring to before confession – כָּאן קוֹדֶם וִידּוּי: The Rambam writes: With regard to the two goats of Yom Kippur that were slaughtered outside the Temple courtyard: If one slaughtered them before confession was recited upon them he is liable to receive *karet* for both of them, since they are fit to come before the Lord for confession. If one slaughtered them after confession had been recited he is exempt for slaughtering the scapegoat. This ruling is based on the conclusion of the discussion here, though it appears that the Rambam had a different version of the Gemara. According to the conclusion of the other early commentaries, if one slaughters the goats outside the Temple courtyard before the lottery he is liable for both, while if one slaughters them after the lottery he is exempt for the scapegoat. This is in accordance with the *baraita* on *Yoma* 62b (Rambam *Sefer Avoda, Hilkhot Ma'aseh HaKorbanot* 18:11; see *Likkutei Halakhot*).

HALAKHA

A person does not render forbidden an item that is not his – אֵין אָדָם אוֹסֵר דָּבָר שֶׁאֵינוֹ שֶׁלּוֹ: An animal that actively copulated with a person or an animal that was the object of bestiality is forbidden for the altar, whether the animal belonged to that person or to another, whether the act occurred before or after the animal was consecrated, and whether the act was intentional or unwitting, because a physical act has taken place. With regard to one who set aside an animal for idol worship, if the animal was his, and it was set aside before it was consecrated, it is disqualified. But if one set aside for idol worship either the animal of another or an animal that had already been consecrated, then the animal may be sacrificed, since a person does not render forbidden an item that is not his. If one worshipped an animal as an idol, whether it belonged to him or to another, whether he did so under duress or willingly, intentionally or unwittingly, before it was consecrated or afterward, the animal is forbidden.

The Ra'avad writes that according to the Gemara in *Avoda Zara* (54a), a person does not render forbidden the property of another by worshipping it unless some physical act was performed on it. The Rambam holds that this applies only with regard to rendering it forbidden to its owner, but it is disqualified for Temple service even if no act was performed (Rambam *Sefer Avoda, Hilkhot Issurei Mizbe'aḥ* 4:5–6; see *Sefer HaMadda, Hilkhot Avoda Zara* 8:1).

בִּשְׁלָמָא רוֹבֵעַ וְנִרְבָּע – מַשְׁכַּחַת לֵיהּ דְּאַקְדְּשִׁינְהוּ מֵעִיקָּרָא וַהֲדַר רְבָעוֹ.

Granted, with regard to **an animal that** actively **copulated with a person or an animal that was the object of bestiality, you find** circumstances in which the exemption for one who slaughters it outside the Temple courtyard cannot be based on the fact that it is not fit to be brought to the entrance of the Tent of Meeting, e.g., a case **where one initially consecrated it,** at which point it was fit to be brought to the Temple courtyard, **and then engaged in bestiality with it.** Since it was initially fit to be brought to the Temple courtyard, another verse is needed to exclude it.

אֶלָּא מוּקְצֶה וְנֶעֱבָד – אֵין אָדָם אוֹסֵר דָּבָר שֶׁאֵינוֹ שֶׁלּוֹ! בְּקָדָשִׁים קַלִּים, וְאַלִּיבָּא דְּרַבִּי יוֹסֵי הַגְּלִילִי. דְּאָמַר: קָדָשִׁים קַלִּים מָמוֹן בְּעָלִים הוּא.

But with regard to an animal that was **set aside** for idol worship **or** one that was **worshipped,** this explanation is not tenable, since an animal that was already consecrated would not become disqualified because **a person does not render forbidden an item that is not his.**[H] The Gemara responds that it is possible to disqualify a consecrated item **in the case of offerings of lesser sanctity,** such as a peace offering, **and in accordance with** the opinion **of Rabbi Yosei HaGelili, who says: An offering of lesser sanctity is the property of the owner.**

דְּתַנְיָא: ״וּמָעֲלָה מַעַל בַּה׳״ – לְרַבּוֹת קָדָשִׁים קַלִּים, שֶׁהֵן מָמוֹנוֹ, דִּבְרֵי רַבִּי יוֹסֵי הַגְּלִילִי.

This is **as it is taught** in a *baraita* that the verse states with regard to the obligation to bring a guilt offering for robbery for taking a false oath concerning unlawful possession of the property of another: "If anyone sin, **and commit a trespass against the Lord,** and deal falsely with his neighbor in a matter of deposit, or of pledge, or of robbery, or have oppressed his neighbor" (Leviticus 5:21). The term "against the Lord" serves **to include** one who takes an oath with regard to another's **offerings of lesser sanctity, since they** are **the property of** their owner. This is **the statement of Rabbi Yosei HaGelili.**

הִלְכָּךְ, רוֹבֵעַ וְנִרְבָּע – דְּבַר עֶרְוָה, מוּקְצֶה וְנֶעֱבַד עֲבוֹדָה זָרָה – בְּקָדָשִׁים קַלִּים.

The Gemara summarizes: **Therefore,** all of the cases listed in the mishna are cases in which the animal was initially fit to be brought to the entrance of the Tent of Meeting but was subsequently disqualified as an offering. **An animal that** actively **copulated with a person and an animal that was the object of bestiality** are disqualified after having been consecrated, due to **a matter of forbidden sexual intercourse.** An animal that was **set aside** for idol worship **or** one that **was worshipped** as an object of **idol worship** becomes forbidden after it was consecrated in the case **of an offering of lesser sanctity,** which according to Rabbi Yosei HaGelili is the property of its owner.

אֶתְנָן וּמְחִיר, כִּלְאַיִם, יוֹצֵא דוֹפֶן – בְּוַלְדוֹת קָדָשִׁים,

In the case of an animal that was given as **payment** to a prostitute **or** as the **price** of a dog,[N] or an animal born of a mixture of **diverse kinds,** or an animal **born by caesarean section,** none of which could have occured at a time that the animal was fit to be sacrificed, the mishna is referring **to the offspring of sacrificial** animals that were given as payment to a prostitute or as the price of a dog while in utero. These animals were fit to be brought as a sacrifice while they were still part of a consecrated animal, and only following birth are they considered to be unfit for sacrifice.

NOTES

Payment to a prostitute or as the price of a dog – אֶתְנָן וּמְחִיר: In contrast to the disqualifications of an animal for being set aside for idol worship or having been worshipped, the disqualifications of payment to a prostitute or the price of a dog apply only to non-sacred animals and not to sacred animals, even offerings of lesser sanctity (*Temura* 30b). Consequently, an animal that was given as payment to a prostitute or as the price of a dog was already disqualified, as it is not fit to be brought to the entrance of the Tent of Meeting; it is therefore unnecessary to state that one who slaughters it outside the courtyard is exempt.

But when an animal is given in utero as the payment to a prostitute or the price of a dog, since at that moment it is still fit to be sacrificed, as it is considered part of the mother, one could say that slaughtering it outside the courtyard after birth renders one liable. The Gemara therefore cites the verse: "To present it as an offering to the Lord" (Leviticus 17:4), to exempt one who slaughters such an animal, since at that time it is not fit for sacrifice. The *halakha* is the same for an animal born of a mixture of diverse kinds or an animal born by caesarean section: If it was consecrated after its birth, it is not fit to be brought to the entrance of the Tent of Meeting. If it was consecrated in utero, it is fit to be sacrificed as a part of the mother, as only after birth does it become disqualified.

קָסָבַר: וַלְדֵי קָדָשִׁים בַּהֲוָיָיתָן הֵן קְדוֹשִׁים.

Although these offspring are still part of a consecrated animal while in utero, and as such one might say that the status of payment to a prostitute or the price of a dog should not take effect with rgeard to them, the *tanna* of the mishna **holds** that with regard to **the offspring of sacrificial** animals, **they are sanctified** only **as they are**[N] from the time of birth, but not in utero. Therefore, they can be disqualified by serving as payment to a prostitute or as the price of a dog.

"בַּעֲלֵי מוּמִין וכו' אוֹתוֹ וְאֶת בְּנוֹ" וכו'.

§ The mishna cites a disagreement between the Rabbis and Rabbi Shimon with regard to temporarily **blemished** animals: Rabbi Shimon holds that one who sacrifices them outside the Temple courtyard violates a prohibition, as they will be fit for sacrifice after the passage of time, whereas the Rabbis hold that one is exempt. The mishna cites two similar disagreements: With regard to doves whose time of fitness has not yet arrived that are slaughtered outside the Temple courtyard, and with regard to one who slaughters an animal **itself and its offspring** on one day, where the latter, which is not fit for being sacrificed until the next day, is slaughtered outside the Temple courtyard.

וּצְרִיכִי, דְּאִי תְּנָא בַּעֲלֵי מוּמִין – מִשּׁוּם דְּמָאִיסִי, אֲבָל תּוֹרִין דְּלָא מָאִיסִי – אֵימָא לָא, דְּמוֹדוּ לֵיהּ לְרַבִּי שִׁמְעוֹן.

The Gemara comments: **And** all of these cases **are necessary. As, if** the mishna had **taught** the disagreement only in the case of temporarily **blemished** animals, one would think that the Rabbis deem exempt one who sacrifices outside the Temple courtyard only in that case, **because they are repulsive; but** with regard to **doves** whose time of fitness has not yet arrived, **which are not repulsive** and which will be fit when their time arrives, **I will say** that this is **not** the *halakha*, and **that** the Rabbis **concede to Rabbi Shimon** that one does violate a prohibition.

וְאִי תְּנָא תּוֹרִין – מִשּׁוּם דְּלָא חֲזוּ וְאִידְּחוּ. אֲבָל בַּעֲלֵי מוּמִין דְּאִיחֲזוּ וְאִידְּחוּ – אֵימָא לָא, דְּמוֹדֶה לְהוּ רַבִּי שִׁמְעוֹן לְרַבָּנַן.

And if the mishna had **taught** the disagreement only in the case of **doves** whose time of fitness has not yet arrived, one could say that it is only in this case that Rabbi Shimon holds that one who sacrifices them outside violates a prohibition, **because they are not** defined as: **Fit** for sacrifice **and rejected;**[N] their time of fitness simply has not arrived. **But** with regard to temporarily **blemished** animals, **which were fit** for sacrifice **and** then **disqualified, I will say** that this is **not** the *halakha*, **as Rabbi Shimon concedes to the Rabbis** that one who sacrifices them outside the Temple courtyard does not violate a prohibition, since they are not fit to be sacrificed as offerings.

NOTES

They are sanctified only as they are – בַּהֲוָיָיתָן הֵן קְדוֹשִׁים: In other words, according to this opinion, it can become considered to be consecrated only after it is born; while it is in utero it has no independent sanctity and is sacrificed only as part of its mother. This statement was necessary to explain that although the disqualifications of payment to a prostitute and the price of a dog do not apply to a consecrated animal, they do apply to the fetus of a consecrated animal, as it is not yet sacred. It should be noted that in tractate *Nidda* (41a) Rashi states that this applies only to a fetus of an offering of lesser sanctity, which, in the opinion of Rabbi Yosei HaGelili, is the property of the owner.

According to the opinion that a fetus has independent sanctity while in utero, the disqualifications of payment to a prostitute and the price of a dog do not apply, and the offspring is fit for sacrifice; therefore one who sacrifices it outside the courtyard is liable. The disqualification would still apply to an animal born of a mixture of diverse kinds or to one born of a cesarean section (*Panim Meirot*).

The Rid's version of the Gemara states that the animal had been consecrated before it was used for payment to a prostitute or the price of a dog, or became a *tereifa*, a case mentioned in the mishna but not the Gemara. This is also the opinion of Rabbeinu Hillel in his commentary to *Torat Kohanim*, where he adds that these are animals consecrated as offerings of lesser sanctity, in accordance with the opinion of Rabbi Yosei HaGelili, and the *tanna* of the mishna disagrees with the assumption that consecrated animals cannot be given as payment to a prostitute or as the price of a dog. Only in the case of an animal born by cesarean section does he explain that the mishna is discussing an animal that was consecrated in utero, on the assumption that the offspring of consecrated animals become sacred in utero.

Because they are not defined as fit for sacrifice and rejected – מִשּׁוּם דְּלָא חֲזוּ וְאִידְּחוּ: One can say that according to the opinion of Rabbi Shimon, the reason that one violates a prohibition in the case of doves whose time has not yet arrived is that they are intrinsically fit to be sacrificed and lack only time. In the case of a temporarily blemished animal, though, a physical blemish on the body of the animal disqualifies it. It may therefore be compared to any other animal that is disqualified from sacrifice, for which there is no liability if it is slaughtered outside the courtyard.

NOTES

Where the disqualification comes to it from an external factor I will say the Rabbis concede to Rabbi Shimon – דִּפְסוּלָא מֵעָלְמָא קָאָתֵי לָהּ אֵימָא מוֹדוּ לֵיהּ רַבָּנַן לְרַבִּי שִׁמְעוֹן: It appears that *Tosafot* had a version of the Gemara that reads: I will say that Rabbi Shimon concedes to the Rabbis. This version appears in a small number of manuscripts and is also used by Rabbi Ovadya Bartenura in his commentary on the mishna. The meaning of this version is as follows: In the cases of temporarily blemished animals and doves whose time has not yet arrived, the disqualifications are intrinsic to the body of animal, and when they are no longer relevant, the animal will be fit for sacrifice. By contrast, in the case of an animal and its offspring being sacrificed on the same day, nothing can be done to the body of the animal that will render it fit for sacrifice; it is only the passage of time that will do so. Therefore, perhaps Rabbi Shimon will concede that one who sacrifices the latter outside the courtyard is not in violation of a prohibition.

וְאִי תְּנָא הָנֵי תַּרְתֵּי – מִשּׁוּם דִּפְסוּלָא דְּגוּפַיְיהוּ, אֲבָל אוֹתוֹ וְאֶת בְּנוֹ, דִּפְסוּלָא מֵעָלְמָא קָאָתֵי לָהּ – אֵימָא מוֹדוּ לֵיהּ רַבָּנַן לְרַבִּי שִׁמְעוֹן, צְרִיכָא.

And if the mishna had **taught** only **these two** cases, i.e., temporarily blemished animals and doves whose time of fitness has not yet arrived, I would say that the Rabbis hold that one who slaughters them outside the Temple courtyard is not liable **because their disqualification** is **inherent. But** in the case of the animal **itself and its offspring,** where **the disqualification comes to** the offspring **from an external** factor, i.e., that its parent was slaughtered that day, **I will say** that **the Rabbis concede to Rabbi Shimon**[N] that one who slaughters an animal and its offspring outside the Temple courtyard does violate the prohibition. Therefore, it is **necessary** for the mishna to teach the disagreement in each case.

״שֶׁהָיָה רַבִּי שִׁמְעוֹן אוֹמֵר״. מַאי טַעְמָא דְּרַבִּי שִׁמְעוֹן?

§ The mishna teaches **that Rabbi Shimon says:** In the case of any sacrificial animal that is fit to be sacrificed after the passage of time, if one sacrificed it outside the courtyard, he is in violation of a prohibition but there is no liability for *karet*. Rabbi Shimon did not specify what prohibition is violated. The Gemara therefore asks: **What is the reasoning of Rabbi Shimon?**

אָמַר רַבִּי אִילְעָא אָמַר רֵישׁ לָקִישׁ: דְּאָמַר קְרָא: ״לֹא תַעֲשׂוּן כְּכֹל אֲשֶׁר אֲנַחְנוּ עֹשִׂים פֹּה הַיּוֹם״. אֲמַר לְהוּ מֹשֶׁה לְיִשְׂרָאֵל: כִּי עַיְילִיתוּ לָאָרֶץ – יְשָׁרוֹת תַּקְרִיבוּ, חוֹבוֹת לֹא תַּקְרִיבוּ.

Rabbi Ile'a says that **Reish Lakish says** that **the verse states: "You shall not do all that we do here this day,** every man whatsoever is right in his own eyes. For you have not as yet come to the rest and to the inheritance, which the Lord your God gives you" (Deuteronomy 12:8–9). **Moses said** the following **to the Jewish people: When you enter Eretz** Yisrael, **upright** offerings, i.e., offerings that one believes are proper to bring due to one's own generosity, such as vow offerings and gift offerings, **you may sacrifice,** but **obligatory** offerings **you may not sacrifice,** even in the Tabernacle in Gilgal, until you arrive at "the rest," i.e., Shiloh, at which point you may sacrifice them.

וְגִלְגָּל לְגַבֵּי שִׁילֹה מְחוּסַּר זְמַן הוּא, וְקָאָמַר לְהוּ מֹשֶׁה: ״לֹא תַעֲשׂוּן״.

And since obligatory offerings during the period of **Gilgal, in relation to** the period of **Shiloh,** are considered offerings **whose time has not yet** arrived, **and Moses said to** the Jewish people concerning them: **"You shall not do,"** during that period, it follows that one who sacrifices an offering whose time has not yet arrived is in violation of the prohibition: "You shall not do."

אֲמַר רַבִּי יִרְמְיָה לְרַבִּי זֵירָא: אִי הָכִי,

Rabbi Yirmeya said to Rabbi Zeira: Therefore, it is prohibited to sacrifice offerings whose time has not yet arrived, even if they are sacrificed in the Tabernacle as was the case in Gilgal. **If so,** anyone who sacrifices an offering whose time has not yet arrived, even if he sacrifices it inside the Temple courtyard,

Perek **XIV**
Daf **114** Amud **b**

מִילְקֵי נַמִּי לִילְקֵי! אַלְּמָה אָמַר רַבִּי זֵירָא: הַכָּתוּב נִתְּקוֹ לַעֲשֵׂה?

should also receive lashes for sacrificing it, just as one would for violating other Torah prohibitions. **Why did Rabbi Zeira say** elsewhere that one who slaughters, inside the Temple courtyard, an offering whose time has not yet arrived does not receive lashes for having violated the prohibition of: "It shall not be accepted" (Leviticus 22:23), which is the general prohibition against sacrificing animals that are not fit to be sacrificed. Rabbi Zeira explains that he does not receive lashes because **the verse has transmuted** the negative precept **into** a prohibition that is stated as **a positive mitzva,** in the verse: "But from the eighth day forward it may be accepted" (Leviticus 22:27). There is no punishment of lashes for violating such a prohibition. Rabbi Yirmeya is asking that one should still receive lashes for having violated the prohibition of: "You shall not do."

הָנֵי מִילֵּי לְרַבָּנַן, לְרַבִּי שִׁמְעוֹן – הָכִי נַמִּי.

The Gemara responds: **That statement** of Rabbi Zeira applies only **according to** the opinion of **the Rabbis,**[N] who disagree with Rabbi Shimon in the mishna and hold that the verse that states: "You shall not do," does not indicate that one who slaughters an animal whose time has not yet arrived is in violation of a prohibition. But **according to** the opinion of **Rabbi Shimon,** one would **indeed** receive lashes for slaughtering an animal whose time has not yet arrived inside the Temple.

רַב נַחְמָן בַּר יִצְחָק אֲמַר: פְּנִים דְּגִלְגָּל לְגַבֵּי שִׁילֹה – כְּחוּץ דָּמֵי.

Rav Naḥman bar Yitzḥak said: Rabbi Zeira's statement is even in accordance with the opinion of Rabbi Shimon, who also holds that one would not receive lashes for slaughtering inside the Temple courtyard an offering whose time has not yet arrived. A prohibition cannot be derived from the prohibition stated with regard to the Tabernacle in Gilgal, since **inside** the Tabernacle **in Gilgal, in relation to** the Tabernacle in **Shiloh, is considered like outside,**[N] and the prohibition: "You shall not do," pertains only to sacrificing an offering whose time has not yet arrived outside the Temple courtyard.

רַבָּה אֲמַר: טַעְמֵיהּ דְּרַבִּי שִׁמְעוֹן – כִּדְתַנְיָא, רַבִּי שִׁמְעוֹן אוֹמֵר: מִנַּיִן לַזּוֹבֵחַ פֶּסַח בְּבָמַת יָחִיד בִּשְׁעַת אִיסּוּר הַבָּמוֹת שֶׁהוּא בְּלֹא תַעֲשֶׂה? תַּלְמוּד לוֹמַר: "לֹא תוּכַל לִזְבֹּחַ אֶת הַפָּסַח".

Rabba said: The reason of Rabbi Shimon is not based upon: "You shall not do," as Reish Lakish claims, but upon another verse. **As it is taught** in a *baraita* that **Rabbi Shimon says: From where** is it derived **that one who slaughters** his **Paschal offering on a private altar**[H] **at a time** when it is **prohibited** to sacrifice offerings on private **altars** violates **a prohibition? The verse states: "You may not sacrifice the Paschal offering** within any of your gates; but at the place that the Lord your God shall choose to cause His name to dwell in, there you shall sacrifice the Paschal offering" (Deuteronomy 16:5–6).

יָכוֹל אַף בִּשְׁעַת הֶיתֵּר הַבָּמוֹת כֵּן? תַּלְמוּד לוֹמַר: "בְּאַחַד שְׁעָרֶיךָ", לֹא אָמַרְתִּי לְךָ אֶלָּא בְּשָׁעָה שֶׁכׇּל יִשְׂרָאֵל נִכְנָסִין בְּשַׁעַר אֶחָד.

One **might** have thought that **even at a time** when it is **permitted** to sacrifice offerings on private **altars** this is **so.** Therefore, **the verse states: "Within any [*be'aḥad*] of your gates,"** which indicates that **I said** this prohibition **to you only when all of the Jewish people enter** the Temple **through one [*eḥad*] gate** in order to sacrifice their offerings. When there is no permanent communal altar, it is permitted to slaughter the Paschal offering on a private altar.

אֵימַת? אִי נֵימָא אַחַר חֲצוֹת – כָּרֵת נַמִּי מִחַיַּיב! אֶלָּא לָאו – קוֹדֶם חֲצוֹת!

Rabba analyzes the *baraita*: **When** was this Paschal offering, for which one violates a prohibition for slaughtering it during a time when it is forbidden to sacrifice on private altars, slaughtered? **If we say** that it was **after midday** on the fourteenth of Nisan, which is the proper time for sacrificing the Paschal offering in the Temple, then one who sacrifices it then violates not only a prohibition, he should also **be deemed liable** to receive ***karet* as well,** as would anyone who slaughters a fit offering outside the Temple courtyard. **Rather, is it not** discussing one who slaughtered the Paschal offering on a private altar on the fourteenth of Nisan **before midday,** when its time had not yet arrived?

לְעוֹלָם לְאַחַר חֲצוֹת, וּבִשְׁעַת הֶיתֵּר הַבָּמוֹת קָאֵי.

The Gemara rejects Rabba's explanation: **Actually,** the Paschal offering may have been sacrificed on a private altar **after midday** of the fourteenth of Nisan, **and** it is **referring to a time** when it is **permitted** to sacrifice on private **altars,**[N] i.e., the periods of Gilgal, Nov, and Gibeon. The verse teaches that although it was permitted to sacrifice voluntary vow offerings and gift offerings on a private altar, the Paschal offering may be sacrificed only on a great public altar.

וְהָא בִּשְׁעַת אִיסּוּר הַבָּמוֹת קָאָמַר! אִיסּוּר בָּמָה לוֹ, הֶיתֵּר בָּמָה לַחֲבֵירוֹ.

The Gemara asks: **But doesn't** the *baraita* **state: At a time** when it is **prohibited** to sacrifice offerings on private **altars?** The Gemara responds: The *baraita* means that it is **prohibited for** one to sacrifice the Paschal offering on a private **altar,** but it is **permitted** to use a private **altar for another** offering,[N] i.e., a voluntary vow offering or gift offering.

NOTES

That statement of Rabbi Zeira applies only according to the opinion of the Rabbis – הָנֵי מִילֵּי לְרַבָּנַן: The opinion of the Rabbis may be identical to that of Rabbi Yehuda, who holds that any offering that could be sacrificed in the Tabernacle in the wilderness could be sacrificed in the Tabernacle in Gilgal, including obligatory offerings (see 117a). Therefore, this is not considered to be an offering whose time has not yet arrived.

Inside the Tabernacle in Gilgal in relation to the Tabernacle in Shiloh is considered like outside – פְּנִים דְּגִלְגָּל לְגַבֵּי שִׁילֹה כְּחוּץ דָּמֵי: According to Rabbi Shimon, it may be derived from here that one is liable for sacrificing any offering whose time has not yet arrived outside the Temple courtyard. The Rabbis, who disagree with Rabbi Shimon, hold that a broad prohibition against sacrificing an offering whose time has not yet arrived outside the Temple courtyard cannot be derived from a prohibition that was unique to the period of Gilgal. In their opinion, this is not a prohibition against slaughtering an offering outside the Temple courtyard but a specific prohibition against sacrificing obligatory offerings in Gilgal (*Sefat Emet*).

And it is referring to a time when it is permitted to sacrifice on private altars – וּבִשְׁעַת הֶיתֵּר הַבָּמוֹת קָאֵי: The Rambam holds that the prohibition against sacrificing on a private altar during the period when private altars were permitted is unique to the Paschal offering, as with regard to other offerings the mishna teaches that if one consecrated them during the period when private altars were permitted and sacrificed them during that period, he is exempt (*Kesef Mishne*, citing Rabbi Avraham ben HaRambam). Rashi indicates that one who sacrifices any obligatory offering on a private altar rather than on a great public altar violates this prohibition.

It is prohibited…on a private altar but is permitted to use a private altar for another offering – אִיסּוּר בָּמָה...הֶיתֵּר בָּמָה לַחֲבֵירוֹ: Consequently, the statement in the continuation of the *baraita*, that during a time when private altars are permitted there is no prohibition, is referring to a time when one is also permitted to bring the Paschal offering on a private altar, e.g., before midday on the fourteenth of Nisan, when it is fit as a peace offering (Rashi).

HALAKHA

Paschal offering on a private altar – פֶּסַח בְּבָמַת יָחִיד: The Paschal offering may be slaughtered only in the Temple courtyard, like other offerings. Even during the period when private altars were permitted, the Paschal offering is not sacrificed on a private altar, and whoever sacrifices it there is liable to receive lashes. This is in accordance with the opinion of Rabbi Shimon in the *baraita* (Rambam *Sefer Avoda*, *Hilkhot Korban Pesaḥ* 1:3).

״מְחוּסַּר זְמַן״ כו׳. וְהָנֵי בְּנֵי אֲשָׁמוֹת נִינְהוּ? אֲמַר זְעֵירִי: תְּנֵי ״מְצוֹרָע״ בַּהֲדַיְיהוּ.

§ The mishna teaches that with regard to an offering **whose time has not yet** arrived because it is premature for its owner, one who sacrifices it outside the Temple courtyard is exempt. This category includes a *zav*, a *zava*, and a woman after childbirth, any of whom sacrificed a sin offering or guilt offering outside the Temple courtyard during the days that they are counting toward purification. The Gemara asks: **And are these** individuals **subject to** the obligation to bring **guilt offerings? Ze'eiri said:** The text of the mishna should **teach: Leper, together with** the *zav*, *zava*, and woman after childbirth.[H] A leper brings a guilt offering as part of his purification process.

״עוֹלוֹתֵיהֶן וְשַׁלְמֵיהֶן״. וְהָנֵי בְּנֵי שְׁלָמִים נִינְהוּ? אֲמַר רַב שֵׁשֶׁת: תְּנֵי ״נָזִיר״. דִּזְעֵירִי קְבָעוּהָ תַּנָּאֵי, דְּרַב שֵׁשֶׁת לָא קְבָעוּהָ תַּנָּאֵי.

The mishna also teaches that if those whose time has not yet arrived sacrifice **their burnt offerings or their peace offerings** outside the Temple courtyard, they are liable. The Gemara asks: **And are these** individuals **subject to** the obligation to bring **peace offerings? Rav Sheshet said: Teach** the case of **a Nazirite** as part of the list in the mishna. A nazirite brings a peace offering at the conclusion of his term of naziriteship. The Gemara notes that the addition **of Ze'eiri** to the text of the mishna, i.e., the case of a leper, was **fixed** by **the *tanna'im***[N] in the version of the mishna that they would teach, while the addition **of Rav Sheshet,** i.e., the case of a nazirite, was **not fixed** by **the *tanna'im***[N] in the mishna that they would teach.

אָמַר רַבִּי חִלְקִיָּה (דְּבֵי) רַב טוֹבִי: לֹא שָׁנוּ אֶלָּא לִשְׁמוֹ, אֲבָל שֶׁלֹּא לִשְׁמוֹ – חַיָּיב, הוֹאִיל וְרָאוּי לְשֶׁלֹּא לִשְׁמוֹ בִּפְנִים.

§ The mishna teaches that if one whose days of purification are not complete, e.g., a leper, slaughters his guilt offering outside the courtyard, he is exempt, since the offering is not fit for sacrifice at that time. With regard to this, **Rabbi Ḥilkiya,** a Sage **from the school of Rav Tovi, says: They taught** this **only** with regard to one who slaughters a guilt offering outside the Temple courtyard **for its own sake. But** if he slaughtered it outside the Temple courtyard **not for its own sake** but for the sake of a different offering, he is **liable**[HN] for having sacrificed outside the courtyard. This is **because** it was **fit to** be sacrificed **not for its own sake inside** the Temple courtyard, as a guilt offering that was slaughtered not for its own sake is fit for sacrifice (see 2a).

אִי הָכִי, לִשְׁמוֹ נַמִי נִיחַיַּיב, הוֹאִיל וְרָאוּי לְשֶׁלֹּא לִשְׁמוֹ בִּפְנִים! בָּעֵי עֲקִירָה.

The Gemara asks: **If so,** one who slaughtered the guilt offering **for its own sake should also be liable** for having slaughtered it outside the Temple courtyard, **since** it was **fit** to be slaughtered **not for its sake inside** the Temple courtyard. The Gemara answers: In order for a guilt offering that was slaughtered outside the Temple courtyard to be considered fit to be sacrificed inside it, it first **requires uprooting** of its status, i.e., the one who slaughters it should intend explicitly that it be a different sacrifice. If its status as a guilt offering has not been uprooted, it is not considered fit to be sacrificed inside.

מַתְקִיף לַהּ רַב הוּנָא: וְכִי יֵשׁ לְךָ דָּבָר שֶׁאֵינוֹ כָּשֵׁר לִשְׁמוֹ, וְכָשֵׁר שֶׁלֹּא לִשְׁמוֹ? וְלָא? וַהֲרֵי

Rav Huna objects to Rabbi Ḥilkiya's statement that a guilt offering whose time has not yet arrived is fit to be sacrificed inside if it is slaughtered not for its own sake: **And is there anything that is not fit** if its action is performed **for its own sake, but is fit** if its action is performed **not for its sake?** The Gemara replies: **And is there not? But** there is

HALAKHA

Teach leper together with them – תְּנֵי מְצוֹרָע בַּהֲדַיְיהוּ: A leper who slaughtered his sin offering or guilt offering outside the Temple courtyard during his days of purification is exempt. The same applies to a nazirite who sacrificed his sin offering outside the Temple courtyard during his days of purification. This is because they are not yet fit to sacrifice the offering. But if either of them sacrificed his burnt offering or peace offering outside the courtyard he is liable, since the burnt offering is a gift and the peace offering is not an essential component of the process of atonement (Rambam *Sefer Avoda, Hilkhot Ma'aseh HaKorbanot* 18:9).

If he slaughtered it not for its own sake he is liable – שֶׁלֹּא לִשְׁמוֹ חַיָּיב: One who slaughters a leper's guilt offering not for its own sake outside the Temple courtyard is liable, since it is fit to be sacrificed inside the courtyard not for its own sake. This ruling is in accordance with the opinion of Rabbi Ḥilkiya. Although Rav Huna disagrees with the opinion of Rabbi Ḥilkiya, Rav Ashi, who came later, accepted it (Rambam *Sefer Avoda, Hilkhot Ma'aseh HaKorbanot* 18:10; see *Likkutei Halakhot*).

NOTES

The addition of Ze'eiri was fixed by the *tanna'im* – דִּזְעֵירִי קְבָעוּהָ תַּנָּאֵי: Consequently, the standard text of the mishna contains the word leper. In his commentary on the mishna, Rashi claims the word leper should be removed from the text of the mishna, since the talmudic discussion proves it was not present before the amoraic period. *Tosefot Yom Tov* maintains that since the change was made to the text of the mishna during talmudic times, it should appear in the standard version of the mishna as well. Rashi's methodology in his commentary on the Talmud is to utilize the original version of the text and to interpret the mishna in accordance with the way that it was initially understood prior to the discussion in the Gemara.

The addition of Rav Sheshet was not fixed by the *tanna'im* – דְּרַב שֵׁשֶׁת לָא קְבָעוּהָ תַּנָּאֵי: Rashi explains that because none of the other cases cited by the mishna of one whose time has not yet arrived requires a peace offering, the mishna must be alluding to a nazirite. Nevertheless, the case of a nazirite was not added to the text of the mishna, but was included in the explanation of the mishna by the *amora'im*. This concept is akin to when the Talmud states: The text of the mishna is incomplete and this is what it is teaching. *Tosafot* explain that the absence of the case of a nazirite is due to the fact that the mishna contains a list of ritually impure individuals: A *zav*, a *zava*, a woman after childbirth, and a leper. The nazirite is not impure, and therefore the *halakha* with regard to him is only alluded to by the mention of peace offerings but is not explicitly stated.

If he slaughtered it not for its own sake he is liable – שֶׁלֹּא לִשְׁמוֹ חַיָּיב: Rashi notes that while the mishna makes reference to both sin offerings and guilt offerings, Rabbi Ḥilkiya speaks exclusively about guilt offerings, since a sin offering that was slaughtered not for its own sake is disqualified and therefore not fit to be sacrificed inside the Temple courtyard (see 2a).

פֶּסַח בִּשְׁאָר יְמוֹת הַשָּׁנָה, דְּאֵינוֹ כָּשֵׁר לִשְׁמוֹ, וְכָשֵׁר שֶׁלֹּא לִשְׁמוֹ! פֶּסַח בִּשְׁאָר יְמוֹת הַשָּׁנָה שְׁלָמִים נִינְהוּ.

the **Paschal offering during the rest of the days of the year,**[H] i.e., not on the fourteenth of Nisan after midday, when it is fit to be sacrificed, **which is not fit** if it was sacrificed **for its sake, but is fit** if it was sacrificed **not for its sake.** The Gemara responds: The **Paschal offering during the rest of the days of the year is** considered to be **a peace offering,**[N] not a Paschal offering that was slaughtered not for its sake.

לֵימָא מְסַיֵּיעַ לֵיהּ: יָכוֹל שֶׁאֲנִי מוֹצִיא אַף עוֹלַת מְחוּסַר זְמַן בִּבְעָלִים, וַאֲשַׁם נָזִיר וַאֲשַׁם מְצוֹרָע?

The Gemara suggests: **Let us say** that the following *baraita* **supports** the opinion of Rabbi Ḥilkiya, who holds that one who slaughters a guilt offering whose time has not yet arrived, outside the courtyard, not for its own sake, is liable: One **might** have thought **that I exclude** from the category of those who are liable for slaughtering outside the courtyard **even** one who slaughters **a burnt offering whose time has not yet** arrived **due to** its being premature **for its owner,** e.g., a woman after childbirth whose term of impurity is not yet finished, **and** one who slaughters **the guilt offering of a nazirite and the guilt offering of a leper**[H] before they are fit to sacrifice their offerings.

תַּלְמוּד לוֹמַר: ״שׁוֹר״ – מִכׇּל מָקוֹם, ״כֶּשֶׂב״ – מִכׇּל מָקוֹם, ״עֵז״ – מִכׇּל מָקוֹם. וְאִילּוּ חַטָּאת שַׁיְירָא.

To counter this, **the verse states** with regard to slaughter outside the courtyard: "Whatever person there be of the house of Israel that slaughters an ox, or lamb, or goat, in the camp, or that slaughters it outside the camp" (Leviticus 17:3). **"Ox"** indicates **in any case** of an ox, **"lamb"** indicates **in any case** of a lamb, and **"goat"** indicates **in any case** of a goat, that one is liable for slaughtering them outside the courtyard; **while a sin offering** was **omitted** from the cases in the *baraita* where one who slaughters the offering outside the courtyard is liable.

בְּמַאי עָסְקִינַן? אִילֵימָא בִּזְמַנּוֹ – מַאי אִירְיָא אָשָׁם? אֲפִילּוּ חַטָּאת נָמֵי! אֶלָּא שֶׁלֹּא לִזְמַנּוֹ.

The Gemara clarifies: **What are we dealing with**[N] in this *baraita* when it discusses the guilt offering of a nazirite and the guilt offering of a leper? **If we say** that it is dealing with a guilt offering that was slaughtered outside the courtyard **at its** proper **time, why** state that one is liable **specifically** for **a guilt offering?** One would be liable for slaughtering **a sin offering** outside the courtyard at its time **as well. Rather,** it is discussing a guilt offering that was slaughtered **not at its time,** i.e., when the nazirite or leper's time had not yet arrived.

וּבְמַאי? אִילֵימָא לִשְׁמוֹ – אָשָׁם אַמַּאי חַיָּיב? אֶלָּא לָאו – שֶׁלֹּא לִשְׁמוֹ! לְעוֹלָם בִּזְמַנּוֹ וְשֶׁלֹּא לִשְׁמוֹ,

The Gemara explains: **And what** is the *baraita* dealing **with? If we say** that it is dealing with one who slaughtered it **for its sake, why** would he be **liable** for **a guilt offering** that was slaughtered outside the courtyard if it is not fit for sacrifice? **Rather, is** the *baraita* **not** dealing with one who slaughtered it **not for its sake,**[N] and the *baraita* states that one would be liable, in accordance with the opinion of Rabbi Ḥilkiya? The Gemara rejects this: **Actually,** the *baraita* is dealing with one who slaughtered a guilt offering outside the courtyard **at its** proper **time and not for its sake.**[N]

וְרַבִּי אֱלִיעֶזֶר הִיא. דְּאָמַר: מַקְשִׁינַן אָשָׁם לְחַטָּאת,

And although there is ostensibly no need for an additional verse from which to derive the *halakha* in this case, as a guilt offering that was slaughtered not for its sake inside the courtyard is fit for sacrifice, the *baraita* **is** in accordance with the opinion of **Rabbi Eliezer, who says: We juxtapose a guilt offering with a sin offering** in the verse: "As is the sin offering, so is the guilt offering; there is one law for them" (Leviticus 7:7), from which it may be derived that they have equivalent halakhic status. Therefore, a guilt offering that was slaughtered not for its sake is disqualified, and consequently one might say that one who slaughters a guilt offering not for its sake outside the Temple courtyard is exempt, as it is not fit for sacrifice. Therefore, the derivation from the verse is necessary.

וּתְנָא טָפֵל וְהוּא הַדִּין עִיקָּר.

And the *tanna* of the *baraita* **taught:** Guilt offering, which, in this context, is **secondary** to the sin offering, as it is derived from the latter. **But the same is true** of the **primary,** i.e., the sin offering: One who slaughters it outside the courtyard not for its sake is liable.

HALAKHA

The Paschal offering during the rest of the days of the year – **פֶּסַח בִּשְׁאָר יְמוֹת הַשָּׁנָה**: A Paschal offering that was slaughtered not for its own sake is disqualified. This statement applies when the offering was slaughtered at its proper time, i.e., the fourteenth of Nisan, even before midday. But if it was slaughtered not at its proper time it is fit. If it was slaughtered for its own sake on the fourteenth of Nisan before midday it is disqualified, as this is not its proper time (Rambam *Sefer Avoda, Hilkhot Pesulei HaMukdashin* 15:11–12).

The guilt offering of a nazirite and the guilt offering of a leper – **אֲשַׁם נָזִיר וַאֲשַׁם מְצוֹרָע**: If the guilt offering of a nazirite or the guilt offering of a leper is slaughtered not for its sake the offering does not satisfy the obligation of its owner, but its meat may be eaten by the priests (Rambam *Sefer Avoda, Hilkhot Pesulei HaMukdashin* 15:20).

NOTES

The Paschal offering during the rest of the days of the year is a peace offering – **פֶּסַח בִּשְׁאָר יְמוֹת הַשָּׁנָה שְׁלָמִים נִינְהוּ**: At a time other than the proper time for slaughtering the Paschal offering, the Paschal offering has the status of a peace offering with all the relevant *halakhot* pertaining to its slaughter and consumption. Therefore, if it was slaughtered without specification, or even as a different offering (see 8b), it is not considered a Paschal offering slaughtered not for its own sake, but rather a peace offering.

What are we dealing with, etc. – **בְּמַאי עָסְקִינַן וכו׳**: The basis for this question is that with regard to a burnt offering the *baraita* notes that it is referring to the offering of one whose time has not yet arrived, but does not mention this with regard to the guilt offering of a nazirite and the guilt offering of a leper. Therefore, it would appear that in the case of a guilt offering the *baraita* is not discussing one whose time has not yet arrived.

Is it not slaughtered not for its sake – **לָאו שֶׁלֹּא לִשְׁמוֹ**: One would be liable only for a guilt offering that was slaughtered prematurely, not for its sake, and outside the Temple courtyard, since in that case it would be fit to be slaughtered inside the Temple. By contrast, a sin offering is disqualified if slaughtered not for its sake, and therefore one who slaughters a sin offering not for its sake outside the courtyard would not be liable.

At its proper time and not for its sake – **בִּזְמַנּוֹ וְשֶׁלֹּא לִשְׁמוֹ**: Although a guilt offering or sin offering that was slaughtered not for its sake is ostensibly disqualified, nevertheless the *baraita* rules one liable for slaughtering it outside the Temple courtyard for the following reason: Had an animal that was consecrated for the purpose of this offering been slaughtered inside the Temple without specification, it would have been fit. Therefore, at the time of its slaughter outside the courtyard it is still fit for sacrifice inside. Only after it was slaughtered as a different sacrifice, and its initial status is uprooted, is it deemed unfit for sacrifice inside the Temple (Rashi).

תָּא שְׁמַע: יָכוֹל שֶׁאֲנִי מְרַבֶּה עוֹלַת מְחוּסַּר זְמַן בְּגוּפָהּ, וְחַטָּאת בֵּין בְּגוּפָהּ בֵּין בַּבְּעָלִים?

The Gemara suggests: **Come** and **hear** a *baraita* in support of Rabbi Ḥilkiya: One **might** have thought **that I include** in liability even one who slaughters **a burnt offering whose time has not yet** arrived because it is **intrinsically** lacking, i.e., eight days have not yet passed; **and** one who slaughters **a sin offering** whose time has not yet arrived, **whether** because it is **intrinsically** lacking **or** because it is premature for **the owner.**

תַּלְמוּד לוֹמַר: ״וְאֶל פֶּתַח אֹהֶל מוֹעֵד״, כָּל שֶׁאֵינוֹ רָאוּי לָבֹא בְּפֶתַח אֹהֶל מוֹעֵד – אֵין חַיָּיבִין עָלֶיהָ. וְאִילּוּ אָשָׁם שַׁיְּירָא.

To counter this, **the verse states** with regard to one who slaughters outside the courtyard: **"And** has not brought it **to the entrance of the Tent of Meeting"** (Leviticus 17:4), which teaches that for **any** sacrifice **that is unfit to be brought to the entrance of the Tent of Meeting, one is not liable for** slaughtering it outside the courtyard. **But a guilt offering** whose time has not yet arrived was **omitted** by the *tanna*, from which it can be inferred that one who slaughters a guilt offering outside the courtyard is liable.

בְּמַאי עָסְקִינַן? אִילֵּימָא לִשְׁמוֹ – אָשָׁם נַמִי לִיפְטְרֵיהּ! אֶלָּא לָאו – שֶׁלֹּא לִשְׁמוֹ!

The Gemara asks: **What are we dealing with? If we say** that the *baraita* is dealing with a case where one slaughtered a sin offering whose time has not yet arrived, outside the courtyard **for its sake,** then one who slaughters **a guilt offering should also be exempt,** as it is an offering whose time has not yet arrived. **Rather, is it not** dealing with a case of one who slaughtered a sin offering whose time has not yet arrived, outside the courtyard **not for its sake?** In this case, one would be exempt for slaughtering it outside the courtyard, as if it is slaughtered inside the courtyard not for its sake it is disqualified. But in the case of a guilt offering whose time has not yet arrived one would be liable, since it is fit for sacrifice, in accordance with the opinion of Rabbi Ḥilkiya.

לְעוֹלָם שֶׁלֹּא לִשְׁמוֹ, וְרַבִּי אֱלִיעֶזֶר הִיא, דְּמַקִּישׁ אָשָׁם לְחַטָּאת, תְּנָא עִיקָּר וְכָל שֶׁכֵּן לְטָפֵל.

The Gemara responds: **Actually,** the *baraita* is dealing with one who slaughtered a sin offering whose time has not yet arrived, outside the courtyard **not for its sake. And** nevertheless, it may not be inferred that in the case of a guilt offering one would be liable, as this *baraita* may **be** in accordance with the opinion of **Rabbi Eliezer, who juxtaposes a guilt offering with a sin offering;** and one who slaughters a guilt offering is also exempt. The *tanna* of the *baraita* omitted mention of a guilt offering because he **taught:** Sin offering, which is the **primary** case of the disqualification of an offering slaughtered not for its sake, **and all the more so** it applies **to** the **secondary** case, i.e., the guilt offering.

תָּא שְׁמַע, דְּכִי אֲתָא רַב דִּימִי אָמַר, תָּנָא דְּבֵי רַבִּי לִיוַאי: יָכוֹל שֶׁאֲנִי מוֹצִיא אַף עוֹלַת מְחוּסַּר זְמַן בַּבְּעָלִים, אֲשַׁם נָזִיר וַאֲשַׁם מְצוֹרָע מִנַּיִן? וְנָסֵיב לְהוּ תַּלְמוּדָא לְחִיּוּבָא, וְלָא יָדַעְנָא מַאי הִיא.

The Gemara suggests: **Come** and **hear** another proof for the opinion of Rabbi Ḥilkiya, **as when Rav Dimi came** to Babylonia from Eretz Yisrael **he said** that **the school of Rabbi Livai taught** a *baraita*: One **might** have thought **that I exclude** from the category of those who are liable for slaughtering offerings outside the Temple courtyard **even** one who slaughters **a burnt offering whose time has not yet** arrived **due to** its being premature **for its owner,** or who slaughters **a guilt offering of a nazirite or the guilt offering of a leper** whose time has not yet arrived due to its being premature for its owner. **From where** is it derived that one is liable for doing so? Rav Dimi added: **And** the Sages **brought a derivation** from a verse to prove that one is **liable, but I do not know what** the derivation **is.**

מַאי תַּלְמוּדָא? אֲמַר רָבִינָא: ״שׁוֹר״ – מִכָּל מָקוֹם, ״כֶּשֶׂב״ – מִכָּל מָקוֹם, ״עֵז״ – מִכָּל מָקוֹם. הָא מַאי רוּמְיָא? כִּדַאֲמַרְתְּ!

The Gemara clarifies: **What is the** biblical **derivation? Ravina said** that it is derived from the verse cited above with regard to offerings that are slaughtered outside the courtyard, where **"ox"** indicates **in any case** of an ox, **"lamb"** indicates **in any case** of a lamb, and **"goat"** indicates **in any case** of a goat. This supports the opinion of Rabbi Ḥilkiya, as the *baraita* is discussing a guilt offering whose time has not yet arrived that is slaughtered not for its sake, and contradicts the opinion of Rav Huna. The Gemara asks: **What contradiction is this?** It can be resolved **as you stated** earlier: That the *baraita* is dealing with a guilt offering that was slaughtered not for its sake at the proper time, and is accordance with the opinion of Rabbi Eliezer.

אָמַר רַב נַחְמָן: מִשּׁוּם [דְּרָמֵי] דְּתָנָא דְּבֵי רַבִּי לִיוַאי אַדְּתָנֵי לֵוִי: אֲשַׁם נָזִיר וַאֲשַׁם מְצוֹרָע שֶׁשְּׁחָטָן שֶׁלֹּא לִשְׁמָן – כְּשֵׁירִין, וְלֹא עָלוּ לַבְּעָלִים לְשׁוּם חוֹבָה.

Rav Naḥman said that according to the opinion of Rav Dimi, the *baraita* cannot be interpreted as dealing with a guilt offering that was slaughtered at its proper time, **because he raises a contradiction between** the *baraita* **that the school of Rabbi Livai taught** and a *baraita* **that Levi taught: The guilt offering of a nazirite and the guilt offering of a leper that one slaughtered not for their sakes are fit, but they do not satisfy the obligation of the owner.**

שְׁחָטָן מְחוּסַּר זְמַן בַּבְּעָלִים, אוֹ שֶׁהָיוּ בְּנֵי שְׁתֵּי שָׁנִים וּשְׁחָטָן – פְּסוּלִין.

If one **slaughtered them** in a case where the offering was **premature due to its owner, or** if the lambs **were in their second year** when one **slaughtered them,** and not in their first year as required, they **are disqualified,** and one who slaughters them outside the Temple courtyard is not liable. This contradicts the *baraita* taught by the school of Rabbi Livai.

וּמְשַׁנֵּי רַב דִּימִי: לָא קַשְׁיָא; כָּאן – לִשְׁמוֹ, כָּאן – שֶׁלֹּא לִשְׁמוֹ.

And Rav Dimi answers: This is **not difficult. Here,** in the *baraita* that states that one who slaughters outside the courtyard is exempt, it is referring to a case where the animal whose time has not yet arrived was slaughtered **for its sake; there,** in the *baraita* that teaches that one who slaughters outside the courtyard is liable, it is referring to a case where the offering was slaughtered **not for its sake.**

רַב אַשִׁי רָמֵי מַתְנִיתִין אַבָּרַיְיתָא, וּמְשַׁנֵּי: כָּאן – לִשְׁמוֹ, וְכָאן – שֶׁלֹּא לִשְׁמוֹ.

Likewise, **Rav Ashi raises a contradiction between the mishna,** which teaches that one who slaughters a guilt offering whose time has not yet arrived outside the courtyard is exempt, **and the** ***baraita*****,** which teaches that one who does so is liable. **And** Rav Ashi **answers: Here,** the mishna that teaches that one is exempt is referring to a case where the offering was slaughtered **for its sake. And there,** the *baraita* that teaches that one is liable is referring to a case where the offering was slaughtered **not for its sake,** in accordance with the opinion of Rabbi Ḥilkiya.

לֵימָא תֶּיהֱוֵי תְּיוּבְתֵּיהּ דְּרַב הוּנָא?

The Gemara says: If so, **shall we say** that this **is a conclusive refutation** of the opinion **of Rav Huna,** who holds that one who slaughters a guilt offering whose time has not yet arrived not for its sake outside the courtyard is exempt?

אָמַר לָךְ רַב הוּנָא: הָכָא בְּמַאי עָסְקִינַן – כְּגוֹן שֶׁהִפְרִישׁ שְׁתֵּי אֲשָׁמוֹת לְאַחֲרָיוּת, דְּחַד מִינַּיְיהוּ מֵעִיקָּרָא עוֹלָה הִיא.

The Gemara replies that **Rav Huna** could have **said to you: What are we dealing with here,** in the *baraita* that deems one liable for a guilt offering that was slaughtered not for its sake? We are dealing with a case **where** one **separated two guilt offerings as a guarantee,** so that atonement would be achieved through the sacrifice of the second if the first was lost, but before the proper time arrived he slaughtered one of them as a burnt offering rather than as a guilt offering. In this case there would be liability for slaughtering outside the courtyard, as is the case with one who slaughters a burnt offering outside the courtyard, **since one of them,** i.e., the one that will not effect atonement, **is a burnt offering from the outset.**

Perek **XIV**
Daf **115** Amud **b**

כִּדְרַב הוּנָא אָמַר רַב. דְּאָמַר רַב הוּנָא אָמַר רַב: אָשָׁם שֶׁנִּיתַּק לִרְעִיָּה וּשְׁחָטוֹ סְתָם – כָּשֵׁר לְעוֹלָה.

This is **in accordance with** the statement that **Rav Huna** says that **Rav says. As Rav Huna says** that **Rav says:** With regard to **a guilt offering** whose owner died or achieved atonement through a different guilt offering and which **was consigned to grazing** in the field until it develops a blemish, **and** prior to its being consigned one **slaughtered it without specification** of its purpose, it is **fit as a burnt offering.**

"הַמַּעֲלֶה מִבְּשַׂר חַטָּאת" [וכו׳]. תָּנוּ רַבָּנַן: מִנַּיִן לַמַּעֲלֶה מִבְּשַׂר חַטָּאת, וּמִבְּשַׂר אָשָׁם, וּמִבְּשַׂר קָדְשֵׁי קָדָשִׁים, וּמִבְּשַׂר קָדָשִׁים קַלִּים, וּמִמּוֹתַר הָעוֹמֶר, וּשְׁתֵּי הַלֶּחֶם, וְלֶחֶם הַפָּנִים, וּשְׁיָרֵי מְנָחוֹת שֶׁפָּטוּר?

§ The mishna teaches: **One who offers up** outside the Temple courtyard a portion **of the meat of a sin offering** that is eaten, or who offers up a portion of several other items, is exempt. With regard to the reasoning behind this *halakha*, **the Sages taught** in a *baraita*: **From where** is it derived **that one who offers up** outside the Temple courtyard a portion **of the meat of a sin offering, or** a portion **of the meat of a guilt offering, or** a portion **of the meat of offerings of the most sacred order, or** a portion **of the meat of offerings of lesser sanctity, or** a portion **of the surplus of the *omer* offering, or the two loaves, or the shewbread, or the remainder of meal offerings** is **exempt,** as all these are eaten by the priests and not sacrificed on the altar?

תַּלְמוּד לוֹמַר: "עוֹלָה", מָה עוֹלָה שֶׁהִיא רְאוּיָה לְהַעֲלָאָה – אַף כָּל שֶׁרְאוּיָה לְהַעֲלָאָה.

The verse states with regard to the prohibition against sacrificing outside the Temple courtyard: "Whatever man…that sacrifices **a burnt offering** or sacrifice, and brings it not to the entrance of the Tent of Meeting, to sacrifice it to the Lord, that man shall be cut off from his people" (Leviticus 17:8–9). The term "burnt offering" teaches: **Just as a burnt offering is fit for offering up** upon the altar, **so too, anything that is fit for offering up** is included in the prohibition. All of the offerings listed in the *baraita* are not sacrificed upon the altar but given to the priests.

מִנַּיִן שֶׁאַף הַיּוֹצֵק, וְהַבּוֹלֵל, וְהַפּוֹתֵת, וְהַמּוֹלֵחַ, וְהַמֵּנִיף, וְהַמַּגִּישׁ, וְהַמְסַדֵּר הַשֻּׁלְחָן, וְהַמֵּטִיב אֶת הַנֵּרוֹת, וְהַקּוֹמֵץ, וְהַמְקַבֵּל בַּחוּץ, שֶׁפָּטוּר?

From where is it derived **that even** with regard to **one who pours** oil onto the meal offering, **and one who mixes** the oil into the flour of the meal offering, **and one who breaks** the loaves of the meal offering into pieces, **and one who salts** the meal offering or other offerings, **and one who waves** the meal offering, **and one who brings** the meal offering to the corner of an altar that he constructs outside the courtyard, **and one who arranges** the shewbread on **the table** outside the Sanctuary, **and one who removes the ashes** from **the lamps** of the Candelabrum, **and one who removes a handful** from a meal offering, **and one who collects the blood** of an offering in a vessel, if he did so **outside** the Temple courtyard he is **exempt.**

תַּלְמוּד לוֹמַר: "אֲשֶׁר יַעֲלֶה עוֹלָה אוֹ זָבַח", מַה הַעֲלָאָה שֶׁהִיא גְּמַר עֲבוֹדָה – אַף כָּל שֶׁהוּא גְּמַר עֲבוֹדָה.

The verse states: "That sacrifices a burnt offering or sacrifice" (Leviticus 17:8). **Just as sacrificing is the conclusion of** the sacrificial **service, so too, any** rite **that is the conclusion of** a sacrificial **service**[N] is included. All of these are excluded from the prohibition, as there are rites that follow them.

"עַד שֶׁלֹּא הוּקַם הַמִּשְׁכָּן" [וכו׳]. יָתֵיב רַב הוּנָא בַּר רַב קְטִינָא קַמֵּיהּ דְּרַב חִסְדָּא, וְקָא קָרֵי: "וַיִּשְׁלַח אֶת נַעֲרֵי בְּנֵי יִשְׂרָאֵל". אֲמַר לֵיהּ: הָכִי אֲמַר רַבִּי אַסִּי קָרְבוּ וּפָסְקוּ.

§ The mishna teaches: **Until the Tabernacle was established,** private altars were permitted and the sacrificial service was performed by the firstborn. The Gemara relates that **Rav Huna bar Rav Ketina was sitting before Rav Ḥisda and was reading** this verse with regard to the revelation at Sinai: **"And he sent the young men of the children of Israel,**[N] who offered burnt offerings and sacrificed peace offerings of oxen to the Lord" (Exodus 24:5). The young men referred to in the verse were the firstborn of the Jewish people. Rav Ḥisda **said to him: This** is what **Rabbi Asi said: They sacrificed** the offerings **and then ceased**[NB] to serve; after that day, the firstborn no longer performed the sacrificial service.

סָבַר לְאוֹתוּבֵיהּ מִמַּתְנִיתִין, שַׁמְעֵיהּ דְּקָאָמַר מִשְּׁמֵיהּ דְּרַב אַדָּא בַּר אַהֲבָה: עוֹלָה שֶׁהִקְרִיבוּ יִשְׂרָאֵל בַּמִּדְבָּר אֵינָהּ טְעוּנָה הֶפְשֵׁט וְנִיתּוּחַ. אוֹתְבֵיהּ בָּרַיְיתָא דְּשַׁוְיָא בְּכוּלְּהוּ.

Rav Huna **thought to raise a contradiction from the mishna,** which states that the firstborn performed not only the sacrificial service on that day, but also did so until the Tabernacle was established the following year. In the meanwhile, **he heard** Rav Ḥisda **say in the name of Rav Adda bar Ahava** that the **burnt offering that the** children of **Israel sacrificed in the wilderness** before the establishment of the Tabernacle **did not require flaying** of the skin **and cutting** into pieces; it was sacrificed as it was. He therefore **raised the contradiction** from **a *baraita* that is equal with regard to both of them,** i.e., from which Rav Huna could raise a contradiction to both of Rav Ḥisda's statements.

NOTES

So too any rite that is the conclusion of a sacrificial service – אַף כָּל שֶׁהוּא גְּמַר עֲבוֹדָה: Most of the rites listed here are associated with the meal offering, whose sacrifice concludes with the burning of the handful upon the altar. Likewise, the conclusion of the shewbread service is the burning of the bowls of frankincense. In the case of collecting the blood of an offering in a vessel, the conclusion of the service is the sprinkling of the blood upon the altar. With regard to the removal of ashes from the lamps of the Candelabrum, see 114b.

And was reading, and he sent the young men of the children of Israel – וְקָא קָרֵי וַיִּשְׁלַח אֶת נַעֲרֵי בְּנֵי יִשְׂרָאֵל: The standard text of the Gemara states that Rav Huna bar Rav Ketina was reading the verse, and Rav Ḥisda cited statements that he heard from Rav Asi. Rashi's version of the Gemara differs in that Rav Ḥisda read the verse, and Rashi explains that Rav Huna bar Rav Ketina cited the statement of Rav Asi. The version of the Gemara quoted in *Tosafot* reads simply: And he was sitting and said: "And he sent," which is explained as referring to Rav Huna.

And then ceased [*ufasku*] – וּפָסְקוּ: From that time, the third month after the Exodus from Egypt, until the Tabernacle was constructed in the first month of the second year, Nadav and Avihu served as priests, as the Gemara proceeds to state. Rashi cites another version of the Gemara that reads: And stop it [*ufaskah*]. According to this version, Rav Asi holds that the firstborn did not sacrifice the burnt offerings or peace offerings during the revelation at Sinai. This is because the phrase: And stop it, means that when this verse is read there should be a break between: "And he sent the young men of the children of Israel," and: "Who offered burnt offerings," the reason being that the latter does not refer to the young men of the children of Israel, who were sent only as representatives of the people, to stand alongside the offerings when they were sacrificed. Rather, that phrase refers to the priests Nadav and Avihu. According to this version, the question discussed is whether the firstborn ever performed the service before the Tabernacle was constructed.

BACKGROUND

And then ceased – וּפָסְקוּ: This version of the text includes the term: They sacrificed [*karvu*], before the words: And ceased [*ufasku*]. According to this reading, the term *karvu* can mean either they, the firstborn, sacrificed (see Rashi), or they, the burnt offerings, were sacrificed. According to the *Shita Mekubbetzet*, this word should be removed from the text.

דתניא: עד שלא הוקם המשכן – הבמות מותרות, ועבודה בבכורות, והכל כשירין להקריב בהמה חיה ועוף, זכרים ונקבות, תמימין ובעלי מומין, טהורין אבל לא טמאין.

As it is taught in a *baraita*: **Until the Tabernacle was established,** private **altars** were **permitted, the** sacrificial **service** was performed **by the firstborn, and all** animals were **fit to be sacrificed: A domesticated animal, an undomesticated animal, or a bird; males and females; unblemished and blemished** animals. All animal sacrifices were brought from animals and birds that were **kosher, but not** from **non-kosher** species.

והכל קרבו עולות. ועולה שהקריבו ישראל במדבר טעונה הפשט וניתוח. וגוים בזמן הזה רשאין לעשות כן!

And all offerings brought before the construction of the Tabernacle were **sacrificed** as **burnt offerings. And the burnt offering that the Jewish people sacrificed in the wilderness** before the Tabernacle was established **required flaying** of the skin **and cutting** into pieces. **And today, gentiles are permitted to** sacrifice offerings on private altars. The *baraita* states explicitly that until the Tabernacle was constructed, the sacrificial service was performed by the firstborn, and the burnt offering required flaying and cutting.

תנאי היא, דתניא: "וגם הכהנים הנגשים אל ה׳ יתקדשו" – רבי יהושע בן קרחה אומר: זו פרישות בכורות. רבי אומר: זו פרישות נדב ואביהוא.

Rav Ḥisda replied that with regard to the firstborn, **it is a dispute** between ***tanna'im*, as it is taught** in a *baraita*: God said to Moses on Mount Sinai: **"And let the priests also that come near to the Lord sanctify themselves,** lest the Lord break forth upon them" (Exodus 19:22). In other words, they should separate themselves and not approach the mountain. This command was given one day after the burnt offerings and peace offerings were sacrificed in anticipation of the revelation at Sinai. With regard to this command, **Rabbi Yehoshua ben Korḥa says: This** command is a reference to **the separation of** the **firstborn,**[N] as they functioned as priests. **Rabbi** Yehuda HaNasi **says: This** command is a reference to **the separation of Nadav and Avihu,** who were priests.

בשלמא למאן דאמר: זו פרישות נדב ואביהוא – היינו דכתיב: "הוא אשר דבר ה׳ לאמר בקרבי אקדש",

The Gemara asks: **Granted, according to the one who says** that the command for the priests to sanctify themselves is referring to **the separation of Nadav and Avihu, this is** the meaning of that **which is written** after their death on the eighth day of the inauguration of the Tabernacle: "Then Moses said to Aaron: **This is it that the Lord spoke, saying: Through them that are near to Me I will be sanctified...** and Aaron held his peace" (Leviticus 10:3). Nadav and Avihu had already been warned not to draw too close: "Lest the Lord break forth upon them."

אלא למאן דאמר: זו פרישות בכורות, היכא רמיזא? דכתיב: "ונעדתי שמה לבני ישראל ונקדש בכבדי", אל תקרי "בכבודי" אלא: "במכובדיי".

But according to the one who says that the command for the priests to sanctify themselves is referring to **the separation of the firstborn, where is the allusion** to the fact that God would be sanctified through Nadav and Avihu? The Gemara replies: **As it is written: "And there I will meet with the children of Israel; and it shall be sanctified by My glory"** (Exodus 29:43). **Do not read** it as **"by My glory [*bikhvodi*]"; rather,** read it as: **By My honored ones [*bimekhubadai*].** God will be sanctified by those considered honored by God when He reveals Himself in the Tabernacle.

דבר זה אמר הקדוש ברוך הוא למשה, ולא ידעו עד שמתו בני אהרן. כיון שמתו בני אהרן אמר לו: אהרן אחי, לא מתו בניך אלא להקדיש שמו של הקדוש ברוך הוא. כיון שידע אהרן שבניו ידועי מקום הן – שתק וקבל שכר, שנאמר: "וידם אהרן".

The Holy One, Blessed be He, said this statement to Moses, but Moses **did not know** its meaning[N] **until the sons of Aaron died. Once the sons of Aaron died,** Moses **said to him: Aaron, my brother, your sons died only to sanctify the name of the Holy One, Blessed be He. When Aaron knew that his sons were beloved by the Omnipresent, he was silent and received a reward,**[N] **as it is stated: "And Aaron held his peace [*vayidom*]."**

וכן בדוד הוא אומר: "דום לה׳ והתחולל לו", אף על פי שמפיל לך חללים חללים – את שתוק. וכן בשלמה הוא אומר: "עת לחשות ועת לדבר", פעמים ששותק ומקבל שכר על השתיקה, פעמים מדבר ומקבל שכר על הדבור.

And likewise in a verse written by **David** it **states: "Resign yourself [*dom*] to the Lord, and wait patiently [*vehitholel*] for Him"** (Psalms 37:7). **Although He strikes down many corpses [*ḥalalim*]** around **you, you be silent** and do not complain. **And likewise in** a verse written by **Solomon** it **states: "A time to keep silence, and a time to speak"** (Ecclesiastes 3:7). There are **times that** one **is silent and receives reward for the silence,** and at **times** one **speaks and receives reward for the speech.**

NOTES

That come near to the Lord sanctify themselves...this is the separation of the firstborn – הנגשים אל ה׳ יתקדשו...זו פרישות בכורות: Even those who intend to approach the Lord to sacrifice upon the altar should sanctify themselves in their places, and separate, not drawing near to Mount Sinai (Rashi's commentary on the Torah). According to Rashi and others, this statement, which was made on the sixth of the Hebrew month of Sivan, was after the covenant with God was entered into, when the "young men of the children of Israel," i.e., the firstborn, sacrificed the burnt offerings and peace offerings, which occurred on the fourth of Sivan. Although the covenant appears later (Exodus 24:1), there is no absolute chronological order in the Torah.

Others say the covenant was entered into after the giving of the Torah (see, e.g., Ramban on Exodus 24:1); the issue is also disputed in the *Mekhilta*, as noted by the Ramban. According to this latter opinion, the phrase "that come near to the Lord" refers to those who performed the service before the people arrived at Sinai, as when Moses built an altar after the war with Amalek (Exodus 17:15; Ibn Ezra on Exodus 19:22).

And it shall be sanctified by My glory...but Moses did not know its meaning – ונקדש בכבדי...ולא ידעו: The term "and it shall be sanctified" ostensibly refers to the Tabernacle. Rashi explains that Moses did not know the meaning of this statement until he understood that: "Shall be sanctified," refers not to the Tabernacle but to God, Who will be sanctified by His honored ones. This seems to be the meaning of the continuation of the discussion in the Gemara.

A midrash (*Vayikra Rabba* 12:2) cited by *Tosafot* indicates that Moses knew from the outset that the Tabernacle would be sanctified by the glory of God through a great person, but he thought that it would be him or Aaron and did not know that it would be Nadav and Avihu. According to this explanation as well, it is possible that Moses did not know in what manner God would be sanctified through those that are near to Him, and did not realize that this would occur through the death of these individuals (*Yad David*).

He was silent and received a reward – שתק וקבל שכר: The Sages (*Vayikra Rabba* 12:2) infer that the reward was Aaron's being exclusively addressed by God in the following passage: "And the Lord spoke to Aaron, saying" (Leviticus 10:8).

BACKGROUND

The plains of Moab – עַרְבוֹת מוֹאָב:

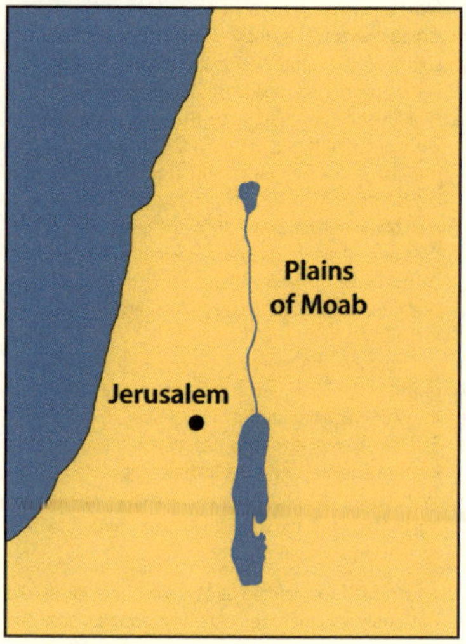

Location of the plains of Moab

וְהַיְינוּ דְּאָמַר רַבִּי חִיָּיא בַּר אַבָּא אָמַר רַבִּי יוֹחָנָן: מַאי דִּכְתִיב ״נוֹרָא אֱלֹהִים מִמִּקְדָּשֶׁךָ״, אַל תִּיקְרֵי ״מִמִּקְדָּשֶׁךָ״ – אֶלָּא: ״מִמְּקוּדָּשֶׁיךָ״, בְּשָׁעָה שֶׁעוֹשֶׂה הַקָּדוֹשׁ בָּרוּךְ הוּא דִּין בִּקְדוֹשָׁיו – מִתְיָירֵא וּמִתְעַלֶּה וּמִתְהַלֵּל.

And this is what Rabbi Ḥiyya bar Abba says that Rabbi Yoḥanan says: What is the meaning of that **which is written: "Awesome is God out of your holy places"** (Psalms 68:36)? **Do not read** it as: **"From your holy places [*mimikdashekha*]"; rather,** read it as: **From your holy ones [*mimekudashekha*]. When the Holy One, Blessed be He, carries out judgment upon His holy ones, He is feared, and exalted, and praised** by all. In any event, there is no contradiction from the *baraita* which teaches that the firstborn performed the sacrificial service before the Tabernacle was established, as this matter is the subject of a dispute between *tanna'im*.

אֶלָּא קַשְׁיָא עוֹלָה! תְּרֵי תַּנָּאֵי הִיא. דְּתַנְיָא, רַבִּי יִשְׁמָעֵאל אוֹמֵר: כְּלָלוֹת נֶאֶמְרוּ בְּסִינַי, וּפְרָטוֹת בְּאֹהֶל מוֹעֵד.

But there is still **a difficulty** with regard to the **burnt offering,** as it was stated in the name of Rav Adda bar Ahava that the burnt offering that the Jewish people sacrificed in the wilderness did not require flaying of the skin or cutting into pieces, while the *baraita* states that it did. The Gemara replies: This **is** a dispute between the opinions of **two *tanna'im*. As it is taught** in a *baraita* that **Rabbi Yishmael says:** The **general statements,** i.e., the principles of the Torah, **were said at Sinai, and** the **details** of the mitzvot that are explicated in Leviticus were said to Moses **in the Tent of Meeting.** This includes the *halakha* that the burnt offering must be flayed and cut into pieces. Consequently, it could not have been in effect before the construction of the Tabernacle.

רַבִּי עֲקִיבָא אוֹמֵר: כְּלָלוֹת וּפְרָטוֹת נֶאֶמְרוּ בְּסִינַי, וְנִשְׁנוּ בְּאֹהֶל מוֹעֵד, וְנִשְׁתַּלְּשׁוּ בְּעַרְבוֹת מוֹאָב.

Rabbi Akiva says: Both **general statements and** the **details** of mitzvot **were said at Sinai and** later **taught again in the Tent of Meeting,** and taught **a third time** by Moses to the Jewish people **in the plains of Moab,**[B] when he taught the Torah to the people (see Deuteronomy 1:1). According to Rabbi Akiva's opinion, the *halakha* of flaying and cutting into pieces was in effect when the Torah was given, even before the construction of the Tabernacle.

NOTES

Ḥayya is included in the term *behema* – חַיָּה בִּכְלַל בְּהֵמָה: The Gemara (34a) proves this assertion from the verse: "These are the animals [*habehema*] that you may eat" (Deuteronomy 14:4), which is followed by a list that includes undomesticated animals, such as the hart, the gazelle, and the roebuck (Rashi).

אָמַר מָר: הַכֹּל כְּשֵׁירִין לְהַקְרִיב. מְנָא הָנֵי מִילֵּי? אָמַר רַב הוּנָא, דְּאָמַר קְרָא ״וַיִּבֶן נֹחַ מִזְבֵּחַ לַה׳ וַיִּקַּח מִכֹּל הַבְּהֵמָה הַטְּהוֹרָה וּמִכֹּל עוֹף הַטָּהוֹר״, ״בְּהֵמָה״ – כְּמַשְׁמָעוֹ, חַיָּה – בִּכְלַל בְּהֵמָה.

§ **The Master said** in the *baraita*: Before the Tabernacle was established, **all** animals were **fit to be sacrificed:** A domesticated animal, an undomesticated animal, or a bird. The Gemara asks: **From where are these matters** derived? **Rav Huna said: As the verse states** with regard to the offering that was sacrificed after the flood: **"And Noah built an altar to the Lord, and took of every pure animal, and of every pure fowl,** and offered burnt offerings on the altar" (Genesis 8:20). The Gemara explains: **"Animal [*behema*],"** is understood **in accordance with its plain meaning,** a domesticated animal, and the same is true of fowl; **an undomesticated animal [*ḥayya*]** is **included in** the term **"*behema*"**[N] that is stated in the verse.

Perek **XIV**
Daf **116** Amud **a**

NOTES

Unblemished status and male status apply to animal offerings but…do not apply to birds – תַּמּוּת וְזַכְרוּת בִּבְהֵמָה וְאֵין...בְּעוֹפוֹת: With regard to animals that are fit for use as a burnt offering, the verse states: "That you may be accepted, you shall offer a male without blemish, of the herd, of the sheep, or of the goats" (Leviticus 22:19). Based on the fact that the verse mentions only animals, the Sages in *Torat Kohanim* inferred that these *halakhot* pertain only to animals that are sacrificed, but not to birds. Nevertheless, major blemishes, e.g., a missing limb, disqualify even birds, as the verse states: "Present it now to your governor; will he be pleased with you?" (Malachi 1:8).

זְכָרִים וּנְקֵבוֹת, תְּמִימִין וּבַעֲלֵי מוּמִין – דְּאָמַר מָר: תַּמּוּת וְזַכְרוּת בִּבְהֵמָה, וְאֵין תַּמּוּת וְזַכְרוּת בְּעוֹפוֹת.

That which was taught in the *baraita*: All animals were fit to be sacrificed: **Males and females, unblemished and blemished** animals, pertains to **that** which **the Master said** as a principle concerning the *halakhot* of sacrifices: The requirements that an offering must have **unblemished status and** that a burnt offering must have **male status** apply **to animal** offerings, **but** the requirements of **unblemished status and male status do not** apply **to birds.**[N]

וְאִיתַּקַּשׁ בְּהֵמָה לְעוֹף.

And in the verses that recount Noah's sacrifices upon exiting the ark, **a domesticated animal is juxtaposed with a bird,** in the verse: "Of every pure animal, and of every pure fowl" (Genesis 8:20), which teaches that kosher animals had a status identical to that of birds, and could be sacrificed whether male or female, unblemished or blemished.

תְּמִימִין וּבַעֲלֵי מוּמִין – לְאַפּוּקֵי מְחוּסַּר אֵבֶר דְּלָא. אָמַר רַבִּי אֶלְעָזָר: מִנַּיִן לִמְחוּסַּר אֵבֶר שֶׁנֶּאֱסַר לִבְנֵי נֹחַ – תַּלְמוּד לוֹמַר "וּמִכָּל הָחַי מִכָּל בָּשָׂר", אָמְרָה תּוֹרָה: הָבֵא בְּהֵמָה שֶׁחַיִּין רָאשֵׁי אֵיבָרִין שֶׁלָּהּ.

The Gemara adds: That which was taught in the *baraita*: **Unblemished and blemished** animals, serves **to exclude** animals that are **lacking a limb, which** were **not** fit for sacrifice. As **Rabbi Elazar says: From where** is it derived **that** an animal that is **lacking a limb is forbidden to the descendants of Noah,** i.e., gentiles, to be used as a sacrifice? **The verse states** with regard to Noah: **"And of every living being of all flesh,** two of every sort shall you bring into the ark" (Genesis 6:19). With regard to the phrase: "And of every living being," which is superfluous, **the Torah stated: Bring an animal whose limbs are all living,** not one lacking a limb, as that animal is disqualified from sacrifice.

וְדִילְמָא לְמַעוּטֵי טְרֵיפָה! הַהוּא מִ"לְּחַיּוֹת זֶרַע" נָפְקָא.

The Gemara challenges: **But perhaps** this phrase: "And of every living being," serves **to exclude an animal with a wound that will cause it to die within twelve months [*tereifa*]**[N] from being fit as a sacrifice. The Gemara explains: The disqualification of a *tereifa* **is derived from** the phrase: **"To keep seed alive"** (Genesis 7:3), as a *tereifa* cannot propagate.

הָנִיחָא לְמַאן דְּאָמַר: טְרֵיפָה אֵינָהּ יוֹלֶדֶת, אֶלָּא לְמַאן דְּאָמַר: טְרֵיפָה יוֹלֶדֶת, מַאי אִיכָּא לְמֵימַר? הָאָמַר קְרָא: "אִתָּךְ" – בְּדוֹמִין לָךְ.

The Gemara challenges: **This works out well according to the one who says** that **a *tereifa* cannot give birth.** In this case the disqualification of the *tereifa* is derived from the verse: "To keep seed alive," while the disqualification of the animal lacking a limb is derived from the verse: "And of every living being." **But according to the one who says** that **a *tereifa* can give birth, what can be said?** According to this opinion, a *tereifa* cannot be excluded by the phrase: "To keep seed alive." The Gemara explains: **Doesn't the verse state** with regard to the animals that were brought by Noah into the ark: "You shall bring into the ark, to keep them alive **with you"** (Genesis 6:19)? The term "with you" indicates that the verse is stated **with regard to** animals that are **similar to you,** not a *tereifa*.

וְדִילְמָא נֹחַ גּוּפֵיהּ טְרֵיפָה הֲוָה! "תָּמִים" כְּתִיב בֵּיהּ. וְדִילְמָא תָּמִים בִּדְרָכָיו! "צַדִּיק" כְּתִיב בֵּיהּ.

The Gemara asks: **But perhaps Noah himself was a *tereifa*.** If so, one cannot exclude a *tereifa* from the comparison of animals to Noah. The Gemara answers: **It is written about** Noah that he was **"complete"** (Genesis 6:9), which indicates that he was physically whole and unblemished. The Gemara challenges: **But perhaps** the verse means that **his ways were complete,** and it is not referring to Noah's physical attributes. The Gemara explains: **It is** already **written about him** that he was **"righteous"** (Genesis 6:9), which means that his actions were perfect. Consequently, when the verse says that he was also complete, it must be referring to his body.

וְדִילְמָא תָּמִים בִּדְרָכָיו, צַדִּיק בְּמַעֲשָׂיו! אִי סָלְקָא דַּעְתָּךְ דְּנֹחַ גּוּפֵיהּ טְרֵיפָה הֲוָה, מִי קָאָמַר לֵיהּ לְנֹחַ: דִּכְוָותָךְ עַיֵּיל, שְׁלֵמִים לָא תְּעַיֵּיל?

The Gemara challenges: **But perhaps** the verse means that Noah was **complete in his manner,** and he was **righteous** in his good **deeds.** Accordingly, the verse would not exclude the possibility that Noah himself was a *tereifa*. The Gemara responds: **If it enters your mind** to say **that Noah himself was a *tereifa*, would the Merciful One have said to him: Bring in** *tereifot* **like you** to the ark, but **do not bring in whole** and perfect animals? It is not reasonable to say that there would be a preference for him to bring *tereifot*. Rather, Noah was certainly not a *tereifa*, and the fact that a *tereifa* is disqualified for sacrifice is derived from "with you."

וּמֵאַחַר דְּנָפְקָא לָן מֵ"אִתָּךְ", "לְחַיּוֹת זֶרַע" לָמָּה לִי? מַהוּ דְּתֵימָא: "אִתָּךְ" – לְצַוְותָּא בְּעָלְמָא, אֲפִילּוּ זָקֵן אֲפִילּוּ סָרִיס, קָמַשְׁמַע לָן.

The Gemara asks: **And once we derive** the disqualification of a *tereifa* **from** the term **"with you," why do I** need the phrase **"to keep seed alive"?** The Gemara answers: If one could derive only from **"with you," you would say** that Noah brought the animals to the ark **only for** the purpose of **companionship,**[N] and therefore **even** an animal that is **old** or **even one who is castrated** can come into the ark, provided that it is not a *tereifa*. Therefore, the Merciful One writes: "To keep seed alive," which **teaches us** that only animals that can bear offspring were allowed to be brought into the ark.

NOTES

But perhaps…a *tereifa* – וְדִילְמָא...טְרֵיפָה: A *tereifa* cannot be classified as included in "every living being." It is logical to exclude only a *tereifa* from the category of "every living being," and not an animal that was missing a limb, since the purpose of bringing animals onto the ark was to reestablish life on earth after the flood. While a *tereifa* could not serve this purpose, an animal that was missing a limb could.

NOTES

If one could derive only from "with you" you would say he brought them only for companionship – מַהוּ דְּתֵימָא אִתָּךְ לְצַוְותָּא בְּעָלְמָא: Rashi explains that had the verse not stated: "To keep seed alive," the term "with you" would not have been interpreted to mean that the animals must be like you, i.e., not *tereifa*; it would have been interpreted to mean that the animals were with Noah for companionship. The phrase: "To keep seed alive," therefore teaches that the purpose of bringing the animals onto the ark was not companionship for Noah but preservation of life on Earth. The term "with you" is consequently interpreted to mean: Like you, disqualifying a *tereifa*.

In his commentary on tractate *Avoda Zara* (51a), Rashi explains that had the verse stated only "with you" it would be possible to infer that animals that were not like you, such as a *tereifa*, would be excluded from the ark, but it would still be possible to say that an animal that was not a *tereifa* could be brought onto the ark, even if it was infertile. The verse therefore states: "To keep seed alive," to teach that an animal that was infertile, even one that was not a *tereifa*, could not be brought onto the ark.

״טְהוֹרִין אֲבָל לֹא טְמֵאִין״. וּמִי הָווּ טְמֵאִין וּטְהוֹרִין בְּהַהִיא שַׁעְתָּא? אָמַר רַבִּי שְׁמוּאֵל בַּר נַחְמָנִי אָמַר רַבִּי יוֹנָתָן: מֵאוֹתָן שֶׁלֹּא נֶעֶבְדָה בָּהֶן עֲבֵירָה.

§ The *baraita* also teaches that before the Tabernacle was constructed, sacrifices were brought from animals and birds that were **kosher, but not** from **non-kosher** species. This is based on the verse that describes what Noah sacrificed when he exited the ark: "And he took of every pure animal and of every pure fowl and offered burnt offerings on the altar" (Genesis 8:20). The Gemara asks: **And were there pure and impure** species **at that time,** during the period of Noah? The distinction between pure, i.e., kosher species, and impure, i.e., non-kosher species, was introduced only after the Torah was given (see Leviticus, chapter 11). **Rabbi Shmuel bar Naḥmani says** that **Rabbi Yonatan says:** The pure animals that Noah took were **from those that had not been used in the performance of sin.**[N]

מְנָא הֲווּ יָדְעִי? כִּדְרַב חִסְדָּא, דְּאָמַר רַב חִסְדָּא: הֶעֱבִירָן לִפְנֵי הַתֵּיבָה, כׇּל שֶׁהַתֵּיבָה קוֹלַטְתָּן – בְּיָדוּעַ שֶׁהוּא טָהוֹר, אֵין הַתֵּיבָה קוֹלַטְתָּן – בְּיָדוּעַ שֶׁהֵן טְמֵאִין.

The Gemara asks: **From where did** Noah and his sons **know** which animals had been used in the performance of a sin, in order to prevent them from entering the ark? The Gemara answers that it is **in accordance with** the statement **of Rav Ḥisda. As Rav Ḥisda says:** Noah caused all of the animals to **pass before the ark. All** animals **that the ark accepted,** i.e., drew in, was **known to be pure;** if **the ark did not accept them,** it was **known that they** were **impure.**

רַבִּי אַבָּהוּ אָמַר, אָמַר קְרָא: ״וְהַבָּאִים זָכָר וּנְקֵבָה״ – הַבָּאִין מֵאֲלֵיהֶן.

Rabbi Abbahu says there is a different explanation as to how Noah knew which animals were pure or impure. **The verse states: "And they that went in,** went in **male and female** of all flesh" (Genesis 7:16), which means: Those **that went in on their own.** Consequently, Noah did not need to distinguish between pure and impure animals, as only the pure ones approached.

אָמַר מָר: וְהַכֹּל קָרְבוּ עוֹלוֹת. עוֹלוֹת – אִין, שְׁלָמִים – לָא. וְהָא כְּתִיב: ״וַיִּזְבְּחוּ זְבָחִים שְׁלָמִים לַה׳ פָּרִים״! אֶלָּא אֵימָא: הַכֹּל קָרְבוּ עוֹלוֹת [וּשְׁלָמִים.

§ In describing the sacrificial service before the Tabernacle was constructed, **the Master said: And all** offerings brought before the construction of the Tabernacle were **sacrificed** as **burnt offerings.** The Gemara infers: **Burnt offerings, yes,** were sacrificed, but **peace offerings** were **not** sacrificed. The Gemara challenges: **But** with regard to the offerings that were sacrificed at Mount Sinai at the time of the giving of the Torah, **it is written:** "And they offered burnt offerings, **and sacrificed peace offerings of oxen to the Lord"** (Exodus 24:5). This event occurred prior to the construction of the Tabernacle. **Rather, say** that the *baraita* means: **All** offerings **sacrificed** were either **burnt offerings or peace offerings.**[N]

וְהָתַנְיָא: אֲבָל שְׁלָמִים לֹא, כִּי אִם עוֹלוֹת]; עוֹלוֹת – אִין, שְׁלָמִים – לָא! כְּמַאן דְּאָמַר: לֹא קָרְבוּ שְׁלָמִים בְּנֵי נֹחַ. דְּאִיתְּמַר, רַבִּי אֶלְעָזָר וְרַבִּי יוֹסֵי בַּר חֲנִינָא, חַד אָמַר: קָרְבוּ [שְׁלָמִים בְּנֵי נֹחַ], וְחַד אָמַר: לֹא קָרְבוּ.

The Gemara challenges: **And isn't it taught** in another *baraita*: **But peace offerings** were **not** sacrificed before the construction of the Tabernacle; **rather, only burnt offerings** were sacrificed? Clearly, **burnt offerings, yes,** were sacrificed, but **peace offerings** were **not** sacrificed. The Gemara answers that this *baraita* is **in accordance with** the opinion of **the one who says** that **peace offerings were not sacrificed** by the **descendants of Noah. As it was stated** that there is a dispute between **Rabbi Elazar and Rabbi Yosei bar Ḥanina** with regard to this: **One says** that **the descendants of Noah sacrificed peace offerings, and one says** that **they did not sacrifice** peace offerings.

NOTES

From those that had not been used in the performance of sin – מֵאוֹתָן שֶׁלֹּא נֶעֶבְדָה בָּהֶן עֲבֵירָה: This refers to animals that engaged in intercourse only with their mates, and were not included in the statement: "For all flesh had corrupted their way upon the earth" (Genesis 6:12; see Rashi on *Sanhedrin* 108b). The Sages elsewhere also use the word sin, without qualification, to denote forbidden sexual intercourse. Consequently, according to Rabbi Yonatan, the term pure animals means those that did not commit this sin, while the word impure refers to those that did (*Ḥizkuni*).

Rather, say: All [*hakol*] offerings sacrificed were burnt offerings or peace offerings, etc. – אֶלָּא אֵימָא הַכֹּל קָרְבוּ עוֹלוֹת וּשְׁלָמִים וכו׳: This version of the text is that of the version of the Gemara in *Ein Ya'akov*, which follows the Sephardic tradition and differs on occasion from the standard version (see *Birkat HaZevaḥ*).

The version of the Gemara used by Rashi and Rabbeinu Ḥananel, as well as the version found in the old printed editions of the Gemara, reads: Rather, say: For all [*lakol*], burnt offerings were sacrificed. The term: For all, indicates that for all people, burnt offerings were sacrificed until the construction of the Tabernacle. Once the Jews were no longer categorized as descendants of Noah, i.e., after the giving of the Torah, they began to sacrifice peace offerings, as is mentioned in the context of the revelation at Sinai.

Alternatively, Rabbeinu Ḥananel explains that the phrase: For all burnt offerings were sacrificed, means that the peace offerings that were sacrificed by the descendants of Noah were also burned completely, like a burnt offering. In contrast to a burnt offering, the sacrificial portions and the meat of the offering were burned separately, and the Jews began partaking of the meat of the peace offerings after the giving of the Torah.

מַאי טַעְמָא דְּמַאן דְּאָמַר: קָרְבוּ שְׁלָמִים בְּנֵי נֹחַ? דִּכְתִיב: "וְהֶבֶל הֵבִיא גַם הוּא מִבְּכוֹרוֹת צֹאנוֹ וּמֵחֶלְבֵהֶן", אֵיזֶהוּ דָּבָר שֶׁחֶלְבּוֹ קָרֵב לְגַבֵּי מִזְבֵּחַ וְאֵין כּוּלּוֹ קָרֵב לְגַבֵּי מִזְבֵּחַ – הֱוֵי אוֹמֵר: זֶה שְׁלָמִים.

The Gemara explains the two opinions: **What is the reasoning of the one who says that the descendants of Noah sacrificed peace offerings? As it is written: "And Abel, he also brought of the firstborn of his flock and of the fat thereof"** (Genesis 4:4). Abel, like all gentiles, is categorized as a descendant of Noah. The verse emphasizes that the fat was sacrificed. The Gemara analyzes: **What is an item,** i.e., an offering, **the fat of which is sacrificed upon the altar, but** that **is not sacrificed in its entirety upon the altar? You must say: This is the peace offering,** the meat of which is consumed.

מַאי טַעְמָא דְּמַאן דְּאָמַר: לֹא קָרְבוּ? דִּכְתִיב: "עוּרִי צָפוֹן וּבוֹאִי תֵימָן", תִּתְנָעֵר אוּמָּה שֶׁמַּעֲשֶׂיהָ בַּצָּפוֹן, וְתָבוֹא אוּמָּה שֶׁמַּעֲשֶׂיהָ בַּצָּפוֹן וּבַדָּרוֹם.

What is the reasoning of the one who says that **they did not sacrifice** peace offerings? **As it is written: "Awake [*uri*], O north; and come, south…** Let my beloved come into his garden, and eat his precious fruits" (Song of Songs 4:16). The Gemara interprets this homiletically: The **nation,** i.e., the nations of the world, who are the descendants of Noah, **whose acts,** i.e., sacrifices, are only **in the north,** i.e., they sacrifice only burnt offerings, which are slaughtered and their blood collected in the north of the Temple courtyard, **shall be removed [*titna'er*], and** in its place **shall come** the Jewish **nation, whose acts,** i.e., sacrifices, are **in the north and in the south,** as they sacrifice burnt offerings, whose rites are performed in the north, and peace offerings, whose rites may also be performed in the south, as the entire courtyard is fit for their rites.

וּמָר נַמִי, הָכְתִיב: "וּמֵחֶלְבֵהֶן"! מִשְּׁמֵנֵיהֶן [דִּידְהוּ].

The Gemara asks: **And also** according to **the Master** who holds that the descendants of Noah did not sacrifice peace offerings, **isn't it written: "And of the fat thereof,"** from which it may be derived that Abel sacrificed a peace offering? The Gemara answers: "The fat thereof," does not mean that Abel sacrificed only the fats of his offerings; rather, it means that he sacrificed **the fattest of them,** i.e., the fattest and choicest of his animals.

וּמָר נַמִי, הָכְתִיב: "עוּרִי צָפוֹן"! [הַהוּא] בְּקִיבּוּץ גָּלֻיּוֹת הוּא דִּכְתִיב.

The Gemara asks: **And also** according to **the Master** who holds that the descendants of Noah did sacrifice peace offerings, **isn't it written: "Awake, O north,"** from which it may be derived that the nations of the world do not sacrifice peace offerings? The Gemara answers: In his opinion, **that** verse **is written with regard to the ingathering of the exiles,** i.e., the Jewish exiles will come from the north and the south.

וְהָא כְּתִיב: "וַיֹּאמֶר מֹשֶׁה גַּם אַתָּה תִּתֵּן בְּיָדֵינוּ זְבָחִים וְעֹלֹת וְעָשִׂינוּ לַה׳ אֱלֹהֵינוּ"! זְבָחִים – לַאֲכִילָה, וְעוֹלוֹת – לְהַקְרָבָה.

With regard to the opinion that the descendants of Noah did not sacrifice peace offerings, the Gemara asks: **But isn't it written: "And Moses said: You must also give into our hand sacrifices [*zevaḥim*] and burnt offerings, that we may sacrifice to the Lord our God"** (Exodus 10:25)? This indicates that sacrifices [*zevaḥim*], i.e., peace offerings, were sacrificed before the Torah was given. The Gemara answers: In this context, "***zevaḥim***" is referring to animals to be used **for consumption,** as the word *zevaḥ* can also be translated as an animal for slaughter, **and "burnt offerings"** is referring to animals to be used **for sacrifice.**

וְהָא כְּתִיב: "וַיִּקַּח יִתְרוֹ [חֹתֵן מֹשֶׁה] עֹלָה וּזְבָחִים"! הַהוּא לְאַחַר מַתַּן תּוֹרָה הוּא דִּכְתִיב.

The Gemara asks: **But isn't it written** before the giving of the Torah: **"And Yitro, Moses' father-in-law, took a burnt offering and sacrifices [*zevaḥim*]** for God" (Exodus 18:12)? Since the word *zevaḥim* there is referring to sacrifices, as the verse clearly states that Yitro took them for God, evidently peace offerings were sacrificed before the giving of the Torah. The Gemara answers: **That** verse **was written** with regard to the period **after the giving of the Torah,** when the Jewish people were permitted to sacrifice peace offerings.

הָנִיחָא לְמַאן דְּאָמַר: [יִתְרוֹ] אַחַר מַתַּן תּוֹרָה הָיָה, אֶלָּא לְמַאן דְּאָמַר: [יִתְרוֹ] קוֹדֶם מַתַּן תּוֹרָה הָיָה, מַאי אִיכָּא לְמֵימַר? דְּאִיתְּמַר, בְּנֵי רַבִּי חִיָּיא וְרַבִּי יְהוֹשֻׁעַ בֶּן לֵוִי, חַד אָמַר: יִתְרוֹ קוֹדֶם מַתַּן תּוֹרָה הָיָה, וְחַד אָמַר: יִתְרוֹ אַחַר מַתַּן תּוֹרָה הָיָה. לְמַאן דְּאָמַר: יִתְרוֹ קוֹדֶם מַתַּן תּוֹרָה הָיָה – קָסָבַר: שְׁלָמִים הִקְרִיבוּ בְּנֵי נֹחַ.

The Gemara notes: **This works out well according to the one who says** that the episode with **Yitro was after the giving of the Torah. But according to the one who says** that the episode with **Yitro was before the giving of the Torah, what can be said? As it was stated: The sons of Rabbi Ḥiyya and Rabbi Yehoshua ben Levi** engage in a dispute concerning this issue. **One says** that the episode with **Yitro was before the giving of the Torah, and one says** that the episode with **Yitro was after the giving of the Torah.** The Gemara answers: **The one who says** that the episode with **Yitro was before the giving of the Torah maintains** that **the descendants of Noah did sacrifice peace offerings.**

כְּתַנָּאֵי: ״וַיִּשְׁמַע יִתְרוֹ כֹהֵן מִדְיָן״, מָה שְׁמוּעָה שָׁמַע וּבָא וְנִתְגַּיֵּיר? רַבִּי יְהוֹשֻׁעַ אוֹמֵר: מִלְחֶמֶת עֲמָלֵק שָׁמַע, שֶׁהֲרֵי כְּתִיב בְּצִדּוֹ: ״וַיַּחֲלֹשׁ יְהוֹשֻׁעַ אֶת עֲמָלֵק וְאֶת עַמּוֹ לְפִי חָרֶב״.

§ The Gemara notes that the disagreement between *amora'im* with regard to when Yitro came to Mount Sinai is **like** a dispute between *tanna'im*: The Torah states with regard to Yitro, before he came to Mount Sinai: **"Now Yitro, the priest of Midian, Moses' father-in-law, heard** of all that God had done for Moses, and for Israel His people, how the Lord had brought Israel out of Egypt" (Exodus 18:1). **What tiding did he hear that he came and converted? Rabbi Yehoshua says: He heard** about **the war with Amalek, as it is written adjacent to** the verses that state that Yitro came: **"And Joshua weakened Amalek and his people with the edge of the sword"** (Exodus 17:13).

רַבִּי אֶלְעָזָר הַמּוֹדָעִי אוֹמֵר: מַתַּן תּוֹרָה שָׁמַע [וּבָא]. שֶׁכְּשֶׁנִּיתְּנָה תּוֹרָה לְיִשְׂרָאֵל הָיָה קוֹלוֹ הוֹלֵךְ מִסּוֹף הָעוֹלָם וְעַד סוֹפוֹ, וְכׇל [מַלְכֵי] אוּמּוֹת הָעוֹלָם אֲחָזָתַן רְעָדָה בְּהֵיכְלֵיהֶן וְאָמְרוּ שִׁירָה, שֶׁנֶּאֱמַר: ״וּבְהֵיכָלוֹ כּוּלּוֹ אוֹמֵר כָּבוֹד״.

Rabbi Elazar HaModa'i says: He heard about **the giving of the Torah and came. As when the Torah was given to the Jewish people, the voice of** the Holy One, Blessed be He, **went from** one **end of the world to the** other **end, and all of the kings of the nations of the world were overcome with trembling in their palaces and recited a song** of praise, **as it is stated:** "The voice of the Lord makes the hinds to calve… **and in his palace all say: Glory"** (Psalms 29:9), i.e., each king in his own palace recited songs of praise to God.

נִתְקַבְּצוּ כּוּלָּם אֵצֶל בִּלְעָם הָרָשָׁע, וְאָמְרוּ לוֹ: מָה קוֹל הֶהָמוֹן אֲשֶׁר שָׁמַעְנוּ? שֶׁמָּא מַבּוּל בָּא לָעוֹלָם? (אָמַר לָהֶם) ״ה׳ לַמַּבּוּל יָשָׁב״? [אָמַר לָהֶם]: ״וַיֵּשֶׁב ה׳ מֶלֶךְ לְעוֹלָם״ – כְּבָר נִשְׁבַּע הַקָּדוֹשׁ בָּרוּךְ הוּא שֶׁאֵינוֹ מֵבִיא מַבּוּל לָעוֹלָם.

At that time, **all of** the kings **gathered around Balaam the wicked,** who was the greatest gentile prophet, **and said to him: What is the tumultuous sound,** i.e., the loud noise, **that we have heard? Perhaps a flood is coming to** destroy **the world, as it is stated: "The Lord sat enthroned at the flood"** (Psalms 29:10)? Balaam **said to them: "The Lord sits as King forever"** (Psalms 29:10), which means that **the Holy One, Blessed be He, already took an oath** after the flood **never to bring a flood to the world,** as it is stated: "And the waters shall no more become a flood" (Genesis 9:15).

אָמְרוּ לוֹ: מַבּוּל שֶׁל מַיִם אֵינוֹ מֵבִיא, אֲבָל מַבּוּל שֶׁל אֵשׁ מֵבִיא, שֶׁנֶּאֱמַר: ״כִּי (הִנֵּה) בָאֵשׁ ה׳ נִשְׁפָּט״! אָמַר לָהֶן: כְּבָר נִשְׁבַּע שֶׁאֵינוֹ מַשְׁחִית כׇּל בָּשָׂר.

The kings **said to him: He will not bring a flood of water,** as he vowed, **but** perhaps **He will bring a flood of fire,** as in the future the Lord will punish the nations with fire, **as it is stated: "For by fire will the Lord contend,** and by His sword with all flesh; and the slain of the Lord shall be many" (Isaiah 66:16). Balaam **said to them: He already took an oath that He will not destroy all flesh** in any manner, as it is stated: "To destroy all flesh" (Genesis 9:15). Therefore, there will not be a flood of fire.

וּמָה קוֹל הֶהָמוֹן הַזֶּה שֶׁשָּׁמַעְנוּ? אָמַר לָהֶם: חֶמְדָּה טוֹבָה יֵשׁ לוֹ בְּבֵית גְּנָזָיו שֶׁהָיְתָה גְּנוּזָה אֶצְלוֹ תְּשַׁע מֵאוֹת שִׁבְעִים וְאַרְבָּעָה דּוֹרוֹת קוֹדֶם שֶׁנִּבְרָא הָעוֹלָם, וּבִיקֵּשׁ לִיתְּנָהּ לְבָנָיו, שֶׁנֶּאֱמַר: ״ה׳ עֹז לְעַמּוֹ יִתֵּן״. [מִיָּד] פָּתְחוּ כּוּלָּם וְאָמְרוּ: ״ה׳ יְבָרֵךְ אֶת עַמּוֹ בַשָּׁלוֹם״.

They asked: **And** if so, **what is this tumultuous sound that we have heard?** Balaam **said to them: He has a good** and **precious item in His treasury, that was hidden away with Him** for **974 generations before the world was created, and He seeks to give it to his children, as it is stated: "The Lord will give strength to His people"** (Psalms 29:11). "Strength" is a reference to the Torah, which is the strength of the Jewish people. **Immediately, they all began to say: "The Lord will bless His people with peace"** (Psalms 29:11).

רַבִּי אֱלִיעֶזֶר אוֹמֵר: קְרִיעַת יַם סוּף שָׁמַע וּבָא, שֶׁנֶּאֱמַר: ״וַיְהִי כִשְׁמֹעַ כׇּל מַלְכֵי הָאֱמֹרִי״. וְאַף רָחָב הַזּוֹנָה אָמְרָה לִשְׁלוּחֵי יְהוֹשֻׁעַ: ״כִּי שָׁמַעְנוּ אֵת אֲשֶׁר הוֹבִישׁ ה׳ אֶת מֵי יַם סוּף״.

The Gemara offers another explanation of what Yitro heard: **Rabbi Eliezer says: He heard** about **the splitting of the Red Sea and came, as it is stated** in a similar context with regard to the splitting of the Jordan in the days of Joshua: **"And it came to pass, when all the kings of the Amorites,** that were beyond the Jordan westward, and all the kings of the Canaanites, that were by the sea, **heard** how that the Lord had dried up the waters of the Jordan from before the children of Israel, until they were passed over, that their heart melted, neither was there spirit in them anymore, because of the children of Israel" (Joshua 5:1). **And even Rahab the prostitute said to Joshua's messengers: "For we have heard how the Lord dried up the water of the Red Sea** before you" (Joshua 2:10).

מַאי שְׁנָא הָתָם דְּאָמַר (לֵיהּ): ״וְלֹא הָיָה בָם עוֹד רוּחַ״, וּמַאי שְׁנָא הָכָא דְּקָאָמַר: ״וְלֹא קָמָה עוֹד רוּחַ בְּאִישׁ״?

The Gemara asks: **What is different there,** i.e., with regard to the splitting of the Jordan, **where** the verse **states: "Neither was there spirit in them anymore," and what is different here,** i.e., in the statement of Rahab, **where** the verse **states: "Neither did there remain [*kama*] any more spirit in any man"** (Joshua 2:11)?

דַּאֲפִילּוּ אִקְשׁוּיֵי נַמִּי לָא אִקַּשׁוּ. וּמְנָא יָדְעָה? דְּאָמַר מָר: אֵין לְךָ כָּל שַׂר וְנָגִיד שֶׁלֹּא בָּא עַל רָחָב הַזּוֹנָה.

The Gemara replies that Rahab used this phrase euphemistically, to say that their fear was so great **that** their male organs **were not even** able to **become erect,** as "*kama*" also means rise. The Gemara asks: **And how did** Rahab **know** this? The Gemara replies: **As the Master said: You do not have any prince or ruler**[N] at that time **who did not engage in intercourse with Rahab the prostitute.**

אָמְרוּ: בַּת עֶשֶׂר שָׁנִים הָיְתָה כְּשֶׁיָּצְאוּ יִשְׂרָאֵל מִמִּצְרַיִם, וְזָנְתָה [כָּל] אַרְבָּעִים שָׁנָה שֶׁהָיוּ יִשְׂרָאֵל בַּמִּדְבָּר. אַחַר חֲמִישִּׁים שָׁנָה נִתְגַּיְּירָה, אָמְרָה: יְהֵא מָחוּל לִי בִּשְׂכַר חֶבֶל חַלּוֹן וּפִשְׁתִּים.

The Gemara adds that the Sages **said** with regard to Rahab: **She was ten years old when the Jewish people left Egypt, and she engaged in prostitution all forty years that the Jewish people were in the wilderness. After** that, when she was **fifty years** old, she **converted** when the two spies visited her. **She said: May** all of my sins of prostitution **be forgiven me as a reward** for having endangered myself with the **rope, window, and flax,** by means of which I saved Joshua's two spies. Rahab first concealed the spies in stalks of flax, and later assisted them in exiting her home by lowering them from the window with a rope (see Joshua 2:6 and 2:15).

אָמַר מָר: וְגוֹיִם בַּזְּמַן הַזֶּה רַשָּׁאִין לַעֲשׂוֹת כֵּן. מְנָא הָנֵי מִילֵּי? דְּתָנוּ רַבָּנַן: "דַּבֵּר אֶל בְּנֵי יִשְׂרָאֵל" – בְּנֵי יִשְׂרָאֵל מְצוּוִּין עַל שְׁחוּטֵי חוּץ, וְאֵין הַגּוֹיִם מְצוּוִּין עַל שְׁחוּטֵי חוּץ.

§ **The Master said** in the *baraita* that discussed the sacrifice of offerings before the construction of the Tabernacle: **And today gentiles are permitted to do so,**[NH] i.e., to sacrifice offerings outside the Temple courtyard, despite the fact that this is forbidden for the Jews. The Gemara asks: **From where are these matters** derived? **As the Sages taught** with regard to the verses that prohibit the slaughter of offerings outside the Temple: "**Speak** to Aaron, and to his sons, and **to all the children of Israel**" (Leviticus 17:2). This indicates that only **Jews are commanded with regard to** offerings **slaughtered outside** the Temple, **but gentiles are not commanded with regard to** offerings **slaughtered outside** the Temple.

לְפִיכָךְ, כָּל אֶחָד וְאֶחָד בּוֹנֶה לוֹ בָּמָה לְעַצְמוֹ וּמַקְרִיב עָלֶיהָ כָּל מַה שֶּׁיִּרְצֶה. אָמַר רַבִּי יַעֲקֹב בַּר אַחָא אָמַר רַב אַסִי: אָסוּר לְסַיְּיעָן וְלַעֲשׂוֹת שְׁלִיחוּתָן. אֲמַר רַבָּה: וּלְאוֹרִינְהוּ [לְהוּ] שָׁרֵי.

Therefore, each and every gentile may, if he desires, **construct a** private **altar for himself, and sacrifice upon it whatever he desires. Rabbi Ya'akov bar Aḥa says** that **Rav Asi says:** Although it is permitted for gentiles to sacrifice offerings outside the Temple courtyard, it is **prohibited** for a Jew **to assist them or to fulfill their agency** in this matter, as sacrificing in this manner is forbidden for a Jew. **Rabba said: But to instruct them** how to sacrifice outside the Temple is **permitted.**

כִּי הָא דְּאִיפְרָא הוּרְמִיז אִימֵּיהּ דְּשָׁבוּר מַלְכָּא שַׁדַּרָה קוּרְבָּנָא לְרָבָא, שְׁלַחָה לֵיהּ: אַסְקוּהּ נִיהֲלֵיהּ לְשֵׁם שָׁמַיִם. אֲמַר לְהוּ לְרַב סָפְרָא וּלְרַב אַחָא בַּר הוּנָא: זִילוּ וּדְבַרוּ תְּרֵי עוּלְמֵי גּוּלָאֵי, וַחֲזוּ הֵיכָא דְּמַסְּקָא יַמָּא שִׁירְטוֹן, וּשְׁקַלוּ צִיבֵי חֲדַתֵי וְאַפִּיקוּ נוּרָא מִמָּרָא חַדְתָּא, וְאַסְקוּהּ נִיהֲלֵיהּ לְשֵׁם שָׁמַיִם.

This is **similar to that** incident **in which Ifera Hurmiz,**[P] **the mother of King Shapur** of Persia, **sent an offering to Rava,** with which **she** sent this message **to him: Sacrifice this for me, for the sake of Heaven. Rava said to Rav Safra and to Rav Aḥa bar Huna: Go, take two** gentile **youths of the same age,** i.e., similar to one another, so that the sacrifice will be performed with maximal beauty, **and see where the sea** currently **raises silt** [*sirton*],[L] which is a place that no one has used before. **And take new wood and bring out fire from new vessels, and** the two youths will **sacrifice** the offering **for her, for the sake of Heaven.**

אֲמַר לֵיהּ אַבַּיֵי: כְּמַאן – כְּרַבִּי אֶלְעָזָר בֶּן שַׁמּוּעַ? דְּתַנְיָא, רַבִּי אֶלְעָזָר בֶּן שַׁמּוּעַ אוֹמֵר: מַה מִּזְבֵּחַ שֶׁלֹּא יִשְׁתַּמֵּשׁ בּוֹ הֶדְיוֹט – אַף עֵצִים שֶׁלֹּא יִשְׁתַּמֵּשׁ בָּהֶן הֶדְיוֹט. וְהָא מוֹדֶה רַבִּי אֶלְעָזָר בֶּן שַׁמּוּעַ בְּבָמָה.

Abaye said to Rava: **In accordance with whose** opinion was the instruction to sacrifice exclusively with new wood? Was it **in accordance with** the opinion of **Rabbi Elazar ben Shammua? As it is taught** in a *baraita* that **Rabbi Elazar ben Shammua says: Just as** the **altar** is a place **that is not used by an ordinary** person, **so too,** the **wood** that will be used **must not be used by an ordinary** person.[H] The Gemara asks: **But doesn't Rabbi Elazar ben Shammua concede** that **in** the case of a private **altar** the wood need not be new?

NOTES

You do not have any prince or ruler – אֵין לְךָ כָּל שַׂר וְנָגִיד: The verse therefore states: "Neither did there remain any more spirit in any man [*be'ish*]," as the word "man [*ish*]" refers to a person of high stature.

And today gentiles are permitted to do so – וְגוֹיִם בַּזְּמַן הַזֶּה רַשָּׁאִין לַעֲשׂוֹת כֵּן: This applies not only to sacrificing upon a private altar but also to the other *halakhot* mentioned in this regard: They may sacrifice domesticated animals, undomesticated animals, and birds; male and female animals; and blemished and unblemished animals.

HALAKHA

Sacrifice by gentiles – קָרְבְּנוֹת הַגּוֹיִם: It is permitted for gentiles to sacrifice burnt offerings to the Lord in any place, provided the offerings are sacrificed upon a private altar that was built by the gentile. It is prohibited for a Jew to assist in this sacrificial service or to act as the gentile's agent, but a Jew may instruct the gentile in the proper procedure for sacrifice. A Jew who slaughters a gentile's offering outside the Temple courtyard is liable (Rambam *Sefer Avoda, Hilkhot Ma'aseh HaKorbanot* 19:16).

The wood must not be used by an ordinary person – עֵצִים שֶׁלֹּא יִשְׁתַּמֵּשׁ בָּהֶן הֶדְיוֹט: Wood salvaged from a demolished building is permanently disqualified for the arrangement of wood on the altar; only new wood that has never been used for any other purpose is fit. This ruling is in accordance with the *Tosefta* (*Menaḥot* 9:4) and the opinion of Rabbi Elazar ben Shammua (Rambam *Sefer Avoda, Hilkhot Issurei Mizbe'aḥ* 6:2 and *Leḥem Mishne* there; see *Shulḥan Arukh, Oraḥ Ḥayyim* 147:1 and the commentaries there).

LANGUAGE

Silt [*sirton*] – שִׁירְטוֹן: From the Greek συρτός, *surtos*, meaning swept, washed down by a river.

PERSONALITIES

Ifera Hurmiz – אִיפְרָא הוּרְמִיז: Queen Ifera Hurmiz was the mother of Shapur II, king of Persia, 309–379 CE. Since Shapur became king as a child, his mother maintained considerable influence over him for many years. Ifera Hurmiz is mentioned on several occasions in the Gemara as an admirer of Judaism and the Sages. She even gave money to several Sages to distribute as charity and for the performance of mitzvot.

דְּתַנְיָא, כָּתוּב אֶחָד אוֹמֵר: ״וַיִּתֵּן דָּוִד לְאָרְנָן בַּמָּקוֹם שִׁקְלֵי זָהָב מִשְׁקַל שֵׁשׁ מֵאוֹת״ וגו׳, וּכְתִיב: ״וַיִּקֶן דָּוִד אֶת הַגֹּרֶן וְאֶת הַבָּקָר בְּכֶסֶף שְׁקָלִים חֲמִשִּׁים״, הָא כֵּיצַד?

As it is taught in a *baraita*: With regard to David's purchase of the site of the Temple, when he wished to build an altar there at God's instruction, **one verse states: "So David gave to Ornan for the place six hundred shekels of gold by weight.** And David built there an altar to the Lord, and offered burnt offerings and peace offerings" (I Chronicles 21:25–26). **And it is written** elsewhere: **"So David bought the threshing floor and the oxen for fifty shekels of silver.** And David built there an altar to the Lord, and offered burnt offerings and peace offerings" (II Samuel 24:24–25). **How can these** texts be reconciled?

גּוֹבֶה מִכָּל שֵׁבֶט וְשֵׁבֶט חֲמִשִּׁים, שֶׁהֵן שֵׁשֶׁת מֵאוֹת. רַבִּי אוֹמֵר מִשּׁוּם אַבָּא יוֹסֵי בֶּן דּוֹסְתַּאי: בָּקָר [וְעֵצִים] וּמְקוֹם מִזְבֵּחַ – בַּחֲמִשִּׁים, וְכָל הַבַּיִת כּוּלּוֹ בְּשֵׁשׁ מֵאוֹת.

David would **collect from each tribe** of the twelve tribes **fifty** shekels, **which are** a sum of **six hundred** shekels. **Rabbi** Yehuda HaNasi **says in the name of Abba Yosei ben Dostai** that there is another explanation: David purchased the **cattle and the wood and the site of** the **altar for fifty** shekels,[N] **and** he purchased the site of **the entire Temple for six hundred** shekels.

רַבִּי אֶלְעָזָר בֶּן שַׁמּוּעַ אוֹמֵר: בָּקָר וְעֵצִים וּמְקוֹם מִזְבֵּחַ – בַּחֲמִשִּׁים, וְכָל הַבַּיִת כּוּלּוֹ בְּשֵׁשׁ מֵאוֹת, דִּכְתִיב: ״וַיֹּאמֶר אֲרַוְנָה אֶל דָּוִד יִקַּח וְיַעַל אֲדוֹנִי הַמֶּלֶךְ [הַטּוֹב בְּעֵינָיו] רְאֵה הַבָּקָר לָעֹלָה וְהַמֹּרִגִּים [וּכְלֵי הַבָּקָר] לָעֵצִים״. וְרָבָא אָמַר לָךְ: הָתָם נַמִּי בַּחֲדָתֵי.

Rabbi Elazar ben Shammua says likewise: David purchased the **cattle and** the **wood and the site of** the **altar for fifty** shekels, **and** the site of **the entire Temple for six hundred** shekels, **as it is written: "And Araunah said to David: Let my lord the king take and offer that which is good in his eyes; see the cattle for the burnt offering, and the threshing tools, and the implements of the cattle for the wood"** (II Samuel 24:22), to which David replied: "No, but I will buy it from you at a price" (II Samuel 24:24). Consequently, according to the opinion of Rabbi Elazar ben Shammua, David purchased the threshing instruments and the furniture of the oxen for use as wood. **And Rava** could have **said to you** in response: **There too,** in the case of David, the verse is dealing **with new** vessels that had not yet been used.

מַאי ״מֹרִגִּים״? אֲמַר עוּלָּא: מִטָּה שֶׁל טוּרְבָּל. מַאי מִטָּה שֶׁל טוּרְבָּל? אֲמַר אַבַּיֵי: עִיזָּא דְּקַרְקְסָא דְּדַיְישִׁן דִּישָׁאֵי. אֲמַר אַבַּיֵי: מַאי קְרָא? ״הִנֵּה שַׂמְתִּיךְ לְמוֹרַג חָרוּץ חָדָשׁ בַּעַל פִּיפִיּוֹת״.

The Gemara asks: **What** are **"the threshing instruments [*morigim*]"** mentioned in the verse? **Ulla said:** It is a ***turbal***[L] **bed.** The Gemara asks: **What is a *turbal* bed? Abaye said:** It **is a heavy, serrated board [*dekurkesa*],**[L] used **for threshing. Abaye said: What is the verse** from which the meaning of *morigim* is derived? **"Behold, I have made you a new threshing board [*morag*] having sharp teeth; you shall thresh the mountains, and beat them small, and shall make the hills as chaff"** (Isaiah 41:15). This verse indicates that a *morag* has grooves and teeth, and is used for threshing.

מַקְרֵי לֵיהּ רָבָא לִבְרֵיהּ, וְרָמֵי לֵיהּ קְרָאֵי אַהֲדָדֵי: כְּתִיב ״וַיִּתֵּן דָּוִד לְאָרְנָן״ וגו׳, וּכְתִיב ״וַיִּקֶן דָּוִד״ וגו׳, הָא כֵּיצַד? גּוֹבֶה מִכָּל שֵׁבֶט וְשֵׁבֶט חֲמִשִּׁים, שֶׁהֵן שֵׁשׁ מֵאוֹת.

With regard to the contradiction between the verses that relate the sum of shekels paid by David, the Gemara says that **Rava** was **teaching** these verses **to his son, and raised a contradiction between verses: It is written: "So David gave to Ornan**…six hundred shekels of gold by weight" (I Chronicles 21:25), **and it is written: "So David bought**…fifty shekels of silver" (II Samuel 24:24). **How can these** texts be reconciled? David would **collect from each tribe** of the twelve tribes **fifty** shekels, **which are** a sum **of six hundred** shekels.

וְאַכַּתִּי קַשְׁיָין אַהֲדָדֵי, הָתָם כֶּסֶף הָכָא זָהָב! אֶלָּא הָכִי קָאָמַר: גּוֹבֶה כֶּסֶף בְּמִשְׁקַל שֵׁשׁ מֵאוֹת זָהָב.

The Gemara asks: **But** these verses **are still difficult,** as they contradict **one another,** since **there** in the book of Samuel it is stated that David paid **silver** shekels, while **here** in Chronicles it is stated that he paid **gold** shekels. The Gemara replies: **Rather, this** is what the verses are **saying:** David would **collect** from each tribe **silver** shekels that had the value of fifty gold shekels in weight, so that the value of the final sum was equal to **six hundred gold** shekels.

LANGUAGE

Turbal – טוּרְבָּל: Apparently from the Greek τρίβολος, *tribolos*. Among its meanings is: Sledge or threshing machine. In essence, it is a heavy wooden board that contains notches or spikes on its underside so that when it is dragged by an animal over grain on the threshing floor, the act of threshing, i.e., the separation of the grain kernels from the stalks, takes place.

Threshing board

Serrated board [*kurkesa*] – קַרְקְסָא: Apparently from the Greek κίρκος, *kirkos*; or κρίκος, *krikos*, meaning circle, circular object, or ring. Among its meanings is: A wheel used for threshing.

Wheeled threshing board from the mishnaic period

NOTES

The cattle and the wood and the site of the altar for fifty shekels – **בָּקָר וְעֵצִים וּמְקוֹם מִזְבֵּחַ בַּחֲמִשִּׁים**: According to the standard version of the text, there is no difference between the opinion of Abba Yosei ben Dostai and that of Rabbi Elazar ben Shammua. Rashi suggests that this version is erroneous and that the text should follow the version in the *Sifrei*, according to which, in the opinion of Rabbi Elazar ben Shammua, the site of the altar was included in the six hundred shekels; only the cattle, their instruments and the threshing instruments were purchased for fifty shekels. He interprets the verses as comprising two separate clauses: "So David bought the threshing floor and the oxen for fifty shekels of silver" (II Samuel 24:24), to mean that only the cattle and its accessories were purchased for fifty shekels, while the threshing floor was purchased for six hundred shekels, as stated in Chronicles. This is the explanation given by Rabbeinu Ḥananel as well.

״קָדָשִׁים קַלִּים נֶאֱכָלִים [בְּכָל מַחֲנֵה יִשְׂרָאֵל]״. אָמַר רַב הוּנָא: בְּכָל מְקוֹמוֹת יִשְׂרָאֵל, אֲבָל מַחֲנֶה לָא הֲוֵי.

§ The mishna teaches that once the Tabernacle was established in the wilderness, **offerings of lesser sanctity** were **eaten throughout the camp of Israel. Rav Huna says:** This means that offerings of lesser sanctity were eaten **in any of the places** that **an Israelite** would be found. **But there was no** actual **camp,**[N] outside of which it was prohibited to eat the offerings.

אֵיתִיבֵיהּ רַב נַחְמָן לְרַב הוּנָא: וּמַחֲנוֹת בַּמִּדְבָּר לָא הֲוַאי? וְהָא תַּנְיָא: כְּשֵׁם שֶׁמַּחֲנֶה בַּמִּדְבָּר כָּךְ מַחֲנֶה בִּירוּשָׁלַיִם; מִירוּשָׁלַיִם לְהַר הַבַּיִת – מַחֲנֵה יִשְׂרָאֵל, מֵהַר הַבַּיִת לְשַׁעַר נִקָּנוֹר – מַחֲנֵה לְוִיָּה,

Rav Naḥman raised an objection to Rav Huna: And were there not camps when the Jews were **in the wilderness?**[H] **But isn't it taught** in a *baraita* (see *Tosefta, Kelim Bava Kamma* 1:12): **Just as** there was **a camp in the wilderness** that was divided into different sections, with each section having particular *halakhot* pertaining to the consumption of offerings and to the ritually impure individuals who were prohibited from entering there, **so too,** there is a corresponding **camp in Jerusalem:** The area **from** the walls of **Jerusalem to the Temple Mount** has the status of **the Israelite camp.** The area **from the Temple Mount to Nicanor's Gate** at the entrance to the Temple courtyard has the status of **the Levite camp.**

מִכָּאן וְאֵילָךְ – מַחֲנֵה שְׁכִינָה, וְהֵן הֵן קְלָעִים שֶׁבַּמִּדְבָּר!

From that point **onward,** i.e., from the entrance to the Temple courtyard, the area has the status of **the camp of the Divine Presence; and** the Temple courtyard has the same status as the area within **the curtains** surrounding the courtyard of the Tabernacle **in the wilderness.**

אֶלָּא אֵימָא: בְּכָל מָקוֹם מַחֲנֵה יִשְׂרָאֵל. פְּשִׁיטָא! מַהוּ דְּתֵימָא: אִיפְּסְלוּ בְּיוֹצֵא, קָא מַשְׁמַע לָן.

The Gemara replies: **Rather, say** that Rav Huna meant that when the Tabernacle was in the wilderness, offerings of lesser sanctity could be consumed **wherever the Israelite camp** was located.[N] The Gemara asks: Isn't that **obvious?** Wherever the Jews were located in the wilderness was where the Israelite camp was. The Gemara responds: **Lest you say** that during the periods of travel between encampments the offerings were taken outside the Israelite camp, and **were** thereby **disqualified due to** the meat's **leaving** the area within the partitions, Rav Huna **teaches us** that the meat is not disqualified.

וְאֵימָא הָכִי נַמִּי! אָמַר קְרָא: ״וְנָסַע אֹהֶל מוֹעֵד״ אַף עַל פִּי שֶׁנָּסַע – אֹהֶל מוֹעֵד הוּא.

The Gemara asks: **But** why not **say** that this is **indeed so,** i.e., that the meat is disqualified because it left the camp? The Gemara answers that **the verse states: "Then the Tent of Meeting,** with the camp of the Levites, **shall travel** in the midst of the camps; as they encamp, so shall they travel" (Numbers 2:17), which indicates that **although it traveled** from its place **it is** still **the Tent of Meeting.**[N] Similarly, the Israelite camp retains its status even while traveling.

HALAKHA

Camps in the wilderness – מַחֲנוֹת בַּמִּדְבָּר: There were three camps in the wilderness: The Israelite camp; the Levite camp; and the camp of the Divine Presence, which was located from the entrance of the courtyard of the Tent of Meeting and inward. In the time of the Temple there was a corresponding division: The area from the entrance to Jerusalem until the Temple Mount had the status of the Israelite camp, the area from the entrance of the Temple Mount until the entrance to the Temple courtyard, i.e., Nicanor's gate, had the status of the Levite camp, and the area from the entrance of the Temple courtyard and inward had the status of the camp of the Divine Presence. In addition, the women's courtyard and the rampart had additional elevated sanctity in the Temple (Rambam *Sefer Avoda, Hilkhot Beit HaBeḥira* 7:11; see 7:16–17).

NOTES

But there was no actual camp – אֲבָל מַחֲנֵה יִשְׂרָאֵל לָא הֲוֵי: According to Rashi, this means that an Israelite who left the camp was still permitted to consume the meat of offerings of lesser sanctity. Rabbeinu Ḥananel interprets this in the opposite manner: With regard to the consumption of offerings, there was no Israelite camp, only a Levite camp and the camp of the Divine Presence, and offerings of lesser sanctity could be consumed only in the Levite camp.

Say they could be consumed wherever the Israelite camp was located – אֵימָא בְּכָל מָקוֹם מַחֲנֵה יִשְׂרָאֵל: Rashi interprets this to mean that the offerings were not disqualified during their periods of travel, although they did not actually consume offerings while traveling. According to this interpretation, the phrase: Wherever the Israelite camp was located, means: Wherever the Israelites encamped, since it was only at that point that they were permitted to consume offerings. *Tosafot* hold that the Gemara indicates earlier (61b) that offerings of lesser sanctity could be consumed during periods of travel. This appears to be the opinion of Rabbeinu Ḥananel as well. Rashi there interprets the Gemara differently from *Tosafot*.

Although it traveled from its place it is still the Tent of Meeting – אַף עַל פִּי שֶׁנָּסַע אֹהֶל מוֹעֵד הוּא: The same is true of the entire camp of the Divine Presence: Anything that had initially been within the curtains, e.g., the shewbread, was not disqualified due to having left the designated area (Rid, citing *Menaḥot* 95a). The same *halakha* applies to the Israelite camp as well. This explanation is in accordance with Rashi's opinion (61a and here), that it was permitted to eat offerings of the most sacred order after the Tabernacle and curtains were dismantled prior to traveling but while the altar was still standing, as well as during the next encampment after the Tabernacle was reassembled and the curtains erected. In both cases, the offerings were not considered disqualified due to having left the designated area.

Tosafot (here and *Menaḥot* 95a) hold that the conclusion of the discussion in *Menaḥot* indicates that the Gemara here is referring only to offerings of lesser sanctity in the Israelite camp, not the camp of the Divine Presence, which existed only when a partition was present. Therefore, even after encampment, with regard to offerings of the most sacred order, only new offerings were permitted to be eaten, and only after the curtains surrounding the Tabernacle courtyard were erected. Any shewbread that did not remain on the Table during the time of travel was disqualified due to having left the designated area. The statement: Although it traveled from its place it is still the Tent of Meeting, refers, as the Gemara in *Menaḥot* notes, to the position of the tribes, teaching that the place of the Tent of Meeting constituted the center of the camp of Israel, and the tribes all remained in their positions relative to it during the time of travel as well. With regard to the camp of the Divine Presence, a partition was necessary, which was lacking during their travel.

תַּנְיָא, רַבִּי שִׁמְעוֹן בֶּן יוֹחַאי אוֹמֵר: עוֹד אַחֶרֶת הָיְתָה, וְחֵיל עֶזְרַת נָשִׁים הִיא, וְלֹא הָיוּ עוֹנְשִׁין עָלֶיהָ. וּבְשִׁילֹה לֹא הָיוּ אֶלָּא שְׁנֵי מַחֲנוֹת בִּלְבָד.

§ With regard to the division of Jerusalem into three camps, **it is taught** in a *baraita* that **Rabbi Shimon ben Yoḥai says: There was an additional** camp in Jerusalem, within the area of the Temple Mount, **and it** was **the rampart of the women's courtyard.**[N] The Sages rendered it prohibited for certain ritually impure individuals to enter that area, **but they would not punish** them **for** entering **it,** as by Torah law it does not constitute a distinct section of the Temple Mount but has the status of the Levite camp. The *baraita* adds: **And** when the Tabernacle was **in Shiloh there were only two camps.**

הֵי מִינַּיְיהוּ לָא הֲוָה? אָמַר רַבָּה: מִסְתַּבְּרָא דְּמַחֲנֵה לְוִיָּה הֲוַאי. דְּאִי סָלְקָא דַּעְתָּךְ מַחֲנֵה לְוִיָּה לָא הֲוַאי,

The Gemara asks: **Which of** the three camps that were present in the wilderness **was not** present in Shiloh? **Rabba said: It stands to reason that the Levite camp was** present, but the Israelite camp was not. **As, if it enters your mind to say** that **the Levite camp was not** present in Shiloh,

NOTES

There was an additional camp in Jerusalem and it was the rampart of the women's courtyard – עוֹד אַחֶרֶת הָיְתָה וְחֵיל עֶזְרַת נָשִׁים הִיא: This version of the text in the Gemara appears to be somewhat difficult. Rashi, who interprets the word additional as meaning an additional camp, probably had a version that read: And it was the women's courtyard, as the singular language indicates there is only one camp mentioned in the *baraita*; this is the version of the *Shita Mekubbetzet* as well. This interpretation understands the Gemara as follows: There is a distinction between the city of Jerusalem, i.e., the Israelite camp, and the Temple Mount, i.e., the Levite camp, in that it is prohibited for a *zav*, a *zava*, a menstruating woman, and a woman who has recently given birth to enter the Temple Mount while in a state of ritual impurity, just as it was prohibited for them to enter the Levite camp in the wilderness. The Sages demarcated additional areas within the Temple Mount, one of which was the women's courtyard, into which, according to tradition, Jehoshaphat and his court decreed that one who immersed on that day may not enter it, despite the fact that by Torah law they were permitted to do so (see *Kelim* 1:8).

A different version of the text of the Gemara reads: There was an additional camp in Jerusalem, and it was the rampart and the women's courtyard. This is in accordance with the version in the *Tosefta* (*Kelim Bava Kamma* 1:8): Rabbi Shimon says: The rampart and the women's courtyard have an elevated level of stringency within the Temple. This version refers to the rampart as well, which was another small area that was surrounded by a wall. That wall was the latticed gate mentioned in the Mishna (see *Middot* 2:3), and it was forbidden for gentiles and those who contracted impurity from a corpse to enter that area. According to this version, the word: Additional, refers in the singular to the elevated level of stringency associated with those two areas (see Rabbeinu Ḥananel).

Perek **XIV**
Daf **117** Amud **a**

נִמְצְאוּ זָבִין וּטְמֵאֵי מֵתִים מִשְׁתַּלְּחִין חוּץ לְמַחֲנֶה אַחַת, וְהַתּוֹרָה אָמְרָה: ״וְלֹא יְטַמְּאוּ אֶת מַחֲנֵיהֶם״

it would consequently be **found** that both ***zavim* and** those who are **ritually impure** from impurity imparted by **a corpse are sent out of one camp,** i.e., the camp of the Divine Presence, and both are permitted in the Israelite camp. **But the Torah said** with regard to sending the ritually impure out of the camp: "Outside the camp you shall put them; **that they will not defile their camps**" (Numbers 5:3).

תֵּן מַחֲנֶה לָזֶה וּמַחֲנֶה לָזֶה.

The use of the plural "camps" indicates: **Give** a specific **camp to this** group, i.e., those who are ritually impure from impurity imparted by a corpse, who may enter the Levite camp but are forbidden to enter the camp of the Divine Presence, **and** give a specific **camp to this** group, i.e., those who are *zavim,* who may enter the Israelite camp but are forbidden to enter the camp of the Divine presence or the Levite camp. If there were no Levite camp in Shiloh, it would follow that both a *zav* and one who is ritually impure from the impurity imparted by a corpse are sent out of only one camp, and there is no distinction between them.

אֲמַר לֵיהּ רָבָא: אֶלָּא מַאי, מַחֲנֵה יִשְׂרָאֵל לָא הֲוַאי? נִמְצְאוּ זָבִין וּמְצוֹרָעִין מִשְׁתַּלְּחִין לְמָקוֹם אֶחָד, וְהַתּוֹרָה אָמְרָה: ״בָּדָד יֵשֵׁב״ – שֶׁלֹּא יֵשֵׁב טָמֵא אַחֵר עִמּוֹ!

Rava said to him: Rather, what would you say instead? Would you say that **the Israelite camp was not** present in Shiloh? If so, it would be **found** that ***zavim* and lepers are** both **sent to one place,** i.e., outside the Levite camp. **But the Torah said** with regard to the leper: **"He shall dwell alone;** outside the camp shall his dwelling be" (Leviticus 13:46). The word "alone" teaches **that another ritually impure person should not dwell with him.**

אלא: לעולם כולהו תלתא הוו, ומאי לא היו אלא שתי מחנות – לקליטה. מכלל דבמדבר הואי קלטה מחנה לויה?

Rather, it must be that **actually, all three** camps **were** present in Shiloh, **and what** is the meaning of that which was taught with regard to Shiloh: **There were only two camps? It is with regard to** the fact that the Levite camp did not provide **refuge**[B] to one who unintentionally killed another. The Gemara asks: **By inference,** does this mean **that in the wilderness the Levite camp did provide refuge** to those who unintentionally killed others?

אין, והא תניא: "ושמתי לך מקום" – בחייך, "מקום" – מקומך, "אשר ינוס שמה" – מלמד שמגלין במדבר. להיכן גולין – למחנה לויה.

The Gemara replies: **Yes, and so it is taught** in a *baraita* with regard to the verse concerning the cities of refuge. The verse states: "And one who did not lie in wait… **and I will appoint for you a place** where he may flee" (Exodus 21:13). The phrase "I will appoint for you" teaches that God said to Moses: There will be a place that provides refuge for unintentional murderers even **during your lifetime.**[N] The term **"a place"** means that it will be from **your place,**[N] meaning the Levite camp served as the place that provided refuge in the wilderness. **"Where he may flee" teaches that** the Jews **would exile** unintentional murderers **in the wilderness** as well, before they entered the land. **To where did they exile** unintentional murderers when they were in the wilderness? They exiled them **to the Levite camp,** which provided refuge.

מכאן אמרו: בן לוי שהרג – גולה מפלך לפלך, ואם גלה לפלכו – פלכו קולטו.

From here the Sages **said: A Levite who killed** unintentionally[H] **is exiled from** one Levite **city to** another Levite **city. And if he was exiled to** another area within **his city, he is admitted to his city,**[N] i.e., it provides him with refuge.

מאי קרא? אמר רב אחא בריה דרב איקא: "כי בעיר מקלטו ישב" – עיר שקלטתו כבר.

The Gemara asks: **What is the verse** from which the principle is derived that one who was already exiled to a city of refuge and who then killed another person is exiled to another area in that same city? **Rav Aḥa, son of Rav Ika, says** that the verse: **"For in his city of refuge he shall dwell"** (Numbers 35:28), indicates that he can be exiled to **a city in which he was already admitted,** as the verse is referring to it as his city, and he shall continue to reside there.

"באו לגלגל". תנו רבנן: כל נידר ונידב היה קרב בבמה, שאין נידר ונידב – אין קרב בבמה. מנחה ונזירות קריבין בבמה, דברי רבי מאיר. וחכמים אומרים: לא קרבו יחיד אלא עולות ושלמים בלבד.

§ The mishna teaches that when the Jewish people **arrived at Gilgal** private altars were permitted. The Gemara elaborates: **The Sages taught** in a *baraita*: **Any** offering that was brought due to **a vow,**[N] **or contributed** voluntarily, **was sacrificed on** a private **altar;** and **any** offering **that is neither** brought due to **a vow nor contributed** voluntarily, but rather is compulsory, was **not sacrificed on** a private **altar.** Therefore, **a meal offering,** which is generally brought voluntarily, **and** offerings of **a nazirite,** which have the status of vow offerings as no one is compelled to become a nazirite, were **sacrificed upon** a private **altar.** This is **the statement of Rabbi Meir. And the Rabbis say: Only burnt offerings and peace offerings were sacrificed** upon **a private** altar, not meal offerings or offerings of a nazirite.

BACKGROUND

City of refuge – עיר מקלט: The Torah prescribes the mitzva of establishing cities of refuge to protect those who unwittingly kill another (see Numbers 35:10–34 and Deuteronomy 19:1–13). The Sages explain that anyone who causes another's death must flee to a city of refuge. From there, he is taken to his trial. If he is convicted of intentional murder, he is executed. If the victim's death was a complete accident, the killer is released. If the court decides that he is guilty of negligent manslaughter, he must return to the city of refuge and remain there throughout the lifetime of the High Priest. If he leaves the city of refuge for any reason, he may be killed by the blood redeemer, who is the closest relative of the victim. After the death of the High Priest, he may return to his own city.

The Torah mandates the establishment of six cities of refuge, three west of the Jordan River and three east of the Jordan. The six cities were among the forty-eight cities given to the Levites. The Sages explain that the other forty-two cities given to the Levites (see Numbers 35:2–8) also served as cities of refuge.

HALAKHA

A Levite who killed unintentionally – בן לוי שהרג: A Levite who kills unintentionally while in his own Levite city, which is a city of refuge, is exiled to another city. If he killed outside a Levite city and fled to his own city, his city provides refuge, since all Levite cities provide refuge (Rambam *Sefer Nezikin, Hilkhot Rotze'aḥ UShmirat HaNefesh* 7:5, 8:9).

NOTES

And I will appoint for you a place during your lifetime – ושמתי לך מקום בחייך: Rashi explains that this refers to the cities of refuge that Moses established in his lifetime, as stated in the verse: "Then Moses separated three cities beyond the Jordan" (Deuteronomy 4:41). The Ritva on tractate *Makkot* (12b) maintains that it is more reasonable to interpret that statement in the context of the Gemara's discussion, i.e., that the *halakhot* of exile were in effect in the Levite camp in the wilderness.

A place, your place – מקום מקומך: Rashi's version of the text of the Gemara apparently read: For you a place, your place. In other words, the place referred to by the verse is your place, i.e., the Levite camp. This serves as the source for the *halakha* that all Levite cities in Eretz Yisrael provide refuge.

There are also other versions of the text (see *Makkot* 12b) which indicate not only that the towns provide refuge but also that Levites can be exiled, and that the Levite cities provide refuge to them as well. It is with regard to this that the Gemara says: From here the Sages said that a Levite who killed unintentionally is exiled from one Levite city to another Levite city. The Ritva on tractate *Makkot* suggests that according to Rashi, the words: From here the Sages said, refer to the latter part of the sentence, which states that if a Levite was exiled to his own city, his city provides refuge, as the Levite camp provided refuge in the wilderness despite the fact that the Levites were all located there.

And if he was exiled to his city he is admitted to his city – ואם גלה לפלכו פלכו קולטו: *Tosafot* note that from the manner in which this *halakha* is formulated, it seems that a Levite should be exiled to a different city *ab initio*, and it is only if he stayed within his city that he is allowed to remain there. Alternatively, it is merely a recommendation that the Levite be exiled to another city, so that he will be afforded a greater range of area in which he can reside (see *Makkot* 12b). The Ritva, citing Rashi, explains that the case discussed in the Gemara is one of a Levite who was already in exile for an unintentional killing, who then killed unintentionally again within his city of exile (see *Sefat Emet*).

Any offering that was brought due to a vow, etc. – כל נידר וכו׳: The mishna in tractate *Kinnim* (1:1) explains the distinction between a vow offering and a voluntary offering: In the case of a vow offering, one states: It is incumbent upon me to bring an offering, and the donor bears financial responsibility for the loss or death of the animal. In the case of a voluntary offering, one states: It is incumbent upon me to bring this animal as an offering. In that case, if the animal dies or is stolen the donor is no longer obligated to bring an offering.

רַבִּי יְהוּדָה אוֹמֵר: כׇּל שֶׁהַצִּבּוּר וְהַיָּחִיד מַקְרִיבִין בְּאֹהֶל מוֹעֵד שֶׁבַּמִּדְבָּר – מַקְרִיבִין בְּאֹהֶל מוֹעֵד שֶׁבְּגִלְגָּל. מַה בֵּין אֹהֶל מוֹעֵד שֶׁבַּמִּדְבָּר לְבֵין אֹהֶל מוֹעֵד שֶׁבְּגִלְגָּל? אֹהֶל מוֹעֵד שֶׁבַּמִּדְבָּר – לֹא הָיוּ בָּמוֹת מוּתָּרוֹת, אֹהֶל מוֹעֵד שֶׁבְּגִלְגָּל – הָיוּ הַבָּמוֹת מוּתָּרוֹת. וּבָמָתוֹ שֶׁבְּרֹאשׁ גַּגּוֹ לֹא הָיָה מַקְרִיב עָלֶיהָ אֶלָּא עוֹלָה וּשְׁלָמִים.

Rabbi Yehuda says: Any offering **that the public or an individual** could **sacrifice**[N] **in the Tent of Meeting in the wilderness** could also be **sacrificed in the Tent of Meeting in Gilgal. What,** then, is the difference **between the Tent of Meeting in the wilderness and the Tent of Meeting in Gilgal?** During the period of **the Tent of Meeting in the wilderness** private **altars were not permitted** and offerings could be sacrificed only in the Tabernacle, while during the period of **the Tent of Meeting in Gilgal** private **altars were permitted. But** even if one desired to sacrifice an offering upon **his** private **altar on his roof,** he could still **sacrifice upon it only burnt offerings and peace offerings.**

וַחֲכָמִים אוֹמְרִים: כׇּל שֶׁהַצִּבּוּר מַקְרִיבִין בְּאֹהֶל מוֹעֵד שֶׁבַּמִּדְבָּר – מַקְרִיבִין בְּאֹהֶל מוֹעֵד שֶׁבְּגִלְגָּל, וְכָאן וְכָאן לֹא קָרְבוּ יָחִיד אֶלָּא עוֹלָה וּשְׁלָמִים בִּלְבָד. רַבִּי שִׁמְעוֹן אוֹמֵר: אַף צִבּוּר לֹא הִקְרִיבוּ אֶלָּא פְּסָחִים

And the Rabbis say: Any offering **that the public** could **sacrifice in the Tent of Meeting in the wilderness** could also be **sacrificed in the Tent of Meeting in Gilgal, and here,** in the Tabernacle in Gilgal, **and there,** upon private altars, **only burnt offerings and peace offerings were sacrificed** for an **individual. Rabbi Shimon says:** Even the **public** did not sacrifice every type of offering in the Tent of Meeting in Gilgal; they **sacrificed only Paschal offerings**

NOTES

Any offering that the public or an individual could sacrifice – כׇּל שֶׁהַצִּבּוּר וְהַיָּחִיד מַקְרִיבִין: Based on Rabbi Yehuda's statement, which does not distinguish between the public and an individual with regard to a public altar, it may be inferred that according to the opinion of Rabbi Meir and the Rabbis, the distinction between individual offerings and communal ones extends to a great public altar as well: The public sacrifices obligatory offerings upon a great public altar, while an individual may sacrifice upon it only vow offerings and gift offerings. The Paschal offering was sacrificed in Gilgal despite the fact that it is an individual obligation, both because the entire Jewish people sacrifice it on the same day and because it is eaten in groups; this confers upon it the status of a communal offering (Rashi).

Perek **XIV**
Daf **117** Amud **b**

וְחוֹבוֹת שֶׁקָּבוּעַ לָהֶן זְמַן.

and compulsory public offerings **that have a set time**[N] to be sacrificed, e.g., daily offerings and additional offerings. Public offerings that do not have a set time were not sacrificed upon the great public altar in Gilgal.

מַאי טַעְמָא דְּרַבִּי מֵאִיר? דְּאָמַר קְרָא: ״לֹא תַעֲשׂוּן כְּכֹל אֲשֶׁר אֲנַחְנוּ עֹשִׂים פֹּה הַיּוֹם״,

§ The Gemara explains the various opinions cited in the *baraita*: **What is the reason** for the opinion **of Rabbi Meir** that only vow offerings and gift offerings, such as nazirite offerings and meal offerings, were sacrificed upon a private altar during the period of Gilgal? It is **as the verse states: "You shall not do all that we do**[N] **here this day,** every man whatsoever is fitting in his own eyes. For you have not as yet come to the rest and to the inheritance" (Deuteronomy 12:8–9).

אָמַר לָהֶן מֹשֶׁה לְיִשְׂרָאֵל: כִּי עַיְילִיתוּ לָאָרֶץ, יְשָׁרוֹת תַּקְרִיבוּ, חוֹבוֹת לֹא תַּקְרִיבוּ; מְנָחוֹת וּנְזִירוּת יְשָׁרוֹת נִינְהוּ.

Moses said the following **to the Jewish people: When you enter Eretz** Yisrael but have not yet arrived at Shiloh or Jerusalem and are therefore permitted to sacrifice upon private altars, you may not sacrifice whatever has been sacrificed in the wilderness, i.e., both obligatory offerings and gift offerings. Rather, the phrase "every man whatsoever is fitting [*hayashar*] in his own eyes," means that **fitting** offerings [*yesharot*], i.e., offerings that are fitting in one's eyes and are brought due to one's own benevolence, **you may sacrifice,** but **you may not sacrifice obligatory** offerings. **Meal offerings and** offerings of **a nazirite are** included in the category of **fitting** offerings: Meal offerings are sacrificed as vow offerings or gift offerings while offerings of a nazirite are considered a vow offering, as becoming a nazirite is not compulsory.

NOTES

And compulsory public offerings that have a set time – וְחוֹבוֹת שֶׁקָּבוּעַ לָהֶן זְמַן: Rashi explains that these words exclude communal sin offerings, e.g., the bull for an unintentional communal sin, which are not bound to a particular date.

You shall not do all that we do, etc. – לֹא תַעֲשׂוּן כְּכֹל אֲשֶׁר אֲנַחְנוּ עֹשִׂים וכו׳: Although the disagreement in the *baraita* between Rabbi Meir and the Rabbis concerns private altars, Rashi comments that the interpretation of the verse that is cited here pertains not only to actual private altars but to the period in which those altars were permitted, when an individual was not even allowed to sacrifice compulsory offerings on a great public altar. This is evident from the fact that the verse does not distinguish between types of altars. On the contrary, in its most straightforward sense the verse appears to refer to the great public altar that took the place of the altar in the Tabernacle in the wilderness, as it is stated: "That we do here this day," at which point there were no other public or private altars.

In *Torat Kohanim* Rabbi Meir derives this *halakha* from a different verse, which pertains to offerings that are slaughtered outside the Temple: "To the end that the children of Israel may bring their offerings, which they sacrifice in the open field, that they may bring them to the Lord, to the entrance of the Tent of Meeting, to the priest, and sacrifice them for sacrifices of peace offerings to the Lord" (Leviticus 17:5). From the words: "Which they sacrifice in the open field," the Sages infer (see 106a) that the verse speaks of offerings that were consecrated at a time that private altars were permitted in order that the offerings could be sacrificed during that time. From the fact that peace offerings were mentioned in that context, Rabbi Meir derives that just as peace offerings are permitted during a period when private altars are permitted, so too are any vowed or voluntarily contributed offerings.

וְרַבָּנַן? אֵין מִנְחָה בְּבָמָה, נְזִירוּת – חוֹבוֹת נִינְהוּ.

And what is the reason that **the Rabbis** disagree with Rabbi Meir and state that meal offerings and offerings of a nazirite were not sacrificed on a private altar? They hold that **a meal offering is not** ever sacrificed **upon** a private **altar**[N] and that offerings of a **nazirite are** considered **compulsory.** While one assumes the status of a nazirite voluntarily, once he has become a nazirite he is required to bring the offering.

אָמַר שְׁמוּאֵל: מַחֲלוֹקֶת בְּחַטָּאת וְאָשָׁם, אֲבָל בְּעוֹלוֹת וּשְׁלָמִים – דִּבְרֵי הַכֹּל יְשָׁרוֹת נִינְהוּ, וְקָרְבִי.

With regard to this, **Shmuel says** that **the disagreement** between Rabbi Meir and the Rabbis pertains only **to the sin offering and the guilt offering**[N] brought by the nazirite. **But with regard to the burnt offering and the peace offering** that the nazirite brings, **all agree** that **they are** considered offerings that one deems **fitting** to sacrifice **and are** therefore **sacrificed** on a private altar.

מוֹתִיב רַבָּה: חָזֶה וָשׁוֹק וּתְרוּמַת לַחְמֵי תוֹדָה – נוֹהֲגִין בְּבָמָה גְּדוֹלָה וְאֵין נוֹהֲגִין בְּבָמָה קְטַנָּה, וְאִילּוּ הַזְּרוֹעַ בְּשֵׁלָה שַׁיְּירָהּ;

Rabba raises an objection from a *baraita*: The *halakha* of **the breast and thigh** portions of peace offerings, which are given to the priests (see Leviticus 7:34), **and** the *halakha* of **the *teruma* of the loaves of the thanks offering**, i.e., the bread that was given to the priests from each of the four types of loaves that were brought with the thanks offering (see Leviticus 7:14), **apply** only **with regard to a great** public **altar, and do not apply with regard to a small** private **altar.**[N] Rabba comments: **By contrast,** another of the priestly gifts, **the cooked foreleg** of the nazirite's ram (see Numbers 6:19–20) was **omitted** by the *tanna*.

אִי אָמְרַתְּ בִּשְׁלָמָא בְּעוֹלָה וּשְׁלָמִים פְּלִיגִי, הָא מַנִּי? רַבָּנַן הִיא. אֶלָּא אִי אָמְרַתְּ בְּחַטָּאת וְאָשָׁם פְּלִיגִי, הָא מַנִּי?

Rabba notes: **Granted, if you say** that Rabbi Meir and the Rabbis **disagree** even **with regard to** whether **a burnt offering and peace offering** of a nazirite may be sacrificed upon a private altar, then in accordance with **whose** opinion **is this** *baraita* that omits the nazirite's ram? It **is** in accordance with the opinion of **the Rabbis,** who hold that the peace offering of the nazirite was not sacrificed upon a private altar. **But if you say** that **they disagree** only **with regard to a sin offering and guilt offering,** while the Rabbis agree that the peace offering and burnt offering of a nazirite were sacrificed on a private altar, then in accordance with **whose** opinion **is this** *baraita*?

אֶלָּא אִי אִיתְּמַר הָכִי אִיתְּמַר, אֲמַר שְׁמוּאֵל: מַחֲלוֹקֶת בְּעוֹלָה וּשְׁלָמִים, אֲבָל בְּחַטָּאת וְאָשָׁם – דִּבְרֵי הַכֹּל חוֹבוֹת נִינְהוּ, וְלָא קָרְבִי.

Rather, if this **was stated,** it **was stated like this: Shmuel said** that the **disagreement** between Rabbi Meir and the Rabbis pertains only **to the burnt offering and peace offering** that were brought by the nazirite. **But with regard to the sin offering and guilt offering, all agree that they are compulsory, and** even according to the opinion of Rabbi Meir they **are not sacrificed** upon a private altar.

אָמַר מָר: וַחֲכָמִים אוֹמְרִים: כָּל שֶׁהַצִּבּוּר מַקְרִיבִין בְּאֹהֶל וכו׳.

§ The Gemara continues to clarify the opinions in the *baraita*: **The Master,** i.e., Rabbi Yehuda, **said** that any offering that the public or an individual could sacrifice in the Tent of Meeting in the wilderness, including vow offerings, gift offerings, and compulsory offerings, could also be sacrificed in the Tent of Meeting in Gilgal. It was only on a private altar that the individual was limited to sacrificing burnt offerings and peace offerings. **And the Rabbis say:** Any offering **that the public** could **sacrifice in the Tent** of Meeting in the wilderness could also be sacrificed in the Tent of Meeting in Gilgal. An individual could sacrifice only burnt offerings and peace offerings, whether on a great public altar or on a private altar.

מַאי טַעֲמַיְיהוּ דְּרַבָּנַן? אָמַר קְרָא: "אִישׁ הַיָּשָׁר בְּעֵינָיו יַעֲשֶׂה", אִישׁ – יְשָׁרוֹת הוּא דְּלִיקְרוּב, חוֹבוֹת לָא לִיקְרוּב, וְצִבּוּר – אֲפִילּוּ חוֹבוֹת לִיקְרוּב.

The Gemara clarifies the two opinions: **What is the reason** for the opinion **of the Rabbis** that only the public could sacrifice compulsory offerings on a great public altar? **The verse states** with regard to the period in which private altars were permitted: "You shall not do all that we do here this day, every **man whatsoever is fitting in his own eyes**" (Deuteronomy 12:8). This indicates that it is **"a man,"** i.e., an individual, **who may sacrifice only** offerings that he deems **"fitting,"** i.e., voluntary offerings, but **may not sacrifice compulsory** offerings. **But the public may sacrifice even compulsory** offerings.

NOTES

A meal offering is not ever sacrificed upon a private altar – אֵין מִנְחָה בְּבָמָה: This is derived (see 119b) from the same verse that serves as the source for Rabbi Meir's opinion as cited in *Torat Kohanim*: "To the end that the children of Israel may bring their offerings, which they sacrifice in the open field, that they may bring them to the Lord, to the entrance of the Tent of Meeting, to the priest, and sacrifice them for sacrifices of peace offerings to the Lord" (Leviticus 17:5). The Rabbis infer from the words: "Which they sacrifice [*zovehim*]," that this pertains only to animal offerings, not to bird offerings or meal offerings, for which the term *zevah* is not generally used; that term connotes slaughtering. This *halakha* can also be derived from the fact that the verse discusses peace offerings, which are brought only from animals (see the commentary of Rabbeinu Hillel on *Torat Kohanim*). Additionally, Rashi on 69a derives this *halakha* from the use of the word "sacrifices" in the context of the revelation at Sinai (Exodus 24:5), which was before the construction of the Tabernacle.

The disagreement pertains only to the sin offering and the guilt offering – מַחֲלוֹקֶת בְּחַטָּאת וְאָשָׁם: A nazirite who has completed his term of naziriteship is obligated to bring a burnt offering, a sin offering, and a peace offering (see Numbers 6:14). By contrast, a nazirite who has become ritually impure brings a ram as a guilt offering, a bird for a burnt offering, and another bird for a sin offering (see Numbers 6:10–12).

The breast and thigh portions of peace offerings and the *teruma* of the loaves of the thanks offering…do not apply with regard to a small private altar – חָזֶה וָשׁוֹק וּתְרוּמַת לַחְמֵי תוֹדָה...אֵין נוֹהֲגִין בְּבָמָה קְטַנָּה: Rashi explains, citing 119b, that this is due to the Torah's mandate that these offerings be waved "before the Lord," and a private altar is not considered to be "before the Lord."

וְרַבִּי יְהוּדָה אָמַר לָךְ: כִּי כְּתִיב "הַיָּשָׁר" – בְּעֵינָיו הוּא דִּכְתִיב, אֲבָל בְּבָמָה גְּדוֹלָה – אֲפִילּוּ חוֹבוֹת נָמֵי לִיקְרוּב.

And Rabbi Yehuda, who holds that an individual may also sacrifice compulsory offerings on a great public altar, could have **said to you** that **when** the phrase "whatsoever **is fitting" is written,** indicating that individuals may sacrifice only vow offerings and gift offerings, **it is** with regard to **"in his own eyes" that it is written.** In other words, it is referring to a location that is fitting in his eyes for sacrifice, i.e., a private altar. **But on a great** public **altar, even compulsory** offerings **may be sacrificed.**

אֶלָּא הָא כְּתִיב "אִישׁ", לָאו לְמֵימְרָא דְּאִישׁ יְשָׁרוֹת הוּא דְּלִיקְרוּב, הָא חוֹבוֹת לָא לִיקְרוּב? כִּי כְּתִיב "אִישׁ" – לְהַכְשִׁיר אֶת הַזָּר.

The Gemara asks: **But** even if that derivation is correct, **isn't "man" written** in that verse? **Isn't that to say that** with regard to **"a man,"** i.e., an individual, **only** offerings that one deems **fitting** to sacrifice **may be sacrificed, but compulsory** offerings **may not be sacrificed?** The Gemara replies: **When "man" is written** in this verse, it is **to qualify a non-priest** to perform the sacrificial service on a private altar.

זָר, מִ"וְזָרַק הַכֹּהֵן אֶת הַדָּם עַל מִזְבַּח ה'" נָפְקָא!

The Gemara challenges: But the fact that **a non-priest** is qualified to perform the sacrificial service on a private altar is **derived from** the verse: **"And the priest shall dash the blood against the altar of the Lord** at the entrance of the Tent of Meeting" (Leviticus 17:6). The verse indicates that service at a great public altar may be performed only by a priest, from which it is inferred that the service on a private altar may be performed by a non-priest as well.

מַהוּ דְּתֵימָא: לִיבָּעֵי קִדּוּשׁ בְּכוֹרוֹת כְּמֵעִיקָּרָא, קָא מַשְׁמַע לַן.

The Gemara replies: **Lest you say** that whereas that verse indicates it is not required that the service on a private altar be performed by a priest, nevertheless **consecration of** the **firstborn is required** for this purpose, **as** was the case **initially,** i.e., before the Tabernacle was constructed. Perhaps the only non-priests who may perform the service on private altars are the firstborn sons. Therefore, the verse states: "Every man whatsoever is fitting in his own eyes," which **teaches us** that with regard to private altars, each person may sacrifice his own offerings.

חֲכָמִים הַיְינוּ תַּנָּא קַמָּא!

§ The Gemara clarifies the opinion of the Rabbis, who disagree with Rabbi Yehuda, by questioning: But the statement of **the Rabbis is** identical to the statement of **the first** ***tanna*****,** i.e., the Rabbis cited at the beginning of the *baraita*, who say that on a private altar an individual sacrificed only burnt offerings and peace offerings. What is the difference between the first *tanna* and the Rabbis?

אָמַר רַב פַּפָּא: קָרְבוּ נְסָכִים בְּמִדְבָּר אִיכָּא בֵּינַיְיהוּ.

Rav Pappa said: The difference **between them** is whether **libations were offered in the wilderness**[N] along with burnt offerings and peace offerings. According to the opinion of the first *tanna*, libations were not offered in the wilderness, nor were they offered in Eretz Yisrael during the period of Gilgal. According to the Rabbis in the latter section of the *baraita*, libations were offered in the wilderness and in Gilgal.

NOTES

The difference between them is whether libations were offered in the wilderness – קָרְבוּ נְסָכִים בְּמִדְבָּר אִיכָּא בֵּינַיְיהוּ: When disagreeing with the opinion of Rabbi Yehuda, the Rabbis state: Any offering that the public could sacrifice in the Tent of Meeting in the wilderness could also be sacrificed in the Tent of Meeting in Gilgal, but there is no similar statement made by the Rabbis when disagreeing with the opinion of Rabbi Meir. In addition, this statement was unnecessary even when responding to Rabbi Yehuda, as it was already made by Rabbi Yehuda himself, and the Rabbis merely add a *halakha* that pertains to an individual. Evidently, the Rabbis' intention in disagreeing with Rabbi Yehuda was to add a type of offering that in their opinion was sacrificed in both the Tabernacle in the wilderness and Gilgal, i.e., libations.

The issue of whether libations were sacrificed in the wilderness is the subject of a dispute between Rabbi Yishmael and Rabbi Akiva (see 111a). The Torah's discussion of libations opens by stating: "Speak to the children of Israel, and say to them: When you come to the land of your habitation, which I give unto you" (Numbers 15:2). Rabbi Yishmael infers from the word "habitation" that libations were not brought with burnt offerings or peace offerings in the wilderness, nor were they brought immediately upon entering Eretz Yisrael. Only once the people were settled and inhabited the land, i.e., after the fourteen years of conquest and division, and the Tabernacle was erected in Shiloh, were libations brought. According to Rabbi Akiva, libations were brought in the Tabernacle in the wilderness. The Torah's statement: "When you come to the land of your habitation," indicates that upon entering the land, libations were offered not only upon a great public altar, i.e., the Tabernacle, but also upon private altars, i.e., altars that are built in the place of an individual's "habitation." This opinion is identical to that of the Rabbis in the *baraita*, although according to this interpretation, the statement: Any offering that the public could sacrifice in the Tent of Meeting, is not precise, as an individual could offer libations upon a private altar. It must, therefore, refer to the period of the Tabernacle in the wilderness and Gilgal, rather than to the location of the offering (see Rashi).

אָמַר מָר: רַבִּי שִׁמְעוֹן אוֹמֵר וכו׳. מַאי טַעְמֵיהּ דְּרַבִּי שִׁמְעוֹן? דִּכְתִיב: ״וַיַּעֲשׂוּ בְנֵי יִשְׂרָאֵל אֶת הַפֶּסַח בַּגִּלְגָּל״;

§ The Master said in the *baraita*: **Rabbi Shimon says** that even the public did not sacrifice all offerings in the Tent of Meeting in Gilgal; they sacrificed only Paschal offerings and compulsory public offerings that have a set time. The Gemara asks: **What is the reason** for the opinion **of Rabbi Shimon? As it is written: "And the children of Israel** encamped **in Gilgal; and they kept the Passover** on the fourteenth day of the month at evening in the plains of Jericho" (Joshua 5:10).

פְּשִׁיטָא! אֶלָּא הָא קָא מַשְׁמַע לָן: דְּחוֹבוֹת כְּעֵין פֶּסַח הוּא דְּקָרֵב, הָא לָאו כְּעֵין פֶּסַח – לָא קָרֵב. וְאִידָךְ?

The Gemara asks: Isn't it **obvious** that they brought the Paschal offering? The Paschal offering is compulsory. **Rather, this** verse **teaches us that** in Gilgal, **only compulsory** offerings **similar to** the **Paschal** offering, i.e., that have a set time, **were sacrificed, but** offerings that are **not similar to the Paschal** offering **were not sacrificed.** The Gemara asks: **And** how does **the other** *tanna*, i.e., the Rabbis who disagree with Rabbi Shimon and hold that during the period of Gilgal other offerings were sacrificed by the public, interpret the verse?

מִיבָּעֵי לֵיהּ לְכִדְרַבִּי יוֹחָנָן. דְּאָמַר רַבִּי יוֹחָנָן מִשּׁוּם רַבִּי בְּנָאָה: עָרֵל מְקַבֵּל הַזָּאָה.

The Gemara responds: **It is necessary for the** *halakha* **that** was taught **by Rabbi Yoḥanan. As Rabbi Yoḥanan says in the name of Rabbi Bena'a:** If **an uncircumcised** Jew contracted ritual impurity from a corpse, he **may receive sprinkling**[HN] of the water containing the ashes of the red heifer on the third and seventh days of his purification, despite the fact that he is uncircumcised. In the time of Joshua, the Jewish people became circumcised after they were purified from impurity imparted by a corpse.

תָּנֵי תַּנָּא קַמֵּיהּ דְּרַב אַדָּא בַּר אַהֲבָה: אֵין בֵּין בָּמָה גְּדוֹלָה לְבָמָה קְטַנָּה אֶלָּא פֶּסַח וְחוֹבוֹת הַקָּבוּעַ לָהֶן זְמַן. אֲמַר לֵיהּ: יָחִיד חוֹבוֹת שֶׁקָּבוּעַ לָהֶן זְמַן מְנָא לֵיהּ?

§ With regard to the Paschal offering and compulsory public offerings that have a set time mentioned by Rabbi Shimon, the Gemara relates that **a** *tanna* **taught** a *baraita* **in the presence of Rav Adda bar Ahava: The difference between a great** public **altar**, e.g., the altar in Gilgal, **and a small** private **altar is only** that the **Paschal offering and compulsory** offerings **that have a set time** may be sacrificed upon a great public altar, but not upon a private altar. Rav Adda bar Ahava **said to him: From where** would **an individual** sacrifice **compulsory** offerings **that have a set time?**[N] There is no such offering brought by an individual. It was therefore unnecessary for the *tanna* to state that this type of offering is not sacrificed on a private altar.

HALAKHA

An uncircumcised Jew may receive sprinkling – עָרֵל מְקַבֵּל הַזָּאָה: An uncircumcised Jew who contracted ritual impurity imparted by a corpse and was sprinkled with the water of purification on the third and seventh days has been purified from the impurity imparted by a corpse. If he becomes circumcised and immerses, he may consume sacrificial food in the evening. This ruling is in accordance with the opinion of Rabbi Yoḥanan (Rambam *Sefer Tahara*, *Hilkhot Para Aduma* 11:3).

NOTES

An uncircumcised Jew may receive sprinkling – עָרֵל מְקַבֵּל הַזָּאָה: This is derived from the verse in Joshua (5:10), which states that the Jewish people sacrificed the Paschal offering, which indicates that they did so in accordance with the *halakha*, i.e., in a state of ritual purity (Rashi). The evidence of this is as follows: The Jewish people emerged from the Jordan River on the tenth of Nisan, and they were not circumcised until the next day, the eleventh of Nisan. If they did not receive their first sprinkling, which is performed on the third day of the purification process, until the eleventh of Nisan, then the seventh and final day of their purification would have been the fifteenth of Nisan and they would not have been able to sacrifice the Paschal offering on the fourteenth. Rather, it must be that the third day of their purification, on which the water of purification was first sprinkled upon them, was before the eleventh of Nisan, and therefore before they were circumcised.

According to the opinion of Rabbi Shimon, the verse need not be interpreted in this way, as in his opinion the people were circumcised on the tenth of Nisan, not the eleventh. See *Or HaYashar*, where it is noted that there is a similar opinion in the Jerusalem Talmud. Alternatively, Rabbi Shimon agrees that an uncircumcised Jew may receive sprinkling, but holds it is not necessary to derive this from a verse (see *Sefat Emet*).

Rav Adda bar Ahava said to him, from where would an individual sacrifice compulsory offerings that have a set time – אֲמַר לֵיהּ יָחִיד חוֹבוֹת שֶׁקָּבוּעַ לָהֶן זְמַן מְנָא לֵיהּ: There are two variations of the text with regard to this discussion. The first is essentially the version that appears in the standard text, but the phrase: As there is a voluntary burnt offering, should be replaced with: As there is the burnt offering of appearance in the Temple brought on the pilgrimage Festivals. *Tzon Kodashim* and *Ḥok Natan* explain this to mean that the *baraita* comparing a great public altar to a private altar with regard to compulsory offerings that have a set time assumes that individuals also bring compulsory offerings that have a set time, but those offerings are sacrificed only upon a great public altar. Consequently, examples of this type of offering must be identified, with the exception of the Paschal offering, which is listed explicitly in the *baraita* and which, in any event, has the status of a communal offering in this context.

There is a difficulty according to this version: It is consistent only with the opinion of Rabbi Yehuda, who holds that an individual may sacrifice compulsory offerings upon a great public altar. This opinion is not shared by the other *tanna'im*, nor is it the opinion of Rabbi Shimon, which is ostensibly the subject of the Gemara's discussion (*Ḥok Natan*).

The early commentaries (Rashi; *Tosafot*; Rabbeinu Ḥananel) had a different version of the text, according to which Rav Adda bar Ahava says that this *baraita* is in accordance with the opinion of Rabbi Shimon, and there is no mention of individual compulsory offerings. That version reads as follows: Rav Adda bar Ahava said to him: That which you have been told, in accordance with whose opinion is it? It is in accordance with the opinion of Rabbi Shimon, who said that the difference between a great public altar and a private altar is only Paschal offerings and compulsory communal offerings for which there is a set time; and interpret your mishna as referring to a compulsory burnt offering, as there is a voluntary burnt offering. As if you were to say that it is a sin offering brought by an individual, are there voluntary sin offerings?

According to Rashi and Rabbeinu Ḥananel, this essentially means that the statement of the *baraita*, that the difference between a great public altar and a small private altar is only compulsory offerings that have a set time, assumes that there is a similar voluntary offering that can be sacrificed on both a public altar and a private altar, even if it has no set time, which must refer to a burnt offering. See *Tosafot*, who offer a different interpretation that is based on the fact that the Paschal offering is mentioned in this *baraita*, despite its already being included in the category of compulsory offerings that have a set time. It is mentioned in this *baraita* in order to teach that according to Rabbi Shimon, the offerings in the discussion must be similar to the Paschal offering in that they were brought by individuals during the period in which personal altars were permitted.

אֲמַר לֵיהּ: אִסְמְיֵיהּ? אֲמַר לֵיהּ: תְּתַרְגֵּם מַתְנִיתָךְ בְּעוֹלַת חוֹבָה, דְּאִיכָּא עוֹלַת נְדָבָה. דְּאִי חַטַּאת יָחִיד הוּא – חוֹבוֹת דִּקְבִיעַ לֵיהּ זְמַן מִי אִיכָּא?

The *tanna* **said to him:** If so, **shall I remove it** from the text of the mishna, and teach only: Paschal offerings? Rav Adda bar Ahava **said to him:** That is not necessary; **interpret your mishna** as referring **to a compulsory burnt offering,**[B] i.e., the burnt offering of appearance brought on the pilgrimage Festivals by every individual, which is not sacrificed on a private altar, **as there is,** conversely, **a voluntary burnt offering** that may be sacrificed on a private altar. This *baraita* must be discussing a burnt offering brought by an individual, **as if it is** referring to **a sin offering** brought by **an individual, are there compulsory** sin offerings **that have a set time?**

וְלוֹקְמָהּ בְּמִנְחַת חוֹבָה, דְּהָא אִיכָּא חֲבִיתִּין! קָא סָבַר: אֵין מִנְחָה בְּבָמָה.

The Gemara asks: **And let him establish** the *baraita* as referring **to** the **compulsory meal offering** of an individual, which has a set time, **as there is** the **griddle-cake** offering that the High Priest was obligated to sacrifice every day and that may be sacrificed only upon a great public altar, not upon a private altar. The Gemara replies: Rav Adda bar Ahava **holds** that **there is no meal offering** sacrificed **upon an altar** outside the Temple, even a great public altar.

״בָּאוּ לְשִׁילֹה״ וכו׳. מְנָא הָנֵי מִילֵּי? אָמַר רַבִּי חִיָּיא בַּר אַבָּא אָמַר רַבִּי יוֹחָנָן: כָּתוּב אֶחָד אוֹמֵר: ״וַתְּבִאֵהוּ בֵית ה׳ שִׁילֹה״, וְכָתוּב אֶחָד אוֹמֵר ״וַיִּטֹּשׁ (אֶת) מִשְׁכַּן שִׁילֹה אֹהֶל שִׁכֵּן בָּאָדָם״, וּכְתִיב: ״וַיִּמְאַס בְּאֹהֶל יוֹסֵף וּבְשֵׁבֶט אֶפְרַיִם לֹא בָחָר״,

§ The mishna teaches that when **they arrived at Shiloh,** private altars were prohibited. There was no roof of wood or stone in the Tabernacle in Shiloh; there was only a building of stone below, and the curtains of the roof of the Tabernacle were spread above it. The Gemara asks: **From where are these matters** derived? **Rabbi Ḥiyya bar Abba says** that **Rabbi Yoḥanan says: One verse states,** with regard to Hannah bringing Samuel to the Tabernacle: **"And she brought him to the house of the Lord in Shiloh"** (I Samuel 1:24), **and one verse states: "And He forsook the Tabernacle of Shiloh, the tent that He had made to dwell among men"** (Psalms 78:60). **And** in addition, **it is written: "Moreover he abhorred the tent of Joseph and chose not the tribe of Ephraim"** (Psalms 78:67).

הָא כֵּיצַד? לֹא הָיְתָה שָׁם תִּקְרָה, אֶלָּא אֲבָנִים מִלְּמַטָּן וִירִיעוֹת מִלְמַעְלָן, וְהִיא הָיְתָה ״מְנוּחָה״.

One verse describes the Tabernacle in Shiloh as a house, while the other describes it as a tent. **How** can **these** texts be reconciled? As the mishna states: **There was no roof**[H] of wood or stone **there; rather,** there was **stone below,** and it was therefore described as a house, **and the curtains** of the Tabernacle were spread **above it,** and it was therefore described as a tent. **And** the period that the Tabernacle was in Shiloh **was** characterized in the Torah as **"rest"** in the verse: "For you have not as yet come to the rest and to the inheritance, which the Lord your God has given you" (Deuteronomy 12:9).

״קָדְשֵׁי קָדָשִׁים״. מְנָא הָנֵי מִילֵּי? אָמַר רַבִּי אוֹשַׁעְיָא, דְּאָמַר קְרָא: ״הִשָּׁמֶר לְךָ פֶּן תַּעֲלֶה עֹלֹתֶיךָ בְּכָל מָקוֹם אֲשֶׁר (אַתָּה) תִּרְאֶה״, בְּכָל מָקוֹם אֲשֶׁר תִּרְאֶה – אִי אַתָּה מַעֲלֶה, אֲבָל אַתָּה אוֹכֵל בְּכָל מָקוֹם שֶׁאַתָּה רוֹאֶה.

§ The mishna teaches that during the period of Shiloh, **offerings of the most sacred order** were eaten within the curtains, and offerings of lesser sanctity and second tithe were eaten in any place that overlooks Shiloh. The Gemara asks: **From where are these matters** derived? **Rabbi Oshaya said: As** in the context of the prohibition against sacrificing outside the Tabernacle, **the verse states: "Take heed to yourself that you do not offer your burnt offerings in every place that you see"** (Deuteronomy 12:13),[N] from which it may be inferred: **You may not offer up in every place that you see, but you may eat** the offerings **in every place that you see.**

אֵימָא: בְּכָל מָקוֹם שֶׁאַתָּה רוֹאֶה – אִי אַתָּה מַעֲלֶה, אֲבָל אַתָּה זוֹבֵחַ בְּכָל מָקוֹם שֶׁתִּרְאֶה!

The Gemara challenges: **Say** instead the following inference: **You may not offer up** offerings upon an altar **in every place that you see, but you may slaughter** offerings **in every place that you see.** It would therefore be permitted to slaughter offerings in any place that overlooks Shiloh.

אֲמַר רַבִּי יַנַּאי: אָמַר קְרָא ״שָׁם תַּעֲלֶה... וְשָׁם תַּעֲשֶׂה״.

Rabbi Yannai said that **the** subsequent **verse states:** "But in the place that the Lord shall choose in one of your tribes, **there you shall offer** your burnt offerings, **and there you shall do** all that I command you" (Deuteronomy 12:14). This verse teaches that all of the sacrificial service is performed in the place that the offering is burned, and only the consumption of offerings of lesser sanctity is permitted in any place that overlooks Shiloh.

רַבִּי אַבְדִּימִי בַּר חָסָא אֲמַר, אָמַר קְרָא:

Rabbi Avdimi bar Ḥasa said that when describing the boundaries of the portions of Eretz Yisrael of the children of Joseph, wherein Shiloh was located, **the verse states:**

BACKGROUND

Compulsory burnt offering – עוֹלַת חוֹבָה: This refers to the burnt offering brought to the Temple by celebrants on the three pilgrimage Festivals. It is prohibited by Torah law to come to the Temple on these Festivals empty-handed (see Deuteronomy 16:16–17).

Family on pilgrimage to Jerusalem with their offerings

HALAKHA

There was no roof – לֹא הָיְתָה שָׁם תִּקְרָה: The Tabernacle in Shiloh was a building constructed of stone, and it had no roof; rather, the curtains of the Tabernacle were spread atop it (Rambam *Sefer Avoda, Hilkhot Beit HaBeḥira* 1:2).

NOTES

Take heed to yourself that you do not offer your burnt offerings in every place that you see – הִשָּׁמֶר לְךָ פֶּן תַּעֲלֶה עֹלֹתֶיךָ בְּכָל מָקוֹם אֲשֶׁר תִּרְאֶה: This verse must be interpreted as referring to Shiloh. It cannot be referring to Jerusalem, where offerings of the most sacred order are eaten within the walls of Jerusalem, and with regard to which the verse states: "But you shall eat them before the Lord your God in the place that the Lord your God shall choose" (Deuteronomy 12:18). Nor can it be referring to the period of Nov and Gibeon, as during that time offerings of lesser sanctity were consumed in every city in Eretz Yisrael, as explained on 119a (Rid).

״וְלוֹ תַּאֲנַת שִׁלֹה״ – מָקוֹם שֶׁכׇּל הָרוֹאֶה אוֹתוֹ מִתְאַנֵּחַ עָלָיו עַל אֲכִילַת קֳדָשִׁים שֶׁלּוֹ.

"**And the border turned about eastward to Taanath Shiloh**" (Joshua 16:6),[B] a place adjacent to Shiloh. Why did it bear the name of Taanath Shiloh? It is because it was the **place from which whoever saw** the Tabernacle in Shiloh after its destruction would **moan** [***mitane'aḥ***] **for it with regard to the consumption of sacrificial** animals from offerings of lesser sanctity that had been previously permitted there, but was now no longer permitted.

רַבִּי אַבָּהוּ אָמַר, אָמַר קְרָא: ״בֵּן פֹּרָת יוֹסֵף בֵּן פֹּרָת עֲלֵי עָיִן״, עַיִן שֶׁלֹּא רָצְתָה לָזוּן וְלֵיהָנוֹת מִדָּבָר שֶׁאֵינוֹ שֶׁלּוֹ – תִּזְכֶּה וְתֹאכַל כִּמְלֹא עֵינֶיהָ.

Rabbi Abbahu says that a different biblical allusion may be found in what **the verse states** in the context of Jacob's blessing to Joseph: "**Joseph is a fruitful vine, a fruitful vine by a fountain** [***ayin***]" (Genesis 49:22).[N] The Gemara interprets the word fountain homiletically: **An eye** [***ayin***] **that did not wish to partake or derive benefit from something that was not his,** i.e., the wife of Potiphar, **shall merit** to have offerings of lesser sanctity **consumed** in Shiloh, in Joseph's portion of Eretz Yisrael, **to the fullest** extent **of its eyes,** i.e., from wherever Shiloh can be seen.

רַבִּי יוֹסֵי בְּרַבִּי חֲנִינָא אָמַר: ״וּרְצוֹן שֹׁכְנִי סְנֶה״, עַיִן שֶׁלֹּא רָצְתָה לֵיהָנוֹת מִדָּבָר שֶׁאֵינוֹ שֶׁלּוֹ – תִּזְכֶּה וְתֹאכַל בֵּין הַשְּׂנוּאִין.

Rabbi Yosei, son of Rabbi Ḥanina, says that another allusion may be found in the context of Moses' blessing to Joseph: "**And the good will of Him Who dwelt in the bush** [***seneh***]" (Deuteronomy 33:16). The Gemara interprets the word "*seneh*" homiletically: **An eye that did not wish to derive benefit from something that was not his shall merit** to have offerings of lesser sanctity **consumed among the haters** [***senu'in***].[N] In other words, offerings of lesser sanctity may be consumed in any place that overlooks Shiloh, even in the portions of the other tribes, who are described by the Torah as hating Joseph (see Genesis, chapter 37).

תָּנָא: ״רוֹאֶה״ שֶׁאָמְרוּ – רוֹאֶה כּוּלּוֹ, וְלֹא הַמַּפְסִיק בֵּינוֹ לְבֵינוֹ. אֲמַר לֵיהּ רַבִּי שִׁמְעוֹן בֶּן אֶלְיָקִים לְרַבִּי אֶלְעָזָר, אַסְבְּרָא לָךְ: כְּגוֹן בֵּי כְנִישְׁתָּא דְּמָעוֹן. אָמַר רַב פָּפָּא: ״רוֹאֶה״ שֶׁאָמְרוּ – לֹא רוֹאֶה כּוּלּוֹ, אֶלָּא רוֹאֶה מִקְצָתוֹ.

§ With regard to the *halakha* that during the period of Shiloh offerings of lesser sanctity could be eaten in any place that overlooks Shiloh, it was **taught:** The term: **Overlooks, that** was **stated** in the mishna, means that one **sees** it in **its entirety, and** there is **nothing that obstructs between** the seer **and** the surrounding area. **Rabbi Shimon ben Elyakum said to Rabbi Elazar: I shall explain** this type of seeing **to you: For example, the synagogue of Maon,** which was adjacent to the city of Tiberias, and from where Tiberias could be seen. **Rav Pappa said** that the term: **Overlooks, that was stated** does **not** mean that one must **see** the Tabernacle in Shiloh in **its entirety, but** rather even if one **sees** it **partially,** offerings of lesser sanctity may be consumed there.

בָּעֵי רַב פָּפָּא: עוֹמֵד וְרוֹאֶה, יוֹשֵׁב וְאֵינוֹ רוֹאֶה, מַאי? בָּעֵי רַבִּי יִרְמְיָה: עוֹמֵד עַל גַּבֵּי הַנַּחַל וְרוֹאֶה, (יוֹשֵׁב) בְּתוֹךְ הַנַּחַל וְאֵינוֹ רוֹאֶה מַאי? תֵּיקוּ.

With regard to the definition of overlooking, **Rav Pappa raises a dilemma:** If one is in a place where he **stands and sees** Shiloh, but if he **sits** he **does not see** Shiloh,[N] **what** is the *halakha*? Is this considered overlooking? Likewise, **Rabbi Yirmeya raises a dilemma:** If one is in a place where he can **stand upon** the bank of **the stream and see** Shiloh, but if he is **in the stream he does not see** Shiloh, **what** is the *halakha*? No resolution is found for either of these questions, and the Gemara concludes: These dilemmas **shall stand** unresolved.

כִּי אֲתָא רַב דִּימִי אָמַר רַבִּי: בִּשְׁלֹשָׁה מְקוֹמוֹת שָׁרְתָה שְׁכִינָה עַל יִשְׂרָאֵל: בְּשִׁילֹה, וְנוֹב וְגִבְעוֹן, וּבֵית עוֹלָמִים, וּבְכוּלָּן לֹא שָׁרְתָה אֶלָּא בְּחֵלֶק בִּנְיָמִין, שֶׁנֶּאֱמַר: ״חֹפֵף עָלָיו כׇּל הַיּוֹם״ – כׇּל חֲפִיפוֹת לֹא יְהוּ אֶלָּא בְּחֶלְקוֹ שֶׁל בִּנְיָמִין.

§ **When Rav Dimi came** from Eretz Yisrael to Babylonia, **he said** that Rabbi Yehuda HaNasi said: **The Divine Presence rested upon the Jewish people in three places:**[N] **In Shiloh, and Nov and Gibeon,**[B] **and the Eternal House, and in all of those** the Divine Presence **rested only in the portion** of the tribe **of Benjamin,**[N] **as it is stated** in Moses' blessing to Benjamin: "The beloved of the Lord shall dwell in safety by Him; **He covers him all the day** and He dwells between his shoulders" (Deuteronomy 33:12), meaning: **All coverings,** i.e., times of resting of the Divine Presence upon the Jewish people, **shall be only in the portion of Benjamin.**

BACKGROUND

Taanath Shiloh – **תַּאֲנַת שִׁלֹה**: This place is mentioned in the description of the northern boundary of the portion of the tribe of Ephraim. It is identified today with either the village of upper Khirbet Tana, which is approximately 15 km northeast of Shiloh, or lower Khirbet Tana, approximately 5 km southeast of Shiloh.

Nov and Gibeon – **נוֹב וְגִבְעוֹן**: There is a difference of opinion as to the precise location of Nov in the portion of Benjamin. Based on the description in Isaiah (10:32), one who stands in Nov can see and wave his hand at Jerusalem. Consequently, there are those who have claimed the location of Nov was either Mount Scopus or the Mount of Olives, both east of the Old City of Jerusalem. Others believe it was located in the modern neighborhood of Shuafat, north of the Old City. Gibeon, the ruins of which are located near the modern village of al-Jib, 10 km northwest of the Old City of Jerusalem, was a major city, located along the road ascending to Beit Ḥoron, which was the primary artery connecting the land of Benjamin to the lowlands.

NOTES

A fruitful [*porat*] vine by a fountain – **בֵּן פֹּרָת עֲלֵי עָיִן**: The word "fruitful" in this context denotes expansion and spreading out, akin to the use of the word fruitful [*porat*] in the context of procreation (Rashi).

Shall merit to have offerings of lesser sanctity consumed among the haters [*senu'in*] – **תִּזְכֶּה וְתֹאכַל בֵּין הַשְּׂנוּאִין**: The interpretation given in the commentary is that of Rashi. Accordingly, the area classified as: Any place that overlooks Shiloh, includes some land of other tribes. Rabbeinu Ḥananel, quoting the *Agron*, a dictionary composed by Rav Se'adya Gaon, says that the text of the Gemara should read *sena'im*, spelled with the letter *samekh*, meaning bushes, rather than *senu'im*, spelled with the letter *sin*. According to this version, the Gemara's interpretation means: In the merit of Joseph's actions, offerings of lesser sanctity were consumed throughout his portion, even in the fields among the bushes, and were not limited to the Tabernacle.

He stands and sees Shiloh, but if he sits he does not see Shiloh – **עוֹמֵד וְרוֹאֶה יוֹשֵׁב וְאֵינוֹ רוֹאֶה**: The question is: If one can see Shiloh from this location only while standing, can he also consume offerings while seated? Or, alternatively, perhaps he cannot consume offerings even while standing, as when seated he cannot see Shiloh, and the standard way to eat is while seated (*Sefat Emet*).

The Divine Presence rested upon the Jewish people in three places – **בִּשְׁלֹשָׁה מְקוֹמוֹת שָׁרְתָה שְׁכִינָה עַל יִשְׂרָאֵל**: Nov and Gibeon are counted as a single location because the period of both was between the period of Shiloh and that of Jerusalem; during that time sacrifices outside the Temple were permitted (see Rashi on 119a).

Shiloh and Nov and Gibeon and the Eternal House… in the portion of Benjamin – **שִׁילֹה וְנוֹב וְגִבְעוֹן וּבֵית עוֹלָמִים...בְּחֵלֶק בִּנְיָמִין**: The Gemara discusses only the location of Shiloh. Nov, which was a city of priests (see I Samuel 21:2, 22:19), and where the Table, the shewbread, and the ephod were located, is mentioned in the book of Nehemiah (11:32) as being in the portion of Benjamin, and Gibeon was listed as such in the book of Joshua (18:25). With regard to the Temple in Jerusalem, see 54b.

כִּי אֲזַיל אַבַּיֵי אֲמָרָהּ קַמֵּיהּ דְּרַב יוֹסֵף. אֲמַר: חַד בְּרָא הֲוָה לֵיהּ לְכַיְילִיל, וְלָא מִיתַּקַּן! וְהָכְתִיב: ״וַיִּטֹּשׁ אֶת מִשְׁכַּן שִׁילוֹ״, וּכְתִיב: ״וַיִּמְאַס בְּאֹהֶל יוֹסֵף וּבְשֵׁבֶט אֶפְרַיִם לֹא בָחָר״!

The Gemara relates that **when Abaye went** to study Torah with Rav Yosef, **he said** the statement of Rav Dimi **before Rav Yosef.** Rav Yosef **said** in response: **Kaylil,** Abaye's father, **had one son,**[N] **and he is not proper. But isn't it written** with regard to the Tabernacle in Shiloh: **"And He forsook the Tabernacle of Shiloh"** (Psalms 78:60); **and it is written: "Moreover He abhorred the tent of Joseph, and chose not the tribe of Ephraim"** (Psalms 78:67)? These verses indicate that the Tabernacle in Shiloh was in the portion of Joseph, not of Benjamin.

אֲמַר רַב אַדָּא: מַאי קָא קַשְׁיָא לֵיהּ? דִּלְמָא שְׁכִינָה בְּחֵלֶק בִּנְיָמִין, וְסַנְהֶדְרִי גְּדוֹלָה בְּחֵלֶק יוֹסֵף. מִדְּמָצִינוּ בְּבֵית עוֹלָמִים, דִּשְׁכִינָה בְּחֶלְקוֹ שֶׁל בִּנְיָמִין וְסַנְהֶדְרִין בְּחֵלֶק יְהוּדָה!

Rav Adda said: What is Rav Yosef's **difficulty** from that verse? **Perhaps** the Tabernacle was in both the portion of Benjamin and that of Joseph. The **Divine Presence** was **in the portion of Benjamin, and the Great Sanhedrin,** which sits adjacent to the location of the Divine Presence, was **in the portion of Joseph.** This is similar to **what we found** in the case of **the Eternal House,**[N] **where** the **Divine Presence** was **in the portion of Benjamin and** the **Sanhedrin** was **in the portion of Judah.**

אֲמַר לֵיהּ: הָכִי הָשְׁתָּא?! הָתָם – מִיקַּרְבָן נַחֲלוֹת גַּבֵּי הֲדָדֵי, הָכָא – מִי מִקַּרְבָן? הָכָא נַמִי מִקַּרְבָן, כִּדְאָמַר רַבִּי חָמָא בְּרַבִּי חֲנִינָא: רְצוּעָה הָיְתָה יוֹצֵאת מֵחֶלְקוֹ שֶׁל יְהוּדָה וְנִכְנֶסֶת לְחֶלְקוֹ שֶׁל בִּנְיָמִין, וּבָהּ הָיָה מִזְבֵּחַ בָּנוּי, וְהָיָה בִּנְיָמִין הַצַּדִּיק מִצְטַעֵר עָלֶיהָ לְבָלְעָהּ.

Rav Yosef **said to him** in response: **How can these cases be compared? There,** in the Temple in Jerusalem, **the portions** of Benjamin and Judah were **close to each other,** and a division in which the Temple was located in the portion of one tribe while the Sanhedrin was located in the portion of another was possible. **Here,** with regard to Shiloh, **are** Shiloh and the portion of Benjamin **close** to each other? The Gemara replies: **Here too they are close, as Rabbi Ḥama, son of Rabbi Ḥanina, says: A strip** of land **protruded from the portion of Judah**[N] **and entered into the portion of Benjamin, and the altar** in the Temple **was built on** that strip. **And** the tribe of **Benjamin the righteous would agonize over it every day,** desiring **to take it** into its portion, due to its unique sanctity.

הָכָא נַמִי – רְצוּעָה הָיְתָה יוֹצֵאת מֵחֶלְקוֹ שֶׁל יוֹסֵף לְחֶלְקוֹ שֶׁל בִּנְיָמִין. וְהַיְינוּ דִּכְתִיב ״תַּאֲנַת שִׁלֹה״.

Here too, with regard to the Tabernacle in Shiloh, **a strip** of land **protruded from the portion of Joseph** and entered **into the portion of Benjamin,** which connected Shiloh to the portion of Benjamin, and it was upon that strip, which had the status of Benjamin's portion, that the Tabernacle stood. **And that is** what it means concerning that **which is written** with regard to the boundary of Joseph: "And the border turned about eastward to **Taanath Shiloh**" (Joshua 16:6), which in this context, is interpreted as meaning that the tribe of Benjamin would bemoan the fact that the Tabernacle in Shiloh was not located entirely in its portion.

כְּתַנָּאֵי: ״חֹפֵף עָלָיו״ – זֶה מִקְדָּשׁ רִאשׁוֹן, ״כָּל הַיּוֹם״ – זֶה מִקְדָּשׁ שֵׁנִי, ״וּבֵין כְּתֵפָיו שָׁכֵן״ – אֵלּוּ יְמוֹת הַמָּשִׁיחַ.

The Gemara notes that the dispute between the *amora'im* with regard to the tribe in which the Tabernacle in Shiloh was located is **like** a dispute between *tanna'im,* as it is taught with regard to Moses' blessing to Benjamin: **"He covers him"; this** is a reference to the **First Temple. "All the day"; this** is a reference to the **Second Temple. "And He dwells between his shoulders"; this** is a reference to **the messianic era.**

NOTES

Kaylil had one son – **חַד בְּרָא הֲוָה לֵיהּ לְכַיְילִיל:** Rashi explains that Kaylil was the name of Abaye's father. According to other versions of the Gemara, it is possible that he was Rav Dimi's father.

What we found in the Eternal House – **מִדְּמָצִינוּ בְּבֵית עוֹלָמִים:** It is universally accepted that the Sanhedrin is located within the Temple, as the Torah states: "If there arise a matter too hard for you in judgment, between blood and blood, between plea and plea, and between stroke and stroke, matters of controversy within your gates; then you shall arise, and go up to the place that the Lord your God shall choose" (Deuteronomy 17:8). Likewise, in Solomon's prayer the Temple is identified as the location of justice (see I Kings 8:31).

The Sages (54b) state that the site of the Temple was intentionally positioned on the border between Judah and Benjamin for this very reason: The place of the Sanhedrin is the portion of Judah, about which the Torah says (Genesis 49:10): "The scepter shall not depart from Judah, nor the ruler's staff from between his feet, as long as men come to Shiloh; and to him shall the obedience of the peoples be" (see *Panim Meirot*).

A strip of land protruded from the portion of Judah – **רְצוּעָה הָיְתָה יוֹצֵאת מֵחֶלְקוֹ שֶׁל יְהוּדָה:** The western section of the Temple, including the place of the Divine Presence, i.e., the Sanctuary, as well as the external altar, was in the portion of Benjamin. The eastern section of the Temple, up to the altar, was in the portion of Judah. According to the description in this *baraita,* a strip of land entered the portion of Benjamin from the portion of Judah and occupied an area one cubit wide under the eastern and southern sides of the altar (see 54b).

רַבִּי אוֹמֵר: ״חוֹפֵף עָלָיו״ – זֶה הָעוֹלָם הַזֶּה, ״כׇּל הַיּוֹם״ – אֵלּוּ יְמוֹת הַמָּשִׁיחַ, ״וּבֵין כְּתֵפָיו שָׁכֵן״ – זֶה הָעוֹלָם הַבָּא.

Rabbi Yehuda HaNasi **says: "He covers him"; this is** a reference to **this world. "All the day"; this is** a reference to **the messianic era. "And He dwells between his shoulders"; this is** a reference to **the World-to-Come.** According to the opinion of the Rabbis, the Divine Presence dwelled in the portion of Benjamin from the first Temple period and onward, but not during the period of the Tabernacle in Shiloh, when it was in the portion of Joseph. However, according to the opinion of Rabbi Yehuda HaNasi, the entire period that the Divine Presence dwelled in this world, including the period of Shiloh, it did so in the portion of Benjamin.

תָּנוּ רַבָּנַן: יְמֵי אֹהֶל מוֹעֵד שֶׁבַּמִּדְבָּר – אַרְבָּעִים שָׁנָה חָסֵר אַחַת. יְמֵי אֹהֶל מוֹעֵד שֶׁבְּגִלְגָּל – אַרְבַּע עֶשְׂרֵה, שֶׁבַע שֶׁכָּבְשׁוּ וְשֶׁבַע שֶׁחִלְּקוּ. יְמֵי אֹהֶל מוֹעֵד שֶׁבְּנוֹב וְגִבְעוֹן – חֲמִשִּׁים וָשֶׁבַע. נִשְׁתַּיְּירוּ לְשִׁילֹה שְׁלֹשׁ מֵאוֹת וְשִׁבְעִים חָסֵר אַחַת.

§ With regard to the duration of the different periods mentioned in the mishna, **the Sages taught: The days of the Tent of Meeting**[H] **in the wilderness** were **forty** years, **less one** year. **The days of the Tent of Meeting that** were **in Gilgal** were **fourteen** years: **Seven** years during **which** the Jews **conquered** the land **and seven** years during **which they divided** the land among the tribes. **The days of the Tent of Meeting that** were **in Nov and Gibeon** were **fifty-seven** years, until the Temple in Jerusalem was constructed. Since the Temple was constructed 480 years after the Exodus from Egypt (see 1 Kings 6:1), it follows that there **remain for** the period of the Tabernacle in **Shiloh** 370 years **less one.**

יְמֵי אֹהֶל מוֹעֵד שֶׁבַּמִּדְבָּר אַרְבָּעִים חָסֵר אַחַת, מְנָלַן? דְּאָמַר מָר: שָׁנָה רִאשׁוֹנָה עָשָׂה מֹשֶׁה אֶת הַמִּשְׁכָּן, שְׁנִיָּה – הוּקַם הַמִּשְׁכָּן וְשָׁלַח מֹשֶׁה מְרַגְּלִים.

The Gemara asks: **From where do we** derive that **the days of the Tent of Meeting that** were **in the wilderness** were **forty** years **less one? As the Master said** in a *baraita*: In **the first year** after the Exodus from Egypt, **Moses constructed the Tabernacle;** in the **second** year **the Tabernacle was erected, and Moses sent spies.** Because of the sin of the spies, the Jewish people remained in the wilderness for forty years. It follows that the Tabernacle in the wilderness stood for thirty-nine years.

שֶׁבְּגִלְגָּל אַרְבַּע עֶשְׂרֵה, שֶׁבַע שֶׁכָּבְשׁוּ וְשֶׁבַע שֶׁחִלְּקוּ, מְנָלַן? דְּקָאָמַר כָּלֵב: ״בֶּן אַרְבָּעִים שָׁנָה אָנֹכִי בִּשְׁלֹחַ מֹשֶׁה עֶבֶד ה׳ אֹתִי מִקָּדֵשׁ בַּרְנֵעַ לְרַגֵּל אֶת הָאָרֶץ וָאָשֵׁב אוֹתוֹ דָּבָר כַּאֲשֶׁר עִם לְבָבִי״, וּכְתִיב: ״וְעַתָּה הִנֵּה אָנֹכִי הַיּוֹם בֶּן חָמֵשׁ וּשְׁמוֹנִים שָׁנָה״,

From where do we derive **that** the Tabernacle remained **in Gilgal** for **fourteen** years, **seven** years during **which** the Jews **conquered** the land **and seven** years during **which they divided** it? **As Caleb,** son of Jephunneh, **said** to Joshua at the conclusion of the period of conquest before the land was divided: **"Forty years old was I when Moses, the servant of the Lord, sent me from Kadesh Barnea to spy out the land; and I brought him back word as it was in my heart"** (Joshua 14:7), **and it is written: "And now, I am this day eighty and five years old"** (Joshua 14:10).

כִּי עַבְרִיהּ לְיַרְדֵּן בַּר כַּמָּה הֲוַי – בַּר שִׁבְעִין וּתְמָנֵי, וְקָאָמַר: ״בֶּן חָמֵשׁ וּשְׁמוֹנִים שָׁנָה״, הֲרֵי שֶׁבַע שֶׁכָּבְשׁוּ.

When the Jewish people **crossed the Jordan, how old was** Caleb? He was **seventy-eight** years **old:** The spies were sent by Moses in the second year after the Exodus from Egypt, and in the fortieth year they crossed the Jordan. **And** at the time of the division of the Land, **he said** that he was **eighty-five years old.** This indicates that it was **seven years** during **which** the Jews **conquered** the land.

וְשֶׁבַע שֶׁחִלְּקוּ מְנָלַן? אִיבָּעֵית אֵימָא: מִדְּשֶׁבַע שֶׁכָּבְשׁוּ – שֶׁבַע נָמֵי שֶׁחִלְּקוּ.

The Gemara asks: **And from where do we** derive that there were **seven** years during **which they divided** the land? **If you wish, say: Since** it was a period of **seven** years in **which they conquered** the land, it was presumably **also** a period of **seven** years in **which they divided** the land.

וְאִיבָּעֵית אֵימָא: מִדְּלָא מַשְׁכַּחַתְּ לַהּ ״בְּאַרְבַּע עֶשְׂרֵה שָׁנָה אַחַר אֲשֶׁר הֻכְּתָה הָעִיר״.

And if you wish, say instead: **Because** otherwise, **you do not find** any plausible explanation for the date mentioned by the prophet Ezekiel in the verse: "In the beginning of the year, on the tenth day of the month, **in the fourteenth year after that the city was smitten"** (Ezekiel 40:1).[N] This indicates that it was a Jubilee Year, unless capturing and dividing the land took a total of fourteen years, after which point they began to calculate Sabbatical and Jubilee Years.

אֹהֶל מוֹעֵד שֶׁבְּנוֹב וְגִבְעוֹן חֲמִשִּׁים וָשֶׁבַע, מְנָא לַן? דִּכְתִיב: ״וַיְהִי כְּהַזְכִּירוֹ אֶת אֲרוֹן הָאֱלֹהִים״,

§ The *baraita* stated that the period of **the Tent of Meeting that** was **in Nov and Gibeon** was **fifty-seven** years. The Gemara asks: **From where do we** derive this? **As it is written** in the description of the death of Eli the High Priest, upon being informed that the Ark was captured by the Philistines: **"And it came to pass, when he made mention of the Ark of God,** that he fell from off his seat backward by the side of the gate, and his neck broke, and he died" (1 Samuel 4:18).

HALAKHA

The days of the Tent of Meeting – יְמֵי אֹהֶל מוֹעֵד: When the Jews entered Eretz Yisrael they erected the Tabernacle in Gilgal, where it stood for the fourteen years they conquered and divided the land. From there they moved it to Shiloh, where they constructed a building of stone and spread the curtains of the Tabernacle upon it, as there was no roof. The Tabernacle stood in Shiloh for 369 years. When Eli the High Priest died it was destroyed, and they relocated it to Nov, where they built a temple. When Samuel died that temple was destroyed, and they relocated it to Gibeon, where they built a temple, and from Gibeon they moved to the Temple in Jerusalem. The period of Nov and Gibeon lasted fifty-seven years (Rambam *Sefer Avoda*, *Hilkhot Beit HaBeḥira* 1:2).

NOTES

In the fourteenth year after that the city was smitten – בְּאַרְבַּע עֶשְׂרֵה שָׁנָה אַחַר אֲשֶׁר הֻכְּתָה הָעִיר: Rashi explains that this refers to a Jubilee Year due to the description of the tenth day of the month as the "beginning of the year." Although Rosh HaShana is generally referred to as the beginning of the year, during the Jubilee Year the tenth of Tishrei, Yom Kippur, is when the unique *halakhot* of the year begin to take effect (see Leviticus 25:9). Rashi also explains the complex calculations as to how the date given in the verse indicates there were fourteen years of conquest and division of the Land of Israel.

BACKGROUND

Shiloh – שִׁילֹה: Shiloh, which is in the portion of Joseph's son Ephraim (see Judges 21:19), is located approximately 35 km north of Jerusalem and 15 km south of Shechem. Although the destruction of Shiloh is not explicitly mentioned in the book of Samuel when the death of Eli is described, it is found in other verses (see Jeremiah 7:12 and Psalms 78:60), and is corroborated by archaeological evidence.

וְתָנָא: כְּשֶׁמֵּת עֵלִי הַכֹּהֵן – חָרְבָה שִׁילֹה וּבָאוּ לְנוֹב, כְּשֶׁמֵּת שְׁמוּאֵל הָרָמָתִי – חָרְבָה נוֹב וּבָאוּ לְגִבְעוֹן.

And a *tanna* **taught: When Eli the priest died, Shiloh**[B] **was destroyed and** the Jews **arrived at Nov,** where they erected the Tabernacle. At that time, Samuel began to lead the people. **When Samuel from Rama died, Nov was destroyed** by Saul (see I Samuel 22:19) **and they arrived at Gibeon,** where the Tabernacle remained (see I Chronicles 16:39).

וּכְתִיב: "וַיְהִי מִיּוֹם שֶׁבֶת הָאָרוֹן בְּקִרְיַת יְעָרִים וַיִּרְבּוּ הַיָּמִים וַיִּהְיוּ עֶשְׂרִים שָׁנָה וַיִּנָּהוּ כָּל בֵּית יִשְׂרָאֵל אַחֲרֵי ה'";

The Gemara determines the number of years from when the Ark was captured by the Philistines and Shiloh was destroyed: **And it is written: "And it came to pass, from the day that the Ark abode in Kiriath Jearim that the time was long; for it was twenty years; and all the house of Israel yearned after the Lord"** (I Samuel 7:2). The Ark was returned by the Philistines to Kiriath Jearim seven months after it was captured, and it remained there for twenty years, until David brought it to Jerusalem.

הָנֵי עֶשְׂרִים שָׁנָה – עֶשֶׂר שָׁנָה שֶׁמָּלַךְ שְׁמוּאֵל בְּעַצְמוֹ, וְשָׁנָה שֶׁמָּלַךְ שְׁמוּאֵל וְשָׁאוּל, וּשְׁתַּיִם שֶׁמָּלַךְ שָׁאוּל, וְשֶׁבַע דָּוִד,

The Gemara explains that **these twenty years** are calculated as follows: **Ten years that Samuel reigned alone,** from the death of Eli until the coronation of Saul, **and one year that Samuel and Saul reigned,** i.e., Saul reigned for one year during the lifetime of Samuel, **and two** years **that Saul reigned** alone after the death of Samuel. **And** in addition to these thirteen years, there were the **seven** years **of David's** reign in Hebron, before the years of his reign in Jerusalem.

Perek **XIV**
Daf **119** Amud **a**

NOTES

Why does the verse divide them into two terms – לָמָּה חִלְּקָן: Rashi explains that it would have been sufficient to say: "For you have not as yet come to the rest," which would include every location of rest. Although the Gemara will ascribe a particular meaning to each of the terms, the *baraita* is not discussing that at this point. Rabbeinu Ḥananel explains that the verse could have said: The rest of inheritance.

דִּכְתִיב: "וְהַיָּמִים אֲשֶׁר מָלַךְ דָּוִד עַל יִשְׂרָאֵל אַרְבָּעִים שָׁנָה בְּחֶבְרוֹן מָלַךְ שֶׁבַע שָׁנִים" [וגו'].

As it is written: "And the days that David reigned over Israel were forty years: Seven years he reigned in Hebron, and thirty-three years he reigned in Jerusalem" (I Kings 2:11). In the first year that David reigned in Jerusalem he brought the Ark there from Kiriath Jearim. The Ark was therefore in Kiriath Jearim for twenty years. When the thirty-three years of David's reign in Jerusalem are added to these, there are a total of fifty-three years from the destruction of Shiloh. During all of these years, and at the beginning of Solomon's reign, the Tabernacle was in Nov and Gibeon (see I Kings 3:4).

וּבִשְׁלֹמֹה כְּתִיב: "וַיָּחֶל לִבְנוֹתוֹ בִּשְׁנַת אַרְבַּע לְמַלְכוּתוֹ", נִשְׁתַּיְּירוּ לְשִׁילֹה שְׁלֹשׁ מֵאוֹת וְשִׁבְעִים חָסֵר אַחַת.

And with regard to the construction of the Temple in the time of **Solomon, it is written: "And he began to build it** in the second day of the second month, **in the fourth year of his reign"** (II Chronicles 3:2), which was the 480th year following the Exodus (see I Kings 6:1). When the forty years in the wilderness, the fourteen years that the Tabernacle stood in Gilgal, and the fifty-seven years that the Tabernacle stood in Nov and Gibeon, which totals 111 years, are subtracted from the 480, there **remain for Shiloh 370 less one** years in which the Tabernacle stood there.

"בָּאוּ לְנוֹב וְגִבְעוֹן" [וכו']. מְנָא הָנֵי מִילֵּי? דְּתָנוּ רַבָּנַן: "כִּי לֹא בָאתֶם עַד עָתָּה אֶל הַמְּנוּחָה וְאֶל הַנַּחֲלָה",

§ The mishna teaches that when Shiloh was destroyed and they **arrived at Nov and Gibeon,** private altars were permitted and offerings of lesser sanctity could be eaten in any city in Eretz Yisrael. The Gemara asks: **From where are these matters** derived? they are derived **as the Sages taught:** The Jewish people were told that when they enter Eretz Yisrael they would be permitted to sacrifice on private altars, **"for you have not as yet come to the rest and to the inheritance"** (Deuteronomy 12:9), during which time those altars would be prohibited.

"אֶל הַמְּנוּחָה" – זוֹ שִׁילֹה, "נַחֲלָה" – זוֹ יְרוּשָׁלַיִם; לָמָּה חִלְּקָן – כְּדֵי לִיתֵּן הֶיתֵּר בֵּין זֶה לָזֶה.

The Gemara interprets the verse: **"To the rest"; this** is a reference to **Shiloh.** "The **inheritance"; this** is a reference to **Jerusalem.** One may ask: **Why** does the verse **divide them** into two terms,[N] i.e., "rest" and "inheritance"? It is **in order to give permission** to sacrifice on private altars during the period **between this one and that** one. Therefore, it was permitted to sacrifice on private altars during the period of Nov and Gibeon.

אָמַר לֵיהּ רֵישׁ לָקִישׁ לְרַבִּי יוֹחָנָן: מַעֲשֵׂר שֵׁנִי נַמִּי לִיתְנֵי! אֲמַר לֵיהּ: מַעֲשֵׂר – "שָׁם" "שָׁם" מֵאָרוֹן קָא יָלְפִי, כֵּיוָן דְּאָרוֹן לָא הֲוָה – מַעֲשֵׂר נַמִּי לָא הֲוַאי.

Reish Lakish said to Rabbi Yoḥanan: Let the *tanna* of the mishna **teach** the *halakha* with regard to **second tithe as well.**[N] Rabbi Yoḥanan **said to him:** Second **tithe is derived from** what was written with regard to **the Ark,** by means of the verbal analogy between **"there"** and **"there."** With regard to second tithe, the verse states: "And there you shall eat before the Lord your God" (Deuteronomy 12:7), while with regard to the Ark, the verse states: "There you shall place the Ark of the Testimony" (Exodus 40:3). Due to the analogy between second tithe and the Ark, one can infer that **since there was no Ark**[N] in Nov and Gibeon, as at that time it was in Kiriath Jearim, **there was also no** second **tithe**[N] eaten there.

אִי הָכִי, פֶּסַח וְקָדָשִׁים נַמִּי, דְּ"שָׁם" "שָׁם" מֵאָרוֹן יָלְפִי, דְּכֵיוָן דְּאָרוֹן לָא הֲוָה – אִינְהוּ נַמִּי לָא הֲווּ!

Reish Lakish asked: **If** it is **so** that this is the source, then with regard to the **Paschal offering and** other **sacrificial** animals,[N] which everyone agrees were consumed in Nov and Gibeon, it can **also** be said **that they are derived from the Ark** by means of the verbal analogy between **"there"** and **"there,"** and **since the Ark was not** in Nov and Gibeon **they too were not** there.

אֲמַר לֵיהּ: [דְּאָמַר לָךְ] הָא מַנִּי – רַבִּי שִׁמְעוֹן הִיא, דְּאָמַר: אַף צִבּוּר לֹא הִקְרִיבוּ אֶלָּא פֶּסַח וְחוֹבוֹת הַקָּבוּעַ לָהֶן זְמַן, אֲבָל חוֹבוֹת שֶׁאֵין קָבוּעַ לָהֶם זְמַן – הָכָא וְהָכָא לָא קָרֵב; מַעֲשַׂר בְּהֵמָה חוֹבוֹת שֶׁאֵין קָבוּעַ לָהֶן זְמַן הוּא, וְאִיתְקַשׁ מַעֲשַׂר דָּגָן לְמַעֲשַׂר בְּהֵמָה.

Rabbi Yoḥanan **said to him:** With regard to the one **who said this to you,** i.e., the *tanna* of the mishna, from which you inferred that second tithe was not eaten in Nov and Gibeon, in accordance with **whose** opinion **is this** statement of his? **It is** the opinion of **Rabbi Shimon, who says: Even** the **public sacrificed** upon a great public altar, e.g., in Nov and Gibeon, **only Paschal offerings and compulsory public offerings that have a set time. But compulsory** offerings **that do not have a set time were not sacrificed here or there,** i.e., on a great public altar or on a small private altar. This includes **an animal tithe** offering, which **is a compulsory offering that has no set time, and grain tithe is juxtaposed to animal tithe.**[N] Since animal tithe offerings were not brought at that time, second tithe was not eaten there either.

NOTES

Let the mishna teach second tithe as well – מַעֲשֵׂר שֵׁנִי נַמִּי לִיתְנֵי: The formulation that appears here assumes the mishna does not mention the *halakha* of the consumption of second tithe in the context of Nov and Gibeon as it does in the context of Shiloh. This version of the text is consistent with the standard version of the mishna. Accordingly, Reish Lakish's question may be interpreted in two ways. The first, which appears to be the explanation of Rabbeinu Ḥananel, is: Why does the mishna not teach that offerings of lesser sanctity and second tithe were eaten in all the cities of Eretz Yisrael, as it taught with regard to Shiloh that offerings of lesser sanctity and second tithe were eaten in any place that overlooks Shiloh? The second explanation, which is accepted in the *Yad David*, is as follows: The omission of second tithe indicates that it was not eaten at all during that period. Reish Lakish therefore asks why it was not eaten in Nov and Gibeon.

By contrast, the version of the mishna utilized by Rashi and the Rambam states that during this period second tithe was eaten in all the cities of Eretz Yisrael. Additionally, Rashi's version of the Gemara reads: Let second tithe be brought to Nov and Gibeon, meaning: Why was second tithe not brought to Nov and Gibeon in the same manner that it was brought to Shiloh and eaten in any place that overlooks Shiloh? The response is that there is an obligation to bring second tithe only to a place that contains the Ark of the Lord. *Tosefot Rabbeinu Peretz* on *Pesaḥim* 38b explains this version of the question as pertaining to the standard version of the text of the mishna as well: Even if second tithe may not be eaten in all cities in Eretz Yisrael, why is it not at least brought to Nov and Gibeon and eaten there? See also the Jerusalem Talmud (*Megilla* 1:12), which records a discussion similar to this one.

Since there was no Ark – כֵּיוָן דְּאָרוֹן לָא הֲוָה: After the Philistines returned the Ark to the Jewish people it was not in Nov or Gibeon but in Kiriath Jearim, from where David brought it to Jerusalem.

There was also no tithe – מַעֲשֵׂר נַמִּי לָא הֲוַאי: The precise meaning of this phrase depends on the meaning of Reish Lakish's question. According to the explanation of Rabbeinu Ḥananel, it would appear that the *halakha* of second tithe did not apply during this period. Although other tithes took effect beginning in the period of Shiloh, second tithe is different from other tithes in that it is not given to others, i.e., to a Levite or the poor, but it is akin to an offering, which must be eaten by its owner "before the Lord." The great public altars of Nov and Gibeon, where the Ark was not present, did not have the status of "before the Lord," and therefore the *halakha* of second tithe did not apply. This appears to be the meaning of the Talmud's discussion on *Makkot* 19a (see *Tosefot HaRash* on *Pesaḥim* 36b and *Keren Ora*).

Other commentaries hold that once the obligation to separate second tithe took effect, i.e., after the Jewish people conquered and settled in Eretz Yisrael, it never ceased. Consequently, the Gemara's response must be interpreted as meaning the following: Since there was no Ark, it was impossible to eat second tithe in Nov and Gibeon, and the only solution was to redeem it (see *Tosefot Rabbeinu Peretz* on *Pesaḥim* 38b, and *Tosafot* here). According to Rashi, the Gemara's statement that there was also no second tithe means that in the absence of the Ark it was not necessary to bring second tithe to be eaten in Nov and Gibeon; it was possible to eat it in any location.

The Paschal offering and other sacrificial animals – פֶּסַח וְקָדָשִׁים נַמִּי: The meaning of the suggestion is that all offerings are listed together with second tithe in the verses under discussion from which these *halakhot* are derived: "And there you shall bring your burnt offerings, and your sacrifices, and your tithes, and the offering of your hand, and your vows, and your gift offerings, and the firstborn of your herd and of your flock" (Deuteronomy 12:6).

And grain tithe is juxtaposed to animal tithe – וְאִיתְקַשׁ מַעֲשַׂר דָּגָן לְמַעֲשַׂר בְּהֵמָה: This juxtaposition appears in tractate *Bekhorot* (53b), based on the verse: "You shall tithe [*asser te'asser*]" (Deuteronomy 14:22), which, according to the Gemara's homiletical interpretation of the doubled verb, is referring to two types of tithes (Rashi; see *Tosafot*). Rabbeinu Ḥananel does not have this juxtaposition of second tithe to animal tithe in his version of the text, as second tithe itself is a compulsory offering for which there is no set time, and the juxtaposition is therefore unnecessary.

NOTES

But these require the Temple – **והא בעי בירה**: According to Rashi, as understood by *Shita Mekubbetzet*, the Temple is called the *bira*, as David said: "And give to Solomon my son a whole heart, to keep Your commandments, Your testimonies, and Your statutes, and to fulfill all these matters, and to build the Temple [*bira*], for which I have made provision" (I Chronicles 29:19; see 104b). Consequently, the Gemara is saying that second tithe must be eaten in a stone building, not a tent, as only a stone building is defined as "before the Lord your God" in this context. Rabbeinu Ḥananel explains that the word *bira* is an abbreviation of the term *Beit HaBeḥira*, the Chosen House, and alludes to the declaration of tithes that was made in the Temple "before the Lord." This declaration contains the statement: "I have hearkened to the voice of the Lord" (Deuteronomy 26:14), which is interpreted in the Mishna (*Ma'aser Sheni* 5:12) as referring to bringing the tithe to the Temple [*Beit HaBeḥira*].

Inheritance, this is a reference to Jerusalem – **נחלה זו ירושלים**: Jerusalem, like an inheritance, will endure forever without interruption.

מכלל דלרבי יהודה קרב? אין, דהאמר רב אדא בר מתנה: מעשר שני ומעשר בהמה נאכלין בנוב וגבעון לדברי רבי יהודה. והא בעי בירה! ולאו תני רב יוסף: שלש בירות הן: שילה ונוב וגבעון ובית עולמים? הוא תני לה והוא אמר לה: לאכילת מעשר שני, ואליבא דרבי יהודה.

The Gemara asks: Based on this, may it be concluded **by inference that according to** the opinion of **Rabbi Yehuda** that compulsory offerings for which there is no set time were sacrificed upon a great public altar, second tithe was eaten there and animal tithe offerings were **sacrificed?** The Gemara responds: **Yes, as Rav Adda bar Mattana says: Second tithe and animal tithe** offerings **were consumed in Nov and Gibeon according to the statement of Rabbi Yehuda.** The Gemara challenges: **But these require** the **Temple,**[N] not a tent, to which people will come to eat tithes. The Gemara responds: **But didn't Rav Yosef teach** a *baraita* that states: **There were three temples: Shiloh, Nov and Gibeon, and the Eternal House. He teaches it and he says it:** This is referring **to consuming second tithe, and** is **in accordance with** the opinion **of Rabbi Yehuda.**

"באו לירושלים" [וכו']. תנו רבנן: "כי לא באתם עד עתה אל המנוחה ואל הנחלה", "מנוחה" – זו שילה, "נחלה" – זו ירושלים.

§ The mishna teaches that when they **arrived at Jerusalem,** private altars were prohibited and there was no subsequent period in which they were permitted. And the Temple in Jerusalem was characterized as "inheritance." With regard to this, **the Sages taught** in a *baraita*: The verse that discusses the permissibility of private altars states: **"For you have not as yet come to the rest and to the inheritance"** (Deuteronomy 12:9). The Gemara interprets: With regard to **"rest," this** is a reference to **Shiloh,** and with regard to **"inheritance," this** is a reference to **Jerusalem.**[N]

ואומר: "היתה לי נחלתי כאריה ביער", ואומר: "העיט צבוע נחלתי לי העיט סביב עליה", דברי רבי יהודה.

And similarly, the verse that relates a prophecy with regard to Jerusalem **states:** "I have forsaken My house, I have cast off My inheritance… **My inheritance has become to Me as a lion in the forest"** (Jeremiah 12:7–8). **And** additionally, in that same prophecy the verse **states: "Is My inheritance to Me as a speckled bird of prey? Are the birds of prey against her round about?"** (Jeremiah 12:9). This is **the statement of Rabbi Yehuda.**

רבי שמעון אומר: "מנוחה" – זו ירושלים, "נחלה" – זו שילה. ואומר: "זאת מנוחתי עדי עד פה אשב כי אויתיה", ואומר: "כי בחר ה׳ בציון אוה למושב לו".

By contrast, **Rabbi Shimon says:** With regard to **"rest," this** is a reference to **Jerusalem,** and with regard to **"inheritance," this** is a reference to **Shiloh. And** this is evident from the verse that **says: "This is My resting place forever; here will I dwell, for I have desired it"** (Psalms 132:14). **And it states** in the previous verse: **"For the Lord has chosen Zion; He has desired it for His habitation"** (Psalms 132:13), which indicates that the verses are referring to Jerusalem.

בשלמא למאן דאמר: "מנוחה" זו שילה – היינו דכתיב: "אל המנוחה ואל הנחלה". אלא למאן דאמר: "מנוחה" זו ירושלים, "נחלה" זו שילה – "אל הנחלה ואל המנוחה" מיבעי ליה! הכי קאמר: לא מיבעיא מנוחה דלא מטיתו, אלא אפילו לנחלה נמי לא מטיתו.

The Gemara challenges: **Granted, according to the one who says** that with regard to **"rest," this** is a reference to **Shiloh; that is, as it is written: "To the rest and to the inheritance,"** in chronological order, as the period of Shiloh preceded that of Jerusalem. **But according to the one who says** that with regard to **"rest," this** is a reference to **Jerusalem,** and with regard to **"inheritance," this** is a reference to **Shiloh,** the verse **should have stated: To the inheritance and to the rest.** The Gemara explains: **This** is what the verse **is saying:** When you enter Eretz Yisrael private altars will be permitted, and **it is not necessary** to say **that you have not arrived at** the **"rest,"** i.e., the Temple in Jerusalem, **but you have not even arrived at** the **"inheritance,"** i.e., the Tabernacle in Shiloh.

תנא דבי רבי ישמעאל: זו וזו שילה, רבי שמעון בן יוחי אומר: זו וזו ירושלים. בשלמא למאן דאמר: "מנוחה" זו

§ With regard to the words "rest" and "inheritance" in the aforementioned verse, **the school of Rabbi Yishmael taught** that **this and that,** i.e., both terms, are a reference to **Shiloh.**[N] **Rabbi Shimon ben Yoḥai says:**[N] **This and that** are a reference to **Jerusalem.**[N] The Gemara asks: **Granted, according to the one who says** that with regard to **"rest," this** is

NOTES

This and that are a reference to Shiloh – **זו וזו שילה**: According to Rabbi Yishmael, this verse permits private altars only until the period of Shiloh, which is referred to as both "rest" and "inheritance." The Tabernacle at Shiloh can be described as an inheritance, since according to Rabbi Yishmael the word inheritance does not denote something that will endure without interruption.

Rabbi Shimon ben Yoḥai says – **רבי שמעון בן יוחאי אומר**: Apparently there is a disagreement with regard to the opinion of Rabbi Shimon, who is quoted earlier as saying that "inheritance" is a reference to Shiloh.

This and that are a reference to Jerusalem – **זו וזו ירושלים**: According to this opinion, which also disagrees with the mishna, private altars were permitted during the period of Shiloh.

שִׁילֹה, "נַחֲלָה" – זוֹ יְרוּשָׁלַיִם, אִי נַמִּי אִיפְּכָא – הַיְינוּ דִּכְתִיב: "אֶל הַמְּנוּחָה וְאֶל הַנַּחֲלָה". אֶלָּא לְמַאן דְּאָמַר: זוֹ וָזוֹ שִׁילֹה, אוֹ זוֹ וָזוֹ יְרוּשָׁלַיִם, "מְנוּחָה נַחֲלָה" מִיבְּעֵי לֵיהּ! קַשְׁיָא.

a reference to **Shiloh,** and with regard to **"inheritance," this** is a reference to **Jerusalem, or the reverse,** i.e., that "rest" is a reference to Jerusalem and "inheritance" is a reference to Shiloh, **this is as it is written: "To the rest and to the inheritance** [*el hamenuḥa ve'el hanaḥala*]**,"** utilizing two different phrases. **But according to the one,** i.e., the school of Rabbi Yishmael, **who says this and that** are both references to **Shiloh, or** according to the opinion of Rabbi Shimon ben Yoḥai that both **this and that** are references to **Jerusalem,** the verse **should have** stated: For you have not as yet come to the **rest** and **inheritance** [*menuḥa naḥala*]**.**[N] The Gemara concedes that this is **difficult.**

בִּשְׁלָמָא לְמַאן דְּאָמַר: זוֹ וָזוֹ שִׁילֹה, "מְנוּחָה" – דְּנָחוּ מִכִּיבּוּשׁ, "נַחֲלָה" (זוֹ) – דִּפְלַגוּ הָתָם נַחֲלוֹת, דִּכְתִיב: "וַיְחַלֵּק לָהֶם יְהוֹשֻׁעַ וַיַּפֵּל לָהֶם גּוֹרָל בְּשִׁילֹה עַל פִּי ה'".

The Gemara comments: **Granted, according to the one,** i.e., Rabbi Shimon ben Yoḥai, **who says this and that** are references to **Shiloh,** each of the designations may be explained: It is called **"rest" because** during the period of Shiloh they **rested from the conquest** in the time of Joshua, and it is called **"inheritance" because** they **divided** the **portions** of land among the tribes **there, as it is written: "And Joshua divided** the land **for them, and he cast a lot for them in Shiloh according to the Lord"** (Joshua 18:10).

אֶלָּא לְמַאן דְּאָמַר: זוֹ וָזוֹ יְרוּשָׁלַיִם, בִּשְׁלָמָא "נַחֲלָה" – נַחֲלַת עוֹלָמִים, אֶלָּא "מְנוּחָה", מַאי מְנוּחָה? מְנוּחַת אָרוֹן, דִּכְתִיב: "וַיְהִי כְּנוֹחַ הָאָרוֹן".

But according to the one, i.e., the school of Rabbi Yishmael, **who says this and that** are references to **Jerusalem, granted** that **"inheritance"** is a reference to Jerusalem, since it is **an eternal inheritance. But** with regard to **"rest," what rest** was there in the Temple in Jerusalem? The Gemara answers: **The rest of the Ark, as it is written: And when the ark rested.**[N] In other words, verses occasionally refer to the Temple in Jerusalem as the resting place of the Ark.

בִּשְׁלָמָא לְמַאן דְּאָמַר: זוֹ וָזוֹ יְרוּשָׁלַיִם, אֲבָל שִׁילֹה הֲוָה שְׁרֵיָא בָּמוֹת – הַיְינוּ דִּכְתִיב: "וַיִּקַּח מָנוֹחַ אֶת גְּדִי הָעִזִּים וְאֶת הַמִּנְחָה וַיַּעַל עַל הַצּוּר לַה'".

The Gemara comments: **Granted, according to the one,** i.e., Rabbi Shimon ben Yoḥai, **who says** that **this and that** are references to **Jerusalem,** and consequently private altars were forbidden only following the establishment of the Temple in Jerusalem, **but** during the period of the Tabernacle in **Shiloh** private **altars were permitted, this is as it is written: "So Manoah took the kid with the meal offering, and offered them upon the rock to the Lord"** (Judges 13:19),[N] i.e., he sacrificed them upon a private altar and not in Shiloh.

אֶלָּא לְמַאן דְּאָמַר: זוֹ וָזוֹ שִׁילֹה, וּבָמוֹת הֲוָה אֲסִירָן, מַאי "וַיִּקַּח מָנוֹחַ"? הוֹרָאַת שָׁעָה הָיְתָה.

But according to the one, i.e., the school of Rabbi Yishmael, **who says** that **this and that** are references to **Shiloh, and** private **altars were forbidden** during this period, **what is** the meaning of: **"So Manoah took,"** as it was forbidden to sacrifice offerings outside the Temple? The Gemara answers: Permitting this sacrifice **was a provisional edict** issued in exigent circumstances.

תָּנָא דְּבֵי רַבִּי יִשְׁמָעֵאל כְּרַבִּי שִׁמְעוֹן בֶּן יוֹחַי, דְּאָמַר: זוֹ וָזוֹ יְרוּשָׁלַיִם. וְסִימָנָיךְ: מַשְׁכֵי גַּבְרָא לְגַבְרֵי.

The Gemara notes that with regard to the disagreement between the *tanna'im* over the interpretation of the words "rest" and "inheritance," there is another version of that which **the school of Rabbi Yishmael taught,** which is **in accordance with** the opinion of **Rabbi Shimon ben Yoḥai, who says** that **this and that** are references to **Jerusalem. And your mnemonic** to remember this is: **The man pulled the men,**[N] meaning: Rabbi Shimon ben Yoḥai, who is an individual, pulled, i.e., convinced, the members of the school of Rabbi Yishmael to adopt his opinion.

"כָּל הַקֳּדָשִׁים" [וכו']. אָמַר רַב כָּהֲנָא: לֹא שָׁנוּ אֶלָּא בִּשְׁחִיטָה, אֲבָל בְּהַעֲלָאָה – כָּרֵת נַמִּי מִיחַיַּיב.

§ The mishna teaches that with regard to **all offerings** that one consecrated during a period of the permitting of private altars and sacrificed outside their designated area during a period of prohibition of private altars, one is in violation of a positive mitzva and a prohibition, but he is not liable to receive *karet* for sacrificing them. With regard to this, **Rav Kahana says: They taught** that **only with regard to slaughter**[N] of these animals outside the designated area is one not liable to receive *karet.* **But with regard to offering up,** one would **also** be **liable** to receive ***karet.***

NOTES

The verse should have stated rest and inheritance [*menuḥa naḥala*] – מְנוּחָה נַחֲלָה מִיבְּעֵי לֵיהּ: In other words, the verse should have used either the term "rest" or the term "inheritance"; why was it necessary to use both? Alternatively, the difficulty lies in the repetition of the term: "To [*el*]," before the word "inheritance," which divides the two terms and indicates that they refer to two separate places. Had both terms been descriptions of the same place, the verse should have stated: To the rest and the inheritance [*el hamenuḥa vehanaḥala*]," or "to the rest of inheritance [*lemenuḥat hanaḥala*]" (see Rabbeinu Ḥananel).

And when the Ark rested – וַיְהִי כְּנוֹחַ הָאָרוֹן: Rashi notes that this is not a precise quote of a verse, as there is no such verse in the Bible. Likewise, the Gemara in a number of instances in this discussion, including with regard to the division of Eretz Yisrael during the time of Joshua, does not cite verses precisely. In this particular instance, the intention is that there are verses that refer to the fact that the Ark rested in Jerusalem. Rashi references a verse where this concept is alluded to by King Solomon after the construction of the Temple: "Now therefore arise O Lord God in Your resting place, You and the Ark of Your strength" (II Chronicles 6:41). See also *Tosafot*, who suggest other possible verses that the Gemara may be referring to here.

This is as it is written: "So Manoah took…and offered them upon the rock to the Lord" – וַיִּקַּח מָנוֹחַ...וַיַּעַל עַל הַצּוּר לַה': Rabbi Shimon also derives from this verse that a private altar need not be a formal altar, as Manoah sacrificed his offering on a rock, and it was accepted (see 108b).

The man pulled the men – מַשְׁכֵי גַּבְרָא לְגַבְרֵי: *Tosafot* (53b) state that the correct version of the text should read, in accordance with the *Arukh*: The men, i.e., Rabbi Shimon, whose name comprises two names, Shimon and Yoḥai, pulled the man, i.e., Rabbi Yishmael.

They taught only with regard to slaughter – לֹא שָׁנוּ אֶלָּא בִּשְׁחִיטָה: Rav Kahana's statement is based on the *baraita* that was cited on 106b. That *baraita* interprets the verses in Leviticus (17:5–7) that appear in the context of the prohibition against slaughtering offerings outside their designated place as pertaining to offerings that were consecrated during a period of the permitting of private altars. The *baraita* infers from those verses: From the phrase: "And they shall bring them to the Lord," it is derived that there is a positive mitzva to bring these offerings to the Tabernacle.

From where is it derived that one violates a prohibition if he sacrifices animals outside the Tabernacle? The verse states: "And they shall no more slaughter." One might have thought that doing so would be punishable by *karet*. Therefore, the verse states: "This shall be a statute forever for them throughout their generations" (Leviticus 17:7), from which it is derived: This, i.e., a punishment for failing to fulfill a positive mitzva and for violating a prohibition, shall be for them, but another punishment, *karet*, shall not be for them. This is the source of the mishna, to which Rav Kahana adds that from the subsequent verses it may be inferred that these *halakhot* apply only to slaughter and not to offering up.

מַאי טַעְמָא? דְּאָמַר קְרָא: ״וַאֲלֵהֶם תֹּאמַר״ – עַל הַסְּמוּכִין תֹּאמַר.

What is the reason for this? It is **that** immediately following the Torah's description of an offering that was consecrated during a period of the permitting of private altars **the verse states** the penalty for sacrificing outside the designated area: **"And to them [*va'alehem*] you shall say"** (Leviticus 17:8). The term "*alehem*," to them, the first letter of which is the letter *aleph*, is phonetically similar to the term: *Alehem*, about them, the first letter of which is the letter *ayin*. Therefore, the verse can be understood to mean: **About that which is** written in the **adjacent** passage **you shall say.** The preceding passage discusses offerings that were slaughtered outside the Temple, so although there is no penalty of *karet* for their slaughter, one is liable for *karet* for sacrificing them upon a private altar.

מַתְקִיף לַהּ רָבָא: מִי כְּתִיב ״וַעֲלֵיהֶם תֹּאמַר״? ״אֲלֵהֶם״ כְּתִיב, וַ״אֲלֵיהֶם״ קָרֵינַן!

Rava objects to this: Is it written: And about them you shall say? "To them" is written, and we read it as **"to them."** The verse means that the command should be relayed to Aaron, his sons, and the Jewish people, who are mentioned in the beginning of the passage.

וְעוֹד תַּנְיָא: אַרְבָּעָה כְּלָלוֹת הָיָה רַבִּי שִׁמְעוֹן אוֹמֵר בְּקָדָשִׁים: הִקְדִּישָׁן בִּשְׁעַת אִיסּוּר הַבָּמוֹת, וְשָׁחַט וְהֶעֱלָה בִּשְׁעַת אִיסּוּר הַבָּמוֹת בַּחוּץ – הֲרֵי הֵן בַּעֲשֵׂה וְלֹא תַעֲשֶׂה, וְיֵשׁ בָּהֶן כָּרֵת. הִקְדִּישָׁן בִּשְׁעַת הֶיתֵּר הַבָּמוֹת, וְשָׁחַט וְהֶעֱלָה בִּשְׁעַת אִיסּוּר הַבָּמוֹת – הֲרֵי הֵן בַּעֲשֵׂה וְלֹא תַעֲשֶׂה, וְאֵין בָּהֶן כָּרֵת.

And additionally, it is taught in a *baraita*: **Rabbi Shimon would say four principles with regard to sacrificial** animals: With regard to offerings that one **consecrated during a period of prohibition of** private **altars, and slaughtered and offered up outside** their designated area **during a period of prohibition of** private **altars,** for **these** one is **in** violation of **a positive mitzva and a prohibition, and they carry** the punishment of ***karet***.[N] With regard to one who **consecrated them during a period of** the **permitting of** private **altars, and slaughtered and offered** them **up during a period of prohibition of** private **altars,** for **these** one is **in** violation of **a positive mitzva and a prohibition, but they do not carry** the punishment of ***karet***.

הִקְדִּישָׁן בִּשְׁעַת אִיסּוּר הַבָּמוֹת וְשָׁחַט וְהֶעֱלָה בַּחוּץ בִּשְׁעַת הֶיתֵּר הַבָּמוֹת – הֲרֵי הֵן בַּעֲשֵׂה, וְאֵין בָּהֶן בְּלֹא תַעֲשֶׂה.

With regard to one who **consecrated them during a period of prohibition of** private **altars,**[N] **and slaughtered and offered** them **up outside** their designated area **during a period of** the **permitting of** private **altars,** for **these** one is **in** violation of **a positive mitzva, but** one has **not** violated **a prohibition with regard to them.**

הִקְדִּישָׁן בִּשְׁעַת הֶיתֵּר הַבָּמוֹת וְשָׁחַט וְהֶעֱלָה בִּשְׁעַת הֶיתֵּר הַבָּמוֹת – פָּטוּר מִכְּלוּם. תְּיוּבְתָּא דְּרַב כָּהֲנָא! תְּיוּבְתָּא.

With regard to one who **consecrated them during a period of** the **permitting of** private **altars, and slaughtered and offered** them **up during a period of** the **permitting of** private **altars,** he is **exempt from all** violations. The *baraita* states explicitly that there is no distinction between slaughtering and offering up on a private altar: In both cases, one who consecrated the offering during a period of the permitting of private altars and slaughtered or offered it up during a period of prohibition of private altars is exempt from the punishment of *karet*. The Gemara concludes: **The refutation of** the opinion of **Rav Kahana,** who distinguished between slaughter and offering up, is **a conclusive refutation.**

״וְאֵלּוּ קָדָשִׁים״ [וכו׳]. סְמִיכָה – דִּכְתִיב: ״לִפְנֵי ה׳ וְסָמַךְ״.

§ The mishna teaches: **And these are the consecrated** items, and lists components of the sacrificial service that were performed only on a great public altar, i.e., in the Tabernacle, and not on a private altar. The Gemara clarifies the source of each ritual on the list: The source for the *halakha* concerning **placing hands** on the head of an offering is **as it is written:** "If his offering be a burnt offering… he shall bring it to the entrance of the Tent of Meeting, that he may be accepted **before the Lord. And he shall lay** his hand[N] upon the head of the burnt offering" (Leviticus 1:3–4).

שְׁחִיטַת צָפוֹן – דִּכְתִיב: ״צָפוֹנָה לִפְנֵי ה׳״. מַתָּנוֹת סָבִיב – דִּכְתִיב ״וְזָרַק עַל הַמִּזְבֵּחַ סָבִיב (סָבִיב)״.

The source for the *halakha* concerning **slaughtering** offerings of the most sacred order in the **north** is **as it is written:** "And he shall slaughter it on the side of the altar **northward before the Lord**" (Leviticus 1:11). The source for the *halakha* concerning **placement** of the blood of a burnt offering **around,** i.e., on all four sides of, the altar, is **as it is written: "And** Aaron's sons, the priests, **shall… sprinkle** the blood **roundabout against the altar** that is at the entrance of the Tent of Meeting" (Leviticus 1:5).

NOTES

One is in violation of a positive mitzva and a prohibition, and they carry the punishment of *karet* – בַּעֲשֵׂה וְלֹא תַעֲשֶׂה וְיֵשׁ בָּהֶן כָּרֵת: According to Rashi, the positive mitzva to sacrifice in the Temple is: "That they may bring them to the Lord, to the entrance of the Tent of Meeting" (Leviticus 17:5). The Rambam cites the verse: "Then it shall come to pass that the place that the Lord your God shall choose to cause His name to dwell there, there you shall bring all that I command you" (Deuteronomy 12:11). Rabbi Ovadya Bartenura, who also cites the latter verse, explains that it is in actuality a prohibition, i.e., not to sacrifice on a private altar, but a prohibition that stems from a positive mitzva is classified as a positive mitzva.

The prohibition is that which is written: "Take heed to yourself that you do not offer your burnt offerings in every place that you see" (Deuteronomy 12:13), as the phrase "take heed" always denotes a prohibition. The liability to receive *karet* is derived from the verses: "And you shall say to them: Whatsoever man there is of the house of Israel, or of the strangers that sojourn among them, that sacrifices a burnt offering or sacrifice and brings it not to the entrance of the Tent of Meeting, to sacrifice it to the Lord, that man shall be cut off from his people" (Leviticus 17:8–9).

One who consecrated them during a period of prohibition of private altars, etc. – הִקְדִּישָׁן בִּשְׁעַת אִיסּוּר הַבָּמוֹת וכו׳: Rashi (112b) explains that one has violated the positive mitzva: "That they may bring them to the Lord" (Leviticus 17:5), by not sacrificing the offering during the period of prohibition of private altars.

The *Sefat Emet* notes that according to this opinion in the *baraita*, there is no need to state that the offering was sacrificed during the period of the permitting of private altars. He therefore suggests that one violates a positive mitzva only if one sacrificed the offering upon a private altar. But if one sacrificed it upon a great public altar the positive mitzva has not been violated, a point that is made explicitly in the *Tosefta* (13:9). For a different analysis of this matter, see the Rashash on 112b.

Placing hands is as it is written, before the Lord and he shall lay his hand – סְמִיכָה דִּכְתִיב לִפְנֵי ה׳ וְסָמַךְ: Rabbeinu Ḥananel explains that a great public altar is classified as: An altar of the Lord, and therefore the Gemara cites verses that make reference to an altar or which say "before the Lord." Rambam's Commentary on the Mishna adds that the same applies to any place designated as: Holy, or: Tent of Meeting (see Rashi).

תְּנוּפָה – דִּכְתִיב: "וְהֵנִיף הַכֹּהֵן לִפְנֵי ה'". הַגָּשָׁה – דִּכְתִיב: "וְהִגִּישָׁהּ אֶל הַמִּזְבֵּחַ".

The source for the *halakha* concerning **waving** of those offerings that require waving is **as it is written: "And the priest** shall take one of the lambs, and offer it for a guilt offering, and the *log* of oil, and **wave** them for a wave offering **before the Lord"** (Leviticus 14:12). The source for the *halakha* concerning **bringing** meal offerings to the corner of the altar before the removal of the handful is **as it is written: "And he shall bring it to the altar"** (Leviticus 2:8). The definite article before the word "altar" indicates that this applies only to the altar in the Tabernacle, and not on a private altar.

"רַבִּי יְהוּדָה אוֹמֵר: אֵין מִנְחָה בְּבָמָה". אָמַר רַב שֵׁשֶׁת: לְדִבְרֵי הָאוֹמֵר יֵשׁ מִנְחָה בְּבָמָה – יֵשׁ עוֹפוֹת בְּבָמָה, לְדִבְרֵי הָאוֹמֵר אֵין מִנְחָה בְּבָמָה – אֵין עוֹפוֹת בְּבָמָה;

§ With regard to the question of whether a meal offering was sacrificed upon an altar outside the Temple, the mishna teaches that **Rabbi Yehuda says: There is no meal offering** sacrificed **on an altar** outside the Temple, even a great public altar, e.g., the Tabernacle in Gilgal, Nov, and Gibeon. **Rav Sheshet says: According to the statement of the one who says there is a meal offering** sacrificed **on an altar** outside the Temple, **there are** also **bird** offerings sacrificed **on an altar** outside the Temple. **According to the statement of the one who says there is no meal offering** sacrificed **on an altar** outside the Temple, **there are** also **no bird** offerings sacrificed **on an altar** outside the Temple.

"זְבָחִים" – וְלֹא מְנָחוֹת, "זְבָחִים" – וְלֹא עוֹפוֹת.

The reason for this is that the Torah is referring to offerings that were sacrificed during the period of the permitting of private altars as: Slaughtered offerings [*zevaḥim*], in the verse: "And sacrifice them for sacrifices of [*vezaveḥu zivḥei*] peace offerings" (Leviticus 17:5), from which it may be inferred: **Slaughtered offerings but not meal offerings; slaughtered offerings but not bird** offerings,[N] i.e., neither meal offerings nor bird offerings were sacrificed on an altar outside the Temple, including a great public altar.

וְכֹהֵן – דִּכְתִיב: "וְזָרַק הַכֹּהֵן", בִּגְדֵי שָׁרֵת – "לְשָׁרֵת בַּקֹּדֶשׁ",

The Gemara continues detailing the distinctions between great public altars and small private altars: **And a priest** is required only at a public altar, **as it is written: "And the priest shall sprinkle** the blood against the altar of the Lord at the entrance of the Tent of Meeting" (Leviticus 17:6). Priestly **service vestments**[N] are required only at a public altar, as it is written: "And they shall be upon Aaron, and upon his sons when they go into the Tent of Meeting or when they come near to the altar **to minister in the sacred place"** (Exodus 28:43).

וּכְלֵי שָׁרֵת – "אֲשֶׁר יְשָׁרְתוּ בָם בַּקֹּדֶשׁ". לְרֵיחַ נִיחוֹחַ – דִּכְתִיב: "לְרֵיחַ נִיחֹחַ לַה'".

And with regard to **service vessels,** it is written: "And they shall take all the service vessels **wherewith they serve in the sacred place"** (Numbers 4:12). With regard **to a pleasing aroma,** i.e., that limbs that had previously been roasted off the altar should not be placed upon the altar, it is required only on a public altar, **as it is written:** "And the priest shall sprinkle the blood against the altar of the Lord at the entrance of the Tent of Meeting, and the priest shall make the fat smoke **for an aroma pleasing to the Lord"** (Leviticus 17:6).

מְחִיצָה בְּדָמִים – דִּכְתִיב: "וְהָיְתָה הָרֶשֶׁת עַד חֲצִי הַמִּזְבֵּחַ". רִיחוּץ יָדַיִם – דִּכְתִיב: "וּבְקָרְבָתָם אֶל הַמִּזְבֵּחַ יִרְחָצוּ".

A partition for the **blood,** i.e., the red line that divides the altar, as the blood of some offerings, e.g., a sin offering, was sprinkled above the line, and the blood of other offerings, e.g., a burnt offering, was sprinkled below the line, was required only on a public altar, **as it is written: "And the net may reach halfway up the altar"** (Exodus 27:5). The definite article before the word "altar" indicates that this applied only to the altar in the Tabernacle. With regard to the requirement for **washing of hands** and feet before the service, it is required only on a public altar, **as it is written:** "When they went into the Tent of Meeting **and when they came near to the altar, they shall wash"** (Exodus 40:32).

אָמַר רָמִי בַּר חָמָא: לֹא שָׁנוּ אֶלָּא בְּקָדְשֵׁי בָּמָה קְטַנָּה וְהִקְרִיבוּם בְּבָמָה קְטַנָּה, אֲבָל בְּקָדְשֵׁי בָּמָה קְטַנָּה דְּקָרְבִינְהוּ בְּבָמָה גְּדוֹלָה – יֵשׁ חִיצּוּי.

§ Concerning the *halakha* requiring a partition for the blood, and other *halakhot* that did not apply to a private altar but did apply to a great public altar, **Rami bar Ḥama said:** The Sages **taught** that there is no requirement for a partition **only with regard to** consecrated **sacrificial** items to be used on **a small** private **altar,**[N] **and** which one **sacrificed upon a small** private **altar. But in** the case of consecrated **sacrificial** items to be used on **a small** private **altar that were sacrificed upon a great** public **altar, there is a partition.**

NOTES

Slaughtered offerings but not bird offerings – זְבָחִים וְלֹא עוֹפוֹת: Rashi on 69a cites as proof the verse that states with regard to the great public altar at Mount Sinai (Exodus 24:5): "And they sacrificed slaughtered offerings of cattle to the Lord" (see 117b).

Priestly service vestments, etc. – בִּגְדֵי שָׁרֵת וכו׳: An alternative version of the text of the Gemara cites the verse: "Seven days shall the son that is priest in his stead put them on" (Exodus 29:30), indicating that only priests are obligated to wear the priestly vestments. Since the sacrificial service on a private altar does not need to be performed by a priest, there is no need for the priestly vestments. The same is true with regard to the washing of hands and feet (*Sefat Emet* and *Or HaYashar*, citing 19b).

With regard to sacrificial items to be used on a small private altar – בְּקָדְשֵׁי בָּמָה קְטַנָּה: Rashi explains that these offerings were slaughtered on a small private altar and then sacrificed on a public altar. The version of Rashi that appears in *Shita Mekubbetzet* reads: That were consecrated, rather than: That were slaughtered.

NOTES

That one brought inside – **שֶׁהִכְנִיסָהּ בִּפְנִים**: Rashi explains that the offering had already been slaughtered outside. *Keren Ora* explains that in Rashi's opinion, an animal can be absorbed by the partitions only once it has been slaughtered and its limbs, which are prepared for sacrifice, have been brought into an area designated for offerings. *Tosafot* explain that the animal was brought inside alive.

Absorbed by the partitions – **קְלָטוּהָ מְחִיצוֹת**: The partitions of the courtyard of the Tabernacle were present at the great public altars, as was taught in the mishna (112b) with regard to offerings of the most sacred order. These were eaten at a great public altar within the curtains surrounding the courtyard of the Tabernacle.

מוֹתִיב רַבָּה: חָזֶה וְשׁוֹק, תְּרוּמַת לַחְמֵי תוֹדָה – נוֹהֲגִין בְּקָדְשֵׁי בָּמָה גְּדוֹלָה, וְאֵין נוֹהֲגִין בְּקָדְשֵׁי בָּמָה קְטַנָּה! אֵימָא: נוֹהֲגִין בְּבָמָה גְּדוֹלָה וְאֵין נוֹהֲגִין בְּבָמָה קְטַנָּה.

Rabba raised an objection from a *baraita*: The *halakha* of waving the **breast and** the **thigh** of a peace offering and **the *teruma* of the loaves of a thanks offering applies with regard to sacrificial** items **of a great** public **altar and does not apply with regard to sacrificial** items **of a small** private **altar**, even if they were sacrificed upon a great public altar. The Gemara responds: **Say** that the text of the *baraita* should be the following: The *halakha* of waving the breast and thigh and the *teruma* of the loaves of a thanks offering **applies to a great** public **altar**, even with regard to a sacrificial item of a small private altar, **but does not apply to a small** private **altar**.

אִיכָּא דְּאָמְרִי: אֲמַר רָמִי בַּר חָמָא: לֹא שָׁנוּ אֶלָּא בְּקָדְשֵׁי בָּמָה גְּדוֹלָה וְהִקְרִיבָן בְּבָמָה גְּדוֹלָה, אֲבָל בְּקָדְשֵׁי בָּמָה קְטַנָּה, אַף עַל גַּב דְּקָרְבִינְהוּ בְּבָמָה גְּדוֹלָה – אֵין חִיצּוּי.

Some say that **Rami bar Ḥama said:** The Sages **taught** that there is a requirement for a partition **only with regard to sacrificial** items **of a great** public **altar that were sacrificed upon a great** public **altar. But in the case of sacrificial** items **of a small** private **altar, even though they were sacrificed upon a great** public **altar, there is no partition.**

לֵימָא מְסַיַּיע לֵיהּ: חָזֶה וְשׁוֹק וּתְרוּמַת לַחְמֵי תוֹדָה – נוֹהֲגִין בְּקָדְשֵׁי בָּמָה גְּדוֹלָה, וְאֵין נוֹהֲגִין בְּקָדְשֵׁי בָּמָה קְטַנָּה.

The Gemara suggests: **Let us say** that the following *baraita* **supports** the opinion **of** Rami bar Ḥama: Waving of the **breast and thigh** of a peace offering **and the *teruma* of the loaves of a thanks offering applies to sacrificial** items **of a great** public **altar, and does not apply to sacrificial** items **of a small** private **altar.**

אֵימָא: נוֹהֲגִין בְּבָמָה גְּדוֹלָה וְאֵין נוֹהֲגִין בְּבָמָה קְטַנָּה. וּפְלִיגָא דְּרַבִּי אֶלְעָזָר, דְּאָמַר רַבִּי אֶלְעָזָר: עוֹלַת בָּמַת יָחִיד שֶׁהִכְנִיסָהּ בִּפְנִים – קְלָטוּהָ מְחִיצוֹת לְכָל דָּבָר.

The Gemara responds: No proof may be brought from here, as **I will say** that it means the *halakha* of waving the breast and thigh and the *teruma* of the loaves of a thanks offering **applies to a great** public **altar**, even with regard to the sacrificial items of a private altar, **and does not apply to a small** private **altar**. The Gemara notes: **And** this latter version of Rami bar Ḥama's statement **disagrees with** the opinion of **Rabbi Elazar, as Rabbi Elazar says: A burnt offering of a private altar that one brought inside,**[N] i.e., into the area of a great public altar, is **absorbed,** i.e., sanctified, by the **partitions**[N] **for all matters.**

בָּעֵי רַבִּי זֵירָא: עוֹלַת בָּמַת יָחִיד

With regard to the previous matter, **Rabbi Zeira raises a dilemma:** With regard to **a burnt offering of a private altar**

שֶׁהִכְנִיסָהּ לִפְנִים וְהוֹצִיאָהּ לַחוּץ, מַהוּ? מִי אָמְרִינַן: כֵּיוָן דְּעַיְּילָא – קָלְטָה לָהּ מְחִיצְתָא, אוֹ דִּלְמָא כֵּיוָן דַּהֲדַר – הֲדַר?

that one brought inside and subsequently **took outside, what is** the *halakha*? Does it have the status of a sacrificial item of a public altar? The Gemara clarifies the question: **Do we say** that **once** it was **brought in the partition** has already **absorbed it,**[N] and all *halakhot* of sacrificial items of a public altar apply; **or perhaps once** it **returns,** i.e., was taken outside again, **it returns** to its prior status as an offering of a private altar?

NOTES

Once brought in the partition absorbed it – **כֵּיוָן דְּעַיְּילָא קָלְטָה לָהּ מְחִיצְתָא**: If so, all the *halakhot* of a great public altar are in effect, e.g., *teruma* of the breast and thigh are required, and the offering must be returned to the great public altar (Rashi). The commentaries question why this offering would not be disqualified due to its being taken outside its boundaries, which is the *halakha* with an offering that is slaughtered inside. Some explain that since this animal was consecrated to be sacrificed upon a private altar and was slaughtered there, it cannot be disqualified if it was taken outside a public altar. Nevertheless, they suggest that perhaps Rabbi Zeira's question concerns this very point: Is this burnt offering rendered invalid after being taken outside or not (*Ḥok Natan*).

לָאו הַיְינוּ פְּלוּגְתָּא דְּרַבָּה וְרַב יוֹסֵף? דִּתְנַן: קׇדְשֵׁי קֳדָשִׁים שֶׁשְּׁחָטָן בַּדָּרוֹם – מוֹעֲלִין בָּהֶן, וְאִם עָלוּ – לֹא יֵרְדוּ.

The Gemara asks: **Isn't this** issue **a disagreement between Rabba and Rav Yosef? As we learned** in a mishna (*Me'ila* 2a): With regard to **offerings of the most sacred order,** e.g., a sin offering or a guilt offering, **that were slaughtered in the south**[NH] of the Temple courtyard, and not in the north as dictated by *halakha*, and are therefore disqualified, one who derives benefit **from** them is liable for **misuse** of consecrated property, **and** despite the fact that they should not ascend the altar, **if they ascended they shall not descend.**[H]

וְאִיבַּעְיָא לְהוּ: יָרְדוּ, מַהוּ שֶׁיַּעֲלוּ? רַבָּה אָמַר: לֹא יַעֲלוּ, וְרַב יוֹסֵף אָמַר: יַעֲלוּ.

And a dilemma was raised before the Sages: If they **did descend** the altar, **what is the** *halakha* with regard to **ascending** again?[N] **Rabba says: They shall not ascend, and Rav Yosef says: They shall ascend.** Consequently, they disagree with regard to the issue of whether an item that is not fit to be sacrificed in a consecrated area acquires the sanctity of that area even if it is removed from there.

תִּיבְּעֵי לְרַבָּה, תִּיבְּעֵי לְרַב יוֹסֵף. תִּיבָּעֵי לְרַבָּה: עַד כָּאן לָא קָאָמַר רַבָּה אֶלָּא בְּמִזְבֵּחַ, דַּחֲזֵי לֵיהּ – מְקַדֵּשׁ, דְּלָא חֲזֵי – לָא מְקַדֵּשׁ. אֲבָל מְחִיצָה, אַף עַל גַּב דְּלָא חֲזֵי לֵיהּ – קָלְטָה.

The Gemara responds: The disagreements are not identical, as **the dilemma can be raised according to** the opinion of **Rabba,** and **the dilemma can be raised according to** the opinion of **Rav Yosef.** The Gemara elaborates: It is possible to **raise the dilemma according to** the opinion of **Rabba,** as **Rabba says** his statement: Offerings of the most sacred order that were slaughtered in the south shall not descend if they ascended, **only with regard to the altar,** as the altar **consecrates that which is fit for it,** while it **does not consecrate that which is not fit for it.**[N] **But** with regard to the **partition** of the public altar, **even though** an offering that was consecrated for a private altar **is not fit for** that altar, the partition nevertheless **absorbs** the offering and it is sacrificed there. Consequently, all the *halakhot* of the public altar apply to that offering, even if it is taken outside.

אוֹ דִּלְמָא אֲפִילּוּ לְרַב יוֹסֵף; עַד כָּאן לָא קָאָמַר רַב יוֹסֵף הָתָם אֶלָּא דְּחַד מָקוֹם הוּא, אֲבָל הָכָא דִּתְרֵי מְקוֹמוֹת נִינְהוּ – לָא. אוֹ דִּלְמָא לָא שְׁנָא? תֵּיקוּ.

Or perhaps the dilemma of the burnt offering of a private altar can be raised **even according to** the opinion of **Rav Yosef. Rav Yosef states** his opinion **there,** that offerings of the most sacred order that were slaughtered in the south of the Temple courtyard and descended the altar shall ascend again, **only because** the altar and the offering are both located in **one place,** i.e., the Temple courtyard. **But here** in Rabbi Zeira's case, **where** the private altar and public altar **are two** separate **places,** the *halakhot* of the public altar do **not** apply if the offering was taken outside the designated location. **Or perhaps** there **is no difference,** and the opinions of Rabba and Rav Yosef in one case are identical to their opinions in the other. The Gemara concludes: The dilemma **shall stand** unresolved.

מִילְּתָא דִּפְשִׁיטָא לֵיהּ לְרַבָּה בְּחַד גִּיסָא, וּלְרַב יוֹסֵף בְּחַד גִּיסָא, מִיבָּעֵי לֵיהּ לְרַבִּי יַנַּאי. דְּבָעֵי רַבִּי יַנַּאי: אֵבְרֵי עוֹלַת בָּמַת יָחִיד שֶׁעָלוּ לַמִּזְבֵּחַ וְיָרְדוּ, מַהוּ? הֵיכָא דְּלֹא מָשְׁלָה בָּהֶן הָאוּר – לָא תִּיבָּעֵי לָךְ. כִּי תִּיבָּעֵי לָךְ – הֵיכָא דְּמָשְׁלָה בָּהֶן הָאוּר, מַאי? תֵּיקוּ.

The Gemara notes that **a matter that is obvious to Rabba on one side,** i.e., that these offerings shall not ascend the altar again, **and to Rav Yosef on the other side,** i.e., that they shall ascend again, **was raised as a dilemma by Rabbi Yannai.**[N] **As Rabbi Yannai raises a dilemma: What is the** *halakha* with regard to **the limbs of a burnt offering of a private altar that ascended the altar and descended?** The Gemara notes: In a case **where the fire has not** yet **taken hold of them, do not raise the dilemma,** as they certainly shall not ascend again. **When should you raise the dilemma?** Raise it in a case **where the fire has taken hold of them: What** is the *halakha*? The Gemara concludes: The dilemma **shall stand** unresolved.

NOTES

Offerings of the most sacred order that were slaughtered in the south, etc. – **קׇדְשֵׁי קֳדָשִׁים שֶׁשְּׁחָטָן בַּדָּרוֹם וכו׳**: In other words, although they have been disqualified by being slaughtered in the incorrect location within the Temple courtyard they do not have the status of consecrated animals that died, for which the *halakha* of misuse of consecrated property would not apply (*Me'ila* 2a).

And a dilemma was raised before them…what is the *halakha* with regard to ascending again – **וְאִיבַּעְיָא לְהוּ...מַהוּ שֶׁיַּעֲלוּ**: Rabbeinu Ḥananel and Rashi maintain that this version of the text is erroneous, as in the parallel discussion in *Me'ila* (2b) the primary disagreement between Rabba and Rav Yosef concerns whether offerings that ascended the altar shall descend. But with regard to whether offerings should ascend if previously they should not have ascended but ascended nevertheless and then descended, even Rav Yosef agrees with the *halakha* stated explicitly in the mishna (84a), that for all offerings about which it is stated that they shall not ascend the altar, if they did ascend they shall not descend, but in any case if they did descend they shall not ascend again.

Therefore, Rashi emends the text to read: And a dilemma was raised before the Sages: What is the *halakha* with regard to descending? According to the opinion of Rabba, they have the status of a consecrated animal that died, and therefore they shall descend. Consequently, one must say the mishna that teaches that one who derives benefit from them is liable for misuse of consecrated property is by rabbinic law. By contrast, according to the opinion of Rav Yosef they have the status of any offering that was disqualified, and if they ascended they shall not descend.

Tosafot explain the standard version of the text as referring to a case where the fire of the altar had already burned some of the flesh of the offerings. In that case, even if they descended they shall ascend again, as they have already become the food of the altar (see 85b).

It does not consecrate that which is not fit for it – **דְּלָא חֲזֵי לָא מְקַדֵּשׁ**: Rabba agrees that if these offerings did ascend the altar they shall not descend, but only where the fire of the altar already burned some of the flesh. Having become food of the altar, they may not descend (*Tosafot*).

A matter that is obvious to Rabba on one side…was raised as a dilemma by Rabbi Yannai – **מִילְּתָא דִּפְשִׁיטָא לֵיהּ לְרַבָּה בְּחַד גִּיסָא...מִיבָּעֵי לֵיהּ לְרַבִּי יַנַּאי**: *Tosafot* explain that this means Rabbi Yannai is unsure whether the limbs of a burnt offering of a private altar have the status of the limbs of offerings of the highest order of sanctity that were slaughtered in the south of the Temple courtyard. Others explain that the limbs of a burnt offering of a private altar do have a status identical to the limbs of offerings of the highest order of sanctity that were slaughtered in the south of the Temple courtyard, and therefore Rabbi Yannai's dilemma is precisely the disagreement between Rabba and Rav Yosef (*Ḥazon Ish*). A third explanation is that Rabbi Yannai disagrees with the *halakha* stated in the name of Rabbi Elazar, and holds that the burnt offering of a private altar that was brought to a public altar is not absorbed by the partitions. He is uncertain if the same is true of the public altar itself, that it does not consecrate what is upon it, or whether the case of the altar itself is different (Ri Ḥaver).

HALAKHA

Offerings of the most sacred order that were slaughtered in the south – **קׇדְשֵׁי קֳדָשִׁים שֶׁשְּׁחָטָן בַּדָּרוֹם**: If offerings of the most sacred order were slaughtered in the south of the Temple courtyard they are disqualified, even if the blood was collected in the north. Moreover, one who derives benefit from them at any time is liable for misuse of consecrated property, as there was never a time that they were fit to be eaten (Rambam *Sefer Avoda, Hilkhot Me'ila* 3:1).

If they ascended they shall not descend – **אִם עָלוּ לֹא יֵרְדוּ**: With regard to offerings of the most sacred order that were slaughtered in the south of the Temple courtyard, or if their blood was collected there, although they are disqualified, if they ascended to the top of the altar they shall not descend. Some say the source of the Rambam's ruling is the version of the text found in the context of the dispute between Rabba and Rav Yosef in this Gemara, rather than that of the primary discussion in tractate *Me'ila* (Rambam *Sefer Avoda, Hilkhot Pesulei HaMukdashin* 3:7 and the commentaries there; and see *Birkat HaZevaḥ* and *Tzon Kodashim*).

אִיתְּמַר, שְׁחִיטַת לַיְלָה בְּבָמַת יָחִיד – רַב וּשְׁמוּאֵל; חַד אָמַר: כְּשֵׁרָה, וְחַד אָמַר: פְּסוּלָה. וְקָא מִיפַּלְגִי בִּדְרַבִּי אֶלְעָזָר.

§ Additionally, with regard to a private altar it **was stated:** With regard to **the slaughter of** offerings at **night on a private altar, Rav and Shmuel** disagree: **One says** that it is **valid, and one says** that it is **not valid.** The Gemara explains: **And they disagree with regard to** the resolution to a contradiction that was raised **by Rabbi Elazar.**

דְּרַבִּי אֶלְעָזָר רָמֵי קְרָאֵי אַהֲדָדֵי, כְּתִיב: ״וַיֹּאמֶר בְּגַדְתֶּם גֹּלּוּ אֵלַי הַיּוֹם אֶבֶן גְּדוֹלָה״,

As Rabbi Elazar raised a contradiction between two verses: **It is written** in the context of Saul's war with the Philistines: "And the people flew upon the spoil and took sheep and cattle and calves and slew them on the ground; and the people ate them with the blood. Then they told Saul, saying: 'Behold, the people sin against the Lord in that they eat with the blood. **And he said: You have dealt treacherously;**[N] **roll a great stone to me this day**" (I Samuel 14:32–33). That stone was made into a private altar upon which offerings could be slaughtered and sacrificed. Evidently, Saul was particular about slaughtering offerings during the day and not at night, despite the fact that it was a private altar and not a public altar.

וּכְתִיב: ״וַיֹּאמֶר שָׁאוּל פֻּצוּ בָעָם וַאֲמַרְתֶּם לָהֶם הַגִּישׁוּ אֵלַי אִישׁ שׁוֹרוֹ וְאִישׁ שֵׂיֵהוּ וּשְׁחַטְתֶּם בָּזֶה וַאֲכַלְתֶּם וְלֹא תֶחֶטְאוּ לַה׳ לֶאֱכוֹל עַל הַדָּם, וַיַּגִּשׁוּ כָל הָעָם אִישׁ שׁוֹרוֹ בְיָדוֹ הַלַּיְלָה וַיִּשְׁחֲטוּ שָׁם״.

And immediately thereafter **it is written: "And Saul said: Disperse yourselves among the people and say to them: Bring me here every man his ox and every man his sheep, and slay them here and eat and sin not against the Lord in eating with the blood. And all the people brought every man his ox with him that night, and slew them there"** (I Samuel 14:34). This verse states explicitly that the slaughter took place at night and not during the day.

מָר מְשַׁנֵּי: כָּאן – בְּחוּלִּין, כָּאן – בְּקָדָשִׁים. וּמָר מְשַׁנֵּי: כָּאן – בְּקָדְשֵׁי בָּמָה גְּדוֹלָה, כָּאן – בְּקָדְשֵׁי בָּמָה קְטַנָּה.

Rav and Shmuel disagree with regard to the resolution of this contradiction: One **Sage answers** that **here,** i.e., when the slaughter took place at night, it was **of non-sacred** animals, while **there,** i.e., when Saul was particular about slaughtering during the day, it was the slaughter **of sacrificial** animals. According to this opinion, the sacrificial service was performed only during the day, even on a private altar. **And** the other **Sage answers** that both verses are referring to the slaughter of offerings: **Here,** in the verse that states that Saul was particular about slaughtering during the day, it is referring **to the sacrificial** animals **of a great** public **altar,**[N] while **there,** in the verse that states that the slaughter took place at night, it is referring **to sacrificial** animals **of a small** private **altar.**

אִיתְּמַר, עוֹלַת בָּמַת יָחִיד – רַב אָמַר: אֵין טְעוּנָה הֶפְשֵׁט וְנִיתּוּחַ, וְרַבִּי יוֹחָנָן אָמַר: טְעוּנָה הֶפְשֵׁט וְנִיתּוּחַ. וְקָא מִיפַּלְגִי בִּדְרַבִּי יוֹסֵי הַגְּלִילִי. דְּתַנְיָא, רַבִּי יוֹסֵי הַגְּלִילִי אוֹמֵר: עוֹלָה שֶׁהִקְרִיבוּ יִשְׂרָאֵל בַּמִּדְבָּר אֵין טְעוּנָה הֶפְשֵׁט וְנִיתּוּחַ, שֶׁאֵין הֶפְשֵׁט וְנִיתּוּחַ אֶלָּא מֵאֹהֶל מוֹעֵד וָאֵילָךְ.

§ **It was stated** that with regard to **the burnt offering of a private altar, Rav says: It does not require flaying and cutting** into pieces, which the Torah requires of a burnt offering (see Leviticus 1:6), **and Rabbi Yoḥanan says: It does require flaying and cutting** into pieces.[N] The Gemara explains: **And they disagree with regard to** the meaning of a statement **of Rabbi Yosei HaGelili. As it is taught** in a *baraita* that **Rabbi Yosei HaGelili says: The burnt offering that the Jewish people sacrificed in the wilderness,** i.e., at Mount Sinai before the establishment of the Tabernacle, **did not require flaying and cutting** into pieces, **because** the requirement of **flaying and cutting** into pieces applied **only from the Tent of Meeting and onward,** as this *halakha* was first taught in the Tent of Meeting.

NOTES

And he said you have dealt treacherously – וַיֹּאמֶר בְּגַדְתֶּם: Rabbi Elazar assumes that Saul was discussing the slaughter of sacrificial offerings, i.e., the people were slaughtering peace offerings after their victory over the Philistines. The earlier statement: "And the people ate them with the blood," means they ate peace offerings without sprinkling the blood, which, as explained, is forbidden on a small private altar. Saul therefore became angry and instructed that a stone be rolled to him so that there would be an altar upon which the blood would be sprinkled (see Radak).

Here it is referring to the sacrificial animals of a great public altar – כָּאן בְּקָדְשֵׁי בָּמָה גְּדוֹלָה: While there was a small private altar there, they were obligated to treat the offerings that were consecrated for the great public altar in accordance with the appropriate *halakha* (see 119b).

Flaying and cutting into pieces – הֶפְשֵׁט וְנִיתּוּחַ: This means that the hide of the animal sacrificed at a private altar is flayed and given to the owners, just as it would be given to a priest at a great public altar. The limbs are then cut into pieces so that they may be sacrificed on the altar. The opinion that says a burnt offering does not require flaying and cutting into pieces holds that the burnt offering can be sacrificed as is (see Jerusalem Talmud, *Megilla* 1:12).

מַר סָבַר: מֵאֹהֶל מוֹעֵד וְאֵילָךְ – לָא שְׁנָא בָּמָה גְדוֹלָה וְלָא שְׁנָא בָּמָה קְטַנָּה. וּמַר סָבַר: בְּבָמָה גְדוֹלָה – אִין, בְּבָמָה קְטַנָּה – לָא.

One Sage, Rabbi Yoḥanan, **holds** that **from the Tent of Meeting and onward** there is a requirement of flaying and cutting into pieces, and there **is no difference** whether the offering is brought upon a **great** public **altar, and** there **is no difference** whether it is brought upon **a small** private **altar. And** one **Sage,** Rav, **holds** that **with regard to a great** public **altar, yes,** flaying and cutting are required, but **with regard to a small** private **altar** they are **not.**

תַּנְיָא כְּוָתֵיהּ דְּרַבִּי יוֹחָנָן: דְּבָרִים שֶׁבֵּין בָּמָה גְדוֹלָה לְבָמָה קְטַנָּה: קֶרֶן וְכֶבֶשׁ וִיסוֹד וְרִיבּוּעַ בְּבָמָה גְדוֹלָה, וְאֵין קֶרֶן וִיסוֹד וְכֶבֶשׁ וְרִיבּוּעַ בְּבָמָה קְטַנָּה; כִּיּוֹר וְכַנּוֹ בְּבָמָה גְדוֹלָה, וְאֵין כִּיּוֹר וְכַנּוֹ בְּבָמָה קְטַנָּה; חָזֶה וָשׁוֹק בְּבָמָה גְדוֹלָה, וְאֵין חָזֶה וָשׁוֹק בְּבָמָה קְטַנָּה.

It is taught in a *baraita* **in accordance with** the opinion **of Rabbi Yoḥanan:** What are the **matters that are different between a great** public **altar and a small** private **altar?**[N] The **corner** of the altar, the **ramp,** the **base** of the altar, **and** the **square** shape are required **in a great** public **altar, but** the **corner,** the **base,** the **ramp, and** the **square** shape **are not** required **in a small** private **altar.** The **Basin and its base** are required **in a great** public **altar, but** the **Basin and its base are not** required **in a small** private **altar.** The **breast and thigh** of a peace offering, which are given to a priest, are waved **at a great** public **altar, but** the **breast and thigh are not** waved at a **small** private **altar.**[N]

דְּבָרִים שֶׁשָּׁוְותָה בָּמָה גְדוֹלָה לְבָמָה קְטַנָּה: שְׁחִיטָה בְּבָמָה גְדוֹלָה וּקְטַנָּה, הֶפְשֵׁט וְנִיתּוּחַ בִּגְדוֹלָה וּקְטַנָּה, דָּם מַתִּיר וּמְפַגֵּל בִּגְדוֹלָה וּקְטַנָּה, מוּמִין וּזְמַן בִּגְדוֹלָה וּקְטַנָּה.

And there are other **matters** in **which a great** public **altar is identical to a small** private **altar: Slaughter** is required **at** both **a great** public **altar and a small** private altar. **Flaying** a burnt offering **and cutting** it into pieces is required **at** both **a great** public altar **and a small** private altar. Sprinkling the **blood permits** the meat to be eaten, **and** if at that time the priest thought of eating or sacrificing this offering outside its appropriate time, this **renders** the offering ***piggul*** both **at a great** public altar **and** at **a small** private altar. Likewise, the *halakha* that **blemishes** disqualify an offering **and** the *halakha* that there is a limited **time** for eating offerings are in effect **at** both **a great** public altar **and a small** private altar.

אֲבָל נוֹתָר וְהַזְּמַן וְהַטָּמֵא שָׁוִין בָּזֶה וּבָזֶה.

§ Following the detailing of the differences between a communal altar and a private altar, the mishna teaches: **But** the *halakha* that portions of the offering **left over** [***notar***] beyond the time it is permitted must be burned and that one who eats them incurs *karet*, **and the** *halakha* that intent to sacrifice or partake of the offering beyond its designated **time** renders the offering *piggul*, **and the** prohibition against performing the sacrificial service or eating consecrated meat while **ritually impure are equal in this,** i.e., a private altar, **and that,** i.e., a public altar.

תָּנוּ רַבָּנַן: מִנַּיִן לַעֲשׂוֹת זְמַן בְּבָמָה קְטַנָּה כְּבָמָה גְדוֹלָה? אָמְרָה תּוֹרָה: לָן יִשָּׂרֵף וּפִיגּוּל יִשָּׂרֵף, מָה פִּיגּוּל פָּסוּל בְּבָמָה – אַף לָן פָּסוּל בְּבָמָה.

With regard to this **the Sages taught** in a *baraita*: **From where** is it derived that **time,** i.e., the *halakha* that an offering left over beyond its designated time is disqualified, in the case **of a small** private **altar should be made equivalent to** the *halakha* in the case **of a great** public **altar? The Torah stated:** An offering that was **left overnight** must **be burned, and** likewise the Torah stated that **an offering that was sacrificed with the intent to consume it after its designated time** [***piggul***] must **be burned.**[N] Therefore, another parallel may be drawn between them: **Just as *piggul* is disqualified** in the case **of a** private **altar, so too,** an offering that was **left overnight** is **disqualified** in the case **of** a private **altar.**

NOTES

Matters that are different between a great public altar and a small private altar – דְּבָרִים שֶׁבֵּין בָּמָה גְדוֹלָה לְבָמָה קְטַנָּה: The reason these matters are not required for a small private altar is that each item listed contains a reference to either the Tent of Meeting or the phrase: "Before the Lord" (see 119b and Rashi here).

But the breast and thigh are not waved at a small private altar – וְאֵין חָזֶה וָשׁוֹק בְּבָמָה קְטַנָּה: In the *Tosefta* (13:7) and the Jerusalem Talmud (*Megilla* 1:12) it is stated that at a small private altar the breast and thigh are kept by the owner.

An offering that was left overnight must be burned and *piggul* must be burned – לָן יִשָּׂרֵף וּפִיגּוּל יִשָּׂרֵף: The *halakha* that an offering left overnight must be burned is derived from the verse: "But that which remains of the flesh of the sacrifice on the third day shall be burned with fire" (Leviticus 7:17). The same is true of offerings that leave the Temple courtyard, as derived from the discussion between Moses and Aaron with regard to the sin offering on the eighth day of the inauguration of the Tabernacle (Leviticus 10:16–20; see *Pesaḥim* 82a).

In the *Birkat HaZevaḥ* the words: An offering that was left overnight must be burned and *piggul* must be burned, are deleted from the text of the Gemara (see *Ḥok Natan* and *Tzon Kodashim*). That is the version of the *baraita* that appears in *Torat Kohanim* as well.

אוֹ כְּלָךְ לְדֶרֶךְ זוֹ: דְּהָא אָמְרָה תּוֹרָה לָן יִשָּׂרֵף וְיוֹצֵא יִשָּׂרֵף, מַה יּוֹצֵא כָּשֵׁר בְּבָמָה – אַף לָן כָּשֵׁר בְּבָמָה. וְלָאו קַל וָחוֹמֶר הוּא מֵעוֹפוֹת?

Or go this way, and say that **because the Torah stated:** An offering that was **left overnight must be burned, and** likewise, the Torah stated that an offering that **leaves** the Temple courtyard **must be burned,** the following conclusion may be drawn: **Just as** an offering that **leaves** the Temple courtyard is **valid in** the case of a private **altar** because it has no set perimeter, **so too,** an offering that was **left overnight** is **valid in** the case of a private **altar,** and it may therefore be concluded that the *halakha* of time does not apply to offerings on a private altar. The Gemara asks: **And is it not an *a fortiori* inference from** the *halakha* of **bird** offerings that in the case of a private altar, time should render an offering disqualified?

Perek **XIV**
Daf **120** Amud **b**

מָה עוֹפוֹת שֶׁאֵין הַמּוּם פּוֹסֵל בָּהֶן – זְמַן פּוֹסֵל בָּהֶן, קָדְשֵׁי בָּמָה קְטַנָּה שֶׁהַמּוּם פּוֹסֵל בָּהֶן – אֵינוֹ דִּין שֶׁזְּמַן פּוֹסֵל בָּהֶן?

If **bird** offerings, whose *halakhot* are more lenient in **that a blemish does not disqualify them,**[H] are nevertheless **disqualified by time,** then with regard to **sacrificial** animals **of a small** private **altar, which are disqualified by a blemish, is it not logical that they** should be **disqualified by time?**

מַה לְעוֹפוֹת שֶׁכֵּן אֵין הַזָּר כָּשֵׁר בָּהֶן, תֹּאמַר בְּבָמָה קְטַנָּה שֶׁהַזָּר כָּשֵׁר בָּהּ, לֹא יְהֵא זְמַן פָּסוּל בָּהּ! תַּלְמוּד לוֹמַר: ״וְזֹאת תּוֹרַת זֶבַח הַשְּׁלָמִים״ – לַעֲשׂוֹת זְמַן בָּמָה קְטַנָּה כִּזְמַן בָּמָה גְּדוֹלָה.

The Gemara questions the inference: **What** is notable **about bird** offerings? They are notable **in that a non-priest is not fit** to sacrifice **them.**[H] **Shall you say** the same **with regard to** offerings sacrificed on **a small** private **altar, where a non-priest is fit?** No, and consequently they **should not be disqualified by time.** Therefore, **the verse states: "And this is the law of the sacrifice of peace offerings"** (Leviticus 7:11), which equates all peace offerings, **to render** the *halakha* of **time** with regard to **a small** private **altar identical to** the *halakha* of **time** with regard to **a great** public **altar.**

הדרן עלך פרת חטאת
וסליקא לה מסכת זבחים

HALAKHA

A blemish does not disqualify them – אֵין הַמּוּם פָּסוּל בָּהֶן: Minor blemishes do not disqualify bird offerings, as the term "without blemish" (see, e.g., Leviticus 1:3) is stated only with regard to sacrificial animals, not birds (Rambam *Sefer Avoda, Hilkhot Issurei Mizbe'ah* 3:1).

A non-priest is not fit to sacrifice them – אֵין הַזָּר כָּשֵׁר בָּהֶן: With regard to anyone disqualified from performing the Temple service, including a non-priest, if he pinched the nape of a bird offering his pinching is not valid (Rambam *Sefer Avoda, Hilkhot Issurei Mizbe'ah* 7:1).

Summary of **Perek XIV**

With regard to the definition of sacrificial animals for which one is not liable for their sacrifice outside the Temple courtyard, the Gemara discusses the case of an animal that is not designated to be sacrificed in the courtyard, referred to by the mishna as: Not fit to come to the entrance of the Tent of Meeting. The Gemara determines that if one sacrifices it outside the Temple courtyard he is not liable, neither to receive *karet* if he sinned intentionally nor to bring a sin offering if he did so unwittingly. This category of animal includes sacrificial animals whose service is to be performed outside the courtyard, i.e., the red heifer of purification and the scapegoat, as well as offerings that were disqualified from sacrifice from the outset.

Likewise, with regard to offerings that became disqualified after they were consecrated, and that were therefore fit at some stage to be sacrificed, since they are at present unfit to be brought as offerings, one is not liable for sacrificing them outside the Temple courtyard. But if the disqualification occurred during the sacrificial process, and it is one of those offerings that shall not descend if it already ascended the altar, one who sacrifices it outside the Temple is liable.

The category of those offerings that are unfit to come to the entrance of the Tent of Meeting and for whose sacrifice outside the Temple one is not liable includes offerings whose time has not yet arrived but which will be fit for sacrifice at a later point. There are two primary types of offerings whose time has not yet arrived: Animals that have not reached the appropriate age for sacrifice and offerings whose owners are as yet unfit to sacrifice them, e.g., a leper whose period of impurity is incomplete. There is an important difference between these two categories: If the reason the offering may not be sacrificed is due to the animal itself, then one who sacrifices it outside is exempt in all cases. In cases where the owner is unready for the sacrifice, potential liability depends on the nature of the offering in question. In the cases of sin offerings and guilt offerings, since at present they may not be sacrificed by that individual at all, one who sacrifices them outside the Temple courtyard is exempt. He is liable in the case of offerings that can be brought as gift offerings, i.e., burnt offerings and peace offerings, as these are fit to be sacrificed at any time.

Another important factor with regard to the prohibition against sacrificing offerings outside the Temple courtyard is that one is liable only for those portions of the offering that are fit for the altar. Concerning the parts designated for consumption, whether by priests or by the Israelite owner, one who sacrifices them outside the Temple courtyard is not liable. Furthermore, one violates this prohibition only for performing the concluding rites of the sacrificial service, such as the sacrifice upon the altar, whereas if the action is not a concluding rite, e.g., pouring oil onto a meal offering, one is not liable.

The second section of this chapter dealt at length with the *halakhot* pertaining to those places, known as private altars, where offerings may be sacrificed outside the Temple and the Tabernacle. The chapter surveyed the various periods relevant to this issue: The period before the construction of the Tabernacle at Sinai, when private altars were permitted; when the Tabernacle was in the wilderness; when the Tabernacle was in Gilgal after the Jews entered Eretz Yisrael until it moved to the "rest" (see Deuteronomy 12:9) in Shiloh; the period when the Tabernacle was in Shiloh, when sacrifice on private altars was prohibited, until the destruction of the Tabernacle in Shiloh; and during the presence of the Tabernacle in Nov and Gibeon, when private altars were again permitted until the building of the Temple in Jerusalem.

There are two basic principles: The first is that any place, whether a Tabernacle or the Temple, where the Ark of the Covenant is found, is considered a dwelling place of the Divine Presence, and it is prohibited to sacrifice outside that place. During a period where there was no Ark, private altars were permitted. The second principle relates to the period when private altars were permitted: Even when such altars were permitted, there was still a difference between the great public altar, where there was a Tent of Meeting and where the service was performed in accordance with all the rites of the Tabernacle, including the requirement that it must be performed by priests; and a private altar, where an individual was allowed to sacrifice vow offerings and gift offerings on his own altar, without all the conditions that apply to a Tabernacle. Nevertheless, with regard to the primary *halakhot* of the offering itself, e.g., the fixed time for its consumption, the prohibition against leaving over any part beyond that time, and the prohibitions of performing the service and partaking of the offering in a state of ritual impurity, a private altar is similar to a public altar.

The chapter also discussed at length the question of which offerings are sacrificed on a private altar, which on a public altar, and which may not be sacrificed in either place. It is accepted that only individuals may sacrifice their vow offerings and gift offerings on a private altar, while on a public altar one would sacrifice individual gift offerings, and compulsory public offerings for which there is a set time. There are differences of opinion among the Sages with regard to the other offerings.

Although it is agreed that nowadays it is prohibited to sacrifice outside the Temple, this prohibition applies only to Jews, to whom the service of the Tent of Meeting and the Temple was given. It does not apply to gentiles, who are permitted to sacrifice burnt offerings to God in all places. Jews may not assist gentiles or sacrifice on their behalf, although they may instruct them in this regard, as occurred in an incident related by the Gemara.

The final section of the chapter dealt with various other aspects of the periods mentioned above. It also cited statements of *aggada* relating to the place of the Tabernacle and the Temple, and the dwelling of the Divine Presence among the Jewish people.

Image **Credits**

My Notes

My Notes

My Notes

My Notes

My Notes

My Notes

תלמוד בבלי

— מהדורת נאה —

זבחים חלק ו

Steinsaltz Center

KOREN

Please note that the number ranges that appear at the bottom of each daf of the Vilna pages indicate the corresponding pages of the Koren Talmud Bavli translation and commentary.

תלמוד בבלי

הוצאת קורן ירושלים

— מהדורת נאה —

מסכת זבחים

דף צח: עד דף קכ:

COMMENTARY BY

Rabbi Adin Even-Israel Steinsaltz

EDITOR-IN-CHIEF

Rabbi Dr Tzvi Hersh Weinreb

EXECUTIVE EDITOR

Rabbi Joshua Schreier

•

STEINSALTZ CENTER
KOREN PUBLISHERS JERUSALEM

עג א מיי' פ"ח מהל' מעה"ק הלכה ט:
עד ב ג מיי' פ"ג מהל' מקוואות הלכה ו ז:
א ד מיי' פ"י מהלכות מעה"ק הלכה יט:
ב ה מיי' פי"ב מהלכות שאר אבות הטומאה הלכה טו ופ"ב מהלכות ביאת מקדש הלכה ח:
ג ו מיי' פ"ב מהלכות ביאת מקדש הל' ו:
ד ז מיי' פ"י מהלכות מעה"ק הלכה יט:
ה ח מיי' שם הל' יז ופ"ו מהלכות ביאת מקדש הל' יב ועי' רש"ק:
ו ט מיי' פ"ו מהלכות ביאת מקדש הלכה ח:
ז י מיי' פ"י מהלכות מעה"ק הלכה יד:
ח כ מיי' שם הל' כח:

דם חטאת לְמַטָּה וְדַם עוֹלָה לְמַעְלָה — טָעוּן כִּיבּוּס. בָּעֵי רָבָא: דַּם עוֹלָה לְמַטָּה, וְדַם חַטָּאת לְמַעְלָה מַהוּ? מִשּׁוּם נוֹגֵעַ הוּא — וְהָא נוֹגֵעַ, אוֹ דִּלְמָא מִשּׁוּם בְּלוּעַ הוּא — וְהָא לֹא בָּלַע א] (הוּא) הֲדַר פַּשְׁטַהּ, דְּאֵין [א]טְעוּנִין כִּיבּוּס. אָמַר רָבָא: פְּשִׁיטָא לִי, דָּם [ב]עַל בִּגְדוֹ — חוֹצֵץ, וְאִם טַבָּח הוּא — אֵינוֹ חוֹצֵץ. רְבָב עַל בִּגְדוֹ — חוֹצֵץ, וְאִם מוֹכֵר רְבָב הוּא — אֵינוֹ חוֹצֵץ. בָּעֵי רָבָא: דָּם וּרְבָב עַל בִּגְדוֹ, מַהוּ? אִם טַבָּח הוּא — תֵּיפּוֹק לִי מִשּׁוּם רְבָב, וְאִי מוֹכֵר רְבָב הוּא — תֵּיפּוֹק לִי מִשּׁוּם דָּם! לָא צְרִיכָא, דְּעָבֵיד הָא וְהָא; אַחֲדָא לָא קָפֵיד, אַתַּרְתֵּי קָפֵיד. אוֹ דִּלְמָא אַתַּרְתֵּי נַמִּי לָא קָפֵיד? [ג]תֵּיקוּ.§

הדרן עלך דם חטאת

טְבוּל [ד]יוֹם וּמְחוּסַּר כִּיפּוּרִים אֵינָן חוֹלְקִין בְּקָדָשִׁים לֶאֱכוֹל לָעֶרֶב. אוֹנֵן ב] (אֵינוֹ) [ה]נוֹגֵעַ [ו]וְאֵינוֹ מַקְרִיב, [ז]וְאֵינוֹ חוֹלֵק לֶאֱכוֹל לָעֶרֶב. [ח]בַּעֲלֵי מוּמִין, בֵּין בַּעֲלֵי מוּמִין ג] עוֹבְרִין בֵּין בַּעֲלֵי מוּמִין קְבוּעִין — חוֹלְקִין וְאוֹכְלִין, [ט]אֲבָל לֹא מַקְרִיבִין. [י]כָּל שֶׁאֵינוֹ רָאוּי לַעֲבוֹדָה — אֵינוֹ חוֹלֵק בַּבָּשָׂר, [כ]וְכָל שֶׁאֵין לוֹ בַּבָּשָׂר — אֵין לוֹ בָּעוֹרוֹת. אֲפִילּוּ טָמֵא בִּשְׁעַת זְרִיקַת דָּמִים וְטָהוֹר בִּשְׁעַת הֶקְטֵר חֲלָבִים — אֵינוֹ חוֹלֵק בַּבָּשָׂר, שֶׁנֶּאֱ': ד] °"הַמַּקְרִיב אֶת דַּם הַשְּׁלָמִים ה] [וְאֶת הַחֵלֶב מִבְּנֵי אַהֲרֹן] לוֹ (יִהְיֶה) [תִּהְיֶה שׁוֹק הַיָּמִין לְמָנָה]".§ (ויקרא ז) גמ'

תורה אור

רש"י

דם חטאת למטה ודם עולה למעלה. נָפַל דַּם חַטָּאת תְּחִילָּה עַל הַבֶּגֶד, וְחָזַר וְנִיתַּז דַּם עוֹלָה עַל אוֹתוֹ כֶּתֶם. טָעוּן כִּיבּוּס. דְּהָא דַּם חַטָּאת נוֹגֵעַ בַּבֶּגֶד וּבָלוּעַ בּוֹ. וְהָא נוֹגֵעַ. שֶׁדַּם עוֹלָה נִבְלַע בַּבֶּגֶד, וּכְשֶׁנָּפַל דַּם חַטָּאת עָלָיו — נוֹגֵעַ הוּא בַּבֶּגֶד, אֲבָל אֵינוֹ נִבְלָע, דְּהָא שָׂבַע לֵיהּ בַּבָּלוּעַ דַּם עוֹלָה. חוֹצֵץ. לְעִנְיַן טְבִילָה בְּבֶגֶד שֶׁנִּטְמָא. וְאִם טַבָּח הוּא. שֶׁאֵינוֹ מַקְפִּיד בַּדָּם שֶׁעַל בִּגְדוֹ. אֵינוֹ חוֹצֵץ. דַּחֲלִילָה בְּקְפִידָא תַּלְיָא י]. רְבָב. כָּל דָּבָר הַנִּיתּוֹךְ, כְּגוֹן שׁוּמָּן וְחֵלֶב וְשַׁעֲוָה. וְתֵיפּוֹק לֵיהּ מִשּׁוּם רְבָב. שֶׁאֵינוֹ רָגִיל בּוֹ, וּמַקְפִּיד עָלָיו, וַהֲוֵי חֲלִילָה! אַתַּרְתֵּי קָפֵיד. [נוֹסַף עַל גַּב] דְּרָגִיל בְּתַרְוַיְיהוּ — גְּנַאי הוּא לוֹ שֶׁיֵּרָאוּ שְׁנֵיהֶם עַל בִּגְדוֹ. אוֹ דִּלְמָא לָא קָפֵיד. הוֹאִיל וּבִשְׁנֵיהֶם רָגִיל.

הדרן עלך דם חטאת

טְבוּל יוֹם וּמְחוּסַּר כִּיפּוּרִים. הוֹאִיל וְאֵין רְאוּיִן לַאֲכִילָה ז]. אֵין חוֹלְקִין לֶאֱכוֹל לָעֶרֶב. לִכְשֶׁיִּטָּהֲרוּ. וּבַגְּמָרָא מְפָרֵשׁ טַעְמָא. אוֹנֵן אֵינוֹ מַקְרִיב. כִּדְאָמַר בְּפֶרֶק שֵׁנִי (לעיל דף טז.). בַּעֲלֵי מוּמִין חוֹלְקִין. טַעְמָא מְפָרֵשׁ בַּגְּמָרָא. כָּל שֶׁאֵינוֹ רָאוּי לַעֲבוֹדָה כו'. בַּגְּמָרָא פָּרֵיךְ: וַהֲרֵי ח] בַּעַל מוּם. וְטָהוֹר בִּשְׁעַת הֶקְטֵר חֲלָבִים. שֶׁהוּא כָּל הַלַּיְלָה, כְּגוֹן שֶׁטָּבַל וְטִיהֵר בְּהֶעֱרֵב שֶׁמֶשׁ. גמ' *מְחַטֵּא. זוֹרֵק אֶת הַדָּם. וּכְלָלָא הוּא. רֵישׁ לָקִישׁ גּוּפֵיהּ יָלֵיף וְאָזֵיל לְמִילְּתֵיהּ. וּפָרֵיךְ לִקְרָא עַד דְּמִמֵּילָא מִיתּוֹקְמָא בַּחֲלוּקָה. מִשְׁמָרָה

[שייך לדף לט.]

תוספות

ושליא דלעיל. ומאן דדריש עצמות מותרין מ"לו יהיה" פרק "המזבח מקדש" (לעיל דף פו.) אית ליה היקישא דאשם לגבי שפיר ושליא. ולפרש"י דאמר דבכל הקדשים מן הדין אסורין העצמות, דלא התיר הכתוב אלא בשר הראוי לאכילה, וגילה לנו באשם "לו יהיה" דמשמע שריותא – נילף כמו כן היתר בכל הקדשים ע"פ זה. הגהה: קשה, דבההוא קרא כתיבי חטאת ואשם, בפרשת "צו את אהרן": "כחטאת כאשם תורה אחת להם הכהן אשר יכפר בו לו יהיה", ולמה נקט אשם? וי"ל: דעיקר פרשה *באשם. ועוד, ד"לו יהיה" נכתב ל' יחיד, שמא לא קאי רק על האשם דסליק מיניה. ולא תקשי ט] (הכי גרסינן) הא דדרשינן לעיל בפרק "המזבח מקדש" (שם): נאמר "לו יהיה" בעולה – "עור העולה אשר הקריב לכהן לו יהיה", ונאמר "לו יהיה" באשם, מה אשם עצמותיו מותרין – אף עולה עצמותיה מותרין. וקאמר התם: מופני. והשתא, למה לי בעולה "לו יהיה"? תיפוק לי מהיקישא דאשם דשמעתין! וי"ל: דלא גמרינן מהיקישא אלא קרבנות הנאכלין. ומ"מ קשה: אי ממשמעותא ד"לו יהיה" דאשם דרשינן עצמותיו מותרין, וילפינן מיניה שאר קרבנות, שלמים חטאת ותודה, הלא בעולה נמי כתיב "לו יהיה", ול"ל גזירה שוה פרק "המזבח מקדש" (שם) למיגמר מאשם? וי"ל: ד"לו יהיה" דעולה קאי על העור, ולא להתיר עצמות. דהכי כתיב קרא "עור העולה לו יהיה"*. הגהה: "לו יהיה" י] לא דריש אלא מייתורא. ושם פירש בקונטרס דפשיטא ליה באשם יותר מעולה, משום דאף בשרו מותר. ואי משום נותר דבשריפה – לא שייך נותר אלא במידי דבר אכילה, כדכתיב "והנותר מבשר הזבח". וא"כ לא צריכנא למגמר אלא עולה דכליל, וזהו כמו שפירש בשמעתין בשם רבותיו.. הגה"ה.: ובפרק "כיצד צולין" (פסחים דף פג.) מוכח בהדיא כדבריו, דאין נותר בעצמות. ובמנחות בסוף "התודה" (דף פג.) פירש בקונטרס דהא דפשיטא ליה באשם יותר משאר קרבנות הנאכלין – משום דכתיב באשם "הוא" לאחר הקטרת אימורין, דמשמע: הוא אשם ואין עצמותיו אשם. וצריך לדקדק: ל"ל תרי קראי לעצמות, היקישא דהכא יא] דאתי מ"הוא", וגזירה שוה ד"לו יהיה" בפרק "המזבח מקדש" (לעיל דף פו.)? ותו קשה לי: ד"הוא" דאשם דרשינן פ"ק (לעיל דף ה:) לאשם שניתק לרעייה! מיהו, תרי "הוא" כתיבי באשם בפרשת ויקרא. ברו"ך.

נ"ל דאשם נקטיה נ"ק

גי' נ"ק לו יהיה ולא דריש אלא מיתורא כו' ועיין רש"ק

הדרן עלך דם חטאת

שיטה מקובצת

טבול יום ומחוסר כיפורים אינם חולקים בקדשים לאכול לערב. משמע הכא דמחסורי כיפורים שהביאו כפרתן בעו עדיין טבילה והערב שמש. וכן משמע פרק "בכל מערבין" (עירובין דף לב.) דמייתי יב] הא מתניתא: האשה שיש עליה לידה או זיבה – מביאה מעות ונותנת בשופר, וטובלת ואוכלת בקדשים לערב. ובריש "תמיד נשחט" (פסחים דף נט.) נמי אמרינן: אף מחוסר כפרה בשאר ימות השנה שטובל ואוכל יג] לערב. ותימה: דתנא פרק "חומר בקודש" (חגיגה דף כא.) ובשמעתין מייתי לה: האונן והמחוסר כיפורים צריכין טבילה לקדש. ובשמעתין נמי בגמ' משמע דטבילה דוקא בעי, דמייתי ההיא דמחוסר כפרה דחגיגה, ופריך בתר הכי: טמא שרץ טמא מעליא הוא והערב שמש בעי! משמע דעד השתא לא איירי כלל בהערב שמש. ועוד אמרינן בפסחים בפ' "האשה" (דף צ:) שוחטין וזורקין על טבול יום ועל מחוסר כיפורים, ואין שוחטין וזורקין על טמא שרץ. ופריך: מאי שנא טבול יום – דחזי לאורתא, טמא שרץ נמי חזי לאורתא! ומשני: מחוסר טבילה, וחיישינן דלמא פשע. אבל במחוסר כיפורים – לא חיישינן, כשמסר קינו לב"ד. וכדרב שמעיה, דאין ב"ד של כהנים מתעצלין. והשתא מחוסר כיפורים יד] הא בעי טבילה, ניחוש דלמא פשע! אלא ודאי בטמא שרץ דבעי הערב שמש – איכא למיחש דלמא פשע ולא טבל עד לאורתא, אבל הא דלא בעי הערב שמש למאי ניחוש ליה? אפילו בלילה יכול לטבול ויאכל. ועוד אמרינן בפרק שני דביצה (דף יח.): כלי שנטמא באב הטומאה – אין מטבילין אותו ביום טוב, בולד הטומאה – מטבילין אותו בי"ט. ואי בטבילה דרבנן בעי הערב שמש – אם כן לא יוכל להשתמש בו טו] ביום עד הלילה, ולצורך חול הוא מטביל ליה! ועוד, תנן במס' פרה (פי"א מ"ה): כל הטעון ביאת מים מדברי סופרים – מטמא את הקדש, ופוסל את התרומה, ומותר בחולין ובמעשר. לאחר ביאתו – הותר בכולן. ובהדיא אמרינן בירושלמי במס' תרומות פ' שני: נפל דלי לתוך הבור, נפלו כליו לתוך הבור – מעריב עליהן ומטבילן. תרין אמוראין, חד אמר: באב הטומאה, וחד אמר: בולד הטומאה. מתיב מ"ד בולד הטומאה למ"ד באב בטומאה: *אף בחול טז] והא צריך הערב שמש! ומשני: ברוצה להשתמש בהן חולין בטהרה. משמע בהדיא דלמ"ד בולד הטומאה ניחא, דלא בעי הערב שמש. ובירושלמי פ' שני דביצה איכא איפכא: מתיב מ"ד באב הטומאה למ"ד בולד הטומאה. ואותה גירסא משובשת, וההיא דמס' תרומות עיקר. ונראה לפרש, דהא דקתני הכא במתניתין "לערב" – לאו משום מחוסר כיפורים, אלא משום טבול יום. ובפ' "בכל מערבין" (עירובין דף לב.) דנקט "לערב" – לאו משום הערב שמש, דאי ידעה שהוקרב קינה – ודאי יז] טובלת ואוכלת לאלתר. אלא התם הוא מטעם חזקה שאין ב"ד של כהנים *מתעצלין עד שיכלו כל מעות שבשופר, ומטעם זה לא תוכל לאכול כל היום. וכי תימא משעה שמתחילין להקריב את התמיד של בין הערבים תהא טובלת ואוכלת – הא אפשר להקריב את הקינים לאחר תמיד, כיון שאין למזבח אלא דמה. כדאמר בריש "תמיד נשחט" (פסחים דף נט.). ובהמה נמי אמרינן התם מעלה ומלינה. וההיא ד"תמיד נשחט" (שם) דמחוסר כיפורים בשאר ימות השנה שטובל ואוכל בקדשים לערב, איידי דנקט התם גבי פסח שטובל ואוכל פסחו לערב, דפסח אינו נאכל אלא בלילה – נקט נמי בההיא "לערב". והא דאמרינן בפסחים

נ"ל אפילו בחול דהא לא כו' נ"ק

[נ"ל שוהין משם שיכלו כו' וכ"ה שם]

א] תיבת הוא נמחק: ב] תיבת אינו נמחק: ג] בין בעלי מומין קבועין בין בעלי מומין עוברין: ד] שנאמר לכהן הזורק את דם השלמים לו יהיה כצ"ל וכן משמע בגמרא (דף קב ע"ב) ואח"כ מצאתי כך בתוס' (דף קג.) [מדפוס שלנו בדף לט ע"א] [כפי הנראה דברים אלו מהגאון רב"א זצ"ל]: ה] השלמים ואת החלב מבני אהרן לו יהיה שוק הימין למנה: ו] תליא מילתא הס"ד: ז] הואיל ואין ראוין לאכילה אין חולקין והד"א: ח] והרי בעלי מומין: ט] תיבות הכי גרסינן נמחק: י] יהיה ולהכי ממשמעות לו לא: יא] תיבות דאתי מהוא נמחק: יב] דמייתי התם מתניתין דהאשה שיש עליה: יג] ואוכל בקדשים לערב ותימה דתנן בפ' חומר בקודש האונן א) תיבות דתנא ובשמעתין מייתי לה נמחק לקדש אבל לא לתרומה ומשמע טבילה אין הערב שמש לא דכה"ג דייק התם גבי כלים הנגמרים בטהרה צריכין טבילה לקודש ובשמעתין מייתי לה כו': יד] כיפורים נמי הא: טו] בו היום אות ב' נמחק: טז] בחול יהא צריך אות ו' נמחק: יז] ודאי היתה טובלת:

א) נראה דל"ל האונן והמחוסר כיפורים צריכים טבילה לקודש אבל לא לתרומה ומשמע וכו' טבילה לקודש ובשמעתין נמי בגמ' משמע וכו' ותיבות ובשמעתין מייתי לה נמחק.

גמ' מנא הני מילי? אמר ר"ל, דאמר קרא: °"הכהן המחטא אותה יאכלנה" (ויקרא ו), כהן המחטא – א] יאכל, שאינו מחטא – אינו אוכל. וכללא הוא? והרי משמרה כולה, דאין מחטאין, ואוכלין! ראוי לחיטוי קאמרינן. הרי קטן, דאינו ראוי לחיטוי, ואוכל! אלא: מאי "יאכלנה" – יחלקנה; אראוי לחיטוי – חולק, שאינו ראוי לחיטוי – אינו חולק. הרי בעל מום, דאינו ראוי לחיטוי, וחולק! בבעל מום. רחמנא רבייה: °"כל זכר בכהנים" (שם) – לרבות בעל מום. ואימא: "כל זכר" לרבות טבול יום! מסתברא, בעל מום ה"ל לרבויי, שכן אוכל. אדרבה, טבול יום הוה ליה לרבויי, דלאורתא ב] מיחזא חזי! השתא מיהא הא לא חזי. רב יוסף אמר: מכדי מאי "יאכלנה" – יחלקנה, לכתוב רחמנא "יחלקנה", מאי "יאכלנה"? ש"מ: ראוי לאכילה – חולק, שאינו ראוי לאכילה – אינו חולק. בעי ר"ל: בעל מום והוא טמא, מהו שיחלקו לו? כיון דלא חזי ורחמנא רבייה – לא שנא, (א) מה לי טמא מה לי בעל מום. או דלמא: ראוי לאכילה – חולק, שאינו ראוי לאכילה – אינו חולק? אמר רבה, ת"ש: *גכהן גדול מקריב אונן, ואינו אוכל, ואינו חולק לאכול לערב. ש"מ: דראוי לאכילה בעינן, ש"מ. בעי רב אושעיא: טמא בקרבנות ציבור, מהו שיחלקו לו? מי אמרינן: ג] "המחטא" אמר רחמנא, והאי נמי מחטא הוא. או דלמא ראוי לאכילה – חולק, שאין ראוי לאכילה – אינו חולק? אמר רבינא, ת"ש: כהן גדול מקריב אונן, ואינו אוכל, ואינו חולק לאכול לערב. ש"מ: הראוי לאכילה בעינן, ש"מ. § "אונן נוגע ואינו מקריב" כו'. § אונן נוגע? ורמינהי: *אונן ומחוסר כיפורים וצריכין טבילה לקודש! א"ר אמי א"ר יוחנן: לא קשיא, כאן – בשטבל, כאן – בשלא טבל. וכי טבל מאי הוי? הא הדרא עליה אנינות. דאמר רבה בר רב הונא: אונן שטבל – אנינותו חוזרת עליו! ד] *ל"ק; הא – דאסח דעתיה, הא – דלא אסח דעתיה. היסח הדעת, ה] שלישי ושביעי בעי. *דא"ר יוסטאי ברבי מתון א"ר יוחנן: זהיסח הדעת צריך הזאה שלישי ושביעי! לא קשיא; הא – דאסח דעתיה מטמא מת, הא – דאסח דעתיה מטמא שרץ. טמא שרץ טמא מעלייא הוא, הערב שמש ו] בעי! ועוד: אפילו תרומה נמי! *א"ר ירמיה, באומר: "נשמרתי מדבר המטמאני, ולא נשמרתי מדבר הפוסלני". ומי איכא נטירותא לפלגא? אין, והתניא: *עודהו הסל על ראשו, ומגריפה

רש"י

משמרה כולה. לא זרקו את הדם, אלא אחד זרק ע"י כולן, וכולן חולקין ואוכלין! קטן. פסול לעבודה, דנפקא לן מ"איש מזרעך לדורותם" בה"כל שוחטין" (חולין דף כד:) (ג) בסיפא. ובקדשים אוכל, דאמרינן במנחות (דף עג.): "איש כאחיו" – איש חולק ואין קטן חולק. ומדמעיט ליה מחלוקה – מכלל דאכיל. ועוד, "כל זכר" כתיב. יחלקנה. ומהכא נפקא לן מתני', דקתני: טבול יום אינו חולק. כל זכר בכהנים יאכל לרבות בעל מום. ולקמן מוקמינן לה בפרקין (ד' קב.) דלחלוקה רבייה. דאי לאכילה – לא אצטריך, דהא בהדיא כתיב ביה (ויקרא כא): "ומן הקדשים יאכל". שכן אוכל. כדכתיב: "ומן הקדשים יאכל". דלאורתא חזי. לעבודה, כגון הקטר חלבים. רב יוסף אמר. לרבות טבול יום לחלוקה לא מצית אמרת, ז] הא אוקימנא: מאי "יאכלנה" – יחלקנה כו'. ראוי לאכילה. בעל מום. כיון דלא חזי. לעבודה ח] לחיטוי, ואפילו מקמי טומאה, ורחמנא רבייה לחלוקה, הלכך מה לי כשהוא בעל מום לחודיה, מה לי כשהוא טמא ובעל מום? דהא לא קרינא ביה "המחטא" מעיקרא ופליג, השתא נמי ניפלוג. מקריב אונן. דכתיב ביה (שם כא): "לאביו ולאמו לא יטמא ומן המקדש לא יצא" – אינו צריך לצאת מן המקדש ביום מיתת אביו ואמו, ט] שעבודתו אינה מחוללת. הא אחר, הדיוט שלא יצא – חילל. ואינו חולק לאכול י] בערב. לכשיפטר מאנינותו. אלמא, אע"ג דקרינן "המחטא אותה" – לא פליג, דעיקר חלוקה באכילה תלי, מדאפקה רחמנא בלשון אכילה. הלכך, מאן דמייתי ראיה מבעל מום קודם טומאה, דפליג אע"ג דאין ראוי לחיטוי, ומהיא טעמא בעית לרבויי אף לאחר טומאה – לאו ראיה היא, דבראוי לאכילה תלוי, ולא בראוי לחיטוי, ובעל מום בלא טומאה ראוי לאכילה הוא. מהו שיחלקו לו. מקרבן ציבור לאכול לערב? ובקרבן ציבור שהקריבוהו טהורים קא מיבעיא ליה אי פלגי מיניה להאי טמא, הואיל וראוי לחיטוי, דקרבן ציבור דוחה טומאה. או דלמא ראוי לאכילה בעינן. אבל בהקריבוהו טמאין – לא מיבעי לן, שהרי אינו נאכל, דקי"ל ב"כיצד צולין" (פסחים דף עו:): קרבנות ציבור באין בטומאה, אבל יא] אין (ג) נאכלין. מתני' דקתני אונן נוגע בשטבל לאנינותו בו ביום. והך טבילה לא בעיא הערב שמש, דמעלה דרבנן בעלמא היא. אונן שטבל. בו ביום. דאנינות בליר מחד יומא ליתיה, כדכתיב: "ואחריתה כיום מר", במ"ק (דף כא.). ה"ג: אלא לא קשיא הא דאסח דעתיה כו'. ההיא ד"חומר בקדש" דמצריך ליה טבילה. בדאסח דעתיה. משמירת גופו, מפני שהוא אסור בקדשים לבו ביום. מטמא מת. מטומאת מת. מטמא שרץ. מטומאת שרץ. ועוד לתרומה נמי. ליבעי טבילה. אלמה תנן התם: צריכין טבילה לקדש אבל לא לתרומה? ה"ג: באומר נשמרתי מדבר המטמאני ולא מדבר הפוסלני ו"מדבר המטמאני" – טומאה דאורייתא, דבעיא הערב שמש. הפוסלני. לאכילת קדשים, מדרבנן, דלא בעי הערב שמש. יב] וכן לגבי תרומה, באומר: [לא] נשמרתי מדבר הפוסלני בתרומה. ושינויא דחיקא הוא, ולא מיתוקם במסקנא הכי. מגריפה

תוספות

בפסחים בפ' "אלו דברים" (דף ע.) סכין שנמצא בי"ד – שוחט בה מיד, בי"ג – שונה ומטביל. פי': בנמצא חוץ לירושלים. דלא גזרו על ספק כלים הנמצאים בירושלים, כדאמר בפ"ק דפסחים (דף יט:): ובי"ד שוחט בה מיד – דמסתמא הטבילוהו מאתמול כדי שיהא לו הערב שמש, ולא חיישינן שמא נטמא בטומאה דרבנן דלא בעי הערב שמש, ולא חש להטביל עד י"ד, ועדיין לא הטביל. היינו משום דכיון דהוזקק להטביל בי"ג משום טומאה דאורייתא – לא חיישינן שמא נטמא אחר כך בשום טומאה. ועוד: כשגזרו על ספק כלים הנמצאים – משום חשש טומאה דאורייתא גזרו, ולא משום טומאה דרבנן. ומיהו, יש טומאה דרבנן דבעיא הערב שמש, כדאשכחן בפסחים בסוף "האשה" (דף צב.): כל הפורש מן הערלה כפורש מן הקבר, דבעי הזאה שלישי ושביעי, וכ"ש הערב שמש. והיא דרבי ישמעאל בן קמחית בפרק "הוציאו לו" (יומא דף מז.) שנתזה צינורא דהגמון על בגדו יג] (לצנורא דערבי). ונכנסו אחיו ושימשו תחתיו, אע"ג דטומאת גוי דרבנן – בעיא הערב שמש. וכי ההיא ד"חומר בקודש" (חגיגה דף כג.) דספופרת שחתכה לחטאת, ר' יהושע אומר: יטמא ויטביל. ופריך: דחתכה מאן? אי דחתכה חבר – ל"ל טבילה? ואי דחתכה עם הארץ – בהא נימא רבי יהושע יטמא ויטביל? משמע בהדיא דטומאת עם הארץ בעיא הערב שמש. והיא דכהן יד] השורף את הפרה שהיו אחיו הכהנים סומכין ידיהן עליו כדי לטמאותו, לעשות טו] *להכעיס לצדוקים שהיו אומרים: במעורבי שמש היתה נעשית. ובגדי אוכלי קודש מדרס לחטאת – ומשמע דבעי הערב שמש. *אינו חולק בבשר שנאמר המקריב את דם השלמים ואת החלב. ר"ת ל"ג ליה, משום דבגמ' (לקמן דף קב:), בדינא דר"א בר"ש דריש ליה מקרא אחרינא, מדכתיב: "הזורק את דם השלמים". והאי קרא טז] ד"מקריב" אתא לכהן שאינו מודה בעבודה, כדדרשינן בחולין בפ' "הזרוע" (דף קלג:), כדפירש בקונטרס בגמ' לת"ק דאבא שאול. ומיהו, י"ל: דכולה מילתא דרשינן מקרא ד"המקריב", דמ"ואת החלב" דרשינן כהן שאינו מודה בעבודה, יז] *ו"המקריב" דרשינן שיהא טהור בשעת זריקה. ושמא הנך תרי קראי צריכי, חד לזריקה וחד לקבלה, ד"המקריב" משמע קבלה, כדדרשינן בפ"ק (לעיל יג.): "והקריבו" – זו קבלת הדם. ומיהו, מדקאמר התם בחולין וב"הקומץ רבה" (מנחות דף יח:): יח] לרבות הקבלות וההזאות – משמע דאכתי לא ידעינן קבלה. **והרי** קטן דאין ראוי לחיטוי ואוכל. וא"ת: אמאי לא משני: קטן רחמנא רבייה, כדמשני בתר הכי גבי בעל מום, לבתר דמסיק מאי "יאכלנה" – יחלקנה? וי"ל: כיון דקטן ובעל מום יט] אוכל, מאי אתא קרא לאשמועינן א) אי נדרוש שאינו מחטא אינו אוכל? אי למעוטי טבול יום ומחוסר כיפורים – הא נפקא לן בפ' "הערל" (יבמות דף עד:) מקרא אחרינא, דהביא כפרתו אוכל בקדשים. ב) הילכך נדרוש: אינו חולק. א"נ: אי הוה משני רבייה קרא – ג) תיקשי ליה אכתי מבעל מום, ד) כדפריך בסמוך. כ] **ה"ג** ראוי לחיטוי חולק. ותימה: הרי כה"ג אונן, וטמא בקרבנות ציבור, דראויין לחיטוי ואינם חולקין, כדבסמוך! י"ל: דעיקר קרא אצטריך לדיוק: שאינו ראוי לחטוי – אינו חולק. כא] **ה"ג:** הא דאסח דעתיה כו'. היסח הדעת פוסל בקדשים. והא דנקט אונן – משום דרגיל לאסוחי דעתיה, לפי שאינו יכול לאכול. **מדבר** המטמאני. טומאה דאורייתא דבעיא הערב שמש, ולא מדבר הפוסלני לאכילת קדשים מדרבנן דלא *בעיא הערב שמש. [ה"ג רש"י. ונראה דה"ג: באומר לא נשמרתי מדבר הפוסלני לקודש, אבל נשמרתי מדבר הפוסלני מתרומה]. דאונן אסור לאכול קודש, ולכך לא שמר עצמו מדבר הפוסלו לקודש, ולא נתן לבו שיהא מותר לערב. אבל לתרומה מותר אפילו [בו] ביום, כדאמרינן: זרות אמרתי לך ולא אנינות, ולכך שמר עצמו מדבר הפוסלו לתרומה. כב] וא"ת: מאי ניהו אותה טומאה דקאמר כג] דטמא בה °לקודש אבל לא לתרומה, דקתני מתני' דחגיגה (דף כ:): צריכין טבילה לקודש אבל לא לתרומה? ומפרש ה"ר חיים: כגון דאכל ככר שלישי של תרומה, כד] שגופו שני לקדש אבל לא לתרומה, כדאמר בפרק שני דחולין (דף לג:). ובסמוך ליכא לפרושי הכי גבי כה] (כלי) "[לבי] על הסל ולא על המגריפה" – טמאה לפסול קודש, ואינה פוסלת פירות תרומה שבסל. דככר אינו פוסל כלי.

א) אי אתא למעוטי שאינו מחטא אינו כו' כצ"ל ל"ק ב) נ"ל הלכך משני אינו חולק ואכתי תיקשי ליה מבעל מום כדפריך בסמוך ומשני רבייה קרא ל"ק ג) נ"א תיפוק ד) נ"א כדפריש'

עין משפט נר מצוה

ט א מיי' פ"י מהל' מעה"ק הלכה יד:
י ב ג מיי' פ"י מהלכות מעה"ק הלכה כ:
יא ד מיי' שם הל' יז:
יב ה מיי' שם הל' כג:
יג ו מיי' פי"ב מהלכות אבות הטומאה הל' טו:
יד ז מיי' שם:

מסורת הש"ס

תוספתא זבחים פי"א יומא יג: הוריות יב: ב"ק קי. [מ"ק יד:]

חגיגה כ. ע"ש

חגיגה כ. ע"ש תוספתא דטהרות פ"ח

גי' רש"ק והג"ה ל"ג תיבת לא

נ"א בעי הערב שמש והא דנקט אונן לאו וכו' ל"ק

היכר ל"ק

[שייך לדף נח ע"ב במתני' ל"ק]

חגיגה כא.

נ"א אלא ל"ק

[יומא ל: ע"ש]

ל"ל ומהמקריב ל"ק

הגהות הב"ח

(א) גמ' לא שנא מה לי בעל מום ומה לי בעל מום והוא טמא או דלמא: (ב) רש"י ד"ה קטן וכו' בסופיה וכו' כל זכר כתיב כל זכר בכהנים יאכל הס"ד ואח"כ מ"ה יחלקנה וכו' חולק הס"ד ואח"כ מ"ה לרבות: (ג) ד"ה או דלמא וכו' אין נאכלין הס"ד ואח"כ מ"ה כאן כשטבל מתני' דקתני:

גליון הש"ס

תוס' ד"ה מדבר וכו' לקדש אבל לא לתרומה. עדיין יקשה למ"ד התם בין לקדש בין לתרומה:

שיטה מקובצת

א] אוכל שאינו אות י' נמחק: ב] דלאורת' מיהת חזי תיבת מיחזא נמחק: ג] אמרינן כהן המחטא: ד] עליו אלא ל"ק: ה] הדעת הזאה שלישי: ו] שמש נמי בעי: ז] אמרת דמכדי הא: ח] תיבת לחיטוי נמחק: ט] ואמו ולא יחלל שהעבודה שיעבוד אינה מחוללת הא הדיוט אחר שלא: י] לאכול לערב: יא] אינן נאכלין: יב] שמש אבל לגבי תרומה ליכא למימר דאמר לא נשמרתי מדבר הפוסלני בתרומה דהא אונן מותר הוא בתרומה כדאי' ביבמות הלכך לא אסח דעתיה ושינויא דחיקא: יג] בגדו וצנורא דערבי: יד] דכהן. עי' בפי' המשניות של ר"ש במס' פרה: טו] לעשות היכרא לצדוקים: טז] קרא דהמקריב אתא: יז] ומהמקריב דרשינן: יח] רבה מנין לרבות: יט] ובעל מום אוכלים מאי: כ] הג"ה תיבת ה"ג נמחק: כא] הג"ה תיבת ה"ג נמחק: כב] לתרומה עכ"ה וא"ת: כג] דקאמר מיטמא בה: כד] תרומה שנעשה גופו שני: כה] גבי לבי על תיבת כלי נמחק:

ומגריפה בתוכו, ואמר: "לבי על הסל ואין לבי על המגריפה" – [א]הסל טהור והמגריפה טמאה. ותטמא מגריפה לסל! אין כלי מטמא כלי. ותטמא מה שבתוכו! אמר רבא, *[ב]באומר: "שמרתיה מדבר המטמאה ולא שמרתיה מדבר הפוסלה". איגלגל מילתא ומטאי לקמיה דרבי אבא בר ממל, א"ל: לא שמיע להו *הא דאמר רבי *יוחנן א"ר: [ג]האוכל שלישי של תרומה – א] אסור לאכול ומותר ליגע. אלמא: באכילה עבוד רבנן מעלה, בנגיעה לא עבוד רבנן מעלה ב]. § "ואינו חולק לאכול" כו'. § מיפלג הוא דלא פליג, וכי מזמני ליה – אכיל. ורמינהי: *[ד]אונן ([ה]ומחוסר כיפורים) טובל ואוכל את פסחו לערב, אבל לא בקדשים! אמר רב ירמיה מדיפתי: לא קשיא, כאן – בפסח, כאן – בשאר ימות השנה. בפסח, °איידי דאכיל פסח – [ו]אכיל נמי ג] קדשים. בשאר ימות השנה, *דלא חזי – לא חזי. ומאי "אבל לא בקדשים" – אבל לא בקדשים של כל השנה. ד] רב אסי אמר: ל"ק, [ז]כאן – שמת לו מת בארבעה עשר וקברו בארבעה עשר, כאן – שמת לו מת בשלשה עשר וקברו בארבעה עשר; ה] יום קבורה לא *תפים לילו מדרבנן. מאן תנא ו] *[ח]אנינות לילה מדרבנן – ר"ש היא. דתניא: אנינות לילה מדברי תורה, דברי רבי יהודה. ר"ש אומר: אונן אינו מדברי תורה אלא מדברי סופרים. תדע, שהרי אמרו: *אונן טובל ואוכל את פסחו לערב, אבל לא בקדשים. וסבר ר"ש אנינות לילה מדרבנן? והתניא, ר"ש אומר: [ט]אונן אינו משלח קרבנותיו; מאי לאו ז] ואפילו בפסח? לא, לבר מפסח. *והתניא, ר"ש אומר: "שלמים" – כשהוא שלם מביא, ואינו מביא כשהוא אונן; מנין לרבות את התודה? מרבה אני את התודה שכן נאכלת בשמחה כשלמים; מנין לרבות את העולה? מרבה אני את העולה, שכן באה בנדר ובנדבה כשלמים; מנין לרבות ח] [בכור ומעשר ופסח? מרבה אני] בכור ומעשר ופסח שכן אינן באין *על חטא; מנין לרבות חטאת ואשם – ת"ל: "זבח". מנין לרבות העופות והמנחות [י]והיין והעצים והלבונה – ת"ל: "שלמים קרבנו", כל קרבנות שהוא מביא, כשהוא שלם ט] מביא, ואינו מביא כשהוא אונן. קתני מיהא פסח! *אמר רב חסדא: פסח כדי נסביה. רב ששת אמר: *מאי "פסח" – שלמי פסח. אי הכי, היינו שלמים! תנא שלמים הבאין מחמת י] פסח, ותנא שלמים הבאין מחמת יא] עצמן. דאי לא תנא שלמים הבאין מחמת פסח – סלקא דעתך אמינא: *הואיל ומחמת פסח אתי – כגופיה דפסח דמי, קמ"ל. רב מרי אמר:
לא

רש"י

מגריפה. כלי ברזל הוא וראשו רחב, ומבדילים בו גרוגרות הנדבקות זו בזו. לבי על הסל. לשומרו. יב] מדבר המטמא – אב הטומאה שמטמא כלי, וכן מטומאות דרבנן המטמאות אותה לטמא חולין ותרומה יג] מדרבנן. ולא מדבר הפוסלה לחולין ולתרומה, ומיהו טמאה היא להשתמש בה קדשים. איגלגל מילתא. הא דרמינהו לעיל מתני' דאונן, יד] דאיבעי לך לשנויי עלה הנך שינויי דאיקי. שלישי של תרומה. עצמה. וכ"ש שלישי של חולין שנעשו על טהרת תרומה. מותר ליגע. בתרומה, דאינו נעשה גופו אלא שלישי טו] כמו המאכל שאכל, ואסור לאכול תרומה, אבל מותר ליגע. אלמא: מעלות עבוד רבנן באכילה דליתנהו בנגיעה. וגבי אונן נמי, הא דתנן אונן צריך טבילה – באכילה תנן, אבל נוגע – אין צריך לטבול. כי מזמני ליה. אם זימנו חבירו כהן לאכול עמו לערב בחלקו בקדשים – אוכל. ורמינהו אונן טובל ואוכל פסחו טז]. משנה היא בפסחים (דף צא:). ולא גרסינן בה "מחוסר כיפורים", דאינו צריך להמתין לערב, אלא מביא כפרתו וטובל ואוכל בקדשים. טובל. כדתנן: אונן צריך טבילה לקדש. ואוכל פסחו לערב. אבל לא בקדשים. מפרש לה בפסחים (דף צב.): קסבר אנינות לילה דרבנן, ואנינות דאורייתא חד יומא הוא, כדכתיב: "ואחריתה כיום מר" (עמוס ח). וגבי פסח לא העמידו דבריהם במקום כרת, גבי קדשים העמידו דבריהם במקום עשה דאכילת *קדשים, יז] כדאמרינן. כאן בפסח. מתני' דקתני אינו חולק, ואי מזמנו ליה יח] לאכילת קדשים אוכל – בלילי פסחים קאי, דמגו דשרו יט] רבנן אכילת פסחים – שרו ליה נמי שאר קדשים. והא דקתני אבל לא בקדשים אשאר ימות השנה קאי. כ] והאי "אבל לא בקדשים" – לאו אלילי פסחים קמהדר, ואע"ג דעליה קאי, אלא: אבל לא בקדשים של כל השנה. וה"ק: טובל ואוכל פסחו בערב, וה"ה לכל הקדשים באותו לילה, אבל לא בקדשים של שאר ימות השנה. רב אסי אמר. אידי ואידי בלילי פסחים, ולא קשיא; ההיא דפסחים – שמת בי"ד וקברו בי"ד. הלכך בפסח אוכל אבל לא בקדשים, דאנינות לילה דיום מיתה דרבנן. ומתני' כשמת בי"ג וקברו בי"ד. דיום קבורה גופיה דרבנן, ולילו לא תפים אפילו מדרבנן. מאן תנא. דתנא להך דפסחים, דאית ליה אנינות ליל כא] יום מיתה דרבנן. מדברי תורה. לקמן יליף לה רבי יהודה בשמעתין מאנינות דאהרן ובניו. תדע שהרי אונן כו'. ואי דאורייתא – פסח נמי לא ליכול! נאכלת בשמחה. יוצא בה ידי חובת שמחה, כב] דכתיב בה שמחה: "וזבחת שלמים ואכלת שם ושמחת" (דברים כז), ותודה "שלמים" כג] איקרי. שאינן באין על חטא. הלכך כשלמים דמי. ת"ל זבח. "אם זבח שלמים קרבנו". והעצים. המתנדב עצים, מביא קרבן עמהן. קתני מיהת פסח. דבשלמא כולהו איכא למימר מדרבנן, וקרא אסמכתא בעלמא. אלא פסח קשיא אדלעיל, דתנא: טובל ואוכל פסחו. שלמי פסח. חגיגת י"ד, כשהחבורה מרובה.
לא

תוספות

ואי משקין דמטמאו כלי, גזירה משום משקה זב וזבה – א"כ אפילו לתרומה נמי! ואי משקין שנגעו לטבול יום, דאינו תחלה אלא לקדש, כדתנן (פרה פ"ח מ"ז): כל הפוסל התרומה מטמא משקין להיות תחילה, חוץ מטבול יום – א"כ אפילו קדש נמי לא מטמא רק לפסול, כדאיתא במעילה ריש פ' "חטאת העוף" (דף ח.). וא"כ לא יטמאו המגריפה לפסול קדש, ד"טמאה" משמע לעשות פסול אחרי כן, מדלא קאמר "מגריפה פסולה". *דכי כד] אמרינן פ"ק דפסחים (דף כ.) גבי הבשר טמא: למאי? אי למנות ראשון ושני בחיבת הקדש – תפשוט דבעי ר"ל צריך של מנחות כו'. לכך נראה לפרש: דמשכחת לה במעת לעת שבנדה, דאמרינן פ"ק דנדה (דף ו.): לקודש, אבל לא לתרומה. א"נ: בבגדי כה] תרומה דמדרס לקודש. והא דאמר "ולא שמרתיה מדבר הפוסלה" אע"פ כו] שמטמאה לקדש – כל דבר שאינו כז] *(עושה שלישי ועושה) אחרי כן לקדש כח] קרי "פוסלה", כמו שלישי של חולין.

ה"ג: ה"נ באכילה עבוד רבנן מעלה. פירש בקונטרס: והא דתנן: אונן צריך טבילה – אאכילה תנן, אבל נוגע א"צ לטבול. והשתא לא קאי שינויא דרבי יוחנן. ונראה דאפשר לקיימו, דלעולם מתני' בשטבל, וההיא דחגיגה – בדלא טבל. אבל הא דאמר: אונן שטבל, כט] דאנינותו חוזרת עליו – היינו באכילה. ופ"ה עיקר.

אונן טובל ואוכל פסחו לערב אבל לא בקדשים. משנה היא בפסחים בפרק "האשה" (דף צא:). ול"ג "מחוסר כיפורים", דאונן דוקא הוא דלא אכיל בקדשים לערב משום אנינות לילה. אבל מחוסר כיפורים, כיון שהביא כפרתו וטבל – למה לא יאכל?.

אמר רב חסדא פסח כדי נסביה. במסקנא משני: ל] כאן קודם ששחטו וזרקו עליו, כאן לאחר ששחטו וזרקו עליו. דההיא לא] לא יביא פסחו – כשמת קודם ששחטו וזרקו עליו, וההיא דטובל ואוכל לערב – כשמת לאחר ששחטו וזרקו עליו. אבל הנך אמוראי לא בעו לשנויי הכי, משום דקסברי: אכילה לא מעכבא. וכיון דלא מעכבא – אמאי דחיא אכילתה אנינות לילה דרבנן טפי משאר קדשים? אבל היכא דמת קודם ששחטו, אף על גב דאכילה לא לב] מעכבת, אי לא שרית לאוכלו – לא מייתי. ויש לתמוה: דמשמע דשרי ר"ש לשחוט ולזרוק אחר שמת לו מת, משום דאנינות לילה דרבנן. והלא אנינות יום דאורייתא, ודל אכילה מהכא – מ"מ הקרבה ביום אסור לג] בחטאת עולה ואשם, דאסור להביא כשהוא אונן, מדכתיב "קרבנו" – כל ששמו קרבן! וכי תימא משום דאתי עשה דפסח לד] ודחי עשה דאנינות דכשהוא שלם מביא – א) א"כ היכי דייק מינה אנינות לילה מדרבנן? אפילו היא דאורייתא דחיא! ומתוך פי' הקונטרס משמע דסבר השתא דכולה אסמכתא בעלמא. ונראה לפרש: כיון דעיקר פסח לא בא אלא לאכילה, כדתנן (פסחים דף עו:): פסח הבא בטומאה – נאכל בטומאה, שעיקרו לא בא אלא לאכילה. הלכך לא חיישינן ביה לאנינות לה] בזמן הקרבה, אלא בזמן אכילה, ואף על גב דאכילה ב) לא מעכבת:

א) עיין רש"ק ב) נ"א לא מעכב' מ"מ אם לא היה ראוי לאכילה גרע

עין משפט נר מצוה

טו א ב מיי' פי"ג מהל' מטמא משכב ומושב הלכה ו:
טז ג מיי' פי"א מהלכות אבות הטומאה הלכה יא:
יז ד מיי' פ"ו מהלכות קרבן פסח הלכה ט:
יח ה מיי' שם הל' ד:
יט ו ז מיי' שם הל' ט:
כ ח מיי' פ"ב מהלכות ביאת מקדש הל' ט:
כא ט י מיי' שם הל' יא:

[נ"ל דכי ה"ג]
נ"א פוסל חולין ופוסל וגירסת הש"ק עושה עכשיו כלום ועושה אחרי כן לקדש
[פסחים צא:]
מ"ק טו:

מסורת הש"ס

חגיגה כ. [ע"ש]
חולין לה.
נ"א יוחנן
רש"ק מ"ז
נ"א דלא חזי לא אכיל
נ"א תפים לילו אפילו מדרבנן
[ברכות טז: וש"נ]
גי' הש"ק קדשים עם כדאמרינן ואכילו את אשר כופר בהם והשם כנ"ל
נ"ל על חטא כשלמים מג כו' נ"ק
[ר"ה ה. וש"נ]
[שם]
[שם]

גליון הש"ס

גמ' אידי דאכיל פסח ע' חגיגה דף כ ע"ב ובטורי אבן שם ד"ה מדמהינן פסח:

שיטה מקובצת

א] תרומה עצמה אסור: ב] מעלה ה"נ באכילה עבוד רבנן מעלה בנגיעה לא עבוד רבנן מעלה: ג] נמי בקדשים בשאר: ד] השנה כולה רב אסי: ה] עשר מת לו מת בארבעה עשר וקברו בי"ד יום מיתה תפים לילו מדרבנן מת לו מת בי"ג וקברו בי"ד יום קבורה: ו] תנא דאמר אנינות: ז] לאו אפילו בפסח אות ו' נמחק: ח] לרבות בכור ומעשר ופסח מרבה אני בכור: ט] שלם הוא מביא: י] מחמת עצמן ותיבת פסח נמחק: יא] מחמת פסח ומתיבות עצמן כו' עד תיבת סלקא נמחק: יב] לשומרו הס"ד ומה"ד מדבר כו': יג] תיבת מדרבנן נמחק: יד] דאונן אהדדי דאיבעי לן לשנויי: טו] שלישי כמות המאכל: טז] פסחו לערב. משנה: יז] תיבת כדאמרינן נמחק: יח] ליה אכיל באכילת קדשים: יט] דשרו ליה רבנן: כ] מתיבת והאי כו' עד תיבות וה"ק טובל בס"א הכל אינו: כא] ליל דיום מיתה: כב] שמחה. ס"א ושלמים כתיב בהו וזבחת כו': כג] איקרי הס"ד: כד] פסולה דכי האי גוונא אמרינן: כה] בבגדי אוכלי תרומה: כו] אע"פ שטמאה לקדש ותיבת שמטמאה ל"ש: כז] שאינו מטמא כלים ועושה אחרי תיבות עושה שלישי ל"ש ונמחק: כח] לקדש נקרא פוסלה: כט] שטבל אנינותו: ל] משני רבא כאן: לא] דההיא דלא יביא: לב] לא מעכבא: לג] אסור כחטאת עולה: לד] דפסח דחמיר ודחי: לה] לאנינות לזמן הקרבה אלא לזמן אכילה ואע"ג דאכילה לא מעכבא מכל מקום הנו לאכילה בעי הס"ד:

לָא קַשְׁיָא, כָּאן – שֶׁמֵּת לוֹ מֵת בְּי"ד וּקְבָרוֹ בְּי"ד, כָּאן – שֶׁמֵּת לוֹ מֵת בְּי"ג וּקְבָרוֹ בְּי"ד. מֵת לוֹ מֵת בְּי"ד וּקְבָרוֹ בְּי"ד – יוֹם מִיתָה א] תּוֹפֵס לֵילוֹ מִדְּאוֹרַיְיתָא. מֵת לוֹ מֵת בְּי"ג וּקְבָרוֹ בְּי"ד – יוֹם קְבוּרָה מִדְּרַבָּנַן, אֵינוֹ ב] תּוֹפֵס לֵילוֹ אֶלָּא מִדְּרַבָּנַן. א"ל רַב אַשִׁי לְרַב מָרִי: וְאֶלָּא הָא דְּקָתָנֵי, אָמַר לוֹ ר"ש: תֵּדַע, שֶׁהֲרֵי אָמְרוּ: אוֹנֵן טוֹבֵל וְאוֹכֵל אֶת פִּסְחוֹ ג] אֲבָל לֹא בְּקָדָשִׁים. נֵימָא לֵיהּ: ד] קָאָמֵינָא לָךְ אֲנָא יוֹם מִיתָה דְּאוֹרַיְיתָא, וְאָמְרַתְּ לִי אַתְּ יוֹם קְבוּרָה דְּרַבָּנַן! קַשְׁיָא. אַבַּיֵי אָמַר: לָא קַשְׁיָא, [א]כָּאן – שֶׁמֵּת קוֹדֶם חֲצוֹת, כָּאן – שֶׁמֵּת לְאַחַר חֲצוֹת. קוֹדֶם חֲצוֹת, דְּלָא אִיחֲזֵי לְפֶסַח – חָיְילָא עֲלֵיהּ אֲנִינוּת, אַחַר חֲצוֹת, דְּאִיחֲזֵי לְפֶסַח – לָא חָיְילָא עֲלֵיהּ אֲנִינוּת. וּמְנָא תֵּימְרָא דְּשַׁנֵּי ה] לֵיהּ בֵּין קוֹדֶם חֲצוֹת בֵּין לְאַחַר חֲצוֹת? *דְּתַנְיָא: °"לָהּ יִטַּמָּא" – מִצְוָה, [ב]לֹא רָצָה – מְטַמְּאִין אוֹתוֹ עַל כָּרְחוֹ. וּמַעֲשֶׂה בְּיוֹסֵף הַכֹּהֵן שֶׁמֵּתָה אִשְׁתּוֹ בְּעֶרֶב הַפֶּסַח וְלֹא רָצָה לִיטַּמֵּא, ו] וְנִמְנוּ אֶחָיו הַכֹּהֲנִים וְטִימְּאוּהוּ בְּעַל כָּרְחוֹ. וּרְמִינְהִי: *°"וְלַאֲחוֹתוֹ" מַה ת"ל? הֲרֵי שֶׁהָלַךְ לִשְׁחוֹט אֶת פִּסְחוֹ וְלָמוּל אֶת בְּנוֹ, וְשָׁמַע שֶׁמֵּת לוֹ מֵת, יָכוֹל יִטַּמֵּא? אָמַרְתָּ: °"לֹא יִטַּמָּא". יָכוֹל כְּשֵׁם ז] שֶׁלֹּא יִטַּמֵּא לַאֲחוֹתוֹ כָּךְ אֵין מְטַמֵּא לְמֵת מִצְוָה? ת"ל: "וְלַאֲחוֹתוֹ" – לַאֲחוֹתוֹ הוּא דְּאֵינוֹ מְטַמֵּא, אֲבָל מְטַמֵּא [ג]הוּא לְמֵת מִצְוָה. ח] לָאו ש"מ: כָּאן – קוֹדֶם חֲצוֹת, כָּאן – לְאַחַר חֲצוֹת? מִמַּאי? דִּילְמָא לְעוֹלָם אֵימָא לָךְ: אִידִי וְאִידִי ט] אַחַר חֲצוֹת, וְהָא – רַבִּי יִשְׁמָעֵאל, וְהָא – ר"ע. דְּתַנְיָא: "לָהּ יִטַּמָּא" – רְשׁוּת, דִּבְרֵי רַבִּי יִשְׁמָעֵאל. ר"ע אוֹמֵר: חוֹבָה! לָא ס"ד, דְּרֵישָׁא דְּהַהִיא ר"ע קָתָנֵי לָהּ. דְּתַנְיָא, *ר"ע אוֹמֵר: °"נֶפֶשׁ" – אֵלּוּ הַקְּרוֹבִים, "מֵת" – אֵלּוּ הָרְחוֹקִים, "לְאָבִיו" – אֵינוֹ מְטַמֵּא, אֲבָל מְטַמֵּא הוּא לְמֵת מִצְוָה. "לְאִמּוֹ" – י] הָיָה כֹּהֵן וְהוּא נָזִיר, לְאִמּוֹ הוּא דְּאֵינוֹ מְטַמֵּא, אֲבָל מְטַמֵּא הוּא לְמֵת מִצְוָה. "לְאָחִיו" – שֶׁאִם הָיָה כ"ג וְהוּא נָזִיר, לְאָחִיו הוּא דְּאֵינוֹ מְטַמֵּא, אֲבָל מְטַמֵּא הוּא לְמֵת מִצְוָה. "וְלַאֲחוֹתוֹ" – מַה ת"ל? הֲרֵי שֶׁהָלַךְ לִשְׁחוֹט אֶת פִּסְחוֹ וְלָמוּל אֶת בְּנוֹ, וְשָׁמַע שֶׁמֵּת לוֹ מֵת, יָכוֹל יִטַּמֵּא? אָמַרְתָּ: "לֹא יִטַּמָּא". יָכוֹל כְּשֵׁם שֶׁאֵין מְטַמֵּא לַאֲחוֹתוֹ כָּךְ אֵינוֹ מְטַמֵּא לְמֵת מִצְוָה? תַּלְמוּד לוֹמַר: "וְלַאֲחוֹתוֹ", לַאֲחוֹתוֹ יא] לֹא יִטַּמֵּא, אֲבָל יִטַּמֵּא הוּא לְמֵת מִצְוָה.

רָבָא

(ויקרא כא; במדבר ו; שם; שם)

רש"י

לא קשיא. דר"ש אדר"ש. הָא דְּקָתָנֵי הָכָא: אוֹנֵן לֹא מַיְיתֵי פֶּסַח – כְּשֶׁמֵּת יב] וּקְבָרוֹ בְּי"ד, דְּיוֹם מִיתָה דְּאוֹרַיְיתָא, וְתָפֵיס לֵילוֹ מִדְּאוֹרַיְיתָא כִּדְיָלֵיף לֵיהּ רַבִּי יְהוּדָה לְקַמָּן. וְהָא דְּקָתָנֵי לְעֵיל: אוֹכֵל פִּסְחוֹ – יג] כְּשֶׁמֵּת בְּי"ג וּקְבָרוֹ בְּי"ד, דְּיוֹם קְבוּרָה גּוּפֵיהּ דְּרַבָּנַן, וְלֹא תָּפֵיס לֵילוֹ אֶלָּא מִדְּרַבָּנַן. וְרוּמְיָא דְּתַרְתֵּי מַתְנִי' קַמַּיְיתָא מְשַׁנֵּי לֵיהּ רַב מָרִי: אִידִי וְאִידִי יד] יוֹם קְבוּרָה, וְכָאן בְּפֶסַח וְכָאן בִּשְׁאָר יְמוֹת הַשָּׁנָה, כִּדְשַׁנֵּינַן לֵיהּ מֵעִיקָּרָא. וּמַאי "אֲבָל לֹא בְּקָדָשִׁים" – אֲבָל לֹא בְּקָדָשִׁים שֶׁל כָּל הַשָּׁנָה כּוּלָּהּ. הָכִי גָּרְסִי: **לא תפים לילו עמו אלא מדרבנן. אמינא לך** אֲנִינוּת יוֹם מִיתָה **דאורייתא.** דְּהָא מֵאֲנִינוּת דְּאַהֲרֹן מַיְיתֵי לֵיהּ לְקַמָּן, וְהָתָם יוֹם מִיתָה הֲוָאי. וְאַתְּ מַהְדְּרַתְּ יוֹם קְבוּרָה. דְּהוּא גּוּפֵיהּ מִדְּרַבָּנַן, וְהָתָם מוֹדֵינָא. **אביי אמר.** אִידִי וְאִידִי בְּיוֹם מִיתָה. וּלְעוֹלָם אֲנִינוּת לַיְלָה לְר"ש דְּרַבָּנַן. וּדְקָתָנֵי בַּבָּרַיְיתָא: פֶּסַח אֵינוֹ בָּא בַּאֲנִינוּת – כְּשֶׁמֵּת קוֹדֶם חֲצוֹת, דְּרַחֲמָנָא דַּחְיֵיהּ מֵהַאי קְרָא דְּדָרְשִׁינַן: כְּשֶׁהוּא שָׁלֵם הוּא מֵבִיא וְלֹא כְּשֶׁהוּא אוֹנֵן. וּדְקָתָנֵי בִּפְסָחִים: טוֹבֵל וְאוֹכֵל פִּסְחוֹ, אַלְמָא מַיְיתֵי לֵיהּ אוֹנֵן – כְּשֶׁמֵּת אַחַר חֲצוֹת, דְּקָדְמָה חוֹבַת שְׁחִיטַת פֶּסַח לַאֲנִינוּת, וְתוּ לָא דַּחְיָא לֵיהּ אֲנִינוּת מִלְּשַׁלֵּחַ טו] קָרְבָּנוֹ. וּמִיהוּ עַל כָּרְחָךְ ש"מ אֲנִינוּת לַיְלָה דְּרַבָּנַן, דְּאִי מִדְּאוֹרַיְיתָא הִיא – טז] הַאי לָא הֲוָה אָכֵיל, נְהִי דְּקָדְמָה חוֹבַת שְׁחִיטָה לַאֲנִינוּת, אֲבָל חוֹבַת אֲכִילָה לָא קָדְמָה לֵיהּ. וַאֲכִילַת פְּסָחִים לָא מְעַכְּבָא לְאַבַּיֵי. יז] אֶלָּא מִשּׁוּם דַּאֲנִינוּת לַיְלָה דְּרַבָּנַן, וְהֵם לֹא הֶעֱמִידוּ דִּבְרֵיהֶם בִּמְקוֹם כָּרֵת, דְּדִילְמָא מִמְּנַע וְלָא שָׁחֵיט. א"נ: כֵּיוָן דְּעַל יח] כָּרְחָךְ שָׁחֲטֵיהּ – לָאו אוֹרַח אַרְעָא דְּנֵימְרוּ יִשְׁחֲטוּ ע"מ לִיפָּסֵל. הִילְכָּךְ, אוֹכֵל פִּסְחוֹ. אֲבָל לֹא שְׁאָר קָדָשִׁים, אֲפִי' לֵיל פֶּסַח, דְּהֶעֱמִידוּ דִּבְרֵיהֶם בִּמְקוֹם עֲשֵׂה. וּמַתְנִי' דְּדָיְיקִינַן: אִי יט] מְזַמְּנוּ לֵיהּ אָכֵיל – בְּיוֹם קְבוּרָה, כִּדְאָמַר רַב אַסִּי לְעֵיל [דְּמֵת בְּי"ג וּקְבָרוֹ בְּי"ד], אֲפִילּוּ מִדְּרַבָּנַן לָא תָּפֵיס לֵילוֹ. דְּשַׁנֵּי לָן. (א) מִדְּאוֹרַיְיתָא. וּרְמִינְהִי כו'. מַסְקָנָא דְּמִילְּתֵיהּ הוּא, דְּבָעֵי לְאַתּוּיֵי מִגּוֹ רוּמְיָא וְשִׁינּוּיֵי. לַאֲחוֹתוֹ מַה ת"ל. בְּנָזִיר קָאֵי, וְכֵיוָן דִּכְתִיב "לְאָבִיו וּלְאִמּוֹ" כ] כ"ש לַאֲחוֹתוֹ. **אָמַרְתָּ לא יטמא.** רֵישָׁא דְּבָרַיְיתָא בְּנָזִיר קָא מַיְירֵי, כִּדְתָנֵי לָהּ לְקַמָּן בִּשְׁמַעְתִּין. וְה"ק סֵיפָא: הֲרֵי שֶׁהָיָה נָזִיר וְהוּא כ"ג, וְהוֹלֵךְ לִשְׁחוֹט אֶת פִּסְחוֹ אוֹ לָמוּל אֶת בְּנוֹ, וְשָׁמַע שֶׁמֵּת לוֹ מֵת, יָכוֹל יִטַּמָּא – אָמַרְתָּ לֹא יִטַּמָּא, אִי מִשּׁוּם נָזִיר, אִי מִשּׁוּם כ"ג, אִי מִשּׁוּם פֶּסַח, וכ"ש הֵיכָא דְּאִיתְנְהוּ לְכוּלְּהוּ. וְלָמוּל אֶת בְּנוֹ. דְּמִילַת זְכָרָיו מְעַכַּבְתּוֹ מִלֶּאֱכוֹל כא] פִּסְחוֹ. **לַאֲחוֹתוֹ אין מטמא.** אַלְמָא אָתְיָא חוֹבָה דְּפֶסַח וְאָסְרָה לֵיהּ לְהִיטַּמֵּא, וּמֵבִיא פֶּסַח *אוֹנֵן. וְקס"ד *דְּתַרְוַיְיהוּ קָתָנֵי אַלִּיבָּא דְּר' עֲקִיבָא, דְּאָמַר: "לָהּ יִטַּמָּא" – מִצְוָה. וְהִילְכָּךְ לָא מִיתּוֹקְמָא הַךְ בַּתְרַיְיתָא אֶלָּא בְּשֶׁמֵּת לְאַחַר חֲצוֹת, דְּאָתְיָא חוֹבַת פֶּסַח וְדָחְיָא לְמִצְוַת טוּמְאָה. וְקַמַּיְיתָא בְּמֵת קוֹדֶם חֲצוֹת, דְּאַפְקַעְתֵּיהּ אֲנִינוּת מִפֶּסַח. **וממאי.** דְּטַעְמָא דְּקַמַּיְיתָא מִשּׁוּם דְּקָדְמָה אֲנִינוּת הוּא, דְּתוֹקְמָא לְר"ש דְּאָמַר לְעֵיל, (ב) אֵין מֵבִיא פֶּסַח אוֹנֵן, בְּמֵת קוֹדֶם חֲצוֹת, וּכְר"ע? **דילמא.** כב] טַעַם דְּר"ע לָאו מִשּׁוּם קוֹדֶם חֲצוֹת הוּא, וְהֵיכָא דְּלָא אִיטַּמֵּי בְּמֵת – וַאֲפִילּוּ כג] קוֹדֶם חֲצוֹת בָּעֵי לְמֶעְבַּד פֶּסַח. וְהָכָא – מִשּׁוּם דְּאִיטַּמֵּי הוּא. וַאֲפִילּוּ מֵת לְאַחַר חֲצוֹת נַמִּי קָאָמַר ר' עֲקִיבָא יִטַּמָּא, מִשּׁוּם דְּקָסָבַר: "לָהּ יִטַּמָּא" מִצְוָה, וְאֵין לָהּ תַּשְׁלוּמִין. הִילְכָּךְ מְטַמְּאִינַן לֵיהּ, וּמִמֵּילָא אָזַל לֵיהּ כָּרֵת, דה"ל טָמֵא, וּפֶסַח יֵשׁ לוֹ תַּשְׁלוּמִין בַּשֵּׁנִי. וְהַךְ דְּקָתָנֵי "לֹא יִטַּמָּא" – רַבִּי יִשְׁמָעֵאל הִיא, דְּאָמַר: רְשׁוּת. הִילְכָּךְ כד] לָא תִּדְחְיֵיהּ מִצְוַת פֶּסַח בִּשְׁבִיל רְשׁוּת דְּטוּמְאָה. וּלְעוֹלָם בֵּין לְרַבִּי יִשְׁמָעֵאל בֵּין לְר"ע, אוֹנֵן שֶׁלֹּא נִטְמָא – מֵבִיא פִּסְחוֹ, וַאֲפִילּוּ מֵת קוֹדֶם חֲצוֹת, דְּטַעַם דְּהָכָא לָאו מִשּׁוּם אֲנִינוּת הוּא כה]. **דרישא.** דְּהַהִיא דְּנָזִיר, ר"ע קָתָנֵי לָהּ, דְּאוֹמֵר מִצְוָה. הִילְכָּךְ לָא מִיתָּרְצֵי אֶלָּא מִשּׁוּם טַעְמָא דְּקוֹדֶם חֲצוֹת וְאַחַר חֲצוֹת: כו] הֵיכָא דְּמֵת קוֹדֶם חֲצוֹת – קָדְמָה לֵיהּ חוֹבַת טוּמְאָה לְפֶסַח וְטָמֵא, וְהוּא הַדִּין לַאֲנִינוּת דְּהָא קָדְמָה. וְהֵיכָא דְּמֵת לְאַחַר חֲצוֹת – קָדְמָה חוֹבַת פֶּסַח וּמַפְקַע לְחוֹבַת טוּמְאָה, וְהוּא הַדִּין לַאֲנִינוּת. **נפש.** בְּנָזִיר כְּתִיב: "כָּל יְמֵי הַזִּירוֹ לַה' עַל נֶפֶשׁ מֵת לֹא יָבֹא", וְסָמֵיךְ לֵיהּ "לְאָבִיו וּלְאִמּוֹ" וגו'. וְכוּלֵּיהּ קְרָא יְתֵירָא הוּא, דְּהָא כְּתִיב כז] לֵיהּ קְרוֹבִים וּרְחוֹקִים. **נפש אלו הקרובים.** לָאו מַשְׁמָעוּתָא הִיא, דְּתִיקְשֵׁי לָךְ: אִם כֵּן לָמָּה נֶאֶמְרוּ רְחוֹקִים. דְּאִי לָא כְּתִיב תַּרְתֵּי קְרָאֵי – הֲוָה מוֹקְמִינַן לֵיהּ בִּרְחוֹקִים. אֲבָל הַשְׁתָּא כח] דְּאִיכְּתִיבָא תְּרֵי קְרָאֵי, "נֶפֶשׁ" – קְרוֹבִים מַשְׁמַע, שֶׁהֵן כְּנַפְשׁוֹ. **לאביו.** מַה ת"ל? אִם לְלַמֵּד שֶׁלֹּא יִטַּמָּא לוֹ – הֲרֵי פֵּירֵשׁ קְרוֹבִים וּרְחוֹקִים. אֶלָּא בָּא לִפְרוֹט כט] אֶת מִי אָסַר – אֶת הַקְּרוֹבִים, אֲבָל לֹא מֵת מִצְוָה. **לאמו.** מַה תַּלְמוּד לוֹמַר? אִם לֶאֱסוֹר – הֲרֵי לָמַדְנוּ, אִם לְהַתִּיר מֵת מִצְוָה – הֲרֵי לָמַדְנוּ. אֶלָּא לֹא הוּצְרַךְ לְנָזִיר לְבַדּוֹ, אֶלָּא לְלַמֶּדְךָ שֶׁאִם הָיְתָה בּוֹ עוֹד קְדוּשָּׁה אַחֶרֶת, כְּגוֹן שֶׁהָיָה כֹּהֵן וְנָזִיר – הִתַּרְתִּי לְךָ בּוֹ מֵת מִצְוָה. ל] מִמִּיעוּט דִּ"לְאִמּוֹ" דָּרְשִׁינַן: לְאִמּוֹ לֹא יִטַּמָּא, אֲבָל מִיטַּמֵּא הוּא לְמ"מ, וְכֵן כּוּלָּם. **הרי שהלך לשחוט את פסחו.** לא] זֶה שֶׁהָיָה כ"ג וְנָזִיר, וְנִיתּוֹסֵף בּוֹ עוֹד דָּבָר אַחֵר הַמְעַכְּבוֹ מִלִּיטַּמֵּא, שֶׁהָיָה צָרִיךְ לִשְׁחוֹט אֶת פִּסְחוֹ. אַף זֶה – לַאֲחוֹתוֹ פָּטַרְתִּי לְךָ בּוֹ, אֲבָל מִיטַּמֵּא הוּא לְמֵת מִצְוָה. דְּאִם אֵינוֹ עִנְיָן לְנָזִיר לְבַדּוֹ – תְּנֵהוּ עִנְיָן לְמִי שֶׁיֵּשׁ בּוֹ כָּל אֵלּוּ.

רבא

תוספות

הרי שהיה הולך לשחוט **את** פסחו ולמול **את** בנו כו'. תימה: היכי דייק מהכא דשחיטת פסח דוחה טומאת מתו? שאני הכא שהוא כ"ג ונזיר! וכי תימא: אי לאו דבאפי נפשיה דחיא מתו, לא היה צריך קרא למת מצוה דדחיא שלשתן, דכיון דכ"ג ונזיר נדחים משום מת מצוה – בשביל שהולך עדיין לשחוט את פסחו לא מימנע. א"א לומר כן, *דהא לכהן הדיוט ונזיר איצטריך קרא, אף על גב דכהן הדיוט לחודיה מיטמא למתו. ויש פירושים שמוגה בהם משום הך קשיא, דלא מיירי *הכא בנזיר אלא בהולך לשחוט פסחו לחודיה. ולא יתכן כלל, דהיינו ברייתא דמייתי בסמוך דמיירי בכהן לב] ונזיר. ונראה דדייק משום דקתני הכא: אמרת "לא יטמא", ובכולהו לא קתני הכי – לג] משמע לא יטמא משום שחיטת פסחו. ולא גרסינן "ת"ל לא יטמא". ועוד נראה לדקדק: אי שחיטת הפסח לחודה לא דחיא טומאת קרובים – ה"ל למתנייה ברישא דהולך לשחוט כו': הרי שהיה כ"ג ונזיר והולך לשחוט כו', כמו כהן הדיוט דתני ברישא. דמעיקרא תני הקל יותר, כי היכי דתני כהן הדיוט לד] קודם לנזיר, ואח"כ כ"ג ונזיר. **הא** רבי ישמעאל הא ר"ע. פי' בקונטרס: ואפילו מת לאחר חצות נמי קאמר ר"ע יטמא, משום דקסבר: "לה יטמא" – מצוה, ואין לה תשלומין. הילכך מטמאינן ליה, וממילא אזל ליה כרת, דה"ל טמא. דפסח יש לו תשלומין בשני, ולא דמי לעשה דהשלמה דאתי עשה דפסח ודחי ליה, כדאמר בריש "תמיד נשחט" (פסחים דף נט. ושם*), אע"פ שיש לה] לו תשלומין בשני.

נפש אלו הקרובים מת אלו הרחוקים. בנזיר בפ' "כ"ג" (דף מח:) גרס איפכא, ועיקר. ועושה שם [אדא] דרשא מ"לאביו ולאמו".

אכילת

עין משפט נר מצוה

כב א מיי' פ"ו מהל' קרבן פסח הל"ט:
כג ב מיי' פ"ב מהל' אבל הל' ז:
כד ג מיי' שם פ"ג הל"ח:

[ובתוס' דברכות לחו זה בשם הר"ש מקוצי ע"ש]

גי' הצ"ק הכא בכהן ונזיר כו'

[קצרו כאן דבריהם וע"ש בתוס' בפסחים ועי' רש"ק]

נ"א דברייתא דקתני לא רצה מטמאין אותו אליבא כו'

מסורת הש"ס

שמחות פ"ד סוטה ג.

מגילה ג: ברכות יט: סנהדרין לה. נזיר מח:

[סוטה ג.]

[נזיר מח:]

גירסת צ"ק באינות וקס"ד דהנך ברייתות תרווייהו קתני אליבא דר"ע כו' וכ"ה בש"י

הגהות הב"ח

(א) רש"י ד"ה דשני לן בדאורייתא: (ב) ד"ה וממאי וכו' לעיל אונן אין מביא פסח במת:

שיטה מקובצת

א] מיתה תפים לילו: ב] אינו תפים לילו: ג] פסחו לערב אבל: ד] אנא קאמינא לך יום: ה] דשני לן בין: ו] ליטמא לה ונמנו: ז] כשם שאינו מטמא לאחותו כך אינו מטמא למת מצוה: ח] מצוה אלא לאו: ט] ואידי לאחר חצות: י] לאמו שאם היה: יא] לאחותו הוא דאינו מטמא אבל מטמא הוא: יב] כשמת בי"ד וקברו בי"ד: יג] פסחו כשמת בי"ג: יד] ואידי ביום קבורה: טו] מלשלח פסחו ומיהו תיבת קרבנו נמחק: טז] היא לא הוה אכיל דנהי דקדמה תיבת האי נמחק: יז] לאביי. ס"א אבל אי סבירא ליה אכילת פסחים מעכבא אז מצי ר"ש למיסבר אנינות לילה דאורייתא ואפ"ה כיון דחל עליו חובת פסח קודם אנינות אכיל פסחו לערב דאי לא אכיל לא מצי להקריב ומיהו אע"ג דלא מעכב אכיל דלא העמידו כו': יח] דעל כרחי' שחיט לאו אורח ארעא דנימרו רבנן ישחטנו: יט] אי מזמני ליה: כ] ולאמו כ"ש ולאחותו ס"א ואמו ואחיו אייתינהו לדרשא דרישא דברייתא למידרש לאחיו לא יטמא אבל מטמא הוא למת מצוה ולקמן בשמעתין מייתי לה וה"ק סיפא ולאחותו מה ת"ל הרי שהיה הולך כו' כלומר אם אינו ענין לנזיר לא לאיסור אחותו ולא להתיר מת מצוה דהא נפקא לן מרישא דקרא תנהיו ענין להולך לשחוט את פסחו ולמול את בנו דמילת זכריו מעכבתו מלאכול פסח הס"ד. ומה"ד אמרת לא יטמא. כי היכא דנזיר אין לו לדחות נזירות מפני טומאת קרוביו כך שוחט פסחו אין לו לדחות פסחו מפני טומאת קרוביו ואינו יכול לפרש אותה בנזיר עצמו ולומר הרי שהיה הולך נזיר זה לשחוט את פסחו דא"כ מאי רומיא דמרמינן לה אדיוסף הכהן דילמא הא דקתני אמרת לא יטמא משום נזירות הוא דנזיר אין מטמא לקרובים: הס"ד ומה"ד לאחותו אינו מטמא אלמא אתיא חובה כו': כא] מלאכול פסח הס"ד ומה"ד ולאחותו אין כו' אתיא חובת פסח ואסרה כו' ומביא פסחו אונן: כב] דילמא טעמא דר"ע: כג] ואפילו מת קודם חצות בעי למעבד פסחו דאנינות לא דחיא והכא: כד] הילכך כיון דלאחר חצות הוא וחיילא עליה חובת פסח לא: כה] הוא ובקודם חצות לא מצינן מוקמי' ליה דא"כ אפי' יטמא רשות אמאי לא יטמא אם ירצה הא לא חיילא עליה חובת פסח וכ"ת משום חומרא דפסח א"כ מאי איו יא ערב פסח אפילו ששה ימים קודם פסח נמי דהא הזאה שלישי ושביעי בעי הס"ד: כו] חצות דהיכא דמת קודם חצות קדמה ליה חובת טומאה לפסח ומטמא והוא הדין: כז] תיבת ליה נמחק: כח] השתא דאיכתבו תרי: כט] לפרט דאת מי אסר: ל] מצוה ממיעוטא דלאמו דדרשינן לאמו: לא] פסחו. ס"א ולמול את בנו אם אינו ענין לנזיר תנהו ענין לכל מי שהולך לשחוט את פסחו ולמול את בנו זה כו': לב] בכהן גדול ונזיר: לג] הכי אלמא משמע: לד] כהן הדיוט ונזיר ואח"כ כ"ג ונזיר: לה] שיש לפסח תשלומין בשני תיבת לו נמחק:

א"ל

תורה אור

רָבָא אֲמַר: אִידִי וְאִידִי אַחַר חֲצוֹת, וְל"ק: אכָּאן — קוֹדֶם שֶׁשָּׁחֲטוּ וְזָרְקוּ עָלָיו, כָּאן — לְאַחַר שֶׁשָּׁחֲטוּ וְזָרְקוּ עָלָיו. א"ל רַב אַדָּא בַּר מַתְּנָה לְרָבָא: אַחַר שֶׁשָּׁחֲטוּ וְזָרְקוּ אֶת דָּמוֹ — מַה דַּהֲוָה הֲוָה! א"ל רָבִינָא: *אֲכִילַת פְּסָחִים מְעַכְּבָא, מִדְּרַבָּה בַּר רַב הוּנָא. א"ל: א] צַיֵּית מַאי דְּקָאָמַר לָךְ רַבָּךְ. מַאי דְּרַבָּה בַּר רַב הוּנָא? *דְּתַנְיָא: ביוֹם שְׁמוּעָה כְּיוֹם קְבוּרָה לְמִצְוַת שִׁבְעָה וּשְׁלֹשִׁים, גוְלַאֲכִילַת פְּסָחִים — כְּיוֹם לִיקּוּט עֲצָמוֹת. אֶחָד זֶה וְאֶחָד זֶה טוֹבֵל וְאוֹכֵל בְּקָדָשִׁים לָעֶרֶב. הָא גּוּפָא קַשְׁיָא: אָמְרַתְּ יוֹם שְׁמוּעָה כְּיוֹם קְבוּרָה לְמִצְוַת שִׁבְעָה וּשְׁלֹשִׁים, וְלַאֲכִילַת פְּסָחִים כְּיוֹם לִיקּוּט עֲצָמוֹת.

מִכְּלָל דְּיוֹם קְבוּרָה — אֲפִילּוּ לָעֶרֶב נַמִי לָא אָכֵיל. וַהֲדַר תָּנֵי: אֶחָד זֶה וְאֶחָד זֶה טוֹבֵל וְאוֹכֵל בְּקָדָשִׁים לָעֶרֶב! אָמַר רַב חִסְדָּא: תַּנָּאֵי הִיא. רַבָּה בַּר רַב הוּנָא אָמַר: ל"ק; כָּאן — שֶׁשָּׁמַע שְׁמוּעָה עַל מֵתוֹ סָמוּךְ לִשְׁקִיעַת הַחַמָּה, וְכֵן שֶׁלִּיקְּטוּ לוֹ עֲצָמוֹת סָמוּךְ לִשְׁקִיעַת הַחַמָּה, וְכֵן שֶׁמֵּת לוֹ מֵת וּקְבָרוֹ סָמוּךְ לִשְׁקִיעַת הַחַמָּה. וְכָאן — לְאַחַר שְׁקִיעַת הַחַמָּה. לְאַחַר שקה"ח מַאי דַּהֲוָה הֲוָה! אֶלָּא ש"מ: אֲכִילַת פְּסָחִים מְעַכְּבָא. רַב אָשֵׁי אָמַר: מַאי "אֶחָד זֶה וְאֶחָד זֶה" — ה"ק: אֶחָד יוֹם שְׁמוּעָה וְאֶחָד יוֹם לִיקּוּט — ב] טוֹבֵל וְאוֹכֵל בְּקָדָשִׁים לָעֶרֶב. וְהָא דְּרַב אָשֵׁי *בְּדוּתָא הִיא; מִכְּדֵי עֲלָהּ קָאֵי, "זֶה וְזֶה" מִיבָּעֵי לֵיהּ? אֶלָּא ש"מ בְּדוּתָא הִיא. וּמַאי תַּנָּאֵי? דְּתַנְיָא: *עַד מָתַי מִתְאוֹנֵן עָלָיו — כָּל הַיּוֹם, רַבִּי אוֹמֵר: כָּל זְמַן דשֶׁלֹּא נִקְבַּר. בְּמַאי עָסְקִינַן? אִילֵימָא בְּיוֹם מִיתָה, מִי אִיכָּא דְּלֵית לֵיהּ ג] דְּיוֹם מִיתָה דְּתָפֵיס לֵילוֹ מִדְּרַבָּנַן? וְתוּ, רַבִּי אוֹמֵר: כָּל זְמַן שֶׁלֹּא נִקְבַּר; ד] הָא קְבָרוֹ — אִישְׁתְּרֵי לֵיהּ. וּמִי אִיכָּא דְּלֵית לֵיהּ *°"וְאַחֲרִיתָהּ כְּיוֹם מָר"? אָמַר רַב שֵׁשֶׁת: אַיוֹם קְבוּרָה קָאֵי. מַתְקִיף (א) רַב יוֹסֵף: אֶלָּא הָא דְּקָתָנֵי: ההַשּׁוֹמֵעַ עַל מֵתוֹ ה] *כִּמְלַקֵּט עֲצָמוֹת, טוֹבֵל וְאוֹכֵל בְּקָדָשִׁים לָעֶרֶב; מִכְּלָל דְּיוֹם קְבוּרָה — אֲפִילּוּ לָעֶרֶב נַמִי לָא אָכֵיל, הָא מַנִּי? אֶלָּא תְּרֵיץ: ו] עַד מָתַי מִתְאוֹנְנִין עָלָיו — כָּל אוֹתוֹ הַיּוֹם וְלֵילוֹ. רַבִּי אוֹמֵר: כָּל זְמַן שֶׁלֹּא נִקְבַּר. [אֲבָל נִקְבַּר] — בְּלֹא לֵילוֹ. אֲמַרוּהָ (ב) קַמֵּיהּ דְּר' יִרְמְיָה, אָמַר: *גַּבְרָא רַבָּה כְּרַב יוֹסֵף לֵימָא הָכִי? ז] לֵימָא דְּרַבִּי לְקוּלָּא? וְהָתַנְיָא: עַד מָתַי מִתְאוֹנֵן עָלָיו — כָּל זְמַן ח] שֶׁאֵינוֹ נִקְבָּר, אֲפִילּוּ מִכָּאן וְעַד עֲשָׂרָה יָמִים, דִּבְרֵי רַבִּי. וַחכ"א: אֵין מִתְאוֹנֵן עָלָיו אֶלָּא אוֹתוֹ הַיּוֹם בִּלְבַד! אֶלָּא תְּרֵיץ הָכִי: עַד מָתַי הוּא מִתְאוֹנֵן עָלָיו — כָּל אוֹתוֹ הַיּוֹם בְּלֹא לֵילוֹ. רַבִּי אוֹמֵר: כָּל זְמַן שֶׁלֹּא נִקְבַּר, (ג) ט] וְאִם נִקְבַּר — תּוֹפֵס לֵילוֹ. אֲמַרוּהָ קַמֵּיהּ דְּרָבָא: מִדְּקָאָמַר רַבִּי יוֹם קְבוּרָה י] תּוֹפֵס לֵילוֹ מִדְּרַבָּנַן — מִכְּלָל דְּיוֹם מִיתָה תּוֹפֵס לֵילוֹ מִדְּאוֹרַיְיתָא. וְסָבַר רַבִּי אֲנִינוּת לַיְלָה דְּאוֹרַיְיתָא? וְהָתַנְיָא: °"הֵן הַיּוֹם" — אֲנִי הַיּוֹם אָסוּר (ד) וְלַיְלָה מוּתָּר, וּלְדוֹרוֹת — בֵּין בַּיּוֹם וּבֵין בַּלַּיְלָה אָסוּר, דִּבְרֵי רַבִּי יְהוּדָה. רַבִּי אוֹמֵר: *אֲנִינוּת לַיְלָה אֵינָהּ מִדִּבְרֵי תוֹרָה אֶלָּא מִדִּבְרֵי סוֹפְרִים! לְעוֹלָם דְּרַבָּנַן הִיא,

וַחֲכָמִים

עמוס ח / ויקרא י / שמחות פ"ד הלכה ד'

רש"י

רָבָא אָמַר כו'. אַמִּילְּתֵיהּ דְּר"ש קָאֵי, לְשַׁנּוּיֵי דְּר"ש אַדְּר"ש. אִידִי וְאִידִי לְאַחַר חֲצוֹת. וַאֲפִילּוּ מֵת לְאַחַר חֲצוֹת קוֹדֶם שֶׁשָּׁחֲטוּ עָלָיו — אִית לֵיהּ לְר"ש לֹא יָבִיא אֶת פִּסְחוֹ. דְּרַחֲמָנָא דַּחְיֵיהּ, כִּדְדָרֵישׁ וְאָזֵיל: "שְׁלָמִים קָרְבָּנוֹ" — כָּל קָרְבְּנוֹתָיו לֹא יָבִיא אֶלָּא כְּשֶׁהוּא שָׁלֵם. וּדְקָתָנֵי: "אוֹנֵן טוֹבֵל וְאוֹכֵל יא] פִּסְחוֹ לָעֶרֶב" — כְּשֶׁמֵּת לְאַחַר שֶׁשָּׁחֲטוּ וְזָרְקוּ עָלָיו. מַאי דַּהֲוָה הֲוָה. הֲרֵי נִפְטַר, וְאַמַּאי דְּחָיָיא אֲכִילָתוֹ אֲנִינוּת לַיְלָה דְּרַבָּנַן טְפֵי מִשְּׁאָר קָדָשִׁים? בִּשְׁלָמָא לְאַבַּיֵי דְּמוֹקֵי לָהּ בְּקוֹדֶם שֶׁשָּׁחֲטוּ וְזָרְקוּ עָלָיו, וּבִלְאַחַר חֲצוֹת — הוֹאִיל וּפֶסַח חָלָה עָלָיו לַהֲבִיא, וְאִי לָא שָׁרֵית לֵיהּ לְאוֹכְלוֹ — לָא מַיְיתֵי, הִילְכָּךְ לֹא הֶעֱמִידוּ דִּבְרֵיהֶם. אֶלָּא לְרָבָא אַמַּאי לֹא הֶעֱמִידוּ? הָא יב] כְּבָר שָׁחַט וְזָרַק! ה"ג: א"ל רָבִינָא אֲכִילַת פְּסָחִים מְעַכְּבָא מִדְּרַבָּה בַּר רַב הוּנָא. וּלְקַמָּן מַיְיתִינַן לָהּ. א"ל רָבָא לְרַב אַדָּא צַיֵּית מַאי דְּאָמַר לָךְ רַבָּךְ. רָבִינָא. שְׁמַע לוֹ, שֶׁיָּפֶה הֱשִׁיבְךָ עַל שְׁאֵלָתְךָ. וּבְמַסֶּכֶת שְׁבוּעוֹת יג] כִּי הַאי סוּגְיָא *דְּרַבָּה וְרָבִינָא וְרַב אַדָּא בְּפֶ' "יְדִיעוֹת הַטּוּמְאָה" (דף יח.). יוֹם שְׁמוּעָה. שֶׁשָּׁמַע שֶׁמֵּת לוֹ מֵת. וּבִשְׁמוּעָה קְרוֹבָה שֶׁתּוֹךְ ל' עָסְקִינַן. כְּיוֹם קְבוּרָה לְמִצְוַת שִׁבְעָה וּשְׁלֹשִׁים. מִיּוֹם שְׁמוּעָה מַתְחִיל לִמְנוֹת ז' לִרְחִיצָה וּנְעִילַת הַסַּנְדָּל, וְל' לְגִיהוּץ. וְלַאֲכִילַת פְּסָחִים. הָוֵי יוֹם שְׁמוּעָה כְּיוֹם לִיקּוּט עֲצָמוֹת, דְּקַיְימָא לָן בִּפְסָחִים בְּפֶרֶק "הָאִשָּׁה" (דף צב.): הַשּׁוֹמֵעַ עַל מֵתוֹ וְהַמְלַקֵּט עֲצָמוֹת — טוֹבֵל וְאוֹכֵל בְּקָדָשִׁים לָעֶרֶב. וְהָוֵינַן בָּהּ: מְלַקֵּט עֲצָמוֹת הַזָּאָה שְׁלִישִׁי וְז' בָּעֵי וּמְשַׁנֵּינַן: אֵימָא שֶׁלִּיקְּטוּ יד] [לוֹ] אֲחֵרִים עֲצָמוֹת. דְּאָמְרִינַן בְּמוֹ"ק (דף ח.): הַמְלַקֵּט עַצְמוֹת אָבִיו וְאִמּוֹ — הֲרֵי זֶה מִתְאַבֵּל עֲלֵיהֶם כָּל הַיּוֹם. וְאַשְׁמוּעִינַן בִּפְסָחִים דְּלָעֶרֶב מוּתָּר בְּקָדָשִׁים. וְהָכָא אַשְׁמוּעִינַן: טו] יוֹם שְׁמוּעָה לְעִנְיַן אֲכִילַת פְּסָחִים לָא כְּיוֹם קְבוּרָה הוּא, דְּאִילּוּ יוֹם קְבוּרָה לָא אָכֵיל פִּסְחוֹ לָעֶרֶב וַאֲפִילּוּ מֵת טז] בְּאֶתְמוֹל בְּי"ג, אֶלָּא כְּיוֹם לִיקּוּט עֲצָמוֹת הָוֵי, וּמוּתָּר בְּכָל הַקֳּדָשִׁים. וְהָא דִּנְקַט פְּסָחִים — מִשּׁוּם יז] דְּיוֹם קְבוּרָה נָקַט לֵיהּ, לְמֵימַר דִּבְיוֹם קְבוּרָה אֲפִילּוּ פֶּסַח נַמִי לָא. אֶחָד זֶה וְאֶחָד זֶה. (ה) עַל כָּרְחָךְ אַיּוֹם קְבוּרָה וְיוֹם לִיקּוּט קָאֵי, וְקַשְׁיָא רֵישָׁא לְסֵיפָא כִּדְלְקַמָּן. דְּאִי אַיּוֹם שְׁמוּעָה וְיוֹם לִיקּוּט — לָא שַׁיָּיךְ לְמִיתְנֵי "אֶחָד זֶה וְאֶחָד זֶה", דְּכֵיוָן דְּמִינַּיְיהוּ סָלֵיק — "זֶה וָזֶה" מִיבָּעֵי לֵיהּ. טוֹבֵל וְאוֹכֵל בְּקָדָשִׁים לָעֶרֶב. וכ"ש פִּסְחוֹ. (ו) כְּיוֹם לִיקּוּט עֲצָמוֹת. מַשְׁמַע: וְלֹא כְּיוֹם קְבוּרָה, דְּאִילּוּ יוֹם קְבוּרָה לָא אָכֵיל פִּסְחוֹ לָעֶרֶב. תַּנָּאֵי הִיא. דִּפְלִיגֵי בְּלֵיל יוֹם קְבוּרָה שֶׁאֵינָהּ יוֹם מִיתָה. דְּאִיכָּא לְמ"ד תָּפֵיס לֵילוֹ מִדְּרַבָּנַן, וְסָבַר: אֲכִילַת פְּסָחִים לָא מְעַכְּבָא, הִילְכָּךְ אֲפִילּוּ פֶּסַח לָא אָכֵיל. וּלְקַמָּן מַיְיתֵי לְהוּ. רַבָּה בַּר רַב הוּנָא אָמַר כָּאן שֶׁשָּׁמַע שְׁמוּעָה אוֹ שֶׁלִּקְּטוּ לוֹ עֲצָמוֹת אוֹ שֶׁקָּבַר מֵתוֹ בְּי"ד סָמוּךְ לִשְׁקִיעַת הַחַמָּה וְכָאן לְאַחַר שְׁקִיעַת הַחַמָּה. סֵיפָא דְּקָתָנֵי: בְּכוּלְּהוּ אוֹכֵל קָדָשִׁים, וכ"ש פִּסְחוֹ — כְּשֶׁבָּא עָלָיו אֶחָד מֵאֵלּוּ לִפְנֵי שְׁקִיעַת הַחַמָּה, דה"ל לָעֶרֶב לֵיל יוֹם קְבוּרָה, וְלֵיל יוֹם שְׁמוּעָה, וְלֵיל יח] (פְּסָחִים) *כְּיוֹם לִיקּוּט עֲצָמוֹת. וְסָבַר: יוֹם קְבוּרָה לָא תָּפֵיס לֵילוֹ אֲפִילּוּ מִדְּרַבָּנַן, וכ"ש יוֹם שְׁמוּעָה וְלִיקּוּט עֲצָמוֹת. וְהָא דְּקָתָנֵי רֵישָׁא: וְלַאֲכִילַת פְּסָחִים כְּיוֹם לִיקּוּט עֲצָמוֹת, דְּאִילּוּ יוֹם קְבוּרָה לָא יט] אָכַל — כְּשֶׁאֵירַע לוֹ אֶחָד מֵאֵלּוּ לְאַחַר שְׁקִיעַת הַחַמָּה, דה"ל לֵילָה זֶה יוֹם קְבוּרָה עַצְמוֹ וְלָא לֵיל יוֹם קְבוּרָה. אע"ג דְּאַף הוּא מִדְּרַבָּנַן — הֶחֱמִירוּ בְּיוֹם קְבוּרָה עַצְמוֹ יוֹתֵר מִיּוֹם שְׁמוּעָה וְלִיקּוּט לְאוֹסְרוֹ בְּפֶסַח. אֲבָל בְּיוֹם לִיקּוּט לָא אֲסָרוּהוּ בְּפֶסַח, אֶלָּא בִּשְׁאָר קָדָשִׁים הִצְרִיכוּהוּ לְהַמְתִּין כ] עַד עֶרֶב. וה"ק: לַאֲכִילַת פְּסָחִים הָוֵי יוֹם שְׁמוּעָה כְּיוֹם לִיקּוּט, וְאוֹכֵל פִּסְחוֹ. וַאֲפִי' שָׁמַע אוֹ לִיקֵּט אַחַר שְׁקִיעָה, דה"ל יוֹם שְׁמוּעָה עַצְמוֹ וְיוֹם לִיקּוּט כא] עֲצָמוֹת — וַאֲפִילּוּ הָכִי שָׁרֵי. מַה שֶּׁאֵין כֵּן בְּיוֹם קְבוּרָה עַצְמוֹ, דְּאִילּוּ מֵת לוֹ מֵת בְּי"ג וּקְבָרוֹ אוֹתוֹ עֲמָמִים לְאַחַר שְׁקִיעָה דְּי"ד — אָסוּר לֶאֱכוֹל בַּפֶּסַח. וְאע"ג דְּחָלָה עָלָיו שִׂמְחַת הָרֶגֶל וְאֵינוֹ נוֹהֵג אֲבֵילוּת בָּרֶגֶל — ה"מ אֲבֵילוּת, דְּמִדְּרַבָּנַן הִיא, וּכְתִיב: "וְשָׂמַחְתָּ בְּחַגֶּךָ", אֲבָל אֲנִינוּת לֵיאָסֵר בְּקָדָשִׁים — חָלָה עָלָיו. וְאֶחָד זֶה (ז) וְאֶחָד זֶה, הֵיכָא דְּבָאוּ עָלָיו מִבְּעוֹד יוֹם — אוֹכֵל בְּקָדָשִׁים לָעֶרֶב, כב] דְּלֵילוֹ לָא תָּפֵיס. וּמִיהוּ, בַּיּוֹם אָסוּר בִּשְׁאָר קָדָשִׁים אֲפִי' כג] יוֹם שְׁמוּעָה וְלִיקּוּט עֲצָמוֹת, בַּר מִפֶּסַח, כִּדְמְפָרֵשׁ טַעְמָא וְאָזֵיל. מַאי דַּהֲוָה הֲוָה. וּמַה לִּי פֶּסַח וּמַה לִּי שְׁאָר קָדָשִׁים? הָא אָמְרַתְּ קָדָשִׁים אָסוּר בְּיוֹם לִיקּוּט לְבוֹ בַּיּוֹם, כִּדְקָתָנֵי "לָעֶרֶב", וּבְפֶסַח אַמַּאי שָׁרֵית לֵיהּ? אֲכִילַת פְּסָחִים מְעַכֶּבֶת. כד] לֹא הֶעֱמִידוּ דִּבְרֵיהֶם בִּמְקוֹם כָּרֵת. וּמִיהוּ, בְּיוֹם קְבוּרָה הֶעֱמִידוּ דִּבְרֵיהֶם, מִשּׁוּם דְּרוּבָּא קָבְרֵי בְּיוֹם מִיתָה, וְאָתֵי לְמִישְׁרֵי יוֹם מִיתָה עַצְמוֹ. וְיֵשׁ מְקוֹמוֹת שֶׁהֶעֱמִידוּ דִּבְרֵיהֶם בִּמְקוֹם כָּרֵת, כִּדְאָמְרִינַן בִּפְסָחִים בְּ"הָאִשָּׁה" (דף צב.). וּמַאי תַּנָּאֵי. דִּפְלִיגֵי בְּיוֹם קְבוּרָה לְמִיתְפַּס לֵילוֹ מִדְּרַבָּנַן, דְּקָאָמַר רַב חִסְדָּא לְעֵיל "תַּנָּאֵי הִיא"? עַד מָתַי מִתְאוֹנֵן. לֵיאָסֵר בְּקָדָשִׁים. כָּל הַיּוֹם. קס"ד בְּלֹא לֵילוֹ. כָּל זְמַן שֶׁלֹּא נִקְבַּר. קָא ס"ד לְקוּלָּא פָּלֵיג, וְאָמַר כה] דְּכָל הַיּוֹם לָא מִיתְּסַר, דְּמִשֶּׁקְּבָרוֹ (ח) הוּתַּר מִיָּד. אִי נֵימָא בְּיוֹם מִיתָה. שֶׁקְּבָרוֹ בַּיּוֹם שֶׁמֵּת. מִי אִיכָּא דְּלֵית לֵיהּ כו'. הָא בֵּין לְר"ש בֵּין לְרַבִּי, דִּפְלִיגֵי עֲלֵיהּ דְּר' יְהוּדָה בַּאֲנִינוּת לַיְלָה דְּיוֹם מִיתָה, מוֹדוּ כו] מִדִּבְרֵי סוֹפְרִים מֵיהָא אָסוּר! אַחֲרִיתָהּ כְּיוֹם מָר. *אַחֲרִיתָהּ שֶׁל זוֹנָה כְּיוֹם מַר, שֶׁמִּתְאַבֵּל וּמֵימַר עַל מֵתוֹ, לְפִי שֶׁסּוֹפוֹ לָמוּת עָלֶיהָ, וְיִתְאַבְּלוּ כז] עֲלֵיהֶן. אַלְמָא מְרִירוּת יוֹם שָׁלֵם הוּא. אַיּוֹם קְבוּרָה. שֶׁמֵּת אֶתְמוֹל וּקְבָרוֹ הַיּוֹם. וְאַכַּתִּי לָא אַסִּיקְנָא מִילְּתֵיהּ לְתַנָּאֵי דְּרַב חִסְדָּא עַד סֵיפָא, דְּתַרְצַהּ ר' יִרְמְיָה. הָא מַנִּי. *) בֵּין לְרַבִּי בֵּין לְרַבָּנַן כח] מוּתָּר. כָּל אוֹתוֹ הַיּוֹם. שֶׁל קְבוּרָה וְלֵילוֹ. רַבִּי אוֹמֵר כָּל זְמַן שֶׁלֹּא נִקְבַּר. אֲבָל קְבָרוֹ — אִישְׁתְּרֵי לֵיהּ בַּלַּיְלָה. וּמִיהוּ, בַּיּוֹם לֵיכָּא לְמֵימַר דְּשָׁרֵי לֵיהּ רַבִּי, דַּאֲפִילּוּ יוֹם כט] דְּלִיקּוּט עֲצָמוֹת אָסוּר כָּל הַיּוֹם, כִּדְאָמְרַתְּ: טוֹבֵל וְאוֹכֵל לָעֶרֶב. וְהָתַנְיָא כו'. אַלְמָא רַבִּי לְחוּמְרָא אֲמָרָהּ. וְכֵיוָן דְּלֵיכָּא לְפָרוּשֵׁי פְּלוּגְתָּא ל] דְּרַבָּנַן (ט) לֶאֱכוֹל בְּעוֹדוֹ מוּטָּל לְפָנָיו — וע"כ בְּלֵיל יוֹם קְבוּרָה פְּלִיגִי, דְּקָאָמַר רַבִּי: אֲפִי' קְבָרוֹ לְסוֹף י' יָמִים — מִתְאוֹנֵן עָלָיו לֵיל יוֹם קְבוּרָה, וחכ"א: אֵינוֹ מִתְאוֹנֵן עָלָיו בְּיוֹם קְבוּרָה אֶלָּא יוֹם עַצְמוֹ, אֲבָל לֹא לֵילוֹ. וְהַיְינוּ תַּנָּאֵי דְּרַב חִסְדָּא. מִדְּקא"ר יוֹם קְבוּרָה. דְּאִיהוּ גּוּפֵיהּ דְּרַבָּנַן, תָּפֵיס לֵילוֹ מִדְּרַבָּנַן, מִכְּלָל דְּיוֹם מִיתָה דְּאוֹרַיְיתָא. תָּפֵיס לֵילוֹ לא] דְּאוֹרַיְיתָא. דְּקָא סָלְקָא דַּעְתָּךְ: לֹא עָשׂוּ חֲכָמִים חִיזּוּק לְדִבְרֵיהֶם, שֶׁעִיקָּרוֹ מִדִּבְרֵיהֶם, יוֹתֵר מִשֶּׁעָשְׂתָה תּוֹרָה לִדְבָרֶיהָ. הֵן הַיּוֹם. "הֵן" מַשְׁמַע דְּאִלּוּ הַקָּרְבָּנוֹת חֲלוּקִין מִשְּׁאָר קָרְבָּנוֹת, שֶׁעֲלֵיהֶן שָׁמַעְתָּ לְאוֹכְלָן בַּאֲנִינוּת לַיְלָה, מִפְּנֵי שֶׁכּוּלָּנוּ אוֹנְנִין וְאֵין כֹּהֵן לְאוֹכְלָן. אֲבָל לְדוֹרוֹת, שֶׁיֵּשׁ כֹּהֲנִים לְאוֹכְלָן — בֵּין בַּיּוֹם וּבֵין בַּלַּיְלָה אָסוּר. לְעוֹלָם דְּרַבָּנַן הִיא. אֲפִילּוּ אֲנִינוּת לַיְלָה דְּיוֹם מִיתָה. וַאֲפִילּוּ הָכִי, יוֹם קְבוּרָה דְּאִיהוּ גּוּפֵיהּ מִדְּרַבָּנַן — לֵילוֹ נַמִי לְרַבִּי אָסוּר מִדְּרַבָּנַן.

וַחֲכָמִים

*) נ"ל בין לרבי בין לרבנן לילה מותר נ"ק

תוספות

אכילת פסחים מעכבא. פלוגתא היא בפרק "כיצד צולין" (פסחים דף עח:) דרבי נתן *ורבנן. ומשמע מתוך פירוש הקונטרס דסבר לה כמ"ד מעכבא לב] לגבי הא [דאפילו למ"ד לא מעכבא] דבעינן גברא ראוי לאכילה, כדמוכח התם, אם כן אכילה לג] היא מצוה, וסברא הוא שדוחה אנינות דרבנן. א"נ, כיון דכתיב "איש לפי אכלו" למצוה, דמצוה בדידיה מבאחריני — סברא הוא דדחיא אנינות דרבנן. ומעכבא דקאמר לאו דוקא.

סמוך לשקיעת החמה. לד] במנחה נקט "סמוך" — נקט נמי הכא "סמוך". דהוה מצי למימר: כאן קודם שקיעה כאן לאחר שקיעה.

ואחריתה כיום מר. פסוק הוא בתרי עשר [עמוס ח']: "ושמתיה כאבל יחיד ואחריתה כיום מר". ולא כמו שפירש בקונטרס.

וחכמים

עין משפט נר מצוה

גי' הל"ק ורבנן ומדלא קתני כס"ל כמ"ד מעכבא משמע דלגבי הא אפי' למ"ד לא מעכבא מודה דבעינן גברא כו'

כה א מיי' פ"ו מהל' קרבן פסח הל"ט:

כו ב מיי' פ"ב מהל' אבל הל"ב טוש"ע יו"ד סי' תב סעי' ה:

כז ג מיי' פ"ו מהל' קרבן פסח הל"ט:

כח ד מיי' פ"ב מהל' ביאת המקדש הלכה ט ו ופ"ד מהל' אבל הל"ז טוש"ע יו"ד סי' שמא סעיף ה:

כט ה מיי' פ"ב מהל' ביאת המקדש הל"י:

ל ו מיי' שם הל"ט [וכרב אלפס ברכות פ"ב דף יב. וע"ש]:

שיטה מקובצת

א] א"ל רבא צייה: ב] ליקוט עצמות טובל: ג] ליה יום מיתה תפיס לילו: ד] הא קבריה אישתרי אות ד' נמחק: ה] מתו והמלקט עצמות: ו] תריץ הכי עד מתי מתאוננין: ז] הכי למימרא דרבי: ח] כל זמן שלא נקבר: ט] [illegible] י] [illegible] יא] ואוכל את פסחו: יב] תיבת כבר ל"ש: יג] שבועות גרסינן כי האי סוגיא דרבא ורבינא [illegible] יד] שליקטו לו: טו] אשמועינן דיום שמועה: טז] מת מאתמול בי"ג: יז] [illegible]

הגהות הב"ח

(א) גמ' מתקיף לה רב יוסף: (ב) שם אמרוה [illegible] (ח) ד"ה כל זמן וכו' דמשקברו מותר מיד: (ט) ד"ה והתניא וכו' פלוגתא דרבנן בעודו כצ"ל ותיבת לאכול נמחק:

מסורת הש"ס

[פסחים עח:]

שמחות פי"ב ע"ש

[נ"ל דרבא]

[נ"א ברותא ערוך ערך בר ד' וע' מ"ש פסחים יח. על הגליון]

מ"ק כה.

גי' הל"ק והמלקט עצמות

[לעיל מז. כתובות מג.]

[ברכות טז: וש"נ]

[כס"י יום]

[ככל המקומות שהביא הש"ס הך קרא ברכות טז: מו"ק כה. סוכה כה: לא פירש רש"י כמו כאן וגם לא נמצא בשום פסוק רק בעמוס ח' כדאיתא בתוס' ד"ה ואחריתה]

*וַחֲכָמִים עָשׂוּ חִיזּוּק לְדִבְרֵיהֶם יוֹתֵר מִשֶּׁל תּוֹרָה. *תָּנוּ רַבָּנַן: °"כִּי כֵן צֻוֵּיתִי", "כַּאֲשֶׁר צִוֵּיתִי", "כַּאֲשֶׁר צִוָּה ה'". "כִּי כֵן צֻוֵּיתִי" — בַּאֲנִינוּת יֹאכְלוּהָ, "כַּאֲשֶׁר צִוֵּיתִי" — בִּשְׁעַת מַעֲשֶׂה א] אָמַר לָהֶן, "כַּאֲשֶׁר צִוָּה ה'" — לֹא מֵאֵלַיי אֲנִי אוֹמֵר. וּרְמִינְהִי: מִפְּנֵי אֲנִינוּת (א) נִשְׂרְפָה, לְכָךְ נֶאֱמַר "כָּאֵלֶּה"! אָמַר שְׁמוּאֵל: לָא קַשְׁיָא; הָא — ב] ר"י, הָא — ר"נ. דְּתַנְיָא: *מִפְּנֵי אֲנִינוּת שְׂרָפוּהָ, לְכָךְ נֶאֱמַר "כָּאֵלֶּה", דִּבְרֵי רַבִּי נְחֶמְיָה. רַבִּי יְהוּדָה וְר"ש אוֹמְרִים: *מִפְּנֵי טוּמְאָה נִשְׂרְפָה, שֶׁאִם אַתָּה אוֹמֵר: מִפְּנֵי אֲנִינוּת נִשְׂרְפָה — הָיוּ ג] לִשְׁלָשְׁתָּן שֶׁיִּשָּׂרְפוּהָ. ד"א: הָיוּ רְאוּיִ לְאוֹכְלָן לָעֶרֶב. ד"א: וַהֲלֹא פִּינְחָס הָיָה עִמָּהֶן. רָבָא אָמַר: אִידִי וְאִידִי רַבִּי נְחֶמְיָה, וְלָא קַשְׁיָא; כָּאן — בְּקָדְשֵׁי שָׁעָה, כָּאן — בְּקָדְשֵׁי דוֹרוֹת. רַבִּי נְחֶמְיָה הֵיכִי מְתָרֵיץ ד] לְהָנֵי קְרָאֵי, וְרַבָּנַן הֵיכִי מְתָרְצִי לְהוּ לְהָנֵי קְרָאֵי? רַבִּי נְחֶמְיָה מְתָרֵיץ לְהוּ הָכִי: "מַדּוּעַ לֹא אֲכַלְתֶּם", ה] *אָמַר לוֹ מֹשֶׁה לְאַהֲרֹן: שֶׁמָּא נִכְנַס דָּמָהּ ו] לִפְנַי וְלִפְנִים? אָמַר לוֹ: °"הֵן לֹא הוּבָא אֶת דָּמָהּ". שֶׁמָּא חוּץ לִמְחִיצָתָהּ יָצָאת? אָמַר לוֹ: בַּקֹּדֶשׁ הָיְתָה. וְדִלְמָא בַּאֲנִינוּת אַקְרִיבְתּוּהָ וּפְסַלְתּוּהָ? אָמַר לוֹ: מֹשֶׁה, וְכִי הֵם הִקְרִיבוּ? אֲנִי הִקְרַבְתִּי! וְא"ל: הֵן לֹא הוּבָא אֶת דָּמָהּ, וּבַקֹּדֶשׁ הָיְתָה — "אָכוֹל תֹּאכְלוּ אוֹתָהּ כַּאֲשֶׁר צִוֵּיתִי" בַּאֲנִינוּת יֹאכְלוּהָ! אָמַר לוֹ: °"וַתִּקְרֶאנָה אוֹתִי כָּאֵלֶּה וְאָכַלְתִּי חַטָּאת הַיּוֹם הַיִּיטַב בְּעֵינֵי ה'"? שֶׁמָּא לֹא שָׁמַעְתָּ אֶלָּא בְּקָדְשֵׁי שָׁעָה. דְּאִי בְּקָדְשֵׁי דוֹרוֹת — *ק"ו מִמַּעֲשֵׂר הַקַּל: וּמָה מַעֲשֵׂר הַקַּל אָמְרָה תּוֹרָה: °"לֹא אָכַלְתִּי בְאוֹנִי מִמֶּנּוּ" — ז] בְּקָדְשֵׁי דוֹרוֹת לֹא כָּל שֶׁכֵּן? מִיָּד — °"וַיִּשְׁמַע מֹשֶׁה וַיִּיטַב בְּעֵינָיו", הוֹדָה וְלֹא בּוֹשׁ ח] מֹשֶׁה לוֹמַר "לֹא שָׁמַעְתִּי", אֶלָּא אָמַר: "שָׁמַעְתִּי וְשָׁכַחְתִּי". ור"י וְר"ש הֵיכִי מְתָרְצִי לְהוּ? ט] הָכִי מְתָרְצִי לְהוּ: °"מַדּוּעַ לֹא אֲכַלְתֶּם אֶת הַחַטָּאת י] (ב) בִּמְקוֹם [הַקּוֹדֶשׁ]" שֶׁמָּא נִכְנַס דָּמָהּ יא] לִפְנַי וְלִפְנִים? אָמַר לוֹ: °"הֵן לֹא הוּבָא אֶת דָּמָהּ (אֶל הַקֹּדֶשׁ פְּנִימָה)". שֶׁמָּא חוּץ יב] לִמְחִיצָתָהּ יָצָאת? אָמַר לוֹ: יג] הֵן בַּקּוֹדֶשׁ הָיְתָה. וְדִילְמָא בַּאֲנִינוּת אַקְרִיבְתּוּהָ וּפְסַלְתּוּהָ? אָמַר לוֹ: מֹשֶׁה, הֵן הִקְרִיבוּהָ דְּפָסְלָה בְּהוּ אֲנִינוּת? אֲנִי הִקְרַבְתִּיהָ! וְדִילְמָא אַגַּב מְרָרַיְיכוּ פְּשַׁעְתּוּ בָּהּ וְאִיטַּמַּאי! אָמַר לוֹ: מֹשֶׁה, כָּךְ אֲנִי בְּעֵינֶיךָ שֶׁאֲנִי מְבַזֶּה קָדְשֵׁי שָׁמַיִם? "וַתִּקְרֶאנָה אוֹתִי כָּאֵלֶּה" — וַאֲפִילּוּ אֵלֶּה וְכָאֵלֶּה — אֵין אֲנִי מְבַזֶּה קָדְשֵׁי שָׁמַיִם! אָמַר לוֹ: וְאִי הֵן לֹא הוּבָא אֶת דָּמָהּ, וּבַקּוֹדֶשׁ הָיְתָה — "אָכוֹל תֹּאכְלוּ אוֹתָהּ בַּקּוֹדֶשׁ כַּאֲשֶׁר צִוֵּיתִי" בַּאֲנִינוּת יֹאכְלוּהָ! אָמַר לוֹ: שֶׁמָּא לֹא שָׁמַעְתָּ אֶלָּא בַּלַּיְלָה, דְּאִי בַּיּוֹם — *ק"ו מִמַּעֲשֵׂר הַקַּל, וּמָה מַעֲשֵׂר הַקַּל אָמְרָה תּוֹרָה: °"לֹא אָכַלְתִּי בְאוֹנִי מִמֶּנּוּ", קוֹדֶשׁ יד] חָמוּר לֹא כָּל שֶׁכֵּן? מִיָּד — "וַיִּשְׁמַע מֹשֶׁה וַיִּיטַב

(ויקרא י — כי כן צויתי; שם — הן לא הובא; שם — ותקראנה; דברים כו — לא אכלתי; ויקרא י — וישמע משה; שם — מדוע לא אכלתם; שם — הן לא הובא; דברים כו — לא אכלתי)

וַחֲכָמִים עָשׂוּ חִיזּוּק לְדִבְרֵיהֶם יוֹתֵר. מִמַּה שֶּׁעָשְׂתָה תּוֹרָה לִדְבָרֶיהָ. כִּי כֵן צֻוֵּיתִי. טו] בְּמִנְחוֹת שְׁמִינִי כְּתִיב: "קְחוּ אֶת הַמִּנְחָה" וגו'. טז] בַּאֲנִינוּת. נָדָב וַאֲבִיהוּא. כַּאֲשֶׁר צִוֵּיתִי. בְּחַטָּאת דְּרֹאשׁ חֹדֶשׁ שֶׁנִּשְׂרְפָה כְּתִיב: "הֵן לֹא הוּבָא אֶת דָּמָהּ" וגו'. בִּשְׁעַת מַעֲשֶׂה. כְּשֶׁאֵירַע לָהֶם אֲנִינוּתָם אָמַר לָהֶם שֶׁלֹּא יִמָּנְעוּ מֵאֲכִילַת קָדָשִׁים הַיּוֹם, תורה אור שֶׁשָּׁמַע מִפִּי הַגְּבוּרָה שֶׁחָלוּק אֲנִינוּת הַיּוֹם בְּקָדָשִׁים מִשְּׁאָר יָמִים. וּכְשֶׁרָאָה שֶׁנִּשְׂרְפָה אָמַר לָהֶם: "אָכוֹל תֹּאכְלוּ אוֹתָהּ" — הָיָה *לָהֶם לְאוֹכְלָהּ כַּאֲשֶׁר צִוֵּיתִי אֶתְכֶם בִּשְׁעַת מַעֲשֶׂה. כַּאֲשֶׁר צִוָּה ה'. בַּאֲכִילַת חָזֶה וְשׁוֹק שֶׁל יז] צִבּוּר שֶׁקָּרְבוּ בּוֹ בַּיּוֹם נֶאֱמַר. וְלֹא מֵאֵלַיי אֲנִי אוֹמֵר. לְאוֹכְלָם בַּאֲנִינוּת. מִפְּנֵי אֲנִינוּת נִשְׂרְפָה. לְכָךְ נֶאֱמַר: "וַתִּקְרֶאנָה אוֹתִי כָּאֵלֶּה". וּמָצִינוּ שֶׁהוֹדָה לוֹ מֹשֶׁה, כִּדְכְתִיב: "וַיִּיטַב בְּעֵינָיו". וְאִם מִפִּי הַגְּבוּרָה שָׁמַע הֶיתֵּר אֲנִינוּת לְבוֹ בַּיּוֹם — לָמָּה הוֹדָה? מִפְּנֵי אֲנִינוּת נִשְׂרְפָה. [illegible] אֲנִינוּת לְבוֹ בַּיּוֹם. וְלֵית לֵיהּ לְרַבִּי נְחֶמְיָה הַךְ דְּרָשָׁא דְּבַאֲנִינוּת יֹאכְלוּהָ, אֶלָּא הָכִי קָאָמַר יח] לוֹ: כִּי כֵן צֻוֵּיתִי — שֶׁאַף מִנְחַת צִבּוּר זוֹ, שֶׁלֹּא מָצִינוּ מִנְחָה קְרֵיבָה לַצִּבּוּר כַּיּוֹצֵא בָּהּ — נֶאֱכֶלֶת. וְעַל הָאֲנִינוּת לֹא הוּזְכַּר לְמֹשֶׁה לִדְרוֹשׁ ק"ו מִמַּעֲשֵׂר, וּכְשֶׁהִזְכִּירוֹ אַהֲרֹן הוֹדָה לוֹ. מִפְּנֵי טוּמְאָה נִשְׂרְפָה. יט] שֶׁנָּגְעָה בָּהּ טוּמְאָה בְּחַטָּאת שֶׁל שְׂעִיר רֹאשׁ חֹדֶשׁ שֶׁקָּרְבָה (לָהֶם) בּוֹ בַּיּוֹם שֶׁהוּקַם הַמִּשְׁכָּן, בְּרֹאשׁ חֹדֶשׁ נִיסָן, וְהוּא הָיָה שְׁמִינִי לַמִּלּוּאִים. וּשְׁלֹשָׁה שְׂעִירִים קָרְבוּ בּוֹ בַּיּוֹם: שְׂעִיר נַחְשׁוֹן, וּשְׂעִיר רֹאשׁ חֹדֶשׁ, וְשָׂעִיר שֶׁבָּא לְשָׁעָה, כִּדְכְתִיב (ויקרא ט): "קְחוּ שְׂעִיר עִזִּים לְחַטָּאת". וְשֶׁל רֹאשׁ חֹדֶשׁ נִשְׂרְפָה, כִּדְאָמְרִינַן לְקַמָּן. הָיָה לָהֶם לִשְׁלָשְׁתָּן. דִּשְׁלֹשָׁה שְׂעִירִים קָרְבוּ לָהֶם, כִּדִלְקַמָּן. הָיָה לָהֶם לְאוֹכְלָם לָעֶרֶב. לְר' יְהוּדָה, אע"ג דְּאָמַר אֲנִינוּת לַיְלָה דְּאוֹרַיְיתָא — מוֹדֶה הוּא דְּלְאוֹתוֹ הַיּוֹם הוּתְּרָה לָהֶן אֲנִינוּת לַיְלָה, וְכָל שֶׁכֵּן לְר"ש, דְּאַף לְדוֹרוֹת אֵינוֹ אֶלָּא מִדִּבְרֵי סוֹפְרִים. וּלְקַמָּן מְפָרֵשׁ טַעַם דְּרַבִּי נְחֶמְיָה. וַהֲלֹא פִּינְחָס הָיָה עִמָּהֶן. שֶׁלֹּא הָיָה אוֹנֵן. וּלְקַמָּן פָּרֵיךְ: שַׁפִּיר קָאָמְרֵי לֵיהּ. אִידִי וְאִידִי רַבִּי נְחֶמְיָה. וְאִית לֵיהּ לְרַבִּי נְחֶמְיָה דְּהוּתְּרָה אֲנִינוּת בְּמִנְחָה, דִּכְתִיב: "כִּי כֵן צֻוֵּיתִי", וַאֲפִי' הָכִי, בְּשָׂעִיר שֶׁל רֹאשׁ חוֹדֶשׁ הוֹדָה לְדִבְרֵי אַהֲרֹן. וְלָא קַשְׁיָא, מִנְחָה קָדְשֵׁי שָׁעָה כ] הִיא, וְהוֹרָאַת שָׁעָה הָיְתָה בָּהּ שֶׁתֵּאָכֵל לְאוֹנְנִין, אֲבָל שָׂעִיר שֶׁל רֹאשׁ חֹדֶשׁ — קָדְשֵׁי דוֹרוֹת הֵן. וּמֹשֶׁה כְּשֶׁקָּצַף טָעָה, כְּסָבוּר: כֵּיוָן שֶׁשָּׁמַעְתִּי הֶיתֵּר אֲנִינוּת בְּמִנְחָה — הוּא הַדִּין לְחַטָּאת. וְאָמַר לוֹ אַהֲרֹן: שֶׁמָּא דַּוְקָא קָדְשֵׁי שָׁעָה שָׁמַעְתָּ, וְהוֹדָה לוֹ. רַבִּי נְחֶמְיָה. דְּאָמַר: מִפְּנֵי אֲנִינוּת נִשְׂרְפָה, הֵיכִי מְתָרֵץ לְהָנֵי קְרָאֵי דְּאוֹתָהּ פָּרָשָׁה? מַאי אָמַר מֹשֶׁה וּמַאי אַהַדְרֵיהּ לְעִנְיַן אֲנִינוּת, וּמַה הָיָה הַקִּפָּפוֹן, וּמַה הִיא הוֹדָאָה? וְרַבָּנַן. כא] רַבִּי יְהוּדָה וְרַבִּי שִׁמְעוֹן, הֵיכִי מְתָרְצֵי לְהוּ לְעִנְיַן טוּמְאָה? שֶׁמָּא נִכְנַס כב] דָּמוֹ לִפְנִים. מִתְּשׁוּבָתוֹ אַתָּה לָמֵד שֶׁכָּךְ אָמַר לָהֶם מִתְּחִילָּה, מִדְּקָאָמַר: "הֵן לֹא הוּבָא וגו' פְּנִימָה". אָמַר לוֹ. אַהֲרֹן לְמֹשֶׁה. מֹשֶׁה הֵן הִקְרִיבוּ. בִּתְמִיָּה. וְכִי בָּנַיי שֶׁהֵם הֶדְיוֹטִים שִׁמְּשׁוּ הַיּוֹם? וַהֲלֹא עָלַי הַטַּלְתָּ כָּל הָעֲבוֹדָה, כִּדְכְתִיב (שם): "קְרַב אֶל הַמִּזְבֵּחַ וַעֲשֵׂה" וגו'. וַאֲנִי כֹּהֵן גָּדוֹל אֲנִי, וּמַקְרִיב אוֹנֵן. כַּאֲשֶׁר צִוֵּיתִי. בְּמִנְחָה. קָדְשֵׁי שָׁעָה. כְּגוֹן מִנְחָה, שֶׁחוֹבַת שָׁעָה הָיְתָה וְאֵינָהּ נוֹהֶגֶת לְדוֹרוֹת. מְרָרַיְיכוּ. צַעֲרֵיכֶם. שֶׁאֲנִי מְבַזֶּה קָדְשֵׁי שָׁמַיִם. לְהַסִּיחַ דַּעְתִּי מֵהֶם. אֲפִי' אֵלֶּה וְכָאֵלֶּה אֲבֵלוּת אֵירְעוּנִי אֵין אֲנִי מְבַזֶּה כו'. וְהַיְינוּ דִּכְתִיב "כָּאֵלֶּה" וְלָא כְּתִיב "אֵלֶּה". טוּמְאָה

וחכמים עשו חיזוק לדבריהם יותר משל תורה. אין פירושו: כג] יותר משל תורה דעלמא. אלא, כלומר: חכמים עשו חיזוק לדבריהם, יותר ממה שעשתה תורה לדבריה.

ורמינהו מפני אנינות נשרפה. לכך נאמר "כאלה". פי' בקונטרס: שהודה לו משה, כדכתיב "וייטב בעיניו". ואם מפי הגבורה שמע היתר אנינות לבו ביום, למה הודה? ומשני שמואל: דההיא כרבי נחמיה, דאמר מפני אנינות נשרפה. ולית ליה לרבי נחמיה דרשא דבאנינות יאכלוה. אלא הכי אמר להן משה: כי כן צויתי — שאף מנחת צבור זו, שלא מצינו מנחה קרבה לצבור כיוצא בה, נאכלת. ועל האנינות לא הזכר לו למשה לדרוש קל וחומר ממעשר, וכשהזכירו אהרן הודה לו, כך פירש בקונטרס. ולא מיסתבר ליה לשמואל לשנויי כדרבא: אידי ואידי רבי נחמיה, כאן — בקדשי שעה, כאן — בקדשי דורות. שמשמע משה היתר אנינות במנחה שהיא קדשי שעה, והיה סבור כמו כן בחטאת דראש חדש שהיא קדשי דורות. דאין סברא שיהא משה טועה בין קדשי שעה לקדשי דורות. וקשה: לשמואל, מאי כד] הוה משני רבי נחמיה *מקושיא דר' יהודה: אם אתה אומר מפני אנינות נשרפה היה לשלשתן שישרפו? ועוד: משמע לקמן דיש חילוק לרבי נחמיה בין קדשי שעה לקדשי דורות, דקאמר: אלא לר' נחמיה מאי היום — חובת היום, היינו דורות! ונראה לפרש, דסלקא דעתך: "כאשר צויתי" דכתיב בשעיר דראש חדש לא בעי למימר: כאשר צויתי במנחה תעשו את החטאת, אלא: כאשר אני מצוה עכשיו תאכלו באנינות. והיה סבור משה דכמו שהותר כה] קדשי דורות אנינות לילה — הוא הדין ביום, ובין יום ללילה היה טועה. לכך פריך: ורמינהי מפני אנינות נשרפה, ואם היתה אנינות לילה מותרת — אמאי נשרפה? היה להם לאכול בלילה! ומשני: הא רבי נחמיה *הא ר' יהודה כו]. (הג"ה). ההיא דלעיל דהותר אנינות לילה בכל הקדשים — לר' יהודה, והא דנשרפה שעיר החדש — מפני טומאה. אבל רבי נחמיה סבר: אף לילה נאסר בקדשי דורות בשעיר החדש, ולא הותרה אנינות אלא בקדשי שעה. אבל משה אמר: כאשר צויתי חטאת החדש לאכול באנינות. דהיה סבור שהתיר לו בכל הקדשים* כז] (הג"ה). והא דלא משני: כולה רבי נחמיה היא, כאן בקדשי שעה כאן בקדשי דורות — היינו משום ד"כאשר צויתי" בחטאת כתיב, דהוי בקדשי דורות. ורבא סבירא ליה: "כאשר צויתי" אמנחה קאי ולא אחטאת. וה"ק: כאשר צויתי במנחה מפי הגבורה, כך אני מצוה מעצמי בחטאת. והשתא ניחא, דלשמואל לא קשיא ליה: היה לשלשתן שישרפו. דיש חילוק לרבי נחמיה בין קדשי שעה לקדשי דורות.

ומה מעשר הקל כו'. (ג) תימה: מה למעשר — שכן טעון כסף צורה! דכה"ג פריך בפרק "אלו הן הלוקין" (מכות דף יז:) א).

דאי ביום קל וחומר ממעשר. *תימה: בלילה נמי נימא קל וחומר, דהא רבי יהודה אית ליה אנינות לילה דאורייתא לדורות!

א) [וע' ביבמות ע: ד"ה דפסח גופיה וכו' כתבו ישוב נכון על זה]

[יבמות לו: וש"נ] [יומא ה:] [נ"ל לכם] [לעיל טז: פסחים פב:] [לעיל טז.] פסחים פב. [אבות דר"נ פרק לז] אבות דר"נ פל"ז

גי' רש"ק: גי' הנ"ק הא ר"י וה"ק ההיא כו' כנ"ל וכן הוא בס"י

נ"ל כמו באלו הב' והאי דלא וכו' ותיבת הגה"ה נמחק נ"ק

[עיין בר"א מזרחי שהקשה קושית התוס' והניח בנ"ע ע"ש ומהתימה שלא הקשה כן בשם תוס' וע' בספר קרבן אהרן דף ס ע"ג שהאריך בזה ליישב ג"כ קושייתם ועיין רש"ק ונ"ק]

הגהות הב"ח

(א) גמ' ורמינהו מפני אנינות שרפוה לכך: (ב) שם מדוע לא אכלתם את החטאת שמא כנ"ל ותיבות במקום [הקדוש] נמחק: (ג) תום' ד"ה ומה מעשר וכו' תימה. נ"ב והתוס' בר"פ הערל תירצו קושיא זו ע"ש בד"ה דפסח בד"ע:

א] תיבות אמר להן נמחק: ב] הא ר' נחמיה הא ר"י ור"ש דתניא: ג] היו להם לשלשתן שישרפוה ד"א היו להם לאוכלן לערב: ד] מתריץ להו להני: ה] אכלתם את החטאת אמר: ו] דמה לפנים אמר תיבת לפני ואות ו' נמחק: ז] ממנו קודש החמור לא כ"ש: ח] הודה ולא בוש לומר לא שמעתי אלא שמעתי ושכחתי: ט] להו להני קראי הכי: י] תיבות במקום הקודש נמחק: יא] דמה לפנים אמר לו: יב] חוץ. עיין בתוס' לעיל דף פב: יג] תיבת הן נמחק: יד] קודש החמור: טו] צויתי. במנחת שמיני: טז] וגו': באנינות. דנדב ואביהוא כתיב כאשר הד"א: יז] של שלמי צבור: יח] קאמר להו כי תיבת לו נמחק: יט] נשרפה שנגע בה: כ] שעה הוא והוראת: כא] ורבנן היינו ר"י: כב] נכנס דמה לפנים: כג] כיותר משל: כד] מאי הוי משני: כה] שהותר לדורות אנינות ותיבת קדשי נמחק: כו] יהודה הג"ה ההיא: כז] הקדשים ע"כ הג"ה:

תורה אור

וַיִּיטַב בְּעֵינָיו", לֹא בּוֹשׁ מֹשֶׁה לוֹמַר: "לֹא שָׁמַעְתִּי", אֶלָּא: "שָׁמַעְתִּי וְשָׁכַחְתִּי". אִיבַּעְיָא לְהוּ: לְשַׁהוּיֵיהּ וּלְמֵיכְלָא א] בְּאוֹרְתָא. טוּמְאָה בְּאוֹנֶס בָּאתָה. בִּשְׁלָמָא לְרַבָּנַן, הַיְינוּ דִּכְתִיב: "הַיּוֹם", אֶלָּא לְרַבִּי נְחֶמְיָה מַאי "הַיּוֹם"? חוֹבַת הַיּוֹם. בִּשְׁלָמָא לְרַבִּי נְחֶמְיָה, הַיְינוּ דִּכְתִיב: "הֵן הַיּוֹם", אֶלָּא לְרַבָּנַן מַאי "הֵן הַיּוֹם"? ה"ק: הֵן הִקְרִיבוּ? אֲנִי הִקְרַבְתִּי. אָמַר מָר: ב] הָיוּ לִשְׁלָשְׁתָּן שֶׁיִּשָּׂרְפוּ. מַאי "שְׁלָשְׁתָּן"? דְּתַנְיָא: °"וְאֵת שְׂעִיר הַחַטָּאת דָּרֹשׁ דָּרַשׁ מֹשֶׁה", "שְׂעִיר" ויקרא י — (א) זוֹ שְׂעִיר נַחְשׁוֹן, "חַטָּאת" — זוֹ חַטַּאת שְׁמִינִי, "דָּרֹשׁ" — ג] שְׂעִיר שֶׁל רֹאשׁ חוֹדֶשׁ. יָכוֹל שְׁלָשְׁתָּן נִשְׂרְפוּ? ת"ל: "וְהִנֵּה שׂוֹרָף" — אֶחָד נִשְׂרַף וְלֹא שְׁלָשְׁתָּן נִשְׂרְפוּ. "דָּרֹשׁ דָּרַשׁ" — שְׁתֵּי דְרִישׁוֹת לָמָּה? אָמַר לְהוּ: מִפְּנֵי מָה חַטָּאת זוֹ נִשְׂרְפָה וְאֵלּוּ מוּנָּחוֹת? וְאֵינִי יוֹדֵעַ אֵיזֶהוּ, כְּשֶׁהוּא אוֹמֵר: °"וְאוֹתָהּ נָתַן לָכֶם לָשֵׂאת אֶת עֲוֹן הָעֵדָה" — ד] הֱוֵי שם אוֹמֵר: זֶה שְׂעִיר שֶׁל רֹאשׁ חוֹדֶשׁ. שַׁפִּיר קָאָמְרִי לֵיהּ! רַבִּי נְחֶמְיָה לְטַעְמֵיהּ, דְּאָמַר: קָדְשֵׁי שָׁעָה לָא פָּסְלָה בְּהוּ אֲנִינוּת. אָמַר מָר: הָיָה ה] לוֹ לְאָכְלָהּ לָעֶרֶב. שַׁפִּיר קָאָמְרִי לֵיהּ! *קָסָבַר: אֲנִינוּת לַיְלָה דְּאוֹרַיְיתָא. דָּבָר אַחֵר: וַהֲלֹא פִּינְחָס הָיָה עִמָּהֶן. שַׁפִּיר קָאָמְרִי לֵיהּ! סָבַר לָהּ ו] כְּרַבִּי אֶלְעָזָר. דְּאָר"א א"ר חֲנִינָא: לֹא נִתְכַּהֵן פִּינְחָס עַד שֶׁהֲרָגוֹ לְזִמְרִי, דִּכְתִיב: °"וְהָיְתָה לּוֹ וּלְזַרְעוֹ במדבר כה אַחֲרָיו בְּרִית כְּהוּנַּת עוֹלָם". רַב אַשִׁי אָמַר: עַד שֶׁשָּׂם שָׁלוֹם בֵּין הַשְּׁבָטִים, שֶׁנֶּאֱמַר: °"וַיִּשְׁמַע יהושע כב פִּינְחָס הַכֹּהֵן וּנְשִׂיאֵי הָעֵדָה וְרָאשֵׁי אַלְפֵי יִשְׂרָאֵל" וגו'. וְאִידָךְ נַמִי, וְהָכְתִיב: "וְהָיְתָה לּוֹ וּלְזַרְעוֹ אַחֲרָיו"! כִּי כְּתִיב הַהוּא — בִּבְרָכָה הוּא דִּכְתִיב. וְאִידָךְ נַמִי, הָא כְּתִיב: "וַיִּשְׁמַע פִּינְחָס הַכֹּהֵן"! הַהוּא לְיַחֵס זַרְעוֹ אַחֲרָיו. ז] אָמַר רַב: *מֹשֶׁה רַבֵּינוּ כֹּהֵן גָּדוֹל, ח] וְחוֹלֵק בְּקָדְשֵׁי שָׁמַיִם הָיָה, שֶׁנֶּאֱמַר: °"מֵאֵיל ויקרא ח הַמִּלֻּאִים לְמֹשֶׁה הָיָה לְמָנָה". מֵיתִיבֵי: וַהֲלֹא פִּינְחָס הָיָה עִמָּהֶן. וְאִם אִיתָא, לֵימָא: "וַהֲלֹא מֹשֶׁה רַבֵּינוּ הָיָה עִמָּהֶן"! דִּילְמָא שָׁאנֵי מֹשֶׁה דִּטְרִיד בַּשְּׁכִינָה, *דְּאָמַר מָר: מֹשֶׁה בְּהַשְׁכָּמָה עָלָה וּבְהַשְׁכָּמָה יָרַד. מֵיתִיבֵי: °"לֶחֶם אֱלֹהָיו מִקָּדְשֵׁי הַקֳּדָשִׁים וּמִן הַקֳּדָשִׁים יֹאכֵל", אִם נֶאֶמְרוּ קָדְשֵׁי קָדָשִׁים, שם כא לָמָּה ט] נֶאֱמַר קָדָשִׁים קַלִּים? וְאִם נֶאֶמְרוּ קָדָשִׁים קַלִּים, לָמָּה י] נֶאֱמַר קָדְשֵׁי קָדָשִׁים? אִילּוּ לֹא נֶאֱמַר קָדָשִׁים קַלִּים — הָיִיתִי אוֹמֵר: קָדְשֵׁי קָדָשִׁים הוּא דְּאוֹכֵל, שֶׁהֲרֵי הוּתְּרוּ לְזָר וְלָהֶן, קָדָשִׁים קַלִּים לֹא יֹאכַל. וְאִילּוּ לֹא נֶאֶמְרוּ קָדְשֵׁי קָדָשִׁים — הָיִיתִי אוֹמֵר: בְּקָדָשִׁים קַלִּים יְהֵא אוֹכֵל שֶׁהֵן קַלִּים, בְּקָדְשֵׁי קָדָשִׁים לֹא יְהֵא אוֹכֵל. לְכָךְ נֶאֶמְרוּ קָדְשֵׁי קָדָשִׁים וּלְכָךְ נֶאֱמַר קָדָשִׁים קַלִּים. קָתָנֵי מִיהָא: "שֶׁהֲרֵי הוּתְּרוּ לְזָר וְלָהֶן", יא] לָאו מֹשֶׁה? אָמַר רַב שֵׁשֶׁת: לָא, בְּבָמָה יב] לְזָר, וּכְדִבְרֵי *הָאוֹמֵר: יֵשׁ מִנְחָה בְּבָמָה. מֵיתִיבֵי: מִרְיָם מִי הִסְגִּירָהּ? א"ת מֹשֶׁה הִסְגִּירָהּ — מֹשֶׁה זָר הוּא, וְאֵין

טוּמְאָה בְּאוֹנֶס. שֶׁרָצוּ לְהַשְׁהוֹתָהּ עַד הַלַּיְלָה וּלְאוֹכְלָן כּוּלָּן יַחַד, וְנִטְמֵאת בְּאוֹנֶס. בִּשְׁלָמָא לְרַבָּנַן. דְּאָמְרִי: אֶחָד קָדְשֵׁי שָׁעָה וְאֶחָד קָדְשֵׁי דוֹרוֹת, לַיְלָה הוּתַּר לָהֶן וְלֹא יוֹם, יג] עַד הַלַּיְלָה הָיוּ רוֹצִין לְהַשְׁהוֹתָהּ – הַיְינוּ דִּכְתִיב: "וְאָכַלְתִּי חַטָּאת הַיּוֹם" אֲנִי אוֹנֵן וְאוֹכֵל הַיּוֹם חַטָּאת? שֶׁמָּא לֹא שָׁמַעְתָּ אֶלָּא בַּלַּיְלָה. אֶלָּא לְרַבִּי נְחֶמְיָה. דְּאָמַר: מַה שֶּׁהוּתַּר לָהֶם – הוּתַּר אֲפִי' בַּיּוֹם, כְּגוֹן קָדְשֵׁי שָׁעָה, וּמַה שֶּׁנֶּאֱסַר – נֶאֱסַר אַף בַּלַּיְלָה. מַאי וְאָכַלְתִּי חַטָּאת הַיּוֹם. בַּלַּיְלָה נַמִי קָדְשֵׁי דוֹרוֹת הָווּ אֲסִירֵי! דְּהָאָמַר: מִפְּנֵי אֲנִינוּת נִשְׂרְפָה, וְלֹא הִמְתִּינוּ עַד הָעֶרֶב וְיֹאכְלוּהָ, אַלְמָא קָסָבַר: אֲנִינוּת לַיְלָה דְּאוֹרַיְיתָא. וְהָכִי אָמַר לְקַמָּן. מַאי הַיּוֹם חוֹבַת הַיּוֹם. כְּלוֹמַר, קָדְשֵׁי דוֹרוֹת, שֶׁהֵן חוֹבַת הַיּוֹם שֶׁל ר"ח, אַתָּה אוֹמֵר לִי לֶאֱכוֹל אוֹנֵן? וְהַיְינוּ "חַטַּאת הַיּוֹם" – חַטָּאת הַקָּבוּעַ לַיּוֹם. בִּשְׁלָמָא לְרַבִּי נְחֶמְיָה הַיְינוּ דִּכְתִיב הֵן הַיּוֹם הִקְרִיבוּ. כְּלוֹמַר, קָרְבָּן זֶה לְחוֹבַת הַיּוֹם קָרֵב, וְקָדְשֵׁי דוֹרוֹת הוּא, יד] וַאֲנִי אוֹכְלָן אוֹנֵן? בִּתְמִיָּה. שֶׁמָּא לֹא שָׁמַעְתָּ אֶלָּא בְּשֶׁל שָׁעָה. אֶלָּא לְרַבָּנַן. דְּאָמְרִי: שֶׁמָּא לֹא שָׁמַעְתָּ אֶלָּא בַּלַּיְלָה קָאָמַר לֵיהּ, מַאי (ב) טו] *הִיא דְּקָאָמַר לֵיהּ "הֵן הַיּוֹם הִקְרִיבוּ"? הָכִי קָאָמַר לֵיהּ. אָמַרְתָּ טז] דִּילְמָא בַּאֲנִינוּת אַקְרִיבְתֵּיהּ, וְכִי הֵן בְּנֵי יז] הֶדְיוֹטוֹת הַיּוֹם הִקְרִיבוּ שׁוּם קָרְבָּן? אֲנִי הִקְרַבְתִּי אֶת הַכֹּל. שְׂעִיר נַחְשׁוֹן. שֶׁאוֹתוֹ הַיּוֹם הָיָה רִאשׁוֹן לְהַקְרָבַת נְשִׂיאִים. דְּתַנְיָא בְּסֵדֶר עוֹלָם: בְּכ"ג בַּאֲדָר הִתְחִילוּ הַמִּלּוּאִים, וְכָל שִׁבְעַת הַיָּמִים הָיָה מֹשֶׁה מַעֲמִיד הַמִּשְׁכָּן, וּמַקְרִיב אֶת קָרְבְּנוֹתָיו בְּכָל בֹּקֶר וּבֹקֶר, יח] וּפָרְקוֹ. וּבַשְּׁמִינִי הֶעֱמִידוֹ וְלֹא פֵּירְקוֹ, וְהוּא רֹאשׁ חֹדֶשׁ נִיסָן. וְאוֹתוֹ הַיּוֹם נָטַל עֶשֶׂר עֲטָרוֹת וכו'. חַטַּאת שְׁמִינִי. שֶׁבָּא חוֹבָה לְשָׁעָה, דִּכְתִיב: "קְחוּ שְׂעִיר עִזִּים לְחַטָּאת". שְׁתֵּי דְרִישׁוֹת. דְּרִישָׁה יט] לַנִּשְׂרָפוֹת, דְּרִישָׁה לַמּוּנָּחוֹת – לָמָּה מוּנָּחוֹת לְהַמְתִּין לָעֶרֶב וְלֹא נֶאֶכְלוּ בַּיּוֹם? וְאֵינִי יוֹדֵעַ אֵיזוֹ הִיא. תַּנָּא דְּמַתְנִיתָא הוּא דְּקָמְהַדַּר לְמִילְּתֵיהּ. הֱוֵי אוֹמֵר זֶה שְׂעִיר ר"ח. שֶׁמְּכַפֵּר עַל טוּמְאַת מִקְדָּשׁ וְקָדָשָׁיו, כִּדְאָמַר בִּשְׁבוּעוֹת (דף ב.). שַׁפִּיר קא"ל. לְעֵיל קָאֵי, דַּאֲמָרַן: לְר' נְחֶמְיָה הָיָה לָהֶן לִשְׁלָשְׁתָּן שֶׁיִּשָּׂרְפוּ. קָסָבַר (ג) לַיְלָה דְּאוֹרַיְיתָא. וּמֵהָכָא נ"ל דְּמִ"וַּתִּקְרֶאנָה אוֹתִי כָּאֵלֶּה" יָלֵיף מִפְּנֵי אֲנִינוּת נִשְׂרְפָה, וּמִדְּלָא אֲכָלוּהָ לָעֶרֶב נָפְקָא לֵיהּ אֲנִינוּת לַיְלָה דְּאוֹרַיְיתָא. וְר' יְהוּדָה לְדוֹרוֹת אִית לֵיהּ אֲנִינוּת לַיְלָה דְּאוֹרַיְיתָא, אֲבָל לְאוֹתוֹ הַיּוֹם הוּתְּרָה, דְּדָרֵישׁ: הַיּוֹם אֲנִי הַיּוֹם אָסוּר וְלַיְלָה מוּתָּר כו'. בְּרִית כְּהוּנַּת עוֹלָם. "תַּחַת אֲשֶׁר קִנֵּא". אַלְמָא: מִכָּאן וְאֵילָךְ הוּא. שֶׁשָּׂם שָׁלוֹם בֵּין הַשְּׁבָטִים. בִּימֵי יְהוֹשֻׁעַ, כְּשֶׁבֶּט בְּנֵי גָד וּבְנֵי רְאוּבֵן שֶׁבָּנוּ אֶת הַמִּזְבֵּחַ בְּעֵבֶר הַיַּרְדֵּן, וּבִקְּשׁוּ שְׁאָר שְׁבָטִים לַעֲלוֹת עֲלֵיהֶם לַצָּבָא, וְשָׁלְחוּ אֶת פִּנְחָס לְדַבֵּר עִמָּהֶם. וַיִּשְׁמַע פִּינְחָס הַכֹּהֵן. בְּכָל מָקוֹם אַתָּה מוֹצֵא "פִּינְחָס בֶּן אֶלְעָזָר בֶּן אַהֲרֹן הַכֹּהֵן" – אֵין כְּהוּנָּה כְּתוּבָה אֶלָּא בְּאֶלְעָזָר, וְכָאן כְּתוּבָה *בְּפִנְחָס. הַהוּא. קְרָא סְתָם – בִּבְרָכָה כְּתִיב, בִּשְּׂרוֹ שֶׁלֹּא תִּפְסוֹק כְּהוּנָּה מִזַּרְעוֹ, אֲבָל עֲדַיִין לֹא נִתְכַּהֵן. לְיַיחֵס זַרְעוֹ אַחֲרָיו כ]. [מִימֵי מֹשֶׁה נִתְכַּהֵן, וּכְשֶׁשָּׂם שָׁלוֹם – נִתְיַיחֵס לִיקָּרֵא "כֹּהֵן", וּלְיַיחֵס זַרְעוֹ בְּמַעֲלוֹת כְּהוּנָּה לִהְיוֹתָם כֹּהֲנִים גְּדוֹלִים, שֶׁלֹּא הָיוּ כֹּהֲנִים גְּדוֹלִים אֶלָּא מִפִּנְחָס]. לְמֹשֶׁה הָיָה לְמָנָה. לְשׁוֹן חֲלוּקָּה כא] בַּכֹּהֲנִים. טָרִיד בַּשְּׁכִינָה. וְלֹא הָיָה עָסוּק בַּאֲכִילַת קָדָשִׁים. שֶׁהַדִּבּוּר טוֹרְדוֹ לִהְיוֹת תָּמִיד בָּהָר מִבֹּקֶר וְעַד עֶרֶב. בְּהַשְׁכָּמָה עָלָה. לָהָר בִּימֵי מַתַּן תּוֹרָה, כְּשֶׁהָיָה עוֹלֶה וְיוֹרֵד לְקַדֵּשׁ אֶת הָעָם וּלְהָשִׁיב אֶת דִּבְרֵי הָעָם אֶל ה', בְּפֶרֶק "רַבִּי עֲקִיבָא" בְּמַסֶּכֶת שַׁבָּת (דף פו.). אַלְמָא טָרוּד הָיָה. לֶחֶם אֱלֹהָיו וגו'. בְּבַעַל מוּם כְּתִיב, לְהַתִּירוֹ בַּקֳּדָשִׁים. שֶׁהֲרֵי הוּתְּרוּ לְזָר וְלָהֶן. קָא ס"ד: כב] הוּתַּר לְזָר – בְּמֹשֶׁה קָאָמַר, שֶׁאָכַל חָזֶה וָשׁוֹק שֶׁל אֵיל הַמִּילּוּאִים. וְקָדְשֵׁי קָדָשִׁים הָיָה, כִּדְכְתִיב בֵּיהּ: "בַּשְּׁלוּ אֶת הַבָּשָׂר פֶּתַח אֹהֶל מוֹעֵד וְשָׁם תֹּאכְלוּ אוֹתוֹ", וְלֹא נֶאֱכַל אֶלָּא לְיוֹם וָלַיְלָה, דִּכְתִיב: (ד) "וְאִם יִוָּתֵר" וגו'. בְּקָדָשִׁים קַלִּים. בְּחָזֶה וָשׁוֹק שֶׁל שַׁלְמֵי יָחִיד – לֹא יַחֲלוֹק עִם אֶחָיו, שֶׁלֹּא מָצִינוּ זָר וּפָסוּל חוֹלֵק כְּהֵן. לָאו מֹשֶׁה. דְּהָא כג] לָאו זָר אוֹכֵל בַּקֳּדָשִׁים אֶלָּא בַּמִּילּוּאִים. לָא בְּבָמָה קָאָמַר. דְּהוּתְּרוּ לְזָר. וּכְדִבְרֵי הָאוֹמֵר בְּפֶרֶק אַחֲרוֹן (דף קיג.): יֵשׁ מִנְחָה בְּבָמָה קְטַנָּה, וּמִנְחָה קָדְשֵׁי קָדָשִׁים הִיא, וְאוֹכְלִין שְׁיָרֶיהָ כד] זָרִים שֶׁהָיוּ עוֹבְדִים בְּבָמָה קְטַנָּה שֶׁהַזָּר עוֹבֵד שָׁם, כִּדְאָמַר בְּפֶרֶק בַּתְרָא. אֲבָל קָדָשִׁים קַלִּים – לֹא יֹאכַל בְּחָזֶה וָשׁוֹק שֶׁל כֹּהֲנִים, שֶׁהֲרֵי לֹא הוּתְּרוּ לְזָר. דְּלָא אַשְׁכַּחַן זָר חוֹלֵק בְּמוּרָם מִשַּׁלְמֵי יָחִיד, דְּאִילּוּ בַּמִּקְדָּשׁ נֶאֱכָל לַכֹּהֲנִים, וּבְבָמָה קְטַנָּה לֹא הָיָה חָזֶה וָשׁוֹק, כה] כִּדְתַנְיָא בְּפֶרֶק בַּתְרָא: חָזֶה וָשׁוֹק בְּבָמָה גְּדוֹלָה, וְאֵין חָזֶה וָשׁוֹק בְּבָמָה קְטַנָּה. וְהַאי דְּבָעֵי לְמִינְקַט כְּדִבְרֵי הָאוֹמֵר יֵשׁ מִנְחָה בְּבָמָה, דְּאִי אֵין מִנְחָה בְּבָמָה – כו] אֵין לְךָ עוֹד קָדְשֵׁי קָדָשִׁים נֶאֱכָלִין בְּבָמָה, דְּאִילּוּ חַטָּאת וְאָשָׁם בְּבָמָה לֹא קָרְבִי, דִּתְנַן מְגִילָּה (דף ט:): כָּל שֶׁאֵין נִידָּר וְנִידָּב – אֵין קָרֵב בְּבָמָה, אֵין לְךָ נֶדֶר וּנְדָבָה בְּקָדְשֵׁי קָדָשִׁים אֶלָּא עוֹלָה וּמִנְחָה. וְאֵין

בשלמא לרבי נחמיה היינו דכתיב הן היום הקריבו. כלומר, קרבן זה לחובת היום קרב, וקדשי דורות הוא, ואכלתי חטאת היום? בתמיה, *לא שמעת אלא בשל שעה. אלא לרבנן דאמרי: שמא לא שמעת אלא בלילה קאמר ליה, מאי (ה) היא דקאמר ליה "הן היום הקריבו"? הכי קאמר ליה: אמרת לי דילמא באנינות אקריבתיה – וכי הן בניי הדיוטות היום הקריבו שום קרבן? אני הקרבתי אותם! זו היא גירסת הקונט' ופירושו. והשתא לפי זה, למ"ד מפני אנינות נשרפה הוי "הן היום" בניחותא, ולמ"ד מפני טומאה הוי בתמיה. וקשה: דלעיל בריש פ"ב (דף טז.) משמע איפכא! ונראה דגרסינן נמי בהך פירכא בתרייתא: בשלמא לרבנן, היינו דכתיב "הן היום", כמו בקמייתא. ובתרווייהו פריך לר' נחמיה מדכתיב "היום", כדמפרש בקונט' בקמייתא ומשני, הכי קאמר: וכי הן כז] הקריבו? אני הקרבתי כל הקרבנות שקרבו היום. **ההוא** בברכה הוא דכתיב. שברכו הקב"ה שיהיה כהן. ומיד היה יכול להיות כהן, אלא שתחילה צריך להלבישו ולמושחו ולחנכו בחביתין, כדין הדיוטות המתחנכים בחביתין, כדאמרינן בסוף "התכלת" (מנחות דף נא:). אבל שמא לא נתרצו לו כל ישראל באותה שעה מפני שהרג נשיא שבט, עד ששם שלום בין השבטים בימי יהושע, ואז נתרצו לו והלבישוהו *[ומשחוהו] וחנכוהו בחביתין. *ואידך נמי הכתיב וישמע פנחס הכהן ההוא לייחס זרעו אחריו. פי': מימי משה נתכהן, וכששם שלום נתייחס ליקרא כהן ולייחס זרעו במעלות כהונה להיותם כהנים גדולים, שכן מצינו בדברי הימים (א' ה') שלא היו כהנים גדולים אלא מפנחס. ובספרי מפיק ליה מ"את בריתי שלום" שעמדו ממנו שמונים כהנים בבית ראשון, ושלש מאות בבית שני, וכולם נמנו בספרי*. אהרן

נ"ל שמא לא

הגהות הב"ח
(א) גמ' שעיר זה שעיר של נחשון החטאת זו חטאת יום שמיני דרש משה זה שעיר של ר"ח: (ב) רש"י ד"ה אלא וכו' מאי האי דקאמר: (ג) ד"ה קסבר אנינות לילה: (ד) ד"ה שהרי וכו' דכתיב והנותר וגו': (ה) תום' ד"ה בשלמא וכו' מאי האי דקאמר:

כ"ה בס"י

[ע' זה באורך בתוס' יומא דף ע ע"ב ד"ה כתוב: ד"ה שמעון]

[ע' תוס' יומא ע. ד"ה ולא וכו' שהעתיקו בשם ספרי נוסחא אחרת]

נ"ל הן דקאמר נ"ק

לעיל קי.

גליון הש"ס
גמ' משה רבינו כה"ג. עי' ע"ז דף לד ע"א תוד"ה במה.

שבת פו.

לקמן קיג.

בפנחס וההוא קרא סתם כתיבא הס"ד ואח"כ מ"ה בברכה כתיב ברכו כו' כנ"ל נ"ק

שיטה מקובצת
א] ולמיכלא לאורתא טומאה: ב] היה להם לשלשתן: ג] דרש זה שעיר: ד] העדה איזה היא שנשא עון העדה הוי: ה] היה להם לאכלה: ו] סבר לה כהא דא"ר אילעי דא"ר אילעי אמר רבי חנינא: ז] אחריו הוא דאתא אמר: ח] גדול היה וחולק בקדשי שמים שנאמר: ט] למה נאמרו קדשים: י] למה נאמרו קדשי כו' לא נאמרו: יא] ולהן מאי זר לאו: יב] תיבת לזר נמחק: יג] יום ועד הלילה: יד] הוא ואכלתי חטאת היום בתמיה כלומר לא שמעת וכו' א) ותיבת שמא נמחק: טו] מאי האי דקאמר: טז] אמרת לי דילמא: יז] בניי שהם הדיוטות: יח] ובקר ומפרקו ובשמיני: יט] דרישה לנשרפת למה נשרפה דרישה: כ] מתיבות מימי כו' עד תיבות למשה נמחק כי כל זה כתוב בתוס': כא] חלוקה בכהנים הס"ד: כב] ס"ד הותרו לזר במשה: כג] דהא לא אשכחן זר: כד] שיריה הזרים שהיו: כה] ושוק נוהג כדתניא: כו] בבמה ואין לך: כז] הן היום הקריבו:

א) נראה דצ"ל ותיבות ואני אוכלן אונן ותיבת שמא נמחק.

וְאֵין אזָר רוֹאֶה אֶת הַנְּגָעִים. וְא"ת: אַהֲרֹן הִסְגִּירָהּ — אַהֲרֹן *קָרוֹב הוּא, וְאֵין בקָרוֹב רוֹאֶה אֶת הַנְּגָעִים! אֶלָּא, כָּבוֹד גָּדוֹל חָלַק לָהּ הקב"ה לְמִרְיָם א] אוֹתָהּ שָׁעָה: אֲנִי כֹּהֵן, וַאֲנִי מַסְגִּירָהּ, אֲנִי חוֹלְטָהּ, וַאֲנִי פּוֹטְרָהּ. קָתָנֵי מִיהַת: מֹשֶׁה זָר, וְאֵין זָר רוֹאֶה אֶת הַנְּגָעִים! אָמַר רַב נַחְמָן בַּר יִצְחָק: שָׁאנֵי מַרְאוֹת נְגָעִים, דְּאַהֲרֹן וּבָנָיו כְּתוּבִין בַּפָּרָשָׁה. מֵיתִיבֵי: *חָמֵשׁ שְׂמָחוֹת הָיְתָה אֱלִישֶׁבַע יְתֵירָה עַל בְּנוֹת יִשְׂרָאֵל: ב] יְבָמָהּ מֶלֶךְ, אִישָׁהּ כֹּהֵן גָּדוֹל, בְּנָהּ סְגָן, בֶּן בְּנָהּ מְשׁוּחַ מִלְחָמָה, וְאָחִיהָ נְשִׂיא שֵׁבֶט — וַאֲבֵילָה עַל שְׁנֵי בָנֶיהָ. קָתָנֵי מִיהַת: "יְבָמָהּ מֶלֶךְ", מֶלֶךְ — אִין, כ"ג — לָא! אֵימָא: אַף מֶלֶךְ. כְּתַנָּאֵי: °"וַיִּחַר אַף ה' בְּמֹשֶׁה", רַבִּי יְהוֹשֻׁעַ בֶּן קָרְחָה אוֹמֵר: *כָּל חֲרוֹן אַף שֶׁבַּתּוֹרָה נֶאֱמַר בּוֹ רוֹשֶׁם, וְזֶה לֹא נֶאֱמַר בּוֹ רוֹשֶׁם. ר"ש בֶּן יוֹחַי אוֹמֵר: אַף זֶה נֶאֱמַר בּוֹ רוֹשֶׁם, שֶׁנֶּאֱמַר: °"הֲלֹא אַהֲרֹן אָחִיךָ הַלֵּוִי", וַהֲלֹא כֹּהֵן הוּא! ג] הָכִי קָאָמַר, אֲנִי אָמַרְתִּי: אַתָּה כֹּהֵן וְהוּא לֵוִי, עַכְשָׁיו הוּא כֹּהֵן וְאַתָּה לֵוִי. וַחֲכָמִים אוֹמְרִים: לֹא נִתְכַּהֵן מֹשֶׁה אֶלָּא שִׁבְעַת יְמֵי הַמִּלּוּאִים בִּלְבַד. וְיֵשׁ אוֹמְרִים: לֹא פָּסְקָה כְּהוּנָּה אֶלָּא מִזַּרְעוֹ שֶׁל מֹשֶׁה, שֶׁנֶּאֱמַר: °"וּמֹשֶׁה אִישׁ הָאֱלֹהִים בָּנָיו יִקָּרְאוּ עַל שֵׁבֶט הַלֵּוִי", וְאוֹמֵר: °"מֹשֶׁה וְאַהֲרֹן בְּכֹהֲנָיו וּשְׁמוּאֵל בְּקוֹרְאֵי שְׁמוֹ". מַאי "וְאוֹמֵר"? וְכִי תֵּימָא ד] לְדוֹרוֹת הוּא דִּכְתִיב — וְאוֹמֵר: "מֹשֶׁה וְאַהֲרֹן בְּכֹהֲנָיו". וְכָל חֲרוֹן אַף שֶׁבַּתּוֹרָה נֶאֱמַר בּוֹ רוֹשֶׁם? וְהָכְתִיב: °"וַיֵּצֵא (מֹשֶׁה) מֵעִם פַּרְעֹה בָּחֳרִי אָף", וְלָא א"ל וְלָא מִידֵּי! אָמַר ר"ל: סְטָרוֹ וְיָצָא. וּמִי אָמַר ר"ל הָכִי? וְהָכְתִיב: °"וְנִצַּבְתָּ לִקְרָאתוֹ עַל שְׂפַת הַיְאוֹר", וְאָמַר ר"ל: ה] מֶלֶךְ הוּא, וְהַסְבִּיר לוֹ פָּנִים. וְרַבִּי יוֹחָנָן אָמַר: רָשָׁע הוּא, וְהָעֵז פָּנֶיךָ בּוֹ! אֵיפוּךְ. *א"ר יַנַּאי: לְעוֹלָם תְּהֵא אֵימַת מַלְכוּת עָלֶיךָ, דִּכְתִיב: °"וְיָרְדוּ כָל עֲבָדֶיךָ אֵלֶּה אֵלַי", וְאִילּוּ לְדִידֵיהּ לָא קָאָמַר לֵיהּ. רַבִּי יוֹחָנָן אָמַר, מֵהָכָא: °"וְיַד ה' הָיְתָה אֶל אֵלִיָּהוּ וַיְשַׁנֵּס מָתְנָיו וַיָּרָץ לִפְנֵי אַחְאָב". אָמַר עוּלָּא: בִּקֵּשׁ מֹשֶׁה מַלְכוּת, וְלֹא נָתְנוּ לוֹ, דִּכְתִיב: °"אַל תִּקְרַב הֲלֹם", וְאֵין "הֲלֹם" אֶלָּא מַלְכוּת, שֶׁנֶּאֱמַר: °"מִי אָנֹכִי ה' אֱלֹהִים ו] [וגו'] כִּי הֲבִיאֹתַנִי עַד הֲלֹם". מְתִיב רָבָא, רַבִּי יִשְׁמָעֵאל אוֹמֵר: יְבָמָהּ מֶלֶךְ! אָמַר ז] רָבָא: לוֹ וּלְזַרְעוֹ קָאָמַר. וְכָל הֵיכָא דִּכְתִיב "הֲלֹם" ח] לְדוֹרוֹת הוּא? וְהָא גַּבֵּי שָׁאוּל, דִּכְתִיב: °"הֲבָא עוֹד הֲלֹם אִישׁ", ט] הוּא — אִין, זַרְעוֹ — לָא! אִיבָּעֵית אֵימָא: הָא הֲוָה אִישׁ בֹּשֶׁת. וְאִיבָּעֵית אֵימָא: שָׁאנֵי שָׁאוּל, דַּאֲפִי' בְּגַוֵּיהּ לָא קָאֵים. *כִּדְר' אֶלְעָזָר אָמַר רַבִּי חֲנִינָא: י] בְּשָׁעָה שֶׁפּוֹסְקִים גְּדוּלָּה לְאָדָם — פּוֹסְקִים לוֹ וּלְזַרְעוֹ עַד סוֹף כָּל הַדּוֹרוֹת, שֶׁנֶּאֱמַר: °"לֹא יִגְרַע מִצַּדִּיק עֵינָיו וְאֶת מְלָכִים לַכִּסֵּא" וגו'. וְאִם הֵגִיס דַּעְתּוֹ — הקב"ה מַשְׁפִּילוֹ, שֶׁנֶּאֱמַר: °"וְאִם אֲסוּרִים בַּזִּקִּים יִלָּכְדוּן בְּחַבְלֵי עֹנִי".§ "בַּעֲלֵי מוּמִין, בֵּין בַּעֲלֵי מוּמִין" כו'.§ מְנָא ה"מ? דְּת"ר: °"כָּל זָכָר" — לְרַבּוֹת בַּעֲלֵי מוּמִין. לְמַאי? אִי לַאֲכִילָה — הֲרֵי כְּבָר נֶאֱמַר: °"לֶחֶם אֱלֹהָיו מִקָּדְשֵׁי הַקֳּדָשִׁים יֹאכֵל". אֶלָּא לַחֲלוּקָה. תַּנְיָא אִידָךְ: "כָּל זָכָר" — לְרַבּוֹת בַּעֲלֵי מוּמִין. לְמַאי? אִי לַאֲכִילָה — הֲרֵי כְּבָר אָמוּר, אִי לַחֲלוּקָה — הֲרֵי כְּבָר *אָמוּר! שֶׁיָּכוֹל אֵין לִי אֶלָּא תָּם וְנַעֲשָׂה בַּעַל מוּם, בַּעַל מוּם מֵעִיקָּרוֹ מִנַּיִן? ת"ל: "כָּל זָכָר". תַּנְיָא אִידָךְ: "כָּל זָכָר" — לְרַבּוֹת בַּעַל מוּם. לְמַאי? אִי לַאֲכִילָה — הֲרֵי כְּבָר אָמוּר, וְאִי לַחֲלוּקָה — הֲרֵי כְּבָר אָמוּר, וְאִי לְבַעַל מוּם מֵעִיקָּרוֹ — הֲרֵי כְּבָר אָמוּר! שֶׁיָּכוֹל אֵין לִי אֶלָּא בַּעַל מוּם קָבוּעַ, בַּעַל מוּם עוֹבֵר מִנַּיִן? ת"ל: "כָּל זָכָר". כְּלַפֵּי לַיָּיא? אָמַר רַב שֵׁשֶׁת: אֵיפוּךְ. רַב אַשִׁי אָמַר: לְעוֹלָם לָא תֵּיפוּךְ. וְאִיצְטְרִיךְ, סָלְקָא דַּעְתָּךְ אָמִינָא: כִּי

וְאֵין זָר רוֹאֶה אֶת הַנְּגָעִים. דִּכְתִיב (ויקרא יג): "וְהוּבָא אֶל אַהֲרֹן" וגו'. וְאֵין קָרוֹב רוֹאֶה אֶת הַנְּגָעִים. כִּדְתַנְיָא בְּסַנְהֶדְרִין (דף לד:): "כָּל רִיב וְכָל נָגַע", מַה רִיבִים שֶׁלֹּא בִּקְרוֹבִים — אַף נְגָעִים שֶׁלֹּא בִּקְרוֹבִים. הָיְתָה אֱלִישֶׁבַע יְתֵירָה. בַּיּוֹם שֶׁהוּקַם הַמִּשְׁכָּן קָאֵי, בְּסֵדֶר עוֹלָם. בְּנָהּ סְגָן. אֶלְעָזָר. בֶּן בְּנָהּ. פִּנְחָס, מְשׁוּחַ מִלְחָמָה, כִּדְאַשְׁכַּחַן בְּמִדְיָן: "אוֹתָם וְאֶת פִּנְחָס בֶּן אֶלְעָזָר הַכֹּהֵן לַצָּבָא", וְהוּא הַמְדַבֵּר אֶל הָעָם: "שְׁמַע יִשְׂרָאֵל אַתֶּם קְרֵבִים הַיּוֹם לַמִּלְחָמָה עַל אוֹיְבֵיכֶם". אָחִיהָ. נַחְשׁוֹן. כְּתַנָּאֵי. אִם מֹשֶׁה כֹּהֵן הָיָה. נֶאֱמַר בּוֹ רוֹשֶׁם. סִימָן מַה שֶּׁל חָרוֹן הָיָה שָׁם: פְּעָמִים הַכָּאָה, פְּעָמִים נְזִיפָה, פְּעָמִים קְלָלָה וְגִידּוּף. כְּגוֹן (שמואל א כ) "וַיִּחַר אַף שָׁאוּל" — כְּתִיב בַּתְרֵיהּ: "בֶּן נַעֲוַת הַמַּרְדּוּת", "וַיִּחַר אַף אֱלִיהוּא" (איוב לב) — "לֹא רַבִּים יֶחְכָּמוּ" (שם), "וַיִּחַר אַף יַעֲקֹב בְּרָחֵל הֲתַחַת אֱלֹהִים" (בראשית ל) — לְשׁוֹן נְזִיפָה הוּא. הֲלֹא אַהֲרֹן אָחִיךָ. שֶׁהָיָה רָאוּי לִהְיוֹת לֵוִי, יָדַעְתִּי כִּי דַּבֵּר יְדַבֵּר הוּא. וּמִשָּׁם זָכָה לִכְהוּנָּה. לֹא נִתְכַּהֵן מֹשֶׁה. וְלֹא פָּסְקוּ לוֹ כְּהוּנָּה מֵעוֹלָם. וְיֵשׁ אוֹמְרִים. לֹא פָּסְקָה כְּהוּנָּה אֶלָּא מִזַּרְעוֹ, אֲבָל הוּא כָּל יָמָיו כֹּהֵן הָיָה. וְרַב דְּאָמַר כְּיֵשׁ אוֹמְרִים. בָּנָיו יִקָּרְאוּ עַל שֵׁבֶט הַלֵּוִי. אֲבָל הוּא כֹּהֵן. וְכִי תֵּימָא יא] לְדוֹרוֹת הוּא דִּכְתִיב. לְאַחַר זְמַן נִכְתַּב, כְּשֶׁהָיוּ מְיַיחֲסִים אֶת הַכְּהוּנָּה וְאֶת הַלְּוִיָּה, וּלְהָכִי נָקַט "בָּנָיו יִקָּרְאוּ" — דְּלָא הֲוָה לֵיהּ לְמֵימַר "מֹשֶׁה יִקָּרֵא עַל שֵׁבֶט הַלֵּוִי", שֶׁהֲרֵי *לֹא יב] קַיָּים, וְאֵין לוֹ לוֹמַר אֶלָּא עַל הַמִּתְיַיחֲסִים. סְטָרוֹ. = הִכָּהוּ עַל לֶחְיוֹ. הִסְבִּיר לוֹ פָּנִים. וְהַיְינוּ "וְנִצַּבְתָּ לִקְרָאתוֹ" — לְפִי גְּדוּלָּתוֹ הִכּוֹן לִקְרָאתוֹ. הָעֵז בּוֹ פָּנֶיךָ. הַיְינוּ "וְנִצַּבְתָּ לִקְרָאתוֹ" — לְמִלְחָמָה וּלְדַבֵּר עַזּוּת. וְאִילּוּ לְדִידֵיהּ לָא קָאָמַר לֵיהּ. "וְיָרַדְתָּ אֵלַי וְהִשְׁתַּחֲוִיתָ לִי לֵאמֹר" וגו', וְאע"ג דְּמַסְקָנָא הָכִי הֲוָה, דִּכְתִיב (שמות יב): "וַיִּקְרָא לְמֹשֶׁה וּלְאַהֲרֹן לַיְלָה וַיֹּאמֶר קוּמוּ" וגו'. וַיָּרָץ לִפְנֵי אַחְאָב. אַחְאָב רוֹכֵב, וְהוּא רָץ לְפָנָיו. שֶׁהָיָה אַחְאָב יְחִידִי, וְלָאו אוֹרַח אַרְעָא. מִי אָנֹכִי. דָּוִד אֲמָרָהּ. שָׁאנֵי שָׁאוּל דַּאֲפִי' בְּגַוֵּיהּ *לָא קָמָא. וּמִיהוּ, "הֲלוֹם" — מַלְכוּת עוֹלָמִית הוּא, וּכְשֶׁפָּסְקוּ לוֹ לְשָׁאוּל — מַלְכוּת עוֹלָמִית פָּסְקוּ לוֹ. אֲבָל הוּא גָּרַם לְעַצְמוֹ שֶׁתִּבָּטֵל הֵימֶנּוּ. כִּדְרַבִּי אֶלְעָזָר. דְּאָמַר: "אִם הֵגִיס כו' וַיִּגְבָּהוּ וְאִם אֲסוּרִים בַּזִּקִּים" — גַּבְהוּת לִבָּם גּוֹרֵם לָהֶם לִהְיוֹת אֲסוּרִים בַּזִּקִּים, יג] יִלָּכְדוּ בְּחַבְלֵי עֹנִי. כָּל זָכָר. קַמָּא בְּמִנְחָה כְּתִיב בְּ"צַו אֶת אַהֲרֹן". אִם לַאֲכִילָה. לְהַתִּירוֹ לֶאֱכוֹל מֵחֵלֶק חֲבֵירָיו אִם יְזַמְּנוּהוּ עִמָּהֶם, אֲבָל הוּא לֹא יַחֲלוֹק. לַחֲלוּקָה. לִיטּוֹל חֵלֶק כְּאַחַד הַכְּשֵׁרִים. כָּל זָכָר. תִּנְיָינָא בְּחַטָּאת כְּתִיב, וְהַשְּׁלִישִׁי בְּאָשָׁם. וּבָרַיְיתוֹת הַלָּלוּ בְּת"כ בְּמִדְרַשׁ הַמִּקְרָאוֹת. כְּלַפֵּי לַיָּיא. בַּעַל מוּם עוֹבֵר מַשְׁמַע לְהַתִּירוֹ טְפֵי מִבַּעַל מוּם קָבוּעַ! לָא תֵּיפוּךְ. וְאִיצְטְרִיךְ קְרָא לְמִידְרְשֵׁיהּ הָכִי. מַהוּ דְּתֵימָא: קְרָא קַמָּא קָבוּעַ הוּא דְּאַכְשַׁר, דְּרַחֲמָנָא יד] חַס עֲלֵיהּ מִשּׁוּם דְּלֵית לֵיהּ הֵיתֵּירָא לְמָחָר וּלְיוֹמָא אַחֲרִינָא. אֲבָל עוֹבֵר, דְּאִית לֵיהּ הֵיתֵּירָא לְמָחֳרַת — אֵימָא

אהרן קרוב הוא ואין קרוב רואה את הנגעים. פלוגתא היא במסכת נגעים פ"ב (מ"ה). דתנן: כל הנגעים אדם רואה, חוץ מנגעי עצמו. ר"מ אומר: אף לא נגעי קרוביו. טו] ותנא ברייתא דהכא כרבי מאיר. וטעמא דרבי מאיר כדמפרש ב"אחד דיני ממונות":* מקיש ריבים לנגעים,* מה נגעים ביום — אף ריבים ביום, ומה ריבים שלא בקרובים — אף נגעים שלא בקרובים. ורבנן לא מקשי, דסברי: דיני ממונות בלילה.

אני מסגירה אני חולטה אני פוטרה. בספרי תניא: אמר אהרן: נמצאת מפסיד לאחותנו, טז] שאינו יכול להסגירה ולא לטמאה ולא לטהרה. יז] לפי *דבריו למדנו שהיה אהרן דורש: אין אדם רואה בנגעי קרובו. ותימה: במה היה מפסידה הא יח] דאין אדם רואה את הנגעים? כל שכן שהיתה טהורה!

בעל

לא א מיי' פ"ט מהל' טומאת צרעת הל' ב:
לב ב מיי' שם הלכה א ופסק דקרוב רואה:

[סנהדרין לד.]
נ"ל ונגעים לריבים נ"ק
נ"ל לפי דרכנו נ"ק
עיין רש"ק מה שהקשה על רש"י בחומש מסוגיא דהכא
תהלים נט
ויקרא כא
אמור אלא לבעל מום מעיקרא שיכול אין לי כו' כנ"ל נ"ק

נגעים פ"ב מ"ה [ע"ש בר"ש]
סדר עולם פ"ד
[נ"א לא היה קיים]
מנחות לח.
[מגילה יג: ע"ש]
[נ"א לא קיימא]

שמות ד; שם; דה"א כג; שמות יא; שם ז; שם יא; מ"א יח; שמות ג; ש"ב ז; שמואל א י; איוב לו; שם; ויקרא ו

שיטה מקובצת

א] למרים ים באותה שעה אמר אני: ב] ישראל ואבל אחד. יבמה: ג] הוא אלא ה"ק ליה אני אמרתי: ד] וכ"ת ההוא לדורות: ה] ר"ל אמר לו הקב"ה למשה מלך: ו] אלהים ומי ביתי כי: ז] אמר רבה בר עולא ותיבת רבא נמחק: ח] הלום עד עולם הוא ותיבת לדורות נמחק: ט] איש והוא: י] חנינא דאמר ר' אלעזר אמר ר' חנינא בשעה: יא] וכ"ת ההוא לדורות הוא: יב] לא היה קיים: יג] בזקים וילכדו: יד] רחמנא דחס עליה: טו] קרוביו ואתא תנא ברייתא דהכא: טז] לאחותנו שאיני יכול: יז] ולפי דרכינו למדנו: יח] הא כיון דאין:

דלא

כִּי טָמֵא, מַה טָמֵא כַּמָּה דְּלָא טָהוֹר לָא אָכֵיל, אַף הַאי נַמִי, כַּמָּה דְּלָא א] מִתְקַן לָא אָכֵיל, קָא מַשְׁמַע לָן.§ "כָּל שֶׁאֵינוֹ רָאוּי" וכו'.§ וְלָא? וַהֲרֵי בַּעַל מוּם, דְּלָא רָאוּי לַעֲבוֹדָה, וְחוֹלֵק! וְתוּ: הָא רָאוּי לַעֲבוֹדָה חוֹלֵק; הֲרֵי טָמֵא בְּקָרְבְּנוֹת צִיבּוּר, דְּרָאוּי לַעֲבוֹדָה, וְאֵינוֹ חוֹלֵק! רָאוּי לַאֲכִילָ' קָאָמַר. ב] וַהֲרֵי קָטָן, דְּרָאוּי לַאֲכִילָה, וְאֵינוֹ חוֹלֵק! הָא לָא קָתָנֵי. הַשְׁתָּא דְּאָתֵית לְהָכִי, לְעוֹלָם ג] כִּדְקָאָמַר מֵעִיקָּרָא: אִי מִשּׁוּם טָמֵא — טָמֵא לָא קָתָנֵי, וְאִי מִשּׁוּם בַּעַל מוּם — רַחֲמָנָא רַבְּיֵיהּ.§ "אֲפִי' טָמֵא בִּשְׁעַת זְרִיקַת דָּמִים וְטָהוֹר בִּשְׁעַת הֶקְטֵר חֲלָבִים אֵינוֹ חוֹלֵק".§ הָא טָהוֹר בִּשְׁעַת זְרִיקַת דָּמִים וְטָמֵא בִּשְׁעַת הֶקְטֵר חֲלָבִים — חוֹלֵק. מַתְנִיתִין דְּלָא כְּאַבָּא שָׁאוּל, *דְּתַנְיָא, אַבָּא שָׁאוּל אוֹמֵר: [א]לְעוֹלָם אֵינוֹ אוֹכֵל עַד שֶׁיְּהֵא טָהוֹר מִשְּׁעַת זְרִיקָה עַד שְׁעַת הֶקְטֵר חֲלָבִים, דְּאָמַר קְרָא: °"הַמַּקְרִיב אֶת דַּם הַשְּׁלָמִים וְאֶת הַחֵלֶב" — דַּאֲפִי' הֶקְטֵר חֲלָבִים נַמִי בָּעֵי.§ בָּעֵי רַב אַשִׁי: נִטְמָא בֵּינְתַיִם, מַהוּ? בִּשְׁעַת זְרִיקָה וּבִשְׁעַת הַקְטָרָה בָּעֵינַן — וְהָאִיכָּא, אוֹ דִּלְמָא: עַד שֶׁיְּהֵא טָהוֹר מִשְּׁעַת זְרִיקָה וְעַד שְׁעַת הֶקְטֵר חֲלָבִים? [ב]תֵּיקוּ. אָמַר ד] *רָבָא: הַאי דִּינָא מֵרַבִּי אֶלְעָזָר בְּרַבִּי שִׁמְעוֹן גְּמִירְנָא, ה] דַּאֲמַר בְּבֵית הַכִּסֵּא: דַּנְתָּה, בָּא ו] טְבוּל יוֹם וְאָמַר: "תֵּן לִי ז] מִמִּנְחָה וְאוֹכַל". אָמַר לוֹ: וּמָה אִם בְּמָקוֹם שֶׁיָּפֶה כֹּחֲךָ, בְּחַטָּאתְךָ — דְּחִיתִיךָ מֵחַטַּאת יִשְׂרָאֵל, מָקוֹם שֶׁהוּרַע כֹּחֲךָ, בְּמִנְחָתְךָ — אֵינוֹ דִּין שֶׁאַדִּיחֲךָ מִמִּנְחַת יִשְׂרָאֵל? ח] וּמָה אִם דְּחִיתָנִי מֵחַטַּאת יִשְׂרָאֵל, שֶׁכְּשֵׁם שֶׁיָּפֶה כֹּחִי — כָּךְ יָפֶה כֹּחֲךָ, תִּדְחֵינִי ט] מִמִּנְחָה? שֶׁכְּשֵׁם שֶׁהוּרַע כֹּחִי — כָּךְ הוּרַע כֹּחֲךָ! — הֲרֵי הוּא אוֹמֵר: °"לַכֹּהֵן הַמַּקְרִיב אוֹתָהּ לוֹ תִהְיֶה", בֹּא הַקְרֵב וֶאֱכוֹל. י] "תֵּן לִי מֵחַטַּאת יִשְׂרָאֵל וְאוֹכַל". א"ל: וּמָה בְּמָקוֹם שֶׁהוּרַע כֹּחִי, בְּמִנְחָתִי — דְּחִיתִיךָ מִמִּנְחַת יִשְׂרָאֵל, מָקוֹם שֶׁיָּפֶה כֹּחִי, בְּחַטָּאתִי — אֵינוֹ דִּין שֶׁאַדִּיחֲךָ מֵחַטַּאת יִשְׂרָאֵל? א"ל: וּמָה אִם שֶׁדְּחִיתָנִי מִמִּנְחַת יִשְׂרָאֵל — שֶׁכְּשֵׁם שֶׁהוּרַע כֹּחֲךָ כָּךְ הוּרַע כֹּחִי, תִּדְחֵינִי מֵחַטַּאת יִשְׂרָאֵל? שֶׁכְּשֵׁם שֶׁיָּפֶה כֹּחֲךָ כָּךְ יָפֶה כֹּחִי! יא] הֲרֵי הוּא אוֹמֵר: °"הַכֹּהֵן הַמְחַטֵּא אוֹתָהּ יֹאכְלֶנָּה", בֹּא יב] חַטֵּא וֶאֱכוֹל. אָמַר לֵיהּ: תֵּן לִי מֵחָזֶה וְשׁוֹק וְאוֹכַל. אָמַר לֵיהּ: וּמָה בְּמָקוֹם שֶׁיָּפֶה כֹּחֲךָ בְּחַטָּאתְךָ — דְּחִיתִיךָ יג] [מֵחַטַּאת יִשְׂרָאֵל] (מֵחָזֶה וְשׁוֹק) מָקוֹם שֶׁהוּרַע כֹּחֲךָ בִּשְׁלָמִים, שֶׁאֵין לְךָ בָּהֶן אֶלָּא חָזֶה וְשׁוֹק — אֵינוֹ דִּין שֶׁאַדִּיחֲךָ? יד] מָה אִם דְּחִיתָנִי מֵחַטָּאת — טו] שֶׁכֵּן הוּרַע כֹּחִי אֵצֶל נָשַׁיי וַעֲבָדַיי, תִּדְחֵינִי מֵחָזֶה וְשׁוֹק? שֶׁכֵּן יָפֶה כֹּחִי אֵצֶל נָשַׁיי וַעֲבָדַיי! טז] הֲרֵי הוּא אוֹמֵר: °"לַכֹּהֵן הַזּוֹרֵק אֶת דַּם הַשְּׁלָמִים לוֹ יִהְיֶה", בֹּא זְרוֹק וֶאֱכוֹל. יָצָא טְבוּל יוֹם קוּלָּיו וַחֲמוּרָיו עַל רֹאשׁוֹ, אוֹנֵן מִימִינוֹ, מְחוּסַּר כַּפָּרָה מִשְּׂמֹאלוֹ. *פָּרֵיךְ רַב אַחַאי, לֵימָא לֵיהּ: תֵּן לִי מִבְּכוֹר וְאוֹכַל! מִשּׁוּם דְּא"ל: וּמָה בְּמָקוֹם שֶׁהוּרַע כֹּחִי בְּחַטָּאת אֵצֶל נָשַׁיי וַעֲבָדַיי — דְּחִיתִיךָ מֵחַטַּאת יִשְׂרָאֵל, מָקוֹם שֶׁיָּפֶה כֹּחִי בִּבְכוֹר, דְּכוּלֵּיהּ דִּילִי יז] הִיא — אֵינוֹ דִּין שֶׁאֲדַחֲךָ מִמֶּנּוּ? וּמָה אִם דְּחִיתָנִי מֵחַטָּאת — שֶׁכְּשֵׁם שֶׁהוּרַע כֹּחֲךָ כָּךְ הוּרַע כֹּחִי, תְּדִיחֵנִי מִבְּכוֹר? שֶׁכְּשֵׁם שֶׁיָּפֶה כֹּחֲךָ כָּךְ יָפֶה כֹּחִי! הֲרֵי הוּא אוֹמֵר: °"אֶת דָּמָם תִּזְרוֹק עַל הַמִּזְבֵּחַ וְאֶת חֶלְבָּם תַּקְטִיר וּבְשָׂרָם יִהְיֶה לָּךְ", בֹּא זְרוֹק וֶאֱכוֹל. וְאִידָךְ פָּרֵיךְ: מִי כְּתִיב "וּבְשָׂרָם לַכֹּהֵן הַזּוֹרֵק"? "וּבְשָׂרָם יִהְיֶה לָּךְ" כְּתִיב, אֲפִי' לְכֹהֵן אַחֵר. וְהֵיכִי עֲבִיד הָכִי? וְהָאָמַר *רַבָּה בַּר בַּר חָנָה א"ר יוֹחָנָן: [ג]בְּכָל מָקוֹם מוּתָּר לְהַרְהֵר, חוּץ מִמֶּרְחָץ וּמִבֵּית הַכִּסֵּא! לְאוֹנְסוֹ שָׁאנֵי.§

מתני'

בעל מום עובר מנין ת"ל כל זכר. תימה: דלמא איצטריך לבעל מום מעיקרו, חד לאכילה וחד לחלוקה. דאי מחד ה"א: דוקא אכילה ולא חלוקה. כמו קטן דאוכל ואינו חולק! וי"ל: כיון דאשכחן תם ונעשה בעל מום, דאין חילוק בין אכילה לחלוקה. דבהמתא ה"ה לבעל מום מעיקרו. *וא"ת: דהכא מייתרי ליה הנך תלתא "כל זכר" דכתיבי במנחה וחטאת ואשם, משמע דילפי מהדדי. וגבי טבול יום בדינא דר"א בר' שמעון מצריך תלת קראי למנחת ישראל וחטאת וחזה ושוק!. **הרי** טמא בקרבנות ציבור דראוי לעבודה ואינו חולק. תימה: דפריך מטמא בקרבנות ציבור שהיא בעיא לעיל. והוה מצי למיפרך מכהן גדול אונן כח] וראוי לעבודה דאינו חולק, דפשיטא לן לעיל בריש פירקין, כדתניא בהדיא!. **מה** אם דחיתני מחטאת שכן הורע כחי אצל נשיי ועבדיי. תימה: אמאי לא קאמר כדקאמר לעיל: ומה אם דחיתני מחטאת, שכשם שיפה כחי כך יפה כחך, תדיחני מחזה ושוק, שכשם שהורע כחי כך הורע כחך?. **פריך** רב אחאי. בכל מקום לשונו משונה, כדאשכחן בריש כתובות (דף ב:): "פשיט רב אחאי". ומתוך כך היה אומר רבינו שמואל דהוא רב אחאי שעשה השאלתות, שהיה מרבנן סבוראי דבתר רבינא ורב אשי כט] *דהוסיף הוראה, וכתבו אחרי כן דבריו ל] בסוף התלמוד. ומיהו בהדיא דכתובות אשכח רב אשי דמיירי בתריה*.

הניחא

יח] (אֵימָא כִּי טָמֵא כו'). [הָרֵי] טָמֵא בְּקָרְבְּנוֹת צִיבּוּר. אֲמָרַן לְעֵיל בְּרֵישׁ פִּירְקִין (דף לט:) דְּאֵין חוֹלֵק. קָטָן אֵינוֹ חוֹלֵק. דִּכְתִיב: "אִישׁ כְּאָחִיו", וְדָרְשִׁינַן יט] לֵיהּ בִּמְנָחוֹת (דף עג.) וּבְקִדּוּשִׁין (דף נג.): אִישׁ חוֹלֵק אֲפִילּוּ בַּעַל מוּם, וְאֵין קָטָן חוֹלֵק אֲפִילּוּ תָּם. הָא לָא קָתָנֵי. כ] "הָא רָאוּי לַאֲכִילָה חוֹלֵק" דְּדָיְיקַתְּ — לָא קָתָנֵי, כא] דְּתִיקְשֵׁי לָךְ קָטָן. לָא תָּדוּק מִינֵּיהּ הָכִי, דְּהָא גּוּפָהּ אִיצְטְרִיךְ, לְאַשְׁמוּעִינַן דְּכָל שֶׁאֵינוֹ רָאוּי אֵינוֹ חוֹלֵק, וְלָאו כב] דִּיוּקָא תָּנֵי. כִּדְאָמְרִינַן מֵעִיקָּרָא. רָאוּי לַעֲבוֹדָה. הָא לָא קָתָנֵי. "הָא רָאוּי לַעֲבוֹדָה חוֹלֵק", דְּקָא דָּיְיקַתְּ וְקַשְׁיָא לָךְ עֲלָהּ טָמֵא בְּקָרְבְּנוֹת צִיבּוּר — לָא קָתָנֵי לָהּ מַתְנִיתִין. וְאַתְּ לָא תֵּיתֵי מִדִּיּוּקָא, דִּלְאַשְׁמוּעִינַן הִיא גּוּפָהּ אֲתָאִי מַתְנִי', וְלָאו לְדִיּוּקָא דִּילָהּ. דַּאֲפִילּוּ הֶקְטֵר חֲלָבִים נַמִי בָּעֵי. שֶׁיְּהֵא רָאוּי לְהַקְטִיר. וְת"ק סָבַר: "לוֹ תִהְיֶה שׁוֹק הַיָּמִין לְמָנָה" — אַהַמַּקְרִיב דַּם הַשְּׁלָמִים קָאֵי, כִּדְאַשְׁכַּחַן קְרָא אַחֲרִינָא: "לַכֹּהֵן הַזּוֹרֵק אֶת דַּם הַשְּׁלָמִים לוֹ יִהְיֶה" (ויקרא ז), וְלָא כְּתִיב כג] מַקְטִיר חֲלָבִים. וְהָכָא דִּכְתִיב: "אֶת הַחֵלֶב" — לָא לְרָאוּי אַתָּא, אֶלָּא לְמוֹדֶה בַּעֲבוֹדוֹת, כִּדְדָרֵישׁ לֵיהּ בִּשְׁחִיטַת חוּלִּין (דף קלג:), רַבִּי שִׁמְעוֹן אוֹמֵר: כָּל כֹּהֵן שֶׁאֵינוֹ מוֹדֶה בַּעֲבוֹדָה — אֵינוֹ חוֹלֵק בִּכְהוּנָּה, שֶׁנֶּאֱמַר "הַמַּקְרִיב אֶת דַּם הַשְּׁלָמִים". אֵין לִי אֶלָּא זְרִיקָה, מִנַּיִן לְרַבּוֹת הֶקְטֵר חֲלָבִים — ת"ל: "וְאֶת הַחֵלֶב". מִנַּיִן לְרַבּוֹת שְׁאָר כָּל עֲבוֹדוֹת — ת"ל: "מִבְּנֵי אַהֲרֹן", עֲבוֹדָה הַמְּסוּרָה לִבְנֵי אַהֲרֹן, כָּל כֹּהֵן שֶׁאֵינוֹ מוֹדֶה בָּהּ — אֵינוֹ חוֹלֵק בִּכְהוּנָּה. בָּעֵי רַב אַשִׁי. אַלִּיבָּא דְּאַבָּא שָׁאוּל. דַּנְתָּה. יָכוֹל אַתָּה לָדוּן. בָּא טְבוּל יוֹם וְאָמַר. לַחֲבֵירוֹ טָהוֹר, שֶׁל בֵּית אָב שֶׁלּוֹ. תֵּן לִי. כד] בְּחֵלֶק מִן הַמִּנְחָה שֶׁל יִשְׂרָאֵל, וְאוֹכֵל לָעֶרֶב. א"ל. טָהוֹר לִטְבוּל יוֹם. כְּלוֹמַר, כֵּן יֵשׁ לוֹ לַהֲשִׁיבוֹ. וּמָה אִם בְּמָקוֹם שֶׁיָּפֶה כֹּחֲךָ בְּחַטָּאתְךָ. דְּכֹהֵן הַמְחוּיָּב חַטָּאת מְבִיאוֹ וּמַקְרִיב אֲפִילּוּ בְּמִשְׁמָר שֶׁאֵינוֹ שֶׁלּוֹ, וַעֲבוֹדָתָהּ וְעוֹרָהּ שֶׁלּוֹ. כה] בְּפֶרֶק "הַגּוֹזֵל" בְּבָ"ק (דף קט:): מִנַּיִן לְכֹהֵן שֶׁבָּא וּמַקְרִיב קָרְבְּנוֹתָיו בְּכָל עֵת וּבְכָל שָׁעָה שֶׁיִּרְצֶה? ת"ל: "וּבָא בְּכָל אַוַּת נַפְשׁוֹ וְשֵׁרֵת". וּמִנַּיִן שֶׁעֲבוֹדָתָהּ וְעוֹרָהּ שֶׁלּוֹ? ת"ל: "וְאִישׁ אֶת קֳדָשָׁיו לוֹ יִהְיוּ". דְּחִיתִיךָ מֵחַטַּאת יִשְׂרָאֵל. דִּטְבוּל יוֹם אֵינוֹ חוֹלֵק בָּהּ, דִּכְתִיב (ויקרא ו): "הַכֹּהֵן הַמְחַטֵּא אוֹתָהּ יֹאכְלֶנָּה", וְאוֹקִימְנָא לְעֵיל (דף לט.) — יְחַלְּקֶנָּה. מָקוֹם שֶׁהוּרַע כֹּחֲךָ בְּמִנְחָתְךָ. שֶׁאִם הִתְנַדַּבְתָּ מִנְחָה וְהִקְרַבְתָּ, אֲפִילּוּ אַתָּה טָהוֹר אִי אַתָּה אוֹכְלָהּ, כִּדְכְתִיב: "כָּל מִנְחַת כֹּהֵן כָּלִיל" וגו' (ויקרא ו). אֵינוֹ דִּין שֶׁאַדִּיחֲךָ. כָּל זְמַן שֶׁאַתָּה טְבוּל יוֹם, וְאֵינְךָ רָאוּי לְהַקְרִיב מִמִּנְחַת יִשְׂרָאֵל. כָּךְ יָפֶה כֹּחֲךָ. בְּחַטָּאתְךָ. לַכֹּהֵן הַמַּקְרִיב אוֹתָהּ לוֹ תִהְיֶה. בְּמִנְחָה כְּתִיב. וּמַה בְּמָקוֹם כו'. טָהוֹר קָמְהַדַּר לֵיהּ לִטְבוּל יוֹם הָכִי, שֶׁלֹּא יַחֲלוֹק עִמּוֹ. *שֶׁכְּשֵׁם שֶׁהוּרַע כֹּחִי. בְּמִנְחָתִי, כָּךְ הוּרַע כֹּחֲךָ בְּמִנְחָתְךָ. תֵּן לִי מֵחָזֶה וְשׁוֹק. חֵלֶק כָּמוֹךָ, וְאוֹכַל לָעֶרֶב. שֶׁכֵּן הוּרַע כֹּחִי אֵצֶל נָשַׁיי וַעֲבָדַיי. אַף כְּשֶׁאֲנִי טָהוֹר, שֶׁאֵינִי רַשַּׁאי לְהַאֲכִילָהּ לָהֶם. יָצָא טְבוּל יוֹם. בְּפַחֵי נֶפֶשׁ. קוּלָּיו וְחוּמְרָיו. שֶׁהָיָה דּוֹרֵשׁ לַהֲנָאָתוֹ, וְאוֹמֵר: כו] לָמָּה דְּחִיתָנִי כו'. אוֹנֵן מִימִינוֹ כו'. שֶׁאַף הֵם נִדְחִים מִן הַמִּקְרָאוֹת הַלָּלוּ, שֶׁאֵינָן רְאוּיִין לַעֲבוֹדָה. פָּרֵיךְ רַב אַחַאי וְלֵימָא. וְלִיתְנֵי כז] ר' אֶלְעָזָר בַּר' שִׁמְעוֹן בְּהַאי דִּינָא. תֵּן לִי מִבְּכוֹר וְאוֹכַל. לָעֶרֶב. אָמַר לוֹ טָהוֹר: מָה אִם בְּמָקוֹם כו'. אֶת דָּמָם תִּזְרוֹק. בִּבְכוֹר כְּתִיב. בֹּא זְרוֹק וֶאֱכוֹל. וְאַע"ג דְּאֵין בְּכוֹר נֶאֱכָל בְּמַחֲלוֹקֶת, שֶׁאֵינוֹ נִיתָּן לְאַנְשֵׁי מִשְׁמָר אֶלָּא לְכָל כֹּהֵן שֶׁיִּרְצֶה, כִּתְרוּמָה וּכְפִדְיוֹן הַבְּכוֹר, מִיהוּ, תִּיפּוֹק לָן מִינֵּהּ דְּלֹא יִתְּנוּ בְּכוֹר אֶלָּא לְמִי שֶׁרָאוּי לַעֲבוֹדָה בְּאוֹתָהּ שָׁעָה. וְהֵיכִי עָבֵיד הָכִי. רַבִּי אֶלְעָזָר בְּרַבִּי שִׁמְעוֹן, דְּאָמַר הַאי דִּינָא בְּבֵית הַכִּסֵּא. לְאוֹנְסוֹ. שֶׁהָיְתָה שְׁמוּעָתוֹ שְׁגוּרָה בְּפִיו וּמְהַרְהֵר בָּהּ עַל כָּרְחוֹ. וְדוּגְמָתוֹ שָׁמַעְתִּי בְּקִדּוּשִׁין (דף לג.).

מתני'

לג א מיי' פ"י מהלכות מעה"ק הלכה כח:
לד ב מיי' שם הל' כב:
ועי' רש"ק מה שתירץ על קושיא זו ועי' בספר פנים מאירות
לה ג מיי' פ"ג מהלכות ק"ש הל' ד טוש"ע א"ח סימן פה סעיף ב:

[ל"ל דכסוף]
[וע"ע תוספות כתובות ב: ד"ה פשיט]
גי' רש"ק ומ"ז
[קדושין יג. וש"נ]

ל"ק מ"ז
תוספתא דמנחות פי"... [ע"ש]
מהרש"ק גרס רב
ברכות כז. שבת מ: קי ע"ז מד: קדושין לג.
ל"ל שכשם שהורע כח במנחתי כך הורע כח במנחתך ל"ק

שיטה מקובצת

א] דלא מתקן לא: ב] קאמר והא קטן ותיבת והרי ל"ש: ג] כדקאמר' מעיקרא אי משום טמא הא לא קתני ואי משום בעל מום רחמנא רבייה: ד] אמר (רב') [רב]: ה] גמירנא ליה דאמר: ו] בא כהן טבול יום: ז] ממנחת ישראל ואוכל: ח] ישראל א"ל ומה: ט] תדחיני ממנחת ישראל שכשם שהורע כו' כחך א"ל הרי הוא אומר לכהן המקריב: י] ואכול א"ל תן. ס"א א"ל אם לאו תן: יא] כחי א"ל הרי: יב] בא חטא: יג] דחיתך מחטאת ישראל ותיבות מחזה ושוק נמחק: יד] שאדיחך מהן א"ל מה טו] מחטאת ישראל שכן: טז] ועבדיי א"ל הרי: יז] דילי הוא אינו: יח] אימא כי טמא כו' טמא ותיבת הרי ל"ש: יט] תיבת ליה נמחק: כ] לא קתני. האי הא: כא] לא קתני ליה בהדיא דתיקשי לך קטן ולא תדוק כב] ולאו לדיוקא: כג] כתיב המקטיר החלבים והכא: כד] לי חלק מן אות ב' נמחק: כה] שלו כדאיתא בפ': כו] ואומר מה אם דחיתני ותיבת למה נמחק: כז] וליתני נמי ר"א: כח] אונן דראוי לעבודה ואינו: כט] אשי דהוו סוף הוראה: ל] בתוך הש"ס:

מתני' אכָּל שֶׁלֹּא זָכָה הַמִּזְבֵּחַ בִּבְשָׂרָהּ — לֹא זָכוּ כֹּהֲנִים בְּעוֹרָהּ, שֶׁנֶּאֱמַר: °"עוֹלַת אִישׁ" — עוֹלָה *שֶׁעָלְתָה לְאִישׁ. בעוֹלָה שֶׁנִּשְׁחֲטָה שֶׁלֹּא לִשְׁמָהּ, אע"פ שֶׁלֹּא עָלְתָה לַבְּעָלִים — עוֹרָהּ לַכֹּהֲנִים. גאֶחָד עוֹלַת הָאִישׁ וְאֶחָד עוֹלַת הָאִשָּׁה — עוֹרוֹתֵיהֶן לַכֹּהֲנִים. דעוֹרוֹת קָדָשִׁים קַלִּים — לַבְּעָלִים, העוֹרוֹת קָדְשֵׁי קָדָשִׁים — לַכֹּהֲנִים. קַל וָחוֹמֶר: וּמָה אִם עוֹלָה שֶׁלֹּא זָכוּ בִּבְשָׂרָהּ — זָכוּ בְּעוֹרָהּ, קָדְשֵׁי קָדָשִׁים שֶׁזָּכוּ בִּבְשָׂרָהּ — אֵינוֹ דִּין שֶׁיִּזְכּוּ א] בְּעוֹרָהּ? אֵין מִזְבֵּחַ יוֹכִיחַ, שֶׁאֵין לוֹ עוֹר בְּכָל מָקוֹם.§ גמ' ת"ר: "עוֹלַת אִישׁ" — ופְּרָט לְעוֹלַת הֶקְדֵּשׁ, דִּבְרֵי ר' יְהוּדָה. רַבִּי יוֹסֵי בַּר' יְהוּדָה אוֹמֵר: פְּרָט לְעוֹלַת גֵּרִים. מַאי "פְּרָט לְעוֹלַת הֶקְדֵּשׁ"? אָמַר רַבִּי חִיָּיא בַּר יוֹסֵף: פְּרָט לְעוֹלָה הַבָּאָה מִן הַמּוֹתָרוֹת. הָנִיחָא לְמ"ד: מוֹתָרוֹת לְנִדְבַת צִיבּוּר אָזְלִי. אֶלָּא לְמ"ד: מוֹתָרוֹת לְנִדְבַת יָחִיד אָזְלִי, מַאי אִיכָּא לְמֵימַר? כִּדְאָמַר רָבָא: "הָעוֹלָה" — עוֹלָה רִאשׁוֹנָה, ה"נ, "הָעוֹלָה" — עוֹלָה רִאשׁוֹנָה. ב] רַבִּי אַיְיבוּ א"ר יַנַּאי: פְּרָט לְמַתְפִּיס עוֹלָה לְבֶדֶק הַבַּיִת. ג] לָא מִיבַּעְיָא לְמ"ד: קָדְשֵׁי בֶּדֶק הַבַּיִת תָּפְסִי מִדְּאוֹרַיְיתָא, אֶלָּא אֲפִילּוּ לְמ"ד: לָא תָּפְסִי — ד] הָנֵי מִילֵּי בָּשָׂר, אֲבָל עוֹר תָּפֵיס. וְכֵן אָמַר רַב נַחְמָן אָמַר רַבָּה בַּר אֲבוּהּ: פְּרָט לְעוֹלָה הַבָּאָה מִן הַמּוֹתָרוֹת. א"ל רַב הַמְנוּנָא לְרַב נַחְמָן: כְּמַאן — כְּרַבִּי יְהוּדָה? הָא הֲדַר בֵּיהּ! דְּתַנְיָא: "שִׁשָּׁה לִנְדָבָה" — לְעוֹלָה הַבָּאָה מִן הַמּוֹתָרוֹת, שֶׁלֹּא יְהוּ ה] כֹּהֲנִים זַכָּאִין בְּעוֹרָהּ, דִּבְרֵי רַבִּי יְהוּדָה. אָמַר לוֹ רַבִּי נְחֶמְיָה, וְאָמְרִי לָהּ ר"ש: אִם כֵּן, בִּיטַּלְתָּ מִדְרָשׁוֹ שֶׁל יְהוֹיָדָע הַכֹּהֵן. *דְּתַנְיָא, *זֶה מִדְרָשׁ דָּרַשׁ יְהוֹיָדָע הַכֹּהֵן: °"אָשָׁם הוּא אָשֹׁם אָשַׁם לַה'" — זכָּל שֶׁבָּא מִשּׁוּם חַטָּאת וּמִשּׁוּם אָשָׁם, יִלָּקַח ו] בּוֹ עוֹלוֹת, הַבָּשָׂר — לַשֵּׁם, חעוֹרָהּ — לַכֹּהֲנִים. א"ל: אֶלָּא מָר בְּמַאי מוֹקִים לָהּ? א"ל: מוֹקְמִינָא לֵיהּ בְּמַקְדִּישׁ נְכָסָיו, וּכְדְרַבִּי יְהוֹשֻׁעַ. *דִּתְנַן: הַמַּקְדִּישׁ נְכָסָיו וְהָיוּ בָּהֶן בְּהֵמוֹת הָרְאוּיוֹת לְגַבֵּי מִזְבֵּחַ, זְכָרִים וּנְקֵבוֹת, ר"א אוֹמֵר: טזְכָרִים — יִמָּכְרוּ לְצוֹרְכֵי עוֹלוֹת, ז] נְקֵבוֹת — יִמָּכְרוּ לְצוֹרְכֵי זִבְחֵי שְׁלָמִים, וּדְמֵיהֶן ח] יִפְּלוּ עִם שְׁאָר נְכָסִים לְבֶדֶק הַבַּיִת. רַבִּי יְהוֹשֻׁעַ אוֹמֵר: זְכָרִים עַצְמָם — יִקְרְבוּ עוֹלוֹת, וּנְקֵבוֹת — יִמָּכְרוּ לְצוֹרְכֵי שְׁלָמִים, וְיָבִיא בִּדְמֵיהֶן עוֹלוֹת, וּשְׁאָר נְכָסִים — יִפְּלוּ לְבֶדֶק הַבַּיִת. וַאֲפִי' לְרַבִּי יְהוֹשֻׁעַ דְּאָמַר אָדָם חוֹלֵק הֶקְדֵּישׁוֹ — הָנֵי מִילֵּי בָּשָׂר, אֲבָל עוֹר תָּפֵיס. רַבִּי יוֹסֵי בְּרַבִּי יְהוּדָה אוֹמֵר: פְּרָט לְעוֹלַת גֵּרִים. אֲמַר לֵיהּ רַב סִימַאי בַּר חִילְקַאי לְרָבִינָא: אַטּוּ גֵּר לָאו "אִישׁ" הוּא? אֲמַר לֵיהּ: פְּרָט לְגֵר שֶׁמֵּת וְאֵין לוֹ יוֹרְשִׁים. תָּנוּ רַבָּנַן: "עוֹלַת אִישׁ" — אֵין לִי אֶלָּא עוֹלַת אִישׁ, יעוֹלַת ט] *גֵּרִים נָשִׁים וַעֲבָדִים מִנַּיִן? ת"ל: "עוֹר הָעוֹלָה" — רִיבָּה. אִם כֵּן, מַה תַּלְמוּד לוֹמַר "עוֹלַת אִישׁ" — עוֹלָה שֶׁעָלְתָה לְאִישׁ, פְּרָט לְשֶׁנִּשְׁחֲטָה חוּץ לִזְמַנָּהּ וְחוּץ לִמְקוֹמָהּ, שֶׁלֹּא יְהוּ הַכֹּהֲנִים זַכָּאִין בְּעוֹרָהּ. יָכוֹל שֶׁאֲנִי *מְרַבֶּה שֶׁנִּשְׁחֲטָה שֶׁלֹּא לִשְׁמָהּ, הוֹאִיל וְלֹא עָלְתָה לַבְּעָלִים

לא

תורה אור: ויקרא ז; ויקרא ה

רש"י

מתני' כָּל שֶׁלֹּא זָכָה הַמִּזְבֵּחַ בִּבְשָׂרָהּ. כְּגוֹן שֶׁאֵירַע בָּהּ פְּסוּל קוֹדֶם זְרִיקָה, דְּלָא הָיְתָה לָהּ שְׁעַת הֶיתֵּר לַמִּזְבֵּחַ. עוֹרָהּ לַכֹּהֲנִים. מִקְּרָאֵי אִיתְרַבַּאי בַּבָּרַיְיתָא בַּגְּמָרָא. וְאֶחָד עוֹלַת הָאִשָּׁה. דְּאִיתְרַבַּאי נַמִּי מִקְּרָא. עוֹרוֹת קָדְשֵׁי קָדָשִׁים. חַטָּאוֹת וַאֲשָׁמוֹת, לַכֹּהֲנִים, כִּדְמְפָרֵשׁ טַעְמָא וְאָזֵיל. אֵין הַמִּזְבֵּחַ מוֹכִיחַ. כְּלוֹמַר, וְאֵין לְךָ לוֹמַר: מִזְבֵּחַ יוֹכִיחַ, שֶׁזָּכָה בִּבְשַׂר הָעוֹלָה וְלֹא זָכָה בְּעוֹרָהּ, וְאַף אַתָּה אַל תִּתְמַהּ בְּקָדְשֵׁי קָדָשִׁים, שֶׁאַע"פ שֶׁזָּכוּ כֹּהֲנִים בִּבְשָׂרָן לֹא יִזְכּוּ בְּעוֹרָן. אֵין זוֹ הוֹכָחָה שֶׁאֵין לַמִּזְבֵּחַ עוֹר בְּכָל מָקוֹם, אֲבָל לַכֹּהֲנִים מָצִינוּ י] שֶׁזָּכוּ בְּעוֹר הָעוֹלָה, וְקַל וָחוֹמֶר שֶׁיִּזְכּוּ בְּעוֹרוֹת קָדְשֵׁי קָדָשִׁים. גמ' פְּרָט לְעוֹלַת הֶקְדֵּשׁ. לְקַמֵּיהּ מְפָרֵשׁ לָהּ. פְּרָט לְעוֹלַת גֵּרִים. לְקַמֵּיהּ פָּרֵיךְ: אַטּוּ גֵּר לָאו אִישׁ הוּא? מִן הַמּוֹתָרוֹת. יא] דְּכָל אֲשָׁמוֹת שֶׁל רְעִיָּיה, כְּגוֹן תְּמוּרַת אָשָׁם, וְאָשָׁם שֶׁמֵּתוּ בְּעָלָיו, וְשֶׁכִּיפְּרוּ בְּעָלָיו בְּאַחֵר, דְּקַיְימָא לָן יב] יִרְעוּ וְיִמָּכְרוּ וְיִפְּלוּ דְּמֵיהֶן לִנְדָבָה. וְהוּא עוֹלַת קַיִץ הַמִּזְבֵּחַ, דְּלָאו עוֹלַת אִישׁ הוּא אֶלָּא נִדְבַת צִבּוּר הִיא, וּנְסָכֶיהָ מִשֶּׁל צִבּוּר, וְאֵין בְּעָלָיו סוֹמֵךְ עָלֶיהָ וְאֵינוֹ שׁוֹחֲטָהּ, כִּדְתְנַן בִּתְמוּרָה (דף כ:). הָנִיחָא כו'. פְּלוּגְתָּא דְּרַבִּי יג] *אֱלִיעֶזֶר וְרַבָּנַן הִיא בִּתְמוּרָה (שם). לְנִדְבַת צִבּוּר. לְקַיִץ הַמִּזְבֵּחַ. לְנִדְבַת יָחִיד. בְּעָלָיו שֶׁל אָשָׁם שֶׁנִּיתּוֹתַר – הוּא עַצְמוֹ מֵבִיא עוֹלָה בִּדְמָיו, וְהוּא סוֹמֵךְ עָלֶיהָ וְשׁוֹחֲטָהּ, וּנְסָכֶיהָ קְרֵיבִין מִשֶּׁלּוֹ. כִּדְאָמַר רָבָא. (יומא דף לד.) גַּבֵּי "וְעָרַךְ עָלֶיהָ הָעוֹלָה" דְּיָלְפִינַן מִינָּהּ: מִנַּיִן שֶׁלֹּא יְהֵא דָּבָר קוֹדֵם לְתָמִיד שֶׁל שַׁחַר – ת"ל: "וְעָרַךְ עָלֶיהָ הָעוֹלָה" וגו'. וְאָמְרִינַן: מַאי תַּלְמוּדָא? וְאָמַר רָבָא: "הָעוֹלָה" מַשְׁמַע – הָעוֹלָה רִאשׁוֹנָה הָאֲמוּרָה בְּסֵדֶר קָרְבְּנוֹת הַיּוֹם. הָכָא נַמִּי "עוֹר הָעוֹלָה" כְּתִיב – הָעוֹלָה רִאשׁוֹנָה, שֶׁהוּפְרְשָׁה מִתְּחִילָּה לְשֵׁם עוֹלָה, וְלֹא הַבָּאָה מִמּוֹתַר אָשָׁם וּמִמּוֹתַר חַטָּאת. וּלְקַמֵּיהּ פָּרֵיךְ: וְהָא קי"ל יד] עוֹרָהּ לַכֹּהֲנִים, מִמִּדְרַשׁ יְהוֹיָדָע הַכֹּהֵן! פְּרָט לְמַתְפִּיס עוֹלָתוֹ לְבֶדֶק הַבַּיִת. שֶׁאֵין עוֹרָהּ לַכֹּהֲנִים. וְלָא מִיבַּעְיָא וכו'. בְּפֶ' בַּתְרָא דִּתְמוּרָה (דף לג:), דְּקָאָמַר עוּלָּא: הַמַּתְפִּיס עוֹלָה לְבֶדֶק הַבַּיִת – אֵין בָּהּ אֶלָּא עִיכּוּב גִּיזְבָּרִים בִּלְבַד. וּמוֹתְבִינַן לְעוּלָּא: הַמַּתְפִּיס עוֹלָה לְבֶדֶק הַבַּיִת – אָסוּר לְשׁוֹחֲטָהּ עַד שֶׁתִּפָּדֶה! וּמְשַׁנֵּי עוּלָּא: הַאי דְּמַצְרִיךְ לֵיהּ פְּדִיָּה – מִדְּרַבָּנַן. מִכְּלָל טו] מַאן דְּמוֹתִיב – בָּעֵי לְמֵימַר דְּאוֹרַיְיתָא. וּלְעִנְיַן עוֹרָהּ, לָא מִיבַּעְיָא לְמ"ד מִדְּאוֹרַיְיתָא תָּפְסָה בָּהּ קְדוּשַּׁת בֶּדֶק הַבַּיִ', דְּאֵין עוֹרָהּ לַכֹּהֲנִים אִם שְׁחָטָהּ עַד שֶׁלֹּא נִפְדֵּית, דְּלָאו "עוֹלַת אִישׁ" הוּא, אֶלָּא עוֹלַת הֶקְדֵּשׁ. אֶלָּא אֲפִי' לְמ"ד. מִדְּרַבָּנַן בְּעָלְמָא, אֲבָל מִדְּאוֹרַיְיתָא לָא – הָנֵי מִילֵּי דְּמִדְּאוֹרַיְיתָא לָא בָּשָׂר, דְּשֶׁל מִזְבֵּחַ הוּא, וְאֵין קְדוּשָּׁה *חָלָה טז] עָלָיו, שֶׁאֵינוֹ שֶׁלּוֹ עַל פִּיו. אֲבָל עוֹר, דְּלָאו מָמוֹן מִזְבֵּחַ הוּא, וְכֹהֲנִים אַכַּתִּי לָא זָכוּ בֵּיהּ – תָּפוּס. כְּמַאן כְּרַבִּי יְהוּדָה. לְקַמָּן מַיְיתֵי לָהּ, דְּאָמַר: אֵין עוֹרָהּ לַכֹּהֲנִים. הָא הֲדַר בֵּיהּ. דְּקָאָמְרִי לֵיהּ: אִם כֵּן בִּטַּלְתָּ מִדְרָשׁוֹ שֶׁל יְהוֹיָדָע הַכֹּהֵן, וְלָא אַהְדַּר לְהוּ מִידֵּי. שִׁשָּׁה לִנְדָבָה. בְּי"ג שׁוֹפָרוֹת שֶׁהָיוּ בַּמִּקְדָּשׁ קָמַיְירֵי, דִּכְתוּב עֲלֵיהֶן: תִּקְלִין חֲדַתִּין, יז] [וְתִקְלִין עַתִּיקִין], קִינִּין, וְגוֹזְלֵי עוֹלָה, עֵצִים, וּלְבוֹנָה, וְזָהָב לַכַּפֹּרֶת, וְשִׁשָּׁה לִנְדָבָה. וּמְפָרֵשׁ מַאי נִיהוּ "שִׁשָּׁה לִנְדָבָה". ה"ג: שִׁשָּׁה לִנְדָבָה לְעוֹלָה הַבָּאָה מִן הַמּוֹתָרוֹת שֶׁאֵין הַכֹּהֲנִים זַכָּאִין בְּעוֹרָהּ יח]. אָשָׁם הוּא אָשָׁם לַה'. אִי אֶפְשָׁר יט] אָשָׁם לַה' – שֶׁכְּבָר נֶאֱמַר אָשָׁם לַכֹּהֵן: "כַּחַטָּאת כָּאָשָׁם תּוֹרָה אַחַת לָהֶם" וגו'. הָא כֵּיצַד? כָּל דָּבָר הַבָּא מִמּוֹתַר חַטָּאת – כְּגוֹן מַפְרִישׁ מָעוֹת לְחַטָּאתוֹ וְנִיתּוֹתַר מֵהֶן, וּמִמּוֹתַר אֲשָׁמוֹת – כְּגוֹן הָנָךְ דְּאָזְלֵי לִרְעִיָּיה, דְּקַיְימָא לָן (תמורה דף יח.): כָּל שֶׁבְּחַטָּאת מֵתָה בְּאָשָׁם רוֹעֶה. יִלָּקַח בָּהֶן כו'. נִמְצְאוּ שְׁנֵי כְתוּבִים כ] מְקוּיָּימִין: אָשָׁם לַה', בָּשָׂר לָעוֹלָה, וְאָשָׁם לַכֹּהֵן – הָעוֹר. וְהַיְינוּ דִּכְתִיב: "כֶּסֶף אָשָׁם וְכֶסֶף חַטָּאוֹת לֹא יוּבָא" וגו'. אֶלָּא מָר בְּמַאי כא] מוֹקֵי לָהּ. לְהָא דְּתָנֵי לְעֵיל: פְּרָט לְעוֹלַת הֶקְדֵּשׁ? וּכְרַבִּי יְהוֹשֻׁעַ. דְּאָמַר: זְכָרִים עַצְמָן יִקְרְבוּ עוֹלוֹת. וְהַךְ עוֹלַת הֶקְדֵּשׁ הִיא, וּכְדִמְסַיֵּים וְאָזֵיל, דְּכִי א"ר יְהוֹשֻׁעַ דְּחָיֵיל שֵׁם מִזְבֵּחַ עֲלַיְיהוּ מֵעִיקָּרָא – אַמַּאי דַּחֲזֵי לַמִּזְבֵּחַ קָאָמַר, אֲבָל בְּעוֹר מוֹדֶה דְּחָיֵיל כב] עֲלֵהּ קְדוּשַּׁת בֶּדֶק הַבַּיִת. הַמַּקְדִּישׁ נְכָסָיו. לְבֶדֶק הַבַּיִת. הָרְאוּיוֹת לַמִּזְבֵּחַ. תְּמִימִים. זְכָרִים יִמָּכְרוּ לְצָרְכֵי עוֹלוֹת כו'. דְּקי"ל בִּתְמוּרָה (דף לג:): הַמַּתְפִּיס תְּמִימִים לְבֶדֶק הַבַּיִת, כְּשֶׁהֵן נִפְדִּין – אֵינָן נִפְדִּין אֶלָּא לַמִּזְבֵּחַ, שֶׁכָּל הָרָאוּי לַמִּזְבֵּחַ – אֵינוֹ יוֹצֵא מִידֵי מִזְבֵּחַ לְעוֹלָם. זְכָרִים עַצְמָן יִקָּרְבוּ עוֹלוֹת. לְשֵׁם אוֹתוֹ הָאִישׁ. דְּקָסָבַר: אָדָם חוֹלֵק הֶקְדֵּשׁוֹ. וְאע"ג כג] דְּמַקְדִּישׁ סְתָמָא – דַּעְתֵּיהּ הֲוָה לְהַקְרִיב לַמִּזְבֵּחַ הָרָאוּי לוֹ. וּנְקֵבוֹת יִמָּכְרוּ כו'. אֲבָל הֵן עַצְמָן לֹא יִקְרְבוּ שְׁלָמִים עַד שֶׁיִּמָּכְרוּ. דְּכֵיוָן כד] דְּמַקְדִּישׁ סְתָמָא – הַכֹּל הִקְדִּישׁ, הָרָאוּי לַמִּזְבֵּחַ דּוּמְיָא דְּבֶדֶק הַבַּיִת, שֶׁכּוּלּוֹ קָדוֹשׁ. הִלְכָּךְ לִדְמֵי עוֹלָה אַקְדְּשִׁינְהוּ. וּבְהַךְ עוֹלָה דְּרַבִּי יְהוֹשֻׁעַ – כה] זְכָרִים הַקְּרֵבִים עוֹלוֹת, קא"ר יְהוּדָה לְעֵיל: פְּרָט לְעוֹלַת הֶקְדֵּשׁ. וַאֲפִי' לְרַבִּי יְהוֹשֻׁעַ. כְּלוֹמַר, וְאע"ג דְּאָמַר ר' יְהוֹשֻׁעַ: אָדָם חוֹלֵק הֶקְדֵּשׁוֹ, הָרָאוּי לַמִּזְבֵּחַ לַמִּזְבֵּחַ, וְשֶׁאֵינוֹ רָאוּי לַמִּזְבֵּחַ יְהֵא לְבֶדֶק הַבַּיִת – לֹא שֶׁיְּהוּ כִּשְׁאָר קָדְשֵׁי מִזְבֵּחַ, שֶׁעוֹרוֹתֵיהֶן לַכֹּהֲנִים, דְּמוֹדֶה הוּא שֶׁהָעוֹר נִתְפָּס לְבֶדֶק הַבַּיִת כִּשְׁאָר נְכָסִים שֶׁלּוֹ. וְאֵין לוֹ יוֹרְשִׁין. דְּאֵין לָהּ בְּעָלִים. ה"ג: עוֹלַת אִישׁ אֵין לִי אֶלָּא עוֹלַת נָשִׁים וַעֲבָדִים מִנַּיִן כו] ת"ל כו'. הָעוֹלָה. קְרָא יְתֵירָא הוּא, דְּלָא אִיצְטְרִיךְ לְמִכְתַּב אֶלָּא "הָעוֹר לַכֹּהֵן", אֶלָּא לְרַבּוֹת בָּא. הוֹאִיל וְלֹא עָלְתָה לַבְּעָלִים. וְאַף עַל פִּי שֶׁהִיא כְּשֵׁרָה,

לא

הגהות בגליון רש"י: נ"א שזכה. [פסחים נח: וש"נ] נ"ל אלעזר. נ"ל דתנן. נ"א גוים וטי' בכ"מ ועי' רש"ק וג"ק ובעל פ"מ. גירסת הב"ח ממעט. נ"א חלה על דבר שאינו כו' נ"ק.

מסורת הש"ס: שקלים פ"ד מ"ז ב"ב קנה. תמורה כ. ודף לח:. [ובכ"ח פח. ד"ה יהא עבד תירלו באופן אחר]. שקלים פ"ו מ"ו [תמורה כג: ע"ש].

תוספות

הניחא למ"ד מותרות לנדבת ציבור אזלי. תימה: לדידיה מ"ש דממעט מותרות טפי מעולת תמיד? וי"ל: דסברא הוא למעוטי טפי מותרות, משום דהיו מעיקרא לאיש. אלא למ"ד לנדבת יחיד מאי איכא למימר. תימה: מאי קשיא ליה? הא רבי יהודה דממעט הכא עולת הקדש – הוא דקאמר בסמוך: לנדבת ציבור אזלי. דקתני "ששה לנדבה", ואי לנדבת יחיד – לא היה משימה בשופר, דקרבן יחיד בעי סמיכה! וי"ל: דלא שמיע ליה ההיא ברייתא. תדע, דאי שמיע ליה – הא הדר ביה רבי יהודה ממדרשו של יהוידע. לא מיבעיא למ"ד קדשי בדק הבית תפסי מדאורייתא. תימה: לדידיה, אמאי איצטריך קרא הכא דאם שחט קודם פדייה אין עורה לכהנים? פשיטא, דקדשי בדק הבית היו בכלל העמדה והערכה!. אין לי אלא עולת איש גרים נשים ועבדים מנין. משמע מחד קרא הוה ממעטינן נשים ועבדים. ודין הוא, דהא ילפינן מהדדי בג"ש ד"לה" "לה" מאשה. והקשה הר"ר חיים: דבפרק "החובל" (ב"ק דף פח.) מצריך תרי קראי גבי עדות, חד למעוטי נשים וחד למעוטי עבדים! וי"ל: דגבי מלות הוא דילפינן מהדדי בג"ש ד"לה" "לה". אבל גבי עדות – לא שייך למילף, דאין תלוי בנאמנות, שהרי משה ואהרן לא מעידין לא משום דלא מהימני, הלכך היכא דגלי – גלי*.

ומודה

עין משפט נר מצוה

לו א מיי' פ"ט מהלכות מעשה"ק הל' כ:
לז ב מיי' פ"ט מהל' פסה"מ הל' ט:
לח ג מיי' פ"ה מהלכות מעשה"ק הלכה כא:
לט ד ה מיי' שם הל' יט:
מ ו מיי' שם הל' יב:
מא ז מיי' פ"ה מהל' פסה"מ הל' ט ופ"ד מהל' שקלים הל' יג:
מב ח מיי' פ"ה מהל' מעשה"ק הלכה כא:
מג ט מיי' פ"ה מהל' ערכין הלכה ז:
מד י מיי' פ"ה מהל' מעשה"ק הלכה כא:

שיטה מקובצת

א] שיזכו בעורה אין המזבח מוכיח שאין: ב] ראשונה ר' אילא א"ר ותיבת אייבו ל"ש ונמחק: ג] הבית ולא: ד] תפסי דאורייתא הני: ה] יהו הכהנים זכאין: ו] ילקח בהן עולות הבשר לה' והעורות לכהנים: ז] עולות ונקבות: ח] ודמיהן עם שאר נכסים יפלו לבדק הבית: ט] תיבת גרים נמחק: י] א) מצינו עולה שזכו: יא] המותרות דמי אשמות ותיבת דכל נמחק: יב] דקי"ל בכולן ירעו: יג] אלעזר ורבנן: יד] קי"ל דעורה לכהנים: טו] מכלל דמאן דמותיב: טז] חלה על שאינו: יז] חדתין ועתיקין קינין: יח] בעורה. פי' אלא חוזרין ומוכרין העור ולוקחין בדמיו בהמה לעולה לקייץ המזבח דברי רבי יהודה הס"ד: יט] אפשר לומר אשם: כ] כתובין קיימין אשם לה' בשר עולה ואשם לכהן: כא] במאי מוקים לה: כב] דחייל עליה קדושת: כג] ואע"ג דאקדיש: כד] דכיון דאקדיש סתמא: כה] יהושע של זכרים: כו] תיבות ת"ל נמחק:

א) נראה דצ"ל מצינו עולה שזכו בעורה וקל וחומר וכו'

מה א מיי' פ"ה מהל' מעה"ק הלכה יח:
מו ב מיי' שם הל' כ:
מז ג מיי' פ"ג מהלכות בכורות הל' י ופי"ט מהלכות פסה"מ הל' ט:
מח ד מיי' פ"ה מהל' מעה"ק הל' יח:

תורה אור

לֹא יְהוּ כֹּהֲנִים זַכָּאִין בְּעוֹרָהּ? ת"ל: "עוֹר הָעוֹלָה", מ"מ. "עוֹר הָעוֹלָה" — אֵין לִי אֶלָּא עוֹר הָעוֹלָה, עוֹרוֹת קָדְשֵׁי קָדָשִׁים מִנַּיִן? ת"ל: א] "עוֹר הָעוֹלָה אֲשֶׁר הִקְרִיב". יָכוֹל שֶׁאֲנִי מְרַבֶּה אַף קָדָשִׁים קַלִּים? ת"ל: "עוֹלָה", מָה עוֹלָה קָדְשֵׁי קָדָשִׁים — אַף כָּל קָדְשֵׁי קָדָשִׁים. רַבִּי יִשְׁמָעֵאל אוֹמֵר: "עוֹר הָעוֹלָה" — אֵין לִי אֶלָּא ב] הָעוֹלָה, עוֹרוֹת קָדְשֵׁי קָדָשִׁים מִנַּיִן? וְדִין הוּא: וּמָה עוֹלָה שֶׁלֹּא זָכוּ בִּבְשָׂרָהּ — זָכוּ בְּעוֹרָהּ, קָדְשֵׁי קָדָשִׁים שֶׁזָּכוּ בִּבְשָׂרָן — אֵינוֹ דִּין ג] שֶׁזָּכוּ בְּעוֹרָן? מִזְבֵּחַ יוֹכִיחַ, שֶׁזָּכָה בַּבָּשָׂר וְלֹא זָכָה בָּעוֹר! מַה לְּמִזְבֵּחַ שֶׁכֵּן לֹא זָכָה בְּמִקְצָת, תֹּאמַר בְּכֹהֲנִים שֶׁזָּכוּ בְּמִקְצָת; הוֹאִיל וְזָכוּ בְּמִקְצָת — ד] זָכוּ בְּכוּלֵּיהּ. רַבִּי אוֹמֵר: כָּל ה] עַצְמוֹ לֹא הוּצְרַכְנוּ אֶלָּא לְעוֹר הָעוֹלָה בִּלְבַד. שֶׁבְּכָל מָקוֹם ו] הָעוֹר מְהַלֵּךְ אַחַר הַבָּשָׂר: אפָּרִים הַנִּשְׂרָפִין וּשְׂעִירִים הַנִּשְׂרָפִין — הֵן ז] וְעוֹרוֹתֵיהֶן [נִשְׂרָפִין] נ"ק עִמָּהֶן; חַטָּאת וְאָשָׁם וְזִבְחֵי שַׁלְמֵי צִיבּוּר מַתָּנָה לַכֹּהֵן, רָצוּ — מַפְשִׁיטִין אוֹתָן, לֹא רָצוּ — אוֹכְלִין אוֹתָן ע"ג עוֹרָן; קָדָשִׁים קַלִּים לַבְּעָלִים, רָצוּ — מַפְשִׁיטִין אוֹתָן, רָצוּ — אוֹכְלִין אוֹתָן עַל גַּב עוֹרָן. אֲבָל עוֹלָה נֶאֱמַר בָּהּ: °"וְהִפְשִׁיט אֶת הָעוֹלָה וְנִתַּח אוֹתָהּ לִנְתָחֶיהָ", יָכוֹל לֹא יְהוּ הַכֹּהֲנִים זַכָּאִין בְּעוֹרָהּ? ת"ל: °"עוֹר הָעוֹלָה אֲשֶׁר הִקְרִיב". "לוֹ יִהְיֶה" — פְּרָט לִטְבוּל יוֹם (וּמְחוּסַּר כִּיפּוּרִים) וְאוֹנֵן. שֶׁיָּכוֹל, לֹא יִזְכּוּ בַּבָּשָׂר שֶׁהוּא לַאֲכִילָה, ח] יִזְכּוּ בָּעוֹר שֶׁאֵינוֹ לַאֲכִילָה! ת"ל: "לוֹ יִהְיֶה" — פְּרָט לִמְחוּסַּר כִּיפּוּרִים וּטְבוּל יוֹם וְאוֹנֵן. וְת"ק נַמִּי, תֵּיפּוֹק לִי מִדִּינָא! *מִילְּתָא דְּאָתְיָא בְּקַל וָחוֹמֶר, טָרַח וְכָתַב לָהּ קְרָא. וְרַבִּי יִשְׁמָעֵאל, הַאי "אֲשֶׁר הִקְרִיב" מַאי עָבֵיד לֵיהּ? פְּרָט לִטְבוּל יוֹם וּמְחוּסַּר כִּיפּוּרִים וְאוֹנֵן. וְתֵיפּוֹק לֵיהּ מִ"לוֹ יִהְיֶה"! רַבִּי יִשְׁמָעֵאל לְטַעְמֵיהּ, *דְּאָמַר רַבִּי יוֹחָנָן מִשּׁוּם רַבִּי יִשְׁמָעֵאל: נֶאֱמַר בָּעוֹלָה "לוֹ יִהְיֶה", וְנֶאֱמַר בְּאָשָׁם "לוֹ יִהְיֶה", מַה לְּהַלָּן עַצְמוֹתָיו מוּתָּרִין — אַף כָּאן עַצְמוֹתָיו מוּתָּרִין. מוּפְנֵי, דְּאִי לָא מוּפְנֵי, אִיכָּא לְמִיפְרַךְ: מַה לְּאָשָׁם שֶׁכֵּן בְּשָׂרוֹ מוּתָּר! "לוֹ יִהְיֶה" קְרָא יְתֵירָא הוּא.§ **מתני'** בכָּל הַקֳּדָשִׁים שֶׁאֵירַע בָּהֶן פְּסוּל קוֹדֶם לְהֶפְשֵׁיטָן — אֵין עוֹרוֹתֵיהֶן לַכֹּהֲנִים, לְאַחַר הֶפְשֵׁיטָן — עוֹרוֹתֵיהֶן לַכֹּהֲנִים. *אָמַר רַבִּי חֲנִינָא סְגַן הַכֹּהֲנִים: מִיָּמַי לֹא רָאִיתִי עוֹר שֶׁיּוֹצֵא לְבֵית הַשְּׂרֵיפָה. *אָמַר רַבִּי עֲקִיבָא: מִדְּבָרָיו לָמַדְנוּ, שֶׁהַמַּפְשִׁיט אֶת הַבְּכוֹר וְנִמְצָא טְרֵיפָה — שֶׁיֵּאוֹתוּ הַכֹּהֲנִים בְּעוֹרוֹ. ט] וַחֲכָמִים אוֹמְרִים: אֵין "לֹא י] רָאִינוּ" רְאָיָה, אֶלָּא גיֵצֵא לְבֵית הַשְּׂרֵיפָה.§ **גמ'** כָּל שֶׁלֹּא זָכָה הַמִּזְבֵּחַ בִּבְשָׂרָהּ, לֹא זָכוּ הַכֹּהֲנִים בְּעוֹרָהּ — וְאע"ג דְּאַפְשְׁטֵיהּ לָעוֹר קוֹדֶם זְרִיקָה; מַנִּי — רַבִּי אֶלְעָזָר בְּרַבִּי שִׁמְעוֹן הִיא, דְּאָמַר: אֵין הַדָּם מְרַצֶּה עַל הָעוֹר בִּפְנֵי עַצְמוֹ. אֵימָא סֵיפָא: כָּל הַקֳּדָשִׁים שֶׁאֵירַע בָּהֶן פְּסוּל קוֹדֶם הֶפְשֵׁיטָן — אֵין עוֹרוֹתֵיהֶן לַכֹּהֲנִים, לְאַחַר הֶפְשֵׁיטָן — עוֹרוֹתֵיהֶן לַכֹּהֲנִים; אֲתָאן לְרַבִּי, דְּאָמַר: הַדָּם מְרַצֶּה עַל הָעוֹר בִּפְנֵי עַצְמוֹ. רֵישָׁא רַבִּי אֶלְעָזָר בְּרַבִּי שִׁמְעוֹן, סֵיפָא רַבִּי? אָמַר אַבַּיֵי: מִדְּסֵיפָא רַבִּי הִיא — רֵישָׁא נַמִּי רַבִּי הִיא, וּמוֹדֶה רַבִּי דשֶׁאֵין הֶפְשֵׁט קוֹדֶם זְרִיקָה. רָבָא אָמַר: מִדְּרֵישָׁא ר"א בְּרַבִּי שִׁמְעוֹן — סֵיפָא נַמִּי ר"א בְּר"ש; מַאי "קוֹדֶם הֶפְשֵׁט", וּמַאי

לא יזכו בעורה. אשר הקריב. כל הקרבנות במשמע. שזכה בבשר. *באימורים. שכן לא זכה במקצת. עורות, שלא מצינו עור למזבח. תאמר בכהנים שזכו במקצת בעור העולה. כל יא] עצמו כו'. אין לנו להביא ראיה לשאר עורות מעולה, שפרט בה הכתוב לבדה. מפני שלא הוצרכנו ללמוד על שאר עורות מה תהא עליהן, אלא על של עולה בלבד. ועורותיהן עמהן. כדכתיב: "ואת הפר ואת עורו" וגו'. רצו מפשיטין יב]. שהרי לא הצריכו להפשיט, ונתנו לכהן כמות שהן, כדכתיב: "כחטאת כאשם תורה אחת" וגו'. נאמר בה והפשיט. והבשר למזבח. ועל העור שהזקיקו להפשיט לא אמור מה תהא עליו. ולמזבח אינך יכול להביאו יג] *(זה), דבהדיא פרט לך הקטר באברים מופשטין, ולא פרט לך העור עמהן. לו יהיה. רישיה דקרא: "המקריב את עולת איש", ועליה קאי "לו יהיה". פרט לאונן כו'. דלא חזי להקרבה. שיכול לא יזכו בבשר. כלומר, אע"פ שנתמעטו מלחלוק בבשר יד] מלאכול לערב, הוצרכו למעטן מן העורות. שיכול לא יזכו בבשר. מפני שהוא טו] ראוי לאכילה, והן אינן ראוים טז] לאכילת היום. מדינא. כי היכי דנפקא ליה לרבי ישמעאל. ולמה לי קרא לעורות קדשי קדשים? אשר הקריב. דיליף ת"ק מיניה עורות קדשי קדשים, מאי עביד ליה? תיפוק ליה מלו יהיה. כדנפקא ליה לרבי. רבי ישמעאל לטעמיה. דדריש "לו יהיה" לדרשה אחריתי. קרא יתירא הוא. דמצי למכתב: "עור העולה אשר הקריב לכהן", ולשתוק. **מתני'** אין עורותיהן לכהנים. אלא נשרפים עם עורן. לא ראיתי עור יוצא יז] לשריפה. משהופשט. הכי מפרש לה בגמרא. ונמצא טריפה. ואפילו שפסול זה היה בו קודם הפשט, הואיל ולא ניכר עד לאחר הפשט – יאותו הכהנים בעורו. אין לא *ראיתי ראיה. שמא לא אירע בימיו שימצא טריפה אחר הפשט, ואם אירע ושרפוה – הוא לא ראה. אלא יצא לבית השריפה. הואיל וקודם הפשט הוה ביה יח]. **גמ'** ה"ג בגמ': כל שלא זכה המזבח בבשרה לא זכו הכהנים בעורה ואע"ג דאפשטיה לעור קודם זריקה ול"ג: כל שאין לו בבשר. דהאיך מאי בעיא לענין דם מרצה על העור? הא הוא בכהן טמא קאמר. אלא יט] רישיה דהך דלעיל, מהך נקט ואותיב (א) הכי: קתני רישא: כל שלא זכה המזבח בבשרה – כגון שאירע בו פסול קודם זריקה, דלא היה כ] לה לבשר שעת היתר למזבח – לא זכו הכהנים בעורה. ולא פליג בין שהופשט קודם הפסול, בין לא הופשט. אלמא, אע"ג דאפשטיה לעור קודם זריקה, ונפסל הבשר ואח"כ זרק – קאמר דלא זכו בעורה. מני ר' אלעזר בר' שמעון היא. דאמר לקמן (דף קד.): אין הדם מרצה על עור חלוץ בפני עצמו בלא בשר. כגון אם נפסל הבשר ואין הדם מרצה עליו – אף העור לא יצא מידי מעילה להיות ניתר לכהנים אחר הפשטן. עורותיהן לכהנים. ואפילו אירע פסול זה קודם זריקה. אתאן לרבי. דפליג עליה דרבי אלעזר לקמן (שם), ואמר: הדם מרצה על עור חלוץ בפני עצמו בלא הרצאת בשר. ומודה רבי שאין הפשט קודם זריקה. אע"ג דאמר: הדם מרצה על העור בפני עצמו, היכא דאיתרמי דאיפשט קודם זריקה – מודה הוא שאין כא] כהנים רגילין בכך, שאסור לשהות הדם כל כך. הלכך כב] נמי דקתני: כל שלא זכה המזבח בבשרה לא זכו הכהנים בעורה, טעמא משום דפסול דקודם זריקה – קודם הפשט הוא. כג] ומיהו היכא דאיתרמי דהפשיט קודם זריקה ונפסל אחר הפשט, אע"פ שלא זכה מזבח בבשר – יזכו הכהנים בעורה. ומשנתינו דברה בהוה. קודם שנראו כד] להפשט. קודם זריקה אין עורותיהן לכהנים, ואפי' הופשט ואח"כ נפסל. וכל שכן כשהוא עם הבשר, דאין דם מרצה על העור בלא בשר. לאחר שנראו להפשט. דהיינו לאחר זריקה, עורותיהן לכהנים. ואפי' עורו עם הבשר כשנפסל, כדקאמר רבי אלעזר, דכיון שנזרק הדם והורצה בשר שעה אחת, יפשיטנו ועורו לכהנים. על העור בפני עצמו. אם הופשט ונפסל הבשר קודם זריקה, וזרק הדם – הותר העור. דקסבר רבי: אין עור פסול אלא הנפסל עם הבשר. אבל הופשט קודם פסולו, אפי' כה] קודם זריקה – אתיא זריקה ושריא ליה. וכל שכן כו] אחר הפשט ואחר זריקה. אבל אם קודם הפשט נפסל, ואפילו אחר זריקה – הרי הוא כבשר. רבי

ומודה רבי שאין הפשט קודם זריקה. משמע הכא דלכ"ע, היכא דנולד פסול קודם הפשט וקודם זריקה – אין הדם מרצה על העור. ותימה: דבסוף "הגוזל קמא" (ב"ק דף קיא.) כז] אמר גבי נתן אשם ליהויריב וכסף לידעיה, דאם קדמו בני יהויריב והקריבו את האשם – זכו במה שבידם. ופריך: למאי חזי? אשם פסול הוא! אמר רבא: לעורו. והשתא עורו גופיה הא לא חזי, דהיינו קודם הפשט וזריקה, דתחלת הבאתו בפסול! וי"ל: דהתם לאחר שחיטת האשם יכול להביא כסף קודם זריקה – קרינא ביה "מלבד איל הכפורים אשר יכפר בו", כיון דעדיין כח] לא נכפר, הלכך לא חשיב פסול דקודם זריקה. ומיהו קשה: כיון דאיכא הפסול כט] בידם, מה לי קודם זריקה ומה לי לאחר זריקה? *וי"ל: ל] דהוי כמו שנמצא טריפה בבני מעיים לרבי חנינא סגן הכהנים, הואיל ולא הוכר פסולו קודם הפשט לרבי, וקודם זריקה לרבי אלעזר – מרצה על העור. *(הג"ה) וקשה: דתניא בתוספתא דפסחים: הביא את אשמו קודם גזילו – לא יהא אחר ממרק בדמו עד שיביא גזילו, אלא תעובר צורתו ותצא לבית השריפה. אלמא אין תקנה להביא הגזל לא] קודם *שנשחט! ואין לומר היינו מדרבנן, לב] הא תניא בסיפא גבי מצורע (*לעיל) (*דף ה): הקדיש חטאתו לאשמו – לא יהא אחר ממרק בדמו, אלא תעובר צורתו ותצא לבית השריפה. ומהכא מוכח פ' קמא דמנחות (דף ה.) יש מחוסר זמן לבו ביום. ואע"ג דמן התורה פסול – צריך עבור צורה, כדתניא פרק "כילד צולין" (פסחים דף *ס): כל שפסולו בגופו – ישרף מיד, בדם ובבעלים – תעובר צורתו. ופסולו בגופו הוי כמו פיגול וטריפה ונבלה, אבל הקדמה לא. ברוך.

מאן

נ"א עולה ובאימורי קדשי קדשים נ"ק

ס"א דהא בהדיא

רש"ק מ"ז

[פסחים יח: וש"נ]

ראיט נ"ק

עדיות פ"ב משנה ב

[כתובות כג.]

לעיל פו.

[עי' תוס' לקמן קד. ד"ה א"ר עקיבא]

מנחות ה.

ויקרא ח

ויקרא ז

נ"א וי"ל מידי דהוי כמו נ"ק

נ"א ה"ג וכ"ל כיון דיכול להביא הכסף קודם זריקה הוי לא הוכר פסולו

ס"א שנמצא

[ליתא בס"י]

[נ"ל פב: וכן איתא שם לד:]

הגהות הב"ח

(א) רש"י ד"ה ה"ג וכו' ולותיב הכא קתני:

שיטה מקובצת

א] תיבות עור העולה נמחק: ב] אלא עור העולה: ג] דין שיזכו בעורן: ד] במקצת יזכו בכולן: ה] כל עצמנו לא: ו] עור הולך אחר: ז] הן נשרפין ועורותיהן עמהן: ח] לאכילה אבל יזכו: ט] בעורו. עיין שו"ת מהר"ם בנייר סי' ת"ח ובקלף סי' תע"ב: י] לא ראיתי ראיה: יא] כל עצמנו כו': יב] מפשיטין כו'. שהרי לא הזקיקו להפשיט ונותנן לכהן: יג] להביאו דהא בהדיא פרט לך הקטרה באברים המופשטין ולא פרט לך הכתוב העור עמה: יד] בבשר לאכול: טו] תיבת ראוי נמחק: טז] לאכילה היום: יז] לבית השריפה. משהופשט: יח] ביה פסול הס"ד: יט] אלא רישא דהך: כ] דלא היה לו לבשר: כא] שאין הכהנים רגילין: כב] הילכך מתניתין: כג] הוא דסתם זריקה קודם הפשט הוא ומיהו: כד] להפשט דהיינו קודם: כה] אפילו פסולו קודם: כו] וכל שכן אם אירע הפסול בבשר אחר הפשט ואחר זריקה דהוי עור לכהנים אבל אם קודם: כז] קמא אמרינן: כח] לא כיפר הילכך: כט] הפסול בדם מה לי: ל] וי"ל כגון שנמצא ותיבת דהוי כמו נמחק: לא] הגזל אחר שנשחט ותיבת קודם נמחק: לב] דהא תניא:

קודם

רבי אלעזר ברבי שמעון כו'. קסבר: בזריקה כשרה תליא היתר העור. אבל נפסל בשר קודם זריקה – אין העור מותר, ואפילו הופשט קודם פסולו. מ"ד. הדם מרצה על העור לאחר שנפסל בשר. כרבי אליעזר. דאמר: דם אע"פ שאין בשר. **אליבא דר' אליעזר כ"ע לא פליגי.** כלומר, מילתיה דרבי אלעזר ברבי שמעון דאמר לא הורצה – ודאי פלוגתא היא. דעל כרחך מודה הוא דאילו רבי אליעזר לא קאי כוותיה, דהא קאמר: יזרוק לכתחילה אף ע"פ שאין בשר, כגון אבד או נשרף, אלמא זריקה מעלייתא היא. **כי פליגי אליבא דרבי יהושע.** כלומר, הא דאמר דמ"ד הורצה – כר' אליעזר ולא כרבי יהושע – ליתא, דאפילו אליבא דרבי יהושע אמרה רבי למילתיה. ה"ג: **עד כאן לא א"ר יהושע אלא בבשר דליכא פסידא לכהנים.** ע"כ לא קאמר רבי יהושע אם אין בשר אין דם – אלא לזונן נעוות הרצון לבעלים לחובה. דליכא פסידא לכהנים, והתורה אמרה (דברים יב): "הבשר והדם". אבל לענין עור **דאיכא פסידא** דכהנים אפילו רבי יהושע מודה. דלא מפסידנא להו שלא כדין. ואם נשרף בשר או אבד קודם זריקה – לכתחילה לא יזרוק, וליכא פסידא דכהנים, שהרי לא קרב הקרבן. ואם עבר וזרק הדם – הויא זריקה להתיר העור. אע"פ שלא עלה לו הקרבן – הקרבה הוי, וקרינא ביה "עור העולה אשר הקריב". מידי דהוה יב] **אדיעבד.** דקתני: אם זרק הורצה. הניחא גבי נטמא – איכא למימר הציץ מרצה. אבל גבי יוצא – לא מרצה הציץ, וקאמר: אם זרק הורצה. אלמא יג] *ק"ל היה לו לרבי יהושע בדרשה זו ד"אם אין בשר אין דם", דאם זרק – הורצה. הלכך, גבי אבוד ושרוף נמי, אע"ג דבדיעבד נמי פסול, כדאמרינן ב"כילד צולין" (פסחים עח:), לענין עור מיהא מודה. **למצותן לא קאמר.** דהני הכשר מצותן בכך. וכי קאמר ר' חנינא – בנשרפין מחמת פסולן. **והאיכא** קודם הפשט וקודם זריקה. דבין לרבי בין לרבי אלעזר ברבי שמעון נשרף, לרבי – משום דקודם הפשט, ולרבי אלעזר – משום דקודם זריקה. **חלוץ קאמרי'.** מימי לא ראיתי עור מופשט יוצא לבית השריפה. והנפסל קודם הפשט – עורו נשרף בבשרו, ואין מפשיטים אותו **והאיכא אחר הפשט** קודם זריקה. דלרבי אלעזר ברבי שמעון יד] חלוץ ונשרף הוא.

[לעיל פה.] [דברים יב] [שם] [תוספתא דזבחים פ"ד] [לעיל סב:] [פסחים לד: עז:] [ס"א קל] [פסחים לד: עז:] [ועי' תוס' לעיל עח: סד"ה ובטריפה ותוס' בכורות לב: ד"ה פסק מתני' מני]

תורה אור

ומאי "אחר הפשט" — קודם א] שנראו להפשט, אחר שנראו להפשט. מאי רבי ומאי רבי אלעזר בר' שמעון? דתניא, רבי אומר: הדם מרצה על העור בפני עצמו. וכשהוא עם הבשר, נולד בו פסול, בין קודם זריקה בין לאחר זריקה — הרי הוא כיוצא בו. *רבי אלעזר בר"ש אומר: אין הדם מרצה על העור בפני עצמו. וכשהוא עם הבשר, נולד בו פסול קודם זריקה — הרי הוא כיוצא בו, אחר זריקה — הורצה בשר שעה אחת, יפשיטנו ועורו לכהנים. לימא בדרבי אליעזר ורבי יהושע קמיפלגי; ב] °"ועשית עולותיך הבשר והדם", *רבי יהושע אומר: אם אין דם — אין בשר, אם אין בשר — אין דם. רבי אליעזר אומר: דם אע"פ שאין בשר, שנאמר: °"ודם זבחיך ישפך". א"כ, מה ת"ל "ועשית ג] עולותיך הבשר והדם"? לומר לך: *מה דם בזריקה — אף בשר בזריקה. הא למדת, שריוח יש בין כבש למזבח. לימא מ"ד הורצה — כר"א, ומ"ד לא הורצה — כר' יהושע? אליבא דר"א כ"ע לא פליגי, כי פליגי — אליבא דרבי יהושע; מ"ד לא הורצה — כרבי יהושע. מ"ד הורצה — אמר לך: עד כאן לא קאמר רבי יהושע התם אלא בבשר, דליכא פסידא לכהנים, אבל עור, דאיכא פסידא לכהנים — אפילו רבי יהושע מודה, מידי דהוה ד] אדיעבד. *דתנן: *נטמא ה] בשר או נפסל, או שיצא חוץ לקלעים, ר"א אומר: יזרוק, רבי יהושע אומר: לא יזרוק. ומודה רבי יהושע שאם זרק — הורצה.§ "א"ר חנינא סגן הכהנים" כו'.§ ולא? הרי פרים הנשרפים ושעירים הנשרפים! למצותן לא קאמרינן. ו] הרי קודם הפשט וקודם זריקה! חלוץ קאמרינן. והאיכא אחר הפשט וקודם זריקה, ז] לרבי אלעזר ברבי שמעון, דאמר: אין הדם מרצה על העור בפני עצמו! ח] רבי חנינא כרבי סבירא ליה. ואיבעית אימא: אפילו ט] תוקמא כרבי אלעזר ברבי שמעון, מודה רבי שאין הפשט קודם זריקה. והאיכא נמצאת טריפה בבני מעיים! קסבר: נמצאת טריפה בבני מעיים — מרצה. דיקא נמי, דקתני א"ר עקיבא: מדבריו למדנו, שהמפשיט את הבכור ונמצא טריפה שיאותו הכהנים בעורו, ש"מ. ואלא מאי קמ"ל ר"ע? הא קמ"ל: י] אפילו בגבולין. א"ר חייא בר אבא א"ר יוחנן: הלכה כר"ע. ואף יא] ר"ע לא אמר אלא כשהתירו מומחה, אבל לא התירו מומחה — לא. והלכתא כדברי חכמים, (*בשר בקבורה, והעור בשריפה).§ **מתני'** פרים הנשרפים ושעירים הנשרפים, בזמן שהן נשרפין כמצותן — נשרפים בבית הדשן, ומטמאין בגדים. ואם אינן נשרפין כמצותן — נשרפין בבית הבירה, ואינן מטמאין בגדים.

היו

[דברים יב] [שם] [ע"ש ל"ג]

מאן דאמר לא הורצה כרבי יהושע. תימה: היכי מצי סבר כוותיה? הא קתני: ומודה רבי יהושע דאם זרק הורצה, כדבסמוך! ונראה לפרש: כח] ומ"ד לא הורצה כר' יהושע – דגזר נטמא בשר או נפסל דלא יזרוק, אטו אבוד ושרוף דליכא בשר כלל, דהתם אפילו בדיעבד לא הורצה. והכא נמי, אין הדם מרצה על העור בפני עצמו אפילו בדיעבד בנטמא, גזירה אטו אבוד ושרוף. ולא מיירי הכא באבוד ושרוף, אלא בנטמא או נפסל. ומ"ד הורצה – ע"כ לא קאמר רבי יהושע כט] דגזר אטו אבוד ושרוף, ולא יזרוק – אלא גבי בעלים, דליכא פסידא דכהנים, שעדיין לא זכו בעורו. אבל עור, דאיכא פסידא [דכהנים], דכבר זכו כהנים משנזרק הדם – התם לא גזרינן אטו אבוד ושרוף, מידי דהוה אדיעבד. פי': בפסול יוצא וטומאה, דדיעבד אם זרק הורצה, ולא גזרינן. הכא נמי מרצה הדם על העור דהוי ... דחוק. ***א"ר** עקיבא מדבריו למדנו כו'. משמע: דוקא בעורו יאותו הכהנים, אבל בבשרו – לא, דאפילו לגוים אסור. והקשה ה"ר אפרים: דבפרק "כל פסולי המוקדשים" (בכורות דף לג:) מתיר רבי עקיבא אפילו לגוים, ולעיל פי' בריש פ' *"התערובת" (דף עא:). אבל לא התירו מומחה – לא. משמע דוקא משום טריפות, הא לאו הכי – לא. והיינו דלא כר"מ, דקנים בפ' (*"כל פסולי המוקדשין" (דף לג)) ל] בבכור שנשחט שלא על פי מומחה. מכאן דקדק בהלכות גדולות, דהא דקיימא לן *כרבי מאיר בגזירותיו – דוקא בגזירותיו ולא בקנסיו*.

לא

[שייך לעיל במשנה קג:] גירסת הל"ק התערובת הס"ד ואח"כ מה"ד אבל לא התירו [נ"ל עד כמה בכורות דף כח.] [עירובין מז.] [וע"ע תוספות יבמות לו. ד"ה מי כו' ובב"ק לו: ד"ה וחכמים וב"מ עב. ד"ה קונסין וב"ב לז: ד"ה וחכמים ובכורות כח. ד"ה ר"מ כו']

ומשני: רבי חנינא כרבי ס"ל. דאמר: הדם מרצה על העור. ה"ג: ואב"א אפילו תימא כר' אלעזר בר"ש ומודה רבי שאין הפשט קודם זריקה. אפילו תימא רבי חנינא כרבי אלעזר ס"ל. ודקא קשיא לך: הא איכא אירע בו טו] אחר הפשט קודם זריקה – לא איתרמי בימיו. דאפילו לרבי דאמר: הדם מרצה על העור בפני עצמו – מודה הוא דאין הפשט קודם זריקה טז] (ולא הורגלו בכך), וכל שכן לרבי אלעזר ברבי שמעון לא הורגלו בכך. והאיכא נמצאת טריפה בבני מעיים. יז] לא נמצא פסולו עד שהופשט. ופסול זה קודם זריקה וקודם הפשט היה בו! דקס"ד דבין לרבי ובין לרבי אלעזר נשרף, כדאמרן, לרבי – משום דקודם הפשט, ולרבי אלעזר – משום קודם זריקה. מרצה. הואיל ולא הוכר פסולו, קודם הפשט לרבי, וקודם זריקה לרבי אלעזר – מרצה על העור. והבשר ישרף כשאר פסולי קדשים. אלא מאי קמ"ל רבי עקיבא. כיון דשמעיה לרבי חנינא דאמר בשאר קדשים מרצה – למה לי לאשמועינן יח] בכור? דאפילו בגבולין. בכור בעל מום הנשחט יט] בו במדינה על מומו. ולא התירו הכתוב אלא באכילה, כדכתיב (דברים טו): "בשעריך תאכלנו", אבל אם מת – עורו אסור, וטעון קבורה. ואשמועינן רבי עקיבא דהיכא דלא ניכר כ] טריפתו עד לאחר הפשט, *שראה שחיטתו *) והפשיט עורו – כאילו נזרק דמו במקדש ונמצא טריפה לאחר הפשט. בשר בקבורה. כא] דאין מאכילין קדשים לכלבים. ושריפה ליכא, דאין שריפה בקדשים אלא כב] כשהובאה לעזרה ונפסל לאחר שחיטה. והעור בשריפה. לא ידענא טעמא. ונראה בעיני דל"ג כג] האי פירושא. *אלא ה"ג: והלכה כדברי חכמים, ותו לא מידי. כד] ותוספתא זו גירסא דתלמידי כה] **) תרביצאי היא, וטעו במה ששנינו במשנתינו במילתייהו דרבנן כו] לבית השריפה (א) יצא. ואני אומר: דרבנן לאו אדר"ע קיימי דאיירי בבכור בגבולין, אלא אדרבי חנינא קיימי, דאיירי בקדשי המקדש. **מתני'** נשרפין בבית הדשן. חוץ לג' מחנות, כדיליף לקמן בפירקין. ומטמאין בגדים. כז] לעסוקין בהן, כדכתיב (ויקרא טז): "והשורף אותם" וגו'. שלא במצותן. שנפסלו, טעונין שריפה כשאר פסולי קדשים. בבית הבירה. פעמים בעזרה פעמים בהר הבית, כדאמרינן בגמרא.

היו

[ס"א שרייה] [אבל הרמב"ם גרס לה ומוקי לה בבכור תם ועיין בר"ע ברטנורא ובכ"מ שם פ"ג מהלכות בכורות הלכה י וע' רש"ק ונ"ק]

*) נ"ל והפשטת עורו נ"ק **) פי' בית המדרש [ועיין רש"י במנחות פב:]

הגהות הב"ח

(א) רש"י ד"ה והעור כו' לבית השריפה ואני כצ"ל ותיבת יצא נמחק:

מט א ב ג מיי' פ"א מהלכות פסה"מ הלכה לא:
נ ד ה מיי' פ"ג מהלכות בכורות הלכה י וע"ש בכ"מ:
נא ו מיי' פ"ז מהלכות מעה"ק הלכה ד:
נב ז מיי' פ"ז מהלכות מעה"ק הלכה ד:
נג ח מיי' פ"ז מהלכות מעה"ק הלכה ד ופ"ה מהלכות פרה הלכה ד:

שיטה מקובצת

א] קודם שיראו להפשט: ב] קמיפלגי דתניא ועשית: ג] עולותיך עיין לעיל דף ס"ב ע"ב: ד] דהוה איוצא ותיבת אדיעבד נמחק: ה] נטמא הבשר או שנפסל או: ו] קאמרינן והאיכא קודם ותיבת הרי נמחק: ז] זריקה כר"א בר"ש: ח] עצמו כרבי דאמר הדם מרצה על העור בפני עצמו ותיבות רבי חנינא כרבי ס"ל ל"ש: ט] אפילו תימא כר"א ותיבת תוקמא נמחק: י] קמ"ל דאפי' בגבולין: יא] ואף רבי עקיבא עיין בתוס' בכורות (דף ל"ג ע"ב): יב] דהוה איוצא דקתני גבי יוצא אם זרק הורצה ותיבת אדיעבד נמחק: יג] קל היה: יד] שמעון נשרף וחלוץ הוא הס"ד: טו] בו פסול אחר: טז] תיבות ולא הורגלו בכך ל"ש ונמחק: יז] מעים דלא נמצא פסולו כו' בו וקס"ד דבין: יח] לאשמועינן בבכור הס"ד: יט] תיבת בו נמחק: כ] ניכר טריפותו עד לאחר הפשט שרייה שחיטתו והפשיט לעורו כאילו: כא] בקבורה כדין קדשים בחוץ דאין: כב] אלא כשהובאו: כג] דל"ג להאי פירושא: כד] מידי ותוספת זו אות א' נמחק: כה] דתלמידי דתרביצאי: כו] דרבנן יצא לבית השריפה ואני: כז] בגדים לעוסקים בהן: כח] לפרש מ"ד לא: כט] יהושע גזירה אטו אבוד: ל] המוקדשין בבכור אות ב' נמחק:

נד א מיי' פ"ה מהלכות פרה אדומה הלכה ה:

נ"א טבול יום פסלה נמי לינה כו'

נה ב מיי' פ"ז מהלכות מעשה הקרבנות הלכה ג:

נ"א פרים הנשרפים נהי דלינה פסלה בהו למאי מחשבה לא פסלה בהו וא"ת כו' נ"ק

נו ג מיי' שם הלכה ד:

נז ד מיי' פי"ט מהלכות פסה"מ הלכה ג ולחומרא:

נח ה מיי' שם פי"ד הלכה ח:

נט ו ז מיי' פ"ב מהלכות מעילה הלכה ד:

ס ח ט מיי' פי"ט מהלכות פסה"מ הלכה ג:

תורה אור

א היו *סובלין א] אותו במוטות. (א) יצאו הראשונים חוץ לחומת העזרה והאחרונים לא יצאו — הראשונים מטמאין בגדים, והאחרונים אינן מטמאין בגדים עד שיצאו. יצאו — אלו ב] ואלו מטמאין בגדים. *רבי שמעון אומר: ג] אינן מטמאין עד שיוצת האור ברובן. ניתך הבשר — אין השורף מטמא בגדים.§ גמ' *מאי "בירה"? אמר רבה בר בר חנה אמר רבי יוחנן: מקום יש בהר הבית, ובירה שמו. ור"ל אמר: כל הבית כולו קרוי בירה, שנאמר: °"(ואל) הבירה אשר הכינותי". אמר רב נחמן אמר רבה בר אבוה, ד] שלשה ב בית הדשנין הן: בית הדשן גדול היה בעזרה, ששם שורפין פסולי קדשי קדשים, ואימורי קדשים קלים, ופרים הנשרפין ושעירים הנשרפין שאירע בהן פסול קודם זריקה. ג ובית הדשן אחר היה בהר הבית, ששם שורפין פרים הנשרפים ושעירים הנשרפים שאירע בהן פסול אחר זריקה. ה] וכמצותן — חוץ לשלש מחנות. תני לוי: שלשה בית הדשנין הן: בית הדשן גדול היה בעזרה, ששם שורפין פסולי קדשי קדשים ואימורי קדשים קלים, ופרים הנשרפים ושעירים הנשרפים שאירע בהן פסול, בין קודם זריקה בין לאחר זריקה. ובית הדשן אחר היה בהר הבית, ששם שורפין פרים הנשרפין ושעירים הנשרפין שאירע בהן פסול ביציאתן. ו] וכמצותן — חוץ לשלש מחנות. בעי רבי ז] ירמיה: ד לינה מהו שתועיל בפרים הנשרפים ובשעירים הנשרפים? מי אמרינן: כי מהניא לינה — בבשר דבר אכילה, אבל הני דלאו בני אכילה נינהו — לא. או דלמא לא שנא? אמר רבא: הא מילתא איבעיא ליה לאביי, ופשטנא ליה מהא: ה ושוין *שאם חישב באכילת פרים ובשריפתן — שלא עשה כלום. מאי לאו, מדמחשבה לא פסלה, לינה נמי לא פסלה? ח] ודלמא מחשבה הוא דלא פסלה, אבל לינה פסלה! תא שמע: * ו פרים הנשרפים ושעירים הנשרפין מועלין בהן משהוקדשו. נשחטו — הוכשרו ליפסל בטבול יום ובמחוסר כיפורים ובלינה. מאי לאו לינת בשר? לא, לינת אימורין. והא מדקתני סיפא: ז כולן מועלין בהן בבית הדשן עד שיותך הבשר; מדסיפא בשר — רישא נמי בשר! מידי איריא? סיפא בשר רישא אימורין. תא שמע, דתני לוי: שאירע בהן פסול ביציאתן. מאי לאו ט] לינה? °לא, פסול טומאה ופסול יציאה. בעי ר"א: °יציאה ח מהו שתועיל בפרים הנשרפים ושעירים הנשרפים? מאי קמיבעיא ליה? א"ר ירמיה בר אבא: (ג) י] אליבא דמ"ד *עדיין לא הגיע זמנו לצאת; מי אמרינן: ה"מ — בשר דאין סופו לצאת יא] חובה, אבל הני דסופן לצאת חובה — לא. או דלמא ה"נ לא הגיע זמנו לצאת? ת"ש, דתני לוי: שאירע יב] בו פסול ביציאתו. מאי לאו פסול יציאה? לא, פסול טומאה ופסול לינה. בעי רבי אלעזר: פרים הנשרפים ושעירים הנשרפים* יג] שיצא רובו במיעוט אבר, מהו? הך מיעוטא דאבר בתר רובא שדינן ליה — והא לא נפקא ליה, או דלמא בתר רובא דבהמה שדינן? פשיטא, דלא שבקינן רובא דבהמה ואזלינן בתר רובא יד] דאברים! אלא, ט שיצא חציו ברוב אבר; האי מיעוטא דאבר בתר

[לעיל לה.]

[לעיל פט:]

לא מחשבה הוא דלא פסלה אבל לינה פסלה. תימה: דבריש "הוליאו לו" (יומא דף מח.) בעי רב פפא: חישב בחפינת קטרת מהו? ת"ש, הוסיף רבי עקיבא הקומץ והקטרת כו'. מדפסיל *טבול יום – פסולה נמי מלינה, ומדפסלה לינה – פסלה נמי מחשבה, ולא דמי כדהכא! וי"ל: דהתם דבאכילת מזבח, מה לי מחשבה מה לי לינה. אבל הכא בבשר *פרים הנשרפין. וא"ת: היכי פסלה מחשבה בקטרת? הא תנן לעיל בפרק "ב"ש" (דף מג:) דקטרת ולבונה אין בהן משום פיגול! וי"ל: דנהי דכרת ליכא, מחשבה מיהא פסלה. מידי דהוה אחטאות הפנימיות לרבי שמעון, דאמר בפ"ק (לעיל יד.): מודה היה רבי שמעון לפסול מק"ו משלא לשמו. ובקטרת נמי אהני ג"ש ד"מלא" "מלא" ממנחה. והתם הקשה בקונטרס: אמאי הוצרך לדקדק מטבול יום? הוה ליה לאתויי ממתני' דמעילה (דף י.) דקתני בהדיא: הוכשרו ליפסל בטבול יום ובמחוסר כיפורים ובלינה! ותירץ רבינו יב"א: משום דההיא מיירי בקטרת דכל השנה, כדקתני: קדשו בכלי, וההוא דמיקדש בכלי – פסלה ביה לינה. אבל התם – בקטרת דיום הכיפורים, דעיקרה אינה בכלי אלא משום דלא אפשר, כדאמר התם לעיל לג] *והא אמרי' דלא מיפסלה בלינה. אבל ההיא דרבי עקיבא משמע דמיירי בכל קטרת. ועוד י"ל: דההיא דמעילה איכא לדחויי – מדרבנן. *וכן מחייבין עליה משום פיגול וטמא – הוה אמינא מכת מרדות. כמו *אכל אוכלין טמאין ושתה משקין טמאין ושתה רביעית יין ונכנס למקדש ושהה כדי אכילת פרס חייב – דהיינו מדרבנן, דפסול לד] גויה [הוי דרבנן], כדאמרינן בפרק בתרא דיומא (דף פ:). אבל ההיא דר' עיקבא פשיטא דאורייתא, מדפסל טבול יום ע"י צירוף, דאי מדרבנן – *לא הוה מחמירין נמי האי פסול על ידי צירוף. וא"ת: והיכי דייק מדפסיל טבול יום פסלה נמי לינה? והא משניתנה במכתשת נפסלת בטבול יום, ולינה לא פסלה עד שנתנן במחתה, כדאמר פרק קמא דשבועות (דף יא.)! וי"ל: דהא דנפסלת בטבול יום – *היינו מדרבנן.

לה] שיצא רובו במיעוט אבר. פי' בקונטרס: דמיבעיא ליה לענין טמא המתעסק בהן. וקשה: דבסוף "כילד צולין" (פסחים פה:) אמרינן: המוליא בשר פסח מחבורה לחבורה – אינו חייב עד שינית, הוצאה כתיב ביה כשבת. ופריך ממתני' דהכא, דהיו סובלין אותו במוטות, דקתני: ראשונים מטמאין בגדים אחרונים אין מטמאין בגדים עד שילאו, ואף על גב דלא נח. ומשני: בנגררים. ואם כן רובו במיעוט אבר דהכא – לא מחייב לענין שבת, כיון דאגודו בפנים לא יטמא בגדים! ונראה לפרש דמבעיא ליה לענין לשורפו בפנים.

או

נ"ל והוי

נ"א וכן הא דקתני סיפא וחייבין עליה כו' נ"ק

[כריתות יב:]

נ"ל לא הוי מחמרינן כולי האי לאיטמא ע"י צירוף כו' נ"ק

[פי' ההיא דשבועות למכתשת ועי' בתוספות יומא מח. ד"ה מדפסיל כיתר ביאור]

היו סובלין טו] אותו. הנשרפין כמלותן, במוטות. לקמן יליף לה טז]. הראשונים. בני אדם הנושאין במוט, אותן שבראש האחד יולאים ראשונים. עד שיצאו. האחרונים. בגמרא יליף לה. ניתך הבשר. יז] דגמרה שריפתן, אין המסייע שוב בהן מטמא בגדים. אבל מקמי הכי – כל המסייעין בשעת שריפה מטמאין בגדים. וכולה יליף יח] בגמרא. גמ' ששם שורפים פסולי בשר קדשי קדשים. שמחילת אכילתן בעזרה. ופסולי אימורים – אפילו של קדשים קלים, דהואיל והקטרת הכשירן בעזרה – אף שריפת פסוליהן בעזרה, כדילפינן בפסחים בפרק "כל שעה" (דף כד.) מ"בקדש באש תשרף". קודם זריקה. שלא הגיע יט] זמנו לצאת, לפיכך נשרפין בעזרה. אחר זריקה. שהגיע כ] זמנו לצאת, לפיכך נשרפין חוץ לעזרה. כא] וכמצותן. וכשהן נשרפין כמלותן, שלא אירע בהן שום פסול. נשרפין חוץ לג' מחנות. כדילפינן בפירקין. בין לאחר זריקה. הואיל ועדיין לא יצאו. ביציאתן. לאחר שיצאו. מהו שתועיל. לפוסלן אם לנו. בבשר דבר אכילה. כב] עולה או אימורין, שהן *לאכילת מזבח. (ג) כג] אבל הני דלשריפה קיימי, דלא אשכחן לה אלא או באכילת מזבח כדכתיב (שמות כג): "לא ילין חלב חגי" וגו'. או באכילת אדם כדכתיב (שם יב): "לא תותירו" וגו'. ושוין שאם חישב כו'. ושוין ר"ש וחכמי' שנחלקו בפ' "ב"ש" כד] (לעיל מג.) אם פיגול נוהג בחטאות הפנימיות, (ד) שאם חישב לאכול מבשר הפרים למחר, או אם חישב בשחיטה על מנת לשורפן חוץ לג' מחנות למחר – לא עשה כלום, דמחשבת אכילה בדבר שדרכו לאכול בעינן, והני לאו דרכן לאכול. וגבי שריפה נמי, אע"ג דכי אורחיה חשיב, אכילת מזבח או אכילת אדם בעינן לפגל. ומ"ד פיגול נוהג בפנימיים, כגון אם חישב על הקטרת אימורים כה] להקריבו למחר. לינה נמי לא פסלה. כו] בבשרו. (ה) קס"ד דאי לינה פסלה – מחשבת לינה נמי פסלה. לינת אימורין. דבמידי דהקטרה ודאי פסלה לינה. עד שיותך הבשר. דכל זמן שלא נעשית מלותן מועלין בהן. מדסיפא. לענין מעילה, בבשר איירי. רישא נמי. לענין לינה, כז] לענין בשר קאמר. דתני לוי. במתניתא דלעיל. ופסול יציאה. כגון שילאו לפני זריקת דמים, שעדיין לא הגיע זמנן ללאת כח]. יציאה מהו שתועיל. לפוסלן, אם ילאו מן העזרה לפני זריקת דמים. מאי קמיבעיא ליה. אמאי תיפסול? הרי סופן ללאת. א"ר ירמיה בר אבא. כי קא מיבעיא ליה אליבא דמאן דפסיל בשר קדשים קלים שילא לפני זריקת דמים, משום דעדיין לא הגיע זמנו ללאת, בפרק "כל התדיר" (לעיל פט:). הכא מאי? מי אמרינן: הני מילי בבשר קדשים קלים, דאין סופן חובה ללאת, אבל הני שסופן כט] ללאת חובה – לא מיפסלי ביליאתן. לא פסול טומאה ולינה. דקאי הכא ומדחי ליה, קאי הכא ומדחי ליה. ל] שיצא רובו. ומיעוט אחד מן האברים משלים לרובא של בהמה ליליאתה. מהו. מי הוי יליאה לא] לטמא את המתעסקין בהולאת רובן, או לב] לא הוי יליאה? מי אמרינן: שדי מיעוטא דאבר בתר

פסחים פה.

יומא סז: תוספתא פ"ג

יומא ב:

נ"א לאכילת מזבח או בשר קדשי קדשים שהם אכילת אדם אבל הני כו' דלא אשכחן לינה אלא כו' נ"ק

מעילה ט. לעיל לה:

חולין ס.

הגהות הב"ח

(א) במשנה במוטות הראשוני' ילאו חוץ לחומת: (ב) גמ' אמר רבי ירמיה בר אבא כי קמיבעיא ליה אליבא דמ"ד: (ג) רש"י ד"ה בבשר דבר וכו' לאכילת מזבח או בשר קדשי קדשים שהן אכילת אדם הס"ד ואח"כ מ"ה אבל הני דלשריפה קיימא לא דלא אשכחן להו לפסול בלינה אלא או: (ד) ד"ה ושוין וכו' הפנימיות שוין שאם חישב וכו' על הקטרת אימורין נ"ב דהוא אכילת מזבח: (ה) ד"ה לינה וכו' דקס"ד:

גליון הש"ס

גמ' לא פסול טומאה ופסול יליאה. הא דנקיט פסול יליאה דלמ"ד טומאה הותרה בליבור ל"ש טומאה. וק"ל דאיך נפרש מה דאמר לוי נפסל אחר זריקה שריפתו בעזרה מה פסול משכחת לה אם אין בו פסול לינה ולא נשאר רק פסול יולא וממילא הוי נפסל ביליאתו דשריפתו בבירה: שם יליאה מהו שתועיל בפרים. עיין בירושלמי פרק ו דיומא הלכה ו:

שיטה מקובצת

א] סובלין אותן: ב] אלו. אלו ואלו: ג] אומר אלו ואלו אינן מטמאין עד שיצת: ד] אבוה אמר רב שלשה בית הדשנין היו בית הדשן: ה] ובמצותן חוץ: ו] ביציאתן ובמצותן: ז] רבי אלעזר לינה ותיבת ירמיה נמחק: ח] פסלה. לא מחשבה ותיבת דלמא נמחק: ט] לאו פסול: י] אבא כי קא מיבעיא ליה אליבא: יא] תיבות חובה חובה ל"ש: יב] שאירע בהן פסול ביציאתן: יג] הנשרפין שיצאו רובן במיעוט: יד] רובא דאבר אלא: טו] סובלין אותן את הנשרפין: טז] לה להוציאן לבית השריפה: יז] דגמרה שריפתן:

יח] יליף לה בגמרא: יט] שלא הגיע זמנן: כ] שהגיע זמנן: כא] מה"ד ובמצותן: כב] אכילה כגון בשר עולה: כג] מזבח או בשר קדש קדשים שהן לאכילת אדם אבל הני דלשרפה קיימי לא אשכחן לה: כד] ב"ש בפיגול אם נוהג בחטאות הפנימיות: כה] אימורים להקטירו ותיבת להקריבו נמחק: כו] פסלה בבשר דקס"ד דאי לינה: כז] לינה בבשר קאמר ותיבת לענין נמחק: כח] לצאת ואחר זמנו לא פסלה: כט] שסופן חובה לצאת: ל] מה"ד שיצא רובו במיעוט אבר מיעוט אחד: לא] לטמא ס"א אם נטמא שורפו בהר הבית כדתני לוי: לב] או לאו יציאה היא דאמרינן שדי מיעוטא דאבר: לג] לעיל לא בשאר פסולים מיירי ולא בפסול יוצא: לד] גזירה מדרבנן כדאמרינן: לה] שיצאו רובן במיעוט:

תורה אור

בָּתַר רוֹב אֵבֶר שָׁדֵינַן לֵיהּ, וְהָא נְפַק לֵיהּ, אוֹ דִּלְמָא בָּתַר בְּהֵמָה שָׁדֵינַן לֵיהּ? תֵּיקוּ. רַבָּה בַּר רַב הוּנָא מַתְנֵי לָהּ בְּגַבְרֵי, בְּמִתְעַסְּקִין בּוֹ חֲמִשָּׁה בְּנֵי אָדָם, וּנְפַקוּ תְּלָתָא וּפָשׁוּ לְהוּ תְּרֵי, מַאי? בָּתַר רוֹב מִתְעַסְּקִין אָזְלִינַן, אוֹ א] בָּתַר בְּהֵמָה אָזְלִינַן? תֵּיקוּ. בָּעֵי רַבִּי אֶלְעָזָר: פָּרִים ב] וּשְׂעִירִים הַנִּשְׂרָפִים שֶׁיָּצְאוּ וְחָזְרוּ, מַהוּ? מִי אָמְרִינַן: כֵּיוָן דִּנְפַקִי ג] לְהוּ – אִיטַּמּוּ לְהוּ, אוֹ דִּלְמָא כֵּיוָן דַּהֲדוּר – הֲדוּר? אָמַר ר' אַבָּא בַּר מָמָל: ת"ש, הָיוּ סוֹבְלִין אוֹתָן בְּמוֹטוֹת, ד] הָרִאשׁוֹנִים יָצְאוּ חוּץ לְחוֹמַת הָעֲזָרָה וְהָאַחֲרוֹנִים לֹא יָצְאוּ – הָרִאשׁוֹנִים שֶׁיָּצְאוּ חוּץ לְחוֹמַת הָעֲזָרָה מְטַמְּאִין בְּגָדִים, וְהָאַחֲרוֹנִים ה] אֵין מְטַמְּאִין בְּגָדִים עַד שֶׁיֵּצְאוּ. וְאִי ס"ד כֵּיוָן דִּנְפַקִי לְהוּ אִיטַּמּוּ – הָנָךְ דְּאִיכָּא גַּוָּאֵי (א) לִיטַּמֵּא! אָמַר רָבִינָא: וְתִסְבְּרָא, הָא בָּעֵינָא "וְאַחַר יָבֹא אֶל הַמַּחֲנֶה" (ויקרא טז), וְלֵיכָּא! אֶלָּא רַבִּי אֶלְעָזָר הֵיכִי בָּעֵי לָהּ? כְּגוֹן דִּנְקִיטִי לָהּ בְּבַקּוּלְסֵי. *ת"ר: ו] *פָּרִים וּפָרָה *וְשָׂעִיר הַמִּשְׁתַּלֵּחַ – הַמְשַׁלֵּחַ הַשּׂוֹרְפָן וְהַמּוֹצִיאָן מְטַמֵּא בְּגָדִים, וְהֵן עַצְמָן ז] אֵין מְטַמְּאִין בְּגָדִים, אֲבָל מְטַמְּאִין אוֹכָלִין וּמַשְׁקִין, דִּבְרֵי ר"מ. וַחכ"א: פָּרָה וּפָרִים – מְטַמְּאִין אוֹכָלִין וּמַשְׁקִין, שָׂעִיר הַמִּשְׁתַּלֵּחַ – אֵינוֹ מְטַמֵּא, ח] שֶׁהוּא חַי, וְהַחַי אֵינוֹ מְטַמֵּא אוֹכָלִין וּמַשְׁקִין. בִּשְׁלָמָא לְרַבִּי מֵאִיר – כִּדְתָנָא ט] דְּבֵי ר' יִשְׁמָעֵאל, *דְּתָנָא דְּבֵי רַבִּי יִשְׁמָעֵאל: "עַל כָּל זֶרַע זֵרוּעַ" (שם יא), מַה זְּרָעִים שֶׁאֵין סוֹפָן לִיטַּמֵּא טוּמְאָה חֲמוּרָה י] וּצְרִיכִין הֶכְשֵׁר – אַף כָּל שֶׁאֵין סוֹפָן לִיטַּמֵּא טוּמְאָה חֲמוּרָה צְרִיכִין הֶכְשֵׁר. יָצְתָה נִבְלַת הָעוֹף טָהוֹר, שֶׁסּוֹפָהּ לִיטַּמֵּא טוּמְאָה חֲמוּרָה, *וְאֵין צְרִיכָה הֶכְשֵׁר. אֶלָּא לְרַבָּנַן, אִי אִית לְהוּ דְּתָנָא דְּבֵי רַבִּי יִשְׁמָעֵאל – אֲפִילּוּ שָׂעִיר הַמִּשְׁתַּלֵּחַ, (ב) יא] אִי לֵית לֵיהּ – אֲפִי' פָּרָה וּפָרִים מְנָלַן? כִּי אֲתָא רַב דִּימִי אֲמַר, אָמְרִי בְּמַעֲרָבָא: צְרִיכִין הֶכְשֵׁר טוּמְאָה מִמָּקוֹם אַחֵר. בָּעֵי רַבִּי אֶלְעָזָר: פָּרִים יב] וּשְׂעִירִים הַנִּשְׂרָפִים, מַהוּ שֶׁיְּטַמְּאוּ אוֹכָלִין וּמַשְׁקִין בִּפְנִים כְּבַחוּץ? מְחוּסַּר יְצִיאָה כִּמְחוּסַּר מַעֲשֶׂה דָּמֵי, אוֹ לָא? בָּתַר דְּבַעְיָא הֲדַר פַּשְׁטַהּ: מְחוּסַּר יְצִיאָה כִּמְחוּסַּר מַעֲשֶׂה דָּמֵי. בְּעָא מִינֵּיהּ רַבִּי אַבָּא בַּר יג] שְׁמוּאֵל מֵרַבִּי חִיָּיא בַּר אַבָּא: נִבְלַת עוֹף טָהוֹר לְר' מֵאִיר, מַהוּ יד] שֶׁיְּטַמֵּא בִּכְזַיִת? דְּמַחְתָּא לְאַרְעָא – לָא תִּיבָּעֵי לָךְ, דְּנָקִיט בְּפוּמֵּיהּ – לָא תִּיבָּעֵי לָךְ. כִּי תִּיבָּעֵי לָךְ – דְּנָקִיט לֵיהּ בִּידֵיהּ; מְחוּסַּר קְרִיבָה כִּמְחוּסַּר מַעֲשֶׂה דָּמֵי, אוֹ לָא? טו] (בָּתַר דְּבַעְיָא הֲדַר פַּשְׁטַהּ:)
מְחוּסַּר

בָּתַר רוֹב הָאֵבֶר, וַהֲוָה לֵיהּ כְּמַאן דְּלָא נְפַק, וְאֵין כָּאן רוֹב הַבְּהֵמָה לַחוּץ. וּלְעִנְיַן טוּמְאַת בְּגָדִים מִחוּץ לַמַּחֲנֶה בָּעֵי טז] (*הַאי מִיעוּטָא דְּאֵבֶר שֶׁיָּצָא לַחוּץ). אֶלָּא שֶׁיָּצָא חֶצְיוֹ. שֶׁל פָּר, כְּרוֹב אֵבֶר* בַּחֲצִי הַפָּר יז] (הג"ה), יָצָא רוֹב אֶחָד מִן הָאֵבָרִים וּמִיעוּטוֹ בַּחֲצִי הַפָּר שֶׁבִּפְנִים, הַאי מִיעוּטָא דְּאֵבֶר שֶׁנִּשְׁאַר בִּפְנִים בָּתַר רוּבָּא דְּאֵבֶר שֶׁיָּצָא שָׁדֵינַן לֵיהּ, וַהֲוָה לֵיהּ כְּמַאן דִּנְפַק, וְאִשְׁתַּכַּח רוֹב בְּהֵמָה מִבַּחוּץ. אוֹ דִּלְמָא בָּתַר בְּהֵמָה. דְּמִיחַבַּר בָּהּ, וְהֵיכָא דְּאִיתָא שָׁדֵינַן לָהּ. (ג) וְאע"ג דְּלָאו רוּבָּא דִּבְהֵמָה יח] הִיא אֶלָּא פַּלְגָא, וְלֵיכָּא לְמֵימַר כִּדְאָמְרַן לְעֵיל יט] *"שָׁבְקִינַן רוּבָּא דִּבְהֵמָה", (ד) אֲפִילּוּ הָכִי, כֵּיוָן דְּאֵין הָאֵבֶר נָתוּק – לָא אָזְלִינַן בֵּיהּ בָּתַר רוּבָּא, וְלָא הָוְיָא יְצִיאָה, וְאִם נִטְמָא הַפָּר – שׂוֹרְפוֹ בִּפְנִים. מַתְנֵי לָהּ. לְהַךְ בַּעְיָא, בְּרוּבָּא דִּמְנְיָינָא דְּגַבְרֵי. שֶׁיָּצְאוּ וְחָזְרוּ מַהוּ. קס"ד: לְעִנְיַן טוּמְאַת בְּגָדִים שֶׁל אֵלּוּ שֶׁהוֹצִיאוּם קָמִיבַּעְיָא לֵיהּ. אִיטַּמּוּ לְהוּ. בִּגְדֵיהֶם. כֵּיוָן דַּהֲדוּר הֲדוּר. וְהָווּ לְהוּ כְּמִי שֶׁלֹּא יָצְאוּ. הָנָךְ דְּאִיכָּא גַּוָּאֵי נַמִּי נִטְמְאוּ. דְּהָא יְצִיאָה לְעִנְיַן טוּמְאַת בְּגָדִים בְּפָרִים כְּתִיבָא: "יוֹצִיא אֶל מִחוּץ לַמַּחֲנֶה וְשָׂרְפוּ" וגו', וּמִינֵּיהּ יָלְפִינַן לְקַמָּן בְּפִירְקִין (דף קה:), לוֹמַר לָךְ: כֵּיוָן שֶׁיָּצָא הַפָּר חוּץ לְמַחֲנֶה אַחַת – מְטַמֵּא בְּגָדִים, אע"פ דְּלָא נְפוּק גַּבְרֵי נִטְמְאוּ! אֶלָּא לָאו מִשּׁוּם דְּאָמַר דְּאִי הֲדַר – הֲדוּר, וְכָל שֶׁכֵּן אֵלּוּ שֶׁמּוּחְזָרִים וְעוֹמְדִין, שֶׁהֲרֵי לֹא יָצְאוּ. אָמַר רָבָא וְתִסְבְּרָא. דְּהַךְ כ] דְּקַמַּיְיתֵי רְאָיָה מִילְּתָא הִיא? הָא בָּעֵינַן וְאַחַר יָבֹא אֶל הַמַּחֲנֶה. אַלְמָא קְרָא בִּדְנָפֵיק לִבְרָאֵי קָאֵי, דְּכָל כַּמָּה דְּלָא נָפֵק – לָא קָרֵינָא בֵּיהּ "וְאַחַר יָבֹא". וְכֵיוָן דְּלָא קָרֵינָא בֵּיהּ "וְאַחַר יָבֹא" – לָא קָרֵינָא בֵּיהּ "יְכַבֵּס בְּגָדָיו". וּפָרְכִינַן: אֶלָּא ר' אֶלְעָזָר הֵיכִי בָּעֵי לָהּ. דְּכֵיוָן דִּבְהָכִי תַּלְיָא מִילְּתָא, מִכִּי נָפֵק קָרֵינָא בֵּיהּ "יְכַבֵּס בְּגָדָיו". וְאִי אַהַדְרִינְהוּ וְאָתוּ אַחֲרִינֵי לְאַפּוּקִינְהוּ, אֲפִי' הַשְׁתָּא לְהוּ מוֹצִיאִין – לָא מִטַּמְּאוּ הָנָךְ בַּתְרָאֵי עַד דְּנָפְקִי, דְּהָא לָא קָרֵינָא בְּהוּ "וְאַחַר יָבֹא"! דִּנְקִיטִי לָהּ בְּבַקּוּלְסֵי. שֶׁאֲחוּזִים בְּמַקְלוֹת, וְעוֹמְדִין מִבַּחוּץ לְהוֹצִיאָם לְאַחַר שֶׁחָזְרוּ. וְקָמִיבַּעְיָא לֵיהּ: מִי אָמְרִינַן כֵּיוָן שֶׁיָּצְאוּ חוּץ לָעֲזָרָה, כָּל הָעֲסוּקִים בָּהֶן מִכָּאן וְאֵילָךְ חוּץ לָעֲזָרָה מְטַמְּאִין בְּגָדִים, אוֹ דִּלְמָא כֵּיוָן דַּהֲדוּר – הֲדוּר, וְעַד דְּנָפְקִי לָא מִטַּמְּאוּ. בַּקּוּלְסֵי בִּלְשׁוֹן הַתַּלְמוּד יְרוּשַׁלְמִי: מַקֵּל. וְרָאִיתִי דּוּגְמָתוֹ (ה) כא] *בְּבִילְמֵי תֶּרַח: נָטַל בַּקּוּלְסָא וְתַבְרִינוּן. הַשּׂוֹרֵף פָּרָה אֲדוּמָּה וּפָרִים הַנִּשְׂרָפִים מְטַמְּאִין בְּגָדִים. פָּרָה בְּהֶדְיָא כְּתִיב בָּהּ (במדבר יט). פָּרִים – פַּר כֹּהֵן מָשִׁיחַ וּפַר הָעֵדָה (ו) כב] וּפַר יוֹם הַכִּפּוּרִים – גָּמְרֵי מִקְּרָא יְתֵירָא דְּ"חַטָּאת" "חַטָּאת" בִּשְׁלָהֵי "כָּל הַזְּבָחִים שֶׁנִּתְעָרְבוּ" (לעיל פג.). וּפַר יוה"כ בְּהֶדְיָא כְּתִיב (ויקרא טז). וְהֵן אֵינָן מְטַמְּאִין בְּגָדִים. פָּרָה וּפָרִים עַצְמָן אֵין מְטַמְּאִין בְּגָדִים הַנּוֹגְעִין בָּהֶן בְּלֹא מִתְעַסְּקִין, אֲבָל מְטַמְּאִין אוֹכָלִין וּמַשְׁקִין הַנּוֹגְעִין בָּהֶן. וּלְקַמָּן מְפָרֵשׁ טַעְמָא. כִּדְתָנָא דְּבֵי ר' יִשְׁמָעֵאל מַה זְּרָעִים שֶׁאֵין סוֹפָן לְטַמֵּא טוּמְאָה חֲמוּרָה. כְּגוֹן אָדָם וּבְגָדִים. כג] וּצְרִיכִין הֶכְשֵׁר. דָּבָר הַמַּכְשִׁירָן לְקַבֵּל טוּמְאָה, כְּגוֹן נְתִינַת מַיִם וּמַגַּע שֶׁרֶץ. אַף כֹּל שֶׁאֵין סוֹפוֹ לְטַמֵּא כו'. כְּגוֹן שְׁאָר אוֹכָלִין. אֲבָל הָנֵי פָּרָה וּפָרִים וְשָׂעִיר, הוֹאִיל וְסוֹפָן לְטַמֵּא אָדָם וּבְגָדִים, כְּגוֹן הַמִּתְעַסְּקִין בָּהֶן – אֵין צְרִיכִין הֶכְשֵׁר טוּמְאָה, הִלְכָּךְ מְטַמְּאוּ מֵחַיִּים וְאע"ג *דְּלָא כד] אִיטַּמּוּיֵי שְׁאָר בַּעֲלֵי חַיִּים דְּעָלְמָא. אֶלָּא לְרַבָּנַן אִי דְּאִית לְהוּ דְּתָנָא דְּבֵי רַבִּי יִשְׁמָעֵאל אֲפִי' שָׂעִיר הַמִּשְׁתַּלֵּחַ וְאִי לֵית לְהוּ דְּתָנָא דְּבֵי רַבִּי יִשְׁמָעֵאל פָּרָה וּפָרִים מְנָא לְהוּ. הֲרֵי טְהוֹרִין הֵן, וְלֹא נֶאֶמְרָה בָּהֶן טוּמְאָה אֶלָּא לַמִּתְעַסְּקִים בָּהֶן! אָמְרִי בְּמַעֲרָבָא צְרִיכִין הֶכְשֵׁר טוּמְאָה מִמָּקוֹם אַחֵר. הָא דְּתָנָא דְּבֵי רַבִּי יִשְׁמָעֵאל, ה"ק: כָּל שֶׁאֵין סוֹפוֹ לְטַמֵּא טוּמְאָה חֲמוּרָה צָרִיךְ הֶכְשֵׁר טוּמְאָה מִמָּקוֹם אַחֵר – שֶׁיִּגַּע בַּשֶּׁרֶץ אוֹ בַּנְּבֵלָה, וְלֹא שֶׁיִּטַּמְּאוּ מֵאֵילָיו. אֲבָל מִי שֶׁסּוֹפוֹ לְטַמֵּא טוּמְאָה חֲמוּרָה – אֵין צָרִיךְ לִיגַּע בַּטּוּמְאָה, וּמְטַמֵּא טוּמְאַת אוֹכָלִין מֵאֵילָיו, כְּגוֹן פָּרָה וּפָרִים. אֲבָל חֲזֵי לְטוּמְאָה מִיהַת בְּעָלְמָא בָּעֵינַן, וְלֹא בַּעֲלֵי חַיִּים, דְּלָא אַשְׁכְּחַן בִּבְהֵמוֹת בַּעֲלֵי חַיִּים מְטַמְּאִין. מַהוּ שֶׁיִּטַּמְּאוּ בִּפְנִים אוֹכְלִין וּמַשְׁקִין. הוֹאִיל וַעֲדַיִין לֹא הִגִּיעוּ לִהְיוֹת מְטַמְּאִין טוּמְאָה חֲמוּרָה – לֹא מְטַמְּאוּ טוּמְאָה קַלָּה. אוֹ דִּלְמָא: הוֹאִיל וְסוֹפָן לְטַמֵּא לִכְשֶׁיֵּצְאוּ – מְטַמְּאוּ. נִבְלַת כה] עוֹף טָהוֹר. מְטַמְּאָה טוּמְאָה חֲמוּרָה בְּבֵית הַבְּלִיעָה בִּכְזַיִת. מַהוּ שֶׁיְּטַמֵּא. לְרַבִּי מֵאִיר אוֹכָלִין וּמַשְׁקִין בִּכְזַיִת. לְרַבָּנַן לָא תִּיבָּעֵי לָךְ, דְּאָמְרִי: מִידֵי דַּחֲזֵי לְטוּמְאָה בָּעֵינַן, וּבִכְזַיִת אֵין *לָזוֹ טוּמְאָה אֶלָּא בְּבֵית הַבְּלִיעָה, אֲבָל לְעִנְיַן מַגָּע – לֵיכָּא שִׁיעוּרָא בִּכְזַיִת. אֶלָּא לְרַבִּי מֵאִיר, דְּאָמַר: כָּל שֶׁסּוֹפוֹ לְטַמֵּא טוּמְאָה חֲמוּרָה אֵין צָרִיךְ רְאוּיָה לְטוּמְאָה, מַהוּ שֶׁתְּטַמֵּא בִּכְזַיִת מֵאֵלֶיהָ? דְּמַחְתָּא עַל אַרְעָא לָא תִּיבָּעֵי לָךְ. דְּלָא מִיטַּמְּאָה, דְּהָא אַכַּתִּי לֹא הוּגְעָה לְסוֹף טוּמְאָה חֲמוּרָה, שֶׁמָּא לֹא תִּיכָּנֵס לְבֵית הַבְּלִיעָה לְעוֹלָם. דְּנַקְטָהּ בְּפוּמֵּיהּ לָא תִּיבָּעֵי לָךְ. דְּאִם הָיוּ אוֹכָלִים אֲחֵרִים לְתוֹךְ פִּיו – כו] מְטַמְּאָתָן, דְּהָא הִגִּיעָה לְטוּמְאָה חֲמוּרָה בְּהַאי שִׁיעוּרָא. כִּי תִּיבָּעֵי לָךְ כו'.
הָכִי

או דלמא בתר בהמה אזלינן. תימה: אם הבהמה בפנים פשיטא דגברי טהורים, כדמוכח כולה שמעתין! ויש לומר, דה"ק: בתר בהמה דוקא אזלינן בתר רובא, אבל בגברי לא. **או** דלמא כיון דהדור הדור. פי' בקונטרס: דמבעיא ליה לענין טומאת בגדים של אלו שהוציאו. וקשה: אטו מחילות עזרה *מקום טהרה? דכיון שנטמאו – מי יטהרם? ונראה לפרש דמבעיא ליה לענין הנוגע בפנים, דדלמא כיון דיצאו בחוץ, אע"ג דחזרו – הנוגע בפנים טמא. ומסיק דמיבעיא ליה כז] *כיון דנקטי בבקולסי, ומיירי בעומד בחוץ ואוחז במקלות להוציאם לאחר *שיחזרו, כדפירש בקונטרס. הג"ה.

פרים הנשרפים. שיצאו הפרים והאנשים, וחזרו הפרים וגברי מהו? פשיטא האנשים וגם בגדים שהיו עליהם טמאים, ובחזרתן לא נטהרו. אלא אם אנשים אחרים נכנסו בעזרה ויתעסקו בהוצאתן, או הראשונים לבשו בגדים אחרים – מי הוו טמאים בעסק זה קודם שיצאו חוץ לעזרה, כיון שיצאו הפרים כבר חשוב כאילו מוציאים אותם מפתח עזרה ולחוץ? וקאמר: כח] *מי תלי מילתא בהוצאת הפר לבדו אע"פ שלא יצאו האנשים? א"כ גבי סובלין אותן במוטות, כיון שיצא הפר ולכך נטמאו הראשונים – אם כן גם דגואי נטמאו! ותסברא שיהא תלוי ביציאת הפר לבדו? והא בעינן "ואחר יבא אל המחנה"! אלא פשיטא *דבעיא גם שיצאו האנשים עם הפרים, ולכך דגואי לא מטמאי. וגם בבעיא דילך, אנשים אחרים שמעולם לא יצאו – פשיטא דטהורין, או גברי קדמאי אם לבשו בגדים אחרים! אלא רבי אלעזר הכי בעי: דנקטי בבקולסי, שהפרים יצאו *וחזרו, כט] אנשים אחרים ועמדו חוץ לעזרה, ומוציאין הפרים שבתוך העזרה במקלות. מי אמרינן: כיון שהפרים כבר יצאו, והאנשים עומדים בחוץ – חשוב כאילו מוציאין אותן מפתח עזרה ולחוץ, וטמאין. או חשוב כאילו לא יצאו הפרים מעולם לחוץ, וטהורים? אבל אם נכנסו בפנים גברי חדשים, או הראשונים בבגדים חדשים, כיון שמעולם אלו לא יצאו – פשיטא דטהורים, אע"פ שיצאו כבר הפרים. *מה שבפנים אינו מבואר וזה עיקר, ברוך ד"ך.

מחוסר יציאה כמחוסר מעשה דמי או לא. וא"ת: אי מטמאו בפנים – אם כן יטמאו את האימורים! ויש לומר: דמחוסר חתיכה – פשיטא דהוי כמחוסר מעשה, ולא תטמאו בשעת פרישתן, דמיירי בניתזין *בעל כרחו.
וירושלמי

עין משפט נר מצוה

סא א מיי' פי"ט מהל' פסה"מ הלכה ג:
סב ב ג מיי' פ"ה מהלכות פרה אדומה הלכה ה:
סג ד מיי' שם הלכה ז ופ"ו מהלכות אבות הטומאה הלכה טו:
[צ"ל מקוה]
סד ה מיי' פ"ג מהלכות אבות הטומאה הלכה ב:
נ"א כגון צ"ק
צ"ל שחזרו כו' צ"ק
סה ו מיי' שם הלכה ג:
סו ז עי' בכ"מ בפ"ה הלכות פרה הלכה ז:
צ"ל אי תלי צ"ק
[עי' תוספות ב"ק עז. ד"ה פרה]
צ"ל ושעיר המשתלח השורפן צ"ק
צ"ל דבעינן גם וכו' צ"ק
גי' הצ"ק וחזרו ובאו אנשים
צ"ל אין צ"ק
צ"ל ומה שפירשתי דמיבעיא ליה לענין הנוגעו בפנים אינו מבואר וזה עיקר הס"ד צ"ק
גירסת הצ"ק בכל כוחו
צ"ל דלא מטמאו צ"ק
נ"א לו

מסורת הש"ס

צ"ק מ"ז
צ"ל בחצי הפר שבחוץ יצא רוב כו' צ"ק
צ"ל דלא שבקינן צ"ק
תוספתא דפרה פרק ו [וע"ע תוספתא יומא פרק ג]
חולין קכא. כריתות כא. נדה נא.
[בכ"ר ס"פ נח]

הגהות הב"ח

(א) גמ' הנך דאיכא גואי נמי ליטמא אמר רבא הא בעינא: (ב) שם שעיר המשתלח נמי אי לית להו פרה ופרים מנלן כצ"ל ותיבת אפי' נמחק: (ג) רש"י ד"ה או דלמא וכו' שדינן לה ולאו רובא כצ"ל ותיבת ואע"ג נמחק: (ד) בא"ד אפילו הכי. נ"ב זהו פסק הלכה של רש"י: (ה) ד"ה בקולסי וכו' דוגמתו בירושלמי תרח: (ו) ד"ה השורף וכו' ופר העדה גמרי כצ"ל ותיבות ופר י"ה נמחק:

גליון הש"ס

גמ' צריכין הכשר טומאה. עיין בב"ק דף עז ע"א תוס' ד"ה פרה:

שיטה מקובצת

א] או דלמא בתר: ב] פרים הנשרפין ושעירים: ג] תיבת להו נמחק: ד] במוטות יצאו הראשונים חוץ: ה] והאחרונים אינן מטמאין: ו] ת"ר א) השורף פרה ופרים הנשרפין והמשלח את השעיר והמוציאן מטמאין בגדים כו' והשאר נמחק: ז] עצמן אינן מטמאין: ח] מטמא מפני שהוא חי וכל דבר שהוא חי אינו מטמא: ט] כדתנא עיין תוס' ב"ק דף ע"ז: י] חמורה צריכין הכשר אות ו' נמחק: יא] המשתלח נמי ואי לית להו דתנא דבי ר' ישמעאל אפי' פרה ופרים מנא להו כי אתא: יב] פרים הנשרפין ושעירים: יג] בר ממל תיבת שמואל נמחק: יד] מהו שתטמא בכזית: טו] תיבות בתר כו' פשטה נמחק: טז] בעי הס"ד ומה"ד האי: יז] תיבת הג"ה נמחק: יח] הוא אלא: יט] לעיל לא שבקינן: כ] דהך (דקמיית') [ראיה] מילתא היא: כא] דוגמתו באגדה בצלמי: כב] תיבות ופר יום הכיפורים נמחק: כג] צריכין הכשר אות ו' נמחק: כד] דלא חזי לאיטמויי: כה] נבלת דעוף טהור: כו] פיו מטמאין דהא: כז] כגון דנקטי בבקולסי: כח] וקאמר אי אית ליה מילתא ותיבות אי תלי ל"ש: כט] יצאו וחזרו ובאו אנשים:

א) וכ"ה בתוספתא דפרה פ"ז השורף פרה ועי"ש [illegible] השעיר מטמא בגדים ע"ש.

א] *מְחוּסַּר קְרִיבָה *לָאו כִּמְחוּסַּר מַעֲשֶׂה דָּמֵי. אֵיתִיבֵיהּ: *שְׁלֹשָׁה עָשָׂר דְּבָרִים נֶאֶמְרוּ בְּנִבְלַת עוֹף טָהוֹר, וְזֶה אֶחָד מֵהֶן: צְרִיכָה מַחֲשָׁבָה, וְאֵין צְרִיכָה הֶכְשֵׁר, אוּמְטַמָּא טוּמְאַת אוֹכָלִין בְּכַבֵּיצָה. מַאי לָאו ר"מ הִיא? לָא, רַבָּנַן הִיא. ב] וְהָא קָתָנֵי רֵישָׁא: צְרִיכָה מַחֲשָׁבָה וְאֵין צְרִיכָה הֶכְשֵׁר; *°וּמַאן שָׁמְעַתְּ לֵיהּ הַאי סְבָרָא — ר"מ. וּמִדְּרֵישָׁא ר"מ — סֵיפָא נַמִי ר"מ! מִידֵי אִירְיָא? הָא כִּדְאִיתָא וְהָא כִּדְאִיתָא. וְהָא מִדְּקָתָנֵי סֵיפָא: בשְׁחִיטָתָהּ וּמְלִיקָתָהּ מְטַהֶרֶת טְרֵיפָתָהּ מִטּוּמְאָתָהּ; *מַאן שָׁמְעַתְּ לֵיהּ הַאי סְבָרָא — ר"מ, רֵישָׁא וְסֵיפָא רַבִּי מֵאִיר וּמְצִיעֲתָא רַבָּנַן? אִין, רֵישָׁא וְסֵיפָא רַבִּי מֵאִיר וּמְצִיעֲתָא רַבָּנַן. אֲמַר לֵיהּ רַב הַמְנוּנָא לְרַבִּי זֵירָא: *לָא תֵּיתִיב *אַכַּרְעָךְ עַד דְּאָמַרְתְּ לִי הָא מִילְּתָא: נִבְלַת עוֹף טָהוֹר לְר"מ, מוֹנִין ג] לָהּ רִאשׁוֹן וְשֵׁנִי, אוֹ אֵין מוֹנִין ד] רִאשׁוֹן וְשֵׁנִי? א"ל: כָּל הֵיכָא דִּמְטַמֵּא אָדָם בְּמַגָּע — מוֹנִין בּוֹ רִאשׁוֹן וְשֵׁנִי, כָּל הֵיכָא ה] דְּאֵין מְטַמֵּא אָדָם בְּמַגָּע — אֵין מוֹנִין בּוֹ רִאשׁוֹן וְשֵׁנִי. בְּעָא מִינֵּיהּ רַבִּי זֵירָא ו] מֵרַבִּי אַמִּי בַּר חִיָּיא, וְאָמְרִי לָהּ מֵר' אָבִין בַּר כָּהֲנָא: הָא *דִּתְנַן: *גחִיבּוּרֵי אוֹכָלִין ע"י מַשְׁקִין — חִיבּוּר לְטוּמְאָה קַלָּה וְאֵין חִיבּוּר לְטוּמְאָה חֲמוּרָה; מוֹנִין ז] בּוֹ רִאשׁוֹן וְשֵׁנִי, אוֹ אֵין מוֹנִין בּוֹ רִאשׁוֹן וְשֵׁנִי? א"ל: דכָּל הֵיכָא דִּמְטַמֵּא אָדָם — מוֹנִין בּוֹ רִאשׁוֹן וְשֵׁנִי, ח] אֵין מְטַמֵּא אָדָם — אֵין מוֹנִין בּוֹ רִאשׁוֹן וְשֵׁנִי.§ "יָצְאוּ אֵלּוּ וְאֵלּוּ".§ מה"מ? דת"ר: *לְהַלָּן ט] הוּא אוֹמֵר חוּץ לְג' מַחֲנוֹת, כָּאן — לְמַחֲנֶה אַחַת, לוֹמַר לְךָ: הכֵּיוָן שֶׁיָּצָא חוּץ לְמַחֲנֶה אַחַת — מְטַמֵּא בְּגָדִים. י] וְהִיא גּוּפָהּ מְנָלַן? דת"ר: °"וְהוֹצִיא אֶת כָּל הַפָּר אֶל מִחוּץ לַמַּחֲנֶה" — וחוּץ לְג' מַחֲנוֹת. (ויקרא ד) אַתָּה אוֹמֵר: חוּץ לְג' מַחֲנוֹת, אוֹ אֵינוֹ אֶלָּא יא] מַחֲנֶה אַחַת? כְּשֶׁהוּא אוֹמֵר בְּפַר הָעֵדָה °"מִחוּץ לַמַּחֲנֶה", שֶׁאֵין יב] צָרִיךְ לוֹמַר, שֶׁהֲרֵי (שם) כְּבָר נֶאֱמַר: °"כַּאֲשֶׁר שָׂרַף אֵת הַפָּר הָרִאשׁוֹן" (שם) — יג] לִיתֵּן לוֹ מַחֲנֶה שְׁנִיָּה. כְּשֶׁהוּא אוֹמֵר "מִחוּץ לַמַּחֲנֶה" בַּדֶּשֶׁן, יד] שֶׁאצ"ל, שֶׁהֲרֵי כְּבָר נֶאֱמַר: °"עַל שֶׁפֶךְ הַדֶּשֶׁן יִשָּׂרֵף" (שם) — טו] לִיתֵּן לוֹ מַחֲנֶה שְׁלִישִׁית. וְר"ש, הַאי "מִחוּץ לַמַּחֲנֶה" מַאי עָבֵיד לֵיהּ? מִיבָּעֵי לֵיהּ לִכְדְתַנְיָא, רַבִּי אֱלִיעֶזֶר אוֹמֵר: נֶאֱמַר כָּאן: טז] "חוּץ לַמַּחֲנֶה" וְנֶאֱמַר לְהַלָּן: °"חוּץ לַמַּחֲנֶה" (במדבר יט), *מַה לְּהַלָּן חוּץ לְג' מַחֲנוֹת — אַף כָּאן חוּץ לְג' מַחֲנוֹת. וּמַה לְּהַלָּן לְמִזְרָחָהּ שֶׁל יְרוּשָׁלַיִם — אַף

רש"י

הָכִי גָּרְסִינַן: אֲמַר לֵיהּ מְחוּסַּר קְרִיבָה לָאו כִּמְחוּסַּר מַעֲשֶׂה דָּמֵי. יז] °צְרִיכָה מַחֲשָׁבָה. לְהִצְטָרֵף פָּחוֹת מִכַּזַּיִת מִמֶּנָּה לְהַשְׁלִים פָּחוֹת מִכַּבֵּיצָה אוֹכָלִין, לְקַבֵּל טוּמְאַת אוֹכָלִין בְּמַגָּע. וְאֵינָהּ צְרִיכָה הֶכְשֵׁר. לְטַמֵּא, לֹא לְמַיִם וְלֹא לְמַגַּע שֶׁרֶץ. שֶׁמֵּאֵלֶיהָ מְטַמְּאָה, הוֹאִיל וְסוֹפָהּ לְטַמֵּא טוּמְאָה חֲמוּרָה. וּמְטַמְּאָה טוּמְאַת אוֹכָלִין בְּכַבֵּיצָה. מִדְּקָתָנֵי צְרִיכָה מַחֲשָׁבָה וְאֵינָהּ צְרִיכָה הֶכְשֵׁר — אַלְמָא בִּדְנָקֵיט לֵיהּ בְּיָדֵיהּ עָסְקִינַן. דְּאִי מַחְתָּא אַאַרְעָא — אַמַּאי אֵינָהּ צְרִיכָה הֶכְשֵׁר? וְאִי דְּנָקֵט לָהּ בְּפוּמֵּיהּ — אַמַּאי צְרִיכָה מַחֲשָׁבָה? אֵין לְךָ מַחֲשָׁבָה גְּדוֹלָה מִזּוֹ! וְקָתָנֵי: כַּבֵּיצָה — אִין, כַּזַּיִת — לָא. ה"ג: שְׁחִיטָתָהּ וּמְלִיקָתָהּ מְטַהֶרֶת טְרֵיפָתָהּ מִטּוּמְאָתָהּ. הַאי סְבָרָא ר' מֵאִיר. בְּפֶרֶק "חַטַּאת הָעוֹף" (לעיל סט.). נִבְלַת עוֹף טָהוֹר לְר' מֵאִיר. דִּמְטַמֵּא טוּמְאַת אוֹכָלִין מֵאֵלֶיהָ בְּכַזַּיִת, מוֹנִין בּוֹ רִאשׁוֹן וְשֵׁנִי אוֹ לֹא? כָּל הֵיכָא דְּלֹא מְטַמֵּא אָדָם בְּמַגָּע אֵין מוֹנִין בּוֹ רִאשׁוֹן וְשֵׁנִי. דְּגָמַר מִשֶּׁרֶץ, דִּכְתִיב בֵּיהּ מִנְיַן רִאשׁוֹן וְשֵׁנִי דִּכְתִיב (ויקרא יא): "כֹּל אֲשֶׁר בְּתוֹכוֹ יִטְמָא", דַּהֲוָה לֵיהּ הַכְּלִי רִאשׁוֹן וְהָאוֹכֶל שֵׁנִי. וְנִבְלַת עוֹף טָהוֹר לֹא מְטַמֵּא אָדָם בְּמַגָּע. חִיבּוּרֵי אוֹכָלִין עַל יְדֵי מַשְׁקִין. חֲצִי זַיִת נְבֵלָה מִכָּאן וַחֲצִי זַיִת נְבֵלָה מִכָּאן, וּמַשְׁקֶה טוֹפֵחַ בָּאֶמְצַע וְנוֹגֵעַ בִּשְׁנֵיהֶם — מְחַבְּרָן לְטַמֵּא אוֹכָלִין וּמַשְׁקִין הַנּוֹגְעִים בְּאֶחָד מִן הַחֲצָאִין הָאֵלּוּ. וְאֵין חִיבּוּר לְטוּמְאָה חֲמוּרָה. לְטַמֵּא אָדָם וְכֵלִים. וְטַעְמָא לָא יָדַעְנָא. ה"ג: לְהַלָּן אַתָּה נוֹתֵן לָהֶם שָׁלֹשׁ מַחֲנוֹת וְכָאן מַחֲנֶה אַחַת א"כ לָמָּה נֶאֱמַר אֶל מִחוּץ לַמַּחֲנֶה לוֹמַר לְךָ כֵּיוָן שֶׁיָּצָא חוּץ לְמַחֲנֶה אַחַת מְטַמְּאִים בְּגָדִים וְהָא מַתְנִיָּא בְּת"כ גַּבֵּי פַּר יוה"כ, דִּכְתִיב (ויקרא טז): "וְאֵת פַּר הַחַטָּאת וְאֵת שְׂעִיר הַחַטָּאת אֲשֶׁר הוּבָא" וגו'. וְקַמְתַמַּהּ תַּנָּא יח] וְאָמַר: לְהַלָּן בְּפַר הָעֵדָה וְכֹהֵן מָשִׁיחַ אַתָּה נוֹתֵן לָהֶם מְקוֹם שְׂרֵיפָתָן חוּץ לְשָׁלֹשׁ מַחֲנוֹת, כִּדְיָלֵיף לְקַמֵּיהּ. וְכָאן אַתָּה אוֹמֵר "אֶל מִחוּץ לַמַּחֲנֶה וְשָׂרְפוּ", דְּמַשְׁמַע שֶׁשּׂוֹרְפָן חוּץ לָעֲזָרָה מִיָּד בְּהַר הַבַּיִת. וַהֲלֹא אַף אֵלּוּ פְּנִימִיִּים, וְאַיְיתֵי לְכוּלְּהוּ כִּי הֲדָדֵי בְּרִיבּוּיָא דְ"חַטַּאת הַחַטָּאת" בִּשְׁלָהֵי "כָּל הַזְּבָחִים", וְאָמַר נַמִי בְּפֶ' "בֵּית שַׁמַּאי" (לעיל לט.) "לְפַר" — זֶה פַּר יוֹם הַכִּיפּוּרִים. אִם כֵּן לָמָּה נֶאֱמַר אֶל מִחוּץ לַמַּחֲנֶה. לְעִנְיַן טוּמְאַת בְּגָדִים דִּכְתִיבִי בִּקְרָא דְּבָתְרֵיהּ קָאָמַר (ויקרא טז): "אֶל מִחוּץ לַמַּחֲנֶה וְהַשּׂוֹרֵף אוֹתָם יְכַבֵּס בְּגָדָיו". לוֹמַר לְךָ כֵּיוָן שֶׁיָּצְאוּ חוּץ לָעֲזָרָה. הַמִּתְעַסְּקִין בָּהֶן, מְטַמְּאִין בְּגָדִים. מִחוּץ לַמַּחֲנֶה בַּדֶּשֶׁן. בְּהוֹצָאַת דֶּשֶׁן הַמִּזְבֵּחַ: "וְהוֹצִיא אֶת הַדֶּשֶׁן אֶל מִחוּץ לַמַּחֲנֶה" (שם ו). שֶׁאֵין ת"ל. אֵין מְלַמֵּד כְּלוּם, דַּהֲוָה יָדַעְנָא דְּאֶל מִחוּץ לַמַּחֲנֶה מוֹלִיאִין אוֹתוֹ, דִּכְתִיב בְּפָרִים הַנִּשְׂרָפִים (שם ד): "אֶל שֶׁפֶךְ הַדֶּשֶׁן", וּכְתִיב בְּהוּ "אֶל (א) מִחוּץ" יט]. וְר' שִׁמְעוֹן. דְּאָמַר בְּמַתְנִי': אֵין מְטַמְּאִין בְּגָדִים עַד שֶׁיּוּצַּת הָאוּר בְּרוּבּוֹ, הַאי "מִחוּץ לַמַּחֲנֶה" דִּכְתִיב בְּפַר וְשָׂעִיר שֶׁל יוֹם הַכִּיפּוּרִים מַאי עָבֵיד לֵיהּ? נֶאֱמַר כָּאן. בְּפַר יוֹם הַכִּיפּוּרִים. וְנֶאֱמַר לְהַלָּן. בְּפָרָה אֲדוּמָּה (במדבר יט): "וְהוֹצִיא אוֹתָהּ אֶל מִחוּץ". מַה כָּאן. בְּפָרִים הַנִּשְׂרָפִים חוּץ לְג' מַחֲנוֹת, אַף *שְׁחִיטַת פָּרָה אֲדוּמָּה חוּץ לְג' מַחֲנוֹת. מַה לְּהַלָּן. בְּפָרָה אֲדוּמָּה — בְּמִזְרָחוֹ שֶׁל יְרוּשָׁלַיִם, דִּכְתִיב בָּהּ: "וְהִזָּה אֶל נוֹכַח פְּנֵי אֹהֶל מוֹעֵד", אַלְמָא, עוֹמֵד בַּמִּזְרָח וּפָנָיו לַמַּעֲרָב, כְּנֶגֶד פִּתְחוֹ שֶׁל הֵיכָל, שֶׁהוּא בְּכוֹתֶל מִזְרָחִי וּפִתְחוֹ לַמִּזְרָח, אַף

תוספות

ובירושלמי גרסינן בסוף פרק "שני שעירים": רבי אליעזר שאל: פרים הנשרפין ושעירים הנשרפים, מהו שיטמאו בגדים בלא הכשר ובלא טומאה, מפני שסופן לטמאות טומאה חמורה? השיב רבי שמואל קפודקיא: מעתה יטמאו אימורים! אלא כשפרשו. ואפילו תימא דלא פירשו, כהדא: אין מי חטאת מטמאין דבר לחזור ולטמאות ממנו.

ומטמא טומאת אוכלין בכביצה. פי' בקונטרס: מדקתני צריכה מחשבה ואין צריכה הכשר — אלמא בדנקיט ליה בידיה עסקינן. דאי מחתא אארעא — אמאי אינה צריכה הכשר? ואי דנקיט ליה בפומיה — אמאי צריכה מחשבה? אין לך מחשבה גדולה מזו! וקתני כביצה — אין, כזית — לא. וקשה: כיון דיש בו כביצה, אע"ג דמחית אארעא — מטמא בלא הכשר, משום דסופו לטמא טומאה חמורה. ולא דמי למחוסר יציאה, דבפנים אין ראוי כלל לטמא. ומשום הכי לא מבעיא ליה לרבנן בכביצה דנקיט בידיה! ונראה לפרש דהיינו טעמא: דמשמע ליה דמיירי בנקיט בידיה משום דאז איכא חידוש, לאשמועינן דבעי כביצה ולא חשיב כנקיט בפומיה. אבל במחית אארעא — פשיטא דבעי כביצה. (*ופי' הקונטרס יש ליישב כמו שפירשתי לעיל בהגהה, וכן עיקר).

ומדסיפא ר"מ רישא נמי ר"מ. הוה מצי למימר: וליטעמיך, הא קתני מציעתא: האוכל אבר מן החי ממנה סופג את הארבעים. והיינו דלא כרבי מאיר, דקסבר אינו נוהג אלא *בטהורה, בפרק "גיד הנשה" (חולין דף קב*:) (כדפרישית לעיל).

חיבורי אוכלין ע"י משקין. פי' בקונט': חצי זית נבלה מכאן, וחצי זית נבלה מכאן, ומשקה טופח באמצע ונוגע בשניהן — מחברן לטמא אוכלין ומשקין הנוגעין באחד מן החצאין האלו. ואין חיבור לטומאה חמורה — לטמא אדם וכלים. וטעמא לא ידענא. וכענין זה פירש ב"הקומץ רבה" (מנחות דף כד.) גבי צירוף כלי וחיבור מים מהו. דפירש התם בקונטרס: כלומר, חצי עשרון שנטמא בצירוף כלי, מהו שמטמא אחר בחיבור מים? כגון אם יש שתי חצאי עשרון בכלי ואין נוגעין, וחצי עשרון יש *חוץ לכלי השני. וחיבור מים, כגון ניצוק או צינור, מחבר את של חוץ לכלי ואת שבתוך הכלי, ונגע טומאה לזה שבכלי שאין נוגע במים, ונטמא חבירו משום צירוף כלי — מהו שיטמא זה את של חוץ בחיבור מים? ודבר תימה הוא לומר שמשקין מחברין אוכלין לקבל טומאה ולטמא אחרים. דאפילו עור אין מצרפו, כדאיתא ב"העור והרוטב" (חולין דף קיז:). ועוד: שפירש שמחברין ע"י ניצוק, והלא אפי' למים עצמן קי"ל *דאין ניצוק חיבור לטומאה! וקלת היה נראה לפרש: דמיירי בשנימוחו ע"י המים ונדבקו יחד. ומיהו, כעין פירוש הקונטרס יש משנה אחת במסכת טהרות (פ"ח מ"ח): עריבה שהיא קטפרס *וניצוק מלמעלן ומשקה טופח מלמטן, וג' חתיכות כביצה — אינן מצטרפות, וב' מצטרפות. ור' יוסי אומר: אף שתים אינן מצטרפות אלא א"כ רוצצות משקה. ואם היה משקה עומד, אפי' כעין החרדל — מצטרף. ובתוספתא *תניא: אתרוג שנפרך ותחבו בכוש או בקיסם — אינו חיבור, שאין חיבורי אדם חיבור. עיסה שנילושה במי פירות — טהורה, שאין לך דבר שהוא מחבר את האוכלין אלא שבעה משקין. *ודבר תימה הוא, אם אין לישת *)פירות מועלת לחבר את הקמח! ושמא לשה לאו דוקא, אלא אורחא דמילתא נקט, [דבר שאדם] לש במי פירות, פעמים שמי פירות מחברים שני חצאי זיתים של עיסה במשקים הבאים מזה לזה.

מה כאן חוץ לשלש מחנות ביום הכיפורים אף כ] להלן בפרה אדומה כן. תימה: הא בפר יוה"כ לא ידעי' שלש מחנות אלא מהיקשא ד"לפר" — זה פר יום הכיפורים, בפרק "ב"ש" (לעיל דף לט.) כדפירש בקונט'. ומספקינן אי דבר הלמד בהיקש חוזר ומלמד בג"ש או לא. ואפי' תימלי לומר דאתא מריבוי דחטאת דבסוף "התערובת" (לעיל פג.) — ההוא נמי היקשא הוא! ושמא ג"ש הוא. *ויש לפרש דפרה קדשי בדק הבית היא. והשתא נמי אתי שפיר, דיליף בג"ז מזרחה של ירושלים, אע"ג דשריפת פרה ילפא מהזאתה, לקמן בפרק בתרא (דף קיג.).

*) מי פירות. יעב"ץ

הדרן עלך טבול יום

עין משפט נר מצוה

סז א מיי' פ"ג מהלכות אבות הטומאה הלכה יז:

סח ב מיי' שם הלכה יב אבל לא מליקתה:

סט ג מיי' פ"א מהלכות אבות הטומאה הלכה ו:

ע ד שם בהגהות:

עא ה מיי' פ"ה מהלכות פרה הלכה ו:

עב ו מיי' פ"ג מהלכות פרה הלכה ב:

[נ"ל אמר ליה מחוסר כו']

[עי' תוס' נזיר כד: בד"ה אמר שמואל וכו' וכתבו פירוש על זה]

עיין נ"ק

[נ"ל בבהמה טהורה]

נ"ל חוץ לכלי וחיבור מים כו' נ"ק

[פרק ה דמכשירין וכן פ"ח דטהרות מ"ח]

נ"ל והבלק מלמעלן נ"ק

[דעוקלין פ"א]

מסורת הש"ס

[חולין קכ:]

נדה ג: טהרות פ"א משנה א בכורות ו.

[נ"ל דתניא]

[קושיא בזה תמצא בתוס' חולין קכ. סד"ה ורבי מאיר וכו"ש ועי"ע תוספות ב"ק עז. ד"ה פרה]

[קדושין לו: וש"נ]

(טהרות פ"ח)

סנהדרין מב. יומא סח.

[כס"י שריפת פרה כו']

עיין נ"ק שהאריך

נ"ל ועוד יש לפרש כו' נ"ק

נ"ל מה כאן חוץ לשלש מחנות אף להלן חוץ לשלש מחנות נ"ק

הגהות הב"ח

(א) רש"י ד"ה שאין ת"ל וכו' מחוץ למחנה הס"ד:

גליון הש"ס

גמ' ומאן שמעת ליה וכו' ר"מ. יש לעיין הא מסקינן לעיל דגם לרבנן ס"ל כתנא דבי ר"י ורק בשעור משתלמת לקבל טומאה. רש"י ד"ה צריכה מחשבה להצטרף פחות מכזית. ק"ל אמאי לא כפשוטו לצריך מחשבה דעי"ז יש לו טומאת עצמו לטמא אוכלין ומשקין כיון דסופו לטמא טומאה חמורה. ובנדה באמת לא כתב רש"י כן:

שיטה מקובצת

א] א"ל מחוסר: ב] היא והא מדקתני סיפא שחיטתה ומליקתה מטהרת טריפתה מטומאתה מאן שמעת ליה האי סברא ר' מאיר מדסיפא ר"מ רישא נמי ר"מ מידי אירייא סיפא ר"מ רישא רבנן א"ל רב כו' כן גירסת ס"י וכן משמע ברש"י ז"ל והגירסא בעמוד קשה לעמוד עליה: ג] מונין בו ראשון תיבת לה נמחק: ד] מונין בו ראשון: ה] דלא מטמא תיבת דאין נמחק: ו] מר' אבין בר חייא תיבת אמי נמחק: ז] מונין בהן ראשון ושני או אין מונין בהן ראשון ושני: ח] ושני כל היכא דלא מטמא אדם תיבת אין נמחק: ט] להלן אתה נותן להם ג' מחנות וכאן מחנה אחת א"כ למה נאמר מחוץ למחנה לומר לך כיון: י] בגדים אמר מר להלן אתה נותן כו' מנ"ל תיבות והיא גופא נמחק: יא] אלא חוץ למחנה: יב] שאין ת"ל שהרי תיבות צ"ל נמחק: יג] הראשון תן לו: יד] בדשן שאין ת"ל ותיבות שאצ"ל נמחק: טו] ישרף תן לו: טז] כאן מחוץ למחנה ונאמר להלן מחוץ למחנה מה כאן חוץ לג' מחנות אף להלן חוץ לג' מחנות: יז] צריכה. עיין במס' נדה דף ג ברש"י ובתוס': יח] תנא ואומר להלן: יט] מחוץ למחנה ה"ד: כ] הכיפורים. עיין בתוס' יומא (דף ס"ח):

אַף כָּאן לְמִזְרָחָהּ שֶׁל יְרוּשָׁלַיִם. א] אֶלָּא לְרַבָּנַן הֵיכָא שָׂרֵיף לְהוּ? כִּדְתַנְיָא: הֵיכָן נִשְׂרָפִין — לִצְפוֹן יְרוּשָׁלַיִם, חוּץ לְשָׁלֹשׁ מַחֲנוֹת. רַבִּי יוֹסֵי הַגְּלִילִי אוֹמֵר: אאַבֵּית הַדֶּשֶׁן ב] נִשְׂרָפִין. אָמַר רָבָא: מַאן תַּנָּא דְּפָלֵיג עֲלֵיהּ דְּר' יוֹסֵי הַגְּלִילִי — ר' אֱלִיעֶזֶר בֶּן יַעֲקֹב ג] הִיא. דְּתַנְיָא: °"עַל שֶׁפֶךְ הַדֶּשֶׁן יִשָּׂרֵף" — שֶׁיְּהֵא שָׁם דֶּשֶׁן (שֶׁיַּקְדִּים לְשָׁם דֶּשֶׁן). ר' אֱלִיעֶזֶר בֶּן יַעֲקֹב אוֹמֵר: שֶׁיְּהֵא מְקוֹמוֹ מְשׁוּפָּךְ. אֲמַר לֵיהּ אַבַּיֵי: ד] דִּילְמָא בִּמְקוֹמוֹ מְשׁוּפָּךְ פְּלִיגִי! תָּנוּ רַבָּנַן: הַשּׂוֹרֵף ה] מְטַמֵּא בְגָדִים, בוְלֹא הַמַּצִּית אֶת הָאוּר ו] מְטַמֵּא בְגָדִים, וְלֹא הַמְסַדֵּר אֶת הַמַּעֲרָכָה מְטַמֵּא בְּגָדִים. וְאֵיזֶהוּ הַשּׂוֹרֵף — ז] הַמְסַיֵּיעַ בִּשְׁעַת שְׂרֵיפָה. יָכוֹל אַף מִשֶּׁנַּעֲשׂוּ אֵפֶר מְטַמֵּא בְּגָדִים? תַּלְמוּד לוֹמַר: "אוֹתָם", אוֹתָם מְטַמְּאִין בְּגָדִים, גוּמִשֶּׁנַּעֲשׂוּ אֵפֶר אֵין מְטַמְּאִין בְּגָדִים. *רַבִּי שִׁמְעוֹן אוֹמֵר: אוֹתָם מְטַמְּאִין בְּגָדִים, נִיתַּךְ הַבָּשָׂר — אֵין מְטַמְּאִין בְּגָדִים. מַאי בֵּינַיְיהוּ? אָמַר רָבָא: אִיכָּא בֵּינַיְיהוּ דְּשָׁוְיָיהּ חֲרוּכָא.§

הדרן עלך טבול יום

הַשּׁוֹחֵט דוְהַמַּעֲלֶה בַּחוּץ — חַיָּיב עַל הַשְּׁחִיטָה, וְחַיָּיב עַל הָעֲלָאָה. רַבִּי יוֹסֵי הַגְּלִילִי אוֹמֵר: השָׁחַט בִּפְנִים וְהֶעֱלָה בַּחוּץ.* שָׁחַט בַּחוּץ וְהֶעֱלָה בַּחוּץ — פָּטוּר, שֶׁלֹּא הֶעֱלָה אֶלָּא דָּבָר פָּסוּל. אָמְרוּ לוֹ: אַף הַשּׁוֹחֵט בִּפְנִים וּמַעֲלֶה בַּחוּץ, כֵּיוָן שֶׁהוֹצִיאוֹ — פְּסָלוֹ. *הַטָּמֵא שֶׁאָכַל בֵּין קֹדֶשׁ טָמֵא בֵּין קֹדֶשׁ טָהוֹר — וחַיָּיב. רַבִּי יוֹסֵי הַגְּלִילִי אוֹמֵר: טָמֵא שֶׁאָכַל טָהוֹר — חַיָּיב. וְטָמֵא שֶׁאָכַל טָמֵא — פָּטוּר, שֶׁלֹּא אָכַל אֶלָּא דָּבָר טָמֵא. אָמְרוּ לוֹ: אַף טָמֵא שֶׁאָכַל אֶת הַטָּהוֹר, כֵּיוָן שֶׁנָּגַע בּוֹ — טִמְּאוּהוּ. וְטָהוֹר שֶׁאָכַל טָמֵא — זפָּטוּר, שֶׁאֵינוֹ חַיָּיב אֶלָּא עַל טוּמְאַת הַגּוּף.§ **גמ'** בִּשְׁלָמָא ח] הֶעֱלָה — כְּתִיב עוֹנֶשׁ וּכְתִיב אַזְהָרָה; עוֹנֶשׁ — דִּכְתִיב: °"וְאֶל פֶּתַח אֹהֶל מוֹעֵד לֹא ט] *הֱבִיאוֹ", אַזְהָרָה — דִּכְתִיב: °"הִשָּׁמֶר לְךָ פֶּן תַּעֲלֶה עוֹלוֹתֶיךָ". וְכִי הָא *דְּא"ר אָבִין א"ר *אֶלְעָזָר: כָּל מָקוֹם שֶׁנֶּאֱמַר "הִשָּׁמֵר" "פֶּן" וְ"אַל" — אֵינוֹ אֶלָּא לֹא תַעֲשֶׂה. אֶלָּא שְׁחִיטָה, בִּשְׁלָמָא עוֹנֶשׁ — דִּכְתִיב: °"וְאֶל פֶּתַח אֹהֶל מוֹעֵד לֹא הֱבִיאוֹ", אֶלָּא אַזְהָרָה מְנָלַן? אָמַר קְרָא: °"וְלֹא יִזְבְּחוּ עוֹד". י] הַאי מִיבָּעֵי לֵיהּ לִכְדְר"א, *דְּאָמַר: יא] חמִנַּיִן לַזּוֹבֵחַ בְּהֵמָה לְמַרְקוּלִיס שֶׁהוּא חַיָּיב — דִּכְתִיב: "וְלֹא יִזְבְּחוּ עוֹד אֶת זִבְחֵיהֶם", אִם אֵינוֹ עִנְיָן לִכְדַרְכָּהּ, יב] דִּכְתִיב: °"אֵיכָה יַעַבְדוּ" — תְּנֵהוּ עִנְיָן לְשֶׁלֹּא כְּדַרְכָּהּ! אָמַר רַבָּה, קְרֵי בֵּיהּ: "וְלֹא יִזְבְּחוּ", וּקְרֵי בֵּיהּ: "וְלֹא עוֹד". אַכַּתִּי מִיבָּעֵי לֵיהּ לִכְדְתַנְיָא: עַד כָּאן הוּא מְדַבֵּר בְּקָדָשִׁים שֶׁהִקְדִּישָׁן בִּשְׁעַת אִיסּוּר הַבָּמוֹת, וְהִקְרִיבָן בִּשְׁעַת אִיסּוּר הַבָּמוֹת, שֶׁהֲרֵי

ויקרא ו · ויקרא יז · שם יז · דברים יב · ויקרא יז · שם · דברים יב · גי' יעב"ץ · [נ"ל סמנים]

רש"י

אַף כָּאן כו'. יג] וְרַבָּנַן. דְּמַפְּקִי לֵיהּ לִקְרָא לְטוּמְאַת בְּגָדִים, וְלֵית לְהוּ ג"ש. הֵיכָא שָׂרֵיף לְהוּ. לְאֵיזוֹ רוּחַ שֶׁל יְרוּשָׁלַיִם. לִצְפוֹנָהּ שֶׁל יְרוּשָׁלַיִם. שֶׁכָּל מַעֲשֵׂה חַטָּאת בַּצָּפוֹן. אַבֵּית הַדֶּשֶׁן. צָרִיךְ שֶׁיַּקְדִּים לְשָׁם דֶּשֶׁן יד] מִזְבֵּחַ, שֶׁיְּהֵא נִקְרָא קוֹדֶם לָכֵן "מְקוֹם שֶׁפֶךְ הַדֶּשֶׁן". מִכְּלָל דְּלְת"ק לֹא צָרִיךְ. רַבִּי אֱלִיעֶזֶר בֶּן יַעֲקֹב הִיא. דְּאָמַר: לֹא מַשְׁמוּעִינַן "עַל שֶׁפֶךְ" אֶלָּא שֶׁיְּהֵא מְקוֹמוֹ מִדְרוֹן, שֶׁיְּהֵא דִּשְׁנוֹ מִשְׁתַּפֵּךְ. וְדִילְמָא בִּמְקוֹמוֹ מְשׁוּפָּךְ הוּא דִּפְלִיגִי. וּמוֹדֶה רַבִּי אֱלִיעֶזֶר בֶּן יַעֲקֹב שֶׁיַּקְדִּים שָׁם דֶּשֶׁן, אֶלָּא דְּבָעֵי נַמִי מְקוֹמוֹ מְשׁוּפָּךְ! (א). הַשּׂוֹרֵף. הַמִּתְעַסֵּק בְּצָרְכֵי שְׂרֵיפָתָן, טו] כְּגוֹן הַמְסַיֵּיעַ בִּשְׁעַת שְׂרֵיפָה. וְהַאי תַּנָּא אִית לֵיהּ כְּרַבִּי שִׁמְעוֹן, דְּאֵין מְטַמְּאִין בְּגָדִים עַד שֶׁיּוּצַּת בָּהֶן הָאוּר. דְּשָׁוְיָיהּ חֲרוּכָא. דְּהָוֵי נִיתַּךְ הַבָּשָׂר, וְאֵפֶר מִיהָא לֹא טז] הָוֵה. לְתַנָּא קַמָּא מְטַמְּאִין עַד שֶׁיֵּעָשׂוּ אֵפֶר, דְּ"אוֹתָם" קָרֵינָא בְּהוּ, אֲבָל אֵפֶר לֹא מִיקְרֵי. וּלְרַבִּי (ב) יז] אֶלְעָזָר בְּרַבִּי שִׁמְעוֹן — אֵין מְטַמְּאִין בְּגָדִים.

הדרן עלך טבול יום

הַשּׁוֹחֵט. קָדָשִׁים בַּחוּץ יח] וְהֶעֱלָה בַּחוּץ. בְּהֶעְלֵם אֶחָד. חַיָּיב עַל הַשְּׁחִיטָה וְחַיָּיב עַל הָעֲלִיָּיה. שֶׁהֵן שְׁנֵי גוּפֵי עֲבֵירָה, דְּתַרְוַיְיהוּ כְּתִיבִי, "אֲשֶׁר יִשְׁחַט" וַ"אֲשֶׁר יַעֲלֶה" (ויקרא יז). שֶׁלֹּא הֶעֱלָה אֶלָּא דָּבָר פָּסוּל. וַאֲנַן מִתְקַבֵּל בִּפְנִים בָּעֵינַן, דִּכְתִיב: "וְאֶל פֶּתַח אֹהֶל מוֹעֵד לֹא יְבִיאֶנּוּ" (שם). כֵּיוָן שֶׁהוֹצִיאוֹ פְּסָלוֹ. וַאֲפ"ה חַיָּיב, וְה"ה לְשׁוֹחֵט בַּחוּץ וּמַעֲלֶה בַּחוּץ. הַטָּמֵא שֶׁאָכַל כו'. מִשּׁוּם דִּפְלִיגִי ר' יוֹסֵי הַגְּלִילִי וְרַבָּנַן בְּתַרְוַיְיהוּ, וְדָמוּ הָנָךְ פְּלוּגְתָּא לַהֲדָדֵי, תְּנֵינְהוּ גַּבֵּי הֲדָדֵי. כֵּיוָן שֶׁנָּגַע בּוֹ טִמְּאוּהוּ. וַאֲפ"ה יט] [כִּי] הֲדַר אָכֵיל לֵיהּ מִחַיַּיב. וּמַה לִּי נִטְמָא בָּשָׂר עַל יָדוֹ, מַה לִּי נִטְמָא ע"י אֲחֵרִים. שֶׁאֵינוֹ חַיָּיב אֶלָּא עַל טוּמְאַת הַגּוּף. כִּדְכְתִיב: "וְטוּמְאָתוֹ עָלָיו וְנִכְרְתָה" וְדָרְשִׁינַן בְּפֶ' "בֵּית שַׁמַּאי" (לעיל דף מג.): בְּטוּמְאַת הַגּוּף הַכָּתוּב מְדַבֵּר, מִי שֶׁטּוּמְאָה פּוֹרַחַת מִמֶּנּוּ. **גמ'** שְׁחִיטָה וְהַעֲלָאָה ב' פָּרָשִׁיּוֹת סְמוּכוֹת זוֹ לָזוֹ בְּ"אַחֲרֵי מוֹת". אֶלָּא אַזְהָרָה מְנָלַן. דְּקָא מְחַיְּיבִינַן לֵיהּ כ] עֲלֵיהּ חַטָּאת? שֶׁאֵין חַטָּאת בָּאָה אֶלָּא עַל לָאו וְכָרֵת, כִּדְתְנַן: (ג) הַפֶּסַח וְהַמִּילָה מִצְוַת עֲשֵׂה וְאֵין חַיָּיבִין עֲלֵיהֶן חַטָּאת, בְּמַסֶּכֶת כְּרֵיתוֹת (דף ב.). לְמַרְקוּלִים. אע"פ שֶׁעֲבוֹדָתוֹ דֶּרֶךְ בִּזָּיוֹן לְסָקְלוֹ בַּאֲבָנִים, וְזֶה עוֹבְדוֹ דֶּרֶךְ כָּבוֹד, וְלָא קָרֵינָא בֵּיהּ "אֵיכָה יַעַבְדוּ (ד) וְאֶעֱשֶׂה כֵּן", וַאֲפ"ה מִנַּיִן שֶׁהוּא חַיָּיב? קְרֵי בֵּיהּ וְלֹא יִזְבְּחוּ וּקְרֵי בֵּיהּ וְלֹא עוֹד. דְּאִי לִכְדְרַבִּי אֶלְעָזָר — לִכְתּוֹב "וְלֹא עוֹד אֶת זִבְחֵיהֶם לַשְּׂעִירִים". וְהַאי דִּכְתִיב "וְלֹא יִזְבְּחוּ" — לְאַזְהָרַת שׁוֹחֲטֵי חוּץ אֲתָא, דְּסָמִיךְ לְהַהִיא פָּרָשָׁה. ע"כ. עַד הַמִּקְרָא הַזֶּה דְּ"לֹא יִזְבְּחוּ", כָּל הָעִנְיָן הָעֶלְיוֹן, כא] *שֶׁנֶּעֱנָשׁ כָּרֵת עַל שְׁחִיטַת חוּץ וְעַל הַעֲלָאַת חוּץ. מְדַבֵּר בְּקָדָשִׁים שֶׁהִקְדִּישָׁן בִּשְׁעַת אִיסּוּר הַבָּמוֹת. מִשֶּׁהוּקַם הַמִּשְׁכָּן. דְּאִילּוּ הָנָךְ דְּהוּקְדְּשׁוּ מֵעִיקָּרָא, אִי לָא מְרַבֵּי לְהוּ קְרָא בְּהֶדְיָא — מִסְּתַמָּא לָא שָׁמְעִינַן לְהוּ.

ראב"ש רש"ק · נ"ל והעלה בחוץ חייב וכ"ה במשנה שבמשניות]

תוספות

כיון שנגע בו טימאהו. אע"ג דמשכחת לה כשתחב לו חבירו בבית הבליעה – סתמא דמילתא איירי קרא אפילו בנותן לתוך פיו*. **אזהרה** מנלן. פי' בקונטרס: דקא מחייבי ליה עלה *[חטאת]. שאין חטאת באה אלא על לאו וכרת, כדתנן: הפסח והמילה מצות עשה ואין חייבין עליהן חטאת, במסכת כריתות (דף ב.). וקשה לפי': דבריש "אלו הן הלוקין" (מכות דף יג:) משמע דקרבן לא בעי אזהרה, דפריך התם: ודילמא אזהרה לקרבן הוא, דהא פסח ומילה דלית בהו אזהרה לא מייתי קרבן! ומשני: התם היינו טעמא משום דאיתקוש כל התורה כולה לעבודה זרה, מה עבודה זרה שב ואל תעשה – לאפוקי הני דקום עשה נינהו! ונראה לפרש: דהאי דבעי הכא אזהרה מנא לן, היינו משום דחשיב ליה בפרק "אלו הן הלוקין" (שם.): השוחט והמעלה בחוץ. ולאו אמתני'* קאי. והאי דקתני בכריתות (דף ב.): הפסח והמילה מצות עשה – היינו כלומר דקום עשה נינהו, ולהכי לית בהו חטאת. ומיהו, לקמן בשמעתין משמע דלאפוקי לאו קאתיא. דפריך רבא: הא דתנן פסח ומילה מצות עשה, תיתי בק"ו ממותיר: ומה מותיר שלא ענש הזהיר כו'. וכן פ' "המוצא תפילין" (עירובין דף צו.) יצא פסח [ומילה] שהן מצות עשה. [ופריך]: הא כתיב "ושמרת את החוקה", וא"ר אילעאי: כל מקום שנאמר השמר פן ואל הוי לא תעשה! אלמא הוי פירושא יצא פסח [ומילה] שיש בעשה היינו שאין בהן לאו ואזהרה! ואין לומר דסוגיא דידן כרבינא, דמשני שינויא אחרינא בפרק "אלו הן הלוקין" (מכות דף יג:), ומצי למימר אליביה דקרבן קבעי אזהרה. דמ"מ קשיא דרבא אדרבא, דהיינו רבא בשמעתין, ושסיא מסקנא דמכות דקרבן לא בעי אזהרה אליבא דרבא. ולפירוש הקונטרס נמי קשה קצת: דהאי תלי טעמא דפסח ומילה משום דלית בהו לאו? תיפוק ליה משום דלית בהו מעשה. דאפילו לר"ע דאמר לא בעי מעשה – הא אמר ריש לקיש בריש כריתות (דף ג:): נהי דלא בעי ר"ע מעשה רבה, מעשה זוטא בעי! מיהו, איכא לאוקמה שמעתין כרבי יוחנן, דאמר: ר"ע לא בעי מעשה כלל. ונראה לפרש: דלישנא דמתני' קא דייק, דקתני: פסח ומילה מצות עשה – היינו שהם בקום עשה. ומשמע נמי הלשון דלית בהו אזהרה כלל.

מניין לזובח בהמה למרקולים שהוא חייב. פי' בקונטרס: אע"פ שעבודתו דרך בזיון, לסקלו באבנים, וזה עובדו דרך כבוד, ולא קרינא ביה "איכה יעבדו הגוים האלה את אלהיהם ואעשה כן", אפ"ה מניין שחייב? ונראה דכל הנהו דלאו אורחייהו בזביחה, אע"ג דמכובדים נינהו – לא נפקא מ"איכה יעבדו", כדמוכח בפרק "ארבע מיתות" (סנהדרין דף סג.). דאמר אביי: שלש השתחואות בעבודה זרה [למה]? אחת לכדרכה, ואחת לשלא כדרכה, ואחת לחלק. ופריך: כדרכה מאיכה

נ"ל אמתני' דהכא קאי נ"ק · גי' יעב"ץ · נ"ק · חולין קח. · נ"א אילעאי · [נ"ל סמנים]

עין משפט נר מצוה

[ועי' תוס' חולין קח. ד"ה ספיר ותוס' סנהדרין פג: ד"ה פרט]

עג א מיי' פ"ז מהל' מעשה הקרבנות הלכה ז:

עד ב ג מיי' פ"ה מהל' פרה אדומה הל"ה:

ד ה מיי' פי"ח מהל' מעשה הקרבנות הל"ה:

ו מיי' פי"ח מהלכות פסולי המוקדשין הלכה יג:

ז מיי' שם הל' יב:

ח מיי' פ"ג מהלכות ע"ז הל' ג:

הגהות הב"ח

(א) רש"י ד"ה ודלמא וכו' סופך הס"ד ואח"כ מה"ד מסייע כגון המתעסק: (ב) שם ד"ה לשויא וכו' לא מיקרי ולר"ש כנ"ל ותיבת אליעזר ברבי נמחק: (ג) שם ד"ה אלא וכו' כדתנן במס' כריתות פסח וכו' חטאת הס"ד: (ד) שם ד"ה למרקולים וכו' איכה יעבדו ואפ"ה נ"ל ותיבות ואעשה כן נמחק:

[נ"ל יביאנו]

עירובין צו: סוטה ה. ע"ז מ: שבועות ז. לו: מכות יג: מנחות לו: לט:

[סנהדרין סא: ע"ז נא.]

גליון הש"ס

תוס' ד"ה אזהרה וכו' קרבן לא בעי אזהרה. עיין בב"ק דף קה ע"ב תוס' ד"ה מאי לאו ושבועות דף יח ע"ב תוס' ד"ה ל"ת:

שיטה מקובצת

א] ירושלים ולרבנן תיבת אלא נמחק: ב] הדשן הן נשרפין. עי' בכפתור ופרח דף כ"א ע"ב: ג] תי' היא נמחק: ד] אביי ודלמא: ה] השורף והמתעסק בצרכי שריפה מטמא בגדים: ו] תיבות מטמא בגדים נמחק: ז] השורף זה המסייע: ח] בשלמא העלאה כתיב: ט] יביאנו אזהרה תיבת הביאו נמחק: י] עוד את זבחיהם לשעירים האי: יא] דאמר ר"א מנין: יב] לכדרכה דנפקא לן מאיכה יעבדו: יג] מה"ד לרבנן דמפקי: יד] המזבח שיהא: טו] שריפתן בגוף דכתיב אותם כגון: טז] לא הוי לתנא: יז] תיבות אליעזר ברבי נמחק: יח] בחוץ והמעלה בחוץ: יט] ואפ"ה כי הדר: כ] ליה עלה: כא] שענש כרת:

תורה אור

ויקרא יז · דברים יב · ויקרא יז · שם · שם · שם

שֶׁהֲרֵי עוֹנְשָׁן אָמוּר — °"וְאֶל פֶּתַח אֹהֶל מוֹעֵד", אַזְהָרָה — א] דִּכְתִיב: °"הִשָּׁמֶר לְךָ פֶּן תַּעֲלֶה עוֹלוֹתֶיךָ". מִכָּאן וָאֵילָךְ — ב] בִּזְבָחִים שֶׁהִקְדִּישָׁן בִּשְׁעַת הֶיתֵּר הַבָּמוֹת וְהִקְרִיבָן בִּשְׁעַת אִיסּוּר הַבָּמוֹת, ג] שֶׁנֶּאֱ': °"לְמַעַן אֲשֶׁר יָבִיאוּ בְּנֵי יִשְׂרָאֵל אֶת זִבְחֵיהֶם אֲשֶׁר הֵם זוֹבְחִים" — זְבָחִים שֶׁהִתַּרְתִּי לְךָ כְּבָר, "עַל פְּנֵי הַשָּׂדֶה" — לוֹמַר לְךָ: הַזּוֹבֵחַ בִּשְׁעַת אִיסּוּר הַבָּמוֹת מַעֲלֶה עָלָיו הַכָּתוּב כְּאִילּוּ הִקְרִיב עַל פְּנֵי הַשָּׂדֶה. °"וֶהֱבִיאוּם לַה'" — זוֹ מִצְוַת עֲשֵׂה, ד] לֹא תַעֲשֶׂה מִנַּיִן? ת"ל: °"וְלֹא יִזְבְּחוּ עוֹד". יָכוֹל יְהֵא עָנוּשׁ כָּרֵת? ת"ל: °"חוּקַּת עוֹלָם תִּהְיֶה זֹּאת לָהֶם לְדוֹרוֹתָם", "זֹאת לָהֶם" — וְלֹא אַחֶרֶת לָהֶם! אֶלָּא אָמַר (א) ה] (ר' אָבִין): ק"ו, וּמַה בְּמָקוֹם שֶׁלֹּא עָנַשׁ — הִזְהִיר, מָקוֹם שֶׁעָנַשׁ — אֵינוֹ דִּין שֶׁהִזְהִיר? א"ל רָבִינָא ו] לְרַב אַשִׁי: א"כ, לֹא יֹאמַר לָאו בְּחֵלֶב, וְתֵיתֵי ק"ו מִנְּבֵילָה: מַה נְּבֵילָה שֶׁלֹּא עָנַשׁ — הִזְהִיר, חֵלֶב שֶׁעָנַשׁ — אֵינוֹ דִּין שֶׁהִזְהִיר? אֲתָא לְקַמֵּיהּ דְּרָבָא, א"ל: מִנְּבֵלָה ז] נַמִי לָא אָתְיָא, דְּאִיכָּא לְמִיפְרַךְ: מַה לִּנְבֵלָה — שֶׁכֵּן מְטַמָּא. מִשְּׁרָצִים טְמֵאִין! מַה לִּשְׁרָצִים טְמֵאִין שֶׁמְּטַמְּאִין *בְּמַשֶּׁהוּ. מִשְּׁרָצִים טְהוֹרִים! מַה לִּשְׁרָצִים טְהוֹרִים שֶׁאִיסּוּרָן בְּמַשֶּׁהוּ. מֵעָרְלָה וְכִלְאֵי הַכֶּרֶם! מַה לְּעָרְלָה וְכִלְאֵי הַכֶּרֶם שֶׁכֵּן אֲסוּרִין בַּהֲנָאָה. מִשְּׁבִיעִית! מַה לִּשְׁבִיעִית שֶׁכֵּן תּוֹפֶסֶת דָּמֶיהָ. מִתְּרוּמָה! ח] שֶׁכֵּן לֹא הוּתַּר מִכְּלָלָהּ. מִכּוּלְּהוּ נַמִי, שֶׁכֵּן לֹא הוּתְּרוּ מִכְּלָלָן. אֲמַר רָבָא: אִי קַשְׁיָא לִי — הָא קַשְׁיָא לִי, הָא דִּתְנַן: *פֶּסַח וּמִילָה מִצְוֹת עֲשֵׂה — תֵּיתֵי בְּק"ו מִמּוֹתִיר: מַה מּוֹתִיר שֶׁלֹּא עָנַשׁ — הִזְהִיר, פֶּסַח וּמִילָה שֶׁעָנַשׁ — אֵינוֹ דִּין שֶׁהִזְהִיר? אָמַר רַב אַשִׁי: אֲמַרִיתָהּ לִשְׁמַעְתָּא קַמֵּיהּ דְּרַב כָּהֲנָא, וַאֲמַר לִי: מִמּוֹתִיר לָא אָתְיָא, דְּאִיכָּא לְמִיפְרַךְ: מַה לְּמוֹתִיר — שֶׁכֵּן אֵין לוֹ תַּקָּנָה, תֹּאמַר ט] פֶּסַח יֵשׁ לוֹ תַּקָּנָה. וְכִי מַזְהִירִין מִן הַדִּין? אֲפִילּוּ לְמ"ד *עוֹנְשִׁין מִן הַדִּין, אֵין מַזְהִירִין מִן הַדִּין! אֶלָּא *כִּדְרַבִּי יוֹחָנָן, דְּאָמַר: י] אָתְיָא הֲבָאָה הֲבָאָה, מַה לְּהַלָּן לֹא עָנַשׁ אא"כ הִזְהִיר — אַף כָּאן לֹא עָנַשׁ אא"כ הִזְהִיר.

רָבָא

עירובין נו. כריתות ב. · סנהדרין נד. וש"נ מכות · [בילקוט אחרי רמז תקפ הגי' אלא אמר אתיא]

שֶׁהֲרֵי עוֹנְשָׁן אָמוּר. כְּלוֹמַר, דְּמִסְתָּמָא בְּהוּ מִשְׁתָּעֵי קְרָא לֶאֱסוֹר, וַהֲרֵי עוֹנְשָׁן אָמוּר כָּאן. מִכָּאן וְאֵילָךְ כו'. שֶׁנֶּאֱמַר: "לְמַעַן אֲשֶׁר יָבִיאוּ" וגו'. דְּמִדִּכְתִיב "אֲשֶׁר הֵם זוֹבְחִים" מַשְׁמַע שֶׁהָיוּ עוֹמְדִים לִישָּׁחֵט בְּבָמָה, וּמִכָּאן וְאֵילָךְ "וֶהֱבִיאוּם לַה'" (ב). כְּזוֹבֵחַ בַּשָּׂדֶה. שֶׁלֹּא לְשֵׁם שָׁמַיִם. (מִצְוַת)9 לֹא תַעֲשֶׂה. בְּהָנָךְ דְּהוּקְדְּשׁוּ בִּשְׁעַת הֶיתֵּר, מִנַּיִן? ת"ל וְלֹא יִזְבְּחוּ עוֹד. מַשְׁמַע: מֵעַכְשָׁיו אֲסוּרִין, וְעַד עַכְשָׁיו יא] מוּתָּרִין. זֹאת לָהֶם. עוֹנֶשׁ עֲשֵׂה וְלֹא תַעֲשֶׂה. וְלֹא אַחֶרֶת לָהֶם. כָּרֵת. מָקוֹם שֶׁלֹּא עָנַשׁ. כְּגוֹן בְּקָדָשִׁים שֶׁהִקְדִּישָׁן בִּשְׁעַת הֶיתֵּר. הִזְהִיר. כִּדְאָמְרַן יב] כָּאן. יג] שֶׁעָנַשׁ. כְּשֶׁהוּקְדְּשׁוּ בִּשְׁעַת אִיסּוּר. אֵינוֹ דִּין שֶׁהִזְהִיר. וּלְקַמָּן פָּרֵיךְ: וְכִי מַזְהִירִין מִן הַדִּין? מִשְּׁרָצִים. וְא"ת: תֵּיתֵי אַזְהָרָה בְּחֵלֶב בְּק"ו מִשְּׁרָצִים טְמֵאִין, כְּגוֹן שְׁמוֹנָה שְׁרָצִים? בְּמַשֶּׁהוּ. טוּמְאָתָן בְּכַעֲדָשָׁה, אֲבָל חֵלֶב — בְּכַזַּיִת. מִשְּׁרָצִים טְהוֹרִים. שֶׁאֵין מְטַמְּאִין, כְּגוֹן צְפַרְדֵּעַ וּנְמָלָה. שֶׁכֵּן אֲסוּרִין בְּמַשֶּׁהוּ. לַאֲכִילָה בְּכַעֲדָשָׁה, כִּדְתַנְיָא בִּמְעִילָה בַּגְּמָרָא בְּפֶרֶק "קָדְשֵׁי מִזְבֵּחַ" (דף טו:): "וְלֹא תְשַׁקְּצוּ אֶת נַפְשׁוֹתֵיכֶם בַּבְּהֵמָה וּבָעוֹף" וגו', פָּתַח הַכָּתוּב בַּאֲכִילָה וְסִיֵּים בְּטוּמְאָה, לוֹמַר לְךָ: כְּשִׁיעוּר טוּמְאָתָן שֶׁל שְׁרָצִים טְמֵאִים — שִׁיעוּר אֲכִילָתָן שֶׁל כָּל הַשְּׁרָצִים, דְּהָא כּוּלְּהוּ כָּיֵיל לְהוּ בְּהַאי קְרָא: "וּבְכֹל אֲשֶׁר תִּרְמוֹשׂ הָאֲדָמָה" וגו'. וְשִׁיעוּר טוּמְאָתָן נָפְקָא לָן בְּ"הַכֹּל חַיָּיבִים" (חגיגה דף יא:): שֶׁכֵּן חוֹמֶט תְּחִלַּת בְּרִיָּיתוֹ בְּכַעֲדָשָׁה. שֶׁכֵּן תּוֹפֶסֶת אֶת דָּמֶיהָ. בְּאִיסּוּרָא, כִּדְתַנְיָא בְּמַסֶּכֶת סוּכָּה (דף מ:): "קֹדֶשׁ תִּהְיֶה לָכֶם", מַה קֹּדֶשׁ תּוֹפֵס אֶת דָּמָיו — אַף שְׁבִיעִית תּוֹפֶסֶת אֶת דָּמֶיהָ. מִכְּלָלוֹ. חֵלֶב הוּתַּר מִכְּלָלוֹ בְּחַיָּה. וּבְכוּלְּהוּ נַמִי אִיכָּא לְמִיפְרַךְ הָא פִּירְכָא, וּמִשּׁ"ה אִיצְטְרִיךְ אַזְהָרָה בְּחֵלֶב. אִי קַשְׁיָא. יד] בְּהַאי דְּאַיְיתִינָא אַזְהָרָה לִשְׁחוּטֵי חוּץ בְּהַאי ק"ו — הָא קַשְׁיָא לִי: הָא דִּתְנַן בְּפֶרֶק קַמָּא דִּכְרֵיתוֹת (דף ב.), דְּקָחָשֵׁיב ל"ו כָּרֵיתוֹת לְהִתְחַיֵּיב עֲלֵיהֶם חַטָּאת, וְקָתָנֵי: וְהַפֶּסַח וְהַמִּילָה כָּרֵת שֶׁלָּהֶם עַל מִצְוַת עֲשֵׂה הִיא בָּאָה, וְאֵין חַיָּיבִין חַטָּאת עַל שִׁגְגָתָהּ, דְּחַטָּאת אֵינָהּ בָּאָה אֶלָּא עַל לָאו וְכָרֵת, כְּדִכְתִיב: "אֲשֶׁר לֹא תֵעָשֶׂינָה" (ויקרא ד). תֵּיתֵי. בּוֹ אַזְהָרָה טו] מִק"ו, מִמּוֹתִיר מִמֶּנּוּ עַד בּוֹקֶר. שֶׁיֵּשׁ לוֹ תַּקָּנָה. בְּתַשְׁלוּמֵי פֶּסַח שֵׁנִי. וְכִי מַזְהִירִין מִן הַדִּין. לְעֵיל קָאֵי, דְּמַיְיתֵי אַזְהָרָה לִשְׁחוּטֵי חוּץ מִק"ו. אֲפִילּוּ לְמ"ד. בְּמַסֶּכֶת מַכּוֹת: עוֹנְשִׁין מִדִּין ק"ו — מוֹדֶה דְּאֵין מַזְהִירִין מִן הַדִּין. דְּתַנְיָא בְּפ"ק דְּמַכּוֹת (דף ה:): "אִישׁ כִּי יִקַּח אֶת אֲחוֹתוֹ" וגו', אֵין לִי אֶלָּא בַּת אָבִיו שֶׁלֹּא בַּת אִמּוֹ, בַּת אִמּוֹ שֶׁלֹּא בַּת אָבִיו, בַּת אָבִיו וּבַת אִמּוֹ מִנַּיִן? תַּלְמוּד לוֹמַר: "עֶרְוַת אֲחוֹתוֹ גִּילָּה". וַהֲלֹא קַל וָחוֹמֶר הוּא! לִמַּדְתָּה שֶׁאֵין עוֹנְשִׁין מִן הַדִּין. וְכֵן לְעִנְיַן אַזְהָרַת "עֶרְוַת אֲחוֹתְךָ בַת אָבִיךָ" וגו' — אֵין לִי כו', עַד "שֶׁאֵין מַזְהִירִין מִן הַדִּין". וּפְלִיגִי תַּנָּאֵי בְּפֶ' בַּתְרָא, וְאִיכָּא דְּדָרֵישׁ לְהַאי "אֲחוֹתוֹ גִּילָּה" דְּגַבֵּי עוֹנֶשׁ לִדְרָשָׁא, (ג) טז] וְעוֹנֶשׁ דְּבַת אָבִיו וּבַת אִמּוֹ — קָסָבַר עוֹנְשִׁין מִן הַדִּין. וְאִילּוּ "אֲחוֹתְךָ הִיא" דְּגַבֵּי אַזְהָרָה דְּיָלְפִינַן מִינֵּיהּ אֵין מַזְהִירִין מִן הַדִּין, דְּלָא אַפְנְיֵיהּ לִדְרָשָׁא אַחֲרִיתֵי. אָתְיָא הֲבָאָה הֲבָאָה. שְׁחִיטָה מֵהַעֲלָאָה, כְּתִיב בִּשְׁחִיטָה (ויקרא יז): "לֹא הֱבִיאוֹ", וּכְתִיב בְּהַעֲלָאָה (שם): "לֹא יְבִיאֶנּוּ". וּגְזֵירָה שָׁוָה, הוֹאִיל וּמוּפְנָה הִיא לְכָךְ — הֲרֵי הִיא יז] כְּמִי שֶׁמְּפָרֵשׁ בָּהּ, וְאֵין זֶה מִן הַדִּין כְּק"ו שֶׁאָדָם דָּן מֵעַצְמוֹ.

ה"ג

מ"איכה יעבדו" נפקא! אלא: אחת לשלא כדרכה — ואפילו לשלא כדרכה כלל, שעובדין אותה בבזיון כגון פעור ומרקולים. ואחת כדרכה ושלא כדרכה, פי': "כדרכה" — בעבודת כבוד, אלא שאין דרכה בהשתחואה. ואם תאמר: מנלן הכא זובח בהמה למרקולים? אימא כי אתא קרא למכובדים שאין דרכן בזביחה, אבל למבוזין כגון פעור ומרקולים — לא! וי"ל: דגלי ליה בהשתחואה דמכובדים ומבוזין שוין — הוא הדין בזביחה. ור"ת מפרש: דתרי קראי בזביחה כתיבי, האי קרא דהכא "ולא יזבחו", ועוד כתיב "זובח לאלהים יחרם", דדרשינן בפ' "ארבע מיתות" (סנהדרין דף סא.) דילתה זביחה ללמד על הכלל, לחייב בכל עבודת פנים אפילו בשלא כדרכה. וקשה לפי', דמהאי קרא לא שמעינן אלא אזהרה, אל עונש במבוזין מנא לן? ועוד: תרוייהו למכובדין צריכי, חד לעונש וחד לאזהרה! ועוד: דלא ה"ל לאיתויי "איכה יעבדו". אלא הוה ליה למימר: אם אינו ענין לכדרכה של מכובדין, דכתיב "זובח לאלהים יחרם" — תנהו ענין לשלא כדרכה, כלומר: מבוזין! אלא כמו שפירשנו נראה, דרבי אלעזר אכל שלא כדרכה אתא לאשמועי' דחייב, אלא דנקט מרקולים לרבותא. ומהשתחואה נפקא לן דאין חילוק בין מכובדין למבוזין, כדפרי'. תדע, דהא אמר בפרק "ד' מיתות" (שם דף סד:): ג' כריתות בעבודה זרה למה? אחת לכדרכה, ואחת לשלא כדרכה, ואחת למולך. ולא מיבעיא לן קרא אחרינא חד למכובדין וחד למבוזין. וק"ק: הא דפריך בפ' "ד' מיתות": אימא ילתה השתחואה ללמד על הכלל כולו, ודקאמרת זובח למה לי — לגופיה דמחשבין מעבודה לעבודה. ומתמה עליה הש"ס: אלא הא דקאמר רבי אלעזר מניין לזובח בהמה למרקולים כו', מהשתחואה נפקא. מאי קושיא? דילמא איצטריך לאזהרה במחשב מעבודה לעבודה. דהא לעולם הוא כך, ד"לא יזבחו" אזהרה לעונש ד"זובח לאלהים יחרם"! וי"ל: דאם איתא דהשתחואה ללמד על הכלל, א"כ "לא תעבדם" דאוקמינן (סנהדרין דף ס:) למגפף ומנשק, הוה מייתר לן לאזהרה *אזביחה, דמהשתחואה הוה ילפינן אפילו חיוב מיתה במגפף ומנשק. **אזהרה** מניין ת"ל השמר לך פן תעלה עולותיך. הא דמייתי אזביחה אזהרה דהעלאה — אמסקנא סמיך, דילפי "הבאה" "הבאה", או "שם שם". אבל לאביי דבסמוך קשה: דק"ו הו"ל לאתויי! **מקום** שענש אינו דין שהזהיר. ולא שייך למימר: פסח ומילה יוכיחו. דאיכא למיפרך: שכן קום עשה. **מה** לשרצים טהורים שכן אסורין במשהו. פי' בקונטרס: דתניא במסכת מעילה בפר "קדשי מזבח" (דף טו:): "ולא תשקצו את נפשותיכם בבהמה ובעוף" וגו', פתח הכתוב באכילה וסיים בטומאה, לומר: כשיעור טומאתן של שרצים טמאים — שיעור אכילתן של כל השרצים, דהא כולהו כייל להו בהאי קרא "ובכל אשר תרמוש" וגו'. ושיעור טומאתן נפקא לן ב"הכל חייבין" (חגיגה דף יא:) שכן חומט תחילת ברייתו בכעדשה. עד כאן לשון הקונטרס. ואגב חורפיה לא עיין בה ובהדיא מסיק התם: דוקא בשרצים טמאים ולא בטהורים, דאמרינן: במובדלין דיבר הכתוב, דכתיב בסיפיה דקרא "אשר הבדלתי לכם לטמא". ונ"ל ד"כל שהוא" דהכא — בבריה קמיירי, דבכל שהוא מיחייב משום בריה, כדאמרינן בפ"ק דחגיגה (דף י.) ובפ' "כהן גדול ונזיר" (נזיר דף נב.), ובמכות (דף יז.), ובפ' "גיד הנשה" (חולין דף צו.*). **מכולהו** שכן לא הותר מכללן. תימה: נילף בכולהו כרת בק"ו מחלב, שהותר מכללו! **תיתי** בק"ו ממותיר. הא דנקט מותיר טפי מגזל וגניבה וכמה לאוין שבתורה — משום דמותיר לא עביד מעשה, דומיא דפסח ומילה. ומש"ה לא נקט נמי הנך דלעיל, דאיכא למיפרך: שכן יש בהן מעשה.

ה"ג

גי' רש"ק אביי

[עי' תוס' חולין קכ. ד"ה שכן וכו' דמה דאיתא הכא (מה לשרצים טמאים שמטמאין) בכל שהוא לא גרסי' לה וסופרים שכתבו משום דבתר הכי קאמר מה לשרצים טהורים שאיסורן במשהו ע"ש ומעתה הבבלית דמה דאיתא בפירש"י ד"ה משרצים וכו' וכן בד"ה במשהו וכו' לאו רש"י כתבו אלא תלמיד אחר פי' כן ע"פ הגי' שכתבו הסופרים ותדע דכך היא דאם מפי רש"י יצאו הדברים תמוה טובא במ"ש ד"ה במשהו כו' אבל חלב בכזית הלא ידענא דחלב אינו מטמא כלל וטהור לגמרי כמבואר הכא דקאמר מה לנבלה שכן מטמא כלומר אבל חלב אינו מטמא וכן נתבאר להדיא בפסחים כג.]

נ"ל אמחשב מעבודה לעבודה דמהשתחואה כו' נ"ק

[ועי' תוס' יבמות ק ד"ה משום ותוס' חולין ד"ה שכן]

הגהות הב"ח

(א) גמ' אלא אמר אביי ק"ו. נ"ב כצ"ל וכן הוא בילקוט רמז תקפ"ח*) מבואר בתוס' ד"ה אזהרה וכן משמע להדיא מג (ב) רש"י ד"ה מכאן וכו' לה' הס"ד ואח"כ מה"ד כאילו הקריב על השדה: (ג) שם ד"ה אזהרה למ"ד כו' דילפינן מי בת אביו ובת אמו ועונש וכו':

*) [לפנינו בילקוט איתא ר' אבין]

שיטה מקובצת

א] אזהרה מנין דכתיב: ב] ואילך הוא מדבר בזבחים: ג] הבמות שהרי נאמר למען ותיבת שנאמר נמחק: ד] עשה מצות ל"ת: ה] אמר אביי ק"ו ותיבות ר' אבין נמחק: ו] רבינא לאביי א"כ ותיבות לרב אשי נמחק: ז] תיבת נמי נמחק: ח] מתרומה מה לתרומה שכן לא הותר מכולהו מה לכולהו שכן תיבת נמי נמחק: ט] תאמר בפסח שיש לו: י] דאמר ר' יוחנן אתיא: יא] עכשיו היו מותרין: יב] תיבת כאן נמחק: יג] מה"ד מקום שענש: יד] קשא לי בהא דאייתינן אזהרה: טו] אזהרה בק"ו ואות מ' נמחק: טז] לדרשה אחריתי ועונש: יז] כמו שמפורש בה:

רָבָא אָמַר: כִּדְרַבִּי יוֹנָה, דְּאָמַר רַבִּי יוֹנָה: אאָתְיָא "שָׁם" "שָׁם", מַה לְּהַלָּן לֹא עָנַשׁ אֶלָּא א"כ הִזְהִיר – אַף כָּאן לֹא עָנַשׁ אֶלָּא אִם כֵּן הִזְהִיר. אַשְׁכַּחַן מוּקְטְרֵי פְּנִים שֶׁהֶעֱלָן א] לַחוּץ, מוּקְטְרֵי חוּץ שֶׁהֶעֱלָן לַחוּץ מְנַיִן? אָמַר רַב כָּהֲנָא, אָמַר קְרָא: °"וַאֲלֵיהֶם תֹּאמַר" – *עַל ב] הַסְּמוּכִין תֹּאמַר. מַתְקִיף לָהּ ג] רָבָא: מִי כְּתִיב "וַעֲלֵיהֶם"? "וַאֲלֵיהֶם" כְּתִיב! אֶלָּא כִּדְתָנָא דְּבֵי ר' יִשְׁמָעֵאל: "וַאֲלֵיהֶם תֹּאמַר" – לְעָרֵב פָּרָשִׁיּוֹת. *ר' יוֹחָנָן אָמַר: אָתְיָא "הֲבָאָה" "הֲבָאָה", מַה לְּהַלָּן מוּקְטְרֵי חוּץ – אַף כָּאן מוּקְטְרֵי חוּץ. מַתְקִיף לָהּ רַב בֵּיבָי: ד] הָא דִּתְנַן *שְׁלֹשִׁים וָשֵׁשׁ כְּרֵיתוֹת בַּתּוֹרָה – תְּלָתִין וְשַׁב הָוְיָין, דְּאִיכָּא הַמַּעֲלֶה וְהַמַּעֲלֶה! קַשְׁיָא. וְהָדְתְנַן:* בהַזּוֹרֵק מִקְצָת דָּמִים בַּחוּץ – חַיָּיב, מְנָלַן? נָפְקָא לֵיהּ מִדְּתַנְיָא: *°"דָּם יֵחָשֵׁב" – לְרַבּוֹת הַזּוֹרֵק, דִּבְרֵי רַבִּי יִשְׁמָעֵאל. ר"ע אוֹמֵר: °"אוֹ זָבַח" – לְרַבּוֹת אֶת הַזּוֹרֵק. וְרַבִּי יִשְׁמָעֵאל, הַאי "אוֹ זָבַח" מַאי עָבֵיד לֵיהּ? ה] לְחַלֵּק. וְר' עֲקִיבָא לְחַלֵּק מְנָא לֵיהּ? נָפְקָא לֵיהּ °מִ"לֹּא יְבִיאֶנּוּ". וְרַבִּי יִשְׁמָעֵאל: הַהוּא מִיבְּעֵי לֵיהּ: * געַל הַשָּׁלֵם הוּא חַיָּיב, וְאֵינוֹ חַיָּיב עַל הֶחָסֵר. וְרַבִּי עֲקִיבָא? נָפְקָא לֵיהּ °מִ"לַּעֲשׂוֹת אוֹתוֹ". וְר' יִשְׁמָעֵאל: חַד לְמוּקְטְרֵי פְנִים שֶׁחֲסֵרוּ ו] וְהֶעֱלוּ בַּחוּץ, וְחַד לְמוּקְטְרֵי חוּץ שֶׁחֲסֵרוּ וְהֶעֱלוּ בַּחוּץ. וְהָא תַּנְיָא, רַבִּי יִשְׁמָעֵאל אוֹמֵר: יָכוֹל מוּקְטְרֵי פְּנִים שֶׁחֲסֵרוּ ז] וְהֶעֱלוּ בַּחוּץ חַיָּיב? דת"ל: "לַעֲשׂוֹת אוֹתוֹ" – עַל הַשָּׁלֵם חַיָּיב, וְאֵינוֹ חַיָּיב עַל הֶחָסֵר. וְרַבִּי עֲקִיבָא: ח] מוּקְטְרֵי פְּנִים שֶׁחֲסֵרוּ וְהֶעֱלוּ בַּחוּץ חַיָּיב. וְרַבִּי עֲקִיבָא, הַאי "דָּם יֵחָשֵׁב" מַאי עָבֵיד לֵיהּ? הלְרַבּוֹת שְׁחִיטַת הָעוֹף. וְרַבִּי יִשְׁמָעֵאל? נָפְקָא לֵיהּ °מֵ"אוֹ אֲשֶׁר יִשְׁחַט". וְרַבִּי עֲקִיבָא אָמַר לָךְ, הַהוּא מִיבְּעֵי לֵיהּ: עַל הַשּׁוֹחֵט הוּא חַיָּיב, ט] וְלֹא עַל הַמּוֹלֵק. וְר' יִשְׁמָעֵאל? נָפְקָא לֵיהּ מִ"זֶּה הַדָּבָר". דְּתַנְיָא: "אֲשֶׁר יִשְׁחַט" – אֵין לִי אֶלָּא שׁוֹחֵט בְּהֵמָה, שָׁחַט עוֹף מנ"ל? ת"ל: "אוֹ אֲשֶׁר יִשְׁחַט". יָכוֹל י] אַף הַמּוֹלֵק? וְדִין הוּא: מַה שְּׁחִיטָה דְּאֵין דֶּרֶךְ הֶכְשֵׁירָהּ בִּפְנִים – חַיָּיב, מְלִיקָה שֶׁדֶּרֶךְ הֶכְשֵׁירָהּ בִּפְנִים – אֵינוֹ דִּין שֶׁהוּא חַיָּיב? ת"ל: °"זֶה הַדָּבָר". וְרַבִּי עֲקִיבָא אָמַר לָךְ: הַהוּא מִיבְּעֵי לֵיהּ *לִגְזֵירָה שָׁוָה. וְהָא דִּתְנַן: יהַקּוֹמֵץ וְהַמְקַבֵּל דָּמִים בַּחוּץ – פָּטוּר, מְנָלַן? וּמֵהֵיכָא תֵּיתֵי דְּחַיָּיב? תֵּיתֵי מִשְּׁחִיטָה – *מַה לִּשְׁחִיטָה חשֶׁכֵּן יא] נִפְסֶלֶת שֶׁלֹּא לָאוֹכְלִין בְּפֶסַח! תֵּיתֵי מִזְּרִיקָה – מַה לִּזְרִיקָה שֶׁכֵּן זָר חַיָּיב עָלֶיהָ מִיתָה!

תֵּיתֵי

רש"י

ה"ג: דְּאָמַר רַבִּי יוֹנָה אָמַר קְרָא שָׁם תַּעֲלֶה עוֹלוֹתֶיךָ וְשָׁם תַּעֲשֶׂה. אִיתְקַשׁ שְׁאָר עֲשִׂיּוֹת לְהַעֲלָאָה מָה הַעֲלָאָה לֹא עָנַשׁ אֶלָּא אִם כֵּן הִזְהִיר אַף שְׁחִיטָה לֹא עָנַשׁ אֶלָּא א"כ הִזְהִיר. אַשְׁכַּחַן מוּקְטָרֵי יב] בִּפְנִים שֶׁהֶעֱלָן בַּחוּץ. שְׁחוּטֵי פְנִים, שֶׁהָיוּ עוֹמְדִים לְהַקְטִירָן בִּפְנִים יג] וְהֶעֱלוּ בַּחוּץ – חַיָּיב, כִּדְכְתִיב בְּהַעֲלָאָה (ויקרא יז): "וְאֶל פֶּתַח אֹהֶל מוֹעֵד לֹא יְבִיאֶנּוּ" – בִּרְאוּיִין לְהָבִיאָן לִפְנִים וּלְהַעֲלוֹתָן הַכָּתוּב מְדַבֵּר. מוּקְטָרֵי חוּץ. שְׁחוּטֵי חוּץ, שֶׁעוֹמְדִין לִיקָטֵר בַּחוּץ וְלֹא בִּפְנִים. וַאֲלֵיהֶם תֹּאמַר. זֶהוּ תְּחִלַּת פָּרָשַׁת הַעֲלָאָה, וּסְמוּכָה לְפָרָשַׁת שְׁחוּטֵי חוּץ. עַל הָרִאשׁוֹנִים, דְּמִשְׁתָּעֵי בִּשְׁחוּטֵי חוּץ, יד] *שֶׁאָמַר שֶׁאִם הֶעֱלוּ בַּחוּץ חַיָּיב, "וַעֲלֵיהֶם" קָרֵינַן. וַאֲלֵיהֶם כְּתִיב טו]. לְשׁוֹן קוּשְׁיָא הוּא. ה"ג: אֶלָּא כִּדְתָנָא דְּבֵי ר' יִשְׁמָעֵאל וַאֲלֵיהֶם תֹּאמַר לְעָרֵב פָּרָשִׁיּוֹת. וָי"ו מוֹסִיף עַל עִנְיָן רִאשׁוֹן וּמְעָרֵב הַפָּרָשִׁיּוֹת, לוֹמַר שֶׁאַף שְׁחוּטֵי חוּץ שֶׁהֶעֱלָן בַּחוּץ חַיָּיב. ל"ו כְּרֵיתוֹת בַּתּוֹרָה. וְקָחָשֵׁיב הָתָם הַמַּעֲלֶה בַּחוּץ. וְהָוֵינַן בָּהּ: מִנְיָינָא לָמָּה לִי? וְאָמַר רַבִּי יוֹחָנָן: שֶׁאִם עֲשָׂאָן כּוּלָּן בְּהֶעְלֵם אֶחָד – חַיָּיב עַל כָּל אַחַת וְאַחַת. הָא תַּרְתֵּי נִינְהוּ לְחִיּוּבָא, הַמַּעֲלֶה אֵיבְרֵי פְנִים, וְהַמַּעֲלֶה אֵיבְרֵי חוּץ. דְּכֵיוָן דְּגָמְרַתְּ לְהוּ בְּהֶיקֵּשָׁא אוֹ בִּגְזֵירָה שָׁוָה – הֲוָה לֵיהּ כָּל חַד וְחַד גּוּף עֲבֵירָה, וְחַיָּיב עַל כָּל אַחַת וְאַחַת אֲפִילּוּ בְּהֶעְלֵם אֶחָד. וְנִיתְנֵי שְׁלֹשִׁים וָשֶׁבַע! וְהָא לֵיכָּא לְשַׁנּוּיֵי: שֵׁם הַעֲלָאָה קָתָנֵי, כִּי הֵיכִי דְּקָא חָשֵׁיב הַמְחַלֵּל אֶת הַשַּׁבָּת טז] וְהָעוֹבֵד עֲבוֹדָה זָרָה בַּחֲדָא, וְאַע"ג דְּטוּבָא חִיּוּבֵי אִיכָּא. דְּהָכִי שָׁנִינוּ בִּכְרֵיתוֹת, וְאַקְשִׁינַן עֲלָהּ (א) שַׁבָּת יז] וַעֲבוֹדָה זָרָה, [וּמְשַׁנֵּי]: תָּנָא חִילּוּקִין שֶׁלָּהֶן בִּמְקוֹמָן, דִּתְנַן בְּמַסֶּכֶת שַׁבָּת (דף עג.): אֲבוֹת מְלָאכוֹת אַרְבָּעִים חָסֵר אַחַת, וּדַעֲבוֹדָה זָרָה תָּנֵינָא בְּסַנְהֶדְרִין (דף ס:): אֶחָד הָעוֹבֵד וְאֶחָד הַזּוֹבֵחַ וְאֶחָד הַמְקַטֵּר וְאֶחָד הַמְנַסֵּךְ. אֲבָל יח] הָכָא לָא תָּנָא בְּהֶדְיָא "הַמַּעֲלֶה אֵיבְרֵי פְנִים, וְהַמַּעֲלֶה אֵיבְרֵי חוּץ". וְאַף עַל גַּב דְּאִיכָּא לְמִשְׁמַע מִפְּלוּגְתָּא דְּרַבִּי יוֹסֵי הַגְּלִילִי וְרַבָּנַן – בְּהֶדְיָא מִיהָא לָא תָּנֵינְהִי בִּתְרָתֵּי. וְהָא דִּתְנַן. לְקַמָּן בְּמַתְנִיתִין (דף קי.): הַזּוֹרֵק יט] [מִקְצָת] דָּמִים בַּחוּץ, שֶׁלֹּא נָתַן אַרְבַּע מַתָּנוֹת אֶלָּא מַתָּנָה אַחַת – חַיָּיב, דְּהָוְיָא זְרִיקָה בִּפְנִים דְּכְוָותֵיהּ, דִּתְנַן (לעיל דף לו:): כָּל הַנִּיתָּנִין עַל מִזְבֵּחַ הַחִיצוֹן שֶׁנְּתָנָן בְּמַתָּנָה אַחַת – כִּיפֵּר. מְנָלַן. דְּאִיחַיֵּיב אַזְּרִיקַת דָּם בַּחוּץ? הָא שְׁחִיטָה וְהַעֲלָאָה הוּא דִּכְתִיבָן! דָּם יֵחָשֵׁב דָּם שָׁפָךְ. לְרַבּוֹת אֶת הַזּוֹרֵק. וְהַאי כ] קְרָאֵי בִּשְׁחוּטֵי חוּץ כְּתִיבִי. אוֹ זָבַח. כְּתִיב גַּבֵּי הַעֲלָאָה. "אוֹ" – לְרַבּוֹת אֶת הַזּוֹרֵק. לְחַלֵּק. דְּלָא תֵּימָא: עַד דְּמַסֵּיק עוֹלָה וּשְׁלָמִים. לֹא יְבִיאֶנּוּ. מַשְׁמַע חַד. וְאֵינוֹ חַיָּיב עַל הֶחָסֵר. לְקַמָּן פְּלִיגֵי בָּהּ, אִיכָּא לְמַאן דְּאָמַר: עַל אֵבֶר חָסֵר, וְאִיכָּא לְמַאן דְּאָמַר: עַל בְּהֵמָה חֲסֵירָה, עַד שֶׁיַּעֲלֶה כא] כָּל הַבְּהֵמָה, וְאִיכָּא לְמַאן דְּאָמַר: עַל הַקְטָרָה חֲסֵירָה, כְּגוֹן פָּחוֹת מִכַּזַּיִת. אוֹתוֹ. שָׁלֵם מַשְׁמַע. חַד לְמוּקְטְרֵי פְּנִים כו'. דְּאִי כָּתַב חַד, הֲוָה אָמֵינָא: הָנֵי מִילֵּי מוּקְטָרֵי חוּץ. אֲבָל מוּקְטָרֵי פְּנִים – מִיחַיֵּיב, דְּהָא מְהַדְּרִינַן פּוֹקְעִין (ב) דְּחָסְרוּ, אַלְמָא הַקְטָרָה הִיא. וְהָא תַּנְיָא. כְּנִיחוּתָא. ור"ע סָבַר מוּקְטָרֵי פְּנִים. שְׁחוּטֵי פְנִים שֶׁחָסְרוּ, כְּגוֹן פָּקְעוּ מֵעַל הָאוּר וְהֶעֱלָן בַּחוּץ – חַיָּיב, דְּהָא מְהַדְּרִינַן פּוֹקְעִין. וְר' יִשְׁמָעֵאל נָפְקָא לֵיהּ מֵאוֹ אֲשֶׁר יִשְׁחַט. אַע"ג דְּאִיצְטְרִיךְ "מִחוּץ לַמַּחֲנֶה" כִּדְלְקַמָּן, אֲפִילּוּ הָכִי "אֲשֶׁר יִשְׁחַט" יְתֵירָא הוּא, דְּמָצֵי לְמִיכְתַּב כב] "אֶל מִחוּץ לַמַּחֲנֶה", אַיְּיתַר לֵיהּ "אֲשֶׁר יִשְׁחַט" לְרַבּוֹת שְׁחִיטַת הָעוֹף. הַהוּא מִיבְּעֲיָא לֵיהּ כג] הַשּׁוֹחֵט הָעוֹף חַיָּיב וְאֵינוֹ חַיָּיב עַל הַמּוֹלֵק. וְהִילְכָּךְ אִיצְטְרִיכוּ תַּרְוַיְיהוּ. דְּאִי כְּתִיב "אֲשֶׁר יִשְׁחַט" לְרַבּוֹת שְׁחִיטַת הָעוֹף, הֲוָה אָמֵינָא: כָּל שֶׁכֵּן מְלִיקָה שֶׁהִיא דֶּרֶךְ הֶכְשֵׁירוֹ בִּפְנִים – לְהָכִי כְּתִיב *"דָּם שָׁפָךְ" לְרַבּוֹת אֶת הָעוֹף. וַהֲדַר כְּתִיב "אֲשֶׁר יִשְׁחַט" לְמַעוּטֵי מוֹלֵק. אֵין לִי אֶלָּא שׁוֹחֵט בְּהֵמָה. כִּדְכְתִיב: "אֲשֶׁר יִשְׁחַט שׁוֹר אוֹ כֶשֶׂב". וּמָה שְׁחִיטָה. שֶׁאֵין זֶה דֶּרֶךְ הֶכְשֵׁירוֹ שֶׁל עוֹף בִּפְנִים, חַיָּיב עָלֶיהָ בַּחוּץ – מְלִיקָה לֹא כ"שׁ? ת"ל זֶה הַדָּבָר. "אֲשֶׁר נִוָּה" וגו', וְסָמֵיךְ לֵיהּ "אֲשֶׁר יִשְׁחַט" – שְׁחִיטָה וְלֹא מְלִיקָה. לִגְזֵירָה שָׁוָה. מְפוֹרֶשֶׁת בְּ"יֵשׁ נוֹחֲלִין" (ב"ב דף קכ:) וּבִנְדָרִים בְּפֶרֶק *בַּתְרָא (דף עח.). הַקּוֹמֵץ מִנְחָה בַּחוּץ. וְלֹא הִקְטִיר, פָּטוּר. מְנָא לֵיהּ. דְּפָטוּר. וּפָרְכִינַן: מֵהֵי תֵּיתֵי לְחִיּוּבָא. דְּאִיצְטְרִיךְ קְרָא לְמִיפְטְרֵיהּ. מַה לִּשְׁחִיטָה שֶׁכֵּן פּוֹסֶלֶת בְּפֶסַח שֶׁשְּׁחָטוֹ שֶׁלֹּא לָאוֹכְלִין. כְּגוֹן לְחוֹלֶה וְזָקֵן שֶׁאֵין יָכוֹל לֶאֱכוֹל כַּזַּיִת, כִּדְכְתִיב (שמות יב): "אִישׁ לְפִי אָכְלוֹ תָּכוֹסּוּ". תֹּאמַר בְּקוֹמֵץ מִנְחָה דְּלָא שַׁיָּיךְ כד] פְּסוּל שֶׁלֹּא לְאוֹכְלָיו. וּבְקַבָּלָה נַמִי אֲפִילּוּ בְּפֶסַח לָא מִיפַּסְלָא, כִּדְאַמְרַן בְּפֶרֶק "תָּמִיד נִשְׁחָט" (פסחים דף סא.), רַבִּי אוֹמֵר: לְשׁוֹן סוּרְסִי הוּא זֶה, כְּאָדָם שֶׁאוֹמֵר כה] "כּוֹס לִי טָלֶה זֶה". דִּבִשְׁחִיטָה לְחוּדָהּ הוּא דִּפְסָלָהּ מַחֲשֶׁבֶת אוֹכְלִין. תֵּיתֵי מִזְּרִיקָה. דְּלָא פְּסָלָהּ שֶׁלֹּא לְשֵׁם אוֹכְלִין בְּפֶסַח, וּמְחַיֵּיב עֲלָהּ בַּחוּץ, וְה"ה לִקְמִיצָה וְקַבָּלָה. שֶׁכֵּן זָר חַיָּיב עָלֶיהָ מִיתָה. מַה שֶּׁאֵין כֵּן בִּקְמִיצָה וְקַבָּלָה. דְּבָעֵינַן עֲבוֹדָה תַּמָּה, וְלֹא עֲבוֹדָה שֶׁיֵּשׁ אַחֲרֶיהָ עֲבוֹדָה, כִּדְאָמְרִינַן פֶּרֶק "בָּרִאשׁוֹנָה" בְּסֵדֶר יוֹמָא (דף כד.), וְהָנֵי תַּרְוַיְיהוּ יֵשׁ אַחֲרֵיהֶן עֲבוֹדָה.

תֵּיתֵי

תוספות

ה"ג: **דאמר** רבי יונה. בפ"ק דכריתות (דף ג:) מהיקשא יליף. **הני** תלתין ושב הויין **דאיכא המעלה והמעלה**. דכיון דגמרת להו בהיקשא או בגזירה שוה – הוה ליה כל חד וחד גוף עבירה, וחייב על כל אחת ואחת אפי' כו] *בהעלמה אחת. "והשוחט ומעלה" נמי דקתני התם בתרתי – לא ידעינן בהו תרתי לאוי אלא בגזירה שוה. פי' בקונטרס: והא ליכא לשנויי שם העלאה קתני, כי היכי דקא חשיב המחלל את השבת בחדא ואע"ג דטובא חיובי איכא. דהכי שנינן לה בכריתות (דף ג:), דאקשינן עליה: שבת ועבודה זרה תנא חלוקין שלהן במקומן, דתנן במס' שבת (דף עג:): אבות מלאכות מ' חסר אחת. ודעבודה זרה תנינן בסנהדרין (דף ס:): אחד העובד ואחד הזובח ואחד המקטר ואחד המנסך. אבל הני לא תנא הכא בהדיא: המעלה איברי פנים והמעלה איברי חוץ. ואע"ג דאיכא למשמע מפלוגתא דרבי יוסי הגלילי ורבנן – בהדיא מיהא לא תנהי בתרתי, עכ"ל. וקשה תימה: גבי עבודה זרה היכי קאמר התם בפ' קמא דכריתות (דף ג:): דקתני יתהון אבינכיהון, פירוש: במקומן? הא ליכא למשמע ממתני' דד' מיתות אלא חיוב חטאת אהנך עבודות, אבל חילוק חטאות לא שמעינן מינה!

דאיכא המעלה והמעלה קשיא. כז] קשה מהא דלא משני: ההיא דכריתות (ג"ז שם) כרבי יוסי הגלילי, דפטר מוקטרי חוץ.

מאי עביד ליה לחלק. *תימה: דהך סוגיא דלא כרבא אלא כאביי דפ' "השואל" (ב"מ דף לה:), דסבר לה כרבי יאשיה דפ' "ד' מיתות" (סנהדרין דף סו:) דבעי קרא לחלק גבי אביו ואמו.

חד למוקטרי פנים שחסרו וחד למוקטרי חוץ שחסרו. הכא לא שייך למילף מ"ואליהם תאמר", או "הבאה" "הבאה". משום דבפנים טעמא דמהדרינן פוקעין וחשיבה הקטרה, ולא שייך למילף למוקטרי חוץ.

להכי

ה א מיי' פי"ח מהלכות מעשה הקרבנות הל"ד:

ו ב מיי' פי"ט שם הל"ג:

[בס"י אי' בהעלם אחת]

ז ג מיי' שם הלכה יא:

ח ד מיי' שם הל' ט:

ט ה ו מיי' פי"ח שם הלכה יח:

י ז מיי' פי"ט שם הל"ו:

יא ח מיי' פ"ב מהלכות קרבן פסח הל' ג:

בילקוט רמז תקפ"ב פרשת אחרי מות השמיט [מתיבת ר"י עד מה להלן ושם הגי' מה להלן בשחוטי חוץ אף כאן בשחוטי חוץ] ועי' רש"ק ול"ק

עיין ל"ק

שיטה מקובצת

א] שהעלן בחוץ מוקטרי חוץ שהעלן בחוץ מנלן אמר כו': ב] על הראשונים תאמר תיבת הסמוכין נמחק: ג] לה רבה מי כתיב ועליהם תאמר ואליהם כתיב ואליהם קרינא אלא כדתנא דבי רבי ישמעאל דתנא דבי ר' ישמעאל ואליהם תאמר: ד] ביבי בר אביי הא: ה] ליה מבעי ליה לחלק: ו] והעלן בחוץ וחד כו' שחסרו והעלן בחוץ: ז] שחסרו והעלן בחוץ יהא חייב: ח] עקיבא סבר מוקטרי פנים שחסרו והעלן בחוץ: ט] חייב ואינו חייב על כו' תיבת ולא נמחק: י] יכול שאני מרבה אף: יא] שכן פוסלת שלא לשום אוכלין בפסח: יב] מוקטרי פנים: יג] בפנים והעלן בחוץ: יד] חוץ תאמר שאם: טו] כתיב ואליהם קרינן: טז] השבת בחדא והעובד: יז] תיבות ועבודה זרה נמחק ותיבת ומשני ל"ש: יח] אבל הני לא תנא הכא בהדיא: יט] הזורק מקצת דמים: כ] והאי קרא בשחוטי: כא] שיעלה את כל: כב] למיכתב או מחוץ תיבת אל נמחק: כג] ליה על השוחט חייב תיבת העוף נמחק: כד] שייך בה פסול שלא לאוכלין ובקבלה: כה] שאומר לחברו כום: כו] אפי' בהעלם אחד: כז] תימה מהא תיבת קשה נמחק:

ויקרא יז

שם

שם

שם

שם

שם

[לקמן קיט:]

נ"ל תאמר

כריתות ב.

לקמן קי.

סנהדרין לד: ע"ש

[לקמן קח: קט:]

נ"ק

[נדרים עח. ב"ב קכ:]

[לעיל ז.]

נ"ל דם יחשב נ"ק

[נ"ל בפרק נערה]

הגהות הב"ח

(א) רש"י ד"ה ל"ו כריתות וכו' ושבת וע"ז תנא. נ"ב זהו תירוץ של רש"י: (ב) שם ד"ה חד למוקטרי וכו' פוקעין שנפקעו מעל מזבח לחסרו:

תֵּיתֵי מִבֵּינַיָּיא א"כ, לֹא יֹאמַר בִּזְרִיקָה, א] וְתֵיתֵי מִבֵּינַיָּיא: וְתֵיתֵי מִשְּׁחִיטָה — מַה לִּשְׁחִיטָה שֶׁכֵּן נִפְסֶלֶת שֶׁלֹּא לְשֵׁם אוֹכְלִין בְּפֶסַח! תֵּיתֵי מֵהַעֲלָאָה — מַה לְּהַעֲלָאָה שֶׁכֵּן יֶשְׁנָהּ בְּמִנְחָה! (א) וְתֵיתֵי מִבֵּינַיָּיא — ב] לְהָכִי כְּתִיב קְרָא, לְמֵימַר דְּלָא אָתְיָא מִבֵּינַיָּיא. *אָמַר ר' אַבָּהוּ: שָׁחַט וְזָרַק, ג] לְדִבְרֵי ר' יִשְׁמָעֵאל — חַיָּיב אַחַת, לְדִבְרֵי ר"ע — חַיָּיב שְׁתַּיִם. *אַבַּיֵי אָמַר: אֲפִי' [לְדִבְרֵי] ר"ע אֵינוֹ חַיָּיב אֶלָּא אַחַת, דְּאָמַר קְרָא: "שָׁם ד] תַּעֲשֶׂה" — הַכָּתוּב עֲשָׂאָן לְכוּלָּן עֲבוֹדָה אַחַת. זָרַק וְהֶעֱלָה, לְדִבְרֵי ר' יִשְׁמָעֵאל — חַיָּיב שְׁתַּיִם, לְדִבְרֵי ר"ע אֵינוֹ חַיָּיב אֶלָּא אַחַת. אַבַּיֵי אָמַר: אֲפִי' ה] [לְדִבְרֵי] ר"ע אחַיָּיב שְׁתַּיִם, לְהָכִי פַּלְגִינְהוּ קְרָא °"שָׁם תַּעֲלֶה וְשָׁם תַּעֲשֶׂה". שָׁחַט וְזָרַק וְהֶעֱלָה — לְדִבְרֵי הַכֹּל חַיָּיב שְׁתַּיִם. ת"ר: *("בַּמַּחֲנֶה", יָכוֹל הַשּׁוֹחֵט עוֹלָה בַּדָּרוֹם יְהֵא חַיָּיב? ת"ל: ו] "(אֶל) מִחוּץ לַמַּחֲנֶה". יָכוֹל חוּץ לְשָׁלֹשׁ מַחֲנוֹת? ז] [ת"ל: °"אוֹ עֵז בַּמַּחֲנֶה".] (מִנַּיִן אַף בְּמַחֲנֵה לְוִיָּה? ת"ל: "בַּמַּחֲנֶה".) אִי "בַּמַּחֲנֶה", יָכוֹל הַשּׁוֹחֵט עוֹלָה בַּדָּרוֹם יְהֵא חַיָּיב? ת"ל: "אוֹ ח] אֶל מִחוּץ לַמַּחֲנֶה". מַה חוּץ לַמַּחֲנֶה מְיוּחָד, שֶׁאֵין רָאוּי לִשְׁחִיטַת קָדָשִׁים וְלִשְׁחִיטַת כָּל זֶבַח; יָצָא דָּרוֹם, שֶׁאע"פ שֶׁאֵין רָאוּי לִשְׁחִיטַת קָדְשֵׁי קָדָשִׁים — רָאוּי לִשְׁחִיטַת קָדָשִׁים קַלִּים. אָמַר עוּלָּא: הַשּׁוֹחֵט עַל גַּגּוֹ שֶׁל הֵיכָל — חַיָּיב, הוֹאִיל וְאֵין רָאוּי לִשְׁחִיטַת כָּל זֶבַח. מַתְקִיף לָהּ רָבָא: א"כ, נִיכְתּוֹב קְרָא: ט] "(אֶל) מִחוּץ לַמַּחֲנֶה" וְלָא בָּעֵי "אֶל פֶּתַח אֹהֶל מוֹעֵד", "אֶל פֶּתַח אֹהֶל מוֹעֵד" ל"ל? לָאו בלְמַעוּטֵי גַּגּוֹ? וּלְרָבָא, א"כ נִכְתּוֹב: "אֶל פֶּתַח אֹהֶל מוֹעֵד", י] "בַּמַּחֲנֶה" (וְ"אֶל) מִחוּץ לַמַּחֲנֶה" ל"ל? לָאו לְאַתּוּיֵי גַּגּוֹ? אָמַר רַב מָרִי: יא] לְאִיתּוּיֵי גכּוּלָּהּ בִּפְנִים וְצַוָּארָהּ בַּחוּץ. [צַוָּארָהּ] בַּחוּץ יב] פְּשִׁיטָא, אַמַּאי קָפֵיד רַחֲמָנָא — אַשְּׁחִיטָה, וּשְׁחִיטָה בַּחוּץ הִיא! אֶלָּא לְאִיתּוּיֵי דכּוּלָּהּ בַּחוּץ וְצַוָּארָהּ בִּפְנִים. אִיתְּמַר, הַמַּעֲלֶה בַּזְּמַן הַזֶּה, ר' יוֹחָנָן אָמַר: החַיָּיב, רֵישׁ לָקִישׁ אָמַר: פָּטוּר. ר' יוֹחָנָן אָמַר: חַיָּיב, *קְדוּשָּׁה רִאשׁוֹנָה קִידְּשָׁה לִשְׁעָתָהּ וְקִידְּשָׁה לֶעָתִיד לָבֹא. רֵישׁ לָקִישׁ אָמַר: פָּטוּר, קְדוּשָּׁה רִאשׁוֹנָה קִידְּשָׁה לִשְׁעָתָהּ וְלֹא קִידְּשָׁה לֶעָתִיד לָבֹא. יג] נֵימָא דִּבִפְלוּגְתָּא דר"א וְר' יְהוֹשֻׁעַ קָמִיפַּלְגִי. *דִּתְנַן, א"ר אֱלִיעֶזֶר: יד] כְּשֶׁהָיוּ בּוֹנִין בַּהֵיכָל, הָיוּ עוֹשִׂים וקְלָעִים בַּהֵיכָל קְלָעִים בָּעֲזָרוֹת, אֶלָּא שֶׁבַּהֵיכָל בּוֹנִין מִבַּחוּץ טו] וּבָעֲזָרָה בּוֹנִין מִבִּפְנִים. א"ר יְהוֹשֻׁעַ: שָׁמַעְתִּי זשֶׁהָיוּ *מַקְרִיבִין אע"פ שֶׁאֵין בַּיִת, חוְאוֹכְלִים קָדְשֵׁי קָדָשִׁים אע"פ שֶׁאֵין קְלָעִים, קָדָשִׁים קַלִּים וּמַעֲשֵׂר שֵׁנִי אע"פ שֶׁאֵין חוֹמָה, מִפְּנֵי שֶׁקְּדוּשָּׁה רִאשׁוֹנָה קִידְּשָׁה לִשְׁעָתָהּ וְקִידְּשָׁה לֶעָתִיד לָבֹא. לָאו מִכְּלָל דר"א סָבַר לֹא קִידְּשָׁה? טז] א"ל רָבִינָא לְרַב אַשִׁי: מִמַּאי? דִּלְמָא דְּכוּלֵּי עָלְמָא קְדוּשָּׁה רִאשׁוֹנָה קִידְּשָׁה לִשְׁעָתָהּ וְקִידְּשָׁה לֶעָתִיד לָבֹא, וּמָר מַאי דְּשָׁמִיעַ לֵיהּ קָאָמַר, וּמָר מַאי דְּשָׁמִיעַ לֵיהּ קָאָמַר! וְכִי תֵּימָא, קְלָעִים לְר' אֱלִיעֶזֶר לָמָּה לִי — לִצְנִיעוּתָא בְּעָלְמָא. אִיתְּמַר, *הַמַּעֲלֶה יז] וְאֵין בּוֹ כַּזַּיִת, וְעֶצֶם מַשְׁלִימוֹ לְכַזַּיִת, רַבִּי יוֹחָנָן אָמַר: טחַיָּיב, רֵישׁ לָקִישׁ אָמַר: פָּטוּר. ר' יוֹחָנָן אָמַר: חַיָּיב — חִיבּוּרֵי עוֹלִין כְּעוֹלִין דָּמֵי. רֵישׁ לָקִישׁ אָמַר: פָּטוּר — חִיבּוּרֵי עוֹלִין לָאו כְּעוֹלִין דָּמוּ. בָּעֵי רָבָא: יהַמַּעֲלֶה

ראש

תֵּיתֵי מִבֵּינַיָּיא. מִשְּׁחִיטָה וּזְרִיקָה. דְּכִי פָּרְכַתְּ: מַה לִּשְׁחִיטָה שֶׁכֵּן פּוֹסֶלֶת שֶׁלֹּא לְשֵׁם אוֹכְלִין בְּפֶסַח — זְרִיקָה תּוֹכִיחַ. מַה לִּזְרִיקָה שֶׁכֵּן זָר חַיָּיב עָלֶיהָ מִיתָה — שְׁחִיטָה תּוֹכִיחַ. וְחָזַר הַדִּין, הַצַּד הַשָּׁוֶה שֶׁבָּהֶן: שֶׁהֵן עֲבוֹדָה וְחַיָּיבִין עֲלֵיהֶן בַּחוּץ, אַף אֲנִי אָבִיא קְמִיצָה וְקַבָּלָה, שֶׁהֵן עֲבוֹדָה, וְיִתְחַיֵּיב עֲלֵיהֶן בַּחוּץ. אִם כֵּן. יח] דְּמַיְיתֵי מִבֵּינַיָּיא לְחַיֵּיב בַּחוּץ עַל עֲבוֹדוֹת שֶׁאֵינָם מְפוֹרָשׁוֹת בַּפָּרָשָׁה, וְיֵשׁ לַהֲבִיאָן בְּ"מַה הַצַּד" — לֹא יֵאָמֵר בִּזְרִיקָה וְתֵיתֵי מִבֵּינַיָּיא מִשְּׁחִיטָה וְהַעֲלָאָה! ה"ג: לְהָכִי כְּתָבָהּ קְרָא דְּלָא אָתְיָא מִבֵּינַיָּיא. לְמֵימַר: דְּאַע"ג דְּאָתְיָא מִבֵּינַיָּיא לָא תֵּיתֵי מִבֵּינַיָּיא. שָׁחַט וְזָרַק בְּהֶעְלֵם אֶחָד לְר' יִשְׁמָעֵאל. דְּנָפְקָא לֵיהּ זְרִיקָה מִ"דָּם *שָׁפָךְ" יט] בְּעוֹנֶשׁ שֶׁל שְׁחִיטָה. אֵינוֹ חַיָּיב אֶלָּא אַחַת. דְּחַד כָּרֵת וְחַד לָאו הוּא. לְר"ע. יט] נָפְקָא לֵיהּ מֵ"אוֹ זֶבַח" דִּכְתִיב (ויקרא יז) גַּבֵּי הַעֲלָאָה. חַיָּיב שְׁתַּיִם. מִשּׁוּם דְּשֵׁמוֹת מוּחְלָקִין. שָׁם תַּעֲלֶה וְשָׁם תַּעֲשֶׂה. הִזְכִּיר הַעֲלָאָה לְבַדָּהּ, וְהַשְּׁאָר כְּלָלָן בַּעֲשִׂיָּה אַחַת, לְמֵימְרָא דְּלָא מְחַיֵּיב אַכּוּלְּהוּ אֶלָּא חֲדָא. (ג) פַּלְגִינְהוּ קְרָא. הוֹצִיא הַעֲלָאָה מִכְּלָל שְׁאָר עֲשִׂיּוֹת, לְמֵימְרָא דִּמְחַיֵּיב עֲלָהּ בְּאַפֵּי נַפְשָׁהּ, וְאַשְּׁאָרָא בְּאַפֵּי נַפְשַׁיְיהוּ. שָׁחַט וְזָרַק וְהֶעֱלָה לְד"ה. בֵּין לְר' יִשְׁמָעֵאל בֵּין לְר"ע חַיָּיב שְׁתַּיִם. לְר' יִשְׁמָעֵאל, כֵּיוָן כ] דְּכוּלָּם בְּהֶעְלֵם [אֶחָד] — מְחַיֵּיב בְּהַעֲלָאָה חֲדָא דְּאִית לָהּ קְרָא בְּהֶדְיָא, וְאַשְּׁחִיטָה וּזְרִיקָה חֲדָא, דְּמֵחַד קְרָא נָפְקֵי. וּלְר"ע, אַשְּׁחִיטָה מִיחַיֵּיב חֲדָא, כא] וְהַעֲלָאָה וּזְרִיקָה חֲדָא. וּבְהָא לָא פָּלֵיג אַבַּיֵי אַדְּר' אַבָּהוּ. דִּלְאַבַּיֵי נָמֵי, לְדִבְרֵי הַכֹּל חַיָּיב שְׁתַּיִם, חֲדָא אַהַעֲלָאָה וַחֲדָא אַשְּׁאָר עֲשִׂיּוֹת. כב] ת"ר אוֹ אֲשֶׁר יִשְׁחַט מִחוּץ לַמַּחֲנֶה יָכוֹל עַד שֶׁיִּשְׁחַט חוּץ לְשָׁלֹשׁ מַחֲנוֹת. וְנֵילַף גז"ש מִפָּרִים הַנִּשְׂרָפִים, כִּדְיָלְפִינַן בַּהֲרוּגֵי ב"ד בְּסַנְהֶדְרִין (דף מב:). ת"ל. בְּרֵישֵׁיהּ דִּקְרָא: "אוֹ עֵז בַּמַּחֲנֶה". אִי בַּמַּחֲנֶה יָכוֹל אַף בְּמַחֲנֵה שְׁכִינָה. אֶלָּא שֶׁשִּׁינָּה מְקוֹם שְׁחִיטָתוֹ, כְּגוֹן שָׁחַט עוֹלָה בַּדָּרוֹם יְהֵא חַיָּיב? ת"ל מִחוּץ לַמַּחֲנֶה. דְּמַשְׁמַע: חוּץ לְשָׁלֹשׁ מַחֲנוֹת. מַה לְהַלָּן. מְיוּחָד שֶׁאֵינוֹ רָאוּי לִשְׁחִיטַת שׁוּם זֶבַח, אַף בַּמַּחֲנֶה — כְּגוֹן בְּמַחֲנֵה לְוִיָּה, שֶׁאֵינוֹ רָאוּי לִשְׁחִיטָה כג] לְשׁוּם זֶבַח. נִכְתּוֹב קְרָא בַּמַּחֲנֶה וְאֶל מִחוּץ לַמַּחֲנֶה. "חוּץ" — לְמַעוּטֵי עוֹלָה בַּדָּרוֹם, וּ"בַמַּחֲנֶה" — לְפָרוּשֵׁי דְּלָא בָּעֵינַן חוּץ לְשָׁלֹשׁ מַחֲנוֹת. "וְאֶל פֶּתַח אֹהֶל מוֹעֵד לֹא הֱבִיאוֹ" לָמָּה לִי? לָאו לְמַעוּטֵי גַּגּוֹ שֶׁל הֵיכָל. דְּהָכִי מַשְׁמַע: כד] שֶׁלֹּא הֱבִיאוֹ לְפֶתַח אֹהֶל מוֹעֵד, יָצָא זֶה שֶׁהֱבִיאוֹ לָעֲזָרָה. וּפָרְכִינַן: וּלְרָבָא. דְּפָטַר אַגַּגּוֹ, דְּמַשְׁמַע כה] כָּל חֲלָלָהּ שֶׁל עֲזָרָה קָרֵי "אֶל פֶּתַח". נִיכְתּוֹב אֶל פֶּתַח. לְמַעוּטֵי גַּגּוֹ וּלְמַעוּטֵי עוֹלָה בַּדָּרוֹם, שֶׁהֲרֵי בָּאוּ אֶל פֶּתַח. וּמִמֵּילָא מִשְׁתַּמַּע חִיּוּבָא בְּמַחֲנֵה לְוִיָּה, שֶׁלֹּא הֱבִיאוֹ אֶל פֶּתַח. מִחוּץ לַמַּחֲנֶה וּבַמַּחֲנֶה ל"ל לָאו לְאִיתּוּיֵי גַּגּוֹ. אֲתָא "בַּמַּחֲנֶה", וַהֲדַר אֲתָא "מִחוּץ", דְּלָא תֵּימָא: מִ"בַּמַּחֲנֶה" אִיתְרַבֵּי נָמֵי שׁוֹחֵט עוֹלָה בַּדָּרוֹם — ת"ל: "מִחוּץ", לְמִידְרַשׁ דְּבָעֵינַן מָקוֹם שֶׁאֵינוֹ רָאוּי לִשְׁחִיטַת שׁוּם זֶבַח. וְ"אֶל פֶּתַח" אִיצְטְרִיךְ לִדְרָשָׁא אַחֲרִיתִי: הָרָאוּי לְפֶתַח אֹהֶל מוֹעֵד חַיָּיבִין עָלָיו בַּחוּץ, יָצְאוּ פָּרַת חַטָּאת וְקָדְשֵׁי בֶּדֶק הַבַּיִת. כו] (לָאו) לְאִיתּוּיֵי [כּוּלָּהּ] בִּפְנִים כו'. לְעוֹלָם גַּג הֵיכָל לָא מִיחַיַּיב, דְּלָא קְרִינָא בֵּיהּ "וְאֶל פֶּתַח אֹהֶל מוֹעֵד לֹא הֱבִיאוֹ", שֶׁהֲרֵי הֱבִיאוֹ. אֶלָּא לְאִיתּוּיֵי הִיא בִּפְנִים וְצַוָּארָהּ בַּחוּץ, דְּלָא תֵּימָא: פֶּתַח אֹהֶל מוֹעֵד הוּא, לְכָךְ נֶאֱמַר "בַּמַּחֲנֶה" — לְחִיּוּבָא. וַהֲדַר אֲתָא "מִחוּץ" — דְּלָא תֵּרַבֵּי מִ"בַּמַּחֲנֶה" שׁוֹחֵט עוֹלָה בַּדָּרוֹם, כז] וּמַהוּ "אֶל פֶּתַח אֹהֶל מוֹעֵד לֹא הֱבִיאוֹ" — שֶׁלֹּא הֱבִיאוֹ כְּדֶרֶךְ כח] הֲבָאַת קָדְשֵׁי קָדָשִׁים בַּצָּפוֹן — תַּלְמוּד לוֹמַר "מִחוּץ", דְּלָא חַיָּיב אֶלָּא מִשּׁוּם חוּץ דְּאֵינוֹ רָאוּי לְשׁוּם זֶבַח, יָצָא זֶה. וְאָתָא "אֶל פֶּתַח" — לְמַעוּטֵי גַּגּוֹ, דְּלָא תַּרְבֵּי כִּדְקָאָמְרַתְּ שֶׁהוּא מָקוֹם שֶׁאֵינוֹ רָאוּי לִשְׁחִיטַת כָּל זֶבַח. דִּכְיוָן דְּאַשְׁמְעִינַן "מִחוּץ" דְּעוֹלָה בַּדָּרוֹם פָּטוּר, שְׁמַע מִינָּהּ: "אֶל פֶּתַח אֹהֶל מוֹעֵד" לֹא כְּדַרְכּוֹ הֲבָאָתוֹ קָפֵיד, אֶלָּא הֲבָאָה כָּל דְּהוּ, וּבִלְבַד שֶׁיְּהֵא כּוּלּוֹ תּוֹךְ חֲלַל הָעֲזָרָה. שְׁחִיטָה בַּחוּץ הִיא. וַהֲרֵי לֹא הֱבִיאוֹ לְבֵית הַשְּׁחִיטָה אֶל פֶּתַח, וּמִ"אֶל פֶּתַח" נַפְקָא. הַמַּעֲלֶה בַּזְּמַן הַזֶּה. בַּחוּץ. וְקִידְּשָׁה לֶעָתִיד לָבֹא. וְקִדְּשָׁה לֹא קִידְּשָׁה יְרוּשָׁלַיִם בֵּית הַבְּחִירָה, וּשְׁעַת אִיסּוּר הַבָּמוֹת הִיא. כְּשֶׁהָיוּ בּוֹנִין בַּהֵיכָל. בִּימֵי עֶזְרָא. לָאו מִכְּלָל דר' אֱלִיעֶזֶר סָבַר לֹא קִידְּשָׁה. הִלְכָּךְ עוֹשִׂין קְלָעִים בִּמְקוֹם חוֹמָה. וְחָזְרוּ וְקִדְּשׁוּ בְּקִידּוּשׁ הַמְפוֹרָשׁ בְּמַסֶּכֶת שְׁבוּעוֹת (דף יד.). עֶצֶם. אֵין מַגִּיָּה לְהַעֲלוֹתוֹ אִם פֵּירַשׁ, כִּדְאָמְרִינַן בְּפֶרֶק "הַמִּזְבֵּחַ מְקַדֵּשׁ" (לעיל דף פה:).

ראש

להכי כתביה קרא דלא תיתי מבינייא. *תימה על סוגיא זו דבפ' בתרא (דף קטו:) דרשינן: "אשר יעלה עולה", מה העולה שהיא גמר עבודה — אף כל שהיא גמר עבודה למעוטי קומץ ומקבל והיולק והבולל והפותת והמולח כו'. **יכול** חוץ לשלש מחנות. ונילף גז"ש מפרים הנשרפים, כדילפי' בהרוגי ב"ד, בפ' "נגמר הדין" (סנהדרין דף סב:) ואפי' אינה מופנה — ילפינן בגילוי מלתא, כיון דלא אשכחן "מחוץ למחנה" אלא חוץ לשלש מחנות.

ולא בעי אל פתח אהל מועד. אע"ג דאיצטריך לקמן (דף קיג:) למעוטי רובע ונרבע ופרת חטאת וקדשי בדק הבית — טובא "פתח אהל מועד" כתיבי.

ה"ג: **ולרבא** נכתוב רחמנא ואל פתח אהל מועד מחוץ למחנה ובמחנה למה לי. וקא קשיא ליה לרבא: נ"ל דכתב רחמנא כלל "מחוץ למחנה" ו"במחנה"? וכן פי' הקונט'.

המעלה בזמן הזה. לעיל פירשתי בריש "קדשי קדשים" (דף ס.) גבי מזבח שנפגם. ופירשתי מ"ט [נקט] הכא, "המעלה", ולא נקט "השוחט".

ריש לקיש אמר פטור קדושה ראשונה כו'. תימה: דלא פריך עליה מהנך משניות דפריך בפ"ק דמגילה (דף י.) אר' יצחק, דאמר: שמעתי שמקריבין בבית חוניו.

רבי יוחנן אמר חייב חיבורי עולין כעולין דמו. וא"ת: למה לי חיבורי? הא שמעינן ליה לר' יוחנן דאמר בפ' "הקומץ רבה" (מנחות דף כו:): יש הקטרה בפחות מכזית, וכיון דחשיב הקטרה בפנים — מחייב בחוץ, כדאמר לקמן (דף קח:) גבי מוקטרי פנים שחסרו דחייבין עליהם בחוץ, כיון דבפנים הויא הקטרה, דמהדרינן פוקעין! וי"ל: הא דחשיב ליה לר' יוחנן הקטרה — היינו לענין מקטיר לחצאין, שמשלים אח"כ. ואע"ג דבפרק "כל המנחות באות מצה" (מנחות דף נח.) חשיב ליה הקטרה גבי שאור ודבש, דאמרי': יש קומץ פחות משני זיתים, ויש הקטרה פחות מכזית — שאני התם דכתיב קרא. ועוד: דבשחוטי חוץ מיפטר טפי, כדדרשינן הכא: על השלם הוא חייב ואינו חייב על החסר. ועוד: דהא איתקש מחשבות זו לזו, אכילת מזבח לאכילת אדם. ומדחשב על מנת להקטיר חוץ למקומו לא מיפסלא בפחות מכזית — ש"מ דמקטיר בחוץ לא מחייב בפחות מכזית.

שחיטת

עיין נ"ק

יב א מיי' פי"ט מהל' מעשה הקרבנות הלכה יא ועי' רש"ק:

יג ב ג ד מיי' פי"ח שם הלכה טו:

יד ה מיי' שם פרק י"ט הל' טו:

טו ו מיי' פ"א מהל' בית הבחירה הל"ה:

טז ז מיי' פ"ו שם הלט"ו:

יז ח מיי' פי"ט מהל' מעשה הקרבנות הל' טו ופ"ו מהלכות בית הבחירה הל' טו:

יח ט י מיי' פי"ט מהל' מעשה הקרבנות הלכה י:

שיטה מקובצת

א] מתיבת ותיתי כו' עד תיבת אלא להכי רש"י לא גריס זה וכן בס"י ליתא: ב] אלא להכי כתיב קרא ולא אתיא מבינייא למימר דאע"ג דאתיא מבינייא לא תיתי מבינייא אמר: ג] לר' ישמעאל אינו חייב אלא אחת לר"ע חייב שתים אביי אמר אפי' לר"ע אינו חייב: ד] שם תעלה ושם תעשה כל אשר אנכי מצוך הכתוב עשאן עשיה אחת זרק והעלה לר' ישמעאל חייב שתים לר"ע אינו חייב כו': ה] אפי' לר"ע חייב: ו] ת"ל מחוץ למחנה תיבת אל נמחק: ז] תיבות ת"ל או עז במחנה ל"ש ונמחק: ח] או אשר ישחט מחוץ למחנה מה חוץ למחנה מיוחד שאין ראוי לשחיטת כל זבח אף במחנה שאין ראוי לשחיטת כל זבח יצא דרום: ט] קרא במחנה ואל מחוץ: י] מועד ומחוץ למחנה ובמחנה למה לי: יא] מרי לא לאתויי: יב] צוואורה בחוץ אמאי קא קפיד תיבת פשיטא ל"ש: יג] לימא דבפלוגתא: יד] אליעזר שמעתי כשהיו: טו] מבחוץ ובעזורות: טז] קידשה לעתיד לבא א"ל: יז] המעלה אבר שאין בו כזית: יח] כן דמייתינן: יט] שפך הכתוב בעונש: יט] דנפקא ליה: כ] כיון דעשה כולם בהעלם אחד מחייב: כא] חדא ואהעלאה וזריקה: כב] מה"ד אי אשר ישחט תיבות ת"ר או נמחק: כג] שום זבח אות ל' נמחק: כד] משמע מי שלא: כה] דמשמע אל פתח כל חללה של עזרה הס"ד ותיבות קרי אל פתח נמחק: כו] מה"ד לא לאתויי היא בפנים: כז] בדרום ומאי אל: כח] כדרך הבאתו:

נ"ק מ"ז

סנהדרין לד:

שם ע"ש

נ"ל ת"ר או אשר ישחט מחוץ למחנה יכול חוץ כו' נ"ק

הגהות הב"ח

(א) גמ' שכן ישנה במנחה. שחיטה תוכיח תיתי מבינייא: (ב) רש"י ד"ה פלגינהו נ"ל קודם ד"ה שם תעלה:

[לעיל ס. חגיגה ג: מגילה י. מכות יט. שבועות טז. חולין ז. תמורה כא. ערכין לב:]

מגילה י: שבועות טז. עדיות פ"ח מ"ו

[לעיל סב.]

מנחות כו.

גליון הש"ס

גמ' דלא אתא מבינייא. עי' יומא דף סג ע"ב תוס' ד"ה זריקה:

כ"ח יחסב נ"ק

דברים יב

ויקרא יז

ראש בן יונה שאין בו כזית, ומלח משלימו לכזית, מהו? א"ל רבא מפרזקיא לרב אשי: לאו היינו פלוגתייהו דר' יוחנן ור"ל? תיבעי לרבי יוחנן, ותיבעי לר"ל; תיבעי לר' יוחנן: ע"כ לא קאמר ר' יוחנן התם אלא עצם, דמינא דבשר הוא, אבל מלח דלאו מינא דבר יונה הוא — לא. א] תיבעי לר"ל: ע"כ לא קאמר ר"ל התם אלא דאי פריש ב] מינה לאו מצוה לאסוקי, אבל הכא, דאי פריש ג] מצוה לאסוקי — לא. או דלמא, ל"ש? תיקו.§ "ר' יוסי הגלילי אומר" כו'.§ השיב רבי תחת רבי יוסי הגלילי: מה לשוחט בפנים ומעלה בחוץ — ד] שהיתה לו שעת הכושר, תאמר בשוחט ה] חוץ ומעלה בחוץ — שלא היתה לו שעת הכושר? השיב ר"א בר' שמעון תחת ר"י הגלילי: מה לשוחט בפנים ומעלה בחוץ — שכן קודש מקבלו, תאמר בשוחט בחוץ — ו] שאין קודש מקבלו? מאי בינייהו? *אמר זעירי: אשחיטת לילה איכא ביניהו. *רבה אמר: בקבלה בכלי חול איכא בינייהו.§ "טמא שאכל בין קודש" כו'.§ שפיר קאמרי ליה רבנן לרבי יוסי הגלילי! *אמר רבא: כל היכא דנטמא ז] טומאת הגוף ואחר כך נטמא בשר — דכולי עלמא לא פליגי דחייב, שכן טומאת הגוף בכרת. כי פליגי — בשנטמא בשר ואח"כ נטמא הגוף, דרבנן סברי: אמרינן מיגו, ור' יוסי הגלילי סבר: לא אמרינן מיגו. ורבי יוסי, ח] נהי דמיגו לא אמרינן, תיתי טומאת הגוף דחמירא ותחול על טומאת בשר! אמר רב אשי: ממאי דטומאת הגוף חמורה? דלמא טומאת בשר חמורה, שכן אין לה טהרה במקוה!§ **מתני'** חומר בשחיטה מבעלייה, ובעלייה מבשחיטה. חומר בשחיטה: גשהשוחט להדיוט — חייב, דוהמעלה להדיוט — פטור. חומר בעלייה: השנים *שאחזו בסכין ושחטו — פטורים, ואחזו באבר ט] והעלו — חייבין. העלה, חזר והעלה, וחזר והעלה — חייב על כל עלייה, י] דברי ר"ש. ר' יוסי אומר: זאינו חייב אלא אחת. חואינו חייב עד שיעלה לראש המזבח, *ר"ש אומר: אפילו העלה על הסלע או על האבן — חייב.§ **גמ'** מאי שנא המעלה להדיוט דפטור — דכתיב °"לה'", בשחיטה נמי הכתיב "לה'"! שאני התם, דאמר קרא: °"איש איש". גבי העלאה נמי כתיב: "איש איש"! יא] °מיבעי ליה *לשנים יב] שהעלו באבר — חייבין. אי הכי, ה"נ מיבעי ליה לשנים שאחזו בסכין ושחטו שחייבין! שאני התם, דאמר קרא: "ההוא" — אחד ולא שנים. אי הכי, גבי העלאה נמי, הא כתיב: "ההוא"! יג] מיבעי ליה למעוטי

ויקרא יז / שם

רש"י

ראש יונה. של עולת העוף והעלו בחוץ. מלח, אי פריש – מצוה לחזור ולמולחו, כדכתיב (ויקרא ב): "ולא תשבית מלח ברית". שעת הכושר. ליקרב בפנים. שכן קדש מקבלו. אע"פ שהוציאו, אם חזר והכניסו והעלהו – *לא ירד, כדאמרן ב"המזבח מקדש" (לעיל דף פד.): הלן והיוצא כו'. שחיטת לילה איכא ביניהו. לרבי שחט בהמה בלילה בפנים והעלה בחוץ – פטור, שלא היתה לה שעת הכושר, דבשחיטתה נפסלה. לר"א – חייב, שהרי הקדש מקבלו, שאם עלה לא ירד. רבה אמר קבלה בכלי חול איכא ביניהו. שעת הכושר – ליכא, קדש מקבלו – איכא, דכל שפסולו בקדש הקדש מקבלו. כל היכא דנטמא גופו של זה ואח"כ נטמא הבשר. ואפילו ע"י אחרים, מודה ר' יוסי הגלילי דחייב, כדאמרן, מה לי על ידו מה לי ע"י אחרים. דטעמא דר' יוסי משום דאין איסור חל על איסור הוא, וכאן איסור טומאת הגוף קודם. כי פליגי בשנטמא בשר תחילה. ונאסר על זה משום טומאת בשר, שאין חייבין עליו חטאת. וכי הדר נטמא הגוף – אית ליה לר' יוסי אין איסור טומאת הגוף חל על איסור זה. ואע"ג דאיסור כולל הוא, דאיכא למימר דמיגו דמיתסר בשאר חתיכות טהורות משום טומאת הגוף נתסר נמי בהך – לא אמרינן האי מיגו. הלכך, אין ראיה מטמא שאכל את הטהור לכאן, דהתם טומאת הגוף קדים. ורבנן סברי אמרינן מגו. ואיסור כולל חל על איסור אחר. דהא דאמרינן אין איסור חל על איסור – באיסורי דעלמא קאמרינן. נהי דלא אמרינן מגו. לחול איסור על איסור ואפילו הוא כולל, מיהו, הני מילי – היכא דשניהן שוין, *אבל הכא איתי טומאת הגוף דחמירא, וניחול בכולל על טומאת בשר דקילא. דהכי אמרינן בשחיטת חולין בפרק "גיד הנשה" (דף קא.) דרבי יוסי הגלילי לית ליה איסור חל על איסור אפילו ע"י כולל, ובאיסור חמור אית ליה איסור חל על איסור כשהוא איסור כולל, גבי אוכל גיד הנשה של עולה דאוקימנא כרבי יוסי הגלילי דקתני: חייב שתים. **מתני'** השוחט קדשים בחוץ. לאכילת הדיוט – חייב. והמעלה להדיוט פטור. משום העלאת חוץ, וחייב משום עובד עבודה זרה. ואם הזיד בעבודה זרה ושגג בהעלאת חוץ – אינו מביא יד] על שגגתו חטאת. וטעמא מפרש בגמ'. שנים שאחזו. בגמרא מפרש לה. העלה ונודע לו, וחזר והעלה. מאותה בהמה עצמה. ובגמרא מפרש פלוגתייהו. שיעלה לראש המזבח. שיבנה מזבח לשם כך ויעלה. וטעמא מפרש בגמ'. **גמ'** דכתיב לה'. "ואל פתח אהל מועד לא יביאנו לעשות אותו לה'" (ויקרא יז) – מכלל דבעושה לשם הכתוב מדבר. בשחיטת חוץ נמי כתיב. (שם) "ואל פתח אהל מועד לא הביאו להקריב קרבן לה'": איש איש. להביא איש ששחט לאיש. שאני התם. בשחיטה לא מלית למידרש "איש איש" לחייב שנים שאחזו בסכין ושחטו. דהא כתיב ההוא. וקא סלקא דעתך "ונכרת האיש ההוא" (שם). למעוטי

תוספות

שחיטת לילה איכא בינייהו. לכאורה רבי ורבי אלעזר בר"ש סברי כר"ש, דאמר בפרק "המזבח מקדש" (לעיל דף פד.): נשחטה בלילה, אם עלתה – לא תרד. דהשתא קדש מקבלו, ולא היתה לו שעת הכושר. אבל לרבי יהודה, דאמר: אם עלתה תרד, בין לרבי בין לרבי אלעזר בר"ש, שחט בלילה בפנים והעלה בחוץ, לא מבעיא (ליה) לרבי יוסי הגלילי דפטור, אלא אפילו לרבנן נמי פטור. כדמוכח בסוף פירקין (לקמן קיא:) גבי הא דתנן, ר"ש אומר: כל שחייבין עליו בחוץ חייבין על כיוצא בו בפנים שהעלה בחוץ. ומפרש זעירי גופיה, שחיטת בהמה בלילה איכא בינייהו. וה"ק: השוחט בהמה בלילה בפנים והעלה בחוץ – פטור. פירוש: דאין מתקבל בפנים, כר' יהודה דאמר: אם עלה (לא) ירד. שחט בחוץ והעלה בחוץ – חייב. אלמא, דאפילו לרבנן דמחייבי שוחט בחוץ ומעלה בחוץ – מודו בשוחט בלילה בפנים ומעלה בחוץ, דפטור לר' יהודה. וקצת תימה: זעירי ורבה אמאי נקטי הכא שחיטת לילה וקבלה בכלי חול, דהיינו כמו נשפך דמה, דלא הוי אלא לר"ש, דלרבי יהודה תרוייהו ירדו? הוי להו למימר: איכא בינייהו נשחטה חוץ לזמנו וחוץ למקומו, דלכולי עלמא לא ירד, דהרי קדש מקבלו ולא היתה לו שעת הכושר! ושמא אגב דנקטי רבה וזריעי בסוף פירקין (שם) גבי פלוגתא דר"ש ורבנן שחיטת לילה וקבלה בכלי חול – נקטי נמי הכא. וצריך לדקדק: לר' יהודה דאמר (לעיל דף פד.) בילא דמה, אם עלה – ירד, הרי זורק מקלת דמים בחוץ דחייב, אע"ג דאין קדש מקבלו! ושמא לרבי יהודה לא היה חייב. והא דדרשינן מקרא לרבות הזורק – דלמא בשחוטי חוץ ולא בשחוטי פנים, מידי דהוה אשחיטת לילה בסוף פירקין. אבל לרבי יוסי הגלילי אליבא דרבי יהודה – ודאי לא משכחת לה זורק בחוץ דחייב. ועוד נראה: דהא דמיפטר לר' יהודה משום דאין קדש מקבלו – היינו כשאין קדש מקבלו מחמת פסול אחר, מלבד פסול זה שיצא לחוץ והעלהו. וניחא נמי, דמתני' מחייב הקומץ והלבונה והקטרת ומנחת כהנים שהעלן בחוץ, אף על גב דאמרינן בריש "המזבח" (לעיל דף פג:) דמנחות לר"י הגלילי ירדו. וכן נסכים הבאים עם הזבח, דאמרינן: לדברי כולן ירדו. וברייתא דבסמוך (דף קט.) דמרבי פסולין – לא חשיב נשחטה בלילה ונשפך דמה, שמע מינה דרבי יהודה היא. ולא מחייבי אהני משום דירדו, ואפילו הכי מחייב אקומץ ומנחת נסכים וניסוך היין והמים. והיינו טעמא כדפרישית. וקצת קשה: דלרבי יהודה אין מתיישב מה שהשיב ר' אלעזר בר"ש תחת ר"י הגלילי, דאכתי תיקשי ליה: אף הקומץ בפנים והעלה בחוץ, כיון שהוציאו – פסלו. **רבנן** סברי מיגו. באיסור כולל פליגי, כדמפרש בסוף "גיד הנשה" (חולין דף קא.).

שוגג

עין משפט נר מצוה

יט א ב מיי' פי"ח מהל' מעה"ק הלכה יז וע"ש בכ"מ וכו':
כ ג מיי' פי"ח מהל' מעה"ק הלכה טז:
כא ד מיי' פי"ט שם הלכה א:
כב ה מיי' שם הלכה יב ופי"ח הלכה טז:
כג ו מיי' פי"ט שם הלכה יב:
כד ז מיי' שם הל' יא עי' כ"מ:
כה ח מיי' שם הל' א:

[גי' הרש"ש לשנים שאחזו באבר והעלוהו שחייבין אי הכי ה"נ כו']

מסורת הש"ס

נ"ל לא ירדו כדאמרינן כו' צ"ק

[לקמן קיא:]

[שם ע"ש]

חולין קא. ע"ש

גי' הג"ק אבל הכא שאין שניהם שוין איתי כו'

קדושין נג.

[לקמן קי.]

גליון הש"ס

גמ' מיבעי ליה לשנים שהעלו. עי' תשובות שער הלכות שחיטה סי' ב ס"ק כב:

שיטה מקובצת

א] לא או דלמא לא שנא תיבעי: ב] פריש מיניה לאו: ג] פריש מיניה מצוה: ד] בחוץ שכן היתה לו: ה] תיבות חוץ ל"ש: ו] בחוץ ומעלה בחוץ ואין: ז] דנטמא הגוף ואח"כ נטמא הבשר: ח] יוסי הגלילי נהי: ט] והעלוהו חייבין העלה וחזר: י] עלייה ועלייה חטאת דברי: יא] ההוא מיבעי: יב] לשנים שאחזו באבר והעלוהו שחייבין ה"נ מיבעי ליה לשנים שאחזו בסכין תיבות שהעלו אי הכי ל"ש ונמחק: יג] ההוא ההוא מיבעי: יד] אינו מביא חטאת על שגגתו:

כו א מיי' פי"ח מהלכות מעשה הקרבנות הל' יא ופי"ט הלכה ז:
כז ב מיי' שם פי"ט הלכה יא:
שייך מעל"ד
כח ג מיי' פי"ט שם הלכה ח:

*לְמַעוּטֵי שׁוֹגֵג, אָנוּס וּמוּטְעֶה. אִי הָכִי, הָכָא נַמִי מִיבָּעֵי לְמַעוּטֵי אָנוּס שׁוֹגֵג וּמוּטְעֶה! תְּרֵי "הַהוּא" כְּתִיבִי. וְאֶלָּא "לַה'" לָמָּה לִי? אלְהוֹצִיא שָׂעִיר הַמִּשְׁתַּלֵּחַ.§ "חוֹמֶר בְּהַעֲלָאָה" כו'.§ ת"ר: °"אִישׁ (ויקרא יז) א] אִישׁ" מַה ת"ל? לְרַבּוֹת שְׁנַיִם שֶׁאָחֲזוּ בְּאֵבָר וְהֶעֱלוּ — שֶׁחַיָּיבִין. שֶׁיָּכוֹל, וַהֲלֹא דִּין הוּא: וּמַה הַשּׁוֹחֵט לְהֶדְיוֹט שֶׁחַיָּיב, שְׁנַיִם שֶׁאָחֲזוּ בְּסַכִּין וְשָׁחֲטוּ — פְּטוּרִין. הַמַּעֲלֶה לְהֶדְיוֹט שֶׁפָּטוּר — אֵינוֹ דִּין שֶׁשְּׁנַיִם שֶׁאָחֲזוּ ב] פְּטוּרִין? ת"ל: "אִישׁ אִישׁ", דִּבְרֵי ר"ש. רַבִּי יוֹסֵי אוֹמֵר: "הַהוּא" — אֶחָד וְלֹא שְׁנַיִם. א"כ, מַה ת"ל "אִישׁ אִישׁ"? *דִּבְּרָה תוֹרָה כִּלְשׁוֹן בְּנֵי אָדָם. וְר"ש? הַאי "הַהוּא" ג] מִיבָּעֵי לֵיהּ לְמַעוּטֵי שׁוֹגֵג אָנוּס מוּטְעֶה. וְרַבִּי יוֹסֵי: מֵ"הוּא" "הַהוּא". וְר"ש: "הוּא" "הַהוּא" לָא דָּרֵישׁ. וְרַבִּי יוֹסֵי, מִדְּהַאי "אִישׁ אִישׁ" דִּבְּרָה תּוֹרָה כִּלְשׁוֹן בְּנֵי אָדָם, ד] הַהוּא "אִישׁ אִישׁ" נַמִי דִּבְּרָה תּוֹרָה כִּלְשׁוֹן בְּנֵי אָדָם, וְאֶלָּא הַשּׁוֹחֵט לְהֶדְיוֹט ה] מְנָא לֵיהּ דְּחַיָּיב? נָפְקָא לֵיהּ °מִ"דָּם יֵחָשֵׁב לָאִישׁ הַהוּא דָּם שָׁפָךְ" (שם) — וַאֲפִילּוּ הַשּׁוֹחֵט לְאִישׁ.§ "הֶעֱלָה וְחָזַר וְהֶעֱלָה" כו'.§ אָמַר ר"ל: מַחֲלוֹקֶת בְּד' וְה' אֵבָרִים, דְּמָר סָבַר: כִּי כְּתִיב "לַעֲשׂוֹת אוֹתוֹ", *עַל הַשָּׁלֵם הוּא חַיָּיב וְאֵינוֹ חַיָּיב עַל הֶחָסֵר — אַכָּל בְּהֵמָה כְּתִיב. וּמָר סָבַר: אַכָּל אֵבָר וְאֵבָר כְּתִיב. אֲבָל ו] אֵבָר אֶחָד — דִּבְרֵי הַכֹּל אֵינוֹ חַיָּיב אֶלָּא אַחַת. וְר' יוֹחָנָן אָמַר: מַחֲלוֹקֶת בְּאֵבָר אֶחָד, דְּמָר סָבַר: מוּקְטְרֵי פְּנִים שֶׁחֲסְרוּ ז] וְהֶעֱלָה בַּחוּץ — חַיָּיב, וּמָר סָבַר: בפָּטוּר. אֲבָל בְּד' וְה' אֵיבָרִין — דִּבְרֵי הַכֹּל חַיָּיב עַל כָּל אֵבָר וְאֵבָר. וּפְלִיגָא דְּעוּלָּא, דְּאָמַר עוּלָּא: הַכֹּל מוֹדִים בְּמוּקְטְרֵי פְּנִים שֶׁחֲסְרוּ וְהֶעֱלוּ בַּחוּץ — שֶׁחַיָּיב, לֹא נֶחְלְקוּ אֶלָּא בְּמוּקְטְרֵי ח] בַּחוּץ שֶׁחָסְרוּ וְהֶעֱלוּ בַּחוּץ, דְּמָר סָבַר: פָּטוּר, וּמ"ס: חַיָּיב. אִיכָּא דְּאָמְרִי, אָמַר עוּלָּא: הַכֹּל מוֹדִים בְּמוּקְטְרֵי חוּץ שֶׁחָסְרוּ וְהֶעֱלוּ בַּחוּץ — שֶׁהוּא פָּטוּר. לֹא נֶחְלְקוּ אֶלָּא בְּמוּקְטְרֵי פְּנִים שֶׁחָסְרוּ וְהֶעֱלוּ בַּחוּץ, דְּמ"ס פָּטוּר וּמ"ס חַיָּיב. וּפְלִיגִי דַּאֲבוּהּ דִּשְׁמוּאֵל אַלִּישָּׁנָא קַמָּא דְּעוּלָּא, דְּאָמַר אֲבוּהּ דִּשְׁמוּאֵל: כְּמַאן מְהַדְּרִינַן פּוֹקְעִין לְגַבֵּי מִזְבֵּחַ? כְּמַאן — דְּלָא כְּר' יוֹסֵי.§ "וְאֵינוֹ חַיָּיב עַד שֶׁיַּעֲלֶה" כו'.§ אָמַר רַב הוּנָא: מַאי טַעְמָא דְּרַבִּי יוֹסֵי? גדִּכְתִיב: °"וַיִּבֶן נֹחַ מִזְבֵּחַ לַה'" (בראשית ח). א"ר יוֹחָנָן: מ"ט דְּר"ש? דִּכְתִיב: °"וַיִּקַּח מָנוֹחַ אֶת גְּדִי הָעִזִּים (שופטים יג) וְאֶת הַמִּנְחָה וַיַּעַל עַל הַצּוּר לַה'". וְאִידָךְ נַמִי, וְהָכְתִיב: "וַיִּבֶן מִזְבֵּחַ לַה'"! הַהוּא גּוֹבְהָה בְּעָלְמָא. וְאִידָךְ נַמִי, הָא כְּתִיב "וַיִּקַּח מָנוֹחַ"! הוֹרָאַת שָׁעָה הָיְתָה. וְאִיבָּעֵית אֵימָא: ה"ט דְּר"ש — כִּדְתַנְיָא, ר"ש אוֹמֵר: °"מִזְבַּח פֶּתַח אֹהֶל מוֹעֵד" (ויקרא יז) וְאֵין מִזְבֵּחַ בְּבָמָה. לְפִיכָךְ, הֶעֱלָה עַל הַסֶּלַע אוֹ עַל הָאֶבֶן — חַיָּיב; (א) "יָצָא" מִיבָּעֵי לֵיהּ! ה"ק: לְפִיכָךְ בִּשְׁעַת אִיסּוּר הַבָּמוֹת הֶעֱלָה עַל הַסֶּלַע אוֹ עַל הָאֶבֶן — חַיָּיב. בָּעֵי רַבִּי יוֹסֵי בְּר' חֲנִינָא: קֶרֶן וְכֶבֶשׁ וִיסוֹד וְרִיבּוּעַ, מַהוּ שֶׁיְּעַכְּבוּ בְּבָמָה? א"ל רַבִּי יִרְמְיָה: תַּנְיָא, *קֶרֶן וְכֶבֶשׁ וְרִיבּוּעַ וִיסוֹד מְעַכְּבִין בְּבָמָה גְּדוֹלָה, וְאֵין מְעַכְּבִין בְּבָמָה קְטַנָּה.§
מתני'

רש"י

לְמַעוּטֵי שׁוֹגֵג אָנוּס וּמוּטְעֶה. דְּהָכִי דָּרֵישׁ בְּת"כ כָּל "הַהוּא" דְּגַבֵּי "וְנִכְרַת" — כְּשֶׁיֶּשְׁנוֹ בַּהֲוָויָיתוֹ וּבְדַעְתּוֹ, וְלֹא אָנוּס, וְלֹא שׁוֹגֵג — מֵאֵלָיו, אוֹ מוּטְעֶה — ע"י אֲחֵרִים. תְּרֵי הַהוּא כְּתִיבִי. "דָּם יֵחָשֵׁב לָאִישׁ הַהוּא" בִּשְׁחִיטָה כְּתִיב (ויקרא יז). אֶלָּא לַה'. דִּכְתִיב גַּבֵּי שְׁחִיטָה. ל"ל לְהוֹצִיא שָׂעִיר הַמִּשְׁתַּלֵּחַ. דְּמַשְׁמַע: הָרָאוּי לִיקָּרֵב לַשֵּׁם — חַיָּיבִין עָלָיו בַּחוּץ, וְשֶׁאֵינוֹ עוֹמֵד לַשֵּׁם אֵין חַיָּיבִין עָלָיו בַּחוּץ. וּלְקַמָּן בְּפ' בַּתְרָא (דף קיג:) דָּרֵישׁ לָהּ תַּנָּא דְּבָרַיְיתָא הָכִי. וְגַלֵּי בִּשְׁחִיטָה וְהוּא הַדִּין לְהַעֲלָאָה, דְּהָא מִיגְמַר גָּמְרֵי מֵהֲדָדֵי, כְּדַאֲמָרַן: לְעָרֵב פָּרָשִׁיּוֹת, בַּר מֵהָנָךְ תְּרֵי חוּמְרֵי דְּמַתְנִי', דִּמְפָרְשִׁי קְרָאֵי בְּכוּלְּהוּ, בֵּין לְחִיּוּבָא בֵּין לִפְטוּרָא. מַה ת"ל אִישׁ אִישׁ. גַּבֵּי הַעֲלָאָה. וְשָׁחֲטוּ פְּטוּרִין. כִּדְיָלְפִינַן לְעֵיל, דִּכְתִיב: "הַהוּא". אַכָּל בְּהֵמָה כְּתִיב. עַל כָּל הַבְּהֵמָה הוּא חַיָּיב, וְאֵינוֹ חַיָּיב עַל אֵבֶר אֶחָד. הִלְכָּךְ, כּוּלָּהּ חֲדָא הַעֲלָאָה הִיא. אֲבָל בְּאֵבֶר אֶחָד. וְהִקְרִיבוֹ לַחֲנָאִין, לְאַחַר שֶׁהִקְרִיב שְׁאָר הָאֵיבָרִים. דְּאִילּוּ עָלָיו לְבַדּוֹ — אֲפִילּוּ הִקְרִיב שָׁלֵם פָּטַר לֵיהּ ר' יוֹסֵי. אוֹ מַיְירֵי שֶׁפָּקַע מֵעַל הָאֵשׁ וְחָזַר וְהֶחֱזִירוֹ. דִּבְרֵי הַכֹּל הַעֲלָאָה אַחַת הִיא. דְּהָא "אוֹתוֹ" כְּתִיב, שָׁלֵם וְלֹא חָסֵר. וְר' יוֹחָנָן אָמַר מַחֲלוֹקֶת בְּאֵבֶר אֶחָד. וּדְכוּלֵּי עָלְמָא "אוֹתוֹ" אַכָּל אֵבֶר וְאֵבֶר כְּתִיב. וּמַאן דִּמְחַיֵּיב סָבַר: מוּקְטָרֵי פְּנִים שֶׁחָסְרוּ וְהֶעֱלוּ בַּחוּץ — חַיָּיב, דְּהָא מְהַדְּרִינַן פּוֹקְעִין לַמִּזְבֵּחַ, דְּהָווּ לְהוּ חָסֵר. וְכִי כְּתִיב "אוֹתוֹ" — אַמּוּקְטָרֵי חוּץ כְּתִיב. וּמ"ס פָּטוּר. דְּנָפְקָא לֵיהּ מִ"לֹא יְבִיאֶנּוּ" כְּר' יִשְׁמָעֵאל. לֹא נֶחְלְקוּ אֶלָּא בְּמוּקְטָרֵי חוּץ כו'. מָר סָבַר חַיָּיב, דְּכִי כְּתִיב "אוֹתוֹ" — וְכִדְדָרֵישׁ לֵיהּ לְקַמָּן. פּוֹקְעִין. שֶׁפּוֹקְעִין מֵעַל הָאֵשׁ. דְּלָא כְּר' יוֹסֵי. ט] דְּכֵיוָן דִּבִפְנִים בְּנֵי הַקְטָרָה נִינְהוּ, וְאַע"ג דְּחָסְרוּ — בַּחוּץ נַמִי י] מִיחַיֵּיב בְּמוּקְטָרֵי פְּנִים שֶׁחָסְרוּ וְהֶעֱלוּ בַּחוּץ. אַלְמָא קָסָבַר אֲבוּהּ דִּשְׁמוּאֵל דְּרַבִּי יוֹסֵי אַמּוּקְטָרֵי פְּנִים שֶׁחָסְרוּ וְהֶעֱלוּ בַּחוּץ פָּלֵיג. וַיִּבֶן נֹחַ מִזְבֵּחַ. אַלְמָא יא] אֲפִילּוּ בָּמַת יָחִיד שֶׁהִיא בַּחוּץ אֵינָהּ הַעֲלָאָה בְּלֹא מִזְבֵּחַ. עַל הַצּוּר. בְּלֹא בִּנְיַן מִזְבֵּחַ לְשֵׁם כָּךְ, וְקָרֵי לֵיהּ הַעֲלָאָה. גּוֹבְהָה בְּעָלְמָא. כְּדֶרֶךְ כָּל הָאָרֶץ, שֶׁיְּהֵא נוֹחַ לְהִשְׁתַּמֵּשׁ, וְלֹא לְחוֹבַת מִזְבֵּחַ. מִזְבֵּחַ פֶּתַח אֹהֶל מוֹעֵד כו'. הַאי קְרָא דָּרֵישׁ לֵיהּ ר"ש בְּת"כ הָכִי: "וְזָרַק הַכֹּהֵן אֶת הַדָּם עַל מִזְבַּח ה' פֶּתַח אֹהֶל מוֹעֵד" — וְלֹא מִזְבֵּחַ בְּבָמַת יָחִיד בִּשְׁעַת הֶיתֵּר הַבָּמוֹת. וּבְפֶ' "הַמַּעֲלֶה בַּחוּץ" כְּתִיב. ה"ג: חַיָּיב יָצָא מִיבָּעֵי לֵיהּ ה"ק לְפִיכָךְ בִּשְׁעַת אִיסּוּר הַבָּמוֹת הֶעֱלָה ע"ג הַסֶּלַע אוֹ עַל גַּבֵּי הָאֶבֶן חַיָּיב. יָצָא מִיבָּעֵי לֵיהּ. כֵּיוָן דְּאָמַר: אֵין מִזְבֵּחַ בְּבָמָה — בִּשְׁעַת הֶיתֵּר הַבָּמוֹת קָאֵי, הִילְכָּךְ "יָצָא" מִיבָּעֵי לֵיהּ! ה"ק לְפִיכָךְ. הוֹאִיל וּבְבָמָה בִּשְׁעַת הֶיתֵּר הַבָּמוֹת הָוְיָא הַקְטָרָה — בִּשְׁעַת יב] אִיסּוּרוֹ אִם הֶעֱלוּ עַל הַסֶּלַע חַיָּיב. קֶרֶן וְכֶבֶשׁ וִיסוֹד וְרִיבּוּעַ. דְּקַיְ"ל דִּמְעַכְּבִי בְּמִזְבַּח הַמִּשְׁכָּן, בְּפֶרֶק "קָדְשֵׁי קָדָשִׁים" (לעיל דף סב.), מַהוּ שֶׁיְּעַכְּבוּ בְּבָמַת יָחִיד? בְּבָמָה גְּדוֹלָה. אַף נוֹב וְגִבְעוֹן שֶׁהָיוּ בָּמוֹת צִיבּוּר. וְכָל שֶׁכֵּן שִׁילֹה וּבֵית עוֹלָמִים.
מתני'

תוספות

שׁוֹגֵג אנוס ומוטעה. קלא קשה: אנוס ל"ל קרא? פשיטא, דאונס רחמנא פטריה! ושמא האי אנוס פרט לאומר מותר. ותימה: ל"ל קרא למיפטריה מכרת כשהוא שוגג? פשיטא, בר קרבן הוא! וי"ל: ס"ד אמינא, אי לא מייתי קרבן — ליהוי בכרת, דהא לאחר הבאת קרבן דוקא כתיב "ונסלח לו".

*והמעלה להדיוט פטור. פי' בקונטרס: פטור משום העלאת חוץ, וחייב משום עובד עבודה זרה. ואם הזיד בעבודה זרה ושוגג בהעלאת חוץ — אינו מביא על שגגתו חטאת. ותימה: אמאי יתחייב מעלה לחבירו משום מעלה בחוץ? כיון דמזיד בעבודה זרה — לאו שב מידיעתו הוא, דמומר לעבודה זרה מומר לכל התורה כולה! ובחנם דחק עצמו בקונטרס, דמעלה לחבירו אין שייך לחייבו משום עבודה זרה, כיון דאין מתכוין לשם עבודה זרה.

להוציא שעיר המשתלח. היינו לאחר הגרלה. דקודם הגרלה מיחייב אתרוייהו, כדמוכח פרק "שני שעירי" (יומא דף סג:).

דברה תורה כלשון בני אדם. בפרק "אלו מציאות" (ב"מ דף לא:) פירשתי.

אכל בהמה כתיב. לפיכך העלה כמה אברים זה אחר זה אינו חייב אלא אחת, אקמא *מיחייב — דאיתיה לכולה בהמה, ואאחריני פטור — דכבר חסרה, דמה שהעלה הרי הוא כנאבד. ומ"ס: אכל אבר ואבר. אבל אבר אחד שהעלה לחצאין — לכ"ע לא מיחייב אלא אחת, ומיחייב אזית קמא. ורבי יוחנן אמר: מחלוקת באבר אחד, דמר סבר: מוקטרי פנים שחסרו והעלן בחוץ — חייב, וכי כתיב "לעשות אותו" — אשחוטי חוץ, אבל לא אשחוטי פנים, דהא מהדרינן פוקעין. ומר סבר: פטור, כר' ישמעאל דלעיל, וקסבר דלא מהדרינן פוקעין. [אבל בד' וה' אברים — חייב על כל אבר] לכ"ע. וא"ת: מאי טעמא לא מיחייב אכזית שני? נהי דלא מהדרינן פוקעין, מ"מ אם מחתך אבר אחד לכמה זיתים — חייב להעלות את כולן. א"כ הקטרה הוא, ואמאי לא מיחייב עלה בחוץ? וי"ל: דהא *מיחייב להקטיר הכל — לאו משום דתיהוי חשובה הקטרה בחצי אבר, אלא משום דכולה חדא הקטרה היא, וכיון שהתחיל בה — גומר. *אבל אי מהדרי פוקעין, שחסרה ונקטרה שאר מזה — יש ללמוד דחשיבא הקטרה בחצי אבר. וכ"נ שיטה זו, ובקונטרס פי' בע"א.

לא נחלקו אלא במוקטרי חוץ שחסרו והעלן בחוץ מר סבר חייב. פי' בקונטרס: וכי כתיב "אותו" — למעוטי פחות מכזית אתא, שאין הקטרה שלימה, וכדדריש לקמן. וא"ת: ומאי טעמא בעי קרא למעוטי פחות מכזית? היכן מצינו שחייבה תורה בחצי שיעור? וחצי זית חצי שיעור הוא, דלא מצינו הקטרה להתחייב בפחות מכזית, לא לענין מחשבה ושום דבר. אלא דוקא גבי שאור ודבש, דחייב בפחות מכזית למאן דאית ליה מכח קראי! ויש לומר: דשמא כיון דמהדרי' פוקעין פחות מכזית — הוה אמינא דמחייב בחוץ, אי לאו דכתיב "אותו". כמאן מהדרינן פוקעין כו'. הא דמיחייבינן בריש פירקין (דף קז.) לר"ע מוקטרי פנים שחסרו והקריבן בחוץ — היינו דוקא כגון אימורי או איברי עולה שחסרו, דלא מפסלי בהכי. אבל מנחה שחסרה, וקטרת ולבונה שחסרו, דמיפסלי מחמת חסרון — פטור. כדתנן לקמן (דף קט:): וכולן שחסרו כל שהוא והקריבן בחוץ — פטור. *וגבי עולה קתני: המעלה *(עולה כזית) חייב, ומצטרפין לכזית להעלותן בחוץ וליחייב עליהן משום פיגול נותר וטמא (ואימוריס ומן האימורין בחוץ חייב), ומשמע בגמרא דבניתותרו מיירי, דקתני בברייתא: עולה ואימורין — אין, שלמים ואימוריהן — לא

[קדושין מג.]
[שם יז: וש"נ]
[לעיל קז. לקמן קט:]
[לעיל סב. לקמן קכ.]

נ"ל מיחייב דעדיין איתא לכולה בהמה כו' נ"ק
נ"ל דמחייב נ"ק
נ"א אבל אי מהדרין פוקעין שחסרה ונקטרה עם השאר מזה כו' נ"ק
נ"א כזית מן העולה ומן האימורין בחוץ
גי' נ"ק וגבי עולה קתני עולה ואימוריהן מצטרפין לכזית להעלותן בחוץ ולחייב עליהן משום פיגול נותר וטמא ומשמע בגמרא דבניתותרו מיירי דקתני וכו'

הגהות הב"ח

(א) גמ' על האבן חייב חייב יצא מיבעי:

שיטה מקובצת

א] ת"ר איש מה ת"ל איש איש לרבות: ב] שאחזו באבר והעלוהו שפטורין ת"ל: ג] ההוא מאי עביד ליה מיבעי: ד] הך איש איש דשחיטה נמי ותיבת ההוא נמחק: ה] להדיוט דחייב מנא ליה נפקא ליה: ו] אבל באבר אחד: ז] שחסרו והעלו בחוץ: ח] במוקטרי חוץ: ט] יוסי. דאי כר' יוסי כיון דבפנים: י] נמי ניחייב במוקטרי: יא] תיבת אפילו נמחק: יב] איסורן אם העלו:

מתני' אאחד קדשים כשרין, ואחד קדשים פסולין שהיה פסולן בקודש, והקריבן בחוץ חייב. בהמעלה כזית מן העולה א] ומן האימורין בחוץ – חייב.§ **גמ'** ת"ר: °"אשר יעלה עולה ב] או זבח", אין לי אלא עולה, מנין גלרבות אימורי אשם, ואימורי חטאת, ואימורי קדשי קדשים, ואימורי קדשים קלים? ת"ל "זבח". ג] מנין דלרבות הקומץ, והלבונה, והקטורת, ומנחת כהנים, ומנחת כהן משיח, והמנסך שלשת לוגין יין ושלשת לוגין מים? ת"ל: °"ואל פתח אהל מועד לא יביאנו", כל הבא לפתח אהל מועד – חייבין עליו בחוץ, ואין לי אלו קדשים כשרים, מנין לרבות פסולין, הכגון הלן, והיוצא, והטמא, ושנשחט חוץ לזמנו, וחוץ למקומו, ושקבלו פסולין וזרקו את דמו, והניתנין למטה שנתנן למעלה, והניתנין למעלה שנתנן למטה, והניתנין בחוץ שנתנן בפנים, והניתנין בפנים שנתנן בחוץ, ופסח וחטאת ד] *שנתנן שלא לשמן, מנין? ת"ל: "לא יביאנו לעשות", וכל המתקבל בפתח אהל מועד – חייבין עליו בחוץ.§ "המעלה כזית מן העולה" כו'.§ עולה ואימוריה – אין, שלמים ואימוריהן – לא. תנינא להא דת"ר: *עולה ואימוריה מצטרפין לכזית להעלותן בחוץ, ולחייב עליהן משום פיגול נותר וטמא. בשלמא *העלאת עולה דכליל – אין, שלמים – לא. אלא פיגול ונותר וטמא מ"ט? ה] והא *תנן: זכל הפגולין מצטרפין, וכל הנותרין מצטרפין; קשיא פיגול אפיגול, קשיא נותר אנותר! פיגול אפיגול לא קשיא: כאן – בפיגול, כאן – במחשבת פיגול. נותר אנותר לא קשיא: כאן – בנותר, כאן – בשניתותרו עד שלא נזרק הדם. ומני – רבי יהושע היא. *דתניא, ר' יהושע אומר: כל הזבחים שבתורה, שנשתייר ו] בהן כזית בשר וכזית

(ויקרא יז; שם – מקור הפסוקים בגליון)

רש"י

מתני' ואחד קדשים פסולין שהיה פסולן בקדש. הואיל ובפנים אם עלו לא ירדו – מתקבל בפנים קרינא ביה, וחייבין עליהן בחוץ, כדיליף בגמ'. המעלה כזית מן העולה ומאימוריה. חצי זית מזה וחצי זית מזה – חייב דכולה כליל. **גמ'** ואימורי קדשים. כבשי עצרת. הלבונה. של מנחת נדבה. ומנחת כהנים. שהיא כליל, וראויה להעלאה כקומץ מנחת ישראל. אבל שירי מנחת ישראל – אינו חייב על העלאתם. מנחת כהן משיח. עשירית האיפה שהוא מביא בכל יום. ושלשת לוגין יין. שהוא פחות שבנסכים. ושלשת לוגין מים. בחג קאמר, ובמוקדשין לחג, שאין העלאת חוץ נוהגת בחולין. מנין לרבות פסולין. הנך דאם עלו לא ירדו, דלא מתרבו מ"לא יביאנו" דהא אינם ראויין להביא לכתחילה. ת"ל לעשות. משמע: הראויין ז] לעשות, אפילו אינו ראוי לבא מחוץ לפנים. והני נמי, כיון דאם עלו לא ירדו, וכהן נזקק להפך בהם בצינורא או להעלותן מראש המזבח למערכה – ראויין ליעשות קרינא ביה. שלמים לא. אין בשרן מצטרף עם אימוריהן לכזית העלאת חוץ, משום דבשר שלמים לאו בר הקטרה הוא, ולא קרינא ביה "אל פתח אהל מועד לא יביאנו". ולחייב עליהן משום פיגול ונותר וטמא. קא ס"ד: באוכל כזית בשר ואימורין מעולת פיגול או נותר, או בטומאת הגוף אכלו. מאי טעמא. לא מצטרף נמי בשר שלמים עם אימוריו לפיגול ונותר וטמא? הא בין בבשר בין באימורין שייך פיגול נותר וטמא. כדאמר בפ' "בית שמאי" (לעיל דף מג.) דכל שיש לו מתירין, בין לאדם בין למזבח – חייבין עליו משום פיגול. והרי הדם מתיר את הבשר לאדם, ואת האימורין למזבח. ותנן נמי התם: דברים שאין חייבין עליהם משום פיגול, כגון הקומץ והלבונה והקטרת, שאין להם מתירין אלא הם עצמן מתירין – חייבין עליהן משום נותר ומשום טמא. וכל שכן אימורין שהפיגול נוהג בהן, ומקראי ילפינן להו. כל הפיגולין מצטרפין. משנה היא במעילה. כאן בפיגול כאן במחשבת פיגול. הא דקתני: מצטרפין – באוכל פיגול קאמר, ולהתחייב חטאת. והא דקתני: עולה אין, שלמים לא – במחשבת פיגול. שאם שחט או זרק על מנת להקטיר חצי זית בשר עולה וחצי זית מאימורין חוץ לזמנו – פיגל. אבל בשלמים, ח] חישב לאכול או להקטיר חצי זית בשר וחצי זית אימורין – לא פיגל, שאין מחשבת אכילה בנקטרין, ואין מחשבת הקטרה בנאכלין. כאן בנותר כאן בשניתותרו עד שלא נזרק הדם. הא דקתני: מצטרפין – באוכל נותר קאמר. והא דקתני: עולה אין, שלמים לא – בשניתותרו מאיבוד ושריפה, כגון אבדו הבשר והאימורין קודם זריקה, ונשתייר חצי זית מזה וחצי זית מזה, בעולה דכולה כליל – הויא זריקת דם זריקה, דהא איכא אכילת מזבח, וכר' יהושע, דאמר בפרק "טבול יום" (לעיל דף קד.): אם אין בשר – אין דם. וכיון דזריקה היא – (א) חייבין עליו משום נותר אם ניתותרו ואכל ממנו, כדאמרן (לעיל דף מה:): דברים שאין חייבין עליהם משום פיגול חייבין ט] משום נותר, כגון קומץ שהוא אכילת מזבח כעולה, וכל שכן דברים שחייבין עליהן משום פיגול, כגון בשר עולה. אבל שלמים – אין חצי זית מבשרן וחצי זית מאימוריהן מצטרפין להיות שיור לזרוק עליהם את הדם, דלא אכילת אדם איכא ולא אכילת מזבח איכא. וכיון דלא הויא זריקה, אם זרק – אין חייבין עליהן משום נותר וטמא. דקי"ל (מנחות דף כה:): י] כל הניתר לטהורין – חייבין עליו משום טומאה. ובפ' "ב"ש" (לעיל דף מה:) אתי נותר "חילול" "חילול" מטומאה, ובמס' מעילה (דף ו:) לענין יוצא אמרינן: יא] לר"א דאמר: אין זריקה מועלת ליוצא – אין חייבין עליו משום נותר וטמא. כל הזבחים. בר מעולה. יב] *אין זורק את הדם. דאית ליה לר' יהושע:* אם אין בשר אין דם, מ"ועשית עולותיך הבשר והדם". ובזבחים כתיב (דברים יב): "ודם זבחיך ישפך והבשר תאכל" – הזקיקן הכתוב זה לזה.

תוספות

לא, ומוקי לה בניתותרו, וכר' יהושע. וקצת תימה: קומץ ולבונה אמאי לא מיחייב עלייהו בחוץ כשחסרו? נהי דמיפסלי לכתחילה – מ"מ מתקבלין הם בפנים, דאם עלו לא ירדו, דהוה ליה פסולו בקדש כשחסר בין קמילה להקטרה! ולמאן דחשיב במנחות פ' קמא (דף ט:) חסרון כבעל מום – ניחא. וי"ל: דאפילו תמצא לומר דאם עלה לא ירד, מ"מ סברא הוא למעוטיה מדכתיב "אותו" – על השלם הוא חייב, ואינו חייב על החסר, כיון דלכתחילה לא יעלה. *וצריך לדקדק אי מהדרינן פוקעין דידהו. *ובפרק "המזבח מקדש" (לעיל דף פג:) איכא כמה קראי לרבן גמליאל מ"היא העולה על מוקדה" ולאידך מ"אשר תאכל האש". ועוד: דדרשינן לעיל (דף פו.) "ועשית עולותיך הבשר והדם" – עיכולי עולה אתה מחזיר, ואי אתה מחזיר עיכולי גידין ועצמות. *משמע: הא בשר דומיא דגידים ועצמות מהדרינן אפילו במקצת. ותימה אי פליג עליה רבי יוסי. **ומנחת** כהנים ומנחת כהן משיח. הא דפלגינהו, משום דמנחת כהנים באה עשרון, ומנחת כהן משיח חצי עשרון. ותימה דלא תני מנחת נסכים. **עולה** ואימורין מצטרפין לכזית להעלותן בחוץ ולחייב עליהם משום פיגול נותר וטמא. במסכת מעילה פרק "קדשי מזבח" (דף טו:) תנן: חמשה דברים בעולה מצטרפין זה עם זה: הבשר, והחלב, והסלת, והיין, והשמן. וששה בתודה, דאיכא לחם. ותימה: לענין מאי קאמר? אי לענין מעילה – הא תנא ליה רישא (שם.): קדשי מזבח מצטרפין זה עם זה למעילה כו'! ועוד: דתודה אין בה מעילה כי אם לאחר זריקה באימורין, אבל בלחם – לא! ואי *(לא יתחייב) בחוץ – הא לא תני בשמעתין אלא עולה ואימורין, אבל חמשה דברים – לא. דאף על גב דמיחייבי בחוץ, כדדריש לעיל מקרא – הני מילי בפני עצמן, אבל אילטרופי – לא! ועוד: דלא מיחייב בחוץ אלחם שבתודה! ועוד: חלב ויין היאך מצטרפין, והא אין שיעורן שוה, שזה בכזית וזה בשלשה לוגין, ואי לענין לזרוק עליהן הדם – הא אמר: ובמנחה אפילו כולה קיימת – לא יזרוק. ואי לענין מחשבת פיגול – אין אכילה והקטרה מצטרפין! ונראה דמיירי לענין אכילה, דמיחייב האוכל משום פיגול נותר וטמא. ואי מרישא, דקתני: קדשי מזבח מצטרפין – הוה אמינא במין אחד, קמ"ל אפילו בכמה מינין. ועוד: תניינהו למעוטי דאין דם חייבין עליו משום פיגול. ועוד: אשמעינן דחל פיגול אהנך דברים חמשה וששה. וצריך לומר דאתיא כר"מ, דתנן לעיל בפרק "ב"ש" (דף מג:) [ואלו] דברים שאין חייבין עליהן משום פיגול: מנחת נסכים, והנסכים הבאין בפני עצמן דברי ר"מ. וחכ"א: אף הבאים עם הבהמה. וב"הקומץ זוטא" (מנחות דף טו:) תנן נמי: הזבח מפגל את הנסכים *משקדש בכלי, דברי ר"מ. והא דחלב ויין מצטרפין, אע"ג דחלב בכזית ומשקין ברביעית – ה"מ בשתיה. אבל דרך אכילה, שׁרה פתו ביין – שיעורו בכזית. וקצת תימה: מאי איריא דנקט "חמשה דברים בעולה"? הא בשלמים נמי מצטרפין לחייב משום פיגול! ויש לומר: דנקט עולה משום דאיירי נמי במעילה, אף על גב דבתודה לא איירי במעילה.

כל הפיגולין מצטרפין. תימה: דלא מייתי מרישא, דקתני (מעילה דף טו.): קדשי מזבח מצטרפין לפיגול! ויש לומר: דהוה מוקמינן לה בעולה, דהא תני נמי מעילה. אבל הך משמע טפי. וכל הנותרות מצטרפין. תימה: דלא תני "כל הטומאות מצטרפין"! ויש לומר: דהוה משמע, אפילו שרץ ונבלה ובשר המת, והנהו לא מצטרפין, כדתנן התם (דף יז:). כאן או

גליון הש"ס / מסורת הש"ס

ע' רש"ק וצ"ק

צ"ל דבפרק צ"ק

גירסת צ"ק משמע הא דומיא דבשר ודם אפילו דחוקא מהדרינן וחוזה היכא פליג ר"י

גירסת צ"ק להתחייב

צ"ל משקדשו

צ"ל ששחטן צ"ק

תוספתא דמעילה פ"א

נ"א להעלותן צ"ק

מעילה טו.

מעילה שם מנחות ט. כו. תוספתא דפסחים פ"ו [פסחים עט. בכורות לט: לעיל כה: תוספתא זבחים פרק ז]

שייך לע"ב צ"ק

[לעיל קד.]

עין משפט נר מצוה

כט א מיי' פי"ט מהל' מעה"ק הלכה ז:
ל ב מיי' שם הל' י:
לא ג ד מיי' שם הל' ג:
לב ה מיי' שם הל' ז:
לג ו מיי' שם הלכה ג:
לד ז מיי' פי"ח מהל' פסה"מ הלכה יח:

שיטה מקובצת

א] העולה ומאימוריה תיבות ומן האימורין נמחק: ב] תיבות או זבח נמחק: ג] זבח מנין לרבות את הדם ת"ל או זבח מנין: ד] וחטאת ששחטן שלא: ה] מ"ט לא והא: ו] שנשתייר מהן כזית: ז] הראויין ליעשות אפילו: ח] בשלמים אם חישב: ט] חייבין עליהן: י] תיבת כל נמחק: יא] אמרינן נמי לר"א: יב] מה"ד אינו זורק:

הגהות הב"ח

(א) רש"י ד"ה כאן בנותר וכו' דזריקה היא אבל עולה חייבין:

*וְכַזַּיִת חֵלֶב – אזוֹרֵק אֶת הַדָּם, חֲצִי זַיִת בָּשָׂר וַחֲצִי זַיִת חֵלֶב – אֵינוֹ זוֹרֵק אֶת הַדָּם. בוּבְעוֹלָה, חֲצִי זַיִת בָּשָׂר וַחֲצִי זַיִת חֵלֶב – זוֹרֵק אֶת הַדָּם, מִפְּנֵי שֶׁכּוּלָּהּ כָּלִיל. וּמִנְחָה, אֲפִילּוּ כּוּלָּהּ קַיֶּימֶת – לֹא יִזְרוֹק. מִנְחָה מַאי עֲבִידְתָּהּ? אָמַר רַב פַּפָּא: מִנְחַת נְסָכִים הַבָּאָה עִם הַזֶּבַח.§ **מתני'** *הַקּוֹמֶץ, וְהַלְּבוֹנָה, וְהַקְּטֹרֶת, וּמִנְחַת כֹּהֲנִים, וּמִנְחַת כֹּהֵן מָשִׁיחַ, וּמִנְחַת נְסָכִים א] שֶׁהִקְרִיב מֵאַחַת מֵהֶן גכַּזַּיִת בַּחוּץ – חַיָּיב. ר"א פּוֹטֵר עַד שֶׁיַּקְרִיב אֶת כּוּלָּן. דוְכוּלָּן ב] שֶׁהִקְרִיב בִּפְנִים, וְשִׁיֵּיר מֵהֶן כַּזַּיִת וְהִקְרִיבוֹ בַּחוּץ – חַיָּיב. הוְכוּלָּן שֶׁחָסְרוּ כָּל שֶׁהוּ וְהִקְרִיבוֹ בַּחוּץ – פָּטוּר. (א) הַמַּקְרִיב קָדָשִׁים וְאֵימוּרִים בַּחוּץ – חַיָּיב.§ **גמ'** ת"ר: והַמַּקְטִיר כַּזַּיִת ג] בַּחוּץ – חַיָּיב, חֲצִי פְרָס בִּפְנִים – פָּטוּר. קס"ד, מַאי "פָּטוּר" – פָּטוּר זָר. אַמַּאי? ד] הַקְטָרָה הִיא! א"ר זֵירָא אָמַר רַב חִסְדָּא אָמַר רַב יִרְמְיָה בַּר אַבָּא אָמַר רַב: מַאי "פָּטוּר" – פָּטוּר צִיבּוּר. א"ר זֵירָא: אִי קַשְׁיָא לִי – הָא קַשְׁיָא לִי, הָא דְּאָמַר רַב עֲלָהּ: בְּהָא אֲפִילּוּ ר' ה] אֱלִיעֶזֶר מוֹדֶה. דְּהָא ר' אֱלִיעֶזֶר לָאו הַקְטָרָה הִיא קָאָמַר! אָמַר רַבָּה: בְּהַקְטָרָה דְּהֵיכָל – דְּכוּלֵּי עָלְמָא לָא פְּלִיגִי. כִּי פְּלִיגִי – בְּהַקְטָרָה דִּפְנִים, דְּמָר סָבַר: °"מְלֹא חָפְנָיו" דַּוְקָא, ומ"ס: "מְלֹא חָפְנָיו" לָאו דַּוְקָא. א"ל אַבַּיֵי: וְהָא כִּי קָא כְּתִיבָא "חוּקָּה" – בְּהַקְטָרָה דִּפְנִים הוּא דִּכְתִיב! אֶלָּא אָמַר אַבַּיֵי: בְּהַקְטָרָה ו] זבִּפְנִים – כ"ע לָא פְּלִיגִי. כִּי פְּלִיגִי – בְּהַקְטָרָה דְּחוּץ, מ"ס: יָלְפִינַן פְּנִים מֵחוּץ, ומ"ס לָא יָלְפִינַן. אָמַר רָבָא: הַשְׁתָּא חוּץ מֵחוּץ לָא יָלְפִי רַבָּנַן, פְּנִים מֵחוּץ מִיבָּעֵי?! מַה הִיא? דְּתַנְיָא: יָכוֹל הַמַּעֲלֶה פָּחוֹת מִכַּזַּיִת קוֹמֶץ, וּפָחוֹת מִכַּזַּיִת אֵימוּרִין, וְהַמְנַסֵּךְ פָּחוֹת מִשְּׁלֹשֶׁת לוּגִּין יַיִן, ז] [פָּחוֹת] מִג' לוּגִּין מַיִם, יְהֵא חַיָּיב? תַּלְמוּד לוֹמַר: "לַעֲשׂוֹת" – ח] *עַל הַשָּׁלֵם חַיָּיב, וְאֵינוֹ חַיָּיב עַל הֶחָסֵר. וְהָא פָּחוֹת מִשְּׁלֹשֶׁת לוּגִּין, דְּאִית בְּהוּ כַּמָּה זֵיתִים, וְלָא יָלְפִי רַבָּנַן חוּץ מֵחוּץ! אֶלָּא אָמַר רָבָא: כְּגוֹן דְּקַבְעִינְהוּ ט] שְׁנֵי חֲצָאֵי פְרָס בְּמָנָא

תורה אור: ° ויקרא טז

או כַּזַּיִת חֵלֶב. דִּכְתִיב: "וְזָרַק הַכֹּהֵן אֶת הַדָּם וגו' וְהִקְטִיר הַחֵלֶב", אע"פ שֶׁאֵין בָּשָׂר – זוֹרֵק עָלָיו אֶת הַדָּם. וְהָכִי מְפָרֵשׁ בִּמְנָחוֹת בְּ"הַקּוֹמֵץ רַבָּה" (דף כו.). *י] וּבְמִנְחָה מַאי עֲבִידְתָּהּ. מַאי זְרִיקַת דָּם אִיכָּא בְּמִנְחָה? מִנְחַת נְסָכִים שֶׁבָּאָה עִם הַזֶּבַח. וְאָבַד בְּשַׂר הַזֶּבַח, וְהַמִּנְחָה קַיֶּימֶת – לֹא יִזְרוֹק אֶת הַדָּם בִּשְׁבִילָהּ. דְּלָאו גּוּפָא דִּזְבִיחָה הוּא. **מתני'** הַלְּבוֹנָה. שֶׁל מִנְחָה. וְהַקְּטֹרֶת. שֶׁבְּכָל יוֹם, פְּרָס [שֶׁל] שַׁחֲרִית וּפְרָס שֶׁל בֵּין הָעַרְבַּיִם שֶׁהִקְטִיר יא] כַּזַּיִת מֵהֶן בַּחוּץ – חַיָּיב. קָסָבַר: כִּי כְּתִיב "אוֹתוֹ" – עַל הַשָּׁלֵם הוּא חַיָּיב וְאֵינוֹ חַיָּיב עַל הֶחָסֵר – אַשִּׁיעוּר הַקְטָרָה כְּתִיב, וְהַיְינוּ *כַּזַּיִת. וְרַבִּי יב] אֱלִיעֶזֶר נַמִי, מִדְּלָא פָּלֵיג אַרֵישָׁא גַּבֵּי עוֹלָה, הָכִי נַמִי דָּרֵישׁ לֵיהּ "אוֹתוֹ" אַשִּׁיעוּר הַקְטָרָה כְּרַבָּנַן. וּמִיהוּ, עוֹלָה דְּלָא מִיפַּסְלָא בְּחִסָּרוֹן, דְּכָל עַצְמָהּ בְּדָם תְּלוּיָה כַּפָּרָתָהּ – חַיָּיב בְּכַזַּיִת, אֲבָל בְּהָנֵי פָּלֵיג, דְּקָא סָבַר: קוֹמֶץ כּוּלֵּיהּ – הַיְינוּ שִׁיעוּר הַקְטָרָתוֹ אַף בִּפְנִים, דְּהָא מִיפְּסָל בְּחִסָּרוֹן. וְכֵן כּוּלָּם, שֶׁכּוּלָּם מַתִּירִין הֵם, כָּל זְמַן שֶׁלֹּא קָרְבוּ כּוּלָּם – לָא הָוְיָא הַקְטָרָה לָצֵאת בְּעָלִים יְדֵי חוֹבָתָן. וּלְרַבָּנַן בְּהָנֵי נַמִי הָוְיָא הַקְטָרָתָן בְּכַזַּיִת, הֵיכָא דְּכוּלֵּיהּ קַיָּים וְלֹא חָסְרוּ קוֹדֶם הַקְטָרָה, וּתְנַן מְנָחוֹת (דף כו.): הִקְטִיר קוּמְצָהּ פַּעֲמַיִם – כְּשֵׁירָה. הִילְכָּךְ הַקְטָרָה הִיא. וְכוּלָּן שֶׁהִקְרִיבָן בִּפְנִים וְשִׁיֵּיר מֵהֶן כו'. חַיָּיב, שֶׁהֲרֵי בָּזֶה נִגְמְרָה הַקְטָרָתָן. וּלְר' אֱלִיעֶזֶר נַמִי, כִּי דָּרֵישׁ "אוֹתוֹ" – אַשִּׁיעוּר הַקְטָרָה דָּרֵישׁ לֵיהּ, וְשִׁיעוּר הַקְטָרָה בְּכַזַּיִת הֵיכָא דִּבְפְנִים הָוְיָא הַקְטָרָה גְּמוּרָה. וְכוּלָּן שֶׁחָסְרוּ כָּל שֶׁהוּא. קוֹדֶם הַקְטָרָה ע"י אִיבּוּד אוֹ שְׂרֵיפָה – נִפְסְלוּ בְּחֶסְרוֹנָן, כִּדְאָמַר בִּמְנָחוֹת (דף ט:): "מִן הַמִּנְחָה" – פְּרָט לְשֶׁחָסְרָה הִיא וְשֶׁחָסַר קוּמְצָהּ. וְהַאי "וְכוּלָּן" – לָאו אַלְּבוֹנָה קָאֵי, דְּהָא מִיפְלִיג פְּלִיגֵי בָּהּ בִּמְנָחוֹת בְּפֶרֶק קַמָּא (דף יא:) בִּלְבוֹנָה שֶׁחָסְרָה, דִּלְר"ש כְּשֵׁירָה אֲפִילּוּ עָמְדָה עַל קוֹרֶט אֶחָד, וּלְר' יְהוּדָה בִּשְׁנֵי קְרָטִין. וְאִי אַלְּבוֹנָה נַמִי קָאֵי – מַיְירֵי שֶׁחָסְרָה מִשִּׁיעוּר הֶכְשֵׁרָהּ, לְמָר כִּדְאִית לֵיהּ וּלְמָר כִּדְאִית לֵיהּ. וְהִקְרִיבוֹ בַּחוּץ פָּטוּר. הוֹאִיל וְאֵין יג] מִתְקַבְּלִין בִּפְנִים. *הַמַּעֲלֶה קָדָשִׁים וְאֵימוּרֵיהֶן. שֶׁהִקְרִיב הַבָּשָׂר וְהָאֵימוּרִין מְחוּבָּרִין בּוֹ – חַיָּיב מִשּׁוּם אֵימוּרִין. **גמ'** חֲצִי פְּרָס בִּפְנִים. לָאו דַּוְקָא חֲצִי פְּרָס נָקַט, דה"ה לְכַזַּיִת. אֶלָּא פָּחוֹת מִכְּשִׁיעוּר הֶכְשֵׁר מִנְחָתָהּ נָקַט. קס"ד מַאי פָּטוּר פָּטוּר זָר. דְּאִי לָאו בְּזָרוּת קָאָמַר – מַאי "פָּטוּר" שַׁיָּיךְ לְמֵימַר בִּפְנִים, וְאַמַּאי פָּטוּר? הָא הַקְטָרָה הִיא, דְּהָא הַאי תַּנָּא דְּקָמְחַיֵּיב עֲלָהּ בַּחוּץ! מַאי פָּטוּר פָּטוּר צִיבּוּר. דְּיָצְאוּ יְדֵי חוֹבָתָן, דְּכַזַּיִת הָוְיָא הַקְטָרָה. בְּהָא אֲפִילּוּ רַבִּי יד] אֱלִיעֶזֶר מוֹדֶה. וְאע"ג דְּפָלֵיג בְּמַתְנִי' אַבַּחוּץ – מוֹדֶה הוּא לְהַאי תַּנָּא בְּהַאי סֵיפָא דְּפָטוּר צִיבּוּר. וְקַשְׁיָא לִי עֲלָהּ: אַמַּאי מוֹדֶה? וְהָא רַבִּי אֱלִיעֶזֶר לָאו הַקְטָרָה הִיא קָאָמַר, מִדְּפָטַר עֲלָהּ בַּחוּץ! **אָמַר רַבָּה** בְּהַקְטָרָה דְּהֵיכָל. שֶׁבְּכָל יוֹם, שֶׁלֹּא נֶאֱמַר בּוֹ שִׁיעוּר, וְהַאי פְּרָס שִׁיעוּר דְּרַבָּנַן הוּא – מוֹדֶה רַבִּי טו] אֱלִיעֶזֶר דְּבְכַזַּיִת הָוְיָא הַקְטָרָה לְחַיֵּיב עָלֶיהָ בַּחוּץ, וּלְהוֹצִיא לַצִּיבּוּר יְדֵי חוֹבָתָן בִּפְנִים. *וּמַתְנִי' כּוּלָּהּ, רֵישָׁא וְסֵיפָא – דִּבְרֵי הַכֹּל הִיא, וּבְהַקְטָרָה דְּהֵיכָל מַיְירֵי. כִּי פְּלִיגֵי. בְּמַתְנִי', בְּהַקְטָרָה דְּיוֹם הַכִּפּוּרִים דְּלִפְנַי וְלִפְנִים, שֶׁנֶּאֱמַר בָּהּ שִׁיעוּר (ויקרא טז). מְלֹא חָפְנָיו דַּוְקָא. וּכְבַת אַחַת, הִילְכָּךְ בַּחוּץ נַמִי לָא מִיחַיֵּיב אֶלָּא אַשְּׁלֵימָה. וְהָא כִּי כְּתִיבָא חוּקָּה בִּפְנִים כְּתִיבָא. כִּדִכְתִיב (שם): "וְהָיְתָה (זֹאת) לָכֶם לְחוּקַּת עוֹלָם לְכַפֵּר" וגו' – דְּבָרִים שֶׁאֵין נַעֲשִׂין אֶלָּא *אַחַת בַּשָּׁנָה, וְ"חוּקָּה" – עִיכּוּבָא הוּא! ה"ג: **אֶלָּא אָמַר אַבַּיֵי** בְּהַקְטָרָה דִּפְנִים דְּכוּלֵּי עָלְמָא לָא פְּלִיגִי כִּי פְּלִיגִי בְּהַקְטָרָה דְּחוּץ. אַבַּיֵי נַמִי כְּרַבָּה מְתָרֵץ לָהּ, דְּבָרַיְיתָא דְּמוֹדֶה בָּהּ רַבִּי אֱלִיעֶזֶר – בְּהַקְטָרָה דְּהֵיכָל, וּמַתְנִיתִין – בְּהַקְטָרָה דִּפְנִים. וּמִיהוּ, לָא כְּטַעֲמָא דְּרַבָּה דְּאָמַר: לְרַבָּנַן מְלֹא חָפְנָיו לָאו דַּוְקָא. דְּכוּלֵּי עָלְמָא מְלֹא חָפְנָיו דַּוְקָא, וּבִפְנִים – דְּכ"ע לָא פְּלִיגֵי דִּשְׁלֵימָה בָּעֵינַן. כִּי פְּלִיגֵי – כְּגוֹן שֶׁהִקְטִיר כַּזַּיִת מִן הַקְּטֹרֶת שֶׁל חֲפִינַת פְּנִים בַּחוּץ. מָר סָבַר: יָלְפִינַן פְּנִים מֵחוּץ – יָלְפִינַן קְטֹרֶת שֶׁל פְּנִים מִקְּטֹרֶת שֶׁל הֵיכָל, מָה הַקְטָרָה שֶׁל הֵיכָל טז] בְּבָמָה בַּחוּץ בְּכַזַּיִת – אַף הַקְטָרָה שֶׁל פְּנִים חַיָּיבִין עָלֶיהָ בְּבָמָה בְּכַזַּיִת. וְאע"ג דִּבְדוּכְתָּהּ לָא הָוְיָא הַקְטָרָה, הוֹאִיל וּבַהֵיכָל הָוְיָא הַקְטָרָה. וְר' אֱלִיעֶזֶר סָבַר לָא יָלְפִינַן פְּנִים מֵחוּץ. הַקְטָרָה דְּהֵיכָל הוּא דְּמִיחַיֵּיב עֲלָהּ בַּחוּץ בְּכַזַּיִת, דְּהָא בְּדוּכְתָּהּ בְּהָכִי חֲשִׁיבָא. אֲבָל יז] הַקְטָרַת פְּנִים – לָא מִיחַיֵּיב עֲלָהּ בַּחוּץ בְּכַזַּיִת, הוֹאִיל וּבְדוּכְתָּהּ לָאו הַקְטָרָה הִיא. הַשְׁתָּא חוּץ מֵחוּץ. כְּגוֹן נִיסּוּךְ הַיַּיִן שֶׁהוּא עַל הַמִּזְבֵּחַ הַחִיצוֹן – לָא יָלְפִי רַבָּנַן מֵהֶקְטֵר חֲלָבִים שֶׁהוּא עַל הַמִּזְבֵּחַ הַחִיצוֹן, לְחַיֵּיב עַל פָּחוֹת מִשְּׁלֹשָׁה לוּגִּין בַּחוּץ, אע"פ שֶׁיֵּשׁ שָׁם כַּמָּה זֵיתִים, וְגַבֵּי כָּל הַקְטָרוֹת שֶׁל מִזְבֵּחַ הַחִיצוֹן הַקְטָרָה הִיא. הוֹאִיל וְגַבֵּי נִיסּוּךְ שִׁיעוּרָא אַחֲרִינָא הוּא – לָא מִיחַיֵּיב עֲלֵיהּ אֶלָּא בִּכְשִׁיעוּר. פְּנִים מֵחוּץ. לְחַיֵּיב עַל קְטֹרֶת שֶׁלִּפְנַי וְלִפְנִים בְּבָמָה בַּחוּץ, יָלְפִינַן מֵהַקְטָרָה דְּהֵיכָל? פָּחוֹת מִכַּזַּיִת קוֹמֶץ. עַל כָּרְחָךְ רַבָּנַן הִיא. דְּאִי רַבִּי יח] אֱלִיעֶזֶר – אֲפִילּוּ אַכַּזַּיִת לָא מִיחַיֵּיב, דְּהָא אָמַר: עַד שֶׁיַּקְרִיב אֶת כּוּלָּן. **אֶלָּא אָמַר רָבָא** כְּגוֹן דְּקַבְעִינְהוּ בְּמָנָא. לְעוֹלָם מַתְנִיתִין וּבָרַיְיתָא בְּהַקְטָרָה דְּהֵיכָל הָוְיָא הַקְטָרָה בְּדוּכְתָּהּ בְּכַזַּיִת. וּמִשּׁוּם הָכִי קָתָנֵי לָהּ בַּבָּרַיְיתָא חַיָּיב, יט] וְר' אֱלִיעֶזֶר מוֹדֶה בָּהּ, כִּדְרַב. וּפְלוּגְתָּא דְּמַתְנִיתִין – כְּגוֹן *דְּקַבְעֵיהּ (דְּכוּלָּהּ) שְׁנֵי חֲצָאֵי פְרָס בְּמָנָא וְקָסָבַר

---

*כאן בשניתותרו [עד] שלא נזרק הדם ומני רבי יהושע. ה"ג לה במעילה בפ' "קדשי מזבח" (דף טו:): אלא אימא עולה ואימורים מצטרפין זה עם זה לכזית לזרוק עליהם את הדם, ומאן קתני לה – רבי יהושע. וגירסא דשמעתין נמי יש ליישב, דהכי נמי קאמר. *וקשה לישנא דברייתא, דקתני "ולחייב עליהם משום פיגול נותר וטמא"! ויש לפרש: דכשניתותרו כזית מעולה ואימורין אשמעינן דזריקה מעלייתא היא לאיחויבי משום פיגול נותר וטמא, דקרבו מתיריו קרינא ביה. והשתא לא צריכי להא דקאמר הכא: פיגול אפיגול לא קשיא, כאן בפיגול, כאן במחשבת פיגול. דבשינויא דניתותרו מתרצי תרוייהו, פיגול ונותר. ובמסכת מעילה לא גרסינן ליה. *ויש מוחקין "טמא" מן הברייתא, משום דמטמא לא משני מידי. אבל לפי מה שפירשתי ניחא, דכולהו מיתרצי. וע"כ גרסינן ליה, דאי לא גרסינן ליה – הא דקאמר התם במעילה: תנינא להא דתנו רבנן – מנא ליה הא דקתני בברייתא דמצטרפין לענין אכילה? *ואימא פיגול אפיגול לא קשיא – כאן בפיגול כאן במחשבת פיגול. ונותר אנותר לא קשיא – כאן בנותר, כאן בשניתותרו. דלמא איירי "להצטרף" – לענין להכשיר הקרבן ולזרוק עליהם את הדם, אבל לאכילה – לא מצטרפין! אבל מכיון דתני טמא – על כרחין לענין אכילה קאמר דמצטרפין, דהיינו "תנינא להא דתנו רבנן". **ומר** סבר מלא חפניו לאו דוקא. תימה: למה לי למימר "לאו דוקא"? אפילו יהא דוקא הוו מחייבי רבנן אכזית ממנו בחוץ, מידי דהוה אקומץ! וכמו כן קשה בסמוך: למה לי למימר דסברי רבנן קביעות דמנא לאו כלום היא? ויש לומר: דעד כאן לא מחייבי רבנן בקומץ – אלא משום דחשיב להתפגל על מנת להקטיר כזית מקומצה בחוץ, הלכך חשיבא נמי הקטרה לחייב אכזית ממנו בחוץ. ומנחת כהנים ומנחת כהן משיח, אע"ג דלא שייך בהם פיגול, כיון דמנחה נינהו ומלינו במנחה דכזית נמי חשיבא הקטרה – שם מנחה אחד הוא. אבל קטרת לא אשכחן דחשיב הקטרה בכזית, דלא שייך ביה פיגול. ועוד: דהא א"ר יוסי דאין פיגול אלא בדבר שהוא על מזבח החיצון. הלכך הא דמחייבי רבנן בקטרת בכזית – על כרחין משום דמלא חפניו לאו דוקא, וקביעות מנא לאו כלום היא. *דקבעינהו במנא. למאי דאסיקנא (למאי) דקבעינהו במנא – הוי לבונה דמתניתין שיעור שלם, ופטור בחוץ לרבי אליעזר, הואיל וקבעינהו במנא. אבל

שייך לעיל מעל"ד

לה א ב מיי' פ"א מהל' פסה"מ הלכה ל:

נ"ל וקשה לישנא דברייתא דלא קתני לזרוק עליהם את הדם ולחייב עליהם כו' נ"ק

לו ג ד ה מיי' פי"ט מהל' מעה"ק הל' ח:

לז ו מיי' שם:

לח ז מיי' פ"ט מהלכות ביאת מקדש הל' ז:

[לעיל מב. מנחות יב:]

[וע' תוספות מנחות נח: ד"ה ואיכא דאמרי]

קאמר ואימא כו' נ"ק

עיין רש"ק וג"ק

שיטה מקובצת

א] נסכים שהקטיר ותיבת שהקריב נמחק: ב] וכולן שהקריבן בפנים: ג] כזית קטורת בחוץ: ד] אמאי הא הקטרה היא: ה] ר' אלעזר מודה והא ר' אלעזר לאו: ו] דפנים כ"ע: ז] ופחות מג': ח] לעשות אותו על: ט] תיבות שני חצאי פרס נמחק: י] מה"ד מנחה מאי: יא] שהקטיר מהן כזית בחוץ: יב] ורבי אלעזר: יג] ואין מתקבל בפנים: יד] ר' אלעזר מודה כו' והא ר' אלעזר לאו: טו] רבי אלעזר דבכזית כו' דהיכל קא מיירי הס"ד: טז] היכל חייבין עליהן בבמה: יז] אבל קטרת פנים: יח] רבי אלעזר אפילו: יט] ורבי אלעזר מודה כו' כגון דקבעיה לכולה חצי פרס תיבת שני נמחק:

כאן שייך ד"ה אין זורק כו' שמעל"ד נ"ק

נ"ל או כזית

כזית הס"ד ואח"כ מ"ה ור"א פוטר ומדלא פליג ארישא גבי עולה ה"נ דר"א וכו' כנ"ל נ"ק

הגהות הב"ח

(א) במשנה בחוץ פטור המעלה קדשים:

[לעיל קז. קח:]

נ"ל המקריב קדשים ואימוריהן כו' נ"ק

ס"א וברייתא

נ"ל פעם אחת בשנה כו' נ"ק

גי' נ"ק כגון דקבעי' לכול' פרס במנא

בְּמָנָא; מָר סָבַר: קְבִיעוּת מָנָא מִילְּתָא הִיא, וּמָר סָבַר: לָאו מִילְּתָא הִיא. אָמַר רָבָא: הָשְׁתָּא א] לְמַאן דְּאָמַר קְבִיעוּתָא דְּמָנָא וְלָא כְּלוּם הוּא, קָבַע שִׁשָּׁה לְפָר, וּמָשַׁךְ מֵהֶן אַרְבָּעָה וְהִקְרִיבָן בַּחוּץ — חַיָּיב, ב] שֶׁרְאוּיִין לְאַיִל. קָבַע אַרְבָּעָה לְאַיִל, וּמָשַׁךְ מֵהֶן שְׁלֹשָׁה וְהִקְרִיבָן בַּחוּץ — חַיָּיב, ג] שֶׁרְאוּיִין לְכֶבֶשׂ. חָסְרוּ כָּל שֶׁהוּא, וְהִקְרִיבָן בַּחוּץ — פָּטוּר. רַב אַשִׁי אָמַר: נִיסּוּךְ מֵהַקְטָרָה לָא יָלְפִי רַבָּנַן. אַף עַל גַּב דְּחוּץ מֵחוּץ ד] לָא יָלְפִי, הַקְטָרָה מֵהַקְטָרָה — יָלְפִי, *אַף עַל גַּב ה] דְּחוּץ מִפְּנִים.§ "וְכוּלָּן ו] שֶׁחָסְרוּ".§ אִיבַּעְיָא לְהוּ: אחִסָּרוֹן דְּחוּץ שְׁמֵיהּ חִסָּרוֹן, אוֹ לָא שְׁמֵיהּ חִסָּרוֹן? מִי אָמְרִינַן: כֵּיוָן דִּנְפַק ז] אִיפַּסְלוּ לְהוּ, מַה לִּי חָסֵר מַה לִּי *יָתֵר. אוֹ דִילְמָא: יוֹצֵא דְּאִיתֵיהּ בְּעֵינֵיהּ — אִין, דְּלֵיתֵיהּ בְּעֵינֵיהּ — לָא? אָמַר אַבַּיֵי: ת"ש, ר' אֱלִיעֶזֶר פּוֹטֵר, עַד שֶׁיַּקְרִיב אֶת כּוּלָּן. אֲמַר לֵיהּ רַבָּה בַּר רַב חָנָן לְאַבַּיֵי: מִדְּר' אֱלִיעֶזֶר פָּשֵׁיט מָר? אֲמַר לֵיהּ: בְּפֵירוּשׁ שְׁמִיעַ לִי מִינֵּיהּ ח] דְּרַב: עַד כָּאן לָא פְּלִיגִי רַבָּנַן עֲלֵיהּ דְּר' ט] אֱלִיעֶזֶר — אֶלָּא דְּאִיתֵיהּ בְּעֵינֵיהּ, אֲבָל בְּחִסָּרוֹן — מוֹדוּ לֵיהּ; לָאו דְּחָסַר בַּחוּץ? לָא, דְּחָסַר בִּפְנִים. ת"ש: וְכוּלָּן שֶׁחָסְרוּ י] וְהִקְרִיבָן בַּחוּץ — פָּטוּר; לָאו דְּחָסַר בַּחוּץ? לָא, דְּחָסַר בִּפְנִים.§ "הַמַּקְרִיב קָדָשִׁים".§ אַמַּאי? וְהָאִיכָּא חֲצִיצָה! אָמַר שְׁמוּאֵל: כְּשֶׁהֲפָכָן. וְר' יוֹחָנָן אָמַר: אֲפִילּוּ תֵּימָא שֶׁלֹּא הֲפָכָן, וְהָא מַנִּי — רַבִּי שִׁמְעוֹן הִיא, דְּאָמַר: *אֲפִילּוּ הֶעֱלָה עַל הַסֶּלַע — יא] חַיָּיב. רַב אָמַר: *מִין בְּמִינוֹ אֵינוֹ חוֹצֵץ.§ **מתני'** במִנְחָה שֶׁלֹּא נִקְמְצָה, וְהִקְרִיבָהּ בַּחוּץ — פָּטוּר. גקְמָצָהּ, וְחָזַר קוּמְצָהּ לְתוֹכָהּ יב] וְהִקְרִיבוֹ בַּחוּץ — חַיָּיב.§ **גמ'** יג] וְאַמַּאי? לִיבַטְּלִי שִׁירַיִם לַקּוֹמֶץ! *אָמַר רַבִּי זֵירָא: נֶאֶמְרָה הַקְטָרָה בַּקּוֹמֶץ וְנֶאֶמְרָה הַקְטָרָה בַּשִּׁירַיִם, מַה יד] הַקְטָרַת קוֹמֶץ — אֵין קוֹמֶץ מְבַטֵּל חֲבֵירוֹ, אַף הַקְטָרַת שִׁירַיִם — אֵין שִׁירַיִם מְבַטְּלִין קוֹמֶץ.§ **מתני'** *דהַקּוֹמֶץ וְהַלְּבוֹנָה שֶׁהִקְרִיב אֶת אֶחָד מֵהֶן בַּחוּץ — חַיָּיב, ר' אֱלִיעֶזֶר פּוֹטֵר עַד שֶׁיַּקְרִיב אֶת הַשֵּׁנִי. האֶחָד בִּפְנִים וְאֶחָד בַּחוּץ — חַיָּיב, ושְׁנֵי בְזִיכֵי לְבוֹנָה שֶׁהִקְרִיב אֶת אֶחָד מֵהֶם בַּחוּץ — חַיָּיב, ר' אֱלִיעֶזֶר פּוֹטֵר עַד שֶׁיַּקְרִיב אֶת הַשֵּׁנִי. זאֶחָד בִּפְנִים וְאֶחָד בַּחוּץ — חַיָּיב.§ **גמ'** בָּעֵי ר' יִצְחָק נַפָּחָא: קוֹמֶץ מַהוּ שֶׁיַּתִּיר כְּנֶגְדּוֹ בַּשִּׁירַיִם? מִישְׁרָא שָׁרֵי, אוֹ טו] קָלוֹשֵׁי מִיקְלַשׁ? אַלִּיבָּא דְּמַאן? אִי אַלִּיבָּא *דְּרַבִּי מֵאִיר דְּאָמַר: מְפַגְּלִין בַּחֲצִי מַתִּיר — מִישְׁרָא שָׁרֵי! אִי אַלִּיבָּא דְּרַבָּנַן דְּאָמְרִי: אֵין מְפַגְּלִין בַּחֲצִי מַתִּיר — לָא מִישְׁרָא שָׁרֵי וְלָא טז] מִקְלַשׁ קָלֵישׁ! אֶלָּא, אַלִּיבָּא דְּרַבִּי אֱלִיעֶזֶר — ר"א כְּרַבָּנַן סְבִירָא לֵיהּ, דְּאָמַר: אֵין מְפַגְּלִין בַּחֲצִי מַתִּיר! (א) אֶלָּא, אַלִּיבָּא דְּרַבָּנַן דְּהָכָא, מַאי? מִישְׁרָא שָׁרֵי, אוֹ יז] קָלֵישׁ מִקְלַשׁ? תֵּיקוּ.§ **מתני'** ח*הַזּוֹרֵק מִקְצָת יח] דָּם בַּחוּץ —
חַיָּיב

וְקָסָבַר ר"א: יט] [קְבִיעוּתָא] דְּמָנָא מִילְּתָא הוּא, הוֹאִיל וְנָתַן שְׁנֵי חֲצָאֵי פְרָס בִּכְלִי כ] הַקְטָרַת הֵיכָל – קַבְעֵיהּ מָנָא, וְאִי חַסִּיר כָּל שֶׁהוּא – מִיפְּסָל. הִילְכָּךְ בַּחוּץ לָא מִיחַיֵּיב עַד שֶׁיַּקְרִיב אֶת כּוּלּוֹ. וְרַבָּנַן סָבְרִי. קְבִיעוּתָא דְּמָנָא לָאו כְּלוּם הִיא. קָבַע שִׁשָּׁה לוּגִּין. דְּהוּא חֲצִי הַהִין לְנִסְכֵּי פָר, וּנְתָנָן בִּכְלִי. וּמָשַׁךְ אַרְבָּעָה מֵהֶן וְהִקְרִיבָן בַּחוּץ – חַיָּיב, שֶׁהֲרֵי רְאוּיִין בִּפְנִים לְאַיִל. פָּטוּר. דְּאַיִל מִשְּׁלֹשֶׁת לוּגִּין לָא חֲזוּ בִּפְנִים. רַב אַשִׁי אָמַר. לְעוֹלָם כִּדְתַרְגְּמָהּ אַבַּיֵי, דִּבְהַקְטָרָה שֶׁל פְּנִים בַּחוּץ פְּלִיגִי, וּמְיַלַּף פְּנִים מִחוּץ. וּדְקָא קַשְׁיָא לָךְ: הַשְׁתָּא חוּץ מִחוּץ לָא יָלְפִי רַבָּנַן כו' – לָא דָּמֵי נִיסּוּךְ לְהַקְטָרָה. דְּנִיסּוּךְ מֵהַקְטָרָה לָא יָלְפִי רַבָּנַן, וְאע"ג דְּחוּץ מִחוּץ. אֲבָל קְטֹרֶת שֶׁל פְּנִים מִקְטֹרֶת שֶׁל הֵיכָל יָלְפִי, וְאע"ג דִּפְנִים מִחוּץ. חִסָּרוֹן דְּחוּץ. הוֹצִיאָן שְׁלֵימִים לַחוּץ, וְחָסְרוּ לְאִיבּוּד. שְׁמֵיהּ חִסָּרוֹן. וְאִם הֶעֱלָה אֶת הַמְשׁוּיָּיר בַּחוּץ – פָּטוּר. אוֹ לָאו שְׁמֵיהּ חִסָּרוֹן, וְחַיָּיב לְרַבָּנַן, כְּאִילּוּ כּוּלּוֹ קַיָּים. אִיפְּסִיל כא] לֵיהּ. וַאֲפִי' הָכִי מִיחַיֵּיב עֲלֵיהּ בַּחוּץ, וּמַה לִּי יוֹצֵא וּמַה לִּי חִסָּרוֹן? עַד שֶׁיַּקְרִיב כב] כּוּלּוֹ. אַלְמָא: כּוּלֵּיהּ בָּעֵינַן. מִדְּרַבִּי כג] אֱלִיעֶזֶר פָּשֵׁיט מָר. בִּתְמִיָּה. רַבִּי אֱלִיעֶזֶר אֲפִי' בְּכוּלּוֹ קַיָּים נַמִי פָּטַר. וַאֲנַן לְרַבָּנַן מִיבָּעֵי לָן, דִּמְחַיְּיבִי בְּכוּלּוֹ קַיָּים, וּמוֹדוּ בְּשֶׁחָסַר בִּפְנִים. וְהָאִיכָּא חֲצִיצָה. שֶׁהַבָּשָׂר כד] אֵינוֹ רָאוּי לְהַקְטָרָה חוֹצֵץ בֵּין אֵימוּרִין לַמַּעֲרָכָה. וְדִכְוָותֵיהּ בִּפְנִים לָאו הַעֲלָאָה הִיא, דְּרַחֲמָנָא אָמַר (ויקרא א): "עַל הָעֵצִים אֲשֶׁר עַל הָאֵשׁ". וְקס"ד דְּמַתְנִי' רַבִּי יוֹסֵי הִיא, דְּאָמַר: אֵינוֹ חַיָּיב עַד שֶׁיַּעֲלֶה לְרֹאשׁ הַמִּזְבֵּחַ, כְּהַקְטָרַת פְּנִים. כְּשֶׁהֲפָכָן. הַחֲלָבִים לְמַטָּה. **מתני'** מִנְחָה שֶׁלֹּא נִקְמְצָה. לָא חֲזִי לִפְנִים, הִילְכָּךְ הַמַּקְרִיבָהּ בַּחוּץ פָּטוּר. קְמָצָהּ וְחָזַר קוּמְצָהּ לְתוֹכָהּ וְהִקְרִיבָהּ בַּחוּץ חַיָּיב. שֶׁכַּיּוֹצֵא בָּהּ בִּפְנִים כְּשֵׁירָה, כִּדְתְנַן בְּ"הַקּוֹמֵץ" (מנחות דף כג.): נִתְעָרֵב קוּמְצָהּ בִּשְׁיָרֶיהָ – לֹא יַקְטִיר, וְאִם הִקְטִיר – עָלְתָה לַבְּעָלִים. **גמ'** וְנִיבַטְּלִי שִׁירַיִם לַקּוֹמֶץ. בְּרוּבָּא, וְהָוֵי כְּמַאן דְּלֵיתֵיהּ, וְלָא נִיחַיֵּיב עֲלֵיהּ. וּבִמְנָחוֹת (דף כג.) נַמִי פָּרְכִינַן לָהּ גַּבֵּי הַקְטָרַת פְּנִים. נֶאֱמַר הַקְטָרָה בַּקּוֹמֶץ. "וְקָמַץ וְהִקְטִיר" (ויקרא ב). וְנֶאֱמַר הַקְטָרָה בַּשִּׁירַיִם. "לֹא תַקְטִירוּ מִמֶּנּוּ אִשֶּׁה לַה'" (שם), כָּל שֶׁמִּמֶּנּוּ לָאִשִּׁים – הֲרֵי הוּא בְּבַל תַּקְטִירוּ, דְּהַיְינוּ שִׁירַיִם. אֵין קוֹמֶץ מְבַטֵּל קוֹמֶץ. וַאֲפִי' רַבָּה עָלָיו, כִּדְאָמְרִינַן בְּ"הַקּוֹמֵץ רַבָּה" (מנחות דף כב.): "וְלָקַח מִדַּם הַפָּר וּמִדַּם הַשָּׂעִיר" – הַדָּבָר יָדוּעַ שֶׁדַּם הַפָּר מְרוּבֶּה מִדַּם הַשָּׂעִיר, מִכָּאן לָעוֹלִין שֶׁאֵין מְבַטְּלִין זֶה אֶת זֶה. **מתני'** הַקּוֹמֶץ וְהַלְּבוֹנָה. שֶׁל מִנְחַת נְדָבָה, שְׁנֵיהֶם מַתִּירִין אֶת שְׁיָרֶיהָ לַאֲכִילָה. הִילְכָּךְ רַבִּי אֱלִיעֶזֶר פּוֹטֵר, דְּבָעֵי הַקְטָרַת כָּל הַמַּתִּיר. אֶחָד בִּפְנִים. תְּחִילָּה, וְאַחַר כָּךְ הַשֵּׁנִי בַּחוּץ. חַיָּיב. שֶׁזֶּה גָּמַר, וּבוֹ הַכֹּל תָּלוּי. שְׁנֵי בְזִיכֵי לְבוֹנָה. מַתִּירִין לֶחֶם הַפָּנִים, דִּכְתִיב (ויקרא כד): "וְהָיְתָה לַלֶּחֶם לְאַזְכָּרָה", וְאָמְרִינַן: נֶאֱמַר כָּאן אַזְכָּרָה וְנֶאֱמַר לְהַלָּן אַזְכָּרָה – מַה לְּהַלָּן קוֹמֶץ מַתִּיר אֶת הַשִּׁירַיִם, אַף הַלְּבוֹנָה מַתֶּרֶת אֶת הַלֶּחֶם, וּבִשְׁיָרֵי מִנְחָה כְּתִיב (ויקרא ו): "יֹאכְלוּ אַהֲרֹן וּבָנָיו קֹדֶשׁ קָדָשִׁים מֵאִשֵּׁי ה'" – אֵין כה] לָנוּ אֶלָּא לְאַחַר מַתְּנוֹת הָאִשִּׁים. **גמ'** מַהוּ שֶׁיַּתִּיר כְּנֶגְדּוֹ בַּשִּׁירַיִם. הִקְטִיר קוֹמֶץ לְבַדּוֹ עַל מְנָת לְהַתִּיר חֲצִי הַשִּׁירַיִם, כו] וּבוֹרְרָן לְחֶלְקָן. מַהוּ. לְאוֹכְלָן. מִישְׁרָא שָׁרֵי. פַּלְגָא לְגַמְרֵי. אוֹ אַקְלוּשֵׁי מַקְלִישׁ. לְאִיסּוּרָא דְּכוּלְּהוּ שִׁירַיִם. כז] וְקוֹמֶץ וּלְבוֹנָה תַּרְוַיְיהוּ אַכּוּלְּהוּ שִׁירַיִים *דָּמוּ, וְכִי מַקְטִיר לְחַד – מַקְלִישׁ לֵיהּ אִיסּוּרַיְיהוּ, וּמִיהוּ לָא אִישְׁתְּרֵי מִידֵי מִינַּיְיהוּ לְגַמְרֵי. פְּלוּגְתָּא דְּרַבִּי מֵאִיר וְרַבָּנַן בִּמְנָחוֹת בְּ"הַקּוֹמֵץ זוּטָא" (דף טז.). מְפַגְּלִין בַּחֲצִי מַתִּיר. פִּיגֵּל בַּקּוֹמֶץ כח] אוֹ בַּלְּבוֹנָה, שֶׁהִקְטִיר קוֹמֶץ ע"מ לֶאֱכוֹל זַיִת מִן הַשִּׁירַיִם חוּץ לִזְמַנּוֹ – פִּיגּוּל. מֵישְׁרָא שָׁרֵי. דְּאִי כִּי מַקְטִיר לֵיהּ בִּשְׁתִיקָה לָא שָׁרֵי כַּזַּיִת מִינַּיְיהוּ לְגַמְרֵי, הֵיכִי הָוְיָא מַחֲשָׁבָה בְּהַהוּא זַיִת? הָא דּוּמְיָא דִּזְרִיקָה בָּעֵינַן, דְּשָׁרֵי לְגַמְרֵי! לא מִישְׁרָא שָׁרֵי כו'. כְּלוֹמַר, דִּילְמָא לָא הָא וְלָא הָא וְהֵיכִי פְּשִׁיטָא לֵיהּ לְר' יִצְחָק נַפָּחָא דְּאוֹ הָא אוֹ הָא עָבֵיד? אֶלָּא אַלִּיבָּא דְּר"א. קָמִיבַּעְיָא, דְּאָמַר: לָא מִחַיֵּיב עֲלָהּ לְחוּדֵיהּ בַּחוּץ, וּמִשּׁוּם הָכִי מְסַפְּקָא לֵיהּ לְרַבִּי יִצְחָק דִּילְמָא שָׁרֵי. ר"א כְּרַבָּנַן ס"ל. וְלָא שַׁרְיָא וְלָא מִיקְלַשׁ. לְשׁוֹן קוּשְׁיָא הוּא: אַמַּאי פְּשִׁיטָא לֵיהּ אַלִּיבֵּיהּ דְּאוֹ הָא אוֹ הָא? וְהָא ר"א, מִדְּקָאָמַר: לָאו הַקְטָרָה הוּא, כְּרַבָּנַן דִּפְלִיגִי עֲלֵיהּ דְּר"מ סְבִירָא לֵיהּ! אֶלָּא אַלִּיבָּא דְּרַבָּנַן דְּהָכָא. דִּמְחַיְּיבִי אַחַד מִינַּיְיהוּ, אַלְמָא הַקְטָרָה הִיא בִּפְנִים. וְקָא מִיבָּעֵי לֵיהּ: לְמַאי הִילְכְתָא הָוְיָא הַקְטָרָה, לְמִישְׁרֵי פַּלְגָא אוֹ לְאַקְלוּשֵׁי? וְהָכָא לֵיכָּא לְמִיפְשַׁט: מִדִּמְחַיְּיבִי עֲלָהּ בַּחוּץ – ש"מ מֵישְׁרָא שָׁרֵי. דְּאִי נַמִי לְאַקְלוּשֵׁי חָתֵיהּ – הָוְיָא הַקְטָרָה לְחַיּוּבֵי בַּחוּץ עֲלַהּ. **מתני'** הַזּוֹרֵק מִקְצָת דָּמִים. כְּגוֹן מַתָּנָה אַחַת. וַאֲפִילּוּ מֵחַטָּאוֹת הַפְּנִימִיּוֹת, שֶׁכָּל מַתְּנוֹתֵיהֶן מְעַכְּבוֹת.

חייב

אבל בחסרון מודו ליה. ומסיק: בחסרו מבפנים. ותימה: מאי קא משמע לן? תנינא לעיל (דף קט:): וכולן שחסרו כל שהוא כו', וכל הפחות – היינו חסרו מבפנים! **אמר** שמואל כשהפכן. וכי תימא: מאי קמ"ל? סד"א דאין דרך הקטרה בכך.

מין במינו אינו חוצץ. והא דאמרינן לעיל (דף טו:): גבי רגל חבירו פסול – *אין דרך שירות בכך.

קומץ מהו שיתיר כנגדו בשירים. פירש בקונטרס: דהקטיר קומץ לבדו על מנת להתיר חלי השירים, ובוררן לחלקן, מהו לאוכלן? מישרא שרי פלגא לגמרי, או אקלושי מקלש לאיסורא דכולהו שירים. וקומץ ולבונה תרוייהו אכולהו שירים *דמו, וכי מקטיר חד – איקליש ליה איסורייהו, ומיהו לא אישתרי מידי מינייהו לגמרי. עכ"ל. והא דתנן ב"הקומץ רבה" (מנחות דף כז.): הקומץ והלבונה מעכבין זה את זה – [illegible], דלא לייתי מנחה בלא לבונה, ובעי קמילה. ומכל מקום תימה: דאפילו למאן דאמר כט] *מישרא שרי לה, היאך מתברר חלקו של קומץ? ונראה לפרש: דלאו לאשתרויי באכילה קאמר, אלא דאי משרא שרי פלגא אידך פלגא, באיסורי' קיימא, ואי אכיל לה – לקי, כמו אוכל בשר חטאת ואשם קודם זריקה. ואי איקלושי מקליש לכולה מנחה – לא לקי כלל, אי נמי: לענין מעילה. וכי האי גוונא בנדרים בפרק "נערה" (דף סח.): בעל מיגז גייז או אקלושי מיקליש, כגון דנדרה מן תרין זיתין ושמע ארוס והפר לה ואכלתינון, אי אמר מיגז גייז – לקיא, אי אמר מקלש קליש – איסורא בעלמא הוא. **ואי אליבא** דר"מ דאמר מפגלין בחצי מתיר. הך סוגיא דלא כריש לקיש, דאמר לעיל בפרק "בית שמאי" (דף מא:): טעמא דרבי מאיר, משום דכל העושה – על דעתו ראשונה הוא עושה. ול"ע: אי שחט סימן אחד, *וקבל אחד דמו וזרקו, כיון דחשיב חלי מתיר אי אמרינן מישרא שרי. ומיהו, הא פשיטא: אי לא גמר אחר כך שחיטתו – לא שרי.

ומודה

לט א מיי' פי"ט מהל' מעשה"ק הל"ט והדבר ספק:
מ ב ג מיי' שם הל"ט:
מא ד ה ו ז מיי' שם הל"ז:
מב ו מיי' פט"ז מהל' פסה"מ הל"ח:
מג ח מיי' פי"ט מהל' מעשה"ק הל"ג:

נ"ל רמו נ"ק
נ"א יוצא
נ"א יש ברירה היאך מתברר מתברר כו' נ"ק וע"ש
נ"ל וקבל את דמו נ"ק

הגהות הב"ח

(א) גמ' ר"א כרבנן וכו' בחצי מתיר ולא שרי ולא מקלש אלא אליבא דרבנן:

גליון הש"ס

תוס' ד"ה מין וכו' אין דרך שירות בכך. עיין יומא דף נח ע"ב:

שיטה מקובצת

א] השתא דאמרי' למאן: ב] חייב שהרי ראוין לאיל: ג] חייב שהרי ראוין לכבש: ד] תיבות לא ילפי נמחק: ה] אע"ג דפנים מחוץ: ו] שהקריבן כו' ותיבת שחסרו ל"ש: ז] דנפק איפסל להו מה לי פסול יוצא מה לי חסרון: ח] מיניה דמר עד כאן ותיבת דרב נמחק: ט] דר' אלעזר וכצ"ל לקמן: י] שחסרו כל שהוא והקריבן: יא] הסלע או על האבן חייב: יב] לתוכה והקריבה בחוץ: יג] וניבטלו שירים תיבת ואמאי ואות ל' נמחק: יד] מה הקטרה האמורה בקומץ אין קומץ כו' אף הקטרה האמורה בשירים אין שירים מבטלים את הקומץ: טו] או אקלושי מיקלש: טז] ולא אקלושי מיקלש: יז] או אקלושי מיקלש: יח] מקצת דמים חוץ: יט] ר"א קביעותא דמנא: כ] בכלי הקטרת היכל קבעי מנא: כא] איפסל להו ואפי' תיבת ליה נמחק: כב] שיקריב את כולן: כג] מדר' אלעזר וכצ"ל לקמן: כד] שאינו ראוי: כה] אין להם אלא ותיבת לנו נמחק: כו] ובירר לחלקן: כז] שירים דקומץ ולבונה כו' שירים דמו וכו': כח] בקומץ ולא בלבונה ותיבת או ל"ש: כט] דאמר יש ברירה היאך תיבות משרא שרי לה ל"ש:

[מרש"ל נראה שגרסתו היתה בגמרא ואע"ג דפנים מחוץ ועיין משנה למלך פי"ט מהל' מעשה"ק ה"ו היתה כמו שהוא לפנינו וע"ש]
[לעיל קח.]
[סוכה לז: ע"ש בכורות טו:]
[מנחות כג:]
מנחות יב: לעיל קז.
[פסחים סג. וש"נ]
[לעיל קז.]
נ"ל רמו נ"ק

מד א מיי' פי"ט מהל' מעה"ק הל"ג:
מה ב מיי' שם ולא פסק כמותו:
מו ג מיי' פ"ג מהל' שמיטה ויובל הל"ה:
מז ד מיי' פ"ז מהל' לולב הל"כ:
מח ה מיי' פ"י מהל' תמידין ומוספין הל"ו:
מט ו מיי' פי"ט מהל' מעה"ק הל"ג:

חַיָּיב. ר"א אוֹמֵר: אאַף *הַמְנַסֵּךְ מֵי הֶחָג בֶּחָג בַּחוּץ חַיָּיב. רַבִּי *נְחֶמְיָה אוֹמֵר: שְׁיָרֵי הַדָּם שֶׁהִקְרִיבוֹ בַּחוּץ — חַיָּיב.§ **גמ'** באָמַר רָבָא: וּמוֹדֶה רַבִּי אֱלִיעֶזֶר בְּדָמִים. *דְּתַנְיָא, *רַבִּי אֱלִיעֶזֶר וְרַבִּי שִׁמְעוֹן אוֹמְרִים: מִמָּקוֹם שֶׁפָּסַק הוּא מַתְחִיל.§ "רַבִּי אֱלִיעֶזֶר אוֹמֵר: אַף הַמְנַסֵּךְ מֵי הֶחָג [בֶּחָג] בַּחוּץ" א].§ א"ר יוֹחָנָן מִשּׁוּם רַבִּי *מְנַחֵם יוֹדְפָאָה: רַבִּי אֱלִיעֶזֶר בְּשִׁטַּת רַבִּי עֲקִיבָא רַבּוֹ אֲמָרָהּ, דְּאָמַר: נִיסּוּךְ הַמַּיִם דְּאוֹרַיְיתָא. דְּתַנְיָא, *רַבִּי עֲקִיבָא אוֹמֵר: °"וּנְסָכֶיהָ" — בִּשְׁנֵי נִיסּוּכִים הַכָּתוּב מְדַבֵּר, אֶחָד נִיסּוּךְ הַמַּיִם וְאֶחָד נִיסּוּךְ הַיַּיִן. אֲמַר לֵיהּ רֵישׁ לָקִישׁ לְר' יוֹחָנָן: אִי מַה לְּהַלָּן שְׁלֹשֶׁת לוּגִּין — אַף כָּאן שְׁלֹשֶׁת לוּגִּין; וְהָא ר"א "מֵי הֶחָג" קָאָמַר! אִי מַה לְּהַלָּן בִּשְׁאָר יְמוֹת הַשָּׁנָה — אַף כָּאן בִּשְׁאָר יְמוֹת הַשָּׁנָה; [וְר"א] בֶּחָג קָאָמַר! אִישְׁתְּמִיטְתֵיהּ הָא דְּאָמַר רַבִּי אַסִי, ב] *דְּאָמַר רַבִּי אַסִי אָמַר רַבִּי יוֹחָנָן מִשּׁוּם רַבִּי נְחוּנְיָא אִישׁ בִּקְעַת בֵּית חוֹרְתָן: געֶשֶׂר נְטִיעוֹת, דעֲרָבָה הוְנִיסּוּךְ הַמַּיִם הֲלָכָה לְמֹשֶׁה מִסִּינַי. תָּנוּ רַבָּנַן: והַמְנַסֵּךְ שְׁלֹשֶׁת לוּגִּין מַיִם בֶּחָג בַּחוּץ — חַיָּיב. ר"א (בְּר"ש) אוֹמֵר: ג] אִם מִלְּאָן לְשֵׁם חָג — חַיָּיב. (א) מַאי בֵּינַיְיהוּ? אָמַר רַב נַחְמָן בַּר יִצְחָק: בְּיֵשׁ שִׁיעוּר בַּמַּיִם קָמִיפַּלְגִי. רַב פַּפָּא אָמַר:

בְּקָרְבוֹ

במדבר כט לא

חַיָּיב. לְרַבָּנַן, דְּלָא בָּעוּ כּוּלּוֹ מַתִּיר. וְרַבִּי אֱלִיעֶזֶר נַמִי מוֹדֶה בָּהּ, כִּדְאָמְרִינַן בַּגְּמָרָא. מֵי הֶחָג. שֶׁנִּתְמַלְּאוּ לְשֵׁם נִיסּוּךְ הַמַּיִם בְּחַג הַסּוּכּוֹת. שְׁיָרֵי הַדָּם. שֶׁל חַטָּאוֹת, הַטְּעוּנִין שְׁפִיכָה לַיְסוֹד, ד] שֶׁהִקְרִיב בַּחוּץ — חַיָּיב. דְּקָסָבַר: שִׁירַיִם מְעַכְּבִין, הִילְכָּךְ מִתְקַבְּלִים בִּפְנִים, וּזְרִיקָה גְּמוּרָה הֵן. **גמ'** מוֹדֶה ר' אֱלִיעֶזֶר בְּדָמִים. וַאֲפִי' בַּחַטָּאוֹת הַפְּנִימִיּוֹת. דְּהָא בִּפְנִים, אִם נִשְׁפַּךְ הַדָּם אַחַר שֶׁנָּתַן מַתָּנָה אַחַת — מְהַנְּיָא הַךְ דְּיָהֲבָהּ, וּמֵבִיא פַּר אַחֵר, וּמַתְחִיל מִמָּקוֹם שֶׁפָּסַק. דְּתְנַן כו'. בְּמַסֶּכֶת יוֹמָא בְּ"הוֹצִיאוּ לוֹ" (דף ס.). יוֹדְפָאָה. דְּמִן יוֹדְפַת*. נִיסּוּךְ הַמַּיִם דְּאוֹרַיְיתָא. הִילְכָּךְ בַּחוּץ נַמִי מִיחַיֵּיב עֲלָהּ. אֲמַר לֵיהּ רֵישׁ לָקִישׁ. אִי רַבִּי אֱלִיעֶזֶר מֵהַהוּא קְרָא יָלֵיף, ה] וּבְהַהוּא קְרָא מַיִם וְיַיִן אִיתְקוּשׁ — אַלְמָא שְׁלֹשֶׁת לוּגִּין בָּעֵינַן, כְּנִסְכֵּי יַיִן שֶׁל עוֹלַת הַתָּמִיד. וְהָא ר' אֱלִיעֶזֶר מֵי הֶחָג קָאָמַר. וַאֲפִילּוּ פָּחוֹת מִשְּׁלֹשֶׁת לוּגִּין. דְּאִיכָּא לְמַאן דְּאָמַר סוּכָּה (דף מח.): בְּלוֹג *הָיָה מְנַסֵּךְ! בֶּחָג קָאָמַר. בִּלְשׁוֹן קוּשְׁיָא גָּרְסִינַן לֵיהּ. אִישְׁתַּמִּיטְתֵיהּ. לִמְנַחֵם יוֹדְפָאָה. הָא דְּא"ר יוֹחָנָן כו'. אַלְמָא לְכוּלֵּי עָלְמָא דְּאוֹרַיְיתָא הוּא. הִילְכָּךְ, אִיכָּא לְמ"ד בְּלוֹג גְּמִירִי לָהּ, אוֹ אֵין לָהֶם שִׁיעוּר. [מַאי בֵּינַיְיהוּ]. בְּמַאי קָמִיפַּלְגִי, וּמַאי קָא אָתֵי רַבִּי אֱלִיעֶזֶר לְמֵימַר? בְּיֵשׁ שִׁיעוּר לַמַּיִם. דְּקָאָמַר תַּנָּא קַמָּא: הַמְנַסֵּךְ שְׁלֹשֶׁת לוּגִּין חַיָּיב — וְהוּא הַדִּין ו] יוֹתֵר מִשְּׁלֹשֶׁת לוּגִּין, דְּיֵשׁ בִּכְלַל מָאתַיִם מָנֶה. וְאַף עַל גַּב דְּמַלְיַנְהוּ בִּכְלִי גָּדוֹל — קַדְּשִׁינְהוּ כְּלִי, דְּאֵין שִׁיעוּר לְמֵי הֶחָג לְמַעְלָה. וְאָתָא רַבִּי אֱלִיעֶזֶר לְמֵימַר: וְהוּא שֶׁמִּילְּאָן לְשֵׁם חַג, כְּדֶרֶךְ מִילּוּאָן, דְּהַיְינוּ שְׁלֹשֶׁת לוּגִּין וְתוּ לָא, כִּדְתְנַן (שם): צְלוֹחִית שֶׁל זָהָב מַחֲזֶקֶת שְׁלֹשֶׁת לוּגִּין מְמַלֵּא מִן הַשִּׁילוֹחַ. אֲבָל אִי הָוֵי טְפֵי — לָא קַדְּשִׁינְהוּ כְּלִי, דְּלָא חֲזוּ לֵיהּ. דְּיֵשׁ שִׁיעוּר לַמַּיִם, וְאֵין כְּלֵי שָׁרֵת מְקַדְּשִׁין אֶלָּא הָרָאוּי לָהֶם.

בְּקָרְבוֹ

ומודה רבי אלעזר בדמים. תימה: מאי קמ"ל רבא? מתניתין היא! דהא תנן: רבי אלעזר אומר אף המנסך כו'. שמע מינה דמודה ברישא! וי"ל: דסלקא דעתך דרבי אלעזר קאי אהנהו דלעיל, ולא אמקבלת דמים. ועוד י"ל: דמתניתין איכא לאוקומי בדמים החיצונים דבמתנה אחת כיפר, ואתא רבא לאשמועינן דאפילו בפנימיים, דכל מתנות מעכבות — אפ"ה מודה ר"א דחייב על מקבלת בחוץ, *דתניא, ר"א אומר: ממקום שפסק הוא מתחיל. ולעיל נמי בפרק "בית שמאי" (דף מב.) דאמר: והאמר רבא מודה ר"א בדמים — גבי חטאות פנימיות מייתי לה. **אי** מה להלן בשאר ימות השנה אף כאן בשאר ימות השנה. תימה: דהא רבי עקיבא מודה דאין ניסוך המים אלא בחג! ויש ספרים דגרסי: "הסך נסך" — בשני ניסוכים. וההוא קרא בתמיד כתיב. וליתא, דר' נתן גריס הכי בריש מסכת תענית (דף ג.). ואפילו לרבי נתן נמי — לא מישתמיט תנא דלימא ניסוך המים כל השנה כולה. ואמר רבינו תם דמצא בספרים ישנים: "אי מה להלן בשאר ימות החג לא", דלרבי עקיבא לא רמזה אלא בששי. ואמרינן במסכת תענית (שם): אלא הך דתנן "ניסוך המים כל שבעה" מני? אי רבי עקיבא האמר בששי מזכיר — תרי יומי הוו. ורבי אלעזר "בחג" קאמר, משמע כל ימות החג. ונראה שפיר ליישב גרסת הספרים, דאף על גב דאין ניסוך המים אלא בחג — מכל מקום חייבין עליו בחוץ כל השנה. כדאשכחן בשמעתין למאן דאמר קרבו נסכים במדבר, דמחייב בלא כלי שרת אע"ג דאין מתקבל בפנים, הואיל ובשעת היתר הבמות קריבים בלא קדושת כלי. וכדאמרינן לעיל (דף קח:) במעלה על גבי הסלע, דמשום דהויא הקטרה בבמת יחיד — מחייב עליו בחוץ בשעת איסור הבמות. ומיהו, לא דמי, דאין לך מחוסר זמן גדול מזה, וכיון דהשתא לא חזו בפנים — היכי מיחייב? ואמרינן ביומא בריש פרק "שני שעירי" (דף סג:): שלמים ששחטן בחוץ קודם שיפתחו דלתות ההיכל — פטור, מ"ט? מחוסר פתיחה כמחוסר *מעשה דמי. וא"ת: ומאי שנא נסכים בכלי חול מקבלת דם בכלי חול, דאמר רבא לעיל דקבלה בכלי חול לרבי פטור? ויש לומר: דלא דמי לקבלה בכלי חול בפנים וזרק בחוץ אין לנו לחייב מחמת דכשר בבמה, הואיל וכבר נפסל בפנים. ולא דמי לנסכים שמקריבין בחוץ בכלי חול, דלא נפסלו בפנים. **אישתמיטתיה** כו'. פי' בקונטרס: למנחם יודפאה. ותימה: דהא רבי יוחנן אמרן לתרווייהו! ושמא לבתר הכי שמעה רבי יוחנן. *וי"ל: דאישתמיטתיה לריש לקיש, דאי הוה שמעה — לא היה מקשה כלום, דהוי מצי לפרושי: בשיטת רבי עקיבא רבו אמרה, דאמר ניסוך המים דאורייתא, ולאו מטעמיה. *ולפי זה משמע דאיכא למאן דאמר ניסוך המים דרבנן. וזהו תימה, דאפילו למאן דאמר (מנחות דף קו.): חולין בעזרה לאו דאורייתא שתקנו חכמים לנסך חולין בעזרה! *שמא לפי שהוא אז זמן גשמים, כדי שיזכרו לפני המקום להתברך במי גשמים. *וקצת משמע בריש "לולב וערבה" (סוכה דף מד.) דריש לקיש הוה ידע להא דר' יוחנן דעשר נטיעות ערבה וניסוך המים, גבי הא דאמר ריש לקיש התם: כהנים בעלי מומין היו נכנסים בין האולם ולמזבח כדי לצאת בערבה. ושמא, נהי דשמיע ליה ערבה — ניסוך המים לא שמיע ליה. ומיהו, לא יתכן פי' זה לפי' הקונטרס במעילה פרק "ולד חטאת" (דף יג:), דתנן התם, נתנן לצלוחית — מועלין בהן. אמר ריש לקיש: אין מועלין אלא בשלשת לוגין, ורבי יוחנן אמר: מועלין בכולן. ופריך: למימרא דקסבר ריש לקיש יש שיעור למים? והא תנן, רבי אלעזר אומר: אף המנסך מי החג בחוץ — חייב. ואמר רבי יוחנן משום ר' מנחם יודפאה: רבי אלעזר בשיטת רבי עקיבא אמרה, דדריש "ונסכיה" — אחד נסכי יין ואחד נסכי מים. ואמר ליה ריש לקיש: אי מה יין שלשת לוגין — אף מים נמי שלשת לוגין. מכלל דקסבר ריש לקיש: אין שיעור למים! ומשני: לטעמיה דמנחם יודפאה קאמר. *ופי' בקונטרס: דריש לקיש דאמר יש שיעור למים — היינו לטעמיה דמנחם, דאמר: רבי אלעזר בשיטת רבי עקיבא. אבל איהו סבירא ליה כרבי יוחנן רביה, דאין שיעור למים. ומיהו לא יתכן אותו פי' דמעילה, דלמה ליה למימר "לטעמא דמנחם יודפאה"? הוה ליה למימר "לטעמיה דרבי עקיבא ורבי אלעזר ור' נתן"! ונראה לפרש: לטעמיה דמנחם יודפאה — היינו מה שהקשה אי מה להלן שלשת לוגין, דלרבי עקיבא יש שיעור. ורבי אלעזר "מי החג" קאמר, אלמא סבירא ליה אין שיעור. ולא משום דסבירא ליה כרבי אלעזר, דר"ל קסבר יש שיעור. אלא לאפוקי ממנחם יודפאה קאתי, דאמר: רבי אלעזר בשיטת רבי עקיבא.

ביש שיעור במים קא מיפלגי. פירש בקונטרס: דקאמר תנא קמא המנסך שלשת לוגין — חייב — והוא הדין יותר מג' לוגין, דיש בכלל מאתים מנה. ואע"ג דמלינהו בכלי גדול — קדשינהו כלי, דאין שיעור למי החג למעלה. ואתא רבי אלעזר למימר: והוא שמלאן לשם חג כדרך מילואן, דהיינו שלשת לוגין ותו לא, כדתנן: צלוחית של זהב מחזקת שלשת לוגין ממלא מן השילוח. אבל אי הוו טפי — לא קדשינהו כלי, דלא חזו ליה, דיש שיעור למי החג, ואין כלי שרת מקדשין אלא הראויין להן. עד כאן לשונו. וקשה: דהא רבי אלעזר "מי החג" קאמר לעיל, דאין שיעור למים כלל לא למעלה ולא למטה כדמוכחא נמי הסיא דמעילה (שם)! ומפרש הר' חיים איפכא: דתנא קמא סבר יש שיעור, דנקט שלשת לוגין — לא פחות ולא יותר. ואתא רבי אלעזר למימר: והוא שמלאן לשם חג — דקבעינהו מנא, דרבי אלעזר לטעמיה, דאמר לעיל: קביעותא דמנא מילתא הוא. אבל לא קבעינהו מנא — חייב בפחות משלשת לוגין, דאין שיעור למים. ור' אלעזר לטעמיה, דאמר במתני' "מי החג".

בקרבו

שיטה מקובצת
א] בחוץ חייב. אמר ר"י משום מנחם ותיבת רבי נמחק: ב] אסי אמר ר' יוחנן דאמר: ג] אומר והוא שמלאן לשם חג ותיבת חייב נמחק: ד] ליסוד שהקריבן: ה] יליף לה ובההוא: ו] ליותר משלשת לוגין:

נ"ל דתנן
נ"ל דתנן
רש"ק מ"ז
גי' הל"ק ויש מפרשים
נ"ל וקצת קשה למשמע כו' נ"ק

מעילה יג:
[לעיל לח: לט. לקמן קי
יומא ס: לעיל מב.
[שם עיר ערכין לג.]
מעילה יג:
תענית ב: שבת קג:
נ"ל היה מנסך כל שמונ נ"ק
תענית ג. ע"ש מו"ק סוכה לד. ע"ש מד.

הגהות הב"ח
(א) גמ' לשם חג חייב במאי קמיפלגי אמר רב נחמן בר יצחק:

בְּקָרְבוּ נְסָכִים בַּמִּדְבָּר א] פְּלִיגֵי. רָבִינָא אָמַר: בִּלְמֵדִין נִיסּוּךְ הַמַּיִם מִנִּיסּוּךְ הַיַּיִן ב] פְּלִיגֵי. ת"ר: אהַמְנַסֵּךְ שְׁלֹשָׁה לוּגִּין יַיִן בַּחוּץ — חַיָּיב, ר' אֶלְעָזָר בְּר"ש אוֹמֵר: וְהוּא שֶׁקִּדְּשָׁן בִּכְלִי. מַאי בֵּינַיְיהוּ? אָמַר רַב אַדָּא ג] בַּר רַב יִצְחָק: בֵּירוּצֵי מִידּוֹת אִיכָּא בֵּינַיְיהוּ. ד] רָבָא בְּרֵיהּ דְּרַבָּה אָמַר: קָרְבוּ נְסָכִים בַּבָּמָה אִיכָּא בֵּינַיְיהוּ. וּבִפְלוּגְתָּא דְּהָנֵי תַּנָּאֵי, דְּתַנְיָא: בָּמַת יָחִיד אֵינָהּ צְרִיכָה נְסָכִים, דִּבְרֵי רַבִּי. וַחכ"א: טְעוּנָה נְסָכִים. וְהָנֵי תַּנָּאֵי כְּהָנֵי תַּנָּאֵי, דְּתַנְיָא: °"כִּי תָבֹאוּ" — לְהַטְעִינָהּ נְסָכִים בְּבָמָה גְּדוֹלָה הַכָּתוּב מְדַבֵּר. אַתָּה אוֹמֵר בְּבָמָה גְּדוֹלָה, אוֹ אֵינוֹ אֲפִי' בְּבָמָה קְטַנָּה? כְּשֶׁהוּא אוֹמֵר: ה] °"אֶל אֶרֶץ מוֹשְׁבוֹתֵיכֶם וגו' אֲשֶׁר אֲנִי נוֹתֵן לָכֶם" — ו] הֲרֵי בְּבָמָה הַנּוֹהֶגֶת לְכוּלְּכֶם הַכָּתוּב מְדַבֵּר, דִּבְרֵי רַבִּי יִשְׁמָעֵאל. ר"ע אוֹמֵר: "כִּי תָבֹאוּ" — לְהַטְעִינָהּ נְסָכִים בְּבָמָה קְטַנָּה הַכָּתוּב מְדַבֵּר. אַתָּה אוֹמֵר לְבָמָה קְטַנָּה, אוֹ אֵינוֹ אֶלָּא לְבָמָה גְּדוֹלָה? כְּשֶׁהוּא אוֹמֵר: "אֶל אֶרֶץ מוֹשְׁבוֹתֵיכֶם" — הֲרֵי בְּבָמָה הַנּוֹהֶגֶת בְּכָל מוֹשָׁבוֹת הַכָּתוּב מְדַבֵּר. כְּשֶׁתִּמְצָא לוֹמַר, לְדִבְרֵי רַבִּי יִשְׁמָעֵאל — לֹא *קָרְבוּ נְסָכִים בַּמִּדְבָּר, וּלְדִבְרֵי ר"ע — קָרְבוּ נְסָכִים בַּמִּדְבָּר.§ רַבִּי נְחֶמְיָה אוֹמֵר: שְׁיָרֵי הַדָּם שֶׁהִקְרִיבָן בַּחוּץ — חַיָּיב.§ א"ר יוֹחָנָן: ז] [תָּנָא] רַבִּי נְחֶמְיָה *כְּדִבְרֵי הָאוֹמֵר (א) שִׁירַיִים מְעַכְּבִין. מֵיתִיבֵי, רַבִּי נְחֶמְיָה אוֹמֵר: שְׁיָרֵי הַדָּם שֶׁהִקְרִיבָן בַּחוּץ — חַיָּיב. אָמַר לוֹ ר"ע: וַהֲלֹא שְׁיָרֵי הַדָּם שְׁיָרֵי מִצְוָה הֵם! אָמַר לוֹ: אֵיבָרִין וּפְדָרִין יוֹכִיחוּ, שֶׁהֵן שְׁיָרֵי מִצְוָה וְהַמַּקְרִיבָן בַּחוּץ חַיָּיב. אָמַר לוֹ: לֹא, אִם אָמַרְתָּ בְּאֵיבָרִים וּפְדָרִים — שֶׁהֵן תְּחִלַּת עֲבוֹדָה, תֹּאמַר בִּשְׁיָרֵי הַדָּם ח] שֶׁאֵינָן תְּחִלַּת עֲבוֹדָה? וְאִם אִיתָא, לֵימָא לֵיהּ: הָנֵי נַמִי ט] מְעַכְּבִי! תְּיוּבְתָּא. וְהַשְׁתָּא דְּאָמַר רַב אַדָּא בַּר אַהֲבָה: מַחֲלוֹקֶת בְּשִׁירַיִים הַפְּנִימִיִּים, אֲבָל בְּשִׁירַיִים הַחִיצוֹנִים — בדִּבְרֵי הַכֹּל לָא מְעַכְּבִי; כִּי קָאָמַר רַבִּי נְחֶמְיָה — בְּשִׁירַיִים הַפְּנִימִים, כִּי תַּנְיָא הַהִיא — בְּשִׁירַיִים הַחִיצוֹנִים. י] *(וְרַבִּי עֲקִיבָא לָא יָדַע מַאי קָאָמַר רַבִּי נְחֶמְיָה. הוּא סָבַר: רַבִּי נְחֶמְיָה שִׁירַיִים חִיצוֹנִים אָמַר, וְקָא מְהַדַּר לֵיהּ שִׁירַיִים הַחִיצוֹנִים. וְרַבִּי נְחֶמְיָה) לְדְבָרָיו דְּר' עֲקִיבָא קָאָמַר.§

מתני' גהַמּוֹלֵק אֶת הָעוֹף בִּפְנִים וְהֶעֱלָה בַּחוּץ — חַיָּיב, דמָלַק בַּחוּץ וְהֶעֱלָה בַּחוּץ — פָּטוּר. *ההַשּׁוֹחֵט אֶת הָעוֹף בִּפְנִים וְהֶעֱלָה בַּחוּץ — פָּטוּר, שָׁחַט

במדבר טו | שם

בְּקָרְבוּ נְסָכִים בַּמִּדְבָּר קָמִיפַּלְגֵי. וְתַרְוַויְיהוּ אִית לְהוּ יֵשׁ שִׁיעוּר לַמַּיִם, יא] וְכִי מַלֵּי טְפֵי – לָא קַדְּשִׁינְהוּ כְּלִי. וְתַנָּא קַמָּא דִּמְחַיֵּיב – לָא בָּעֵי בִּנְסָכִים קְדוּשַּׁת כְּלִי לְחַיֵּיב עֲלֵיהֶן בַּחוּץ, דְּקָסָבַר: קָרְבוּ נְסָכִים בְּאֹהֶל מוֹעֵד שֶׁבַּמִּדְבָּר כָּל אַרְבָּעִים שָׁנָה. הִילְכָּךְ, בִּיאַת הָאָרֶץ הָאֲמוּרָה בְּפָרָשַׁת נְסָכִים בְּ"שְׁלַח לְךָ" לְלַמְּדֵנוּ בָּא שֶׁבְּשֶׁבַע תורה אור שֶׁל כִּיבּוּשׁ הָאָרֶץ וְשֶׁבַע שֶׁל חִילּוּק הָאָרֶץ, כְּשֶׁהָיוּ בַּגִּלְגָּל וְהוּתְּרוּ הַבָּמוֹת, כְּדִתְנַן בְּפֶרֶק בַּתְרָא (לקמן דף קיב:) תְּהֵא בָּמָה קְטַנָּה שֶׁל כָּל יָחִיד טְעוּנָה נְסָכִים. דְּמִשּׁוּם בָּמַת צִיבּוּר לָא אִיצְטְרִיךְ לְמֵימַר בִּיאַת הָאָרֶץ, דְּהָא מִן הַמִּדְבָּר נִתְחַיְּיבוּ בְּכָךְ. וְכֵיוָן דְּבָמוֹת יָחִיד טְעוּנִין נְסָכִים, וְהָתָם כְּלִי שָׁרֵת לֵיכָּא, כִּדְאָמַר בְּפֶרֶק בַּתְרָא (לקמן דף קיג.) – בַּחוּץ נַמִי מִיחַיֵּיב עֲלַיְיהוּ בִּשְׁעַת אִיסּוּר הַבָּמוֹת בְּלָא קִידּוּשׁ כְּלִי, הוֹאִיל וּבִשְׁעַת הֶיתֵּר הַבָּמוֹת קְרֵיבִין בְּלָא קְדוּשַּׁת כְּלִי. כִּדְאָמְרַן לְעֵיל בְּמַעֲלָן עַל גַּבֵּי סֶלַע, מִשּׁוּם דְּהָוְיָא הַקְרָבָה בְּבָמַת יָחִיד בִּשְׁעַת הֶיתֵּר הַבָּמוֹת – מִיחַיֵּיב עֲלָהּ בִּשְׁעַת אִיסּוּר. דְּהָא בִּפְנִים אִם עָלָה לֹא יֵרֵד, כִּדְאָמְרַן לְעֵיל (דף פד:): מִנַּיִן לַיּוֹצֵא אִם עָלָה לֹא יֵרֵד – שֶׁהֲרֵי יוֹצֵא כָּשֵׁר בְּבָמָה. וְר' אֶלְעָזָר סָבַר: לֹא קָרְבוּ נְסָכִים בַּמִּדְבָּר. וּבִיאַת הָאָרֶץ הָאָמוּר בִּנְסָכִים – לְאַחַר יְרוּשָּׁה וִישִׁיבָה, לְאַחַר שֶׁקָּבְעוּ מִשְׁכָּן בְּשִׁילֹה יב] הוּא דְּנִתְחַיְּיבוּ. לְפִיכָךְ הוּזְכְּרָה בִּיאַת הָאָרֶץ יג] לִכְתּוֹב, מִשּׁוּם שֶׁכָּל אַרְבָּעִים שָׁנָה שֶׁבַּמִּדְבָּר לֹא קָרְבוּ בַּמִּשְׁכָּן, וּבָא הַכָּתוּב לְחַיְּיבוֹ בְּשִׁילֹה וּבֵית עוֹלָמִים, יד] וְלֹא בִּשְׁנוֹת הַכִּיבּוּשׁ וְהַחִילּוּק בַּבָּמוֹת הַקְּטַנּוֹת. הִילְכָּךְ, לֹא קָרְבוּ נְסָכִים בְּבָמָה קְטַנָּה שֶׁהִיא טו] שֶׁלֹּא בִּכְלִי שָׁרֵת, וְאִי אַסְּקִינְהוּ כְּשֶׁאֵין מוּקְדָּשִׁין בַּחוּץ – לָא מִיחַיֵּיב עֲלַיְיהוּ. וְהָכִי נַמִי אָמְרִינַן לְקַמָּן, דְּמַאן דְּבָעֵי קְדוּשַּׁת כְּלִי בִּנְסָכִים סָבַר לֹא קָרְבוּ נְסָכִים בַּמִּדְבָּר. רָבִינָא אָמַר בִּלְמֵדִין נִיסּוּךְ הַמַּיִם כו'. וּדְכ"ע קָרְבוּ נְסָכִים בַּמִּדְבָּר. וּבִיאַת הָאָרֶץ הָאָמוּר בִּנְסָכִים – לְבָמָה קְטַנָּה אָתָא, וְקָרְבוּ בְּבָמָה בְּלָא קִידּוּשׁ כְּלִי. וּמִיהוּ, בְּנִיסּוּךְ הַיַּיִן אַשְׁכְּחַן, בְּנִיסּוּךְ הַמַּיִם לָא אַשְׁכְּחַן, דְּהָא חוֹבַת צִיבּוּר הֵן, וְלֹא קָרְבוּ אֶלָּא בְּבָמַת צִיבּוּר בִּכְלִי שָׁרֵת. וּבְהָא פְּלִיגִי; תַּנָּא קַמָּא סָבַר: לְמֵידִין נִיסּוּךְ הַמַּיִם מִנִּיסּוּךְ הַיַּיִן לְחַיֵּיב בַּחוּץ, וַאֲפִי' לֹא קִדְּשׁוֹ בִּכְלִי. וְרַבִּי אֶלְעָזָר סָבַר: אֵין לְמֵידִין, וְנִיסּוּךְ הַיַּיִן הוּא דְּמִתְחַיֵּיב בַּחוּץ בְּלָא כְּלִי, אֲבָל נִיסּוּךְ הַמַּיִם, קִדְּשׁוֹ – אִין, לֹא קִדְּשׁוֹ – לָא. מַאי בֵּינַיְיהוּ. בְּמַאי פְּלִיגִי. בֵּירוּצֵי הַמִּדּוֹת. מַה שֶּׁצָּף עַל שְׂפַת הַכְּלִי. וְתַרְוַויְיהוּ קְדוּשַּׁת כְּלִי בָּעוּ. מִיהוּ, רַבָּנַן סָבְרִי: בֵּירוּצֵי מִדּוֹת שֶׁל לַח נִתְקַדְּשׁוּ. וְרַבִּי אֶלְעָזָר סָבַר: לֹא נִתְקַדְּשׁוּ, וְתוֹךְ כְּלִי בָּעֵינַן. וּפְלוּגְתָּא דְּתַנָּאֵי הִיא בִּמְנָחוֹת (דף פח.). רַבָּה בְּרֵיהּ דְּרָבָא אָמַר. תַּנָּא קַמָּא לָא בָּעֵי קְדוּשַּׁת כְּלִי. וּבְקָרְבוּ נְסָכִים בַּמִּדְבָּר קָמִיפַּלְגֵי, לְתַנָּא קַמָּא קָרְבוּ, לְרַבִּי אֶלְעָזָר בְּר"ש לֹא קָרְבוּ, כִּדְפָרֵישִׁית. וּבִפְלוּגְתָּא דְּהָנֵי תַּנָּאֵי. ר"א בְּר"ש טז] [כְּרַבִּי] דְּאָמַר: אֵין נְסָכִים בְּבָמָה קְטַנָּה, הִילְכָּךְ לָא אַשְׁכְּחַן נִיסּוּךְ בְּלָא קִידּוּשׁ כְּלִי. וְת"ק כְּרַבָּנַן ס"ל, דְּאָמְרִי: יֵשׁ נְסָכִים בְּבָמַת יָחִיד, וְאַשְׁכְּחַן לֵיהּ בְּלָא כְּלִי שָׁרֵת. כִּי תָבֹאוּ. בְּפָרָשַׁת נְסָכִים כְּתִיב בְּ"שְׁלַח לְךָ". לְהַטְעִינָהּ נְסָכִים בְּבָמָה גְּדוֹלָה. בָּא הַכָּתוּב לְלַמֶּדְךָ שֶׁלֹּא קָרְבוּ נְסָכִים בַּמִּדְבָּר, וּמִשֶּׁבָּאוּ לָאָרֶץ נִתְחַיְּיבוּ בָּהֶן וּבְבָמַת צִיבּוּר וְלֹא בְּבָמַת יָחִיד. אוֹ אֵינוֹ אֶלָּא בְּבָמָה קְטַנָּה. דְּאִילּוּ בְּבָמָה גְּדוֹלָה בַּמִּדְבָּר נַמִי קָרְבִי. וּמִיהוּ, עַד הַשְׁתָּא בָּמָה קְטַנָּה לָא הֲוַאי, דְּכָל מ' שָׁנָה נֶאֶסְרוּ הַבָּמוֹת מִשֶּׁהוּקַם הַמִּשְׁכָּן. וּכְשֶׁנִּכְנְסוּ לָאָרֶץ – הוּתְּרוּ בַּשָּׁנִים שֶׁכִּיבְּשׁוּ וְחִילְּקוּ. וּבָא הַכָּתוּב לְהַטְעִינָם נְסָכִים לְקָדְשֵׁי בָּמַת יָחִיד. כְּשֶׁהוּא אוֹמֵר (ב) "אֲשֶׁר אֲנִי נוֹתֵן לָכֶם" כו'. וְרַבִּי עֲקִיבָא יז] אוֹמֵר לְהַטְעִינָהּ נְסָכִים לְבָמָה קְטַנָּה. דְּאַגְּדוֹלָה לָא אִיצְטְרִיךְ, דְּהָא בַּמִּדְבָּר נַמִי קָרְבִי. אוֹ אֵינוֹ אֶלָּא לְבָמָה גְּדוֹלָה. וְאַשְׁמוּעִינַן קְרָא דְּלֹא קָרְבוּ נְסָכִים בַּמִּדְבָּר. בְּכָל מוֹשָׁבוֹת. דְּהַיְינוּ בָּמַת יָחִיד, דְּאִילּוּ בָּמַת צִיבּוּר יח] אֵינָהּ אֶלָּא בְּמָקוֹם אֶחָד. וְר' יִשְׁמָעֵאל מַשְׁמַע לֵיהּ "מוֹשָׁבוֹת" – לְאַחַר יְרוּשָּׁה וִישִׁיבָה. תְּנָא ר' נְחֶמְיָה. בְּמַתְנִי' כְּדִבְרֵי הָאוֹמֵר בְּ"אֵיזֶהוּ מְקוֹמָן" (לעיל דף נג.) שְׁיָרֵי הַדָּם מְעַכְּבִין בְּחַטָּאת. הִילְכָּךְ עֲבוֹדָה הִיא לְהִתְחַיֵּיב עָלֶיהָ בַּחוּץ, כִּשְׁאָר זוֹרֵק מְקַבֵּלַת דָּמִים. שְׁיָרֵי מִצְוָה הֵן. שֶׁאֵין מְעַכְּבִין אֶת הַכַּפָּרָה, כִּדְאָמַר בְּ"אֵיזֶהוּ מְקוֹמָן" (שם): יָכוֹל יְעַכְּבוּ? תַּלְמוּד לוֹמַר "וְאֶת כָּל הַדָּם", נִתְּקוֹ הַכָּתוּב וַעֲשָׂאוֹ שְׁיָרֵי מִצְוָה. הֶקְטֵר אֵיבָרִים וּפְדָרִים. אֵין מְעַכְּבִין אֶת הַכַּפָּרָה, דְּאֵין כַּפָּרָה אֶלָּא בְּדָם. וְאִם אִיתָא. דִּלְרַבִּי נְחֶמְיָה מְעַכְּבִין – נֵימָא לֵיהּ: הָנֵי נַמִי (ג) יט] כִּתְחִילַּת עֲבוֹדָה הֵן כִּשְׁאָר מַתָּנוֹת. (ד) בְּ"אֵיזֶהוּ מְקוֹמָן" מַחֲלוֹקֶת. בְּשִׁירַיִים. בַּחַטָּאוֹת הַפְּנִימִיּוֹת. כָּל מַתְּנוֹתֵיהֶן מְעַכְּבוֹת. וְכִי תַּנְיָא הַהִיא. דְּאוֹדֵי לֵיהּ רַבִּי נְחֶמְיָה דִּשְׁיָרֵי מִצְוָה הֵן – בַּשִּׁירַיִם הַחִיצוֹנִים, וּמוֹדֶה בְּהוּ דְּהַמַּקְרִיבָן בַּחוּץ פָּטוּר. אִי הָכִי. אַמַּאי אַהְדַּר לֵיהּ "הֶקְטֵר אֵיבָרִים יוֹכִיחַ"? נֵימָא לֵיהּ: כִּי אָמְרִי כ] בַּפְּנִימִים וְלֹא בַּחִיצוֹנִים, וְאַתְּ חִיצוֹנִים! ה"ג: אֶלָּא לִדְבָרָיו דְּרַבִּי עֲקִיבָא קא"ל. לְדִידִי שִׁירַיִם מְעַכְּבִין. לְדִידָךְ נַמִי דְּאָמְרַתְּ שְׁיָרֵי מִצְוָה הֵן – הֶקְטֵר אֵיבָרִים יוֹכִיחַ. מַתְנִי' מָלַק בַּחוּץ. נְבֵלָה הִיא, שֶׁאֵין מְלִיקָה אֶלָּא בִּפְנִים, לְפִיכָךְ פָּטוּר עַל הַעֲלָאָתוֹ. וְעַל מְלִיקָתוֹ נַמִי פָּטוּר, כִּדְאָמְרַן בְּרֵישׁ פִּירְקִין (דף קז.): שְׁחוּטֵי חוּץ וְלֹא הַמּוֹלֵק. הַשּׁוֹחֵט אֶת הָעוֹף בִּפְנִים. פָּסוּל, וְשׁוּב אֵינוֹ רָאוּי בִּפְנִים – לְפִיכָךְ פָּטוּר עַל הַעֲלָאָתוֹ בַּחוּץ. וְאִם תֹּאמַר: וַהֲלֹא כָּל הָעוֹלִין פְּסוּלִין בְּיִלָּתָן, כא] וְכָל הַשּׁוֹחֵט בַּחוּץ פָּסוּל הוּא וְחַיָּיבִין עַל הַעֲלָאָתוֹ! הָתָם רַחֲמָנָא רַבְּיֵיהּ, אֲבָל לְעִנְיַן שְׁאָר פְּסוּלִין – מִתְקַבֵּל בִּפְנִים בָּעֵינַן. שְׁחָטוֹ

בקרבו נסכים במדבר קא מיפלגי. פי' בקונטרס: ותרווייהו אית להו יש שיעור למים. ואי אפשר לומר כן, דר"א על כרחין סבר אין שיעור! אלא תרווייהו סברי אין שיעור, ושלשת לוגין דתנא קמא לאו דוקא*. **במה** גדולה ובמה קטנה. יש מפרשים דבמה גדולה קרי שעת איסור הבמות, ובמה קטנה שעת היתר. ופירוש הקונטרס עיקר, דתרווייהו היתר הבמות, אלא דבמה גדולה היא במת ציבור, ובמה קטנה היא במת יחיד. ואע"ג דרבי ישמעאל אמר: להטעינה נסכים לבמה גדולה, ודריש "מושבות" לאחר ירושה וישיבה, כדפירש בקונטרס, וכדתניא בספרי ובפרק קמא דקדושין (דף לז.), ואז נאסרו הבמות שבאו לשילה – *ומ"מ, אף כשהותרו אחרי כן בנוב וגבעון מודה רבי ישמעאל דבמת ציבור טעונה נסכים. **לדברי** רבי ישמעאל לא קרבו נסכים. בשריפה, בקדושין (ג"ז שם) פירש בקונטרס לכולי עלמא קרבו בקרבן ציבור. ואיני יודע מי הזקיקו לכך. ושמא משום דקתני בספרי: אמר אחד מתלמידי רבי ישמעאל: בא הכתוב ללמדך על הנסכים שלא נתחייב יחיד על הנסכים, אלא מביאתן לארץ. וזה לשון הקונטרס דפירש בקדושין (ג"ז שם) ר' ישמעאל סבר לא קרבו נסכים במדבר. ואף על גב דכתיב במילואים "וזה אשר תעשה על המזבח", וכתיב בה נסכים בעולת תמיד – בקרבן ציבור הוא דהוי, אבל היחידים לא נתחייבו בנסכים אלא מביאת הארץ, לאחר ירושה וישיבה. ורבי עקיבא סבר: קרבו נסכים ליחיד במדבר. **כי** קאמר רבי נחמיה בשיריים הפנימיים. לעיל בפרק "ב"ש" (דף לט.) משמע דרבי נחמיה איירי בשיריים החיצונים, ושם פירשתי. **וכי** תניא ההיא בשיריים החיצונים. ומה שהשיב לו "איברים יוכיחו", אע"ג דאיהו גופיה לא חייש בהאי טעמא – אורחיה דתנא הכי, כדפרישית בפרק "התערובת" (לעיל דף עז:*). השוחט

נ א ב מיי' פי"ט מהל' מעה"ק הל"ג ד:

נא ג ד ה מיי' שם פי"ח הל' יח:

עיין נ"ק בגם ס"י

נ"ל מ"מ אף כו' נ"ק

[ד"ה אולו]

[לקמן קיח:] קדושין לז.

יומא ס: [לעיל מב: נב: מנחות עז:]

גירסת רש"י אי הכי נימא ליה כי אמרי אנא בפנימים אלא לדבריו כו'

לעיל פה.

נ"ק

הגהות הב"ח

(א) גמ' כדברי האומר שירי הדם מעכבי: (ב) רש"י ד"ה כשהוא אומר אל ארץ מושבותיכם אשר אני: (ג) ד"ה ואם איתא וכו' הני נמי עבודה כצ"ל ותיבת כתחילת נמחק: (ד) ד"ה מחלוקת דעיכוב שירים באיזהו מקומן בשיריים הפנימיים בחטאות הפנימיות:

שיטה מקובצת

א] במדבר קא מיפלגי רבינא אמר: ב] היין קא מיפלגי: ג] אדא בריה דרב יצחק: ד] בינייהו רבה בריה דרבא אמר בקרבו נסכים: ה] תיבות אל ארץ מושבותיכם וגו' נמחק: ו] תיבת הרי נמחק: ז] יוחנן תנא רבי: ח] הדם שהן סוף העבודה ותיבות שאינן תחילת עבודה ל"ש: ט] נמי תחילת עבודה הן ותיבת מעכבי ל"ש: י] החיצונים. אי הכי נימא ליה כי אמרי אנא בפנימים אלא לדבריו ומתיבות ורבי כו' עד תיבת לדבריו בס"א אינו: יא] למים ואין כלי שרת מקדשין אלא הראוי להן: יב] בשילה ובית עולמים הוא דנתחייבו ולא בשעת כיבוש: יג] הארץ לכתב אות ו' ל"ש: יד] ולא בשעת ותיבת בשנות נמחק: טו] שהיא בלא כלי שרת וכי אסקינהו בשאינו מקודשין בחוץ: טז] בר"ש כרבי דאמר: יז] ור"ע אמר: יח] ציבור לא היתה אלא ותיבת אינה ל"ש: יט] נמי תחילת: כ] אמרי אנא בפנימים: כא] ביציאתן וכן השוחט בחוץ פסול הוא וחייבין על העלאתו התם:

נב א מיי' פי"ח מהל' מעה"ק הל' יח:
נג ב ג ד מיי' שם פי"ח הלכה יז:
נד ה ו מיי' שם הלי"ח:
נה ז מיי' פי"ט מהל' מעה"ק הלי"ג:
[עיין לעיל דף סט ע"א תוס' ד"ה לאתויי כו']

אשָׁחַט בַּחוּץ וְהֶעֱלָה בַחוּץ — חַיָּיב. נִמְצָא, דֶּרֶךְ הֶכְשֵׁירוֹ בִּפְנִים — פְּטוּרוֹ בַּחוּץ, דֶּרֶךְ הֶכְשֵׁירוֹ מִבַּחוּץ — פְּטוּרוֹ בִּפְנִים. ר"ש אוֹמֵר: כָּל שֶׁחַיָּיבִין עָלָיו בַּחוּץ — חַיָּיבִין עַל כַּיּוֹצֵא בוֹ בִּפְנִים שֶׁהֶעֱלָה בַחוּץ, חוּץ מִן הַשּׁוֹחֵט בִּפְנִים וּמַעֲלֶה בַחוּץ.§ **גמ'** הַאי "הֶכְשֵׁירוֹ", "חִיּוּבוֹ" הוּא! תְּנִי: "חִיּוּבוֹ".§ "ר"ש אוֹמֵר" א] [וכו'].§ אַהֵיכָא קָאֵי? אִילֵימָא אַרֵישָׁא קָאֵי: הַמּוֹלֵק עוֹף בִּפְנִים וְהֶעֱלָה בַחוּץ — חַיָּיב, מָלַק בַּחוּץ וְהֶעֱלָה בַחוּץ — פָּטוּר; וְא"ל ר"ש: כִּי הֵיכִי ב] דִּפְנִים מִיחַיַּיב — בַּחוּץ נַמִּי מִיחַיַּיב. ג] הַאי "כָּל שֶׁחַיָּיבִין עָלָיו בַּחוּץ", "כָּל שֶׁחַיָּיבִין עָלָיו בִּפְנִים" מִיבָּעֵי לֵיהּ! ד] אֶלָּא: כִּי הֵיכִי דְּבַחוּץ לָא מִיחַיַּיב — בִּפְנִים נַמִּי לָא ה] לִיחַיַּיב. הַאי "כָּל שֶׁאֵין חַיָּיבִין עָלָיו בַּחוּץ" ו] מִיבָּעֵי לֵיהּ! אֶלָּא אַסֵּיפָא קָאֵי: הַשּׁוֹחֵט עוֹף בִּפְנִים וְהֶעֱלָה בַחוּץ — פָּטוּר, שָׁחַט בַּחוּץ וְהֶעֱלָה בַחוּץ — חַיָּיב; וְאָמַר לֵיהּ ר"ש: כִּי הֵיכִי דְּבִפְנִים לָא מִיחַיַּיב — בַּחוּץ נַמִּי לָא מִיחַיַּיב. ז] הַאי "כָּל שֶׁאֵין חַיָּיבִין" מִיבָּעֵי לֵיהּ! אֶלָּא, כִּי הֵיכִי דְּבַחוּץ מִיחַיַּיב — בִּפְנִים נַמִּי מִיחַיַּיב. הָא קָתָנֵי: חוּץ מִן הַשּׁוֹחֵט בִּפְנִים וְהַמַּעֲלֶה בַחוּץ! *אָמַר זְעֵירִי: שְׁחִיטַת (א) בְּהֵמָה בַּלַּיְלָה אִיכָּא בֵּינַיְיהוּ, וְהָכִי קָאָמַר: [וְכֵן] בהַשּׁוֹחֵט ח] *בְּהֵמָה בִּפְנִים בַּלַּיְלָה וְהֶעֱלָה בַחוּץ — פָּטוּר, גשָׁחַט בַּחוּץ בַּלַּיְלָה וְהֶעֱלָה בַחוּץ — חַיָּיב. ר"ש אוֹמֵר: כָּל שֶׁחַיָּיבִין עָלָיו בַּחוּץ — חַיָּיבִין עַל כַּיּוֹצֵא בוֹ בִּפְנִים וְהֶעֱלָה בַחוּץ, חוּץ מִן הַשּׁוֹחֵט עוֹף בִּפְנִים וְהֶעֱלָה בַחוּץ. *רָבָא אָמַר: קַבָּלָה בִּכְלֵי חוֹל אִיכָּא בֵּינַיְיהוּ, וה"ק: [וְכֵן] דהַמְקַבֵּל בִּכְלֵי חוֹל בִּפְנִים וְהֶעֱלָה בַחוּץ — פָּטוּר, הַמְקַבֵּל בִּכְלֵי חוֹל בַּחוּץ וְהֶעֱלָה בַחוּץ — חַיָּיב. ר"ש אוֹמֵר: כָּל שֶׁחַיָּיבִין עָלָיו בַּחוּץ — חַיָּיבִין עַל כַּיּוֹצֵא בוֹ בִּפְנִים וְהֶעֱלוֹ בַחוּץ, חוּץ מִן הַשּׁוֹחֵט עוֹף בִּפְנִים ט] וְהֶעֱלוֹ בַחוּץ. הַשְׁתָּא דְּתָנֵי אֲבוּהּ דִּשְׁמוּאֵל בַּר רַב יִצְחָק: ההַמּוֹלֵק עוֹף בִּפְנִים וְהֶעֱלוֹ בַחוּץ — חַיָּיב, ומָלַק בַּחוּץ וְהֶעֱלָה בַחוּץ — פָּטוּר, וְר"ש מִיחַיַּיב; י] ר"ש הָתָם קָאֵי, וְתָנֵי: כָּל שֶׁחַיָּיבִין עָלָיו בִּפְנִים וְהֶעֱלָה בַחוּץ — חַיָּיבִין עָלָיו בַּחוּץ.§ **מתני'** זחַטָּאת שֶׁקִּבֵּל דָּמָהּ בְּכוֹס אֶחָד; נָתַן בַּחוּץ וְחָזַר וְנָתַן בִּפְנִים, בִּפְנִים וְחָזַר וְנָתַן בַּחוּץ — חַיָּיב, שֶׁכּוּלּוֹ רָאוּי יא] בִּפְנִים. קִבֵּל דָּמָהּ בִּשְׁתֵּי כוֹסוֹת; נָתַן שְׁנֵיהֶם בִּפְנִים — פָּטוּר, שְׁנֵיהֶם בַּחוּץ — חַיָּיב. אֶחָד בִּפְנִים וְאֶחָד בַּחוּץ — פָּטוּר. אֶחָד בַּחוּץ וְאֶחָד בִּפְנִים — חַיָּיב עַל הַחִיצוֹן, וְהַפְּנִימִי מְכַפֵּר. לְמָה הַדָּבָר דּוֹמֶה? *לְמַפְרִישׁ חַטָּאתוֹ וְאָבְדָה, וְהִפְרִישׁ אַחֶרֶת תַּחְתֶּיהָ, וְאח"כ נִמְצֵאת הָרִאשׁוֹנָה, וַהֲרֵי שְׁתֵּיהֶן עוֹמְדוֹת; שָׁחַט שְׁתֵּיהֶן בִּפְנִים — פָּטוּר, שְׁתֵּיהֶן בַּחוּץ — חַיָּיב, אַחַת בִּפְנִים וְאַחַת בַּחוּץ — פָּטוּר, אַחַת בַּחוּץ וְאַחַת בִּפְנִים — חַיָּיב עַל הַחִיצוֹנָה, וְהַפְּנִימִית מְכַפֶּרֶת. *כְּשֵׁם שֶׁדָּמָהּ פּוֹטֵר אֶת בְּשָׂרָהּ כָּךְ הִיא פּוֹטֶרֶת אֶת בְּשַׂר חֲבֵירְתָּהּ.§
גמ'

השוחט בלילה בהמה כו'. ואם תאמר שחט בחוץ בלילה והעלה בחוץ, אמאי חייב? ומאי שנא משלמים ששחטן בחוץ קודם פתיחת דלתות ההיכל דפטור, כדאיתא בפרק "שני שעירי" (יומא דף סג:)! ויש לומר: דלילה אין מחוסר זמן, אבל התם מחוסר מעשה. ואם תאמר: לר"ש, מאי שנא שוחט בהמה בלילה בפנים משוחט עוף בפנים? *ויש לומר: דשוחט עוף בפנים – מקטל קטליה, ואם עלה – ירד, אפי' לר"ש. אע"ג דלא מטמא בגדים אבית הבליעה, שאין שום שחיטה מטמא בגדים אבית הבליעה, אפילו טרפה או נרבע. אלא

שָׁחַט בַּחוּץ וְהֶעֱלָה בַחוּץ חַיָּיב. אַף עַל הַעֲלָאָה. שְׁחִיטָה בַּחוּץ בָּעוֹף יב] רַבְּיֵיהּ רַחֲמָנָא (ויקרא יז) מֵ"אוֹ אֲשֶׁר יִשְׁחַט",* וְאַהַעֲלָאָתוֹ נַמִּי אָמְרִינַן לְקַמָּן (דף קיט:): "וַאֲלֵיהֶם תֹּאמַר" לְעָרֵב פָּרָשִׁיּוֹת, דְּכָל שֶׁמִּתְחַיֵּיב עַל שְׁחִיטָתוֹ בַּחוּץ, אִם חָזַר וְהֶעֱלָן אוֹ הוּא אוֹ אַחֵר – חַיָּיב. נִמְצָא דֶּרֶךְ הֶכְשֵׁירוֹ בִּפְנִים כו'. בַּגְּמָרָא פָּרֵיךְ אַסֵּיפָא: דֶּרֶךְ הֶכְשֵׁירוֹ בַּחוּץ, חִיּוּבוֹ הוּא! דְּעוֹף קָדָשִׁים אֵין לוֹ הֶכְשֵׁר בַּחוּץ בִּשְׁחִיטָה. וְהָכִי אִיבָּעֵי לְמִיתְנֵי: דֶּרֶךְ חִיּוּבוֹ בַּחוּץ יג] *פְּטוּרוֹ בִּפְנִים, דֶּרֶךְ חִיּוּבוֹ בִּפְנִים פְּטוּרוֹ בַּחוּץ. כְּגוֹן, שָׁחַט בִּפְנִים וְהֶעֱלָה בַּחוּץ – פָּטוּר, יד] שָׁחַט בַּחוּץ וְהֶעֱלָה בַּחוּץ – חַיָּיב. מָלַק בִּפְנִים וְהֶעֱלָה בַּחוּץ – חַיָּיב, מָלַק בַּחוּץ וְהֶעֱלָה בַּחוּץ – פָּטוּר. נִמְצָא בְּמָקוֹם שֶׁמִּתְחַיֵּיב עַל הַעֲלָאָתוֹ *אִם נַעֲשֵׂית עֲבוֹדָה הָרִאשׁוֹנָה בִּפְנִים, כְּגוֹן בִּמְלִיקַת פְּנִים – פָּטוּר עַל הַעֲלָאָתוֹ אִם נַעֲשֵׂית עֲבוֹדָה רִאשׁוֹנָה בַּחוּץ. וְדֶרֶךְ שֶׁמִּתְחַיֵּיב עַל הַעֲלָאָה אִם נַעֲשֵׂית הָעֲבוֹדָה רִאשׁוֹנָה בַּחוּץ, כְּגוֹן בִּשְׁחִיטָה – פְּטוּרוֹ בִּפְנִים אִם נִשְׁחַט בִּפְנִים וְהֶעֱלָה בַּחוּץ. ר"ש אוֹמֵר כָּל שֶׁחַיָּיבִין עָלָיו בַּחוּץ חַיָּיבִין עַל כַּיּוֹצֵא [בוֹ] בִּפְנִים וְהֶעֱלָה בַּחוּץ כו'. בַּגְּמָרָא מְפָרֵשׁ לָהּ. וּמִיהוּ, הָכִי מַשְׁמַע: כָּל שֶׁחַיָּיבִין עַל הַעֲלָאָתוֹ טו] כו' אִם נַעֲשֵׂית עֲבוֹדָתוֹ כּוּלּוֹ בַּחוּץ – חַיָּיבִין עָלָיו כְּנַעֲשֵׂית עֲבוֹדָתוֹ רִאשׁוֹנָה בִּפְנִים וְאח"כ טז] הֶעֱלָהוּ בַּחוּץ. חוּץ מִן הַשּׁוֹחֵט עוֹף בִּפְנִים וְהֶעֱלָה בַּחוּץ, דְּפָטוּר, וְאִילּוּ דְּכְוָותֵיהּ בַּחוּץ – הֲוָה מִתְחַיֵּיב אַף בְּהַעֲלָאָה. **גמ'** הֶכְשֵׁרוֹ חִיּוּבוֹ הוּא. דְּבַחוּץ מַאי הֶכְשֵׁר שַׁיָּיךְ לְמֵימַר? "חִיּוּבוֹ" שַׁיָּיךְ לְמֵימַר, כִּדְפָרִישִׁית לְעֵיל. ר"ש אַהַיָּיא. פָּלֵיג. בַּחוּץ נַמִּי מִיחַיַּיב. אִם מְלָקוֹ בַּחוּץ נַמִּי מְחַיֵּיב אַהַעֲלָאָתוֹ בַּחוּץ. שְׁחִיטַת לַיְלָה בִּבְהֵמָה יז] וְהֶעֱלָה בַּחוּץ אִיכָּא בֵּינַיְיהוּ. וְחַסּוֹרֵי מִחַסְּרָא מַתְנִיתִין בְּמִילְּתֵיהּ דְּתַנָּא קַמָּא, וְהָכִי קָאָמַר: וְכֵן הַשּׁוֹחֵט בְּהֵמָה בַּלַּיְלָה בִּפְנִים וְהֶעֱלָה בַּחוּץ – פָּטוּר, דְּאֵינָהּ מִתְקַבֶּלֶת בִּפְנִים, דִּכְתִיב (ויקרא יט): "בְּיוֹם זִבְחֲכֶם", וַאֲפִי' עָלְתָה תֵּרֵד. וְרַבִּי יְהוּדָה הִיא, דְּאָמַר בְּפֶרֶק "הַמִּזְבֵּחַ" יח] (לעיל דף פד.): פְּרָט לְנִשְׁחֲטָה בַּלַּיְלָה.

שָׁחַט בַּחוּץ וְהֶעֱלָה בַּחוּץ חַיָּיב. דְּבִשְׁחִיטַת חוּץ לָא שְׁנָא לַיְלָה מִיּוֹם, דְּהָא רָאוּי הוּא לָבֹא אֶל פֶּתַח אֹהֶל מוֹעֵד לְמָחָר. וּבְהַעֲלָאָתוֹ נַמִּי חַיָּיב, דְּהָא כְּתִיב (ויקרא יז): "וַאֲלֵיהֶם תֹּאמַר". חַיָּיבִין עַל כַּיּוֹצֵא יט] בִּפְנִים וְהֶעֱלָה בַּחוּץ. וְהַשּׁוֹחֵט בְּהֵמָה בַּלַּיְלָה בִּפְנִים וְהֶעֱלָה בַּחוּץ – חַיָּיב, כְּאִילּוּ כ] שׁוֹחֲטָהּ בַּחוּץ. דְּהָא בִּפְנִים אִם עָלְתָה לֹא תֵּרֵד אִית לֵיהּ, בְּפֶרֶק "הַמִּזְבֵּחַ מְקַדֵּשׁ" (שם), דְּקָתָנֵי, ר"ש אוֹמֵר: "עוֹלָה", אֵין לִי אֶלָּא עוֹלָה כְּשֵׁרָה, מִנַּיִן לְרַבּוֹת שֶׁנִּשְׁחֲטָה בַּלַּיְלָה כו'. חוּץ מִן הַשּׁוֹחֵט כא] הָעוֹף בִּפְנִים וְהֶעֱלָה בַּחוּץ. דְּהָא מִיקְטַל קַטְלֵיהּ, כִּדְאָמְרִי' בְּ"הַמִּזְבֵּחַ מְקַדֵּשׁ" (לעיל דף פה.). [וְכֵן] הַמְקַבֵּל בִּכְלֵי חוֹל בִּפְנִים וְהֶעֱלָה בַּחוּץ פָּטוּר. דְּהָא בִּפְנִים אִם עָלָה יֵרֵד, דה"ל כְּנִשְׁפַּךְ דָּמוֹ. וְרַבִּי יְהוּדָה הִיא, דְּלֵית לֵיהּ אִם עָלוּ לֹא יֵרְדוּ אֶלָּא לָן וְיוֹצֵא וְנִשְׁחַט חוּץ לִזְמַנּוֹ וְחוּץ לִמְקוֹמוֹ, וְשֶׁקִּיבְּלוּ פְּסוּלִין אֶת דָּמוֹ, בְּהָנָךְ פְּסוּלִין דַּחֲזוּ לַעֲבוֹדַת צִבּוּר, כִּדְמְפָרֵשׁ בְּ"הַמִּזְבֵּחַ מְקַדֵּשׁ" (שם דף פד:). רַבִּי שִׁמְעוֹן אוֹמֵר כו'. דְּהָא בִּפְנִים נַמִּי אִית לֵיהּ אִם עָלְתָה לֹא תֵּרֵד, וַאֲפִי' נִשְׁפַּךְ דָּמָהּ, כִּדְקָתָנֵי הָתָם. וְהַשְׁתָּא דְּתָנֵי אֲבוּהּ דִּשְׁמוּאֵל. דְּרַבִּי שִׁמְעוֹן מְחַיֵּיב אַמּוֹלֵק בַּחוּץ וְהֶעֱלָה בַּחוּץ – תָּנֵי בְּמִילְּתֵיהּ דר"ש בְּמַתְנִי': כָּל שֶׁחַיָּיבִין עָלָיו בִּפְנִים, כְּגוֹן הַמּוֹלֵק בִּפְנִים וְהַמַּעֲלֶה בַּחוּץ – חַיָּיבִין עָלָיו בַּחוּץ. וּדְקָתָנֵי סֵיפָא: חוּץ מִן הַשּׁוֹחֵט בִּפְנִים וּמַעֲלֶה בַּחוּץ – אַדִּיּוּקָא קָאֵי, דְּאִיכָּא לְמֵידַק מִמִּילְּתָא דר"ש: הָא כָּל שֶׁאֵין חַיָּיבִין עָלָיו בִּפְנִים וְהֶעֱלָה בַּחוּץ, כְּגוֹן קָדָשִׁים פְּסוּלִין שֶׁלֹּא הָיָה פְּסוּלָן בַּקֹּדֶשׁ, כְּגוֹן הָרוֹבֵעַ וְהַנִּרְבָּע כו' – אֵין חַיָּיבִין עֲלֵיהֶן אִם שְׁחָטָן בַּחוּץ וְהֶעֱלָן בַּחוּץ. אַשְּׁחִיטָתָן לָא מִיחַיַּיב – דְּלָא קְרֵינָא בֵּיהּ "וְאֶל פֶּתַח אֹהֶל מוֹעֵד לֹא הֱבִיאוֹ". וְהַעֲלָאָתָן – מֵהֵיכָא תֵּיתֵי? כב] דְּהָא לָא קְרֵינָא בֵּיהּ נַמִּי "אֶל פֶּתַח אֹהֶל מוֹעֵד לֹא יְבִיאֶנּוּ". חוּץ מִן הַשּׁוֹחֵט עוֹף בִּפְנִים וְהֶעֱלוּ בַּחוּץ, שֶׁאַף עַל פִּי שֶׁפָּטוּר עַל הַעֲלָאָתוֹ בַּחוּץ – חַיָּיבִין עַל כַּיּוֹצֵא בוֹ בְּשׁוֹחֵט בַּחוּץ וְהֶעֱלָה בַּחוּץ, דְּהָא אִיתְרַבַּאי לְעֵיל (דף קז.) שְׁחִיטָתוֹ מֵ"אוֹ אֲשֶׁר יִשְׁחַט", וְהַעֲלָאָתוֹ מִ"וַאֲלֵיהֶם תֹּאמַר". **מתני'** נָתַן בַּחוּץ וְחָזַר וְנָתַן בִּפְנִים חַיָּיב. כְּדֵי נַסְכָּהּ. אֶלָּא מִשּׁוּם סֵיפָא, דְּבָעֵי מִיתְנֵי: בִּפְנִים וְחָזַר וְנָתַן בַּחוּץ. וְאַשְׁמְעִינַן דְּאע"ג דְּשִׁירַיִים נִינְהוּ – מִיחַיַּיב עֲלַיְיהוּ. וּסְתָמָא כְּרַבִּי נְחֶמְיָה. שְׁנֵיהֶם בַּחוּץ חַיָּיב. אַחַת. וְאִם הָיְתָה לוֹ יְדִיעָה בֵּינְתַיִים – חַיָּיב שְׁתַּיִם. אֶחָד בִּפְנִים וְאח"כ הַשֵּׁנִי בַּחוּץ פָּטוּר. וַאֲפִילּוּ לְרַבִּי נְחֶמְיָה, כִּדְמְפָרֵשׁ בַּגְּמָרָא, דְּקָסָבַר: כּוֹס אֶחָד עוֹשֶׂה אֶת חֲבֵירוֹ דָּחוּי. הִילְכָּךְ אֲפִילּוּ שִׁירַיִים לָא הָוֵי. וְהַפְּנִימִי מְכַפֵּר. לְהַכְשִׁיר הַזֶּבַח, כְּדַאֲמָרַן בְּ"כָל הַזְּבָחִים שֶׁנִּתְעָרְבוּ" (שם דף פב.) דְּלֹא עָשָׂה אֶת הַמְשׁוּיָּיר כַּיּוֹצֵא בוֹ. לְמָה הַדָּבָר דּוֹמֶה. בַּגְּמָרָא מְפָרֵשׁ לָמָּה לִי לְדַמּוֹיֵינְהוּ, וּמַאי גָּמְרִי מֵהֲדָדֵי. שְׁתֵּיהֶן בַּחוּץ חַיָּיב. עַל כָּל אַחַת וְאַחַת, דְּבִשְׁעַת שְׁחִיטָה כָּל אַחַת הָיְתָה רְאוּיָה לִפְנִים. אַחַת בִּפְנִים וְהַשְּׁנִיָּה כג] בַּחוּץ פָּטוּר. דַּהֲוְיָא לָהּ חַטָּאת שֶׁכִּיפְּרוּ בְּעָלֶיהָ, וּלְמִיתָה אָזְלָא, וְאֵינָהּ מִתְקַבֶּלֶת בִּפְנִים. חַיָּיב עַל הַחִיצוֹנָה. דְּהָא חַזְיָא לִפְנִים, דְּאֵיזוֹ מֵהֶן שֶׁיִּרְצֶה יַקְרִיב. וְהַפְּנִימִית מְכַפֶּרֶת. עַל הַבְּעָלִים. כְּשֵׁם שֶׁדָּמָהּ פּוֹטֵר כד] בְּשָׂרָהּ. מִן הַמְּעִילָה, דִּזְרִיקַת דַּם מוֹצִיאָה בְּשַׂר קָדְשֵׁי קָדָשִׁים *מִן הַמְּעִילָה, דְּיֵהָא בָּהּ שְׁעַת הֵיתֵּר לַכֹּהֲנִים – כָּךְ הִיא פּוֹטֶרֶת אֶת בְּשַׂר חֲבֶרְתָּהּ, וְאע"פ שֶׁפְּסוּלָה. וְאַ"שָׁחַט שְׁתֵּיהֶם בִּפְנִים" קָאֵי, וְאַשְׁמְעִינַן דְּהֵיכָא דְּמוּנָּח בְּכוֹסוֹת וְקָדַם וְזָרַק אֶת דַּם הָאַחַת – פּוֹטֶרֶת אֶת חֲבֶרְתָּהּ מִן הַמְּעִילָה מִשּׁוּם חַטָּאת שֶׁכִּיפְּרוּ בְּעָלֶיהָ, דְּקַיְימָא לָן *חַטָּאוֹת הַמֵּתוֹת לֹא נֶהֱנִין וְלֹא מוֹעֲלִין. אֲבָל מִשּׁוּם שְׁחוּטֵי חוּץ – לָא אִיצְטְרִיכָא לֵיהּ, דְּכִמְאן כה] דְּקַטְלִינְהוּ דָּמֵי, וְלֵית בְּהוּ מְעִילָה, כִּדְאָמְרִינַן כו] בִּשְׁמַעְתָּא קַמַּיְיתָא: קָדָשִׁים שֶׁמֵּתוּ יָצְאוּ מִידֵי מְעִילָה. וְאַגַּב גְּרָרָא נַסְבָהּ הָכָא, חַיְּידֵי כז] דְּנַקְטָא מִשּׁוּם שְׁחִיטַת חוּץ. וּבְפֶרֶק קַמָּא דִּמְעִילָה (דף ו:) נַמִּי קָתָנֵי לָהּ לְכוּלָּהּ.
גמ'

שיטה מקובצת

א] אומר אהייא אילימא תיבת כו' ל"ש ותיבות אהיכא קאי נמחק: ב] היכי דבפנים: ג] מחייב כל שחייבין עליו בפנים חייבין עליו בחוץ מיבעי: ד] ליה ואלא כי: ה] לא מחייב כל ואות ל' ותיבת האי נמחק: ו] בחוץ אין חייבין עליו בפנים מיבעי ליה ואלא: ז] מיחייב. כל שאין חייבין עליו בפנים אין חייבין עליו בחוץ מיבעי ליה ואלא כי: ח] השוחט בלילה בפנים והעלה בחוץ פטור שחט בלילה בחוץ והעלה: ט] והעלה בחוץ והשתא דתני אבוה דרב שמואל המולק אות ו' ותיבות בר רב יצחק נמחק: י] תיבות ר' שמעון התם קאי נמחק: יא] ראוי לבא בפנים קבל דמו בשני כוסות: יב] רחמנא רביה מאו: יג] (בחוץ פטורו בפנים אות ו' נמחק): יד] תיבות שחט בחוץ והעלה בחוץ חייב ל"ש: טו] תיבת כו' נמחק: טז] העלה בחוץ אות ו' נמחק: יז] בבהמה בפנים והעלה: יח] המזבח מקדש: יט] כיוצא בו בפנים: כ] כאילו שחטה בחוץ: כא] השוחט עוף בפנים אות ה' נמחק: כב] דלא קרינא ותיבת דהא ל"ש: כג] והשניה אחריה בחוץ: כד] פוטר את בשרה: כה] דכמאן דחנקינהו דמי תיבת דקטלינהו ל"ש: כו] כדאמרי' במעילה בשמעתא: כז] איידי דנקט שחיטת אות א' ותיבת משום נמחק:

[לעיל קז.]

נ"ל פטורו בפנים שחיטה דרך חיובו בפ[נים] פטורו בחוץ מליקה [...] שחט כו'

גי' הל"ק אם נע[שית] עבודה הראשונה בפ[נים] כגון במליקה פטור [על] העלאתו אם נע[שית] המליקה בחוץ ו[דרך] שמתחייב כו'

[לעיל קח.]

[לעיל פד: ע"ש]

[לעיל קח.]

מעילה ו:

[שם]

הגהות הב"ח

(א) גמ' אמר זעירי שחיטת לילה בבהמה איכ[א] בינייהו:

מן המעילה דהיה בה שעת כו' כנ"ל

[מעילה ג.]

גמ' בשלמא בחוץ וחזר ונתן בפנים – שכולו ראוי א] להיות בפנים. אבל בפנים והעלן בחוץ – שיריים נינהו! *הא מני – רבי נחמיה היא, דאמר: שירי הדם שהקריבן בחוץ – חייב. אי רבי נחמיה, אימא סיפא: קבל דמה בשני כוסות, נתן שניהם בפנים – פטור, שניהם בחוץ – חייב, אחד בפנים ואחד בחוץ – פטור. והאמר רבי נחמיה: שירי הדם שהקריבן בחוץ – חייב! ב] סיפא אתאן לתנא קמא דרבי אלעזר ברבי שמעון,* דאמר: *כוס עושה דחוי לחבירו.§ "למה הדבר דומה? למפריש חטאתו ואבדה והפריש אחרת תחתיה ואחר כך נמצאת הראשונה".§ ג] "למה הדבר דומה" למה לי? הא מני – רבי *היא, דאמר: אאבודה בשעת הפרשה – מתה. והכי קאמר: טעמא דאבדה, הא הפריש שתי חטאות לאחריות – חדא מינייהו מעיקרא עולה היא. וכדרב הונא אמר רב, *דאמר רב הונא אמר רב: באשם שניתק לרעייה ושחטו סתם – כשר לעולה. מי דמי? התם אשם זכר ועולה זכר, אבל ד] חטאת נקבה היא! א"ר חייא מיוסתיניא: בשעיר נשיא.§

הדרן עלך השוחט והמעלה

פרת גחטאת ה] ששרפה חוץ מגתה, וכן שעיר המשתלח ו] שהקריב בחוץ – פטור, שנאמר: °"ואל פתח אהל מועד לא הביאו", דכל שאין ראוי לבא אל פתח אהל מועד – אין חייבין עליו. ז] ההרובע, והנרבע, והמוקצה, והנעבד, והמחיר, ח] [והאתנן] והכלאים, והטריפה, ויוצא דופן, שהקריבן בחוץ – פטור, שנאמר: °"לפני משכן ה'", דכל שאין ראוי לבא לפני משכן ה' – אין חייבין עליו. בעלי מומין, בין בעלי מומין קבועין בין בעלי

ויקרא יז | שם

רש"י

גמ' מאן תנא דפליג עליה דר' אלעזר בר' שמעון. בפרק "כל הפסולין" (לעיל דף לד:) ואומר: כוס עושה חבירו דחוי. דקתני: חטאת שקבל דמה בארבע כוסות, ונתן ארבע מתנות מאחד מהם – הוא לבדו נשפך ליסוד והן נשפכין לאמה. ורבי אלעזר ב"ר שמעון אמר התם: כולן נשפכין ליסוד, דקסבר: כוס אחד עושה את חבירו שירים. רבי נחמיה הוא. דפליג עליה. דאמר הכא: קבל דמה בכוס אחד, נתן בפנים וחזר ונתן בחוץ – חייב, דשירים נינהו, ושירי הדם ט] שהקריבו בחוץ חייב. והיכא דקיבלו בשני כוסות אמר: פטור. אלמא כוס שני לאו שירים חשיב ליה, אלא דחוי י] הויה לשפוך לאמה, הלכך לא מיחייב עליה בחוץ. (א) מאי למה הדבר דומה. למאי הלכתא דמינהו, ומאי גמר מינה? הא מני רבי היא דאמר. במסכת תמורה (דף כב:): אבודה בשעת הפרשה – מתה, כחטאת שכיפרו בעליה, דקיימא לן (שם דף כא:) דאזלא למיתה. אפילו לא היתה ראשונה אבודה בשעה שמתכפר בשניה אלא בשעת הפרשה, ומשהפריש זו תחתיה נמצאת, קיימא לן בה דאם נתכפר באחת מהן – שניה מתה. והכי קאמר תנא דמתני': טעמא דאבדה, כלומר זו שהופרשה על ידי איבוד חבירתה הוא דכי שוחט אחת מהן בחוץ אחר שקרבה חבירתה – יא] פטור, דדמיא לכוס דחוי. משום דכרבי סבירא ליה, דאמר למיתה אזלא. אבל המפריש שתי חטאות לאחריות מעיקרא, שאם תאבד האחת יתכפר בחבירתה, דאפי' רבי מודה יב] בו דמתכפר באחת מהן, והשניה תרעה ודמיה לעולת קיץ המזבח. וכן לרבנן, באבודה בשעת הפרשה, דאית להו תרעה – בההוא לא אמרינן דאם שחטה בחוץ לשניה דנפטר. ואף על גב דלכתחילה לא קרבה היא גופה עולה, אלא יג] דמיהן – חייב עליה בחוץ, דאי מקרבה לדידה גופה עולה בפנים – מתקבלת היא. כדרב הונא [א"ר] אשם שניתק לרעייה. כגון תמורת אשם, ואשם שמתו בעליו או נתכפרו באחר, וקיימא לן (שם דף יח.): כל שבחטאת מתה – באשם רועה. ונמלך בב"ד, ואמרו לו: ירעה, ושחטו סתם – כשר לעולה. ודוקא ניתק, אבל לא ניתק – לא, כדאמר בפ"ק (לעיל ד' ה:): "הוא" – בהווייתו יהא. מי דמי. מתני' לדרב הונא, לחיובי אחטאת שניה בחוץ מהאי טעמא? הא לא חזיא היא גופה לעולה כלל, דהא נקבה היא! מיוסתיניא. מקום. בשעיר נשיא. שהפריש שנים לאחריות. דהתם זכר הוא.

הדרן עלך השוחט והמעלה

פרת חטאת. חוץ מגתה. בגמרא מפרש היכא. גתה. לשון גת, כלומר יד] מקום עמוק. "ששחטה חוץ מגתה" גרסי'. פטור. ולא אמרינן: שוחט קדשים בחוץ טו] שלא במקום מצוה. דרחמנא פטריה מ"ואל פתח אהל מועד" וגו' – הראוי לפתח אהל מועד, שחובה עליו להביאו שם. דמקפיד קרא לענשו על שלא הביאו, ש"מ בעומד להביאו שם משתעי קרא. כל שאינו ראוי. כל שאינו עתיד [לבא]. ובגמרא פריך: הא שעיר המשתלח עתיד לבא להגריל ולהתוודות! שנאמר לפני משכן. "להקריב קרבן לפני משכן", אע"פ שכשר לבא, הואיל ואינו כשר ליקרב. ובגמרא פריך: הני נמי תיפוק לי מ"ואל פתח אהל מועד"! עובר בל"ת. הואיל וראוי לבא לאחר זמן, כדקתני בסיפא: שהיה

תוספות

אלא בפנים וחזר ונתן בחוץ שיריים נינהו. אע"ג דאית לאוקומא בג' מתנות שבחטאת, דאמרינן בפ' "ב"ש" (לעיל דף לח:) דלענין חוץ הוי כתחילתן – לא משמע ליה אלא בשיריים, דומיא דסיפא דשני כוסות אחד בפנים ואחד בחוץ, שלא היה עושה חבירו דחוי אא"כ נתן לכולם. *כשם שדמה פוטר את בשרה מן המעילה – דזריקת דם מוציאה בשר קדשי קדשים מן המעילה, כך הוא פוטר את בשר חבירתה מן המעילה. ופי' בקונטרס: משום חטאת שכיפרו בעליה, דקי"ל חטאות המתות לא נהנין ולא מועלין. וקשה לפירושו, דבסוף פרק קמא דמעילה (דף ו:) תנן: אמר רבי עקיבא: והרי מפריש חטאתו ואבדה, והפריש אחרת תחתיה, ואחר כך נמצאת הראשונה – הרי שניהם עומדים, לא כשם שדמה פוטר את בשרה כך פוטר את בשר חבירתה? ואמרינן בגמרא, *אמר רבי אלעזר: לא אמר רבי עקיבא אלא ששחט שניהם בבת אחת, רצה – מזה זורק, רצה – מזה זורק. אבל בזה אחר זה – לא. ואי חשיב כחטאות המתות – אפילו בזה אחר זה נמי! אלא ודאי, כיון שנשחטה קודם זריקת דמה של חבירתה, שראוי להתכפר – לא הויא חטאת המתה. והיינו טעמא דיש חילוק בין בת אחת לזה אחר זה, דבבת אחת חשיבי תרוייהו כחד גופא, ולכך פוטר את בשר חבירתה. וכן מוכחת הסוגיא. **הא** מני רבי היא דאמר אבודה בשעת הפרשה מתה. למאן דאמר בפרק "ולד חטאת" (תמורה דף כג.) דהכל מודים במתכפר בשאינה אבודה, דאבודה מתה – מיירי הכא בכל ענין, דהשניה מתה לרבי. ואיכא למאן דאמר התם דבבא לימלך פליגי, והיכא דמשך מדעתו אחת מהן והקריב – השניה מתה לכולי עלמא, דנתכוין לדחותה. והיכא דנמלך – מודה רבי *דנתכפר באבודה, דשאינה אבודה רועה. והכא מיירי בשחט שאינה אבודה בפנים ואבודה בחוץ. וקשה קצת: מאי "רבי היא"? רבנן נמי לא פליגי בהכי! **והכי** קאמר טעמא דאבדה אבל הפריש שתי חטאות לאחריות כו'. משמע: היכא דקתני אבדה – הוי אבדה דוקא. ותימה: דבסוף פ"ק דמעילה (דף ז.) תניא, אמר רבי שמעון: כשהלכתי לכפר (בגא) [פאגי] כו' עד אמר לי: בני אתה אומר כן? והרי מפריש חטאת ואבדה והפריש אחרת תחתיה כו'. ולר"ש על כרחין לא מחלק, דרועה לר' שמעון לית ליה כלל, כדאיתא בפרק "מי שהיה טמא" (פסחים דף צז:) ובתמורה פרק *ולד חטאת (תמורה דף י)! וי"ל: דבמעילה אינו יורד לחידוש זה, אלא לאשמועינן דזריקה מועלת ליוצא, וחד מינייהו נקט. אבל מתני' דהכא לחידוש תנייה, דאין זה דמיון כ"כ, ולא נקטה אלא לאשמועינן *דרבי היא. חדא מינייהו מעיקרא עולה היא. ואפילו למ"ד בעי עקירה – חסרון עקירה לא שמיה חסרון בהאי, דעומד ליעקר. ולא דמי להא דאמרינן בפ' בתרא (לקמן דף קיד:): אי הכי לשמו ליחייב הואיל וראוי שלא לשמו! ומשני: מחוסר עקירה. דהתם אינו עומד ליעקר. **בשעיר** נשיא. וא"ת: לר"ש, חטאת זכר אמאי מתה? הא אמרי' בפרק קמא דהוריות (דף ו:) ובפרק שני דתמורה (דף טו:) דחמש חטאות בחד מקום גמירי להו, ולא משכחת ולד חטאת בחטאת זכר! וי"ל: דמתני' דלא כר"ש. והא דאמרינן בפ' "ולד חטאת" (שם דף כג.) גבי שעירי יום הכיפורים: והשני ירעה לרבי שמעון. ודייקא: הא ביחיד מתה – לאו בזכר כיוצא באלו, אלא בנקבה.

הדרן עלך השוחט והמעלה

פרת חטאת ששחטה חוץ מגתה. ברוב ספרים *גרסינן "ששרפה". וכן במסכת פרה פרק ד' (מ"ג) תנן: שרפה חוץ לגתה פסולה. והוא הדין בשחיטה, דאין חיוב חוץ לא בשחיטה ולא בהעלאה, כדמוכח בגמרא. ועיקר גת ניתקן לשריפה, שהוא כעין גומא כדפירש בערוך, ושורפין אותה שם ואוספין אפרה.

[וכן גי' הערוך ערך גת א']

חוץ

מסורת הש"ס

[לעיל לח. לט. קי.]

כ"ה ומאן תנא דפליג עליה דראב"ש ר' נחמיה היא וכ"ה בכ"י ל"ק

[תמורה כב:]

הגהות הב"ח

(א) רש"י ד"ה למה הדבר דומה לי למאי הלכתא:

עין משפט נר מצוה

שייך למתני' דלעיל

נו א מיי' פ"ד מהלכות פסה"מ הלכה ג:

נז ב מיי' שם הל' טו:

א ג ד מיי' פי"ט מהל' מעה"ק הלכה ז:

ב ה ו מיי' שם ופי"ח הלכה ו:

[יומא נז: לעיל לח: תמורה כב:]

[מעילה ז.]

לעיל ה: [וש"נ]

נ"ל דאם נתכפר באבודה נ"ק

[נ"ל יש בקרבנות טו.]

דרבי היא הס"ד ואח"כ מה"ד חדא נ"ק

שיטה מקובצת

א] ראוי לבא בפנים אלא בפנים וחזר ונתן בחוץ שירים נינהו אמרי הא מני: ב] חייב אמרי מאן תנא דפליג עליה דר"א בר"ש כוס עושה חבירו דיחוי ר' נחמיה היא: ג] מאי למה הדבר דומה הא מני ותיבות למה לי נמחק: ד] אבל הכא חטאת:

ה] חטאת ששחטה חוץ ותיבת ששרפה נמחק: ו] המשתלח שהקריבו: ז] הרובע. עי' תוס' תמורה (דף כד): ח] והמחיר והאתנן והכלאים: ט] שהקריבן בחוץ: י] הוה לשפוך: יא] חבירתה בפנים פטור דדמיא לכוס משום ותיבת דחוי נמחק: יב] בה דמתכפר: יג] אלא דמיה חייב: יד] כלומר א) מקומה ששחטה תיבות מקום עמוק ל"ש: טו] בחוץ הוא שלא:

עוברין

א) נראה דל"ל חוץ ממקומה ששחטה חוץ וכו' תיבות מקום עמוק ל"ש:

בַּעֲלֵי מוּמִין עוֹבְרִין, שֶׁהִקְרִיבָן בַּחוּץ – פָּטוּר. ר"ש אוֹמֵר: בַּעֲלֵי מוּמִין קְבוּעִין – פָּטוּר, בַּעֲלֵי מוּמִין עוֹבְרִין (א) – א] חַיָּיב בְּלֹא תַעֲשֶׂה. [א]תּוֹרִים שֶׁלֹּא הִגִּיעַ זְמַנָּן, וּבְנֵי יוֹנָה שֶׁעָבַר זְמַנָּן, שֶׁהִקְרִיבָן בַּחוּץ – פָּטוּר; ר"ש אוֹמֵר: בְּנֵי יוֹנָה שֶׁעָבַר זְמַנָּן – פָּטוּר, וְתוֹרִים שֶׁלֹּא הִגִּיעַ זְמַנָּן – בְּלֹא תַעֲשֶׂה. *אוֹתוֹ וְאֶת בְּנוֹ וּמְחוּסַּר זְמַן – פָּטוּר, ר"ש אוֹמֵר: הֲרֵי זֶה בְּלֹא תַעֲשֶׂה. ב] *שֶׁר"ש אוֹמֵר: כָּל שֶׁהוּא רָאוּי לָבֹא לְאַחַר זְמַן – ה"ז בְּלֹא תַעֲשֶׂה, וְאֵין בּוֹ כָּרֵת. וַחכ"א: כָּל שֶׁאֵין בּוֹ כָּרֵת – אֵין בּוֹ לֹא תַעֲשֶׂה. *[ב]מְחוּסַּר זְמַן, בֵּין בְּגוּפוֹ בֵּין בִּבְעָלָיו. ג] [ג]אֵיזֶהוּ מְחוּסַּר זְמַן בִּבְעָלָיו – הַזָּב וְהַזָּבָה וְהַיּוֹלֶדֶת וְהַמְּצוֹרָע שֶׁהִקְרִיבוּ חַטָּאתָם וַאֲשָׁמָם בַּחוּץ – פְּטוּרִין, עוֹלוֹתֵיהֶן וְשַׁלְמֵיהֶן בַּחוּץ – חַיָּיבִין. [ד]הַמַּעֲלֶה מִבְּשַׂר חַטָּאת, מִבְּשַׂר אָשָׁם, מִבְּשַׂר קׇדְשֵׁי קֳדָשִׁים, מִבְּשַׂר קָדָשִׁים קַלִּים, וּמוֹתַר הָעוֹמֶר, וּשְׁתֵּי הַלֶּחֶם, וְלֶחֶם הַפָּנִים, וּשְׁיָרֵי מְנָחוֹת, *[ה]וְהַיּוֹצֵק, ד] וְהַפּוֹתֵת, וְהַבּוֹלֵל, וְהַמּוֹלֵחַ, וְהַמֵּנִיף, וְהַמַּגִּישׁ, וְהַמְסַדֵּר אֶת הַשּׁוּלְחָן, וְהַמֵּטִיב אֶת הַנֵּרוֹת, וְהַקּוֹמֵץ, וְהַמְקַבֵּל דָּמִים, בַּחוּץ – פָּטוּר, (ב) [ו]וְאֵין חַיָּיבִין עָלָיו לֹא מִשּׁוּם זָרוּת, [ז]וְלֹא מִשּׁוּם טוּמְאָה, וְלֹא מִשּׁוּם מְחוּסַּר בְּגָדִים, וְלֹא מִשּׁוּם [שֶׁלֹּא] רָחוּץ יָדַיִם וְרַגְלַיִם. עַד *שֶׁלֹּא הוּקַם הַמִּשְׁכָּן – הָיוּ הַבָּמוֹת מוּתָּרוֹת, וַעֲבוֹדָה בַּבְּכוֹרוֹת, וּמִשֶּׁהוּקַם הַמִּשְׁכָּן – נֶאֶסְרוּ הַבָּמוֹת, וַעֲבוֹדָה בְּכֹהֲנִים. קׇדְשֵׁי קָדָשִׁים נֶאֱכָלִין לִפְנִים מִן הַקְּלָעִים, וְקָדָשִׁים קַלִּים בְּכׇל מַחֲנֵה יִשְׂרָאֵל. בָּאוּ לְגִלְגָּל – הוּתְּרוּ הַבָּמוֹת, קׇדְשֵׁי קָדָשִׁים נֶאֱכָלִין לִפְנִים מִן הַקְּלָעִים, וְקָדָשִׁים קַלִּים בְּכׇל מָקוֹם. *בָּאוּ לְשִׁילֹה – נֶאֶסְרוּ הַבָּמוֹת. *וְלֹא הָיָה שָׁם תִּקְרָה, אֶלָּא בֵּית אֲבָנִים ה] בִּלְבַד מִלְּמַטָּן, (ג) וְהַיְרִיעוֹת מִלְּמַעְלָן. וְהִיא הָיְתָה "מְנוּחָה". קׇדְשֵׁי קָדָשִׁים נֶאֱכָלִין לִפְנִים מִן הַקְּלָעִים, וְקָדָשִׁים קַלִּים וּמַעֲשֵׂר שֵׁנִי בְּכׇל הָרוֹאֶה. *בָּאוּ לְנוֹב וְגִבְעוֹן – הוּתְּרוּ הַבָּמוֹת: קׇדְשֵׁי קָדָשִׁים נֶאֱכָלִין לִפְנִים מִן הַקְּלָעִים, קָדָשִׁים קַלִּים ו] *בְּכׇל עָרֵי יִשְׂרָאֵל. *[ח]בָּאוּ לִירוּשָׁלַיִם – נֶאֶסְרוּ הַבָּמוֹת, וְלֹא הָיָה לָהֶן ז] *הֶיתֵּר, וְהִיא הָיְתָה "נַחֲלָה". [ט]קׇדְשֵׁי קָדָשִׁים נֶאֱכָלִין לִפְנִים מִן הַקְּלָעִים, [י]קָדָשִׁים קַלִּים וּמַעֲשֵׂר שֵׁנִי לִפְנִים מִן הַחוֹמָה. כׇּל הַקֳּדָשִׁים שֶׁהִקְדִּישָׁן בִּשְׁעַת אִיסּוּר הַבָּמוֹת וְהִקְרִיבָן בִּשְׁעַת אִיסּוּר הַבָּמוֹת ח] מִבַּחוּץ – [כ]הֲרֵי אֵלּוּ בַּעֲשֵׂה וְלֹא תַעֲשֶׂה, וְחַיָּיבִין ט] עָלָיו כָּרֵת. הִקְדִּישָׁן בִּשְׁעַת הֶיתֵּר הַבָּמוֹת וְהִקְרִיבָן בִּשְׁעַת אִיסּוּר הַבָּמוֹת בַּחוּץ – הֲרֵי אֵלּוּ בַּעֲשֵׂה וְלֹא תַעֲשֶׂה, וְאֵין חַיָּיבִין עֲלֵיהֶן כָּרֵת. הִקְדִּישָׁן בִּשְׁעַת אִיסּוּר הַבָּמוֹת וְהִקְרִיבָן בִּשְׁעַת הֶיתֵּר הַבָּמוֹת – הֲרֵי אֵלּוּ בַּעֲשֵׂה, וְאֵין בָּהֶן לֹא תַעֲשֶׂה. וְאֵלּוּ קָדָשִׁים קְרֵבִין בַּמִּשְׁכָּן: קָדָשִׁים שֶׁהוּקְדְּשׁוּ לַמִּשְׁכָּן. קׇרְבְּנוֹת צִיבּוּר קְרֵבִין בַּמִּשְׁכָּן, וְקׇרְבְּנוֹת הַיָּחִיד בְּבָמָה. קׇרְבְּנוֹת הַיָּחִיד שֶׁהוּקְדְּשׁוּ לַמִּשְׁכָּן – יַקְרִיבוּ בַּמִּשְׁכָּן, וְאִם הִקְרִיבָן בְּבָמָה – פָּטוּר. וּמָה בֵּין בָּמַת יָחִיד לְבָמַת צִיבּוּר? סְמִיכָה, וּשְׁחִיטַת צָפוֹן, וּמַתַּן

וּמַתָּן

(ד) שֶׁהָיָה ר"ש אוֹמֵר כו'. בַּגְּמָרָא מְפָרֵשׁ לָא תַעֲשֶׂה דִּידְהוּ. תּוֹרִין שֶׁלֹּא הִגִּיעַ זְמַנָּן. כִּדְתְנַן י] בְּחוּלִּין (דף כב:): מִשֶּׁיַּזְהִיבוּ כְּשֵׁרִין, וּמִקַּמֵּי הָכִי פְּסוּלִין. דְּתוֹרִין מַשְׁמַע גְּדוֹלִים וְלֹא קְטַנִּים. בְּנֵי יוֹנָה – קְטַנִּים מַשְׁמַע וְלֹא גְּדוֹלִים, וּפְסוּלִין מִתְּחִלַּת הַצִּיהוּב וְאֵילָךְ. בְּלֹא תַעֲשֶׂה. הוֹאִיל וּרְאוּיִן לְאַחַר זְמַן – יֵשׁ יא] בּוֹ לָא תַעֲשֶׂה לְשׁוֹחֲטָן בַּחוּץ. מְחוּסַּר זְמַן. שֶׁאָמַרְנוּ פָּטוּר – בֵּין שֶׁהוּא מְחוּסַּר זְמַן בְּגוּפוֹ, בֵּין שֶׁהוּא מְחוּסַּר זְמַן בִּבְעָלִים, שֶׁלֹּא הִגִּיעַ זְמַן יב] בְּעָלִים לְהַקְרִיב קׇרְבְּנוֹתֵיהֶם.. וְהַמְּצוֹרָע לָא גָּרְסִי' בְּמַתְנִי'. שֶׁהִקְרִיבוּ. בְּתוֹךְ יְמֵי סִפְרָן. וְיוֹלֶדֶת. בְּתוֹךְ מְלֹאת. וַאֲשָׁמָם. בַּגְּמָרָא פָּרֵיךְ: מַאי אָשָׁם אִיכָּא בְּהָנֵי? פָּטוּר. שֶׁאֵין מִתְקַבְּלִין בִּפְנִים, לֹא לְחוֹבָה וְלֹא לִנְדָבָה. עוֹלוֹתֵיהֶן. דְּזָב וְזָבָה – (ה) דְּעוֹף, וּדְיוֹלֶדֶת – בְּהֵמָה. חַיָּיבִין. שֶׁהֲרֵי מִתְקַבְּלוֹת בִּפְנִים נְדָבָה לִשְׁמָן. וְשַׁלְמֵיהֶן. בַּגְּמָ' פָּרֵיךְ: מַאי שְׁלָמִים אִיכָּא בְּהָנֵי? קׇדְשֵׁי קָדָשִׁים. כִּבְשֵׂי עֲצֶרֶת. וּמוֹתַר הָעוֹמֶר. לְאַחַר קְמִיצָה. הַיּוֹצֵק. שֶׁמֶן עַל הַמִּנְחָה, כְּדִכְתִיב (ויקרא ב): "וְיָצַקְתָּ" וגו'. וְהַפּוֹתֵת. מִנְחַת מַאֲפֶה, כְּדִכְתִיב (שם): "פָּתוֹת אוֹתָהּ פִּתִּים". וְהַמַּגִּישׁ. מִנְחָה בַּחוּץ. וְהִיא טְעוּנָה הַגָּשָׁה בִּפְנִים, בְּקֶרֶן מַעֲרָבִית דְּרוֹמִית כְּמִשְׁפָּטָהּ. הַמֵּטִיב אֶת הַנֵּרוֹת. מְדַשֵּׁן אֶת הַמְּנוֹרָה בַּבֹּקֶר. פָּטוּר. טַעְמָא יָלֵיף בְּבָרַיְיתָא בַּגְּמָ'. אֵין בָּהֶן מִשּׁוּם זָרוּת. חִיּוּב מִיתָה. כָּל הָנָךְ הַקְטָרוֹת בְּדָבָר שֶׁדַּרְכָּן לֶאֱכוֹל – לָאו הַקְטָרָה נִינְהוּ, וְכָל הָנָךְ עֲבוֹדוֹת, הוֹאִיל וְיֵשׁ אַחֲרֵיהֶן עֲבוֹדָה – אֵין זָר חַיָּיב עָלֶיהָ מִיתָה, כִּדְאָמְרִינַן בְּפֶרֶק "בָּרִאשׁוֹנָה" (יומא דף כד.): עֲבוֹדַת מַתָּנָה וְלֹא עֲבוֹדַת סִילּוּק, עֲבוֹדָה תַּמָּה וְלֹא עֲבוֹדָה שֶׁיֵּשׁ אַחֲרֶיהָ עֲבוֹדָה. וְלֹא מִשּׁוּם טוּמְאָה. כֹּהֵן טָמֵא שֶׁשִּׁימֵּשׁ. דְּאַזְהָרַת זָרוּת וְשִׁימּוּשׁ בְּטוּמְאָה מֵחַד קְרָא נָפְקִי, מִ"וְיִנָּזְרוּ וְלֹא יְחַלְּלוּ" בְּ"כָל הַזְּבָחִים" תַּנְיָא (לעיל יז.) מַאי דְּמִחַיַּיב אַזָּרוּת מְחַיֵּיב אַשִּׁימּוּשׁ טוּמְאָה. וְלֹא מִשּׁוּם מְחוּסַּר בְּגָדִים. דְּאִינְהוּ נַמִי כְּזָר, בִּזְמַן שֶׁאֵין בִּגְדֵיהֶן עֲלֵיהֶם – אֵין כְּהוּנָּתָם עֲלֵיהֶם, וְהָווּ לְהוּ זָרִים. הָכִי נָפְקָא לָן בְּפֶרֶק שֵׁנִי (שם יז:). וְלֹא מִשּׁוּם שֶׁלֹּא רָחוּץ יָדַיִם וְרַגְלַיִם. גָּמַר "חוּקָּה" "חוּקָּה" מִמְּחוּסַּר בְּגָדִים הָתָם לְעִנְיַן חִלּוּלֵי עֲבוֹדָה, וּלְעִנְיַן מִיתָה נַמִי אֲנַן גָּמְרִינַן לָהּ מֵהָתָם. וַעֲבוֹדָה בִּבְכוֹרוֹת. כְּדִכְתִיב: "וַיִּשְׁלַח אֶת נַעֲרֵי בְּנֵי יִשְׂרָאֵל" וגו' (שמות כד). נֶאֶסְרוּ הַבָּמוֹת. כְּדִכְתִיב בִּשְׁחוּטֵי חוּץ. וַעֲבוֹדָה בְּכֹהֲנִים. כְּדִכְתִיב "קְרַב אֶל הַמִּזְבֵּחַ". לִפְנִים מִן הַקְּלָעִים. דִּכְתִיב בְּחַטָּאת וְאָשָׁם וּמִנְחָה (ויקרא ו): "בַּחֲצַר אֹהֶל מוֹעֵד". קָדָשִׁים קַלִּים בְּכָל מַחֲנֵה יִשְׂרָאֵל. כְּמוֹת שֶׁהֵן שְׁרוּיִין בְּדִגְלֵיהֶם. וְהָא יָלְפִינַן יג] בְּ"אֵיזֶהוּ מְקוֹמָן" (לעיל נה.) מִקְּרָאֵי. בָּאוּ לְגִלְגָּל. כְּשֶׁעָבְרוּ אֶת הַיַּרְדֵּן, וְהוּקְבַּע אֹהֶל מוֹעֵד שָׁם שֶׁבַע שָׁנִים שֶׁכָּבְשׁוּ וְשֶׁבַע שֶׁחָלְקוּ. הוּתְּרוּ הַבָּמוֹת. כְּדִילְפִינַן לְקַמָּן מֵ"אִישׁ כָּל הַיָּשָׁר בְּעֵינָיו". קׇדְשֵׁי קָדָשִׁים. יד] הַנֶּאֱכָלִין לָא קָרֵב בְּבָמַת יָחִיד, טו] *כָּל שֶׁאֵין נִידָּר וְנִידָּב – אֵין קָרֵב בְּבָמָה קְטַנָּה, וְאֵין מִנְחָה בְּבָמָה. הִלְכָּךְ עוֹלָה הוּא דַּהֲוַאי, וְאֵין נֶאֱכֶלֶת. וְחַטָּאת וְאָשָׁם בְּבָמַת צִיבּוּר הוּא דְּקָרְבֵי, וְנֶאֱכָלִין לִפְנִים מִן הַקְּלָעִים. קָדָשִׁים קַלִּים בְּכָל מָקוֹם. דְּכֵיוָן שֶׁבָּטְלוּ הַדְּגָלִים, כּוּלְּהוּ יָלֵיף בַּגְּמָרָא דְּלָא נְהִיגֵי בְּבָמַת יָחִיד. בָּמַת צִיבּוּר. גִּלְגָּל נוֹב וְגִבְעוֹן (ח).

קַלִּים

וְהֵן הָיוּ הוֹלְכִים בְּכָל הָאָרֶץ לְכׇבְשָׁהּ, וְלֹא הָיְתָה חֲנִיָּיתָן סְבִיבוֹת הַמִּשְׁכָּן – בָּטְלָה קְדוּשַּׁת מַחֲנֵה יִשְׂרָאֵל. מַעֲשֵׂר שֵׁנִי לֹא הוּזְכַּר כָּאן, לְפִי שֶׁלֹּא נָהֲגוּ מַעַשְׂרוֹת עַד לְאַחַר יְרוּשָּׁה וִישִׁיבָה. בָּאוּ לְשִׁילֹה. לְאַחַר *חִילּוּקוֹ מִיָּד קְבָעוּהוּ בְּשִׁילֹה. נֶאֶסְרוּ הַבָּמוֹת. כְּדְקָתָנֵי: וְהִיא הָיְתָה "מְנוּחָה". וּכְתִיב: "כִּי לֹא בָאתֶם עַד עָתָּה" וגו'. כְּלוֹמַר, כְּשֶׁתַּעַבְרוּ אֶת הַיַּרְדֵּן לֹא טז] תַּקְרִיבוּ בַּבָּמוֹת כְּכָל אֲשֶׁר אֲנַחְנוּ עוֹשִׂים פֹּה הַיּוֹם, שֶׁאָנוּ מַקְרִיבִין בַּמִּשְׁכָּן חַטָּאוֹת וַאֲשָׁמוֹת, אֶלָּא אִישׁ כָּל הַיָּשָׁר בְּעֵינָיו תַּעֲשׂוּ – דְּהַיְינוּ נְדָרִים וּנְדָבוֹת, שֶׁאֵינָן עֲלֵיכֶם חוֹבָה, אֶלָּא לְפִי מַה שֶּׁיָּשָׁר בְּעֵינֵיכֶם. כִּי בְּעוֹד שֶׁתִּכְבְּשׁוּ וְתַחְלְקוּ לֹא בָּאתֶם עַד עָתָּה אֶל הַמְּנוּחָה. יז] "וַעֲבַרְתֶּם אֶת הַיַּרְדֵּן וִישַׁבְתֶּם בָּאָרֶץ" – הַיְינוּ לְאַחַר יְרוּשָּׁה וִישִׁיבָה, "וְהָיָה הַמָּקוֹם וגו' הִשָּׁמֶר לְךָ וגו'" – הַיְינוּ אִיסּוּר הַבָּמוֹת. תִּקְרָה. יח] (שֶׁל) גַּג שֶׁל נְסָרִים. וִירִיעוֹת מִלְּמַעְלָן. בַּגְּמָרָא יָלֵיף לָהּ. בְּכָל הָרוֹאֶה. בְּמָקוֹם שֶׁרוֹאִין מִשָּׁם אֶת שִׁילֹה. וּבַגְּמָרָא יָלֵיף לָהּ. בָּאוּ לְנוֹב וְגִבְעוֹן. כְּשֶׁחָרְבָה שִׁילֹה וְנִלְקַח הָאָרוֹן בִּימֵי עֵלִי – בָּאוּ לְנוֹב יט] וְגִבְעוֹן, כְּמוֹ שֶׁנֶּאֱמַר: "אֵין לֶחֶם חוֹל [וגו'] כִּי אִם לֶחֶם קֹדֶשׁ כ] אֲשֶׁר מִלִּפְנֵי ה'" (שמואל א כא) אַלְמָא: שׁוּלְחָן וּמִזְבֵּחַ הָתָם הֲוָה. חָרְבָה נוֹב בִּימֵי שָׁאוּל – בָּאוּ לְגִבְעוֹן, כְּדִכְתִיב בִּמְלָכִים (א ג): "כִּי (ו) שָׁם הַבָּמָה גְּדוֹלָה". הוּתְּרוּ הַבָּמוֹת. יָלֵיף בַּגְּמָרָא. קָדָשִׁים קַלִּים בְּכָל עָרֵי יִשְׂרָאֵל. דְּהָא בְּכָל מָקוֹם שֶׁהוּא שָׁם עוֹשֶׂה בָּמָה (ז) וּמַקְרִיבוֹ. וּמַעֲשֵׂר שֵׁנִי. פָּרֵיךְ בַּגְּמָרָא: נַסְּקֵיהּ לְהָתָם. וְהִיא הָיְתָה נַחֲלָה. הַהִיא דִּכְתִיב בִּקְרָא, דְּמִשֶּׁבָּאוּ אֶל הַמְּנוּחָה וְאֶל הַנַּחֲלָה יֶאֶסְרוּ הַבָּמוֹת. לִפְנִים מִן הַחוֹמָה. שֶׁל יְרוּשָׁלַיִם, שֶׁהִיא בִּמְקוֹם מַחֲנֵה יִשְׂרָאֵל שֶׁבַּמִּדְבָּר, כְּדִכְתִיב: "וְאָכַלְתָּ שָּׁם לִפְנֵי ה'" (דברים יב). בַּעֲשֵׂה. "וֶהֱבִיאוּם לַה'" וגו' (ויקרא יז). וְלֹא תַעֲשֶׂה. כְּדִילְפִי' מִ"שָּׁם תַּעֲלֶה" כא] לִשְׁחִיטָה, וְאַזְהָרָה דְּהַעֲלָאָה – "הִשָּׁמֶר לְךָ פֶּן תַּעֲלֶה עוֹלוֹתֶיךָ" וגו' (דברים יב). וְחַיָּיבִין עֲלֵיהֶן כָּרֵת. כְּדִכְתִיב (ויקרא יז): "וְאֶל פֶּתַח אֹהֶל מוֹעֵד לֹא הֱבִיאוֹ". וְאֵין חַיָּיבִין עֲלֵיהֶן כָּרֵת. כְּדַאֲמָרַן בְּ"הַשּׁוֹחֵט" (לעיל קו:) עַד כָּאן הוּא מְדַבֵּר בְּקָדָשִׁים שֶׁהִקְדִּישָׁן כו'. וְקָתָנֵי סֵיפָא: יָכוֹל יְהוּ חַיָּיבִין עֲלֵיהֶן כָּרֵת – תַּלְמוּד לוֹמַר: "זֹאת לָהֶם" וְאֵין אַחֶרֶת לָהֶם. הִקְדִּישָׁן בִּשְׁעַת אִיסּוּר הַבָּמוֹת. מֵהַהִיא שַׁעְתָּא קָרֵינָא בֵּיהּ "וֶהֱבִיאוּם לַה'", וְכֵיוָן שֶׁהִמְתִּין עַד שֶׁלֹּא כב] יָבֹא לְקַיְּימוֹ – נִתְבַּטֵּל הָעֲשֵׂה עַל יָדוֹ. אֲבָל לָאו וְכָרֵת לֵיכָּא, דְּאַזְהָרָה וְעוֹנֶשׁ בִּשְׁעַת הַקְרָבָה כְּתִיבִי, וַהֲרֵי הוּתְּרוּ הַבָּמוֹת. וְאֵלּוּ קָדָשִׁים קְרֵבִין בַּמִּשְׁכָּן. קָדָשִׁים שֶׁהוּקְדְּשׁוּ לַמִּשְׁכָּן בִּזְמַן שֶׁהָיָה הַמִּשְׁכָּן בַּגִּלְגָּל, וְהוּתַּר בָּמָה, אֵלּוּ קָדָשִׁים צְרִיכִין לְהַקְרִיבָן בַּמִּשְׁכָּן וְלֹא יִקְרְבוּ בַּבָּמָה – אוֹתָם שֶׁהוּקְדְּשׁוּ לְשֵׁם מִשְׁכָּן. כג] מְפָרֵשׁ וְאָזֵיל. קׇרְבְּנוֹת צִיבּוּר. סְתָמָן כד] לַמִּקְדָּשׁ. קׇרְבְּנוֹת יָחִיד. סְתָמָן בַּבָּמָה. קׇרְבְּנוֹת יָחִיד שֶׁהוּקְדְּשׁוּ לַמִּשְׁכָּן. שֶׁפֵּירֵשׁ בִּשְׁעַת הֶקְדֵּישָׁן עַל מְנָת לְהַקְרִיבָן לַמִּשְׁכָּן. פָּטוּר. מֵאַזְהָרָה וּמֵעוֹנֶשׁ, שֶׁהֲרֵי הוּתְּרוּ הַבָּמוֹת. וּמִיהוּ אָסוּר לְשַׁנּוֹת, מִשּׁוּם "כַּאֲשֶׁר נָדַרְתָּ תִּשְׁמוֹר וְעָשִׂיתָ" (דברים כג). וּמָה בֵּין בָּמַת יָחִיד כו'.

עין משפט נר מצוה

ג א מיי' פי"ח מהלכות מעה"ק הלכה ח:
ד ב מיי' שם הלכה ז:
ה ג מיי' שם הלכה ט:
ו ד מיי' שם פרק יט הלכה ד:
ז ה מיי' שם הלכה ו:
ח ו מיי' פ"ט מהלכות ביאת מקדש הלכה ה:
ט ז מיי' שם הלכה י:
י ח מיי' פ"א מהלכות בית הבחירה הלכה ג:
יא ט מיי' פ"ו מהלכות בית הבחירה הל' יא ופ"י מהלכות מעה"ק הל' ג ופי"א שם הל' ה:
יב י מיי' פ"ו מהלכות בית הבחירה הל' טו ופ"י שם הלכה יד ופ"י מהלכות מעה"ק הל' ה:
יג כ מיי' פי"ח מהלכות מעה"ק הלכה ב:

יומא סג.

[עי' תוס' לקמן קיט. ד"ה באו ותוס' לעיל ס: ד"ה מאי קסבר]

נ"א ומעשר שני

מסורת הש"ס

[נ"ל חלוקו]

חולין פא.

[מעילה יב. חולין ... ונזכר ג"כ תמורה יט:]

סנהדרין פב: [וע' בתוספות הקטן הרבה]

[בכורות ז:]

מגילה י.

סדר עולם פי"ח

מגילה י.

[נ"ל עוד היתר כך איתא במגילה י. וכן במשנ' שבמשניות]

הגהות הב"ח

(א) במשנה ר"ש אומר וכו' מומין עוברין עובר בלא תעשה: (ב) שם ואין חייבין עליו בהם משום זרות כצ"ל ותיבות חייבין עליו לא נמחק: (ג) שם וידיעות מלמעלן: (ד) רש"י ד"ה (בע"א) עובר וכו' בסיפא שר"ש אומר כצ"ל ותיבת שהיה נמחק: (ה) ד"ה עולותיהן דזב וזבה עוף: (ו) ד"ה באו לנוב וכו' במלכים כי היא הבמה גדולה: (ז) ד"ה קדשים קלים וכו' ומקריב ובגמרא פריך מעשר שני נסקיה להתם כצ"ל והד"א: (ח) ד"ה במת ציבור וכו' וגבעון הס"ד ואח"כ מ"ה מתן סביב ותיבות מתן סובב נמחק:

שיטה מקובצת

א] עוברין עובר בלא תעשה תיבת חייב נמחק: ב] בלא תעשה שהיה ר"ש אומר: ג] בבעליו ואיזהו מחוסר: ד] והיוצק והבולל והפותת והמולח: ה] תיבת בלבד נמחק: ו] בכל. עיין לעיל בתוס' (דף ס ע"ב): ז] להן עוד היתר: ח] הבמות בחוץ: ט] וחייבין עליהן כרת: י] כדתנן בשחיטת חולין משיזהיבו: יא] יש בה: יב] זמן הבעלים להקריב: יג] ילפינן לה באיזהו: יד] קדשי קדשים נאכלין לפנים מן הקלעים. שאין לך קדשי קדשים א) אות ה' נמחק: טו] יחיד דכל שאין: טז] לא תעשון בבמות תיבת תקריבו נמחק: יז] המנוחה אבל ועברתם: יח] תקרה גג של נסרים: יט] תיבת וגבעון נמחק: כ] קדש המוסרים מלפני תיבת אשר נמחק: כא] תעלה ושם תעשה לשחיטה: כב] שלא יכול לקיימו: כג] משכן ומפרש ואזיל: כד] סתמן למשכן הס"ד ותיבת למקדש נמחק:

א) אולי צ"ל שאין לך קדשי קדשים נאכלין שקרבין בבמת יחיד:

מן

ומתן סביב, ותנופה והגשה. ר"י אומר: *אין מנחה בבמה. וכיהון, ובגדי שרת, וכלי שרת, וריח ניחוח, ומחיצה לדמים, וריחוץ ידים ורגלים. אבל הזמן, הנותר והטמא – שוין בזה ובזה.§ **גמ'** מאי "חוץ מגתה"? אמר ר"ל: חוץ ממקום הבדוק לה. אמר לו רבי יוחנן: והלא כל א"י בדוקה היא! אלא א"ר יוחנן: כגון ששחטה לפנים מן א] חומת ירושלים. ולוקמה כגון ששחטה חוץ לחומה שלא כנגד הפתח. דאמר רב אדא בר אהבה: שחטה שלא כנגד הפתח – פסולה, שנאמר: °"ושחט והזה", מה הזאתה כנגד הפתח – אף *שחיטתה כנגד הפתח! ורי תימא דלא מקיש – והא אתמר: ב] (שחטה שלא כנגד הפתח, רבי יוחנן אמר: אפסולה – "ושחט והזה". ר"ל אמר: כשרה – °"אל מחוץ למחנה ושחט". ואיתמר נמי:) שרפה שלא כנגד הפתח, רבי יוחנן אמר: בפסולה, ור' אושעיא אמר: כשרה. ר' יוחנן אמר פסולה – "ושרף והזה", ורבי אושעיא אמר: כשרה – ג] °"על פרשה ישרף", מקום שפורשת למיתה שם תהא שריפתה! אמרי: לא מיבעיא קאמר; לא מיבעיא חוץ לחומה דרחוקי רחקה, אלא אפי' לפנים מן החומה, דקרובי קרבה, ואימא תתכשר – קמ"ל. אמר מר, אמר לו רבי יוחנן: והלא כל א"י בדוקה היא. במאי קמיפלגי? מר סבר: ירד מבול לא"י, ומר סבר: לא ירד. אר"נ בר יצחק, ושניהם מקרא אחד דרשו: °"בן אדם אמר לה את ארץ לא מטוהרה היא לא גושמה ביום זעם". רבי יוחנן סבר אתמוהי מתמה קרא: ד] א"י מי לא ה] מטוהרה את? כלום ירדו עליך גשמים ביום זעם? ור"ל סבר כפשטיה: ארץ לא ו] מטוהרה את, מי לא ירדו עליך גשמים ביום זעם? איתיביה ר"ל לר' יוחנן: *גחצירות היו בירושלים בנויות על ז] הסלע, ותחתיהן חלול מפני קבר התהום, ומביאין נשים מעוברות ויולדות ומגדלות שם בניהם לפרה, ומביאין שוורים ועל גביהן דלתות, ותינוקות יושבין עליהן וכוסות של אבן ח] בידן. ומלאו, וישבו במקומן! אמר רב הונא בריה דרב יהושע: דמעלה עשו בפרה. איתיבי' רבי יוחנן לריש לקיש: ט] *פעם אחד מצאו עצמות בלשכת דיר העצים ובקשו לגזור טומאה על ירושלים. עמד רבי יהושע על רגליו ואמר: לא בושה וכלימה היא לנו שנגזור טומאה על עיר אבותינו? איה מתי מבול, איה מתי נבוכדנצר? י] מדקאמר הכי, לאו למימרא דלא הוו? ולטעמיך, הרוגי נבוכדנצר הכי נמי דלא הוו? אלא, הוו (א) ופנינהו. הכא נמי – הוו ופנינהו. יא] ואי אפנו, הא

תורה אור: במדבר יט | רש"ק מ"ז | שם | שם | יחזקאל כב

רש"י

יב] ומתן סובב – מתן סביב, שתהא נראית המתנה לשתי רוחות המזבח, דהיינו ב' מתנות שהן ארבע. תנופה והגשה. דמנחות. אין מנחה בבמה. מפרש בגמ' מנא ליה. וכיהון. כהונה, דאפי' זר בבמת יחיד כשר. בגדי שרת. בגדי כהונה. ריח ניחוח. כדאמרינן בפרק "בית שמאי" (לעיל דף מו:): לשם ששה דברים הזבח נזבח לשם ריח – לאפוקי אברים שצלאן והעלן, שאין בהם משום "ריח ניחוח". ומחיצה לדמים. חוט הסיקרא, להבדיל בין דמים העליונים לדמים התחתונים. הזמן. שנפסלין במחשבת חוץ לזמנו, וחייבין על קדשים משום נותר וטמא – שוין בשתיהם. **גמ'** ממקום הבדוק לה. לשוחטה שם, שאין תחתיה קבר התהום. בדוקה היא. לקמן מפרש פלוגתייהו. לפנים מן החומה. של ירושלים. דכתיב בה (במדבר יט): "והוציא אותה" וגו'. שלא כנגד הפתח. של היכל. הזאה. יג] מפרש בה: "אל נוכח" וגו'. ושרף והזה. בתר "והזה" סמך "ושרף". מקום שפורשת למיתה. מקום שנפשה יוצאה, בגמר פירכוסה וליציאת נפשה, שלא קבע לה הכתוב מקום. לא מיבעיא יד] לחוץ לחומה. שלא כנגד הפתח. דרחוקי רחקה. מכנגד (ג) הקדושה. ר"ל סבר ירד מבול לא"י. ונשקעו בה עצמות המתים. ותחתיהן חלל. שאם יש קבר – מפסיק החלל, ושוב אין טומאה בוקעת למעלה מן החלל. אבל טומאה רצוצה בוקעת ועולה עד לרקיע. ומגדלות שם בניהם. לפרה. דמשום דמטמאין את הכהן השורף את הפרה מפני הצדוקים, עשו בה שאר מעלות הרבה, שאין אחיו הכהנים נוגעין בו כל שבעת ימי טו] פרישתו, *והוו אלו תינוקות נוגעין בו ומזין עליו. ועל גביהן דלתות. להפסיק בין התינוקות לקרקע, שלא יאהילו על קבר התהום בלכתם למלאות מים חיים לקידוש מן השילוח. אלמא, לאו כולה בדוקה היא. וכוסות של אבן. שכל מעשה פרה בכלי גללים בכלי אבנים שאין מקבלים טומאה, כדאמר טעמא בשמעתא קמייתא דסדר יומא (דף ב.). מעלה עשו בפרה. משום קולא דאקילו בה, משום צדוקין שהיו אומרים: במעורבי שמש היתה נעשית, והיו מטמאין את הכהן ומטבילין אותו, ושרפה טבול יום – עשו בה מעלות אחרות דלא לזלזלו בה. ומיהו, אם שחטה במקום שאין בדוק לה – לא מיפסלא בהכי, דכל א"י בדוקה היא. איה מתי מבול. שנמצאים בשאר מקומות, וכאן אינן נמצאין. איה הרוגי נבוכדנאצר. שהרג בה. *והופנו כולם, ואין אחד מצוי בה. על כרחינו: בדוקה היא. נהי

תוספות

חוץ ממקום הבדוק לה. קסבר דבעי בדיקה, משום דירד מבול לא"י. תימה: *וכי מדאורייתא בעי בדיקה? וי"ל: דאיצטריך קרא (שלא) לשרפה במקום טומאה, דאסור מדאורייתא. דבעי' שחיטה ושריפה במקום טהור כשריפת פרים, דאיתקוש אהדדי, כדמשמע לעיל בסוף "טבול יום" (דף קה:). ואם תאמר: אמאי לא מיחייב משום חוץ כששחטה חוץ למקומה, כיון דתמימה היא וראויה לשאר קרבנות? כדאמרינן בפרק "שני שעירי" (יומא דף סב:) גבי שעירי יום הכפורים ששחטן בחוץ – דחייב על שניהם, הואיל וראויין לשעיר הנעשה בחוץ! ויש לומר: דלא דמי, דיכול לשנותם, דאין עליהם קריאת שם עד שעת הגרלה. ועוד: דאין קרבן שתהא פרה זו ראויה, דאי לשלמים – אין שלמים בציבור. ועוד: דפרה קדשי בדק הבית היא, ואין יכול לשנותה בקדשי מזבח.

שנאמר ושחט והזה מה הזאה כנגד הפתח וכו'. יש ספרים דגרסי: "ושרף והזה". וכן משמע, מדמייתי עלה מפלוגתא דרבי יוחנן ור' אושעיא. ומיהו, אפי' גרסינן הכא "ושחט והזה" – ניחא, דמשמע ליה דאי מקשינן שריפה להזאה – ה"ה שחיטה.

אבל לפנים מן החומה דקרובי קרבה אימא תתכשר קא משמע לן. דפסולה, משום דבעיא חוץ לשלש מחנות.

לא ירד מבול לא"י. תימה: והכתיב (בראשית ז) "ויכסו כל ההרים הגבוהים אשר תחת כל השמים". ובבראשית *רבה אמרינן דר' ישמעאל ב"ר יוסי ובהמי אחד היו הולכין בדרך. פירוש "בהמי" – שומר בהמות. אמר להו ההוא כותאה: איתו לצלויי על טורא גריזים, דלא נחית עליה טופנא. אמר אותו בהמי לפני ר' ישמעאל בר' יוסי: רבי, תן לי רשות להשיב לו תשובה. א"ל: השב. א"ל: הר גריזים תחת כל השמים הוא? א"ל: הן. ולא כתיב "ויכסו כל ההרים הגבוהים אשר תחת כל השמים"? קרא עליו: "לא יהיה בך עקר ועקרה ובבהמתך" – אפי' הבהמי בך לא יתעקר מן התשובה! ושמא י"ל ד"ויכסו כל ההרים" – היינו ששלט הבל המבול בכל מקום, כדאמרינן לקמן דמתו בהבלא. ואותו כותי היה ר"ל שלא היה שם לא הבל, ולא שום דבר. אי נמי: לאותו כותי נתכונו לדחות בקש. וקרא (להכא) ל"ק, דמקום שירד מבול – התם קאמר שנתכסו ההרים.

ומביאין נשים עוברות ויולדות שם. אף על פי שהתינוקות טמאין בנדה ויולדות – לא היו חוששין אלא לשמרן מטומאת מת דבעי הזאה, ומטומאה היוצאה מגופן, כגון בעל קרי*.

ועל גביהן דלתות. מאן דאמר בפ' קמא דגיטין (דף ח:) ובנזיר פרק "כ"ג" (דף נה.) ובפ' "בכל מערבין" (עירובין דף ל:) ובפ' בתרא דחגיגה (דף כה.): אהל זרוק לא שמיה אהל – סבר כר' יהודה דאמר בריש "הישן" (סוכה דף כא.): לא היו מביאין דלתות, אלא שוורים שכריסן רחבה. והתם טעמא משום דכתיב קרא (איוב י): "ובעצמות וגידים תסוככני", אע"ג דבעלמא אהל שאינו עשוי בידי אדם לא שמיה אהל. ומיהו, רבי יהודה ודאי סבר שמיה אהל, דהא קא אמר טעמא: מפני שדעתו של תינוק גסה עליו.

ומלאו ועלו וישבו במקומן. קצת תימה: מה מועיל בתינוקות? דסוף סוף בעינן "איש" בשעת קידוש שנותנין האפר במים או בשעת הזאה, לרבי יהודה או לרבנן, כדמוכח *בפרק "טרף בקלפי" (יומא דף מג.)?*

מעלה עשו בפרה. ר"ל נמי ידע דמעלה עשו, אלא דאי לא ירד מבול לא"י – אין ראוי לעשות מעלה זו. ומיהו, קצת קשה: דהא מודה רבי יוחנן דמתו בהבלא, כדלקמן.

מדקאמר איה מתי מבול מכלל דלא הוו. תימה: דלרבי יוחנן גופיה תקשי ליה הכא, דמתו בהבלא!

היינו

עין משפט נר מצוה

גי' נ"ק וכי מדאורייתא בעי בדיקה דאיצטריך קרא לפוטרה וי"ל דכיון דמדאוריית' אסור לשורפה במקום טומאה דבעינן שחיטה כו'

יד א ב מיי' פ"ד מהל' פרה אדומה הל' ה:

טו ג ד מיי' פ"ב מהל' פרה הלכה ז:

שיטה מקובצת

א] מן החומה ולוקמה תיבות חומת ירושלים נמחק: ב] מן תיבת שחטה עד תיבת שרפה רשום עליו קו שהוא נמחק: ג] כשרה אמר קרא על: ד] קרא ארץ ארואו וחורות א"ו חו נמחק: ה] לא טהורה את: ו] לא טהורה תיבת מטוהרה ל"ש: ז] על גבי סלע: ח] אבן בידם הגיעו לשילוח ירדו ומלאו עלו וישבו: ט] לקיש מעשה ומצאו: י] מדקאמר איה מתי מבול לאו ותיבת הכי נמחק: יא] תיבות ואי אפנו נמחק: יב] תיבות ומתן סובב נמחק: יג] הזאה מפורש בה אל נוכח פני וגו': יד] מיבעי' חוץ לחומה אות ל' נמחק: טו] ימי פרישותו:

[סדר נח פרשה לב וע"ש כמה וכמה שינויים ועיין עוד בדברים רבה סדר עקב פ' ג' בנוסחא אחרת]

תוספתא דעדיות פ"ג

[וע"ע בתוס' סוכה כא.]

[וע"ע בתוס' סוכה כא. כתבו ישוב לזה]

מסורת הש"ס

[עי' תוס' לקמן קיט: ד"ה אין מנחה]

ס"א והיו אלו תינוקות ממלאין מי חטאת ומזין עליו

סוכה כא. תוספתא דפרה פ"ב [משנה דפרה פ"ג מ"ב]

הס"ד ואח"כ מה"ד הא איפני כולם ואין כו' כצ"ל נ"ק

גי' נ"ק בפ' טרף בקלפי וי"ל דמה שהיה יכול לתקן מתקני' משום מעלה דכולה מילתא מעלה בעלמא כדמשני מעלה עשו בפרה וריש לקיש נמי ידע כו' והד"א

הגהות הב"ח

(א) גמ' אלא הוו והופנו הכא נמי הוו והופנו וא"י: (ב) רש"י ד"ה לרחוקי וכו' הקדושה הס"ד ואח"כ מ"ה מ"ס ירד מבול ר"ל סבר:

גליון הש"ס

גמ' שחיטתה כנגד הפתח. עיין לעיל דף נג ע"ב תוס' ד"ה אלא:

א] הָא אִיפַּנִי! נְהִי דְּאִיפַּנִי מִירוּשָׁלַיִם, מִכּוּלָּהּ א"י לָא אִיפַּנִי. אִיכָּא דְּאָמְרִי, אֵיתִיבֵיהּ ר"ל לְרַבִּי יוֹחָנָן: "אַיֵּה מֵתֵי מַבּוּל אַיֵּה מֵתֵי נְבוּכַדְנֶאצַּר"? מַאי לָאו מִדְּהָנֵי הֲווּ — הָנֵי נַמִי הָווּ? מִידֵי אִירְיָ'? הָא כִּדְאִיתֵיהּ וְהָא כִּדְאִיתֵיהּ. אֵיתִיבֵיהּ: ב] °"מִכֹּל אֲשֶׁר בֶּחָרָבָה מֵתוּ"; בִּשְׁלָמָא לְדִידִי דְּאָמִינָא יָרַד מַבּוּל לְא"י — מִשּׁוּם הָכִי מֵתוּ, אֶלָּא לְדִידָךְ אַמַּאי מֵתוּ? ג] מִשּׁוּם הַבְלָא, כִּדְרַב חִסְדָּא. דְּאָמַר רַב חִסְדָּא: *בְּרוֹתְחִין קִלְקְלוּ וּבְרוֹתְחִין נִידּוֹנוּ, ד] דִּכְתִיב הָכָא: °"וַיָּשֹׁכּוּ הַמָּיִם", וּכְתִיב הָתָם: °"וַחֲמַת הַמֶּלֶךְ שָׁכָכָה". אִיכָּא דְּאָמְרִי, אֵיתִיבֵיהּ רַבִּי יוֹחָנָן לְר"ל: "מִכֹּל אֲשֶׁר בֶּחָרָבָה מֵתוּ"; בִּשְׁלָמָא לְדִידִי דְּאָמִינָא לֹא יָרַד מַבּוּל לְא"י — ה] מִשּׁוּם הָכִי הֲוֵי חָרָבָה, אֶלָּא לְדִידָךְ מַאי חָרָבָה? חָרָבָה שֶׁהָיְתָה מֵעִיקָּרָא. וְאַמַּאי קָרֵי לֵיהּ חָרָבָה — כִּדְרַב חִסְדָּא. דְּאָמַר רַב חִסְדָּא: בְּדוֹר הַמַּבּוּל *לֹא נִגְזְרָה גְּזֵרָה עַל דָּגִים שֶׁבַּיָּם, שֶׁנֶּאֱמַר: "מִכֹּל אֲשֶׁר בֶּחָרָבָה מֵתוּ", וְלֹא דָּגִים שֶׁבַּיָּם. בִּשְׁלָמָא לְמ"ד לֹא יָרַד מַבּוּל לְא"י — הַיְינוּ דְּקָם רֵימָא הָתָם. אֶלָּא לְמ"ד יָרַד, רֵימָא הֵיכָא קָם? א"ר יַנַּאי: גּוּרִיּוֹת הִכְנִיסוּ בַּתֵּיבָה. *וְהָאָמַר רַבָּה בַּר בַּר חָנָה: לְדִידִי חֲזִי לִי אוּרְזִילָא דְּרֵימָא בַּת יוֹמָא, וַהֲוֵי כְּהַר תָּבוֹר, וְהַר תָּבוֹר כַּמָּה הָוְיָא — אַרְבְּעִין פַּרְסֵי. מַשְׁכָּא דְּצַוָּארֵיהּ — תְּלָתָא פַּרְסֵי, ו] מַרְבַּעְתָּא דְּרֵישָׁא — פַּרְסָא וּפַלְגָּא, רָמָא ז] *כָּבָא וּסְכַר יַרְדְּנָא! א"ר יוֹחָנָן: רֹאשׁוֹ הִכְנִיסוּ לַתֵּיבָה. וְהָאָמַר מָר: מַרְבַּעְתָּא דְּרֵישָׁא פַּרְסָא וּפַלְגָּא! אֶלָּא: ח] רֹאשׁ חוֹטְמוֹ הִכְנִיסוּ לַתֵּיבָה. וְהָא א"ר יוֹחָנָן: לֹא יָרַד מַבּוּל לְא"י! לְדִבְרֵי ר"ל קָאָמַר. וְהָא קָסַגְיָא תֵּיבָה! אָמַר ר"ל: קַרְנָיו קָשְׁרוּ בַּתֵּיבָה. *וְהָאָמַר רַב חִסְדָּא: אַנְשֵׁי דּוֹר הַמַּבּוּל בְּרוֹתְחִין קִלְקְלוּ, וּבְרוֹתְחִין נִידּוֹנוּ! וּלְטַעֲמֵיךְ, תֵּיבָה הֵיכִי סַגְיָא? וְעוֹד, עוֹג מֶלֶךְ הַבָּשָׁן הֵיכָא קָאֵי? אֶלָּא, נֵס נַעֲשָׂה לָהֶם, שֶׁנִּצְטַנְּנוּ בְּצִידֵּי הַתֵּיבָה. וּלְר"ש ט] [בֶּן לָקִישׁ], נְהִי נַמִי דְּיָרַד מַבּוּל לְא"י, וְהָא לָא פַּשׁ! י] דְּאָמַר ר"ל: *לָמָּה נִקְרָא שְׁמָהּ "מְצוּלָה" — שֶׁכָּל מֵתֵי מַבּוּל נִצְטַלְּלוּ יא] שָׁם. וְרַבִּי יוֹחָנָן אָמַר: לָמָּה נִקְרָא שְׁמָהּ "שִׁנְעָר" — שֶׁכָּל מֵתֵי מַבּוּל נִנְעֲרוּ שָׁם! אִי אֶפְשָׁר דְּלָא אִידַּבְקוּ. א"ר אַבָּהוּ: לָמָּה נִקְרָא שְׁמָהּ "שִׁנְעָר" — שֶׁמְּנֻעֶרֶת עֲשִׁירֶיהָ. וְהָא קָחָזֵינַן יב] דְּהָווּ! תְּלָתָא דָּרֵי לָא מָשְׁכִי. א"ר אַמִּי: *כָּל הָאוֹכֵל מֵעֲפָרָהּ שֶׁל בָּבֶל, כְּאִילּוּ אוֹכֵל בְּשַׂר אֲבוֹתָיו. תנ"ה: כָּל הָאוֹכֵל מֵעֲפָרָהּ שֶׁל בָּבֶל — כְּאִילּוּ אוֹכֵל בְּשַׂר אֲבוֹתָיו, וי"א: כְּאִילּוּ אוֹכֵל שְׁקָצִים וּרְמָשִׂים.§ יג] "שָׂעִיר הַמִּשְׁתַּלֵּחַ".§ *וּרְמִינְהִי: *°"אוֹ קָרְבָּן", שׁוֹמֵעַ אֲנִי אֲפִילּוּ קָדְשֵׁי בֶּדֶק הַבַּיִת שֶׁנִּקְרְאוּ קָרְבָּן, שֶׁנֶּאֱמַר: °"וַנַּקְרֵב אֶת קָרְבַּן ה'" ת"ל: "וְאֶל פֶּתַח אֹהֶל מוֹעֵד לֹא הֱבִיאוֹ" — מִי שֶׁרָאוּי לָבֹא יד] בְּאֹהֶל מוֹעֵד, יָצְאוּ קָדְשֵׁי בֶּדֶק הַבַּיִת שֶׁאֵינָן רְאוּיִן. טו] אוֹצִיא אֶת אֵלּוּ שֶׁאֵינָן רְאוּיִן, וְלֹא אוֹצִיא אֶת שָׂעִיר הַמִּשְׁתַּלֵּחַ שֶׁהוּא רָאוּי לָבֹא אֶל פֶּתַח אֹהֶל מוֹעֵד! ת"ל: "לַה'", *לְהוֹצִיא שָׂעִיר הַמִּשְׁתַּלֵּחַ שֶׁאֵינוֹ מְיוּחָד לַה'! לָא קַשְׁיָא, כָּאן — קוֹדֶם הַגְרָלָה, כָּאן — לְאַחַר הַגְרָלָה. אַחַר הַגְרָלָה נַמִי, הָאִיכָּא וִידּוּי! אֶלָּא אָמַר רַב מָנִי, לָא קַשְׁיָא: כָּאן — אקוֹדֶם וִידּוּי, כָּאן — לְאַחַר וִידּוּי.§ "הָרוֹבֵעַ וְהַנִּרְבָּע".§ וְהָא נַמִי תֵּיפּוֹק לִי מִ"פֶּתַח אֹהֶל מוֹעֵד"! בִּשְׁלָמָא

רש"י

נְהִי דְּאִיפַּנִי מִירוּשָׁלַיִם. כּוּלָּהּ ר"ל קָאָמַר לָהּ. מֵהַבְלָא מֵתוּ. וּקְבָרוּם הַבָּאִים אַחֲרֵיהֶם בְּבָתֵּי קְבָרוֹת. וְאֵין לָחוּשׁ לְכָל הָאָרֶץ, אֶלָּא לִשְׁאָר אֲרָצוֹת שֶׁהָיָה שָׁם מַבּוּל וְנִשְׁקְעוּ בַּטִּיט. חָרָבָה דְּמֵעִיקָּרָא. קוֹדֶם מַבּוּל טז]. מִכֹּל אֲשֶׁר בֶּחָרָבָה. לְאַפּוּקֵי דָּגִים שֶׁבַּיָּם. יז] דְּהַיְינוּ דְּקָם רֵימָא הָתָם. הָרְאֵם זָכָר וּנְקֵבָה, שֶׁהוּא גָּדוֹל וְאֵינוֹ יָכוֹל לִיכָּנֵס לַתֵּיבָה, עָמְדוּ שָׁם. גּוּרִיּוֹת. הִכְנִיסָם לַתֵּיבָה. אוּרְזִילָא. הוּא רְאֵם. דְּרֵימָא שֶׁהוּא עַל שְׂפַת הַיָּם. בַּר יוֹמָא. בַּיּוֹם שֶׁנּוֹלַד. מַשְׁכָא דְּצַוָּארֵי'. מֶשֶׁךְ צַוָּארוֹ. בֵּי מַרְבַּעְתָּא דְּרֵישֵׁיהּ. בֵּי מַרְבֵּץ שֶׁל רֹאשׁוֹ. רְמָא יח] כָּבָא וּסְכַר לְיַרְדְּנָא. הֵטִיל גְּלָל בַּיַּרְדֵּן וְסָכַר הַיַּרְדֵּן, וְסָתַם הִילּוּךְ מֵימָיו. יט] כָּבָא – כְּמוֹ (עירובין דף כט:): "כִּיבּוּי דְּרַעֲוָתָא דְּנִיסָן". חוֹטְמוֹ. שֶׁיּוּכַל לְהַנְשִׁים. לֹא יָרַד מַבּוּל לְא"י. וְלָמָּה לֵיהּ לְשַׁנּוּיֵי הָכִי? "לֵימָא דְּהָתָם קָם" כ"ל דְּל"ג. וְהָא קָא סַגְיָא תֵּיבָה. וְהָא הַתֵּיבָה מְהַלֶּכֶת עַל פְּנֵי הַמַּיִם מִגָּבוֹהַּ לְנָמוּךְ, נִמְצָא חוֹטְמוֹ נִשְׁמֶטֶת מִן הַתֵּיבָה וּמֵת! וּמְשַׁנֵּי: קַרְנָיו קָשְׁרוּ לַתֵּיבָה. בְּרוֹתְחִין נִידּוֹנוּ. וְנִמְצָא נִמְלָג בְּרוֹתְחִין. וְלִיטַעֲמִיךְ תֵּיבָה הֵיכִי סַגְיָא. וַהֲלֹא זְפוּתָה הִיא מִבַּיִת וּמִבַּחוּץ, כִּדְכְתִיב: "וְכָפַרְתָּ אוֹתָהּ" וגו' (בראשית ו), וְכֵיוָן דְּרוֹתְחִין הֵן – הֵיאַךְ כ] מְהַלֶּכֶת שֶׁאֵין זִפְתָּהּ נִפְשָׁר? עוֹג מֶלֶךְ הַבָּשָׁן. דִּכְתִיב בֵּיהּ: "וַיָּבֹא הַפָּלִיט", וְא"ר יוֹחָנָן (נדה דף סא.): זֶה עוֹג שֶׁפָּלַט מֵאַנְשֵׁי דוֹר הַמַּבּוּל. נֵס נַעֲשָׂה וְנִצְטַנְּנוּ הַמַּיִם. שֶׁבְּצִידֵּי הַתֵּיבָה, וְשָׁם עָמַד עוֹג וְהָרְאֵם. וְגַם הַזֶּפֶת לֹא נִפְשַׁר. וְהָרְאֵם לֹא הוּלַךְ לְתֵיבָה, וּמִפְּנֵי גּוֹדְלָן לֹא טָבְעוּ. הָא לָא פַּשׁ. מִן הַמֵּתִים שָׁם כְּלוּם, דְּאַיְּידֵי דְּגָבוֹהַּ הִיא – הִשְׁפִּילוּם הַמַּיִם לְבָבֶל, שֶׁהִיא מְצוּלָּה! לָמָּה נִקְרָא שְׁמָהּ מְצוּלָה. דִּכְתִיב (ישעיה מד): "הָאוֹמֵר לַצּוּלָה חֳרָבִי". אִי אֶפְשָׁר דְּלָא אִדַּבִּיקוּ. בַּטִּיט. שֶׁמְּנֻעֶרֶת עֲשִׁירֶיהָ. כא] מִפְּנֵי שֶׁאֵינָן מְרַחֲמִים עַל הַבְּרִיּוֹת, כִּדְאָמְרִינַן בְּמַסֶּכֶת בֵּיצָה (דף לב:): עֲשִׁירֵי בָבֶל יוֹרְדֵי גֵיהִנָּם הֵן. כְּאִילּוּ אוֹכֵל שְׁקָצִים וּרְמָשִׂים. שֶׁל מַבּוּל. אוֹ קָרְבָּן שׁוֹמֵעַ אֲנִי כו'. "קָרְבָּן" דִּכְתִיב בִּשְׁחוּטֵי חוּץ (ויקרא יז): "לְהַקְרִיב קָרְבָּן" וגו', דָּרֵישׁ לֵיהּ בְּת"כ: עַל הַקָּרְבָּן כב] חַיָּיב, וְאֵינוֹ חַיָּיב עַל הַשּׁוֹחֵט חוּלִּין בִּפְנִים. אוֹ "קָרְבָּן" לָאו לְהָכִי אֲתָא אֶלָּא לְחַיֵּיב עַל קָדְשֵׁי בֶּדֶק הַבַּיִת שֶׁשְּׁחָטָן בַּחוּץ! שֶׁאַף הֵן נִקְרְאוּ קָרְבָּן, כְּעִנְיָן שֶׁנֶּאֱמַר (במדבר לא): "וַנַּקְרֵב אֶת קָרְבַּן ה' אִישׁ אֲשֶׁר מָצָא כְלִי זָהָב אֶצְעָדָה וְצָמִיד", וְאֵין זֶה אֶלָּא לְבֶדֶק הַבַּיִת. שֶׁאֵין רְאוּיִן לְפֶתַח אֹהֶל מוֹעֵד. אֲנִי שָׁמַעְתִּי בְּסֵדֶר יוֹמָא: לְפִי שֶׁסְּתָמָן בַּעֲלֵי מוּמִין, דְּקַיְ"ל: הַמַּתְפִּיס תְּמִימִים לְבֶדֶק הַבַּיִת עוֹבֵר בַּעֲשֵׂה, בְּמַס' תְּמוּרָה (דף ז:). אֲבָל לְעִנְיַן הַסּוּגְיָא אֲנִי לָמֵד כָּאן דַּאֲפִילּוּ תָּמִים נַמִי קָרֵי "אֵינוֹ רָאוּי", כג] דְּלָא הוּעֲמַד לָבֹא אֶל אֹהֶל מוֹעֵד, דְּהָא פָּרַת חַטָּאת תְּמִימָה הִיא, וְקָרֵי לָהּ "אֵינוֹ רָאוּי". אוֹצִיא אֶת אֵלּוּ שֶׁאֵין עֲתִידִין כד] לְאֹהֶל מוֹעֵד. וְלֹא אוֹצִיא שָׂעִיר הַמִּשְׁתַּלֵּחַ דְּרָאוּי הוּא – שֶׁהוּא תָּמִים, דְּבָעֵינַן שֶׁיְּהֵא רָאוּי לַשֵּׁם, דְּלָא יָדְעִינַן הֵי מִתְרְמֵי. כה] זֶה שָׁמַעְתִּי. וּלְפִי סוּגְיָא שֶׁל שְׁמוּעָה זוֹ מַשְׁמַע דְּקָרֵי לֵיהּ רָאוּי וְעָתִיד לִיכָּנֵס מִשּׁוּם הַגְרָלָה וּוִידּוּי. ת"ל לַה'. "לְהַקְרִיב קָרְבָּן לַה'" – הַמְיוּחָד לַה', לְהוֹצִיא שָׂעִיר הַמִּשְׁתַּלֵּחַ שֶׁאֵינוֹ מְיוּחָד לַשֵּׁם. קוֹדֶם הַגְרָלָה. הֲוֵי רָאוּי וְעָתִיד לִיכָּנֵס מִשּׁוּם הַגְרָלָה, וְאִי לָאו דְּמַעֲטִינַן מִ"לַה'" – ה"א: לְחַיֵּיב. כו] אַחַר הַגְרָלָה. לֹא רָאוּי לָבֹא הוּא, וּמִתְמְעִיט מֵ"אֶל פֶּתַח". הָא אִיכָּא וִידּוּי. דְּבָעֵי לִיכָּנֵס לְהִתְוַדּוֹת עָלָיו. תֵּיפּוֹק לִי מֵאֶל פֶּתַח אֹהֶל מוֹעֵד. דְּהָא לָאו רְאוּיִן הֵן לָבֹא לַעֲזָרָה. בִּשְׁלָמָא

תוספות

הַיְינוּ דקם רימא התם. ואע"ג דכל השאר מתו בהבלא, מחמת שהיה גדול וגבור לא הזיק לו ההבל. **אורזילא** דרימא. גר' ר"ת פי': עופר של ראם. ד"עופר האילים" מתרגמי': אורזילא דאיילא (שיר ב). ורימא הוא ראם. ולא כרבי שמואל דגורס ב"המוכר את הספינה" (ב"ב דף עג:): אורזילא דימא, ומפרש דג של ים. ואגב ריהטיה לא דק, דהא אמר הכא: לא נגזרה גזרה על דגים שבים. ואותם בופל"ש שאנו קורין ראם — ליתא, וחלבם אסור. דראם ודאי מין חיה הוא וחלבו מותר, כדכתיב "אקו ודישון", ומתרגמינן: יעלא ורימא. ובופל"ש שבמקומינו קטנים. דאין לומר שהוא מין ראם, ויש במינו גדול — דא"כ, מאי קשיא ליה היכא קם? הא לא קשיא ליה *אריה דבי עילאי בפרק "אלו טריפות" (חולין דף נט:) היכא קם — *שהיו אריות אחרים קטנים שיכול להכניס. ועוד, הא קא חזינן דאותן בופל"ש בני מלאכה נינהו, ומושכין בקרון וחורשין בהן. וראם לאו בר מלאכה הוא, דכתיב: "התקשר ראם בתלם עבותו אם ישדד עמקים אחריך" (איוב לט). **יצאו** קדשי בדק הבית. בלשון אחר פי' בקונטרס: דממעט אפי' תמימים, דהא פרת חטאת תמימה, וממעטא משום דאינה ראויה לפתח אהל מועד. ונראה דאין זו ראיה, דפרת חטאת לא קיימא למזבח. *ולאו מתפיס תמימים לבדק הבית — *הא אמר בסוף תמורה (דף לג:) דכל הראוי למזבח אינו יוצא מידי מזבח לעולם, ונמכרו לצורכי עולות ושלמים. וא"ת: מאי שנא קדשי בדק הבית תמימים משעירי יוה"כ, דאמר בפ' "שני שעירי" (יומא דף סג:) דחייב על שניהם בחוץ, הואיל וראויים לשעיר הנעשה בחוץ, וכ"ש הנך דאין יוצאין מידי מזבח! וי"ל: כיון דעדיין לאו קדשי מזבח נינהו — לא חשיבי "ראוין לפתח אהל מועד"*. **כאן** קודם הגרלה כו'. בפ' "שני שעירי" (יומא דף סג:) אמרי' דחייב על שניהם. והיינו למסקנא דשמעתין, דמשני: כאן קודם וידוי וכו'. אבל קודם הגרלה — חייב, דראוי לשעיר הנעשה בחוץ. **כאן** קודם וידוי כאן לאחר וידוי. ומדפטר קרא קודם וידוי — כ"ש לאחר וידוי. וכי איצטריך "פתח אהל מועד" — משום פרה ומשום קדשי בדק הבית. ומיהו, היא גופה תימה: אמאי לא ממעטינן מ"לה'"? ובפ"ק דתמורה (דף יג.) גרס בכל הספרים: ולא אוציא פרת חטאת ושעיר המשתלח שהם ראוין לפתח אהל מועד, ת"ל: "לה'" — שמיוחדים לה', יצאו אלו שאין מיוחדין לה'. ומיהו, קדשי בדק הבית שפיר מיקרו מיוחדין לה', דכולם לשמים! וע"כ נמי לא גרס פרת חטאת בברייתא, דלא תיקשי מתני'. ועוד אצטריך "אל פתח אהל מועד" למעוטי גגו, כדאמרינן לעיל בפ' "השוחט והמעלה" (דף קז:).

עין משפט נר מצוה

טז א מיי' פי"ח מהלכות מעה"ק הלכה יח:

מהריא כצ"ל נ"ק

אלא שהיו כו' כצ"ל נ"ק

נ"ל אבל

גי' נ"ק קיימא למזבח כדאמרינן בסוף תמורה כו'

[ועי' תוס' יומא סג: ד"ה וכל שאין]

[שבת קג: ע"ש דברי ר"ל וכו"י בהפך]

[יומא סג: תמורה ו: יג. ושם איתא אי קרבן וע"ש ברש"י]

מסורת הש"ס

[ר"ה יב. סנהדרין קח:]

סנהדרין קח. קדושין יג.

ב"ב עג: ע"ש

[בב"ב איתא כופתא וע"ש ברשב"ם ותוס' וכן מוכח ברש"י סנהדרין לח: ד"ה בטולא וקלת נ"ע רש"י דהכא]

ר"ה יב. סנהדרין קח:

[שבת קיג:]

[הגי' בת"כ כך היא אוציא הקדש בדק הבית שאינו בא אל אהל מועד ולא אוציא רובע ונרבע וכו' ת"ל להקריב הכשרים ליקרב אוציא את אלו שאינם כשרים ליקרב ולא אוציא שעיר המשתלח ת"ל לה' המיוחדים לשם יצאו אלו שאין מיוחדים לשם. והקושיא נמלא שעיר המשתלח לא ממועט מן ואל פתח אהל מועד לא הביאו רק לריך קרא אחרינא לה' המיוחדים לשם ובמתניתין ממעט שעיר המשתלח מפסוק ואל פתח אהל מועד ועי' רש"ק]

תורה אור: בראשית ז; בראשית ח; אסתר ז; ויקרא יז; במדבר לא

שיטה מקובצת

א] תיבות הא איפני נמחק: ב] איתיביה ר"ל לר"י מכל: ג] מתו מהבלא כדרב חסדא תיבת משום נמחק: ד] נידונו ברותחין קלקלו בשכבת זרע וברותחין נידונו כתיב הכא: ה] לא"י אמטול כתיב חרבה דהוי חרבה בעולם אלא לדידך מאי חרבה חרבה דמעיקרא דאמר רב חסדא והשאר נמחק: ו] פרסי בי מרבעתא דרישא: ז] רמא כבא וסכר תיבת כבא וי"ג כופתא נמחק: ח] תיבת ראש נמחק: ט] שמעון בן לקיש: י] פש תמן מיתא דאמר ר"ל: יא] נצתללו לשם: יב] קחזינן דאיכא עד תלתא ותיבת דהוו נמחק: יג] וכן שעיר המשתלח שעיר המשתלח לאו ראוי לפתח אהל מועד הוא והתניא ותיבת ורמינהי נמחק: יד] לבא לפתח אהל מועד: טו] ראויין לפתח אהל מועד יכול שאני אוציא את אלו ולא אוציא את שעיר המשתלח ת"ל והשאר ל"ש: טז] מבול כלומר כל אשר ביבשה לאפוקי והד"א ותיבות מכל אשר בחרבה ל"ש: יז] מה"ד היינו דקם: יח] רמא כבא וסכריה: יט] כבא כמו כיבוי דרעיתא: כ] היאך היא: כא] עשיריה אין מתקיימין מפני: כב] הקרבן הוא חייב: כג] ראוי דאין עתידין לבא: כד] שאין עתידין לבא אל פתח אהל מועד: כה] מתרמי לשם חטאת זה: כו] מה"ד לאחר הגרלה:

בשלמא רובע ונרבע – משכחת ליה דאקדשינהו מעיקרא והדר א] רבעו. אלא מוקצה ונעבד – *אאין אדם אוסר דבר שאינו שלו! בקדשים קלים, *ואליבא דר' יוסי הגלילי. דאמר: קדשים קלים ממון בעלים ב] הוא. *דתניא: °"ומעלה מעל בה'" (ויקרא ה) – לרבות קדשים קלים, שהן ממונו, דברי רבי יוסי הגלילי. הלכך, רובע ונרבע – דבר ערוה, ג] מוקצה ונעבד עבודה זרה – בקדשים קלים. אתנן ומחיר, כלאים, יוצא דופן – בולדות קדשים, קסבר: *ולדי קדשים בהווייתן הן קדושים.§ "בעלי מומין וכו' אותו ואת בנו" וכו'.§ וצריכי. דאי תנא בעלי מומין – משום דמאיסי, אבל תורין דלא מאיסי – אימא ד] (לא,) דמודו ליה לר"ש. ואי תנא תורין – משום דלא חזי ואידחו. אבל בעלי מומין דאיחזו ואידחו – אימא ה] (לא,) דמודה להו ר"ש לרבנן. ואי תנא הני תרתי – משום דפסולא דגופייהו, אבל אותו ואת בנו, דפסולא מעלמא קאתי ו] לה – אימא מודו ליה רבנן לר"ש, צריכא.§ "שהיה רבי שמעון אומר".§ מאי טעמא דר"ש? אמר רבי אילעא אמר ריש לקיש, דאמר קרא: °"לא תעשון ככל אשר אנחנו עושים פה היום" (דברים יב). אמר להו משה לישראל: כי עייליתו לארץ – ישרות תקריבו, חובות לא תקריבו. וגלגל לגבי שילה מחוסר זמן הוא, וקאמר להו משה: "לא תעשון". אמר רבי ירמיה לרבי זירא: אי הכי, מילקי

רש"י

בשלמא רובע ונרבע משכחת לה. דאיצטריך למעוטינהו מ"להקריב", דאקדשינהו והדר נרבעו. וכיון דחזו כבר ואידחו – לאו יש קרינא בהו, שנרבעו כבר, ולא מימעטי מ"אל פתח". דאיכא למימר, הכי אמר קרא: "ואל פתח אהל מועד לא הביאו" – כשנראה לבא ואחר כך שחטו בחוץ – חייב. אבל שעיר המשתלח לאחר וידוי – מימעיט מ"אל פתח", שהרי זה הביאו כשנראה לבא, ומשיצא לאחר וידוי לא נראה לבא. אלא מוקצה ונעבד. על כרחך מקמי דאקדשינהו הוו להו מוקצה ונעבד. דאי לבתר דאקדשינהו – תו לא מיתסרי בהקצאה ועבודה, דאין אדם אוסר דבר שאינו שלו. בה'. "וכחש בעמיתו" – דברים שיש בהם לשם ולעמיתו. לרבות קדשים קלי'. *שהכופר כהן ונשבע והודה – חייב עליהם אשם גזילות, שהן ממון בעלים, דקרינא ביה "וכחש בעמיתו". דבר ערוה. וחייל אף על המוקדשים כבר. הלכך ממעטי בחוץ מ"להקריב קרבן", דלאו בני הקרבה נינהו, דכתיב (ויקרא כב) "כי משחתם בהם", וכל מקום שנאמר השחתה אינו אלא דבר ערוה ועבודה זרה. נראה לי דה"ג: אתנן ומחיר וכלאים ויוצא דופן בולדות קדשים. כלומר, הנך דאצרכנו למעוטינהו מ"להקריב קרבן" ולא נפקי מ"אל פתח", על כרחך כשנראו כבר מיירי – לא משכחת ז] אלא בולדות קדשים ואירע להו פסול במעי אמן, דנראו לבא אל פתח אהל מועד קודם שנעשו אתנן ומחיר, אם בא להקריב את אמן – היו הן באין אל פתח. דאי בדאקדשינהו – לא משכחת לה, דאין אתנן ומחיר חל על המוקדשין, לפי שאינן שלו, ומקרא נפקא לן בתמורה (דף ל:). ואי בדהוו אתנן והדר אקדשינהו – מ"אל פתח" נפקי. וכן כלאים ויוצא דופן, דאי אקדשינהו משנולדו – מ"אל פתח" נפקי. אלא בולדות קדשים, דמעיקרא עם אמן נראו לבא. וקסבר ולדות קדשים בהווייתן הן קדושין. בלידתן מתקדשות. הלכך, חל אתנן ומחיר עליהן אם נתן לה עובר של ח] מוקדשין באתנן, דלא קדיש עד שנולד. בהווייתן ט] (הן). לשון "הוייה" נקט בהו משום ד"אשר יהיה לך" נפקי לן ולדות קדשים ליקרב: י] "רק קדשיך" – אלו התמורות, "אשר יהיו לך" – אלו הוולדות, במסכת תמורה (דף יז:). וצריכי. הנך תלת פלוגתא דר' שמעון ורבנן במתני'. משום דמאיסי. בעודן במומן פטרי רבנן בחוץ, דלא מתקבלין *בפנים. מודו ליה. יא] דהואיל וחזו לאחר זמן, קאי בלא תעשה. "ובני יונה" לא גרסינן. דאיחזו ואידחו. אימא: אע"ג דכי עבר מומן ירצו, השתא מיהא דחויין נינהו, ונפטר בחוץ. לא תעשון כן. בספרי דריש ליה בתחילת ביאת הארץ: היום אנו מטלטלין את המשכן ואנו אסורין בבמה, ואין אנו מקריבין אלא במשכן, לפיכך כל הקרבנות כשרים להקריב. משנבוא לארץ, י"ד שנים של כיבוש וחילוק – אנו מותרין בבמה, ושם "לא תעשון ככל אשר אנחנו עושים פה" יב] להקריב חובות. ומה אנו מותרין בה – "איש כל הישר בעיניו", נדרים ונדבות שאינן חובה עליו, אלא שישרו בעיניו להתנדב. "כי לא באתם עד עתה" וגו' – עד שתבאו אל המנוחה לשילה. שאע"פ שנכנסתם לארץ בעברכם את הירדן, עדיין לא באתם אל המנוחה. כי עייליתו לארץ. י"ד שנים שתכבשו ותחלקו. ישרות תקריבו. נדרים ונדבות יג] הקרב בבמת ציבור. חובות לא תקריבו. איש איש שבכם לא יקריב שום חובה, ואפילו בבמת ציבור, עד שתבאו אל המנוחה ותקריבום. אלמא, חובות דגלגל מחוסרי זמן הם, עד כי יבא שילה ויקריבום שם. וקאמר רחמנא: לא תעשון אותם בגלגל, ומשמע, בין בבמת ציבור בין בבמת יחיד. אלמא מחוסר זמן בבמה בלא תעשה. אי הכי. דהנך דגלגל "מחוסרי זמן" קרית להו. מילקי

תוספות

אתנן ומחיר יוצא דופן וכלאים בוולדות קדשים. אתנן ומחיר לא מיתוקם בקדשים קלים אפילו לרבי יוסי הגלילי. דאף על גב דממונו הוי – אינו חל עליו, כדדרשינן פ' "כל האסורין" (תמורה ל:): "לכל נדר" – פרט לנדור. **וקסבר** ולדות קדשים בהווייתן הן קדושים. וא"ת: למה לי קרא למעוטי? הלא חולין גמורים נינהו, ודינם כשאר חולין לישחט בחוץ, דאפילו פדיון לא בעו, דאין קדושה חלה עליהן כלל, כדמוכח בתמורה בפרק "כילד מערימין" (דף כד:). דתנן: "אם זכר – עולה, ואם נקבה – זבחי שלמים". ופריך בגמ': ל"ל למימר "אם נקבה – זבחי שלמים"? נקבה מי קדשה בבכורה? ומשני: סיפא אתאן לבהמה דהקדש. וקתני סיפא: ילדה טומטום או אנדרוגינוס, רשב"ג אומר: אין קדושה חלה עליהן. ומפרש בגמ': *משום דסבר בהוייתן הן קדושים, ואין קדושה חלה בדבר שאין ראוי ליקרב. א"כ, הכא נמי לא תיילא אאתנן ומחיר וכלאים ויוצא דופן! וי"ל: דהא דאמר רשב"ג: אין קדושה חלה עליהן – היינו קדושת הגוף (לפדות) וליאסר בגיזה ועבודה. אבל קדושת דמים איכא ליפדות שלא במום, ולכך בעי האי קרא דלא ממעטי מ"פתח אהל מועד" *בקדשי בדק הבית. *ולמאן דאמר במעי אמן הן קדושים – אפילו קדושת הגוף נחתא עלייהו, דתפסתינהו קדושה דאימיה. וא"ת: למאן דאמר "בהוייתן" נמי נימא: מיגו דנחתא להן קדושת דמים נחתא להן קדושת הגוף, כדאמר בתמורה בפרק "אלו קדשים" (דף יט: ושם) גבי מפריש נקבה לאשם! ודוחק לומר: רשב"ג סבר לה כרבי שמעון דלית ליה "מיגו". דאמר: תמכר שלא במום. ועוד: דאי כרבי שמעון, אפילו סבר במעי אמן קדושים לא חיילא עליה קדושת הגוף, כדמפרש התם: רבי שמעון לטעמיה דאמר: כל מידי דלא חזי לגופיה – לא נחתא ליה קדושת הגוף! וגם אין לפרש: דשאני מפריש נקבה, דחזי לשאר קרבנות, ושייך "מגו" טפי. דהא אפילו בטרפה אשכחן דאמרינן "מגו", בסוף "יש בקרבנות" (שם דף יז.)! ונראה לפרש: דהכא מיירי כגון דלאחר שנעשו אתנן ומחיר הקדישן, או בעודן במעי אמן או אחר שנולדו, דכיון שהקדישן בפירוש – חיילא עלייהו קדושה. וא"ת: ולוקמה נמי הכא כמ"ד במעי אמן הן קדושים, וכגון שהקדיש בהמה מעוברת ושייר העובר. כר' יוחנן, דאמר בפ' "כילד מערימין" (תמורה כה.): אם שייר – משוייר. ועשה העובר אתנן ומחיר, ואחר כך הקדישן. ואע"ג דרבי יוחנן איתותב התם – הא לבסוף *מסיק כתנאי. ועוד: מאי לאוקומה בבהמה של חולין מעוברת, ועשה העובר אתנן ומחיר, ואחר כך הקדישה! וי"ל: דניחא ליה לאוקומה בפשיטות כמאן דאמר בהוייתן הן קדושים והקדישן ואח"כ נתעברה. ואם תאמר: בההיא ד"כילד מערימין" (ג"ז שם) דדייק אליבא דרשב"ג דסבר בהוייתן הן קדושין – מרישא נמי הוה מצי למידק הכי, ד"אם נקבה זבחי שלמים" דאוקימנא בבהמה דהקדש, ואי במעי אמן הן קדושות – לא היה יכול להפקיע קדושת הולד! ויש לומר: דנקט עד סיפא ומפרש לה, וה"ה לרישא. ואם תאמר: בסוף "בהמה המקשה" (חולין עז.) דתנן: המבכרת שהפילה שליא – ישליכנה לכלבים, ובמוקדשין – תקבר. ומפרש בגמ' (שם:): משום דרובא בר מיקדש היא. על כרחך מדקאמר תקבר – קסבר: במעי אמן הן קדושין, דאי בהוייתן – אמאי תקבר? הא לא חיילא קדושה אלא בחזי להקרבה, כדפרישית. ואם כן – כולה בר מיקדש היא, ואמאי נקט רובא? דאפי' אכלאים ונדמה תפסה קדושת אימיה, אי במעי אמן הן קדושים. כדאשכחן בתמורה בסוף "יש בקרבנות" (דף יז.) דאמרינן גבי כלאים טומטום ואנדרוגינוס – דאי אתה מוצא אלא בולדות קדשים. ולכל הפחות אתיא כמאן דאמר במעי אמן הן קדושים! ⊕ויש לומר: דנקט רובא ולא כולה – משום דאיכא דמות יונה, או קלוט, לר' שמעון. דכיון דלא מישתרי באכילה – לא מיסתבר דתפסינהו קדושת אמן, אף על גב דבמעי אמן הן קדושין.

משום דפסולא דגופייהו. בכל דוכתי משמע דפסול הגוף חמיר מפסולא דאתי מעלמא, כדאמרינן בפרק קמא (לעיל דף ז.): מה לשינוי קודש שכן פסולו בגופו, ובפסחים בסוף "אלו דברים" (דף עג:) נמי אמרינן: כל שפסולו בגופו ישרף מיד.* *דהא דמשמע הכא איפכא – לאו משום דפסול הגוף קיל, אלא הכי קאמר: דמום עובר ותורין שלא הגיע זמנן – הפסול תלוי בגופו, ואם היה מום עובר מיד, והתורים גדילין לאלתר – היו ראויין. אבל אותו ואת בנו – אין הפסול תלוי בגופו שיועיל לו שום תיקון, דלכולי יומא לא חזי. אלמה

עין משפט נר מצוה

יז א מיי' פ"ד מהלכות איסורי מזבח הל' ה:

[פסחים ל. ב"ק יב: עו. סנהדרין קיב:]

[שם כה.]

נ"ל כקדשי נ"ק

[עי' בתוספות לתמורה כד: ד"ה קסבר דמתרלו בע"א ע"ש]

[עי' תוס' ב"ק מז. ד"ה מ"ט ותוס' סנהדרין פ: ד"ה עובר]

והא כנ"ל נ"ק

שיטה מקובצת

א] והדר רבען אלא: ב] בעלים הן דתניא: ג] תיבות מוקצה ונעבד עבודה זרה נמחק ותיבות בקדשים קלים ל"ש: ד] תיבת לא נמחק: ה] תיבת לא נמחק: ו] קאתי להו: ז] משכחת לה אלא: ח] מוקדשים באתננה דלא: ט] תיבת הן נמחק: י] ליקרב דכתיב רק: יא] ליה לר"ש דהואיל: יב] פה היום: יג] ונדבות הקריבו בבמת צבור:

מסורת הש"ס

[עי' תוספות חולין מח. ד"ה כיון]

[קדושין נב: ב"ק יב: ב"ב קכג: בכורות נג: תמורה ח.]

נ"א שאם כפר בהם

[תמורה יח: כה. מנחות פג. לעיל לח. חולין ל. כריתות כג: נדה מא.]

ליתא בח"ג

גליון הש"ם

תוס' ד"ה וקסבר וכו' וי"ל דנקט רובא. עיין לעיל דף פד ע"ב תוס' ד"ה ומוליך:

[לפי שיטתם משמע שגורסים בפנים אימא מודה ליה ר"ש לרבנן וכ"ה גי' ר"ע ברטנורא]

מִילְקֵי נַמִּי לִילְקֵי! אַלְמָה *אָמַר רַבִּי זֵירָא: הַכָּתוּב נִתְּקוֹ לַעֲשֵׂה? א] הָנֵי מִילֵּי לְרַבָּנַן, לְרַבִּי שִׁמְעוֹן — הָכִי נַמִּי. רַב נַחְמָן בַּר יִצְחָק אָמַר: פְּנִים דְּגִלְגָּל לְגַבֵּי שִׁילֹה — כְּחוּץ דָּמֵי. רַבָּה אָמַר: טַעְמֵיהּ דְּרַבִּי שִׁמְעוֹן — *כִּדְתַנְיָא, רַבִּי שִׁמְעוֹן אוֹמֵר: מִנַּיִן לַזּוֹבֵחַ אפֶּסַח בְּבָמַת יָחִיד בִּשְׁעַת אִיסּוּר הַבָּמוֹת שֶׁהוּא בְּלֹא תַעֲשֶׂה? ת״ל: °״לֹא תוּכַל לִזְבּוֹחַ אֶת הַפָּסַח״. יָכוֹל אַף בִּשְׁעַת הֶיתֵּר הַבָּמוֹת כֵּן? ת״ל: ״בְּאַחַד שְׁעָרֶיךָ״, לֹא אֲמַרְתִּי לְךָ אֶלָּא בְּשָׁעָה שֶׁכָּל יִשְׂרָאֵל נִכְנָסִין בְּשַׁעַר אֶחָד. אֵימַת? אִי נֵימָא אַחַר חֲצוֹת — כָּרֵת נַמִּי ב] מִחַיַּיב! אֶלָּא לָאו — קוֹדֶם חֲצוֹת! ג] לְעוֹלָם לְאַחַר חֲצוֹת, בוּבִשְׁעַת הֶיתֵּר הַבָּמוֹת קָאֵי. וְהָא בִּשְׁעַת אִיסּוּר הַבָּמוֹת קָאָמַר! אִיסּוּר בָּמָה לוֹ, הֶיתֵּר בָּמָה לַחֲבֵירוֹ.§ ״מְחוּסַּר זְמַן״ כו׳.§ וְהָנֵי בְּנֵי אֲשָׁמוֹת נִינְהוּ? אָמַר זְעֵירִי: גתְּנֵי ״מְצוֹרָע״ בַּהֲדַיְיהוּ.§ ״עוֹלוֹתֵיהֶן וְשַׁלְמֵיהֶן״.§ וְהָנֵי בְּנֵי שְׁלָמִים נִינְהוּ? אָמַר רַב שֵׁשֶׁת: תְּנֵי ד״נָזִיר״. דִּזְעֵירִי קְבָעוּהָ תַּנָּאֵי, דְּרַב שֵׁשֶׁת לָא קְבָעוּהָ תַּנָּאֵי. א״ר ד] *חִלְקִיָּה (דְּבֵי) רַב טוֹבִי: לֹא שָׁנוּ אֶלָּא לִשְׁמוֹ, האֲבָל שֶׁלֹּא לִשְׁמוֹ — חַיָּיב, הוֹאִיל וְרָאוּי לְשֶׁלֹּא לִשְׁמוֹ בִּפְנִים. אִי הָכִי, לִשְׁמוֹ נַמִּי נִיחַיַּיב, הוֹאִיל וְרָאוּי לְשֶׁלֹּא לִשְׁמוֹ בִּפְנִים! (א) ה] בָּעֵי עֲקִירָה. מַתְקִיף לָהּ רַב הוּנָא: וְכִי יֵשׁ לְךָ *דָּבָר שֶׁאֵינוּ כָּשֵׁר לִשְׁמוֹ, וְכָשֵׁר שֶׁלֹּא לִשְׁמוֹ? וְלָא? וַהֲרֵי

פֶּסַח

דברים טז

רש״י

מִילְקֵי נַמִּי לִילְקֵי. הַשּׁוֹחֵט מְחוּסַּר זְמַן. ו] דְּהָא מִשְׁכַּן דְּגִלְגָּל דְּהָיָה בָּמַת צִיבּוּר – פְּנִים הוּא, שֶׁאֹהֶל מוֹעֵד שֶׁל מִדְבָּר הָיָה שָׁם, וְקָאָמַר רַחֲמָנָא בֵּיהּ נַמִּי ״לֹא תַעֲשׂוּן״. אַלְמָה אָמַר רַבִּי זֵירָא. בְּפֶ׳ ״אוֹתוֹ וְאֶת בְּנוֹ״ (חולין פ:), דְּקָתָנֵי: קָדָשִׁים בִּפְנִים ז] סוֹפֵג אֶת הָאַרְבָּעִים מִשּׁוּם לָאו דְ״אוֹתוֹ וְאֶת בְּנוֹ״. וְהָוֵינַן בָּהּ: וְנִילְקֵי נַמִּי מִשּׁוּם לָאו דִּמְחוּסַּר זְמַן. דְּתַנְיָא: מִנַּיִן שֶׁכָּל הַפְּסוּלִים שֶׁבְּשׁוֹר וְשֶׂבְּשֶׂה, שֶׁהֵן בְּ״לֹא יֵרָצֶה״ – ת״ל: ״וְשׁוֹר וָשֶׂה שָׂרוּעַ וְקָלוּט״, וּמְחוּסַּר זְמַן פָּסוּל הוּא! וּמְשַׁנֵּי ר׳ זֵירָא: ח] הַאי לָאו דִּמְחוּסַּר זְמַן דְּהַכָּתוּב נִתְּקוֹ לַעֲשֵׂה, דִּכְתִיב בֵּיהּ עֲשֵׂה יְתֵירָא, כִּדְמְפָרֵשׁ הָתָם – לְמֵימְרָא שֶׁהוֹצִיאוֹ וְנִתְּקוֹ מִכְּלַל לָאו, דְּלָא קָאֵי עֲלֵיהּ (ב) בְּלָאו דִּשְׁאָר פְּסוּלִין. וְהָשְׁתָּא דְּאָמְרַתְּ הָכָא: לָאו בַּהֲדְיָא כְּתִיב בֵּיהּ – נִילְקֵי עֲלֵיהּ! (דִּלְמָא) ה״מ. דִּמְשַׁנֵּי נַמִּי הָתָם דְּלָא לָקֵי – לְרַבָּנַן דִּפְלִיגֵי עֲלֵיהּ דְּרַבִּי שִׁמְעוֹן, דְּלָא דָּרְשֵׁי לְהַאי לֹא תַעֲשֶׂה לִמְחוּסַּר זְמַן. דְּהַהוּא דְּאוֹתוֹ וְאֶת בְּנוֹ דְּשַׁנֵּי ר׳ זֵירָא עֲלָהּ, מִיתּוֹקְמָא הָתָם דְּלָא כְּר״ש. אֲבָל לְר׳ שִׁמְעוֹן ה״נ דְּלָקֵי אַלָּאו דִּמְחוּסַּר זְמַן בִּפְנִים. רַב נַחְמָן בַּר יִצְחָק אָמַר. לְר׳ שִׁמְעוֹן נַמִּי לָא לָקֵי אַמְחוּסַּר (ג) זְמַן. בִּפְנִים דְּגִלְגָּל לְגַבֵּי שִׁילֹה – חוּץ הוּא לְגַבֵּי חוּבוֹת, הוֹאִיל ט] דְּאֵינוֹ כָּשֵׁר לְהַקְרָבָתוֹ. הִלְכָּךְ בַּחוּץ הוּא דְּאַשְׁכַּחַן בֵּיהּ לֹא תַעֲשֶׂה מִשּׁוּם אִיסּוּר בָּמָה, וְלֹא בִּפְנִים. בִּשְׁעַת אִיסּוּר הַבָּמוֹת. קס״ד: בַּמִּדְבָּר וְשִׁילֹה וּבֵית עוֹלָמִים. אַחַר חֲצוֹת. דְּי״ד, דְּמָטֵי זִימְנֵיהּ. כָּרֵת נַמִּי נִיחַיַּיב. דְּהָא מִתְקַבֵּל בִּפְנִים. קוֹדֶם חֲצוֹת. דַּהֲוֵי מְחוּסַּר זְמַן לִשְׁמוֹ. בִּשְׁעַת הֶיתֵּר הַבָּמוֹת קָאָמַר. כְּמוֹ בַּגִּלְגָּל וְנוֹב וְגִבְעוֹן, דְּהוּתְּרוּ בָּמוֹת יָחִיד לְעוֹלָה וּשְׁלָמִים, וְאַשְׁמְעִינַן קְרָא דִּלְגַבֵּי חוֹבוֹת אִיכָּא לֹא תַעֲשֶׂה. וְלָאו מִשּׁוּם מְחוּסַּר זְמַן, דְּהָא חֲזוּ הָשְׁתָּא בְּבָמָה גְּדוֹלָה. אִיסּוּר בָּמָה לוֹ. לְקָרְבָּן זֶה. הֶיתֵּר בָּמָה לַחֲבֵירוֹ. לְעוֹלָה וּשְׁלָמִים דְּנֶדֶר וּנְדָבָה. וְסֵיפָא ה״ק: יָכוֹל אַף בְּשָׁעָה שֶׁהוּא מוּתָּר בְּבָמָה, כְּגוֹן קוֹדֶם חֲצוֹת שֶׁהוּא י] לִשְׁלָמִים – *ת״ל כו׳. בְּשַׁעַר אֶחָד – בְּבָמָה גְּדוֹלָה לִשְׁחוֹט פִּסְחֵיהֶם. דִּזְעֵירִי קְבָעוּהָ תַּנָּאֵי. לְמִיתְנֵי בְּמַתְנִיתִין מְצוֹרָע בַּהֲדְיָא. דְּרַב שֵׁשֶׁת לֹא קְבָעוּהָ תַּנָּאֵי. וּמִיהוּ, אֲנַן מְשַׁנִּינַן לָהּ בַּגְּמָרָא וְקָבְעִינַן לָהּ בַּגְּמָ׳ הָכִי, כְּכָל ״חַסּוּרֵי מִחַסְּרָא״ דְּהַתַּלְמוּד. רַב חִלְקִיָּה. אַאָשָׁם קָאֵי וְלָא אַחַטָּאת. דְּאִילּוּ חַטָּאת פְּסוּלָה שֶׁלֹּא לִשְׁמוֹ בִּפְנִים. לֹא שָׁנוּ. דְּפָטוּר בַּחוּץ. אֶלָּא לִשְׁמוֹ. וַאֲפִילּוּ סְתָמָא. דִּבְהַאי שְׁמָא אֵינוֹ מִתְקַבֵּל עַכְשָׁיו בִּפְנִים. אֲבָל שֶׁלֹּא לִשְׁמוֹ. כְּגוֹן לְשֵׁם עוֹלָה. וּבְשֵׁם זֶה הוּא רָאוּי לָבֹא לִפְנִים, דְּכָל הַזְּבָחִים שֶׁנִּזְבְּחוּ שֶׁלֹּא לִשְׁמָן כְּשֵׁרִין, חוּץ מִן הַפֶּסַח וְהַחַטָּאת. אִי הָכִי כִּי שָׁחֵיט לֵיהּ לִשְׁמוֹ בַּחוּץ נַמִּי נִיחַיַּיב. דְּהָא רָאוּי הָיָה לַעֲקוֹר שֵׁם זֶה מִמֶּנּוּ וְלָבֹא לִפְנִים. מְחוּסַּר עֲקִירָה. וְכָל כַּמָּה דְּלָא אִיעֲקַר שֵׁם אָשָׁם מִינֵּיהּ – סְתָמֵיהּ לָאו לְמִיעֲקַר קָאֵי, וְלָא רָאוּי הוּא. וְכִי יֵשׁ לְךָ דָּבָר שֶׁאֵינוֹ כָּשֵׁר לִשְׁמוֹ. לִפְנִים. וְכָשֵׁר שֶׁלֹּא לִשְׁמוֹ. *אֲפִי׳ דְּקי״ל לְעֵיל (דף ב.): כָּל הַזְּבָחִים כְּשֵׁרִין שֶׁלֹּא לִשְׁמָן – ה״מ הֵיכָא דִּכְשֵׁרִין לִשְׁמָן. אֲבָל מְחוּסַּר זְמַן בִּבְעָלִים זֶה, שֶׁאֵינוֹ כָּשֵׁר לִשְׁמוֹ – הֵיאַךְ יוּכְשַׁר שֶׁלֹּא לִשְׁמוֹ!

פֶּסַח

תוספות

אלמה אמר רבי זירא הכתוב נתקו לעשה. אין זה כשאר ״לאו הניתק לעשה״ דבפ׳ בתרא דחולין (דף קמא.) ובפ׳ ג׳ דמכות (דף יד. טו. טז.), כגון לאו דגזילה ולקט שכחה ופיאה ונותר, *ו״לא יוכל לשלחה כל ימיו״. דא״כ, מאי פריך דלילקי משום לאו ד״לא תעשון״? והא ניתק לעשה הוא! אלא הוי כמו ״נתקו הכתוב מטומאה חמורה לטומאה קלה״. דב״אותו ואת בנו״ (חולין פ:) דרשינן ״ולנדר לא ירצה״ – לימד על כל הפסולים שבשור ושה שהם ב״לא ירצה״. וכתב רחמנא במחוסר זמן: ״מיום השמיני והלאה ירצה״ – להוציאו מכלל שאר פסולים שהם ב״לא ירצה״, ולומר דבהאי ליכא אלא עשה, כעין דבר שהיה בכלל ויצא לידון בדבר החדש, בסוף פ״ק דתמורה (דף יג:). וכענין זה הוי ״בדד ישב״ דמצורע בפ׳ ״אלו דברים״ (פסחים סז.) דאמרי׳ שהכתוב נתקו לעשה והוציאו מכלל שאר טמאים שהם בלאו ד״לא יטמאו את מחניהם״. ולהכי פריך דלילקי, משום דמפורש בגופיה לאו בהדיא, כדדרשינן מ״לא תעשון״, וכן פי׳ בקונטרס. אבל בפרק ״אותו ואת בנו״ (חולין פא.) פירש בקונטרס דהוי כשאר לאו הניתק לעשה דעלמא, ד״מיום השמיני והלאה ירצה״ משמע: קודם זמנו – לא ירצה, והניחהו עד שיעבור זמנו. *וקשה מהך דשמעתא! וכי תימא, דהכי פריך: משום דאיכא נמי לאו ד״לא תעשון״ לא אמרינן דאתי חד עשה ועקר תרי לאוי, כדאמרי׳ בפ״ק דתמורה (דף ד:) – לא דמי, דהני מילי התם, דסמיכי גבי הדדי הלאוין אצל העשה. תדע, דהא בפרק ג׳ דמכות (ד׳ טו. ושם ד״ה ״תנינא״) חשיב ״לא יטמאו את מחניהם״ ניתק לעשה אי לאו משום דקדמו עשה, אף על גב דאיכא לאו נמי ד״ואל המקדש לא תבא״. ומיהו, התם איכא למימר משום דאיכא תרי עשה, דכתיב ״מחוץ למחנה תשלחום״. אבל אשכחן גזלה דאיכא תרי לאוי, לאו ד״לא תעשוק״ ו״לא תגזול״, דבפרק ״המקבל״ (ב״מ קיא.) אמר רבא: זהו עושק זהו גזל. וחשבי ליה ניתק לעשה במכות (דף יד:) ובחולין (דף פ:). הלכך צריך לחלק בההיא דתמורה (דף ד:) כדפרישית: דלכך סמך שני הלאוין אצל העשה – לומר שאין העשה מנתקם.

רב נחמן בר יצחק אמר פנים דגלגל כו׳. שינויא הוא דקמשני (התם), דאפילו לר״ש לא לקי במחוסר זמן בפנים כי אם בחוץ, כדפי׳ בקונטרס. ויש גירסא אחרת בספרים: לרבי שמעון ה״נ. והא גלגל פנים הוא! אמר רב נחמן בר יצחק: פנים דגלגל כו׳. *וריש לקיש פריך, דנפקא ליה מ״לא תעשון״ לאו במחוסר זמן. דהאי קרא בגלגל קאי, ופנים הוא. וכי תימא קל וחומר בחוץ – הא אין מזהירין מן הדין! ומשני: פנים דגלגל לגבי שילה כחוץ דמי. **אלא** לאו קודם חצות. ואע״ג דחזי בפנים שלא לשמו – לא מיחייב כרת, כיון דמחוסר עקירה, ואין עומד האי ליעקר קודם זמנו. **היתר** במה לחבירו. ו״שעת היתר הבמות״ דקתני – היינו קודם חצות, דכשר בבמה שלא לשמו. וא״ת: דמשמע הכא דתורין שלא הגיע זמנן לרבי שמעון חיילא קדושה עלייהו, והשוחטן בחוץ – בלאו. ובמעילה בפרק ״ולד חטאת״ (דף יב.) נמי אמר רבי שמעון דמועלין, משום דראוין לאחר זמן. ובתמורה בפרק ״אלו קדשים״ (דף יט:) גבי אשם בן שתים והביאו בן שנה, אמר ר׳ שמעון דכל עצמן אינן קדושים, משום דכל מידי דלא חזי ליה *לגופיה – לא נחתא ליה קדושת הגוף. ופריך התם: מאי שנא ממחוסר זמן דלא חזי ליה לגופיה, (לא נחתא ליה קדושת הגוף) ואמר ר״ש דקדוש! פירוש: במתני׳ דהכא, דתנן: מחוסר זמן, רבי שמעון אומר בלא תעשה! ומשני: דאיתקוש לבכור, דקדוש לפני זמנו וקרב לאחר זמן. והשתא תינח מחוסר זמן, תורין שלא הגיע זמנן מאי טעמא? וי״ל: דדבר שאינו ראוי לשם קרבן – ילפינן ממחוסר זמן שאין ראוי לשום קרבן. אבל דבר שראוי לקרבן אחר, ולקרבן זה שהוא מקדישו אינו ראוי – לא נחתא ליה קדושת הגוף. ופסח קודם חצות דקדוש לר׳ שמעון, וכן חטאת ואשם דזב וזבה ויולדת ומצורע דקדושים קודם זמנן, כדתנן בפירקין (לעיל קיב.) ולא פליג ר׳ שמעון, ובתורת כהנים בפ׳ ״אחרי מות״ קאמר נמי רבי שמעון: והשוחטן בחוץ בלאו – הני אין מחוסר זמן בגופן. ולא דמי לאשם בן שנה והביאו בן שתים, בן שתים והביאו בן שנה – דמחוסרי זמן בגופן. וא״ת: דמחוסר זמן היאך קדוש? הא אמרינן לעיל בפ״ק (דף יב.): לילה – לקדושה יום – להרצאה, אבל ביום שביעי – לא. ובבכורות פרק ״הלוקח בהמה״ (דף כא.) קאמר ר״ש: מחוסר זמן נכנס לדיר להתעשר, יליף מבכור דקדוש לפני זמנו. ופריך: ואדיליף מבכור, לילף מקדשים! אלמא משמע דקדשים קודם זמנן לא קדשי! וי״ל: דאסור להקדישם, אבל אם הקדישם תוך זמנם – קדושין, אלא דעבד איסור, דרחמנא אמר ״מיום השמיני״ – אין, הא קודם לכן – לא. אבל מעשר לרבי שמעון שרי להכניסו תוך זמנו לדיר להתעשר כדיליף התם מעשר ״העברה״ ״העברה״ מבכור. והא דלא ניחא ליה למילף ״תחת״ ״תחת״ מקדשים – דניחא ליה למילף ״העברה״ טפי, משום ד״העברה״ דתרוייהו משתעי, שמעבירה להקדישה. ויש ליתן טעם לרבא דריש תמורה (דף ד:), היאך מחוסר זמן קדוש קדושת הגוף? דכל היכא דאמר רחמנא לא תעביד אי עביד לא מהני! ושמא לענין זה יליף ״תחת״ ״תחת״ ממעשר, או שמא יש טעם אחר. **דזעירי** קבעוה תנאי. משום דמצורע יש בו טומאה כעין זב וזבה ויולדת. אבל נזיר דלא דמי להו – שייריה. וכן בכריתות בפרק ״ארבעה מחוסרי כפרה״ (דף ח:) נמי אשכחן, דתני: זב וזבה ויולדת ומצורע. והתם מפרש: מאי טעמא לא תני מצורע ומצורעת, כדקתני זב וזבה. וניחא השתא לזעירי, דבנזיר בלא מצורע סגי, דאיכא תרתי בנזיר, דנזיר טמא מביא אשם*.

פסח

עין משפט נר מצוה

יח א ב מיי׳ פ״א מהל׳ קרבן פסח הל׳ ג:

נ״ל ומחזיר גרושתו ואנוסתו דלא יוכל כו׳ נ״ק

יט ג ד מיי׳ פי״ח מהל׳ מעה״ק הלכה ט:

כ ה מיי׳ שם הלכה י:

שיטה מקובצת

א] לעשה דלמא הני מילי לרבנן אבל לרבי: ב] נמי ניחייב אלא: ג] חצות לא לעולם: ד] חלקיה בר טובי ותיבות דבי רב נמחק: ה] בפנים מחוסר עקירה תיבת בעי נמחק: ו] זמן בפנים דהא: ז] בפנים השני סופג: ח] ר׳ זירא הך לאו דמחוסר זמן הכתוב נתקו לעשה: ט] הואיל ואינו כשר להקרבתן הלכך: י] שהוא כשר לשלמים:

עיין נ״ק

נ״ל ולריש לקיש כו׳ נ״ק

נ״ל לגופיה ונחתא ליה קדושת הגוף לאמר ר״ש כו׳

מסורת הש״ס

[חולין פ:]

פסחים לא. תוספתא פי״

[יומא סג.]

[מנחות מז:]

ת״ל כו׳ הס״ד ואח״כ מ״ה בשער נ״ק

נ״ל אע״פ נ״ק

עיין רש״ק

הגהות הב״ח

(א) גמ׳ וראוי לשלא לשמו בפנים (בעי) תא״מ ונ״ב גירסת רש״י מחוסר: (ב) רש״י ד״ה אלמה וכו׳ דלא קאי עליה לאו כל׳ ואות ב׳ נמחק: (ג) ד״ה רב נחמן וכו׳ זמן הס״ד ואח״כ מ״ה פנים:

גליון הש״ס

תום׳ ד״ה היתר וכו׳ מיום השמיני אין הא קודם לכן לא. עיין יומא דף ס׳ ע״ב:

כא א מיי' פט"ו מהל' פסה"מ הלכה יא:
כב ב מיי' שם הל' כ:

תורה אור

אפֶּסַח בִּשְׁאָר יְמוֹת הַשָּׁנָה, דְּאֵינוֹ כָּשֵׁר לִשְׁמוֹ, וְכָשֵׁר שֶׁלֹּא לִשְׁמוֹ! פֶּסַח בִּשְׁאָר יְמוֹת הַשָּׁנָה שְׁלָמִים נִינְהוּ. לֵימָא מְסַיַּיע לֵיהּ: יָכוֹל שֶׁאֲנִי מוֹצִיא אַף א] עוֹלַת מְחוּסַּר זְמַן בַּבְּעָלִים, וַאֲשַׁם נָזִיר וַאֲשַׁם מְצוֹרָע? ת"ל: °"שׁוֹר" – מ"מ, "כֶּשֶׂב" – מ"מ, "עֵז" – מ"מ. (ויקרא יז) וְאִילּוּ חַטָּאת שַׁיְּירָא. בְּמַאי עָסְקִינַן? אִילֵימָא בִּזְמַנּוֹ – מַאי אִירְיָא אָשָׁם? אֲפִילּוּ חַטָּאת נַמִי! אֶלָּא שֶׁלֹּא ב] לִזְמַנּוֹ. וּבְמַאי? אִילֵימָא לִשְׁמוֹ – אָשָׁם אַמַּאי חַיָּיב? אֶלָּא לָאו – שֶׁלֹּא לִשְׁמוֹ! לְעוֹלָם בִּזְמַנּוֹ וְשֶׁלֹּא לִשְׁמוֹ, *וְרַבִּי ג] אֱלִיעֶזֶר הִיא. דְּאָמַר: מַקְּשִׁינַן אָשָׁם לְחַטָּאת, וּתְנָא טָפֵל וְה"ה עִיקָּר. ת"ש: *יָכוֹל שֶׁאֲנִי מְרַבֶּה ד] עוֹלַת מְחוּסַּר זְמַן בְּגוּפָהּ, וְחַטָּאת בֵּין בְּגוּפָהּ בֵּין בַּבְּעָלִים? ת"ל: °"וְאֶל פֶּתַח אֹהֶל מוֹעֵד", (שם טז) כׇּל שֶׁאֵינוֹ רָאוּי לָבֹא בְּפֶתַח אֹהֶל מוֹעֵד – אֵין חַיָּיבִין עָלֶיהָ. וְאִילּוּ אָשָׁם שַׁיְּירָא. בְּמַאי עָסְקִינַן? אִילֵימָא לִשְׁמוֹ – אָשָׁם נַמִי לִיפְטְרֵיהּ! אֶלָּא לָאו – שֶׁלֹּא לִשְׁמוֹ! ה] לְעוֹלָם שֶׁלֹּא לִשְׁמוֹ, וְר"א הִיא, דְּמַקִּישׁ אָשָׁם לְחַטָּאת, תְּנָא עִיקָּר וְכ"ש לְטָפֵל. ת"ש, דְּכִי אֲתָא רַב דִּימִי אֲמַר, תָּנָא דְּבֵי ו] ר' לִיוָאי: יָכוֹל שֶׁאֲנִי מוֹצִיא אַף עוֹלַת מְחוּסַּר זְמַן בַּבְּעָלִים, ז] אֲשַׁם נָזִיר וַאֲשַׁם מְצוֹרָע (מִנַּיִן? וְנָסֵיב לְהוּ תַּלְמוּדָא לְחִיּוּבָא, וְלָא יָדְעָנָא מַאי הִיא.) מַאי תַּלְמוּדָא? אָמַר רָבִינָא: "שׁוֹר" – מִכׇּל מָקוֹם, "כֶּשֶׂב" – מִכׇּל מָקוֹם, "עֵז" – מִכׇּל מָקוֹם. ח] הָא מַאי רוּמְיָא? כְּדַאֲמַרְתְּ! אָמַר ר"נ: (א) מִשּׁוּם (רס"ק) [דְּרָמֵי] דִּתְנָא דְּבֵי ר' לִיוָאי *)אַדִּתְנֵי לֵוִי: ט] באֲשַׁם נָזִיר וַאֲשַׁם מְצוֹרָע שֶׁשְּׁחָטָן שֶׁלֹּא לִשְׁמָן – כְּשֵׁירִין, וְלֹא עָלוּ לַבְּעָלִים לְשׁוּם חוֹבָה. שְׁחָטָן מְחוּסַּר זְמַן בַּבְּעָלִים, אוֹ שֶׁהָיוּ בְּנֵי שְׁתֵּי שָׁנִים וּשְׁחָטָן – פְּסוּלִין. י] וּמְשַׁנֵּי רַב דִּימִי: לָא קַשְׁיָא; כָּאן – לִשְׁמוֹ, כָּאן – שֶׁלֹּא לִשְׁמוֹ. רַב אַשִׁי רָמֵי מַתְנִי' אַבָּרַיְיתָא, וּמְשַׁנֵּי: כָּאן – לִשְׁמוֹ, וְכָאן – שֶׁלֹּא לִשְׁמוֹ. לֵימָא תֶּיהֱוֵי תְּיוּבְתֵּיהּ דְּרַב הוּנָא? אָמַר לָךְ רַב הוּנָא: הָכָא בְּמַאי עָסְקִינַן – כְּגוֹן שֶׁהִפְרִישׁ שְׁתֵּי אֲשָׁמוֹת לְאַחֲרָיוּת, דְּחַד מִינַּיְיהוּ יא] מֵעִיקָּרָא עוֹלָה הִיא.

כִּדְרַב

*) מנחות מח.

פֶּסַח בִּשְׁאָר יְמוֹת הַשָּׁנָה. אֵינוֹ כָּשֵׁר לִשְׁמוֹ, דִּתְנַן: *שְׁחָטוֹ קוֹדֶם חֲצוֹת – פָּסוּל, שֶׁנֶּאֱמַר: "בֵּין הָעַרְבַּיִם". שְׁלָמִים הוּא. וְאֵין זֶה אֶלָּא לִשְׁמוֹ. לֵימָא מְסַיַּיע לֵיהּ. לְרַב חִלְקִיָּה. יָכוֹל שֶׁאֲנִי מוֹצִיא. מֵ"אֶל פֶּתַח" שֶׁלֹּא יִתְחַיֵּיב בַּחוּץ עַל עוֹלַת מְחוּסַּר זְמַן בַּבְּעָלִים, כְּגוֹן שֶׁל יוֹלֶדֶת וּמְצוֹרָע, הוֹאִיל וְאֵינָהּ רְאוּיָה לָבֹא לִפְנִים לְמִצְוָתָהּ. וַאֲשַׁם נָזִיר וַאֲשַׁם מְצוֹרָע. שֶׁיֵּשׁ בָּהּ פְּסוּל. וּלְקַמֵּיהּ מְפָרֵשׁ וְאָזֵיל מַאי פְּסוּלָהּ. שׁוֹר מ"מ כו'. דְּמָצֵי לְמֵימַר "אֲשֶׁר יִשְׁחַט בַּמַּחֲנֶה אוֹ אֲשֶׁר יִשְׁחַט מִחוּץ לַמַּחֲנֶה וְאֶל פֶּתַח" וגו', וַאֲנָא יָדַעְנָא דְּשׁוֹר אוֹ כֶּשֶׂב אוֹ עֵז הוּא. וְאִילּוּ חַטָּאת שַׁיְּירֵיהּ. וְלָא רַבְּיֵיהּ לְחִיּוּבָא. אִי נֵימָא בִּזְמַנּוֹ. וְלִשְׁמוֹ. מַאי אִירְיָא. אָשָׁם דְּרַבְּיֵיהּ? חַטָּאת נַמִי מְחַיֵּיב! יב] דְּלָא בָּעֵי רִבּוּיָא, וַאֲפִילּוּ אָשָׁם, דְּהָא חֲזִי בִּפְנִים! אֶלָּא שֶׁלֹּא בִּזְמַנּוֹ. רַבְּיֵיהּ לְחִיּוּבָא בְּאָשָׁם. אִי לִשְׁמוֹ אָשָׁם אַמַּאי חַיָּיב. וְהָא אֵינוֹ כָּשֵׁר לִיקְרַב, יג] וּמַתְנִי' תָּנָא פָּטוּר. וְאִי מִשּׁוּם דְּרָאוּי לְשֶׁלֹּא לִשְׁמוֹ בִּפְנִי' – הָא מְחוּסַּר עִיקָּר', וְכוּלְּהוּ מוֹדוּ בּוֹ! אֶלָּא לָאו שֶׁלֹּא לִשְׁמוֹ רַבִּי לְחִיּוּבָא בַּחוּץ, כְּרַב חִלְקִיָּה. אַלְמָא דָּבָר שֶׁאֵינוֹ כָּשֵׁר לִשְׁמוֹ בִּפְנִים – כָּשֵׁר לְשֶׁלֹּא לִשְׁמוֹ, וּמְחַיֵּיב עָלֶיהָ שֶׁלֹּא לִשְׁמוֹ בַּחוּץ. ה"ג: "לְעוֹלָם בִּזְמַנּוֹ וְשֶׁלֹּא לִשְׁמוֹ". א"נ, ה"ג: "לְעוֹלָם בִּזְמַנּוֹ" וְתוּ לָא, וּמִמֵּילָא אַשֶּׁלֹּא לִשְׁמוֹ דְּאוֹקִימְנָא קָאֵי. יד] וְשֶׁכָּתְבוּ בַּסְּפָרִים "וְלִשְׁמוֹ" – (ב) מְפָרֵשׁ טוֹעֶה כְּתָבוֹ, וְלִפּוּס רִיהֲטָא, מִשּׁוּם דְּפָרְכִינַן לְעֵיל: אִי נֵימָא בִּזְמַנּוֹ מַאי אִירְיָא כו', וְקָא בָּעֵי לְשַׁנּוּיֵי: לְעוֹלָם בִּזְמַנּוֹ וְלִשְׁמוֹ, וּדְקָא קַשְׁיָא לָךְ: אִי הָכִי חַטָּאת נַמִי – אֵין ה"נ, וְתָנָא אָשָׁם וְהוּא הַדִּין לְחַטָּאת. וְלָאו מִילְּתָא הִיא, דְּא"כ ר"א מַאי בָּעֵי הָכָא? מִכְּדֵי ר"א לְעִנְיַן שֶׁלֹּא לִשְׁמוֹ אַקְּשֵׁיהּ בְּפ"ק (לעיל י:), בִּפְסוּל אָשָׁם שֶׁלֹּא לִשְׁמוֹ כְּחַטָּאת, אֲבָל לְעִנְיַן לִשְׁמוֹ מַאי עִיקָּר וּמַאי טָפֵל אִיכָּא? תַּרְוַיְיהוּ כְּתִיבִי לְהַכְשִׁיר בִּפְנִים וְחִיּוּב בַּחוּץ! וְתוּ: ל"ל לְרַבּוּיֵי לְהַאי מִשּׁוֹר וְכֶשֶׂב וָעֵז? הֲרֵי כָּשֵׁר לִיקְרַב, וּכְמִצְוָתוֹ בִּפְנִים הוּא שׁוֹחֲטוֹ בַּחוּץ! אֶלָּא קָא מְשַׁנֵּי: לְעוֹלָם בִּזְמַנּוֹ וְשֶׁלֹּא לִשְׁמוֹ, וְאִיצְטְרִיךְ לְרַבּוּיֵיהּ מִשּׁוּם דְּשֶׁלֹּא לִשְׁמוֹ פָּסוּל הוּא. וְר"א הִיא. דְּמַקִּישׁ אָשָׁם לְחַטָּאת, דְּמִיפְסִיל בְּשֶׁלֹּא לִשְׁמוֹ בִּפְנִים טו] *בָּאֲשָׁמוֹת, דְּאַפ"ה מְחַיֵּיב עָלָהּ בַּחוּץ. אע"ג דְּעָקַר מִינֵּיהּ שֵׁם אָשָׁם, הַכְּתִי אִי הֲוָה מְעַיֵּיל לֵיהּ לִפְנִים – הֲוָה כָּשֵׁר לְמִישְׁחֲטֵיהּ סְתָמָא, וְכָשֵׁר לְשֵׁם אָשָׁם, וְעוֹלֶה (ג) לְשֵׁם חוֹבָה. דְּמִשּׁוּם דִּיבּוּרֵיהּ לָא מִיעֲקַר שְׁמֵיהּ מִינֵּיהּ, וְכׇל כַּמָּה דְּלָא שָׁחֲטֵיהּ טז] *בְּעִיקָּרֵהּ קָאֵי סְתָמָא לִשְׁמוֹ. הִלְכָּךְ, כִּי שָׁחֵיט לֵיהּ – רָאוּי לִפְנִים לִשְׁמוֹ הָיָה. וְה"ה דְּחַטָּאת שֶׁלֹּא לִשְׁמוֹ נַמִי חַיָּיב. אֶלָּא תָּנָא טָפֵל, וְאַשְׁמְעִינַן אע"ג דְּהָכָא פָּסוּל בִּפְנִים – מִיחַיֵּיב עָלֶיהָ בַּחוּץ, וְה"ה לְעִיקָּר, דְּמ"ש? סוֹף סוֹף תַּרְוַיְיהוּ פְּסִילֵי שֶׁלֹּא לִשְׁמָן. וּבְת"כ קָתָנֵי בָּהּ בְּהֶדְיָא שֶׁלֹּא לִשְׁמוֹ, וְע"כ מוֹקֵי לָהּ כְּר"א, דְּאִילּוּ לְרַבָּנַן – לָא אִיצְטְרִיךְ לֵיהּ לְרַבּוּיֵי, דְּהָא כִּי הַאי גַּוְונָא מִתְקַבֶּלֶת בִּפְנִים הִיא. ת"ש. סַיַּיעְתָּא לְרַב חִלְקִיָּה, וּתְיוּבְתָּא דְּרַב הוּנָא. בְּגוּפָהּ. כְּגוֹן תּוֹךְ שְׁמוֹנָה לְלֵידָתָהּ. יָכוֹל שֶׁאֲנִי מְרַבֶּה יז] גָּרֵס הָכָא, דְּרֵישָׁא דִּלְעֵיל הִיא. וּבְתוֹרַת כֹּהֲנִים הָכִי תַּנְיָא לָהּ: אוֹצִיא אֶת אֵלּוּ שֶׁאֵינָן מְיוּחָדִין לַשֵּׁם, וְלֹא אוֹצִיא עוֹלָה מְחוּסֶּרֶת זְמַן בְּגוּפָהּ, וְחַטָּאת בֵּין בְּגוּפָהּ כו'. וְהַגַּרְסָנִין שִׁינּוּ אֶת הַלָּשׁוֹן יח] וְגָרְסִינַן הָכָא "יָכוֹל שֶׁאֲנִי מְרַבֶּה אֶת" כו', *לְפִי שֶׁהֱבִיאוּהָ יט] בְּלִימּוּדָא אַחֲרִינָא, וּסְבָרֵי דְּסֵיפָא דְּהַהִיא דִּלְעֵיל הִיא. יָכוֹל שֶׁאֲנִי מְרַבֶּה כ] *)מִשּׁוּם מכ"מ אַף עוֹלָה מְחוּסַּר זְמַן וכו'. וְחַטָּאת בֵּין בְּגוּפָהּ בֵּין בַּבְּעָלִים. כְּגוֹן שֶׁל נָזִיר וּמְצוֹרָע שֶׁלֹּא מָלְאוּ יְמֵיהֶם. וְאִילּוּ אֲשַׁם נָזִיר וּמְצוֹרָע מְחוּסְּרֵי זְמַן בְּעָלִים – שַׁיְּירֵיהּ, וְלָא רַבְּיֵיהּ לִפְטוֹרָא. שְׁמַע מִינַּהּ ס"ל דְּחַיָּיב. וּבְמַאי אִי נֵימָא בְּלִשְׁמוֹ אָשָׁם נַמִי נִיפְטְרֵיהּ. דְּהָא לָא חֲזִי. אֶלָּא שֶׁלֹּא לִשְׁמוֹ. הִלְכָּךְ, חַטָּאת פָּטוּר – דְּלָא חֲזֵי לִפְנִים, וְאָשָׁם חַיָּיב – דַּחֲזֵי לִפְנִים, וְאַף עַל גַּב דְּאֵין כא] רָאוּי לִשְׁמוֹ. וְהַיְינוּ כְּרַב חִלְקִיָּה, וּדְלָא כְּרַב הוּנָא. ה"ג: הָא מַנִּי ר"א הִיא כו' וְלָא גָּרְסִינַן "לְעוֹלָם בְּלִשְׁמוֹ". הָא מַנִּי ר"א הִיא. כְּלוֹמַר, וַדַּאי בְּשֶׁלֹּא לִשְׁמוֹ הִיא, כִּדְקָאָמְרַתְּ. הִלְכָּךְ, חַטָּאת פָּטוּר – דְּלָא חֲזֵי בִּפְנִים, לָא בְּלִשְׁמוֹ וְלָא בְּשֶׁלֹּא לִשְׁמוֹ, דִּמְחוּסַּר זְמַן הוּא. וְאָשָׁם נַמִי פָּטוּר – דְּלָא חֲזֵי לִפְנִים לִשְׁמוֹ בִּמְחוּסַּר זְמַן, וְלָא לְשֶׁלֹּא לִשְׁמוֹ, דְּר"א קָאָמַר דְּפָסוּל בְּאָשָׁם שֶׁלֹּא לִשְׁמוֹ. וְהַאי דְּשַׁיְּירֵיהּ לְאָשָׁם – לָאו דְּס"ל דְּחַיָּיב. אֶלָּא כֵּיוָן דְּחַד טַעְמָא הוּא, מִשּׁוּם דְּתַרְוַיְיהוּ פְּסוּלִין שֶׁלֹּא לִשְׁמוֹ בִּפְנִים הוּא, תָּנָא עִיקָּר חַטָּאת דְּפָטוּר, וְכ"ש טָפֵל אָשָׁם. וְהַאי "כ"ש" גִּמְגּוּם. וְדוֹחֲקֵיהּ דְּרַב הוּנָא לְאוֹקְמֵיהּ כְּר"א – מִשּׁוּם סֵיפָא, דְּעַל כׇּרְחָךְ כְּרַבִּי אֱלִיעֶזֶר מִיתּוֹקְמָא, כִּדְפָרֵישְׁנָא לְעֵיל. וְעוֹד: מִשּׁוּם דִּלְרַבָּנַן כב] לָא יָלְפִינַן אָשָׁם מֵחַטָּאת לֵיכָּא לְמֵימַר "תָּנָא הַאי וְהוּא הַדִּין לְהַאי". וְאַף עַל גַּב דִּלְרַבָּנַן נַמִי קָאָמַר דְּפָטוּר, דְּאֵין לָךְ דָּבָר שֶׁאֵינוֹ כָּשֵׁר לִשְׁמוֹ וְכָשֵׁר שֶׁלֹּא לִשְׁמוֹ – לָא מָצֵי לְאוֹקוּמָהּ כְּרַבָּנַן, דְּא"כ כג] נַשְׁמְעִינַן אָשָׁם דְּפָטוּר, דְּנַשְׁמְעִינַן בָּהּ תַּרְתֵּי, וְכ"ש חַטָּאת. ת"ש דְּכִי אֲתָא רַב דִּימִי כו' וְאִילּוּ חַטָּאת שַׁיְּירָא וּבְמַאי כו'. כד] כִּדְאוֹתִיבְנָא (ד) בְּקַמַּיְיתָא. וּמַאי קוּשְׁיָא. לְסַיּוּעָהּ לְרַב חִלְקִיָּה? דִּלְמָא ה"נ כִּדְאָמְרִינַן, דְּבִזְמַנּוֹ קָאֵי כִּדְאוֹקְמָא בְּקַמַּיְיתָא לְעֵיל, וְר"א הִיא! אָמַר ר"נ בַּר יִצְחָק. לָא מָצֵי לְאוֹקוּמֵי לְהָא בִּזְמַנּוֹ, מִשּׁוּם דְּרַב דִּימִי קַשְׁיָא לֵיהּ דְּתָנֵי כה] (לֵיהּ) בַּר לִיוָאי אַדְּתָנֵי לֵוִי: שְׁחָטָן מְחוּסַּר זְמַן בַּבְּעָלִים פְּסוּלִין, וּבַחוּץ נַמִי נִפְטָר. וּמְשַׁנֵּי כו] לֵיהּ רַב דִּימִי. הָא דְּתָנֵי חַיָּיב – שֶׁלֹּא לִשְׁמוֹ. וְהָא דְּתָנֵי פְּסוּלִין, וְדִכְוָותֵיהּ בַּחוּץ פָּטוּר – בְּשֶׁשְּׁחָטָן לִשְׁמוֹ. וּמִדְּקַשְׁיָא לֵיהּ דְּתָנֵי לֵוִי אַבַּר לִיוָאי – ש"מ שְׁמִיעַ לֵיהּ לְרַב דִּימִי דְּמַתְנִי' דְּבַר לִיוָאי נַמִי בִּמְחוּסַּר זְמַן, וְקָאָמַר: חַיָּיב. וְאע"ג דְּאֵינוֹ רָאוּי לִשְׁמוֹ בִּפְנִים, רָאוּי לְשֶׁלֹּא לִשְׁמוֹ, וְסַיַּיעְתָּא לְרַב חִלְקִיָּה. רַב אַשִׁי רָמֵי מַתְנִי'. דְּקָתָנֵי: לִשְׁמוֹ פָּטוּר – אַבָּרַיְיתָא קַמַּיְיתָא דְּתַנְיָא לְעֵיל: חַיָּיב. וּמְשַׁנֵּי: מַתְנִי' לִשְׁמוֹ וּבָרַיְיתָא שֶׁלֹּא לִשְׁמוֹ. כְּרַב חִלְקִיָּה. נֵימָא תֶּהֱוֵי תְּיוּבְתֵּיהּ דְּרַב הוּנָא. כז] מ"ד דְּכִי אֲתָא רַב דִּימִי. כִּדְאָמְרָן, דְּלֵיכָּא לְאוֹקוּמָא בִּזְמַנּוֹ, מִדְּקַשְׁיָא לֵיהּ תְּנֵי לֵוִי אַדְּתָנֵי בַּר לִיוָאי. הָכָא בְּמַאי עָסְקִינַן. דִּמְחוּסַּר זְמַן חַיָּיב בְּשֶׁלֹּא לִשְׁמוֹ. כְּגוֹן שֶׁהִפְרִישׁ שְׁנֵי אֲשָׁמוֹת לְאַחֲרָיוּת. שֶׁאִם יֹאבַד הָאֶחָד יִתְכַּפֵּר בַּשֵּׁנִי, וְשָׁחַט אֶחָד מֵהֶם בַּחוּץ קוֹדֶם זְמַנּוֹ לְשֵׁם עוֹלָה. דְּהַאי כֵּיוָן דִּמְוֹתוֹ לִרְעִיָּיה קָאֵי, דְּאָשָׁם שֶׁכִּיפְּרוּ בְּעָלָיו רוֹעֶה, וְדָמָיו לְקַיִץ הַמִּזְבֵּחַ שֶׁהִיא עוֹלָה – חֲזֵי לְדוּכְתֵּיהּ בִּפְנִים, אִי שָׁחֵיט לְגוּפֵיהּ לְעוֹלָה.

כִּדְרַב

*) ס"א משור

פסח בשאר ימות השנה שלמים הוא. פי' בקונטרס: ואין זה אלא לשמו. משמע שרוצה לומר דכיון דשלמים הוא, כששוחטו לשם שלמים – היינו לשמו. וא"ת: והלא כששחטו לשם עולה או לשם זבח אחר – הוי נמי שלמים, כדאמרי' בפ"ק (לעיל ח:): לכל דשחיט ליה – שלמים ליהוי! וי"ל: דמ"מ, כיון דשלמים הוא – הרי הוא כשר לשמו ושלא לשמו, כגון לשם שלמים ולשם זבח אחר.

מחוסר זמן בבעלים. אעולה דוקא קאי, ולא אאידך.

או שהיו בני שתי שנים ושחטן פסולין. הך ברייתא איתא בפ' "התכלת" (מנחות מח:), והכא והתם קתני "פסולין". ועוד תניא התם באידך ברייתא: פסולין, ותעובר צורתן ויצאו לבית השריפה. ותימה: דבתמורה בפ' "אלו קדשים" (דף יט:) תניא: אשם בן שנה והביאו בן שתים, בן שתים והביאו בן שנה – כשרים, ולא עלו *לשם בעלים לשם חובה. [נ"ל לבעלים] ר"ש אומר: כל עצמן אינן קדושים! וי"ל: דכאן – לשמו, כאן – שלא לשמו, כדמשני הכא. ומיהו קשה: דא"כ קשיא לרב הונא, הא איכא האי דפסול לשמו וכשר שלא לשמו! ועוד: דאי בשלא לשמו מיירי בתמורה – ל"ל למיתני "ולא עלו לשם חובה"? הא אפי' במלותו נמי, דכיון דשלא לשמו הוא – אין עולה לשם חובה!

שיטה מקובצת

א] אף עולה מחוסר: ב] שלא בזמנו ובמאי: ג] ור' אלעזר אות י' נמחק: ד] מרבה עולה מחוסר זמן: ה] שלא לשמו הא מני ר' אלעזר היא ותיבות לעולם שלא לשמו ואות ו' נמחק: ו] דבי בר לואי תיבת ר' נמחק: ז] בבעלים ואשם נזיר ואשם מצורע ונסיב לה תלמודא לחיובא ולא ידענא מאי תלמודא אמר רבינא מאי טעמא לא ידעת שור מ"מ. והשאר נמחק: ח] מ"מ ומאי קשיא דלמא כדאמרת אמר רב נחמן בר יצחק משום דקשיא ליה דתני דבי בר לואי ותיבות רומיא דרמי ל"ש וגם מה שיש גורסים הא אמאי תרמיה דבעי למרמי ר' נמחק: ט] לוי דתני לוי אשם: י] תיבות ומשני רב דימי ל"ש: יא] תיבת מעיקרא נמחק: יב] נמי מחייב ואפילו אשם לא בעי רבוייא דהא: יג] ליקרב ובמתני': יד] קאי ושכתוב: טו] בפנים ואשמועינן דאפ"ה: טז] ליה בעקירה קאי: יז] מרבה לא גרס הכא דרישא דההיא דלעיל היא: יח] הלשון וגרסי הכא: יט] שהביאוה בתלמודא אחרונה וסברי תיבת בלימודא ל"ש ותיבת אחרינא נמחק: כ] מרבה משור תיבת משום ל"ש: כא] ראויה לשמו והיינו: כב] דלרבנן דלא ילפי אשם: כג] דא"כ נשמעינה אשם: כד] כדאוקמא ברייתא לעיל ותיבת בקמייתא נמחק: כה] תיבת ליה נמחק: כו] ומשני לה רב דימי: כז] הונא הא דבי אות ה' נמחק:

פסחים סה.

לעיל י: מנחות כח.

(יומא סג.)

ס"א אינו

ס"א עז מ"מ ואילו חטאת כו' הא אמאי תרמייה דלמא ה"נ וכדאמרת בקמייתא אמר ר"נ כו'

ס"א ולשמעינן

נ"א בעקירת שמו עדיין קאי סתמא

נ"ל לפי שהביאוה התלמוד אחרונה וסברי דסיפא כו'

הגהות הב"ח

(א) גמ' א"ר נחמן ב"י משום: (ב) רש"י ד"ה ה"ג לעולם וכו' ולשמו מספר טעות כתבו: (ג) ד"ה ור"א היא וכו' ועולה לבעלים לשם חובה: (ד) ד"ה ת"ש וכו' בקמייתא הס"ד ואח"כ מ"ה הא אמאי כו' ומאי קושיא וכו' כדאוקמא בקושייתא לעיל.

גמרא

כְּדְרַב הוּנָא אָמַר רַב. דְּאָמַר *רַב הוּנָא אָמַר רַב: אָשָׁם שֶׁנִּיתַּק לִרְעִיָּה וּשְׁחָטוֹ סְתָם — כָּשֵׁר לְעוֹלָה.§ "הַמַּעֲלֶה מִבְּשַׂר חַטָּאת" [וכו'].§ ת"ר: מִנַּיִן לַמַּעֲלֶה מִבְּשַׂר חַטָּאת, וּמִבְּשַׂר אָשָׁם, וּמִבְּשַׂר קָדְשֵׁי קָדָשִׁים, וּמִבְּשַׂר קָדָשִׁים קַלִּים, וּמִמּוֹתַר הָעוֹמֶר, וּשְׁתֵּי הַלֶּחֶם, וְלֶחֶם הַפָּנִים, וּשְׁיָרֵי מְנָחוֹת שֶׁפָּטוּר? ת"ל: "עוֹלָה", מָה עוֹלָה שֶׁהִיא רְאוּיָה לְהַעֲלָאָה — אַף כֹּל שֶׁרְאוּיָה לְהַעֲלָאָה. מִנַּיִן שֶׁאַף הַיּוֹצֵק, וְהַבּוֹלֵל, וְהַפּוֹתֵת, וְהַמּוֹלֵחַ, וְהַמֵּנִיף, וְהַמַּגִּישׁ, וְהַמְסַדֵּר הַשֻּׁלְחָן, וְהַמֵּטִיב אֶת הַנֵּרוֹת, וְהַקּוֹמֵץ, וְהַמְקַבֵּל א] בַּחוּץ, שֶׁפָּטוּר? ת"ל: °"אֲשֶׁר יַעֲלֶה עוֹלָה אוֹ זָבַח", מַה הַעֲלָאָה שֶׁהִיא גְּמַר עֲבוֹדָה — אַף כֹּל שֶׁהוּא גְּמַר עֲבוֹדָה.§ "עַד שֶׁלֹּא הוּקַם הַמִּשְׁכָּן" [וכו'].§ יָתֵיב רַב (א) ב] הוּנָא בַּר רַב קְטִינָא קַמֵּיהּ *דְּרַב חִסְדָּא, וְקָא קָרֵי: °"וַיִּשְׁלַח אֶת נַעֲרֵי בְּנֵי יִשְׂרָאֵל". א"ל: הָכִי אָמַר ר' אַסִי ג] (קָרְבוּ) וּפָסְקוּ. סָבַר לְאוֹתוּבֵיהּ מִמַּתְנִיתִין, שַׁמְעֵיהּ דְּקָאָמַר מִשְּׁמֵיהּ דְּרַב אַדָּא בַּר אַהֲבָה: *עוֹלָה שֶׁהִקְרִיבוּ יִשְׂרָאֵל בַּמִּדְבָּר אֵינָהּ טְעוּנָה הֶפְשֵׁט וְנִיתּוּחַ. ד] אוֹתְבֵיהּ בָּרַיְיתָא דְּשַׁוְיָא בְּכוּלְּהוּ. דְּתַנְיָא: עַד שֶׁלֹּא הוּקַם הַמִּשְׁכָּן — ה] הַבָּמוֹת מוּתָּרוֹת, וַעֲבוֹדָה בִּבְכוֹרוֹת, וְהַכֹּל כְּשֵׁירִין ו] לְהַקְרִיב בְּהֵמָה חַיָּה וְעוֹף, זְכָרִים וּנְקֵבוֹת, תְּמִימִין וּבַעֲלֵי מוּמִין, טְהוֹרִין אֲבָל לֹא טְמֵאִין. וְהַכֹּל קָרְבוּ עוֹלוֹת. וְעוֹלָה שֶׁהִקְרִיבוּ יִשְׂרָאֵל בַּמִּדְבָּר טְעוּנָה הֶפְשֵׁט וְנִיתּוּחַ. וְגוֹיִם בַּזְּמַן הַזֶּה רַשָּׁאִין לַעֲשׂוֹת כֵּן! תַּנָּאֵי הִיא, דְּתַנְיָא: °"וְגַם הַכֹּהֲנִים הַנִּגָּשִׁים אֶל ה' יִתְקַדָּשׁוּ" — ר' יְהוֹשֻׁעַ בֶּן קָרְחָה אוֹמֵר: זוֹ פְּרִישׁוּת בְּכוֹרוֹת. רַבִּי אוֹמֵר: זוֹ פְּרִישׁוּת נָדָב וַאֲבִיהוּא. בִּשְׁלָמָא לְמ"ד: זוֹ פְּרִישׁוּת נָדָב וַאֲבִיהוּא — הַיְינוּ דִּכְתִיב: °"הוּא אֲשֶׁר דִּבֶּר ה' לֵאמֹר בִּקְרֹבַי אֶקָּדֵשׁ", אֶלָּא לְמ"ד: זוֹ פְּרִישׁוּת בְּכוֹרוֹת, הֵיכָא רְמִיזָא? דִּכְתִיב: °"וְנֹעַדְתִּי שָׁמָּה לִבְנֵי יִשְׂרָאֵל וְנִקְדַּשׁ בִּכְבֹדִי", אַל תִּקְרֵי "בִּכְבוֹדִי" אֶלָּא: ז] "בִּמְכוּבָּדַיי". דָּבָר זֶה אָמַר הקב"ה לְמֹשֶׁה, וְלֹא יָדְעוּ עַד שֶׁמֵּתוּ בְּנֵי אַהֲרֹן. כֵּיוָן שֶׁמֵּתוּ בְּנֵי אַהֲרֹן אָמַר לוֹ: אַהֲרֹן אָחִי, לֹא מֵתוּ בָּנֶיךָ אֶלָּא לְהַקְדִּישׁ ח] שְׁמוֹ שֶׁל הקב"ה. כֵּיוָן שֶׁיָּדַע אַהֲרֹן שֶׁבָּנָיו יְדוּעֵי מָקוֹם הֵן — שָׁתַק וְקִבֵּל שָׂכָר, ט] שֶׁנֶּאֱמַר: °"וַיִּדֹּם אַהֲרֹן". וְכֵן *בְּדָוִד הוּא אוֹמֵר: °"דּוֹם לַה' וְהִתְחוֹלֵל לוֹ", *אע"פ שֶׁמַּפִּיל לְךָ חֲלָלִים חֲלָלִים — אַתְּ י] שְׁתוֹק. וְכֵן יא] *בִּשְׁלֹמֹה הוּא אוֹמֵר: °"עֵת לַחֲשׁוֹת וְעֵת לְדַבֵּר", פְּעָמִים יב] שֶׁשּׁוֹתֵק וּמְקַבֵּל שָׂכָר עַל הַשְּׁתִיקָה, יג] פְּעָמִים מְדַבֵּר וּמְקַבֵּל שָׂכָר עַל הַדִּבּוּר. וְהַיְינוּ דְּא"ר חִיָּיא בַּר אַבָּא א"ר יוֹחָנָן, מַאי דִּכְתִיב: °"נוֹרָא אֱלֹהִים מִמִּקְדָּשֶׁיךָ", אַל תִּיקְרֵי "מִמִּקְדָּשֶׁיךָ" — אֶלָּא: "מִמְּקוּדָּשֶׁיךָ", בְּשָׁעָה יד] *שֶׁעוֹשֶׂה הקב"ה דִּין בִּקְדוֹשָׁיו — מִתְיָירֵא וּמִתְעַלֶּה וּמִתְהַלֵּל. אֶלָּא קַשְׁיָא עוֹלָה! תְּרֵי תַּנָּאֵי הִיא. *דְּתַנְיָא, ר' יִשְׁמָעֵאל אוֹמֵר: כְּלָלוֹת נֶאֶמְרוּ בְּסִינַי, וּפְרָטוֹת טו] בְּאֹהֶל מוֹעֵד. ר"ע אוֹמֵר: כְּלָלוֹת וּפְרָטוֹת נֶאֶמְרוּ בְּסִינַי, וְנִשְׁנוּ בְּאֹהֶל מוֹעֵד, וְנִשְׁתַּלְּשׁוּ בְּעַרְבוֹת מוֹאָב. אָמַר מָר: הַכֹּל כְּשֵׁירִין לְהַקְרִיב. מְנָא הָנֵי מִילֵּי? אָמַר רַב הוּנָא, דְּאָמַר קְרָא: °"וַיִּבֶן נֹחַ מִזְבֵּחַ לַה' וַיִּקַּח מִכֹּל הַבְּהֵמָה הַטְּהוֹרָה וּמִכֹּל עוֹף הַטָּהוֹר", "בְּהֵמָה" — טז] כְּמַשְׁמָעוֹ, *חַיָּה — בִּכְלַל בְּהֵמָה. זְכָרִים

(מראי מקומות בשולי הגמרא: ויקרא טז; שמות כד; שם יט; ויקרא י; שמות כט; ויקרא י; תהלים לז; קהלת ג; תהלים סח; בראשית ח)

תוספות

מה העלאה שהיא גמר עבודה כו'. סוגיא זו קשה אההיא דלעיל בריש "השוחט" (דף קו: ושם) דדרשינן: להכי כתב רחמנא "או" — לרבות את הזורק דלא תיתי מיניה, ומשום הכי פטור מקבל בחוץ.

ויתיב וקאמר וישלח וגו'. פירש בקונטרס: ויתיב רב חסדא וקאמר *ונראה לפרש: ד"יתיב וקאמר" ארב הונא קאי. **א"ל** הכי אמר רב אסי ופסקוהו. פי': כמו שאמרת אמר רב אסי ד"וישלח" היינו עבודה בבכורות. אבל חכמים הפסיקוהו ומנעוהו מלומר כן. ושני לשונות שבקונטרס עיקר.

רמזו הקב"ה למשה ולא ידעו. פי': ולא ידע במי. אבל היה יודע שעתיד הקב"ה לקדש את המשכן באדם גדול, דאמרי' במדרש,* שאמר לו משה לאהרן: הייתי סבור כי או בך.

וקיבל שכר על שתיקתו. תניא בתורת כהנים: שבשכר זה נתייחד אליו הדיבור, דכתיב בפרשת "יין ושכר אל תשת": "וידבר ה' אל אהרן", ולא כתיב "אל משה". ותימה: דבסיפרי דריש בפרשת קרח, דכתיב "וידבר אל אהרן": שומע אני שהדיבור אל אהרן, ת"ל "כאשר דבר ה' ביד משה לו" בפרשת מחתות השרופים. הא למדנו שהדיבור למשה שיאמר לאהרן! ושמא זה קורא "נתייחד" — הא דכתיב "אל אהרן", ולא שיאמר לבני ישראל.

כללות נאמרו בסיני כו'. הוה מצי לאיתויי מדר' יוסי הגלילי דאמר בפ"ק דחגיגה (דף ו: ולקמן קכ.) דאין טעונה הפשט וניתוח. ודלמא

רש"י

כְּדְרַב הוּנָא אָמַר רַב כו' שֶׁנִּיתַּק לִרְעִיָּה. שֶׁנִּיתַּק מִדִּין הַקְרָבָה וּמְסָרוּהוּ לְרוֹעֶה עַד שֶׁיִּסְתָּאֵב, דְּקי"ל (תמורה דף יח.): כָּל שֶׁבְּחַטָּאת מֵתָה בְּאָשָׁם רוֹעֶה. עוֹלָה. "אֲשֶׁר יַעֲלֶה עוֹלָה". גְּמַר עֲבוֹדָה. שֶׁאֵין אַחֲרֶיהָ עֲבוֹדָה. וְאִיתְרַבּוּ לְהוּ בְּ"אַף כֹּל" כְּגוֹן הַמְנַסֵּךְ וּמַקְטִיר קְטֹרֶת וּמַקְטִיר קְמָצִים יז] וּמַקְטִיר מִנְחַת כֹּהֲנִים. וְיָתֵיב רַב חִסְדָּא וְקָאָמַר וַיִּשְׁלַח אֶת נַעֲרֵי בְּנֵי יִשְׂרָאֵל. נִרְאֶה בְּעֵינַי שֶׁהַסְּפָרִים חֲסֵרִים כָּאן, וְלֹא יָדַעְתִּי מָה. וְאִם אֵין חֲסֵרִין זֶהוּ פֵּירוּשׁוֹ: יָתֵיב רַב חִסְדָּא וְקָאָמַר לְהַאי קְרָא "וַיִּשְׁלַח אֶת נַעֲרֵי" וגו', וּמְפָרֵשׁ דְּאֵלּוּ הַבְּכוֹרוֹת. א"ל רַב הוּנָא הָכִי אָמַר רַב אַסִי וּפָסְקוּ. אוֹתוֹ הַיּוֹם פָּסְקָה עֲבוֹדָה מִן הַבְּכוֹרוֹת. שֶׁמִּסִּינַי נִלְוּוּ עַל הַכְּהוּנָּה כִּדְיָלֵיף לְקַמָּן, וְשִׁמְּשׁוּ נָדָב וַאֲבִיהוּא כָּל אוֹתָהּ שָׁנָה רִאשׁוֹנָה עַד שֶׁהוּקַם הַמִּשְׁכָּן, וּמֵתוּ. לִישָּׁנָא אַחֲרִינָא: הָכִי אָמַר רַב אַסִי וּפְסָקֵיהּ. צָרִיךְ לְהַפְסִיק כָּאן יח] נְגִינַת טַעַם הַמִּקְרָא בְּאֶתְנַחְתָּא, וְלֹא יִקְרָא בְּטַעַם פַּשְׁטָא כְּמוֹ שֶׁאָנוּ קוֹרִין אוֹתוֹ. דִּכְשֶׁהוּא נִקְרָא בְּטַעַם פַּשְׁטָא מַשְׁמַע שֶׁקְּרִיאַת "נַעֲרֵי בְּנֵי יִשְׂרָאֵל" דָּבֵק עַל "וַיַּעֲלוּ עוֹלוֹת", מַשְׁמַע שֶׁהֵם הֶעֱלוּם. אֲבָל כְּשֶׁאַתָּה קוֹרֵהוּ בְּאֶתְנַחְתָּא — עוֹמֶדֶת הַתֵּיבָה לְבַדָּהּ וְאֵינָהּ דָּבֵק עַל "וַיַּעֲלוּ", וְי"ל שֶׁלֹּא שְׁלָחָם אֶלָּא לְהָבִיא הַקָּרְבָּנוֹת וְלַעֲמוֹד עֲלֵיהֶם. "וַיַּעֲלוּ עוֹלוֹת" — אוֹתָם שֶׁכְּשֵׁרִים לְהַעֲלוֹתָם, דְּהַיְינוּ נָדָב וַאֲבִיהוּא, שֶׁמִּשֶּׁבָּאוּ לְסִינַי הוּפְרְשׁוּ הַכֹּהֲנִים, כִּדְיָלֵיף לְקַמָּן. סָבַר רַב חִסְדָּא יט] לְאוֹתְבֵיהּ מַתְנִי'. דְּקָתָנֵי שֶׁנָּהֲגוּ עֲבוֹדָה בִּבְכוֹרוֹת עַד יוֹם הֲקָמַת הַמִּשְׁכָּן. שַׁמְעֵיהּ. רַב חִסְדָּא, לְרַב *חָנָא דְּיָתֵיב וְקָאָמַר תּוּ מִשְּׁמֵיהּ דְּרַב אַדָּא כו'. כ] אֵיתִיבֵיהּ מִבָּרַיְיתָא דְּשַׁוְיָא בְּכוּלְּהוּ. שֶׁתְּהֵא שָׁוָה לְהָשִׁיב עַל כָּל דְּבָרָיו. עוֹלָה שֶׁהִקְרִיבוּ יִשְׂרָאֵל בְּמִדְבַּר סִינַי. קוֹדֶם מַתַּן תּוֹרָה: "וַיִּשְׁלַח אֶת נַעֲרֵי" וגו'. וְהַכֹּל כְּשֵׁרִין לִיקְרַב. כִּדְמְפָרֵשׁ וְאָזֵיל: בְּהֵמָה וְחַיָּה וְעוֹף כו'. וְהַכֹּל קָרְבוּ עוֹלוֹת. הַשְׁתָּא מַשְׁמַע שֶׁלֹּא הָיוּ מַקְרִיבִין אֶלָּא עוֹלוֹת. וּלְקַמֵּיהּ פָּרֵיךְ עֲלֵיהּ. רַשָּׁאִין לַעֲשׂוֹת כֵּן. דְּלֹא נֶאֶסְרוּ לָהֶן הַבָּמוֹת. יִתְקַדָּשׁוּ. מִלַּעֲלוֹת. וְאע"פ שֶׁרְגִילִין לָגֶשֶׁת אֵלַי וּלְהַעֲלוֹת — הָעֵד בָּהֶן שֶׁלֹּא יַעֲלוּ בָּהָר. זוֹ פְּרִישַׁת בְּכוֹרוֹת. הִזְהִיר אֶת הַבְּכוֹרוֹת כא] לְהַפְרִישׁ מִן הָהָר. זוֹ פְּרִישַׁת נָדָב וַאֲבִיהוּא. כְּלוֹמַר, לֹא נִקְרְאוּ בְּכוֹרוֹת כֹּהֲנִים. אֶלָּא מִי הֵן הַכֹּהֲנִים הַנִּגָּשִׁים, שֶׁהוּזְהֲרוּ כָּאן לִפְרוֹשׁ מִן הָהָר — זֶה נָדָב וַאֲבִיהוּא, שֶׁנַּעֲשׂוּ כב] בְּסִינַי כֹּהֲנִים, וְהֵן הַכֹּהֲנִים הַנִּגָּשִׁים אֶל ה' לְהַקְרִיב קָרְבָּנוֹת. הַיְינוּ דִּכְתִיב. כְּשֶׁמֵּתוּ נָדָב וַאֲבִיהוּא: "אֲשֶׁר דִּבֶּר" וגו' — כִּדְקָאָמַר בְּסִינַי (שמות יט): "פֶּן יִפְרוֹץ (ב) בָּהֶם ה'". וְכֵיוָן שֶׁלֹּא נִזְהֲרוּ לִפְרוֹשׁ מִן הַהֵיכָל בַּהֲקָמַת הַמִּשְׁכָּן — פָּרַץ בָּהֶם. אֶלָּא לְמ"ד זוֹ פְּרִישַׁת בְּכוֹרוֹת הֵיכָא רְמִיזָא. ה"ג. וְלָא גָּרְסִי': פְּרִישַׁת נָדָב וַאֲבִיהוּא. הֵיכָא רְמִיזָא — מִיתַת נָדָב וַאֲבִיהוּא הֵיכָא רְמָזָהּ לְמֹשֶׁה קוֹדֶם לָכֵן. דְּקָאָמַר: "הוּא אֲשֶׁר דִּבֶּר". וְנִקְדַּשׁ בִּכְבוֹדִי. נֶאֶמְרָה לוֹ לְמֹשֶׁה בַּיּוֹם שֶׁנִּצְטַוָּוה עַל מְלֶאכֶת הַמִּשְׁכָּן, וְרָמַז לוֹ שֶׁבַּיּוֹם שֶׁיַּשְׁרֶה שְׁכִינָתוֹ עַל הַבַּיִת יִתְקַדֵּשׁ בִּכְבוֹדָיו, וְלֹא נִרְמַז לְהָבִין מַה הוּא עַד שֶׁמֵּתוּ. אֶלָּא כְּדֵי לְהִתְקַדֵּשׁ כְּבוֹדוֹ שֶׁל מָקוֹם עֲלֵיהֶם. לְהוֹדִיעַ שֶׁהוּא נוֹרָא עַל יְרֵאָיו וּמְיוּדָּעָיו. וְזֶהוּ "הוּא אֲשֶׁר דִּבֶּר" אֵלַי — בַּיּוֹם שֶׁנִּצְטַוֵּיתִי עַל הַמִּשְׁכָּן "וְנִקְדַּשׁ בִּכְבוֹדִי" — בְּאוֹתָם הַנִּכְבָּדִים וּקְרוֹבִים לִי אֶקָּדֵשׁ. שֶׁנֶּאֱמַר וַיִּדֹּם אַהֲרֹן. הֲרֵי שֶׁשָּׁתַק. וְקִבֵּל הַשָּׂכָר — מְפָרֵשׁ בְּת"כ: שֶׁמִּתּוֹךְ כָּךְ זָכָה וְנִתְיַיחֵד אֵלָיו הַדִּיבּוּר, שֶׁנֶּאֱמַר אַחֲרֵי אוֹתוֹ עִנְיָן פָּרָשַׁת שְׁתוּיֵי יַיִן, וְלֹא הוּזְכַּר בְּאוֹתוֹ דִּיבּוּר מֹשֶׁה אֶלָּא אַהֲרֹן. נוֹרָא אֱלֹהִים מִמִּקְדָּשֶׁךָ. "אֱלֹהִים" זוֹ מִדַּת הַדִּין. אֵימָתַי הוּא נוֹרָא — ע"י שֶׁהוּא עוֹשֶׂה דִּין בִּמְקוּדָּשָׁיו. אֶלָּא עוֹלָה קַשְׁיָא. דְּקָתָנֵי הָכָא כג] [דִּטְעוּנָה הֶפְשֵׁט] וְנִיתּוּחַ. כְּלָלוֹת נֶאֶמְרוּ בְּסִינַי. כְּגוֹן "מִזְבַּח אֲדָמָה תַּעֲשֶׂה לִּי וְזָבַחְתָּ עָלָיו" וגו', וְלֹא נִתְפָּרְשׁוּ הִלְכוֹת עוֹלָה וּשְׁלָמִים שָׁם. וּפְרָטוֹת בְּאֹהֶל מוֹעֵד. לְאַחַר שֶׁהוּקַם הַמִּשְׁכָּן נֶאֶמְרָה ת"כ לְמֹשֶׁה, וְשָׁם נִתְפָּרְשׁוּ "וְהִפְשִׁיט וְנִתַּח". (ג) לְרַבִּי יִשְׁמָעֵאל שָׁמְעִי' דְּעוֹלָה שֶׁהִקְרִיבוּ בְּסִינַי לֹא הוּטְעֲנָה הֶפְשֵׁט וְנִיתּוּחַ. כד] נִשְׁתַּלְּשׁוּ בְּעַרְבוֹת מוֹאָב. מִשְׁנֵה תּוֹרָה, שֶׁחָזַר מֹשֶׁה וַאֲמָרָהּ לָהֶם עַל הַסֵּדֶר, כִּדְכְתִיב (דברים א): "בְּעֵבֶר הַיַּרְדֵּן בְּאֶרֶץ מוֹאָב הוֹאִיל מֹשֶׁה" וגו'. חַיָּה בִּכְלַל בְּהֵמָה. דִּכְתִיב: "זֹאת הַבְּהֵמָה אֲשֶׁר תֹּאכֵלוּ" וגו' וְסָמֵיךְ לֵיהּ: "אַיָּל וּצְבִי וְיַחְמוּר" וגו' (שם יד). ה"ג

הערות בשוליים

תורה אור

נ"א ולי נראה לפרש כו' נ"ק

[רבה שמיני פרשה יב]

[שהקב"ה עושה דין במקודשיו כך גירסת הילקוט]

נ"א בהמה ועוף כמשמעו נ"ק

לעיל ה: קיב. נזיר כה: ע"... מנחות ז. פסחים ע... תמורה יח.

[לפי גי' רש"י צ"ל דר"... ויתיב רב חסדא וק... קרי]

חגיגה ו: ע"ש תוספתא דפרה פ"ג [לקמן קכ. ע"...]

[צ"ל הונא]

[גרסת הילקוט ע"י דוד

מוגהין סולקוש ע"י שלמה

חגיגה ו. סוטה לז:

[נדרים פא. וש"נ]

שיטה מקובצת

א] והמקבל דמים בחוץ: ב] רב חנא בר רב קטינא קמיה דרב חסדא ויתיב וקאמר וישלח את: ג] תיבת קרבו נמחק: ד] וניתוח אותביה מברייתא דשויא: ה] המשכן היו הבמות: ו] כשרין ליקרב אות ה' נמחק: ז] אלא בכבודי דבר זה רמז הקב"ה ואות מ' ל"ש ותיבת אמר נמחק: ח] להקדיש כבודו של מקום עליהם כיון שידע תיבות שמו של הקב"ה הוא טעות הדפוס: ט] שכר על שתיקתו שנאמר: י] את דום תיבת שתוק נמחק: יא] וכן שלמה הוא אומר: יב] פעמים שאדם שותק ומקבל אות ש' נמחק: יג] השתיקה ופעמים שמדבר ומקבל: יד] בשעה שהקב"ה עושה דין בקדושיו: טו] ופרטות נאמרו באהל מועד: טז] בהמה ועוף כמשמעו חיה הרי היא בכלל: יז] קמצים של מנחות: יח] כאן טעם נגינת המקרא: יט] לאותובי' ממתני': כ] כו' הס"ד ומה"ד עולה ואח"כ מה"ד איתיבי': כא] הבכורות לפרוש מן: כב] כהנים בסיני והן: כג] הכא דטעונה הפשט וניתוח: כד] מה"ד ונשתלשו בערבות.

הגהות הב"ח

(א) גמ' יתיב רב חנה ב... רב קטינא: (ב) רש"י ד"... היינו וכו' פן יפרוץ בם ה'... (ג) ד"ה ד"ה ופרטות וכו... ונתח שמעינן לרב... ישמעאל דעולה:

[תורה אור]

זְכָרִים וּנְקֵבוֹת, תְּמִימִין וּבַעֲלֵי מוּמִין — א] (*דְּאָמַר מָר: א*תַּמּוּת וְזַכְרוּת בִּבְהֵמָה, וְאֵין תַּמּוּת וְזַכְרוּת בְּעוֹפוֹת. וְאִיתַּקַּשׁ בְּהֵמָה לְעוֹף. תְּמִימִין וּבַעֲלֵי מוּמִין) — לְאַפּוּקֵי מְחוּסַּר אֵבֶר דְּלָא. ב] א"ר אֶלְעָזָר: *מִנַּיִן לִמְחוּסַּר אֵבֶר שֶׁנֶּאֱסַר לִבְנֵי נֹחַ — ת"ל: °"וּמִכָּל הָחַי מִכָּל בָּשָׂר", ג] אָמְרָה תּוֹרָה: הָבֵא בְּהֵמָה שֶׁחַיִּין רָאשֵׁי אֵיבָרִין שֶׁלָּהּ. וְדִילְמָא ד] לְמַעוּטֵי טְרֵיפָה! הַהוּא מִ"לְחַיּוֹת זֶרַע" נָפְקָא. הָנִיחָא *לְמ"ד: טְרֵיפָה אֵינָהּ יוֹלֶדֶת, אֶלָּא לְמ"ד: טְרֵיפָה יוֹלֶדֶת, מַאי אִיכָּא לְמֵימַר? הָאָמַר קְרָא: "אִתָּךְ" — בְּדוֹמִין לָךְ. וְדִילְמָא נֹחַ גּוּפֵיהּ טְרֵיפָה הֲוָה! "תָּמִים" כְּתִיב בֵּיהּ. וְדִילְמָא תָּמִים בִּדְרָכָיו! "צַדִּיק" כְּתִיב בֵּיהּ. וְדִילְמָא תָּמִים בִּדְרָכָיו, צַדִּיק בְּמַעֲשָׂיו! אִי סָלְקָא דַּעְתָּךְ דְּנֹחַ גּוּפֵיהּ טְרֵיפָה הֲוָה, מִי קָאָמַר לֵיהּ ה] לְנֹחַ: דִּכְוָותָךְ עַיֵּיל, שְׁלֵמִים לָא תְּעַיֵּיל? וּמֵאַחַר דְּנָפְקָא לָן מֵ"אִתָּךְ", "לְחַיּוֹת זֶרַע" לָמָּה לִי? מַהוּ דְּתֵימָא: "אִתָּךְ" — לְצַוְתָּא בְּעָלְמָא, אֲפִי' זָקֵן אֲפִילּוּ סָרִיס, קָמַשְׁמַע לָן.§ ו] "טְהוֹרִין אֲבָל לֹא טְמֵאִין".§ וּמִי הֲווּ טְמֵאִין וּטְהוֹרִין בְּהַהִיא שַׁעְתָּא? א"ר *שְׁמוּאֵל בַּר נַחְמָנִי א"ר יוֹנָתָן: *מֵאוֹתָן שֶׁלֹּא נֶעֶבְדָה בָּהֶן עֲבֵירָה. ז] מְנָא הֲווּ יָדְעִי? כִּדְרַב חִסְדָּא, דְּאָמַר רַב חִסְדָּא: הֶעֱבִירָן לִפְנֵי הַתֵּיבָה, כָּל שֶׁהַתֵּיבָה קוֹלַטְתָּן — בְּיָדוּעַ שֶׁהוּא טָהוֹר, אֵין הַתֵּיבָה קוֹלַטְתָּן — בְּיָדוּעַ שֶׁהֵן טְמֵאִין. רַבִּי אַבָּהוּ אָמַר, אָמַר קְרָא: °"וְהַבָּאִים זָכָר וּנְקֵבָה" — הַבָּאִין מֵאֲלֵיהֶן. אָמַר מָר: וְהַכֹּל קָרְבוּ עוֹלוֹת. עוֹלוֹת — אִין, שְׁלָמִים — לָא. וְהָא כְּתִיב: °"וַיִּזְבְּחוּ זְבָחִים שְׁלָמִים לַה' פָּרִים"! אֶלָּא אֵימָא: ח] הַכֹּל קָרְבוּ עוֹלוֹת [וּשְׁלָמִים. וְהָתַנְיָא: אֲבָל שְׁלָמִים לֹא, כ"א עוֹלוֹת]; עוֹלוֹת — אִין, שְׁלָמִים — לָא! כְּמ"ד: לֹא קָרְבוּ שְׁלָמִים ט] בְּנֵי נֹחַ. דְּאִיתְּמַר, ר"א וְר' יוֹסֵי בַּר חֲנִינָא, חַד אָמַר: קָרְבוּ [שְׁלָמִים י] בְּנֵי נֹחַ], וְחַד אָמַר: לֹא קָרְבוּ. מ"ט דְּמ"ד: קָרְבוּ שְׁלָמִים בְּנֵי נֹחַ? דִּכְתִיב: °"וְהֶבֶל הֵבִיא גַם הוּא מִבְּכוֹרוֹת צֹאנוֹ וּמֵחֶלְבֵיהֶן", אֵיזֶהוּ דָּבָר שֶׁחֶלְבּוֹ קָרֵב לְגַבֵּי מִזְבֵּחַ וְאֵין כּוּלּוֹ קָרֵב לְגַבֵּי מִזְבֵּחַ — הֱוֵי אוֹמֵר: זֶה שְׁלָמִים. מ"ט דְּמ"ד: לֹא קָרְבוּ? יא] דִּכְתִיב: °"עוּרִי צָפוֹן וּבוֹאִי תֵימָן", יב] תִּתְנָעֵר אוּמָּה שֶׁמַּעֲשֶׂיהָ בַּצָּפוֹן, וְתָבוֹא אוּמָּה שֶׁמַּעֲשֶׂיהָ בַּצָּפוֹן וּבַדָּרוֹם. וּמָר נַמִי, הָכְתִיב: "וּמֵחֶלְבֵיהֶן"! יג] מִשְּׁמֵנֵיהֶן [דִּידְהוּ]. וּמָר נַמִי, הָכְתִיב: "עוּרִי צָפוֹן"! [הַהוּא] בְּקִיבּוּץ גָּלֻיּוֹת הוּא דִּכְתִיב. וְהָא כְּתִיב: °"וַיֹּאמֶר מֹשֶׁה גַּם אַתָּה תִּתֵּן בְּיָדֵינוּ זְבָחִים וְעוֹלוֹת וְעָשִׂינוּ לַה' אֱלֹהֵינוּ"! זְבָחִים — לַאֲכִילָה, וְעוֹלוֹת — לְהַקְרָבָה. וְהָא כְּתִיב: °"וַיִּקַּח יִתְרוֹ יד] [חוֹתֵן מֹשֶׁה] עוֹלָה וּזְבָחִים"! הַהוּא לְאַחַר מַתַּן תּוֹרָה הוּא דִּכְתִיב. הָנִיחָא *לְמ"ד: [יִתְרוֹ] אַחַר מַתַּן תּוֹרָה הָיָה, אֶלָּא לְמ"ד: [יִתְרוֹ] קוֹדֶם מַתַּן תּוֹרָה הָיָה, מַאי אִיכָּא לְמֵימַר? דְּאִיתְּמַר, *בְּנֵי ר' חִיָּיא וְר' יְהוֹשֻׁעַ בֶּן לֵוִי, חַד אָמַר: יִתְרוֹ קוֹדֶם מַתַּן תּוֹרָה הָיָה, וְחַד אָמַר: יִתְרוֹ אַחַר מַתַּן תּוֹרָה הָיָה. לְמ"ד: יִתְרוֹ קוֹדֶם מַתַּן תּוֹרָה הָיָה — קָסָבַר: שְׁלָמִים הִקְרִיבוּ בְּנֵי נֹחַ. כְּתַנָּאֵי: °"וַיִּשְׁמַע יִתְרוֹ כֹּהֵן מִדְיָן", מַה שְּׁמוּעָה שָׁמַע וּבָא וְנִתְגַּיֵּיר? ר' יְהוֹשֻׁעַ אוֹמֵר: מִלְחֶמֶת עֲמָלֵק שָׁמַע, (א) שֶׁהֲרֵי טו] כְּתִיב בְּצִדּוֹ: °"וַיַּחֲלֹשׁ יְהוֹשֻׁעַ אֶת עֲמָלֵק וְאֶת עַמּוֹ לְפִי חָרֶב". ר"א הַמּוֹדָעִי אוֹמֵר: מַתַּן תּוֹרָה שָׁמַע [וּבָא]. שֶׁכְּשֶׁנִּיתְּנָה תּוֹרָה לְיִשְׂרָאֵל הָיָה קוֹלוֹ הוֹלֵךְ מִסּוֹף הָעוֹלָם וְעַד סוֹפוֹ, וְכָל [מַלְכֵי] גוֹיִם אֲחָזָתַן רְעָדָה בְּהֵיכְלֵיהֶן וְאָמְרוּ שִׁירָה, שֶׁנֶּאֱמַר: °"וּבְהֵיכָלוֹ כּוּלּוֹ אוֹמֵר כָּבוֹד". נִתְקַבְּצוּ כּוּלָּם אֵצֶל בִּלְעָם הָרָשָׁע, וְאָמְרוּ לוֹ: מַה קּוֹל הֶהָמוֹן אֲשֶׁר שָׁמַעְנוּ? שֶׁמָּא מַבּוּל בָּא לָעוֹלָם? טז] (אָמַר לָהֶם) °"ה' לַמַּבּוּל יָשָׁב"? [אָמַר לָהֶם]: "וַיֵּשֶׁב ה' מֶלֶךְ לְעוֹלָם" — *כְּבָר נִשְׁבַּע הקב"ה שֶׁאֵינוֹ מֵבִיא מַבּוּל לָעוֹלָם. יז] אָמְרוּ לוֹ: מַבּוּל שֶׁל מַיִם אֵינוֹ מֵבִיא, אֲבָל מַבּוּל שֶׁל אֵשׁ מֵבִיא, שֶׁנֶּאֱ': °"כִּי (הִנֵּה) בָאֵשׁ ה' נִשְׁפָּט"! אָמַר לָהֶן: כְּבָר נִשְׁבַּע שֶׁאֵינוֹ יח] מַשְׁחִית כָּל בָּשָׂר. וּמַה קּוֹל הֶהָמוֹן הַזֶּה שֶׁשָּׁמַעְנוּ? אָמַר לָהֶם: חֶמְדָּה טוֹבָה יֵשׁ לוֹ בְּבֵית גְּנָזָיו שֶׁהָיְתָה גְּנוּזָה אֶצְלוֹ *תתקע"ד דּוֹרוֹת קוֹדֶם שֶׁנִּבְרָא הָעוֹלָם, וּבִיקֵּשׁ לִיתְּנָהּ לְבָנָיו, שֶׁנֶּאֱמַר: °"ה' עֹז לְעַמּוֹ יִתֵּן". יט] [מִיָּד] פָּתְחוּ כּוּלָּם וְאָמְרוּ: °"ה' יְבָרֵךְ אֶת עַמּוֹ בַשָּׁלוֹם". *)ר"א אוֹמֵר: קְרִיעַת יַם סוּף שָׁמַע וּבָא, שֶׁנֶּאֱ': °"וַיְהִי כִשְׁמוֹעַ כָּל מַלְכֵי הָאֱמוֹרִי". וְאַף רָחָב הַזּוֹנָה אָמְרָה לִשְׁלוּחֵי יְהוֹשֻׁעַ: °"כִּי שָׁמַעְנוּ אֵת אֲשֶׁר הוֹבִישׁ ה' אֶת מֵי יַם סוּף". מַאי שְׁנָא הָתָם כ] **)דְּאָמַר (לֵיהּ): °"וְלֹא הָיָה בָם עוֹד רוּחַ", וּמ"ש הָכָא***) דְּקָאָמַר: °"וְלֹא קָמָה עוֹד רוּחַ בְּאִישׁ"?

דַּאֲפִילּוּ

*) נ"א ר"א בן יעקב **) נ"א דכתיב ***) נ"א דכתיב

[רש"י]

ה"ג: זְכָרִים וּנְקֵבוֹת תְּמִימִים וּבַעֲלֵי מוּמִין לְאַפּוּקֵי מְחוּסַּר אֵבֶר דְּלָא. *וְלָא (ב) גָּרְסִי': "תַּמּוּת וְזַכְרוּת בִּבְהֵמוֹת" כו', דְּמַאי אִירְיָא קוֹדֶם מַתַּן תּוֹרָה? לְאַחַר הֲקָמַת הַמִּשְׁכָּן נַמִי אִיתָא לְהָא, וְעוֹד: מִדְּקָאָמַר "אֲבָל מְחוּסַּר אֵבֶר לָא" — מִכְּלָל דְּבַעֲלֵי מוּמִין לֹא נִפְסְלוּ לֹא בִּבְהֵמָה וְלֹא בְּעוֹף. שֶׁנֶּאֱסַר לִבְנֵי נֹחַ. לְהַקְרִיב לַגָּבוֹהַּ. שֶׁחַיִּין רָאשֵׁי אֵיבָרִים. וְלָמָּה לִי לְאַזְהוּרֵי עֲלַיְיהוּ אִי לָאו מִשּׁוּם הַקְרָבָה, שֶׁהִקְרִיב מֵהֶן בְּצֵאתוֹ מִן הַתֵּיבָה. מִלְּחַיּוֹת זֶרַע נָפְקָא. דִּטְרֵיפָה אֵינָהּ יוֹלֶדֶת. בְּדוֹמִין לָךְ. לְמַעוּטֵי טְרֵיפָה. תָּמִים בִּדְרָכָיו. עָנָיו וְסַבְלָן. מַהוּ דְּתֵימָא אִתָּךְ. לָאו לְמִידְרַשׁ: בְּדוֹמִין לָךְ, אֶלָּא כא] שֶׁהוֹדִיעַ שֶׁאֵינוֹ עוֹשֶׂה אֶלָּא לִכְבוֹדוֹ לִהְיוֹת לוֹ לְוַוְתָּא. קמ"ל "לְחַיּוֹת זֶרַע". לָאו לְוַוְתָּא בָּעֵי לְהוּ. וּמֵהָשְׁתָּא עַל כָּרְחָךְ "אִתְּךָ" יְתֵירָא הוּא, לְמִידְרַשׁ בֵּיהּ: בְּדוֹמִין לָךְ. מִי הָווּ. הֲרֵי לֹא נִתְּנָה תּוֹרָה! הַבָּאִין מֵאֲלֵיהֶן. וְכָל אוֹתָן שֶׁבָּאוּ אֶל הַתֵּיבָה מֵאֲלֵיהֶן בָּאוּ, וּבָהֶן הִכִּיר: אוֹתָם שֶׁבָּאוּ שִׁבְעָה שִׁבְעָה — יָדַע שֶׁהֵן טְהוֹרִין, וְשֶׁבָּאוּ שְׁנַיִם שְׁנַיִם — שֶׁהֵן טְמֵאִין. וַיִּזְבְּחוּ זְבָחִים שְׁלָמִים. וְסִינַי קוֹדֶם הֲקָמַת הַמִּשְׁכָּן הֲוָה. וְאַתְּ אָמְרַתְּ דְּעַד [שֶׁלֹּא] הוּקַם הַמִּשְׁכָּן לֹא קָרְבוּ שְׁלָמִים כְּלָל. *לַכֹּל. בֵּין לְיִשְׂרָאֵל בֵּין לִבְנֵי נֹחַ קָרְבוּ עוֹלוֹת. אֲבָל שְׁלָמִים לֹא קָרְבוּ לִבְנֵי נֹחַ. וּמִשְּׁעַת מַתַּן תּוֹרָה שֶׁנִּבְחֲרוּ יִשְׂרָאֵל קָרְבוּ לָהֶם שְׁלָמִים. כב] תִּתְנָעֵר. לְשׁוֹן (שמות יד) "וַיְנַעֵר ה' אֶת מִצְרַיִם". שֶׁמַּעֲשֶׂיהָ בַּצָּפוֹן. הַיְינוּ עוֹלָה שֶׁטְּעוּנָה צָפוֹן. כג] וְתָבֹא. אֶל מֶלֶךְ הַמָּשִׁיחַ. אוּמָּה שֶׁמַּעֲשֶׂיהָ צָפוֹן וְדָרוֹם. דְּהַיְינוּ יִשְׂרָאֵל, שֶׁמַּקְרִיבִין עוֹלוֹת וּשְׁלָמִים. מִשְּׁמֵנֵיהוֹן דִּידְהוּ. מִן הַשְּׁמֵנִין שֶׁבָּהֶן. וּמִיהוּ, עוֹלוֹת הָווּ. בְּקִיבּוּץ גָּלֻיּוֹת. [וְה"ק]: עוּרִי רוּחַ צְפוֹנִית וּבוֹאִי רוּחַ דְּרוֹמִית לְקַבֵּץ גָּלֻיּוֹת הַמְפוּזָּרוֹת בָּכֶם. זְבָחִים וְעוֹלוֹת. זְבָחִים הַיְינוּ שְׁלָמִים. וְקוֹדֶם מַתַּן תּוֹרָה כּוּלְּהוּ בְּנֵי נֹחַ! וּמְשַׁנֵּי: זְבָחִים אֵינָן שְׁלָמִים, אֶלָּא לְשׁוֹן שְׁחִיטָה בְּעָלְמָא, וְלַאֲכִילָה. הָנִיחָא לְמ"ד כו'. פְּלוּגְתָּא לְקַמָּן. כְּתַנָּאֵי. אִי קוֹדֶם מַתַּן תּוֹרָה הֲוָה [יִתְרוֹ], אִי לְאַחַר. וּבְהֵיכָלוֹ כּוּלּוֹ אוֹמֵר כָּבוֹד כו'. רֵישָׁא דִּקְרָא: "קוֹל ה' יְחוֹלֵל אַיָּלוֹת", וּבְמַתַּן תּוֹרָה מִשְׁתָּעֵי, וּבְהֵיכָלוֹ שֶׁל כָּל מֶלֶךְ וּמֶלֶךְ כּוּלּוֹ אוֹמֵר כָּבוֹד לְהַקב"ה. אָמַר לָהֶם וַיֵּשֶׁב ה' מֶלֶךְ לְעוֹלָם. כְּבָר נִשְׁבַּע שֶׁיְּהֵא מֶלֶךְ לְעוֹלָם עַל בְּרִיּוֹתָיו, וְלֹא יַשְׁחִיתֵם. תְּשַׁע מֵאוֹת וְשִׁבְעִים וְאַרְבָּעָה דּוֹרוֹת קוֹדֶם שֶׁנִּבְרָא הָעוֹלָם. וְכ"ו מֵאָדָם וְעַד מֹשֶׁה רַבֵּינוּ, הֲרֵי "דָּבָר צִוָּה לְאֶלֶף דּוֹר" (תהלים קה). עֹז. הַתּוֹרָה, שֶׁהִיא מָעוּזָן שֶׁל יִשְׂרָאֵל. דַּאֲפִי'

[תוספות]

ודילמא למעוטי טריפה. תימה דבפ' "שילוח הקן" (חולין דף קמ. ושם) גבי "שתי לפרים חיות" דרשי' מינה תרתי: שחיין ראשי איבריה שלה, ולמעוטי טריפה! וי"ל: דשאני ציפורי מצורע שהוא כעין קרבן, ושניהן שוין לענין פסול. אבל גבי נח, דשאר מומין כשרין — הו"ל לאוקמיה למעוטי טריפה דוקא.

אבל למ"ד טריפה יולדת מאי איכא למימר. פי': דלדידיה לא מייתר ליה "מכל החי" למחוסר אבר, ואיצטריך למעוטי טריפה. וא"ת: כיון דטריפה חיה ויולדת, היכי מימעט מ"כל החי"? הא בפ' "שילוח הקן" (ג"ז שם) לא ממעט מ"חיות" טריפות למ"ד טריפה חיה! ויש לומר: דשאני הכא, ד"מכל החי" מיותר, ושפיר משתמע למעוטי טריפה אע"ג דחיה, דמשתמע חיות גמורה. ומסתבר למעוטי טריפה אע"ג דחיה ויולדת, טפי ממחוסרת אבר, דמ"מ אין טריפה בריאה כשאר, ולא חזיא לקיום העולם כולי האי. **אתך** בדומין לך. וא"ת: א"כ האי "מכל החי" למה לי? דתרוייהו מ"אתך" נפקא! וכי תימא: דלמא נח גופיה מחוסר אבר הוה — מי קאמר רחמנא. דכוותך עייל, שלמים לא תעייל? *וי"ל: דמוקמא קרא בדדמי לטריפה ולא דמי למחוסרת אבר, דלענין קיום העולם לא חיישינן.

דילמא נח גופיה טריפה הוה. וא"ת: והלא חי אחרי כן ג' מאות שנה! וי"ל: דשמא לא היה בכח ובריאות כראוי לו. וסוגיין כמ"ד טריפה חיה. *ור"ת היה רגיל לחלק בין טריפות דאדם לטריפות דבהמה, משום דאדם אית ליה מזלא. וקשה: דבריש "אלו טריפות" (חולין דף מג.) מייתי ראיה מאיוב אטריפות דבהמה*. אסור

[עין משפט נר מצוה]

כג א מיי' פ"ג מהל' איסורי מזבח הל' ח:

[מסורת הש"ס]

עיין בפנים מאירות

קדושין כב: מנחות ו. כה. תמורה יד. [חולין כג.]

ע"ז ה: ודף נא. כל הענין

[חולין נז:]

ס"א הכל

[סנהדרין קח: ע"ש]

[נ"א מאותן העתידין ליטהר כו' ועי' מהרש"א בח"א שכך הוא גירסא נכונה]

[ע"ז כב.]

כתב רש"י בע"ז מו. ד"ה בני ר"ח. יהודה וחזקיה שמן

[סוטה יא. ע"ש]

[תגיגה יג. שבת פח:]

עי' בתוס' מס' ע"ז ו. דמתרלו קושיא זו בענין אחר

עי' בכ"מ בפי"ג מהל' גירושין מה שהקשה על הרמב"ם ועי' בבה"ז ובפ"מ

וע"ע תוס' חולין מב: ד"ה ואמר רב יהודה ותוס' עירובין ז. ד"ה כגון שדרה ומיהו וכו' ותוס' גיטין נו: ד"ה וניקר ותוס' ב"ק נא. ד"ה נעבד ותוס' בכורות לז: ד"ה כדי

[מקורות הפסוקים]

בראשית ו | שם | שמות כד | גי' רש"ק | בראשית ד | שיר ד | שמות י | שם יח | שם | שם יז | תהלים כט | שם | ישעיהו סו | תהלים כט | שם | יהושע ה | שם ב | שם ה | שם ב

הגהות הב"ח

(א) גמ' שמע ובא שהרי: (ב) רש"י ד"ה ה"ג זכרים וכו' ולא (אמרי') [גרסי' דאמר מר] תמות וזכרות בבהמות (לאפוקי לא בעופות) כו' דמאי איריא:

שיטה מקובצת

א] מתיבת דאמר כו' עד תיבת לאפוקי נמחק: ב] דלא דאר"א: ג] בשר אמר הקב"ה לנח הבא. תיבות אמרה תורה נמחק: ד] ודילמא ההיא למעוטי: ה] ליה רחמנא לנח: ו] לן. אמר מר טהורין: ז] עבירה. ל"א מאותן שעתידין ליטהר: ח] אימא לכל קרבו עולות ולבני נח עולות אין שלמים לא והשאר נמחק: ט] שלמים לבני נח: י] קרבו שלמים לבני נח וח"א לא קרבו שלמים לבני נח מ"ט דמ"ד קרבו שלמים לבני נח: יא] קרבו שלמים לבני נח דכתיב: יב] תימן התנערי: יג] מחלביהן משמני דידהו: יד] יתרו חותן משה עולה וזבחים יתרו לאחר מתן תורה הוה הניחא למ"ד יתרו לאחר מתן תורה הוה אלא למ"ד יתרו קודם מתן תורה הוה מאי כו' קודם מתן תורה הוה וח"א יתרו לאחר מתן תורה הוה ומ"ד יתרו קודם מתן תורה הוה קסבר קרבו שלמים: טו] שהרי כתוב בצידו: טז] לעולם שנאמר ה' למבול ישב אמר להם וישב ה' מלך לעולם: יז] לעולם שנאמר כי מי נח זאת לי אשר נשבעת[י] אמרו לו שמא מבול של מים כו' שנאמר ה' באש יבא ותיבות כי הנה באש ה' נשפט נמחק: יח] שאינו מביא מבול כל עיקר שנאמר ולא יהיה עוד מבול לשחת כל בשר ואלא מה קול ההמון הזה: יט] יתן מיד פתחו: כ] התם דכתיב ולא היה בהם עוד רוח ומ"ש הכא דכתיב ולא קמה. חומה דף ל"ד ר"א] אלא להודיעו: כב] מה"ד התנערי לשון וינער: כג] ותבוא אל:

כד א ב ג מיי' פי"ט מהל' מעשה הקרבנות הלכה טז:
כה ד מיי' פ"ו מהל' איסורי מזבח הל"ג:
כו ה מיי' פ"ז מהל' בית הבחירה הל' יא:

אסור לסייען ואסור לעשות שליחותן. תימה: לר' יוסי דאמר לעיל בפרק "ב"ש" (דף מה.) דקדשי גוים השוחטן בחוץ חייב – לא ה"ל למיתני הכא לשון "אסור", כדמוכח בריש פ' בתרא דיומא (דף עג:) לד] דחיוב כרת לית ליה למיתני אסור! וי"ל: דקתני אסור לפי שיש כמה עבודות דלא מחייב עלייהו בחוץ, דאסור לסייען, דגזרינן אטו עבודה דבת חיובא. **כמאן** כרבי אלעזר בן שמוע כו'. עיקר מילתיה במנחות, ב"הקומץ רבה" (דף כב.). **גבה** חמשים מכל שבט ושבט שהן שש מאות. הא דכתיב הכא כסף והכא זהב – מפרש לקמיה דה"ק: גבה כסף שוה נ' שקלים של זהב לכל שבט, דהיינו שוה שש מאות זהב לכל השבטים. ור"ת אומר: שיש במדרש דנתן לו חמשים שקלי זהב, דהיינו שש מאות שקלי כסף. וקשה: דבפ' "שור שנגח" (ב"ק דף לו.) משמע דדינר של זהב שוה כ"ה של כסף! ואומר ר"ת: דדינר של זהב עב כפלים משל כסף. ותדע, מדאמרי' בפ' "אלו טריפות" (חולין דף נה:) גדי טחול: ואי אשתייר ביה כעובי דינר זהב – כשירה. משמע דמשונה בעוביו משל כסף*. **אימא** בכל מקומות מחנה ישראל. שאפילו בשעת

דאפי' אקשויי. אבל לתשמיש לא אקשו. והיא שהיתה יודעת בדבר אמרה לשלוחי יהושע בלשון זה. דאמר מר. במכילתא בפ' יתרו. אמרה כד] ימחל לי בשביל חבל ופשתים וחלון. במכילתא תניא הכי: אמרה, רבש"ע, בג' דברים חטאתי בג' ימחל, כה] בחבל ופשתים וחלון. שהיו מנאפים עולין אליה בחבלים דרך החלון ויורדים, וגם טמנתם בפשתי העץ. ובאותן שלשה דברים עלמן זכתה להציל השלוחים. אסור לסייען. בשעת איסור הבמות, כגון בזמן הזה, דקדושת ירושלים אין אחריה היתר. אורויי להן. היאך יעשו. זילו כו] דברו תרין עולמי גילאי. לכו כז] וקחו שני גוים, בחורים בני גיל אחד, שכן נוי לדבר. דמספקא ימא שירטון. *לימו"ן בלע"ז, ומתייבש ונעשה קרקע. דבעינן שלא נשתמש הדיוט במזבח. ואייתו ציבי חדתי. שלא נשתמש בהן אדם, שלא יהא שברי כלים. ואפקו נורא כח] ממרא חדתא. נ"ל שהוא *פויישי"ר של איסתמא = *אלייי"ר בלע"ז, שמוציאין בו אש מן האבנים. ה"ג: כמאן כר"א בן שמוע דתניא ר"א בן שמוע אומר מה מזבח כו'. ובת"כ היא שנויה, בפרשה ראשונה. כתוב אחד אומר. ברייתא זו משובשת בספרים, ושנויה היא בספרי בברכת כהנים, וכך היא שנויה: הא כילד? מקום מזבח בחמשים, וכל הבית בשש מאות. רבי אומר בשם אבא יוסי בן דוסתאי: גבה מכל שבט חמשים, שהן שש מאות. ר"א בן שמוע אומר: "ויקן דוד את הגורן" – כדמפרש בענין: כט] "ויתן דוד לארונה במקום [שקלי] זהב משקל שש מאות". אבל הבקר לעולה והמוריגים וכלי הבקר לעצים – בכסף שקלים חמשים, ל] "ויאמר ארונה" וגו' (ע"כ הגי'). והכי פירושא דקרא: "ויקן דוד את הגורן" – ולא פירש במה קנאו, שהרי פירשו במקום אחר כבר (דה"א כא), "ויתן דוד לארונה במקום וגו' ואת הבקר קנה בכסף שקלים חמשים" לא] (זהב). (ג) הא מודה ר' אלעזר בבמה. דקתני: המוריגים לקח דוד לעצים כדבר ארונה. משקל שש מאות. לקמיה מפרש: כסף שוה משקל שש מאות זהב. מטה של טורבל. כך נקרא במסכת פרה (פי"ב מ"ט). עיזא דקורקסא. כמין עז של עץ, ויש בו יתידות חדים, לב] [וגם עשוי] חרילים = *קרני"ש ומוליכו ומביאו על הקשים של דישה לאחר שנידושה, ומתחתכין ונעשין *תבן. מאי קרא. דהוא עשוי חרילים ומוכן לדוך ולדוק. בכסף שש מאות שקלי זהב. וה"ק: כסף שוה שקלים חמשים של זהב גבה מכל שבט ושבט. בכל מקומות ישראל. קא סלקא דעתך השתא דאפי' יצא אחד מהן חוץ למחנה ישראל, אוכל קדשים קלים שם. שער נקנור. של עזרה לג] היה, שער המזרח. והן הן קלעים שבמדבר. לפנים משער נקנור הוה, כמקום לפנים מן הקלעים במשכן. אימא בכל מקומות מחנה ישראל. שאפי' בשעת סילוק מסעות אין נפסלים, אלא מוליכן עמו, ובמקום חנייתן אוכלין במחנה. עוד אחרת היתה. מחנה רביעית, חלוקה מהר הבית ומעזרה, ולא היו עונשין עליה על הנכנס לה בטומאה. במסכת כלים (פ"א מ"ח) מפרש מה היא חלוקתו מהר הבית. דמחנה לויה מיהא הואי. ומחנה ישראל הוא דחסר. דאם לא כן, דמחנה ישראל הואי ולא מחנה לויה. נמלאו

תורה אור

דאפילו אקשויי נמי לא אקשו. ומנא ידעה? דאמר מר: אין לך כל שר ונגיד שלא בא על רחב הזונה. אמרו: בת י' שנים היתה כשיצאו ישראל ממצרים, וזנתה א] [כל] מ' שנה שהיו ישראל במדבר. אחר נ' שנה נתגיירה, אמרה: ב] יהא מחול לי בשכר חבל חלון ופשתים.§ אמר מר: וגוים בזמן הזה רשאין לעשות כן. מנא ה"מ? דת"ר: °"דבר אל בני ישראל" – בני ישראל מצווין על שחוטי חוץ, אואין הגוים מצווין על שחוטי חוץ. לפיכך, כל אחד ואחד בונה לו במה לעצמו ומקריב עליה כל מה שירצה. א"ר יעקב בר אחא אמר רב אסי: באסור לסייען ולעשות שליחותן. אמר ג] רבה: גולאורינהו [להו] שרי. כי הא *דאיפרא הורמיז *אימיה דשבור מלכא שדרה ד] קורבנא לרבא, שלחה ליה: אסקוה ניהליה לשם שמים. *אמר להו לרב ספרא ולרב אחא בר הונא: זילו ודברו תרי עולמי גולאי, וחזו היכא דמסקא ימא שירטון, ושקלו ציבי חדתי ואפיקו נורא ה] ממרא חדתא, ואסקוה ניהליה לשם שמים. א"ל אביי: כמאן – כר"א ו] בן שמוע. *דתניא, ר' אלעזר בן שמוע אומר: מה מזבח שלא ישתמש בו הדיוט – דאף עצים שלא ישתמש בהן הדיוט? והא מודה ר"א בן שמוע בבמה. דתניא, כתוב אחד אומר: °"ויתן דוד ז] לארנן במקום שקלי זהב משקל שש מאות" וגו', וכתיב: °"ויקן דוד את הגרן ואת הבקר בכסף שקלים חמשים", הא כיצד? ח] גובה מכל שבט ושבט חמשים, שהן שש מאות. רבי אומר משום אבא יוסי בן דוסתאי: בקר [*ועצים] ומקום מזבח – בנ', וכל הבית ט] כולו בשש מאות. ר"א בן שמוע אומר: בקר ועצים ומקום מזבח – בנ', וכל הבית כולו בשש מאות, דכתיב: °"ויאמר ארונה אל דוד יקח ויעל אדוני המלך [הטוב בעיניו] ראה הבקר לעולה והמורגים [וכלי הבקר] לעצים". ורבא אמר לך: התם נמי בחדתי. מאי "מוריגים"? אמר עולא: מטה של טורבל. מאי מטה של טורבל? אמר *אביי: עיזא דקרקסא דדיישן י] דישאי. אמר אביי: מאי קרא? °"הנה שמתיך למורג חרוץ חדש בעל פיפיות". מקרי ליה יא] רבא לבריה, ורמי ליה קראי אהדדי, כתיב: "ויתן דוד יב] לארנן" וגו', וכתיב: "ויקן דוד" וגו', הא כיצד? גובה מכל שבט ושבט חמשים, שהן שש מאות. ואכתי קשיין יג] אהדדי, התם כסף הכא זהב! אלא יד] ה"ק: גובה כסף במשקל שש מאות זהב.§ "קדשים קלים טו] נאכלים [בכל מחנה ישראל]"§ אמר רב הונא: בכל מקומות ישראל, טז] אבל מחנה לא הוי. איתיביה יז] ר"נ לרב הונא: ומחנות במדבר לא הואי? והא תניא: *כשם יח] השמחנה במדבר כך מחנה בירושלים; מירושלים להר הבית – מחנה ישראל, מהר הבית לשער נקנור – מחנה לויה, מכאן ואילך – מחנה שכינה, והן הן קלעים שבמדבר! יט] אלא אימא: בכל מקום מחנה ישראל. פשיטא! מהו דתימא: איפסלו ביוצא, קמ"ל. ואימא ה"נ! אמר קרא: °"ונסע אהל מועד" *אע"פ שנסע – אהל מועד הוא. תניא, רשב"י אומר: עוד אחרת היתה, כ] וחיל עזרת נשים היא, ולא היו עונשין עליה. ובשילה לא היו אלא שני מחנות בלבד. הי מינייהו לא הוה? אמר כא] רבה: מסתברא דמחנה לויה (א) כב] הואי. דאי סלקא דעתך מחנה לויה לא כג] הואי, נמצאו

ויקרא יז · דה"א כא · ש"ב כד · שם · ישעיהו מא · במדבר ב

ב"ב ח. · נ"א אמר להו רבא · מנחות כב. · ג"ז שם וע"ז כד: · [במנחות שם איתא ר' יהודה ובע"ז הוא סתם ע"ש] · תוספתא דכלים פ"ק · לעיל סה: [מנחות לה.] · נ"א תרין

עי' מ"ש רש"י נדה כ: וע"ע תוס' ב"ב ח. ד"ה איפרא ותוס' סנהדרין לט. ד"ה דהורמיז · [וע"ע תוס' כתובות לט: ד"ה נתן ובב"מ מד: ד"ה אחד מכ"ה ובשבועות מד: ד"ה התקבלת] · ועי' רש"י בח"א

הגהות הב"ח

(א) גמ' דמחנה לויה מיה הואי: (ב) רש"י ד"ה כמאן כו' מודה נ"ל קודם ד"ה כתוב אחד כו' (ג) [וכו נ"ל ויתן דוד לארנן במקום שקלי זהב משקל וכו' בכסף שקלי חמשים שנאמר' (ויקן [ויאמר] דוד וגו' וה' פירושו לקרא וכו' ולא פירש במה וכו' חמשים הס"ד

שיטה מקובצת

א] וזנתה כל מ': ב] אמרה ימחול לי בשביל חבל ופשתים וחלון: ג] אמר רבא אות ה' נמחק: ד] שדרה עגלא תילתא לקמיה דרבא שלחה: ה] נורא ממגנא חדתא תיבת ממרא ל"ש: ו] אלעזר בר שמוע. וכצ"ל לקמן: ז] דוד לארונה תיבת לארנן נמחק: ח] הא כיצד מקום מזבח בחמשים ומה שבנתים נמחק: ט] הבית בשש מאות רבי אומר משום אבא יוסי בן דוסתאי גובה מכל שבט ושבט חמשים שהן ש מאות ר"א בר שמוע אומר ויקן דוד את הגורן כדמפרש בענין ומה מפורש ויתן דוד לארונה במקום זהב משקל שש מאות אבל את הבקר לעולה והמורגים וכלי הבקר לעצים בכסף שקלים חמשים שנאמר ויאמר ארונ וגו' ורבא אמר לך: י] דדיישן דשתאי: יא] ליה רחבה לבריה תיבת רבא נמחק: יב] דוד לארונא תיבת לארנן נמחק: יג] קשיין קראי אהדדי: יד] אלא אימא גובה תיבות ה"ק נמחק: טו] קדשים קלים נאכלי בכל מחנה ישראל: טז] מתיבת אבל עד תיבת ר"נ נמחק: יז] א"ל ר"נ לרב הונא: יח] כשם שהיה מחנות במדבר כך היה מחנה בירושלים: יט] שבמדבר אימא בכל מקומות מחנה ישראל ותיבת אלא נמח כ] היתה שם עזרת נשים ולא היו עונשין עליה: כא] אמר אביי תיבת רבה נמחק: כב] לויה מיהא הואי: כג] לא הוה דא"כ נמצאו. תיבת הואי נמחק: כד] אמרה ימחול לי: כה] יחמול לי בחבל: כו] זילו ודברו תרי כז] לכו ודברו שני תיבת קחו ל"ש: כח] נורא ממגנא תיבת ממרא ל"ש: כט] בענין ומה מפורש ויתן: ל] חמשים שנאמר ויאמר: לא] חמשים הוא סה"ד ואח"כ מה"ד זהב משקל שש מאות לקמיה מפרש כסף שו משקל שש מאות זהב ואח"כ מה"ד הא: לב] חדים וגם עשוי חריצים: לג] עזרה הוא תיבת היה נמחק: לד] דיומא דבחיוב כרת:

כז א מיי' פ"ז מהלכות רוצח הלכה ה:

נִמְצְאוּ זָבִין וּטְמֵאֵי מֵתִים מִשְׁתַּלְּחִין חוּץ לַמַּחֲנֶה אַחַת, וְהַתּוֹרָה אָמְרָה: °"וְלֹא יְטַמְּאוּ אֶת מַחֲנֵיהֶם" – *תֵּן מַחֲנֶה לָזֶה וּמַחֲנֶה לָזֶה. א"ל רָבָא: אֶלָּא מַאי, מַחֲנֵה יִשְׂרָאֵל לָא הֲוַאי? א] נִמְצְאוּ זָבִין וּמְצוֹרָעִין מִשְׁתַּלְּחִין ב] לְמָקוֹם אֶחָד, וְהַתּוֹרָה אָמְרָה: °"בָּדָד יֵשֵׁב" – *שֶׁלֹּא יֵשֵׁב טָמֵא אַחֵר עִמּוֹ! אֶלָּא: לְעוֹלָם כּוּלְּהוּ תְּלָתָא הֲווּ, וּמַאי לֹא הָיוּ אֶלָּא שְׁתֵּי מַחֲנוֹת – לִקְלִיטָה. מִכְּלָל דְּבַמִּדְבָּר הֲוַאי קָלְטָה מַחֲנֶה לְוִיָּה? אִין, *וְהָא תַּנְיָא: °"וְשַׂמְתִּי לְךָ ג] מָקוֹם" – בְּחַיֶּיךָ, "מָקוֹם" – מְקוֹמְךָ, °"אֲשֶׁר יָנוּס שָׁמָּה" – מְלַמֵּד שֶׁמַּגְלִין בַּמִּדְבָּר. לְהֵיכָן גּוֹלִין – לְמַחֲנֵה לְוִיָּה. מִכָּאן אָמְרוּ: בֶּן לֵוִי "שֶׁהָרַג – גּוֹלֶה מִפֶּלֶךְ לְפֶלֶךְ, וְאִם גָּלָה ד] לְפִלְכּוֹ – פִּלְכּוֹ קוֹלְטוֹ. מַאי קְרָא? אָמַר רַב אַחָא בְּרֵיהּ דְּרַב אִיקָא: °"כִּי בְעִיר מִקְלָטוֹ יֵשֵׁב" – עִיר שֶׁקְּלָטַתּוּ כְּבָר.§ "בָּאוּ לְגִלְגָּל".§ ת"ר: *כָּל נִידָּר וְנִידָּב ה] הָיָה קָרֵב בְּבָמָה, שֶׁאֵין נִידָּר וְנִידָּב – אֵין קָרֵב בְּבָמָה. ו] *מִנְחָה וּנְזִירוּת קְרֵיבִין בְּבָמָה, דִּבְרֵי ר"מ. וַחכ"א: לֹא קָרְבוּ ז] יָחִיד אֶלָּא עוֹלוֹת וּשְׁלָמִים בִּלְבָד. ר' יְהוּדָה אוֹמֵר: כָּל שֶׁהַצִּבּוּר וְהַיָּחִיד מַקְרִיבִין בְּאֹהֶל מוֹעֵד שֶׁבַּמִּדְבָּר – מַקְרִיבִין בְּאֹהֶל מוֹעֵד שֶׁבְּגִלְגָּל. מַה בֵּין אֹהֶל מוֹעֵד שֶׁבַּמִּדְבָּר לְבֵין אֹהֶל מוֹעֵד שֶׁבְּגִלְגָּל? אֹהֶל מוֹעֵד שֶׁבַּמִּדְבָּר – לֹא הָיוּ בָּמוֹת מוּתָּרוֹת, אֹהֶל מוֹעֵד שֶׁבְּגִלְגָּל – הָיוּ הַבָּמוֹת מוּתָּרוֹת. וּבָמָתוֹ שֶׁבְּרֹאשׁ גַּגּוֹ לֹא הָיָה מַקְרִיב עָלֶיהָ אֶלָּא עוֹלָה וּשְׁלָמִים. ח] וַחכ"א: כָּל שֶׁהַצִּבּוּר מַקְרִיבִין בְּאֹהֶל מוֹעֵד שֶׁבַּמִּדְבָּר – מַקְרִיבִין בְּאֹהֶל מוֹעֵד שֶׁבְּגִלְגָּל, וְכָאן וְכָאן *לֹא קָרְבוּ ט] יָחִיד אֶלָּא עוֹלָה וּשְׁלָמִים בִּלְבָד. *ר' שִׁמְעוֹן אוֹמֵר: אַף צִבּוּר לֹא הִקְרִיבוּ אֶלָּא פְּסָחִים וְחוֹבוֹת

תורה אור: במדבר ה / ויקרא יג / שמות כא / שם / במדבר לה / [מגילה ט:]

רש"י

נִמְצְאוּ זָבִין וּטְמֵאֵי מֵתִים מִשְׁתַּלְּחִין חוּץ לַמַּחֲנֶה. שְׁכִינָה לְבַדָּהּ. דְּהָא שְׁנֵיהֶם מוּתָּרִין בְּמַחֲנֵה יִשְׂרָאֵל, כִּדְאָמְרִי' בִּפְסָחִים בְּפ' "אֵלּוּ דְּבָרִים" (דף סז.). מַחֲנֵיהֶם. שְׁנֵי מַחֲנוֹת מַשְׁמַע, אַחַת י] לְכָל זָב וְאַחַת לְכָל טְמֵא נֶפֶשׁ! אֶלָּא וַדַּאי הֲוַאי מַחֲנֶה לְוִיָּה, וּמְשַׁלְּחִין טְמֵאֵי מֵתִים מִמַּחֲנֵה שְׁכִינָה וּמוּתָּרִין בְּמַחֲנֵה לְוִיָּה, וְזָבִין וּבַעֲלֵי קְרָיִין מְשַׁלְּחִין חוּץ לְמַחֲנֵה לְוִיָּה. אֶלָּא מַאי מַחֲנֵה יִשְׂרָאֵל לָא הֲוַאי. וּמִשֶּׁיָּצָא חוּץ לְמַחֲנֵה לְוִיָּה שׁוּב אֵין שָׁם יא] קֶבַע מַחֲנֶה, וַהֲרֵי הוּא כְּשָׂדֶה בְּעָלְמָא וּמוּתָּרִין מְצוֹרָעִין לֵישֵׁב שָׁם, הַצְּרִיכִין לְהִשְׁתַּלֵּחַ מִמַּחֲנֵה יִשְׂרָאֵל, וְיָשְׁבוּ עַכְשָׁיו עִם הַזָּבִין. א"כ נִמְצְאוּ זָבִין וּמְצוֹרָעִים. חוּץ לְמַחֲנֵה לְוִיָּה בִּלְבַד. אֶלָּא כּוּלְּהוּ הָווּ. וּדְקָתָנֵי: לֹא הָיוּ אֶלָּא שְׁתֵּי מַחֲנוֹת – לְעִנְיַן קְלִיטָה הוּא, דְּנִסְתַּלְּקָה תּוֹרַת מַחֲנֵה לְוִיָּה מִלִּקְלוֹט אֶת הַהוֹרְגִים שׁוֹגֵג. וְשַׂמְתִּי לְךָ יב] מָקוֹם בְּחַיֶּיךָ. רָמַז לוֹ הקב"ה לְמֹשֶׁה בְּמַתַּן תּוֹרָה שֶׁיִּזְכֶּה לְתַקָּנָה זוֹ, כִּדְכְתִיב (דברים ד): "אָז יַבְדִּיל מֹשֶׁה שָׁלֹשׁ עָרִים" בְּסוֹף אַרְבָּעִים שָׁנָה. לְךָ מָקוֹם. הַמָּקוֹם שֶׁלְּךָ, דְּהַיְינוּ מַחֲנֵה לְוִיָּה, אַף הוּא נִקְלָט. מִכָּאן אָמְרוּ בֶּן לֵוִי. *שֶׁהָיָה דָּר בְּעָרֵי מִקְלָט. שֶׁכָּל אַרְבָּעִים וּשְׁמֹנֶה עֲיָירוֹת שֶׁל לְוִיִּם עָרֵי מִקְלָט הָיוּ, כִּדְאָמְרִי' בְּמַסֶּ' מַכּוֹת (דף יד.). וְאִם הָרַג בְּשׁוֹגֵג – גּוֹלֶה לְאֶחָד מֵעָרֵי חֲבֵירָיו. דְּדָרֵישׁ בֵּיהּ נַמִי הָכִי: "וְשַׂמְתִּי לְךָ מָקוֹם" – אַף הַלְוִיִּם גּוֹלִים. וְאִם גָּלָה בְּפִלְכּוֹ. עַצְמוֹ, כְּגוֹן מִשְּׁכוּנָה לִשְׁכוּנָה. פִּלְכּוֹ קוֹלְטוֹ. דּוּמְיָא דְּמִדְבָּר, יג] שֶׁהָיָה מַחֲנֵה לְוִיָּה קוֹלֶטֶת. כָּל הַנִּידָּר וְהַנִּידָּב קָרֵב בְּבָמָה. קְטַנָּה. דְּאִילּוּ בְּבָמָה גְּדוֹלָה – ע"כ קָרְבוּ חוֹבַת צִבּוּר, דִּכְתִיב: "וַיַּעֲשׂוּ אֶת הַפֶּסַח בַּגִּלְגָּל". אֶלָּא בִּקְטַנָּה. *וְאָמַר דְּקָרְבִי נְדָרִים וּנְדָבוֹת, וְלֹא חוֹבוֹת. וּבְתוֹרַת כֹּהֲנִים תָּנֵי לָהּ בְּהֶדְיָא לְר' מֵאִיר. מְנָחוֹת וּנְזִירוּת. נִידָּר וְנִידָּב יד] הוּא, וְקָרְבִי. כָּל שֶׁאֵין נִידָּר וְנִידָּב אֵין קָרֵב בְּבָמָה קְטַנָּה. כִּדְיָלֵיף טַעְמֵיהּ לְקַמֵּיהּ – שֶׁאֵין יָחִיד מַקְרִיב חוֹבָה בִּשְׁעַת הֶיתֵּר הַבָּמוֹת וַאֲפִילּוּ בִּגְדוֹלָה, וְצִבּוּר בִּקְטַנָּה לָא מַקְרְבִי טו] כו', אִישְׁתַּכַּח דְּאֵין חוֹבוֹת קְרֵיבִין בִּקְטַנָּה. וְאִי קַשְׁיָא לְר' מֵאִיר: א"כ יָחִיד לֹא עָשָׂה פִּסְחוֹ בַּגִּלְגָּל, וּקְרָא כְּתִיב: *"וַיַּעֲשׂוּ אֶת הַפֶּסַח" (במדבר ט)! פֶּסַח "קָרְבַּן צִבּוּר" קָרֵי לֵיהּ, דְּאָתֵי בִּכְנוּפְיָא, בְּמַסֶּ' יוֹמָא (דף נא.). וְהָכִי נַמִי בְּדְר"ש קָתָנֵי: אַף צִבּוּר לֹא הִקְרִיבוּ אֶלָּא טז] פְּסָחִים. אַלְמָא קָרְבַּן צִבּוּר קָרֵי לֵיהּ. לְקַמָּן יז] יָלֵיף טַעְמָא דְּכוּלְּהוּ. לֹא יח] קָרְבִי כו'. לְאַפּוּקֵי מְנָחוֹת וּנְזִירוּת, דְּלָא יט] קָרְבִי בְּבָמָה קְטַנָּה. כָּל שֶׁהַצִּבּוּר וְהַיָּחִיד מַקְרִיבִין בְּאֹהֶל מוֹעֵד שֶׁבַּמִּדְבָּר. דְּהַיְינוּ כָּל הַקָּרְבָּנוֹת כּוּלָּן, נְדָרִים וּנְדָבוֹת וְחוֹבוֹת (שֶׁקָּבוּעַ לָהֶם זְמַן) מַקְרִיבִין בְּאֹהֶל מוֹעֵד שֶׁבַּגִּלְגָּל, דְּהִיא בָּמָה גְּדוֹלָה. וְהַשְׁתָּא פָּלֵיג אַדְּר"מ וְאַדְּרַבָּנַן. דְּמִדְּקָתָנֵי: "כָּל שֶׁהַצִּבּוּר" כו', לְאַשְׁמוּעִינַן דְּאֵין חִילּוּק כ] בְּאֹהֶל מוֹעֵד שֶׁבַּמִּדְבָּר לְאֹהֶל מוֹעֵד שֶׁבַּגִּלְגָּל – מִכְּלָל דְּשַׁמְעִינְהוּ לְר"מ וְרַבָּנַן דְּאָמְרִי יֵשׁ חִילּוּק. כא] *וּמַה חִילּוּקוֹ – שֶׁאֵין יָחִיד מַקְרִיב בּוֹ חוֹבוֹת. וְטַעֲמַיְיהוּ נַמִי שָׁמְעִינַן לְקַמָּן, דַּאֲפִי' בְּבָמָה גְּדוֹלָה לָא קָרְבִי לְיָחִיד אֶלָּא נְדָרִים וּנְדָבוֹת, וּלְר' מֵאִיר מְנָחוֹת וּנְזִירוּת בִּכְלָל (א). בָּמוֹת מוּתָּרוֹת. בָּמוֹת יָחִיד. וּבָמָתוֹ שֶׁבְּרֹאשׁ הַגַּג. הִיא בָּמַת יָחִיד. אֶלָּא עוֹלָה וּשְׁלָמִים. וְלֹא מְנָחוֹת וּנְזִירוּת. וְכָאן וְכָאן. בָּמַת צִבּוּר וּבָמַת יָחִיד, לֹא קָרְבוּ בָּהֶן לְיָחִיד אֶלָּא עוֹלוֹת וּשְׁלָמִים. וּלְקַמָּן פָּרֵיךְ: הַיְינוּ תַּנָּא קַמָּא! דְּהָא חֲכָמִים דִּלְעֵיל נַמִי הָכִי קָאָמְרִי. ר' שִׁמְעוֹן פָּלֵיג אַכּוּלְּהוּ, דְּכוּלְּהוּ סְבִירָא לְהוּ דְּאֵין חִילּוּק לַצִּבּוּר בֵּין מִדְבָּר לְגִלְגָּל בְּבָמָה גְּדוֹלָה, וְרַבִּי שִׁמְעוֹן אוֹמֵר: אַף צִבּוּר עַצְמָם לֹא הִקְרִיבוּ בַּגְּדוֹלָה יוֹתֵר מִיָּחִיד בִּקְטַנָּה. אֶלָּא פְּסָחִים כו'. אֲבָל לֹא פַּר הֶעְלֵם דָּבָר וּשְׂעִירֵי עֲבוֹדָה זָרָה, לֹא קָרְבוּ לָהֶם בַּגִּלְגָּל.

מסורת הש"ס: [פסחים סז.] / שם / מכות יב: ע"ש / ס"א לך מקום המקום שלך / מגילה ט: / אע"פ שהיה נ"ק / [תמורה יד:] / קאמר דקרבו נ"ק / בתוספתא פי"ג הגי' אין היחיד מקריב עליה אלא כו'] / צ"ל ויחנו בני ישראל בגלגל ויעשו את הפסח (יהושע ה)] / מהו חילוקו נ"ק

תוספות

בשעת סילוק המסעות אין נפסלין, אלא מוליכן עמו, ובמקום חנייתן אוכלין במחנה. כך פירש בקונטרס. ונראה דאף שעת הליכתם שרי, כיון דאמרי' לעיל (דף סא.): אע"פ שנסע – אהל מועד הוא. ודוקא לקדשים קלים, אע"פ שנסע אהל מועד הוא, אבל קדשי קדשים דבעי מחיצה, כיון דנסתלקו מסעות – אין מחנה שכינה קיים, ולחם הפנים ושאר קדשי קדשים מיפסלי ביוצא, כדמוכח במנחות בפ' "שתי הלחם" (דף נה.). ולעיל בפ' "קדשי קדשים" (דף ס:), *דאמר: בשני מקומות קדשים נאכלין, ומוקי לה בקדשי קדשים ולאחר שיפרקו לוים את המשכן – היינו כל זמן שלא נסע מכל וכל, דעדיין המזבח וקלעי החצר במקומן. וא"ת: בריש "שתי הלחם" (מנחות דף נה.) דפליגי בלחם הפנים אם נפסל במסעות. ומפרש: דבמסודר כ"ע לא פליגי דלא מיפסיל, כי פליגי – במסולק. מאן דאמר אינו נפסל – כדדרשינן, דאע"פ שנסע אהל מועד הוא. ואידך ההוא לדגלים הוא דאתא. פי': להודיע איזה דגל יסע תחלה. והשתא, אמאי לא משני דאתא לקדשים קלים ולקדשי קדשים קודם סילוק הקלעים?*. **והתורה** אמרה בדד ישב. שלא יהו טמאים אחרים יושבים עמו. אע"ג דהך סוגיא לר"ש והך דרשא לר' יהודה, דלר"ש דריש ליה מקרא אחרינא, בפסחים בריש "אלו דברים" (דף סו.) – ניחא ליה להתלמוד לאתויי דרשא הפשוטה והקלרה*. **פלכו** קלטתו. כך דגושה בנחמיה, (ג) כמו נסך נסכו. **עיר** שקלטתו כבר. עיקר קרא ברוצח שהרג בעיר מקלטו. ותרוייהו תניגהו במכות פ"ב (דף יב:): הרג באותה העיר – גולה משכונה לשכונה, ולוי גולה מעיר לעיר. ושמא היינו לכתחלה, דבן לוי גולה מעיר לעיר, אבל דיעבד – הא אמרי' דאם גולה לתוך פלכו פלכו קולטו. ומפלך לפלך – היינו מעיר לעיר. ואם גולה לתוך פלכו – כגון משכונה לשכונה. וכן משמע פי' הקונטרס. אי נמי: גם לכתחלה אין זקוק לצאת מן העיר. והא דגולה לעיר אחרת – כדי להלך כולה ובתחומה. דאי בעירו משכונה לשכונה, אם חזר לשכונתו – כילא חוץ לתחום. **כל** הנידר ונידב קרב בבמה. אפי' מנחות ונזירות קרב בבמה קטנה, כדמפרש. ושאין נידר ונידב אין קרב בבמה קטנה, דאילו לצבור אין מקריבין בקטנה. וחובות דיחיד אפי' בגדולה לא קרבי בשעת היתר הבמות לר' מאיר, כדמוכח מלתא דר' יהודה. כדפי' בקונטרס, דמדקאמר ר' יהודה כל שהצבור ויחיד מקריבין כו' – מכלל דשמעינהו לר' מאיר ורבנן שיש חילוק, וזהו חלוקו: שאין יחיד מקריב חובות בגלגל אפי' בבמה גדולה. דר' מאיר ורבנן דרשי: לא תעשו בגלגל ככל אשר אנחנו עושים פה היום חובות, ואפי' בבמה גדולה. אלא איש הישר בעיניו יעשה – ישרות, דהיינו נדבות. ר' יהודה סבר דכי כתיב "הישר" – א"בעיניו" קאי, דהיא במת יחיד. **רבי** שמעון אומר אף צבור לא הקריבו כו'. פי' בקונטרס: ר"ש פליג אכולהו. דכולהו סבירא להו דאין חילוק לצבור בין מדבר לגלגל בבמה גדולה, ור"ש אומר: אף צבור עצמן לא הקריבו בגדולה יותר מיחיד בקטנה, אלא פסחים כו' וחובות

לא

דאמרינן נ"ק

[ועיין מה שהירלו תוס' בזבחים סא: ד"ה אע"פ וכו' ובמנחות נה. ד"ה מר וכו' ועי' מ"ש לעיל מא. בתוס' ד"ה ואתא]

[וכ"כ תוס' שבת קכח: ועי' מה שרשמתי שם על לדו]

שיטה מקובצת

א] הואי א"כ נמצאו: ב] משתלחין חוץ למחנה אחת והתורה אמרה בדד ישב לבדו ישב שלא יהא טמאים אחרים יושבים עמו אלא כולהו הוו ומחנה לויה לא הוה קלטה ומאי לא היו: ג] לך בחייך לך מקום במקומך אשר ינום שמה מלמד שהיו ישראל גולין במדבר להיכן: ד] גלה לתוך פלכו: ה] תיבת היה נמחק: ו] בבמה מנחות ומתיבות מנחות ונזירות קריבין בבמה בס"א אינו אלא רש"י ז"ל מביאו מת"כ וק"ל: ז] קרבו ליחיד אלא: ח] ושלמים בלבד וחכ"א: ט] ליחיד אלא: י] אחת זב ואחת טמא נפש: יא] שם עוד מחנה תיבת קבע נמחק: יב] לך בחייך. תיבת מקום נמחק: יג] דמדבר שהיתה מחנה: יד] הן וקרבי תיבת הוא נמחק: טו] מקרבי כלל אשתכח תיבת כו' נמחק: טז] אלא פסחים אות ה' נמחק: יז] ילפי טעמייהו דכולהו: יח] לא קרבו: יט] קרבו בבמה: כ] בין אהל מועד: כא] חילוק ומהו חילוקן שאין:

הגהות הב"ח

(א) (רש"י ד"ה וכל שהצבור וכו' בכלל מותרות במות יחיד כצ"ל והד"א):

תורה אור

וְחוֹבוֹת א] שֶׁקָּבוּעַ לָהֶן זְמַן. מַאי טַעְמָא דְּר"מ? דְּאָמַר קְרָא: °"לֹא תַעֲשׂוּן כְּכֹל אֲשֶׁר אֲנַחְנוּ עוֹשִׂים פֹּה הַיּוֹם", אָמַר לָהֶן מֹשֶׁה לְיִשְׂרָאֵל: כִּי עַיְילִיתוּ לָאָרֶץ, יְשָׁרוֹת תַּקְרִיבוּ, חוֹבוֹת לֹא תַּקְרִיבוּ; מְנָחוֹת וּנְזִירוּת יְשָׁרוֹת נִינְהוּ. וְרַבָּנַן? ב] אֵין מִנְחָה בְּבָמָה, נְזִירוּת – חוֹבוֹת נִינְהוּ. אָמַר שְׁמוּאֵל: מַחֲלוֹקֶת בְּחַטָּאת וְאָשָׁם, אֲבָל בְּעוֹלוֹת וּשְׁלָמִים – דִּבְרֵי הַכֹּל יְשָׁרוֹת נִינְהוּ, וְקָרְבִי. מוֹתִיב רַבָּה: *חָזֶה וָשׁוֹק וּתְרוּמַת לַחְמֵי תוֹדָה – נוֹהֲגִין בְּבָמָה גְּדוֹלָה וְאֵין נוֹהֲגִין בְּבָמָה קְטַנָּה, וְאִילּוּ הַזְּרוֹעַ בְּשֵׁלָה שַׁיְּירָהּ; אִי אָמְרַתְּ בִּשְׁלָמָא בְּעוֹלָה וּשְׁלָמִים פְּלִיגִי, הָא מַנִּי? רַבָּנַן הִיא. אֶלָּא אִי אָמְרַתְּ בְּחַטָּאת וְאָשָׁם פְּלִיגִי, הָא מַנִּי? אֶלָּא אִי אִיתְּמַר הָכִי אִיתְּמַר, אָמַר שְׁמוּאֵל: מַחֲלוֹקֶת בְּעוֹלָה וּשְׁלָמִים, אֲבָל בְּחַטָּאת וְאָשָׁם – דִּבְרֵי הַכֹּל חוֹבוֹת נִינְהוּ, וְלָא קָרְבִי. אָמַר מָר, וַחֲכָמִים אוֹמְרִים: כֹּל שֶׁהַצִּבּוּר מַקְרִיבִין בְּאֹהֶל וכו'. מַאי טַעֲמַיְיהוּ דְּרַבָּנַן? אָמַר קְרָא: *°"אִישׁ הַיָּשָׁר בְּעֵינָיו יַעֲשֶׂה", אִישׁ – יְשָׁרוֹת הוּא דְּלִיקְרוּב, חוֹבוֹת לָא לִיקְרוּב, וְצִבּוּר – אֲפִי' חוֹבוֹת ג] לִיקְרוּב.
וְרַבִּי

דברים יב
שופטים יז

לא תַעֲשׂוּן וגו'. לְאַחַר בִּיאַת הָאָרֶץ מִשְׁתָּעֵי, וְקָאָמַר: לֹא תַעֲשׂוּן כְּשֶׁתָּבֹאוּ בַּגִּלְגָּל. כְּכֹל אֲשֶׁר אֲנַחְנוּ עוֹשִׂים פֹּה הַיּוֹם. שֶׁאָנוּ בֵּין לַצִּבּוּר בֵּין יָחִיד מַקְרִיבִין חַטָּאוֹת וַאֲשָׁמוֹת וּבְכוֹר וּמַעֲשֵׂר, שֶׁהֵן חוֹבוֹת שֶׁאֵין קָבוּעַ לָהֶם זְמַן, וְכ"ש חוֹבוֹת הַקָּבוּעַ לָהֶם זְמַן. אֲבָל מַה אָנוּ עוֹשִׂים שָׁם – "אִישׁ כָּל הַיָּשָׁר בְּעֵינָיו", הַיָּחִיד לֹא יַקְרִיב שָׁם אֶלָּא נְדָרִים וּנְדָבוֹת שֶׁיָּשְׁרוּ בְּעֵינָיו לִנְדּוֹר וְלִנְדּוֹב. עַד מָתַי – "כִּי לֹא בָאתֶם" וגו', עַד שֶׁתָּבֹאוּ לְשִׁילֹה. יְשָׁרוֹת תַּקְרִיבוּ. נְדָרִים וּנְדָבוֹת. חוֹבוֹת לֹא תַקְרִיבוּ. הַיְּחִידִים. דְּ"אִישׁ" כְּתִיב, וְלָא פָּלֵיג קְרָא בֵּין גְּדוֹלָה בֵּין קְטַנָּה, דְּלְיָחִיד לֹא קָרֵב אֶלָּא נִידָּר וְנִידָּב. הִלְכָּךְ, שֶׁאֵין נִידָּר וְנִידָּב – אֵין קָרֵב בְּבָמַת יָחִיד, דְּהָא אֵין קָדְשֵׁי לַצִּבּוּר קְרֵיבִין, ד] כִּדְתְנַן בְּמַתְנִי' (דף קיב:): קָרְבָּנוֹת לַצִּבּוּר קְרֵיבִין בַּמִּשְׁכָּן, קָרְבְּנוֹת יָחִיד קְרֵיבִין בְּבָמָה. מְנָחוֹת וּנְזִירוּת יְשָׁרוֹת נִינְהוּ. דְּאע"ג דִּבְמְלֹאת נִזְרוֹ הָוְיָין קָרְבְּנוֹתָיו ה] חוֹבָה עָלָיו, מִיהוּ ע"י נֶדֶר בָּאוּ עָלָיו. אֵין מִנְחָה בְּבָמָה. כִּדְאָמְרִי' לְקַמָּן: "זְבָחִים" וְלֹא מְנָחוֹת. [דִּכְתִיב]: "לְמַעַן אֲשֶׁר יָבִיאוּ בְּנֵי יִשְׂרָאֵל וגו' עַל פְּנֵי הַשָּׂדֶה" – הַיְינוּ ו] בָּמוֹת, שְׁעַת הֶיתֵּר שֶׁלָּהֶם. "וֶהֱבִיאוּם לַה'" – אוֹתָם שֶׁהוּקְדְּשׁוּ בִּשְׁעַת הֶיתֵּר וְלֹא הִסְפִּיק לַהֲבִיאָם עַד שֶׁנֶּאֶסְרוּ, כְּדַאֲמַרַן בְּ"הַשּׁוֹחֵט" לְעֵיל (דף קו:) דְּפָסוּק זֶה בְּקָדְשֵׁי קָדָשִׁים שֶׁהוּקְדְּשׁוּ בִּשְׁעַת הֶיתֵּר וְהִקְרִיבוּם בִּשְׁעַת אִיסּוּר קָאֵי. "וְזָבְחוּ זִבְחֵי שְׁלָמִים" – וּמְפָרֵשׁ בְּת"כ: אֵין לִי שֶׁקָּרְבוּ בְּבָמָה אֶלָּא שְׁלָמִים, דְּהָא אוֹקִימְנָא בְּקָדְשֵׁי בָמָה, מִנַּיִן אַף עוֹלָה? ת"ל: "זְבָחִים". יָכוֹל אַף חַטָּאת וְאָשָׁם? ת"ל: "אוֹתָם". וּמָה רָאִיתָ? אַחֲרֵי שֶׁרִיבָּה וּמִיעֵט, אָמַרְתָּ: מַה שְּׁלָמִים הַבָּאִים בְּנֶדֶר וּנְדָבָה – אַף כָּל הַבָּא בְּנֶדֶר וּנְדָבָה. וּלְר"מ אִיתְרַבּוּ נַמִי מְנָחוֹת וּנְזִירוּת. וְרַבָּנַן דָּיְיקִי: "זְבָחִים" וְלֹא מְנָחוֹת, אֶלָּא דָּבָר הַנִּזְבָּח. נְזִירוּת חוֹבָה הִיא. דְּהוּא לֹא הִתְנַדֵּב ז] *[אֵלּוּ] הַקָּרְבָּנוֹת, אֶלָּא אָסַר עַצְמוֹ בְּיַיִן וּבְתִגְלַחַת, וּמֵאֵלָיו נִתְחַיֵּיב בְּקָרְבָּנוֹת. מַחֲלוֹקֶת. דְּר"מ וְרַבָּנַן בִּנְזִירוּת – בְּחַטָּאת וְאָשָׁם שֶׁבָּהּ. אֲבָל עוֹלוֹת וּשְׁלָמִים דְּנָזִיר – דִּבְרֵי הַכֹּל קָרְבִי. חָזֶה וָשׁוֹק. הַמּוּרָם מִשְּׁלָמִים וְתוֹדָה, (א) וְאַרְבַּע חַלּוֹת הַמּוּרָמוֹת לַכֹּהֵן מֵאַרְבַּע מִינֵי חַלּוֹת שֶׁבַּתּוֹדָה, כִּדְכְתִיב: "וְהִקְרִיב מִמֶּנּוּ אֶחָד מִכָּל קָרְבָּן" וגו' (ויקרא ז). וְאֵין נוֹהֲגִין בְּבָמָה קְטַנָּה. גָּרְסִינַן בְּסוֹף פִּירְקִין (דף קיט:), דִּכְתִיב בְּהוּ: "לְהָנִיף תְּנוּפָה לַה'" – וְלֹא בְּבָמָה. וְאִילּוּ מוּרָם מֵאֵיל נָזִיר, דְּהַיְינוּ זְרוֹעַ בְּשֵׁלָה – שַׁיְּירָהּ וְלָא תְּנָיֵיהּ. שְׁמַע מִינַּהּ: לָא קָרְבִי שַׁלְמֵי נָזִיר בְּבָמָה, דְּאִי הָווּ קָרְבִי – הֲוָה תָּנֵי דְּלָא נָהֵיג בֵּיהּ נַמִי תְּרוּמָה דִּידֵיהּ (ב). אֶלָּא אִי אָמְרַתְּ בְּחַטָּאת וְאָשָׁם הוּא דִּפְלִיג. אֲבָל שַׁלְמֵי נָזִיר דִּבְרֵי הַכֹּל קָרְבִי, הָא מַנִּי? אִישׁ הוּא דְּחוֹבוֹת לא הִקְרִיבוּ. וַאֲפִי' בִּגְדוֹלָה, אֲבָל לַצִּבּוּר מַקְרִיבִים חוֹבוֹת.
וְרַבִּי

וחובות הקבוע להם זמן. אבל פר העלם דבר ושעירי עבודה זרה – לא קרבו להם בגלגל, עכ"ל. ובחנם הזכיר פר העלם דבר ושעירי עבודה זרה שהן חטאות שאין קבוע להם זמן, דאפי' חטאות הקבוע להם זמן, כגון שעירי הרגלים, לא קרבו לר"ש, כדמסיק לקמן: תתרגם מתני' בעולה. (הג"ה: וא"כ ביוה"כ לא קרבו לצבור באהל מועד* בנוב וגבעון לא פרים ולא שעירים כי אם *תמידים. והא דאמרי' בתוספתא ר' יהודה אומר: אבשלום נזיר היה, שנאמר "ויאמר אבשלום אלכה נא ואשלם נדרי אשר נדרתי בחברון כי נדר נדר עבדך בשבתי בגשור". והאי קרא בהיותם בגבעון כתיב, ומפרש פ"ב דתמורה (דף יד:) שהקריבם בחברון בבמת יחיד. דאי הלך בחברון להביא כבשים טובים ולהקריבם בבמה גדולה – א"כ "מחברון" מיבעי ליה. והשתא לר' יהודה, אי נזירות נידר ונידב הוא – אתי שפיר שהקריבן בבמת יחיד בחברון. ואי נזירות חובה הוי – א"כ הקריבן בגבעון באהל מועד שהיה שם, *דלר' יהודה יחיד נמי מצי מקריב חובות בבמה גדולה, אף בשעת היתר הבמות. ולא דייק בין "מחברון" "ובחברון". אבל רבנן דאמרי: נזירות חובה הוא, ולא קרב יחיד חובות אף בבמת צבור בנוב וגבעון – א"כ אבשלום לא נזיר היה. והא קרא ד"אלכה ואשובה ואשלם נדרי" מיירי בנדרים ונדבות. הג"ה).

רבי שמעון אומר אף צבור לא הקריבו כו'. לכאורה ר"ש אדרבנן דלעיל מייניה קאי. ואינהו סברי כרבנן קמאי דמנחות ונזירות לא קרבו בבמה, דליכא בינייהו אלא נסכים, כדמפרש לקמיה ש"מ דלר"ש נמי לא קרבו, דהא אפי' בלבור ממעט יותר משאר תנאים. ותימה: דבפ"ק דמגילה (דף ט:) [במתני' דקתני]: אין בין במה גדולה לבמה קטנה אלא פסחים, זה הכלל כל הנידר ונידב קרב כו'. ומפרש בגמ': כעין פסחים, דהיינו חובות הקבוע להם זמן, אבל שאין קבוע להם זמן – הכא והכא לא קרב. ומוקי לה כר"ש. אלמא ר"ש תני האי כללא, א"כ מנחות ונזירות קרבי לר"ש, וכדאמרינן הכא לר"מ דתני האי כללא! ואי הוה גרסי' במגילה "זה הכלל נידר ונידב", בלא "כל" – הוה ניחא ליה, ד"כל" דר"מ אתי לרבויי מנחות ונזירות. ועוד יש לומר: דהא דפשיטא ליה לר"מ דמנחות ונזירות ישרות – משום דתניא בת"כ בפרשת "אחרי מות": מה שלמים מיוחדין שהם נידר ונידב קריבין בבמה – אף כל נידר ונידב קרב בבמה, אף המנחות והנזירות, דברי ר"מ. וקלת תימה אי אההיא סמיך, דלא מייתי לה. ועוד: לר"ש דמגילה, מי נפקא מנחה מכלל נידר ונידב? ונראה ליישב מתניתין דהכי קאמר: דאין חילוק בין במה גדולה לבמה קטנה אלא פסחים. כל הנידר ונידב הקרב בבמה גדולה – קרב בקטנה, וכל שאין נידר ונידב שאין קרב בגדולה – אין קרב בקטנה. ולא נחת אלא לפרש מה ששוותה הגדולה והקטנה. אבל *יש נידר ונידב שאין קרב לא בזו ולא בזו, כגון מנחות ונזירות. אבל לנידר ונידב דר"מ אין לפרש דלא איירי במנחות ונזירות, דספיר מישתמע מלישנא ד"נידב". ועוד: דקתני לה בהדיא בת"כ. וכן נראה ודאי לפרש דאההיא דתורת כהנים סמיך, אע"ג דלא מייתי לה. דבתמורה מייתי לה בפ"ב (דף יד:) דאמרי' התם, אמר ליה אביי: ולימא מר שלמי פסח, דאי שלמי נזיר – נידר ונידב הוא. דהא תניא: זה הכלל כל הנידר ונידב – קרב בבמת יחיד, וכל שאינו נידר ונידב – אינו קרב בבמת יחיד. ותניא: המנחות ונזירות קריבות בבמת יחיד, דברי ר"מ. משמע דמההיא דייק, ולא מלישנא. ומאן דלא חשיב התם נזירות נידר ונידב – קמשני: סמי מכאן נזירות. **ורבנן** מנחות אין מנחה בבמה ליחיד. בין בבמה גדולה בין בבמה קטנה קאמר, כדתניא אידך רבנן: כאן וכאן לא קרבו (נסכים) ליחיד אלא עולה ושלמים בלבד. ואמרי' דנסכים איכא בינייהו ותו לא. וה"ה דעופות נמי לא קרבו לרבנן, כדאמרי' בסוף פירקין (דף קיט.): לדברי האומר אין מנחה בבמה – אין עופות בבמה. מ"ט? "זבחים" – ולא עופות, "זבחים" – ולא מנחות. דאוקימנא ההוא קרא לעיל בריש "השוחט" (דף קו:) בקדשים שהקדישן בשעת היתר הבמות. ותימה: *דבסוף פירקין (קיג.) תנן, ר' יהודה אומר: אין מנחה בבמה. והכא קא"ר יהודה: כל שהצבור והיחיד מקריבין באהל מועד שבמדבר – מקריבין באהל מועד שבגלגל. והרי מנחות ועופות, דבגלגל כאן וכאן לא קרבו! ולא מיסתבר למימר דנהי דלרבנן כאן וכאן לא קרבו, לר' יהודה קרבו *בבמה לצבור. דמהיכי תיתי הך דרשא למר ולמר? ועוד, א"כ לקמן דפריך: חכמים היינו תנא קמא! ומשני: קרבו נסכים במדבר איכא בינייהו. לימא דמנחה קריבה בבמת צבור איכא בינייהו, דלרבנן קדמאי קרבה ולבתראי לא קרבה!

מחלוקת בחטאת ואשם. בחטאת ואשם של נזירות איירי.

ואין נוהגין בבמה קטנה. פי' בקונטרס: דכתיב בהו "להניף תנופה לה'". וא"ת: הרי מנחה לת"ק דר' יהודה דמתני', דאיתא בבמה קטנה, ואין תנופה והגשה בה. וא"כ הנך נמי ליהוי בבמה ולא ליבעי תנופה! ויש לומר: דהני חזה ושוק ותרומת לחמי תודה – עיקר מלותן בתנופה, הלכך בטלה תנופה בטלי אינהו. אבל מנחה – עיקר מלותה קמילה והקטרה.

מחלוקת בעולה (ואשם) [ושלמים]. של נזירות קאמר. *ותימה: דמאן דאמר לא קרבו ואפ' בבמה גדולה, היכי משני קרא דאבשלום, דכתיב (שמואל ב טו) "ואשלם נדרי"? דליכא למימר בשאר נדרים, דבפרק שני דתמורה (דף יד:) משמע דאיירי בקרבן נזירות!
ותתרגם

[לקמן קיט: ע"ש]

ל"ק

אבל מודה ר"ש דיש ל"ק

נ"ל דבמתני' תנן ל"ק

נ"ל בבמת לצבור

הגהות הב"ח

(א) רש"י ד"ה חזה ו[...] ותודה הס"ד ואח"כ מה[...] ותרומת לחמי תודה ארב[...] (ב) ד"ה ואין נוהגין ו[...] תרומה דידיה בבמת יח[...] הס"ד:

מועד שבגלגל ובנוב ל"ק

דומיא דתמידים ל"ק

ולר"י ל"ק

[איש כל הישר בעיניו (דברים יב) כל"ל]

שייך לע"א

שיטה מקובצת

א] וחובות הקבוע להן: ב] ורבנן מנחות אין מנחה: ג] חובות נמי ליקריב: ד] קריבין ביה כדתנן: ה] קרבנותיו עליו חובה מיהו: ו] היינו במה בשעת היתר: ז] התנדב את הקרבנות:

אע"פ שקרב בבמה גדולה ל"ק

רש"ק מ"ז

ובהג"ה דלעיל לא כתבו כן ועי' בתוס' דתמורה דף יד ע"ב ד"ה סמי דמתרצו תמיה ז

וְרַבִּי יְהוּדָה אָמַר לָךְ: כִּי כְּתִיב "הַיָּשָׁר" – (*בְּעֵינָיו) הוּא דִּכְתִיב, אֲבָל בְּבָמָה גְּדוֹלָה – אֲפִילּוּ חוֹבוֹת נַמִי לִיקְרוּב. אֶלָּא הָא כְּתִיב "אִישׁ", לָאו לְמֵימְרָא דְּאִישׁ יְשָׁרוֹת הוּא דְּלִיקְרוּב, הָא חוֹבוֹת לָא לִיקְרוּב? כִּי כְּתִיב "אִישׁ" – לְהַכְשִׁיר אֶת הַזָּר. זָר, °מִ"וְזָרַק הַכֹּהֵן אֶת הַדָּם עַל מִזְבַּח ה'" נָפְקָא! מַהוּ דְּתֵימָא: לִיבָּעֵי קִדּוּשׁ בְּכוֹרוֹת כְּמֵעִיקָּרָא, קָא מַשְׁמַע לָן. חֲכָמִים הַיְינוּ תַּנָּא קַמָּא! אָמַר רַב פַּפָּא: *קָרְבוּ נְסָכִים בַּמִּדְבָּר אִיכָּא בֵּינַיְיהוּ.§ אָמַר מָר: רַבִּי שִׁמְעוֹן אוֹמֵר וכו'.§ מ"ט דְּרַבִּי שִׁמְעוֹן? דִּכְתִיב: °"וַיַּעֲשׂוּ בְנֵי יִשְׂרָאֵל אֶת הַפֶּסַח בַּגִּלְגָּל"; פְּשִׁיטָא! אֶלָּא א] הָא קמ"ל: דְּחוֹבוֹת כְּעֵין פֶּסַח הוּא דְּקָרֵב, הָא לָאו כְּעֵין פֶּסַח – לָא קָרֵב. וְאִידָךְ? מִיבָּעֵי לֵיהּ לְכִדְרַבִּי יוֹחָנָן. *דְּא"ר יוֹחָנָן מִשּׁוּם רַבִּי בְּנָאָה: אעָרֵל מְקַבֵּל הַזָּאָה. תָּנֵי תַּנָּא קַמֵּיהּ דְּרַב אַדָּא בַּר אַהֲבָה: *אֵין בֵּין בָּמָה גְּדוֹלָה לְבָמָה קְטַנָּה אֶלָּא ב] פֶּסַח וְחוֹבוֹת הַקָּבוּעַ לָהֶן *זְמַן. (א"ל: יָחִיד חוֹבוֹת שֶׁקָּבוּעַ לָהֶן זְמָן מְנָא לֵיהּ? א"ל: אַסְמְיֵיהּ?) א"ל: תְּתַרְגֵּם מַתְנִיתָךְ בְּעוֹלַת חוֹבָה, דְּאִיכָּא עוֹלַת נְדָבָה. ג] *דְּאִי חַטָּאת יָחִיד הוּא – חוֹבוֹת דְּקָבִיעַ לֵיהּ זְמַן מִי אִיכָּא? וְלוֹקְמַהּ בְּמִנְחַת חוֹבָה, דְּהָא אִיכָּא חֲבִיתִּין! קָא סָבַר: *אֵין מִנְחָה בְּבָמָה.§ "בָּאוּ לְשִׁילֹה" וכו'.§ מְנָא הָנֵי מִילֵּי? א"ר חִיָּיא בַּר אַבָּא אָמַר רַבִּי יוֹחָנָן: כָּתוּב אֶחָד אוֹמֵר: °"וַתְּבִיאֵהוּ בֵית ה' שִׁלֹה", ד] וְכָתוּב אֶחָד אוֹמֵר °"וַיִּטֹּשׁ (אֶת) מִשְׁכַּן שִׁלֹה ה] אֹהֶל שִׁכֵּן בָּאָדָם", וּכְתִיב: °"וַיִּמְאַס בְּאֹהֶל יוֹסֵף וּבְשֵׁבֶט אֶפְרַיִם לֹא בָחָר", הָא כֵּיצַד? בלֹא הָיְתָה שָׁם תִּקְרָה, אֶלָּא אֲבָנִים מִלְּמַטָּן וִירִיעוֹת ו] מִלְּמַעְלָן, וְהִיא הָיְתָה "מְנוּחָה".§ "קָדְשֵׁי קָדָשִׁים".§ מְנָא הָנֵי מִילֵּי? ז] א"ר אוֹשַׁעְיָא, דְּאָמַר קְרָא: °"הִשָּׁמֶר לְךָ פֶּן תַּעֲלֶה עֹלֹתֶיךָ בְּכָל מָקוֹם אֲשֶׁר (אַתָּה) תִּרְאֶה", בְּכָל מָקוֹם ח] אֲשֶׁר תִּרְאֶה – אִי אַתָּה מַעֲלֶה, אֲבָל אַתָּה אוֹכֵל בְּכָל מָקוֹם שֶׁאַתָּה רוֹאֶה. אֵימָא: בְּכָל מָקוֹם שֶׁאַתָּה רוֹאֶה – אִי אַתָּה מַעֲלֶה, אֲבָל אַתָּה זוֹבֵחַ בְּכָל מָקוֹם ט] שֶׁתִּרְאֶה! א"ר יַנַּאי, אָמַר קְרָא: °"שָׁם תַּעֲלֶה וְשָׁם תַּעֲשֶׂה". רַבִּי אַבְדִּימִי בַּר י] חַסָּא אָמַר, אָמַר קְרָא:

וְלוֹ

תורה אור: ויקרא יז | יהושע ה | ש"א א | תהלים עח | שם | דברים יב | שם

רש"י

וְרַבִּי יְהוּדָה. דְּאָמַר יָחִיד נַמִי מַקְרִיב חוֹבוֹת בַּגְּדוֹלָה, אָמַר לָךְ: כִּי כְּתִיב "הַיָּשָׁר" דְּמְמַעֵט יָחִיד מֵהַקְרָבַת חוֹבוֹת – אַ"בְּעֵינָיו" כְּתִיב יא]. אֶלָּא לְרַבִּי יְהוּדָה הָא כְּתִיב אִישׁ. וְאִי לָאו לְמַעוּטֵי אַף מִבָּמָה גְּדוֹלָה אָתָא, לָמָּה לִי דִּכְתִיב "אִישׁ"? נִכְתּוֹב: "כָּל הַיָּשָׁר בְּעֵינָיו", וְכֵיוָן דִּ"בְּעֵינָיו" הַיְינוּ יב] קְטַנָּה, פְּשִׁיטָא דְּאִישׁ הוּא דְּמִימְעִיט, דְּהָא צִבּוּר לָא מַקְרְבֵי בָּהּ! לְהַכְשִׁיר אֶת הַזָּר. לַעֲבוֹדַת בָּמָה. זָר מִוְּזָרַק הַכֹּהֵן נָפְקָא לָן. לְקַמָּן בְּפִירְקִין, דִּכְתִיב (ויקרא יז): "וְזָרַק הַכֹּהֵן אֶת הַדָּם עַל מִזְבַּח ה' פֶּתַח אֹהֶל מוֹעֵד" – כֹּהֵן פֶּתַח אֹהֶל מוֹעֵד, וְאֵין כֹּהֵן בְּבָמָה, אֶלָּא אֲפִי' זָר וַאֲפִי' עֶבֶד. הָכִי דָּרֵישׁ לֵיהּ בְּתוֹרַת כֹּהֲנִים. חֲכָמִים הַיְינוּ תַּנָּא קַמָּא. רַבָּנַן בַּתְרָאֵי הַיְינוּ רַבָּנַן קַמָּאֵי, דְּהָא אִינְהוּ נַמִי הָכִי אָמְרִי, דְּיָחִיד לָא קָרְבוּ אֶלָּא עוֹלוֹת וּשְׁלָמִים וְצִבּוּר קָרְבִי [נַמִי חוֹבוֹת], דְּהָא מֵ"אִישׁ" נָפְקָא לְהוּ מִיעוּטָא. קָרְבוּ נְסָכִים בַּמִּדְבָּר אִיכָּא בֵּינַיְיהוּ. לְרַבָּנַן קַמָּאֵי לָא קָרְבוּ נְסָכִים בַּמִּדְבָּר, וְעוֹלָה וּשְׁלָמִים גְּרֵידָא בְּלָא נְסָכִים קָא גָּמְרִי דְּקָרְבִי בְּבָמָה, דְּבַמִּדְבָּר לָא קָרְבִי דְּ"כִּי תָבֹאוּ" דְּפָרָשַׁת נְסָכִים (במדבר טו) לְהַטְעִינָהּ נְסָכִים בְּמִשְׁכַּן שִׁילֹה אָתָא, לְאַחַר יְרוּשָּׁה וִישִׁיבָה, כִּדְאָמְרַן בְּ"הַשּׁוֹחֵט" (לעיל קיא.). וְרַבָּנַן בַּתְרָאֵי לְטְפוּיֵי אָתוּ, מִדְּתְנַן מִשְׁנָה יְתֵירָא: "כָּל שֶׁהַצִּבּוּר מַקְרִיבִין בְּאֹהֶל מוֹעֵד שֶׁבַּמִּדְבָּר מַקְרִיבִין בַּגִּלְגָּל". לָמָּה לְהוּ לְמִיתְנֵי? הָא רַבִּי יְהוּדָה נַמִי בְּצִבּוּר כְּוָותַיְיהוּ קָאָמַר, וְהָכִי אִיבָּעֵי לְהוּ לְמֵימַר: "כָּאן וְכָאן לָא קָרְבוּ לְיָחִיד אֶלָּא עוֹלָה וּשְׁלָמִים"! אֶלָּא לְטְפוּיֵי אַדְּרַבָּנַן קַמָּאֵי אָתוּ, וְאָמְרִי: כָּל שֶׁהַצִּיבּוּר צְרִיכִין לְהַקְרִיב (א) מַקְרִיבִין בְּאֹהֶל מוֹעֵד שֶׁבַּמִּדְבָּר, יג] מַקְרִיבִין בְּאֹהֶל מוֹעֵד שֶׁבַּגִּלְגָּל. וּלְטְפוּיֵי נְסָכִים אָתוּ, וּלְמֵימַר דְּקָרְבוּ בַּמִּדְבָּר לְצִבּוּר וּלְיָחִיד, וְכֵן בַּגִּלְגָּל (ב) לִשְׁתֵּי הַבָּמוֹת. וּלְמַאן דְּאִית לֵיהּ קָרְבוּ בַּמִּדְבָּר – אִית לֵיהּ דְּקָרְבוּ בְּבָמַת יָחִיד בַּגִּלְגָּל, דְּ"כִי תָבֹאוּ" לָא אָתָא אֶלָּא לְהַטְעִינָהּ נְסָכִים לְבָמָה קְטַנָּה, דְּהָא בַּגְּדוֹלָה כְּבָר הָיוּ קְרֵבִין. פְּשִׁיטָא. דְּבָעוּ לְמֶיעֱבַד פֶּסַח. עָרֵל. שֶׁנִּטְמָא בְּמֵת, מְקַבֵּל הַזָּאָה וְטָהוֹר מִטּוּמְאַת מֵת לִיגַּע בַּקֳּדָשִׁים. וְיָלֵיף מֵהָכָא דִּכְתִיב (יהושע ה): "וַיַּעֲשׂוּ אֶת הַפֶּסַח בַּגִּלְגָּל" – דְּמַשְׁמַע שֶׁעֲשָׂאוּהוּ כְּהִלְכָתוֹ בְּמִילָה בְּטָהֳרָה. וְרוּבָּן עֲרֵלִים הָיוּ בַּמִּדְבָּר, דִּכְתִיב (שם): "לֹא מָלוּ". וְאָמְרִינַן בִּיבָמוֹת: בַּעֲשָׂרָה בְּנִיסָן שֶׁעָבְרוּ אֶת הַיַּרְדֵּן לָא מְהוּל מִשּׁוּם חוּלְשָׁא דְאוֹרְחָא, אֶלָּא בְּחַד סְרֵי הוּא דְמָהוּל. וְאִשְׁתַּכַּח דִּטְמֵאֵי מֵתִים שֶׁהָיוּ בָּהֶם, שֶׁהֲרֵי רוּבָּן טְמֵאֵי מֵתִים הָיוּ, שֶׁמֵּתוּ אֲבוֹתֵיהֶם כָּל אַרְבָּעִים שָׁנָה בַּמִּדְבָּר וְנִטְמְאוּ בָּהֶם, וְאִם לֹא קִבְּלוּ הַזָּאָה וְנִטְהֲרוּ בְּעַרְלוּתָן – אֵין לָהֶם שְׁהוּת לִהְיוֹת מִשֶּׁמָּלוּ, דְּהָא צָרִיךְ לְהַפְרִישׁ שְׁלֹשָׁה יָמִים בֵּין הַזָּאָה לְהַזָּאָה: רְבִיעִי, חֲמִישִׁי, וְשִׁשִּׁי. וְהָכָא, אִי לָא הִזּוּ עַד יוֹם אַחַד עָשָׂר בְּנִיסָן הַזָּאָה רִאשׁוֹנָה לְאַחַר שֶׁמָּלוּ – תּוּ לָא מָטֵי זְמַן הַזָּאָה שְׁנִיָּה עַד יוֹם חֲמִשָּׁה עָשָׂר. וּבִיבָמוֹת אִיתֵיהּ לְהָא דְּרַבִּי יוֹחָנָן בְּפֶרֶק "הֶעָרֵל" (דף עא:). יד] וְתִתַרְגֵּם מַתְנִיתָךְ. דְּקָתָנֵי: חוֹבוֹת הַקָּבוּעַ לָהֶם זְמַן קָרְבוּ בַּגְּדוֹלָה. בְּעוֹלָה. כְּגוֹן עוֹלוֹת שֶׁל תְּמִידִין וּמוּסָפִין לַצִּבּוּר קָרְבוּ בָּהּ. טו] [אֲבָל] חַטָּאוֹת הַקָּבוּעַ לָהֶם זְמַן, כְּגוֹן שְׂעִירֵי הָרְגָלִים שֶׁל צִבּוּר – לֹא קָרְבוּ בָּהּ. דְּאִי בְּחַטָּאת. דְּאִי חוֹבוֹת הַקָּבוּעַ לָהֶם זְמַן בְּחַטָּאת נַמִי קָאָמַר. חַטָּאת נְדָבָה מִי אִיכָּא. לִיקְרַב כַּיּוֹצֵא בָּהּ בַּקְּטַנָּה? וְעַל כָּרְחָךְ טז] מַתְנִיתִין קמ"ל דְּלֹא קָרְבוּ לר"ש בַּגְּדוֹלָה לְבַד מִפְּסָחִים אֶלָּא חוֹבוֹת שֶׁיֵּשׁ כַּיּוֹצֵא בָּהֶן נְדָבָה. מִדְּקָתָנֵי "אֶלָּא פְּסָחִים וְחוֹבוֹת הַקָּבוּעַ לָהֶם זְמַן", וְאִי ס"ד כָּל חוֹבוֹת הַקָּבוּעַ לָהֶם זְמַן קָאָמַר – פְּסָחִים דְּקָתָנֵי לָמָּה לִי? הָכִי הֲוָה לֵיהּ לְמֵימַר: אֵין בֵּין בָּמָה גְּדוֹלָה לְבָמָה קְטַנָּה אֶלָּא חוֹבוֹת הַקָּבוּעַ לָהֶם זְמַן, וְהָווּ לְהוּ פְּסָחִים בִּכְלָל! אֶלָּא ה"ק: אֶלָּא פְּסָחִים – שֶׁקָּרְבוּ בַּגְּדוֹלָה וְלֹא קָרְבוּ בַּקְּטַנָּה כְּלָל. וּשְׁאָר דְּבָרִים שֶׁקָּרְבוּ כָּאן וְכָאן – אֵין חִילּוּק בָּהֶן, אֶלָּא שֶׁבְּזוֹ לֹא קָרְבוּ אֶלָּא נְדָבוֹת, וּבְזוֹ קָרְבוּ אַף חוֹבוֹת הַקָּבוּעַ לָהֶם זְמַן. וְנוֹקְמַהּ נַמִי בְּמִנְחָה. דְּמַשְׁכַּחַתְּ לָהּ כָּאן יז] מִנְחַת נְדָבָה בַּקְּטַנָּה, וּבַגְּדוֹלָה עוֹדֶפֶת מִנְחַת חֲבִיתִּין שֶׁהִיא יח] חוֹבוֹת הַקָּבוּעַ לָהֶן זְמַן בְּכָל יוֹם. קָא סָבַר רַב אַדָּא בַּר אַהֲבָה אֵין מִנְחָה בְּבָמָה. דְּ"זְבָחִים" כְּתִיב. וּבִשְׁלָמֵי צִבּוּר דַּעֲצֶרֶת לֵיכָּא לְאוֹקְמַהּ, מִשּׁוּם דְּשַׁלְמֵי בָּמָה קְטַנָּה לָא דָּמֵי לְהוּ, שֶׁאֵלּוּ קָדְשֵׁי קָדָשִׁים וְאֵלּוּ קָדָשִׁים קַלִּים. מנה"מ. דְּבֵית אֲבָנִים לְמַטָּן וִירִיעוֹת לַגַּג. וַיִּטֹּשׁ מִשְׁכַּן שִׁילֹה אֹהֶל שִׁכֵּן בָּאָדָם. הִשָּׁמֶר לְךָ. מִשֶּׁבָּאוּ אֶל הַמְּנוּחָה קָאֵי קְרָא.

וְלוֹ

תוספות

ותתרגם מתניתך בעולה. פירוש: כגון עולות תמידין ומוספין שיש כיולא בהם נדבות. אבל חטאות הלבור, כגון שעירי הרגלים, אע"ג דקבוע להם זמן – לא קרבו. והא מילתא דייק לה מדקתני פסחים. דליתני "קבוע להם זמן" ותו לא, והוו להו פסחים בכלל! אלא על כרחך: מתניתין קמ"ל דלא קרבו לרבי שמעון בגדולה לבד מפסחים, אלא שיש כיולא בהם בבמה. והכי קאמר: אלא פסחים שקרבו בגדולה לא קרבו בקטנה כלל, ושאר דברים שקרבו כאן וכאן – אין חילוק בהם, אלא שבזה לא הקריבו אלא נדבות ובזה קרבו חובות הקבוע להם זמן, כדפירש בקונטרס. והכי נמי הוה מצי למידק אברייתא דלעיל, דקאמר ר"ש: אף לבור לא הקריבו כו'. *ואי משום דלא איירי התם רבי שמעון בחילוק שבין במה גדולה לבמה קטנה, כדאיירי הכא – מ"מ על אגב הזכיר פסחים, דהא הוו בכלל חובות הקבוע להם זמן. ותימה: מנא ליה לר' שמעון הא מילתא, דחטאת דקבוע להם זמן לא קרב? דהא לעיל מפרשינן טעמא דרבי שמעון דיליף מפסח גלגל, והא ליכא למילף מפסח, דפסח נמי אין כיולא בו נדבה! ואי הוה מפרשינן כן, דפסח חשיב כיולא בו נדבה, משום דהוי קדשים קלים כעין שלמים – הוה ניחא. אבל בקונטרס לא פירש כן. וע"ק: היכי דייק מדקתני פסחים? דלמא הא דקתני פסחים – משום דעיקר טעמא מפסח יליף! וכן בפ"ק דמגילה (דף ט:) תני פסחים לחוד. ופריך בגמרא: פסחים ותו לא? אלא: כעין פסחים. ע"כ, מה שהזכיר פסחים טפי מאינך – משום דכולהו מפסח ילפינן! לכן נראה לפרש, דקא אמר: תתרגם מתניתך בעולה – היינו משום דכיון דמפסח יליף אית לן למימר: מה פסח שקבוע לו זמן וישנו בלבור כביחיד בשעת היתר הבמות, לבור בפסח ראשון ויחיד בפסח שני, כדאמרי' פסחים (דף סו.): איש נדחה ואין לבור נדחין – אף כל שקבוע להם זמן, וישנו בלבור כביחיד בשעת היתר הבמות, דהיינו עולות שישנן בלבור בתמידין ומוספין וביחיד בנדבה. אבל חטאת לא משכחת ביחיד בשעת היתר הבמות, דאפילו בבמה גדולה לא קרבו חובות דיחיד לרבי שמעון, כמו לר"מ ורבנן. והכי פירושו דשמעתא: ותתרגם מתניתך בעולה – דאיכא עולת נדבה ונדבות דיחיד קרבו, והוי דומיא דפסח. דאי בחטאת – חטאת נדבה מי איכא דמשכחת ביה חטאת ביחיד? דאילו חובות דיחיד לא קרבו לא עולות ולא חטאות. ופריך: ונוקמה במנחה, דאיכא חביתים! ומשני: אין מנחה בבמה. וא"ת: ונוקמה בשלמים, כגון כבשי עלרת, דהא איכא ביה שלמי נדבה! וי"ל, כדפרש"י: דכבשי עלרת קק"ד נינהו, ושלמי יחיד קדשים קלים, ולא משכחת כיולא בהן ביחיד.

באו

מסורת הש"ס: [צ"ל אבעיניו] | [לעיל קיא. קידושין לז:] | יבמות עא: | מגילה ט: ע"ש | ס"א דאי חטאת חטאת נדבה מי איכא | [לעיל קיג.] | רש"ק ול"ק מ"ז

עין משפט נר מצוה

כח א מיי' פ"א מהל' פרה אדומה הל' ג:

כט ב מיי' פ"א מהלכות בית הבחירה הל' ב:

נ"א ואע"ג דלא איירי כו' ל"ק

[בקרא כתיב ויחנו בני ישראל בגלגל ויעשו את הפסח]

ס"א זמן א"ל דאמר לך מני רבי שמעון היא דאמר אין בין במה גדולה לבמה קטנה אלא פסח וחובות הקבוע להן זמן ותתרגם מתני' כו' ועיין ל"ק ועיין בספר פנים מאירות

הגהות הב"ח

(א) רש"י ד"ה קרבו נסכים וכו' כל שהלבור לריכין להקריב באהל מועד כל"ל ותיבת מקריבין נמחק: (ב) בא"ד וכן בגלגל בשעת הבמות:

שיטה מקובצת

א] אלא לאו הא: ב] אלא פסחים וחובות הקבוע להן זמן א"ל דאמר לך מני ר' שמעון היא דאמר אין בין במה גדולה לבמה קטנה אלא פסחים וחובות הקבוע להן זמן תתרגם מתניתך א) בעולת נדבה: ג] דאי בחטאת נדבה מי איכא ולוקמה נמי במנחה דהא איכא חביתין והשאר נמחק: ד] שילה אלמא בית הוא: ה] שילה אלמא אהל הוא הא כיצד מלמד שלא היתה שם תקרה והשאר נמחק: ו] מלמעלן: קדשים קלים בכל הרואה ותיבות והיא היתה מנוחה קדשי קדשים נמחק: ז] א"ר אלעזר א"ר אושעיא: ח] מקום שאתה רואה תיבות אשר תראה נמחק ותיבת אתה ל"ש: ט] שאתה רואה תיבת שתראה נמחק: י] בר חמא תיבת חסא נמחק: יא] כתיב אבמה קטנה שהיא לפניו בכל אשר יבחר אבל בגדולה אף היחיד מקריב חובות הס"ד: יב] היינו במה קטנה: יג] שבמדבר ומקריבין באהל: יד] מה"ד תתרגם: טו] בה אבל חטאות: טז] תיבת מתניתין נמחק: יז] כאן וכאן מנחת: יח] שהיא חובה הקבוע:

א) נראה דל"ל בעולת חובה.

תורה אור

"ולו א] תאנת שילה" – מקום שכל הרואה אותו מתאנח עליו על אכילת קדשים שלו. רבי אבהו אמר, אמר קרא: °"בן פרת יוסף בן פרת עלי עין", עין שלא רצתה לזון וליהנות מדבר שאינו ב] שלו – תזכה ותאכל כמלא עיניה. רבי יוסי ברבי חנינא אמר: °"ורצון שוכני סנה", עין שלא רצתה ליהנות מדבר שאינו ג] שלו – תזכה ותאכל בין השנואין. ד] תנא: "רואה" שאמרו – ה] רואה כולו, ולא המפסיק בינו לבינו. אמר ליה רבי שמעון בן אליקום לר' אלעזר, °אסברא ו] לך: כגון בי כנישתא דמעון. אמר רב פפא: "רואה" שאמרו – לא ז] רואה כולו, אלא רואה מקצתו. בעי רב פפא: עומד ורואה, יושב ואינו רואה, מאי? בעי ר' ירמיה: עומד על ח] גבי הנחל ורואה, (יושב) בתוך הנחל ואינו רואה מאי? תיקו. כי אתא רב דימי אמר ט] רבי: *בשלשה מקומות שרתה שכינה על ישראל: בשילה, ונוב וגבעון, ובית עולמים, ובכולן לא שרתה אלא בחלק בנימין, שנאמר: °"חופף עליו כל היום" – כל חפיפות לא יהו אלא בחלקו של בנימין. י] כי אזיל אביי אמרה קמיה דרב יוסף. אמר: חד ברא הוה ליה לביליל, ולא מיתקן! והכתיב: °"ויטש (את) משכן שילה", יא] וכתיב: °"וימאס באהל יוסף ובשבט אפרים לא בחר"! אמר רב אדא: יב] מאי קא קשיא ליה? דלמא שכינה בחלק בנימין, יג] וסנהדרי גדולה בחלק יוסף. יד] מדמצינו בבית עולמים, דשכינה בחלקו של בנימין וסנהדרין בחלק יהודה! אמר ליה: הכי השתא?! התם – מיקרבן נחלות גבי הדדי, הכא – מי מקרבן? טו] הכא נמי מקרבן, *כדאמר רבי חמא בר' חנינא: רצועה היתה יוצאת מחלקו של יהודה ונכנסת לחלקו של בנימין, ובה היה מזבח בנוי, והיה בנימין הצדיק מצטער עליה לבלעה. ה"נ – רצועה היתה יוצאת מחלקו של יוסף לחלקו של בנימין. והיינו דכתיב °"תאנת שילה". כתנאי: "חופף עליו" – זה מקדש ראשון, "כל היום" – זה מקדש שני, "ובין כתיפיו שכן" – אלו ימות המשיח. רבי אומר: "חופף עליו" – זה העולם הזה, "כל היום" – אלו ימות המשיח, "ובין כתיפיו שכן" – זה העולם הבא. *ת"ר: ימי אהל מועד שבמדבר – ארבעים שנה חסר אחת. ימי אהל מועד שבגלגל – ארבע עשרה, ז' שכבשו וז' שחלקו. ימי אהל מועד שבנוב וגבעון – חמשים ושבע. נשתיירו לשילה ג' מאות ושבעים חסר אחת. ימי אהל מועד שבמדבר ארבעים חסר אחת, מנלן? דאמר מר: *שנה ראשונה עשה משה את המשכן, שניה – הוקם המשכן ושלח משה מרגלים. שבגלגל ארבע עשרה, שבע שכבשו ושבע שחלקו, מנלן? דקאמר כלב: °"בן ארבעים שנה אנכי בשלוח משה עבד ה' אותי מקדש ברנע לרגל את הארץ ואשיב אותו דבר כאשר עם לבבי", וכתיב: "ועתה הנה אנכי היום בן חמש ושמונים שנה", כי עבריה לירדן בר כמה הוי – בר שבעין ותמני, וקאמר: "בן חמש ושמונים שנה", הרי שבע שכבשו. ושבע שחלקו מנלן? איבעית אימא: מדשבע טז] שכבשו – שבע נמי שחלקו. ואיבעית אימא: מדלא משכחת לה °"בארבע עשרה שנה אחר אשר הוכתה העיר". § אהל מועד שבנוב וגבעון חמשים ושבע, מנ"ל? דכתיב: °"ויהי כהזכירו את ארון האלהים", יז] *)ותנא: כשמת עלי הכהן – חרבה שילה ובאו יח] לנוב, כשמת שמואל הרמתי – חרבה נוב ובאו לגבעון. וכתיב: °"ויהי מיום שבת הארון בקרית יערים וירבו הימים ויהיו עשרים שנה וינהו כל בית ישראל אחרי ה'"; הני עשרים שנה – יט] עשר שנה *שמלך שמואל בעצמו, ושנה שמלך שמואל ושאול, ושתים שמלך שאול, ושבע כ] דדוד, דכתיב:

*) סדר עולם פרק יא

ולו תאנת שילה. תפשתיו ולא מלאתיו במקרא, אבל מלאתיו *(ועבר) "מזרחה תאנת שילה" (יהושע טז). תאנת. לשון "תאניה ואניה" (איכה ב) שהיו מתאננין ורואין, שמשם היו זוכרין אכילת קדשים שהיתה במקום מראיתו. (א) כא] שאינו שלו. אשת אדוניו. בן פרת יוסף. לשון פריה ורביה, מקום אכילת קדשים נתרבה לו על ידי העין. ושילה בחלקו של יוסף היתה, כדכתיב (תהלים עח): "וימאס באהל יוסף" וגו', כב] אחר "ויטש משכן שילה" כתיב. ורצון. ע"י רצון, שלא רצה ליזון ממה שאינו שלו. בין השנואים. שילה קדשיו נאכלין אף בגבולי שאר שבטים שמשנאוהו. אסברא (ב) לי. הראני דוגמא לדבר. בי כנישתא דמעון. משם היו רואין את שילה, ולא היה דבר מפסיק. לא רואה את כולה. לראות משם את כל שילה, אלא מקצת. חד ברא הוה ליה לביליל ולא מיתקן. נראה בעיני כי אביו של אביי "ביליל" שמו. מי מקרבן. שילה וגבול נחלת בנימין? תאנת שילה. על כג] שהיה בנימין מתאונן עליה. העולם הזה. כל מקום ששרתה שכינה, ואף שילה ונוב וגבעון. נשתיירו לשילה. מארבע מאות ושמונים מיציאת מצרים לבנין הבית שס"ט. שניה הוקם המשכן. דכתיב: "ויהי בשנה השנית בחדש הראשון" וגו' (שמות מ). וקאמר כלב. בשעת חילוק, כשבא לתבוע חברון: "בן מ' שנה" וגו', והיא היתה השנה השניה. נתעכבו במדבר עוד שלשים ושמונה שנה, נמצא כלב בן ע"ח שנים כשעברו הירדן. וקאמר בשעת חילוקה "בן חמש ושמונים שנה" – הרי שבע נשתהו לכיבוש. מדשבע כיבשו שבע חילקו. סברא בעלמא היא. ואיבעית אימא מדלא כד] אשכח י"ד שנה אחר(ג) שהוכתה העיר. דלא מיתוקם קרא דכתיב ביחזקאל (מ) "בארבע עשרה שנה אחר אשר הוכתה העיר", בראש השנה כה] שנאמר: "בעשור לחדש היה דבר ה' אלי" וגו', ודרשינן במסכת ערכין כו] (דף יב.): איזה היא שנה שראש השנה בעשור לחדש – הוי אומר זה יובל. ולא מנו שמיטין ויובלות אלא לאחר ירושה וישיבה. וכי אמרת דשנות כיבוש וחילוק י"ד היו, ודלית להו ממנין היובלות – משכחת לה דחרב הבית בשנת ל"ו ליובל, והוה ליה שנת היובל שנת י"ד שנה אחר כז] שנה שהוכתה העיר, ואי לא – לא משכחת לה. כיצד? "ויהי בשמונים שנה וד' מאות שנה וגו' ויבן הבית לה'", לא מהן מ' שהיו במדבר – נמצא משבאו לארץ עד שנבנה הבית ארבע מאות וארבעים. והבית עמד ד' מאות ועשר – הרי ח' מאות וחמשים, הרי י"ז יובלות שלימים. לא מהן י"ד שכבשו ושחלקו, שלא מנו יובלות – נמצא בית חרב קודם השלמת היובל י"ד שנה. והכי תניא בהדיא בערכין (שם:): י"ז יובלות מנו ישראל משנכנסו לארץ עד שיצאו. ואי אתה יכול לומר משנכנסו מנו, שאם אתה אומר כן נמצא בית חרב בתחילת היובל, ואי אתה מוצא "י"ד שנה אחרי אשר הוכתה העיר". אלא לא מהן שבע שכבשו ושבע שחלקו, ואתה מוצא ארבע עשרה שנה אחר שהוכתה העיר. חרבה נוב. ע"י שאול. בקרית יערים. שם נתנוהו לסוף ד' חדשים שעמד בשדה פלשתים, שנאמר (שמואל א ה): "ותכבד יד ה' אל האשדודים", והחזירוהו בעגלה חדשה ונתנוהו שם. ועשה שם עשרים שנה עד שהביאו דוד משם בשנה ראשונה שנעשה מלך על כל ישראל, שהיא שנה שמינית למלכו על יהודה. הכי גרסינן: עשרה דשמואל עצמו. שהיה שופט לבדו משמת עלי עד שמלך שאול. ובמסכת תמורה (דף יד: טו.) ה"ג לה: עשר שנים שמלך שמואל לעצמו. דאותה שנה ששאלו להם מלך היא שנה עשירית לשמואל הרמתי. ושנה אחת מלכו שמואל ושאול יחד, שהיה שאול הולך אחר עצת שמואל, עד שסרח במעשה אגג וסר שמואל מעליו, כדכתיב (שמואל א טו): "ולא יסף שמואל לראות את שאול" וגו'. ומלך עוד שאול שתי שנים, והן שכתב במקרא (שם יג): "ושתי שנים מלך על ישראל", דלא חשיב כח] אותם דמלך שמואל בהדיה. והיינו דאמרינן במסכת תענית (דף ה:): מי גרם לשאול שישב בגבעה שתי שנים ומחצה – תפלתו של שמואל ברמה. דבחלי שנה ראשונה סרח, ונגזרה עליו מיתה, אלא שעמדה לו תפלת שמואל. ושבע שמלך דוד בחברון על יהודה, ולכשהמליכוהו כל ישראל עליהם הביא את הארון מקרית יערים כט] עיר דוד – הרי עשרים. דכתיב

שיטה מקובצת

א] ולו. ס"א ועלה הגבול מזרחה תאנת שילה: ב] שאינו שלה תזכה ותאכל בקדשים כמלא עיניה שלה: ג] שאינו שלה: ד] השנואין שלה: ה] שאמרו כל שרואה ואין דבר מפסיק א"ל והשאר נמחק: ו] אסברא לי אמר ליה כגון כו': ז] לא שרואה כולו אלא אפילו מקצתו: ח] על שפת הנחל ורואה בתוך הנחל: ט] אמר בשלשה תיבת רבי נמחק: י] תיבת כי נמחק: יא] משכן שילה וגו' וכתיב: יב] אדא בר מתנה מאי: יג] בנימין וסנהדרין בחלק תיבת גדולה נמחק: יד] יוסף כדרך שמצינו בבית עולמים שכינה בחלק בנימין וסנהדרין בחלק יהודה אמרי הכי השתא: טו] מקרבן אמרי הכא: טז] מדשבע כיבשו שבע חילקו: יז] האלהים וגו' ותנא: יח] ובאו להם לנוב: יט] עשרים שנה אחת עשרה שנה שמלך שמואל בעצמו ותיבות עשרה ושנה שמלך שאול ושמואל ל"ש (רק רש"י ז"ל הוא דגרים הכי עכ"ה): כ] ושבע שמלך דוד בחברון דכתיב: כא] מה"ד שאינה שלה: כב] וגו' בתר ויטוש כו' ותיבת אחר ל"ש: כג] על שם שהיה: כד] מדלא משכחת י"ד אחר שהוכתה העיר מדלא מיתוקם ותיבת שנה נמחק: כה] תיבת שנה נמחק: כו] ערכין בפרק שני איזה היא שראש השנה שלה בעשור לחדש: כז] אותו דמלך שמואל: כח] ... כט] יערים לעיר ד...

עין משפט נר מצוה

ל א מיי' פ"א מהלכות בית הבחירה הל' ב:

[בארבע כן הוא בע"י וע' רש"י לקמן קיט. ד"ה טוב ונבעון תלת חשיב להו]

מסורת הש"ס

בראשית מט; דברים לג; שם; תהלים עח; שם; יהושע טז; סדר עולם פרק יא; [תענית כט. סנהדרין כ... ערכין יג.]; יהושע יד; יחזקאל מ; שמואל ד; שם ז; [תמורה יד: טו.]; לעיל נג. מגילה כו. יומא יב.

נ"ל רואה שאמרו שהוא רואה ואין ד... מפסיק בינו לבינו וכן ... כס"י

הגהות הב"ח

(א) רש"י ד"ה שאינו ... נ"ל אחר ד"ה בן פ... (ב) ד"ה אסברא הראנך: (ג) ד"ה ואיבע... אימא וכו' אחר א... הוכתה העיר:

גליון הש"ס

גמ' אסברא לך. ב... הגי' אסברא לי. וב... הדורות בהקדמה אות ... כתב שכן עיקר:

גמרא

דכתיב: °"והימים אשר מלך דוד על ישראל מ' שנה בחברון מלך ז' שנים" א] [וגו']. ובשלמה כתיב: °"ויחל לבנותו בשנת ארבע למלכותו", *נשתיירו לשילה שלש מאות ושבעים חסר אחת.§ "באו לנוב וגבעון" ב] [וכו'].§ מנא ה"מ? דת"ר: °"כי לא באתם עד עתה אל המנוחה ואל הנחלה", "אל המנוחה" — זו שילה, "נחלה" — זו ירושלי'; למה חלקן — ג] כדי ליתן היתר בין זה לזה. א"ל ריש לקיש לר' יוחנן: (א) ד] מעשר שני נמי ליתני! א"ל: מעשר — "שם" "שם" מארון קא ילפי, כיון דארון לא הוה — מעשר נמי לא הואי. אי הכי, פסח וקדשים נמי, ד"שם" "שם" מארון ילפי, הכיון דארון לא הוה — אינהו נמי לא הוו! א"ל: ה] [דאמר לך] הא מני — ר"ש היא, דאמר: אף צבור לא הקריבו אלא פסח וחובות הקבוע להן זמן, אבל חובות שאין קבוע להם זמן — הכא והכא לא קרב; ו] מעשר בהמה חובות שאין קבוע להן זמן הוא, ואיתקש מעשר דגן למעשר בהמה. מכלל דלרבי יהודה קרב? אין, דהאמר רב אדא בר מתנה: מעשר שני ומעשר בהמה נאכלין בנוב וגבעון לדברי רבי יהודה. והא בעי בירה! ולאו תני רב יוסף: שלש בירות הן: שילה ונוב וגבעון ובית עולמים? הוא תני לה והוא אמר לה: לאכילת מעשר שני, ואליב' דרבי יהודה.§ "באו לירושלים" ז] [וכו'].§ ת"ר: כי לא באתם עד עתה אל המנוחה ואל הנחלה", "מנוחה" — זו שילה, "נחלה" — זו ירושלים. ח] ואומר: °"היתה לי נחלתי כאריה ביער", ואומר: °"העיט צבוע נחלתי לי העיט סביב עליה", דברי רבי יהודה. ר"ש אומר: "מנוחה" — זו ירושלים, "נחלה" — זו שילה. ואומר: °"זאת מנוחתי עדי עד פה אשב כי אויתיה", ואומר: °"כי בחר ה' בציון אוה למושב לו". בשלמא למ"ד: "מנוחה" זו שילה — היינו דכתיב: "אל המנוחה ואל הנחלה". אלא למ"ד: "מנוחה" *זו ירושלים, "נחלה" זו שילה — "אל הנחלה ואל המנוחה" מיבעי ליה! הכי קאמר: לא מיבעיא מנוחה דלא מטיתו, אלא אפילו לנחלה נמי לא מטיתו. תנא דבי רבי ישמעאל: זו וזו שילה, רבי שמעון בן יוחי אומר: זו וזו ירושלים. בשלמא למאן דאמר: "מנוחה" זו שילה

מ"א ב | דה"ב ג | דברים יב | ירמיהו יב | שם | תהלים קלב | שם

רש"י

דכתיב והימים אשר מלך וגו'. *ל"ג שנה – הרי כ"ג. וארבע שמלך שלמה לפני בנין הבית, והותה שנה שלמו ארבע מאות ושמונים ליציאת מצרים – נשתיירו לשילה שס"ט. מנהני מילי. שהיה היתר לבמות אחר קדושת שילה משחרבה. כי לא באתם. בימי גלגל, אל המנוחה וגו'. ולמה חלקן. הכתוב, לכתוב את שניהם? ליתן היתר במה בין זה לזה. דהא קרא בהיתר במות דגלגל משתעי, וקאמר: עד מתי אני אומר לכם איש כל הישר בעיניו – כי לא באתם עד עתה וגו', אבל לא משבאתם. ואי אין היתר בין זו לזו – לא ה"ל למיכתב אלא "מנוחה", ומדכתיב "נחלה" ש"מ דה"ק להו: אחר קדושת המנוחה תחזרו להיתר הראשון עד שתבאו אל הנחלה. אי הכי. דשעת היתר הואי – נייתי נמי מעשר שני לנוב וגבעון. שהרי ט] נסתלקו כל קדושת שילה, ואמאי טעם לא תנן במתני' לאוכלו שם? שם שם. "ואכלתם שם" (דברים יב). אי נמי: *(כי אם) "לפני ה' אלהיך (תאכלנו) במקום אשר יבחר לשכן שמו שם" (שם יד). ובארון כתיב (שמות מ): י] "[ונתת] שם את הארון" וגו'. וכיון דארון לא הוה. דכל ימי נוב וגבעון היה הארון בקרית יערים כ' שנה, ובעיר דוד עד שנבנה הבית. פסח וקדשים נמי. דהא "ואכלתם שם" בהו נמי כתיב (דברים יב). מני. הך מתני' דקתני: מעשר שני בכל ערי ישראל, ולא היה צריך להביאן שם. ר"ש היא. דאמר: חובות שאין קבוע להם זמן לא קרבו בנוב וגבעון, והיינו בכורות ומעשר בהמה. ויליף טעמא כדאמרן לעיל בגלגל. וכיון דמעשר בהמה לא הוה התם – מעשר דגן נמי לא בעי לאיתויי התם, דאיתקוש להדדי, דכתיב (שם יד): "עשר תעשר" ואמרינן: בשתי מעשרות הכתוב מדבר, במסכת בכורות (דף נג:). ה"ג: אבל לר' יהודה ה"נ דאמר רב אדא *בר אהבה מעשר שני נאכל בנוב וגבעון לדברי ר' יהודה. והא בעינן בירה. יא] דכתיב (דברים יב): "לפני ה' אלהיכם". נוב וגבעון. חדא חשיב לה. זו וזו שילה. ואפי' הכי יב] *יש היתר בתרה. דקסבר: קדושה ראשונה קדשה לשעתה ולא קדשה לעתיד לבא. ובקדושת ירושלים גופה סבירא ליה דיש אחריה היתר, כדאמרינן במגילה (דף י.): שמעתי שמקריבין בבית חוניו בזמן הזה. ואוקימנא כר' ישמעאל. זו וזו ירושלים. ועד שיבנה הבית לא נאסרו הבמות.

ויהי

תורה אור

תוספות

באו לנוב וגבעון [כו'] קדשים קלים ומעשר שני בכל ערי ישראל. ברים פירקין במתניתין (דף קיב:) פירש בקונטרס, דלעיל ב"באו לגלגל" לא הוזכר מעשר שני לפי שלא נהגו מעשרות עד לאחר ירושה וישיבה. ותימה: דהא פריך הכא בגמרא דמעשר שני נמי נסקיה להתם בנוב וגבעון. ומסיק דמתני' ר' שמעון היא, דאמר: חובות שאין קבוע להם זמן לא קרבו – דהיינו בבכור ומעשר בהמה, וכיון דמעשר בהמה לא הוה התם – מעשר דגן לא בעי לאתויי התם, דאיתקוש להדדי. והשתא, מהאי טעמא דאיתקש למעשר – לא יהא נאכל כלל, כמו מעשר בהמה *בנוב וגבעון למ"ד לא קרבו חובות, והיו צריכין להמתין בבכור ומעשר עד שיוממו, ונאכלין במומן לבעלים. ומעשר שני לא יהא לו תקנה אלא בפדיון! ויש ספרים דלא גרסי במתניתין מעשר שני כלל גבי נוב וגבעון. ונראה לפרש: דלענין הבאה הוא שייך להקיש, דאי האי טעון הבאת מקום – גם זה יהא טעון הבאת מקום כדקאמר לר' יהודה דאמר חובות קרבו, דבנוב וגבעון נאכל – גם מעשר שני נאכל שם. אבל מה שאין מעשר בהמה קרב לרבי שמעון משום דחובות לא קרבו – לענין זה אין שייך להקיש מעשר שני שלא יהא נאכל בכל מקום. דהא דאין מעשר בהמה נאכל – משום דבעי מתן דמים ואימורים ולא אפשר, אבל מעשר שני – שרי. ומיהו, קשה: דלעיל בפרק "קדשי קדשים" (דף ס:) ילפינן מעשר מבכור דאין נאכל בזמן הזה. ויש גירסות בספרים. ושם פירשתי. *ועוד קשה: אי משכחת מעשר דנאכל בכל ערי ישראל, א"כ הא דאמר בפרק "כל שעה" (פסחים דף לו:): מרבה אני מעשר שיש לו היתר בכל מושבות, דאמר ר' אלעזר: מנין למעשר שנטמא כו'. למה לי דרבי אלעזר? הא כיון דבנוב (נאכל) וגבעון נאכל בכל ערי ישראל, א"כ יש היתר בכל מושבות, כדאמר התם (דף לח:) לקמיה בההוא פירקא, גבי חלות תודה ורקיקי נזיר נאכלין בנוב וגבעון! וי"ל: דאיצטריך התם דרבי אלעזר משום רבי יהודה, דאמר בשמעתין: שלש בירות הן, של שילה ושל נוב וגבעון ושל בית עולמים, לאכילת מעשר שני, ואליבא דרבי יהודה. וא"ת: והיכי קאמר התם: "ומוציא אני בכורים שאין להם היתר בכל מושבות"? והלא נאכלין בנוב וגבעון בכל ערי ישראל כמעשר שני! ויש לומר: דבכורים לא אפשר, משום דבעו הנחה אצל המזבח, *ובנוב וגבעון ממטו להו התם, כדאמרינן לעיל בפרק "קדשי קדשים" (דף ס:) ובפרק בתרא דמכות (דף יט:) ובתמורה בפרק "אלו קדשים" (דף כא.) דבכורים אינם שלא בפני הבית משום דבעי הנחה. ועוד: מידי דהוה אחזה ושוק ותרומת לחמי תודה, דאמרי' לעיל (דף קיז:) נוהגין בבמה גדולה ואין נוהגין בבמה קטנה משום דבעו תנופה, ובכורים נמי בעו תנופה. דלא דמי למנחה, דקרבה בבמה בלא תנופה, לרבנן דפליגי עליה דר' יהודה במתניתין בפירקין, כדפרישית לעיל: דמנחה – עיקר מצותה *(סמיכה) והקטרה, הלכך משום תנופה לא בטלה. אבל הני, דעיקר מצותן תנופה, בטלה תנופה – בטלי אינהו. **הא** מני רבי שמעון היא. הכי נמי מצי למימר: רבנן היא, דאמרי: חובות ליחיד לא קרבו בשעת היתר הבמות אף בבמת צבור. וכן רבי מאיר. אלא נקט ר' שמעון משום דעביד הך דרשא: "עשר תעשר" בשני מעשרות הכתוב מדבר. הג"ה **ואיתקש** [מעשר] דגן למעשר בהמה. לעיל בפרק "קדשי קדשים" (דף ס:) נקט היקשא דמעשר לבכור, והכא והתם סגי בחדא. **זו** וזו שילה. פירש בקונטרס: ואפילו הכי הוי היתר בתרה, דקסבר: קדושה ראשונה קדשה לשעתה ולא קדשה לעתיד לבא. ובקדושת ירושלים גופה סבירא ליה דיש אחריה היתר, כדאמרינן במגילה (דף י.): שמעתי שמקריבין בבית חוניו בזמן הזה, ואוקימנא כרבי ישמעאל, עכ"ל. ולא דק, דהתם רבי ישמעאל ב"ר יוסי, דהוא בתראה, בימי רבי. והכא – רבי ישמעאל בן אלישע, בר פלוגתיה דר' עקיבא רבו של ר' שמעון בן יוחי. והשתא אסיקנא לעיל לפום חד גירסא דכולי עלמא קידשה. ומיהו, אי אפשר לומר לדידיה שלא יהא היתר אחר שילה, דהא

מצינו

מסורת הש"ס

גי' הל"ק ל"ג שנה שמלך על כל ישראל וז' שנים מלך בחברון הרי כ"ג וכו'

סדר עולם פי"א

[מגילה י.]

נ"ל ואכלת

[בפנים איתא בר מתנה]

[מגילה י.]

נ"ל הוא היתר כו' נ"ק

[וע' תוס' פסחים לו: ד"ה דאמר ר"א]

[נ"ל קמיצה]

הגהות הב"ח

(א) גמ' א"ל ר"ל לר' יוחנן אי הכי מעשר שני:

גליון הש"ס

תום' ד"ה זו וכו' ולא דק. עיין לעיל דף ס ע"ב תוס' ד"ה קסבר:

עין משפט נר מצוה

לא א מיי' פ"ג מהלכות מעילה הלכה א:

לב ב מיי' פ"ג מהלכות פסה"מ הלכה ז:

נ"ל כנוב וגבעון דלא קרבו והיו כו' נ"ק

עיין נ"ק

שיטה מקובצת

א] שנים ובירושלים מלך ל"ג שנים וארבע דשלמה דכתיב: ב] וגבעון וכו' מנא ה"מ: ג] חלקן הכתוב כדי: ד] יוחנן אי הכי מעשר: ה] א"ל דאמר לך הא מני: ו] קרב ומעשר בהמה: ז] לירושלים כו': ח] ירושלים וכן הוא אומר היתה: ט] נסתלקה כל: י] כתיב ונתת שם: יא] בירה מקדש דכתיב: יב] הכי הוי היתר:

(תורה אור)

שִׁילֹה, "נַחֲלָה" — זוֹ יְרוּשָׁלַיִם, אִי נַמִּי אִיפְּכָא — הַיְינוּ דִּכְתִיב: °"אֶל הַמְּנוּחָה וְאֶל הַנַּחֲלָה" (דברים יב). אֶלָּא לְמַאן דְּאָמַר: זוֹ וָזוֹ שִׁילֹה, אוֹ זוֹ וָזוֹ יְרוּשָׁלַיִם, "מְנוּחָה *נַחֲלָה" מִיבָּעֵי לֵיהּ! קַשְׁיָא. בִּשְׁלָמָא לְמ"ד: זוֹ וָזוֹ שִׁילֹה, "מְנוּחָה" — דְּנָחוּ מִכִּיבּוּשׁ, "נַחֲלָה" א] (זו) — דִּפְלַגוּ הָתָם נְחָלוֹת, דִּכְתִיב: °"וַיְחַלֵּק לָהֶם יְהוֹשֻׁעַ וַיַּפֵּל לָהֶם גּוֹרָל בְּשִׁילֹה עַל פִּי ה'" (יהושע יח). אֶלָּא לְמ"ד: זוֹ וָזוֹ יְרוּשָׁלַיִם, בִּשְׁלָמָא "נַחֲלָה" — נַחֲלַת עוֹלָמִים, אֶלָּא "מְנוּחָה", ב] מַאי מְנוּחָה? מְנוּחַת אָרוֹן, דִּכְתִיב: "וַיְהִי כְּנוֹחַ הָאָרוֹן". בִּשְׁלָמָא לְמ"ד: זוֹ וָזוֹ יְרוּשָׁלַיִם, אֲבָל שִׁילֹה הֲוָה שַׁרְיָא בָּמוֹת — הַיְינוּ דִּכְתִיב: °"וַיִּקַּח מָנוֹחַ אֶת גְּדִי הָעִזִּים וְאֶת הַמִּנְחָה וַיַּעַל עַל הַצּוּר לַה'" (שופטים יג). אֶלָּא לְמ"ד: זוֹ וָזוֹ שִׁילֹה, וּבָמוֹת הֲוָה אֲסִירָן, מַאי "וַיִּקַּח מָנוֹחַ"? הוֹרָאַת שָׁעָה הָיְתָה. תָּנָא דְּבֵי רַבִּי יִשְׁמָעֵאל כְּרַבִּי שִׁמְעוֹן בֶּן יוֹחַי, דְּאָמַר: זוֹ וָזוֹ יְרוּשָׁלַיִם. *וְסִימָנֵיךְ: ג] מָשְׁכֵי גַּבְרָא לְגַבְרֵי.§ "כָּל הַקֳּדָשִׁים" ד] [וכו'].§ אָמַר רַב כָּהֲנָא: לֹא שָׁנוּ אֶלָּא בִּשְׁחִיטָה, אֲבָל בְּהַעֲלָאָה — כָּרֵת נַמִּי מִיחַיַּיב. מַאי טַעְמָא? דְּאָמַר קְרָא: °"וַאֲלֵיהֶם תֹּאמַר" (ויקרא יז) — עַל ה] *הַסְּמוּכִין תֹּאמַר. מַתְקִיף לָהּ רַבָּה: מִי כְּתִיב "וַעֲלֵיהֶם תֹּאמַר"? ו] "אֲלֵיהֶם" כְּתִיב, (וַ"אֲלֵיהֶם" קָרֵינַן!) וְעוֹד תַּנְיָא: אַרְבָּעָה כְּלָלוֹת הָיָה רַבִּי שִׁמְעוֹן אוֹמֵר בְּקָדָשִׁים: הִקְדִּישָׁן בִּשְׁעַת אִיסּוּר הַבָּמוֹת, וְשָׁחַט וְהֶעֱלָה בִּשְׁעַת אִיסּוּר הַבָּמוֹת בַּחוּץ — הֲרֵי הֵן בַּעֲשֵׂה וְלֹא תַעֲשֶׂה, וְיֵשׁ בָּהֶן כָּרֵת. הִקְדִּישָׁן בִּשְׁעַת הֶיתֵּר הַבָּמוֹת, וְשָׁחַט וְהֶעֱלָה בִּשְׁעַת אִיסּוּר הַבָּמוֹת — ז] הֲרֵי הֵן בַּעֲשֵׂה וְלֹא תַעֲשֶׂה, וְאֵין בָּהֶן כָּרֵת. הִקְדִּישָׁן בִּשְׁעַת אִיסּוּר הַבָּמוֹת וְשָׁחַט וְהֶעֱלָה בַּחוּץ בִּשְׁעַת הֶיתֵּר הַבָּמוֹת — הֲרֵי הֵן בַּעֲשֵׂה, וְאֵין בָּהֶן בְּלֹא תַעֲשֶׂה. הִקְדִּישָׁן בִּשְׁעַת הֶיתֵּר הַבָּמוֹת וְשָׁחַט וְהֶעֱלָה בִּשְׁעַת הֶיתֵּר הַבָּמוֹת — פָּטוּר מִכְּלוּם. תְּיוּבְתָּא דְּרַב כָּהֲנָא! תְּיוּבְתָּא.§ "וְאֵלּוּ קָדָשִׁים" ח] [וכו'].§ סְמִיכָה — דִּכְתִיב: °"לִפְנֵי ה' וְסָמַךְ" (שם א). שְׁחִיטַת צָפוֹן — דִּכְתִיב: "צָפוֹנָה לִפְנֵי ה'". מַתָּנוֹת סָבִיב — דִּכְתִיב: °"וְזָרַק (שם יז) ט] עַל הַמִּזְבֵּחַ סָבִיב (סָבִיב".) תְּנוּפָה — דִּכְתִיב: °"וְהֵנִיף הַכֹּהֵן לִפְנֵי ה'" (שם י). הַגָּשָׁה — דִּכְתִיב: °"וְהִגִּישָׁהּ אֶל הַמִּזְבֵּחַ" (שם ב).§ "רַבִּי יְהוּדָה אוֹמֵר: אֵין מִנְחָה בְּבָמָה".§ *אָמַר רַב שֵׁשֶׁת: לְדִבְרֵי הָאוֹמֵר י] יֵשׁ מִנְחָה בְּבָמָה — יֵשׁ עוֹפוֹת בְּבָמָה, לְדִבְרֵי הָאוֹמֵר אֵין מִנְחָה בְּבָמָה — אֵין עוֹפוֹת בְּבָמָה; °"זְבָחִים" (ויקרא יז) — וְלֹא מְנָחוֹת, "זְבָחִים" — וְלֹא עוֹפוֹת. וְכֹהֵן — דִּכְתִיב: °"וְזָרַק הַכֹּהֵן" (ויקרא יז), בִּגְדֵי שָׁרֵת — °"לְשָׁרֵת בַּקֹּדֶשׁ" (שמות כח), וּכְלֵי שָׁרֵת — °"אֲשֶׁר יְשָׁרְתוּ בָם בַּקּוֹדֶשׁ" (במדבר ד).§ לְרֵיחַ נִיחוֹחַ — דִּכְתִיב: °"לְרֵיחַ נִיחוֹחַ לַה'" (ויקרא א).§ מְחִיצָה יא] *בְּדָמִים — דִּכְתִיב: °"וְהָיְתָה הָרֶשֶׁת עַד חֲצִי הַמִּזְבֵּחַ" (שמות כז).§ רִיחוּץ יָדַיִם — יב] דִּכְתִיב: °"וּבְקָרְבָתָם אֶל הַמִּזְבֵּחַ יִרְחָצוּ" (שם מ). אָמַר רָמִי בַּר חָמָא: *לֹא שָׁנוּ אֶלָּא בְּקָדְשֵׁי בָּמָה יג] קְטַנָּה וְהִקְרִיבוּם בְּבָמָה קְטַנָּה, אֲבָל בְּקָדְשֵׁי בָּמָה קְטַנָּה דְּקָרְבִינְהוּ בְּבָמָה גְּדוֹלָה — יד] יֵשׁ חִיצּוּי. מוֹתִיב רַבָּה: *חָזֶה וָשׁוֹק, טו] תְּרוּמַת לַחְמֵי תוֹדָה — נוֹהֲגִין בְּקָדְשֵׁי בָמָה גְּדוֹלָה, וְאֵין נוֹהֲגִין בְּקָדְשֵׁי בָּמָה קְטַנָּה! אֵימָא: נוֹהֲגִין בְּבָמָה גְּדוֹלָה וְאֵין נוֹהֲגִין בְּבָמָה קְטַנָּה. אִיכָּא דְּאָמְרֵי: אָמַר רָמִי בַּר חָמָא: לֹא שָׁנוּ אֶלָּא טז] בְּקָדְשֵׁי בָּמָה גְּדוֹלָה וְהִקְרִיבָן בְּבָמָה גְּדוֹלָה, אֲבָל בְּקָדְשֵׁי בָּמָה קְטַנָּה, אַף עַל גַּב דְּקָרְבִינְהוּ בְּבָמָה גְּדוֹלָה — אֵין חִיצּוּי. יז] לֵימָא מְסַיַּיע לֵיהּ: חָזֶה וָשׁוֹק וּתְרוּמַת לַחְמֵי תוֹדָה — נוֹהֲגִין יח] בְּקָדְשֵׁי בָּמָה גְּדוֹלָה, וְאֵין נוֹהֲגִין בְּקָדְשֵׁי בָּמָה קְטַנָּה. אֵימָא: נוֹהֲגִין בְּבָמָה גְּדוֹלָה וְאֵין נוֹהֲגִין בְּבָמָה קְטַנָּה. וּפְלִיגָא דְּרַבִּי אֶלְעָזָר, דְּאָמַר רַבִּי אֶלְעָזָר: *עוֹלַת בָּמַת יָחִיד שֶׁהִכְנִיסָהּ בִּפְנִים — יט] קְלָטוּהָ מְחִיצוֹת לְכָל דָּבָר. בָּעֵי רַבִּי זֵירָא: עוֹלַת בָּמַת יָחִיד שֶׁהִכְנִיסָהּ

וַיְהִי כְּנוֹחַ הָאָרוֹן. חִיפַּשְׂתִּיו וְלֹא מְצָאתִיו. וְאִם אֵינוֹ בַּכְּתוּבִים יֵשׁ לִי מִקְרָא אַחֵר בְּדִבְרֵי הַיָּמִים (ב ו) בִּשְׁלֹמֹה: *"קוּמָה ה' אֱלֹהִים לְנוּחֶךָ אַתָּה וַאֲרוֹן עֻזֶּךָ". מָנוֹחַ. בִּימֵי שִׁילֹה הָיָה, שֶׁהֲרֵי לֹא חָרְבָה עַד שֶׁמֵּת עֵלִי. הָכִי גָּרְסִינַן: תָּנָא דְּבֵי ר' יִשְׁמָעֵאל כְּר' שִׁמְעוֹן בֶּן יוֹחַי. בָּרַיְיתָא נִמְצֵאת בְּבֵית מִדְרָשׁוֹ שֶׁל ר' כ] שִׁמְעוֹן, שֶׁהָיוּ תַּלְמִידֵי ר' יִשְׁמָעֵאל שׁוֹנִים כְּמוֹתוֹ. מַשְׁכִינְהוּ גַּבְרָא לְגַבְרֵי. ר' שִׁמְעוֹן שֶׁהוּא יְחִידִי מָשַׁךְ אֶת תַּלְמִידֵי ר' יִשְׁמָעֵאל, לְהַנִּיחַ דִּבְרֵי רַבָּם שֶׁאָמַר: זוֹ וָזוֹ שִׁילֹה. לֹא שָׁנוּ. הָא דְּקָתָנֵי דְּהִקְדִּישָׁן בִּשְׁעַת הֶיתֵּר וְהִקְרִיבָם בִּשְׁעַת אִיסּוּר אֵין בָּהֶם כָּרֵת. כא] אֶלָּא בִּשְׁחִיטָה. כִּדְתַנְיָא בְּ"הַשּׁוֹחֵט" (לעיל דף קז:): יָכוֹל יְהֵא חַיָּיבִין כב] עָלָיו כָּרֵת? תַּלְמוּד לוֹמַר: "זֹאת לָהֶם" וְאֵין אַחֶרֶת לָהֶם. וַאֲלֵיהֶם תֹּאמַר. גַּבֵּי הַעֲלָאָה כְּתִיב, וּבָתַר כג] קְרָא דְּאַיְירֵי בְּשׁוֹחֵט קָדָשִׁים שֶׁהִקְדִּישָׁן בִּשְׁעַת הֶיתֵּר כד] וּשְׁחָטָן בִּשְׁעַת אִיסּוּר — "וְלֹא יִזְבְּחוּ עוֹד" וגו', דְּאוֹקִימְנָא בְּהָכִי. וְשָׁחַט וְהֶעֱלָה. כה] *אֶחָד שָׁחַט וְהֶעֱלָה, אֶחָד שָׁחַט וַחֲבֵירוֹ הֶעֱלָה. אַלְמָא, בְּהַעֲלָאָה נַמִּי קָתָנֵי דְּאֵין בָּהּ כָּרֵת. לִפְנֵי ה' וְסָמַךְ. "לִרְצוֹנוֹ לִפְנֵי ה'", וְסָמֵיךְ לֵיהּ (ויקרא א): "וְסָמַךְ אֶת יָדוֹ". צָפוֹנָה לִפְנֵי ה'. וְלֹא צְפוֹנָה בְּבָמָה. וְהָכִי דָּרֵישׁ לֵיהּ נַמִּי בְּתוֹרַת כֹּהֲנִים. עַל הַמִּזְבֵּחַ סָבִיב. וּמֵהָכָא נָפְקָא לָן מַתַּן סוֹבֵב בְּ"אֵיזֶהוּ מְקוֹמָן" (לעיל דף נג:), וְסֵיפֵיהּ דִּקְרָא: "אֲשֶׁר פֶּתַח אֹהֶל מוֹעֵד". נִרְאֶה בְּעֵינַי דְּהָכִי גָּרְסִינַן: הַגָּשָׁה דִּכְתִיב (ויקרא ו) הַקְרֵב אוֹתָהּ לִפְנֵי ה' וגו' וּמֵהַאי קְרָא נָפְקָא לָן הַגָּשָׁה בְּקֶרֶן מַעֲרָבִית דְּרוֹמִית בְּמַסֶּכֶת סוֹטָה (דף יד:), וּבִמְנָחוֹת כו] (דף יט:). זְבָחִים. כז] "(וַיִּזְבְּחוּ זְבָחִים) שְׁלָמִים לַה' אוֹתָם", וְאוֹקִימְנַן לְעֵיל (דף קו:) לְהַאי קְרָא בְּקָדָשִׁים שֶׁהִקְדִּישָׁן בִּשְׁעַת הֶיתֵּר בָּמוֹת. וּכְתִיב "אוֹתָם" — מִיעוּטָא. אַלְמָא זְבָחִים הוּא דַּהֲווּ נָהֲגֵי בְּהוּ, וְלָא עוֹפוֹת וּמְנָחוֹת. וְזָרַק הַכֹּהֵן — "אֶת הַדָּם עַל מִזְבַּח ה' פֶּתַח" וגו' (ויקרא יז) — וְדָרְשִׁינַן לֵיהּ בְּת"כ בְּפָרָשַׁת שְׁחוּטֵי חוּץ: זְרִיקַת כֹּהֵן פֶּתַח אֹהֶל מוֹעֵד, וְאֵין זְרִיקַת כֹּהֵן בְּבָמָה, אֶלָּא אַף הַזָּרִים וְהָעֲבָדִים. יְשָׁרְתוּ בָם בַּקֹּדֶשׁ. הַיְינוּ מִשְׁכָּן. רֵיחַ נִיחוֹחַ. בְּהַהוּא קְרָא כח] נַמִּי: "וְהִקְטִיר הַחֵלֶב לְרֵיחַ נִיחוֹחַ לַה'". עַד חֲצִי הַמִּזְבֵּחַ. מֵהָכָא נָפְקָא לָן מְחִיצָה לְדָמִים, בְּפֶרֶק "אֵיזֶהוּ מְקוֹמָן" (לעיל דף נג.). וּכְתִיב "הַמִּזְבֵּחַ" — הַיְינוּ מִיעוּטָא, בְּהַהוּא מִזְבֵּחַ לְחוּדֵיהּ דְּאַיְירֵי בֵּיהּ קְרָא, וְהַיְינוּ מִזְבֵּחַ שֶׁל מִשְׁכָּן. לֹא שָׁנוּ. דְּיֵשׁ מְחִיצָה לְדָמִים בְּבָמָה גְּדוֹלָה. אֶלָּא קָדָשִׁים. שֶׁהוּקְדְּשׁוּ כט] לִשְׁמוֹ, וְהִקְרִיבוּ בָּהּ. אֲבָל קָדָשִׁים ל] שֶׁשְּׁחָטָן לְבָמָה קְטַנָּה. וְהִכְנִיסָן וְהִקְרִיבָן בִּגְדוֹלָה — אֵין חִיצּוּי. וְאִם בָּא לִיתֵּן עוֹלָה לְמַעְלָה מִן הַחוּט — יִתֵּן. וְאֵין נוֹהֲגִין בִּקְטַנָּה. דִּכְתִיב בְּהוּ "תְּנוּפָה לַה'". מִכָּל מָקוֹם בְּבָמָה גְּדוֹלָה אִיתְנְהוּ, וַאֲפִילּוּ בְּקָדְשֵׁי בָמָה קְטַנָּה, וְה"ה לְכוּלְּהוּ. *לֹא שָׁנוּ. דְּיֵשׁ חִיצּוּי בְּבָמָה גְּדוֹלָה, אֶלָּא בִּזְמַן בָּמָה גְּדוֹלָה, כְּלוֹמַר — בִּשְׁעַת אִיסּוּר הַבָּמוֹת. אֲבָל בִּזְמַן הֶיתֵּר הַבָּמוֹת אֵין חִילּוּק בֵּין זוֹ לָזוֹ בְּדָבָר הַקָּרֵב בִּשְׁתֵּיהֶן. הִלְכָּךְ, *אֲפִילּוּ לא] גְּדוֹלָה הַקְרֵיבִין לִגְדוֹלָה — אֵין חִיצּוּי. שֶׁהִכְנִיסָהּ

מלינו אבשלום שהקריב בחברון, כדכתיב (שמואל ב טו): "אלכה נא ואשלמה את נדרי אשר נדרתי לה' בחברון", וכתיב (שם): "כי נדר נדר עבדך בשבתי בגשור". דאין לומר דהוה מפרש דלא הלך אבשלום אלא להביא כבשים מחברון שהיו שם טובים, ולהקריבם בגבעון בבמה גדולה באהל מועד, כדבעי למימר בריש פרק שני דתמורה (דף יד.). דהא מסקינן התם על כרחין דלאקרובי בחברון בבמת יחיד אזל, דאי להביא – "מחברון" מיבעי ליה. ועוד: כתיב בשמואל (א ט): "כי הוא יברך הזבח". ובשאול כתיב (שם יג): "הגישו אלי העולה והשלמים ויעל העולה. ובסמוך מייתי לה קרא שהקריב בלילה בבמה. **ויהי** כנוח הארון. פירש רש"י: פסוק בדברי הימים (ב ו): "קומה ה' אלהים לנוחך אתה וארון עוזך". והוה מצי להביא פסוק דכתיב ביהושע: (ג) "והיה כנוח כפות רגלי הכהנים נושאי הארון", א"נ (במדבר י): "ויהי בנסוע הארון וגו' ובנוחה יאמר" וגו'.

ה"ג: **משכינהו** גברא לגברי. פירשתילעילבפ' "איזהו מקומן" (דף נג:) גבי זה וזה יסוד דרומי. לג] **ואליהם** כתיב. והא דאמרן לעיל: "ואליהם" לערב פרשיות – היינו שחיטה והעלאה. אבל כולי האי לא אמרן, לערב היתר הבמות על איסור הבמות.

ה"ג: **הקדישן** בשעת היתר הבמות ושחט והעלה בשעת היתר הבמות פטור מכלום. וקשה: היאך שייך א) למיתני בדבר שמצותו בכך? וכי תימא דאיצטריך משום חובות דאין קריבין בבמה, או משום קרבנות צבור ואם שחט והעלה בחוץ פטור מכלום – הא איכא לאו הבא מכלל עשה! ונראה לפרש: דמיירי בעולת במת יחיד, דאפילו הקדישה על מנת להקריבה ב) בבמה גדולה, ואפי' הכניסה בפנים דקלטוה מחילות כדבסמוך, אפי' הכי, אם חזר והוציאה ושחט והעלה בחוץ – פטור מכלום.

***אין** מנחה בבמה וכיהון ובגדי שרת כו'. מנחה לא הויא דומיא דאינך. דמאן *דלית ליה מנחה בבמה – היינו דלא קרבה כלל, אפילו בבמה גדולה, כגון מזבח הנחושת שבנוב וגבעון. וכולהו נהגו, דכולי עלמא מודו דבקדשי במה גדולה יש חילוי. **בעי** רב *אדא עולת במת יחיד שהכניסה בפנים וחזר והוציאה לחוץ מהו, מי אמרינן כיון דעיילא לה קלטה להו מחילות או דלמא כיון דהדור הדור. לאו היינו דרבה ורב יוסף, דתנן: קדשי קדשים ששחטן בדרום מועלין בהן, ואיבעיא להו: *מהו שירדו? רבה אמר ירדו רב יוסף אמר לא ירדו. תיבעי לרבה תיבעי לרב יוסף, כך גירסת רש"י ז"ל

א) גירסת הנ"ק למיתני פטור מכלום בדבר כו'
ב) נ"ל בבמה גדולה והכניסה בפנים כו' נ"ק

שייך לעיל במשנה קיג.
ס"י דמאן דלית ליה אין מנחה כו'
[בגמ' ר' זירא]
נ"ל עלו מהו כו' נ"ק

א] תיבת זו נמחק: ב] מנוחה אמאי מנוחת ארון דכתיב: ג] וסימניך משכינהו: ד] הקדשים וכו': ה] על הראשונים ותיבת הסמוכין נמחק: ו] ואלהם כתיב ואליהם קרינן: ז] הבמות בחוץ הרי: ח] קדשים וכו' סמיכה: ט] וזרק את הדם על המזבח סביב תנופה: י] האומר אין מנחה בבמה אין עופות בבמה לדברי האומר יש מנחה בבמה יש עופות בבמה מאי טעמא זבחים: יא] מחיצה לדמים: יב] ידים ורגלים דכתיב: יג] במה גדולה והקריבו בבמה גדולה: יד] גדולה אין חיצוי: טו] ושוק ותרומות לחמי תודה נוהגין בבמה גדולה ואין נוהגין בבמה קטנה אימא נוהגין בקדשי במה גדולה ואין נוהגין בקדשי במה קטנה איכא דאמרי: טז] אלא בזמן במה והקריבן: יז] חיצוי מתיב רבה תיבות לימא מסייע נמחק: יח] נוהגין בבמה גדולה ואין נוהגין בבמה קטנה אימא נוהגין בזמן במה גדולה ואין נוהגין בזמן במה קטנה: יט] קלטה לה מחיצות: כ] ר' ישמעאל תיבת שמעון נמחק: כא] כרת כדתניא והד"א תיבות אלא בשחיטה נמחק: כב] חייבין עליה כרת: כג] ובתר האי קרא: כד] היתר במות ושחטן: כה] והעלה אחד שחט והעלה אחד שחט: כו] ובמנחות ובהאי מכילתא בפרק קדשי קדשים (דף סג): כז] זבחים וזבחו זבחי שלמים: כח] קרא כתיב ותיבת נמי נמחק: כט] שהוקדשו לשמה והקריבו: ל] קדשים שהוקדשו לבמה ותיבת ששחטן נמחק: לא] אפי' קדשי גדולה והקריבו בגדולה אין חיצוי: לב] מה"ד מי כתיב ועליהם והא תיבת ואליהם ל"ש ותיבת כתיב נמחק:

נ"ל לא שנו אלא בקדשי במה גדולה והקריבו בבמה גדולה אבל בקדשי במה קטנה וקרבינהו בבמה גדולה אין חיצוי מתיב רבה חזה ושוק ותרומות לחמי תודה נוהגים בבמה גדולה ואין נוהגין בבמה קטנה אימא נוהגין בקדשי במה גדולה ואין נוהגין בקדשי במה קטנה איכא דאמרי אמר רמב"ח לא שנו אלא בזמן במה גדולה אבל בזמן במה קטנה אע"ג דקרבינהו בבמה גדולה אין חיצוי מתיב רבה חזה ושוק ותרומות לחמי תודה נוהגין בבמה גדולה ואין נוהגין בבמה קטנה אימא נוהגין בזמן גדולה ואין נוהגין בזמן קטנה ופליגא דר"א

[מקרא זה הוא נמי בכתובים בתהלים סימן קלב ע"ש ויש להביא ראיה מן פסוק אחר בד"ה א סי' כח גבי דוד כתיב אני עם לבבי גו' בית מנוחה לארון ברית ה' ע"ש]
[נ"ל ונחלה וכ"ה בס"י]
[ביהושע יח פ"י כתיב וישלך להם יהושע גורל בשילה לפני ה' אבל קרא ויחלק וגו' לא מצאתי]
נ"ל אחד שחט והעלה הוא ואחד שחט כו' נ"ק
[יומא נט.] לעיל נג:
[לעיל קז. ע"ש]
[וזבחו זבחי]
[לעיל סט.]
נ"ל מחילה לדמים דכתיב כו' נ"ק
[לעיל קיז: ע"ש]
עיין נ"ק
נ"ל אפילו קדשי גדולה הקריבן בגדולה נ"ק
מעילה ג.

שהכניסה לפנים והוציאה לחוץ, מהו? מי אמרי': כיון דעיילא — קלטה לה מחיצתא, או דלמא כיון דהדר — הדר? א] לאו היינו פלוגתא דרבה ורב יוסף? דתנן: *אקדשי קדשים ששחטן בדרום — מועלין בהן, ב] ב(*ואם עלו — לא ירדו.) *ואיבעיא להו: ג] (א) *ירדו, מהו שיעלו? רבה אמר: לא יעלו, ורב יוסף אמר: יעלו. תיבעי לרבה, תיבעי לרב יוסף. תיבעי לרבה: עד כאן לא קאמר רבה אלא במזבח, ד] דחזי ליה — מקדש, דלא חזי — לא מקדש. אבל מחיצה, אע"ג דלא חזי ליה — קלטה. או דלמא ה] אפי' לרב יוסף; עד כאן לא קאמר רב יוסף התם אלא דחד מקום הוא, אבל הכא דתרי מקומות נינהו — לא. או דלמא לא שנא? תיקו. ו] מילתא דפשיטא ליה לרבה בחד גיסא, ולרב יוסף בחד גיסא, מיבעי ליה לרבי ינאי. דבעי רבי ינאי: אברי עולת במת יחיד שעלו למזבח וירדו, מהו? ז] היכא דלא משלה בהן האור — לא תיבעי לך. כי תיבעי לך — היכא דמשלה בהן האור, מאי? תיקו. איתמר, שחיטת לילה בבמת יחיד — רב ושמואל; *חד אמר: כשרה, וחד אמר: פסולה. וקא מיפלגי בדרבי אלעזר. דרבי אלעזר רמי קראי אהדדי, כתיב: ש"א יד °"ויאמר בגדתם גלו אלי היום אבן גדולה", וכתיב: שם °"ויאמר שאול פוצו בעם ואמרתם להם הגישו אלי איש שורו ואיש ח] שיהו ושחטתם בזה ואכלתם ולא תחטאו לה' לאכול על הדם, ויגישו כל העם איש שורו בידו הלילה וישחטו שם". מר משני: כאן — בחולין, כאן — בקדשים. ומר משני: כאן — בקדשי במה גדולה, כאן — בקדשי במה קטנה. איתמר, עולת במת יחיד — רב אמר: אין טעונה הפשט וניתוח, ורבי יוחנן אמר: טעונה הפשט וניתוח. וקא מיפלגי בדר"י הגלילי. *דתניא, ר"י הגלילי אומר: *עולה שהקריבו ישראל במדבר אין טעונה הפשט וניתוח, שאין הפשט וניתוח אלא מאהל מועד ואילך. מר סבר: מאהל מועד ואילך — לא שנא במה גדולה ולא שנא במה קטנה. ומר סבר: בבמה גדולה — אין, בבמה קטנה — לא. תניא כותיה דרבי יוחנן: דברים שבין במה גדולה לבמה קטנה: *קרן וכבש ויסוד וריבוע בבמה גדולה, ואין קרן ויסוד וכבש וריבוע בבמה קטנה; כיור ט] וכנו בבמה גדולה, ואין כיור וכנו בבמה קטנה; חזה ושוק בבמה גדולה, ואין חזה ושוק בבמה קטנה. דברים ששוותה במה גדולה לבמה קטנה: שחיטה בבמה גדולה וקטנה, הפשט וניתוח בגדולה וקטנה, דם מתיר ומפגל בגדולה וקטנה, מומין וזמן בגדולה וקטנה.§ אבל י] (ב) נותר והזמן והטמא שוין בזה ובזה.§ ת"ר: מנין לעשות זמן בבמה קטנה כבמה גדולה? יא] (אמרה תורה: לן ישרף ופיגול ישרף, מה פיגול פסול בבמה — אף לן פסול בבמה. או כלך לדרך זו:) דהא אמרה תורה לן ישרף ויוצא ישרף, מה יוצא כשר בבמה — אף לן כשר בבמה. ולאו ק"ו הוא מעופות?

מה

רש"י

שהכניסה. גרס בדרבי אלעזר. שהכניסה לאחר ששחטה בחוץ — קלטוה מחילות לכל דבר. גרס במסכת מעילה (דף ג.). אלמא: אף קדשים שנשחטו בבמה קטנה שהקריבן בגדולה — כל דין במה גדולה נוהג בהן. ושמעינן מינה נמי, דבשעת היתר במה נמי לא נשתנה דין גדולה מהלכתא. יב] ושתיהן הלשונות דרמי בר תורה אור חמא פליגי אדרבי אלעזר. שהכניסה לפנים. אחר ששחטה בחוץ, וחזר והוציאה. מהו. מי נהוג בה דין קדשי במה גדולה ליטעון בתרומת חזה ושוק, וצריך להחזירה לפנים, או לא? ה"ג: דתנן קדשי קדשים כו'. ולא גרסינן "דאיתמר", ולא גרס "אם עלו לא ירדו". ומשנה היא במסכת מעילה. מועלין בהן. ולא אמרינן: כמאן דחנקינון דמי, והוי להו כקדשים שמתו, דיצאו מידי מעילה, כדתניא במסכת מעילה. ה"ג *במסכת מעילה, והכי נמי גרסינן לה: יג] לאו היינו דרבה ורב יוסף דתנן קדשי קדשים ששחטן בדרום מועלין בהם ואיבעיא להו עלו מהו שירדו רבה אמר ירדו ורב יוסף אמר יד] אם עלו לא ירדו — רבה אמר ירדו, דלא דמו לשאר פסולין שפסולן בקדש, אלא כמאן דחנקינון דמי. אלמא, לרבה לא אמרינן קלוט, לרב יוסף אמרינן קלוט. דלא חזי לא מקדש. דתניא בפ' "המזבח [מקדש]" (לעיל פג:): מתוך שנאמר "כל הנוגע במזבח יקדש" שומע אני בין ראוי בין שאינו ראוי — ת"ל "עולה". *והני לאו "ראוי" נינהו, טו] דלרבה כמאן דחנקינון דמי. דחד מקום הוא. שהרי בעזרה נשחטו. דבעי רבי ינאי אברי עולת במת יחיד שעלו למזבח מהו שירדו. ה"ג. ובמעילה (דף ג:) נמי הכי גרס לה, אבל לא ברבי ינאי טז] גרס לה *התם. אברי עולה שנשחטה בבמת יחיד. שלא במקומה הוא לגבי במה גדולה, כקדשי קדשים ששחטן בדרום. ה"ג: איתמר עולת במת יחיד ששחטה בלילה רב אמר כשר ושמואל אמר פסול וקמיפלגי בהא דרבי אלעזר רמי כתיב גולו אלי היום אבן גדולה — בעוד שהוא יום. אלמא דלילה פסולה בבמה קטנה. והתם במה קטנה הואי, שהרי במלחמה היו רודפים אחרי פלשתים. וכתיב סיפא דקרא: "ויגישו כל העם איש שורו בידו הלילה". רב משני כאן בקדשי במה גדולה. שהוקדשו ליקרב בבמה גדולה, ואע"ג דאקרבינהו בבמה קטנה בעינן יום. כאן בקדשי במה קטנה. קרבו בלילה. ושמואל משני — הא דכתיב יום — אקדשים קאי, ואפילו בקדשי במה קטנה בעינן יום. הא דכתיב לילה — בחולין. במדבר. יז] *סיני. מאהל מועד ואילך. שמשם נאמר, בויקרא. קרן וכבש ויסוד וריבוע. ילפינן להו בפרק "קדשי *קדשים" (לעיל סב.). ובמזבח של משכן כתיב כיור, וכן "בין אהל מועד ובין המזבח" כתיב ביה (שמות ל). חזה ושוק. "תנופה לפני ה'" כתיב בהו (ויקרא ז). שחיטה הפשט וניתוח כו'. דלא אשכחן בהו מיעוטא. דם. לזריקה. מתיר את הבשר בזריקה, ומקמי זריקה אסירא. ומפגל. פיגול נוהג בהן, כדיליף לקמן. ומומין. דלא אשכחן דשרינהו בקטנה. וזמן. לאכילה. אבל הזמן והנותר והטמא כו'. סיפא דמתני' היא, ולא בברייתא הוא. מנין לעשות זמן. להיות נפסל בנותר. הלן. היינו נותר. והיוצא ישרף. נפקא לן בפסחים (דף פב.) מ"הן לא הובא את דמה אל הקדש", פנימה היתה, לפיכך "אכל תאכלו אותה". הא (ג) אם לא היתה פנימה — ראויה היא לישרף. מה יוצא כשר בבמה. קטנה, שהרי כשירה בלא מחילות — אף לן כשר. ומעתה לא יהא הזמן פוסל, דהא אתיא מהאי דינא כדאמרן. ודין הוא. מדרך אחרת, שיהא הזמן פוסל בה.

ומה

תוספות

אבל בספרים ישנים גרסינן: קדשי קדשים ששחטן בדרום מועלין בהן, אם עלו לא ירדו. ואיבעיא להו: ירדו מהו שיעלו? רבה אמר: לא יעלו, רב יוסף אמר: יעלו. תיבעי לרבה כו'. ומיירי במשלה בהן האור, להכי לכ"ע אם עלו לא ירדו ובריש מעילה (דף ג:) דאמר רבה אם עלו ירדו — מיירי בלא משלה בהן האור. ותדע, בלא ההיא דמעילה צריך לאוקמא הכא במשלה בהן האור. דאי בלא משלה — אמאי אמר רב יוסף אם ירדו יעלו? הא אמרינן פרק "ב"ש" (לעיל מג.): כשם שאם עלו לא ירדו — כך אם ירדו לא יעלו. וכל שכן בשחיטת דרום, דגרוע משאר פסולין. והכא מיירי בהכניסה חיה, וקלטוה כדין במה גדולה, להצריך כיהון וריחוץ ידים ורגלים מן הכיור, ואם היא שלמים — בעי תנופת חזה ושוק. ולפי גירסא זו גרסינן בסמוך: אברי עולת במת יחיד שעלו למזבח של במה גדולה וירדו, מהו שיעלו? פירוש: דכיון דשחטן בחוץ — שמא הוי כמו שחטן בדרום. *וגם שמא כיון ששחטה בהיתר בחוץ בבמת יחיד, שלכך הקדישה תחילה, לכולי עלמא היכא דמשלה האור — יעלה. *אבל ללשון ראשון דמבעיא ליה בלא משלה, ומדמי ליה לשחיטת דרום — הלא פשיטא, אפי' שאר פסולין דלא גריעי כמו שחיטת דרום, אם עלו וירדולא יעלו, כדאמר עולא פרק "ב"ש" (שם): אם לא משלה בהן האור, כשם שאם עלו לא ירדו — כך אם ירדו לא יעלו! *וצריך לומר, הא דקאמר: מילתא דפשיטא לרבה ורב יוסף מיבעיא ליה לרבי ינאי — היינו לאיכא דאמרי.

הדרן עלך פרת חטאת
וסליקא לה מסכת זבחים

מעילה ב.

גי' הספרים הוא גירסת הרמב"ם ועי' ברכ"ש גירסא אחרת

מעילה ב:

[עיין תוספות לעיל יד. ד"ה הג"ה תוך עזרה]

נ"ל במסכת מעילה וה"ג במס' מעילה וה"נ גרסי' הכי לאו היינו כו' מועלין בהן ולא אמרו' כמאן דחנקינון דמי והוה ליה קדשים שמתו דילאו מידי מעילה כדתניא במסכת מעילה ואיבעיא להו עלו כו' נ"ק

נ"א או שמא כו' נ"ק

נ"ל וללשון ראשון דמיבעיא ליה כו' ול"נ אבל ללשון ראשון נ"ק

לפי גי' רש"י נ"ל רב אמר כשרה ושמואל אמר פסולה

נ"ל והכנהו לאו כו' נ"ק

עי' רש"ק

נ"ל התם אלא רבי אלעזר

חגיגה ו:

[לעיל קטו.]

[לעיל סב. קח:]

רש"ק מ"ז

הגהות הב"ח

(א) גמ' ואיבעיא להו עלו מהו שירדו רבה אמר: (ב) שם אבל הזמן ונותר וטמא: (ג) רש"י ד"ה והיוצא ישרף וכו' הא אם היתה הוכה פנימה ראויה:

נ"ל בסיני נ"ק

נ"ל קדשים הס"ד ואח"כ ד"ה כיור וכנו במזבח של משכן כתיב כיור ובין אהל מועד ובין המזבח כתיב ביה הס"ד וכנ"ל נ"ק

שיטה מקובצת

א] לאו היינו פלוגתא דרבה ורב יוסף וכו' ואיבעיא להו עלו מהו שירדו וכו' פי' אע"ג דפלוגתא דרבה ורב יוסף לאו בהוציאה לחוץ וא"כ היכי בעי למפשט מהתם מ"מ שפיר מצי למיפשט דדוקא התם דלא חזר והוציאה ס"ל לרב יוסף אם עלו לא ירדו אבל הכא דהדר והוציא אפילו רב יוסף מודה דלא קלטוהו מחיצות ולרבה פשיט מכ"ש ומה התם דלא חזר והוציאה ס"ל ירדו כ"ש הכא דאמרינן כיון דהדר הדר א"נ דלרב יוסף פשיט אם בקדשים פסולין דהיינו ששחטן בדרום דהו"ל כמאן דחנקינהו ס"ל דאם עלו לא ירדו כ"ש הכא דקדשים כשרין הן דאמרינן קלטוהו מחיצות ולא מיפסל להו מה שחזר והוציאה לחוץ וכה"ג אפשר דגם רבה מודה דקלטוהו מחיצות ודו"ק: ב] תיבות ואם עלו לא ירדו נמחק: ג] להו עלו מהו שירדו רבה אמר ירדו ורב יוסף אמר לא ירדו: ד] במזבח מאי דחזי ליה מקדש מאי דלא חזי ליה לא מקדש: ה] דלמא לא שנא תיבעי לרב יוסף: ו] מילתא דפשיטא ליה לרבה וכו' מיבעי לר' ינאי הקשו חכמי ישיבה יצ"ו דהיכא קאמר פשיטא לרב יוסף דלא ירדו הא לעיל אמר דבתרי מקומות אפילו לרב יוסף מיבעי והכי תרי מקומות נינהו אברי עולת במת יחיד שעלו למזבח במת גדולה ונראה לפע"ד דמתרצא במאי דכתיבנא אם בקדשים פסולים אמרינן למר כדאית ליה ולמר כדאית ליה כ"ש הכא דקדשים כשרין הן דאפילו רבה מודה דלא ירדו א"נ לעיל ששחטו בחוץ והכניסו לפנים לעזרה דבודאי ממקום הפסול דהיינו מחוץ לעזרה שהוא מקום קדוש תרי מקומות נינהו אבל הכא מבמה קטנה לבמה גדולה כיון דמשם אחד הן וגם בהרבה דברים ששוו זו לזו כדבסמוך דברים ששותה במה גדולה וכו' כחד מקום דמי ודו"ק: ז] מהו שירדו היכא דמשלה בהן האור לא תיבעי לך כי תיבעי לך היכא דלא משלה בהן האור איכא דאמרי היכא: ח] ואיש שיהו: ט] כיור וכן ואות ג' ו' נמחק: י] אבל זמן ונותר וטמא: יא] מתיבת אמרה עד תיבת אמרה בס"י כל זאת אינו אלא כתוב מיד אמרה תורה לן ישרף כו' עד כשר בבמה יכול לא יהא זמן פוסל בה ודין הוא ומה עופות: יב] ושתי הלשונות: יג] לה הכא לאו: יד] תיבות אם עלו נמחק: טו] נינהו לרבה דכמאן: טז] ינאי כו'. פי' דהתם לא מבעיא דבעייא משם ר' ינאי כדהכא וכו' וק"ל: יז] במדבר במדבר סיני:

מָה עוֹפוֹת אשֶׁאֵין הַמּוּם פּוֹסֵל בָּהֶן — בזְמַן פּוֹסֵל בָּהֶן, קָדְשֵׁי בָּמָה קְטַנָּה שֶׁהַמּוּם פּוֹסֵל בָּהֶן — אֵינוֹ דִּין שֶׁזְּמַן פּוֹסֵל בָּהֶן? מַה לְּעוֹפוֹת שֶׁכֵּן גאֵין הַזָּר כָּשֵׁר בָּהֶן, תֹּאמַר בְּבָמָה קְטַנָּה שֶׁהַזָּר כָּשֵׁר א] בָּהּ, לֹא יְהֵא זְמַן פָּסוּל בָּהּ! ת"ל: °"וְזֹאת תּוֹרַת זֶבַח הַשְּׁלָמִים" — לַעֲשׂוֹת זְמַן בָּמָה קְטַנָּה כִּזְמַן בָּמָה גְּדוֹלָה.§

ויקרא ז

הדרן עלך פרת חטאת וסליקא לה מסכת זבחים

וּמָה עוֹפוֹת שֶׁאֵין הַמּוּם פּוֹסֵל בָּהֶן. דְּאָמַר מָר (תמורה דף יד.): אֵין תַּמּוּת וְזַכְרוּת בְּעוֹפוֹת. זְמַן פּוֹסֵל בָּהֶן. דְּהָא רַבִּינְהוּ לְהוּ גַּבֵּי פִּיגּוּל בְּפ' "בֵּית שַׁמַּאי" (לעיל מד.), אַלְמָא פָּסוּל בְּהוּ זְמַן. תּוֹרַת זֶבַח הַשְּׁלָמִים. תּוֹרָה אַחַת לְכָל הַשְּׁלָמִים, וַאֲפִילּוּ לְשַׁלְמֵי בָּמָה קְטַנָּה לְמַה שֶּׁאָמוּר בָּעִנְיָן, וּמָה אָמוּר בְּאוֹתוֹ עִנְיָן — זְמַן לְתוֹדָה, וּזְמַן לִשְׁלָמִים, וּמַחֲשֶׁבֶת פִּיגּוּל. וְהָא דְּאִיצְטְרִיךְ לְרַבּוּיִינְהוּ — מִשּׁוּם דְּאָתֵי מִבְּנְיַן אָב דְּהָלָן יִשָּׂרֵף וְהַיּוֹצֵא יִשָּׂרֵף, דְּלָא יִפְסוֹל בָּהּ זְמַן, לְפִיכָךְ הוּצְרַךְ לְרַבּוֹתוֹ. לַעֲשׂוֹת זְמַן ב] בָּמָה קְטַנָּה כִּזְמַן בָּמָה גְּדוֹלָה. לְתוֹדָה יוֹם וְלַיְלָה, וְלִשְׁלָמִים שְׁנֵי יָמִים וְלַיְלָה אֶחָד. וְנוֹתָר נַמִי מִפִּיגּוּל יָלֵיף (שם) מִג"ש דְּ"עָוֹן" "עָוֹן", וְטָמֵא נַמִי בְּהַהִיא פָּרָשָׁתָא כְּתִיב (ויקרא ז): "וְהַנֶּפֶשׁ אֲשֶׁר תֹּאכַל" וגו'.

הדרן עלך פרת חטאת וסליקא לה מסכת זבחים

לג א מיי' פ"ג מהל' איסורי מזבח הלכה ח:

לד ב מיי' פי"ח מהל' פסה"מ הל' ז:

לה ג מיי' פ"ז מהלכות פסה"מ הלכה ח:

שיטה מקובצת

א] כשר בה הואיל וחזר כשר בה לא: ב] זמן בבמה קטנה:

The following paragraph is recited three times:

הַדְרָן עֲלָךְ מַסֶּכֶת זְבָחִים וְהַדְרָךְ עֲלָן, דַּעְתָּן עֲלָךְ מַסֶּכֶת זְבָחִים וְדַעְתָּךְ עֲלָן, לָא נִתְנְשֵׁי מִנָּךְ מַסֶּכֶת זְבָחִים וְלָא תִתְנְשֵׁי מִנָּן, לָא בְּעָלְמָא הָדֵין וְלָא בְּעָלְמָא דְאָתֵי.

יְהִי רָצוֹן מִלְּפָנֶיךָ יהוה אֱלֹהֵינוּ וֵאלֹהֵי אֲבוֹתֵינוּ, שֶׁתְּהֵא תוֹרָתְךָ אֻמָּנוּתֵנוּ בָּעוֹלָם הַזֶּה, וּתְהֵא עִמָּנוּ לָעוֹלָם הַבָּא. חֲנִינָא בַּר פָּפָּא, רָמֵי בַּר פָּפָּא, נַחְמָן בַּר פָּפָּא, אֲחָאי בַּר פָּפָּא, אַבָּא מָרִי בַּר פָּפָּא, רַפְרָם בַּר פָּפָּא, רָכִישׁ בַּר פָּפָּא, סוּרְחָב בַּר פָּפָּא, אַדָּא בַּר פָּפָּא, דָּרוּ בַּר פָּפָּא.

הַעֲרֶב נָא יהוה אֱלֹהֵינוּ אֶת דִּבְרֵי תוֹרָתְךָ בְּפִינוּ וּבְפִי עַמְּךָ בֵּית יִשְׂרָאֵל, וְנִהְיֶה אֲנַחְנוּ וְצֶאֱצָאֵינוּ (וְצֶאֱצָאֵי צֶאֱצָאֵינוּ) וְצֶאֱצָאֵי עַמְּךָ בֵּית יִשְׂרָאֵל, כֻּלָּנוּ יוֹדְעֵי
תהלים קיט שְׁמֶךָ וְלוֹמְדֵי תוֹרָתְךָ לִשְׁמָהּ. מֵאֹיְבַי תְּחַכְּמֵנִי מִצְוֹתֶךָ
כִּי לְעוֹלָם הִיא־לִי: יְהִי־לִבִּי תָמִים בְּחֻקֶּיךָ לְמַעַן לֹא אֵבוֹשׁ: לְעוֹלָם לֹא־אֶשְׁכַּח פִּקּוּדֶיךָ כִּי־בָם חִיִּיתָנִי: בָּרוּךְ אַתָּה יהוה לַמְּדֵנִי חֻקֶּיךָ: אָמֵן אָמֵן אָמֵן סֶלָה וָעֶד.

מוֹדִים אֲנַחְנוּ לְפָנֶיךָ יהוה אֱלֹהֵינוּ וֵאלֹהֵי אֲבוֹתֵינוּ שֶׁשַּׂמְתָּ חֶלְקֵנוּ מִיּוֹשְׁבֵי בֵּית הַמִּדְרָשׁ, וְלֹא שַׂמְתָּ חֶלְקֵנוּ מִיּוֹשְׁבֵי קְרָנוֹת. שֶׁאָנוּ מַשְׁכִּימִים וְהֵם מַשְׁכִּימִים, אָנוּ מַשְׁכִּימִים לְדִבְרֵי תוֹרָה, וְהֵם מַשְׁכִּימִים לִדְבָרִים בְּטֵלִים. אָנוּ עֲמֵלִים וְהֵם עֲמֵלִים, אָנוּ עֲמֵלִים וּמְקַבְּלִים שָׂכָר, וְהֵם עֲמֵלִים וְאֵינָם מְקַבְּלִים שָׂכָר. אָנוּ רָצִים וְהֵם רָצִים, אָנוּ רָצִים לְחַיֵּי הָעוֹלָם הַבָּא, וְהֵם רָצִים
תהלים נה לִבְאֵר שַׁחַת, שֶׁנֶּאֱמַר: וְאַתָּה אֱלֹהִים תּוֹרִדֵם לִבְאֵר
שַׁחַת אַנְשֵׁי דָמִים וּמִרְמָה לֹא־יֶחֱצוּ יְמֵיהֶם וַאֲנִי אֶבְטַח־בָּךְ:

יְהִי רָצוֹן מִלְּפָנֶיךָ יהוה אֱלֹהַי, כְּשֵׁם שֶׁעֲזַרְתַּנִי לְסַיֵּם מַסֶּכֶת זְבָחִים כֵּן תְּעַזְרֵנִי לְהַתְחִיל מַסֶּכְתּוֹת וּסְפָרִים אֲחֵרִים וּלְסַיְּמָם, לִלְמֹד וּלְלַמֵּד לִשְׁמֹר וְלַעֲשׂוֹת וּלְקַיֵּם אֶת כָּל דִּבְרֵי תַלְמוּד תּוֹרָתְךָ בְּאַהֲבָה, וּזְכוּת כָּל הַתַּנָּאִים וְאָמוֹרָאִים וְתַלְמִידֵי חֲכָמִים יַעֲמֹד לִי וּלְזַרְעִי שֶׁלֹּא תָמוּשׁ הַתּוֹרָה מִפִּי וּמִפִּי זַרְעִי וְזֶרַע זַרְעִי
משלי ו עַד עוֹלָם, וְיִתְקַיֵּם בִּי: בְּהִתְהַלֶּכְךָ תַּנְחֶה אֹתָךְ בְּשָׁכְבְּךָ
משלי ט תִּשְׁמֹר עָלֶיךָ וַהֲקִיצוֹתָ הִיא תְשִׂיחֶךָ: כִּי־בִי יִרְבּוּ יָמֶיךָ
משלי ג וְיוֹסִיפוּ לְךָ שְׁנוֹת חַיִּים: אֹרֶךְ יָמִים בִּימִינָהּ בִּשְׂמֹאולָהּ
תהלים כט עֹשֶׁר וְכָבוֹד: יהוה עֹז לְעַמּוֹ יִתֵּן יהוה יְבָרֵךְ אֶת־עַמּוֹ בַשָּׁלוֹם:

The following paragraph is recited three times:

הַדְרָן We shall return to you, tractate *Zevaḥim,* and your glory is upon us. Our thoughts are upon you, tractate *Zevaḥim,* and your thoughts are upon us. We will not be forgotten from you, tractate *Zevaḥim,* and you will not be forgotten from us; neither in this world nor in the World-to-Come.

יְהִי רָצוֹן May it be Your will, Lord our God and God of our ancestors, that Your Torah will be our avocation in this world and will accompany us to the World-to-Come. Ḥanina bar Pappa, Ramei bar Pappa, Naḥman bar Pappa, Aḥai bar Pappa, Abba Mari bar Pappa, Rafram bar Pappa, Rakhish bar Pappa, Surḥav bar Pappa, Adda bar Pappa, Daru bar Pappa.

הַעֲרֶב נָא Please, Lord our God, make the words of Your Torah sweet in our mouths and in the mouths of Your people, the house of Israel, so that we, our descendants (and their descendants), and the descendants of Your people, the house of Israel, may all know Your name and
study Your Torah for its own sake. Your commandments Psalms 119
make me wiser than my enemies, for they are ever with me. Let my heart be undivided in Your statutes, in order that I may not be put to shame. I will never forget Your precepts, for with them You have quickened me. Blessed are You, O Lord; teach me Your statutes. Amen, Amen, Amen, Selah, Forever.

מוֹדִים We give thanks before You, Lord Our God and God of our ancestors, that You have placed our lot among those who sit in the study hall and that you have not given us our portion among those who sit idly on street corners. We rise early and they rise early. We rise early to pursue matters of Torah and they rise early to pursue frivolous matters. We toil and they toil. We toil and receive a reward and they toil and do not receive a reward. We run and they run. We run to the life of the World-to-Come and they run to the pit of destruction,
as it is stated: But You, God, will bring them down into Psalms 55
the pit of destruction; men of blood and deceit shall not live out half their days; but as for me, I will trust in You.

יְהִי רָצוֹן May it be Your will, Lord my God, just as you have assisted me in completing tractate *Zevaḥim* so assist me to begin other tractates and books and conclude them to learn and to teach, to observe and to perform, and to fulfill all the teachings of Your Torah with love. And may the merit of all the *tanna'im* and *amora'im* and Torah scholars stand for me and my descendants so that the Torah will not move from my mouth and from the mouths of my descendants and the descendants of my
descendants forever. And may the verse: When you Proverbs 6
walk, it shall lead you, when you lie down, it shall watch over you; and when you awaken, it shall talk with you
be fulfilled in me. For in the Torah your days shall be Proverbs 9
multiplied, and the years of your life shall be increased.
Length of days is in her right hand; in her left hand are Proverbs 3
riches and honor. May the Lord give strength to His Psalms 29
people; the Lord will bless His people with peace.

The following קדיש *requires the presence of a* מנין.

יִתְגַּדַּל וְיִתְקַדַּשׁ שְׁמֵהּ רַבָּא
בְּעָלְמָא דְּהוּא עָתִיד לְאִתְחַדָּתָא
וּלְאַחֲיָאָה מֵתַיָּא, וּלְאַסָּקָא יָתְהוֹן לְחַיֵּי עָלְמָא
וּלְמִבְנֵא קַרְתָּא דִירוּשְׁלֵם, וּלְשַׁכְלָלָא הֵיכְלֵהּ בְּגַוַּהּ
וּלְמֶעְקַר פָּלְחָנָא נֻכְרָאָה מֵאַרְעָא
וְלַאֲתָבָא פָּלְחָנָא דִשְׁמַיָּא לְאַתְרֵהּ
וְיַמְלִיךְ קֻדְשָׁא בְּרִיךְ הוּא בְּמַלְכוּתֵהּ וִיקָרֵהּ
(נוסח ספרד: וְיַצְמַח פֻּרְקָנֵהּ וִיקָרֵב מְשִׁיחֵהּ)
בְּחַיֵּיכוֹן וּבְיוֹמֵיכוֹן וּבְחַיֵּי דְכָל בֵּית יִשְׂרָאֵל
בַּעֲגָלָא וּבִזְמַן קָרִיב, וְאִמְרוּ אָמֵן.

יְהֵא שְׁמֵהּ רַבָּא מְבָרַךְ לְעָלַם וּלְעָלְמֵי עָלְמַיָּא.

יִתְבָּרַךְ וְיִשְׁתַּבַּח וְיִתְפָּאַר וְיִתְרוֹמַם וְיִתְנַשֵּׂא
וְיִתְהַדָּר וְיִתְעַלֶּה וְיִתְהַלָּל
שְׁמֵהּ דְּקֻדְשָׁא בְּרִיךְ הוּא
לְעֵלָּא מִן כָּל בִּרְכָתָא
/בעשרת ימי תשובה: לְעֵלָּא לְעֵלָּא מִכָּל בִּרְכָתָא/
וְשִׁירָתָא, תֻּשְׁבְּחָתָא וְנֶחֱמָתָא, דַּאֲמִירָן בְּעָלְמָא
וְאִמְרוּ אָמֵן. (קהל: אָמֵן)

עַל יִשְׂרָאֵל וְעַל רַבָּנָן
וְעַל תַּלְמִידֵיהוֹן וְעַל כָּל תַּלְמִידֵי תַלְמִידֵיהוֹן
וְעַל כָּל מָאן דְּעָסְקִין בְּאוֹרַיְתָא
דִּי בְּאַתְרָא (בארץ ישראל: קַדִּישָׁא) הָדֵין, וְדִי בְּכָל אֲתַר וַאֲתַר
יְהֵא לְהוֹן וּלְכוֹן שְׁלָמָא רַבָּא
חִנָּא וְחִסְדָּא, וְרַחֲמֵי, וְחַיֵּי אֲרִיכֵי, וּמְזוֹנֵי רְוִיחֵי
וּפֻרְקָנָא מִן קֳדָם אֲבוּהוֹן דִּי בִשְׁמַיָּא
וְאִמְרוּ אָמֵן.

יְהֵא שְׁלָמָא רַבָּא מִן שְׁמַיָּא
וְחַיִּים (טוֹבִים) עָלֵינוּ וְעַל כָּל יִשְׂרָאֵל
וְאִמְרוּ אָמֵן.

Bow, take three steps back, as if taking leave of the Divine Presence, then bow, first left, then right, then center, while saying:

עֹשֶׂה שָׁלוֹם/ בעשרת ימי תשובה: הַשָּׁלוֹם/ בִּמְרוֹמָיו
הוּא יַעֲשֶׂה בְרַחֲמָיו שָׁלוֹם, עָלֵינוּ וְעַל כָּל יִשְׂרָאֵל
וְאִמְרוּ אָמֵן.

The following Kaddish requires the presence of a minyan.

Magnified and sanctified may His great name be,
in the world that will in future be renewed,
reviving the dead and raising them up to eternal life.
He will rebuild the city of Jerusalem
and in it re-establish His Temple.
He will remove alien worship from the earth
and restore to its place the worship of Heaven.
Then the Holy One, blessed be He,
will reign in His sovereignty and splendor.
May it be in your lifetime and in your days,
(*Nusaḥ Sepharad:* make His salvation flourish,
and hasten His messiah,)
and in the lifetime of all the House of Israel,
swiftly and soon – and say: Amen.

May His great name be blessed for ever and all time.

Blessed and praised,
glorified and exalted,
raised and honored,
uplifted and lauded
be the name of the Holy One,
blessed be He,
beyond any blessing,
song, praise and consolation uttered in the world –
and say: Amen.

To Israel, to the teachers,
their disciples and their disciples' disciples,
and to all who engage in the study of Torah,
in this (*in Israel add:* holy) place or elsewhere,
may there come to them and you great peace,
grace, kindness and compassion,
long life, ample sustenance and deliverance,
from their Father in Heaven –
and say: Amen.

May there be great peace from heaven,
and (good) life for us and all Israel –
and say: Amen.

Bow, take three steps back, as if taking leave of the Divine Presence, then bow, first left, then right, then center, while saying:

May He who makes peace in His high places,
in His compassion make peace for us and all Israel –
and say: Amen.